Fromm

POSTCARDS

FROM

SPAIN

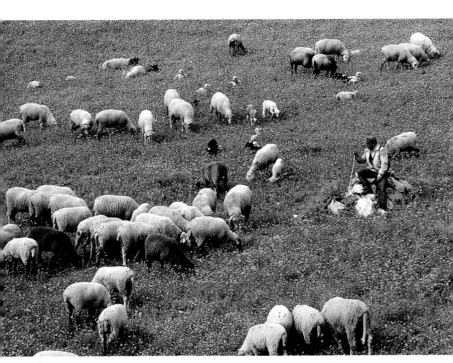

Driving through Andalusia, you may come across bucolic scenes like this one of a shepherd tending his flock. See chapter 7. © Anthony Cassidy/Tony Stone Images.

Just inland from the overdeveloped beach resorts of the Costa del Sol is lovely unspoiled country-side and farmland. © Thomas Kanzler/The Viesti Collection, Inc.

The little town of Ronda, one of the oldest and most aristocratic in Spain, is a fantastic place to explore. See chapter 7. © Thomas Kanzler/The Viesti Collection, Inc.

Córdoba's whitewashed dwellings boast flower-filled patios and balconies. See chapter 7. © A.S.K./Viesti Associates, Inc.

Visit one of Jerez's bodegas (wineries) to taste the golden sherry that has been called the lifeblood of Spain. See chapter 7. © Degas-Parra/ Ask Images/Viesti Collection, Inc.

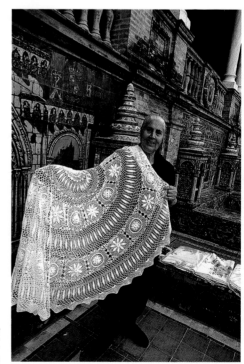

A woman sells crafts on Plaza de España in Seville. See chapter 7. © Kindra Clineff Photography.

Follow the sounds of castanets to Seville's Club Los Gallos for an evening of flamenco dancing. See chapter 7. © Kelly/Mooney Photography.

At Seville's landmark square, the Plaza de España, you can rent rowboats for excursions. See chapter 7. © P & G Bowater/The Image Bank.

If you visit only a few Spanish cities in your lifetime, make beautiful, romantic Seville one of them. See chapter 7. © P & G Bowater/The Image Bank.

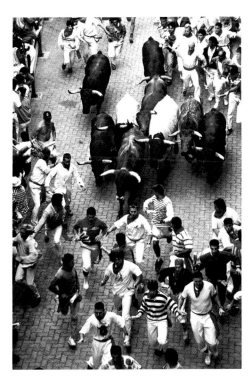

The running of the bulls at Pamplona's Fiesta de San Fermín is one of the most popular events in Europe. See chapter 14. © Oliver Benn/Tony Stone Images.

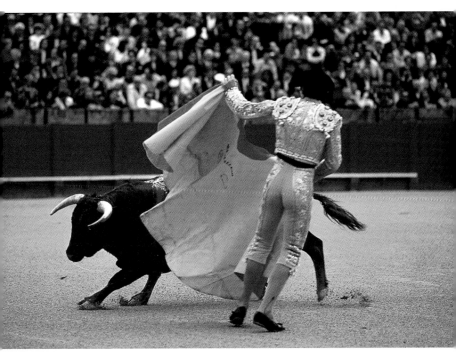

From Easter until late October, some of Spain's best bullfighters appear at the Maestranza bullring in Seville. See chapter 7. © J. Du Boisberran/The Image Bank.

The Mezquita (mosque) in Córdoba is a fantastic labyrinth of red-and-white peppermint-striped pillars. See chapter 7. © Bill Wassman/The Stock Market.

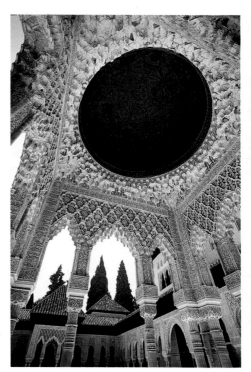

The Alhambra, a lavish palace in Granada, is one of the most exotic settings in Europe. See chapter 7. © Nik Wheeler Photography.

On a hiking tour, you might discover a forgotten village nestled into the valleys of the Pyrenees. See chapters 1 and 2. © Ric Ergenbright Photography.

Gaudí's La Sagrada Familia in Barcelona is a bizarre wonder that has yet to be completed. See chapter 10. © Kindra Clineff Photography.

Street entertainers, flower vendors, café patrons, and strollers congregate on Barcelona's Les Rambles, the most famous promenade in Spain. See chapter 10. © Robert Frerck/Odyssey/ Chicago.

Drink in Madrid's vibrant nightlife surrounded by the elaborately tiled walls of historic Los Gabrieles. See chapter 3. © Robert Frerck/Odyssey/Chicago.

Madrid's Museo del Prado houses one of the most important art collections in the world. See chapter 3. © Nik Wheeler Photography.

Filled with taverns and bars, the Plaza Mayor is the heart of Old Madrid. See chapter 3. © Robert Frerck/Odyssey/Chicago.

With its 12th-century walls and fishing boats, Tossa de Mar makes a delightful base for a Costa Brava vacation. See chapter 12. © Tom Benoit/Tony Stone Images.

The arid plains of New Castile are visible from Toledo's lofty hilltop position. See chapter 4.
© Nik Wheeler Photography.

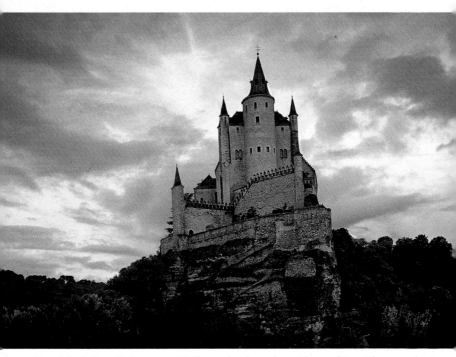

Segovia's glorious 12th-century El Alcázar has been the residence of Spanish monarchs since the days of Ferdinand and Isabella. See chapter 4. © Michael Busselle/Tony Stone Images.

Harborside houses reflected in the water on the island of Majorca. See chapter 18. © David C. Tomlinson/Tony Stone Worldwide.

Set against a backdrop of olive-green mountains, the area around Deià in Majorca is beautiful and serene. See chapter 18. © *Michael Defreitas Photography.*

Frommer's® 2000

Spain

by Darwin Porter & Danforth Prince

with Online Directory by Michael Shapiro

MACMILLAN • USA

ABOUT THE AUTHORS

North Carolina–born **Darwin Porter,** and **Danforth Prince,** a native of Ohio, are the coauthors of several best-selling Frommer's guides, including those that cover the Caribbean, England, France, Italy, and Germany. Darwin, who worked in television advertising and was a former bureau chief for the *Miami Herald,* wrote the first-ever Frommer's guide to Spain while still a student. Danforth, who began writing with Darwin in 1982, worked for the Paris bureau of the *New York Times.*

MACMILLAN TRAVEL USA

Macmillan General Reference USA, Inc.
1633 Broadway
New York, NY 10019
Find us online at **www.frommers.com**

ISBN 0-02-863088-2
ISSN 1091-2827

Editors: Matthew Garcia, Marie Morris
Thanks to Nicole Daro
Production Editor: Donna Wright
Design by Michele Laseau
Staff Cartographers: John Decamillis and Roberta Stockwell
Photo Editor: Richard Fox
Page Creation by: Peter Lippincott, Judith McMullen, and Linda Quigley

SPECIAL SALES

Bulk purchases (10+ copies) of Frommer's and selected Macmillan travel guides are available to corporations, organizations, mail-order catalogs, institutions, and charities at special discounts, and can be customized to suit individual needs. For more information write to Special Sales, Macmillan General Reference, 1633 Broadway, New York, NY 10019.

Manufactured in the United States of America

5 4 3 2 1

Contents

5   Old Castile & León   178

6   Extremadura   204

7   Andalusia   222

8   The Costa del Sol   293

9   Valencia & the Costa Blanca   333

List of Maps

AN INVITATION TO THE READER

In researching this book, we discovered many wonderful places—hotels, restaurants, shops, and more. We're sure you'll find others. Please tell us about them, so we can share the information with your fellow travelers in upcoming editions. If you were disappointed with a recommendation, we'd love to know that, too. Please write to:

Frommer's Spain 2000
Macmillan Travel
1633 Broadway
New York, NY 10019

AN ADDITIONAL NOTE

Please be advised that travel information is subject to change at any time—and this is especially true of prices. We therefore suggest that you write or call ahead for confirmation when making your travel plans. The authors, editors, and publisher cannot be held responsible for the experiences of readers while traveling. Your safety is important to us, however, so we encourage you to stay alert and be aware of your surroundings. Keep a close eye on cameras, purses, and wallets, all favorite targets of thieves and pickpockets.

WHAT THE SYMBOLS MEAN

✪ Frommer's Favorites

Our favorite places and experiences—outstanding for quality, value, or both.

The following abbreviations are used for credit cards:

AE	American Express	EURO	Eurocard
CB	Carte Blanche	JCB	Japan Credit Bank
DC	Diners Club	MC	MasterCard
DISC	Discover	V	Visa
ER	EnRoute		

FIND FROMMER'S ONLINE

Arthur Frommer's Budget Travel Online (**www.frommers.com**) offers more than 6,000 pages of up-to-the-minute travel information—including the latest bargains and candid, personal articles updated daily by Arthur Frommer himself. No other Web site offers such comprehensive and timely coverage of the world of travel.

The Best of Spain

Spain is one of the most diverse and visually stunning nations of Europe. As you begin to plan your trip, you may find yourself overwhelmed with so many fascinating sights, beautiful landscapes, and charming towns to fit into your limited time. So let us give you a hand. We've scoured the country in search of the best places and experiences, and we've chosen our very favorites below, admittedly very personal and opinionated choices.

Seek out a Picasso masterwork. Check out the "hanging houses" in cliff-top Cuenca. Run from a charging bull down the cobblestone streets of Pamplona (scratch that: from the safety of protective barricades, watch the *locals* elude the bulls). Enjoy fresh seafood paella in a picture-perfect fishing village. We hope that these picks, everything from the sultry sound of flamenco to tapas tasting, will get you started on the road to planning the trip that's right for you.

1 The Best Travel Experiences

- **Sitting in *Sol* or *Sombra* at the Bullfights:** With origins as old as pagan Spain, the art of bullfighting is the expression of Iberian temperament and passions. Detractors object to the sport as cruel, bloody, violent, hot, and savage. Fans, however, view bullfighting as a microcosm of death, catharsis, and rebirth. These philosophical underpinnings may not be immediately apparent, but if you strive to understand the bullfight, it can be one of the most evocative and memorable events in Spain. Head for the *plaza de toros* (bullring) in any major city, but particularly in Madrid, Seville, or Granada. Tickets are either *sol* (sunny side) or *sombra* (in the shade); you'll pay more to get out of the sun. Observe how the feverish crowds appreciate the ballet of the *banderilleros,* the thundering fury of the bull, the arrogance of the matador—all leading to "death in the afternoon."
- **Feasting on Tapas in the Tascas:** Tapas, those bite-size portions washed down with wine, beer, or sherry, are reason enough to go to Spain! Tapas bars, called *tascas,* are a quintessential Spanish experience. Originally tapas were cured ham or *chorizo* (spicy sausage). Today they are likely to include everything—*gambas* (deep-fried shrimp), anchovies marinated in vinegar, stuffed peppers, a cool, spicy gazpacho, or hake salad. These dazzling spreads will hold you over until the fashionable 10pm dining hour.

Spain

- **Getting Caught Up in the Passions of Flamenco:** It's best heard in some old tavern, in a neighborhood like the Barrio de Triana in Seville. From the lowliest *taberna* to the poshest nightclub, you can hear the staccato heel clicking, foot stomping, castanet rattling, hand clapping, and sultry guitar and tambourine sound. Some say its origins lie deep in Asia, but the Spanish gypsy has given the art form, which dramatizes inner conflict and pain, an original style. Performed by a great artist, flamenco can tear your heart out with its soulful and throaty singing.
- **Seeing the Masterpieces at the Prado:** It's one of the world's premier art museums, home to some 4,000 masterpieces, many of them acquired by Spanish kings. The wealth of Spanish art is staggering—everything from Goya's *Naked Maja* to the celebrated *Las Meninas* (*The Maids of Honor*) by Velázquez (our favorite). Masterpiece after masterpiece unfolds before your eyes: You can imagine your fate in Hieronymus Bosch's *Garden of Earthly Delights* or recoil from the horror of Goya's *Disasters of War* etchings. When the Spanish artistic soul gets too dark, escape to the Italian salons and view canvases by Caravaggio, Fra Angelico, and Botticelli. See chapter 3.
- **Sipping Sherry at Jerez de la Frontera:** In Spain, sherry is called Jerez, and it's a major industry and subculture in its own right. Hispanophiles compare its complexities to the finest wines produced in France and make pilgrimages to the *bodegas* (wineries) in Andalusia that ferment this amber-colored liquid. More than 100 bodegas are available for visits, tours, and tastings, and most open their gates to visitors interested in a process that dates from the country's Roman occupation. See chapter 7.
- **Wandering the Crooked Streets of Barcelona's Gothic Quarter:** Long before Madrid was even founded, the kingdom of Catalonia was a bastion of art and architecture. Whether the Barri Gòtic, as it's called in Catalán, is truly Gothic is the subject of endless debate, but the Ciutat Vella, or old city, of Barcelona is one of the most evocative neighborhoods in Spain. Its richly textured streets, with their gurgling fountains, vintage stores, and ancient fortifications, inspired such artists as Pablo Picasso (a museum of his work is found here) and Joan Miró (who was born in this neighborhood). See chapter 10.
- **Going Gaga Over Gaudí:** No architect in Europe was as fantastical as Antoni Gaudí y Cornet, the foremost proponent of Catalan *modernismo*. Barcelona is studded with the works of this extraordinary artist—in fact, UNESCO now lists all his creations among the World Trust Properties. This eccentric genius conceived buildings as "visions." A recluse and a celibate bachelor, as well as a fervent Catalan nationalist, he lived out his own fantasy. Nothing is more stunning than his Sagrada Familia, Barcelona's best-known landmark, a cathedral on which Gaudí labored for the last 43 years of his life before he was killed tragically by a tram in 1926. The landmark cathedral was never completed, though believe it or not, they're still working on it. If it's ever finished, "The Sacred Family" will be Europe's largest cathedral. See chapter 10.
- **Running with the Bulls in Pamplona:** Okay, maybe it's smarter to watch, not actually participate in, the running of the bulls. The Fiesta de San Fermín in July is the most dangerous ritual in Spain, made even worse by the copious amounts of wine consumed by participants and observers. Broadcast live on TV throughout Spain and the rest of Europe, and originally introduced to North American audiences by Ernest Hemingway, the festival features herds of furious bulls that charge down medieval streets, sometimes trampling and goring some of the hundreds of people who run beside them. Few other rituals in Spain are as breathtaking and foolhardy. And few others as memorable. See chapter 14.

Impressions

Three Spaniards, four opinions.

—Old Spanish proverb

- **Following the Ancient Pilgrim Route to Santiago:** Tourism as we know it began during the Middle Ages, as thousands of European pilgrims journeyed to the shrine of Santiago (Saint James) in Galicia in northwestern Spain. Even if you're not motivated by faith, you should come to see some of the most dramatic landscapes and the grandest scenery in Spain, by crossing the northern tier of the country—all the way from the Pyrenees to Santiago de Compostela. Some of the country's most stunning architecture can be viewed along the way, including gems in Roncevalles, Burgos, and León. The deluxe Hostal de Los Reyes Católicos in Santiago awaits the weary pilgrim at the end of the journey. See chapter 17.

2 The Best Small Towns

- **Cuenca:** Set amid a landscape of rugged limestone outcroppings at the junction of two rivers, Cuenca is a fascinating combination of medieval masonry and cantilevered balconies that seem to float above the steep gorges below. The angularity of the architecture here is said to have inspired early versions of cubism, a fact commemorated in Cuenca's Museo de Arte Abstracto Español. This museum is considered by some to be one of the finest modern art museums in Spain. See chapter 4.
- **Zafra:** Zafra's 15th-century castle is the largest and best preserved in the region. The castle is set within the angular, stark white architecture of Zafra, which is said to have inspired the cubists. See chapter 6.
- **Baeza:** After it was wrenched away from the Moors in 1227, Baeza became a frontier town between the Christian and Moorish worlds, a diehard symbol of the Catholic ambition to occupy all of Iberia. Today a wealth of architecture survives as evidence of the splendor of Iberian dynasties in the past. See chapter 7.
- **Carmona:** Pint-sized, sleepy Carmona—usually visited as a side trip from Seville—packs a historical wallop, evoking the Roman occupation of Iberia. The town claims an architectural legacy from every occupying force dating from 206 B.C., when a Roman general demolished the resident Carthaginian army. See chapter 7.
- **Arcos de la Frontera:** Parts of Andalusia are very overcrowded, so you may want to stretch out and relax when you arrive at this ancient Arab town. Now a historical monument, Arcos de la Frontera is 20 miles (32km) east of Jerez de la Frontera—the town that sherry put on the map. The place to stay is the Parador Casa del Corregidor (an old vicar's home). From there you can set out to explore this lofty town, hemmed in on three sides by the Guadalete River. The parador is perched along the edge of a cliff, and walks from there in almost any direction offer spectacular views of this *pueblo blanco* (white village) of whitewashed Andalusian houses. See chapter 7.
- **Ronda:** The site appears inhospitable—a gorge slices through the town center and its twin halves are interconnected with bridges that are antiques in their own right. But the winding streets of this old Moorish town are perfect for wandering, and the views of the surrounding Andalusian countryside are stupendous. Ronda is also revered by bullfighting fans, because of both its bullring (the oldest and

most beautiful in Spain) and the region's skill in breeding what are the fiercest bulls in the country. See chapter 7.

- **Mijas:** Wander through streets and alleys that were once trod by the Phoenicians, the Celts, and the Moors. Today, the town offers a welcome dose of medieval flair on the Costa del Sol, a region otherwise filled with modern, anonymous, and often ugly resort hotels. See chapter 8.

- **Nerja:** On the Costa del Sol at the Balcón de Europa (Balcony of Europe), this is a Mediterranean gem, with a palm-shaded promenade jutting out into the sea. Lined with antique iron lampposts, the village overlooks a pretty beach and the fishing fleet. The resort town lies on a sloping site at the foot of a wall of jagged coastal mountains. You can snuggle up in the parador or lodge in one of the little inns on the narrow streets. See chapter 8.

- **Elche:** Although famed as a charming medieval village, Elche is best known as the excavation site of one of the premier sculptures of the Roman Empire in Iberia, *La Dama de Elche*, now exhibited in Madrid's archaeological museum. These days, you can still see date palms planted originally by the Phoenicians and a mystery play celebrating the Assumption of the Virgin, which has been performed in the village church every year since the 1300s. See chapter 9.

- **Sitges:** South of Barcelona is Spain's most romantic Mediterranean beach town, with a 1½-mile-long sandy beach and a promenade studded with flowers and palm trees. Sitges is a town with a rich connection to art; Picasso and Dalí both spent time here. Wander its little lanes and inspect the old villas of its Casco Antiguo, the old quarter. When not at the beach, you can view three good art museums, including one in the former studio of artist Santiago Rusiñol (1861–1931). Nowadays, thousands of gay men and lesbians flock to Sitges, but there's a wide spectrum of visitors of all persuasions. See chapter 11.

- **Cadaqués:** The 16th-century church that dominates this town from a nearby hilltop isn't particularly noteworthy. But Cadaqués—on the Costa Brava near the French border—still charms, with whitewashed, fishing-village simplicity. The azure waters of the Mediterranean appealed to surrealist master Salvador Dalí, who built a suitably bizarre villa in the adjoining hamlet of Lligat. See chapter 12.

- **Santillana del Mar:** Jean-Paul Sartre called it "the prettiest village in Spain." Only 6 blocks long and just 3 miles (5km) from the sea, Santillana del Mar perfectly captures the spirit of Cantabria. It's also near the Cuevas de Altamira, often called "the Sistine Chapel of prehistoric art." Romanesque houses and mansions line the ironstone streets. People still sell fresh milk from their stable doors, as if the Middle Ages had never ended, but you can live in comfort at one of Spain's grandest paradors, Parador de Santillana, a converted 17th-century mansion. See chapter 16.

- **Deià:** On the island of Majorca, you'll find this lovely old village (also spelled Deyá), where the poet Robert Graves lived until his death in 1985. Following in his footsteps, artists and writers flock to this haven of natural beauty, 17 miles (27km) northwest of Palma. The views of the sea and mountains are panoramic. Gnarled and ancient olive trees dot the landscape. You can book into cozy nests of luxury like La Residencia or Es Molí. See chapter 18.

3 The Best Beaches

Spain may be flanked to the east by France and the Pyrenees and to the west by Portugal, but most of the country is ringed with sand, rock, and seawater. That, coupled with almost year-round sunshine, has attracted many millions of beachgoers.

- **Costa de la Luz:** This stretch of coastline in southwestern Andalusia boasts long stretches of sand and almost-constant sunshine. The blue, sometimes rough, Atlantic waters are enticement enough, as is the region's proximity to several historic cities. Foremost among coastal cities is Cádiz, and Seville is just a short drive inland. This area is less developed than the more popular Costa del Sol. See chapter 7.
- **Costa del Sol:** Stretching east from Gibraltar along the southernmost coast of Spain, the Costa del Sol is the most famous, party-hearty, and overdeveloped string of beaches in Iberia. The beaches feature superb sand, and the Mediterranean waters are calm and warm throughout most of the year. But these charms have brought throngs of visitors, making this the most congested string of coastal resorts in Europe. The most important resorts here are Marbella, Torremolinos, Málaga, and Nerja. Look for soaring skyscrapers; eye-popping bikinis; some sophisticated resorts and restaurants alongside hotels that cater to tour groups; lots of sunshine; and interminable traffic jams. See chapter 8.
- **Costa Blanca:** This southeastern coast embraces the industrial city of Valencia, but its best-known resorts, Benidorm and Alicante, are packed with northern-European sun-seekers every year. The surrounding scenery isn't particularly dramatic—flat, sunbaked terrain bathed in a stark white light. But the water is turquoise, the sand is white, and a low annual rainfall virtually guarantees a sunny vacation. See chapter 9.
- **Costa Brava:** Rockier, more serpentine, and without the long stretches of sand that mark the Costa Blanca, the cliff-edged Costa Brava stretches from Barcelona to the French border. Look for the charming, sandy-bottomed coves that dot the coast. Although there are fewer undiscovered beaches here than along Spain's Atlantic coast, the Costa Brava still retains a sense of rocky wilderness. One of the more eccentric-looking villas along this coast belonged to the late Salvador Dalí, the region's most famous modern son who lived much of his life near Cadaqués. See chapter 12.
- **Costa Verde:** Radically different from the dry and sunbaked coastline of Andalusia, the rocky Costa Verde (Green Coast) resembles a sunny version of Ireland's western shore. It's temperate in summer, when the rest of Spain can be unbearably hot. Much of the coast is contained within the ancient province of Asturias, a region rife with Romanesque architecture and medieval pilgrimage sites—and one that has not yet been overwhelmed with tourism. Premier resorts include some districts of Santander, Gijón, and, a short distance inland, Oviedo. See chapter 16.
- **The Balearic Islands:** Just off the coast of Catalonia and a 45-minute flight from Barcelona, this rocky, sand-fringed archipelago has attracted urban refugees seeking the sun, jet-set glitterati, and exhibitionists in scanty beachwear. The Mediterranean climate is warmer here than on the mainland. Majorca in particular has been targeted by northern Europeans, many of whom have bought vacation homes there. The city of Palma de Majorca has the greatest number of high-rises and the most crowded shorelines. Much of Ibiza is party central for young people and gay visitors during the summer. Sleepy Minorca offers more isolation. See chapter 18.

4 The Best Castles & Palaces

- **The Palacio Real** (Madrid): No longer occupied by royalty, but still used for state occasions, the Royal Palace sits in the heart of Madrid on the bank of the Manzanares River. It was built in the mid–18th century over the site of a former palace. It's not Versailles, but it's still mighty impressive, with around 2,000 rooms. No one has lived here since the king fled in 1931, but the chandeliers, marble columns, and ornate, gilded borders, paintings, and objets d'art, including Flemish tapestries and Tiepolo ceiling frescoes, are still well preserved. The empty thrones of King Juan Carlos and Queen Sofia are among the highlights of the tour. See chapter 3.

- **El Alcázar** (Segovia): Once the most impregnable castle in Spain, it rises dramatically from a rock spur near the ancient heart of town. Isabella married Ferdinand at this foreboding site, surrendering rights that eventually led to the unification of Spain. Today, it's the single most photographed and dramatic castle in Iberia. See chapter 4.

- **The Palacio Real** (Aranjuez): Built at enormous expense by the Bourbon cousins of the rulers of France, it was designed to emulate the glories of Versailles in its 18th-century neoclassicism. The gardens are even more fascinating than the palace. The gem of the complex is the Casita del Labrador, an annex as rich and ornate as its model—Marie Antoinette's Petit Trianon at Versailles. See chapter 4.

- **The Alhambra** (Granada): One of Spain's grandest sights, the Alhambra was originally conceived by the Muslims as a fortified pleasure pavilion. Its allure was instantly recognized by Catholic monarchs after the Reconquest. Despite the presence of a decidedly European palace in its center, the setting remains one of the most exotic (and Moorish) in all of Europe. See chapter 7.

- **The Alcázar** (Seville): The oldest royal residence in Europe still in use was built by Peter the Cruel (1350–69) in 1364, 78 years after the Moors left Seville. Ferdinand and Isabella once lived here. One of the purest examples of the Mudéjar, or Moorish, style, its decoration is based on that of the Alhambra in Granada. A multitude of Christian and Islamic motifs are combined architecturally in this labyrinth of gardens, halls, and courts, none more notable than the Patio de las Doncellas (Court of the Maidens). See chapter 7.

5 The Best Museums

The spectacular **Prado** in Madrid is no mere museum, but a travel experience. It's worth a journey to Spain just to visit it (see "The Best Travel Experiences" above).

- **Museo Lázaro Galdiano** (Madrid): This rare collection demonstrates the evolution of enamel and ivory crafts from the Byzantine era to 19th-century Limoges. Of almost equal importance are the displays of superb medieval gold and silver work along with the Italian Renaissance jewelry. The museum also contains galleries with rare paintings, everything from Flemish primitives to works by Spanish masters of the golden age, including El Greco, Murillo, and Zurbarán. There are also paintings from Goya's "Black Period" and from the English and Italian masters Constable and Tiepolo. See chapter 3.

- **Thyssen-Bornemisza Museum** (Madrid): Madrid's acquisition of this treasure trove of art in the 1980s was one of the greatest coups in European art history. Amassed by a central European collector beginning around 1920, and formerly displayed in Lugano, Switzerland, its 700 canvases are arranged in chronological order in a way that rivals the legendary holdings of the queen of England herself. Works by artists ranging from El Greco to Picasso decorate the walls. See chapter 3.

- **Museo de Arte Abstracto Español** (Cuenca): The angular medieval architecture of the town that contains it is an appropriate foil for a startling collection of modern masters. A group of some of Spain's most celebrated artists settled in

Cuenca, in the 1950s and 1960s, and their works are displayed here. They included Fernando Zobel, Antoni Tàpies, Eduardo Chillida, Luis Feito, and Antonio Saura—still the big names in the Spanish art world. See chapter 4.

- **Museo de Santa Cruz** (Toledo): Built as a hospital for the poor and orphaned by the archbishop of Toledo, this is the most important museum in New Castile. The Santa Cruz museum is known for its plateresque architecture, notably for its intricate facade, and for the wealth of art inside. Among its noteworthy collection of 16th- and 17th-century paintings are 18 works by El Greco. Especially evocative is his *Altarpiece of the Assumption,* completed in 1613 during his final period. The gallery also contains a collection of primitive paintings. See chapter 4.

- **Museo Nacional de Escultura** (Valladolid): The greatest collection of gilded polychrome sculpture—an art form that reached its pinnacle in Valladolid—is on display here in the 15th-century San Gregorio College. Figures are first carved in wood, then painted with great artistry to achieve a lifelike appearance. The most remarkable exhibit is an altarpiece designed by Alonso Berruguete for the Church of San Benito. Be sure to see his *Martyrdom of St. Sebastian.* See chapter 5.

- **Museo Nacional de Arte Romano** (Mérida): A museum that makes most archaeologists salivate, this modern building contains hundreds of pieces of ancient Roman sculpture discovered in and around this dried-out, sunbaked Extremaduran town. The treasures built here by the Romans include theaters, amphitheaters, racecourses, and hundreds of tombs full of art objects, many of which are on display here. In 1986 the well-known and award-winning architect Rafael Moneo created a stir in architectural circles when he designed this ambitious and innovative brick building. Designing the building on a grand scale, he freely borrowed from Roman motifs and daringly incorporated an ancient Roman road, which had been discovered when the foundations were dug. See chapter 6.

- **Museo Provincial de Bellas Artes de Sevilla** (Seville): The Prado doesn't own all the great Spanish art in the country. Located in the early 17th-century convent of La Merced, this Andalusian museum is famous for its works by such Spanish masters as Valdés Leal, Zurbarán, and Murillo. Spain's golden age is best exemplified by Murillo's monumental *Immaculate Conception* and Zurbarán's *Apotheosis of St. Thomas Aquinas.* See chapter 7.

- **Museu Picasso** (Barcelona): Picasso, who spent many of his formative years in Barcelona, donated some 2,500 of his paintings, drawings, and engravings to launch this museum in 1970. It's second only to the Picasso Museum in Paris. Seek out his notebooks, which contain many sketches of Barcelona scenes. Here is a rare chance to see the development of Picasso's genius in his early works; since the pieces are arranged in rough chronological order, you'll discover that he completely mastered traditional representational painting before tiring of it and beginning to experiment. Watch for numerous portraits of his family, as well as examples from both his Blue Period and Rose Period. His obsessive *Las Meninas* series—painted in 1959—offers exaggerated variations of the theme of the famous picture by Velázquez hanging in Madrid's Prado Museum. See chapter 10.

- **Teatre Museu Dalí** (Figueres): The eccentric Salvador Dalí is showcased here as nowhere else. The surrealist artist—known for everything from lobster telephones to *Rotting Mannequin in a Taxicab*—conceived of his art partly as theater. But, be warned: As Dalí's final joke, he wanted the museum to spew forth "false information." See chapter 12.

6 The Best Cathedrals & Churches

- **Catedral de Ávila:** One of the earliest Gothic cathedrals in Castile, this rugged and plain edifice was called "a soldier's church." A brooding, granite monolith, which in some ways resembles a fortress, it is the centerpiece of a city that produced St. Teresa, the most famous mystic of the Middle Ages. In contrast with the foreboding exterior, the interior of the cathedral, with its High Gothic nave, is filled with notable works of art, including many plateresque statues. See chapter 4.
- **Catedral de Toledo:** Ranked among the greatest of all Gothic structures, this cathedral was built on the site of an old Arab mosque. A vast pile from the 13th through the 15th centuries, it has an interior filled with masterpieces—notably an immense polychrome retable carved in the flamboyant style and magnificent 15th- and 16th-century choir stalls. In the treasury is a splendid 16th-century silver and gilt monstrance, weighing about 500 pounds. See chapter 4.
- **Real Monasterio de San Lorenzo de El Escorial** (near Madrid): Philip II, who commissioned this monastery in the 1530s, envisioned it as a monastic fortress against the distractions of the secular world. Frightening in its severe dignity, and more awesome than beautiful, it's the world's best example of the religious devotion of Renaissance Spain. This huge granite fortress, the burial place for Spanish kings, houses a wealth of paintings and tapestries—works by everyone from Titian to Velázquez. See chapter 4.
- **Catedral de León:** Filled with more sunlight than any other cathedral in Spain, it was begun in 1250 with a design pierced with 125 stained-glass windows and 57 oculi, the oldest of which date from the 13th century. This architectural achievement, unique in Spain, is stunning but also dangerous. The sheer mass endangers the resistance of the walls. Architects fear that an urgent restoration is needed to strengthen the walls to prevent collapse. The well-preserved cloisters are well worth a visit. See chapter 5.
- **Catedral de Santa María de Burgos:** After its cornerstone was laid in 1221, this cathedral became the beneficiary of creative talent imported from England, Germany, and France. It is the third-largest cathedral in Spain, after Seville and Toledo. Art historians claim that among medieval religious buildings, it has the most diverse spectrum of sculpture in Gothic Spain—so diverse that a special name has been conjured up to describe it: the School of Burgos. El Cid is buried here. See chapter 5.
- **Catedral de Sevilla:** The Christians are not the only occupants of Seville who considered this site holy; an enormous mosque stood here before the Reconquista. To quote the Christians who built the cathedral, they planned one "so immense that everyone, on beholding it, will take us for madmen." They succeeded. After St. Peter's in Rome and St. Paul's in London, the cathedral of this Andalusian capital is the largest in Europe. Among its most important features are the tomb of Columbus, the Patio de los Naranjos (Courtyard of the Orange Trees), the Giralda Tower, and the Capilla Real (Royal Chapel). See chapter 7.
- **Mezquita-Catedral de Córdoba:** In the 1500s, the Christian rulers of Spain tried to gracefully convert one of the largest and most elaborate mosques in the Muslim world, the Mezquita, into a Catholic cathedral. The result, a bizarre amalgam of Gothic and Muslim architecture, is an awesomely proportioned cultural compromise that defies categorization. In its 8th-century heyday, the Mezquita was the crowning Muslim architectural achievement in the West, rivaled only by the Mosque at Mecca. See chapter 7.

- **Catedral de Barcelona:** Completed in 1450, this cathedral grew to represent the spiritual power of the Catalan empire. With its 270-foot facade and flying buttresses and gargoyles, it is the Gothic Quarter's most stunning monument. The interior is in the Catalan Gothic style with slender pillars. See chapter 10.
- **Montserrat** (near Barcelona): Since its inauguration in the 9th century by Benedictine monks, Montserrat has been the preeminent religious shrine of Catalonia and the site of the legendary statue of La Moreneta (the Black Madonna). Its glory years ended abruptly in 1812, when it was sacked by the armies of Napoléon. Today, sitting atop a 4,000-foot mountain, 7 miles long and 3½ miles wide, it is one of the three most important pilgrimage sites in Spain and the most popular day excursion from Barcelona. See chapter 11.
- **Catedral de Santiago de Compostela:** During the Middle Ages, this verdant city on the northwestern tip of Iberia attracted thousands of religious pilgrims, who walked from as far away as Italy through hostile terrain to seek salvation at the tomb of St. James. The cathedral itself shows the architectural influences of nearly 800 years of religious conviction, much of it financed by donations from exhausted pilgrims. Its two most stunning features are its Obradoiro facade, a baroque masterpiece, and its carved Doorway of Glory behind the facade. An enormous silver censor called the *Botafumeiro* swings from the transept during major liturgical ceremonies. Although the original need for this swinging incense ceremony is no longer necessary—to overpower the stench of faithful pilgrims, not known for their excessive bathing habits—tradition lives on. See chapter 17.

7 The Best Vineyards & Wineries

Spanish wines are some of the best in the world and, especially in Spain, they're remarkably affordable. Here's a list of *bodegas* (wineries) that receive visitors—some old favorites as well as some bright newcomers that are quickly gaining international recognition. For more information about the 10 wine regions—and the 39 officially recognized wine-producing *Denominaciones de Origen* scattered across those regions—contact **Wines from Spain,** ℅ the Commercial Office of Spain, 405 Lexington Ave., 44th Floor, New York, NY 10174-0331 (☎ **212/661-4959**).

RIBERA DEL DUERO

Halfway between Madrid and Santander, this region near Burgos is the fastest developing wine district in the country and the beneficiary of massive investments in the last few years. Cold nights, sunny days, the highest altitudes of any wine-producing region in Spain, and a fertile alkaline soil produce flavorful, award-winning wines. Among the noteworthy individual vineyards is:

- **Bodegas Señorío de Nava** (Nava de Roa; ☎ **947-55-00-03**): This is one of the region's best examples of a once-sleepy and now-booming vintner. Merlot and Cabernet Sauvignon grapes are cultivated, as are more obscure local varieties such as *Tinta del país* (also known as *Tempranillo*) and *Garnacha* (or *Grenache,* as it's called across the border in France). Some of the wines bottled here are distributed under the brand name Vega Cubillas.

JEREZ DE LA FRONTERA

This town of 200,000 (most of whom work in the wine trade) is surrounded by a sea of vineyards, which thrive in the hot, chalky soil. Ninety-five percent of the region is planted with the hardy and flavorful *Palomino fino* to produce sherry, a wine fortified by high-alcohol additives, which has long been one of the most beloved products of

Spain. Few other regions contain so many bodegas, any of which can be visited as part of active public relations programs that are the most accommodating in Spain. See chapter 7 for more information, but some of the outstanding choices include:

- **Hijos de Agustín Blazquez** (Jerez de la Frontera; ☎ **956-15-15-00**): Established in 1795, its products have been judged among the finest in the region since the 1980s. Connoisseurs consider this sherry a perfect accompaniment for tapas, for which the town of Jerez is also well known.

- **Emilio Hidalgo** (Jerez de la Frontera; ☎ **956-34-15-97**): This bodega was established in 1896 by a local lawyer, and ever since it has produced exotic forms of sherry snapped up as collectors' items by aficionados everywhere.

- **Antonio Barbadillo** (Sanlúcar de Barrameda; ☎ **956-36-08-94**): This firm controls 70% of the sherry produced in the region around Sanlúcar, a town just 15 miles (25km) north of Jerez. Venerable and respected, it boasts one of the most impressive headquarters of any distillery in the south—a palace originally conceived as a residence for a local bishop. Although established in 1821, it remained a sleepy, small-time player until the 1960s, when production and quality zoomed upward. Some of its wine is distributed in Britain as Harvey's of Bristol.

- **González Byass** (Jerez de la Frontera; ☎ **956-35-70-00**): Flourishing since 1835, this bodega has gained enormous recognition from one of the most famous brand names and the world's best-selling sherry, Tío Pepe. It isn't as picturesque as you might have hoped, since modernization has added some rather bulky concrete buildings to its historic core. Nonetheless, it's one of the most visible names in the industry.

- **Pedro Domecq** (Jerez de la Frontera; ☎ **956-15-15-00**): The oldest of all the large sherry houses was established by an Irishman, Patrick Murphy, in 1730. Its bodega contains casks whose contents were once destined for such sherry lovers as William Pitt, Lord Nelson, and the duke of Wellington. If you visit this sprawling compound, look for *La Mezquita* bodega, whose many-columned interior somewhat resembles the famous mosque in Córdoba.

PENEDÉS

In ancient times, thousands of vessels of wine were shipped from this region of Catalonia, to fuel the orgies of the Roman Empire. Much of the inspiration for the present industry was developed in the 19th century by French vintners, who found the climate and soil similar to those of Bordeaux. The region produces still wines, as well as 98% of Spain's sparkling wine (*cava*), which stands an excellent chance of supplanting French champagne in the minds of celebrants throughout the world. In fact, Freixenet is the largest selling sparkling wine in the world.

- **Cordoníu** (Sant Sadurní d'Anoia; ☎ **93-818-32-32**): With a history dating from the mid-1500s, this vineyard became famous after its owner, Josep Raventós, produced Spain's first version of sparkling wine. During the harvest, more than 2.2 million pounds of grapes, collected from about 1,000 growers, are pressed daily. The company's headquarters, designed around the turn of the century by Puig i Cadafalch, a contemporary of Gaudí, sits above the 19 miles of underground tunnels where the product is aged.

- **Freixenet** (Sant Sadurní d'Anoia; ☎ **93-891-70-00**): Cordoníu's largest and most innovative competitor began in 1889 as a family run wine business that quickly changed its production process to incorporate the radical developments in sparkling cava. Today, although still family owned, it's an awesomely efficient factory pressing vast numbers of grapes, with at least a million cases sold to the United States every year. Award-winning brand names include Cordon Negro Brut and Carta Nevada Brut. The company now operates a vineyard in California, which produces the sparkling wine Gloria Ferrer, which has won awards in the United States.

- **Miguel Torres** (Vilafranca del Penedés; ☎ 93-817-74-00): This winery was established in 1870 by a local son (Jaime Torres), who returned to his native town after making a fortune trading petroleum and oil in Cuba. Today, you can see what was once the world's largest wine vat (132,000 gallons); its interior was used as the site of a banquet held in honor of the Spanish king. Thanks to generations of management by French-trained specialists, it is now one of the most sophisticated and advanced vineyards in the region. Like the others, it's also close enough to Barcelona, the beach resort of Sitges, and the ancient monastery of Montserrat to permit a side trip.

LA RIOJA

Set in the foothills of the Pyrenees, close to the French border, La Rioja turns out wines that compete with the best in the world. Rioja is what most people have in mind when they think of Spanish wines. The region produced millions of gallons during the regime of the ancient Romans, and it boasts quality-control laws promulgated by a local bishop in the 9th century. Here are some of the best vineyards for a visit:

- **Hérederos de Marqués de Riscal** (Elciego; ☎ 941-60-60-00): This vineyard was founded around 1850 by a local entrepreneur who learned wine-growing techniques after a prolonged exile in France. The modern-day enterprise still bases most of its income on the 492 acres acquired by the organization's founding father. Despite several disappointing years between 1975 and 1985, the site is still one of the most respected in the region.

- **Bodegas Riojanas** (Cenicero; ☎ 941-45-40-50): Set on the main street of the wine-growing hamlet of Cenicero, this century-old bodega expanded massively in the 1980s, and upgraded its visitor information program. You'll be received in a mock-feudal tower where you can grasp the nuances of the wine industry.

- **Bodegas Muga** (Haro; ☎ 941-31-18-25): This bodega adheres more to the 19th-century old-world craftsmanship than any of its competitors. The winery contains an assortment of old-fashioned casks made from American or French oak. Production is small, eclectic, and choice.

- **La Rioja Alta** (Haro; ☎ 941-31-03-46): Another bodega in the wine-growing community of Haro, La Rioja Alta is set near the railway station. Founded in 1890, it has all the dank and atmospheric cellars you'd expect, and was graced in 1984 by a visit from Spain's royal family. About 85% of the production at this small but quality outfit is bottled as *reservas* (aged at least 3 years) and *gran reservas* (aged at least 5 years).

GALICIA

This Celtic outpost, set in the northwestern corner of Spain, produces white wines that connoisseurs praise as the perfect accompaniment to local seafood. The marketing name for the product, appropriately, is "El Vino del Mar" ("Sea Wine"), although the *Denominación de Origen* includes the appellations "Rias Baixas" and "Ribeiro." Per capita wine consumption in Galicia is significantly higher than anywhere in Spain, and formerly a majority of the wine produced here was consumed locally. Massive investments during the 1980s changed all that, as you'll note after visits to the region's most viable wineries, such as:

- **Bodega Morgadio** (Albeos-Crecente; ☎ **986-66-61-50**): This vineyard, near Pontevedra, launched the Denominación de Origen "Rias Baixas" in 1984. Four friends whom locals referred to as "madmen" bought 70 acres of land that, with the Albariño grape, they transformed into one of the most respected and award-winning vineyards in the district. Fertilizers for each year's crop comes from the bodega's own flock of sheep. The success of old-fashioned farming methods coupled with state-of-the-art fermentation tanks is a model of entrepreneurial courage in an otherwise economically depressed outpost of Spain.

8 The Best Festivals

- **The Autumn Festival** (Madrid; ☎ **91-580-25-75**): Held in October and November, the Festival de Otoño is the best music festival in Spain, with a lineup that attracts the cream of the European and South American musical communities. The usual roster of chamber music, symphonic pieces, and orchestral works is supplemented by a program of zarzuela (musical comedy), as well as Arabic and Sephardic pieces that were composed during the Middle Ages. See chapter 3.
- **Feria del Caballo** (Jerez de la Frontera; ☎ **95-633-11-50**): Few events show off Spain's equestrian traditions in such flattering light. Costumes are appropriately ornate; riders demonstrate the stern, carefully controlled movements developed during countless medieval battles; and the entire city of Jerez (otherwise famous for its sherry) becomes one enormous riding ring for the presentation of dressage and jumping events. Horse buying and trading is commonplace at this May event; especially coveted is a graceful type of white horse (*Cartujanos*) first bred by the Moors. See chapter 2.
- **Las Hogueras de San Juan** (Alicante; ☎ **96-520-00-00**): Bonfires blaze through the night on June 20 as a celebration of a festival revered by the Celtic pagans and Romans alike—the summer solstice. Stacks of flammable objects, including discarded finery and cardboard replicas of sinners and witches, are set ablaze in a ceremony that reminds some observers of the *auto da fés* during the Inquisition. The bonfire signals the beginning of five days of nightly fireworks and daily parades during which normal business comes virtually to a standstill. See chapter 2.
- **Misteri d'Elx** (Elche; ☎ **96-545-38-31**): Based on the reputed mystical powers of an ancient, black-faced statue of the Virgin, the citizens of Elche have staged a mystery play in the local church every year for more than 6 centuries. The chanting and songs that accompany the plot line are in an archaic dialect that even the Castilians can barely understand. Competition is fierce for seats during the August event, and celebrations precede and follow the play. See chapter 9.
- **Moros y Cristianos** (Alcoy, near Alicante; ☎ **96-520-00-00**): The agonizing, century-long process of evicting the Moors from Iberia is re-created during 2 days of simulated, vaudeville-style fighting between "Moors" and "Christians" every April (dates vary). Circus-style costumes worn by the Moors are as absurdly anachronistic as possible. When the Christians win, a statue of the Virgin is carried proudly through the city as proof of Alcoy's staunchly passionate defense of its role as a bastion of Christianity. See chapter 2.
- **La Tomatina** (Buñol, Valencia): Held every year on the last Wednesday in August, nearly everyone in the town along with thousands from neighboring towns and villages join this 2-hour-long tomato war (11am to 1pm). The local government organizes and sponsors the festival, bringing in four truckloads of

tomatoes totaling more than 88,000 pounds of vegetable artillery. Two local bands provide the music for dancing and singing and plenty of drinking. Portable showers are installed for the participants. See chapter 2.

- **A Rapa das Bestas—The Capture of the Beasts** (San Lorenzo de Sabuceno, Galicia; ☎ 986-85-08-14): In the verdant hills of northwestern Spain, horses graze at will, oblivious to boundary markers and borders. On the first weekend of July, they are rounded up and herded into a corral, in a ritual that evokes the Wild West. Here, each is branded, then released back into the wild after a few days of medical observation. For information, contact the Office of Tourism in Pontevedra. See chapter 2.

9 The Best Paradors

Funded and maintained by the government, Spain's paradors (*paradores* in Spanish) are hostelries that showcase a building or setting of important cultural and historic interest. Some are, admittedly, much older, grander, and more interesting than others. Here are the country's most interesting and unusual.

- **Parador de Ávila** (Ávila; ☎ 920-21-13-40): Built as an enlargement of a 15th-century palace (Palacio de Piedras Albas, also known as the Palacio de Benavides), this parador features gardens that flank the northern fortifications of this well-preserved 11th-century walled city. While only some of the comfortable, airy bedrooms lie within the original palace, it's still the region's most intriguing hotel. In the parador restaurant, try the roast suckling pig, a regional specialty. See chapter 4.
- **Parador de Turismo de Cuenca** (Cuenca; ☎ 969-23-23-20): This 16th-century building, once a Dominican convent, is one of the newer paradors in Spain. Like the medieval houses for which Cuenca is famous, the balconies here jut out over rocky cliffs, overlooking swift-moving rivers below. The sight of the *casas colgadas,* or "suspended houses," is unforgettable. An adjoining restaurant specializes in seasonal wild game. See chapter 4.
- **Parador Nacional de Conde Orgaz** (Toledo; ☎ 925-22-18-50): Though this is a relatively modern building, the architecture subtly evokes much older models. Views from the windows, boasting a faraway glimpse of the city's historic core, evoke the scenes El Greco painted in his *View of Toledo.* A swimming pool comes as a welcome relief in blistering Toledo. Such regional dishes as stewed partridge are featured in the hotel restaurant. See chapter 4.
- **Parador San Marcos** (León; ☎ 987-23-73-00): Originally home to the Order of Santiago—a group of knights charged with protecting pilgrims who journeyed across northern Spain in the 12th century—the building was expanded and embellished into a monastery some 400 years later. These days, set beside the Bernesga River and with a lavishly decorated church on the grounds, it's one of Spain's most deluxe paradors. The public areas are pure medieval grandeur: a dramatic lobby, grand entranceway, huge cast-iron chandelier, and stone staircases. See chapter 5.
- **Parador Turístico de Zamora** (Zamora; ☎ 980-51-44-97): Among the most beautiful and richly decorated paradors in Spain is this onetime Moorish fortress-turned-Renaissance palace. A medieval aura is reflected in the details: armor, coats-of-arms, tapestries, and attractive four-poster beds. A swimming pool enhances the tranquil back garden. Castilian fare such as stuffed roast veal typifies the restaurant's offerings. See chapter 5.

- **Parador de Cáceres** (Cáceres; ☎ 927-21-17-59): Live like royalty at this palace, built in the 1400s on the site of Arab fortifications. The parador lies in the city's old quarter, recently declared a World Heritage Site. The spacious public areas are decorated with soft cream shades and rough-hewn ceiling beams. Venison with goat cheese and roast kid with rosemary are typical of the varied Extremaduran cuisine served in the parador restaurant. See chapter 6.
- **Parador Nacional de Trujillo** (Trujillo; ☎ 927-32-13-50): A parador set in the inviting 16th-century convent of Santa Clara, this was originally built in a combination of medieval and Renaissance styles. The building was transformed into a hotel in 1984. The bedrooms are considerably more lavish than they were during their stint as nuns' cells. The cuisine is the best in town. See chapter 6.
- **Parador Vía de la Plata** (Mérida; ☎ 924-31-38-00): A 16th-century building that was at various times a convent and a prison, this parador once hosted a meeting between the much-hated dictators of Spain (Franco) and Portugal (Salazar) in the 1960s. Mudéjar, Roman, and Visigothic elements adorn the interior in unusual but stunning juxtaposition. The inner courtyard and Mozarabic gardens add a grace note. The kitchen serves the best of the area, including gazpacho, *calderetas extremeñas* (stews), and the famous Almoharin figs. See chapter 6.
- **Parador Castillo de Santa Catalina** (Jaén; ☎ 953-23-00-00): In the 10th century, Muslims built this foreboding fortress on a cliff high above town. After the Reconquista, the Christians added Gothic vaulting and touches of luxury, which remain in place thanks to a renovation by the government. Bedrooms provide sweeping views over Andalusia. A swimming pool is a welcome retreat from the burning sun. Sample such dishes as cold garlic soup and partridge salad in the panoramic restaurant. See chapter 7.
- **Parador de Santillana del Mar** (Santillana del Mar; ☎ 942-81-80-00): This bucolic parador recalls the manor houses that dotted northern Spain's verdant hillsides more than 400 years ago. Composed of thick stone walls and heavy timbers, it's pleasantly isolated and elegantly countrified. An added bonus is its proximity to what has been called "the Sistine Chapel of prehistoric art"—the Caves of Altamira. See chapter 16.
- **Parador El Molino Viejo** (Gijón; ☎ 98-537-05-11): As the name implies, this hotel grew up around the decrepit remains of a *molino,* a cider mill (and the antique presses are still on hand). Close to San Lorenzo Beach, it's the only parador in the northern province of Asturias. The dining room serves up typical Asturian cuisine, including the famous *fabada,* a rich white bean and pork stew. See chapter 16.
- **Parador Nacional Casa del Barón** (Pontevedra; ☎ 986-85-58-00): The building is a 16th-century Renaissance palace built on foundations that are at least 200 years older than that. It's famous as one of Spain's first paradors. Inaugurated in 1955, its success led to the amplification of the parador program. The hotel is still alluring today, with its delightful terrace garden and stately dining room, which serves the fresh fish and seafood for which Galicia is known. See chapter 17.
- **Hostal de Los Reyes Católicos** (Santiago de Compostela; ☎ 981-58-22-00): The best is saved for last—this is one of the most spectacular hotels in Europe. Originally a hospice for wayfaring pilgrims, it boasts a lavish 16th-century facade, four open-air courtyards, and a bedchamber once occupied by Franco. Today the hotel is a virtual museum, with Gothic, Renaissance, and baroque architectural elements. There are four cloisters of immense beauty, elegant public areas, and spectacular bedrooms. See chapter 17.

10 The Best Luxury Hotels

- **Park Hyatt Villa Magna** (Madrid; ☎ **91-587-12-34**): Although it looks like a House of Parliament, this elegant hotel is regal and sedate, giving off the aura of a country estate. Fine furnishings, beautiful linen, and such designer toiletries as fragrant Maja soaps are part of the exquisite guestrooms. The hotel is surrounded by beautiful gardens. See chapter 3.

- **The Ritz** (Madrid; ☎ **91-521-28-57**): Flawless service is the hallmark of Madrid's most distinguished hotel. Antiques, gracious marble bathrooms, and elegant detailing characterize the bedrooms. This Edwardian grand hotel is more relaxed than it once was, the old haughtiness of former management gone with the wind—it long ago rescinded its policy of not allowing movie stars as guests. You still may have to wear a coat and tie, however. See chapter 3.

- **Hotel Alfonso XIII** (Seville; ☎ **95-422-28-50**): This is where the royal family stayed when the Infanta Elena, daughter of Juan Carlos, married in Seville in 1995. Built to house visitors for the Iberoamerican Exposition of 1929, this grand hotel features Moorish-style rooms, with doors opening onto little balconies overlooking a Spanish courtyard with a bubbling fountain and potted palms. Set in front of the city's fabled Alcázar, the Alfonso XIII is one of the most legendary hotels of Spain. See chapter 7.

- **La Bobadilla** (Loja; ☎ **958-32-18-61**): The most luxurious retreat in the south of Spain, this secluded oasis lies in the foothills of the Sierra Nevada, an hour's drive northeast of Málaga. Whitewashed *casas* (small individual villas) cluster around a tower and a church. Each individually designed casa is complete with a roof terrace and balcony overlooking olive groves. Guests live in luxury within the private compound of 1,750 acres. See chapter 8.

- **Marbella Club** (Marbella; ☎ **95-282-22-11**): Built during the "golden age" of the Costa del Sol (the 1950s), this bastion of chic is composed of ecologically conscious clusters of garden pavilions, bungalows, and small-scale annexes. The luxurious rooms are modeled after pages of a European design magazine. It has many competitors but remains an elite retreat. See chapter 8.

- **Puente Romano** (Marbella; ☎ **95-282-09-00**): On manicured and landscaped grounds facing the beach, Puente Romano evokes a highly stylized Andalusian village. Exotic bird life flutters its way through the lush gardens, planted with banana trees and other vegetation. Villas are spacious and beautifully furnished, with marble floors and bathrooms, big mirrors, and tasteful wood furnishings. In the summer, flamenco dancers entertain here. See chapter 8.

- **Hotel Ritz** (Barcelona; ☎ **93-318-52-00**): A 1919 *grand luxe* hotel formerly known as the Palace, this is one of the finest hotels in Spain, if not all of Europe. Guests are enveloped in dazzling elegance, with all the gilt, marble, and fresh flowers they would ever want. Classic belle epoque detailing extends to the plush guest quarters, many of which have high, ornate ceilings and gold bathroom fixtures. See chapter 10.

- **Hotel María Cristina** (San Sebastián; ☎ **943-42-49-00**): One of the country's great belle epoque treasures, this old-world seafront hotel has sheltered discriminating guests since 1912. Oriental rugs, antiques, potted palms, high ceilings, formal lounges, marble pillars, and marble floors show off a turn-of-the-century glamour. The bedrooms are traditional with wood furnishings and tasteful pastel fabrics. Nothing else in the Basque country quite measures up to this old charmer. See chapter 15.

- **La Residencia** (Deià, Majorca; ☎ 971-63-90-11): Set amid 30 acres of citrus and olive groves, this tranquil hotel was converted from two Renaissance-era manor houses. Jasmine-scented terraces open onto panoramic views of the surrounding villages and mountains. Pampered guests are served a creative cuisine that features local produce. Leisure facilities include a swimming pool fed by mountain spring water. Many of the bedrooms have regal four-poster beds. It's a haven from the rest of the overcrowded Majorca. See chapter 18.

11 The Best Hotel Bargains

- **Hostal del Cardenal** (Toledo; ☎ 925-22-49-00): The summer residence of Toledo's 18th-century Cardinal Lorenzano, built into the walls of the old city next to the Bisagra Gate, just happens to be Toledo's best restaurant. But the setting—rose gardens, cascading vines, and Moorish fountains—makes it an ideal place to stay as well. Spanish furniture and a scattering of antiques recapture the aura of old Castile. See chapter 4.
- **Posada de San José** (Cuenca; ☎ 969-21-13-00): This hotel, located in the oldest part of medieval Cuenca, is a remarkable bargain. In the 17th century it was a convent, but the rooms have been converted to receive guests, and are now decorated in a rustic style. The posada sits atop a cliff, overlooking the forbidding depths of a gorge and the river below; views are superb. See chapter 4.
- **Hostería Real de Zamora** (Zamora; ☎ 980-53-45-45): Once the dreaded headquarters of the local Spanish Inquisition, today this hotel offers a far friendlier welcome. Hotel guests enjoy coffee on the patio and the pleasure of a garden planted along the city's medieval fortifications. Imagine if these 15th-century walls could talk. See chapter 5.
- **Hotel Doña María** (Seville; ☎ 95-422-49-90): Near the fabled cathedral, this hotel boasts a rooftop terrace with unmatched views of the Andalusian capital. A private villa that dates from the 1840s, the Doña María has a swimming pool ringed with garden-style lattices and antique wrought-iron railings. Bedrooms are uniquely designed with tasteful Iberian antiques. See chapter 7.
- **Hotel Reina Victoria** (Ronda; ☎ 95-287-12-40): This country-style hotel is best known as the place where the German poet Rainer Maria Rilke wrote *The Spanish Trilogy*. Its terrace, perched on a dramatic precipice, offers commanding views of the countryside. An Englishman built this Victorian charmer in 1906 to honor his recently deceased monarch, Queen Victoria. See chapter 7.
- **Hotel América** (Granada; ☎ 958-22-74-71): This onetime private villa, located within the walls of the Alhambra, is one of the most popular small hotels in Granada. Its cozy bedrooms are filled with reproductions of Andalusian antiques. Plants cascade down the white plaster walls the ornate grillwork on the shady patio. Good-tasting, inexpensive meals are served in the hotel restaurant. See chapter 7.
- **Hotel Mijas** (Mijas; ☎ 95-248-58-00): This is the most charming of affordable hotels along the Costa del Sol. It's designed in typical Andalusian style, with flowering terraces, wrought-iron accents, and sun-flooded bedrooms. Though built in the 1970s, it blends in perfectly with the region's gleaming white buildings. See chapter 8.
- **Huerto del Cura** (Elche; ☎ 96-545-80-40): From your bedroom you'll have a panoramic view of Priest's Grove, a formidable date-palm forest. Between Alicante and Murcia, this is one of the choice addresses in the south of Spain. Bedrooms are handsomely maintained and beautifully furnished, and a swimming

pool separates the palm grove from the rooms. The regional cuisine in the hotel's restaurant is excellent. See chapter 9.

- **Mesón Castilla** (Barcelona; ☎ 93-318-21-82): This two-star charmer with an art nouveau facade is right in the heart of Barcelona. It is well maintained and well managed, with prices that are blessedly easy on the wallet. Comfortable rooms often come with large terraces. Only breakfast is served, but there are many nearby taverns with excellent food. See chapter 10.

- **Hotel Pampinot** (Fuenterrabía; ☎ 943-64-06-00): The Infanta María Teresa stayed at this 16th-century aristocratic mansion on a journey to France for her eventual marriage to the Sun King, Louis XIV. Now a stately hotel, it's on a quiet side street in this Basque seaside resort, near the French border. Behind a richly textured stone facade and Renaissance detailing are bedrooms furnished with both antiques and reproductions. See chapter 15.

12 The Best Restaurants

- **El Amparo** (Madrid; ☎ 91-431-64-56): In the old days of Franco, gastronomes flocked to Jockey or Horcher. Today their savvy sons and daughters head to El Amparo, the trendiest of Madrid's gourmet restaurants. It serves mainly haute Basque cuisine, against a backdrop of cosmopolitan glamour. Patrons sample everything from cold marinated salmon with a tomato sorbet to ravioli stuffed with seafood. See chapter 3.

- **Sobrino de Botín** (Madrid; ☎ 91-366-42-17): Since 1725, this restaurant has been celebrated for its roast suckling pig, prepared in a 200-year-old tile oven. Hemingway even mentioned it in *The Sun Also Rises*. The roast Segovian lamb is equally delectable. There is little subtlety of flavor here—only food prepared by time-tested recipes that have appealed to kings as well as Castilian peasants. The aromas waft clear across Madrid's old town. See chapter 3.

- **Mesón de Cándido** (Segovia; ☎ 921-42-59-11): Gastronomes from around the country flock to this 19th-century Spanish inn, "The House of Candido," for one dish: roast suckling pig, acclaimed the best in Spain (even by Hemingway, who might otherwise be seen at Botín in Madrid). In Spanish it's called *cochinillo asado,* and it's delectable—prepared according to a century-old recipe. Here's a secret: The *cordero asado,* or roast baby lamb, is equally flavorful. See chapter 4.

- **Mesón Casa Colgadas** (Cuenca; ☎ 969-22-35-09): Without a doubt, this is the most spectacularly situated restaurant in Spain—a "hanging house" suspended over a precarious precipice. The cookery is Spanish and international, with an emphasis on regional ingredients. The dishes can be ingenious, but the culinary repertoire usually reflects proven classics that might have pleased your grandparents. See chapter 4.

- **Chez Victor** (Salamanca; ☎ 923-21-31-23): In the historic center of this university town, this is the most glamorous continental restaurant around. Chef Victoriano Salvador gives customers terrific value for their pesetas with his imaginative, oft-renewed menus. The freshly prepared fish and his traditional version of roast lamb are especially tempting. Regionally rooted but modern in outlook, Salvador has a finely honed technique and isn't afraid to be inventive on occasion. See chapter 5.

- **El Caballo Rojo** (Córdoba; ☎ 957-47-53-75): Begin your evening with a sherry in the popular bar, followed by a visit to the traditional dining room. Not only Andalusian dishes are served here; some classics are based on ancient Sephardic and Mozarabic specialties. Most guests begin with a soothing gazpacho and wash everything down with sangría. Finish off the meal with one of the homemade ice creams—we recommend pistachio. See chapter 7.

- **El Plat** (Valencia; ☎ 96-374-12-54): No Spanish dish is more famous than paella, and Valencia is where this culinary delight originated. Locals maintain that it tastes better on its home turf than anywhere else in the world, and we concur. In Valencia, El Plat is known as "El Rey del Arroz" (The Rice King). Each day of the week chefs prepare a different version of this succulent dish, often studded with shellfish. See chapter 9.

- **Jaume de Provença** (Barcelona; ☎ 93-430-00-29): The Catalan capital has more great restaurants than even Madrid. At the western end of the Eixample district, this Catalan/French restaurant is the domain of one of the city's most talented chefs, Jaume Bargués. He serves modern interpretations of traditional Catalan and southern French cuisine—such dishes as pig's trotters with plums and truffles or crabmeat lasagna. His personal cooking repertoire is distinctive, and he has been known to create new taste sensations when he's feeling experimental. See chapter 10.

- **Botafumeiro** (Barcelona; ☎ 93-218-42-30): The city's finest seafood is prepared here, in a glistening, modern kitchen visible from the dining room. The King of Spain is a frequent patron, enjoying paellas, *zarzuelas,* or any of the 100 or so ultrafresh seafood dishes. The chef's treatment of the fish is the most intelligent and subtle in town—but don't expect such quality to come cheap. See chapter 10.

- **Los Caracoles** (Barcelona; ☎ 93-302-31-85): Locals say this restaurant is so old it was around to welcome the Roman armies. Actually it's been feeding hungry Catalans only since 1835. But any restaurant that has thrived that long must be doing something right. These days, a young, sophisticated crowd of food lovers has discovered the full array of hearty Catalan and Spanish dishes served here. The namesake snails are always worth a try. See chapter 10.

- **Empordá** (Figueres; ☎ 972-50-05-62): Although ordinary on the outside, this hotel restaurant is one of the finest on the Costa Brava. It was a favorite of Salvador Dalí, who once wrote his own cookbook. Haute Catalan cuisine is the specialty—everything from duck foie gras with Armagnac to supreme of sea bass with flan. The flavors are refined yet definite. See chapter 12.

- **Akelare** (San Sebastián; ☎ 943-21-20-52): The Basques are renowned for their cooking, and the owner/chef of this San Sebastián restaurant, Pedro Sabijana, pioneered the school of *nueva cocina vasco* (modern Basque cuisine). His restaurant has attracted gourmets from around Europe. Sabijana transforms such seemingly simple dishes as fish cooked on a griddle with garlic and parsley into something magical. No other eatery in northern Spain comes close to equaling the superb viands dispensed here. There are those (and we are among them) who consider Subijana the best chef in Spain. See chapter 15.

Planning a Trip to Spain 2

In this chapter, you'll find everything you need to plan your trip, from a sketch of Spain's various regions to tips on when to go and how to get the best airfare.

1 The Regions in Brief

Three times the size of Illinois, with a population of approximately 40 million, Spain faces the Atlantic Ocean and the Bay of Biscay to the north and the Mediterranean Sea to the south and east. Portugal borders on the west, whereas the Pyrenees separate Spain from France and the rest of Europe. The southern coastline is only a few sea miles from the north coast of Africa. It's difficult to generalize about Spain because it is composed of so many regions—50 provinces in all—each with its own physical makeup, history, and culture. The country's topography divides it into many regions: The Cantabrian mountains in the north, those of Cuenca in the east, and the Sierra Morena in the south mark off a high central tableland that itself is cut across by other hills.

MADRID & ENVIRONS   Set on a high and arid plateau near the geographic center of Iberia, Madrid was created by royal decree in the 1600s, long after the much older kingdoms of León, Navarre, Aragón, and Catalonia, and long after the final Moor was ousted by Catholic armies. Since its birth, all roads within Spain have radiated outward from its precincts, and as the country's most important airline and railway hub, it's likely to be your point of arrival (although many international flights and European trains now arrive in Barcelona as well).

Despite the city's increasingly unpleasant urban sprawl, its paralyzing traffic jams, and skyrocketing prices, Madrid remains one of Europe's great cities. Take in the Prado, the Thyssen-Bornemisza Museum, and perhaps the Royal Palace. Walk through historic neighborhoods around the Plaza Mayor (though beware of muggers). Devote time to one of the city's greatest pastimes, a round of tapas tasting.

Plan on at least 2 days to explore the city and another 3 for trips to the attractions beyond the capital. Perhaps as important as a visit to Madrid is a day trip to the imperial city of **Toledo,** which brims with monuments and paintings by El Greco and is home to one of Spain's greatest cathedrals. Other worthy excursions include a view of the Roman aqueduct at **Segovia,** tours through such monuments as

El Escorial, and a visit to the "hanging village" of **Cuenca,** site of a world-class museum of modern art.

OLD CASTILE & LEÓN   The proud kingdoms of Castile and León in north-central Iberia are part of the core from which modern Spain developed. Some of their greatest cathedrals and monuments were erected when each was staunchly independent. But León's annexation by Queen Isabella of Castile in 1474 (5 years after her politically advantageous but unhappy marriage to Ferdinand of Aragón) irrevocably linked the two regions.

Even Spaniards are sometimes confused about the terms *Old Castile* (see chapter 5) and *New Castile,* a modern linguistic and governmental concept that includes a territory much larger than the medieval entity known by Isabella and her subjects. Though it's easy to take a train to and from Madrid, we don't recommend that you try to see the regions' highlights as day trips from Madrid; it's better to treat them as overnight destinations in their own right.

Highlights include **Burgos** (the ancient "cradle" of Castile), **Salamanca** (a medieval Castilian university town), and **León,** capital on the northern plains of the district bearing its name and site of one of the most unusual cathedrals in Iberia. If time remains, consider an overnight at the extraordinary parador in **Ciudad Rodrigo,** as well as trips to **Zamora,** known for its stunning Romanesque churches, and **Valladolid.**

EXTREMADURA   Far from the mainstream of urbanized Spain, fascinating Extremadura lives within a time warp where hints of the Middle Ages and ancient Rome crop up unexpectedly beside sun-baked highways. Many conquistadors who pillaged the Indian civilizations of the New World came from this hard, granite land.

Be prepared for hot, arid landscapes and smoking diesel trucks carrying heavy loads across this once-turbulent corridor between Madrid and Lisbon. You can see a lot in about 2 days, stopping off at such sites as **Guadalupe,** whose Mudéjar monastery revolves around the medieval cult of the Dark (or Black) Virgin, and **Trujillo,** where many of the monuments were built with gold sent home by native sons like Pizarro, Peru's conqueror. **Cáceres** is a beautiful, fortified city with one foot planted firmly in the Middle Ages, while **Zafra** displays greater evidence of the Moorish occupation than anywhere in Spain outside of Andalusia.

ANDALUSIA   In A.D. 711 Muslim armies swept into Iberia from strongholds in what is now Morocco. Since then, Spain's southernmost district has been enmeshed in the mores, art, and architecture of the Muslim world. During the 900s, *Andalucía* blossomed into a sophisticated society—advanced in philosophy, mathematics, and trading—that far surpassed a feudal Europe still trapped in the Dark Ages. Moorish domination ended completely in 1492, when Granada was captured by the armies of Isabella and Ferdinand, but even today, the region offers echoes of this Muslim occupation. Andalusia is an arid district that, despite such economically rejuvenating events as Seville's Expo, isn't highly prosperous.

The major cities of Andalusia deserve at least a week, with overnights in **Seville** (hometown of Carmen, Don Giovanni, and the barber); **Córdoba,** site of the Mezquita, one of history's most versatile religious edifices; and **Cádiz,** a venerable seaport where thousands of ships embarked on their colonization of the New World. Perhaps greatest of all is **Granada,** a town of such impressive artistry that it inspired many of the works by the 20th-century romantic poet Federico García Lorca.

THE COSTA DEL SOL   The Costa del Sol sprawls across the southernmost edge of Spain between Algeciras to the west—a few miles from the rocky heights of British-controlled Gibraltar—and Almería to the east. Think traffic jams, suntan oil, sun-bleached high-rises, and almost-naked flesh. The beaches here are some of the best in Europe, but this can be an overly crowded, crime-filled region.

Unless you travel by car or rail from Madrid, chances are that you'll arrive by plane via **Málaga,** the district's most historic city. The coast's largest resort town is distinctive, Renaissance-era **Marbella,** the centerpiece of 17 miles of beaches. Today it's a chic hangout for the tanned and wealthy. **Nerja** is just one of the booming resorts that has kept an out-of-the-way, fishing-village feel. The most overcrowded and action-packed resort is **Torremolinos.** One modern development that has managed to remain distinctive is **Puerto Banús,** a neo-Moorish village that curves around a sheltered marina, where the wintering rich dock their yachts.

VALENCIA & THE COSTA BLANCA **Valencia,** the third-largest city in Spain, is rarely visited by foreign tourists because of the heavy industry that surrounds its inner core. More alluring are such resorts as **Alicante** and **Benidorm** or the medieval town of **Elche** (where some of the world's most famous ancient Roman statues were discovered). Unless you opt to skip Valencia completely, plan to see the city's cathedral, the exterior of its Palacio de la Generalidad, and as many of its three important museums as you can fit into a 1-day trip. For the Costa Blanca, allow as much or as little time as you want to spend on the beach.

BARCELONA & CATALONIA Its history is older than that of its rival, Madrid, and its streets filled with the Gothic and medieval buildings that Spain's relatively newer capital lacks. During the 1200s, **Barcelona** rivaled the trading prowess of such cities as Genoa and Pisa, and it became the Spanish city that most resembled other great cities of Europe. Allow yourself at least 3 days to explore the city, with stops at the Picasso Museum, the Joan Miró foundation, the Gothic quarter, and a crowning triumph of early *modernista* architecture, the Eixample District, where you'll find many of Antoni Gaudí's signature works. Make time for a stroll along Les Rambles, one of the most delightful outdoor promenades in Spain.

Don't overlook Catalonia's other attractions, all within easy reach of Barcelona. A short drive to the south is **Sitges,** a stylish beach resort that caters to a diverse clientele ranging from freewheeling nudists and gay party crowds to fun-seeking families. Other destinations are **Tarragona,** one of ancient Rome's district capitals, and **Montserrat,** the "Serrated Mountain," site of one of Europe's best-preserved medieval monasteries.

THE COSTA BRAVA It's Spain's other Riviera, a region with a deep sense of medieval history and a topography that's rockier and more interesting than that of the Costa del Sol. The "Wild Coast" stretches from the resort of Blanes, just north of Barcelona, along 95 miles (153km) of dangerously winding cliff-top roads that bypass peninsulas and sheltered coves on their way to the French border. Despite hordes of Spanish and Northern European midsummer visitors, the Costa Brava resorts still manage to feel less congested and less spoiled than those along the Costa del Sol.

Sun worshippers usually head for the twin beachfront resorts of **Lloret de Mar** and **Tossa de Mar.** Travelers interested in the history of 20th-century painting go to **Figueres;** Salvador Dalí was born here in 1904, and a controversial and bizarre museum of his design is devoted exclusively to his surrealist works.

ARAGÓN Except for Aragón's association with Ferdinand, the unsavory, often unethical husband of Queen Isabella, few foreign visitors ever thought much about this northeastern quadrant of Iberia. A land of ancient references, noteworthy Mudéjar architecture, and high altitudes that guarantee cool midsummer temperatures, it's also one of the foremost bull-breeding regions of Spain.

Aragón is best visited as a stopover between Barcelona and Madrid. Stay overnight in **Zaragoza,** the district capital, and take a series of day trips to **Tarazona** ("The Toledo of Aragón"), **Calatayud,** and **Daroca,** all important Moorish and Roman military outposts; and **Nuévalos/Piedra,** the site of an extraordinary riverside hotel built in 1194 as a Cistercian monastery. Also worth a trip is **Sos del Rey Católico,** the rocky, relatively unspoiled village where Ferdinand was born.

NAVARRE & LA RIOJA   This strategic province, one of the four original Christian kingdoms in Iberia, shares a border, and numerous historical references, with France. One of France's Renaissance kings, Henri IV "de Navarre," was linked to the province's royal family. Many Navarre customs, and some of its local dialect, reflect the influence of its passionately politicized neighbors, the Basques. Celtic pagans, Romans, Christians, and Arabs have all left architectural reminders of their presence. The province contains nine points where traffic is funneled into and out of Spain, so if you're driving or riding the train, say, from Paris to Madrid, chances are you'll get a fast overview of Navarre. The province's best-known destination is **Pamplona,** the district capital and annual host for the bull-running Fiesta de San Fermín.

One small corner of Navarre is comprised of **La Rioja,** the smallest *autonomía* (semiautonomous province) of Spain. Irrigated by the Ebro River, it produces some of the country's finest wines. If wine tasting appeals to you, head for the town of **Haro,** and drop in on several bodegas (wineries) to sample local vintages.

THE BASQUE COUNTRY   This is the native land of Europe's oldest traceable ethnic group. The Basque people have been more heavily persecuted than any other within Spain, by Madrid regimes determined to shoehorn their unusual language and culture into that of mainstream Spain. The region of rolling peaks and fertile, sunny valleys hugs the Atlantic coast adjacent to the French border. It also boasts the best regional cuisine in Spain.

Unless you want to spend more time relaxing on the beach, allow 3 leisurely days for this unusual district. Visit **San Sebastián** (Donostia) for its international glamour, **Fuenterrabía** (Hondarribía) for its medieval history, **Guernica** for a sobering reminder of past atrocity evoked by Picasso's famous painting, and Lekeitio for its simple fishing-village charm.

CANTABRIA & ASTURIAS   Positioned on Iberia's north-central coastline, these are the most verdant regions of Spain. In the Middle Ages pilgrims passed through here on their way to **Santiago de Compostela**—a legacy evident from the wealth of Romanesque churches and abbeys in the vicinity. Come for beaches that are rainier, but much less crowded, than those along Spain's southern coasts.

Enjoy such beach resorts as **El Sardinero** and **Laredo,** as well as the rugged beauty of **Los Picos de Europa,** a dramatic mountain range that is home to rich colonies of wildlife. Sites of interest include the **Caves of Altamira** (called "the Sistine Chapel of prehistoric art," though admission is strictly regulated), the pre-Romanesque town of **Oviedo,** and the architecturally important old quarter of **Gijón.** The region's largest city, **Santander,** lies amid a maze of peninsulas and estuaries favored by boaters. In summer it becomes a major beach resort, although **San Sebastián** is more fashionable.

GALICIA   A true Celtic outpost in northwestern Iberia, Galicia's landscape is often compared to rainy, windswept Ireland. Known for a spectacular, dramatic coastline, the region is wild and relatively underpopulated.

Spend at least 2 days here, enjoying some of the most scenic drives in Iberia. Stop at such historic and religious sites as Santiago de Compostela. An ancient Roman outpost, **Lugo,** also merits a visit. Perhaps the region's greatest city is **La Coruña,** the point of embarkation for Spain's tragic Armada, sunk by the English army on its way to invade Britain in the late l6th century.

THE BALEARIC ISLANDS   "Discovered" by English Romantics in the early 19th century, and long known as a strategic naval outpost in the western Mediterranean, these islands are sunny, subtropical, mountainous, and more verdant than the Costa del Sol. They have their pockets of style and posh, although **Majorca** and **Ibiza** are overrun in summer, especially by British and German travelers on package tours. Ibiza also attracts a large gay crowd. **Minorca** is more fashionable, although more inconvenient to get to.

2 Visitor Information, Entry Requirements & Customs

VISITOR INFORMATION

The official Web site for the Spanish tourist office is **www.okspain.org.** See the online directory at the end of this book for tips on where to find lots of other help and information on the Internet.

IN THE UNITED STATES   For information before you go, contact the **Tourist Office of Spain,** 666 Fifth Ave., 35th Floor, New York, NY 10103 (☎ 212/265-8822), which can provide sightseeing information, calendars of events, train and ferry schedules, maps, and much, much more. Elsewhere in the United States, branches of the Tourist Office of Spain are located at 8383 Wilshire Blvd., Suite 960, Beverly Hills, CA 90211 (☎ 213/658-7188); 845 N. Michigan Ave., Suite 915 E., Chicago, IL 60611 (☎ 312/642-1992); and 1221 Brickell Ave., Suite 1850, Miami, FL 33131 (☎ 305/358-1992).

IN CANADA   Contact the **Tourist Office of Spain,** 102 Bloor St. W., 34th Floor, Toronto, ON M5S 1M9 (☎ 416/961-3131).

IN GREAT BRITAIN   Contact the **Spanish Tourist Office,** 57–58 St. James's St., London SW1A 1LD (☎ 0171/499-0901).

ENTRY REQUIREMENTS

Visas are not needed by U.S., Canadian, Irish, Australian, New Zealand, or British citizens for visits of less than 3 months. You do need a valid passport unless you're a citizen of another EU country (in which case you only need an identity card, although we always recommend that you carry a passport anyway).

Safeguard your passport in an inconspicuous, inaccessible place like a money belt. If you lose it, visit the nearest consulate of your native country as soon as possible for a replacement.

CUSTOMS

You can take into Spain most personal effects and the following items duty free: two still cameras and 10 rolls of film per camera, tobacco for personal use, one liter each of liquor and wine, a Walkman or portable CD player, a tape recorder, a laptop, a bicycle, sports equipment, fishing gear, and two hunting weapons with 100 cartridges each.

WHAT YOU CAN BRING HOME TO THE U.S.   Returning U.S. citizens who have been away for 48 hours or more are allowed to bring back, once every 30 days, $400 worth of merchandise duty-free. You'll be charged a flat rate of 10% duty on the next $1,000 worth of purchases. Be sure to have your receipts handy. On gifts, the duty-free limit is $100. You cannot bring fresh foodstuffs into the United States; tinned foods, however, are allowed. For more information, contact the **U.S. Customs Service,** 1301 Constitution Ave. (P.O. Box 7407), Washington, DC 20044 (☎ **202/ 927-6724**) and request the free pamphlet *Know Before You Go.* It's also available on the Web at **www.customs.ustreas.gov/travel/kbygo.htm**.

WHAT YOU CAN BRING HOME TO THE U.K.   Citizens of the United Kingdom who are returning from a European Community (EC) country will go through a separate Customs Exit (called the "Blue Exit") especially for EC travelers. In essence, there is no limit on what you can bring back from an EC country, as long as the items are for personal use (this includes gifts), and you have already paid the necessary duty and tax. However, customs law sets out guidance levels. If you bring in more than these levels, you may be asked to prove that the goods are for your own use. Guidance levels on goods bought in the EC for your own use are 800 cigarettes, 200 cigars, 1 kilogram smoking tobacco, 10 liters of spirits, 90 liters of wine (of this not more than 60 liters can be sparkling wine), and 110 liters of beer. For more information, contact **HM Customs & Excise,** Passenger Enquiry Point, 2nd Floor Wayfarer House, Great South West Road, Feltham, Middlesex, TW14 8NP (☎ **0181/ 910-3744;** from outside the U.K. 44/181-910-3744), or consult their Web site at www.open.gov.uk.

WHAT YOU CAN BRING HOME TO CANADA   For a clear summary of Canadian rules, write for the booklet *I Declare,* issued by **Revenue Canada,** 2265 St. Laurent Blvd., Ottawa K1G 4KE (☎ **613/993-0534**). Canada allows its citizens a $500 exemption, and you're allowed to bring back duty-free 200 cigarettes, 2.2 pounds of tobacco, 40 imperial ounces of liquor, and 50 cigars. In addition, you're allowed to mail gifts to Canada from abroad at the rate of Can$60 a day, provided they're unsolicited and don't contain alcohol or tobacco (write on the package "Unsolicited gift, under $60 value"). All valuables should be declared on the Y-38 form before departure from Canada, including serial numbers of valuables you already own, such as expensive foreign cameras. *Note:* The $500 exemption can only be used once a year and only after an absence of 7 days.

WHAT YOU CAN BRING HOME TO AUSTRALIA   The duty-free allowance in Australia is A$400 or, for those under 18, A$200. Personal property mailed back from England should be marked "Australian goods returned" to avoid payment of duty. Upon returning to Australia, citizens can bring in 250 cigarettes or 250 grams of loose tobacco, and 1,125 milliliters of alcohol. If you're returning with valuable goods you already own, such as foreign-made cameras, you should file form B263. A helpful brochure, available from Australian consulates or Customs offices, is *Know Before You Go.* For more information, contact **Australian Customs Services,** GPO Box 8, Sydney NSW 2001 (☎ **02/9213-2000**).

WHAT YOU CAN BRING HOME TO NEW ZEALAND   The duty-free allowance for New Zealand is NZ$700. Citizens over 17 can bring in 200 cigarettes, or 50 cigars, or 250 grams of tobacco (or a mixture of all three if their combined weight doesn't exceed 250 grams); plus 4.5 liters of wine and beer, or 1.125 liters of liquor. New Zealand currency does not carry import or export restrictions. Fill out a certificate of export, listing the valuables you are taking out of the country; that way, you can bring them back without paying duty. Most questions are answered in a free pamphlet available at New Zealand consulates and Customs offices: *New Zealand Customs Guide for Travellers, Notice no. 4.* For more information, contact **New Zealand Customs,** 50 Anzac Ave., P.O. Box 29, Auckland (☎ **09/359-6655**).

3 Money

CASH/CURRENCY

The basic unit of Spanish currency is the **peseta** (abbreviated pta.), currently worth about $7/10$ of a cent in U.S. currency. One dollar was worth about 150 pesetas at press time. Coins come in 1, 5, 25, 50, 100, 200, and 500 pesetas. Notes are issued in 500, 1,000, 5,000, and 10,000 pesetas.

All world currencies fluctuate, so you should be aware that the amounts appearing in this book are not exact. Currency conversions are presented only to give you a rough idea of the price you'll pay in U.S. dollars. There is no way to predict exactly what the rate of exchange will be when you visit Spain. Check the newspaper or ask at your bank for last-minute quotations.

Be advised that rates of exchange vary, depending on where you convert your money. In general, you'll get the best exchange rate by using your credit card or withdrawing cash from an ATM machine. Banks also offer competitive rates, but keep in mind they charge a commission for cashing traveler's checks. You'll get the worst rates of exchange at your hotel, as well as at point-of-entry sites like an airport or train station.

THE EURO

The euro, the new single European currency, became the official currency of Spain and 10 other countries on January 1, 1999, but not in the form of cash. (There are still no euro banknotes or coins in circulation—payment in euros can only be made by check, credit card, or some other bank-related system.)

The Spanish peseta will remain the only currency in France for cash transactions until December 21, 2001, when more and more businesses will start posting their prices in euros alongside those in pesetas, which will continue to exist for a while longer. Over a maximum 6-month transition period, peseta banknotes will be withdrawn from circulation.

The symbol of the euro is a stylized E, which actually looks like an uppercase C with a horizontal double bar through the middle €; its official abbreviation is EUR.

Although at this time, very few, if any, Spanish hotel and restaurant bills are actually paid in euros, there will be an increasing emphasis on the new pan-European currency during the lifetime of this edition.

ATM NETWORKS

PLUS, Cirrus, and other networks connecting automated-teller machines operate in Spain. If your bank card has been programmed with a PIN (personal identification number), it is likely that you can use your card at ATMs abroad to withdraw money directly from your home bank account. Check with your bank to see if your PIN code must be reprogrammed for usage in Spain. Before leaving, always determine the frequency limits for withdrawals and what fees, if any, your bank will assess. For **Cirrus** locations abroad, call ☎ **800/424-7787;** also, Cirrus ATM locations in selected cities are available on MasterCard's Internet site (www.mastercard.com). For **PLUS** usage abroad, contact your local bank or check Visa's page on the World Wide Web (www.visa.com).

TRAVELER'S CHECKS

Traveler's checks are something of an anachronism from the days before the ATM made cash accessible at any time. These days, traveler's checks seem less necessary, but some people still prefer the security of knowing they can recover their money if it's stolen.

The Spanish Peseta

For American Readers   At this writing, $1 = approximately 150 pesetas (or 1 peseta = $^7/_{10}$ of 1 U.S. cent). This was the rate of exchange used to calculate the dollar equivalents given throughout this edition.

For British Readers   At this writing, £1 = approximately 250 pesetas (or 1 peseta = $^4/_{10}$ of 1 pence). This was the rate of exchange used to calculate the pound values in the table below.

The Euro   At this writing, one euro equaled approximately 166 pesetas, a rate that is likely to remain constant throughout the life of this edition. Although it wasn't in particularly widespread use at the time of the compilation of this chart, look for an increasing emphasis on the euro and its applicability to daily life within Spain.

Note: Because the exchange rate fluctuates from time to time according to a complicated roster of political and economic factors, this table should be used only as a general guide.

Peseta	U.S.$	U.K.£	Euro	Peseta	U.S.$	U.K.£	Euro
50	0.34	0.20	0.30	20,000	134.00	80.00	120.00
100	0.67	0.40	0.60	25,000	167.50	100.00	150.00
300	2.01	1.20	1.80	30,000	201.00	120.00	180.00
500	3.35	2.00	3.00	35,000	234.50	140.00	210.00
700	4.69	2.80	4.20	40,000	268.00	160.00	240.00
1,000	6.70	4.00	6.00	45,000	301.50	180.00	270.00
1,500	10.05	6.00	9.00	50,000	335.00	200.00	300.00
2,000	13.40	8.00	12.00	100,000	670.00	400.00	600.00
3,000	20.10	12.00	18.00	125,000	837.50	500.00	750.00
4,000	26.80	16.00	24.00	150,000	1005.00	600.00	900.00
5,000	33.50	20.00	30.00	200,000	1340.00	800.00	1200.00
7,500	50.25	30.00	45.00	250,000	1675.00	1000.00	1500.00
10,000	67.00	40.00	60.00	500,000	3350.00	2000.00	3000.00
15,000	100.50	60.00	90.00	1,000,000	6700.00	4000.00	6000.00

You can get traveler's checks at almost any bank. American Express offers denominations of $10, $20, $50, $100, $500, and $1,000. You'll pay a service charge ranging from 1% to 4%. You can also get **American Express traveler's checks** over the phone by calling ☎ 800/221-7282; by using this number, Amex gold and platinum card-holders are exempt from the 1% fee. AAA members can obtain checks without a fee at most AAA offices.

Visa offers traveler's checks at Citibank locations nationwide, as well as several other banks. The service charge ranges between 1.5% and 2%; checks come in denominations of $20, $50, $100, $500, and $1,000. **MasterCard** also offers traveler's checks. Call ☎ 800/223-9920 for a location near you.

If you opt to carry traveler's checks, be sure to keep a record of their serial numbers, separately from the checks of course, so you're ensured a refund in just such an emergency.

CREDIT CARDS

Credit cards are invaluable when traveling. They are a safe way to carry money and provide a convenient record of all your expenses. You can also withdraw cash advances from your credit cards at any bank (though you'll start paying hefty interest on the advance the moment you receive the cash, and you won't receive frequent-flyer miles on an airline credit card). At most banks, you don't even need to go to a teller; you can get a cash advance at the ATM if you know your PIN number.

Note, however, that at press time, some credit cards companies were discussing plans to increase fees for foreign currency transactions. Citibank, in particular, was considering adding a whopping 4% fee onto the 1% to 2% fee already charged by Visa or MasterCard. Ask you bank about these fees before you go.

4 When to Go

CLIMATE

Spring and fall are ideal times to visit nearly all of Spain, with the possible exception of the Atlantic coast, which experiences heavy rains in October and November. May and October are the best months, in terms of both weather and crowds.

In summer it's hot, hot, and hotter still, with the cities in Castile (Madrid) and Andalusia (Seville and Córdoba) stewing up the most scalding brew. Madrid has dry heat; the temperature can hover around 84°F in July and 75° in September. Seville has the dubious reputation of being about the hottest part of Spain in July and August, often baking under temperatures that average around 93°.

Barcelona, cooler in temperature, is often quite humid. Midsummer temperatures in Majorca often reach 91°. The overcrowded Costa Brava has temperatures around 81° in July and August. The Costa del Sol has an average of 77° in summer. The coolest spot in Spain is the Atlantic coast from San Sebastián to La Coruña, with temperatures in the 70s in July and August.

August remains the major vacation month in Europe. The traffic from France, the Netherlands, and Germany to Spain becomes a veritable migration, and low-cost hotels along the coastal areas are virtually impossible to find. To compound the problem, many restaurants and shops also decide that it's time for a vacation, thereby limiting the visitors' selections for both dining and shopping.

In winter, the coast from Algeciras to Málaga is the most popular, with temperatures reaching a warm 60° to 63°. Madrid gets cold, as low as 34°. Majorca is warmer, usually in the 50s, but it often dips into the 40s. Some mountain resorts can experience extreme cold.

HOLIDAYS

Holidays include January 1 (New Year's Day), January 6 (Feast of the Epiphany), March 19 (Feast of St. Joseph), Good Friday, Easter Monday, May 1 (May Day), June 10 (Corpus Christi), June 29 (Feast of St. Peter and St. Paul), July 25 (Feast of St. James), August 15 (Feast of the Assumption), October 12 (Spain's National Day), November 1 (All Saints' Day), December 8 (Immaculate Conception), and December 25 (Christmas).

No matter how large or small, every city or town in Spain also celebrates its local saint's day. In Madrid it's May 15 (St. Isidro). You'll rarely know what the local holidays are in your next destination in Spain. Try to keep money on hand, because you may arrive in town only to find banks and stores closed. In some cases, intercity bus services are suspended on holidays.

Spain Calendar of Events

The dates given below may not be precise. Sometimes the exact days are not announced until 6 weeks before the actual festival. Check with the National Tourist Office of Spain (see "Visitor Information, Entry Requirements & Customs," earlier in this chapter) if you're planning to attend a specific event.

January

- **Granada Reconquest Festival,** Granada. The whole city celebrates the Christians' victory over the Moors in 1492. The highest tower at the Alhambra is open to the public on January 2. For information, contact the Tourist Office of Granada (☎ **958-22-66-88**). January 2.
- **Día de los Reyes (Three Kings Day),** throughout Spain. Parades are held around the country on the eve of the Festival of the Epiphany. Various "kings" dispense candy to all the kids. January 6.
- **Día de San Antonio (St. Anthony's Day),** La Puebla, Majorca. Bonfires, dancing, revelers dressed as devils, and other riotous events honor St. Anthony on the eve of his day. January 17.

February

- **ARCO** (Madrid's International Contemporary Art Fair), Madrid. One of the biggest draws on Spain's cultural calendar, this exhibit showcases the best in contemporary art from Europe and America. At the Crystal Pavilion of the Casa de Campo, the exhibition draws galleries from throughout Europe, the Americas, Australia, and Asia, who bring with them the works of regional and internationally known artists. To buy tickets, you can contact El Corte Ingles at ☎ **91-556-23-03,** or Madrid Rock at ☎ **91-547-24-23.** The cost is between 5,000 and 6,000 ptas. ($33.50–$40.20). You can get schedules from the tourist office closer to the event. Dates vary.
- **Bocairente Festival of Christians and Moors,** Bocairente (Valencia). Fireworks, colorful costumes, parades, and a reenactment of the struggle between Christians and Moors mark this exuberant festival. A stuffed effigy of Mohammed is blown to bits. February 2 to 5.
- **Carnavales de Cádiz,** Cádiz. The oldest and best-attended carnival in Spain is a freewheeling event full of costumes, parades, strolling troubadours, and drum beating. February 11 to March 21.
- **Madrid Carnaval.** The carnival kicks off with a big parade along the Paseo de la Castellana, culminating in a masked ball at the Círculo de Bellas Artes on the following night. Fancy-dress competitions last until February 28, when the festivities end with a tear-jerking "burial of a sardine" at the Fuente de los Pajaritos in the Casa de Campo. This is followed that evening by a concert in the Plaza Mayor. Dates vary.

March

- **Fallas de Valencia,** Valencia. Dating from the 1400s, this fiesta centers around the burning of papier-mâché effigies of winter demons. Burnings are preceded by bullfights, fireworks, and parades. March 12 to 19.

April

- ✪ **Feria de Sevilla (Seville Fair).** This is the most celebrated week of revelry in all of Spain, with all-night flamenco dancing, entertainment booths, bullfights, horseback riding, flower-decked coaches, and dancing in the streets. You'll need to reserve a hotel early for this one. For general information and exact festival dates, contact the Office of Tourism in Seville (☎ 95-422-14-04). April 20 to 25.

- **Moros y Cristianos (Moors and Christians),** Alcoy, near Alicante. During two days every April (dates vary), the centuries-old battle between the Moors and the Christians is restaged with soldiers in period costumes. Naturally, the Christians who drove the Moors from Spain always win. The simulated fighting takes on almost a circus-like flair, and the costumes worn by the Moors are always absurd and anachronistic. Call ☎ 96-520-00-00 for more information.

✪ **Semana Santa (Holy Week),** Seville. Though many of the country's smaller towns stage similar celebrations (especially notable in Zamora), the festivities in Seville are by far the most elaborate. From Palm Sunday until Easter Sunday, a series of processions with hooded penitents moves to the piercing wail of the *saeta,* a love song to the Virgin or Christ. *Pasos* (heavy floats) bear images of the Virgin or Christ. Again, make hotel reservations way in advance. Call the Seville Office of Tourism for details (☎ 95-422-14-04). March 28 to April 4.

May

- **Festival de los Patios,** Córdoba. At this famous fair, residents flamboyantly decorate their patios with cascades of flowers. Visitors wander from patio to patio. First 2 weeks in May.

- **Romería del Roćo (Pilgrimage of the Virgin of the Dew),** El Roćo (Huelva). The most famous pilgrimage in Andalusia attracts a million people. Fifty men carry the statue of the Virgin 9 miles to Almontc for consecration. May14 to 24.

✪ **Fiesta de San Isidro,** Madrid. Madrileños run wild with a 10-day celebration honoring their city's patron saint. Food fairs, Castilian folkloric events, street parades, parties, music, dances, bullfights, and other festivities mark the occasion. Make hotel reservations early. Expect crowds and traffic (and beware of pickpockets). For information, write to Oficina Municipal de Información y Turismo, Plaza Mayor, 3, 28014 Madrid. May 12 to 21.

✪ **Feria del Caballo (Horse Fair),** Jerez de la Frontera. "Horses, wine, women, and song," according to the old Andalusian ditty, make this a stellar event at which some of the greatest horses in the world go on parade. Call ☎ 956-33-11-50 for more information. May 9 to 16.

June

- **Veranos de la Villa,** Madrid. This program presents folkloric dancing, pop music, classical music, zarzuelas, and flamenco at various venues throughout the city. Open-air cinema is a feature in the Parque del Retiro. Ask at the various tourist offices for complete details (the program changes every summer). Sometimes admission is charged, but often these events are free. All summer long.

- **Corpus Christi,** all over Spain. A major holiday on the Spanish calendar, this event is marked by big processions, especially in Toledo, Málaga, Seville, and Granada. June 6.

✪ **International Music and Dance Festival,** Granada. About to celebrate its 50th year in 2000, Granada's prestigious program of dance and music attracts international artists who perform at the Alhambra and other venues. It's a major event on the cultural calendar of Europe. Reserve well in advance. For a complete schedule and tickets, contact El Festival Internacional de Música y Danza de Granada (☎ 958-22-18-44). June 18 to July 4.

✪ **Las Hogueras de San Juan (St. John's Bonfires),** Alicante. On June 20, during the summer solstice, bonfires blaze through the night to honor the event, just as they did in Celtic and Roman times. The bonfire signals the launching of 5 days of gala celebrations, with fireworks and parades. Business in Alicante comes to a standstill. Call ☎ **96-520-00-00** for more information.

- **Verbena de Sant Joan,** Barcelona. This traditional festival occupies all Catalans. Barcelona literally lights up—with fireworks, bonfires, and dances until dawn. The highlight of the festival is the fireworks show at Montjuïc. June 24.

July

- **A Rapa das Bestas (The Capture of the Beasts),** San Lorenzo de Sabuceno, Galicia. Spain's greatest horse round-up attracts equestrian lovers from throughout Europe. Horses in the verdant hills of northwestern Spain are rounded up, branded, and medically checked before their release into the wild again. For more information, phone ☎ **986-85-08-14.** First weekend in July.
- **Festival of St. James,** Santiago de Compostela. Pomp and ceremony mark this annual pilgrimage to the tomb of St. James the Apostle in Galicia. Galician folklore shows, concerts, parades, and the swinging of the botafumeiro (a mammoth incense burner) mark the event. Mid- to late July.
- **San Sebastián Jazz Festival,** San Sebastián. Celebrating its 35th year (2000), this festival brings together the jazz greats of the world at the pavilion of the Anoeta Sport Complex. Other programs take place al fresco at the Plaza de Trinidad in the old quarter. The Office of the San Sebastian Jazz Festival (☎ **943-48-11-79**) can provide schedules and tickets. Over 1 week in late July.
- ✪ **Fiesta de San Fermín,** Pamplona. Vividly described in Ernest Hemingway's novel *The Sun Also Rises,* the running of the bulls through the streets of Pamplona is the most popular celebration in Spain. The celebration also includes wine tasting, fireworks, and, of course, bullfights. Reserve many months in advance. For more information, such as a list of accommodations, contact the Office of Tourism, Duque de Ahumada, 3, 31002 Pamplona (☎ **948-22-07-41**). Early to mid-July.

August

- **Santander International Festival of Music and Dance,** Santander. The repertoire includes classical music, ballet, contemporary dance, chamber music, and recitals. Most performances are staged at the Plaza de la Porticada. For further information, contact Festival Internacional de Santander (☎ **942-210-508**). Throughout August.
- **Fiestas of Lavapiés and La Paloma,** Madrid. These two fiestas begin with the Lavapiés on August 1 and continue through the hectic La Paloma celebration on August 15, the day of the Virgen de la Paloma. Thousands of people race through the narrow streets. Apartment dwellers hurl buckets of cold water onto the crowds below to cool them off. There are children's games, floats, music, flamenco, and zarzuelas, along with street fairs. August 1 to 15.
- **The Mystery Play of Elche.** This sacred drama is reenacted in the 17th-century Basilica of Santa María in Elche (near Alicante). It represents the Assumption and the Crowning of the Virgin. For tickets, call the Office of Tourism in Elche (☎ **96-545-38-31**). August 11 to 15.
- **Feria de Málaga (Málaga Fair).** One of the longest summer fairs in southern Europe (generally lasting for 10 days), this celebration kicks off with fireworks displays and is highlighted by a parade of Arabian horses pulling brightly decorated carriages. Participants are dressed in colorful Andalusian garb. Plazas rattle with castanets, and wine is dispensed by the gallon. Usually begins around mid-August.
- ✪ **La Tomatina (Battle of the Tomatoes),** Buñol, Valencia. One of the most photographed festivals in Spain, and growing in popularity every year, this festival

takes place the last Wednesday in August. Truckloads of tomatoes are shipped into Buñol, where they become "vegetable missiles" between warring towns and villages. Portable showers are brought in for the cleanup, followed by music for dancing and singing.

September

- **Diada,** Barcelona. This is the most significant festival in Catalonia. It celebrates the region's autonomy from the rest of Spain, following years of repression under the dictator Franco. Demonstrations and other flag-waving events take place. The *senyera,* the flag of Catalonia, is everywhere. Not your typical tourist fare, but interesting. September 11.
- **Festival Setmana Cran,** Barcelona. This celebration honors Nostra Senyora de la Merced, the city's patron saint, known for her compassion for animals. Beginning after dark, and after a mass in the Iglesia de la Merced, a procession of as many as 50 "animals" (humans dressed like tigers, lions, and horses) proceeds with lots of firecrackers and sparklers to the Cathedral of Santa Eulalia, then on to the Plça de Sant Jaume, and eventually into the Rambles, Plça de Catalunya, and the harbor front. September 24.
- **International Film Festival San Sebastián.** The premier film festival of Spain takes place in the Basque capital, often at the Victoria Eugenia Theater, a belle epoque masterpiece. Retrospectives are often featured, and weeklong screenings are shown. Second half of September (dates vary).
- **Setmana Cran,** Barcelona. Barcelona stages week-long *verbenas* (carnivals) and *sardana* (dances) to honor its patron saint, the Virgin of Merced. Parades, concerts, theater, and bullfighting mark this event. Look for the "parade of giants" through the streets, culminating at Plça de Sant Jaume in front of the city hall. Dates vary.

October

- **St. Teresa Week,** Ávila. Verbenas (carnivals), parades, singing, and dancing honor the patron saint of this walled city. Dates vary.
- ☼ **Autumn Festival,** Madrid. Both Spanish and international artists participate in this cultural program, with a series of operatic, ballet, dance, music, and theatrical performances. From Strasbourg to Tokyo, this event is a premier attraction, yet tickets are reasonable. Make hotel reservations early. For tickets, contact Festival de Otoño, Plaza de España, 8, 28008 Madrid (☎ **91-580-25-75**). Late October to late November.
- **Grape Harvest Festival,** Jerez de la Frontera. The major wine festival in Andalusia honors the famous sherry of Jerez, with 5 days of processions, flamenco dancing, bullfights, livestock on parade, and, of course, sherry drinking. Mid-October (dates vary).

November

- **All Saints' Day,** all over Spain. This public holiday is reverently celebrated, as relatives and friends lay flowers on the graves of the dead. November 1.

December

- **Día de los Santos Inocentes,** all over Spain. This equivalent of April Fools' Day is an excuse for people to do loco things. December 28.

5 Special-Interest Vacations

Spain is one of the best destinations in Europe for enjoying the outdoors. Lounging on the beach leads the list of activities for most travelers, but there's lots more to do.

Spain's sierra lures thousands of mountaineers and hikers, and fishing and hunting are long-standing Spanish obsessions. The Pyrenees of Catalunya and Aragón, plus the Guadarramas outside Madrid, attract devoted skiers in the winter. Water sports ranging from sailing to windsurfing are prime summer attractions.

In addition to sports and adventures, we've also detailed some of the best educational and cultural programs below.

Note: The inclusion of an organization in this section is in no way to be interpreted as a guarantee. This information is presented only as a preview, to be followed by your own investigation.

BIKING

The tawny-colored landscape of Andalusia is perfect mountain-biking country. One of the best outfitters is **Mountain Bike Aventura,** Pueblo Platero, 8, Bloque 1, Elviria–Las Chapas, 29600 Marbella (Málaga; ☎ **95-283-12-04**). The leading U.S.-based competitor is **Easy Rider Tours,** P.O. Box 228, Newburyport, MA 01950 (☎ **800/488-8332** or 978/463-6955). Their tours average between 30 and 50 miles a day; the most appealing follows the route trod by medieval pilgrims on their way to Santiago. The bike tours offered by **Backroads,** 801 Cedar St., Berkeley, CA 94710 (☎ **800/GO-ACTIVE**), take you through the verdant countryside of Galicia and into Portugal's Minho region. Companies that specialize in bike tours of Camino de Santiago include **Camino Tours,** Seattle, WA 98115 (☎ **800/938-9311** or 206/523-8256); and **Saranjan Tours,** 18665 NE St., Suite 102, Kirkland, WA 98033 (☎ **800/858-9594** or 425/869-8636).

In England, the **Cyclists' Touring Club,** 60 Meadrow, Godalming, Surrey GU7 3HS, UK (☎ **01483/417-217**), charges £25 a year for membership; part of the fee provides for information and suggested cycling routes through Spain and dozens of other countries.

GOLF

In recent decades, thousands of British retirees have settled in Spain, and their presence has sparked the development of dozens of new golf courses. Although the Costa Blanca has become an increasingly popular setting for golf, more than a third of the country's approximately 160 courses lie within its southern tier, within a short drive of the Costa del Sol.

Packages that include guaranteed playing time on some of the country's finest courses, as well as airfare and accommodations, can be arranged through such firms as **Golf International** (☎ **800/833-1389** in the U.S.), **Spanish Golf Adventures** (☎ **800/772-6465** in the U.S. and Canada), **Central Holidays** (☎ **800/935-5000** in the U.S. and Canada), **PGA Travel** (☎ **800/283-4653** in the U.S., or 770/455-8019), and **Comtours** (☎ **800/248-1331** in the U.S.).

What are the two most talked-about golf courses in Spain? The well-established **Valderrama** on the Costa del Sol, a Robert Trent Jones–designed course carved out of an oak plantation in the 1980s, and Hyatt's new **La Manga Club** on the Costa Blanca near Murcia. It's the site of three golf courses, one of which was recently remodeled by Arnold Palmer. The Ryder Cup between Spain and the U.S. was held in 1997 at Valderrama, Apt. des Correos 1, 11310 Sotogrande (on the western tip of the Costa del Sol, near Gibralter; ☎ **956-795-775**), which is emerging as the premier course in Spain.

HIKING & WALKING

If you're drawn to the idea of combining hiking with stopovers at local inns, contact **Winetrails,** Greenways, Vann Lake, Ockley, Dorking EH5 5NT, UK

(☎ **01306/712-111**). This U.K.-based company conducts 10-day treks through northern Spain's wine districts.

To venture into the more rugged countryside of Catalonia, Andalusia's valley of the Guadalquivir, or the arid, beautiful Extremaduran plains, contact **Ramblers Holidays,** P.O. Box 43, Welwyn Garden AL8 6PQ, UK (☎ **01707/331-133**). Walking tours through the Pyrenees, the region around Alicante, and across the eerie volcanic expanses of the Canary Islands are conducted by **Waymark Holidays,** 44 Windsor Rd., Slough SL1 2EJ, UK (☎ **01753/516-477**).

An outfit known for its extremely luxurious and extremely pricey tours is **Abercrombie & Kent International,** 1520 Kensington Rd., Oak Brook, IL 60521 (☎ **800/323-7308** or 630/954-2944). They conduct a 9-day "Walking the Pyrenees" tour on the Spanish side of the mountainous border with France. Special emphasis is placed on the medieval churches that provided rest and hope to 10th-century pilgrims on their way to Santiago.

HORSEBACK RIDING

You can take a tour that winds across Asturia and Galicia on your way to the medieval religious shrine at Santiago de Compostela. Lodging, the use of a horse, and all necessary equipment are included in the price. For information and reservations, contact the **Centro Hípico "O Castelo,"** calle Urzáiz, 91, no. 5-A Vigo, Spain (☎ **986-42-59-37**).

A well-known equestrian center that conducts tours of the arid Alpujarras highlands is **Cabalgar,** Rutas Alternativas, Bubión, Granada (☎ **958-76-31-35**). The farm is best known for its weekend treks through the scrub-covered hills of southern and central Spain, though longer tours are also available.

SAILING

An agency based in Seville offers weeklong cruises along the coast of Andalusia and the Algarve. Its three-masted, 42-foot sailing yacht departs from the Andalusian port of Huelva. For reservations and information, contact **Alventus,** calle Imagen, 6, 41003 Sevilla (☎ **95-421-00-62**).

In northern Spain, consider a journey with **Voyages Jules Verne,** 21 Dorset Sq., London NW1 6QG, UK (☎ **0171/616-1000**). Its guided vacations take in Galicia, its Portuguese neighbors, Trás-os-Montes and the Minho district, and Porto, the second-largest city in Portugal. The trips end with a boat ride up the Douro River back into Spain.

SKIING

You wouldn't think there'd be good skiing in a country that's often so blazing hot. But Iberia's mountain ranges provide some surprising opportunities for schussing downhill. And because skiers in Spain also tend to keep the same late hours at resorts, slopes are noticeably less crowded between 9 and 11am, and between 1 and 3pm—presumably the time when skiers are sleeping off a night of clubbing or enjoying a late lunch.

Besides the usually crowded facilities in Andorra, Spain's most successful and best-equipped resorts include **Sierra Nevada,** an Andalusian ski resort that was formally launched in the 1960s; **Baqueira-Beret,** in the Pyrenees, a favorite of Spain's royal family; and **Alto Campo,** in Cantabria.

For information about how and where to ski, call the **Ski Resort's Association of Spain (ATUDEM)** in Madrid (☎ **91-350-20-20**). For information from Spain's oldest ski club, contact the **Sierra Nevada Club,** Edificio Cetursa, Plaza de Andalucía, 18196 Sierra Nevada (Granada; ☎ **958-24-91-11**). For information on the slopes in Andorra, contact **Andorra's Oficina de Turismo,** Dr. Vilanova (☎ **00376/820214**).

LEARNING VACATIONS

See section 7, later in this chapter, for details on Interhostel and Elderhostel programs for seniors.

STUDYING SPANISH **Salminter,** calle Toro, 34-36, 37002 Salamanca (☎ **923-21-18-08;** fax 923-26-02-63), conducts courses in conversational Spanish, with optional courses in business Spanish, translation techniques, and Spanish culture. Classes contain no more than 10 persons. There are courses of 2 weeks, 1 month, and 3 months at seven progressive levels. The school can arrange housing with Spanish families or in furnished apartments shared with other students.

Another good source of information about courses in Spain is the **American Institute for Foreign Study (AIFS),** 102 Greenwich Ave., Greenwich, CT 06830 (☎ **800/727-2437** or 203/869-9090). This organization can set up transportation and arrange for summer courses, with bed and board included. It can help you arrange study programs at either the University of Salamanca, one of Europe's oldest academic centers, or the University of Granada.

The biggest organization dealing with higher education in Europe is the **Institute of International Education (IIE),** 809 United Nations Plaza, New York, NY 10017 (☎ **212/883-8200;** www.iie.org). A few of its booklets are free; but for $44.95, plus $6 for postage, you can purchase the more definitive *Vacation Study Abroad.* To order the book, call ☎ **800/445-0443.**

One well-recommended clearinghouse for academic programs throughout the world is the **National Registration Center for Study Abroad (NRCSA),** 823 N. 2nd St., P.O. Box 1393, Milwaukee, WI 53201 (☎ **414/278-0631;** www.nrcsa.com). The organization maintains language-study programs throughout Europe, including those within about 10 cities throughout Spain. Most popular are the organization's programs in Seville, Salamanca, and Málaga, where language courses last between 4 and 6 hours a day. With lodgings in private homes included as part of the price and part of the experience, tuition begins at around $615 for an intensive 2-week language course. Courses accept participants aged 17 to 80.

A clearinghouse for information on at least nine different Spain-based language schools is **Lingua Service Worldwide,** 216 E. 45th St., 17th Floor, New York, NY 10017 (☎ **800/394-LEARN** or 212/867-1225). Maintaining information about learning programs in 10 languages in 17 countries outside the United States, it represents organizations devoted to the teaching of Spanish and culture in 11 cities of Spain, including one in the Canary Islands.

One well-recommended language school that manages to combine a resort setting with intensive linguistic immersion is the **Escuela de Idiomas Nerja,** calle Almirante Ferrándiz, 73, 29780 Nerja, Málaga (☎ **952-52-16-87**). It offers a 2-week Spanish course for 47,000 ptas. ($314.90) and a 4-week course for 71,400 ptas. ($478.40). Also offered are one-on-one courses, refresher course for teachers, and Spanish for business. Classes are limited to a maximum of 10 students each.

For more information about study abroad, contact the **Council on International Educational Exchange (CIEE),** 205 E. 42nd St., New York, NY 10017 (☎ **800/226-8624** or 212/822-2700; www.ciee.com).

"EARTHWATCHING" **Earthwatch,** 680 Mount Auburn St., P.O. Box 403, Watertown, MA 02272-9924 (☎ **617/926-8200**), is a nonprofit organization that recruits ordinary people to work as paying volunteers for university professors on field expeditions throughout the world. Volunteers are almost never specialists in any particular field but interested "intergenerational" participants. Note that only 10% of volunteers are students; many are senior citizens. Ongoing projects in Spain include monitoring the S'Albufera wetlands on the island of Majorca, excavating a prehistoric cluster of Copper Age villages on Majorca, researching the remains of a Bronze Age Iberian village near Borja in Aragón, and participating in the Spanish dolphin project off the southern coast.

Participation in Earthwatch's 2- or 3-week Spanish projects involves a tax-deductible contribution of between $1,600 and $2,000, depending on the project, plus airfare to Spain. Living arrangements, as well as all meals and drinks at the organization's Saturday-night beer parties, are provided.

BIRDING   The Iberian Peninsula lies directly across migration routes of species that travel with the seasons between Africa and Europe. Some of the most comprehensive studies on these migratory patterns are conducted by Spain's **Centro de Migración de Aves,** SEO/BirdLife, Carretera de Humera 63-1, 28224 Pozuelo (Madrid; ☎ **91-434-09-10**). Based at a rustic outpost near Gibraltar, their summer work camps and field projects appeal to participants who want to identify, catalog, and "ring" (mark with an identifying leg band) some of the millions of birds that nest on Spanish soil every year. Participants are expected to pay for their "tuition," room, and board, but can often use the experience toward university credits, especially in such fields as zoology and ecology.

BOTANIC TOURS   Travel specialist **Cox & Kings,** Gordon House, 10 Green Coat Place, London SW7P 1PH, UK (☎ **0171/873-5000**), leads 2-week treks in search of wild orchids, unusual ferns, and samples of the varied flora that grow in the damp but sunny foothills of the Pyrenees in Aragón. The firm also conducts other organized tours through Spain.

COOKING SCHOOLS   One organization devoted to the fine art of creating the nation's cuisine is the **Escuela de Cocina Juan Altimiras,** Plaza de la Incarnación, 2, Madrid (☎ **91-547-88-27**). Established by Clara María González de Amezúa in 1973, it offers a series of lectures and demonstrations that benefit even professional chefs.

6 Health & Insurance

STAYING HEALTHY

Spain should not pose any major health hazards. The rich cuisine—garlic, olive oil, and wine—may give some travelers mild diarrhea, so take along some antidiarrhea medicine, moderate your eating habits, and even though the water is generally safe, drink mineral water only. Fish and shellfish from the horrendously polluted Mediterranean should only be eaten cooked.

If you are traveling around Spain (particularly southern Spain) over the summer, limit your exposure to the sun, especially during the first few days of your trip and, thereafter, from 11am to 2pm. Use a sunscreen with a high protection factor and apply it liberally. Remember that children need more protection than adults do.

If you suffer from a chronic illness, consult your doctor before your departure. For conditions like epilepsy, diabetes, or heart problems, wear a **Medic Alert Identification Tag** (☎ **800/825-3785;** www.commedicalert.org), which will immediately alert doctors to your condition and give them access to your records through Medic Alert's 24-hour hot line. Membership is $35, plus a $15 annual fee.

Pack prescription medications in your carry-on luggage. Carry written prescriptions in generic, not brand-name form, and dispense all prescription medications from their original labeled vials. Also bring along copies of your prescriptions in case you lose your pills or run out.

Contact the **International Association for Medical Assistance to Travelers (IAMAT)**, (☎ **716/754-4883** or 416/652-0137; www.sentex.net/~iamat). This organization offers tips on travel and health concerns in the countries you'll be visiting, and lists many local English-speaking doctors.

INSURANCE

There are three kinds of travel insurance: trip-cancellation, medical, and lost luggage coverage.

Trip-cancellation insurance is a good idea if you have paid a large portion of your vacation expenses up front, say by purchasing a tour. Trip-cancellation insurance should cost approximately 6% to 8% of the total value of your vacation. (Don't buy it from your tour operator, though—talk about putting all your eggs in one basket!)

Your existing health insurance should cover you if you get sick while on vacation (though if you belong to an HMO, you should check to see whether you are fully covered when away from home). If you need hospital treatment, most health insurance plans and HMOs will cover out-of-country hospital visits and procedures, at least to some extent. However, most make you pay the bills up front at the time of care, and you'll get a refund after you've returned and filed all the paperwork. Members of **Blue Cross/Blue Shield** can now use their cards at select hospitals in most major cities worldwide (☎ **800/810-BLUE** or www.bluecares.com/blue/bluecard/wwn for a list of hospitals). **Medicare** only covers U.S. citizens traveling in Mexico and Canada. For independent travel health-insurance providers, see below.

Your homeowner's insurance should cover stolen luggage. The airlines are responsible for $1,250 on domestic flights if they lose your luggage; if you plan to carry anything more valuable than that, keep it in your carry-on bag.

Check your existing policies before you buy additional insurance you might not need. But if you do require additional insurance, try one of the following: **Access America** (☎ **800/284-8300**), **Travel Guard International** (☎ **800/826-1300**), and **Travelex Insurance Services** (☎ **800/228-9792**). In the United Kingdom, there's **Columbus Travel Insurance** (☎ **0171/375-0011** in London; www.columbusdirect. co.uk). Companies specializing in accident and medical care include: **MEDEX International** (☎ **888/MEDEX-00** or 410/453-6300; fax 410/453-6301; www. medexassist. com); and **Travel Assistance International** (Worldwide Assistance Services; ☎ **800/821-2828** or 202/828-5894; fax 202/828-5896).

7 Tips for Travelers with Special Needs

TIPS FOR TRAVELERS WITH DISABILITIES

Because of Spain's many hills and endless flights of stairs, visitors with disabilities may have difficulty getting around the country. But conditions are slowly improving. Newer hotels are more sensitive to the needs of those with disabilities, and the more expensive restaurants, in general, are wheelchair-accessible. (In Madrid, there's even a museum designed for the sightless and sight impaired, called the **Museo Triflológico**—see chapter 3.) However, since most places have limited, if any, facilities for people with disabilities, you might consider taking an organized tour specifically designed to accommodate travelers with disabilities.

There are more resources out there than ever before. *A World of Options,* a 658-page book of resources for disabled travelers, covers everything from biking trips to scuba outfitters. It costs $35 ($30 for members) and is available from **Mobility International USA,** P.O. Box 10767, Eugene, OR 97440 (☎ **541/343-1284,** voice and TDD; www.miusa.org). Annual membership for Mobility International is $35, which includes their quarterly newsletter, *Over the Rainbow.*

The **Moss Rehab Hospital** (☎ **215/456-9600**) has been providing friendly and helpful phone advice and referrals to disabled travelers for years through its **Travel Information Service** (☎ **215/456-9603;** www.mossresourcenet.org).

You can join the **Society for the Advancement of Travel for the Handicapped (SATH),** 347 Fifth Ave. Suite 610, New York, NY 10016 (☎ **212/447-7284;** fax 212-725-8253; www.sath.org), for $45 annually, $30 for seniors and students, to gain access to their vast network of connections in the travel industry. They provide information sheets on travel destinations, and referrals to tour operators that specialize in traveling with disabilities. Their quarterly magazine, *Open World for Disability and Mature Travel,* is full of good information and resources. A year's subscription is $13 ($21 outside the U.S.).

Travelers with disabilities may also want to consider joining a tour that caters specifically to them. One of the best operators is **Flying Wheels Travel,** 143 West Bridge (P.O. Box 382), Owatonna, MN 55060 (☎ **800/535-6790**). They offer various escorted tours and cruises, with an emphasis on sports, as well as private tours in minivans with lifts. Other reputable specialized tour operators include **Access Adventures** (☎ **716/889-9096**), which offers sports-related vacations; **Accessible Journeys** (☎ **800/TINGLES** or 610/521-0339), for slow walkers and wheelchair travelers; **The Guided Tour** (☎ **215/782-1370**); and **Directions Unlimited** (☎ **800/533-5343**).

Vision-impaired travelers should contact the **American Foundation for the Blind,** 11 Penn Plaza, Suite 300, New York, NY 10001 (☎ **800/232-5463**), for information on traveling with Seeing Eye dogs.

British travelers with disabilities can contact **Radar (Royal Association for Disability and Rehabilitation),** Unit 12, City Forum, 250 City Rd., London EC1V 8AF (☎ **0171/250-3222**), for useful annual holiday guides. *Holidays and Travel Abroad* costs £5, *Holidays in the British Isles* goes for £7, and *Long Haul Holidays and Travel* is £5. RADAR also provides holiday information packets on such subjects as sports and outdoor holidays, insurance, and financial arrangements for people with disabilities. Each of these fact sheets is available for £2. All publications can be mailed outside the United Kingdom for a nominal fee.

Another good British service is the **Holiday Care Service,** 2nd Floor Imperial Buildings, Victoria Road, Horley, Surrey RH6 7PZ (☎ **01293/774-535;** fax 01293/784-647), which advises on accessible accommodations. Annual membership costs £15 (U.K. residents) and £30 (abroad) and includes a newsletter and access to a free reservations network for hotels throughout Britain and, to a lesser degree, Europe and the rest of the world.

TIPS FOR GAY & LESBIAN TRAVELERS

In 1978, Spain legalized homosexuality among consenting adults. In April 1995, the parliament of Spain banned discrimination based on sexual orientation. Madrid and Barcelona are the major centers of gay life in Spain, and the most popular resorts for gay travelers are Sitges (south of Barcelona), Torremolinos, and Ibiza.

The **International Gay & Lesbian Travel Association (IGLTA),** (☎ **800/ 448-8550** or 954/776-2626; fax 954/776-3303; www.iglta.org), links travelers up with the appropriate gay-friendly service organization or tour specialist. With around 1,200 members, it offers quarterly newsletters, marketing mailings, and a membership directory that's updated quarterly. Membership often includes gay or lesbian businesses but is open to individuals for $150 yearly, plus a $100 administration fee for new members. Members are kept informed of gay and gay-friendly hoteliers, tour operators, and airline and cruise-line representatives. Contact the IGLTA for a list of its member agencies, who will be tied into IGLTA's information resources.

General gay and lesbian travel agencies include **Family Abroad** (☎ **800/999-5500** or 212/459-1800; gay and lesbian); **Above and Beyond Tours** (☎ **800/397-2681;** mainly gay men); and **Yellowbrick Road** (☎ **800/642-2488;** gay and lesbian).

We're biased, of course, but we'd recommend that you pick up the brand-new *Frommer's Gay & Lesbian Guide to Europe,* which is packed with sightseeing tips, hotel and restaurant reviews, shopping, and lots of nightlife suggestions.

There are also two good, biannual English-language gay guidebooks, both focused on gay men but including information for lesbians as well. You can get the *Spartacus International Gay Guide* or *Odysseus* from most gay and lesbian book stores, or order them from **Giovanni's Room** (☎ **215/923-2960**), or **A Different Light Bookstore** (☎ **800/343-4002** or 212/989-4850). Both lesbians and gays might want to pick up a copy of *Gay Travel A to Z* ($16). The *Ferrari Guides* (www.q-net.com) is yet another very good series of gay and lesbian guidebooks.

Out and About, 8 W. 19th St. no. 401, New York, NY 10011 (☎ **800/929-2268** or 212/645-6922), offers guidebooks and a monthly newsletter packed with good information on the global gay and lesbian scene. A year's subscription to the newsletter costs $49. *Our World,* 1104 North Nova Rd., Suite 251, Daytona Beach, FL 32117 (☎ **904/441-5367**), is a slicker monthly magazine promoting and highlighting travel bargains and opportunities. Annual subscription rates are $35 in the United States, $45 outside the United States.

TIPS FOR SENIORS

Don't be shy about asking for discounts, but always carry some kind of identification, such as a driver's license, that shows your date of birth. Also, mention the fact that you're a senior citizen when you first make your travel reservations. For example, many hotels and airlines offer senior discounts. In most cities, people over the age of 60 qualify for reduced admission to theaters, museums, and other attractions, and discounted fares on public transportation.

Members of the **American Association of Retired Persons (AARP),** 601 E St. NW, Washington, DC 20049 (☎ **800/424-3410** or 202/434-2277), get discounts not only on hotels but on airfares and car rentals, too. AARP offers members a wide range of special benefits, including *Modern Maturity* magazine and a monthly newsletter.

The **National Council of Senior Citizens,** 8403 Colesville Rd., Suite 1200, Silver Spring, MD 20910 (☎ **301/578-8800**), a nonprofit organization, offers a newsletter six times a year (partly devoted to travel tips) and discounts on hotel and auto rentals; annual dues are $13 per person or couple.

Mature Outlook, P.O. Box 9390, Des Moines, IA 50306 (☎ **800/336-6330**), began as a travel organization for people over 50, though it now caters to people of all ages. Members receive discounts on hotels and receive a bimonthly magazine. Annual membership is $19.95, which entitles members to discounts and, often, free coupons for discounted merchandise from Sears.

Golden Companions, P.O. Box 5249, Reno, NV 89513 (☎ **702/324-2227**), helps travelers 45-plus find compatible companions through a personal voice-mail service. Contact them for more information.

Another helpful publication is *101 Tips for the Mature Traveler*, available from **Grand Circle Travel,** 347 Congress St., Suite 3A, Boston, MA 02210 (☎ **800/221-2610** or 617/350-7500).

Grand Circle Travel is also one of the hundreds of travel agencies specializing in vacations for seniors. Many of these packages, however, are of the tour-bus variety, with free trips thrown in for those who organize groups of 10 or more. Seniors seeking more independent travel should probably consult a regular travel agent. **SAGA International Holidays,** 222 Berkeley St., Boston, MA 02116 (☎ **800/343-0273**), offers inclusive tours and cruises for those 50 and older. SAGA also sponsors the more substantial "Road Scholar Tours" (☎ **800/621-2151**), which are fun-loving but with an educational bent.

If you want something more than the average vacation or guided tour, try **Elderhostel** (☎ **877/426-8056;** www.elderhostel.org) or the University of New Hampshire's **Interhostel** (☎ **800/733-9753**), both variations on the same theme: educational travel for senior citizens. On these escorted tours, the days are packed with seminars, lectures, and field trips, and the sightseeing is all led by academic experts. **Elderhostel,** 75 Federal St., Boston, MA 02110-1941 (☎ **877/426-8056;** www.elderhostel.org), arranges study programs for those aged 55 and over (and a spouse or companion of any age). Most courses last about 3 weeks and many include airfare, accommodations in student dormitories or modest inns, meals, and tuition. Write or call for a free catalog, which lists upcoming courses and destinations. Interhostel takes travelers 50 and over (with companions over 40), and offers two- and three-week trips, mostly international. The courses in both these programs are ungraded, involve no homework, and often focus on the liberal arts. They're not luxury vacations, but they're fun and fulfilling.

British travelers can contact **Wasteels,** Victoria Station, opposite Platform 2, London SW1V 1JY, UK (☎ **0207/834-6744**), for a Rail Europe Senior pass, sold to British residents 60 years of age and older for £5. The pass entitles seniors to discounted rail tickets on many of the rail lines of Europe. To qualify, British residents must present a valid British Senior Citizen rail card, available for £16 at any BritRail office if proof of age and British residency are presented.

TIPS FOR FAMILIES

Several books on the market offer tips to help you travel with kids. Most concentrate on the United States, but two, *Family Travel* (Lanier Publishing International) and *How to Take Great Trips with Your Kids* (The Harvard Common Press), are full of good general advice that can apply to travel anywhere. Another reliable tome, with a worldwide focus, is *Adventuring with Children* (Foghorn Press).

Family Travel Times is published 6 times a year by **TWYCH (Travel with Your Children),** (☎ **888/822-4388** or 212/477-5524), and includes a weekly call-in service for subscribers. Subscriptions are $40 a year for quarterly editions. A free publication list and a sample issue are available by calling or sending a request, 40 Fifth Ave., New York, NY 10011.

Families Welcome!, 92 N. Main, Ashland, OR 97520 (☎ **800/326-0724** or 541/482-6121), a travel company specializing in worry-free vacations for families, offers "City Kids" packages to certain European cities.

The University of New Hampshire runs **Familyhostel** (☎ **800/733-9753**), an intergenerational alternative to standard guided tours. You live on a European college campus for the 2- or 3-week program, attend lectures, seminars, go on lots of field trips, and do all the sightseeing—all of it guided by a team of experts and academics. It's designed for children (aged 8 to 15), parents, and grandparents.

The best deals for British families are often package tours, especially those offered by Thomsons Holidays through its subsidiary, **Skytours** (☎ **0207/387-9321**). It offers dozens of air/land packages to Spain that have a predesignated number of airline seats reserved for free use by children under 18 who accompany their parents. To qualify, parents must book airfare and hotel accommodations lasting 2 weeks or more, and book as far in advance as possible. Savings for families with children can be substantial.

8 Getting There

BY PLANE
FROM NORTH AMERICA

Flights from the U.S. east coast to Spain take 6 to 7 hours.

The national carrier of Spain, **Iberia Airlines** (☎ 800/772-4642; www.iberia. com), has more routes into and within Spain than any other airline. It offers daily nonstop service to Madrid from New York, Chicago, and Miami. In addition, Iberia has service to Madrid from Toronto (through Montréal), which is provided between two and three times a week, depending on the season. Also available are attractive rates on fly-drive packages within Iberia and Europe; these can substantially reduce the cost of both the air ticket and the car rental.

A good money-saver to consider is **Iberia's EuroPass.** Available only to passengers who simultaneously arrange for transatlantic passage on Iberia and a minimum of two additional flights, it allows passage on any flight within Iberia's European or Mediterranean dominion for $250 for the first two flights and $125 for each additional flight. This is especially attractive for passengers wishing to combine trips to Spain with, for example, visits to such far-flung destinations as Cairo, Tel Aviv, Istanbul, Moscow, and Munich. For details, ask Iberia's phone representative. The EuroPass can be purchased as a part of an Iberian Air itinerary from your home country only.

Iberia's main Spain-based competitor is **Air Europa** (☎ 888/238-7672), which offers nonstop service from New York's JFK Airport to Madrid, with continuing service to major cities within Spain. Fares are usually lower than Iberia's.

The latest Spanish airline in the market is **Spanair** (☎ 888/545-5757), which is the only airline to service the Washington, D.C., area. Spanair flies directly from Washington's Dulles Airport to Madrid five times a week, with services continuing on to many of the main cities in Spain.

TWA (☎ 800/221-2000; www.twa.com) operates separate daily nonstop flights to both Barcelona and Madrid from JFK. Like its competitors, TWA offers access to its trip-planning service (in this case, the Getaway Vacation desk) and can arrange independent packages with car rentals and hotels or escorted motor coach tours.

American Airlines (☎ 800/433-7300; www.aa.com) offers daily nonstop service to Madrid from its massive hub in Miami, as well as from New York (JFK) and Chicago, where it's easy to make a connection from elsewhere in the United States.

Delta (☎ 800/241-4141; www.delta-air.com) runs daily nonstop service from Atlanta (its worldwide hub) and New York (JFK) to both Madrid and Barcelona. Delta's Dream Vacation department offers independent fly-drive packages, land packages, and escorted bus tours.

United Airlines (☎ 800/538-2929; www.ual.com) does not fly into Spain directly. They do, however, offer airfares from the United States to Spain with United flying as far as Zurich, and then using another carrier to complete the journey. United also offers fly-drive packages and escorted motor coach tours.

Continental Airlines (☎ 800/231-0856; www.continental.com) offers between six and seven nonstop flights per week, depending on the season, to Madrid from Newark, New Jersey.

US Airways (☎ **800/428-4322**; www.usairways.com) offers daily nonstop service between Philadelphia and Madrid. The carrier also has connecting flights to Philadelphia from more than 50 cities throughout the United States, Canada, and The Bahamas.

FLY FOR LESS: TIPS FOR GETTING THE BEST AIRFARES

1. Keep your eyes peeled for **sales.** Check your newspaper for advertised discounts or call the airlines directly and ask if any promotional rates or special fares are available. You'll almost never see a sale during the peak summer vacation months of July and August, or during the Thanksgiving or Christmas seasons; but in the off-season, there have been astoundingly low European fares in the last few years. If you already hold a ticket when a sale breaks, it may even pay to exchange your ticket, which usually incurs a $50 to $75 charge.

2. **Ask the reservations agent lots of questions.** If your schedule is flexible, ask if you can secure a cheaper fare by staying an extra day or by flying midweek. Many airlines won't volunteer this information, so you've got to be persistent on the phone.

3. **Consolidators,** also known as bucket shops, are a good place to find low fares. Consolidators buy seats in bulk from the airlines and then sell them back to the public at prices below even the airlines' discounted rates. Their small boxed ads usually run in the Sunday travel section at the bottom of the page. Before you pay a consolidator, however, ask for a record locator number and confirm your seat with the airline itself. Be prepared to book your ticket with a different consolidator—there are many to choose from—if the airline can't confirm your reservation. Also be aware that bucket shop tickets are usually nonrefundable or rigged with stiff cancellation penalties, often as high as 50% to 75% of the ticket price.

   Council Travel (☎ **800/226-8624**; www.counciltravel.com) and **STA Travel** (☎ **800/781-4040**; www.sta.travel.com) cater especially to young travelers, but their bargain basement prices are available to people of all ages. **Travel Bargains** (☎ **800/AIR-FARE**; www.1800airfare.com) was formerly owned by TWA but now offers the deepest discounts on many other airlines, with a 4-day advance purchase. Other reliable consolidators include **1-800/FLY-CHEAP** (www.1800flycheap.com); **TFI Tours International** (☎ **800/745-8000** or 212/736-1140), which serves as a clearinghouse for unused seats; or "rebators" such as **Travel Avenue** (☎ **800/333-3335** or 312/876-1116) and the **Smart Traveller** (☎ **800/448-3338** in the U.S., or 305/448-3338), which rebate part of their commissions to you.

4. **Surf the Web for bargains** (but always check the lowest published fare before you shop for flights on-line, so you know if you're getting a deal). See the Online Directory at the end of this book for lots of advice on how to use the Internet to its fullest; it goes into much greater detail than we can here. However, just to mention a couple of sites briefly, good bets include **Arthur Frommer's Budget Travel** (www.frommers.com), **Microsoft Expedia** (www.expedia.com), **Yahoo's Travel Page** (www.yahoo.com), **Travelocity** (www.travelocity.com), and **Trip.com** (www.trip.com). Several major airlines offer a free e-mail service known as **E-Savers,** via which they'll send you their best bargain airfares on a regular basis. It's really a service for the spontaneously inclined and travelers looking for a quick getaway. But the fares are cheap, so it's worth taking a look. See the Web addresses given above for each airline.

5. **Consider a charter flight.** Discounted fares have pared the number available, but they can still be found. Most charter operators advertise and sell their seats through travel agents, thus making these local professionals your best source of

information for available flights. Before deciding to take a charter flight, however, check the restrictions on the ticket: You may be asked to purchase a tour package, to pay in advance, to be amenable if the day of departure is changed, to pay a service charge, to fly on an airline you're not familiar with (this usually is not the case), and to pay harsh penalties if you cancel—but be understanding if the charter doesn't fill up and is canceled up to 10 days before departure. Summer charters fill up more quickly than others and are almost sure to fly, but if you decide on a charter flight, seriously consider cancellation and baggage insurance.

Among charter-flight operators is **Council Charter,** a subsidiary of the Council on International Educational Exchange (CIEE), 205 E. 42nd St., New York, NY 10017 (☎ **212/822-2700**). This outfit can arrange charter seats to most major European cities, including Madrid, on regularly scheduled aircrafts. Another big charter operator is **Travac,** 989 Sixth Ave., 16th floor, New York, NY 10018 (☎ **800/TRAV-800** or 212/563-3303).

Be warned: Some charter companies have proved unreliable in the past.

FROM THE UNITED KINGDOM

British Airways (BA) (☎ **0345/222-747,** or 0181/759-5511 in London) and **Iberia** (☎ **0207/830-0011** in London) are the two major carriers flying between England and Spain. More than a dozen daily flights, either on BA or Iberia, depart from London's Heathrow and Gatwick airports. The Midlands is served by flights from Manchester and Birmingham, two major airports that can also be used by Scottish travelers flying to Spain. There are about seven flights a day from London to Madrid and back and at least six to Barcelona (trip time: 2 to 2½ hours). From either the Madrid airport or the Barcelona airport, you can tap into Iberia's domestic network—flying, for example, to Seville or the Costa del Sol (centered at the Málaga airport). The best air deals on scheduled flights from England are those requiring a Saturday night stopover.

British newspapers are always full of classified advertisements touting "slashed" fares to Spain. A good source is *Time Out.* London's *Evening Standard* has a daily travel section, and the Sunday editions of most papers are full of charter deals. A travel agent can always advise what the best values are at the time of your intended departure.

Charter flights leave from most British regional airports with a destination in mind (for example, Málaga), bypassing the congestion at the Barcelona and Madrid airports. Figure on saving approximately 10% to 15% on regularly scheduled flight tickets. But check carefully into the restrictions and terms; read the fine print, especially in regard to cancellation penalties. One recommended company is **Trailfinders** (☎ **0207/ 937-5400** in London) which operates charters.

In London, there are many bucket shops, around Victoria Station and Earls Court, that offer cheap fares. Make sure that the company you deal with is a member of the IATA, ABTA, or ATOL. These umbrella organizations will help you out if anything goes wrong.

CEEFAX, the British television information service, runs details of package holidays and flights to Europe and beyond. Just switch to your CEEFAX channel and you'll find travel information.

FROM AUSTRALIA

From Australia, there are a number of options to fly to Spain. The most popular is Qantas/British Airways, which flies daily via Asia and London. Other popular and cheaper options are Qantas/Luftansa via Asia and Frankfurt, Qantas/Air France via

Asia and Paris, and Alitalia via Bangkok and Rome. The most direct option is on Singapore Airlines, with only one stop in Singapore. Alternatively, there are flights on Thai Airways via Bangkok and Rome but the connections are not always good.

BY TRAIN

If you're already in Europe, you may want to go to Spain by train, especially if you have a EurailPass. Even without a pass, you'll find that the cost of a train ticket is relatively moderate. Rail passengers who visit from Britain or France should make couchette and sleeper reservations as far in advance as possible, especially during the peak summer season.

Since Spain's rail tracks are of a wider gauge than those used for French trains (except for the TALGO and Trans-Europe-Express trains), you'll probably have to change trains at the border unless you're on an express train (see below). For long journeys on Spanish rails, seat and sleeper reservations are mandatory.

The most comfortable and the fastest trains in Spain are the TER, TALGO, and Electrotren. However, you pay a supplement to ride on these fast trains. Both first- and second-class fares are sold on Spanish trains. Tickets can be purchased in either the United States or Canada at the nearest office of Rail Europe, or from any reputable travel agent. Confirmation of your reservation will take about a week.

If you want your car carried aboard the train, you must travel Auto-Expreso in Spain. This type of auto transport can be booked only through travel agents or rail offices once you arrive in Europe.

To go from London to Spain by rail, you'll need to change not only the train but also the rail terminus in Paris. In Paris it's worth the extra bucks to purchase a TALGO express or a "Puerta del Sol" express—that way, you can avoid having to change trains once again at the Spanish border. Trip time from London to Paris is about 6 hours; from Paris to Madrid, about 15 hours or so, which includes 2 hours spent in Paris just changing trains and stations. Many different rail passes are available in the United Kingdom for travel in Europe. Call or stop in at **Wasteels,** at Victoria Station, opposite platform 2, London, SW1V 1JZ (☎ **0207/834-6744**). They can help you find the best option for the trip you're planning.

BY BUS

Bus travel to Spain is possible but not popular—it's quite slow (service from London will take 24 hours or more). But coach services do operate regularly from major capitals of western Europe, and once in Spain, usually head for Madrid or Barcelona. The major bus lines running from London to Spain are **Eurolines Limited,** 52 Grosvenor Gardens, London SW1W 0AU, UK (☎ **0990/143-219** or 0171/730-8235), and **Aerolineas** (☎ **93-490 40-00** in Barcelona, or 01582/40-4511 in Britain).

BY CAR

If you're touring the rest of Europe in a rented car, you might, for an added cost, be allowed to drop off your vehicle in a major city such as Madrid or Barcelona.

Highway approaches to Spain are across France on expressways. The most popular border crossing is near Biarritz, but there are 17 other border stations between Spain and France. If you're planning to visit the north or west of Spain (Galicia), the Hendaye-Irún border is the most convenient frontier crossing. If you're going to Barcelona or Catalonia and along the Levante coast (Valencia), take the expressway in France to Toulouse, then the A-61 to Narbonne, and then the A-9 toward the border crossing at La Junquera. You can also take the RN-20, with a border station at Puigcerdá.

If you're driving from Britain, make sure you have a cross-Channel reservation, as traffic tends to be very heavy, especially in summer.

The major ferry crossings connect Dover and Folkestone with Dunkirk. Newhaven is connected with Dieppe, and the British city of Portsmouth with Roscoff. To take a car on the ferry from Dover to Calais costs £104.50 ($172.45) and takes 4½ hours. This cost includes the car and two passengers.

One of the fastest crossings is by Hovercraft from Dover to Boulogne or Calais. It costs more than the ferry, but it takes only about half an hour. For reservations and information, call **Hoverspeed** (☎ **800/677-8585** for reservations in North America, or 08705/240-241 in England). The Hovercraft takes 35 minutes and costs £115 ($189.75) for the car and two passengers. The drive from Calais to the border would take about 15 hours.

You can take the "Chunnel," the underwater Channel Tunnel linking Britain (Folkestone) and France (Calais) by road and rail. **Eurostar** tickets, for train service between London and Paris or Brussels, are available through Rail Europe (☎ **800/ 4-EURAIL** for information). In London, make reservations for Eurostar at ☎ **0990/300003** (accessible in the United Kingdom only); in Paris at ☎ 01-44-51-06-02, and in the United States, at ☎ 800/EUROSTAR. The tunnel also accommodates passenger cars, charter buses, taxis, and motorcycles, transporting them under the English Channel from Folkestone, England, to Calais, France. It operates 24 hours a day, 365 days a year, running every 15 minutes during peak travel times, and at least once an hour at night. Tickets may be purchased at the toll booth at the tunnel's entrance. With "Le Shuttle," gone are the days of weather-related delays, seasickness, and advance reservations.

The cost is £120 ($198) for the car and up to seven passengers. Once you land, you'll have about a 15-hour drive to Spain.

If you plan to transport a rental car between England and France, check in advance with the rental company about license and insurance requirements and additional drop-off charges. And be aware that many car-rental companies, for insurance reasons, forbid transport of one of their vehicles over the water between England and France.

BY ESCORTED TOUR

An escorted tour may not be the option for you if you like to strike out on your and value spontaneity. But some people love escorted tours. They let you relax and take in the sights while a bus driver fights traffic for you; they spell out your costs up front; and they take you to the maximum number of sights in the minimum amount of time with the least amount of hassle.

If you do choose an escorted tour, you should ask a few simple questions before you buy:

1. What is the cancellation policy? Do they require a deposit? Can they cancel the trip if they don't get enough people? Do you get a refund if they cancel? If you cancel? How late can you cancel if you are unable to go? When do you pay in full?
2. How busy is the schedule? How much sightseeing do they plan each day? Do they allow ample time for relaxing by the pool, shopping, or wandering?
3. What is the size of the group? The smaller the group, the more flexible the itinerary, and the less time you'll spend waiting for people to get on and off the bus. Tour operators may be evasive about this, but they should be able to give you a rough estimate. Some tours have a minimum group size and may cancel the tour if they don't book enough people.
4. What is included in the price? Don't assume anything. You may have to pay for transportation to and from the airport. A box lunch may be included in an

excursion, but drinks might cost extra. Beer might be included, but wine might not. Can you opt out of certain activities, or does the bus leave once a day, with no exceptions? Are all your meals planned in advance? Can you choose your entree at dinner, or does everybody get the same chicken cutlet?

Note: If you choose an escorted tour, think strongly about purchasing travel insurance from an independent agency, especially if the tour operator asks you to pay up front. See the section on insurance, earlier in this chapter. One final caveat: Since escorted tour prices are based on double occupancy, the single traveler is usually penalized.

There are many escorted tour companies to choose from, each offering transportation to and within Spain, prearranged hotel space, and such extras as bilingual tour guides and lectures. Many of these tours to Spain include excursions to Morocco or Portugal.

Some of the most expensive and luxurious tours are run by **Abercrombie & Kent International** (☎ **800/323-7308** or 630/954-2944; www.abercrombiekent.com), including deluxe 13- or 19-day tours of the Iberian Peninsula by train. Guests stay in fine hotels, ranging from a late medieval palace to the exquisite Alfonso XIII in Seville.

American Express Vacations (☎ **800/446-6234** in the U.S. and Canada), offers many options in Spain, and can also arrange nonescorted package deals.

Trafalgar Tours (☎ **800/626-6604** or 212/689-8977; www.trafalgartours.com) offers a number of tours of Spain. One of the most popular offerings is a 16-day trip called "The Best of Spain" (this land-only package is $1,425; with land and air, it's $2,085 to $2,300).

Insight International's "Highlights of Spain" is a 10-day tour that begins in Madrid, sweeps along the southern and eastern coasts, and concludes in Madrid. The company offers the tour for $1,863 to $2,023 including airfare, accommodations, and some meals. For information, contact your travel agent or Insight International (☎ **800/582-8380**).

Alternative Travel Group Ltd. (☎ **01865/310-399**) is a British firm that organizes walking and cycling vacations, plus wine tours in Spain, Italy, and France. Tours explore the scenic countryside and medieval towns of each country. If you'd like a brochure outlining the tours, call ☎ **01865/315-665.**

PACKAGE DEALS

Package tours are not the same thing as escorted tours. They are simply a way to buy airfare and accommodations at the same time. For popular destinations like Spain, they can save you a ton of money. In many cases, a package that includes airfare, hotel, and transportation to and from the airport will cost you less than just the hotel alone would have, had you booked it yourself. That's because packages are sold in bulk to tour operators—who resell them to the public at a cost that drastically undercuts standard rates.

Packages, however, vary widely. Some offer a better class of hotels than others. Some offer the same hotels for lower prices. Some offer flights on scheduled airlines, while others book charters. In some packages, your choice of accommodations and travel days may be limited. Some packages let you choose between escorted vacations and independent vacations; others will allow you to add on just a few excursions or escorted day trips (also at lower prices than you could locate on your own) without booking an entirely escorted tour. Each destination usually has one or two packagers that are usually cheaper than the rest because they buy in even greater bulk. If you spend the time to shop around, you will save in the long run.

The best place to start your search is the travel section of your local Sunday newspaper. Also check the ads in the back of national travel magazines like *Travel & Leisure, National Geographic Traveler,* and *Condé Nast Traveller.* One of the biggest packages in the Northeast, **Liberty Travel** (☎ 888/271-1584; www.libertytravel.com), usually boasts a full-page ad in Sunday papers. You won't get much in the way of service, but you will get a good deal. **American Express Vacations** (☎ 800/241-1700; www.leisureweb.com) is another option.

Another good resource is the airlines themselves, which often package their flights together with accommodations. Among the airline packagers, **Iberia Airlines** (☎ 800/772-4642; www.iberia.com) leads the way. Other packages for travel in Spain are offered by **TWA** (☎ 800/221-2000; www.twa.com), **United Airlines** (☎ 800/538-2929; www.ual.com), **American Airlines FlyAway Vacations** (☎ 800/321-2121; www.aa.com), and **Delta Dream Vacations** (☎ 800/872-7786; www.delta-air.com).

9 Getting Around

BY PLANE

Two affiliated airlines operate within Spain: **Iberia** and its smaller cousin, **Aviaco.** (For reservations on either of these airlines, call ☎ 800/772-4642 in the U.S.) By European standards, domestic flights within Spain are relatively inexpensive, and considering the vast distances within the country, flying between distant points sometimes makes sense.

If you plan to travel to a number of cities and regions, Iberia's "Visit Spain" ticket, priced between $240 and $260 ($299 and $349 to include the Canary Islands), depending on the season, can be a good deal. Sold only in conjunction with a transatlantic ticket and valid for any airport within Spain and the Balearic Islands, it requires that you choose up to four different cities in advance, in the order you'll visit them. Restrictions forbid flying immediately back to the city of departure, instead encouraging far-flung visits to widely scattered regions of the peninsula. Only one change within the preset itinerary is permitted once the ticket is issued. The dates and departure times of the actual flights, however, can be determined or changed without penalty once you arrive in Spain. Also, passengers who want to exceed the predesignated number of stops (four) included within the basic ticket can add additional cities to their itineraries for $50 each. Children under 2 travel for 10% of the adult fare, and children 2 to 11 travel for 50% of the adult fare. The ticket is valid for up to 60 days after your initial transatlantic arrival in Spain.

BY TRAIN

Spain is crisscrossed with a comprehensive network of rail lines. Hundreds of trains depart every day for points around the country, including the fast TALGO and the newer, faster AVE trains, which reduced rail time between Madrid and Seville to only 2½ hours.

If you plan to travel a great deal on the European railroads, it's worth buying a copy of the ***Thomas Cook European Timetable of European Passenger Railroads.*** It's available exclusively in North America from **Forsyth Travel Library,** 226 Westchester Ave., White Plains, NY 10604 (☎ 800/FORSYTH), at a cost of $27.95, plus $4.95 postage priority airmail in the United States plus $2 (U.S.) for shipments to Canada.

The most economical way to travel in Spain is on the Spanish State Railways (RENFE). Most main long-distance connections are served with night express trains having first- and second-class seats as well as beds and bunks. There are also comfortable high-speed daytime trains of the TALGO, TER, and Electrotren types. There is a general fare for these trains; bunks, beds, and certain superior-quality trains cost extra. Nevertheless, the Spanish railway is one of the most economical in Europe; in most cases, this is the best way to go.

RAIL PASSES

RENFE, the national railway of Spain, offers the **Spain Flexipass,** a discounted rail pass. Flexipasses permit a predesignated number of travel days within a predetermined time block—for example, 3 or 5 days in 1 month or 10 days in 2 months. You must buy these passes in the United States prior to your departure. For more information, consult a travel agent or **Rail Europe (☎ 800/4-EURAIL).**

VE Tours offers a computerized link to RENFE with its "instant purchase ticketing." By calling ☎ **800/222-8383,** travelers can reserve seats for travel between various cities within Spain and on journeys on RENFE to neighboring countries. The network includes access to the Intercity, Estrella, and Tren Hotel lines, as well as access to the AVE, Spain's high-speed network.

THE EURAILPASS   The EurailPass is one of Europe's greatest travel bargains, offering unlimited first-class travel in any country in western Europe, except the British Isles (good in Ireland). You must buy these passes in the United States prior to your departure; call your travel agent or **Rail Europe (☎ 800/4-EURAIL).**

The EurailPass also entitles you to discounts on some bus and steamship lines. Passes are available for 15 days or as long as 3 months and are strictly nontransferable. Children under 4 travel free, provided they don't occupy a seat of their own (otherwise, they're charged half fare); children 4 to 12 pay half fare. If you're under 26, you can purchase a Eurail Youthpass, which entitles you to unlimited second-class travel, for either 15 days, 1 month, or 2 months.

The **Eurail Saverpass** provides discounted 15-day travel for groups of three people traveling continuously together between April and September or two people between October and March. The price of a Saverpass, valid all over Europe, is good for first class only.

The **Eurail Flexipass** allows passengers to visit Europe with more flexibility. It's valid in first class and offers the same privileges as the EurailPass. However, it provides a number of individual travel days that can be used over a much longer period of consecutive days. That makes it possible to stay in one city and yet not lose a single day of travel. The pass entitles you, within a 2-month period, to 10 or 15 days of travel.

With similar qualifications and restrictions, travelers under 26 can purchase a **Eurail Youth Flexipass.** It also allows, within a 2-month period, for 10 or 15 days of travel.

EUROPASS   Like the EurailPass, the Europass offers the most favorable rates only to buyers who purchase it outside of Europe. Europasses can be purchased from any travel agent, or arranged over the phone by dialing ☎ **800/4-EURAIL.**

Depending on the fee, Europass allows unlimited rail travel within and between three and five European countries with shared (contiguous) borders, arranged into several different price tiers. The countries participating in the Europass plan include Italy, France, Germany, Switzerland, and Spain. The terrain covered by the Europass plan is deliberately less broad-based than that honored by the 17 countries within the Eurail network.

If you opt for 5 to 7 days of first-class train travel in three of the above-mentioned countries (Italy plus two contiguous countries on the list), you'll have up to 2 months to complete your travel.

If you opt for 8 to 10 days of travel within any 2-month period, you'll be able to add a fourth country from the above-cited list, and if you opt for 11 to 15 days of travel within any 2-month period, you can travel through all five of the above-mentioned countries while using the pass.

Riding the Rails in Style

Al Andalus Expreso (or simply Al Andalus) is a restored vintage train that travels through some of the most historic destinations in Andalusia. The train retains an atmosphere and level of service that you just don't see very often these days. The passenger and dining cars boast panels of inlaid marquetry, hardwoods, brass fittings, and etched glass that could well be found in the Edwardian parlor of a private mansion; beneath the antique veneers, state-of-the-art engineering maintains comfortably high speeds. The train offers fine dining and such amenities as individual showers on wheels.

Al Andalus consists of 13 carriages manufactured in Britain, Spain, or France between 1929 and 1930. These carriages were collected and restored by railway historians at RENFE. Included are two restaurant cars, a games and lounge car, a bar car where live piano music and evening flamenco dances are presented, five sleeping carriages, and two shower cars. All carriages (except the shower cars) are air-conditioned and heated.

For reservations, contact your travel agent. For additional brochures and information, contact **Marketing Ahead,** 433 Fifth Ave., New York, NY 10016 (☎ **800/223-1356** or 212/686-9213).

You can reduce costs with this means of transport by sharing your trip with another adult, who will receive a 50% discount on each of the above-mentioned fares.

Note: You can add what Europass refers to as an "associate country" (Austria, Benelux, Greece, or Portugal) to the reach of your Europass by paying a surcharge.

BY CAR

A car offers the greatest flexibility while you're touring, even if you're just doing day trips from Madrid. Don't, however, plan to drive in Madrid or Barcelona for city sightseeing; it's too congested. Theoretically, rush hour is Monday to Saturday from 8 to 10am, 1 to 2pm, and 4 to 6pm. In reality, it's always busy.

CAR RENTALS

Many of North America's biggest car-rental companies, including Avis, Budget, and Hertz, maintain offices throughout Spain. Although several Spanish car-rental companies exist, we've gotten lots of letters from readers of previous editions telling us that they've had a hard time resolving billing irregularities and insurance claims, so you may want to stick with the U.S.-based rental firms.

Note that tax on car rentals is a whopping 15%; don't forget to factor that into your travel budget. Usually, prepaid rates do not include taxes, which will be collected at the rental kiosk itself. Be sure to ask explicitly what's included when you're quoted a rate.

Avis (☎ 800/331-2112; www.avis.com) maintains about 100 branches throughout Spain, including about a dozen in Madrid, eight in Barcelona, a half dozen in Seville, and four in Murcia. If you reserve and pay your rental by telephone at least 2 weeks before your departure from North America, you'll qualify for the company's best rate, with unlimited kilometers included. You can usually get competitive rates from **Hertz** (☎ 800/654-3001; www.hertz.com) and **Budget** (☎ 800/472-3325; www.budget.com); it always pays to comparison shop. Budget doesn't have a drop-off charge if you pick up in one Spanish city and return to another. All three companies require that drivers be at least 21 years of age and, in some cases, not older than 72. To be able to rent a car, you must have a passport and a valid driver's license;

you must also have a valid credit card or a prepaid voucher. An international driver's license is not essential, but you might want to present it if you have one; it's available from any North American office of the American Automobile Association (AAA).

Two other agencies of note include **Kemwel Holiday Autos** (☎ **800/678-0678;** www.kemwel.com) and **Auto Europe** (☎ **800/223-5555;** www.autoeurope.com).

Many packages are available that include airfare, accommodations, and a rental car with unlimited mileage. Compare these prices with the cost of booking airline tickets and renting a car separately to see if these offers are good deals. Internet resources can make comparison shopping easier. **Microsoft Expedia** (www.expedia.com) and **Travelocity** (www.travelocity.com) help you compare prices and locate car rental bargains from various companies nationwide. They will even make your reservation for you once you've found the best deal. See the Online Directory at the end of this book for tips.

INSURANCE   Before you drive off in a rental car, be sure you're insured. Hasty assumptions about your personal auto insurance or a rental agency's additional coverage could end up costing you tens of thousands of dollars—even if you are involved in an accident that was clearly the fault of another driver.

The basic insurance coverage offered by most car-rental companies, known as the **Loss/Damage Waiver (LDW)** or **Collision Damage Waiver (CDW),** can cost as much as $20 a day. It usually covers the full value of the vehicle with no deductions if an outside party causes an accident or other damage to the rental car.

Americans who have their own car insurance policies are most likely covered in the United States for loss of or damage to a rental car, and liability in case of injury to any other party involved in an accident. Coverage probably doesn't extend outside the United States, however. Be sure to find out whether you are covered in the area you are visiting, whether your policy extends to all persons who will be driving the rental car, how much liability is covered in case an outside party is injured in an accident, and whether the type of vehicle you are renting is included under your contract. (Rental trucks, sports utility vehicles, and luxury vehicles may not be covered.)

Most major credit cards provide some degree of coverage as well—provided they were used to pay for the rental. Terms vary widely, however, so be sure to call your credit card company directly before you rent. If you are uninsured or driving abroad, your credit card provides primary collision coverage as long as you decline the rental agency's insurance. This means that the credit card will cover damage or theft of a rental car for the full cost of the vehicle. If you already have insurance, your credit card will provide secondary coverage—which basically covers your deductible.

Credit cards will *not* cover liability, or the cost of injury to an outside party and/or damage to an outside party's vehicle. If you do not hold an insurance policy, or if your policy doesn't cover you outside the United States, you may want to seriously consider purchasing additional liability insurance from your rental company. Be sure to check the terms, however: Some rental agencies only cover liability if the renter is not at fault; even then, the rental company's obligation varies from state to state.

DRIVING RULES

Spaniards drive on the right side of the road. Drivers should pass on the left; local drivers sound their horns when passing another car and flash their lights at you if you're driving slowly (slowly for high-speed Spain) in the left lane. Autos coming from the right have the right-of-way.

Spain's express highways are known as *autopistas,* which charge a toll, and *autovías,* which don't. To exit in Spain, follow the *salida* sign, except in Catalonia, where the word to get off is *sortida.* On most express highways, the speed limit is 75 miles per hour (120 kmph). On other roads speed limits range from 56 miles per hour (90 kmph) to 62 miles per hour (100 kmph). You will see many drivers far exceeding these limits.

Most accidents in Spain are recorded along the notorious Costa del Sol highway, the Carretera de Cádiz.

If you must drive through a Spanish city, try to avoid morning and evening rush hours. Never park your car facing oncoming traffic, as that is against the law. If you are fined by the highway patrol (Guardia Civil de Tráfico), you must pay on the spot. Penalties for drinking and driving are very stiff.

MAPS

Start by checking out the free, color fold-out map at the back of this book.

For one of the best overviews of the Iberian Peninsula (Spain and Portugal), obtain a copy of Michelin map number 990 (for a folding version) or number 460 for the same map in a spiral-bound version. For more detailed looks at Spain, Michelin has a series of six maps (no. 441 to 446), showing specific regions, complete with many minor roads.

For extensive touring, purchase *Mapas de Carreteras-España y Portugal,* published by Almax Editores and available at most leading bookstores in Spain. This cartographic compendium of Spain provides an overview of the country and includes road and street maps of some of its major cities as well.

The **American Automobile Association** (☎ **800/222-4357**) publishes a regional map of Spain that's available free to members at most AAA offices in the United States. Also available free to members is a guide of approximately 60 pages, *Motoring in Europe,* that gives helpful information about road signs and speed limits, as well as insurance regulations and other relevant matters. Incidentally, the AAA is associated with the **Real Automóvil Club de España,** José Abascal, 10, Madrid 28003 (☎ **91-594-74-00**). This organization will provide helpful information about road conditions in Spain, including tourist and travel data. It will also provide limited road service, in an emergency, if your car breaks down.

BREAKDOWNS

These can be a serious problem. If you're driving a Spanish-made vehicle, you'll probably be able to find spare parts, if needed. But if you have a foreign-made vehicle, you may be stranded. Have the car checked out before setting out on a long trek through Spain. On a major motorway you'll find strategically placed emergency phone boxes. On secondary roads, call for help by asking the operator to locate the nearest Guardia Civil, which will put you in touch with a garage that can tow you to a repair shop.

As noted above, the Spanish affiliate of AAA can provide limited assistance in the event of a breakdown.

BY BUS

Bus service in Spain is extensive, low priced, and comfortable enough for short distances. You'll rarely encounter a bus terminal in Spain. The "station" might be a cafe, a bar, the street in front of a hotel, or simply a spot at an intersection.

A bus may be the cheapest mode of transportation, but it's not really the best option for distances of more than 100 miles. On long hauls, buses are often uncomfortable. Another major drawback might be a lack of toilet facilities, though rest stops are frequent. It's best for 1-day excursions outside of a major tourist center such as Madrid. In the rural areas of the country, bus networks are more extensive than the railway system; they go virtually everywhere, connecting every village. In general, a bus ride between two major cities in Spain, such as from Córdoba to Seville or

Madrid to Barcelona, is about two-thirds the price of a train ride and a few hours faster.

10 Tips on Accommodations

From castles converted into hotels to modern high-rise resorts overlooking the Mediterranean, Spain has some of the most varied hotel accommodations in the world—with equally varied price ranges. Accommodations are broadly classified as follows:

ONE- TO FIVE-STAR HOTELS   The Spanish government rates hotels by stars. A five-star hotel is truly deluxe with deluxe prices; a one-star hotel is the most modest accommodation officially recognized as a hotel by the government. A four-star hotel offers first-class accommodations; a three-star hotel is moderately priced; and a one- or two-star hotel is inexpensively priced. The government grants stars based on such amenities as elevators, private bathrooms, and air-conditioning. If a hotel is classified as a *residencia*, it means that it serves breakfast (usually) but no other meals.

HOSTALS   Not to be confused with a hostel for students, a *hostal* is a modest hotel without services, where you can save money by carrying your own bags and the like. You'll know it's a hostal if a small *S* follows the capital letter *H* on the blue plaque by the door. A hostal with three stars is about the equivalent of a hotel with two stars.

PENSIONS   These boarding houses are among the least expensive accommodations, but you're required to take either full board (three meals) or half-board, which is breakfast plus lunch or dinner.

CASAS HUÉSPEDES & FONDAS   These are the cheapest places in Spain and can be recognized by the light-blue plaques at the door displaying *CH* and *F,* respectively. These are invariably basic but respectable establishments.

YOUTH HOSTELS   Spain has about 140 hostels (*albergues de juventud*). In theory, those 25 or under have the first chance at securing a bed for the night, but these places are certainly not limited to young people. Some of them are equipped for persons with disabilities. Most hostels impose an 11pm curfew. For information, contact **Red Española de Alberques Juveniles,** calle José Ortega y Gasset, 71, 28006 Madrid (☎ **91-347-77-00**).

PARADORS   The Spanish government runs a series of unique state-owned inns called paradors (*paradores* in Spanish), which now blanket the country. Deserted castles, monasteries, palaces, and other buildings have been taken over and converted into hotels. Today there are 86 paradors in all, and they're documented in a booklet called *Visiting the Paradors,* available at Spanish tourist offices (see "Information & Required Documents" at the beginning of this chapter).

At great expense, modern bathrooms, steam heat, and the like have been added to these buildings, yet classic Spanish architecture, where it existed, has been retained. Establishments are often furnished with antiques or at least good reproductions and decorative objects typical of the country.

Meals are also served in these government-owned inns. Usually, typical dishes of the region are featured. Paradors are likely to be overcrowded in the summer months, so advance reservations, arranged through any travel agent, are wise.

The government also operates a type of accommodation known as ***albergues:*** these are comparable to motels, standing along the roadside and usually built in hotel-scarce sections for the convenience of passing motorists. A client is not allowed to stay in an albergue for more than 48 hours, and the management doesn't accept reservations.

In addition, the government runs *refugios,* mostly in remote areas, attracting hunters, fishers, and mountain climbers. Another state-sponsored establishment is the *hostería,* or specialty restaurant, such as the one at Alcalá de Henares, near Madrid. Hosterías don't offer rooms; decorated in the style of a particular province, they serve regional dishes at reasonable prices.

The central office of paradors is **Paradores de España,** Requeña, 3, 28013 Madrid (☎ **91-516-66-66**). The U.S. representative for the Paradores of Spain is **Marketing Ahead,** 433 5th Ave., New York, NY 10016 (☎ **800/223-1356** or 212/686/9213). In the United Kingdom, contact **Keytel International,** 402 Edgeware Rd., London W2 1ED (☎ **0171/402-8182**). Travel agents can also arrange reservations. In the United States, you can make a reservation at any parador by calling **Fourth Dimension Tours,** 7101 SW 99th Ave., Suite 105, Miami 33173 (☎ **800/343-0020**).

RENTING A HOUSE OR APARTMENT

If you rent a home or an apartment, you can save money on accommodations and dining and still take daily trips to see the surrounding area.

Apartments in Spain generally fall into two different categories: hotel *apartamentos* and *residencia apartamentos.* The hotel apartments have full facilities, with chamber service, equipped kitchenettes, and often restaurants and bars. The residencia apartments, also called *apartamentos turísticos,* are fully furnished with kitchenettes but lack the facilities of the hotel complexes. They are cheaper, however.

One rental company to try is **Hometours International** (☎ **800/367-4668** or 423/690-8484), which mainly handles properties in Andalusia. Call them, and they'll send you a 40-page color catalog with descriptions and pictures, for $9 to cover postage and handling. Units are rented for a minimum of 7 days.

Another agency is **ILC** (International Lodging Corp.; ☎ **800/SPAIN-44** or 212/228-5900), which rents privately owned apartments, houses, and villas, for a week or more. It also offers access to suites in well-known hotels for stays of a week or longer, sometimes at bargain rates. Rental units, regardless of their size, usually contain a kitchen. The company's listings cover accommodations in Madrid, Barcelona, Seville, Granada, and Majorca.

Fast Facts: Spain

Business Hours Banks are open Monday to Friday from 9:30am to 2pm and Saturday from 9:30am to 1pm. Most offices are open Monday to Friday from 9am to 5 or 5:30pm; the longtime practice of early closings in summer seems to be dying out. In restaurants, lunch is usually 1 to 4pm and dinner 9 to 11:30pm or midnight. There are no set rules for the opening of bars and taverns, many opening at 8am, others at noon; most stay open until 1:30am or later. Major stores are open Monday to Saturday from 9:30am to 8pm; smaller establishments, however, often take a siesta, doing business from 9:30am to 1:30pm and 4:30 to 8pm. Hours can vary from store to store.

Climate See "When to Go," earlier in this chapter.

Currency See "Money," earlier in this chapter.

Customs See "Visitor Information, Entry Requirements & Customs," earlier in this chapter.

Driving Rules See "Getting Around," earlier in this chapter.

Drugstores To find an open pharmacy outside of normal business hours, check the list of stores posted on the door of any drugstore. The law requires drugstores to operate on a rotating system of hours so that there's always a drugstore open somewhere, even Sunday at midnight.

Electricity Most hotels have 220 volts AC (50 cycles). Some older places have 110 or 125 volts AC. Carry your adapter with you, and always check at your hotel desk before plugging in any electrical appliance. It's best to travel with battery-operated equipment, or just to buy a new hair dryer in Spain.

Embassies/Consulates If you lose your passport, fall seriously ill, get into legal trouble, or have some other serious problem, your embassy or consulate can help. These are the Madrid addresses and hours: The **United States Embassy,** calle Serrano, 75 (☎ **91-587-2200;** metro: Núñez de Balboa), is open Monday to Friday from 9am to 6pm. The **Canadian Embassy,** Núñez de Balboa, 35 (☎ **91-423-32-50;** metro: Velázquez), is open Monday to Friday from 8:30am to 5:30pm. The **United Kingdom Embassy,** calle Fernando el Santo, 16 (☎ **91-319-02-00;** metro: Colón), is open Monday to Friday from 9am to 1:30pm and 3 to 6pm. The **Republic of Ireland** has an embassy at Claudio Coello, 73 (☎ **91-576-35-00;** metro: Serrano); it's open Monday to Friday from 9am to 2pm. The **Australian Embassy,** Plaza Diego de Ordas 3, Edificio Santa Engracia 120 (☎ **91-441-93-00;** metro: Rios Rosas), is open Monday through Thursday 8:30am to 5pm, Friday 8:30am to 2:15pm. Citizens of **New Zealand** have an embassy at Plaza de la Lealtad, 2 (☎ **91-523-02-26;** metro: Banco de España); it's open Monday through Friday 9am to 1:30pm and 2:30 to 5:30pm.

Emergencies The national emergency number for Spain (except the Basque country) is ☎ **006;** in the Basque country it is ☎ **088.**

Language The official language in Spain is Castilian (or *Castellano*). Although Spanish is spoken in every province of Spain, local tongues reasserted themselves with the restoration of democracy in 1975. After years of being outlawed during the Franco dictatorship, Catalán has returned to Barcelona and Catalonia, even appearing on street signs; this language and its derivatives are also spoken in the Valencia area and in the Balearic Islands, including Majorca (even though natives there will tell you they speak *Mallorquín*). The Basque language is widely spoken in the Basque region (the northeast, near France), which is seeking independence from Spain. Likewise, the Gallego language, which sounds and looks very much like Portuguese, has enjoyed a renaissance in Galicia (the northwest). Of course, English is spoken in most hotels, restaurants, and shops.

The best phrasebook is *Spanish for Travellers* by Berlitz; it has a menu supplement and a 12,500-word glossary of both English and Spanish.

Liquor Laws The legal drinking age is 18. Bars, taverns, and cafeterias usually open at 8am, and many serve alcohol until around 1:30am or later. Generally, you can purchase alcoholic beverages in almost any market.

Mail Airmail letters to the United States and Canada cost 120 pesetas (80¢) up to 15 grams, and letters to Britain or other EU countries cost 75 ptas. (50¢) up to 20 grams; letters within Spain cost 35 ptas. (25¢). Postcards have the same rates as letters. Allow about 8 days for delivery to North America, generally less to the United Kingdom; in some cases, letters take 2 weeks to reach North America. Rates change frequently, so check at your hotel before mailing anything. As for surface mail to North America, forget it. Chances are that you'll be home before your letter arrives.

Police　The national emergency number is ☎ **006** throughout Spain, except in the Basque country, where it is ☎ **088.**

Rest Rooms　In Spain they're called *aseos* and *servicios* or simply *lavabos* and labeled *caballeros* for men and *damas* or *señoras* for women. If you can't find any, go into a bar, but you should order something.

Safety　Pickpockets and purse snatchers flourish throughout Spain, particularly in Madrid, Barcelona, Seville, and the Costa del Sol. In the wake of so many robberies, visitors have taken to leaving their passports at the hotel. But here's a catch-22 situation: Identification checks are common by Spanish police, who are actually cracking down on illegal immigrants. Police officers or plainclothes agents can stop you at any time of the day or night and demand to see your passport. You can be arrested, as many visitors are, if you can't produce yours. Carry your passport with you but carefully conceal it on your body, perhaps in a safety belt.

Taxes　The internal sales tax (known in Spain as IVA) ranges between 7% and 33%, depending on the commodity being sold. Food, wine, and basic necessities are taxed at 7%; most goods and services (including car rentals) at 13%; luxury items (jewelry, all tobacco, imported liquors) at 33%; and hotels at 7%.

If you are not a European Union resident and make purchases in Spain worth more than 15,000 ptas. ($100.50), you can get a tax refund. To get this refund, you must complete three copies of a form that the store will give you, detailing the nature of your purchase and its value. Citizens of non-EU countries show the purchase and the form to the Spanish Customs Office. The shop is supposed to refund the amount due you. Inquire at the time of purchase how they will do so and discuss in what currency your refund will arrive.

Telephones　If you don't speak Spanish, you'll find it easier to telephone from your hotel, but remember that this is often very expensive because hotels impose a surcharge on every operator-assisted call. In some cases this can be as high as 40% or more. On the street, phone booths (known as *cabinas*) have dialing instructions in English; you can make local calls by inserting a 25 peseta coin (15¢) for 3 minutes.

In Spain many smaller establishments, especially bars, discos, and a few informal restaurants, don't have phones. Further, many summer-only bars and discos secure a phone for the season only, then get a new number the next season. Many attractions, such as small churches or even minor museums, have no staff to receive inquiries from the public.

In 1998, all telephone numbers in Spain changed to a nine-digit system instead of the six- or seven-digit method used previously. Each number is now preceded by its provincial code for local, national, and international calls. For example, when calling to Madrid from Madrid or another province within Spain, telephone customers must dial 91-123-4567. Similarly, when calling Valladolid from within or outside the province, dial 979-123-4567.

To call Spain from another country, first dial the international long-distance code (011) plus the country code (34), followed by the 9-digit number. Hence, when calling Madrid from the United States, dial (011-34) 91-123-4567.

To make an international call from Spain, you must dial 07, followed by the country code, the area code, and the telephone number.

When in Spain, the access number for an **AT&T** calling card is ☎ **900/ 99-010-11.** The access number for **Sprint** is ☎ **800/366-2255;** for **MCI,** it's ☎ **900/990-014.**

More information is also available on the Teléfonica Web site at www. telefonica.es.

Time   Spain is 6 hours ahead of eastern standard time in the United States. Daylight saving time is in effect from the last Sunday in March to the last Sunday in September.

Tipping   Don't overtip. The government requires restaurants and hotels to include their service charges—usually 15% of the bill. However, that doesn't mean you should skip out of a place without dispensing some extra pesetas. The following are some guidelines:

Your hotel porter should get 75 ptas. (50¢) per bag and never less than 100 ptas. (65¢), even if you have only one suitcase. Maids should be given 150 ptas. ($1) per day, more if you're generous. Tip doormen 125 ptas. (85¢) for assisting with baggage and 50 ptas. (35¢) for calling a cab. In top-ranking hotels the concierge will often submit a separate bill, showing charges for newspapers and other services; if he or she has been particularly helpful, tip extra. For cab drivers, add about 10% to the fare as shown on the meter. At airports, such as Barajas in Madrid and major terminals, the porter who handles your luggage will present you with a fixed-charge bill.

In both restaurants and nightclubs, a 15% service charge is added to the bill. To that, add another 3% to 5% tip, depending on the quality of the service. Waiters in deluxe restaurants and nightclubs are accustomed to the extra 5%, which means you'll end up tipping 20%. If that seems excessive, you must remember that the initial service charge reflected in the fixed price is distributed among all the help.

Barbers and hairdressers expect a 10% to 15% tip. Tour guides expect 200 ptas. ($1.35), although a tip is not mandatory. Theater and bullfight ushers get from 50 to 75 ptas. (35¢ to 50¢).

3 Madrid

Madrid was conceived, planned, and built when Spain was at the peak of its confidence and power, and the city became the solid and dignified seat of a great empire stretching around the world. Monumental Madrid glitters almost as much as Paris, Rome, or London—and parties more than any other city on the continent. Although it lacks the spectacular Romanesque and Gothic monuments of older Spanish cities, Madrid never fails to convey its own sense of grandeur.

Madrid has the highest altitude of any European capital and its climate is blisteringly hot in summer but often quite cold in winter. Traffic roars down wide boulevards that stretch for miles from the narrow streets of the city's historic 17th-century core to the ugly concrete suburbs that have spread in recent years.

Don't come to Madrid expecting a city that looks classically Iberian. True, many of the older buildings in the historic core look as Spanish as those you might have encountered in rural towns across the plains of La Mancha. However, a great number of the monuments and palaces mirror the architecture of France—an oddity that reflects the genetic link between the royal families of Spain and France.

Most striking is how the city has blossomed since Franco's demise. Madrid was the epicenter of *la movida* (the movement), a resuscitation of the arts after years of dictatorial creative repression. Today, despite stiff competition from such smaller cities as Barcelona and Seville, Madrid still reigns as the country's artistic and creative centerpiece.

More world-class art is on view in the central neighborhood around the stellar Prado Museum than within virtually any concentrated area in the world: the Caravaggios and Rembrandts at the Thyssen-Bornemisza; the El Grecos and Velázquezes at the Prado itself; and the Dalís and Mirós—not to mention Picasso's wrenching *Guernica*—at the Reina Sofía. Ironically, much of the city's art was collected by 18th-century Spanish monarchs whose artistic sense was frequently more astute than their political savvy.

Regrettably, within the city limits you'll also find sprawling expanses of concrete towers, sometimes paralyzing traffic, a growing incidence of street crime, and entire districts that, as in every other metropolis, bear virtually no historic or cultural interest for a temporary visitor. Many long-time visitors to the city find that its quintessential Spanish feel has subsided somewhat in the face of a Brussels-like "Europeanization" that has occurred since Spain's 1986 induction into the European Union. The city's gems remain the opulence of the **Palacio Real,** the bustle of **El Rastro's** flea market, and the sultry fever of late-night flamenco. When urban commotion starts to overwhelm, seek respite in the **Parque del Retiro,** a vast, verdant oasis in the heart of the city just a stone's throw from the Prado.

If your time in Spain is limited, a stopover in Madrid coupled with day trips to its environs can provide a primer in virtually every major period and school of Spanish art and architecture dating from the Roman occupation. No fewer than nine world-class destinations are within 100 miles. These include **Toledo,** one of the most successful blends of medieval Arab, Jewish, and Christian cultures in the world; **Segovia,** site of a well-preserved ancient Roman aqueduct and monuments commemorating Queen Isabella's coronation in 1474; and **Ávila,** the most perfectly preserved medieval fortified city in Iberia, with its 11th-century battlements and endless references to Catholicism's most down-to-earth mystic, St. Teresa. **El Escorial, El Pardo** (Franco's favorite hangout), and the palace and monuments at **Aranjuez,** reveal the tastes and manias that inspired rulers of Spain throughout history. The neofascist monument at **El Valle de los Caídos** (the Valley of the Fallen) is a powerful testament to those who died in the Spanish Civil War. To see rural Iberia at its most charming, head for **Chinchón** or, better yet, the cliff-top village of **Cuenca,** where a lavish homage to modern art and music has recently been installed. For more information on these day trips, see chapter 4, "Side Trips from Madrid."

1 Orientation

ARRIVING

BY PLANE   Madrid's international airport, **Barajas,** lies 9 miles east of the center and has two terminals—one for international traffic, the other for domestic—connected by a moving sidewalk. For Barajas Airport information, call ☎ **91-305-83-43.**

Air-conditioned yellow airport buses can take you from the arrival terminal to the bus depot under the central Plaza de Colón. You can also get off at stops along the way, provided that your baggage isn't stored in the hold. The fare is 385 ptas. ($2.60); buses leave every 15 minutes, either to or from the airport.

By taxi, expect to pay 2,500 ptas. ($16.75) and up, plus surcharges, for the trip to the airport and for baggage handling. If you take an unmetered limousine, make sure you negotiate the price in advance.

A subway connecting Barajas Airport and central Madrid was completed in 1999, allowing additional ground transportation options.

BY TRAIN   Madrid has three major railway stations: **Atocha** (Avenida Ciudad de Barcelona; metro: Atocha RENFE), for trains to Lisbon, Toledo, Andalusia, and Extremadura; **Chamartín** (in the northern suburbs at Augustín de Foxá; metro: Chamartí), for trains to and from Barcelona, Asturias, Cantabria, Castilla-León, the Basque country, Aragón, Catalonia, Levante (Valencia), Murcia, and the French frontier; and **Estación Príncipe Pío** or Norte (Paseo del Rey 30; metro: Norte), for trains to and from northwest Spain (Salamanca and Galicia). For information about connections from any of these stations, call RENFE (Spanish Railways) at ☎ **91-328-90-20** daily from 7am to 11pm.

For tickets, go to the principal office of **RENFE,** Alcalá 44 (☎ **91-328-90-20;** metro: Banco de España). The office is open Monday to Friday from 9:30am to 8pm.

BY BUS   Madrid has at least eight major bus terminals, including the large **Estación Sur de Autobuses,** calle Méndez Alvaro (☎ **91-468-42-00;** metro: Palos de la Frontera). Most buses pass through this station.

BY CAR   All highways within Spain radiate outward from Madrid. The following are the major highways into Madrid, with information on driving distances to the city:

Highways to Madrid

Route	From	Distance to Madrid
N-I	Irún	315 miles (505km)
N-II	Barcelona	389 miles (622km)
N-III	Valencia	217 miles (347km)
N-IV	Cádiz	388 miles (625km)
N-V	Badajoz	254 miles (409km)
N-VI	Galicia	374 miles (598km)

VISITOR INFORMATION

The most convenient tourist office is near the American Express office, on Duque de Medinaceli 2, Banco de España (☎ **91-429-31-77;** metro: Plaza de España); it's open Monday to Friday from 9am to 7pm and Saturday from 9:30am to 1pm. Ask for a street map of the next town on your itinerary, especially if you're driving. The staff here can give you a list of hotels and hostals but cannot recommend any particular lodging.

CITY LAYOUT

All roads lead to Madrid, which has outgrown its previous boundaries and is branching out in all directions.

MAIN ARTERIES & SQUARES   Every new arrival must find the **Gran Vía,** which cuts a winding pathway across the city beginning at the **Plaza de España,** where you'll find one of Europe's tallest skyscrapers, the Edificio España. This avenue is home to the largest concentration of shops, hotels, restaurants, and movie houses in the city with **calle de Serrano** a close runner-up.

South of the Gran Vía lies the **Puerta del Sol,** which is the starting point for all road distances within Spain. However, its tourism significance has declined, and today it is a prime hunting ground for pickpockets and purse snatchers. **Calle de Alcalá** begins here at **Sol** and runs for 2½ miles.

The **Plaza Mayor** lies at the heart of Old Madrid and is an attraction in itself with its mix of French and Georgian architecture. (Again, be wary of thieves here, especially late at night.) Pedestrians pass under the arches of the huge square onto the narrow streets of the old town, where you can find some of the capital's most intriguing restaurants and tascas, serving tasty tapas and drinks. The colonnaded ground level of the plaza is filled with shops, many selling souvenir hats of turn-of-the-century Spanish sailors or army officers.

The area south of the Plaza Mayor—known as *barrios bajos*—is made up of narrow cobblestone streets lined with 16th- and 17th-century architecture. From the Plaza, take **Arco de Cuchilleros,** a street packed with markets, restaurants, flamenco clubs, and taverns, to explore this district.

Gran Vía ends at calle de Alcalá, and at this juncture lies the grand **Plaza de la Cibeles,** with its fountain to Cybele, "the mother of the gods," and the main city post office (known as "the cathedral of post offices"). From Cibeles, the wide **Paseo de Recoletos** begins a short run north to **Plaza de Colón.** From this latter square rolls the serpentine central artery of Madrid **Paseo de la Castellana,** flanked by expensive shops, apartment buildings, luxury hotels, and foreign embassies.

Heading south from Cibeles is **Paseo del Prado,** where you'll find Spain's major attraction, the Museo del Prado, as well as the Jardín Botánica (Botanical Garden). The *paseo* also leads to the Atocha Railway Station. To the west of the garden lies **Parque del Retiro,** a magnificent park once reserved for royalty, with restaurants, nightclubs, a rose garden, and two lakes.

FINDING AN ADDRESS   Madrid is a city of both grand boulevards extending for long distances and of cramped meandering streets that follow no plan. Finding an address can sometimes be a problem, primarily because of the way buildings are numbered.

On most streets, the numbering begins on one side and runs consecutively until the end, resuming on the other side and going in the opposite direction, rather as a farmer plows a field, up one side, down the other. Thus, number 50 could be opposite number 250. But there are many exceptions to this system of numbering. That's why it's important to know the cross street as well as the number of the address you're looking for. To complicate matters, some addresses don't have a number at all. What they have instead is the designation *s/n,* meaning *sin número* (without number). For example, the address of the Panteón de Goya (Goya's Tomb) is Glorieta de San Antonio de la Florida, s/n. Note also that in Spain, as in many other European countries, the building number comes after the street name.

STREET MAPS   Arm yourself with a good map before setting out. Falk publishes the best, and it's available at most newsstands and kiosks in Madrid. The free maps given away by tourist offices and hotels aren't really adequate for more than general orientation, as they don't list the maze of little streets that is Old Madrid.

Neighborhoods in Brief

Madrid can be divided into three principal districts—Old Madrid, which holds the most tourist interest; Ensanche, the new district, often with the best shops and hotels; and the periphery, which is of little interest to visitors.

Plaza Mayor/Puerta Del Sol   This is the heart of Old Madrid, often called the tourist zone. Filled with taverns and bars, it is bounded by Carrera de San Jerónimo, calle Mayor, Cava de San Miguel, Cava Baja, and calle de la Cruz. From Plaza Mayor, the Arco de Cuchilleros is filled with Castilian restaurants and taverns; more of these traditional spots, called cuevas, line the Cava de San Miguel, Cava Alta, and Cava Baja. To the west of this old district is the Manzanares River. Also in this area, Muslim Madrid is centered on the Palacio de Oriente and Las Vistillas. What is now Plaza de la Paja was actually the heart of the city and its main marketplace during the medieval and Christian period. In 1617 the Plaza Mayor became the hub of Madrid, and it remains to this day the nighttime center of tourist activity, more so than the Puerta del Sol.

The Salamanca Quarter   Ever since Madrid's city walls came tumbling down in the 1860s, the district of Salamanca to the north has been the fashionable address. Calle de Serrano cuts through this neighborhood and is lined with stores and boutiques. Calle de Serrano is also home to the U.S. Embassy.

Gran Vía/Plaza De España   Gran Vía is the city's main street, lined with cinemas, department stores, and the headquarters of banks and corporations. It begins at the Plaza de España, with its bronze figures of Don Quixote and his faithful squire, Sancho Panza.

Arqúelles/Moncloa The university area is bounded by Pintor Rosales, Cea Bermúdez, Bravo Murillo, San Bernardo, and Conde Duque. Students haunt its famous ale houses.

Chueca This old and decaying area north of the Gran Vía includes the main streets of Hortaleza, Infantas, Barquillo, and San Lucas. It is the center of gay nightlife, with dozens of clubs and cheap restaurants. It can be dangerous at night, although police presence is usually notable.

Castellana/Recoletos/Paseo Del Prado Not a real city district, this is Madrid's north-south axis, its name changing along the way. The Museo del Prado and some of the city's more expensive hotels are found here. Many restaurants and other hotels are located along its side streets. In summer its large medians serve as home to open-air terraces filled with animated crowds. The most famous cafe is the Gran Café de Gijón (see "Where to Dine," later in this chapter).

2 Getting Around

Getting around Madrid is not easy, because everything is spread out. Even many Madrileño taxi drivers, often new arrivals themselves, are unfamiliar with their own city once they're off the main boulevards.

BY SUBWAY The metro system is quite easy to learn and use. The fare is 130 ptas. (85¢) for a one-way trip, and the central converging point is the Puerta del Sol. The metro operates from 6am to 1:30am and you should try to avoid rush hours. For information, call ☎ **91-429-31-77.** You can save money on public transportation by purchasing a 10-trip ticket known as a *bonos*—it costs 680 ptas. ($4.55).

BY BUS A bus network also services the city and suburbs, with routes clearly shown at each stop on a schematic diagram. Buses are fast and efficient because they travel along special lanes. Both red and yellow buses charge 130 ptas. (85¢) per ride.

For 645 ptas. ($4.30) you can also purchase a 10-trip bonos ticket (but without transfers) for Madrid's bus system. It's sold at **Empresa Municipal de Transportes,** Alcantara 24 (☎ **91-406-88-00**), where you can also purchase a guide to the bus routes. The office is open daily from 8am to 2pm.

BY TAXI Cab fares are pretty reasonable. When you flag down a taxi, the meter should register 180 ptas. ($1.20); for every kilometer thereafter, the fare increases by 89 ptas. (60¢). A supplement is charged for trips to the railway station or the bullring, as well as on Sundays and holidays. The ride to Barajas Airport carries a 400 ptas. ($2.70) surcharge, and there is a 150 ptas. ($1) supplement from railway stations. In addition, there is a 150 ptas. ($1) supplement on Sundays and holidays, plus a 150 ptas. ($1) supplement at night. It's customary to tip at least 10% of the fare.

Warning: Make sure that the meter is turned on when you get into a taxi. Otherwise, some drivers will assess the cost of the ride, and their assessment, you can be sure, will involve higher mathematics.

Also, there are unmetered taxis that hire out for the day or the afternoon. These are legitimate, but some drivers will operate as gypsy cabs. Since they're not metered, they can charge high rates. They are easy to avoid—always take either a black taxi with horizontal red bands or a white one with diagonal red bands instead.

If you take a taxi outside the city limits, the driver is entitled to charge you twice the rate shown on the meter.

To call a taxi, dial ☎ **91-447-51-80.**

BY CAR Driving in congested Madrid is a nightmare and potentially dangerous. It always feels like rush hour in Madrid, though theoretically, rush hours are 8 to 10am,

Madrid Metro

1 to 2pm, and 4 to 6pm Monday to Saturday. Parking is next to impossible, except in expensive garages. About the only time you can drive around Madrid with a minimum of hassle is in August, when thousands of Madrileños have taken their cars and headed for Spain's vacation oases. Save your car rentals for excursions from the capital. If you drive into Madrid from another city, ask at your hotel for the nearest garage or parking possibility and leave your vehicle there until you're ready to leave.

For more information on renting a car before you leave home see "Getting Around" in chapter 2. If you decide you want to rent one while in Madrid to explore its environs or to move on, you have several choices. In addition to its office at Barajas Airport (☎ 91-393-72-22), Avis has a main office in the city center at Gran Vía, 60 (☎ 91-348-03-48). Hertz, too, has an office at Barajas Airport (☎ 91-393-72-28) and another in the heart of Madrid in the Edificio España, Gran Vía, 88 (☎ 91-542-58-05). Budget Rent-a-Car maintains its headquarters at Gran Vía, 49 (☎ 91-393-7216). It's known in Spain as **Interrent.**

BY BICYCLE   Ever wonder why you see so few people riding bicycles in Madrid? Those who tried were overcome by the traffic pollution. It's better to walk.

ON FOOT   This is the perfect way to see Madrid, especially the ancient narrow streets of the old town. If you're going to another district—and chances are that your hotel will be outside the old town—you can take the bus or metro. For such a large city, Madrid can be covered amazingly well on foot, because so much of what will interest a visitor lies in various clusters.

Fast Facts: Madrid

American Express   For your mail or banking needs, you can go to the American Express office at the corner of Marqués de Cubas and Plaza de las Cortés, 2, across the street from the Palace Hotel (☎ 91-322-55-00 or 91-322-54-24; metro: Gran Vía). Open Monday to Friday from 9am to 5:30pm and Saturday from 9am to noon.

Baby-Sitters   Most major hotels can arrange for baby-sitters, called *canguros* (literally, kangaroos) or *niñeras.* Usually the concierge keeps a list of reliable nursemaids and will contact them for you provided you give adequate notice. Rates vary considerably but are usually fairly reasonable. Although many baby-sitters in Madrid speak English, don't count on it. You may also want to contact **La Casa de la Abuela** (☎ 91-574-30-94). Located in the prestigious Barrio Salamanca, this "grandmother's house" is basically a children's hotel and offers child care combined with creative exercises and workshops in a child-friendly environment. It is open year-round and prices vary.

Currency Exchange   The currency exchange at Chamartín railway station (metro: Chamartín) is open 24 hours and gives the best rates in the capital. If you exchange money at a bank, ask about the minimum commission charged.

Many banks in Spain still charge a 1% to 2% commission with a minimum charge of 500 ptas. ($3.35). However, branches of **Banco Central Hispano** charge no commission. Branches of **El Corte Inglés,** the department store chain, offer currency exchange facilities at various rates. You get the worst rates at street kiosks such as Chequepoint, Exact Change, and Cambios-Uno. Although they're handy and charge no commission, their rates are very low. Naturally, **American Express** offices offer the best rates on their own checks. ATMs are plentiful in Madrid.

Dentist   For an English-speaking dentist, contact the **U.S. Embassy,** Serrano, 75 (☎ **91-587-22-00**); it maintains a list of dentists who have offered their services to Americans abroad. For dental services, also consult **Unidad Médica Anglo-Americana,** Conde de Arandá 1 (☎ **91-435-18-23**). Office hours are Monday to Friday from 9am to 8pm and Saturday from 10am to 1pm, and there is a 24-hour answering service.

Doctor   For an English-speaking doctor, contact the **U.S. Embassy,** Serrano 75 (☎ **91-587-22-00**).

Drugstores   For a late-night pharmacy, dial ☎ **098** or look in the daily newspaper under *Farmacias de Guardia* to learn which drugstores are open after 8pm. Another way to find one is to go to any pharmacy which, even if closed, will always post a list of nearby pharmacies that are open late that day. Madrid has hundreds of pharmacies, but one of the most central is **Farmacia Gayoso,** Arenal 2 (☎ **91-521-28-60;** metro: Puerta del Sol). It is open Monday through Saturday from 9:30am to 9:30pm.

Embassies/Consulates   See "Fast Facts: Spain" in chapter 2.

Emergencies   A centralized number for fire, police, or ambulance is ☎ **112.**

Eyeglasses   Glasses are sold and repaired at branches of **Optica 2000,** the most central of which is at El Corte Inglés, calle Preciados (☎ **91-401-85-00;** metro: Callao).

Hospitals/Clinics   **Unidad Médica Anglo-Americana,** Conde de Arandá, 1 (☎ **91-435-18-23;** metro: Usera), is not a hospital but a private outpatient clinic, offering the services of various specialists. This is not an emergency clinic, although someone on the staff is always available. The daily hours are 9am to 8pm. For a real medical emergency, call ☎ **112** for an ambulance.

Information   See "Visitor Information," earlier in this chapter.

Internet Cafe   Head for **Net Café,** San Bernardo 81 (☎ **91-595-0999;** e-mail: netcafe@netcafe.es), open daily 11am to 2am, if you've just gotta check your e-mail.

Newspapers/Magazines   The Paris-based *International Herald Tribune* is sold at most newsstands in the tourist districts, as is *USA Today,* plus the European editions of *Time* and *Newsweek. Guía del Ocio,* a small magazine sold in newsstands, contains entertainment listings and addresses, though in Spanish only.

Police   Dial ☎ **112.**

Post Office   Madrid's central office is in the Palacio de Comunicaciones at Plaza de la Cibeles (☎ **91-396-20-00**).

Rest Rooms   Some public rest rooms are available, including those in the Parque del Retiro and on Plaza de Oriente across from the Palacio Real. Otherwise, you can always go into a bar or tasca, but you should always order something. All the major department stores, such as Galerías Preciados and El Corte Inglés, have good, clean rest rooms.

Safety   Because of an increasing crime rate in Madrid, the U.S. Embassy has warned visitors to leave valuables in a hotel safe or another secure place when going out. Your passport may be needed, however, as the police often stop foreigners for identification checks. See "Safety" under "Fast Facts: Spain" in chapter 2 for more details about this requirement. The embassy advises against carrying purses and suggests that you keep valuables in front pockets and carry only enough cash for the day's needs. Be aware of those around you and keep a separate record of your passport number, traveler's check numbers, and credit-card numbers.

Purse snatching is common, and criminals often work in pairs, grabbing purses from pedestrians, cyclists, and even from cars. A popular scam involves one robber smearing the back of the victim's clothing, perhaps with mustard, ice cream, or something worse. An accomplice then pretends to help clean up the mess, all the while picking the victim's pockets.

Every car can be a target, parked or just stopped at a light, so don't leave anything in sight in your car. If a vehicle is standing still, a thief may open the door or break a window in order to snatch a purse or package, even from under the seat. Place valuables in the trunk when you park and always assume that someone is watching to see whether you're putting something away for safekeeping. Keep the car locked while driving.

Taxes There are no special city taxes for tourists, except for the value added tax (VAT; known as IVA in Spain) levied nationwide on all goods and services, ranging from 7% to 33%. In Madrid the only city taxes are for home and car owners, which need not concern the casual visitor.

Taxis See "Getting Around," earlier in this chapter.

Telephone To make calls in Madrid, follow the instructions in "Fast Facts: Spain" in chapter 2. However, for long-distance calls, especially transatlantic ones, it may be best to go to the main telephone exchange, **Locutorio Gran Vía,** Gran Vía, 30; or **Locutorio Recoletos,** Paseo de Recoletos, 37-41. You may not be lucky enough to find an English-speaking operator, but you can fill out a simple form that will facilitate the placement of a call.

Transit Information For metro information, call ☎ **91-429-31-77.**

3 Accommodations

Though expensive, Madrid's hotels are among the finest in the world. The city's much-maligned reputation, earned in the days of Franco, is but a distant, unpleasant memory: No more rooms last renovated in 1870 or food that tastes of acidic olive oil left over from the Spanish-American War.

More than 50,000 hotel rooms blanket the city—from *grand luxe* bedchambers fit for a prince to bunker-style beds in the hundreds of neighborhood *hostales* and *pensiones* (low-cost boarding houses). Three-quarters of our recommendations are modern, yet many guests prefer the landmarks of yesteryear, including those grand old establishments, the Ritz and the Palace (ca. 1910–12). *But beware:* Many older hotels in Madrid haven't kept up with the times and a handful haven't added improvements or overhauled bedrooms substantially since the 1960s.

Traditionally, hotels are clustered around the Atocha Railway Station and the Gran Vía. In our search for the most outstanding hotels, we've downplayed these two popular, but noisy, districts. The newer hotels have been built away from the center, especially on residential streets jutting off from Paseo de la Castellana. Bargain seekers, however, will still find great pickings along the Gran Vía and in the Atocha district.

PARKING This is a serious problem, as so few hotels have garages; many buildings turned into hotels were constructed before the invention of the automobile. Street parking is rarely available, and even if it is, you run the risk of having your car broken into. If you're driving into Madrid, most hotels (and most police) will allow you to

---

A Note on Making Hotel Reservations

The telephone area code for Madrid is 91 if you're calling from within Spain. If you're calling from the United States, dial **011,** the country code (**34**), Madrid's city code (**91**), and then the local number.

---

park in front of the hotel long enough to unload your luggage. Someone on the staff can usually pinpoint the location of the nearest garage in the neighborhood, often giving you a map showing the way. So be prepared to walk 2 or 3 blocks to your car. Parking charges given in most hotel listings are the prices these neighborhood garages charge for an average size vehicle. Don't plan on renting a car for your time in Madrid. If you're moving on to explore the countryside, just pick up your rental when you're ready to set out.

NEAR THE PLAZA DE LAS CORTÉS
VERY EXPENSIVE

✪ **Hotel Villa Real.** Plaza de las Cortés, 10, 28014 Madrid. ☎ **91-420-37-67.** Fax 91-420-25-47. www.derbyhotels.es. E-mail: info@derbyhotels.es. 115 units. A/C MINIBAR TV TEL. 39,500 ptas. ($264.65) double; 75,000 ptas. ($502.50) suite. AE, DC, MC, V. Parking 1,600 ptas. ($10.70). Metro: Sevilla, Banco de España.

Until 1989, the Villa Real was little more than a run-down 19th-century apartment house auspiciously located across a three-sided park from the Spanish parliament (Congreso de los Diputados) between Puerta del Sol and Paseo del Prado. Since then, developers have poured billions of pesetas into renovations to produce this stylish hotel today patronized by the cognoscenti of Spain. The facade combines an odd mixture of neoclassical and Aztec motifs and is guarded by footmen and doormen dressed in uniforms of buff and forest green. Rooms at the Villa Real are more consistent in quality than those offered by its neighbor, the Palace (see below), though lack the latter's mellow charm and patina. The interior contains a scattering of modern paintings amid neoclassical detailing.

Each of the accommodations offers a TV with video movies and satellite reception, a safe for valuables, soundproofing, a sunken salon filled with leather-upholstered furniture, and built-in furniture accented with burl-wood inlays. Though rooms are not imaginatively decorated, they're mostly large, with separate sitting areas and big, bright, well-equipped bathrooms with hair dryers.

Dining/Diversions: The social center of the hotel is its high-ceilinged bar. The hotel's formal restaurant Europa serves both lunch and dinner, with a Spanish and international cuisine.

Amenities: 24-hour room service, laundry/valet, baby-sitting, express checkout, sauna, foreign currency exchange, business center.

The Palace. Plaza de las Cortés, 7, 28014 Madrid. ☎ **800/325-3535** in the U.S., 800/325-3589 in Canada, or 91-360-80-00. Fax 91-360-81-00. www.sheraton.com. 440 units. A/C MINIBAR TV TEL. 56,500–75,000 ptas. ($378.55–$502.50) double; from 95,000 ptas. ($636.50) suite. AE, DC, MC, V. Parking 2,500 ptas. ($16.75). Metro: Banco de España.

The Palace is an ornate Victorian wedding cake known as the "grand *dueña*" of Spanish hotels. It had an auspicious beginning, inaugurated personally by King Alfonso XIII in 1912, and covers an entire city block in the historical and artistic area. It faces the Prado and Neptune Fountain, and lies within walking distance of the main shopping center and the best antiques shops. Some of the city's most intriguing tascas and restaurants are only a short stroll away.

Accommodations in Central Madrid

Anaco **16**
Aristos **33**
Casón del Tormes **4**
Castellana Inter-Continental Hotel **33**
Conde Duque **1**
Crowne Plaza Madrid City Centre **3**
Cuzco **33**
Emperatriz **33**
Eurobuilding **33**
Gran Hotel Colón **31**
Gran Hotel Reina Victoria **22**
Grand Hotel Velazquez **32**
Hostal Buenos Aires **6**
Hostal Cervantes **26**
Hostal La Macarena **12**
Hostal La Perla Asturiana **20**
Hostal Nuevo Gaos **13**
Hostal Residencia Americano **18**
Hostal Residencia Continental **10**
Hostal Residencia Don Diego **32**
Hostal Residencia Principado **30**
Hotel Alcázar Regis **5**
Hotel Atlántico **9**
Hotel Chamartín **33**
Hotel Claridge **28**
Hotel Escultor **34**
Hotel Francisco I **11**
Hotel Husa Princesa **1**
Hotel Inglés **23**
Hotel Mercátor **27**
Hotel Monaco **17**
Hotel Nuria **14**
Hotel Opera **8**
Hotel Paris **19**
Hotel Residencia Cortezo **21**
Hotel Residencia Lisboa **24**
Hotel Residencia Santander **23**
Hotel Santo Domingo **7**
Hotel Villa Magna, a Park Hyatt **33**
Hotel Villa Real **25**
Meliá Castilla **33**
Meliá Madrid **2**
The Palace **25**
Residencia Bréton **1**
Residencia Liabeny **15**
The Ritz **29**
Santo Mauro **34**
Tirol **1**
Tryp Ambassador **8**
Wellington **32**

If You Have an Early Flight

Unless absolutely necessary, it's worth making the journey into Madrid rather than stay at rather bleak Barajas, where the airport is located. If you find that you have to stay, the least expensive option is the **Best Western Villa de Barajas,** av. De Logroño 331 (☎ **91-329-2818;** fax 91-329-2704), where double rooms go for 13,400 ptas. ($89.80). Each room has TV, telephone, and offers 24-hour room service. There is also a restaurant offering traditional Spanish food. The hotel runs a free shuttle bus to and from the airport. The trip takes about 5 minutes.

Architecturally, the Palace captures the grand pre–World War I style, with an emphasis on space and comfort. Though it doesn't achieve the snob appeal and chic of its nearby siblings, the Ritz or the Villa Real, it is one of the largest hotels in Madrid and retains first-class service. The air-conditioned hotel has a formal lobby and con-servative, traditional rooms, boasting plenty of space, large bathrooms and lots of amenities such as hair dryers. Accommodations vary widely, with the best rooms found on the fourth, fifth, and sixth floors. Rooms on the side are noisy and also lack views. Many rooms appear not to have been renovated for some time.

Dining/Diversions: The elegant La Cupola serves Italian specialties along with some of the more famous dishes of the Spanish cuisine. Piano music and other enter-tainment are featured.

Amenities: 24-hour room service, laundry/valet, baby-sitting, express checkout, foreign currency exchange, business center.

INEXPENSIVE

Hostal Cervantes. Cervantes, 34, 28014 Madrid. ☎ **91-429-83-65.** Fax 91-429-27-45. 12 units. TV. 6,000 ptas. ($40.20) double. MC, V. Metro: Banco de España.

One of Madrid's most pleasant family run hotels, the Cervantes has been appreciated by our readers for years. You'll take a tiny birdcage-style elevator to the immaculately maintained second floor of this stone-and-brick building. Each room contains a com-fortable bed, rather spartan furniture, and a tiny bathroom with a shower stall. No breakfast is served, but the owners, the Alfonsos, will direct you to a nearby cafe. The establishment is convenient to the Prado, Retiro Park, and the older sections of Madrid.

NEAR THE PLAZA ESPAÑA
EXPENSIVE

Crowne Plaza Madrid City Centre. Plaza de España, 28013 Madrid. ☎ **800/465-4329** or 91-454-85-00. Fax 91-548-23-89. www.crowneplaza.es. E-mail: reservas@crowneplaza.es. 306 units. A/C MINIBAR TV TEL. 34,240 ptas. ($229.40) double; from 41,510 ptas. ($278.10) suite. AE, DC, MC, V. Parking 1,200 ptas. ($8.05). Metro: Plaza de España.

Built in 1953 atop a city garage, the Plaza Hotel could be called the Waldorf-Astoria of Spain. A massive rose-and-white structure, it soars upward to a central tower that's 26 stories high. It is a landmark visible for miles around and one of the tallest sky-scrapers in Europe. Once one of the best hotels in Spain, the Plaza has long since ceased to be a market leader. Its accommodations include conventional doubles as well as luxurious suites, each of which contains a sitting room and abundant amenities such as private safes, luxury mattresses, bedside controls, and trouser presses, even in some cases alcoves for sitting areas. Each room, regardless of its size, has a marble bath-room equipped with a hair dryer. Furniture is usually of a standardized modern style, in harmonized colors. The upper floor rooms are quieter.

Dining/Diversions: Los Lagos is the breakfast room of the hotel and the main restaurant, Mirador de la Plaza de España, offers a tempting regional Spanish cuisine nightly. The Plaza cocktail bar is a major gathering point for business people.

Amenities: Room service, laundry, money exchange, medical service, hairdresser, shopping arcade, gym, Jacuzzi, sauna.

MODERATE

Casón del Tormes. Calle del Río, 7, 28013 Madrid. ☎ **91-541-97-46.** Fax 91-541-18-52. 63 units. A/C TV TEL. 13,300 ptas. ($89.10) double; 16,700 ptas. ($111.90) triple. MC, V. Parking 1,600 ptas. ($10.70). Metro: Plaza de España.

This attractive three-star hotel is around the corner from the Royal Palace and Plaza de España. Set behind a four-story red-brick facade with stone-trimmed windows, it overlooks a quiet one-way street. A long, narrow lobby contains wooden paneling, a marble floor, and a bar opening into a separate room. Guest rooms are generally roomy and comfortable with color-coordinated fabrics and dark wood furnishings, including mahogany headboards. Bathrooms are very small but with adequate shelf space and stall showers. Motorists appreciate the public parking lot near the hotel. Laundry service is provided.

✪ **Hotel Santo Domingo.** Plaza Santo Domingo, 13, 28013 Madrid. ☎ **91-547-9800.** Fax 91-547-5995. 120 units. A/C MINIBAR TV TEL. Mon–Thurs 24,625 ptas. ($165) double. Fri–Sun 19,250 ptas. ($129) double. Breakfast free Sat–Mon mornings, otherwise 1,450 ptas. ($9.70) extra. AE, DC, MC, V. Parking 2,475 ptas. ($16.60). Metro: Santo Domingo.

This stylish, carefully decorated hotel rises five floors from a position adjacent to the Gran Vía, a 2-minute walk from the Plaza de España. It was inaugurated in 1994, after an older building was radically gutted and reconfigured into the comfortable modern structure you'll see today. Rooms are decorated individually, each in a style just a wee bit different from that of its neighbor, in pastel-derived shades of pink, green, blue, and yellow. Some contain gold damask wall coverings, faux tortoiseshell desks, and striped satin bedspreads. Bathrooms are generally spacious and outfitted with ceramics and gray marble slabs. The best units are the fifth-floor doubles, especially those with furnished balconies and views over the tile roofs of Old Madrid. Each is carefully soundproofed to guard against noises from the street and from its neighbors and contains phones with personal answering machines. There's a bar and a restaurant in the hotel's lobby, serving lunch and dinner every day.

ON OR NEAR THE GRAN VÍA
MODERATE

Hotel Atlántico. Gran Vía, 38, 28013 Madrid. ☎ **800/528-1234** in the U.S. and Canada, or 91-522-64-80. Fax 91-531-02-10. www.bestwestern.com. 82 units. A/C MINIBAR TV TEL. 16,547 ptas. ($110.85) double. Rates include breakfast. AE, DC, MC, V. Metro: Gran Vía.

Refurbished in stages between the late 1980s and 1994, this Best Western affiliate occupies five floors of a large turn-of-the-century building on one of Madrid's most impressive avenues. It offers relatively simple but well-maintained, insulated rooms that are small and come with good beds, clean bathrooms, and security boxes. There is an English-inspired bar serving drinks and snacks that's open 24 hours a day.

Residencia Liabeny. Salud, 3, 28013 Madrid. ☎ **91-531-90-00.** Fax 91-532-74-21. 222 units. A/C MINIBAR TV TEL. 15,470 ptas. ($103.65) double; 18,000 ptas. ($120.60) triple. AE, MC, V. Parking 1,500 ptas. ($10.05). Metro: Puerta del Sol or Gran Vía.

The Liabeny, behind an austere stone facade, is in a prime location midway between the Gran Vía and Puerta del Sol. It has seven floors of comfortable, contemporary rooms, which though newly redecorated are a bit pristine. Nonetheless, they are of a good size and functionally furnished with comfortable beds and neatly organized bathrooms, mainly with shower stalls. The cocktail bar is warming, although in a rather macho style, and the dining room is strictly for convenience. Added pluses include personal attention from the staff, a coffee shop, and good laundry service.

INEXPENSIVE

Anaco. Tres Cruces, 3, 28013 Madrid. ☎ **91-522-46-04.** Fax 91-531-64-84. 40 units. A/C TV TEL. 9,950–11,000 ptas. ($66.65–$73.70) double; 13,430–14,850 ptas. ($90–$99.50) triple. AE, DC, MC, V. Parking 1,500 ptas. ($10.05). Metro: Gran Vía, Callao, or Puerta del Sol.

Modest yet modern, the Anaco is just off the Gran Vía but opens onto a tree-shaded plaza. It's for those who want a clean resting place for a good price, and don't expect much more. The rooms are compact and contemporary, with built-in headboards, reading lamps, and lounge chairs. Each has a comfortable bed with a firm mattress, plus a compact tiled bathroom with a shower stall. *A useful tip:* Ask for one of the five terraced rooms on the top floor, which rent at no extra charge. The hotel has a bar/cafeteria/restaurant open daily, and English is spoken here. Nearby is a municipally operated garage.

Hostal Alcázar Regis. Gran Vía, 61, 28013 Madrid. ☎ **91-547-93-17.** 12 units. TV. 5,600 ptas. ($37.50) double; 7,500 ptas. ($50.25) triple. AE. Metro: Plaza de España or Santo Domingo.

Conveniently located amid Madrid's best shops is this post–World War II building, complete with a circular Greek-style temple as its crown. On the building's fifth floor, you'll find long and pleasant public rooms, wood paneling, leaded-glass windows, parquet floors, crystal chandeliers, and high-ceilinged guest rooms, each with comfortable beds and adequate living space. An excellent bargain.

Hostal Buenos Aires. Gran Vía, 61, 28013 Madrid. ☎ **91-542-01-02.** Fax 91-542-28-69. 25 units. A/C TV TEL. 7,500 ptas. ($50.25) double. AE, DC, MC, V. Metro: Plaza de España. Bus: 1, 2, or 44.

To reach this hostal, you pass through a marble-covered street-floor lobby within a 1955 building then take an elevator to the second floor. One of the best features of this two-floor hostal is a wood-paneled cafe/bar that's open 24 hours a day. The simple rooms are comfortable, modern, and clean, though a bit small, with safety deposit boxes, balconies, firm mattresses, and hair dryers.

Hostal Nuevo Gaos. Calle Mesonero Romanos, 14, 28013 Madrid. ☎ and fax **91-532-71-07.** 23 units. A/C TV TEL. 7,200–8,200 ptas. ($48.25–$54.95) double. AE, DC, MC, V. Parking 1,400 ptas. ($9.40). Metro: Callao or Gran Vía.

On the second, third, and fourth floors of a 1930s building just off the Gran Vía, this residencia offers guests the chance to enjoy simple comfort at bargain prices. Rooms are humble and a bit small. The furnishings are plain but quite livable, and you'll have a firm mattress. Bathrooms are cramped but adequate, with stall showers. The place lies directly north of Puerta del Sol, across the street from the popular flamenco club Torre Bermejas. Breakfast can be taken at a nearby cafe.

Hostal-Residencia Continental. Gran Vía, 44, 28013 Madrid. ☎ **91-521-46-40.** Fax 91-521-46-49. 29 units. TV TEL. 5,992 ptas. ($40.15) double. AE, DC, MC, V. Metro: Callao. Bus: 1, 2, 36, or 46.

Sprawling over the third and fourth floors of Gran Vía, 44, this hostal is a bit more expensive than the other accommodations in the building, but the good-size rooms are comfortable, tidy, and renovated. The Continental is in a virtual house of budget hotels, a 19th-century building filled exclusively with small hotels and pensions. If no room is available at the Continental, you can ring the doorbells of the other places, and try your luck. No breakfast is served.

Hotel Monaco. Calle Barbieri, 5, 28004 Madrid. ☎ **91-522-4630.** Fax 91-521-1601. 30 units. A/C TV TEL. 10,700 ptas. ($71.70) double. AE, DC, MC, V. Metro: Chueca.

Originally built in 1890, this was once a well-known and rather stylish bordello (*casa de putas*) until a moral crackdown forced its closure in the late '50s. Today it's a respectable, unpretentious hotel near the postage stamp Plaza de Chueca. Public areas and guest rooms alike are outfitted with lots of mirrors and faux-Louis furniture that hint at the building's long-ago red-light past. Room 20, for example, has a bathtub on a platform in the center of the room, and room 123 treats you to a mirror on the ceiling above the bed. There's a cafeteria and a bar on the premises, and the staff will tell you tales about the building's racy past.

Hotel Nuria. Fuencarral, 52, 28004 Madrid. ☎ **91-531-92-08.** Fax 91-532-90-05. 80 units. TV TEL. 6,500–6,800 ptas. ($43.55–$45.55) double. Rates include breakfast. AE, DC, MC, V. Metro: Gran Vía or Tribunal. Bus: 3, 7, or 40.

The Nuria, just 3 blocks from the Gran Vía, has some rooms with especially interesting views of the capital. Furnishings are simple and functional, but the mattresses are firm. Living space is rather cramped, but everything is clean and well maintained. Bathrooms are barely adequate but the plumbing works; expect a shower stall in lieu of a full bathtub. A bar, restaurant, and TV lounge are available to guests. The hotel was last renovated in 1986.

NEAR THE PUERTA DEL SOL
EXPENSIVE

Gran Hotel Reina Victoria. Plaza Santa Ana, 14, 28012 Madrid. ☎ **91-531-45-00.** Fax 91-522-03-07. 201 units. A/C MINIBAR TV TEL. 26,250 ptas. ($175.90) double; from 62,500 ptas. ($418.75) suite. AE, DC, MC, V. Metro: Tirso de Molina or Puerta del Sol.

This hotel is as legendary as the famous bullfighter Manolete himself, who used to stay here, giving lavish parties and attracting mobs in the square below when he went out on his balcony for morning coffee. Since the recent renovation and upgrading of this property by Spain's Tryp Hotel Group, it's less staid and more impressive than ever.

Originally built in 1923, the hotel sits behind an ornate stone facade, which the Spanish government protects as a historic monument. Although it's located in a congested and noisy neighborhood in the center of town, the Reina Victoria opens onto its own sloping plaza, usually filled with flower vendors, older people reclining in the midafternoon sun, and young persons resting between bouts at the dozens of neighborhood tapas bars.

The soundproof accommodations are midsize and fairly standard, with private safes, quality mattresses, and livable furnishings, plus tidily organized bathrooms with hair dryers and marble vanities.

Dining/Diversions: Guests enjoy the hotel's stylish and popular lobby bar, the Manuel Gonzalez Manolete, filled with lavishly displayed bullfighting memorabilia. The in-house restaurant is El Ruedo.

Amenities: 24-hour room service, concierge, baby-sitting. Because of the hotel's position in one of Madrid's most interesting neighborhoods, almost anything is available within a few minutes' walk.

Tryp Ambassador. Cuesta Santo Domingo, 5 and 7, 28013 Madrid. ☎ **91-541-6700.**
Fax 91-559-1040. E-mail:ambassador@trypnet.com. 182 units. A/C MINIBAR TV TEL. 26,250
ptas. ($175.90) double; from 36,000 ptas. ($241.20) suite. AE, DC, MC, V. Parking 2,500 ptas.
($17.50) per night. Metro: Opera or Santo Domingo.

In the early 1990s the Tryp hotel chain renovated and massively enlarged this late-
19th-century palace of the dukes of Granada. The result today is a lavishly restored,
four-story historic hotel with suitably grand public areas that's interconnected via a
sunny lobby to a six-story annex that contains about 60% of the establishment's
rooms. Regardless of location within the much-expanded premises, all rooms are conservatively modern, and outfitted in a combination of white and salmon accented with
touches of mahogany. Most are large, soundproofed and come with such amenities as
private safes and twin beds fitted with luxury mattresses. Bathrooms are outfitted in
marble with hair dryers, robes, and deluxe toiletries.

Dining/Diversions: There's a restaurant on the premises, El Madroño, that
includes a greenhouse-style bar lavishly filled with plants and caged exotic birds.

Amenities: Room service, dry cleaning/laundry, concierge, baby-sitting.

MODERATE

✪ **Hotel Opera.** Cuesta de Santo Domingo, 2, 28013 Madrid. ☎ **91-541-2800.**
Fax 91-541-6923. E-mail: hotelopera@phoenix.net. 79 units. A/C TV TEL. 14,200 ptas.
($95.15) double. AE, DC, MC, V. Parking 2,000 ptas. ($13.40). Metro: Opera.

Don't judge this little discovery by its dreary gray facade or its narrow little windows;
it livens up considerably once you enter. Set close to the royal palace and the opera
house, this hotel isn't regal, but it offers first-rate comfort and a warm welcome from
its English-speaking staff. Guest rooms range from medium in size to surprisingly spacious, each fitted with first-rate furnishings, including twin or double beds. Bathrooms are also excellent, clad in marble with dual basins. The hotel's lovely El Café de
la Opera is a popular rendezvous point, even if you're not a guest. It's adorned with
fabric-covered walls and horsey art. The Opera remains one of Madrid's relatively
undiscovered boutique hotels.

INEXPENSIVE

Hostal la Macarena. Cava de San Miguel, 8, 28005 Madrid. ☎ **91-365-92-21.**
Fax 91-364-27-57. 18 units. TEL. 7,500 ptas. ($50.25) double; 9,500 ptas. ($63.65) triple;
12,000 ptas. ($80.40) quad. MC, V. Parking 1,000–2,070 ptas. ($6.70–$13.85). Metro: Puerta
del Sol, Opera, or La Latina.

Known for its reasonable prices and praised by readers for its warm hospitality, this
unpretentious, clean hostal is run by the Ricardo González family. Its 19th-century
facade, accented with belle epoque patterns, stands in ornate contrast to the chiseled
simplicity of the ancient buildings facing it. The location is one of the hostal's assets:
it's on a street (an admittedly noisy one) immediately behind Plaza Mayor, near one
of the best clusters of tascas in Madrid. Rooms range in size from small to medium
and they're all well kept, with modest furnishings and comfortable beds. Windows
facing the street have double panes. Bathrooms are tiny and contain stall showers.

Hostal la Perla Asturiana. Plaza de Santa Cruz, 3, 28012 Madrid. ☎ **91-366-46-00.**
Fax 91-366-46-08. www.perlaasturiana.com. E-mail: perlaasturiana@mundivia.es. 33 units.
TV TEL. 5,200 ptas. ($34.85) double; 7,200 ptas. ($48.25) triple. MC, V. Parking 2,400 ptas.
($16.10). Metro: Puerta del Sol.

Ideal for those who want to stay in the heart of old Madrid (1 block off Plaza Mayor
and 2 blocks from Puerta del Sol), this small family run place has a courteous staff

member at the desk 24 hours a day for security and convenience. You can socialize in the small, comfortable lobby that's adjacent to the reception area but stay here for the cheap prices and location, not grand comfort. Each of the small rooms comes with a comfortable bed, plus a simple and barely adequate bathroom with a stall shower. Many inexpensive restaurants and tapas bars are nearby. No breakfast is served.

Hostal Residencia Americano. Puerta del Sol, 11, 28013 Madrid. ☎ **91-522-28-22.** Fax 91-522-11-92. 44 units. TV TEL. 6,000 ptas. ($40.20) double; 8,000 ptas. ($53.60) triple; 9,000 ptas. ($60.30) quad. AE, MC, V. Parking 2,000 ptas. ($13.40). Metro: Puerta del Sol.

Americano, on the third floor of a five-floor building, is suitable for those who want to be right in the thick of Puerta del Sol. Most of the guest rooms are outside chambers with balconies facing the street and all have been refurbished. Though the rooms are small, especially when three or four guests are crowded in, the beds are good. Bathrooms are bleak but clean cubicles with showers. No breakfast is served.

Hostal-Residencia Principado. Zorrilla, 7, 28014 Madrid. ☎ **91-429-81-87.** Fax 91-429-81-87. 15 units. TV. 6,200 ptas. ($41.55) double. AE, MC, V. Parking 2,200 ptas. ($14.75). Metro: Sevilla, Sol, or Banco de España. Bus: 5, 9, or 53.

The two-star Principado is a real find. Located in a well-kept town house, this gracious hotel is clean and inviting. New tiles, attractive bedspreads, and curtains give the small rooms a fresh look. Bathrooms are very tiny and have shower stalls. Safety boxes are provided. For breakfast, you can go to a nearby cafe. English is spoken.

Hotel Francisco I. Arenal, 15, 28013 Madrid. ☎ **91-548-43-14.** Fax 91-542-28-99. 58 units. TV TEL. 10,600 ptas. ($71) double. Rates include breakfast. AE, DC, MC, V. Parking 2,200 ptas. ($14.75). Metro: Puerta del Sol or Opera.

Here you can rent clean, modern rooms. There's a pleasant lounge and a bar, and on the sixth floor you'll find a comfortable, rustically decorated restaurant. The hotel was considerably modernized in 1993, with the addition of new bathrooms as well as air-conditioning in most of the rooms, which range from small to medium. All the bathrooms are small. Nonetheless, all the beds are comfortable with frequently renewed mattresses. The hotel provides limited hours room service and laundry and valet service.

Hotel Inglés. Calle Echegaray, 8, 28014 Madrid. ☎ **91-429-65-51.** Fax 91-420-24-23. 58 units. TV TEL. 11,500 ptas. ($77.05) double; 15,500 ptas. ($103.85) suite. AE, DC, MC, V. Parking 1,300 ptas. ($8.70). Metro: Puerta del Sol or Sevilla.

You'll find this little hotel where Virginia Woolf used to stay on a central street lined with tascas. Behind the redbrick facade is a modern, impersonal hotel, with unpretentious, contemporary, and well-maintained rooms. The lobby is air-conditioned, although guest rooms are not and guests who open their windows at night are likely to hear noise from the enclosed courtyard, so light sleepers beware. Rooms come in a variety of shapes and sizes, most of them small, and some rooms in the back are quite dark. Beds are fitted with fine mattresses and linens and tend to be twins or doubles. Bathrooms are a bit cramped but are tiled and tidily maintained with shower stalls. The hotel operates its own 24-hour cafeteria as well as a TV lounge with comfortable armchairs.

Hotel Paris. Alcalá, 2, 28014 Madrid. ☎ **91-521-6496.** Fax 91-531-0188. 120 units. A/C TV TEL. 12,000 ptas. ($80.40) double. Rates include breakfast. AE, DC, MC, V. Parking 2,200 ptas. ($14.75) per day. Metro: Puerta del Sol.

Originally built in a grandiose style in the 1870s, when it was undoubtedly more chic than it is today, this hotel occupies a prime location adjacent to the hysterical traffic of the Puerta del Sol. It contains five floors of simple but clean and comfortable rooms, each with parquet floors, white walls, plain furnishings, and views that extend either out over the surrounding neighborhood or over a calm and quiet courtyard. Rooms are generally small but with comfortable good beds. Bathrooms are also small with shower stalls. Something about the dark-paneled lobby might remind you of the old-fashioned, hot and somnolent Spain of long ago. There's a high-ceilinged dining room one floor above lobby level, serving wholesome, uncomplicated meals every day at lunch and dinner. This hotel is a good bargain if your tastes aren't too demanding, if you're not a budding decorator, or if you just want a central location.

Hotel Residencia Lisboa. Ventura de la Vega, 17, 28014 Madrid. ☎ **91-429-98-94.** Fax 91-429-46-76. 27 units. 6,800 ptas. ($45.55) double. AE, DC, MC, V. Parking 2,200 ptas. ($14.75). Metro: Puerta del Sol.

Our only complaint about the Lisboa, which sits on Madrid's most famous restaurant street, is that it can be a bit noisy. The hotel is a neat, modernized town house with compact rooms and a staff that speaks five languages. Most of the rooms, which occupy four floors of this old building, are small although a few are comfortably larger. Most come equipped with a double bed, some with twins; all are fitted with firm mattresses. Bathrooms are small, mainly with shower stalls. The Lisboa does not serve breakfast, but budget dining rooms, cafes, and tascas surround the neighborhood.

Hotel Residencia Santander. Calle Echegaray, 1, 28014 Madrid. ☎ **91-429-95-51.** Fax 91-369-10-78. 38 units. TEL. 7,500 ptas. ($50.25) double. MC, V. Parking 2,000 ptas. ($13.40). Metro: Puerta del Sol.

The Santander is a snug little hotel in a refurbished 1930's house with adequate rooms, some of which have TVs. Rooms are small and the mattresses a bit worn, the towels thin, but this is such a bargain price you can't expect great comfort or luxury of any kind. It's on a teeming street but you might appreciate the nonstop local atmosphere. Restaurants and bars in the area are active day and night. No breakfast is served.

NEAR ATOCHA STATION
MODERATE

Hotel Mercátor. Calle Atocha, 123, 28012 Madrid. ☎ **91-429-05-00.** Fax 91-369-12-52. 89 units. MINIBAR TV TEL. 12,200 ptas. ($81.75) double; 13,500 ptas. ($90.45) suite. AE, DC, MC, V. Parking 1,740 ptas. ($11.65). Metro: Atocha or Antón Martín.

Only a 3-minute walk from the Prado, Centro de Arte Reina Sofía, and the Thyssen-Bornemisza Museum, the Mercátor is orderly, well run, and clean, with enough comforts and conveniences to please the weary traveler. Its public rooms are simple, outfitted in a vaguely modern type of minimalism. Some of the guest rooms are more inviting than others, especially those with desks and armchairs. Twenty-one units are air-conditioned. Beds have firm mattresses and fine linen. Bathrooms are usually cramped without adequate shelf space although they are equipped with good showerheads. The Mercátor is a residencia—that is, it offers breakfast only and does not have a formal restaurant for lunch and dinner; however, it has a bar and cafeteria serving light meals, such as *platos combinados* (combination plates). The hotel also has a garage and is within walking distance of American Express. Laundry service is provided, plus room service from 7am to 10pm.

INEXPENSIVE

Hotel Residencia Cortezo. Doctor Cortezo, 3, 28012 Madrid. ☎ **91-369-01-01.** Fax 91-369-37-74. 90 units. A/C MINIBAR TV TEL. 13,750 ptas. ($92.15) double; 16,850 ptas. ($112.90) suite. AE, DC, MC, V. Parking 1,800 ptas. ($12.05). Metro: Tirso de Molina.

Just off calle de Atocha, which leads to the railroad station of the same name, the Cortezo is a short walk from Plaza Mayor and Puerta del Sol. The accommodations are comfortable but simply furnished, with contemporary bathrooms. The beds are springy, the colors are well chosen, and the furniture is pleasantly modern; many rooms have sitting areas with a desk and armchair. The public rooms match the guest rooms in freshness. The hotel was built in 1959 and last renovated in 1997.

NEAR RETIRO/SALAMANCA
VERY EXPENSIVE

✪ **Park Hyatt Villa Magna.** Paseo de la Castellana, 22, 28046 Madrid. ☎ **800/223-1234** in North America, or 91-587-12-34. Fax 91-431-22-86. www.hyattint.com. E-mail: dcourtier @villamagna.es. 182 units. A/C MINIBAR TV TEL. 60,000 ptas. ($402) double; from 90,000 ptas. ($603) suite. AE, DC, MC, V. Parking 3,000 ptas. ($20.10). Metro: Rubén Darío.

One of the finest hotels in Europe, the nine-story Park Hyatt is faced with slabs of rose-colored granite and set behind a bank of pines and laurels on the city's most fashionable boulevard. It's an even finer choice than the Palace or Villa Real and is matched in luxury, ambience, service, and tranquillity only by the Ritz, which has a greater patina since it's much older.

Separated from the busy boulevard by a parklike garden, its facade has contemporary lines. In contrast, its interior recaptures the style of Carlos IV, with paneled walls, marble floors, and bouquets of fresh flowers. Almost every film star shooting on location in Spain stays here. This luxury palace has plush but dignified rooms decorated in Louis XVI, English Regency, or Italian provincial style. Each comes with fresh flowers and a TV with video movies and satellite reception (including news broadcasts from the United States).

Dining/Diversions: A pianist provides entertainment in the lobby-level champagne bar. In his restaurant, LeDivellec, French chef Jacques le Divellec serves international food in a glamorous setting with a summer terrace overlooking the garden. For the more exotic flavors of Chinese cuisine, there is the Tse Yang Restaurant.

Amenities: 24-hour room service, concierge, same-day laundry and dry cleaning, limousine service, baby-sitting, business center, car rentals, barber and beauty shop, the boutique "VillaMagna," availability of both tennis and golf (15 and 25 minutes from the hotel, respectively).

✪ **The Ritz.** Plaza de la Lealtad, 5, 28014 Madrid. ☎ **800/225-5843** in the U.S. and Canada, or 91-521-28-57. Fax 91-532-87-76. www.ritz.es. 154 units. A/C MINIBAR TV TEL. 45,000–58,000 ptas. ($301.50–$388.60) double; from 99,000 ptas. ($663.30) suite. AE, DC, MC, V. Parking 4,000 ptas. ($26.80). Metro: Banco de España.

The Ritz is the most legendary hotel in Spain, constantly hosting celebrity guests. With soaring ceilings and graceful columns, it offers all the luxury and special pampering you'd expect of a grand hotel. Though the building has been thoroughly modernized, great effort was expended to retain its belle epoque character and architectural details.

No other Madrid hotel, except the Palace, has a more varied history. One of *Les Grand Hôtels Européens,* the Ritz was built in 1908 at the command of King Alfonso XIII, with the aid of César Ritz. It looks out onto the circular Plaza de la Lealtad in the center of town, near 300-acre Retiro Park, facing the Prado, the adjacent Palacio de Villahermosa, and the Stock Exchange. The Ritz was constructed when costs were relatively low and when spaciousness, luxury, and comfort were the standard. Its facade has even been designated a historic monument. The glory days of 1910 live on in the rooms with their spacious closets, luxury mattresses, antique furnishings, handwoven carpets, and elegant fabrics. Bathrooms are spacious, with robes, plush towels, dual basins, deluxe toiletries, and hair dryers.

Dining: The hotel maintains a formal dining room, called Restaurante Goya, which is lined with mirrors and 16th-century Flemish tapestries. Chefs present an international menu featuring the most elaborate paella in Madrid. In time-honored Spanish tradition, guests tend to dress up here, sometimes even for breakfast. (Management stresses that this is not a resort hotel.) Guests looking for a more casual eatery usually head for the Jardín Ritz.

Amenities: 24-hour room service with everything from good nutty Jabugo ham to fresh hake, laundry/valet, express checkout, fitness center, car-rental kiosk, business center, foreign currency exchange.

EXPENSIVE

The Emperatriz. López de Hoyos, 4, 28006 Madrid. ☎ **91-563-80-88.** Fax 91-563-98-04. 158 units. A/C MINIBAR TV TEL. 23,500 ptas. ($157.45) double; 37,000–45,000 ptas. ($247.90–$301.50) suite. AE, DC, MC, V. Parking 1,500 ptas. ($10.05) nearby. Metro: Rubén Darío.

This hotel lies just off the wide Paseo de la Castellana. Built in the 1970s, it has been recently renovated in a combination of Laura Ashley and Spanish contemporary by Madrid's trendiest firm, Casa & Jardin. Rooms are comfortable and classically styled in cheery yellows and salmons, with pale striped wallpapers, and come with TVs that receive many different European channels. Ask for a room on the seventh floor, where you'll get a private terrace at no extra charge.

Dining/Diversions: Guests gather in the cozy lobby bar before planning their assault on Madrid for the evening. Standard Spanish and international cuisine is served in the hotel's restaurant, followed by a substantial breakfast buffet in the morning. There is also a moderately priced fixed-price lunch.

Amenities: Beauty salon, barbershop, and laundry/valet service, along with a concierge and room service.

The Wellington. Velázquez, 8, 28001 Madrid. ☎ **91-575-44-00.** Fax 91-576-4164. www.hotel-wellington.com. E-mail: wellin@genio.infor.es. 288 units. A/C MINIBAR TV TEL. 36,000 ptas. ($241.20) double; from 49,500 ptas. ($331.65) suite. AE, DC, MC, V. Parking 2,750 ptas. ($18.45). Metro: Retiro or Velázquez.

The Wellington, with its somber antique-tapestried entrance, is one of Madrid's more sedate deluxe hotels, built in the mid-1950s but substantially remodeled since. Set within the Salamanca residential area near Retiro Park, the Wellington offers redecorated but rather staid guest rooms, each with cable TV and movie channels, music, two phones (one in the bathroom), and a guest-operated combination safe. Units are furnished in English-inspired mahogany reproductions, and the bathrooms are modern and immaculate, with marble sheathing and fixtures. Doubles with private terraces (at no extra charge) are the most sought-after accommodations.

Dining/Diversions: An added bonus here is the El Fogón grill room, styled like a 19th-century tavern, where many of the provisions for the typically Spanish dishes are shipped in from the hotel's own ranch. The pub-style Bar Inglés is a hospitable rendezvous. Lighter meals are served in the Las Llaves de Oro (Golden Keys) cafeteria.

Amenities: 24-hour room service, same-day dry cleaning and laundry, outdoor swimming pool in summer, garage, beauty parlor.

MODERATE

Gran Hotel Velázquez. Calle de Velázquez, 62, 28001 Madrid. ☎ **91-575-28-00.** Fax 91-577-5131. 146 units. A/C MINIBAR TV TEL. 12,570–21,150 ptas. ($84.20–$141.70) double; from 29,160 ptas. ($195.35) suite. AE, DC, MC, V. Parking 2,200 ptas. ($14.75). Metro: Velázquez.

ⓘ Family-Friendly Hotels

Meliá Castilla *(see p. 83)*   Children can spend hours and all their extra energy in the hotel's swimming pool and gymnasium. On the grounds is a showroom exhibiting the latest European automobiles. Hotel services include baby-sitting, providing fun for kids and parents too.

Crowne Plaza Madrid City Centre *(see p. 70)*   Safe and reliable, and located at the very heart of Madrid, this 26-story hotel offers roomy accommodations and good beds and attracts a large family trade to its precincts. It's got location, reasonable prices, and all the services, including laundry, that most family travelers need.

The Tirol *(see p. 84)*   This centrally located three-star hotel is a favorite of families seeking good comfort at moderate price. It also has a cafeteria.

This is one of the most attractive medium-size hotels in Madrid, with plenty of comfort and convenience. Opened in 1947 on an affluent residential street near the center of town, it has a 1930s style art deco facade and a 1940s interior filled with well-upholstered furniture and richly grained paneling. Several public rooms, including a bar, lead off a central oval area. As in many hotels of its era, the rooms vary, some large enough for entertaining, with a small but separate sitting area for reading or watching TV. All contain piped-in music, walk-in closets, and private safes. Bathrooms are decorated in marble or tiles, with either stall showers or tubs. The in-house restaurant, Roceo, features both international and Spanish cuisine. There's also room service (8am to midnight), a beauty salon, dry cleaning, and laundry service.

INEXPENSIVE

Gran Hotel Colón. Pez Volador, 11, 28007 Madrid. ☎ **91-573-59-00.** Fax 91-573-08-09. 370 units. A/C MINIBAR TV TEL. 14,800 ptas. ($99.15) double. AE, DC, MC, V. Parking 1,800 ptas. ($12.05). Metro: Sainz de Baranda.

East of Retiro Park, Gran Hotel Colón is just a few minutes from the city center by subway. Built in 1966, it offers comfortable yet reasonably priced accommodations in a modern setting. More than half of the accommodations have private balconies, and all contain comfortably traditional furniture, much of it built-in. Rooms vary in size but most offer roomy comfort, with firm mattresses resting on dark wood beds. Furnishings are well arranged, and there is adequate closet space. Bathrooms are small, with stall showers, but still have suitable shelf space. Other perks include two dining rooms, a covered garage, and bingo games. One of the Colón's founders was an accomplished interior designer, which accounts for the unusual stained-glass windows and murals in the public rooms and the paintings by Spanish artists in the lounge.

Hotel Claridge. Plaza Conde de Casal, 6, 28007 Madrid. ☎ **91-551-94-00.** Fax 91-501-03-85. 150 units. A/C TV TEL. Mon–Thurs 12,100 ptas. ($81.05), Fri–Sun 9,100 ptas. ($60.95) double; Mon–Thurs 19,000 ptas. ($127.30), Fri–Sun 16,000 ptas. ($107.20) suite. AE, MC, V. Parking 1,000 ptas. ($6.70). Metro: Conde de Casal.

This contemporary building, last renovated in 1994, is beyond Retiro Park, about 5 minutes from the Prado by taxi or subway. The rooms are well organized and pleasantly styled: small and compact, with coordinated furnishings and colors. These include excellent beds and small but well-organized private bathrooms. You can take your meals in the hotel's cafeteria and also relax in the modern lounge.

CHAMBERÍ
VERY EXPENSIVE

Castellana Inter-Continental Hotel. Paseo de la Castellana, 49, 28046 Madrid. ☎ **800/327-0200** in the U.S., or 91-310-02-00. Fax 91-319-58-53. 306 units. A/C MINIBAR TV TEL. 45,800–59,000 ptas. ($306.85–$395.30) double; from 9,000 ptas. ($60.30) suite. AE, DC, MC, V. Parking 2,600 ptas. ($17.40). Metro: Rubén Darío.

Solid, spacious, and conservatively modern, this is one of Madrid's most reliable hotels. Originally built in 1963, the Castellana Inter-Continental lies behind a barrier of trees within a neighborhood of apartment houses and luxury hotels. Its high-ceilinged public rooms are gorgeous, with terrazzo floors and giant angular abstract murals pieced together from multicolored stones and tiles. Most of the accommodations have private balconies and traditional furniture, each with a color TV with in-house videos and many channels from across Europe. Most rooms have generous living space with private safes and very large beds, often king size. Bathrooms are tiled and well equipped with robes, phones, hair dryers, and plush towels.

Dining/Diversions: The La Ronda Bar offers drinks near the elegant Los Continentes Restaurant, serving a creative Mediterranean cuisine. In addition, El Jardín is a retreat in summer, with candlelit dinners and live soft background music. Another restaurant, El Sarracin, provides good food at thrifty prices.

Amenities: There's a helpful concierge and a travel agent who will book theater tickets, rental cars, and airline connections; there's also 24-hour room service, laundry, and baby-sitting, kiosks and boutiques, hairdresser/barbershop, business center, top floor gym with sauna and outdoor solarium.

✪ **Santo Mauro Hotel.** Calle Zurbano, 36, 28010 Madrid. ☎ **91-319-6900.** Fax 91-308-5477. E-mail: santo-mauro@itelco.es. 37 units. A/C MINIBAR TV TEL. 44,000 ptas. ($294.80) double; from 60,000 ptas. ($402) suite. AE, DC, MC, V. Free parking. Metro: Rubén Darío or Alonso Martínez.

This hotel opened in 1991 in what was once a neoclassical villa built in 1894 for the duke of Santo Mauro. Set within a garden and done in a French style, it's decorated with rich fabrics and art deco art and furnishings. Staff members outnumber rooms by two to one. Each of the rooms contains an audio system with a wide choice of tapes and CDs as well as many lovely details, like raw silk curtains, Persian carpets, jewel-toned colors, antique prints, and parquet floors. Rooms are of generous size and come in many combinations ranging from studios to duplex suites.

Dining/Diversions: Restaurante Belagua is reviewed separately, later in this chapter. An elegant bar is located off the main lobby, and tables are set up beneath the garden's large trees for drinks and snacks.

Amenities: 24-hour room service, laundry/valet, reception staff trained in the procurement of practically anything, indoor swimming pool, health club with sauna and massage.

EXPENSIVE

Conde Duque. Plaza Conde Valle de Súchil, 5, 28015 Madrid. ☎ **91-447-70-00.** Fax 91-448-35-69. www.hotelcondeduque.es. E-mail: condeduque@hotelcondeduque.es. 143 units. A/C MINIBAR TV TEL. 26,800 ptas. ($179.55) double; from 31,100 ptas. ($208.35) suite. AE, DC, MC, V. Parking 1,800 ptas. ($12.05). Metro: San Bernardo.

The modern four-star Conde Duque, near a branch of El Corte Inglés department store, opens onto a tree-filled plaza in a residential neighborhood that's near the Glorieta Quevado. The hotel is 12 blocks north of the Plaza de España, off calle de San Bernardo, which starts at the Gran Vía. Furnishings include built-in modern headboards and reproductions of 19th-century English pieces, plus bedside lights and telephones. Rooms contain a lot of thoughtful extras, including private safes, quality mattresses, fax facilities, a tea- or coffeemaker, fireproof materials, and a digital fire warning system. Bathrooms also contain scales, phones, hair dryers, hydromassage showers (suites only), and magnifying mirrors.

Dining/Diversions: The hotel operates a tearoom and cafeteria, plus a full-service restaurant serving regional and international dishes.

Amenities: Concierge, laundry/dry cleaning, and baby-sitting.

Miguel Angel. Miguel Angel, 29–31, 28010 Madrid. ☎ **91-442-81-99.** Fax 91-442-53-20. 304 units. A/C MINIBAR TV TEL. 29,600 ptas. ($198.30) double; 39,600–44,600 ptas. ($265.30–$298.80) suite. AE, DC, MC, V. Parking 2,500 ptas. ($16.75). Metro: Rubén Darío.

Just off Paseo de la Castellana, the sleek, modern Miguel Angel opened its doors in 1975 and has been renovated and kept up to date periodically ever since. It has a lot going for it: ideal location, contemporary styling, good furnishings and art objects, an efficient staff, and plenty of comfort. There's an expansive sun terrace on several levels, with clusters of garden furniture surrounded by paintings of semitropical scenes. The soundproof rooms are done in color-coordinated fabrics and carpets, and in many cases reproductions of classic Iberian furniture, each with a superbly comfortable bed.

Dining/Diversions: The Farnesio bar is decorated in a Spanish Victorian style, with piano music beginning at 8pm. A well-managed restaurant on the premises is the Florencia. Dinner is also served until around 3am in the Zacarías Boîte restaurant, where you can dine while watching an occasional cabaret or musical performance.

Amenities: 24-hour room service, same-day laundry/valet, indoor heated swimming pool, saunas, hairdressers, and a drugstore. Art exhibitions are sponsored in the arcade of boutiques.

MODERATE

Hotel Escultor. Miguel Angel, 3, 28010 Madrid. ☎ **91-310-42-03.** Fax 91-319-25-84. 61 units. A/C MINIBAR TV TEL. From 13,950 ptas. ($93.45) double; from 21,350 ptas. ($143.05) suite. AE, DC, MC, V. Parking 2,300 ptas. ($15.40) nearby. Metro: Rubén Darío.

This comfortably furnished hotel built in 1975 provides fewer services and offers fewer facilities than others within its category, but it compensates with larger rooms, each with its own charm and contemporary styling. Fully air-conditioned, the hotel has a knowledgeable staff, a small but comfortable bar that's open nightly, and a traditional restaurant, the Señorio de Erazu, which closes on Saturday at lunchtime and all day on Sunday. Room service is offered at breakfast only, from 7 to 10:30am.

Residencia Bréton. Bréton de los Herreros, 29, 28003 Madrid. ☎ **91-442-83-00.** Fax 91-441-38-16. 56 units. A/C MINIBAR TV TEL. 17,500 ptas. ($117.25) double; 25,000 ptas. ($167.50) suite. AE, DC, MC, V. Parking 1,500 ptas. ($10.05) nearby. Metro: Ríos Rosas.

You'll find this well-furnished modern hotel on a side street several blocks from Paseo de la Castellana. As a residencia, it doesn't offer a major dining room, but it does have a little bar and breakfast room adjoining the reception lounge. All rooms have wood-frame beds with excellent mattresses, wrought-iron electrical fixtures, mirrored closets, wall-to-wall curtains, comfortable chairs, and ornate tile work in the bathrooms, which also come with hair dryers.

INEXPENSIVE

Hostal Residencia Don Diego. Calle de Velázquez, 45, 28001 Madrid. ☎ **91-435-07-60.** Fax 91-431-42-63. 58 units. A/C TV TEL. 9,630 ptas. ($64.50) double; 13,001 ptas. ($87.10) triple. MC, V. Parking 2,000–2,500 ptas. ($13.40–$16.75). Metro: Velázquez.

On the fifth floor of an elevator building, Don Diego is in a combination residential/commercial neighborhood that's relatively convenient to many of the city monuments. The vestibule contains an elegant winding staircase accented with iron griffin heads supporting its balustrade. The hotel is warm and inviting, filled with leather couches and comfortable, no-nonsense angular but attractive furniture. Rooms are a bit small but comfortable for the price, with excellent beds. Bathrooms are cramped but adequate with shower stalls. The staff is very service oriented and they keep the place humming along efficiently. A bar stands at the far end of the main sitting room. The hotel's cafeteria serves breakfast from 7:45 to 11am. From 7 to 11pm daily, you can also order drinks and snacks, especially sandwiches and omelets. Laundry service is provided, and room service is available daily from 8am to midnight.

CHAMARTÍN
EXPENSIVE

The Cuzco. Paseo de la Castellana, 133, 28046 Madrid. ☎ **91-556-06-00.** Fax 91-556-03-72. 328 units. A/C MINIBAR TV TEL. 25,080 ptas. ($168.05) double; from 31,500 ptas. ($211.05) suite. AE, DC, MC, V. Parking 2,100 ptas. ($14.05). Metro: Cuzco.

Popular with businesspeople and tour groups, the Cuzco lies in a commercial neighborhood of big buildings, government ministries, spacious avenues, and the main Congress Hall. The Chamartín railway station is only a 10-minute walk north, so this is a popular and convenient place to stay. The 15-floor structure, set back from Madrid's longest boulevard, has been redecorated and modernized many times since it was completed in 1967. The rooms are spacious, with separate sitting areas, video movies, modern furnishings, and good beds; bathrooms have hair dryers.

Dining/Diversions: There is a bilevel snack bar and cafeteria. The lounge is a forest of marble pillars and leather armchairs, its ambience enhanced by contemporary oil paintings and tapestries.

Amenities: Beauty parlor, sauna, massage, health club.

The Eurobuilding. Calle Padre Damián, 23, 28036 Madrid. ☎ **91-345-45-00.** Fax 91-345-45-76. 520 units. A/C MINIBAR TV TEL. 29,500 ptas. ($197.65) double; from 34,700 ptas. ($232.50) suite. AE, DC, MC, V. Parking 2,500 ptas. ($16.75). Metro: Cuzco.

Even while the Eurobuilding was on the drawing boards, the rumor was that this five-star sensation of white marble would provide, in the architect's words, "a new concept in deluxe hotels." It is actually two hotels linked by a courtyard, away from the city center but right in the midst of apartment houses, boutiques, nightclubs, first-class restaurants, and the modern Madrid business world.

The more glamorous of the twin buildings is the main one, named Las Estancias de Eurobuilding; it contains only suites, all of which were recently renovated in luxurious pastel shades. Ornately carved gold-and-white beds, background music, large terraces for breakfast and cocktail entertaining—all are tastefully coordinated. Across the courtyard, the neighbor Eurobuilding contains less-impressive, but still very comfortable double rooms, many with views from private balconies of the formal garden and swimming pool below. All the accommodations have TVs with video movies and satellite reception, security doors, and individual safes.

Dining: Le Relais Coffee Shop is suitable for a quick bite, and Le Relais Restaurant offers buffets at both breakfast and lunch. For more formal dining, La Taberna at both lunch and dinner features a selection of Spanish and international cuisine, specializing in seafood and various paella dishes.

Amenities: Laundry/valet, concierge, 24-hour room service, baby-sitting, health club with sauna, outdoor swimming pool.

Meliá Castilla. Calle Capitán Haya, 43, 28020 Madrid. ☎ **800/336-3542** in the U.S., or 91-567-50-00. Fax 91-567-5051. 900 units. A/C MINIBAR TV TEL. 29,900 ptas. ($200.35) double; from 75,000 ptas. ($502.50) suite. AE, MC, V. Parking 2,500 ptas. ($16.75). Metro: Cuzco.

This mammoth hotel is one of the largest in Europe. Loaded with facilities and built primarily to accommodate conventions, Meliá Castilla also caters to the needs of the individual traveler. Everything is larger than life here: You need a floor plan to nego- tiate the place. The lounges and pristine marble corridors are vast—there is even a landscaped garden as well as a showroom full of the latest-model cars. Each good- size room comes with excellent twin beds and contemporary furniture. Note that some lower rooms are quite noisy. Meliá Castilla is in the north of Madrid, about a block west of Paseo de la Castellana, and a short drive from the Chamartín railway station.

Dining/Diversions: The hotel has a coffee shop, a seafood restaurant, a restaurant specializing in paella and other rice dishes, cocktail lounges, and the Trinidad night- club. In addition, there's the restaurant/show Scala Meliá Castilla.

Amenities: 24-hour room service, hairdresser/barbershop, concierge, baby-sitting, laundry/valet, swimming pool, shopping arcade with souvenir shops and bookstore, saunas, gymnasium, parking garage.

MODERATE

The Aristos. Avenida Pío XII, 34, 28016 Madrid. ☎ **91-345-04-50.** Fax 91-345-10-23. 24 units. A/C TV TEL. 20,150–22,850 ptas. ($135–$153.10) double. AE, DC, MC, V. Parking 1,500 ptas. ($10.05). Metro: Pío XII.

This three-star hotel is in an up-and-coming residential area of Madrid, not far from the Eurobuilding (see above). Its main advantage is a garden where you can lounge, have a drink, or order a complete meal. The hotel's restaurant, Aristos Bar, offers breakfast, snacks and informal meals including local specialties, in a pleasant, relaxed atmosphere. Each of the medium-size rooms has a small terrace and an uncomplicated collection of modern furniture.

Hotel Chamartín. Estacíon de Chamartín, 28036 Madrid. ☎ **91-323-30-87** or 91-334- 49-00. Fax 91-733-02-14. www.husa.es. E-mail: chamartin@husa.es. 396 units. A/C MINIBAR TV TEL. 21,900 ptas. ($146.75) double; from 35,000 ptas. ($234.50) suite. AE, DC, MC, V. Parking 2,000 ptas. ($13.40) in nearby garage. Metro: Chamartín. Bus: 5.

This brick-sided hotel soars nine stories above the northern periphery of Madrid. It's part of the massive modern shopping complex attached to the Chamartín railway sta- tion, although once you're inside your soundproofed room, the noise of the railway station will seem far away. The owner of the building is RENFE, Spain's government railway system, but the nationwide chain that administers it is HUSA Hotels. The hotel lies 15 minutes by taxi from both the airport and the historic core of Madrid and sits atop one of the capital's busiest metro stops. The well-appointed rooms are good size, with private safes, quality mattresses, and cushiony furnishings, along with orderly bathrooms with stall showers and hair dryers. Especially oriented to the busi- ness traveler, Chamartín offers a currency exchange kiosk, a travel agency, a car-rental office, and a lobby video screen that posts the arrival and departure of all of Chamartín's trains.

A coffee bar serves breakfast daily, and room service is available from 7am to mid- night. The hotel restaurant, Cota 13, serves an international cuisine. A short walk from the hotel lobby, within the railway-station complex, are a handful of shops and movie theaters, a roller-skating rink, a disco, and ample parking.

ARGÜELLES/MONCLOA
VERY EXPENSIVE

Hotel Husa Princesa. Princesa, 40, 28008 Madrid. ☎ **91-542-35-00.** Fax 91-542-35-01. www.husa.es. E-mail:husaprincesa@husa.es. 275 units. A/C TV TEL. 35,250 ptas. ($236.20) double; from 72,600 ptas. ($486.40) suite. AE, DC, MC, V. Parking 3,500 ptas. ($23.45). Metro: Argüelles.

Originally built during the mid-1970s and radically renovated after its takeover in 1991 by the nationwide chain Husa, the Princesa is a sprawling concrete-and-glass hotel overlooking busy boulevards in the center of Madrid. Business travelers and tour groups make up most of the guest list. The soundproof accommodations are generally roomy, with desk space, good lighting, bedside controls, spacious closets, and quality mattresses, plus a marble bathroom that comes equipped with a phone, robes, a hair dryer, and dual basins.

Dining/Diversions: The hotel's restaurant offers traditional Spanish specialties together with a more international fare. There is also a bar, the Bar Royal.

Amenities: 24-hour room service, concierge, baby-sitting; the interior contains a large assortment of conference rooms, an underground garage, and a hairdressing salon.

Meliá Madrid Princesa. Princesa, 27, 28008 Madrid. ☎ **800/336-3542** in the U.S., or 91-541-82-00. Fax 91-541-19-05. 265 units. A/C MINIBAR TV TEL. 35,595 ptas. ($238.50) double; from 39,500–67,000 ptas. ($264.65–$448.90) suite. AE, DC, MC, V. Parking 2,400 ptas. ($16.10). Metro: Rodríguez.

Here you'll find one of the most modern yet uniquely Spanish hotels in the country. Its 23 floors of wide picture windows have taken a permanent position in the capital's skyline. Each of the bedrooms is comfortable, spacious, and filled with contemporary furnishings, including excellent beds, plus a TV with video movies and many channels from across Europe. Most offer views over the skyline of Madrid. The chalk-white walls dramatize the flamboyant use of color accents; the bathrooms are sheathed in marble and come with a hair dryer.

Dining/Diversions: Restaurante Princesa is elegant and restful; equally popular is Don Pepe Grill. The cuisine in both restaurants is international and includes an array of Japanese and Indian dishes. There are also three bars and a coffee shop.

Amenities: 24-hour room service, concierge, baby-sitting, hairdresser/barber, laundry, a gallery that includes souvenir shops and bookstores, health club with sauna and massage.

MODERATE

The Tirol. Marqués de Urquijo, 4, 28008 Madrid. ☎ **91-548-19-00.** Fax 91-541-39-58. 90 units. A/C TV TEL. 11,475 ptas. ($76.90) double. MC, V. Metro: Argüelles. Bus: 2 or 21.

A short walk from Plaza de España and the swank Meliá Madrid Princesa hotel (see above), the Tirol is a good choice for clean, unpretentious comfort. Furnishings in this three-star hotel are simple, functional, and comfortable. Eight of the guest rooms have private terraces. A cafeteria and a parking garage are within the hotel.

4 Dining

Madrid boasts the most varied cuisine and the widest choice of dining opportunities in Spain. At the fancy tourist restaurants, prices are just as expensive as in New York, London, or Paris, but there are lots of affordable taverns and family restaurants as well.

It's the custom in Madrid to consume the big meal of the day from 2 to 4pm. After a recuperative siesta, Madrileños then enjoy tapas, and indeed, no culinary experience would be complete without a tour of the city's many tapas bars (see "An Early Evening Tapeo," below, and "Our Favorite Tascas," later in this chapter). All this nibbling is followed by light supper in a restaurant, usually from 9:30pm to as late as midnight. Many restaurants, however, start serving dinner at 8pm to accommodate visitors from other countries who don't like to dine so late.

Many of Spain's greatest chefs have opened restaurants in Madrid, energizing the city's culinary scene. Gone are the days when mainly Madrileño food was featured, which meant Castilian specialties such as *cocido* (a chickpea-and-sausage stew) or roasts of suckling pig or lamb. Now you can take a culinary tour of the country while remaining in Madrid—from Andalusia with its gazpacho and braised bull's tails to Asturias with its *fabada* (a rich pork stew) and *sidra* (cider) to the Basque country, which has the most sophisticated cuisine in Spain. There is also a host of Galician and Mediterranean restaurants in Madrid. Amazingly, though Madrid is a landlocked city surrounded by a vast arid plain, you can order some of the freshest seafood in the country here.

Follow the local custom and don't overtip. Theoretically, service is included in the price of the meal, but it's customary to leave an additional 10%.

One way to save money is to order the *menú del día* (menu of the day) or *cubierto* (fixed price)—both fixed-price menus based on what is fresh at the market that day. They are the dining bargains in Madrid, although often lacking the quality of more expensive à la carte dining. Usually each will include a first course, such as fish soup or hors d'oeuvres, followed by a main dish, plus bread, dessert, and the wine of the house. You won't have a large choice. The *menú turístico* is a similar fixed-price menu, but for many it's too large, especially at lunch. Only those with large appetites will find it to be the best bargain.

NEAR THE PLAZA DE LAS CORTÉS
MODERATE

Edelweiss. Jovelianos, T. ☎ **91-521-03-26.** Reservations recommended. Main courses 990–2,500 ptas. ($6.65–$16.75); fixed-price menu 2,300 ptas. ($15.40). AE, DC, MC, V. Daily 1–4pm, Mon–Sat 8pm–midnight. Closed Aug. Metro: Sevilla. Bus: 5. GERMAN/MEDITERRANEAN.

This German standby has provided good-quality food and service at moderate prices since World War II. Edelweiss serves hearty portions of food, mugs of draft beer, and fluffy pastries; that's why there's always a wait. *Tip:* To beat the crowds, go for dinner at un-Spanish hours, say before 9pm, when tables are not at a premium. But even when it's jammed, service is almost always courteous.

Start with Bismarck herring, then dive into goulash with spaetzle or *Eisbein* (pigs' knuckles) with sauerkraut and mashed potatoes, the most popular dish at the restaurant. Finish with the homemade apple tart. The decor is vaguely German, with travel posters and wood-paneled walls. Edelweiss is air-conditioned in summer.

El Espejo. Paseo de Recoletos, 31. ☎ **91-308-23-47.** Reservations required. Menú del día 2,850 ptas. ($19.10). AE, MC, V. Daily 1–4pm and 9pm–midnight. Metro: Colón. Bus: 27. INTERNATIONAL.

Here you'll find good food and one of the most perfectly crafted art nouveau decors in Madrid. If the weather is good, you can choose one of the outdoor tables, served by uniformed waiters who carry food across the busy street to a green area flanked with trees and strolling pedestrians. We prefer a table inside, within view of the tile maidens with vines and flowers entwined in their hair. Upon entering, you'll find yourself in a

Dining in Central Madrid

Alfredo's Barbacoa 41
Alkalde 45
Amparo 15
Antonio Sánchez 14
Arce 28
Bajamar 5
Barraca 25
Bodegón 42
Bola 6
Cabo Mayor 3
Café Balear 36
Café de Oriente 9
Casa Alberto 16
Casa Lucio 13
Casa Mingo 1
Casa Paco 11
Casa Vallejo 33
Cenador del Prado 17
Cervecería Santa Bárbara 35
Chata 13
Chez Lou Crêperie 41
Ciao Madrid 34
Cornucopia 8
Cuatro Estaciones 3
Cuchi 10
Cuevas de Luís Candelas 10
Cuevas del Duque 2
Edelweiss 22
Espejo 40
Foster's Hollywood 44
Galayos 10
Galetta 46
Gamella 47
Goizeko Kabi 41
Gran Café de Gijón 30
Gure-Etxea (Restaurant Vasco) 12
Horcher 47
Hylogui 21
Inca 29
Jockey 38
Lhardy 20
Mad Madrid 24
Mentidero de la Villa 31
Nabucco 32
O'Pazo 3
Olivo Restaurant 41
Paellería Valenciana 23
Pampa de Lavapies 15
Pescador 43
Platerías Comedor 18
Principe de Viana 41
Restaurante Belagu 37
Ríofrío 39
Schotis 13
Sobrino de Botin 10
Taberna Carmencita 27
Taberna del Alabardero 7
Taberna Toscana 21
Terraza 19
Tiendo de Vinos 28
Trainera 42
Trucha 21
V.I.P. 26
Vera Cruz 4
Viridiana 48
Zalacaín 36

Legend
† Church
ℹ Information
Ⓜ Metro
✉ Post Office

86

charming cafe/bar, where many visitors linger before heading toward the spacious dining room. Dishes include grouper ragout with clams, steak tartare, guinea fowl with Armagnac, and lean duck meat with pineapple. Try profiteroles with cream and chocolate sauce for dessert.

La Trucha. Manuel Fernandez González, 3. ☎ **91-429-58-33.** Reservations recommended. Main courses 1,600-2,000 ptas. ($10.70–$13.40). AE, MC, V. Mon–Sat 12:30–4pm and 7:30pm–midnight. Metro: Sevilla. SPANISH/SEAFOOD.

With its Andalusian tavern ambience, La Trucha boasts a street-level bar and small dining room with arched ceiling and whitewashed walls. The festive decor includes hanging braids of garlic, dried peppers, and onions. On the lower level the walls of a second bustling area are covered with eye-catching antiques, bullfight notices, and other bric-a-brac. The specialty here is fish; there's a complete à la carte menu including *trucha* (trout), *verbenas de ahumados* (a selection of smoked delicacies), a glorious stew called *fabada* (made with beans, Galician ham, black sausage, and smoked bacon), and a *comida casera rabo de toro* (home-style oxtail). No one should miss nibbling on the tapas variadas in the bar.

If this Trucha turns out to be too crowded, there's another branch at Núñez de Arce, 6 (☎ **91-532-08-82**).

NEAR THE PLAZA DE ESPAÑA
EXPENSIVE

Bajamar. Gran Vía, 78. ☎ **91-559-59-03.** Reservations recommended. Main courses 5,000–6,500 ptas. ($33.50–$43.55). AE, DC, MC, V. Daily 1–4pm and 8pm–midnight. Metro: Plaza de España. SEAFOOD.

Bajamar is one of best fish houses in Spain. Flown in daily, fish and shellfish are market-priced while lobster, king crab, prawns, and soft-shell crabs are all priced according to weight. There is a large array of reasonably priced dishes as well. The service is smooth and professional and the menu is in English. For an appetizer, order the half-dozen giant oysters or rover crayfish. The special seafood soup is a most satisfying meal in itself. Also try the lobster bisque. Some of the noteworthy main courses include turbot Gallego style, seafood paella, and baby squid cooked in its ink. Desserts are simple, including the chef's custard.

MODERATE

Las Cuevas del Duque. Princesa, 16. ☎ **91-559-50-37.** Reservations required. Main courses 2,700–2,975 ptas. ($18.10–$19.95). AE, DC, MC, V. Mon–Fri 1–4pm, daily 8pm–midnight. Metro: Ventura Rodríguez. Bus: 1, 2, or 42. SPANISH/CASTILIAN.

Located in front of the Duke of Alba's palace, Las Cuevas del Duque has an underground bar and a small, 20-table mesón. Specialties include such simple Spanish fare as roast suckling pig (on which its reputation was built), sirloin, tiny grilled lamb cutlets, and a few seafood dishes, including hake in garlic sauce and sole cooked in cider. In fair weather a few tables are set outside, beside a tiny triangular garden. Other tables line the calle de la Princesa side and make an enjoyable roost for an afternoon drink.

INEXPENSIVE

Vera Cruz. San Leonardo, 5. ☎ **91-597-54-41.** Main courses 400–950 ptas. ($2.70–$6.35); fixed-price menu 950 ptas. ($6.35). No credit cards. Mon–Sat 1–5pm and 8pm–midnight. Metro: Plaza de España. SPANISH.

Behind the landmark Edificio España, you'll find this old standby for hungry budget-minded visitors. It's a simple *económico*, but the food is acceptable and the service polite. The menú del día usually includes soup or appetizer, followed by a meat or fish dish,

An Early Evening Tapeo

What's more fun than a pub crawl in London or Dublin? In Madrid, it's a tapeo, and you can drink just as much or more than in those far northern climes. One of the unique pleasures of Madrid, a tapeo is the act of strolling from one bar to another to keep yourself amused and fed before the fashionable Madrileño dining hour of 10pm.

Most of the world knows that tapas are Spain's delectable appetizers, and hundreds of restaurants in England and the United States now serve them. In Madrid they're served almost everywhere, in tabernas, tascas, bars, and cafes.

Although Madrid took to tapas with a passion, they may have originated in Andalusia, especially around Jerez de la Frontera, where they were traditionally served to accompany the sherry produced there. The first tapa (which means a cover or lid) was probably *chorizo* (a spicy sausage) or a slice of cured ham perched over the mouth of a glass to keep the flies out. Later, the government mandated bars to serve a "little something" in the way of food with each drink to dissipate the effects of the alcohol. This was important when drinking a fortified wine like sherry, as its alcohol content is more than 15% higher than that of normal table wines. Eating a selection of tapas as you drink will help preserve your sobriety.

Tapas can be relatively simple: toasted almonds; slices of ham, cheese, or sausage; potato omelettes; or the ubiquitous olives. They can be more elaborate too: a succulent veal roll; herb-flavored snails; *gambas* (fried or grilled shrimp); a saucer of peppery *pulpo* (octopus); stuffed peppers; delicious *anguila* (eel); *cangrejo* (crabmeat salad); merluza (hake) salad flavored with sweet red peppers, garlic, and cumin; and even bull testicles.

Each bar in Madrid gains a reputation for its rendition of certain favorite foods. One bar, for example, specializes in very garlicky grilled mushrooms, usually accompanied by pitchers of sangría. Another will specialize in gambas. Most chefs are men in Madrid, but at tapas bars or *tascas*, the cooks are most often women—perhaps the mother or sister of the owner, or more usually the wife.

Louis Armstrong, Manolete, Ava Gardner, and even Orson Welles each enjoyed this characteristic culinary feature of Spain in their day. They may no longer be around to accompany you on a tapeo, but the tradition lives on. For a selection of our favorite bars, see "Our Favorite Tascas," later in this chapter. There are literally hundreds of others, many of which you'll discover on your own during your strolls around Madrid.

---

then cheese or fruit, plus bread and wine. The Vera Cruz also has daily specials like paella and *cocido*, a typical Madrid dish made of chickpeas, sausage, cabbage, and potatoes.

ON OR NEAR THE GRAN VÍA
EXPENSIVE

Arce. Augusto Figueroa, 32. ☎ **91-522-59-13.** Reservations recommended. Main courses 2,800–3,500 ptas. ($18.75–$23.45). AE, DC, MC, V. Mon–Fri 1:30–4pm, Mon–Sat 9pm–midnight. Closed the week before Easter and Aug 15–31. Metro: Colón. BASQUE.

Arce has brought some of the best modern interpretations of Basque cuisine to Madrid, thanks to the enthusiasm of owner/chef Iñaki Camba and his wife, Theresa.

Within a comfortably decorated dining room, you can enjoy dishes made of the finest ingredients using flavors designed to dominate your taste buds. Examples include a salad of fresh scallops and an oven-baked casserole of fresh boletus mushrooms, seasoned lightly so the woodsy vegetable taste comes through. Look for unusual preparations of hake and seasonal variations of such game dishes as pheasant and woodcock.

MODERATE

El Mentidero de la Villa. Santo Tomé, 6. ☎ **91-308-12-85.** Reservations required. Main courses 1,750–2,540 ptas. ($11.75–$17); menú del día 1,900 ptas. ($12.75). MC, V. Mon–Fri 1:30–4:30pm, Mon–Sat 9pm–midnight. Closed last 2 weeks of Aug. Metro: Alonso Martínez, Colón. Bus: 37. SPANISH/FRENCH.

The Mentidero ("Gossip Shop" in English) is a truly multicultural experience. The owner describes the cuisine as "modern Spanish with Japanese influence and a French cooking technique." That may sound confusing, but the result is an achievement; each ingredient in every dish manages to retain its distinct flavor. The kitchen plays with such adventuresome combinations as veal liver in sage sauce, a spring roll filled with fresh shrimp and leeks, noisettes of veal with tarragon, fillet steak with a sauce of mustard and brown sugar, and medallions of venison with puree of chestnut and celery. One especially notable dessert is sherry trifle. The postmodern decor includes trompe l'oeil ceilings, exposed wine racks, ornate columns with unusual lighting, and a handful of antique carved merry-go-round horses.

La Barraca. Reina, 29-31. ☎ **91-532-71-54.** Reservations recommended. Main courses 2,000 ptas. ($13.40); fixed-price menu 3,600 ptas. ($24.10). AE, DC, MC, V. Daily 1–4pm and 8:30pm–midnight. Metro: Gran Vía or Banco de España. Bus: 1, 2, or 74. VALENCIAN.

La Barraca is like a country inn right off the Gran Vía, and is a longtime local favorite. The food, frankly, used to be better, but perhaps our tastes have changed since our student days. This Valencian-style restaurant is a well-managed establishment recommended for its tasty Levante cooking. There are four different dining rooms, three of which lie one flight above street level; they're colorfully cluttered with ceramics, paintings, photographs, Spanish lanterns, flowers, and local artifacts. The house specialty, paella à la Barraca, is made with pork and chicken. Specialties in the appetizer category include *desgarrat* (a salad made with codfish and red peppers), mussels in a white-wine sauce, and shrimp sautéed with garlic. In addition to the recommended paella, you can select at least 16 rice dishes, including black rice. Main-dish specialties include brochette of angler fish and prawns and rabbit with fines herbs. Lemon-and-vodka sorbet brings the meal to a fitting finish.

INEXPENSIVE

Paellería Valenciana. Caballero de Gracia, 12. ☎ **91-531-17-85.** Reservations recommended. Main courses 1,250–2,500 ptas. ($8.40–$16.75); fixed-price menus 1,250 ptas. ($8.40). AE, MC, V. Mon–Sat 1:30–4:30pm. Metro: Gran Vía. SPANISH.

This lunch-only restaurant ranks as one of the best values in the city. The specialty is paella, of course, which you must order by phone in advance. Once you arrive, you might begin with a homemade soup or the house salad, then follow with the rib-sticking paella, served in an iron skillet for two or more only. Among the desserts, the chef's special pride is razor-thin orange slices flavored with rum, coconut, sugar, honey, and raspberry sauce. A carafe of house wine comes with the set menu, and after lunch the owner comes around dispensing free cognac.

V.I.P. Gran Vía, 43. ☎ **91-559-64-57.** Main courses 750–1,445 ptas. ($5.05–$9.70). AE, DC, MC, V. Daily 9am–3am. Metro: Callao. FAST FOOD.

Though it looks like a bookstore emporium from the outside, in back is a cafeteria serving fast food. There are more than a dozen V.I.P.s scattered throughout Madrid, but this is the most central one. Hamburgers are the rage here, though you might begin with a cup of soothing gazpacho. The service leaves a lot to be desired.

NEAR THE PUERTA DEL SOL
VERY EXPENSIVE

Lhardy. Carrera de San Jéronimo, 8. ☎ **91-521-33-85.** Reservations recommended in the upstairs dining room. Main dishes 6,000–9,000 ptas. ($40.20–$60.30). AE, MC, V. Mon–Sat 1–3:30pm and 8:30–11pm. Closed Aug. Metro: Puerta del Sol. SPANISH/INTERNATIONAL.

Lhardy has been a Madrileño legend since it opened in 1839 as a gathering place for the city's literati and political leaders. (In 1846 it even entertained Dumas, father, not son.) At street level is what may be the most elegant snack bar in Spain. Within a dignified antique setting of marble and varnished hardwoods, cups of steaming consommé are dispensed from silver samovars into delicate porcelain cups, and rows of croquettes, tapas, and sandwiches are served to stand-up clients who pay for their food at a cashier's kiosk near the entrance. The ground-floor deli and take-out service is open daily from 9am to 3pm and 5 to 9:30pm.

The real culinary skill of the place, however, is found on Lhardy's second floor, where you'll find a formal restaurant decorated in the ornate belle epoque style of Isabel Segunda. Specialties of the house include fish, pork and veal, tripe in a garlicky tomato and onion wine sauce, and cocido, the celebrated chickpea stew of Madrid. *Soufflé sorpresa* (baked Alaska) is the dessert specialty.

Platerías Comedor. Plaza de Santa Ana, 11. ☎ **91-429-70-48.** Reservations recommended. Main courses 4,000–5,000 ptas. ($26.80–$33.50). AE, DC, MC, V. Tues–Sun 1:30–4pm, Tues–Sat 8:30pm–midnight. Metro: Puerta del Sol. SPANISH.

One of the most charming dining rooms in Madrid, Platerías Comedor has richly brocaded walls evocative of 19th-century Spain. Busy socializing may take place on the plaza outside, but this serene oasis makes few concessions to the new generation in its food, decor, or formally attired waiters. Specialties include paella Valenciana, stuffed partridge with cabbage and sausage, duck liver with white grapes, tripe à la Madrid, veal stew with snails and mushrooms, and guinea hen with figs and plums. Follow up any of these with the passion fruit sorbet. Better restaurants have sprouted up in recent years, but Platerías Comedor continues to thrive as a culinary tradition; its old-fashioned atmosphere is hard to come by.

Terraza. Alcala, 15. ☎ **91-521-8700.** Main courses 3,500-4,000 ptas. ($23.45–$26.80); fixed-price menu 9,000 ptas. ($60.30). AE, DC, MC, V. Mon–Fri 1–3:30pm, 9–11:30pm; Sat 9–11pm. Closed Aug. Metro: Sevilla. SPANISH/INTERNATIONAL.

Glamorous in its neobaroque casino location, and with a mouthwatering menu, this restaurant is a perfect example of postmodern Spanish cuisine. The fifth floor restaurant provides a panoramic view of the heart of Madrid and can either be reached by an elevator or by a sweeping 19th-century staircase designed to impress. The decor is classically restrained with high ceilings and crystal chandeliers. The delicious food depends on fresh seasonal ingredients and reinterprets Spanish dishes. An example is raya in oil and saffron with parsley puree and nuts on a bed of finely diced fries. More traditional dishes include the succulent *merluza a la Gallega* (Galician hake), *crema de la fabada asturiana* (creamed Asturian bean soup), and the steeply priced *jamon jabugo* (cured ham from acorn-fed pigs) served with a *menestra* (mixed vegetables) a dente. Only French champagne and Spanish wines are listed and one of the best is the rounded woody red, the Ribeira de Duero from the province of Valladolid.

MODERATE

Café de Oriente. Plaza de Oriente, 2. ☎ **91-541-39-74.** Reservations recommended (in restaurant only). Cafe: tapas 400 ptas. ($2.70). Restaurant: main courses 2,500–3,100 ptas. ($16.75–$20.75). AE, DC, MC, V. Daily 1–4pm and 9pm–midnight. Metro: Opera. SPANISH.

The Oriente is a cafe and restaurant complex, with the former being one of the most popular in Madrid. From the cafe tables on its terrace, there's a spectacular view of the Palacio Real (Royal Palace) and the Teatro Real. The dining rooms—Castilian upstairs, French Basque downstairs—are frequented by royalty and diplomats. Typical of the refined cuisine are vichyssoise, fresh vegetable flan, and many savory meat and fresh-fish offerings. Service is excellent. Most visitors, however, patronize the cafe, trying if possible to get an outdoor table. The cafe is decorated in turn-of-the-century style, with banquettes and regal paneling, as befits its location. Pizza, tapas, and drinks (including Irish, Viennese, Russian, and Jamaican coffees) are served.

Casa Paco. Plaza Puerta Cerrada, 11. ☎ **91-366-31-66.** Reservations required. Main courses 1,100–3,800 ptas. ($7.35–$25.45); fixed-price menu 3,800 ptas. ($25.45). DC. Mon–Sat 1–4pm and 8:30pm–midnight. Closed Aug. Metro: Puerta del Sol, Opera, or La Latina. Bus: 3, 21, and 65. STEAK.

Madrileños defiantly name Casa Paco, just beside the Plaza Mayor, when someone dares to denigrate Spanish steaks. They know that here you can get the thickest, juiciest, tastiest steaks in Spain, which are priced according to weight. Señor Paco was the first in Madrid to sear steaks in boiling oil before serving them on plates so hot that the almost-raw meat continues to cook, preserving the natural juices. Located in the Old Town, this two-story restaurant has three dining rooms but reservations are imperative. If you face a long wait, while away the time sampling the tapas at the bar in front. Around the walls are autographed photographs of notables.

Casa Paco isn't just a steakhouse; you can start with fish soup and proceed to grilled sole, baby lamb, or *Casa Paco cocido*, the house version of Madrid's famous chickpea and pork soup. You might top it off with one of the luscious desserts, but know that Paco no longer serves coffee. It made customers linger, keeping tables occupied while potential patrons had to be turned away.

Cornucopia. Calle Flora, 1. ☎ **91-547-6465.** Reservations recommended. Main courses 1,800–2,600 ptas. ($12.05–$17.40). Fixed-price lunch (Tues–Fri only) 1,600 ptas. ($10.70). AE, DC, MC, V. Tues–Fri 1:30–4pm and Tues–Sun 8:30–11:30pm. Closed 1 week in Aug. Metro: Opera or Callao. EURO-AMERICAN.

Set on a narrow side street adjacent to the medieval Plaza de Descalzas Reales, this restaurant occupies the mezzanine level of what was originally a 19th-century private palace. Its glamour and allure derive from its ownership by four partners, two of whom (North Carolina–born Jennifer Cole and her cohort, Kimberly Manning) are American; the others include French-born François and Spanish-born Fernando. Within a pair of elegant and airy dining rooms whose gleaming parquet floors remain intact from the original decor, you can admire the frequently changing paintings, all available for sale. Menu items include mussels with fennel and a roasted red pepper sauce over black fettuccini; grilled baby hen with mushrooms, flan, and sherry sauce; and grilled pork tenderloin stuffed with brie and bacon, and served with a pomegranate-apple compote and a red wine reduction sauce. Desserts are sumptuous and might include a dollop of such original homemade ice creams as morito. Named after a traditional Cuban cocktail, it's flavored with mint, lemon, and rum. All the food is well prepared, the ingredients are fresh, and the staff is among the most inviting in Madrid.

✪ **El Cenador del Prado.** Calle del Prado, 4. ☎ **91-429-15-61.** Reservations recommended. Jackets and ties are recommended for men. Main courses 1,250–2,200 ptas.

($8.40–$14.75); fixed-price menu 3,325 ptas. ($22.30). AE, DC, MC, V. Mon–Fri 1:45–4pm, Mon–Sat 9pm–midnight. Closed Aug 12–19. Metro: Sevilla. INTERNATIONAL.

In this deceptively elegant restaurant's anteroom, an attendant will check your coat and packages into an elaborately carved armoire before the maître d' ushers you into one of a trio of rooms. Two of the rooms, done in tones of peach and sepia, have cove moldings and English furniture, as well as floor-to-ceiling gilded mirrors. A third room, the most popular, is ringed with lattices and flooded with sun from a skylight.

The imaginative food reflects a French influence, with the occasional Asian flourish. You might enjoy such specialties as crepes with salmon and Iranian caviar, a salad of red peppers and salted anchovies, a casserole of snails and oysters with mushrooms, a ceviche of salmon and shellfish, potato-leek soup studded with tidbits of hake and clams, sea bass with candied lemons, veal scaloppini stuffed with asparagus and garlic sprouts, or medallions of venison served with pepper-and-fig chutney.

✪ **Mad Madrid.** Calle Virgin de los Peligros, 4. ☎ **91-532-6228.** Reservations recommended. Main courses 1,600–2,100 ptas. ($10.70–$14.05); fixed-price menu (at lunch only) 1,500 ptas. ($10.05). AE, DC, MC, V. Mon–Wed 1–4pm and 9:30pm–3am; Thurs–Sat 1–4pm and 9:30pm–4am. Dinner served until 12:30am. Metro: Sevilla, Gran Vía. INTERNATIONAL.

This restaurant bar in the very center of Madrid is a hot spot. Done all in gray and red in stark minimalism (sort of a tongue-in-cheek Soviet style), there's also a garden where you can enjoy a cocktail on a summer night. Taking her inspiration from around the Mediterranean, chef Belen Laguía changes the menu every 3 months. Staples, however, include starters such as goat cheese on caramelized onions and corral salad, which is comprised of wild chicken marinated in vinegar and cream on four types of lettuce. Other dishes to savor are marinated salmon with dill and golden caviar, which is black, from an inland sea in the dry southern province of Murcia. This is served with Japanese seaweed and fresh seasonal vegetables presented al dente. Desserts include an apple tart, not too sweet and topped with egg yolk.

INEXPENSIVE

Casa Alberto. Huertas, 18. ☎ **91-429-93-56.** Reservations recommended. Main courses 650–2,250 ptas. ($4.35–$15.10). AE, DC, MC, V. Tues–Sat 1–4pm, Tues–Sun 8:30pm–midnight. Metro: Antón Martín. CASTILIAN.

One of the oldest *tascas* in the neighborhood, Casa Alberto was originally established in 1827, and has thrived ever since. On the street level of a house where Miguel de Cervantes lived briefly in 1614, it contains an appealing mixture of bullfighting memorabilia, engravings, and reproductions of Old Master paintings. Many visitors opt only for the tapas, continually replenished from platters on the bar, but there's also a sit-down dining area for more substantial meals. Specialties include fried squid, shellfish in vinaigrette sauce, *chorizo* (sausage) in cider sauce, and several versions of baked or roasted lamb.

Hylogui. Ventura de la Vega, 3. ☎ **91-429-73-57.** Reservations recommended. Main courses 1,000–2,200 ptas. ($6.70–$14.75); fixed-price menus 1,400–1,700 ptas. ($9.40–$11.40). AE, MC, V. Daily 1–4:30pm, Mon–Sat 9pm–12:30am. Metro: Sevilla. SPANISH.

Hylogui, a local legend, is one of the largest dining rooms along Ventura de la Vega, though it contains many arches and nooks for privacy. One globe-trotting American wrote enthusiastically that he took all his Madrid meals here, finding the soup pleasant and rich, the flan soothing, and the regional wine dry. The food is old-fashioned Spanish home-style cooking.

Taberna del Alabardero. Felipe V, 6. ☎ **91-547-25-77.** Reservations required for restaurant only. Bar: tapas 300–1,200 ptas. ($2–$8.05); glass of house wine 200 ptas. ($1.35). Restaurant: main courses 1,900–5,500 ptas. ($12.75–$36.85). AE, DC, MC, V. Daily 8am–1am. Metro: Opera. BASQUE/SPANISH.

In close proximity to the Royal Palace, this little Spanish classic is known for its selection of tasty tapas, ranging from squid cooked in wine to fried potatoes dipped in hot sauce. Photographs of famous former patrons, including Nelson Rockefeller and the race-car driver Jackie Stewart, line the walls. The restaurant in the rear is said to be one of the city's best-kept secrets. Decorated in typical tavern style, it serves a savory Spanish and Basque cuisine with market-fresh ingredients.

RETIRO/SALAMANCA
EXPENSIVE

Alkalde. Jorge Juan, 10. ☎ **91-576-33-59.** Reservations required. Main courses 2,000–5,300 ptas. ($13.40–$35.50); fixed-price menu from 6,000 ptas. ($40.20). AE, DC, MC, V. Daily 1:15–4pm and 8:30pm–midnight. Closed Sat–Sun in July–Aug. Metro: Retiro or Serrano. Bus: 8, 20, 21, or 53. BASQUE.

For decades, Alkalde has been known for serving top-quality Spanish food in an old tavern setting. Decorated like a Basque inn, it has beamed ceilings with hams hanging from the rafters. Upstairs is a large típico tavern; downstairs is a maze of stone-sided cellars that are pleasantly cool in summer (though the whole place is air-conditioned).

Basque cookery is the best in Spain, and Alkalde honors that noble tradition. Begin with the cream of crabmeat soup, followed by *gambas a la plancha* (grilled shrimp) or *cigalas* (crayfish). Other recommended dishes include *mero salsa verde* (brill in a green sauce), trout Alkalde, stuffed peppers, and chicken steak. The dessert specialty is copa *Cardinal* (ice cream topped with fruit).

○ **El Amparo.** Callejón de Puigcerdá, 8 (at corner of Jorge Juan). ☎ **91-431-64-56.** Reservations required. Main courses 2,950–4,300 ptas. ($19.75–$28.80). AE, MC, V. Sun–Fri 1:30–3:30pm, daily 9–11:30pm. Closed week before Easter and in Aug. Metro: Serrano. Bus: 21 or 53. BASQUE.

Behind the cascading vines on El Amparo's facade is one of Madrid's most elegant gastronomic enclaves. Inside this converted carriage house, three tiers of roughly hewn wooden beams surround tables set with pink linens and glistening silver for a touch of cosmopolitan glamour. A sloping skylight floods the interior with sun by day; at night, pinpoints of light from the high-tech hanging lanterns create intimate shadows. Polite, uniformed waiters serve well-prepared nouvelle cuisine versions of cold marinated salmon with a tomato sorbet, cold cream of vegetable and shrimp soup, bisque of shellfish with Armagnac, ravioli with crayfish dressed with balsamic vinegar and vanilla-scented oil, roast lamb chops with garlic puree, breast of duck, ragout of sole, steamed fish of the day, roulades of lobster with soy sauce, and steamed hake with pepper sauce.

El Pescador. Calle José Ortega y Gasset, 75. ☎ **91-402-12-90.** Reservations required. Main courses 6,000–15,000 ptas. ($40.20–$100.50); fixed price menu 6,250 ptas. ($41.90). MC, V. Mon–Sat noon–4pm and 8pm–midnight. Closed Aug. Metro: Lista or Diego de Leon. SEAFOOD.

El Pescador is a popular spot that packs in crowds with more than 30 kinds of fish served, all prominently displayed in a glass case. Many of these are unknown in North America, and some originate off the coast of Galicia. The management air-freights them in and prefers to serve them *à la plancha* (grilled). You might start off with spicy fish soup and accompany it with one of the many good wines from northeastern Spain. If you're not sure what to order (even the English translations might sound unfamiliar), try one of the many varieties and sizes of shrimp. These go under the names *langostinos, cigalas, santiaguinos,* and *carabineros.* Many of them are expensive and priced by the gram, so be careful when you order.

Horcher. Alfonso XII, 6. ☎ **91-532-35-96.** Reservations required. Jackets and ties for men. Main courses 3,500–4,500 ptas. ($23.45–$30.15). AE, DC, MC, V. Mon–Fri 1:30–4pm, Mon–Sat 8:30pm–midnight. Metro: Retiro GERMAN/INTERNATIONAL.

Horcher originated in Berlin in 1904. In 1943, prompted by a tip from a high-ranking German officer that Germany was losing the war, Herr Horcher moved his restaurant to Madrid. For years, it was known as the best dining room in the city, though fierce competition has lately stolen that crown. Nevertheless, the restaurant has continued its grand European traditions, including excellent service.

You might try the skate or shrimp tartare or the distinctive warm hake salad. Both the venison stew with green pepper and orange peel and the crayfish with parsley and cucumber are typical of the elegant fare served with impeccable style. Spanish aristocrats often come here in autumn to sample game dishes, including venison, wild boar, and roast wild duck. Other main courses include veal scaloppini in tarragon and sea bass with saffron. For dessert, the house specialty is crepes Sir Holden, prepared at your table with fresh raspberries, cream, and nuts.

✪ **La Gamella.** Alfonso XII, 4. ☎ **91-532-45-09.** Reservations required. Main courses 2,300–4,200 ptas. ($15.40–$28.15). AE, DC, MC, V. Mon–Fri 1:30–4pm, Mon–Sat 9pm–midnight. Closed 2 weeks around Easter and 2 weeks in Aug. Metro: Retiro. Bus: 19. CALIFORNIAN/CASTILIAN.

La Gamella established its gastronomic reputation shortly after it opened several years ago in less imposing quarters in another part of town. In 1988, its Illinois-born owner, Dick Stephens, moved his restaurant into the 19th-century building where the Spanish philosopher Ortega y Gasset was born. The prestigious Horcher, one of the capital's legendary restaurants (see above), is just across the street, but the food at La Gamella is better. The russet-colored, high-ceilinged design invites customers to relax. Mr. Stephens has prepared his delicate and light-textured specialties for the king and queen of Spain, as well as for Madrid's most talked-about artists and merchants, many of whom he knows and greets personally between sessions in his kitchen.

Typical menu items include a ceviche of Mediterranean fish, sliced duck liver in truffle sauce, a dollop of goat cheese served over caramelized endive, duck breast with peppers, and an array of well-prepared desserts, among which is an all-American cheesecake. Traditional Spanish dishes such as chicken with garlic have been added to the menu, plus what has been called "the only edible hamburger in Madrid." Because of the intimacy and the small dimensions of the restaurant, reservations are important.

La Trainera. Calle Lagasca, 60. ☎ **91-576-8035.** Reservations recommended. Main courses 3,000–6,000 ptas. ($20.10–$40.20). Fixed-price menus 7,600–11,500 ptas. ($50.90–$77.05). AE, DC, MC, V. Mon–Sat 1–4pm and 8pm–midnight. Metro: Serrano. SEAFOOD.

This restaurant is more expensive, and more chic, than its sprawling, paneled interior might imply. Suitable for up to 300 diners at a time, it occupies a quartet of dining rooms within a turn-of-the-century building in the glamorous shopping neighborhood of Serrano. Look for vaguely Basque-inspired platters of very fresh seafood, which arrive steaming hot and drizzled with subtle combinations of herbs, wines, and olive oils. No meat of any kind is served here. Instead, you'll find spicy and garlic-enriched versions of fish soup, an *escabeche of bonita* served as an appetizer, fillet of sole prepared in any of several different versions, Cantabrian crayfish, and well-conceived versions of a *salpicon de mariscos* (a platter of shellfish). Other fish include red mullet, swordfish with capers, monkfish, and virtually anything else that swims. Any of these can be preceded with a heaping platter of shellfish set atop a bed of artfully arranged seaweed. Succulent shellfish, including lobster, shrimp, crab, and mussels, plus an array of other items, is market-priced by weight.

✪ **Viridiana.** Juan de Mena, 14. ☎ **91-523-44-78.** Reservations recommended. Main courses 3,000–4,000 ptas. ($20.10–$26.80). AE, MC, V. Mon–Sat 1:30pm–4pm and 9pm–midnight. Closed 1 week at Easter and 2 weeks in Aug. Metro: Banco. INTERNATIONAL.

Viridiana—named after the 1961 Luis Buñuel film classic—is praised as one of the up-and-coming restaurants of Madrid, known for the creative imagination of its chef and part-owner, Abraham García, who has lined the walls with stills from Buñuel films. He is also a film historian, not just a self-taught chef. Menu specialties are contemporary adaptations of traditional recipes, and they change frequently according to availability. Examples of the highly individualistic cooking include a salad of exotic lettuces served with smoked salmon, a chicken pastilla laced with cinnamon, baby squid with curry served on a bed of lentils, roasted lamb served in puff pastry with fresh basil, and the choicest langostinos from Cádiz. The food is sublime, and the inviting ambience makes you relaxed as you sit back to enjoy dishes that often dazzle the eye, notably venison and rabbit arranged on a plate with fresh greens to evoke an autumnal scene in a forest.

MODERATE

Gran Caféde Gijón. Paseo de Recoletos, 21. ☎ **91-521-54-25.** Reservations required for restaurant. Main courses 1,400–2,950 ptas. ($9.40–$19.75); fixed-price menu 1,500 ptas. ($10.05). AE, DC, MC, V. Sun–Fri 7am–1:30am, Sat 7am–2am. Metro: Banco de España, Colón, or Recoletos. SPANISH.

Each of the old European capitals has a coffeehouse that traditionally attracts the literati—in Madrid it's the Gijón, which opened in 1888 in the heyday of the belle epoque. Artists and writers still patronize this venerated old cafe, many of them spending hours over one cup of coffee. Ernest Hemingway made the place famous for Americans, and such notables as Ava Gardner and Truman Capote followed in his footsteps in the 1950s. Open windows look out onto the wide paseo and a large terrace is perfect for sun worshippers and bird-watchers. Along one side of the cafe is a stand-up bar, and on the lower level is a restaurant. Food is prepared the way it used to be in Madrid. In summer, sit in the garden to enjoy a *blanco y negro* (black coffee with ice cream) or a mixed drink.

CHAMBERÍ
VERY EXPENSIVE

✪ **jockey.** Amador de los Ríos, 6. ☎ **91-319-24-35.** Reservations required. Main courses 3,350–6,750 ptas. ($22.45–$45.25). AE, DC, MC, V. Mon–Fri 1–4pm and Mon–Sat 9pm–midnight. Closed Aug. Metro: Colón. INTERNATIONAL.

For decades this was the premier restaurant of Spain. A favorite of international celebrities, diplomats, and heads of state, it was once known as the Jockey Club, although "Club" was eventually dropped because it suggested exclusivity. The restaurant, with tables on two levels, isn't large. Wood-paneled walls and colored linen provide a cozy ambience. Against the paneling are a dozen prints of jockeys mounted on horses—hence the name of the place.

Since Jockey's establishment shortly after World War II, each chef who has come along has prided himself on coming up with new and creative dishes. You can still order Beluga caviar from Iran, but might settle happily for the goose-liver terrine or slices of Jabugo ham. Cold melon soup with shrimp is soothing on a hot day, especially when followed by grill-roasted young pigeon from Talavera or sole fillets with figs in Chardonnay. Stuffed small chicken Jockey style is a specialty, as is tripa *Madrileña,* a local dish. Desserts are sumptuous.

EXPENSIVE

✪ **Las Cuatro Estaciones.** General Ibémñez Ibero, 5. ☎ **91-553-63-05.** Reservations required. Main courses 2,100–3,500 ptas. ($14.05–$23.45); fixed-price dinner 6,150 ptas. ($41.20). AE, DC, MC, V. Mon–Fri 1:30–4pm and Mon–Sat 9–11:30pm. Closed Easter and Aug. Metro: Guzmán el Bueno. MEDITERRANEAN.

Las Cuatro Estaciones is placed by gastronomes and horticulturists alike among their favorite Madrid dining spots, and it is a neck-and-neck rival with the prestigious Jockey. In addition to superb food, the establishment prides itself on the masses of flowers that change with the season. Depending on the time of year, the mirrors surrounding the multilevel bar near the entrance reflect thousands of hydrangeas, chrysanthemums, or poinsettias. Even the napery matches whichever colors the resident florist has chosen as the seasonal motif. Each person involved in food preparation spends a prolonged apprenticeship at restaurants in France before returning home to try their talents on the taste buds of aristocratic Madrid.

Representative specialties include crab bisque, a petite marmite of fish and shellfish, a salad of eels, fresh asparagus and mushrooms in puff pastry with parsley-butter sauce, and a nouvelle cuisine version of blanquette of monkfish so tender that it melts in your mouth. The desserts include daily specials, a selection of which is brought temptingly to your table.

✪ **Restaurante Belagua.** In the Hotel Palacio Santo Mauro, Calle Zurbano, 36. ☎ **91-319-69-00.** Reservations recommended. Main courses 2,900–3,200 ptas. ($19.45–$21.45). AE, DC, MC, V. Daily 1:30–4pm and 8:30–11:30pm. Closed national holidays. Metro: Rubén Darío or Alonso Martínez. BASQUE.

This glamorous restaurant was originally built in 1894 as a small palace in the French neoclassical style. In 1991 Catalan designer Josep Joanpere helped transform the building into a carefully detailed hotel (the Santo Mauro), which we've recommended separately (see above). On the hotel premises is this highly appealing postmodern restaurant, today one of the capital's finest.

Assisted by the well-mannered staff, you'll select from a menu whose inspiration and ingredients change with the seasons. Examples include watermelon-and-prawn salad, light cream of cold ginger soup, haddock baked in a crust of potatoes tinted with squid ink, fillet of monkfish with prawn-and-zucchini sauce, and duck with honey and black cherries. Dessert might include miniature portions of flan with strawberry sauce plus an array of the day's pastries. The restaurant's name, incidentally, derives from a village in Navarre known for its natural beauty.

MODERATE

La Bola. Calle de la Bola, 5. ☎ **91-547-69-30.** Reservations required. Main courses 1,975–2,550 ptas. ($13.25–$17.10). No credit cards. Mon–Sat 1–4:15pm, daily 8:30–11:15pm. Metro: Santo Domingo. Bus: 1 or 2. MADRILEÑA.

This is the taberna in which to savor the 19th century. Just north of the Teatro Real, it's one of the few restaurants (if not the only one) left in Madrid with a blood-red facade; at one time, nearly all fashionable restaurants were so coated. La Bola hangs on to tradition like a tenacious bull. Time has passed, but not inside this restaurant: The soft, traditional atmosphere; the gentle and polite waiters; the Venetian crystal; the carmine-red draperies; and the aging velvet all preserve the 1870 ambience. Ava Gardner, with her entourage of bullfighters, used to patronize this establishment, but that was long before La Bola became so well known to tourists. Grilled sole, fillet of veal, and roast veal are regularly featured. Basque-style hake and grilled salmon also are well recommended. Refreshing dishes to begin your meal include grilled shrimp, red-pepper salad, and lobster cocktail.

INEXPENSIVE

Foster's Hollywood. Velázquez, 80. ☎ **91-435-61-28.** Main courses 950–2,950 ptas. ($6.35–$19.75). AE, DC, MC, V. Sun–Thurs 1pm–midnight, Fri–Sat 1pm–2am. Metro: Serrano. AMERICAN.

When Foster's opened its doors in 1971, it was not only the first American restaurant in Spain, but one of the first in Europe. Since those early days, it has grown to 15 restaurants in Madrid, and has even opened branches in Florida. A popular hangout for both locals and visiting Yanks, it offers a choice of dining venues, ranging from classical club American to a studio, the latter evoking a working movie studio with props. Its varied menu includes Tex-Mex selections, ribs, steaks, sandwiches, freshly made salads, and, as its signature product, hamburgers grilled over natural charcoal in many variations. The *New York Times* once claimed that it had "probably the best onion rings in the world."

Other locations include Paseo de la Castellana, 116-118 (☎ **91-564-63-08**) and Princesa, 13 (☎ **91-559-19-14**), near Plaza de España.

Ríofrío. Centro Colón; Plaza de Colón, 1. ☎ **91-319-29-77.** Main courses 700–3,200 ptas. ($4.70–$21.45); fixed-price menu 2,500 ptas. ($16.75); sandwiches 525–900 ptas. ($3.50–$6.05). AE, DC, MC, V. Daily 7:30am–2am. Metro: Colón. Bus: 5, 14, 21, 27, or 45. INTERNATIONAL.

Overlooking Madrid's version of New York's Columbus Circle, this is a sort of all-purpose place for drinking, eating, dining, or nightclubbing. The least-expensive way to eat here is to patronize one of two self-service cafeterias, where average meals run from 1,200 to 1,800 ptas. ($8.05 to $12.05). There's also a larger restaurant with an international cuisine, serving meals averaging 3,500 ptas. ($23.45), plus yet another dining room for informal lunches, dinners, snacks, or aperitifs. The spacious glassed-in terrace, open year-round, is known for serving some of the best paella in Madrid. Finally, there's even a nightclub, El Descubrimiento, should you desire to make an evening of it. The club serves dinners from 4,500 ptas. ($30.15), which includes not only the meal but a show to follow. Sandwiches are also available throughout the day if you'd like just a light bite in the hot Madrid sun.

NEAR ALONSO MARTÍNEZ
MODERATE

Café Balear. Calle Sagunto, 18. ☎ **91/447-9115.** Reservations recommended. Average cost 4,000 ptas. ($26.80) per person. AE, MC, V. Daily 1:30–4pm, Tues–Sat 8:30–11:30pm. Metro: Iglesia. PAELLA/SEAFOOD

Only a handful of other restaurants in Madrid focuses as aggressively as this one on the national dish of Spain, paella, which here comes in 14 different versions, with permutations that might surprise even the most jaded aficionado of Spanish cuisine. Within a yellow-and-white dining room loaded with verdant potted plants, you can order any of several *calderas* (casseroles) that bubble with all kinds of fish and shellfish. Paella here includes versions with shellfish, with chicken and shellfish, with pork, with crabs, with lobster, and with an all-black version that's tinted with squid ink for extra flavor. There's even a vegetarian version if you absolutely, positively hate fish. Your fellow diners represent many of the creative arts of Spain, with lots of journalists, writers, poets, and artists who seem to have adopted the place.

Casa Vallejo. Calle San Lorenzo, 9. ☎ **91-308-6158.** Reservations recommended. Main courses 1,500–3,200 ptas. ($10.05–$21.45); fixed-price menu (available Mon–Fri only) 1,800 ptas. ($12.05). MC, V. Mon–Sat 2–4pm, Tues–Sat 9:30pm–midnight. Metro: Tribunale or Alonso Martínez. SPANISH.

This hardworking bistro with a not-terribly-subtle staff has less exposure to international clients than some of its competitors. But despite that, you'll find a sense of culinary integrity that's based on a devotion to fresh ingredients and a rigid allegiance to time-tested Spanish recipes. It occupies a turn-of-the-century building and contains room for only 42 diners at a time. Menu items include garlic soup; tartlets layered with tomatoes, zucchini, and cheese; a ragout of clams and artichokes; croquettes of chicken; breast of chicken garnished with a fricassee of fresh wild mushrooms; pork fillet; duck breast in orange or prune sauce; and creamy desserts. Budget gourmands in Madrid praise the hearty flavors here, the robust cookery, and the prices.

Ciao Madrid. Calle Apodaca, 20 (☎ **91-447-0036**; metro: Tribunal); and calle Argensola, 7 (☎ **91-308-2519**; metro: Alonso Martínez). Reservations recommended. Pastas 1,000–1,500 ptas. ($6.70–$10.05); main courses 1,500–2,500 ptas. ($10.05–$16.75). AE, DC, MC, V. Mon–Fri 1:30–3:45pm and Mon–Sat 9:30pm–midnight. The branch at calle Apodaca is closed in Sept; branch at calle Argensola is closed in Aug. ITALIAN.

These are two highly successful all-Italian restaurants established and maintained by extended members of the Laguna family. The older of the two is the branch on calle Apodaca, established about a dozen years ago; its cohort entered the scene in the early 1990s. Both maintain the same hours, prices, menu, and a decor inspired by the tenets of minimalist Milanese decor, with good-tasting food items that include risottos and pastas such as ravioli or tagliatelle with wild mushrooms. No one will mind if you order a pasta as a main course (lots of clients here do, accompanying it with a green salad). If you're in the mood for a more substantial main course, consider osso bucco, veal scaloppini, chicken or veal parmigiana, and any of several kinds of fish.

CHAMARTÍN
VERY EXPENSIVE

✪ **Zalacaín.** Alvarez de Baena, 4. ☎ **91-561-48-40.** Reservations required. Main courses 9,500–11,000 ptas. ($63.65–$73.70). AE, DC, MC, V. Mon–Fri 1:30–3:45pm, Mon–Sat 9–11:45pm. Closed week before Easter and in Aug. Metro: Rubén Darío. INTERNATIONAL.

Outstanding in both food and decor, Zalacaín opened in 1973 and introduced nouvelle cuisine to Spain. It is reached by an illuminated walk from Paseo de la Castellana and housed at the garden end of a modern apartment complex. In fact, it's within an easy walk of such deluxe hotels as the Castellana and the Miguel Angel. The name of the restaurant comes from the intrepid hero of Basque author Pío Baroja's 1909 novel, *Zalacaín El Aventurero.* Zalacaín is small, exclusive, and expensive. It has the atmosphere of an elegant old mansion: The walls are covered with textiles, and some are decorated with Audubon-type paintings. Men should wear jackets and ties.

The menu features many Basque and French specialties, often with nouvelle cuisine touches. It might offer a superb sole in a green sauce, but it also knows the glory of grilled pigs' feet. Among the most recommendable main dishes are oysters with caviar and sherry jelly; crepes stuffed with smoked fish; ravioli stuffed with mushrooms, foie gras, and truffles; Spanish bouillabaisse; and veal escalopes in orange sauce. For dessert, we'd suggest one of the custards, perhaps raspberry or chocolate.

EXPENSIVE

El Bodegón. Pinar, 15. ☎ **91-562-88-44.** Reservations required. Main courses 2,900–5,200 ptas. ($19.45–$34.85); fixed-price dinner 5,500 ptas. ($36.85). AE, DC, MC, V. Mon–Fri 1:30–4pm, Mon–Sat 9pm–midnight. Closed holidays and Aug. Metro: Rubén Darío. INTERNATIONAL/BASQUE/SPANISH.

El Bodegón is imbued with the atmosphere of a gentleman's club for hunting enthusiasts. International globetrotters come here, especially in the evening, as the restaurant is near such deluxe hotels as the Castellana and the Miguel Angel. King Juan Carlos and Queen Sofía have dined here.

Waiters in black and white, with gold braid and buttons, bring dignity to the food service. Even bottled water is served champagne style, chilled in a silver floor stand. There are two main dining rooms, both conservative and oak-beamed in the country-inn style.

We recommend cream of crayfish bisque or velvety vichyssoise to launch your meal. Main-course selections include grilled filet mignon with classic béarnaise sauce and venison bourguignonne. Other main-course selections include shellfish au gratin Escoffier, quails Fernand Point, tartare of raw fish marinated in parsley enriched vinaigrette, and smoked salmon.

✪ **El Olivo Restaurant.** General Gallegos, 1. ☎ **91-359-15-35.** Reservations recommended. Main courses 2,950–3,700 ptas. ($19.75–$24.80); fixed-price meals 3,850–5,700 ptas. ($25.80–$38.20). AE, DC, MC, V. Tues–Sat 1–4pm and 9pm–midnight. Closed Aug 15–31 and 4 days around Easter. Metro: Plaza de Castilla. MEDITERRANEAN.

Locals praise the success of a non-Spaniard (in this case, French-born Jean Pierre Vandelle) in recognizing the international appeal of two of Spain's most valuable culinary resources, olive oil and sherry. His likable restaurant pays homage to the glories of the Spanish olive. Designed in tones of green and amber, it is the only restaurant in Spain that wheels a cart stocked with 40 regional olive oils from table to table. From the cart, diners select a variety to soak up with chunks of rough-textured bread that is, according to your taste, seasoned with a dash of salt.

Menu specialties include grilled fillet of monkfish marinated in herbs and olive oil, then served with black-olive sauce over compote of fresh tomatoes, and four preparations of codfish arranged on a single platter and served with a *pil-pil* sauce. (Named after the sizzling noise it makes as it bubbles on a stove, pil-pil sauce is composed of codfish gelatin and herbs that are whipped into a mayonnaise-like consistency with olive oil.) Dessert might be one of several different chocolate pastries. *Note:* Many clients deliberately arrive early as an excuse to linger within El Olivo's one-of-a-kind sherry bar. Although other drinks are offered, the bar features more than 100 brands of *vino de Jerez,* more than practically any other establishment in Madrid. Priced at 250 to 750 ptas. ($1.70 to $5.05) per glass, they make the perfect aperitif.

✪ **Principe de Viana.** Calle Manuel de Falla, 5. ☎ **91-457-15-49.** Reservations required. Main courses 1,500–2,600 ptas. ($10.05–$17.40); fixed-price menu 7,500–8,000 ptas. ($50.25–$53.60). AE, DC, MC, V. Mon–Fri 1–4pm, 9–11:30pm; Sat 9–11:30pm. Closed in Aug. Metro: Lima. BASQUE.

This place has gotten rave reviews. The decor is neutral yet classical in style. Fish is of course the most important staple of Basque cuisine and there is a wide selection from which to choose. You might go the traditional route, with *bacalao ajoarriera* (cod with red peppers and tomatoes) and *merluza en salsa verde* (hake in parsley, garlic, and olive oil sauce). There are also more adventurous modern concoctions such as a salad with *chipirones* (baby squid) and *mojellas* (sweet meats) in a soya viniagrette. Those with a sweet tooth will be more than satisfied with the dessert of cream cheese and mango sorbet. From the many Spanish and occasional foreign wines to choose from, the Albirino from Galicia is particularly recommended.

MODERATE

✪ **El Cabo Mayor.** Juan Ramón Jiménez, 37. ☎ **91-350-87-76.** Reservations recommended. Main courses 1,850–3,900 ptas. ($12.40–$26.15). AE, DC, MC, V. Mon–Fri

1:30–4pm and Mon–Sat 8:45–11:45pm. Closed 1 week at Easter and Aug 25. Metro: Cuzco. SPANISH.

Not far from Chamartín train station, this is one of the best, most popular, and most stylish restaurants in Madrid, attracting on occasion the king and queen of Spain. An open-air staircase leading to the entranceway descends from a manicured garden on a quiet side street where a battalion of uniformed doormen stands ready to greet arriving taxis. The restaurant's decor is nautically inspired, with hardwood panels, brass trim, old-fashioned pulleys and ropes, a tile floor custom-painted with sea-green and blue replicas of waves, and hand-carved models of fishing boats. Some dozen bronze statues honoring fishers and their craft are displayed in brass portholes in illuminated positions of honor.

Menu choices include paprika-laden peppers stuffed with fish, a salad composed of Jabugo ham and foie gras of duckling, Cantabrian fish soup, stewed sea bream with thyme, asparagus mousse, salmon in sherry sauce, and loin of veal in cassis sauce. Desserts include a rice mousse with pine-nut sauce.

✪ **Goizeko Kabi.** Comandante Zorita, 27. ☎ **91-533-0214.** Reservations recommended. Main courses 1,500–5,000 ptas. ($10.05–$33.50). AE, DC, V. Mon–Sat 1–4pm, 8:30pm–midnight. Metro: Alvarado. BASQUE.

This restaurant serves some of the best Basque dishes in Madrid in a small, intimate, and understated interior. Particularly delicious is the starter of *boquerones,* almost sweet anchovies marinated in garlic and olive oil. We also loved the *bacalao pil-pil vizcaina* (cod in a Basque garlic sauce) and the wonderfully juicy king prawns. Dessert lovers will revel in the orange mousse with a coating of bitter chocolate or the more experimental black bread ice cream with coffee sauce.

✪ **O'Pazo.** Calle Reina Mercedes, 20. ☎ **91-553-23-33.** Reservations required. Main courses 2,000–5,350 ptas. ($13.40–$35.85). MC, V. Mon–Sat 1–4pm and 8:30pm–midnight. Closed Aug. Metro: Nuevos Ministerios or Alvarado. Bus: 3 or 5. GALICIAN/SEAFOOD.

O'Pazo is a deluxe Galician restaurant, viewed by local cognoscenti as one of the top seafood places in the country. The fish is flown in daily from Galicia and much of it priced by weight, at market rates. In front is a cocktail lounge and bar, all polished brass, with low sofas and paintings. Carpeted floors, cushioned Castilian furniture, soft lighting, and colored-glass windows complete the picture.

The fish and shellfish soup is delectable, although others gravitate to the seaman's broth as a beginning course. Natural clams are succulent, as are *cigalas* (a kind of crayfish), spider crabs, and Jabugo ham. Main dishes range from baby eels to sea snails, from Galician style scallops to *zarzuela* (a seafood casserole).

INEXPENSIVE

Alfredo's Barbacoa. Juan Hurtado de Mendoza, 11. ☎ **91-345-16-39.** Reservations recommended. Main courses 695–2,200 ptas. ($4.65–$14.75). AE, MC, V. Mon–Sat 1–4:30pm and 8:30pm–midnight (Fri–Sat until 1am). Metro: Cuzco. AMERICAN.

Alfredo's is a popular rendezvous for Americans longing for home-style food. Al himself arrives at his bar/restaurant wearing boots, blue jeans, and a 10-gallon hat; his friendly welcome has made the place a center for both his friends and newcomers to Madrid. You *can* have hamburgers here, but they are of the barbecued variety, and you might prefer the barbecued spareribs or chicken. The salad bar is an attraction, and it's a rare treat to be able to have corn on the cob in Spain.

The original Alfredo's Barbacoa, Lagasca, 5 (☎ **91-576-62-71;** metro: Retiro), is still in business, and also under Al's auspices.

CHUECA
INEXPENSIVE

El Inca. Gravina, 23. ☎ **91-532-77-45.** Reservations required on weekends. Main courses 1,800–3,500 ptas. ($12.05–$23.45); fixed-price menu 1,800 ptas. ($12.05) available at lunch. AE, DC, V. Tues–Sat 1:30–5pm and 9pm–1am, Sun 1:30–5pm. Closed Sun in Aug. Metro: Chueca. PERUVIAN.

For a taste of South America, try El Inca, decorated with Incan motifs and artifacts. Since it opened in the early 1970s, it has hosted its share of diplomats and celebrities, although you're more likely to see families and local office workers. The house cocktail is a deceptively potent pisco sour—the recipe comes straight from the Andes. Many of the dishes contain potatoes, the national staple of Peru. The salad of potatoes and black olives is given unusual zest with a white-cheese sauce. Other specialties are the *ceviche de merluza* (raw hake marinated with onions) and *aji de gallina* (a chicken-and-rice dish made with peanut sauce), a Peruvian favorite.

Nabucco. Calle Hortaleza, 108. ☎ **91-310-06-11.** Reservations recommended. Pizza 755–935 ptas. ($5.05–$6.25); main courses 870–1,500 ptas. ($5.85–$10.05). AE, DC, MC, V. Daily 1:30–4pm, Sun–Thurs 8:45pm–midnight, Fri–Sat 8:45pm–1am. Metro: Alonso Martínez. Bus: 7 or 36. ITALIAN.

In a neighborhood of Spanish restaurants, the Italian trattoria format here comes as a welcome change. The decor resembles a postmodern update of an Italian ruin, complete with trompe l'oeil walls painted like marble. Roman portrait busts and a prominent bar lend a dignified air. Menu choices include cannelloni, a good selection of veal dishes, and such main courses as osso bucco. You might begin your meal with a selection of antipasti.

○ Taberna Carmencita. Libertad, 16. ☎ **91-531-66-12.** Reservations recommended. Main courses 1,800–2,600 ptas. ($12.05–$17.40); fixed-price menu 1,300 ptas. ($8.70) available only at lunch. AE, DC, MC, V. Mon–Fri 1–4pm, Mon–Sat 9pm–midnight. Metro: Chueca or Banco de España. SPANISH/BASQUE.

Carmencita, founded in 1840 and exquisitely restored, is a street-corner enclave of old Spanish charm, filled with 19th-century detailing and tile work. It was a favorite hangout for the poet Federico García Lorca, as well as a meeting place for intelligentsia in the pre–Civil War days. Meals might include entrecôte with green pepper sauce, escalope of veal, braised mollusks with port, fillet of pork, codfish with garlic, and Bilbao-style hake. Every Thursday the special dish is a complicated version of Madrid's famous cocido. Patrons wax lyrical over this regional stew and the chefs have had decades to get it right.

Tienda de Vinos. Augusto Figueroa, 35. ☎ **91-521-70-12.** Main courses 700–1,200 ptas. ($4.70–$8.05); fixed-price menu 1,200 ptas. ($8.05). No credit cards. Mon–Sat 1–4:30pm and 9pm–midnight. Metro: Chueca. SPANISH.

Officially this restaurant is known as Tienda de Vinos (the Wine Store), but ever since the 1930s, Madrileños have called it "El Comunista" (The Communist). Its now-deceased owner was a fervent Communist, and many locals who shared his political beliefs patronized the establishment. This rickety old wine shop with a few tables in the back is quite fashionable with actors and journalists looking for Spanish fare without frills. There is a menu, but no one ever looks at it—just ask what's available. Nor do you get a bill; you're just told how much to pay. You sit at simple wooden tables with wooden chairs and benches; walls are decorated with old posters, pennants, and clocks. Start with garlic or vegetable soup or lentils, followed by lamb chops, tripe in a spicy sauce, or meatballs and soft-set eggs with asparagus.

OFF THE PLAZA MAYOR
MODERATE

Casa Lucio. Cava Baja, 35. ☎ **91-365-32-52.** Reservations recommended. Main courses 1,400–6,500 ptas. ($9.40–$43.55). AE, DC, MC, V. Sun–Fri 1–4pm, daily 9pm–midnight. Closed Aug. Metro: La Latina. CASTILIAN.

Set on a historic street whose edges once marked the perimeter of Old Madrid, this is a venerable tasca with all the requisite antique accessories. Dozens of cured hams hang from hand-hewn beams above the well-oiled bar. Among the clientele is a stable of sometimes surprisingly well known public figures—perhaps even the king of Spain. The two dining rooms, each on a different floor, have whitewashed walls, tile floors, and exposed brick. A well-trained staff offers classic Castilian food, which might include Jabugo ham with broad beans, shrimp in garlic sauce, hake with green sauce, several types of roasted lamb, and a thick steak served sizzling hot on a heated platter, called *churrasco de la casa.*

El Cuchi. Calle de Cuchilleros, 3. ☎ **91-366-44-24.** Reservations required. Main courses 2,500–3,000 ptas. ($16.75–$20.10). AE, DC, MC, V. Mon–Sat 1pm–midnight; Sun 1–4pm and 8pm–midnight. Metro: Puerta del Sol. MEXICAN/SPANISH.

A few doors down from Sobrino de Botín (see below), El Cuchi defiantly claims that "Hemingway never ate here." However, just about everybody else has, attracted by both its low prices and its labyrinth of dining rooms. A European link in Mexico's famous Carlos 'n Charlie's chain, this Madrid restaurant is a true tourist joint but amazingly popular as it stands off a corner of Plaza Mayor. Ceiling beams and artifacts suggest rusticity. Menu specialties include black bean soup, ceviche, guacamole, stuffed trout, and roast suckling pig (much cheaper than that served at Botín). You've had all this before, and probably in better versions, but the collection of beers from all over the globe and the rainbow-colored margaritas are unequaled in Madrid.

El Schotis. Cava Baja, 11. ☎ **91-365-32-30.** Reservations recommended. Main courses 950–2,900 ptas. ($6.35–$19.45); fixed-price menu 3,250 ptas. ($21.80). AE, DC, MC, V. Daily 1–4pm, Mon–Sat 8:30pm–midnight. Metro: Puerta del Sol or La Latina. SPANISH.

El Schotis was established in 1962 on one of Madrid's oldest and most historic streets. A series of large and pleasingly old-fashioned dining rooms is the setting for an animated crowd of Madrileños and foreign visitors, who receive ample portions of conservative, well-prepared vegetables, salads, soups, fish, and above all, meat. Specialties of the house include roasted baby lamb, grilled steaks and veal chops, shrimp with garlic, fried hake in green sauce, and traditional desserts. Although one reader found everything but the gazpacho ho-hum, this local favorite pleases thousands of diners annually. There's a bar near the entrance for tapas and before- or after-dinner drinks.

Gure-Etxea (Restaurante Vasco). Plaza de la Paja, 12. ☎ **91-365-61-49.** Reservations recommended. Main courses 1,425–2,950 ptas. ($9.55–$19.75); fixed-price menu 3,500 ptas. ($23.45). AE, DC, MC, V. Tues–Sat 1:30–4pm, Mon–Sat 9pm–midnight. Closed Aug. Metro: La Latina. BASQUE.

This restaurant is housed in a stone-walled building that was the convent for the nearby Church of San Andres before the Renaissance. Today, amid a decor enhanced by Romanesque arches, vaulted tunnels, and dark paneling, you can enjoy selections from a small but choice menu. Specialties include *lomo de merluza* (hake), *chipirones en su tinta* (squid in its own ink), Gure-Etxea's special fillet of sole, and *bacalao al pil-pil* (codfish in a fiery sauce).

Las Cuevas de Luís Candelas. Calle Cuchilleros, 1. ☎ **91-366-54-28.** Reservations required. Main courses 1,400–3,500 ptas. ($9.40–$23.45). DC, MC, V. Daily 1–4pm and 8pm–midnight. Metro: Puerta del Sol. SPANISH/INTERNATIONAL.

Right down the steps from the popular but very touristy Mesón del Corregidor, is the even better known and also kitschy Las Cuevas de Luís Candelas, housed in a building dating from 1616. Enter the restaurant, which opened its doors at the turn of the century, through a doorway under an arcade, on steps leading to the calle de Cuchilleros—the nightlife center of Madrid that teems with restaurants, flamenco clubs, and rustic taverns. The restaurant with its hokey Spanish decor is named after an 18th-century bandit who's sometimes known as the Spanish Robin Hood. He is said to have hidden out in this maze of cuevas (dens). Although the menu is in English, the cuisine is authentically Spanish but often overcooked. Specialties include the chef's own style of hake. To begin your meal, you might try another house dish, *sopa de ajo Candelas* (garlic soup). As in the other restaurants on the Plaza Mayor, roast suckling pig and roast lamb are featured, but we prefer these two dishes at Sobrino de Botín (see below). In spite of the tourist trap overtures of this place, so many readers report such hilarious fun here we've included it among our recommendations. It's not really Spanish, merely the mock, but with all that hand kissing of the ladies, music, festive food and drink, it's still a fun night in Old Madrid for those not seeking authenticity.

Los Galayos. Calle Botoneras, 5. ☎ **91-366-30-28.** Reservations recommended. Main courses 1,200–3,500 ptas. ($8.05–$23.45). AE, DC, MC, V. Daily 12:30pm–12:45am. Metro: Puerta del Sol. SPANISH.

Its location is among the most desirable in the city, on a narrow side street about three steps from the arcades of Plaza Mayor. Set within two separate houses, the restaurant has flourished on this site since 1894. In summer, cascades of vines accent a series of tables and chairs on the cobblestones outside, perfect for tapas sampling and people watching. Some visitors consider an evening here among the highlights of their trip to Spain.

The ambience inside evokes Old Castile with vaulted or beamed ceilings in several dining rooms. Your hosts, the Grande family, prepare traditional versions of fish, shell-fish, pork, veal, and beef in time-tested ways. Suckling pig, baby goat, and roasted lamb are almost always featured.

✪ **Sobrino de Botín.** Calle de Cuchilleros, 17. ☎ **91-366-42-17.** Reservations required. Main courses 970–3,150 ptas. ($6.50–$21.10); fixed-price menu 3,945 ptas. ($26.45). AE, DC, MC, V. Daily 1–4pm and 8pm–midnight. Metro: La Latina or Opera. SPANISH.

Ernest Hemingway made this restaurant famous. In the final two pages of his novel, *The Sun Also Rises,* Jake invites Brett to Botín for the Segovian specialty of roast suckling pig, washed down with Rioja Alta.

As you enter, you step back to 1725, the year the restaurant was founded. You'll see an open kitchen with a charcoal hearth, hanging copper pots, an 18th-century tile oven for roasting the suckling pig, and a big pot of regional soup whose aroma wafts across the tables. Painter Francisco Goya was once a dishwasher here. Your host, Antonio, never loses his cool—even when he has 18 guests standing in line waiting for tables.

The two house specialties are roast suckling pig and roast Segovian lamb. From the à la carte menu, you might try the fish-based "quarter-of-an-hour" soup. Good main dishes include baked Cantabrian hake and filet mignon with potatoes. The dessert list features strawberries (in season) with whipped cream. You can accompany your meal with Valdepeñas or Aragón wine, although most guests order sangría.

INEXPENSIVE

La Chata. Cava Baja, 24. ☎ **91-366-14-58.** Reservations recommended. Main dishes 1,500–2,300 ptas. ($10.05–$15.40). AE, MC, V. Daily 12:30–5pm, Mon–Sat 8pm–midnight. Metro: La Latina. SPANISH.

The cuisine here is Castilian, Galician, and northern Spanish. Set behind a heavily ornamented tile facade, the place has a stand-up tapas bar at the entrance and a formal restaurant in a side room. Many locals linger in the darkly paneled bar, which is framed by hanging Serrano hams, cloves of garlic, and photographs of bullfighters. Full meals might include such dishes as roast suckling pig, roast lamb, *calamares en su tinta* (squid in its own ink), grilled fillet of steak with peppercorns, and omelettes flavored with strips of eel.

NEAR PLAZA DE CUZCO

Chez Lou Crêperie. Pedro Munguruza, 6. ☎ **91-350-34-16.** Reservations required on weekends. Crepes 600–900 ptas. ($4–$6.05). No credit cards. Mon–Fri 1:30–4pm and Mon–Sat 8pm–midnight. Metro: Plaza de Castilla. Bus: 27 or 147. FRENCH.

Near the Eurobuilding in the northern sector of Madrid, Chez Lou stands near the huge mural by Joan Miró, which would be worth the trek up here alone. Come if you're seeking a light supper when it's too hot for one of those table-groaning Spanish meals. In this intimate setting, you get well-prepared and reasonably priced French food. The restaurant serves pâté as an appetizer, then a large range of crepes with many different fillings. Folded envelope style, the crepes are not tearoom size, and they're perfectly adequate as a main course. We've sampled several variations, finding the ingredients nicely blended yet distinct enough to retain their identity. A favorite is the large crepe stuffed with minced onions, cream, and smoked salmon. The ham-and-cheese crepe is also tasty.

NEAR RECOLETOS

Antonio Sánchez. Mesón de Parades, 13. ☎ **91-539-78-26.** Tapas (in the bar) 200–600 ptas. ($1.35–$4); main courses 600–1,700 ptas. ($4–$11.40); fixed-price menu 1,000 ptas. ($6.70) available at lunch Mon–Fri. V. Daily noon–2pm, Mon–Sat 8pm–midnight. Metro: Tirso de Molina. SPANISH.

Named in 1850 after the founder's son, who was killed in the bullring, Antonio Sánchez is full of bullfighting memorabilia, including the stuffed head of the animal that gored the young Sánchez. Also featured on the dark paneled walls are three works by the Spanish artist Zuloaga, who had his last public exhibition in this restaurant near Plaza Tirso de Molina. A limited array of tapas, including garlic soup, are served with Valdepeñas wine drawn from a barrel—though many guests ignore the edibles in favor

---

Picnic, Anyone?

On a hot day, do as the Madrileños do: Secure the makings of a picnic lunch and head for Casa de Campo (metro: El Batón), those once-royal hunting grounds in the west of Madrid across the Manzanares River. Children delight in this adventure, as they can also visit a boating lake, the Parque de Atracciones, and the Madrid zoo.

Your best choice for picnic fare is **Rodilla,** Preciados, 25 (☎ **91-522-57-01;** metro: Callao), where you can find sandwiches, pastries, and take-out tapas. Sandwiches, including vegetarian, meat, and fish, begin at 85 ptas. (55¢). It's open Monday and Tuesday from 8:30am to 10:30pm; Wednesday, Thursday, and Sunday from 9am to 11pm; and Friday and Saturday from 9am to 11:30pm.

of smoking cigarettes and arguing the merits of this or that bullfighter. A restaurant in the back serves Spanish food with a vaguely French influence.

La Galette. Conde de Aranda, 11. ☎ **91-576-06-41.** Reservations recommended. Main courses 550–1,985 ptas. ($3.70–$13.30); fixed-price menus 985–1,655 ptas. ($6.60–$11.10) Mon–Fri lunch only. AE, DC, MC, V. Mon–Sat 2–4pm and 9pm–midnight. Metro: Retiro. VEGETARIAN/INTERNATIONAL.

La Galette was one of Madrid's first vegetarian restaurants, and it remains one of the best. Small and charming, it lies in a residential and shopping area in the exclusive Salamanca district, near Plaza de la Independencia and the northern edge of Retiro Park. There is a limited selection of meat dishes, but the true allure lies in this establishment's imaginative preparation of vegetables. Examples include baked stuffed peppers, omelettes, eggplant croquettes, and even vegetarian hamburgers. Some of the dishes are macrobiotic. The place is also noted for its mouth-watering pastries. The same owners also operate La Galette II, in the same complex.

NEAR PLAZA LAVAPIES
INEXPENSIVE

La Pampa de Lavapies. Amparo, 61. ☎ **91/528-0449.** Reservations recommended. Main courses 2,500–3,000 ptas. ($16.75–$20.10). Fixed-price menu for lunch 1,200 ptas. ($8.05). AE, DC, MC, V. Tues–Sun 1:30–4:30pm and 9pm–12:30am. Metro: Lavapies. ARGENTINIAN.

Set in the very heart of old Madrid is an authentic piece of Argentina, complete with assorted memorabilia from the land of the pampas. The restaurant is a replica of those in San Telmo, the oldest and most evocative area of Buenos Aires. Meat eaters can gorge on immense Argentinian steaks cooked traditionally *à la parilla* (on the barbecue), and experience other national dishes such as pickled eggplants, barbecued provolone cheese, and both Argentinian and Chilean *empanadas* (pies) filled with beef, chicken, cheese, or corn. Pasta, a legacy of millions of Italian immigrants, is now considered traditionally Argentinian, and the cannelloni Rossini and the house gnocchi are especially tasty.

OUR FAVORITE TASCAS

Don't starve waiting around for Madrid's fashionable 9:30 or 10pm dinner hour. Throughout the city you'll find tascas, bars that serve wine and platters of tempting hot and cold hors d'oeuvres known as tapas: mushrooms, salads, baby eels, shrimp, lobster, mussels, sausage, ham—and, in one establishment at least, bull testicles. Below we've listed our favorite tapas bars. Keep in mind that you can often save pesetas by ordering at the bar rather than occupying a table.

Casa Mingo. Paseo de la Florida, 2. ☎ **91-547-79-18.** Main courses 250–975 ptas. ($1.70–$6.55). No credit cards. Daily 11am–midnight. Metro: Norte, then 15-min. walk. SPANISH.

Casa Mingo has been known for decades for its cider, both still and bubbly. The perfect accompanying tidbit is a piece of the local Asturian *cabrales* (goat cheese), but the roast chicken is the specialty of the house, with a large number of helpings served daily. There's no formality here, since customers share big tables under the vaulted ceiling in the dining room. In summer, the staff sets up tables and wooden chairs out on the sidewalk. This is not so much a restaurant but a bodega/taverna that serves food.

Cervecería Alemania. Plaza de Santa Ana, 6. ☎ **91-429-70-33.** Beer 200–400 ptas. ($1.35–$2.70); tapas 150–2,000 ptas. ($1–$13.40). No credit cards. Sun–Thurs 11am–12:30am, Fri–Sat 11am–2am. Metro: Alonso Martín or Tirso de Molina. TAPAS.

Hemingway used to frequent this casual spot with the celebrated bullfighter Luís Miguel Domínguín—ask the waiter to point out Hemingway's table. However, it earned its name because of its long-ago German clients. Opening directly onto one of the liveliest little plazas in Madrid, it clings to its turn-of-the-century traditions. Young Madrileños are fond of stopping in for a mug of draft beer. You can sit at one of the tables, leisurely sipping beer or wine, since the waiters make no attempt to hurry you along. To accompany your beverage, try the fried sardines or a Spanish omelette.

Cervecería Santa Bárbara. Plaza de Santa Bárbara, 8. ☎ **91-319-04-049.** Beer 150–300 ptas. ($1–$2); tapas 300–4,000 ptas. ($2–$26.80). V. Daily 11:30am–midnight. Metro: Alonzo Martínez. Bus: 3, 7, or 21. TAPAS.

Unique in Madrid, Cervecería Santa Bárbara is an outlet for a beer factory, and the management has spent a lot to make it modern and inviting. Hanging globe lights and spinning ceiling fans create an attractive ambience, as does the black-and-white checkerboard marble floor. You go here for beer, of course: *cerveza negra* (black beer) or *cerveza dorada* (golden beer). The local brew is best accompanied by homemade potato chips or by fresh shrimp, lobster, crabmeat, or barnacles. You can either stand at the counter or go directly to one of the wooden tables for waiter service.

Taberna Toscana. Manuel Fernandez y Gonzales, 10. ☎ **91-429-60-31.** Beer 130 ptas. (85¢), glass of wine 110 ptas. (75¢); tapas 200–2,000 ptas. ($1.35–$13.40). MC, V. Tues–Sat noon–4pm and 8pm–midnight. Closed Aug. Metro: Puerta del Sol or Sevilla. TAPAS.

Many Madrileños begin their nightly tasca crawl here. The ambience is that of a village inn that's far removed from 20th-century Madrid. You sit on crude country stools, under sausages, peppers, and sheaves of golden wheat that hang from the age-darkened beams. The long, tiled bar is loaded with tasty tidbits, including the house specialties: *lacón y cecina* (boiled ham), *habas* (broad beans) with Spanish ham, and *chorizo* (a sausage of red peppers and pork)—almost meals in themselves. Especially delectable are the kidneys in sherry sauce and the snails in hot sauce.

5 Seeing the Sights

THE TOP ATTRACTIONS

In the heart of Madrid, near the Puerta del Sol metro stop, the **Plaza Mayor** is the city's most famous square. It was known as the Plaza de Arrabal in medieval times, when it stood outside the city wall. The original architect of Plaza Mayor itself was Juan Gómez de Mora, who worked during the reign of Philip III. Under the Hapsburgs, the square rose in importance as the site of public spectacles, including the abominable autos-da-fé, in which heretics were burned. Bullfights, knightly tournaments, and festivals were also staged here.

Three times the buildings on the square burned—in 1631, 1672, and 1790—but each time the plaza bounced back. After the last big fire, it was completely redesigned by Juan de Villanueva. Nowadays a Christmas fair is held around the equestrian statue of Philip III (dating from 1616) in the center of the square. On summer nights, the Plaza Mayor becomes the virtual living room of Madrid, as tourists sip sangría at the numerous cafes and listen to street musicians.

✪ **Museo del Prado.** Paseo del Prado. ☎ **91-330-28-00.** Admission 500 ptas. ($3.35) adults, 250 ptas. ($1.70) students and seniors. Tues–Sat 9am–7pm, Sun and holidays 9am–2pm. Closed Jan 1, Good Friday, May 1, and Dec 25. Metro: Banco de España or Atocha. Bus: 10, 14, 27, 34, 37, or 45.

With more than 7,000 paintings, the Prado is one of the most important repositories of art in the world. It began as a royal collection and was enhanced by the Hapsburgs, especially Charles V, and later the Bourbons. For paintings of the Spanish school, the Prado has no equal; on your first visit, concentrate on the Spanish masters (Velázquez, Goya, El Greco, and Murillo).

Most major works are exhibited on the first floor. You'll see art by Italian masters— Raphael, Botticelli, Mantegna, Andrea del Sarto, Fra Angelico, and Correggio. The most celebrated Italian painting here is Titian's voluptuous Venus being watched by a musician who can't keep his eyes on his work.

The Prado is a trove of the work of El Greco (c. 1541–1614), the Crete-born artist who lived much of his life in Toledo. You can see a parade of "The Greek's" saints, Madonnas, and Holy Families—even a ghostly *John the Baptist.*

You'll find a splendid array of works by the incomparable Diego Velázquez (1599–1660). The museum's most famous painting, in fact, is his *Las Meninas,* a triumph in the use of light effects. The faces of the queen and king are reflected in the mirror in the painting itself. The artist in the foreground is Velázquez, of course.

The Flemish painter Peter Paul Rubens (1577–1640), who met Velázquez while in Spain, is represented by the peacock-blue *Garden of Love* and by the *Three Graces.* Also worthy is the work of José Ribera (1591–1652), a Valencia-born artist and contemporary of Velázquez whose best painting is the *Martyrdom of St. Philip.* The Seville-born Bartolomé Murillo (1617–82)—often referred to as the "painter of Madonnas"—has three *Immaculate Conceptions* on display.

The Prado has an outstanding collection of the work of Hieronymus Bosch (1450?–1516), the Flemish genius. The *Garden of Earthly Delights,* the best-known work of "El Bosco," is here. You'll also see his *Seven Deadly Sins* and his triptych *The Hay Wagon. The Triumph of Death* is by another Flemish painter, Pieter Breughel the Elder (1525?–69), who carried on Bosch's ghoulish vision.

Francisco de Goya (1746–1828) ranks along with Velázquez and El Greco in the trio of great Spanish artists. Hanging here are his unflattering portraits of his patron, Charles IV, and his family, as well as the *Clothed Maja* and the *Naked Maja.* You can also see the much-reproduced *Third of May* (1808), plus a series of Goya sketches (some of which, depicting the decay of 18th-century Spain, brought the Inquisition down on the artist) and his expressionistic "black paintings."

✪ **Thyssen-Bornemisza Museum.** Palacio de Villahermosa, Paseo del Prado, 8. ☎ **91-369-01-51.** Admission 700 ptas. ($4.70) adults, 400 ptas. ($2.70) students and seniors, free for children 11 and under. Tues–Sun 10am–7pm. Metro: Banco de España. Bus: 1, 2, 5, 9, 10, 14, 15, 20, 27, 34, 45, 51, 52, 53, 74, 146, or 150.

Until around 1985, the contents of this museum overflowed the premises of a legendary villa near Lugano, Switzerland; it was a hugely popular attraction there. The collection had been laboriously amassed over a period of about 60 years by the wealthy Thyssen-Bornemisza family, of Holland, Germany, and Hungary. Experts had proclaimed it as one of the world's most extensive and valuable privately owned collections of paintings, rivaled only by the legendary holdings of Queen Elizabeth II. For tax and insurance reasons, and because the collection had outgrown the boundaries of its lakeside villa, the collection was discreetly put on the market in the early 1980s to the world's major museums. Amid endless intrigue, glamorous supplicants from eight different nations came calling. Among them were Margaret Thatcher and Prince Charles; trustees of the Getty Museum in Los Angeles; the president of West Germany; and the duke of Badajoz, brother-in-law of King Carlos II. Even emissaries from Walt Disney World came! Eventually, the collection was awarded to Spain for

$350 million. Controversies over the huge public cost of the acquisition raged for months. Despite the brouhaha, various estimates have placed the value of this collection at anywhere between $1 billion and $3 billion.

To house the collection, an 18th-century building adjacent to the Prado, the Villahermosa Palace, was retrofitted with appropriate lighting and security devices, and renovated at a cost of $45 million. Rooms are arranged numerically so that by following the order of the various rooms (numbers 1 through 48, spread out over three floors), a logical sequence of European painting can be traced from the 13th through the 20th centuries. The nucleus of the collection consists of 700 world-class paintings. They include works by, among others, El Greco, Velázquez, Dürer, Rembrandt, Watteau, Canaletto, Caravaggio, Hals, Memling, and Goya.

Unusual among the world's great art collections because of its eclecticism, the Thyssen group also contains 19th- and 20th-century paintings by many of the notable French impressionists, as well as works by Picasso, Sargent, Kirchner, Nolde, and Kandinsky—artists who had never been well represented in Spanish museums. This museum has attracted many millions of visitors since its long-awaited opening so be prepared for magnificent art but long lines.

✪ **Museo Nacional Centro de Arte Reina Sofía.** Santa Isab-el, 52. ☎ **91-467-50-62.** Admission 500 ptas. ($3.35), free after 2:30pm on Sat and all day Sun. Mon and Wed–Sat 10am–9pm, Sun 10am–2:30pm. Free guided tours Mon and Wed at 5pm, Sat at 11am. Metro: Atocha.

What the Prado is to traditional art, this museum is to modern art. Madrid's "MOMA" (Museum of Modern Art) is the greatest repository of 20th-century works in Spain. Set within the echoing, futuristically renovated walls of the former General Hospital, originally built between 1776 and 1781, the museum is a sprawling, high-ceilinged showplace. Once designated "the ugliest building in Spain" by Catalan architect Oriol Bohigas, the Reina Sofía has a design that hangs in limbo somewhere between the 18th and the 21st centuries. It incorporates a 50,000-volume art library and database, a cafe, a theater, and a bookstore.

Special emphasis is paid to the great artists of 20th-century Spain: Juan Gris, Salvador Dalí, Joan Miró, and Pablo Picasso (the museum has been able to acquire a handful of his works). What many critics feel is Picasso's masterpiece, *Guernica,* now rests at this museum after a long and troubling history of traveling. Banned in Spain during Franco's era (Picasso refused to allow it to be displayed here anyway), it hung until 1980 at New York's Museum of Modern Art. The fiercely antiwar painting immortalizes the town's shameful blanket bombing by the German Luftwaffe, who were fighting for Franco during the Spanish Civil War. Guernica was the cradle of the Basque nation, and Picasso's canvas made it a household name around the world.

✪ **Museo Lázaro Galdiano.** Serrano, 122. ☎ **91-561-60-84.** Admission 500 ptas. ($3.35). Tues–Sun 10am–2pm. Closed holidays and Aug. Metro: Rubén Darío, Núñez de Balboa. Bus: 9, 16, 19, 27, 45, 51, 61, 89, or 114.

Imagine 37 rooms in a well-preserved 19th-century mansion bulging with artworks—including many by the most famous old masters of Europe. Most visitors take the elevator to the top floor and work down, lingering over 15th-century handwoven vestments, swords and daggers, royal seals, 16th-century crystal from Limoges, Byzantine jewelry, Italian bronzes from ancient times to the Renaissance, and medieval armor.

One painting by Bosch evokes his own peculiar brand of horror, the canvas peopled with creepy fiends devouring human flesh. The Spanish masters are the best represented: El Greco, Velázquez, Zurbarán, Ribera, Murillo, and Valdés-Leal.

Madrid Attractions

Biblioteca Nacional ⑲
Campo del Moro ⑤
Casa de Lope
  de Vega ㉓
Casón del
  Buen Retiro ㉕
Catedral de la
  Almudena ⑨
Centro de Arte
  Reina Sofía
  ("The Sofidou") ㉘
Convento de la
  Encarnación ④
Convento de las
  Descalzas Reales ⑭
Museo Arqueológico
  Nacional ⑱
Museo de Cerralbo ②
Museo de la Real Academia
  de Bellas Artes
  de San Fernando ⑮
Museo de las Figuras
  de Cera ⑰
Museo del Ejército ㉔
Museo del Prado ㉖
Museo Nacional de Artes
  Decorativas ⑳
Museo Naval ㉑
Museo Romántico ⑯
Palacio Real ⑦
Palacio Senado ③
Plaza Mayor ⑬
Rastro ⑪
Real Basílica de San
  Francisco el Grande ⑩
Real Jardín Botánico ㉗
San Isidro el Real ⑫
San Nicolás ⑧
Teatro Real ⑥
Templo de Debod ①
Thyssen-Bornemisza
  Museum ㉒

Legend
† Church
ⓘ Information
Ⓜ Metro
✉ Post Office

111

❓ Did You Know?

- Sobrino de Botín, a Hemingway favorite founded in 1725, claims to be the world's oldest restaurant.
- The only public statue anywhere dedicated to the Devil stands in Madrid's Retiro Park.
- A Mexican composer wrote the unofficial anthem "Madrid, Madrid, Madrid"—and he had never been to Madrid.

One section is devoted to works by the English portrait and landscape artists Reynolds, Gainsborough, and Constable. Italian artists exhibited include Tiepolo and Guardi. Salon 30—for many, the most interesting—is devoted to Goya and includes paintings from his "black period."

✪ Palacio Real (Royal Palace). Plaza de Oriente, Calle de Bailén, 2. ☎ **91-454-8700.** Admission 850 ptas. ($5.70) adults, 350 ptas. ($2.35) students and children. Mon–Sat 9am–6pm, Sun 9am–3pm. Metro: Opera or Plaza de España.

This huge palace was begun in 1738 on the site of the Madrid Alcázar, which burned to the ground in 1734. Some of its 2,000 rooms—which that "enlightened despot" Charles III called home—are open to the public; others are still used for state business. The palace was last used as a royal residence in 1931, before King Alfonso XIII and his wife, Victoria Eugénie, fled Spain.

You'll be taken on a guided tour that includes the Reception Room, the State Apartments, the Armory, and the Royal Pharmacy. (To get an English-speaking guide, say *"Inglés"* to the person who takes your ticket.) The Reception Room and State Apartments should get priority here if you're rushed. They embrace a rococo room with a diamond clock; a porcelain salon; the Royal Chapel; the Banquet Room, where receptions for heads of state are still held; and the Throne Room.

The rooms are literally stuffed with art treasures and antiques—salon after salon of monumental grandeur, with no apologies for the damask, mosaics, stucco, Tiepolo ceilings, gilt and bronze, chandeliers, and paintings.

If your visit falls on the first Wednesday of the month, look for the **changing of the guard ceremony,** which occurs at noon and is free to the public.

In the Armory, you'll see the finest collection of weaponry in Spain. Many of the items—powder flasks, shields, lances, helmets, and saddles—are from the collection of Carlos V. From here, the comprehensive tour takes you into the Pharmacy.

Afterward, stroll through the Campo del Moro, the gardens of the palace.

Panteón de Goya (Goya's Tomb). Glorieta de San Antonio de la Florida, s/n. ☎ **91-542-07-22.** Admission 300 ptas. ($2). Free on Wed and Sun. Tues–Fri 10am–2pm and 4–8pm, Sat–Sun 10am–2pm (in summer daily 10am–2pm only). Metro: Norte. Bus: 41, 46, 75, or C.

In a remote part of town beyond the North Station lies Goya's tomb, containing one of his masterpieces: an elaborately beautiful fresco depicting the miracles of St. Anthony on the dome and cupola of the little hermitage of San Antonio de la Florida. This has been called Goya's Sistine Chapel. Already deaf when he began the painting, Goya labored dawn to dusk for 16 weeks, painting with sponges rather than brushes. By depicting common street life—stone masons, prostitutes, and beggars—Goya raised the ire of the nobility who held judgment until the patron, Carlos IV, viewed it. When the monarch approved, the formerly outrageous painting was deemed acceptable.

The tomb and fresco are in one of the twin chapels (visit the one on the right) that were built in the latter part of the 18th century. Discreetly placed mirrors will help you see the ceiling better.

✪ **Monasterio de las Descalzas Reales.** Plaza de las Descalzas Reales, s/n. ☎ **91-542-00-59.** Admission 650 ptas. ($4.35) adults, 350 ptas. ($2.35) children. Sat and Tues–Thurs 10:30am–12:30pm and 4–5pm, Fri 10:30am–12:30pm, Sun 11am–1:15pm. Bus: 1, 2, 5, 20, 46, 52, 53, 74, M1, M2, M3, or M5. From Plaza del Callao, off Gran Vía, walk down Postigo de San Martín to Plaza de las Descalzas Reales; the convent is on the left.

In the mid–16th century, aristocratic women either disappointed in love or wanting to be the "bride of Christ," stole away to this convent to take the veil. Each brought a dowry, making this one of the richest convents in the land. By the mid–20th century, the convent sheltered mostly poor women. True, it still contained a priceless collection of art treasures, but the sisters were forbidden to auction anything; in fact, they were literally starving. The state intervened, and the pope granted special dispensation to open the convent as a museum. Today the public can look behind the walls of what was once a mysterious edifice on one of the most beautiful squares in Old Madrid.

An English-speaking guide will show you through. In the Reliquary are the noblewomen's dowries, one of which is said to contain bits of wood from Christ's Cross; another, some of the bones of St. Sebastian. The most valuable painting is Titian's *Caesar's Money.* The Flemish Hall shelters other fine works, including paintings by Hans de Beken and Breughel the Elder. All of the tapestries were based on Rubens's cartoons, displaying his chubby matrons.

Real Fábrica de Tapices (Royal Tapestry Factory). Fuenterrabía, 2. ☎ **91-551-34-00.** Admission 200 ptas. ($1.35). Mon–Fri 9am–12:30pm. Closed Aug and holidays. Metro: Menéndez Pelayo. Bus: 10, 14, 26, 32, 37, C, or M9.

In this factory the age-old process of making exquisite (and very expensive) tapestries is still carried on with consummate skill. Nearly every tapestry is based on a cartoon of Goya, who was the factory's most famous employee. Many of these patterns, such as *The Pottery Salesman,* are still in production today. (Goya's original drawings are in the Prado.) Many of the other designs are based on cartoons by Francisco Bayeu, Goya's brother-in-law.

THE BULLFIGHT

Madrid draws the finest matadors in Spain. If a matador hasn't proved his worth in the **Plaza Monumental de Toros de las Ventas,** Alcalá, 237 (☎ **91-356-22-00;** metro: Ventas), he just hasn't been recognized as a top-flight artist. The major season begins during the Fiestas de San Isidro, patron saint of Madrid, on May 15. This is the occasion for a series of fights, during which talent scouts are in the audience. Matadors who distinguish themselves in the ring are signed up for Majorca, Málaga, and other places.

The best way to get tickets to the bullfights is at the stadium's box office (open Friday to Sunday 10am to 2pm and 5 to 8pm). Alternatively, you can contact one of Madrid's most competent ticket agents, **Localidades Galicia,** Plaza del Carmen, 1 (☎ **91-531-27-32;** metro: Puerto del Sol). It's open Tuesday to Saturday from 9:30am to 1:30pm, and 4:30 to 7:30pm; Sunday from 9:30am to 1:30pm. Open Monday to Saturday 9:30am to 8pm and Sunday 9:30am to 2pm in May. Regardless of where you buy them, tickets to bullfights range from 2,000 to 20,000 ptas. ($13.40 to $134), depending on the event and the position of your seat within the stadium. Concierges for virtually every reputable upper-bracket hotel in Madrid can also acquire tickets, through inner channels of their own, to bullfights and other sought-after entertainment venues. Front-row seats at the bullfights are known as *barreras*. *Delanteras* (third-row seats)are available in both the *alta* (high) and the *baja* (low) sections. The cheapest seats sold, *filas*, afford the worst view and are in the sun (*sol*) during the entire performance. The best seats are in the shade (*sombra*). Bullfights are held on Sunday and holidays throughout most of the year, and every day during certain festivals, which tend to last around 3 weeks, usually in the late spring. Starting times are adjusted according to the anticipated hour of sundown on the day of a performance, usually 7pm from March through October, and at 5pm during late autumn and early spring. Late-night fights by neophyte matadors are sometimes staged under spotlights on Saturday around 11pm.

IF YOU HAVE MORE TIME
MUSEUMS

Museo Arqueológico Nacional. Serrano, 13. ☎ **91-577-79-12.** Admission 500 ptas. ($3.35), free for children and adults over 65. Free on Sat 2:30–8:30pm and Sun. Tues–Sat 9:30am–8:30pm, Sun 9:30am–2:30pm. Metro: Serrano or Retiro. Bus: 1, 9, 19, 51, 74, or M2.

This stately mansion is a storehouse of artifacts from the prehistoric to the baroque. One of the prime exhibits here is the Iberian statue *The Lady of Elche*, a piece of primitive carving (from the 4th century B.C.), discovered on the southeastern coast of Spain. Finds from Ibiza, Paestum, and Rome are on display, including statues of Tiberius and his mother, Livia. The Islamic collection from Spain is outstanding. There are also collections of Spanish Renaissance lusterware, Talavera pottery, Retiro porcelain, and some rare 16th- and 17th-century Andalusian glassware.

Many of the exhibits are treasures that were removed from churches and monasteries. A much-photographed choir stall from the palace of Palencia dates from the 14th century. Also worth a look are the reproductions of the Altamira cave paintings (chiefly of bison, horses, and boars), discovered near Santander in northern Spain in 1868.

Museo de América (Museum of the Americas). Avenida de los Reyes Católicos, 6. ☎ **91-549-2641.** Admission 500 ptas. ($3.35) adults, 250 ptas. ($1.70) students and children. Tues–Sat 10am–3pm, Sun 10am–2:30pm. Metro: Moncloa.

This museum, situated near the university campus, houses an outstanding collection of pre-Columbian, Spanish-American, and Native American art and artifacts. Various exhibits chronicle the progress of the inhabitants of the New World, from the Paleolithic period to the present day. One exhibit, "Groups, Tribes, Chiefdoms, and States," focuses on the social structure of the various peoples of the Americas. Another display outlines the various religions and deities associated with them. Also included in the museum is an entire exhibit dedicated to communication, highlighting written as well as nonverbal expressions of art.

Museo del Ejército (Army Museum). Méndez Núñez, 1. ☎ **91-522-89-77.** Admission 100 ptas. (65¢) adults, free for children under 18 and adults over 65. Tues–Sun 10am–2pm. Metro: Banco de España, or Retiro. Bus: 10, 19, 27, 34.

This museum, in the Buen Retiro Palace, houses outstanding exhibits from military history, including El Cid's original sword. In addition, you can see the tent used by Charles V in Tunisia, relics of Pizarro and Cortés, and an exceptional collection of armor. Look for the piece of the cross that Columbus carried when he landed in the New World. The museum had a notorious founder: Manuel Godoy, who rose from relative poverty to become the lover of Maria Luisa of Parma, wife of Carlos IV.

Museo de la Real Academia de Bellas Artes de San Fernando (Fine Arts Museum). Alcalá, 13. ☎ **91-522-1491.** Tues–Sat admission 300 ptas. ($2) adults, free for students, children and adults over 60; free on Sun. Tues–Fri 9am–7pm, Sat–Mon 9am–2pm. Metro: Puerta del Sol or Sevilla. Bus: 15, 20, 51, 52, 53, or 150.

An easy stroll from Puerta del Sol, the Fine Arts Museum is located in the restored and remodeled 17th-century baroque palace of Juan de Goyeneche. The collection—more than 1,500 paintings and 570 sculptures, ranging from the 16th century to the present—was started in 1752 during the reign of Fernando VI (1746–59). It emphasizes works by Spanish, Flemish, and Italian artists. You can see masterpieces by El Greco, Rubens, Velázquez, Zurbarán, Ribera, Cano, Coello, Murillo, Goya, and Sorolla.

Museo Municipal. Fuencarral, 78. ☎ **91-588-86-72.** Admission 300 ptas. ($2) adults, 150 ptas. ($1) seniors and children under 18. Free Wed and Sun. Tues–Fri 9:30am–8pm, Sat–Sun 10am–2pm. Metro: Bilbao or Tribunal. Bus: 3, 21, 40, 147, or 149.

After years of restoration, the Museo Municipal again displays collections on local history, archaeology, and art, with an emphasis on the Bourbon Madrid of the 18th century. Paseos with strolling couples are shown on huge tapestry cartoons. Paintings from the royal collections are here, plus period models of the best-known city squares and a Goya that was painted for the Town Hall.

Museo Nacional de Artes Decorativas. Calle de Montalbán, 12. ☎ **91-532-64-99.** Admission 400 ptas. ($2.70) adults, 200 ptas. ($1.35) students, children, and seniors. Tues–Fri 9:30am–3pm, Sat–Sun 10am–2pm. Metro: Banco de España. Bus: 14, 27, 34, 37, or 45.

In 62 rooms spread over several floors, this museum, near the Plaza de la Cibeles, displays a rich collection of furniture, ceramics, and decorative pieces. Emphasizing the 16th and 17th centuries, the eclectic collection includes Gothic carvings, alabaster figurines, festival crosses, elaborate dollhouses, elegant baroque four-poster beds, a chapel covered with leather tapestries, and even kitchens from the 18th century. Two new floors focusing on the 18th and 19th centuries have recently been added to the museum.

Museo Naval. Paseo del Prado, 5. ☎ **91-379-52-99.** Free admission. Tues–Sun 10:30am–1:30pm. Closed Aug. Metro: Banco de España. Bus: 2, 14, 27, 40, 51, 52, or M6.

The history of nautical science and the Spanish navy, from the time of Isabella and Ferdinand until today, comes alive at the Museo Naval. The most fascinating exhibit is the map made by the *Santa María's* first mate to show the Spanish monarchs the new discoveries. There are also souvenirs of the Battle of Trafalgar.

Museo Romántico. San Mateo, 13. ☎ **91-448-10-71.** Admission 400 ptas. ($2.70) adults, 200 ptas. ($1.35) students and children, free for seniors over 65 years. Tues–Sat 9am–3pm, Sun 10am–2pm. Closed Aug. Metro: Alonso Martínez.

Geared toward those seeking the romanticism of the 19th century, this museum is housed in a mansion decorated with numerous period pieces: crystal chandeliers, faded portraits, oils from Goya to Sorolla, opulent furnishings, and porcelain. Many exhibits date from the days of Isabella II, the high-living, fun-loving queen who was forced into exile and eventual abdication.

Museo Sorolla. General Martínez Campos, 37. ☎ **91-310-15-84.** Admission 400 ptas. ($2.70). Tues–Sat 10am–3pm, Sun 10am–2pm. Metro: Iglesia or Rubén Darío. Bus: 5, 16, 61, 40, or M3.

From 1912, painter Joaquín Sorolla and his family occupied this elegant Madrileño town house off Paseo de la Castellana. His widow turned it over to the government, and it is now maintained as a memorial. Much of the house remains as Sorolla left it, right down to his stained paintbrushes and pipes. The museum wing displays a representative collection of his works.

> ### ☆ Frommer's Favorite Madrid Experiences
>
> **Tasca Hopping.** This is the quintessential Madrid experience and the fastest way for a visitor to tap into the local scene. *Tascas* are Spanish pubs serving tapas, those tantalizing appetizers. You can go from one to the other, sampling each tavern's special dishes and wines.
>
> **Eating "Around Spain."** The variety of gastronomic experiences is staggering: You can literally restaurant-hop from province to province without ever leaving Madrid.
>
> **Viewing the Works of Your Favorite Artist.** Spend an afternoon at the Prado, savoring the works of your favorite Spanish artist, devoting all your attention to his work.
>
> **Bargain Hunting at El Rastro.** Madrid has one of the greatest flea markets in Europe, if not the world. Wander through its many offerings to discover that hidden treasure you've been searching for.
>
> **A Night of Flamenco.** Flamenco folk songs (*cante*) and dances (*baile*) are an integral part of the Spanish experience. Spend at least one night in a flamenco tavern, listening to the heart-rending laments of gypsy sorrows, tribulations, hopes, and dreams.
>
> **Outdoor-Cafe Sitting.** This is a famous experience for the summertime, when Madrileños come alive again on their terrazas. The drinking and good times can go on until dawn. From glamorous hangouts to lowly street corners, the cafe scene takes place mainly along the axis formed by the Paseo de la Castellana, Paseo del Prado, and Paseo de Recoletos (all of which make up one continuous street).

Although Sorolla painted portraits of Spanish aristocrats, he was essentially interested in the common people, often depicting them in their native dress. On view are the artist's self-portrait and the paintings of his wife and their son. Sorolla was especially fond of painting beach scenes of the Costa Blanca.

Museo Taurino (Bullfighting Museum). Plaza de Toros de las Ventas, Alcalá, 237. ☎ **91-725-18-57.** Free admission. Mar–Oct, Tues–Fri and Sun 9:30am–2:30pm; Nov–Feb, Mon–Fri 9:30am–2:30pm. Metro: Ventas. Bus: 12, 21, 38, 53, 146, M1, or M8.

This museum might serve as a good introduction to bullfighting for those who want to see the real event. Here you'll see the death costume of Manolete, the *traje de luces* (suit of lights) that he wore when he was gored to death at age 30 in Linares's bullring. Other memorabilia evokes the heyday of Juan Belmonte, the Andalusian who revolutionized bullfighting in 1914 by performing close to the horns. Other exhibits include a Goya painting of a matador, as well as photographs and relics that trace the history of bullfighting in Spain from its ancient origins to the present day.

Museo Tiflológico. La Coruña, 18. ☎ **91-589-42-00.** Free admission. Tues–Fri 10am–2pm and 5–8pm, Sat 10am–2pm. Metro: Estrecho. Bus: 3, 42, 43, 64, or 124.

This museum is designed for sightless and sight-impaired visitors. Maintained by Spain's National Organization for the Blind, it's one of the few museums in the world that emphasizes tactile appeal. All the exhibits are meant to be touched and felt; to that end, the museum provides audiotapes, in English and Spanish, to guide visitors as they move their hands over the object on display. It also offers pamphlets in large type and Braille.

One section of the museum features small-scale replicas of such architectural wonders as the Maya and Aztec pyramids of Central America, the Eiffel Tower, and the Statue of Liberty. Another section contains paintings and sculptures created by blind artists, such as Miguel Detrel and José António Braña. A third section outlines the status of blind people throughout history, with a focus on the sociology and technology that led to the development of Braille during the 19th century.

Real Basílica de San Francisco el Grande, Plaza de San Francisco el Grande, San Buenaventura, 1. ☎ **91-365-38-00.** Admission 50 ptas. (35¢). Tues–Sat 11am–1pm and 4–6:30pm. Metro: La Latina or Puerta del Toledo. Bus: 3, 60, C, or M4.

Ironically, Madrid, the capital of cathedral-rich Spain, does not itself possess a famous cathedral—but it does have an important church, with a dome larger than that of St. Paul's in London. This 18th-century church is filled with a number of ecclesiastical works, notably a Goya painting of St. Bernardinus of Siena. A guide will show you through.

Templo de Debod. Paseo de Rosales. ☎ **91-409-61-65.** Admission 300 ptas. ($2) adults, 150 ptas. ($1) children under 16; free on Wed and Sun. Apr 1–Sept 30, Mon–Fri 10am–2pm and 6–8pm; Oct 1–Mar 31, Mon–Fri 9:45am–1:45pm and 4:15–6:15pm; Sat–Sun 10am–1pm year-round. Metro: Plaza de España or Ventura Rodríguez. Bus: 25, 33, 39, 46, or 74.

This Egyptian temple near Plaza de España once stood in the Valley of the Nile, 19 miles from Aswan. When the new dam threatened the temple, the Egyptian government dismantled and presented it to Spain. Taken down stone by stone in 1969 and 1970, it was shipped to Valencia and taken by rail to Madrid, where it was reconstructed and opened to the public in 1971. Photos upstairs depict the temple's long history.

PARKS & GARDENS

The **Casa de Campo** (metro: Lago or Batán) is the former royal hunting grounds—miles of parkland lying south of the Royal Palace across the Manzanares River. You can see the gate through which the kings rode out of the palace grounds, either on horseback or in carriages, on their way to the tree-lined park. A lake contained within Casa de Campo is usually filled with rowers. You can have drinks and light refreshments around the water or go swimming in a municipally operated pool. Children will love both the zoo and the Parque de Atracciones (see "Especially for Kids," below). The Casa de Campo can be visited daily from 8am to 9pm.

The **Parque de Retiro** (metro: Retiro), originally a royal playground for the Spanish monarchs and their guests, extends over 350 acres. The huge palaces that once stood here were destroyed in the early 19th century; only the former dance hall, the Cáson del Buen Retiro (housing the modern works of the Prado) and the building containing the Army Museum remain. The park boasts numerous fountains and statues, plus a large lake. There are also two exposition centers, the Veláquez and Crystal palaces (built to honor the Philippines in 1887), and a lakeside monument, erected in 1922 in honor of King Alfonso XII. In summer, the rose gardens are worth a visit, and you'll find several places for inexpensive snacks and drinks. The park is open daily 24 hours, but it is safest from 7am to about 8:30pm.

Across calle de Alfonso XII, at the southwest corner of Parque de Retiro, is the **Real Jardín Botánico (Botanical Garden;** ☎ **91-420-30-17;** metro: Atocha; bus: 10, 14, 19, 32, or 45). Founded in the 18th century, the garden contains more than 104 species of trees and 3,000 types of plants. Also on the premises are an exhibition hall and a library specializing in botany. The park is open daily from 10am to 8:30pm; admission is 200 ptas. ($1.35).

Literary Landmarks

Casa de Lope de Vega. Cervantes, 11. ☎ **91-429-92-16.** Admission 200 ptas. ($1.35). Mon–Fri 10am–2pm, Sat 10am–1:30pm. Closed Aug. Metro: Anton Martín.

Felix Lope de Vega, a prolific Madrid-born author, dramatized Hapsburg Spain as no one had before, earning a lasting position in Spanish letters. A reconstruction of his medieval house stands on a narrow street—ironically named for Cervantes, his competitor for the title of the greatest writer of the golden age of Spain. The dank, dark house is furnished with relics of the period, although you can't be sure that any of the furnishings or possessions actually belonged to this 16th-century genius.

Chicote. Gran Vía, 12. ☎ **91-532-67-37.** Beer 550 ptas. ($3.70), whiskey and soda 950 ptas. ($6.35). Mon–Sat 8am–3am (till 3am Fri–Sat). Metro: Gran Vía.

Ernest Hemingway used Chicote as a setting for his only play, *The Fifth Column.* He would sit here night after night, gazing at the *putas* (it was a famed hooker bar back then) as he entertained friends with such remarks as "Spain is a country for living and not for dying." The bar still draws a lively crowd.

Sobrino de Botín. Cuchilleros, 17. ☎ **91-366-42-17**.

In the final two pages of Hemingway's novel *The Sun Also Rises,* Jake invites Brett here for roast suckling pig and red wine. In another book, *Death in the Afternoon,* Hemingway told his mythical "Old Lady": "I would rather dine on suckling pig at Botín's than sit and think of casualties my friends have suffered." Since that time, thousands upon thousands of Americans have eaten at Botín (see "Dining," earlier in this chapter for details), a perennial favorite of all visiting Yankees.

An Architectural Highlight

Puerta de Toledo. Metro: Puerta de Toledo.

Puerta de Toledo is one of the two surviving town gates (the other is Puerta de Alcalá). Constructed during the brief and unpopular rule of Joseph I Bonaparte, this one marks the spot where citizens used to set out for the former imperial capital of Toledo. On an irregularly shaped square, it stands at the intersection of the Ronda de Toledo and calle de Toledo. Its original purpose was a triumphal arch to honor Napoléon Bonaparte. In 1813, it became a symbol of Madrid's fierce independence and the loyalty of its citizens to their Bourbon rulers, who had been restored to the throne in the wake of the Napoleonic invasion.

Especially For Kids

Aquápolis. Villanueva de la Canada, Avenida de la Dehesa (Carretera de El Escorial). ☎ **91-815-69-11.** Admission 1,875 ptas. ($12.55) adults, 1,250 ptas. ($8.40) children. Mon–Fri noon–8pm, Sat–Sun 11am–8pm. Closed Oct–June. Free buses from 11am leaving Madrid from calle de los Reyes, next to Coliseum Cinema, on eastern edge of Plaza de España.

Sixteen miles northwest of Madrid lies a watery attraction where the kids can cool off. Scattered amid shops, a picnic area, and a barbecue restaurant are water slides, wave-making machines, and tall slides that spiral children into a swimming pool below.

Museo de Cera de Madrid (Wax Museum). Paseo de Recoletos, 41. ☎ **91-319-26-49.** Admission 900 ptas. ($6.05) adults, 600 ptas. ($4) children, children 3 and under free. Daily 10am–2pm and 4–8pm. Metro: Colón. Bus: 27, 45, or 53.

The kids will enjoy seeing a lifelike wax Columbus calling on Ferdinand and Isabella, as well as Marlene Dietrich checking out Bill and Hillary Clinton. The 450 wax figures also include heroes and villains of World War II. Two galleries display Romans and Arabs from the ancient days of the Iberian Peninsula; a show in multivision gives a 30-minute recap of Spanish history from the Phoenicians to the present.

Parque de Atracciones. Casa de Campo. ☎ **91-463-29-00.** Admission 600 ptas. ($4). Apr–May Tues–Fri noon–8pm, Sat–Sun noon–10pm; June–Aug Tues–Fri 6pm–1am, Sat 6pm–2am, Sun noon–1am; Sept Tues–Sun (variable hours; call to check before going); Oct–Mar Sat noon–8pm (sometimes 9pm), Sun 11am–8pm (sometimes 9pm). Take the Teleférico cable car (see below); at the end of this ride, microbuses take you the rest of the way. Alternatively, take the suburban train from Plaza de España and stop near the entrance to the park (Entrada de Batán).

The park was created in 1969 to amuse the young at heart with an array of rides and concessions. The former includes a toboggan slide, a carousel, pony rides, an adventure into outer space, a walk through a transparent maze, a visit to jungle land, a motor-propelled series of cars disguised as a tail-wagging dachshund puppy, and a gyrating whirligig clutched in the tentacles of an octopus named El Pulpo. The most popular rides are a pair of roller coasters named 7 Picos and Jet Star.

The park also has many diversions for adults. See the listing for the Auditorio del Parque de Atracciones, under "Madrid After Dark," later in this chapter, for details.

Planetarium. Parque Tierno Galván, Méndez Álvaro. ☎ **91-467-34-61.** Admission 475 ptas. ($3.20) adults, 200 ptas. ($1.35) seniors and children under 14. Shows: winter, Tues–Wed 5:30 and 6:45pm; Apr–Oct, Easter, and Christmas Tues–Sun 11:30am, 12:45pm, 5:30 and 6:45pm; Sat–Sun year-round 11:30am, 12:45pm, 5:30, 6:45 and 8pm. Closed 2 weeks in Jan. Metro: Méndez Álvaro. Bus: 148.

This planetarium has a projection room with optical and electronic equipment, including a multivision system, designed to reproduce outer space.

Teleférico. Paseo del Pintor Rosales, s/n. ☎ **91-541-74-50.** Fare 375 ptas. ($2.50) one way, 520 ptas. ($3.50) round-trip. Apr–Sept, daily 11am–9pm; Oct–Mar, Sat–Sun noon–9pm. Metro: Plaza de España or Argüelles. Bus: 74.

Strung high above several of Madrid's verdant parks, this cable car was originally built in 1969 as part of a public fairgrounds (Parque de Atracciones) modeled vaguely along the lines of Disneyland. Today, even for visitors not interested in visiting the park, the teleférico retains an allure of its own as a high-altitude method of admiring the cityscape of Madrid. The cable car departs from Paseo Pintor Rosales at the eastern edge of Parque del Oeste (at the corner of calle Marqués de Urquijo) and carries you high above two parks, railway tracks, and over the Manzanares River to a spot near a picnic ground and restaurant in Casa de Campo. Weather permitting, there are good views of the Royal Palace along the way. The ride takes 11 minutes.

Zoo Aquarium de la Casa de Campo. Casa de Campo. ☎ **91-512 37 70.** Admission 1,600 ptas. ($10.70) adults, 1,300 ptas. ($8.70) seniors and children 3–8, free for children 2 and under. Daily 10am–sunset. Metro: Batán. Bus: 33.

This modern, well-organized facility allows you to see wildlife from five continents, with about 3,000 animals on display. Most are in simulated natural habitats, with moats separating them from the public. There's a petting zoo for the kids and a show presented by the Chu-Lin band. The zoo/aquarium complex includes a 520,000-gallon tropical marine aquarium, a dolphin aquarium, and an array of colorful parrots.

ORGANIZED TOURS

A large number of agencies in Madrid book organized tours and excursions to sights and attractions both within and outside the city limits. Although it won't exactly be spontaneous, some visitors appreciate the ease, convenience, and efficiency of being able to visit so many sights in a single well-organized day.

Many of the city's hotel concierges, and all of the city's travel agents, will book anyone who asks for a guided tour of Madrid or its environs with one of Spain's largest tour operators, **Pullmantours,** Plaza de Oriente, 8 (☎ **91-541-18-07**). Regardless of their destination and duration, virtually every tour departs from the Pullmantour terminal, at that address. Half-day tours of Madrid include an artistic tour priced at 5,250 ptas. ($35.20) per person, which includes entrance to a selection of the city's museums, and a panoramic half-day tour for 3,000 ptas. ($20.10).

Toledo is the most popular full-day excursion outside the city limits. Trips cost 8,700 ptas. ($58.30). These tours (including lunch) depart daily at 9:45am from the above-mentioned departure point, last all day, and include ample opportunities for wandering at will through the city's narrow streets. You can, if you wish, take an abbreviated morning tour of Toledo, without stopping for lunch, for 5,600 ptas. ($37.50).

Another popular tour stops briefly in Toledo and continues on to visit both the monastery at El Escorial and the Valley of the Fallen (*Valle de los Caídos*) before returning the same day to Madrid. With lunch included, this all-day excursion costs 12,000 ptas. ($80.40).

The third major destination of bus tours from Madrid's center to the city's surrounding attractions is Pullmantour's full-day guided excursion to Ávila and Segovia, which takes in a heady dose of medieval and ancient Roman monuments that are really very interesting. The price, per person, with lunch included is 9,000 ptas. ($60.30).

The hop-off, hop-on **Madrid Vision Bus** lets you set your own pace and itinerary. A scheduled panoramic tour lasts a half hour, provided that you don't get off the bus. Otherwise, you can opt for an unlimited number of stops, exploring at your leisure. The Madrid Vision makes four complete tours daily, two in the morning and two in the afternoon; on Sunday and Monday buses depart only in the morning. Check with Trapsa Tours (☎ **91-767-17-43**) for departure times, which are variable. The full-day tour with unlimited stops, costs 2,200 ptas. ($14.75). You can board the bus at the Madrid tourist office.

6 Shopping

THE SHOPPING SCENE

Spain has always been known for its craftspeople, many of whom still work in the time-honored and labor-intensive traditions of their grandparents. It's hard to go wrong if you stick to the beautiful handcrafted Spanish objects—hand-painted tiles, ceramics, and porcelain; handwoven rugs; handmade sweaters; and intricate embroideries. And, of course, Spain produces some of the world's finest leather. Jewelry, especially gold set with Majorca pearls, represents good value and unquestioned luxury.

Some of Madrid's art galleries are known throughout Europe for discovering and encouraging new talent. Antiques are sold in highly sophisticated retail outlets. Better suited to the budgets of many travelers are the weekly flea markets.

Spain continues to make inroads into the fashion world. Its young designers are regularly featured in the fashion magazines of Europe. Excellent shoes are available, some highly fashionable. But be advised that prices for shoes and quality clothing are generally higher in Madrid than in the United States.

GREAT SHOPPING AREAS

THE CENTER   The sheer diversity of shops in Madrid's center is staggering. Their densest concentration lies immediately north of Puerta del Sol, radiating out from calle del Carmen, calle Montera, and calle Preciados.

In case you want to see the world.

At American Express, we're here to make your journey a smooth one. So we have over 1,700 travel service locations in over 130 countries ready to help. What else would you expect from the world's largest travel agency?

do more

Travel

In case you want to be welcomed there.

We're here to see that you're always welcomed at establishments everywhere. That's why millions of people carry the American Express® Card – for peace of mind, confidence, and security, around the world or just around the corner.

do more

Cards

In case you're running low.

We're here to help with more than 190,000 Express Cash locations around the world. In order to enroll, just call American Express at 1 800 CASH-NOW before you start your vacation.

And in case you'd rather be safe than sorry.

We're here with American Express® Travelers Cheques. They're the safe way to carry money on your vacation, because if they're ever lost or stolen you can get a refund, practically anywhere or anytime. To find the nearest place to buy Travelers Cheques, call 1 800 495-1153. Another way we help you do more.

do more

Travelers Cheques

CALLE MAYOR & CALLE DEL ARENAL   Unlike their more stylish neighbors to the north of Puerta del Sol, shops in this district to the west tend toward the small, slightly dusty enclaves of coin and stamp dealers, family owned souvenir shops, clock makers, sellers of military paraphernalia, and an abundance of stores selling musical scores.

GRAN VÍA   Conceived, designed, and built in the 1910s and 1920s as a showcase for the city's best shops, hotels, and restaurants, the Gran Vía has since been eclipsed by other shopping districts. Its art nouveau/art deco glamour still survives in the hearts of most Madrileños, however. The bookshops here are among the best in the city, as are outlets for fashion, shoes, jewelry, furs, and handcrafted accessories from all regions of Spain.

EL RASTRO   It's the biggest flea market in Spain, drawing collectors, dealers, buyers, and hopefuls from throughout Madrid and its suburbs. The makeshift stalls are at their most frenetic on Sunday morning. For more information, see "Flea Markets" section, below.

PLAZA MAYOR   Under the arcades of the square itself are exhibitions of lithographs and oil paintings, and every weekend there's a loosely organized market for stamp and coin collectors. Within 3 or 4 blocks in every direction you'll find more than the average number of souvenir shops.

ON CALLE MARQUÉS   Viudo de Pontejos, which runs east from Plaza Mayor, is one of the city's headquarters for the sale of cloth, thread, and buttons. Also running east, on calle de Zaragoza, are silversmiths and jewelers. On calle Postas, you'll find housewares, underwear, soap powders, and other household items.

NEAR THE CARRERA DE SAN JERÓNIMO   Several blocks east of Puerta del Sol is Madrid's densest concentration of gift shops, crafts shops, and antiques dealers—a decorator's delight. Its most interesting streets include calle del Prado, calle de las Huertas, and Plaza de las Cortés. The neighborhood is pricey so don't expect bargains here.

NORTHWEST MADRID   A few blocks east of Parque del Oeste is an upscale neighborhood that's well stocked with luxury goods and household staples. Calle de la Princesa, its main thoroughfare, has shops selling shoes, handbags, fashion, gifts, and children's clothing. Thanks to the presence of the university nearby, there's also a dense concentration of bookstores, especially on calle Isaac Peral and calle Fernando el Católico, several blocks north and northwest, respectively, from the subway stop of Argüelles.

SALAMANCA DISTRICT   It's known throughout Spain as the quintessential upper-bourgeois neighborhood, uniformly prosperous, and its shops are correspondingly exclusive. They include outlets run by interior decorators, furniture shops, fur and jewelry shops, several department stores, and design headquarters whose output ranges from the solidly conservative to the high-tech. The main streets of this district are calle de Serrano and calle de Velázquez. The district lies northeast of the center of Madrid, a few blocks north of Retiro Park. Its most central metro stops are Serrano and Velázquez.

HOURS & SHIPPING

Major stores are open (in most cases) Monday to Saturday from 9:30am to 8pm. Many small stores take a siesta between 1:30 and 4:30pm. Of course, there is never any set formula, and hours can vary greatly from store to store, depending on the idiosyncrasies and schedules of the owner.

Many art and antiques dealers will crate and ship bulky objects for an additional fee. Whereas in most cases it pays to have heavy objects shipped by sea, it might surprise you that in some cases it's almost the same price to ship crated goods by airplane. Of course, it depends on the distance your crate will have to travel overland to the nearest international port which, in many cases for the purposes of relatively small-scale shipments by individual clients, is Barcelona. Consequently, it might pay to call two branches of **Emery Worldwide** from within Spain to explain your particular situation, and receive comparable rates. For information about sea transit for your valuables, call **Emery Worldwide Ocean Services** at its only Spanish branch, Barcelona (☎ **93-479-30-50**). For information about **Emery Worldwide Air Freight,** call its main Spanish office in Madrid (☎ **91-747-56-66**) for advice on any of the dozen of air freight pickup stations they maintain throughout Spain. These include, among many others, Barcelona, Alicante, Málaga, Bilbao, and Valencia. For more advice on this, and the formalities that you'll go through in clearing U.S. customs after the arrival of your shipment in the United States, call **Emery Worldwide** in the United States at ☎ **800/488-9451.**

For most small- and medium-size shipments, air freight isn't much more expensive than ocean shipping. **Iberia's Air Cargo Division** (☎ **800/221-6002** in the U.S.) offers air-freight service from Spain to either New York, Chicago, Miami, or Los Angeles. What will you pay for this transport of your treasured art objects or freight? Here's a rule of thumb: For a shipment under 220 pounds (100 kilos), from either Barcelona or Madrid to New York, the cost is approximately 734 ptas. ($4.90) per pound. The per pound price goes down as the weight of the shipment increases, declining to, for example, 254 ptas. ($1.70) per pound for shipments of more than 1,100 pounds (500 kilos). Regardless of what you ship, there's a minimum charge of 7,650 ptas. ($51.25).

For an additional fee, Iberia or one of its representatives will also pick up your package. For a truly precious cargo, ask the seller to build a crate for it. For information within Spain about air-cargo shipments, call Iberia's cargo division at Madrid's Barajas Airport (☎ **91-587-3307**) or at Barcelona's airport (☎ **93-401-3426**).

Remember that your air-cargo shipment will need to clear Customs after it's brought into the United States. This involves some additional paperwork, costly delays, and in some cases a trip to the airport where the shipment first entered the United States. It's usually easier (and in some cases, much easier) to hire a commercial customs broker to do the work for you. Emery Worldwide, a division of CF Freightways, can clear most shipments of goods for around $138, which you'll pay in addition to any applicable duty you owe your home government. For information, you can call ☎ **800/443-6379** within the United States.

SHOPPING A TO Z
ANTIQUES

In addition to the shops listed below, the flea market (see **El Rastro,** below) is also a source of antiques.

Centro de Anticuarios Lagasca. Lagasca, 36. No phone. Metro: Serrano or Velázquez.

You'll find about a dozen antique shops here, clustered into one covered arcade. They operate as individual businesses, although by browsing through each you'll find an impressive assemblage of antique furniture, porcelain, and whatnots. Open Monday to Saturday from 10am to 1:30pm and 5 to 8pm.

Centro de Arte y Antigüedades. Serrano, 5. ☎ **91-576-96-82.** Metro: Retiro. Bus: 9 or 15.

Housed in a mid–19th-century building are several unusual antique dealers (and a large carpet emporium as well) many of whom specialize in antique, sometimes monumental paintings. Each establishment maintains its own schedule, although the center itself has overall hours. Open Monday through Saturday from 10am to 2pm and 5 to 8:15pm.

ART GALLERIES

✪ **Galería Kreisler.** Hermosilla, 8. ☎ **91-431-42-64.** Metro: Serrano. Bus: 27, 45, or 150.

One successful entrepreneur on Madrid's art scene is Ohio-born Edward Kreisler, whose gallery, now run by his son Juan, specializes in figurative and contemporary paintings, sculptures, and graphics. The gallery prides itself on occasionally displaying and selling the works of artists who are critically acclaimed and displayed in museums in Spain. Open Monday through Saturday from 10:30am to 1pm and 5 to 9pm. Closed Saturday afternoon July 15 to September 15 and August.

CAPES

Capas Seseña. Cruz, 23. ☎ **91-531-68-40.** Metro: Sevilla or Puerta del Sol. Bus: 5, 51, or 52.

Founded shortly after the turn of the century, this shop manufactures and sells wool capes for both women and men. The wool comes from the mountain town of Béjar, near Salamanca. Celebrities who have been spotted donning Seseña capes include Picasso, Hemingway, Miró, and recently, Hillary Rodham Clinton and daughter Chelsea. Open Monday through Friday from 10am to 2pm and 4:30 to 8pm, Saturday from 10am to 2pm.

CARPETS

Ispahan. Serrano, 5. ☎ **91-575-20-12.** Metro: Retiro. Bus: 1, 2, 9, and 15.

In this 19th-century building, behind bronze handmade doors, are three floors devoted to carpets from around the world, notably Afghanistan, India, Nepal, Iran, Turkey, and the Caucasus. One section features silk carpets. It's open Monday through Saturday from 10am to 2pm and 4:30 to 8:30pm (till 8pm on Saturday).

CERAMICS

✪ **Antigua Casa Talavera.** Isabel la Católica, 2. ☎ **91-547-34-17.** Metro: Santo Domingo. Bus: 1, 2, 46, 70, 75, or 148.

"The first house of Spanish ceramics" has wares that include a sampling of regional styles from every major area of Spain, including Talavera, Toledo, Manises, Valencia, Puente del Arzobispa, Alcora, Granada, and Seville. Sangría pitchers, dinnerware, tea sets, plates, and vases are all handmade. Inside one of the showrooms is an interesting selection of tiles, painted with reproductions of scenes from bullfights, dances, and folklore. There's also a series of tiles depicting famous paintings in the Prado. At its present location since 1904, the shop is only a short walk from Plaza de Santo Domingo. Open Monday through Friday from 10am to 1:30pm and 5 to 8pm, Saturday from 10am to 1:30pm.

CRAFTS

El Arco de los Cuchilleros Artesania de Hoy. Plaza Mayor, 9 (basement level). ☎ **91-365-26-80.** Metro: Puerta del Sol or Opera.

Set within one of the 17th-century vaulted cellars of Plaza Mayor, this shop is entirely devoted to unusual craft items from throughout Spain. The merchandise is one of a kind, and in most cases contemporary; it includes a changing array of pottery, leather, textiles, wood carvings, glassware, wickerwork, papier mâché, and silver jewelry. The hardworking owners deal directly with the artisans who produce each item, ensuring a wide inventory of handcrafts. The staff is familiar with the rituals of applying for tax-free status of purchases here, and speaks several different languages. It's open Monday through Saturday 11am to 9pm and Sunday 1am to 8pm.

DEPARTMENT STORES

El Corte Inglés. Preciados, 3. ☎ **91-379-80-00.** Metro: Puerta del Sol.

This flagship of the largest department-store chain in Madrid sells hundreds of souvenirs and Spanish handcrafts—damascene steelwork from Toledo, flamenco dolls, and embroidered shawls. Some astute buyers report that it also sells glamorous fashion articles, such as Pierre Balmain designs, for about a third less than equivalent items in most European capitals. Services include interpreters, currency-exchange windows, and parcel delivery either to a local hotel or overseas. Open Monday through Saturday from 10am to 9:30pm.

EMBROIDERIES

Casa Bonet. Núñez de Balboa, 76. ☎ **91-575-09-12.** Metro: Núñez de Balboa.

The intricately detailed embroideries produced in Spain's Balearic Islands (especially Majorca) are avidly sought for bridal chests and elegant dinner settings. A few examples of the store's extensive inventory are displayed on the walls. Open Monday through Friday from 9:45am to 2pm and 5 to 8pm, Saturday from 10:15am to 2pm.

ESPADRILLES

Casa Hernanz. Toledo, 18. ☎ **91-366-54-50.** Metro: Puerta del Sol, Opera, or La Latina.

A brisk walk south of Plaza Mayor delivers you to this store, in business since the 1840s. In addition to espadrilles, they sell shoes in other styles, as well as hats. Open Monday through Friday 9am to 1:30pm and 4:30 to 8pm, Saturday from 10am to 2pm.

FANS & UMBRELLAS

Casa de Diego. Puerta del Sol, 12. ☎ **91-522-66-43.** Metro: Puerta del Sol.

Here you'll find a wide inventory of fans, ranging from plain to fancy, from plastic to exotic hardwood, from cost-conscious to lavish. Some fans tend to be a bit overpriced; shopping around may increase your chances of finding a real bargain. Now open year-round from Monday to Saturday, 9:30am to 8pm.

FASHIONS FOR MEN

For the man on a budget who wants to dress reasonably well, the best outlet for off-the-rack men's clothing is one of the branches of El Corte Inglés department store chain (see above). Most men's boutiques in Madrid are very expensive and may not be worth the investment.

FASHIONS FOR WOMEN

Herrero. Preciados, 7. ☎ **91-521-29-90.** Metro: Puerta del Sol or Callao.

The sheer size and buying power of this popular retail outlet for women's clothing make it a reasonably priced emporium for all kinds of feminine garb as well as various articles for gentlemen. It is open Monday through Saturday from 10:30am to 8:15pm; some Sundays from noon to 8:15pm. An additional outlet lies on the same street at no. 16 (☎ **91-521-15-24**). Both stores are open Monday through Saturday from 10:30am to 8:15pm.

Modas Gonzalo. Gran Vía, 43. ☎ **91-547-12-39.** Metro: Callao or Puerta del Sol.

This boutique's baroque, gilded atmosphere evokes the 1940s, but its fashions are strictly up to date, well made, and intended for stylish adult women. No children's garments are sold. Open Monday through Saturday from 10am to 1:30pm and 4:30 to 8:30pm.

FLEA MARKETS

✪ **El Rastro.** Plaza Cascorro and Ribera de Curtidores. Metro: La Latina. Bus: 3 or 17.

Foremost among markets is El Rastro (translated as either flea market or thieves' market), occupying a roughly triangular district of streets and plazas a few minutes' walk south of Plaza Mayor. Its center is Plaza Cascorro and Ribera de Curtidores. This market will delight anyone attracted to a mishmash of fascinating junk interspersed with antiques, bric-a-brac, and paintings. *Note:* Thieves are rampant here (hustling more than just antiques), so secure your wallet carefully, be alert, and proceed with caution. Insofar as scheduling your visit to El Rastro, bear in mind that this is a flea market involving hundreds of merchants who basically pull up their display tables and depart whenever their goods are sold or they get fed up with the crowds. In theory, vendors are in place, hawking their wares every day from 9:30am to 1:30pm, and after a leisurely lunch, again from 5 to 8pm. But the absolutely best day for scheduling a visit here is Sunday morning, when the neighborhood has a higher percentage of merchants and salespersons than any other time of the week.

FOOD & WINE

Majorca. Velázquez, 59. ☎ **91-431-99-09.** Metro: Velásquez.

Madrid's best-established gourmet shop opened in 1931 as an outlet selling a pastry called *ensaimada,* and this is still one of the store's most famous products. Tempting arrays of cheeses, canapés, roasted and marinated meats, sausages, and about a dozen kinds of pâté accompany a spread of tiny pastries, tarts, and chocolates. Don't overlook the displays of Spanish wines and brandies. A stand-up tapas bar is always clogged with clients three deep, sampling the wares before they buy larger portions to take home. Tapas cost from 150 to 400 ptas. ($2.70) per *ración* (portion). Open daily from 9:30am to 9pm.

HATS & HEADGEAR

Casa Yustas. Plaza Mayor, 30. ☎ **91-366-50-84.** Metro: Puerta del Sol.

Founded in 1894, this extraordinary hat emporium is very popular. Want to see yourself as a Congo explorer, a Spanish sailor, an officer in the kaiser's army, or even Napoléon? Open Monday through Saturday from 9:30am to 9:30pm, Sunday from 11:30am to 9pm.

LEATHER

✪ **Loewe.** Gran Vía, 8. ☎ **91-522-68-15.** Metro: Banco de España or Gran Vía.

Since 1846 this has been the most elegant leather store in Spain. Its gold-medal-winning designers have always kept abreast of changing tastes and styles, but the inventory still retains a timeless chic. The store sells luggage, handbags, and jackets for men and women (in leather or suede). Open Monday through Saturday from 9:30am to 8pm.

PERFUMES

Perfumería Padilla. Preciados, 17. ☎ **91-522-86-29.** Metro: Puerta del Sol.

This store sells a large and competitively priced assortment of Spanish and international scents for women. It also maintains a branch at calle del Carmen, 8 (☎ 91-522-66-83). Both branches are open Monday through Saturday from 10am to 8:30pm.

Oriental Perfumeries. Mayor, 1. ☎ 91-521-59-05. Metro: Puerta del Sol.

Located at the western edge of the Puerta del Sol, this time-tested shop carries one of the most complete stocks of perfume in Madrid—both national and international brands. It also sells gifts, souvenirs, and costume jewelry. Open Monday through Saturday from 10am to 8:30pm.

PORCELAIN

Lasarte. Gran Vía, 44. ☎ 91-521-49-22. Metro: Callao.

This imposing outlet is devoted almost exclusively to Lladró porcelain, and the staff can usually tell you about new designs and releases the Lladró company is planning for the near future. Open Monday through Friday from 9:30am to 8pm, Saturday from 10am to 8pm.

SHOPPING MALLS

ABC Serrano. Serrano, 61 or Castellana, 34. Metro: Serrano.

Set within what used to function as the working premises of a well-known Madrileño newspaper (ABC), this is a complex of about 85 upscale boutiques that emphasize fashion, housewares, cosmetics, and art objects. Although each of the outfitters inside are independently owned and managed, most of them maintain hours of Monday to Saturday from 10am to midnight. On the premises, you'll find cafes and restaurants to keep you fed between bouts of shopping, lots of potted and flowering shrubbery, and acres and acres of Spanish marble and tile.

Galería del Prado. Plaza de las Cortes, 7. Metro: Banco de España or Atocha.

Spain's top designers are represented in this marble-sheathed concourse below the Palace Hotel. It opened in 1989 with 47 different shops, many featuring *moda joven* (fashions for the young). Merchandise changes with the season, but you will always find a good assortment of fashions, Spanish leather goods, cosmetics, perfumes, and jewelry. You can also eat and drink in the complex. The entrance to the gallery is in front of the hotel, facing the broad tree-lined Paseo del Prado across from the Prado itself. Open Monday through Saturday from 10am to 9pm.

7 Madrid After Dark

Madrid abounds with dance halls, *tascas,* cafes, theaters, movie houses, music halls, and nightclubs. Because dinner is served late in Spain, nightlife doesn't really get under way until after 11pm, and it generally lasts until around 3am—Madrileños are so fond of prowling around at night that they are known around Spain as *gatos* (cats). If you arrive at 9:30pm at a club, you'll have the place all to yourself, if it's even open.

In most clubs a one-drink minimum is the rule: Feel free to nurse one drink through the entire evening's entertainment.

In summer Madrid becomes a virtual free festival because the city sponsors a series of plays, concerts, and films. Pick up a copy of the *Guía del Ocio* (available at most newsstands) for listings of these events. This guide also provides information about occasional discounts for commercial events, such as the concerts that are given in Madrid's parks. Also check the program of **Fundación Juan March,** calle Castello, 77

(☎ 91-435-42-40; metro: Núñez dc Balboa). Tapping into funds that were bequeathed to it by a generous financier (Sr. Juan March), it stages free concerts of Spanish and international classical music within a concert hall at its headquarters at calle Castello 77. In most cases, these are 90-minute events that are presented every Monday and Saturday at noon, and every Wednesday at 7:30pm.

Flamenco in Madrid is geared mainly to prosperous tourists with fat wallets, and nightclubs are expensive. But since Madrid is preeminently a city of song and dance, you can often be entertained at very little cost—in fact, for the price of a glass of wine or beer, if you sit at a bar with live entertainment.

Like flamenco clubs, discos tend to be expensive, but they often open for what is erroneously called afternoon sessions (from 7 to 10pm). Although discos charge entry fees, at an afternoon session the cost might be as low as 500 ptas. ($3.35), rising to 2,000 ptas. ($13.40) and beyond for a night session—that is, beginning at 11:30pm and lasting until the early morning hours. Therefore, go early, dance until 10pm, then proceed to dinner (you'll be eating at the fashionable hour).

Nightlife is so plentiful in Madrid that the city can be roughly divided into the following "night zones."

PLAZA MAYOR/PUERTA DEL SOL   The most popular areas from the standpoint of both tradition and tourist interest, they can also be dangerous, so explore them with caution, especially late at night. They are filled with tapas bars and *cuevas* (drinking caves). Here it is customary to begin a tasca crawl, going to tavern after tavern, sampling the wine in each, along with a selection of tapas. The major streets for such a crawl are Cava de San Miguel, Cava Alta, and Cava Baja. You can order *pinchos y raciones* (tasty snacks and tidbits).

GRAN VÍA   This area contains mainly cinemas and theaters. Most of the after-dark action takes place on little streets branching off the Gran Vía.

PLAZA DE ISABEL II/PLAZA DE ORIENTE   Another area much frequented by tourists, many restaurants and cafes flourish here, including the famous Café de Oriente.

CHUECA   Along such streets as Hortaleza, Infantas, Barquillo, and San Lucas, this is the gay nightlife district, with dozens of clubs. Cheap restaurants, along with a few female striptease joints, are also found here. This area can also be dangerous at night, so watch for pickpockets and muggers. As of late, there has been greater police presence at night.

ARGÜELLES/MONCLOA   For university students, this part of town sees most of the action. Many dance clubs are found here, along with ale houses and fast-food joints. The area is bounded by Pintor Rosales, Cea Bermúdez, Bravo Murillo, San Bernardo, and Conde Duque.

THE PERFORMING ARTS

Madrid has a number of theaters, opera companies, and dance companies. To discover where and when specific cultural events are being performed, pick up a copy of *Guía del Ocio* at any city newsstand. The sheer volume of cultural offerings might stagger you; for a concise summary of the highlights, see below.

Tickets to dramatic and musical events usually range in price from 700 to 3,000 ptas. ($4.70 to $20.10), with discounts of up to 50% granted on certain days of the week (usually Wednesday and matinees on Sunday).

The concierges at most major hotels can usually get you tickets to specific concerts, if you are clear about your wishes and needs. They, of course, charge a considerable markup, part of which is passed along to whichever agency originally booked the

The Sultry Sound of Flamenco

The lights dim and the flamenco stars clatter rhythmically across the dance floor. Their lean bodies and hips shake and sway to the music. The word flamenco has various translations, meaning everything from "gypsified Andalusian" to "knife," and from "blowhard" to "tough guy."

Accompanied by stylized guitar music, castanets, and the fervent clapping of the crowd, dancers are filled with tension and emotion. Flamenco dancing, with its flash, color, and ritual, is evocative of Spanish culture though its origins remain mysterious.

Experts disagree as to where it came from, but most claim Andalusia as its seat of origin. It was the gypsy artist who perfected both the song and the dance. Gypsies took to flamenco like "rice to paella," in the words of the historian Fernando Quiñones.

The deep song of flamenco represents a fatalistic attitude to life. Marxists used to say it was a deeply felt protest of the lower classes against their oppressors, but this seems unfounded. Protest or not, over the centuries rich patrons, often brash young men, liked the sound of flamenco and booked artists to stage *juergas* or fiestas where dancer-prostitutes became the erotic extras. By the early 17th century flamenco was linked with pimping, prostitution, and lots and lots of drinking, both from the audience and the artists.

By the mid–19th century, flamenco had gone legitimate and was heard in theaters and *café cantantes*. By the 1920s even the pre-Franco Spanish dictator, Primo de Rivera, was singing the flamenco tunes of his native Cádiz. The poet Federico García Lorca and the composer Manuel de Falla preferred a purer form, attacking what they viewed as the degenerate and "ridiculous" burlesque of *flamenquismo,* the jazzed-up, audience-pleasing form of flamenco. The two artists launched a Flamenco Festival in Grenada in 1922. Of course, in the decades since, their voices have been drowned out, and flamenco is more *flamenquismo* than ever.

In his 1995 book *Flamenco Deep Song,* Thomas Mitchell draws a parallel to flamenco's "lowlife roots" and the "orgiastic origins" of jazz. He notes that early jazz, like flamenco, was "associated with despised ethnic groups, gangsters, brothels, free-spending blue bloods, and whoopee hedonism." By disguising their origins, Mitchell notes, both jazz and flamenco have entered the musical mainstream.

tickets. You'll save money if you go directly to the box office to buy tickets. In the event your choice is sold out, you may be able to get tickets (with a reasonable markup) at **Localidades Galicia** at Plaza del Carmen 1 (☎ **91-531-27-32;** metro: Puerta del Sol). This agency also markets tickets to bullfights and sporting events. It is open Tuesday through Saturday from 9:30am to 1:30pm and 4:30 to 7:30pm; Sunday from 9:30am to 1:30pm; and daily 9:30am to 8pm in May.

Here follows a grab bag of nighttime diversions that might amuse and entertain you. First, the cultural offerings:

MAJOR PERFORMING ARTS COMPANIES

For those who speak Spanish, the **Compañía Nacional de Nuevas Tendencias Escénicas** is an avant-garde troupe that performs new and often controversial works by undiscovered writers. On the other hand, the **Compañía Nacional de Teatro Clásico,** as its name suggests, is devoted to the Spanish classics, including works by the ever-popular Lope de Vega and Tirso de Molina.

Among dance companies, the national ballet of Spain—devoted exclusively to Spanish dance—is the **Ballet Nacional de España.** Their performances are always well attended. The national lyrical ballet company of the country is the **Ballet Lírico Nacional.**

World-renowned flamenco sensation Antonio Canales and his troupe, **Ballet Flamenco Antonio Canales,** offer spirited high-energy performances. Productions are centered around Canales's impassioned *Torero,* his interpretation of a bull-fighter and the physical and emotional struggles within the man. For tickets and information, you can call Madrid's most comprehensive ticket agency, the previously recommended **Localidades Galicia,** Plaza del Carmen, 1 (☎ **91-531-27-32**), for tickets to cultural events and virtually any other event in Castille. Other agencies include **Casa de Catalunya** (☎ **91-538-33-33**) or **Corte Inglés** (☎ **91-432-93-00**). Both Casa de Catalunya and Cortes Inglés have satellite offices located throughout Madrid.

Madrid's opera company is the **Teatro de la Opera,** and its symphony orchestra is the outstanding **Orquesta Sinfónica de Madrid.** The national orchestra of Spain, widely acclaimed on the continent, is the **Orquesta Nacional de España,** which pays particular homage to Spanish composers.

CLASSICAL MUSIC

Auditorio Nacional de Música. Príncipe de Vergara, 146. ☎ **91-337-01-39** or 91-337-01-40. Box office 91-337-03-07. Tickets 1,000–1,200 ptas. ($6.70–$8.05). Metro: Cruz del Rayo.

Sheathed in slabs of Spanish granite, marble, and limestone and capped with Iberian tiles, this hall is the ultramodern home of both the National Orchestra of Spain and the National Chorus of Spain.

Standing just north of Madrid's Salamanca district, it ranks as a major addition to the competitive circles of classical music in Europe. Inaugurated in 1988, it is devoted exclusively to the performances of symphonic, choral, and chamber music. In addition to the Auditorio Principal (Hall A), whose capacity is almost 2,300, there's a hall for chamber music (Hall B), as well as a small auditorium (seating 250) for intimate concerts.

Auditorio del Parque de Atracciones. Casa de Campo. Metro: Lago or Batán.

The schedule of this 3,500-seat facility might include everything from punk-rock musical groups to the more high-brow warm-weather performances of visiting symphony orchestras. Check with Localidades Galicia to see what's on at the time of your visit (see "The Performing Arts," above).

Fundación Juan March. Castelló, 77. ☎ **91-435-42-40.** Metro: Núñez de Balboa.

This foundation sometimes holds free concerts at lunchtime. The advance schedule is difficult to predict, so call for information.

La Fidula. Calle Huerta, 57. ☎ **91-429-29-47.** Cover 500–700 ptas. ($3.35–$4.70). Metro: Antón Martín.

Serving as a bastion of civility in a sea of rock and roll and disco chaos, this club was a converted 1800s grocer. Today, it presents chamber music concerts nightly at 11:30pm with an additional show at 1am on weekends. The club offers the prospect of a tranquil, cultural evening on the town, at a moderate price. They take performances here seriously—late arrivals may not be seated for concerts. It is open Monday through Thursday and Sunday from 7pm to 3am and Friday and Saturday from 7pm to 4am.

Teatro Cultural de la Villa. Plaza de Colón. ☎ **91-575-60-80.** Tickets, depending on event, 1,000–2,500 ptas. ($6.70–$16.75). Metro: Serrano or Colón.

Spanish-style ballet along with *zarzuelas* (musical reviews), orchestral works, and theater pieces, are presented at this cultural center. Tickets go on sale 5 days before the event of your choice, and performances are usually presented at two evening shows (8 and 10:30pm).

○ **Teatro Real.** Plaza Isabel II. ☎ **91-516-06-60.** Tickets 1,000–32,000 ptas. ($6.70–$214.40). Metro: Opera.

Reopened in 1997 after a massive $157 million renovation, this theater is one of the world's finest stage and acoustic settings for opera. Its extensive state-of-the-art equipment affords elaborate stage designs and special effects. Luis Antonio García Navarro, the internationally heralded maestro from Valencia, is the musical and artistic director of the Royal Opera House, at least until 2002, and he works with leading Spanish lyric talents, including Plácido Domingo. Today, the building is the home of the Compañía del Teatro Real, a company specializing in opera, and is also a major venue for classical music. On November 19, 1850, under the reign of Queen Isabel II, the Royal Opera House opened its doors with Donizetti's *La Favorita.*

THEATER

Madrid offers many different theater performances, useful to you only if your Spanish is very fluent. If it isn't, check the *Guía del Ocio* for performances by English-speaking companies on tour from Britain or select a concert or subtitled movie instead.

In addition to the major ones listed below, there are at least 30 other theaters, including one devoted almost entirely to children's plays, the **Sala la Bicicleta,** in the Ciudad de los Niños at Casa de Campo. Nonprofessional groups stage dozens of other plays in such places as churches.

Teatro Calderón. Atocha, 18. ☎ **91-402-36-01.** Tickets 2,000–3,000 ptas. ($13.40–$20.10). Metro: Tirso de Molina.

This is the largest theater in Madrid, with a seating capacity of 2,000. Whereas in the past, this venue included everything from dramatic theater to flamenco, in recent years, it has endorsed a more serious venue that focuses mostly on opera, with performances beginning most evenings at 8pm. At press time, a long-running favorite was Bizet's *Carmen,* whose setting within Spain partly justifies its enduring popularity among Madrileños.

Teatro de la Comedia. Príncipe, 14. ☎ **91-521-49-31.** Tickets 1,300–2,600 ptas. ($8.70–$17.40); 50% discount on Thurs. Metro: Sevilla. Bus: 15, 20, or 150.

This is the home of the Compañía Nacional de Teatro Clásico. Here, more than anywhere else in Madrid, you're likely to see performances from the classic repertoire of such great Spanish dramatists as Lope de Vega and Calderón de la Barca. There are no performances on Wednesday, and the theater is completely shut during July and August. The box office is open daily from 11:30am to 1:30pm and 5 to 6pm, and for about an hour before the performances.

Teatro Español. Príncipe, 25. ☎ **91-429-62-97.** Tickets 200–2,400 ptas. ($1.35–$16.10); 50% discount on Wed. Metro: Sevilla.

This company is funded by Madrid's municipal government, its repertoire a time-tested assortment of great and/or favorite Spanish plays. The box office is open daily from 11:30am to 1:30pm and 5pm to the opening of the show.

Teatro Lírico Nacional de la Zarzuela. Jovellanos, 4. ☎ **91-524-54-00.** Tickets 1,200–4,500 ptas. ($8.05–$30.15). Metro: Sevilla.

Near Plaza de la Cibeles, this theater of potent nostalgia produces ballet and an occasional opera in addition to zarzuela. Show times vary. The box office is open daily from noon to show time.

Teatro María Guerrero. Tamayo y Baus, 4. ☎ **91-319-47-69.** Tickets 1,650–3,600 ptas. ($11.05–$24.10); 50% discount on Wed. Metro: Banco de España or Colón.

Also funded by the government, the María Guerrero (named after a much-loved Spanish actress) works in cooperation with the Teatro Español (see above) for performances of works by such classic Spanish playwrights as Lope de Vega and García Lorca. The box office is open daily from 11:30am to 1:30pm and 5 to 6pm.

Teatro Nuevo Apolo. Plaza de Tirso de Molina, 1. ☎ **91-369-14-67.** Cover usually 2,800 PTAS ($18.75). Metro: Tirso de Molina.

Nuevo Apolo is the permanent home of the renowned Antología de la Zarzuela company. It is on the restored site of the old Teatro Apolo, where these musical variety shows have been performed since the 1930s. Prices and times depend on the show. The box office is open daily from 11:30am to 1:30pm and 5 to 6pm; show times vary.

THE CLUB & MUSIC SCENE
CABARET

Café del Foro. Calle San Andres, 38. ☎ **91-445-37-52.** No cover (but may be imposed for a specially booked act). Metro: Bilboa. Bus: 40, 147, 149, or N19.

This old-time favorite in the Malasaña district has suddenly become hip again. You never know exactly what the show for the evening will be, although live music of some sort generally starts at 11:30pm. Cabaret is often featured, along with live merengue, bolero, and salsa. There's a faux starry sky above the stage area, plus Roman colonnades that justify the name Café del Foro. Open daily from 7pm to 3am.

✪ **Las Noches de Cuplé.** La Palma, 51. ☎ **91-532-71-15.** Cover 7,500 ptas. ($50.25), including dinner, 3,200 ptas. ($21.45) without dinner. Metro: Noviciado.

If you don't mind going to bed at sunrise, you might enjoy this updated version of a once-celebrated Madrileño cabaret. Its entrance is on a narrow, crowded street. Inside, in a long room with a vaulted ceiling and a tiny stage, Señora Olga Ramos conducts an evening of Iberian song in a belle epoque package of castizo songs. The charm of her all-Spanish act is increased by the discreet humor of an octogenarian accompanist with an ostrich-feather tiara and a fuchsia-colored boa. She keeps the Cuplé dances of love and courtship alive, along with tangos and zarzuelas. Open Monday through Saturday from 9:30pm to 2am; shows at 11pm. Drinks begin at 1,100 ptas. ($7.35).

FLAMENCO

Café de Chinitas. Torija, 7. ☎ **91-559-51-35.** Dinner and show 9,800 ptas. ($65.65); cover charge for show without dinner (but with one drink included) 4,450 ptas. ($29.80). Metro: Santo Domingo. Bus: 1 or 2.

One of the best flamenco clubs in town, Café de Chinitas is set one floor above street level in a 19th-century building midway between the Opera and the Gran Vía. It features an array of (usually) gypsy-born flamenco artists from Madrid, Barcelona, and Andalusia, with acts and performers changing about once a month. You can arrange for dinner before the show, although many Madrileños opt for dinner somewhere else and then arrive just for drinks and the flamenco. Open Monday through Saturday, with dinner served from 9 to midnight and the show lasting from 10:30pm to 2am. Reservations are recommended.

Casa Patas. Calle Cañizares, 10. ☎ **91-369-04-96.** Admission 2,500 ptas. ($16.75). Metro: Tirso de Molina.

This club is now one of the best places to see "true" flamenco as opposed to the more touristy version presented at Corral de la Morería (see below). It is also a bar and restaurant, with space reserved in the rear for flamenco. Shows are presented midnight on Thursday, Friday, and Saturday and during Madrid's major fiesta month of May. The best flamenco in Madrid is presented here. Proof of the pudding is that flamenco singers and dancers often hang out here after hours. Tapas—priced at 450 to 2,500 ptas. ($3 to $16.75)—are available at the bar. The club is open daily from 8pm to 2:30am.

Corral de la Morería. Morería, 17. ☎ **91-365-84-46.** Cover one-drink minimum 4,200 ptas. ($28.15); 11,000 ptas. ($73.70) with dinner. Metro: La Latina or Puerta del Sol.

In the old town, the Morería ("where the Moors reside") sizzles with flamenco, though it's definitely a tourist crowd. Colorfully costumed strolling performers warm up the audience around 11pm; a flamenco show follows, with at least 10 dancers. It's much cheaper to eat somewhere else first, paying only the one-drink minimum. Open daily from 9:15pm to 2am.

JAZZ

✪ **Café Central.** Plaza del Angel, 10. ☎ **91-369-41-43.** Cover charge 1,300 ptas. ($8.70), prices can vary depending on show. Metro: Antón Martín.

Off the Plaza de Santa Ana, beside the famed Gran Hotel Victoria, the Café Central has a vaguely turn-of-the-century art deco interior, with an unusual series of stained-glass windows. Many of the customers read newspapers and talk at the marble-top tables during the day, but the ambience is far more animated during the nightly jazz sessions, which are ranked among the best in Spain, often drawing top artists. Open Sunday through Thursday from 1:30pm to 2:30am, Friday and Saturday from 1:30pm to 3:30am; live jazz is offered daily from 10pm to midnight. Beer costs 400 ptas. ($2.70).

Café Populart. Calle Huertas, 22. ☎ **91-429-84-07.** Metro: Antón Martín or Sevilla. Bus: 6 or 60.

This club is known for its exciting jazz groups, which encourage the audience to dance. It specializes in Brazilian, Afro-bass, reggae, and new wave African music. When the music starts, usually around 11pm, the prices of drinks are nearly doubled. Open daily from 6pm to 3 or 4am. Beer costs 350 ptas. ($2.35), whisky with soda 600 ptas. ($4) when live music isn't playing. After the music begins, beer costs 600 ptas. ($4), whisky with soda 950 ptas. ($6.35).

Clamores. Albuquerque, 14. ☎ **91-445-79-38.** Cover Tues–Sat usually 600–1,200 ptas. ($4–$8.05), but varies with act; no cover Sun–Mon. Metro: Bilbao.

With dozens of small tables and a huge bar in its dark and smoky interior, Clamores, which means noises in Spain, is the largest and one of the most popular jazz clubs in Madrid. Established in the early 1980s, it has thrived because of the diverse roster of American and Spanish jazz bands who have appeared here. The place is open daily from 7pm to around 3am, but jazz is presented only Tuesday through Saturday. Tuesday through Thursday, performances are at 11pm and again at 1am; Saturday, performances begin at 11:30pm, with an additional show at 1:30am. There are jam sessions on Sunday night, and no live performances on Monday night, when the format is recorded disco music. Regardless of the night of the week you consume them, drinks begin at around 700 ptas. ($4.70) each.

DANCE CLUBS

The Spanish dance club takes its inspiration from those of other Western capitals. In Madrid, most clubs are open from around 6pm to 9pm, later reopening around 11pm. They generally start rocking at midnight or thereabouts.

Joy Eslava. Arenal, 1. ☎ **91-366-37-33.** Admission 2,000 ptas. ($13.40), including first drink. Metro: Puerta del Sol.

Set near the Puerta del Sol, this place has survived the passing fashions of Madrileño nightlife with more style than many of its (now-defunct) competitors. Virtually everyone in Madrid is likely to show up here, ranging from traveling sales reps in town from Düsseldorf to the youthful members of the Madrileño *movida*. Open nightly from 10pm to 6:30am. Drinks are 1,500 ptas. ($10.05) each.

Kapital. Atocha, 125. ☎ **91-420-29-06.** Admission 2,000 ptas. ($13.40), including first drink. Metro: Antón Martín.

This is the most sprawling, labyrinthine, and multicultural disco in Madrid at the moment. Set within what was originally conceived as a theater, it contains seven different levels, each of which sports at least one bar and an ambience that's often radically different from the one you just left on a previous floor. Voyeurs of any age take heart—there's a lot to see at the Kapital, with a mixed crowd that pursues whatever form of sexuality seems appropriate at the moment. Open Thursday through Sunday 11:30pm to 5:30am. Second drinks from 1,000 ptas. ($6.70) each.

Long Play. Plaza Vasquez de Mella, 2. ☎ **91-532-90-69.** Admission 1,000 ptas. ($6.70), including first drink. Metro: Gran Vía.

Catering to crowds of all ages, and sexual orientations, Long Play manages to combine disco music with long stretches of bars, comfortable tables and chairs, and a crowd with seemingly nothing to do but dance, dance, dance. Recorded music sometimes gives way to live bands. Open Friday and Saturday from midnight to 5:30am.

Pachá. Calle Barcelo, 11. ☎ **91-446-01-37.** Admission 2,000 ptas. ($13.40), including first drink. Metro: Tribunal.

The carefully contrived setting is pseudo-opulent, and the drinks sometimes hard to get because of the milling crowds. Despite that, Pachá thrives as one of the late-night staples in Madrid for the mid-20s to late-40s clientele (a crowd that often segregates itself by age into distinctly different areas of the place). More than other nightclubs in Madrid, this has been the subject of complaints from neighbors about late-night noise. It's open Monday through Saturday 11pm to 6:30am.

A LITTLE BIT OF EVERYTHING

Bagëlus. Calle María de Molina, 25. ☎ **91-561-61-00.** No cover. Metro: Avenida America.

Bagëlus is a bit of an oddity in Madrid, providing entertainment and shopping 24 hours a day, spread over a four-story building. A Spanish adaptation of the American mall theme, restaurants, cafes, bookstores, music stores, discos, and just about everything imaginable can be found. Sip on a drink and book your next vacation at the travel agency, indulge yourself with live music from cabaret to flamenco, or just sit back and observe Madrid's version of yuppies hustling from shop to shop.

THE BAR SCENE
PUBS & BARS

Balmoral. Hermosilia, 10. ☎ **91-431-41-33.** Metro: Serrano.

Its exposed wood and comfortable chairs evoke a London club. The clientele tends toward journalists, politicians, army brass, owners of large estates, bankers, diplomats, and the occasional literary star. *Newsweek* magazine dubbed it one of the "best bars in the world." No food other than tapas is served. Open Monday through Saturday from 12:30pm to 2:30 or 3am. Beer is 500 ptas. ($3.35); drinks are from 900 ptas. ($6.05).

Balneario. Juan Ramón Jiménez, 37. ☎ **91-350-87-76.** Metro: Cuzco.

Clients enjoy potent drinks in a setting with fresh flowers, white marble, and a stone bathtub that might have been used by Josephine Bonaparte. Near Chamartín Station on the northern edge of Madrid, Balneario is one of the most stylish and upscale bars in the city. It is adjacent to and managed by one of Madrid's most elegant and prestigious restaurants, El Cabo Mayor, and often attracts that dining room's clients for aperitifs or after-dinner drinks. Tapas include endive with smoked salmon, asparagus mousse, and anchovies with avocado. Open Monday through Saturday from noon to 2:30am. Drinks are 650 to 1,000 ptas. ($4.35 to $6.70); tapas cost 500 to 1,800 ptas. ($3.35 to $12.05).

Bar Cock. De la Reina, 16. ☎ **91-532-28-26.** Metro: Gran Vía.

This bar on two floors attracts some of the most visible artists, actors, models, and filmmakers in Madrid. The name comes from the word *cocktail,* or so they say. The decoration is elaborate and unique, in contrast to the hip clientele, and the martinis are Madrid's best. Open daily from 7pm to 3am; closed December 24 to 31. Drinks are 1,000 ptas. ($6.70).

Bar Taurino. In the Hotel Reina Victoria, Plaza Santa Ana. ☎ **91-531-45-00.** Metro: Antón Martín.

Ava and Ernesto have long departed, but this bar remains the number one gathering spot for bullfight aficionados. A multitiered place, it is still a shrine to Manolete, the greatest matador of the '50s who was praised by Hemingway. This is no rough-and-tumble bar, but a cultured venue often attracting Madrid society. It reaches the peak of its excitement during the San Isidro bullfighting festival, when Spain's top bullfighters often make appearances here in their full death in the afternoon suits of light. Hours are daily 11:30am to 11:30pm.

✪ Chicote. Gran Vía, 12. ☎ **91-532-67-37.** Metro: Gran Vía.

Beloved by Hemingway, who had quite a few drinks here, this is Madrid's most famous cocktail bar. It's classic retro chic, with the same 1930s interior design it had when the foreign press came to sit out the Civil War, although the sound of artillery shells along the Gran Vía could be heard at the time. Even the seats are the same ones that held such luminaries as Don Ernesto, Luis Buñuel, Gary Cooper, Grace Kelly, and Ava Gardner. Long a favorite of artists and writers, the bar became a haven for prostitutes in the late Franco era. No more. It's back in the limelight again, a sophisticated and much-frequented rendezvous. Open Monday to Saturday 8am to 3am (until 4am on Friday and Saturday). Drinks cost from 1,000 ptas. ($6.70) Monday to Saturday, but the waiters serve them with such grace you don't mind.

Hispano Bar/Buffet. Paseo de la Castellana, 78. ☎ **91-411-48-76.** Metro: Nuevos Ministerios.

This establishment does a respectable lunch trade every day for members of the local business community, who crowd in to enjoy the amply portioned platos del día. These might include a platter of roast duck with figs or orange sauce, or a supreme of hake.

After around 5pm, however, the ambience becomes that of a busy after-office bar, patronized by stylishly dressed women and many local entrepreneurs. The hubbub continues on into the night. Open daily from 1:30pm to 2am. Full meals at lunchtime cost from around 4,500 to 5,000 ptas. ($30.15 to $33.50), while beer, depending on the time of day you order it, costs about 300 ptas. ($2).

La Venencia. Calle Echegary, 7. ☎ **91-429-73-13.** Metro: Sevilla.

On one of the traditional tasca streets in Old Madrid, this tavern has a distinct personality. It is dedicated to the art of serving Spain's finest sherry—and that's it. Don't come in here asking for an extra dry martini. Our favorite remains Manzanilla, a delicate fino with just a little chill on it. If Luis Buñuel were to need extras in a film, surely the patrons here would be an ideal backdrop. To go with all that sherry, the waiters (a little rough around the edges) will serve tapas, especially those garlicky marinated olives, majoama (cured tuna), and blue-cheese canapés. Barrels form the decor, along with antique posters long turned tobacco-gold from the cigarette smoke. Open daily 7:30pm to 1:30am (until 2am on Friday and Saturday).

Los Gabrieles. Echegaray, 17. ☎ **91-429-62-61.** Metro: Puerta de Sol, Sevilla.

Located in the heart of one of Madrid's most visible warrens of narrow streets, in a district that pulsates with after-dark nightlife options, this historic bar served throughout most of the 19th century as the sales outlet for a Spanish wine merchant. Its cellar was once a fabled Gypsy bordello. In the 1980s its two rooms were transformed into a bar and cafe, where you can admire lavishly tiled walls with detailed scenes of courtiers, dancers, and Andalusian maidens peering from behind mantillas and fans. Open daily from noon to 3:30am. Beer costs 275 to 400 ptas. ($2.70).

Palacio Gaviria. Calle del Arenal, 9. ☎ **91-526-6069.** Cover 2,000 ptas. ($13.40), including first drink. Metro: Puerta del Sol or Opera.

Its construction in 1847 was heralded as the architectural triumph of one of the era's most flamboyant aristocrats, the marqués de Gaviria. Famous as one of the paramours of Queen Isabella II, he outfitted his palace with the ornate jumble of neoclassical and baroque styles that later became known as *Isabelino.* In 1993, after extensive renovations, the building was opened to the public as a concert hall for the occasional presentation of classical music and as a late-night cocktail bar. Ten high-ceilinged rooms now function as richly decorated, multipurpose areas for guests to wander in, drinks in hand, reacting to whatever, or whomever, happens to be there at the time. (One room is discreetly referred to as having been the bedroom-away-from-home of the queen herself.) No food is served, but the libations include a stylish list of cocktails and wines. The often-dull music doesn't match the elegance of the decor. Thursdays through Saturdays are usually dance nights, everything from the tango to the waltz. Cabaret is usually featured on most other nights. Open Monday through Friday from 9pm to 3am; Saturday and Sunday from 9pm to 5am. Second drinks start at 1,200 ptas. ($8.05).

Teatriz. Hermosilla, 15. ☎ **91-577-53-79.** Metro: Serrano.

Part of its function is as a restaurant where soft lighting and a decor by world-class decorator Philippe Starck create one of the most stylish-looking and avant-garde environments in Madrid. A meal averages around 3,000 ptas. ($20.10) at lunch and 4,000 ptas. ($26.80) in the evening, but if it's just a drink you're looking for, consider an extended session at any of the site's three bars. Here, within a setting not quite like a disco, but with a sound system almost as good, you'll find a music bar environment where stylish folk of all persuasions enjoy drinks and the gossip that seems to both originate and be magnified at a place like this. The restaurant is open daily from 9am to 1pm and 1:30 to 4pm. The bars are best appreciated every night from 9pm to 3am.

✪ **Viva Madrid.** Manuel Fernández y González, 7. ☎ **91-410-55-35.** Metro: Sevilla.

A congenial and sudsy mix of students, artists, and foreign tourists cram into the turn-of-the-century interior here, where antique tile murals and blatant belle epoque nostalgia contribute to an undeniable charm. In the good old days (the '50s, that is), the fabled beautiful people showed up here, notably Ava Gardner with the bullfighter Manolete, when they couldn't take their hands off each other. But Orson Welles or even Louis Armstrong used to pop in as well. Crowded and noisy, it's a place where lots of beer is swilled and spilled. It's set within a neighborhood of antique houses and narrow streets near the Plaza de Santa Ana. Open Friday from noon to 1am, Saturday from noon to 2am. Beer costs 500 ptas. ($3.35); whisky begins at 875 ptas. ($5.85).

GAY & LESBIAN BARS

Black and White. Gravina (at corner of Libertad). ☎ **91-531-11-41.** Metro: Chueca.

This is the major gay bar of Madrid, located in the center of the Chueca district. A guard will open the door to a large room—painted, as you might expect, black and white. There's a disco in the basement, but the street-level bar is the premier gathering spot, featuring drag shows beginning at 3am Thursday through Sunday, male striptease, and videos. Old movies are shown against one wall. Warning: This bar is frequented by young, potentially dangerous hustlers. Open Monday through Friday from 8pm to 5am; Saturday and Sunday from 8pm to 6am. Beer is 500 ptas. ($3.35); whisky costs 850 ptas. ($5.70).

Café Figueroa. Augusto Figueroa, 17 (at corner of Hortaleza). ☎ **91-521-16-73.** Metro: Chueca.

This turn-of-the-century cafe attracts a diverse clientele, including a large number of gay men and lesbians. It's one of the city's most popular gathering spots for drinks and conversations. Open daily from 12:30pm to 1am. Beer from 400 ptas. ($2.70); whisky costs from 700 ptas. ($4.70).

Cruising. Perez Galdos, 5. ☎ **91-521-51-43.** Metro: Chueca.

One of the landmark gay bars of Madrid, a center for gay consciousness-raising and gay cruising, this place has probably been visited at least once by every gay male in Castile. There are virtually no women inside, but always a hustler looking for a tourist john. It doesn't get crowded or lively until late at night. Open daily from 7pm to 3:30am. Beer costs from 400 to 500 ptas. ($2.70 to $3.35).

New Leather Bar. Calle Pelayo, 42. ☎ **91-308-14-62.** No cover, but a minimum charge of 400 ptas. ($2.70). Metro: Chueca.

This is another of the premier venues for gay men in Madrid, but despite its supposed emphasis on leather and uniforms, only about 25% of the men who show up actually wear them. You'll find two bars on the establishment's street level, and a disco within the basement where same-sex couples can dance. The place can be fun, especially since, in the words of one of the more gregarious bartenders, "I think everybody's gay." Beer costs 450 ptas. ($3). It's open Sunday to Thursday from 9pm to 3am; Friday and Saturday from 9pm to 3:30am.

Olimpo. Calle Aculana, 21. No phone. Metro: Sevilla. Cover 1,000 ptas. ($6.70).

In direct competition with Refugio, Olimpo is the other main nightclub for gay men in Madrid. The crowd is generally young but open to all ages, with the shared goal of dancing and romancing. The club is replete with go-go boys and regularly features drag shows and even the occasional striptease. Olimpo also hosts relatively frequent theme nights, such as a recent underwear evening where patrons were encouraged to wear nothing but their underwear. The disco is open from Wednesday to Sunday from 11pm to 7am.

Refugio. Calle Doctor Cortezo, 1. ☎ **91-369-40-38.** Cover 1,000 ptas. ($6.70); 500 ptas. ($3.35) before 2. Metro: Tirso de Molina.

This is one of the best-established, most deeply entrenched venues for gay men in Madrid, with a strong emphasis on dancing, drinking, and dialogue, or simply standing and cruising whenever it feels appropriate. The interior is like a grotto with nude gladiator statues, equaled only by the caged dancing boys stirring up libidos. Larger than many of its gay competitors within Madrid, it sometimes hosts theme nights (golden oldies nights, merengue nights, and so on), that regrettably, don't really get going until very, very late. It's open nightly from midnight to 6am.

Sutileza. Plaza de Chueca. No phone. Metro: Chueca.

Leading the way as one of the various lesbian bars now established in Plaza de Chueca, the Sutileza is the perfect commencing point for the discerning lesbian on the prowl. The crowd is predominately women with a few gay men thrown in for good measure. From May to September there is an outside terrazza which competes with the other lesbian bars in the square, namely Escape and Truco. The atmosphere at all the bars in the square is friendly and frequently quite cruisey. As with all the bars in the square, Sutileza is open from Tuesday to Thursday and Sunday from 8pm to 3am, and on Friday and Saturday from 9pm to 4am.

Tabata. Vergara, 12. ☎ **91-547-97-35.** Metro: Opera.

This is a very popular bar with more than a few heartbreakers amongst the crowd. The atmosphere is very lively with popular dance music encouraging the patrons to dance wherever possible in the venue's rather limited space. This is one of the friendliest bars in Madrid and full of opportunities to strike up conversation with the locals. It's open from Wednesday to Saturday from 10pm to 6am.

Rick's. Calle Clavel, 8. No phone. Metro: Chueca.

Rick's takes its name from "Everybody Comes to Rick's," the original title of the Bogie classic, *Casablanca*. Many gay bars in the Chueca barrio are sleazy, but this is a classy joint, just like the fictional Rick's in Morocco. It's decorated with Bogie paraphernalia, including marble floors and gilt columns. The only thing missing is a piano player singing *As Time Goes By*, and Bergman, of course. Gay men patronize the place, with the occasional woman showing up, too. Incongruously, it has a foos ball table in the bar but lavender walls. It's open daily from 11:30am "until some time in the morning."

SUMMER TERRAZAS

At the first blush of spring weather, Madrileños rush outdoors to drink, talk, and sit at a string of open-air cafes, called *terrazas*, throughout the city. The best and most expensive ones are along Paseo de la Castellana between Plaza de la Cibeles and Plaza Emilio Castelar, but there are dozens more throughout the city.

You can wander up and down the boulevard, selecting one that appeals to you; if you get bored, you can go on later to another one. Sometimes these terrazas are called *chiringuitos*. You'll also find them along other paseos, the Recoletos and the Prado, both fashionable areas, although not as hip as the Castellana. For old, traditional atmosphere, the terraces at Plaza Mayor win out. Plaza Santa Ana also has several atmospheric choices within the old city. Friday and Saturday are the most popular nights for drinking; many locals sit here all night.

CAVE CRAWLING

To capture a peculiar Madrid joie de vivre of the 18th century, visit some mesones and cuevas, many found in the barrios bajos. From Plaza Mayor, walk down the Arco de Cuchilleros until you find a gypsylike cave that fits your fancy. Young people love to meet in the taverns and caves of Old Madrid for communal drinking and songfests. The sangría flows freely, the atmosphere is charged, and the room usually is packed; the sounds of guitars waft into the night air. Sometimes you'll see a strolling band of singing students going from bar to bar, colorfully attired, with ribbons fluttering from their outfits.

Mesón de la Guitarra. Cava de San Miguel, 13. ☎ **91-559-95-31.** Metro: Puerta del Sol or Opera.

Our favorite cueva in the area, Mesón de la Guitarra is loud and exciting on any night of the week, and it's as warmly earthy as anything you'll find in Madrid. The decor combines terra-cotta floors, antique brick walls, hundreds of sangría pitchers clustered above the bar, murals of gluttons, old rifles, and faded bullfighting posters. Like most things in Madrid, the place doesn't get rolling until around 10:30pm, although you can stop in for a drink and tapas earlier. Don't be afraid to start singing an American song if it has a fast rhythm—60 people will join in, even if they don't know the words. Open daily from 7pm to 2am. Beer is 200 ptas. ($1.35); wine is from 100 ptas. (65¢); tapas are 800 to 1,000 ptas. ($5.35 to $6.70).

Mesón del Champiñón. Cava de San Miguel, 17. No phone. Metro: Puerta del Sol or Opera.

The bartenders keep a brimming bucket of sangría behind the long stand-up bar as a thirst quencher for the crowd. The name of the establishment in English is Mushroom, and that is exactly what you'll see depicted in various sizes along sections of the vaulted ceilings. A more appetizing way to experience a *champiñón* is to order a ración of grilled, stuffed, and salted mushrooms, served with toothpicks. Two tiny, slightly dark rooms in the back are where Spanish families go to hear organ music performed. Unless you want to be exiled to the very back, don't expect to get a seat. Practically everybody prefers to stand. Open daily from 6pm to 2am.

Sesamo. Príncipe, 7. ☎ **91-429-65-24.** Metro: Sevilla or Puerta del Sol.

In a class by itself, this cueva, dating from the early 1950s, draws a clientele of young painters and writers with its bohemian ambience. Hemingway was one of those early visitors (a plaque commemorates him). At first you'll think you're walking into a tiny snack bar—and you are. But proceed down the flight of steps to the cellar. Here, the walls are covered with contemporary paintings and quotations. At squatty stools and tables, an international assortment of young people listens to piano music and sometimes piano or guitar playing. Open daily from 6pm to 2:30am. A pitcher of sangría (for four) is 1,200 ptas. ($8.05); beer costs 300 ptas. ($2).

MORE ENTERTAINMENT

MOVIES Cinematic releases from Paris, New York, Rome, and Hollywood come quickly to Madrid, where an avid audience often waits in long lines for tickets. Most foreign films are dubbed into Spanish, unless they're indicated as VO (original version).

Madrid boasts at least 90 legitimate movie houses (many of which have several theaters under one roof) and many others with adult entertainment only. The premier theaters of the city are the enormous, slightly faded movie palaces of the Gran Vía, whose huge movie marquees announce in lurid colors whichever romantic or adventure espectáculo happens to be playing at the moment. For listings, consult *Guía del Ocio* or *Guía de Diario 16* (both available at newsstands), or a newspaper.

If you want to see a film while in Madrid, one of the best places is the quadruplex **Alphaville,** Martín de los Heroes, 14 (☎ **91-559-38-36;** metro: Plaza de España). Its films come from throughout Spain and the rest of Europe and North America, and include some of the most hip and sometimes controversial films anywhere, as well as good, old-fashioned Hispanic romance films. Admission is 800 ptas. ($5.35). The complex also includes a bookstore and a cafe decorated in art deco style.

For classic revivals and foreign films, check the listings at Filmoteca in the *Cine Doré,* Santa Isabel, 3 (☎ **91-369-11-25;** metro: Antón Martín). One of the best-recommended movie complexes in Madrid, this organization tends to show films (French, American, Spanish, English, and others) in their original version, with Spanish subtitles. Presentations begin every night at 5pm, and continue until the late show every evening between 10pm and 11pm. Tickets cost 225 ptas. ($1.50) each. There's a bar and a simple restaurant on the premises.

A CASINO   Casino Gran Madrid is at km 29 along the Carretera La Coruña (the A6 highway running between Madrid and La Coruña), Apartado 62 (☎ **91-856-11-00).** The largest gambling venue in Madrid, it appeals to nongamblers with a well-choreographed roster of dining and entertainment facilities, including two restaurants, four bars, and a nightclub. And if you happen to enjoy gambling, there are facilities for French and American roulette, blackjack, punto y banco, baccarat, and chemin de fer. Presentation of a passport at the door is essential—without it, you won't be admitted. Entrance costs 500 ptas. ($3.35), although that fee is often waived for residents of some of Madrid's larger hotels who arrive with a ticket that's sometimes provided gratis by the hotel's management. The casino and all of its facilities are open daily from 4pm to 5am.

An à la carte restaurant in the French Gaming Room offers international cuisine, with dinners costing from 7,000 ptas. ($46.90). A buffet in the American Gaming Room will cost around 3,000 ptas. ($20.10). The restaurants are open from 9:15pm to 2am. The casino is about 18 miles (29km) northwest of Madrid, along the Madrid–La Coruña N-VI highway. If you don't feel like driving, the casino has buses that depart from Plaza de España, 6, every afternoon and evening at 4:30, 6, 7:30, and 9pm. Note that between October and June, men must wear jackets and ties; T-shirts and tennis shoes are forbidden in any season. To enter, European visitors must present an identity card and non-European visitors must present a passport.

4

Side Trips from Madrid

Madrid makes an ideal base for excursions because it's surrounded by some of Spain's major attractions. The day trips listed below to both New Castile and Old Castile range from 9 miles to 100 miles (14km to 161km) outside Madrid, allowing you to leave in the morning and be back by nightfall. In case you choose to stay overnight, however, we've included a selection of hotels in each town.

The satellite cities and towns around Madrid include Toledo, with its El Greco masterpieces; the wondrous El Escorial monastery; Segovia's castles that seem to float in the clouds; and the Bourbon palaces at La Granja. Cuenca, which is actually in La Mancha, is the longest excursion; so unless you want to spend a good part of the day getting there and back, you should consider it an overnight trip. For a selection of other cities in Old Castile—each of which is better visited on an overnight stopover rather than a day trip from Madrid—refer to chapter 5.

1 Toledo

42 miles (68km) SW of Madrid, 85 miles (137km) SE of Ávila

If you have only 1 day for an excursion outside Madrid, go to Toledo—a place made special by its Arab, Jewish, Christian, and even Roman and Visigothic elements. A national landmark, the city that so inspired El Greco in the 16th century has remained relatively unchanged. You can still stroll through streets barely wide enough for a man and his donkey—much less for an automobile.

Surrounded on three sides by a bend in the Tagus River, Toledo stands atop a hill overlooking the arid plains of New Castile—a natural fortress in the center of the Iberian Peninsula. It was a logical choice for the capital of Spain, though it lost its political status to Madrid in the 1500s. Toledo has remained the country's religious center, as the seat of the Primate of Spain.

If you're driving, the much-painted skyline of Toledo will come into view about 3½ miles (6km) from the city. When you cross the Tagus River on the 14th-century Puente San Martín, the scene is reminiscent of El Greco's moody, storm-threatened *View of Toledo,* which hangs in New York's Metropolitan Museum of Art. The artist reputedly painted that view from a hillside that is now the site of Parador Nacional de Conde Orgaz. If you arrive at the right time, you can enjoy an apéritif

0   10 mi

0   10 km

N110

Sierra de Guadarrama

Segovia

San Idelfonso
la Granja

604

100

101

Sierra de Gredos

To
Ávila
←

600

607

E5

NI

102   Guadalajara

Colmenar
Viejo

San Lorenzo
de El Escorial

El Pardo

San Sebastián
de los Reyes

E90

Valle de los Caídos

Galapagar

A6

Aravaca

Barajas Airport

Alcalá de
Henares

Las Rozas

Pozuelo

NII

★ MADRID

Mejorada
del Campo

404

602

Alcorcón

C600

Leganés

Arganda

San Martín
de la Vega

Chinchón   NIII

NV

Ciempozuelos

E901

E90

Illescas

N401

To
Cuenca
→

Aranjuez

N400

Ocaña

N400

N403

N301

502

NIV

Toledo

E5

401   N401

Legend

Airport ✈

La
Guarda

on the parador's terrace and watch one of the famous violet sunsets of Toledo (see "Where to Stay," below).

Another Toledan highlight is the **Carretera de Circunvalación,** the route that threads through the city and runs along the Tagus. Clinging to the hillsides are rustic dwellings, the cigarrales of the Imperial City, immortalized by 17th-century dramatist Tirso de Molina, who named his trilogy *Los Cigarrales de Toledo.*

ESSENTIALS

GETTING THERE   RENFE trains run here frequently every day. Those departing Madrid's Atocha Railway Station for Toledo run daily from 7am to 9:50pm; those leaving Toledo for Madrid run daily from 7am to 9pm. Traveling time is approximately 2 hours and a one-way fare costs 630 ptas. ($4.20). For train information in Madrid call ☎ **91-328-90-20;** in Toledo call ☎ **925-22-30-99.**

It's actually easier to take the bus from Madrid than the train. Buses are maintained by several companies, the largest of which include **Continental** or **Galiano.** They depart from Madrid's Estación Sur de Autobuses (South Bus Station), calle Méndez Alvaro (☎ **91-468-42-00** for information), every day between 6:30am and 10pm at 30-minute intervals. The fastest leave Monday through Friday on the hour. Those that depart weekdays on the half hour, and those that run on weekends, take a bit longer. Travel time, depending on whether the bus stops at villages en route, is between 1 hour and 1 hour 20 minutes. One-way transit costs 580 ptas. ($3.90).

Once you reach Toledo, you'll be deposited at the Estación de Autobuses, which lies beside the river, about ¾ mile from the historic center. Although many visitors opt to walk, be ready to climb a hill. Bus numbers 5 and 6 run from the station uphill to the center, charging 115 ptas. (75¢) for the brief ride. Pay the driver directly.

If you're driving, exit Madrid via Cibeles (Paseo del Prado) and take the N-401 south.

VISITOR INFORMATION   The tourist information office is at Puerta de Bisagra (☎ **925-22-08-43**). It's open Monday through Friday from 9am to 6pm, Saturday from 9am to 7pm, and Sunday from 9am to 3pm.

EXPLORING THE TOWN

✪ **Cathedral.** Arco de Palacio. ☎ **925-22-22-41.** Free admission to cathedral; Treasure Room 500 ptas. ($3.35). Daily 10:30am–1:30pm and 3:30–6pm. Bus: 5 or 6.

Ranked among the greatest Gothic structures, the cathedral actually reflects several styles, since more than 2½ centuries elapsed during its construction (1226–1493). Many historic events transpired here, including the proclamation of Joanna the Mad and her husband, Philip the Handsome, as heirs to the throne of Spain.

Among its art treasures, the transparente stands out—a wall of marble and florid baroque alabaster sculpture overlooked for years because the cathedral was too poorly lit. Sculptor Narciso Tomé cut a hole in the ceiling, much to the consternation of Toledans, and now light touches the high-rising angels, a *Last Supper* in alabaster, and a Virgin in ascension.

The 16th-century Capilla Mozárabe, containing works by Juan de Borgona, is another curiosity of the cathedral. Mass is still held here using Mozarabic liturgy.

The Treasure Room has a 500-pound 15th-century gilded monstrance—*allegedly* made with gold brought back from the New World by Columbus—that is still carried through the streets of Toledo during the feast of Corpus Christi.

Other highlights of the cathedral include El Greco's Twelve Apostles and Spoliation of Christ and Goya's Arrest of Christ on the Mount of Olives.

The Alcázar. Calle General Moscardó, 4, near the Plaza de Zocodover. ☎ **925-22-30-38.** Admission 125 ptas. (85¢) adults, free for children under 10. Tues–Sun 10am–2pm and 4–6pm (6:30pm July–Sept). Bus: 5 or 6.

The Alcázar, located at the eastern edge of the old city, dominates the Toledo skyline. It became world famous at the beginning of the Spanish Civil War, when it underwent a 70-day siege that almost destroyed it (see "The Siege of the Alcázar," below). Today it has been rebuilt and turned into an army museum, housing such exhibits as a plastic model of what the fortress looked like after the Civil War, electronic equipment used during the siege, and photographs taken during the height of the battle. A walking tour gives a realistic simulation of the siege. Allow an hour for a visit.

✪ **Museo de Santa Cruz.** Calle Miguel de Cervantes, 3. ☎ **925-22-14-02.** Admission 200 ptas. ($1.35) adults, 100 ptas. (65¢) students, and free for children. Mon–Sat 10am–6pm, Sun 10am–2pm. Bus: 5 or 6. Pass beneath the granite archway on the eastern edge of the Plaza de Zocodover and walk about 1 block.

Today a museum of art and sculpture, this was originally a 16th-century Spanish Renaissance hospice, founded by Cardinal Mendoza, "the third King of Spain," who helped Ferdinand and Isabella gain the throne. The facade is almost more spectacular than any of the exhibits inside. It's a stunning architectural achievement in the classical plateresque style. The major artistic treasure inside is El Greco's *The Assumption of the Virgin,* his last known work. Paintings by Goya and Ribera are also on display along with gold items, opulent antique furnishings, Flemish tapestries, and even Visigoth artifacts. In the patio of the museum you'll stumble across various fragments of carved stone and sarcophagi lids. One of the major exhibits is of a large Astrolablio tapestry of the zodiac from the 1400s. In the basement you can see artifacts, including elephant tusks, from various archaeological digs throughout the province.

Casa y Museo de El Greco. Calle Samuel Leví, 3. ☎ **925-22-40-46.** Admission 200 ptas. ($1.35) adults, free for children under 10. Tues–Sat 10am–2pm and 4–6pm, Sun 10am–2pm. Bus: 5 or 6.

Located in Toledo's *antiguo barrio judío* (the old Jewish quarter, a labyrinth of narrow streets on the old town's southwestern edge), the House of El Greco honors the great master painter, although he didn't actually live here. In 1585 the artist moved into one of the run-down palace apartments belonging to the marqués of Villena. Although he was to live at other Toledan addresses, he returned to the Villena palace in 1604 and remained there until his death. Only a small part of the original residence was saved from decay. In time, this and a neighboring house became the El Greco museum; today it's furnished with authentic period pieces.

You can visit El Greco's so-called studio, where one of his paintings hangs. The museum contains several more works, including a copy of *A View of Toledo* and three portraits, plus many pictures by various 16th- and 17th-century Spanish artists. The garden and especially the kitchen also merit attention, as does a sitting room decorated in the Moorish style.

Sinagoga del Tránsito. Calle Samuel Leví. ☎ **925-22-36-65.** Admission 400 ptas. ($2.70). Tues–Sat 10am–1:45pm and 4–5:45pm, Sun 10am–1:45pm. Closed Jan 1, May 1, Dec 24–25, and Dec 31. Bus: 2.

One block west of the El Greco home and museum stands this once-important house of worship for Toledo's large Jewish population. A 14th-century building, it is noted for its superb stucco Hebrew inscriptions, including psalms inscribed along the top of the walls and a poetic description of the Temple on the east wall. The synagogue is the most important part of the **Museo Sefardí** (Sephardic Museum), which opened in

Toledo

Alcázar **8**
Casa y Museo de El Greco **5**
Catedral **7**
Hospital de Tavera **1**
Iglesia de San Juan de los Reyes **2**
Iglesia de Santo Tomé **6**
Museo de Santa Cruz **9**
Sinagoga de Santa María La Blanca **3**
Sinagoga del Tránsito **4**

C. del Rio Llano

Pza.
del Solar

Bajada de la
Antequeruela

C. de Azacanes

Puente de Azarquiel

Railway
Station

C. Gerardo Lobo

C. de Múñez de Arce

C. Venancio González

C. de
la Silliria

Pza. de
Zocodover

C. Armas

C. Nueva

C. Toledo
Ohio

C. Comercio

Barrio
Rey

Alfereces Provisionales

9

Puente de
Alcántara

C. Martin
Gamero

Pza.
Mayor

8

C. de Capuchinos

C. Pasquales

Puerta
Llana

Puente
Nuevo

Ruinas
Acqueducto
Romano

Pza.
San Justo

C. San Justo

Ronda de Juanelo

Rio Tajo

Pza.
San
Lucas

C. de
San Lucas

C. del Pozo Amargo

Pza.
Don
Fernando

C. del
Plegadero

Pobre

San Sebastián

to Parador

Legend

Bus Stop 🚌
Church ✝
Information ⓘ
Post Office ✉

145

1971 and contains art objects as well as tombstones with Hebrew epigraphy, some of which are dated before 1492.

Monasterio de San Juan de los Reyes. Calle Reyes Católicos, 17. ☎ **925-22-38-02.** Admission 150 ptas. ($1) adults, free for children 8 and under. Winter, daily 10am–1:45pm and 3:30–6pm; summer, daily 10am–1:45pm and 3:30–7pm. Bus: 2.

Founded by King Ferdinand and Queen Isabella to commemorate their triumph over the Portuguese at Toro in 1476, the church was started in 1477 according to the plans of architect Juan Guas. It was finished, together with the splendid cloisters, in 1504, dedicated to St. John the Evangelist, and used from the beginning by the Franciscan friars. An example of Gothic-Spanish-Flemish style, San Juan de los Reyes was restored after the damage caused during Napoléon's invasion and after its abandonment in 1835; since 1954 it has been entrusted again to the Franciscans. The church is located at the extreme western edge of the old town, midway between the Puente (bridge) of San Martín and the Puerta (gate) of Cambrón.

✪ **Iglesia de Santo Tomé.** Plaza del Conde, 2, Vía Santo Tomé. ☎ **925-25-60-98.** Admission 150 ptas. ($1). Daily 10am–6:45pm (closes at 5pm in winter). Closed Dec 25 and Jan 1.

This modest little 14th-century chapel, situated on a narrow street in the old Jewish quarter, might have been overlooked had it not possessed El Greco's masterpiece *The Burial of the Count of Orgaz,* created in 1586.

Sínagoga de Santa María La Blanca. Calle Reyes Católicos, 2. ☎ **925-22-72-57.** Admission 150 ptas. ($1). Apr–Sept, daily 10am–2pm and 3:30–7pm; Oct–Mar, daily 10am–2pm and 3:30–6pm. Bus: 2.

In the late 12th century, the Jews of Toledo erected an important synagogue in the almohada style, which employs graceful horseshoe arches and ornamental horizontal moldings. Although by the early 15th century it had been converted into a Christian church, much of the original remains, including the five naves and elaborate Mudéjar decorations, mosquelike in their effect. The synagogue lies on the western edge of the city, midway between the El Greco museum and San Juan de los Reyes.

Hospital de Tavera. Hospital de Tavera, 2. ☎ **925-22-04-51.** Admission 500 ptas. ($3.35). Daily 10:30am–1:30pm and 3:30–6pm.

This 16th-century Greco-Roman palace north of the medieval ramparts of Toledo was originally built by Cardinal Tavera; it now houses a private art collection. Titian's portrait of Charles V hangs in the banqueting hall. The museum owns five paintings by El Greco: *The Holy Family, The Baptism of Christ,* and portraits of St. Francis, St. Peter, and Cardinal Tavera. Ribera's *The Bearded Woman* also attracts many viewers. The collection of books in the library is priceless. In the nearby church is the mausoleum of Cardinal Tavera, designed by Alonso Berruguete.

ENJOYING THE OUTDOORS

Anglers wanting to try their luck in the Tagus River often head for Toledo, since the river forms a natural moat around the city. The Spanish government has introduced black bass at Finisterra Dam, which lies some 28 miles (45km) southeast of the city. In various reservoirs you can catch large pike and carp. To fish these waters, you must obtain a permit in Madrid at either **ICONA,** Gran Vía de San Francisco, 4 (☎ **91-580-39-09**), or from the **Federación Española de Pesca,** Navas de Tolosa, 3 (☎ **91-532-83-53**).

The best place for swimming is the Parador Nacional de Conde Orgaz (see below), but its pool is available only to guests. The best outdoor pool—and a welcome relief in July and August—is at the **Camping Circo Romano,** calle Circo Romano, 21

(☎ **925-22-04-42**), a campground just north of the old city walls. It's open June to September daily 10am to 8pm. Admission Monday to Friday is 700 ptas. ($4.70); Saturday and Sunday it's 800 pesetas ($5.35).

SHOPPING

In swashbuckling days, the swordsmiths of Toldeo were renowned. They're still around and still turning out swords. Toledo is equally renowned for its *damasquinado,* or damascene work, the Moorish art of inlaying gold, even copper or silver threads, against a matte black steel backdrop. Today Toledo is filled with souvenir shops hawking damascene. The price depends on whether the item is handcrafted or machine made. Sometimes machine-made damascene is passed off as the more expensive handcrafted item, so you have to shop carefully. Bargaining is perfectly acceptable in Toledo, but if you get the price down, you can't pay with a credit card—only cash.

Marzipan (called *mazapán* locally) is often prepared by nuns and is a local specialty. Many shops in town specialize in this treat made of sweet almond paste.

The province of Toledo is also renowned for its pottery, which is sold in so many shops at competitive prices that it's almost unnecessary to recommend specific branches hawking these wares. However, over the years we've found that the large roadside emporiums on the outskirts of town on the main road to Madrid often are better bargains than the shops within the city walls, where rents are higher.

Better yet, for the best deals, and if you're interested in buying a number of items, consider a trip to Talavera la Reina, 47 miles (76km) west of Toledo, where most of the pottery is made. Since Talavera is the largest city in the province, it is hardly a picture-postcard little potter's village. Most of the shops lie along the main street of town, where you'll find store after store selling this distinctive pottery in multicolored designs.

Pottery hunters also flock to Puente del Arzobispo, another ceramic center, known for its green-hued pottery. From Talavera drive west on the N-V to Oropesa, then south for 9 miles (14km) to a fortified bridge across the Tagus. In general, ceramics here are cheaper than those sold in Toledo.

Just past Oropesa at the turnoff to Lagartera is the village where the highly renowned and sought after embroidery of La Mancha originates. Virtually every cottage displays samples of this free-form floral stitching, shaped into everything from skirts to tablecloths. Of course, shops in Toledo are also filled with samples of this unique embroidery.

Established in 1910, **Casa Bermejo,** Calle Airosas, 5 (☎ **925-28-53-67**), is a factory and store that employs almost 50 artisans, and you can watch them at work. The outlet carries a wide array of damascene objects fashioned into Toledo's traditional Mudéjar designs—swords, platters, pitchers, and other gift items. But not all of the items follow the inspiration of the medieval Arabs. The outfit engraves many of the ornamental swords that are awarded to graduates of West Point in the United States, as well as the decorative, full-dress military accessories used by the armies of various countries of Europe, including France. Open Monday through Friday from 9am to 1pm and 3 to 6pm, Saturday 9am to 1pm. Closing times are later in July and August, determined solely by business traffic.

Around since the 1920s, **Felipe Suarez,** Paseo de los Canónigos, 19 (☎ **925-22-56-15**), has manufactured damascene work in various forms ranging from unpretentious souvenir items to art objects of rare museum-quality beauty that sell for as much as 2,000,000 ptas. ($14,000). You'll find swords, straight-edged razors, pendants, fans, and an array of pearls. The shop maintains extended hours throughout the year, daily from 10am to 7pm.

The Siege of the Alcázar

Although the Alcázar of Toledo has suffered many a siege, one particularly dramatic encounter, in 1936, made world headlines. The Republicans were fighting to gain control of conservative, staunchly Catholic Toledo. Franco's rebel troops were commanded by one tough officer, Col. José Moscardó. Not only were his troops inside the Alcázar, but women and children were holed up here as well. The Alcázar, although under heavy attack, withstood 70 days of bombardment.

On July 23, a Republican officer reached Moscardó by telephone within the Alcázar. The colonel was informed that Nationalist forces had kidnapped Luis, his 16-year-old son. Moscardó was told that unless he immediately surrendered the fortress, Luis would be executed.

To show that they did indeed have the child, they put Luis on the phone to his father. "Papá!" he shouted, "They say they are going to shoot me if you don't surrender."

Without hesitation, Moscardó told his son: "Then commend your soul to God, shout 'Viva España!' and die like a hero."

The Republicans were good to their word. Luis was shot in the head. The fortress was surrendered in September of that year. In the Alcázar today the wall phone on which the colonel spoke to his son for the last time still hangs.

You'll also find superb craftsmanship in damascene work at **Santiago Sanchez Martín,** Calle Rio Llano, 15 (☎ **925-22-77-57**), which specializes in the elaborately detailed arabesques whose techniques are as old as the Arab conquest of Iberia. Look for everything from decorative tableware (platters, pitchers, etc.) to mirror frames, jewelry, letter openers, and ornamental swords. It's open Monday through Friday from 9am to 2pm and 5 to 7pm.

Many long-time residents of Toledo remember **Casa Telesforo,** Plaza de Zocodover, 13 (☎ **925-22-33-79**), as the outfit that supplied the marzipan consumed at their childhood birthday parties and celebrations. A specialist in this almond-and-sugar confection, it sells the best marzipan in town, cunningly made into such whimsical shapes as hearts, diamonds, flowers, and fish. It's open daily from 9am to 10pm, later in summer, depending on the crowds.

WHERE TO STAY
EXPENSIVE

✪ **Parador Nacional de Conde Orgaz.** Cerro del Emperador, 45002 Toledo. ☎ **925-22-18-50.** Fax 925-22-51-66. 76 units. A/C MINIBAR TV TEL. 21,000 ptas. ($140.70) double; 26,000 ptas. ($174.20) suite. AE, DC, MC, V. Free parking. Drive across Puente San Martín and head south for 2½ miles (4km).

You'll have to make reservations well in advance to stay at this parador, which is built on the ridge of a rugged hill where El Greco is said to have painted his *View of Toledo.* That view is still here, and it is without a doubt one of the grandest in the world. The main living room/lounge has fine furniture—old chests, brown leather chairs, and heavy tables—and leads to a sunny terrace overlooking the city. On chilly nights you can sit by the public fireplace. The guest rooms are the most luxurious in all of Toledo, far superior to those at Maria Cristina. Spacious and beautifully furnished, they contain reproductions of regional antique pieces. Most of the rooms come with roomy modern baths clad in marble (others are tiled) and equipped with hair dryers and robes.

Dining: The hotel's restaurant, Parador Nacional de Conde Orgaz, serves fine Castilian cuisine. See "Where to Dine," below.

Amenities: Room service, laundry/valet, outdoor swimming pool.

MODERATE

✪ **Hostal del Cardenal.** Paseo de Recaredo, 24, 45003 Toledo. ☎ **925-22-49-00.** Fax 925-22-29-91. 29 units. A/C TV TEL. 9,115–12,150 ptas. ($61.05–$81.40) double; 12,000–16,530 ptas. ($80.40–$110.75) suite. AE, DC, MC, V. Bus: 2 from rail station.

This place has long been acclaimed as the best restaurant in Toledo (see below), but we'll let you in on a secret: You can rent rooms here, too. They're not as grand as those at the Parador, but they're wonderful nevertheless, especially if you want an old Toledan atmosphere. The entrance to this unusual hotel is set into the stone fortifications of the ancient city walls, a few steps from the Bisagra Gate. To enter the hotel, you must climb a series of terraces to the top of the crenellated walls of the ancient fortress. Here, grandly symmetrical and very imposing, is the hostal, the former residence of the 18th-century cardinal of Toledo, Señor Lorenzana. Just beyond the entrance, still atop the city wall, you'll find flagstone walkways, Moorish fountains, rose gardens, and cascading vines. The building has tiled walls; long, narrow salons; dignified Spanish furniture; and a smattering of antiques. Bedrooms are small to medium in size, and each one is well appointed with a firm mattress and quality linen, plus a tidily organized bathroom with a stall shower and adequate shelf space. The only parking is what's available free on the street.

Hotel Carlos V. Calle Trastamara, 1, 45001 Toledo. ☎ **925-22-21-00.** Fax 925-22-21-05. E-mail: alfonsovi@macom.es. 69 units. A/C TV TEL. 13,000–13,500 ptas. ($87.10–$90.45) double. AE, MC, V. Bus: 5 or 6.

In Franco's day, this was *the* place to stay in Toledo. But increasing competition from such newer hotels as Maria Cristina and Alfonso VI has relegated it to second-tier status. It's still going strong and filling up many a night, even though some readers have complained of an unhelpful staff. Whereas the parador (see above) is outside of town, requiring frequent taxi rides, the Carlos V is right in the center of the action, between the cathedral and the Alcázar. Inside a masculine aura prevails, with brown leather chairs in the lounges. Rooms are also decorated in a rather severe masculine style. They range from small to medium, and many have better views than others. Each comes with a firm mattress on a comfortable bed, plus a small and well-maintained bathroom with a hair dryer. An outdoor bar is a summer feature. Standard Castilian meals are served in the dining room, which has a Mudéjar decorative motif. Set menus cost 2,852 ptas. ($19.10) each. Parking is in a nearby garage at a cost of 1,800 ptas. ($12.05) per day.

✪ **Hotel el Pintor El Greco.** Alamillos del Tránsito, 13, 45002 Toledo. ☎ **925-21-42-50.** Fax 925-21-58-19. E-mail: elgreco@estanciases.es. 33 units. A/C TV TEL. 14,000–18,000 ptas. ($93.80–$120.60) double. AE, DC, MC, V. Parking 700 ptas. ($4.70).

In the old Jewish quarter, one of the most traditional and historic districts of Toledo, this hotel was converted from a typical *casa Toledana,* which had once been used as a bakery. With careful restoration, especially of its ancient facade, it was transformed into one of Toledo's best and most atmospheric small hotels—the only one to match the antique charm of Hostal del Cardenal, although it too seems relatively unknown. Decoration in both the public rooms and bedrooms is in a traditional Castilian style. Phones, piped-in music, air-conditioning, satellite TV, and individual security boxes have been added to the immaculately kept bedrooms. Bedrooms come in a variety of shapes and sizes, as befits a building of this age, but all are equipped with firm mattresses and small bathrooms with stall showers and adequate shelf space. At the doorstep of the hotel are such landmarks as the Monasterio de San Juan de los Reyes, Sínagoga de Santa María la Blanca, Sínagoga del Tránsito, Casa y Museo de El Greco, and Iglesia de Santo Tomé. Public parking is available for 700 ptas. ($4.70) per day.

Hotel María Cristina. Marqués de Mendigorría, 1, 45003 Toledo. ☎ **925-21-32-02.** Fax 925-21-26-50. 63 units. A/C MINIBAR TV TEL. 12,200 ptas. ($81.75) double; 22,150 ptas. ($148.40) suite. AE, DC, MC, V. Parking 1,000 ptas. ($6.70).

Adjacent to the historic Hospital de Tavera and near the northern perimeter of the old town, this stone-sided, awning-fronted hotel resembles a palatial country home. If you're willing to forgo the view from the parador and the charm of Hostal del Cardenal, this hotel is a good backup. Originally built as a convent in 1560 and later used as a hospital, it was transformed into this comfortable hotel in the late 1980s. Sprawling, historic, and generously proportioned, it contains clean, amply sized, attractively furnished bedrooms, each with a comfortable bed and an immaculate bathroom, often with a tub and shower combo.

On site is the very large and well-recommended restaurant, El Abside, where fixed-price lunches and dinners are served, ranging in price from 1,825 to 2,500 ptas. ($12.25 to $16.75). There's also a bar. The food is much better, however, at Hostal del Cardenal.

Amenities include 24-hour room service, laundry, concierge, and baby-sitting.

Hotel Residencia Alfonso VI. Calle General Moscardó, 2, 45001 Toledo. ☎ **925-22-26-00.** Fax 925-21-44-58. www.alfonsovi.macom.es. E-mail: alfonsovi@macom.es. 83 units. A/C TV TEL. 13,500–14,500 ptas. ($90.45–$97.15) double; 24,480 ptas. ($164) suite. AE, MC, V. Bus: 5 or 6.

Although built in the early 1970s, this hotel has been kept up to date with frequent renovations. Run by the same management as the Carlos V, it is a superior hotel with better appointments and comfort, though a few of the public rooms appear so faux Castilian they look like movie sets. It sits near a dense concentration of souvenir shops in the center of the old city, at the southern perimeter of the Alcázar. Inside you'll discover a high-ceilinged, marble-trimmed decor with a scattering of Iberian artifacts, copies of Spanish provincial furniture, and dozens of leather armchairs. Rooms, for the most part, are medium in size, each well appointed with cushiony furnishings including comfortable mattresses on the Spanish beds. Bathrooms are tiled and a bit small. There's also a stone-floored dining room, where well-prepared, fixed-price meals range in price from 1,295 to 3,000 ptas. ($8.70 to $20.10) each.

INEXPENSIVE

Hotel Maravilla. Plaza de Barrio Rey, 7, 45001 Toledo. ☎ **925-22-33-04.** Fax 925-22-81-55. 18 units. A/C TV TEL. 6,500 ptas. ($43.55) double. AE, DC, MC, V. Bus: 5 or 6.

If you want lots of local color, then head here. It's only 1 block south of Plaza de Zocodover and opens directly onto its own cobblestone plaza. Semimodernized in 1995, the building has many bay windows; the bedrooms are modest but adequate, the furnishings so-so. Mattresses are a bit worn but still have comfort left in them, and the tiny bathrooms are cramped with showers and rather thin towels. You can hang your laundry on the roof and use an iron in the downstairs laundry room. What parking is available will be on the street.

Hotel Residencia Imperio. Calle de las Cadenas, 5, 45001 Toledo. ☎ **925-22-76-50.** Fax 925-25-31-83. E-mail: parroyo@batch-pc.es. 21 units. A/C TV TEL. 6,200 ptas. ($41.55) double. AE, DC, MC, V.

Just off calle de la Plata, 1 block west of Plaza de Zocodover, the Imperio is the best bet for those on a tight budget. The rooms are clean and comfortable but small and lackluster, showing the wear of their years. Mattresses are a bit thin, but, considering the price, there are few complaints. Bathrooms are mere cubicles with thin towels and showers. Most overlook a little church with a wall overgrown with wisteria. Parking is available on the street.

NEARBY PLACES TO STAY

Hotel los Cigarrales. Carretera Circunvalación, 32, 45004 Toledo. ☎ **925-22-00-53.** Fax 925-21-55-46. 36 units. A/C TV TEL. 6,100 ptas. ($40.85) double. DC, MC, V. Free parking. Bus: Chamartín from rail station.

About a mile south of the city center, this hotel is for those seeking quiet seclusion. Built in the 1960s in traditional red brick, it looks like a private villa with a garden; the friendliness of the family of owners adds to this feeling. The hotel was closed in 1999 for a total renovation but will reopen in spring 2000. Most of the interior is covered with blue and green tiles. The guest rooms are clean, sunny, and decorated with heavy Spanish furniture, a bit sterile but comfortable. Each has been fitted with a new, firm mattress, plus a renovated bathroom with modernized plumbing. Some of the rooms have balconies with panoramic views. From the flower-filled terrace of the cozy bar, you can see the towers of medieval Toledo.

La Almazara. Carretera Toledo-Argés-Cuerva, km 3400, 45080 Toledo. ☎ **925-22-38-66.** 24 units. TEL. 5,500–6,300 ptas. ($36.85–$42.20) double. AE, DC, MC, V. Closed Dec 10–Mar 7. Free parking. Follow the road to the parador of Ciudad Real, then take the C-781 to Cuerva.

For readers who have a car or who don't mind one or two taxi rides a day, there are some excellent lodgings across the Tagus. Taking its name from an olive-oil mill that used to stand here, La Almazara offers some of the most offbeat accommodations around. Hidden away in the hills, this old-fashioned country villa, with its own courtyards and vineyards, exudes the atmosphere of old Spain, far removed from city life. It has an exceptional view of Toledo. Request one of the spacious rooms in the main house rather than the less comfortable annex. Most rooms have balconies, so you can catch the evening breezes. Beds and mattresses are old but still quite comfortable. Come here for the atmosphere of an old Toledo house, far removed from the sterile new choices springing up.

WHERE TO DINE
MODERATE

✪ **Asador Adolfo.** La Granada, 6. ☎ **925-22-73-21.** Reservations recommended. Main courses 2,800–3,500 ptas. ($18.75–$23.45); fixed-price menu 5,500–6,500 ptas. ($36.85–$43.55). AE, DC, MC, V. Daily 1–4pm, Mon–Sat 8pm–midnight. Bus: 5 or 6. SPANISH.

Located less than a minute's walk north of the cathedral, at the corner of calle Hombre de Palo behind an understated sign, Asador Adolfo is one of the finest restaurants in town (though we prefer the Hostal del Cardenal). Sections of the building were first constructed during the 1400s, although the thoroughly modern kitchen has recently been renovated. Massive beams support the dining room ceilings, and here and there the rooms contain faded frescoes dating from the original building.

Game dishes are a house specialty; such dishes as partridge with white beans and venison consistently rate among the best anywhere. Nongame offerings include hake flavored with local saffron as well as a wide array of beef, veal, or lamb dishes. To start, try the *pimientos rellenos* (red peppers stuffed with pulverized shellfish). The house dessert is marzipan, prepared in a wood-fired oven and noted for its lightness.

✪ **Hostal del Cardenal.** Paseo de Recaredo, 24. ☎ **925-22-08-62.** Reservations required. Main courses 1,000–2,600 ptas. ($6.70–$17.40); fixed-price menu 2,700 ptas. ($18.10). AE, DC, MC, V. Daily 1–4pm and 8:30–11:30pm. Bus: 2 from rail station. SPANISH.

Treat yourself to Toledo's best-known restaurant, owned by the same people who run Madrid's Sobrino de Botín, so beloved by Hemingway (see chapter 3). The chef prepares regional dishes with flair and originality. Choosing from a menu very similar to that of the fabled Madrid eatery, begin with "quarter of an hour" (fish) soup or white asparagus, then move on to curried prawns, baked hake, filet mignon, or smoked salmon. Roast suckling pig is a specialty, as is partridge in casserole. Arrive early to enjoy a sherry in the bar or in the courtyard.

Mesón Aurelio. Calle Sínagoga. ☎ **925-22-20-97.** Reservations recommended. Main courses 2,500–3,500 ptas. ($16.75–$23.45); fixed-price menu 3,500 ptas. ($23.45). AE, DC, MC, V. Daily 1–4:30pm and 8–11:30pm. Bus: 5 or 6. CASTILIAN.

Established in the late 1940s, Mesón Aurelio occupies two separate but neighboring dining rooms, with two separate entrances, near the northern edge of the cathedral. It's one of the restaurant staples of Toledo, with its generous portions, Castilian ambience, and efficient service. Traditional versions of *sopa castellana,* grilled hake, *lubina á la sal* (whitefish cooked in salt), fresh salmon, and roast lamb are on the menu. Note that the main outlet of this restaurant (calle Sínagoga 6) is usually closed every Wednesday, the smaller of the restaurant's two branches (calle Sínagoga 1) remains open, opting instead to close every Monday. Despite their different closing days, the food items and prices within the two branches are identical.

Parador Nacional de Conde Orgaz. Cerro del Emperador. ☎ **925-22-18-50.** Reservations not accepted. Main courses 1,100–2,500 ptas. ($7.35–$16.75); fixed-price menu 3,700 ptas. ($24.80). AE, DC, MC, V. Daily 8–10:30am, 1–4pm and 8:30–11pm. Drive across Puente San Martín and head south for 2½ miles (4km). CASTILIAN.

Sturdy Castilian cuisine is enhanced by one of the most panoramic views from any restaurant in Europe. Located in a fine parador (recommended above), this restaurant is on the crest of a hill—said to be the spot that El Greco chose for his *View of Toledo.* The place is tourist trodden, and the food doesn't quite match the view, but it's a worthy choice, nonetheless. The fixed-price meal might include tasty Spanish tapas, hake, then perhaps either veal or beef grilled on an open fire, and dessert. If you're dining lightly, try a local specialty, *tortilla española con magra* (potato omelette with ham or bacon). There is a bar on the upper level.

Venta de Aires. Circo Romano, 35. ☎ **925-22-05-45.** Reservations recommended. Main courses 1,700–2,500 ptas. ($11.40–$16.75); fixed-price menu 2,200–3,400 ptas. ($14.75–$22.80). AE, DC, MC, V. Daily 1–4pm, 8–11pm. SPANISH.

Just outside the city gates, southwest of the Circo Romano (Roman Circus), Venta de Aires has served Toledo's pièce de résistance, *perdiz* (partridge), since 1891, when the place was just a tiny roadside inn. This dish is best eaten with the red wine of Méntrida. For dessert, try the marzipan, an institution in Toledo. On your way out, take note of former Pres. Richard Nixon's entry in the guest book (he dined here in 1963)—believe it or not, they're still talking about the visit.

INEXPENSIVE

El Emperador. Carretera del Valle, 1. ☎ **925-22-46-91.** Reservations recommended. Main courses 1,000–4,000 ptas. ($6.70–$26.80); fixed-price menu 1,100 ptas. ($7.35). V. Tues–Sun 1–3:30pm and 8:30–11pm. Bus: Carretera Valle. SPANISH.

A circa 1974 restaurant on the outskirts of Toledo, 1 mile southwest of the historic core of the town, near the parador, El Emperador is reached via an arched bridge. Its terraces overlook the river and the towers of Toledo; the tavern-style interior has leather-and-wood chairs, heavy beams, and wrought-iron chandeliers. Service at this family owned establishment is attentive. The fixed-price menu might include a choice of soup (beef, vegetable, or noodle), followed by a small steak with french fries, then fresh fruit, plus wine. Although the dishes are decently prepared from fresh ingredients, it is the economical prices that make this such an appealing choice.

La Parilla. Horno de los Bizcochos, 8. ☎ **925-21-22-45.** Reservations not necessary. Main courses 2,100–2,300 ptas. ($14.05–$15.40); fixed-price menu 1,400 ptas. ($9.40). AE, DC, MC, V. Daily 1–4pm and 8–10:30pm. Bus: 5 or 6. SPANISH.

Go here for some real Franco-era dishes. This classic Spanish restaurant, lying within a thick-walled medieval building, stands on a cobbled street near the Hotel Alfonso VI, just east of the cathedral. The menu offers no surprises, but it's reliable. Likely inclusions on the bill of fare are roast suckling pig, spider crabs, Castilian baked trout, stewed quail, baked kidneys, and La Mancha rabbit. This is the type of heavy fare so beloved by Castilians, who still frequent the place in great numbers.

Maravilla. Plaza de Barrio Rey, 7. ☎ **925-22-85-82.** Reservations not accepted. Main courses 1,200–2,200 ptas. ($8.05–$14.75); fixed-price menus 900–2,200 ptas. ($6.05–$14.75). AE, MC, V. Tues–Sun 1–4pm and 7:30–11pm. Bus: 5 or 6. SPANISH.

Maravilla is in the Barrio Rey, a small square off the historic Plaza de Zocodover filled with budget restaurants and cafes that change their names so often it's virtually impossible to keep track. Here, you'll get the best all-around dining bargain. The kitchen serves a typically Castilian menu, specializing in the area's famous *perdiz* (partridge) but also preparing *cordero asado* (roast lamb).

TOLEDO AFTER DARK

Before your nighttime crawl through Toledo, begin with a stop at **Bar Ludeña,** Plaza de la Madelena, 13, Corral de Don Diego, 10 (☎ **925-22-33-84**), where a loyal clientele comes for the delectable tapas served here. Fixed-price menus range from 1,200 to 2,500 ptas. ($8.05 to $16.75). Glasses of wine are sometimes passed through a small window to clients who are standing outside enjoying the view of the square. The bar is little more than a narrow corridor, serving *raciónes* of tapas that are so generous they make little meals, especially when served with bread. The roasted red peppers in olive oil are quite tasty, along with the stuffed crabs and *calamares* (squid). Huge dishes of pickled cucumbers, onions, and olives are available. They also have a tiny dining room behind a curtain at the end of the bar serving inexpensive fare.

Despite the many tourists that throng its streets during the day, Toledo is quiet at night, with fewer dance clubs than you'd expect from a town of its size. If you want to hear some recorded music, head for **Bar La Abadia,** calle Nuñez de Arce, 5 (☎ **925-25-11-40**), where crowds of local residents, many of them involved in the tourism industry, crowd elbow to elbow for pints of beer, glasses of wine, and access to the music of New York, Los Angeles, or wherever. A roughly equivalent competitor is **Bar Camelot,** calle Cristo de la Luz, s/n (no phone), which occupies an old, stone-sided building within the historic core of Toledo. Both are open nightly from 8:30pm to around 4am.

2 Aranjuez

29 miles (47km) S of Madrid, 30 miles (48km) NE of Toledo

This Castilian town at a confluence of the Tagus and Jarama Rivers, was once home to Bourbon kings in the spring and fall. With the manicured shrubbery, stately elms, fountains, and statues of the Palacio Real and surrounding compounds, Aranjuez remains a regal garden oasis in what is otherwise an unimpressive agricultural flatland known primarily for its strawberries and asparagus.

ESSENTIALS

GETTING THERE   Trains depart about every 20 minutes from Madrid's Atocha Railway Station to make the 50-minute trip to Aranjuez, a one-way fare costing 480 ptas. ($3.20). Trains run less often along the east-west route to and from Toledo (a 40-minute ride). The Aranjuez station lies about a mile outside town. For information and schedules, call ☎ **91-891-02-02.** You can walk it in about 15 minutes, but taxis and buses line up on calle Stuart (2 blocks from the city tourist office). The bus that makes the run from the center of Aranjuez to the railway station is marked "N–Z."

Buses for Aranjuez depart every 30 minutes from 7:30am to 10pm from Madrid's Estación Sur de Autobuses, calle Méndez Alvaro. In Madrid, call ☎ **91-468-42-00** for information. Buses arrive in Aranjuez at the City Bus Terminal, calle Infantas, 8 (☎ **91-891-01-83**).

Driving is easy and takes about 30 minutes once you reach the southern city limits of Madrid. To reach Aranjuez, follow the signs to Aranjuez and Granada, taking highway N-IV.

VISITOR INFORMATION   The **tourist information office** is at Plaza de San Antonio, 9 (☎ **91-891-04-27**). Open Monday through Friday from 10am to 2pm and 4 to 6pm.

EXPLORING ARANJUEZ

✪ **Palacio Real.** Plaza Palacio. ☎ **91-891-13-44.** Admission 500 ptas. ($3.35) adults, 250 ptas. ($1.70) students and children. Apr–Sept, Wed–Mon 10am–6:15pm; Oct–Mar, Wed–Mon 10am–5:15pm. Bus: Routes from the rail station converge at the square and gardens at the westernmost edge of the palace.

As you enter a cobblestoned courtyard, you can tell just by the size of the palace that it's going to be spectacular. Ferdinand and Isabella, Philip II, Philip V, and Charles III all made their way through here. The structure you see today dates from 1778 (the previous buildings were destroyed by fire). Its salons show the opulence of a bygone era, with room after room of royal extravagance. Many styles are blended: Spanish, Italian, Moorish, and French. And, of course, no royal palace would be complete without a room reflecting the rage for chinoiserie that once swept over Europe. The Porcelain Salon is also of special interest. A guide conducts you through the huge complex (a tip is expected).

Jardín de la Isla. Directly northwest of the Palacio Real. No phone. Free admission. Apr–Sept, daily 8am–8:30pm; Oct–Mar, daily 8am–6:30pm.

After the tour of the Royal Palace, wander through the Garden of the Island. Spanish impressionist Santiago Rusiñol captured its evasive quality on canvas, and one Spanish writer said that you walk here "as if softly lulled by a sweet 18th-century sonata." A number of fountains are remarkable: the "Ne Plus Ultra" fountain, the black-jasper fountain of Bacchus, the fountain of Apollo, and the ones honoring Neptune (god of the sea) and Cybele (goddess of agriculture).

You may also stroll through the Jardín del Parterre, located in front of the palace. It's much better kept than the Garden of the Island but not as romantic.

Casita del Labrador. Calle Reina, Jardín del Príncipe. ☎ **91-891-03-05.** Admission 550 ptas. ($3.70) adults, 225 ptas. ($1.50) students and children. May–Sept, Tues–Sun 10am–6:30pm; Oct–Apr, Tues–Sun 10am–5:30pm.

"The Little House of the Worker," modeled after the Petit Trianon at Versailles, was built in 1803 by Charles IV, who later abdicated in Aranjuez. The queen came here with her youthful lover, Godoy (whom she had elevated to the position of prime minister), and the feeble-minded Charles didn't seem to mind a bit. Surrounded by beautiful gardens, the "bedless" palace is lavishly furnished in the grand style of the 18th and 19th centuries. The marble floors represent some of the finest workmanship of that day; the brocaded walls emphasize the luxurious lifestyle and the royal toilet is a sight to behold (in those days, royalty preferred an audience). The clock here is one of the treasures of the house. The casita lies half a mile east of the Royal Palace; those with a car can drive directly to it through the tranquil Jardín del Príncipe.

WHERE TO STAY

Hostal Castilla. Carretera Andalucia, 98, 28300 Aranjuez. ☎ **91-891-26-27.** 17 units. TV TEL. 6,950 ptas. ($46.55) double. AE, DC, MC, V.

On one of the town's main streets north of the Royal Palace and gardens, the Castilla consists of the ground floor and part of the first floor of a well-preserved early 18th-century house. Most of the accommodations overlook a courtyard with a fountain and flowers. Owner Joaquin Suarez, who speaks English fluently, suggests that reservations be made at least a month in advance. There are excellent restaurants nearby, and the hostal has an arrangement with a neighboring bar to provide guests with an inexpensive lunch. This is a good location from which to explore either Madrid or Toledo on a day trip. Parking is available along the street.

WHERE TO DINE

Casa Pablo. Almibar, 42. ☎ **91-891-14-51.** Reservations recommended. Main courses 1,900–2,500 ptas. ($12.75–$16.75); four-course fixed-price menu 3,000 ptas. ($20.10). AE, MC, V. Daily 1–4:30pm and 8pm–midnight. Closed Aug. SPANISH.

An unpretentious and well-managed restaurant near the bus station in the town center, Casa Pablo was established in 1941. At tables set outside under a canopy, you can dine while enjoying red and pink geraniums along the tree-lined street; in cooler weather you eat either upstairs or in the cozy and clean rear dining room. The fixed-price menu includes four courses, a carafe of wine, bread, and gratuity. If it's hot and you don't want a heavy dinner, try a shrimp omelette or half a roast chicken; once we ordered just a plate of asparagus in season, accompanied by white wine. If you want a superb dish, try a fish called *mero* (Mediterranean pollack of delicate flavor), grilled over an open fire.

La Rana Verde. Reina, 1. ☎ **91-891-32-38.** Reservations recommended. Main courses 1,000–2,200 ptas. ($6.70–$14.75); fixed-price menu 1,225–3,900 ptas. ($8.20–$26.15). MC, V. Daily 9pm–midnight. SPANISH.

"The Green Frog," just east of the Royal Palace and next to a small bridge spanning the Tagus, is still the traditional choice for many. Opened in 1905 by Tomas Diaz Heredero, it is owned and run by a third-generation member of his family, who has decorated it in 1920s style. The restaurant looks like a summerhouse, with its high-beamed ceiling and soft ferns drooping from hanging baskets. The preferred tables are in the nooks overlooking the river. As in all the restaurants of Aranjuez, asparagus is a special feature. Game, particularly partridge, quail, and pigeon, can be recommended in season; fish, too, including fried hake and fried sole, makes a good choice. Strawberries are served with sugar, orange juice, or ice cream.

✪ **San Jose.** Abastos, 32. ☎ **91-891-14-88.** Main courses 2,000–2,500 ptas. ($13.40–$16.75); fixed-price menu 3,000 ptas. ($20.10). AE, DC, MC, V. Tues–Sun 1–4pm and 8–11pm (closed July 25–Aug 25). INTERNATIONAL/SPANISH.

This relative newcomer to Aranjuez is a pleasant family restaurant with two small dining rooms and a bar where you can choose from a wide variety of tapas, including several types of Manchego, the strong local cheese, and the truly succulent cured ham from Andalusia, *Jamon Jabugo*. Dishes in the restaurant reflect the cooking of Castile and La Mancha in particular but include more international fare. One specialty is the *pocho*, a juicy bean, which is combined with wild mushrooms in fall and with north coast clams in winter and early spring. The usual meats are available and the sea is best represented by a seafood soup packed with maritime goodies ranging from king prawns to razor clams.

3 San Lorenzo de El Escorial

30 miles (48km) W of Madrid, 32 miles (52km) SE of Segovia

Aside from Toledo, the most important excursion from Madrid is to the austere royal monastery of San Lorenzo de El Escorial. Philip II ordered the construction of this granite-and-slate behemoth in 1563, two years after he moved his capital to Madrid. Once the haunt of aristocratic Spaniards, El Escorial is now a resort where hotels and restaurants flourish in summer, as hundreds come to escape the heat of the capital. Aside from the appeal of its climate, the town of San Lorenzo itself is not very noteworthy. But because of the monastery's size, you might decide to spend a night or two at San Lorenzo—or more if you have the time.

San Lorenzo makes a good base for visiting nearby Segovia and Ávila, the royal palace at La Granja, the Valley of the Fallen—and even the more distant university city of Salamanca.

ESSENTIALS

GETTING THERE   More than two dozen trains depart daily from Madrid's Atocha, Nuevos Ministerios, and Chamartín train stations. During the summer extra coaches are added. For schedules and information, call ☎ **91-328-90-20.** A one-way fare costs 780 ptas. ($5.25).

The railway station for San Lorenzo de El Escorial is located about a mile outside of town along Ctra. Estación (☎ **91-890-07-14**). The Herranz bus company meets all arriving trains with a shuttle bus that ferries arriving passengers to and from the Plaza Virgen de Gracia, about a block east of the entrance to the monastery.

Empresa Herranz, calle Reina Victoria, 3, in El Escorial (☎ **91-890-41-22** or 91-890-41-25), runs some 40 buses per day back and forth between Madrid and El Escorial. On Sunday service is curtailed to 10 buses. Trip time is an hour, and a round-trip fare costs 740 ptas. ($4.95). The same company also runs one bus a day to El Valle de los Caídos (The Valley of the Fallen). It leaves El Escorial at 3:15pm with a return at 5:30pm. The ride takes only 15 minutes, and a round-trip fare is 870 ptas. ($5.85), El Valle only.

If you're driving, follow the N-VI highway (marked on some maps as A-6) from the northwest perimeter of Madrid toward Lugo, La Coruña, and San Lorenzo de El Escorial. After about a half hour, fork left onto the C-505 toward San Lorenzo de El Escorial. Driving time from Madrid is about an hour.

VISITOR INFORMATION   The **tourist information office** is at Floridablanca, 10 (☎ **91-890-15-54**). It is open Monday through Friday from 10am to 2pm and 3 to 5pm, Saturday from 10am to 2pm.

SEEING THE SIGHTS

✪ **Real Monasterio de San Lorenzo de El Escorial.** Calle San Lorenzo de El Escorial, 1. ☎ **91-890-59-03.** Comprehensive ticket 850 ptas. ($5.70) adults, 350 ptas. ($2.35) children. Apr–Sept, Tues–Sun 10am–7pm; Oct–Mar, Tues–Sun 10am–6pm.

This huge granite fortress houses a wealth of paintings and tapestries and also serves as a burial place for Spanish kings. Foreboding both inside and out because of its sheer size and institutional look, El Escorial took 21 years to complete, a remarkably short time considering the bulk of the building and the primitive construction methods of the day. After his death, the original architect Juan Bautista de Toledo was replaced by Juan de Herrera, the greatest architect of Renaissance Spain, who completed the structure.

Philip II, who collected many of the paintings exhibited here in the New Museums, did not care for El Greco but favored Titian instead. Still, you'll find El Greco's *The Martyrdom of St. Maurice,* rescued from storage, and also his St. Peter. Other superb works include Titian's Last Supper and Velázquez's *The Tunic of Joseph.*

The Royal Library houses a priceless collection of 60,000 volumes—one of the most significant in the world. The displays range from the handwriting of St. Teresa to medieval instructions on playing chess. See, in particular, the Muslim codices and a Gothic *Cantigas* from the 13th-century reign of Alfonso X ("The Wise").

You can also visit the Philip II Apartments; these are strictly monastic, and Philip called them the "cell for my humble self" in this "palace for God." Philip became a religious fanatic and requested that his bedroom be erected overlooking the altar of the 300-foot-high basilica, which has four organs and whose dome is based on Michelangelo's drawings for St. Peter's. The choir contains a crucifix by Cellini. By comparison, the Throne Room is simple. On the walls are many ancient maps. The Apartments of the Bourbon Kings are lavishly decorated, in contrast to Philip's preference for the ascetic.

Under the altar of the church you'll find one of the most regal mausoleums in the world, the Royal Pantheon, where most of Spain's monarchs, from Charles I to Alfonso XII, including Philip II, are buried. In 1993 Don Juan de Borbón, the count of Barcelona and the father of King Juan Carlos (Franco passed over the count and never allowed him to ascend to the throne) was interred nearby. On a lower floor is the "Wedding Cake" tomb for children.

Allow at least 3 hours for a visit.

Casa de Príncipe (Prince's Cottage). Calle Reina, s/n. ☎ **91-891-03-05.** Admission included in comprehensive ticket to El Escorial, see above. Apr–July and Sept, Sat–Sun and holidays 10am–5:45pm; Aug, Tues–Sun 10am–5:45pm; Oct–Mar, Sat–Sun and holidays 10am–6:45pm.

This small but elaborately decorated 18th-century palace near the railway station was originally a hunting lodge built for Charles III by Juan de Villanueva. Most visitors stay in El Escorial for lunch, visiting the cottage in the afternoon.

El Valle de los Caídos (Valley of the Fallen). ☎ **91-890-56-11.** Admission 650 ptas. ($4.35) adults, 250 ptas. ($1.70) students and children. Apr–Sept, Tues–Sun 9:30am–7pm; Oct–Mar, Tues–Sun 10am–6pm. Bus: Tour buses from Madrid usually include an excursion to the Valley of the Fallen on their 1-day trips to El Escorial (see "By Bus," above). By Car: Drive to the valley entrance, about 5 miles (8km) north of El Escorial in the heart of the Guadarrama Mountains. Once here, drive 3½ miles (6km) west along a wooded road to the underground basilica.

This is Franco's El Escorial, an architectural marvel that took 2 decades to complete, dedicated to those who died in the Spanish Civil War. Its detractors say that it represents the worst of neofascist design; its admirers say they have found renewed inspiration by coming here.

A gargantuan cross nearly 500 feet high dominates the Rock of Nava, a peak of the Guadarrama Mountains. Directly under the cross is a basilica with a vault in mosaic, completed in 1959. When José Antonio Primo de Rivera, the founder of the Falange party and a Nationalist hero, was buried at El Escorial, many, especially influential monarchists, protested that he was not a royal. Infuriated, Franco decided to erect another monument, this one. Originally it was slated to honor the dead on the Nationalist side only, but the intervention of several parties led to a decision to include all the *caídos* (fallen). In time the mausoleum claimed Franco as well; his body was interred behind the high altar.

A funicular extends from near the entrance to the basilica to the base of the gigantic cross erected on the mountaintop above (where there's a superb view). The fare is 350 ptas. ($2.35), and the funicular runs daily from 10:30am to 1:15pm and 4 to 6pm.

On the other side of the mountain is a Benedictine monastery that has sometimes been dubbed "the Hilton of monasteries" because of its seeming luxury.

WHERE TO STAY
MODERATE

Hotel Botánico. Calle Timoteo Padros, 16, 28200 San Lorenzo de El Escorial. ☎ **91-890-78-79.** Fax 91-890-81-58. 20 units. 14,000 ptas. ($93.80) double; 18,700–28,500 ptas. ($125.30–$190.95) suite. AE, V. Free parking.

True to its name, the hotel stands in a lovely manicured garden consisting of both indigenous and exotic shrubbery. Although the building is traditionally Castilian, the decor seems vaguely alpine, with wood paneling and beams in the reception rooms. The clean, well-lit rooms are large and comfortable, with especially good beds. There is a restaurant inside the hotel, which specializes in rice and fish dishes. Main courses range from 1,500 to 2,500 ptas. ($10.05 to $16.75) and there is a fixed-price menu at 5,000 ptas. ($33.50).

Hotel Victoria Palace. Calle Juan de Toledo, 4, 28200 San Lorenzo de El Escorial. ☎ **91-890-15-11.** Fax 91-896-98-96. 96 units. TV TEL. 11,900–17,900 ptas. ($79.75–$119.95) double. AE, DC, MC, V. Free parking.

The Victoria Palace, with its view of El Escorial, is the finest hotel in town, a traditional establishment that has been modernized without losing its special aura of style and comfort. It is surrounded by beautiful gardens and has an outdoor swimming pool. The good-size rooms (some with private terraces) are well furnished and maintained, each with a quality mattress, plus a small, tiled, and immaculately kept bathroom, often with a tub and shower combo. The rates are reasonable enough, and a bargain for a four-star hotel. The dining room serves some of the best food in town.

INEXPENSIVE

✪ **Hostal Cristina.** Juan de Toledo, 6, 28200 San Lorenzo de El Escorial. ☎ **91-890-19-61.** Fax 91-890-12-04. 16 units. TV TEL. 6,200 ptas. ($41.55) double. MC, V.

An excellent budget choice, this hotel is run by the Delgado family, which opened it in the mid-1980s. It doesn't pretend to compete with comfort and amenities of the Victoria Palace or even the Miranda & Suizo (see below), but it has its devotees nonetheless. About 50 yards from the monastery, it stands in the center of town, offering clean and comfortable but simply furnished rooms. The beds have firm mattresses, and accommodations range in size from small to medium, each equipped with a small tiled bathroom with a shower stall. The helpful staff will direct you to the small garden. Since the food served in the restaurant is both good and plentiful, many Spanish visitors prefer to book here for a summer holiday. Parking is available along the street.

Miranda & Suizo. Calle Floridablanca, 20, 28200 San Lorenzo de El Escorial. ☎ **91-890-47-11.** Fax 91-890-43-58. 52 units. TV TEL. 9,300–11,500 ptas. ($62.30–$77.05) double; 16,000–20,000 ptas. ($107.20–$134) suite. AE, DC, MC, V.

On a tree-lined street in the heart of town, within easy walking distance of the monastery, this excellent middle-bracket establishment ranks as a leading two-star hotel. It is the second choice in town, with rooms not quite as comfortable as those at the Victoria Palace. The Victorian-style building has good guest rooms nevertheless, some with terraces; 10 contain TVs. Many of the rooms are rather spacious and each comes with a firm mattress and a well-maintained private bathroom with shower. The furnishings are comfortable, the beds often made of brass; sometimes you'll find fresh flowers on the tables. In summer, there is outside dining. Parking is available nearby for 1,000 ptas. ($6.70) per day.

WHERE TO DINE
MODERATE

Charolés. Calle Floridablanca, 24. ☎ **91-890-59-75.** Reservations required. Main courses 2,800–3,800 ptas. ($18.75–$25.45). AE, DC, MC, V. Daily 1–4pm and 9pm–midnight. SPANISH/INTERNATIONAL.

The thick and solid walls of this establishment date, according to its managers, "from the monastic age"—and probably predate the town's larger and better-known monastery of El Escorial. The restaurant contained within was established around 1980 and has been known ever since as the best dining room in town. It has a flower-ringed outdoor terrace for use during nice weather. The cuisine doesn't quite rate a star, but chances are you'll be satisfied. The wide choice of menu items based entirely on fresh fish and meats includes such dishes as grilled hake with green or hollandaise sauce, shellfish soup, pepper steak, a *pastel* (pie) of fresh vegetables with crayfish, and herb-flavored baby lamb chops. A strawberry or kiwi tart is a good dessert choice.

INEXPENSIVE

Mesón la Cueva. San Antón, 4. ☎ **91-890-15-16.** Reservations recommended. Main courses 950–2,500 ptas. ($6.35–$16.75); *menú del día* 1,800 ptas. ($12.05), *menú especial* 3,500 ptas. ($23.45). No credit cards. Tues–Sun 1–4pm and 8:30–11:30pm. CASTILIAN.

Founded in 1768, this restaurant captures the world of Old Castile, and it lies only a short walk from the monastery. A *mesón típico* built around an enclosed courtyard, "the Cave" boasts such nostalgic accents as stained-glass windows, antique chests, a 19th-century bullfighting collage, faded engravings, paneled doors, and iron balconies. The cooking is on target, and the portions are generous. Regional specialties include Valencian paella and *fabada asturiana* (pork sausage and beans), but the fresh trout broiled in butter is the best of all. The menu's most expensive items are Segovian roast suckling pig and roast lamb (tender inside, crisp outside). Off the courtyard through a separate doorway is La Cueva's tasca, filled with Castilians quaffing their favorite before-dinner drinks.

NEAR THE VALLEY OF THE FALLEN

Hosteleria Valle de los Caídos. Valle de los Caídos. ☎ **91-890-55-11.** Reservations not accepted. Fixed-price menu 1,250 ptas. ($8.40). No credit cards. Daily 9–10am, 2–3:30pm. Closed Dec 15–Jan 15. SPANISH.

Frankly, there aren't a lot of dining options available within the arid landscapes around the Valley of the Fallen, and of the few that exist, this somewhat sterile and grandiose structure is about as good as you'll get. Built in 1956, it's set amid an arid but dramatic landscape halfway along the inclined access road leading to Franco's monuments, and reachable only by car or bus. It's a mammoth modern structure with wide terraces, floor-to-ceiling windows, and a well-established pattern of feeding busloads of foreign tour groups. The menú del día usually includes such dishes as cannelloni Rossini, pork chops with potatoes, a dessert choice of flan or fruit, and wine. The typical fare of roast chicken, roast lamb, shellfish, and paella is somewhat cafeteria-style in nature. View it mainly as a feeding station for the hundreds flocking to this attraction, but don't expect any culinary individuality or any particular deviation from a tried-and-true pattern that has varied little in many years.

EL ESCORIAL AFTER DARK

No longer the dead place it was during the long Franco era, the town comes alive at night, fueled mainly by the throngs of young people who pack into the bars and taverns, especially those along calle Rey and calle Floridablanca. Some of our favorite bars, offering vats of wine or kegs of beer, include the **Piano Bar Regina,** Floridablanca (☎ **91-890-68-43**), **Gurriato,** Leindro Rubio, 3 (☎ **91-890-47-10**), and **Don Felipe II,** Floridablanca (☎ **91-896-07-65**). The hottest disco is **Move it,** Plaza de Santiago, 11 (☎ **91-890-54-91**), which rarely imposes a cover unless some special group is featured.

4 Segovia

54 miles (91km) NW of Madrid, 42 miles (68km) NE of Ávila

Less commercial than Toledo, Segovia, more than anywhere else, typifies the glory of Old Castile. Wherever you look, you'll see reminders of a golden era, whether it's the most spectacular Alcázar on the Iberian Peninsula or the well-preserved, still-functioning Roman aqueduct.

Segovia lies on the slope of the Guadarrama Mountains, where the Eresma and Clamores Rivers converge. This ancient city stands in the center of the most castle-rich part of Castile. Isabella herself was proclaimed queen of Castile here in 1474.

The narrow, winding streets of this hill city must be covered on foot to fully view the Romanesque churches and 15th-century palaces along the way.

ESSENTIALS

GETTING THERE Nine trains leave Madrid's Chamartín Railway Station every day and arrive 2 hours later in Segovia, where you can board bus no. 3, which departs every quarter hour for the Plaza Mayor. A one-way rail fare costs 765 ptas. ($5.15). The station lies on the Paseo Obispo Quesada, s/n (☎ **921-42-07-74**), a 20-minute walk southeast of the town center.

Buses arrive and depart from the Estacionamiento Municipal de Autobuses, Paseo de Ezequile González, 10 (☎ **921-42-77-25**), near the corner of the Avenida Fernández Ladreda and the steeply sloping Paseo Conde de Sepúlveda. There are 10 to 15 buses a day to and from Madrid (which depart from Paseo de la Florida, 11; metro: Norte), and about four a day traveling between Ávila, Segovia, and Valladolid. One-way tickets from Madrid cost around 765 ptas. ($5.15).

If you're driving, take the N-VI (on some maps it's known as the A-6) or the Autopista del Nordeste northwest from Madrid, toward León and Lugo. At the junction with Route 110 (signposted Segovia), turn northeast.

VISITOR INFORMATION The **tourist information office** is at Plaza Mayor, 10 (☎ **921-46-03-34**). It is open daily from 10am to 2pm and 5 to 8pm.

EXPLORING SEGOVIA

You'll find the best **shopping** between the Roman aqueduct, the cathedral, and the Alcázar. Head especially for calle de Juan Bravo, calle Daoiz, and calle Marqués del Arco. Although their merchandise is mirrored in other shops nearby, two of the most appealing shops for ceramic pottery, woodcarvings, wrought-iron, and art objects include **Salvador Lucio,** calle Marqués del Arco, s/n (☎ **921-46-05-52**); and **Kokul Artesania,** calle Marqués del Arco, 20 (☎ **921-46-04-50**).

✪ **El Alcázar.** Plaza de La Reina Victoria Eugenia. ☎ **921-46-07-59.** Admission 375 ptas. ($2.50) adults, 250 ptas. ($1.70) children 8–14, free for children 7 and under. Apr–Sept, daily 10am–7pm; Oct–Mar, daily 10am–6pm. Bus: 3. Take either calle Vallejo, calle de Velarde, calle de Daoiz, or Paseo de Ronda.

View the Alcázar first from below, at the junction of the Clamores and Eresma Rivers. It is on the west side of Segovia, and you may not spot it when you first enter the city. But that's part of the surprise.

The castle dates from the 12th century, but a large segment, which contained its Moorish ceilings, was destroyed by fire in 1862. Restoration has continued over the years.

Royal romance is associated with the Alcázar. Isabella first met Ferdinand here, and today you can see a facsimile of her dank bedroom. Once married, she wasn't foolish enough to surrender her royal rights, as replicas of the thrones attest—both are equally proportioned. Philip II married his fourth wife, Anne of Austria, here as well.

Walk the battlements of this once-impregnable castle, from which its occupants hurled boiling oil onto the enemy below. Ascend the hazardous stairs of the tower, originally built by Isabella's father as a prison, for a panoramic view of Segovia.

✪ **Roman Aqueduct (Acueducto Romano).** Plaza del Azoguejo.

This architectural marvel was built by the Romans nearly 2,000 years ago. Constructed of mortarless granite, it consists of 118 arches, and in one two-tiered section it soars 95 feet to its highest point. The Spanish call it El Puente. It spans the Plaza del Azoguejo, the old market square, stretching nearly 800 yards. When the Moors took Segovia in 1072, they destroyed 36 arches, which were later rebuilt under Ferdinand and Isabella in 1484.

✪ **Cabildo Catedral de Segovia.** Plaza Catedral, Marqués del Arco. ☎ **921-43-53-25.** Free admission to cathedral; cloisters, museum, and chapel room 250 ptas. ($1.70) adults, 50 ptas. (35¢) children. Spring and summer, daily 9am–7pm; Off-season, daily 9:30am–6pm.

Constructed between 1515 and 1558, this is the last Gothic cathedral built in Spain. Fronting the historic Plaza Mayor, it stands on the spot where Isabella I was proclaimed queen of Castile. Affectionately called *la dama de las catedrales*, it contains numerous treasures, such as the Blessed Sacrament Chapel (created by the flamboyant Churriguera), stained-glass windows, elaborately carved choir stalls, and 16th- and 17th-century paintings, including a reredos portraying the deposition of Christ from the cross by Juan de Juni. The cloisters are older than the cathedral, dating from an earlier church that was destroyed in the so-called War of the Communeros. Inside the cathedral museum you'll find jewelry, paintings, and a collection of rare antique manuscripts.

Iglesia de la Vera Cruz. Carretera de Zamarramala. ☎ **921-43-14-75.** Admission 200 ptas. ($1.35). Apr–Sept, Tues–Sun 10:30am–1:30pm and 3:30–7pm; Oct–Mar, Tues–Sun 10:30am–1:30pm and 3:30–6pm.

Built in either the 11th or the 12th century by the Knights Templar, this is the most fascinating Romanesque church in Segovia. It stands in isolation outside the walls of the old town, overlooking the Alcázar. Its unusual 12-sided design is believed to have been copied from the Church of the Holy Sepulchre in Jerusalem. Inside you'll find an inner temple, rising two floors, where the knights conducted nightlong vigils as part of their initiation rites.

Monasterio del Parral. Calle del Marqués de Villena (across the Eresma River). ☎ **921-43-12-98.** Free admission. Mon–Sat 10am–2:30pm and 4–6:30pm; Sun 10–11:30am, 4–6:30pm. Take Ronda de Sant Lucía, cross the Eresma River, and head down calle del Marqués de Villena.

The restored "Monastery of the Grape" was established for the Hieronymites by Henry IV, a Castilian king (1425–74) known as "The Impotent." The monastery lies across the Eresma River about a half mile north of the city. The church is a medley of styles and decoration—mainly Gothic, Renaissance, and plateresque. The facade was never completed, and the monastery itself was abandoned when religious orders were suppressed in 1835. Today it's been restored and is once again the domain of the *jerónimos,* Hieronymus priests and brothers. Inside, a robed monk will show you the various treasures of the order, including a polychrome altarpiece and the alabaster tombs of the Marquis of Villena and his wife—all the work of Juan Rodríguez.

Esteban Vicente Contemporary Art Museum. Plazuela de las Bellas. ☎ **921-46-20-10.** Admission 400 ptas. ($2.70) adults, 200 ptas. ($1.35) seniors and students, free for children under 12. Mon–Sat 11am–2pm and 4–7pm, Sun 11am–2pm.

In the heart of the city, in a newly renovated 15th-century palace, a permanent collection of some 142 works by the abstract-expressionist artist Esteban Vicente has opened. The Spanish-born artist, now in his late 90s, has described himself as "an American painter, with very deep and loving Spanish roots." Born in a small town outside Segovia in 1903, he remained in Spain until 1927, eventually (since 1936) residing in New York where he played a pivotal role in the development of American abstract art. Today, he is one of the last surviving members of the New York School Artists, whose members include Rothko, de Kooning, and Pollock. Vicente's paintings and collages convey his sense of structure and feelings of luminous serenity with colors of astonishing vibrancy, brilliance, and range. His paintings are shown at the Metropolitan Museum of Art, the Museum of Modern Art, and the Whitney, all in New York—and now Segovia.

WHERE TO STAY
EXPENSIVE

✪ **Parador de Segovia.** Carretera Valladolid, s/n (N-601), 40003 Segovia. ☎ **921-44-37-37.** Fax 921-43-73-62. 120 units. A/C MINIBAR TV TEL. 19,795 ptas. ($132.65) double; from 29,425 ptas. ($197.15) suite. AE, DC, MC, V. Covered parking 1,000 ptas. ($6.70), free outside.

This 20th-century tile-roofed parador sits on a hill 2 miles (3km) northeast of Segovia (take the N-601). It stands on an estate called El Terminillo, which used to be famous for its vines and almond trees, a few of which still survive. If you have a car and can get a reservation, book in here; you'll pay more, but it's much more comfortable here than at either Los Arcos or Los Linajes (see below). The good-size rooms are deluxe, containing such extras as private safes and tiled bathrooms with shower/tub combos. Furnishings are tasteful (often in blond pieces), and large windows open onto panoramic views of the countryside. Some of the older rooms here are a bit dated, however, with lackluster decor. The vast lawns and gardens contain two lake-like swimming pools, and there is also an indoor pool. Other facilities include saunas and tennis courts.

MODERATE

Hotel Infanta Isabel. Plaza Mayor, 40001 Segovia. ☎ **921-13-00.** Fax 921-22-17.
29 units. A/C MINIBAR TV TEL. 11,000–13,350 ptas. ($73.70–$89.45) double. AC, DC, MC, V.
Free parking.

Named after Queen Isabel, the great-grandmother of the present-day king, the hotel
stands overlooking the charming central square and is within a stone's throw of the
majestic cathedral. This is where she would stay when on her way to the nearby
summer palace of La Granja. The present owners have modernized the interior considerably but a good deal of the building's 19th-century grandeur, such as the staircase, remain. Each room is decorated in its own style, and each is furnished with an
eye to comfort. Despite its style, the hotel has every convenience; satellite TV and
modern bathrooms strike a reassuring 20th-century note.

Hotel Los Linajes. Dr. Velasco, 9, 40003 Segovia. ☎ **921-46-04-75.** Fax 921-46-04-79.
65 units. A/C TV TEL. 9,900–11,900 ptas. ($66.35–$79.75) double; from 13,200–15,400 ptas.
($88.45–$103.20) suite. AE, DC, V. Parking 800 ptas. ($5.35). Bus: 1.

In the historical district of St. Stephen at the northern edge of the old town stands this
hotel, the former home of a Segovian noble family. While the facade dates from the
11th century, the interior is modern, except for some Castilian decorations. Following
a 1996 renovation, the hotel looks a bit brighter and fresher than Los Arcos. Bedrooms, which come in a range of sizes and shapes, are most comfortable with fine beds
and tidily kept tiled bathrooms. One of the best hotels in town, Los Linajes offers gardens and patios where guests can enjoy a panoramic view over the city. The hotel also
has a bar/lounge, coffee shop, disco, and garage.

Los Arcos. Paseo de Ezequiel González, 26, 40002 Segovia. ☎ **800-528-1234** in the U.S.,
or 921-43-74-62. Fax 921-42-81-61. 59 units. A/C MINIBAR TV TEL. 15,000 ptas. ($100.50)
double. AE, DC, MC, V. Parking 1,000 ptas. ($6.70).

This concrete-and-glass five-story structure opened in 1987 and is generally cited as
the best in town, although you may prefer Los Linajes instead (see above). Well run
and modern, it attracts the business traveler, although tourists frequent the place in
droves as well. Rooms are generally spacious but furnished in a standard international
bland way, except for the beautiful rug-dotted parquet floors. Built-in furnishings and
tiny combination bathrooms with hair dryers are part of the offering, along with private safes. Rooms are well kept, with good beds, although some furnishings look worn.

Even if you don't stay here, consider dining at the hotel's La Cocina de Segovia,
which is the only hotel dining room that competes successfully with Mesón de Cándido (see below). As at the nearby competitors, roast suckling pig and roast Segovia
lamb—perfectly cooked in specially made ovens—are the specialties. There's also a
tavernlike cafe and a bar. In all, it's a smart, efficiently run, and pleasant choice, if not
a terribly exciting one.

INEXPENSIVE

Las Sirenas. Juan Bravo, 30, 40001 Segovia. ☎ **921-46-26-63.** Fax 921-46-26-57. 39 units.
A/C TV TEL. 7,000–8,500 ptas. ($46.90–$56.95) double. AE, DC, MC, V.

Standing on the most charming old plaza in Segovia, opposite the Church of
St. Martín, this hotel was built around 1950, and has been renovated several times.
However, it has long since lost its Franco-era supremacy to Los Arcos (see above).
Modest and well maintained, it is decorated in a conservative style. Each room is filled
with functional, simple furniture, but the beds are good. However, rooms are somewhat small. Breakfast is the only meal served, but the staff at the reception desk can
direct clients to cafes and tascas nearby.

WHERE TO DINE

El Bernardino. Cervantes, 2. ☎ **921-46-24-74.** Reservations recommended. Main courses 1,400–2,500 ptas. ($9.40–$16.75); fixed-price menu 2,800 ptas. ($18.75). AE, DC, MC, V. Daily 1–4pm and 7:30–11:30pm. CASTILIAN.

El Bernardino, a 3-minute walk west of the Roman aqueduct, is built like an old tavern. Lanterns hang from beamed ceilings, and the view over the red-tile rooftops of the city is delightful. There is also a summer terrace. The menú del día might include a huge paella, roast veal with potatoes, flan or ice cream, plus bread and wine. You might begin your meal with *sopa castellana* (soup made with ham, sausage, bread, egg, and garlic). The roast dishes are exceptional here, including roast suckling pig, from a special oven, and roast baby lamb. You can also order grilled rib steak or stewed partridge.

José María. Cronista Lecea, 11. ☎ **921-46-11-11.** Reservations recommended. Main courses 1,500–2,400 ptas. ($10.05–$16.10); fixed-price menu 4,000–6,000 ptas. ($26.80–$40.20). AE, DC, MC, V. Daily 1–4pm and 8–11:30pm. SEGOVIAN.

This centrally located bar and restaurant, 1 block east of the Plaza Mayor, serves quality regional cuisine in a rustic stucco-and-brick dining room. Before dinner, locals crowd in for tapas at the bar, then move into the dining room for such Castilian specialties as roast suckling pig, rural-style conger eel, and freshly caught sea bream. Try the cream of crabmeat soup, roasted peppers, salmon with scrambled eggs, house-style hake, or grilled veal steak. For dessert, a specialty is ice cream tart with a whisky sauce.

✪ **Mesón de Candido.** Plaza del Azoguejo, 5. ☎ **921-42-59-11.** Reservations recommended. Main courses 1,400–2,400 ptas. ($9.40–$16.10); fixed-price menu 3,500 ptas. ($23.45). AE, DC, MC, V. Daily 12:30–4:30pm and 8–11:30pm or midnight. CASTILIAN.

For years this beautiful old Spanish inn, standing on the eastern edge of the old town, has maintained a monopoly on the tourist trade. Apart from the hotel restaurants—specifically La Cocina de Segovia at the Los Arcos—it is the town's finest dining choice. The Candido family took it over in 1905, and fourth- and fifth-generation family members still run the place, having fed, over the years, everybody from Hemingway to Nixon. The oldest part of the restaurant dates from 1822, and the restaurant has gradually been enlarged since then. The proprietor of the House of Candido is known as *mesonero mayor de Castilla* (the major innkeeper of Castile). He's been decorated with more medals and honors than paella has grains of rice. The restaurant's popularity can be judged by the crowds of hungry diners who fill every seat in the six dining rooms. The à la carte menu includes those two regional staples: *cordero asado* (roast baby lamb) and *cochinillo asado* (roast suckling pig).

Mesón el Cordero. Calle de Carmen, 4. ☎ **921-46-33-45.** Reservations recommended. Main courses 1,200–2,000 ptas. ($8.05–$13.40); fixed-price menus 1,200–3,500 ptas. ($8.05–$23.45). AE, DC, MC, V. Daily 12:30–4pm and 8–11:30pm. CASTILIAN/IBERIAN.

Originally constructed in the 1800s as a Carmelite convent, near the base of the town's aqueduct, Mesón el Cordero was substantially enlarged in the 1970s by two hard-working partners who added dozens of rustic artifacts to create the charming eatery you see today. This restaurant is known for its flavorful roasted meats. One noteworthy specialty, *cordero lechal* (roasted suckling lamb), is served on the bone and seasoned with fresh herbs, including ample amounts of rosemary and thyme. The wine list includes an array of suitably robust reds from Rioja, Rivera, and southern France.

A SIDE TRIP TO LA GRANJA

To reach La Granja, 7 miles (11km) southeast of Segovia, you can take a 20-minute bus ride from the center of the city. Six to 10 buses a day leave from Paseo Conde de

Sepulveda at Avenida Fernández Ladreda. A one-way fare costs 105 ptas. (70¢). For information, call ☎ **921-42-77-25.**

✪ **Palacio Real de La Granja.** Plaza de España, 17, San Ildefonso (Segovia). ☎ **921-47-00-19.** Admission 650 ptas. ($4.35) adults, 250 ptas. ($1.70) children 5–14, free for children 4 and under. Apr–May, Mon–Fri 10am–1:30pm and 3–5pm, Sat–Sun 10am–6pm; June–Sept, daily 10am–6pm; Oct–Mar, Mon–Sat 10am–1:30pm and 3–5pm, Sun 10am–2pm.

San Ildefonso de la Granja was the summer palace of the Bourbon kings of Spain, who replicated the grandeur of Versailles in the province of Segovia. Set against the snow-capped Sierra de Guadarrama, the slate-roofed palace dominates the village that grew up around it (which is a summer resort these days).

The founder of La Granja was Philip V, grandson of Louis XIV and the first Bourbon king of Spain (his body, along with that of his second queen, Isabel de Fernesio, is interred in a mausoleum in the Collegiate Church). Philip V was born at Versailles on December 19, 1683, which may explain why he wanted to re-create that atmosphere at Segovia.

At one time a farm stood on the grounds of what is now the palace—hence its totally incongruous name, la granja, meaning "the farm" in Spanish.

The palace was built in the first part of the 18th century. Inside you'll find valuable antiques (many in the Empire style), paintings, and a remarkable collection of Flemish tapestries, as well as those based on Goya cartoons from the Royal Factory in Madrid.

Most visitors, however, seem to find a stroll through the gardens more pleasing, so allow adequate time for that. The fountain statuary is a riot of cavorting gods and nymphs, hiding indiscretions behind jets of water. The gardens are studded with chestnuts and elms. A spectacular display takes place when the water jets are turned on.

SEGOVIA AFTER DARK

Just head for the Plaza Mayor, Plaza Azoguejo, and the busy calle del Carmen that runs into the Plaza Azagejo. You're sure to find some fun in the scattering of simple bars and cafes that grow more crowded at night as the days grow hotter. If you want to go dancing, two of the most popular discos include **Mansion,** calle de Juan Bravo (no phone), which is open nightly from 11pm till dawn for dancing, drinking, and flirting with the 20- to 30-year-old crowd; and the somewhat more stylish competitor, **Sabbat,** Paseo del Salon (no phone), which is open nightly from 8pm till dawn, a bit more atmospheric and frequented by persons from age 25 to around 50.

5 Alcalá de Henares

18 miles (29km) E of Madrid

History has been unfair to this ancient town, which once flourished with colleges, monasteries, and palaces. When a university was founded here in the 15th century, Alcalá became a cultural and intellectual center. Europe's first polyglot Bible (supposedly with footnotes in the original Greek and Hebrew) was published here in 1517. But the town declined during the 1800s when the university moved to Madrid. Today Alcalá is one of the main centers of North American academics in Spain, cooperating with the Fulbright Commission, Michigan State University, and Madrid's Washington Irving Center. Overall, the city has taken on new life. Commuters have turned it into a virtual suburb, dubbing it "the bedroom of Madrid."

ESSENTIALS

GETTING THERE Trains travel between Madrid's Atocha or Chamartín station and Alcalá de Henares every day and evening. Service is every 15 minutes (trip time:

half an hour), and a round-trip fare from Madrid costs 610 ptas. ($4.10). The train station (☎ **91-563-02-02**) in Alcalá is at Paseo Estación.

Buses from Madrid depart from Avenida América, 18 (Metro: América), every 15 minutes. A one-way fare is 250 ptas. ($1.70). Bus service is provided by Continental-Auto, and the Alcalá bus station is on Avenida Guadalajara, 36 (☎ **91-888-16-22**), 2 blocks past calle Libreros.

Alcalá lies adjacent to the main national highway (N-11), connecting Madrid with eastern Spain. As you leave central Madrid, follow signs for Barajas Airport and Barcelona.

VISITOR INFORMATION   The **tourist information office** is at Callejón de Santa María, 1 (☎ **91-899-26-94**). It will provide a map locating all the local attractions. Open daily 10am to 2pm and 4 to 6:30pm (until 7:30pm July to September).

EXPLORING ALCALÁ DE HENARES

Museo Casa Natal de Cervantes. Calle Imagen 2, 48. ☎ **91-889-96-54.** Free admission. Tues–Sun 10:15am–1:30pm and 4:15–6:30pm.

Visitors come to see the birthplace of Spain's literary giant Miguel de Cervantes, the creator of *Don Quixote*, who may have been born here in 1547. This 16th-century Castilian house was reconstructed in 1956 around a beautiful little courtyard, which has a wooden gallery supported by pillars with Renaissance-style capitals, plus an old well. The house contains many Cervantes manuscripts and, of course, copies of *Don Quixote*, one of the world's most widely published books (available here in many languages).

Colegio Mayor de San Ildefonso. Plaza San Diego. ☎ **91-882-13-54.** Admission 300 ptas. ($2). Tours (mandatory) Mon–Fri 11:30am, 12:30, 1:30, 5 and 6pm; Sat–Sun 11 and 11:45am, 12:30, 1:15, 2, 4:30, 5:15, 6, 6:45, and 7:30pm.

Adjacent to the main square, Plaza de Cervantes, is the Colegio Mayor de San Ildefonso, where Lope de Vega and other famous Spaniards studied. You can see some of their names engraved on plaques in the examination room. The old university's plateresque facade dates from 1543. From here you can walk across the Patio of Saint Thomas (from 1662) and the Patio of the Philosophers to reach the Patio of the Three Languages (from 1557), where Greek, Latin, and Hebrew were once taught. Here is the *Paraninfo* (great hall or old examination room), now used for special events. The hall has a Mudéjar carved-panel ceiling. The Paraninfo is entered through a restaurant, Hostería del Estudiante (see "Where to Dine," below).

Capilla de San Ildefonso. Pedro Gumíelz. ☎ **91-882-13-54.** Admission included in tour of Colegio (see above). Hours same as Colegio (see above).

Next door to the Colegio is the Capilla de San Ildefonso, the 15th-century chapel of the old university. It also houses the Italian marble tomb of Cardinal Cisneros, the founder of the original university. This chapel also has an artesonado ceiling and intricately stuccoed walls.

WHERE TO DINE

Hostería del Estudiante. Calle Colegios, 3. ☎ **91-888-03-30.** Reservations recommended. Main courses 3,500–5,000 ptas. ($23.45–$33.50); fixed-price menus 3,500 ptas. ($23.45). AE, DC, MC, V. Daily 1–4pm, Mon–Sat 9–11:30pm, Sun 9–10:30pm. Closed for dinner in July and for all of Aug. CASTILIAN.

Located within the university complex, this remarkable 1510 building is an attraction in its own right. It opened as a restaurant in 1929, and its typically Castilian recipes haven't been altered since. In the cooler months if you arrive early you can lounge in front of a 15-foot open fireplace. Oil lamps hang from the ceiling; pigskins are filled with local wine; and rope-covered chairs and high-backed carved settees capture the spirit of the past. Run by the Spanish parador system, the restaurant offers a tasty (and huge) three-course set-price lunch or dinner featuring such regional specialties as roast suckling lamb, *huevos comigos* (three eggs fried with mushrooms), and trout Navarre style. For dessert, try the cheese of La Mancha.

6 El Pardo

8 miles (13km) N of Madrid

After visiting Alcalá de Henares, spend an afternoon in El Pardo, the place Franco called home. During the Civil War many Spaniards died here, and much of the town was destroyed during the famous advance toward University City. But there's no trace of destruction today, and the countryside, irrigated by the Manzanares River, is lush and peaceful. If possible, go to the top of the hill and take in the view.

ESSENTIALS

GETTING THERE   Local city buses depart every 15 minutes from Madrid's Paseo de Moret (metro: Moncloa). A one-way fare costs 135 ptas. (90¢). Call ☎ **91-376-01-04** for more information.

Driving can be confusing on the minor roads. Head north from the city limits, following signs to La Coruña, then branch off to the west in the direction of "El Monte de El Pardo."

VISITOR INFORMATION   Spring and fall can be chilly, so dress accordingly. The Manzanares River flows nearby, but there are no convenient rail lines and no tourist office.

EXPLORING EL PARDO

Palacio de El Pardo. Avenida de La Guardia. ☎ **91-376-15-00.** Admission 650 ptas. ($4.35) adults, 250 ptas. ($1.70) students and children under 12. Mon–Sat 10:30am–6pm; Sun 9:30am–4pm. Closed during official state visits, or whenever it's being used as a guest house for the housing of top-priority foreign dignitaries.

During the regime of Franco, this was the Spanish equivalent of England's Sandringham Palace or France's Rambouillet—a presidential or royal retreat for the head of state, replete with memories of an Imperial past and the trappings of monarchy. Occupied by Castilian power meisters since medieval times, it was Franco's main residence until his death, when his body lay in state surrounded by all the honors and pageantry his political regime could muster.

When El Pardo was opened to the public in 1976, it quickly became one of the most popular sights around Madrid, replete with lore, legends, and gossip about the quirks, peccadilloes, and marital conflicts of Europe's most durable fascist.

You can visit only as part of a guided tour that's conducted mostly in Spanish with occasional English insertions. Tours depart at 15-minute intervals throughout the opening hours listed above, and last 45 minutes each. Your tour will lead you past lavishly furnished rooms once used for state receptions. Franco's ornate gilt throne reveals some of his royal pretensions. Amid noteworthy collections of Empire furniture are family mementos that include extensive wardrobes of the once-mighty Generalissimo. A collection of wax effigies, at least 10 of them, model some of Franco's state uniforms. Highlights of the tour include a visit to the Tapestry Room, many of whose masterpieces were created in the 18th and early 19th century based on cartoons by Goya, Bayeu, Aguirre, and González Ruiz. The Salon de Consejos features a 19th-century coved ceiling and one of Franco's most prized possessions: a 15th-century sideboard that once belonged to Queen Isabella.

On the grounds of the palace, and closed for an indefinite period at this writing because of restorations, stands the 18th-century **Casita del Príncipe (Prince's Cottage).** Compact and charming, it was built during the reign of Charles III, probably by his son, and frequented by his wife, often as a site for discreet romantic trysts. Also on the grounds, and also closed at this writing for restorations, is the **Palacio de la Quinta,** a satellite palace that was annexed by the crown in 1745 from the duke of Arcos.

WHERE TO DINE

Pedro's. Avenida de la Guardia, s/n. ☎ **91-376-08-83.** Reservations recommended. Main courses 2,000–3,000 ptas. ($13.40–$20.10); fixed-price menus 1,900 ptas. ($12.75). AE, DC, MC, V. Daily 1–5pm and 8pm–2 or 3am. INTERNATIONAL.

Set to the side of El Pardo's monumental facade, this is a low-key, likable restaurant that has been owned and operated since the 1960s by several generations of the Peres family. The three generations of family members who now run it contain three individuals named Pedro, and they all insist that the name of their jointly owned restaurant be spelled with an apostrophe. You can dine within a well-scrubbed interior whose predominant color is red, or move to a flower-ringed terrace in back, where there's a view over a verdant garden. Menu items are influenced by one of the Pedro's culinary sojourns in Switzerland. Thanks to that time abroad, the fricassee of rabbit or the filet mignon in brandy sauce is likely to be as flavorful as the four kinds of paella featured on the menu. These include versions with shellfish; versions tinted black from squid ink; and workaday concoctions layered with chicken, vegetables, and a less dense collection of shellfish. Also look for grilled fillet of veal and roasted lamb and/or pork, and when it's available, roasted wild boar.

7 Chinchón

32 miles (52km) SE of Madrid, 16 miles (26km) NE of Aranjuez

The main attraction of Chinchón is the **cuevas (caves),** where Anis de Chinchón, an aniseed liqueur, is manufactured. You can buy bottles of the liqueur in Plaza Mayor, at the center of town.

Wander along the town's steep and narrow streets, past the houses with large bays and spacious carriageways. Although closed to the public, the 15th-century **Chinchón Castle,** seat of the Condes of Chinchón, can be viewed from outside. The most interesting church, **Nuestra Señora de la Asunción,** dating from the 16th and 17th centuries, contains a painting by Goya.

GETTING THERE

Chinchón is most often visited from Aranjuez (see above), which is only a 15-minute ride away. Buses run twice a day from Aranjuez but only Monday through Friday, leaving from calle Almibar next to the Plaza de Toros in Aranjuez. Schedules tend to be erratic, so call for information at ☎ **91-891-39-37.** A one-way fare costs 175 ptas. ($1.15).

You can drive from Alcalá to Toledo, bypassing Madrid by taking the C-300 in a southwesterly arc around the capital. About halfway here, follow signs to "Cuevas de Chinchón." Another option is to take the E-901 southeast of Madrid toward Valencia, turning southwest at the turnoff for Chinchón.

WHERE TO STAY

Parador de Chinchón. Avenida Generalísimo, 1, Chinchón 28370 Madrid. ☎ **91-894-08-36.** Fax 91-894-09-08. 38 units. A/C MINIBAR TV TEL. 17,500 ptas. ($117.25) double; 22,500 ptas. ($150.75) suite. AE, DC, MC, V. Parking 1,250 ptas. ($8.40).

Set near the town center, this hotel lies within the carefully restored 17th-century walls of what was originally an Augustinian convent. After a stint as both a civic jail and a courthouse, it was transformed in 1972 into a government-run parador and is the only really acceptable place to stay in town. A team of architects and designers converted it handsomely, with glass-walled hallways opening onto a stone-sided courtyard. The hotel contains two bars and two dining halls. Severely dignified rooms still manage to convey their ecclesiastical origins. Rooms range from small to medium, and each is fitted with a quality mattress and fine linen along with well-maintained tiled bathrooms. Facilities include an outdoor swimming pool, open in summertime only.

WHERE TO DINE

Mesón Cuevas del Vino. Benito Horteliano, 13. ☎ **91-894-02-85.** Reservations recommended on holidays. Main courses 1,800–3,600 ptas. ($12.05–$24.10); fixed-price menu 3,750 ptas. ($25.15). No credit cards. Wed–Mon 1:30–4pm and 8–11:30pm. Closed Aug 1–20. SPANISH.

This establishment is famous for its wine cellars, and you can sample the stock at lunch or dinner. Hanging from the rafters are hams cured by the owners, and the flavorful spiced sausages are also homemade. Chunks of ham and sausage cooked in oil, plus olives and crunchy bread, are served. Your meal might begin with sliced *chorizo* (Spanish sausage); blood pudding; slices of La Mancha cheese; *sopa castellana* concocted from garlic, ham, and eggs; and thin-sliced cured ham. Main courses place heavy emphasis on roast suckling lamb and pig that emerge, crackling, from a woodburning oven. Desserts include flan, biscuits coated in cinnamon and sugar, and liquefied and sweetened almonds presented in a soupy mixture, in a bowl.

8 Ávila

68 miles (110km) NW of Madrid, 41½ miles (67km) SW of Segovia

The ancient city of Ávila is completely encircled by well-preserved 11th-century walls, which are among the most important medieval relics in Europe. The city has been declared a national landmark, and there is little wonder why. The walls aren't the only attraction, however. Ávila has several Romanesque churches, Gothic palaces, and a fortified cathedral. It is among some 80 cities or so designated by UNESCO as World Heritage Sites. (Six of these cities are in Spain; the other five are Santiago de Compostela, Segovia, Toledo, Cáceres, and Salamanca.)

Ávila's spirit and legend are most linked to St. Teresa, who was born here in 1515. This Carmelite nun, who helped defeat the Reformation and founded a number of convents, experienced visions of the Devil and angels piercing her heart with burning hot lances. She was eventually imprisoned in Toledo. Many legends sprang up after her death, including the belief that a hand severed from her body could perform miracles. Finally, in 1622, she was declared a saint.

Note: Bring warm clothes if you're visiting in the early spring.

ESSENTIALS

GETTING THERE   There are more than two dozen trains leaving daily from Madrid for Ávila, about a 1½- to 2-hour trip each way. Depending on their schedule, trains depart from Chamartín, Atocha, and Príncipe (Norte) railway stations. The 8am train from Atocha, arriving in Ávila at 9:26am, is a good choice, considering all that there is to see. Tickets cost from 835 to 1,800 ptas. ($5.60 to $12.05). The Ávila station lies at Avenida José Antonio (☎ 920-25-02-02), about a mile east of the Old City. You'll find taxis lined up in front of Ávila's railway station and at the more central Plaza Santa Teresa. For information, call ☎ 920-21-19-59 or 920-22-01-49.

Buses leave Madrid daily from Paseo Florida, 11 (metro: Norte), in front of Norte Railway Station. In Ávila the bus terminal (☎ 920-22-01-54) is at the corner of Avenida Madrid and Avenida Portugal, northeast of the center of town. A one-way ticket from Madrid costs 915 ptas. ($6.15).

To drive there, exit Madrid from its northwest perimeter and head northwest on highway N-VI (A-6), toward La Coruña, eventually forking southwest to Ávila. Driving time is around 1½ hours.

VISITOR INFORMATION   The **tourist information office** is at Plaza Catedral, 4 (☎ 920-21-13-87). It is open April through October Monday through Friday from 10am to 2pm and 4 to 7pm, Saturday 9:30am to 2pm and 4 to 7pm, and Sunday 9:30am to 2pm and 4:30 to 8:30pm. Off-season hours are Monday through Friday from 10am to 2pm and 5 to 8pm and Saturday 9:30am to 2pm.

EXPLORING THE TOWN

Begun on orders of Alfonso VI as part of the general reconquest of Spain from the Moors, the 11th-century ✪ **Walls of Ávila,** built over Roman fortifications, took 9 years to complete. They average 33 feet in height, have 88 semicircular towers, and more than 2,300 battlements. Of the nine gateways, the two most famous are the St. Vincent and the Alcázar, both on the eastern side. In many respects the walls are best viewed from the west. Whatever your preferred point of view, you can drive along their entire length: 1½ miles (2km).

Convento de Santa Teresa. Plaza de la Santa. ☎ 920-21-10-30. Free admission. Convent May–Sept, daily 9:30am–1:30pm and 3:30–9pm; Oct–Apr, daily 9:30am–1:30pm and 3:30–8:30pm. Sala de Reliquias daily 9:30am–1:30pm and 3:30–7:30pm. Bus: 1, 3, or 4.

This 17th-century convent and baroque church, 2 blocks southwest of the Plaza de la Victoria, is at the site of St. Teresa's birth. To the right of the convent is the tiny Sala de Reliquias exhibiting some of her relics, including a finger from her right hand, the sole of one of her sandals, and a cord with which she flagellated herself.

✪ **Catedral de Ávila.** Plaza Catedral. ☎ 920-21-16-41. Admission 300 ptas. ($2) adults, free for children under 8. May–Sept, daily 10am–1:30pm and 3:30–6pm; Oct–Apr, daily 10am–1:30pm and 3:30–5:30pm.

Built into the old ramparts of Ávila, this cold, austere cathedral and fortress (begun in 1099) bridges the gap between the Romanesque and the Gothic, and, as such, enjoys a certain distinction in Spanish architecture. One local writer compared it to a granite mountain. The interior is unusual, built with a mottled red-and-white stone.

Like most European cathedrals, Ávila lost its purity of design through the years as new chapels and wings—one completely in the Renaissance mode—were added. A Dutch artist, Cornelius, designed the seats of the choir stalls, also in Renaissance style, and the principal chapel holds a reredos showing the life of Christ by Pedro Berruguete, Juan de Borgoña, and Santa Cruz. Behind the chapel the tomb of Bishop Alonso de Madrigal—nicknamed "El Tostado" ("The Parched One") because of its brownish color—is Vasco de Zarza's masterpiece. The Cathedral Museum contains a laminated gold ceiling, a 15th-century triptych, a copy of an El Greco painting, as well as vestments and 15th-century songbooks.

Basilica de San Vicente. Plaza de San Vicente. ☎ **920-25-52-30.** Admission 200 ptas. ($1.35). Daily 10am–2pm and 4–8pm.

Outside the city walls, at the northeast corner of the medieval ramparts, this Romanesque-Gothic church in faded sandstone encompasses styles from the 12th to the 14th centuries. It consists of a huge nave and a trio of apses. The eternal struggle between good and evil is depicted on a cornice on the southern portal. The western portal, dating from the 13th century, contains Romanesque carvings. Inside is the tomb of St. Vincent, martyred on this site in the 4th century. The tomb's medieval carvings, which depict his torture and subsequent martyrdom, are fascinating.

Monasterio de Santo Tomás. Plaza Granada, 1. ☎ **920-22-04-00.** Admission to museum 200 ptas. ($1.35); cloisters 100 ptas. (65¢). Museum daily 11am–12:45pm and 4–6pm; cloisters Mon–Sun 10am–1pm and 4–8pm. Bus: 1, 2, or 3.

This 15th-century Gothic monastery was once the headquarters of the Inquisition in Ávila. For 3 centuries it housed the tomb of Torquemada, the first general inquisitor, whose zeal in organizing the Inquisition made him a notorious figure in Spanish history. Legend has it that after the friars were expelled from the monastery in 1836, a mob of Torquemada-haters ransacked the tomb and burned the remains somewhere outside the city walls. His final burial site is unknown.

Prince John, the only son of Ferdinand and Isabella, was also buried here, in a sumptuous sepulcher in the church transept. The tomb was desecrated during a French invasion; now, only an empty crypt remains.

Visit the Royal Cloisters, in some respects the most interesting architectural feature of the place. In the upper part of the third cloister, you'll find the Museum of Far Eastern Art, which exhibits Vietnamese, Chinese, and Japanese art and handcrafts.

Carmelitas Descalzas de San José. Las Madres, 4. ☎ **920-22-21-27.** Admission to museum, 100 ptas. (65¢). Apr–Oct, daily 10am–1:30pm and 4–7pm; off-season, daily 10am–1:30pm and 3–6pm. From Plaza de Santa Teresa and its nearby Church of San Pedro, follow calle del Duque de Alba for about 2 blocks.

Also known as the Convento de las Madres (Convent of the Mothers), this is the first convent founded by St. Teresa, who started the Reform of Carmel in 1562. Two churches are here—the primitive one, where the first Carmelite nuns took the habit; and one built by Francisco de Mora, architect of Philip III, after the saint's death. The museum displays many relics, including, of all things, St. Teresa's left clavicle.

WHERE TO STAY

Ávila is a summer resort—a refuge from Castilian heat—but the hotels are few in number, and the Spanish book nearly all the hotel space in July and August. Make sure to have a reservation in advance. Mesón El Sol y Residencia Santa Teresa (see "Where to Dine," below) also rents rooms.

MODERATE

Gran Hotel Palacio de Valderrábanos. Plaza Catedral, 9, 05001 Ávila. ☎ **800-528-1234** in the U.S. and Canada, or 920-25-51-00. Fax 920-25-16-91. 73 units. A/C MINIBAR TV TEL. 15,000 ptas. ($100.50) double; 25,000 ptas. ($167.50) suite. AE, DC, MC, V. Parking 1,000 ptas. ($6.70) per day. Bus: 1, 2, or 3.

Set immediately adjacent to the front entrance of the cathedral, behind an entryway that is a marvel of medieval stonework, this is one of the most elegant and historic hotels of Castile, very atmospheric. Originally built in the 1300s as a private home by an early bishop of Ávila (and a member of the Valderrábanos family), it contains a once-fortified lookout tower (whose circumference encloses one of the suites), high-beamed ceilings, and intricately chiseled stonework. The public rooms have a somber

A Saint & Her City

The walled city of Ávila is forever linked with the legend of St. Teresa, one of the most famous of all Catholic saints. She is most often cited as a mystic but was an adventurer, pioneer, poet, and reformer. She was born in 1515 into a large Jewish family and named Teresa de Cepeda y Ahumada. Her birth was 12 years before the reign of Philip II, who ruled from 1527 to 1598, presiding over Spain's "Golden Century."

Taking the Carmelite veil at 18, she is reported to have had her first vision at the age of 40. She toured Castile, seeking reforms and hoping to return the Carmelite order to its original vows of poverty and piety. For example, she advocated that the nuns discard shoes and wear sandals, which led to the misnomer "the Barefoot Carmelites." She founded her first Carmelite convent in 1562 and, in time, opened 16 other convents. It is said that her unfailing sense of humor and her abundant gift for friendship saved her from the dreaded Inquisition, which imprisoned her friend, mentor, and fellow Ávilan, St. John of the Cross. Many of her reforms were abandoned upon her death in 1582. The church canonized her although she remained a controversial figure, and many church leaders opposed making her a saint.

Ávila abounds with Teresian memorabilia. She was fond of playing drums and bells and was always proclaiming, "God deliver me from sullen saints." If you'd like to pay homage to St. Teresa, you can order her favorite dish, partridge. It's a local specialty served in many of Ávila's restaurants. A servant was once perplexed at her obvious enjoyment of a large helping of partridge. He felt she was demonstrating too much pleasure in eating it. "My child," she said to him, "there is a time for penitence, but there is also a time for partridge."

But we doubt if the saint herself could have tolerated one highly touted local specialty: a sticky-sweet candy called *yemas de Santa Teresa*. We recommend that you avoid this glob as surely St. Teresa herself would have. She'd probably push it away from the table and order more partridge.

---

elegance, with baronial furniture whose tassels and slightly faded upholstery add to the old-fashioned feeling. If possible, ask for a bedroom overlooking the cathedral. Rooms come in a variety of shapes and sizes, but each is usually medium in size, and each is well furnished with comfortable beds equipped with firm mattresses. Bathrooms are well organized with a hair dryer, plush towels, and adequate shelf space.

Dining: The restaurant El Fogón de Santa Teresa is a high-ceilinged bastion of formality serving traditional Castilian meals, with fixed-price menus at 3,700 ptas. ($24.80) each.

Amenities: Concierge, laundry/valet, baby-sitting.

✪ Meliá Palacio de Los Velada. Plaza de la Catedral, 10, 05001 Ávila. ☎ **800-336-3542** in the U.S. and Canada, or 920-25-51-00. Fax 920-25-49-00. 85 units. A/C MINIBAR TV TEL. 18,500 ptas. ($123.95) double. AE, MC, V. Parking 100 ptas. (65¢).

When the Spanish chain Meliá opened this splendid gem to guests in 1995, it overnight became the most sought-after accommodation in the province, surpassing the government-run paradors. Four centuries ago, this palace sheltered the likes of Charles V and Philip II. Arrayed around a central courtyard, today's hotel offers a luxury that was unimaginable when those kings spent the night.

The styling in the public rooms and the luxuriously furnished guest rooms make even the paradors look like they need a face-lift. Enjoying the best location in town—right in the center near the cathedral—the hotel receives guests in the setting of a medieval palace, with massive stones and antiques throughout. All the modern conveniences, including freshly painted closets and wide, comfortable beds, have been installed along with state-of-the-art plumbing. Each of the tiled bathrooms is equipped with a hair dryer.

Dining: The bright, helpful staff eases your adjustment into Ávila, and the elegant dining room serves some of the town's finest meals, including game (on occasion), succulent lamb, and excellent steaks. Service in the dining room is supremely efficient as well as courtly.

Amenities: Concierge, room service, laundry service, conference rooms, bicycle rentals; a shopping arcade is nearby.

✪ Parador de Ávila. Marqués de Canales de Chozas, 2, 05001 Ávila. ☎ **920-21-13-40.** Fax 920-22-61-66. 61 units. MINIBAR TV TEL. 15,000 ptas. ($100.50) double; 30,000 ptas. ($201) suite. AE, DC, MC, V. Free outside parking, garage 1,200 ptas. ($8.05).

Lying 2 blocks northwest of Plaza de la Victoria, this parador stands on a ridge overlooking the banks of the Adaja River. Once it was known as the Palace of Benavides, dating from the 15th century; its facade forms part of the square. The palace has a dignified entranceway, with most of its public lounges opening onto a central courtyard with an inner gallery of columns. The recently refurbished rooms contain tasteful furnishings: a tall stone fireplace, highly polished tile floors, old chests, leather armchairs, paintings, and sculptures. The rooms, generally medium in size, come with all the modern comforts as well, including good mattresses and spick-and-span bathrooms, each one tiled and equipped with a hair dryer.

Dining: The dining room, with its leaded-glass windows opening onto a terraced garden, serves passable Castilian dishes.

Amenities: Concierge, laundry service, conference rooms, baby-sitting, currency exchange service.

INEXPENSIVE

El Rastro. Plaza del Rastro, 1, 05001 Ávila. ☎ **920-21-12-18.** Fax 920-25-16-26. 10 units. 6,350 ptas. ($42.55) double. No credit cards.

Situated near the junction of calle Caballeros and calle Cepadas is the best choice for the bargain hunter. Few visitors know that they can spend the night at this old Castilian inn built into the city walls. The small guest rooms are basic and clean. We recommend the restaurant here, too (see below).

Gran Hostal San Segundo. San Segundo, 28, 05001 Ávila. ☎ **920-25-25-90.** Fax 920-25-27-90. 14 units. TV TEL. 7,500 ptas. ($50.25) double. AE, DC, MC, V. Free parking on the street.

This small hotel and restaurant is situated just outside the immense walls that surround the historic center of Ávila. The elegant 19th-century building itself has just been renovated with a mind to both maintaining its historical charm and incorporating modern comfort. The reception rooms have high ceilings and are decorated in a soft salmon hue, and the medium-size guest rooms are spotlessly clean and decorated in a simple, unpretentious fashion. The hotel incorporates an Italian restaurant, which also prepares typically regional dishes such as *Carne Avilena,* a T-bone steak, roast lamb, and the rich and tasty *cochinillo* (roasted piglet), cooked in its own juice and served with nothing more than bread. The restaurant is open daily from noon to 4pm and from 8pm to midnight.

✪ **Hosteria de Bracamonte.** Bracamonte, 6, 05001 Ávila. ☎ **920-25-38-38.** 18 units. MINIBAR TV TEL. 8,000–10,000 ptas. ($53.60–$67) double. MC, V.

The most tranquil spot in town is this little gem decorated in a classic Castilian style. It lies 1 block north of Plaza de Victoria, the main square within the city walls. A restful and quiet oasis, it has a number of charming features, including a lovely patio. A dark-wood Castilian motif is used throughout. Converted to a small inn in 1989, the hosteria retains some of its aristocratic origins as the town house of Gov. Don Juan Teherán y Monjaraz. Rooms are spacious and have whitewashed walls; some have fireplaces and four-poster beds. Mattresses and linens are of fine quality. Parking is available along the street.

WHERE TO DINE

El Rastro. Plaza del Rastro, 1. ☎ **920-21-12-19.** Reservations required on weekends only. Main courses 1,800–2,500 ptas. ($12.05–$16.75); fixed-price menu 1,800 ptas. ($12.05). AE, DC, MC, V. Daily 1–4pm and 9–11pm. CASTILIAN.

An old inn built into the 11th-century town walls, El Rastro serves typical Castilian dishes, with more attention given to freshness and preparation than to culinary flamboyance. Specialties include roast baby lamb and tender white veal, raised in the region of Ávila and known for its succulence. It is prepared at least four different ways. Dessert recipes have been passed down from Ávila's nuns. Try, if you dare, the highly touted *yemas de Santa Teresa* (St. Teresa's candied egg yolk), although when we once dined here with travel expert Arthur Frommer, he found this a particularly horrible dessert—and we concur. Yet, Ávila residents keep praising it as a specialty. To our taste, there are far better selections on the menu. They also maintain a small hotel with 10 comfortable rooms, each with TV and bathroom and no phone (see "Where to Stay," above).

Mesón El Sol y Residencia Santa Teresa. Avenida 18 de Julio, 25, 05003 Ávila. ☎ **920-22-02-11.** Fax 920-22-41-13. Reservations recommended. Main courses 950–2,400 ptas. ($6.35–$16.10); fixed-price menu 1,800 ptas. ($12.05). AE, DC, MC, V. Daily 1–4pm and 9–11pm. Bus: 2. CASTILIAN.

Just a short walk from the historic center of town, you may be distracted by the aromas emanating from the kitchen of the lowest-priced inn in Ávila—a place known for its good food, moderate prices, and efficient service. Full meals may include seafood soup, fried hake, veal with garlic, and house-style flan. The inn also rents 18 simply furnished rooms, a double going for 6,000 to 8,000 ptas. ($40.20 to $53.60).

9 Cuenca

100 miles (161km) E of Madrid, 202 miles (325km) SW of Zaragoza

This medieval town, once dominated by the Arabs, is a spectacular sight with its casas colgadas, the cliff-hanging houses set on multiple terraces that climb up the impossibly steep sides of a ravine. The Júcar and Huécar Rivers meet at the bottom.

ESSENTIALS

GETTING THERE   Trains leave Madrid's Atocha Railway Station about eight times throughout the day. Trains arrive in Cuenca at Paseo del Ferrocarril in the new city (☎ 969-22-07-20), after a journey lasting anywhere from 2½ to 3 hours. A one-way ticket from Madrid costs 1,355 ptas. ($9.10).

There are about eight buses from Madrid every day. Buses arrive at calle Fermín Caballero, s/n (☎ 969-22-70-87 for information and schedules). A one-way fare costs from 1,305 to 1,600 ptas. ($8.75 to $10.70).

Cuenca is the junction for several highways and about a dozen lesser roads that connect it to towns within its region. From Madrid, take the N-III to Tarancon, then the N-400, which leads directly into Cuenca.

VISITOR INFORMATION   The city tourist office is at calle San Pedro, 6 (☎ **969-23-21-19**), next to the cathedral off Plaza Mayor. Hours are daily from 9:30am to 2pm and 4 to 7pm.

EXPLORING THE AREA

The chief sight of Cuenca is the town itself. Isolated from the rest of Spain, it requires a northern detour from the heavily traveled Valencia-Madrid road. Deep gorges give it an unreal quality, and eight old bridges spanning two rivers connect the ancient parts of town with the growing new sections. One of the bridges is suspended over a 200-foot drop.

Cuenca's streets are narrow and steep, often cobbled, and even the most athletic tourist will tire quickly. But you shouldn't miss it, even if you have to stop and rest periodically. At night you're in for a special treat when the *casas colgadas* are illuminated. Also, try to drive almost to the top of the castle-dominated hill. The road gets rough as you approach the end, but the view makes the effort worthwhile.

If you have the time, you can easily make a side trip to the ✪ **Ciudad Encantada (Enchanted City),** Carretera de la Sierra, about 25 miles (40km) to the northeast of Cuenca. Storms and underground waters have created a city here out of large rocks and boulders, shaping them into bizarre designs: a seal, an elephant, a Roman bridge. Take CU-912, turning northeast onto CU-913. Ciudad Encantada is signposted.

Catedral de Cuenca Plaza. Pío XII. Free admission. Daily 8:45am–2pm and 4–7pm (closes at 6pm in winter). Bus: 1 or 2.

Begun in the 12th century, this Gothic cathedral was influenced by England's Norman style, becoming the only Anglo-Norman cathedral in Spain. Part of it collapsed in this century, but it has been restored. A national monument filled with religious art treasures, the cathedral is a 10-minute walk from the Plaza Mayor, up calle Palafox. The cathedral's *museo diocesano* exhibits two canvases by El Greco, a collection of Flemish tapestries (some beautifully designed), and a statue of the Virgin del Sagrario from the 1100s.

✪ **Museo de Arte Abstracto Español.** Calle los Canónigos, s/n. ☎ **969-21-29-83.** Admission 500 ptas. ($3.35) adults, 250 ptas. ($1.70) students. Tues–Fri 11am–2pm and 4–6pm, Sat 11am–2pm and 4–8pm, Sun 11am–2:30pm. Bus: 1 or 2.

North of Plaza Mayor, housed in a cliff-hanging dwelling, this ranks as one of the finest museums of its kind in Spain. It was conceived by painter Fernando Zóbel, who donated it in 1980 to the Juan March Foundation. The most outstanding abstract Spanish painters are represented, including Rafael Canogar (especially his *Toledo*), Luís Feito, Zóbel himself, Tápies, Eduardo Chillida, Gustavo Torner, Gerardo Rueda, Millares, Sempere, Cuixart, and Antonio Saura (see his grotesque Geraldine Chaplin and his study of Brigitte Bardot, a vision of horror, making the French actress look like an escapee from Picasso's *Guernica*).

WHERE TO STAY

Hotel Avenida. Carretería, 25, 16002 Cuenca. ☎ **969-21-43-43.** Fax 969-21-23-35. 32 units. TV TEL. 4,500–6,000 ptas. ($30.15–$40.20) double. Parking nearby 900 ptas. ($6.05). AE, MC, V.

A good value for the money, this hotel lies in Cuenca's modern commercial center, about a block southwest of Parque de San Julian. Built in 1971 and renovated in 1991 and 1995, it offers tidy but small rooms with simple amenities and access to a helpful staff. Only a handful of rooms has air-conditioning; the rest are on the shaded side of the building and, at least according to management, don't seem to get very hot. Breakfast is the only meal served, but the staff can direct its clients to the nearby calle Colón, where many different restaurants in various price ranges are ready, willing, and able to feed foreign visitors. Parking, incidentally, is within a nearby parking lot maintained by Cuenca's municipal government.

Hotel Figón de Pedro. Calle Cervantes, 13, 16004 Cuenca. ☎ **969-22-45-11.** Fax 969-23-11-92. 28 units. TV TEL. 5,200–6,000 ptas. ($34.85–$40.20) double. AE, DC, MC, V.

Figón de Pedro lies south of the old city, a short walk north of the bus and rail stations. The hotel (with elevator) is immaculate but not stuffy, since the staff keeps the atmosphere pleasantly informal. On the second floor you'll find a lounge with TV, and the hotel boasts a country-style dining room, with a *tasca* in front. Bedrooms are small but well maintained with comfortable beds and tiny tiled bathrooms with shower stalls. Wood beams, fresh linen on the tables, and personal service all make this an inviting place for meals.

Leonor de Aquitania. Calle San Pedro, 60, 16001 Cuenca. ☎ **969-23-10-00.** Fax 969-23-10-04. 49 units. A/C MINIBAR TV TEL. 8,500–10,900 ptas. ($56.95–$73.05) double; 15,000–21,000 ptas. ($100.50–$140.70) suite. AE, DC, MC, V. Free parking.

Perched high up on the hillside above an almost sheer drop, the hotel enjoys spectacular views of both the old city of Cuenca from one angle and the narrow valley rising from the harsh though beautiful precipice opposite. The reception rooms have been maintained in extremely good, conservative taste, and the hotel evokes an elegantly restrained and comfortable charm. The medium-size rooms are exceedingly well cared for, and each comes with a firm mattress and an immaculate tile bath. The Hebrea Hermosa (the beautiful Jewish maiden) suite is one of the most charming in this quiet medieval city, which lies precariously between two deep gorges. There is a restaurant inside the hotel that operates in the day and serves, among other things, a fixed-price menu for 2,300 ptas. ($15.40).

✪ Parador de Turismo de Cuenca. Convento de San Pablo, Paseo de la Hoz del Huécar, 16001 Cuenca. ☎ **969-23-23-20.** Fax 969-23-25-34. 63 units. A/C MINIBAR TV TEL. 17,500 ptas. ($117.25) double; 29,500 ptas. ($197.65) suite. AE, DC, MC, V. Parking 1,100 ptas. ($7.35).

This government-sponsored hotel occupies the dignified premises of what was originally built, in 1523, as a Dominican monastery. A noteworthy example of late Gothic architecture, it lies on a hillside above Cuenca, about a half mile northwest of the town's historic center. It is clearly the town's prestige address. Opened for business after extensive renovations in 1992, its three stories contain masses of intricately chiseled 16th-century stonework (some enhanced with glass panels overlooking the river), a church, a severely beautiful cloister, a sense of timeless solidity, and a swimming pool. There's a bar, a high-ceilinged restaurant, and two floors of medium-size rooms which, despite comfortably traditional furniture and modern bathrooms, richly convey their ecclesiastical origins.

✪ Posada de San José. Julián Romero, 4, 16001 Cuenca. ☎ **969-21-13-00.** Fax 969-23-03-65. www.arrakis.es/~psanjose. E-mail: psanjose@arrakis.es. 30 units (22 with bathroom). 4,100–4,700 ptas. ($27.45–$31.50) double without bathroom; 7,200–9,100 ptas. ($48.25–$60.95) double with bathroom. AE, DC, MC, V. Bus: 1 or 2.

Posada de San José stands in the oldest part of Cuenca, a short walk north of the cathedral. The 17th-century cells that used to shelter the sisters of this former convent now house overnight guests who consider its views of the old city the best in town. It sits atop a cliff, overlooking the forbidding depths of a gorge. Accommodations are small but are still quite comfortable with very good beds with firm mattresses. Bathrooms are also small with shower stalls. Owners Antonio and Jennifer Cortinas renovated this place into one of the best bargain hotels of the region, with the bar perhaps the most charming of its well-decorated public rooms. Parking is available along the street.

WHERE TO DINE

El Figon de Pedro. Cervantes 13. ☎ **969-22-68-21.** Reservations recommended. Main courses 800–2,000 ptas. ($5.35–$13.40); menú del día 3,000 ptas. ($20.10). AE, DC, MC, V. Daily 1:30–4pm, Mon–Sat 9–11pm. Closed Feb.

Set in the business section of the new town at the foot of the hills that leads you to the wonders of medieval Cuenca, this restaurant belongs to one of Spain's most celebrated restaurateurs, Pedro Torres Pacheco. Given this, and by turning a quick blind eye to the abundance of late '60s concrete, the location is well worth a visit. The air-conditioned restaurant is relatively intimate, with 13 tables and the traditional Castillian decor of plates on walls and folkloric memorabilia. The cuisine, however, is not half as predictable. The *mortuelo* (local pâté made from partridge, pork, ham, and hare) should definitely be sampled as should the gazpacho and *bacalao ajo arriero* (a puree of cod, garlic, eggs, and olive oil). The desserts here are interesting, unlike those in many Spanish restaurants, especially the original Moorish *alaju* (almonds, bread crumbs, honey, and orange water) and the Miguelito, a flat almond cake. When sated you can then toast the meal with a glass of resoli, the strong local liquor.

✪ **Mesón Casa Colgadas.** Canónigos, 3. ☎ **969-22-35-09.** Reservations recommended. Main courses 1,000–2,800 ptas. ($6.70–$18.75); fixed-price menus 3,300–3,800 ptas. ($22.10–$25.45). AE, DC, MC, V. Daily 1:30–4pm, Wed–Mon 9–11pm. SPANISH/INTERNATIONAL.

One of the most spectacular dining rooms in Spain stands on one of the most precarious precipices in Cuenca. Established in the late 1960s, it occupies a 19th-century house, five stories high, with sturdy supporting walls and beams. Pine balconies and windows overlook the ravine below and the hills beyond. In fact, it's the most photographed "suspended house" in town, and dinner here is worth every céntimo. The menu includes regional dishes and a wide variety of well-prepared international favorites. Drinks are served in the tavern room on the street level, so even if you're not dining here, you may want to drop in for a drink and the view. You'll find the Mesón Casa Colgadas just south of the cathedral and near the Museum of Spanish Abstract Art.

Togar. Avenida República Argentina, 3. ☎ **969-22-01 62.** Reservations required. Main courses 800–2,000 ptas. ($5.35–$13.40); fixed-price menu 1,800–3,000 ptas. ($12.05–$20.10). AE, DC, MC, V. Daily 1–4pm, Mon–Sat 8–11pm. Closed 1 week in July (dates vary). Bus: 1 or 6. SPANISH.

Rich with local flavor and aggressively cost-conscious, this is a simple but likable tasca on the southwestern periphery of town. Established in 1955, and set within an angular building erected the same year, it offers homemade cookery whose inspiration derives from the various regions of Spain. One of the specialties is *revuelto Togar,* an egg, ham, and shrimp dish served with herbs and crusty bread. Also available are well-peppered versions of pork, several kinds of rich soups, and various beef and fish dishes.

5 Old Castile & León

Spain owes much to Castile, Aragón, and León, since these three kingdoms helped forge the various regions of the country into a unified whole. Modern Spain was conceived when Isabella of Castile married Ferdinand of Aragón on October 19, 1469. Five years later she was proclaimed queen of Castile and León. The Moors were eventually driven out of Granada, the rest of Spain was conquered, and Columbus sailed to America—all during the reign of these two Catholic monarchs.

This proud but controversial queen and her unscrupulous husband fashioned an empire whose influence extended throughout Spain, Europe, and the New World. The power once held by Old Castile shifted long ago to Madrid, but today there are many reminders of its storied past.

The ancient kingdom of León, which was eventually annexed to Castile, embraced three cities: Salamanca, Zamora, and the provincial capital of León. Today the district is known for its many castles.

In Old Castile, we'll cover the inland provincial capital of Valladolid, where Isabella married Ferdinand and where a brokenhearted Columbus died on May 19, 1506. From here we'll move on to Burgos, once the capital of Old Castile. Vivar, a small town near here, produced El Cid, Spain's greatest national hero, who conquered the Moorish kingdom of Valencia.

For other destinations in the region, refer to chapter 4, "Side Trips from Madrid."

1 Ciudad Rodrigo

54 miles (87km) SW of Salamanca, 177 miles (285km) W of Madrid

A walled town dating from Roman days, Ciudad Rodrigo is known for its 16th- and 17th-century town houses, built by the conquistadors. It was founded in the 12th century by Count Rodriguez González and today has been designated a national monument. Located near the Portuguese frontier, it stands high on a hilltop and is known for the familiar silhouette of the square tower of its Alcázar. This walled part of the city is referred to as the Casco Viejo.

The ramparts were built in the 12th century along Roman foundations. Several stairways lead up to a mile-long sentry path. You can wander these ramparts at leisure and then walk through the streets with their many churches and mansions. It is not one chief monument that is the allure, but rather the city as a whole.

The town's major attraction is its cathedral, Santa María, which is a combination of Romanesque and Gothic styles with a neoclassical tower.

Casco Viejo, mostly built between 1170 and 1230, though subsequent centuries have seen more additions. It can be reached going east of Plaza Mayor through Plaza de San Salvador. The Renaissance altar on the north aisle is an acclaimed work of ecclesiastical art; look also for the Virgin Portal, at the west door, which dates from the 1200s. For 200 ptas. ($1.35), you'll be admitted to the cloisters, which have a variety of architectural styles, including a plateresque door. Hours are daily from 10am to 1pm and 4 to 6:30pm.

The **Plaza Mayor** is a showpiece of 17th-century architecture, with two Renaissance palaces. This is the main square of the city.

Your transportation in Ciudad Rodrigo will be your trusty feet, as walking is the only way to explore the city. Pick up a map at the tourist office (see below).

ESSENTIALS

GETTING THERE   The only real way to get here is from Salamanca. Because train service is infrequent and the train station is a long way from the walls of the old city, it's easier to take the bus from Salamanca; you'll get off at the Ciudad Rodrigo station at calle Campo de Toledo (☎ **923-46-12-17**). Monday through Friday 11 buses arrive from Salamanca; on Saturday and Sunday, five buses. The trip takes 1 hour and costs 730 ptas. ($4.90) one-way.

The N-620 is the main road from both Salamanca and Portugal. Driving time from Salamanca is about 1¼ hours.

VISITOR INFORMATION   The **tourist information office** is at Plaza Amayuelas, 5 (☎ **923-46-05-61**). It is open Monday through Friday from 10am to 2pm and 5 to 8pm; Saturday, 10am to 2pm and 4 to 7pm.

SPECIAL EVENTS   Carnival festivities in February in Ciudad Rodrigo feature a running of the bulls, traditional dances, and costumes.

WHERE TO STAY

Conde Rodrigo I. Plaza de San Salvador, 9, 37500 Ciudad Rodrigo. ☎ **923-46-14-04.** Fax 923-46-14-08. 34 units. A/C MINIBAR TV TEL. 6,000–7,000 ptas. ($40.20–$46.90) double. DC, MC, V. Parking 1,000 ptas. ($6.70).

Its central location next to the cathedral is a big plus for this two-star hotel; try for a room opening onto the square. The recently renovated rooms are small and totally devoid of style, but they're comfortable. The building itself has some medieval flavor, with its thick walls of chiseled stone. The hotel restaurant is a good buy, offering well-prepared Castilian food, such as roast meats, spicy sausages, and fresh fish. Public parking is available off the street.

WHERE TO DINE

Estoril. Traversia Talavera, 1. ☎ **923-46-05-50.** Reservations recommended. Main courses 1,500–1,700 ptas. ($10.05–$11.40); *menú del día* 1,400 ptas. ($9.40). DC, MC, V. Daily noon–4pm and 8:30pm–midnight, and Fri–Sat night until 3 or 4am. CASTILIAN/BASQUE.

Lying only a short walk from Plaza Mayor, this popular restaurant was established in 1967, within a building constructed that year. The air-conditioned interior is decorated in a typical regional style, with bullfight photographs. Specialties of the house include roasted meats, such as roast suckling pig, with a special emphasis on roasted goat. Seafood, such as sole and hake, is presented in the Basque style. The seafood soup is particularly good. Everything is accompanied by a variety of regional wines, including Cosechero Rioja.

Mayton. La Colada, 9. ☎ **923-46-07-20.** Reservations recommended. Main courses 850–2,250 ptas. ($5.70–$15.10); fixed-price menu 1,400 ptas. ($9.40). AE, DC, MC, V. Daily 1–3:30pm and 8–11:30pm. CASTILIAN.

Adjacent to Plaza Mayor, within a 17th-century building, Mayton is the best restaurant in the city. The walls of the antique and well-preserved bodega in which it stands reverberate with atmosphere and legend. The menu specializes in fresh fish and shellfish, and does so exceedingly well. Try the *sopa castellana* (Castilian soup) for an appetizer, followed by *merluza* (hake) in green sauce. You can also order veal, as tender as that of Ávila. The place is air-conditioned.

2 Salamanca

127 miles (204km) NW of Madrid, 73 miles (117km) E of Portugal

This ancient city, famous for the university founded here by Alfonso IX in the early 1200s, is well preserved, with turreted palaces, faded convents, Romanesque churches, and colleges that once attracted scholars from all over Europe. The only way to explore Salamanca conveniently is on foot so arm yourself with a good map and set out to explore the city. Nearly all the attractions are within walking distance of the Plaza Mayor.

In its day, Salamanca was ranked with Oxford, Paris, and Bologna as one of "the four leading lights of the medieval world." The intellectual life continues to this day, and a large invasion of American students brings added life to the town in summer. Its population has swelled to 180,000 but a lingering provincial aura remains.

Still a youthful, spirited place because of the venerable Salamanca University, the city has been named a "World Heritage City" by UNESCO, one of six such cities in Spain. No country can boast of more.

ESSENTIALS

GETTING THERE   Three trains travel directly from Madrid's North Station to Salamanca daily (3½ hours one-way), arriving northeast of the town center, on the Paseo de la Estación de Ferrocarril (☎ **923-12-02-02**). The fare is 2,090 ptas. ($14). More frequent are the rail connections between Salamanca, Ávila, Ciudad Rodrigo, and Valladolid (around six trains each per day).

There's frequent daily bus service from Madrid. The trip takes 2½ hours. Salamanca's bus terminal is at Avenida Filiberto Villalobos, 71 (☎ **923-23-67-17**), northwest of the center of town. There are also buses to Salamanca from Ávila, Zamora, Valladolid, León, and Caceres (2 to 13 per day, depending on the point of departure).

Salamanca is not located on a national highway, but a good network of roads converge there from such nearby cities as Ávila, Valladolid, and Ciudad Rodrigo. One of the most heavily trafficked highways is the N-620, leading into Salamanca from both Barcelona and Portugal. From Madrid, take the N-VI northwest, forking off to Salamanca on the N-501.

VISITOR INFORMATION   The **tourist information office** is at Plaza Mayor 13 (☎ **923-21-83-42**). Open Monday through Saturday from 9am to 2pm and 4:30 to 6:30pm, Sunday 10am to 2pm and 4:30 to 6:30pm.

EXPLORING SALAMANCA

To start, spend as much time as you can at the ✪ **Plaza Mayor,** an 18th-century baroque square acclaimed as the most beautiful public plaza in Spain. No trip to this university town is complete unless you walk through the arcade of shops and feast your eyes on the honey-colored buildings. After this you'll understand why the *plaza mayor*, a town's main square, is an integral part of Spanish life. If it's a hot day and you

Now the traveller has re-entered the bald regions of Old Castile, and the best thing is to get out of them again as quickly as possible.
—Richard Ford, *A Handbook for Travellers in Spain* (1855)

want what everybody else in the Plaza Mayor is drinking, stop in a cafe and order *leche helado,* an icy vanilla and almond milkshake that's very refreshing and not too filling.

Even before reaching Plaza Mayor, you may want to stop and admire the facade of the landmark **Casa de las Conchas,** or House of Shells, which appears as you walk north from the Patio de las Escuelas (site of the Universidad de Salamanca, see below) on calles de Libreros and San Isidro. This much-photographed building is at the corner of Rua Mayor and calle de la Compañía (☎ **923-26-93-17**). The restored 1483 house is noted for its facade of 400 simulated scallop shells. A professor of medicine at the university and a doctor at the court of Isabella created the house as a monument to Santiago de Compostela, the renowned pilgrimage site. The shell is the symbol of the Order of Santiago. You can visit the courtyard Monday through Friday from 9am to 9pm, Saturday 9am to 2pm and 4 to 7pm, and Sunday 10am to 2pm. Admission is free.

Casa Museo Unamuno. Calle de Libreros, 25. ☎ **923-29-44-00.** Free admission. Mon–Fri 9am–1:30pm, 4–6pm; Sat–Sun 10am–1:30pm. July 7–Sept 30, only open mornings. Last tours leave 30 minutes before closing time. Bus: 1.

The poet and philosopher Miguel de Unamuno—one of the world's most renowned scholars—lived from 1900 to 1914 in this 18th-century home beside the university. Here he wrote many of the works that made him famous. You can see some of his notebooks and his library, along with many personal mementos.

Catedral Nueva (New Cathedral). Plaza Juan XXII. ☎ **923-21-74-76.** Admission 300 ptas. ($2). Daily 9am–2pm and 4–8pm. Bus: 1.

The "new" cathedral dates from 1513. It took more than 200 years to complete it, so the edifice represents many styles: It's classified as late Gothic, but you'll see baroque and plateresque features as well. José Churriguera contributed some rococo elements, too. The building has a grand gold-on-beige sandstone facade, elegant chapels, the best-decorated dome in Spain, and bas-relief columns that look like a palm-tree cluster. Unfortunately, its stained glass is severely damaged. The cathedral lies in the southern section of the old town, about 5 blocks south of Plaza Mayor at the edge of Plaza de Anaya.

Catedral Vieja (Old Cathedral). Plaza Juan XXII. ☎ **923-21-74-76.** Admission 300 ptas. ($2). Apr–Sept, daily 10am–1:30pm and 4–7:30pm, Oct–Mar, daily 9am–1pm and 4–6pm. Bus: 1.

Adjoining the New Cathedral is this older Spanish Romanesque version, begun in 1140. Its simplicity provides a dramatic contrast to the ornamentation of its younger but bigger counterpart. After viewing the interior, stroll through the enclosed cloisters with their Gothic tombs of long-forgotten bishops. The chapels are of special architectural interest. In the Capilla de San Martín, the frescoes date from 1242, and in the Capilla de Santa Bárbara, final exams for Salamanca University students were given. The Capilla de Santa Catalina is noted for its gargoyles.

Museo Art Nouveau–Art Deco. Calle Gilbraltar, 14. ☎ **923-12-14-25.** Admission 300 ptas. ($2) adults, 200 ptas. ($1.35) students and children. Tues–Fri 11am–2pm and 5–9pm, Sat–Sun 11am–9pm.

Salamanca

Casa de las Conchas ❷
Casa Museo Unamuno ❹
Catedral Nueva ❻
Catedral Vieja ❼
Convento de las Dueñas ❽
Convento de San Estéban ❾
Museo de Salamanca ❸
Plaza Mayor ❶
Universidad de Salamanca ❺

The Art Nouveau–Art Deco Museum contains more than 1,500 pieces, all part of the collection of the Manuel Ramos Andrade Foundation. Spanning the late 19th century to the 1930s, the collection includes bronze and marble figurines, jewelry, furniture, paintings, and a collection of some 300 porcelain dolls. Numerous works by Emile Gallé and René Lalique are also on display.

Museo de Salamanca (Casa de los Doctores de la Reina). Patio de las Escuelas, 2. ☎ **923-21-22-35.** Admission 200 ptas. ($1.35). Tues–Fri 10am–2pm and 4:30–7:30pm, Sat 10am–2pm. Bus: 1.

Built in the late 15th century by Queen Isabella's physician, this structure, located near the university, is a fine example of the Spanish plateresque style. The Fine Arts

Museum is housed here, boasting a collection of paintings and sculptures dating from the 15th to the 20th centuries.

Convento de las Dueñas. Plaza del Concillo de Trento. ☎ **923-21-54-42.** Admission 200 ptas. ($1.35). June–Sept, daily 10am–1pm and 4–7pm; Oct–May, daily 10:30am–1pm and 4:30–5:30pm.

Across calle Buenaventura from Convento de San Esteban (see below) is one of the most popular sights of Salamanca, a former Mudéjar palace of a court official. The cloisters date from the 16th century, and are, in the opinion of some of Spain's architectural critics, the most beautiful in Salamanca. Climb to the upper gallery for a close inspection of the carved capitals, which are covered with demons and dragons, saints and sinners, and animals of every description—some from the pages of *The Divine Comedy.* There is also a portrait of Dante.

Convento de San Esteban. Plaza del Concilio de Trento. ☎ **923-21-50-00.** Admission 200 ptas. ($1.35). Daily 9:30am–1pm and 4–8pm.

Of all the old religious sites of Salamanca, St. Stephen's Convent is one of the most dramatic. The golden-brown plateresque facade of this late Gothic church competes with the cathedral in magnificence. Inside, José Churriguera in 1693 created a high altar that is one of Salamanca's greatest art treasures. The Claustro de los Reyes (Cloister of the Kings) is both plateresque and Gothic in style. The convent lies 2 blocks east of the New Cathedral on the opposite side of busy calle San Pablo at the southern terminus of calle de España (Gran Vía).

Universidad de Salamanca. Patio de las Escuelas, 1. ☎ **923-29-44-00.** Admission 300 ptas. ($2). Mon–Fri 9:30am–1pm and 4–7pm, Sat 9:30am–1:30pm and 4–6pm, Sun 10am–1pm. Enter from Patio de las Escuelas, a widening of calle de Libreros.

The oldest university in Spain was once the greatest in Europe. In front of the plateresque facade of the building, a statue honors Hebrew scholar Fray Luís de León. Arrested for heresy, Fray Luís was detained for 5 years before being cleared. When he returned, he began his first lecture: "As I was saying yesterday . . ." Fray Luís's remains are kept in the chapel, which is worth a look. You can also visit a dim 16th-century classroom, cluttered with crude wooden benches, but the library upstairs is closed to the public. The university lies 2 blocks from the cathedral in the southern section of the old town.

SHOPPING

The town's two main shopping neighborhoods extend around the calle Melendez and the historic borders of the Plaza Mayor. Both areas are good bets for fashion and housewares. You may also want to head for the town's largest department store, **Corte Fiel,** Plaza Mayor (☎ **923-21-92-40**) or the menswear branch at calle Doro 24 (☎ **923-215290**). And if you're looking for handcrafts, head for **Artesanía Hernandez,** calle Conde de Cadarrus 21 (☎ **923-12-07-98**), whose inventories represent most of the trades that used to proliferate within the region around Salamanca.

WHERE TO STAY
EXPENSIVE

Gran Hotel. Plaza Poeta Iglesias, 5, 37001 Salamanca. ☎ **923-21-35-00.** Fax 923-21-35-00. 136 units. A/C MINIBAR TV TEL. 15,000 ptas. ($100.50) double; 25,000 ptas. ($167.50) suite. AE, DC, MC, V. Parking 2,500 ptas. ($16.75).

Because of both its location and the legends that surround it, this hotel has been a favorite since it was built in 1930. Set on the southeast corner of the Plaza Mayor, it became the traditional favorite of bull breeders and matadors, as well as of the literati of this ancient university town. Because its owners have kept it up-to-date, the hotel is still going strong, although accommodations at the Parador Nacional de Salamanca (see below) are better appointed. In 1994 the hotel was completely renovated, with modern plumbing added, but with much of the old-fashioned charm left intact. Each bedroom is well maintained, with quality mattresses and handsomely equipped bathrooms with hair dryers and plush towels.

Dining: Castilian-style meals are served à la carte in the hotel's Restaurante Feudal. Service in both the hotel and the restaurant could stand some improvement.

Amenities: Concierge, room service, laundry service, baby-sitting, conference rooms.

Hotel Monterrey. Azafranal, 21, 37001 Salamanca. ☎ **923-21-44-01.** Fax 923-21-44-01. 144 units. A/C TV TEL. 15,000 ptas. ($100.50) double; 20,000–30,000 ptas. ($134–$201) suite. AE, DC, MC, V. Parking 2,000 ptas. ($13.40).

Run by the same company that operates the Gran Hotel (see above), this hotel isn't as good as its sibling, but it's an okay backup choice. Its location near the Plaza Mayor is ideal and its wood and velvet lobby is inviting. The conservatively and simply furnished midsized guest rooms, although not as well appointed as those of the Gran, are still quite comfortable, each with a firm mattress. The price, especially of the cheaper rooms, is a good value for Salamanca.

Dining: Many Castilian specialties are served in the fine restaurant, El Fogón; there's also an inviting cafe.

✪ **Hotel Rector.** Rector Esperabé, 10, 37008 Salamanca. ☎ **923-21-84-82.** Fax 923-21-40-08. 14 units. A/C MINIBAR TV TEL. 17,000 ptas. ($113.90) double; 22,000 ptas. ($147.40) suite. Breakfast 1,000 ptas. ($6.70) per person extra. AE, DC, MC, V. Parking 1,000 ptas. ($6.70).

Far better than either the parador or the Gran Hotel, this little inn has become the best place to stay in Salamanca, where nothing matches it in either atmosphere or tranquillity. Located just beyond the Roman bridge, it was a private mansion until the owners, who live on the upper floors, converted it into a hotel in 1990. The rooms are not really hotel quarters, but resemble the elegantly furnished and spacious bedrooms you'd find in the home of a grand Spanish don. Rooms are elegantly appointed with luxury mattresses and beautifully tiled and kept bathrooms complete with thick towels and hair dryers. Don't expect all the amenities found in a full-service hotel (no restaurant, for example), but the staff here is extremely professional and polite. Since this place is such a gem, you have to reserve well in advance.

Amenities: Laundry and dry cleaning service, baby-sitting, concierge.

✪ **NH Palacio de Castellanos.** San Pablo 58-64, 37008 Salamanca. ☎ **923-26-18-18.** Fax 923-26-18-19. www.nh-hoteles.es. 62 units. A/C MINIBAR TV TEL. 19,000 ptas. ($127.30) double; from 21,000 ptas. ($140.70) suite. AE, DC, MC, V. Parking 2,500 ptas. ($16.75).

The grandest palace in Salamanca, this deluxe hotel was built on the site of the original 15th-century Palacio de Castellanos and lies in old Salamanca near the Plaza Mayor, with good views in most directions. We like it much better than the parador. The elegant, marble-floored lobby, supported by towering pillars, sets the posh tone, along with Oriental carpeting. The good-size rooms are state of the art, with sleek modern furnishings and deluxe bedding, bedside controls, and private safes. The tiled bathrooms have tub/shower combos and hair dryers, toiletries, plush towels, scales, and robes.

Dining/Diversions: Locals head here to impress a business client or celebrate a special occasion at the Trento Restaurant, which features specialties from the Basque and Navarre regions. There is also on-site Salamanca's poshest cocktail car.

Amenities: Room service, concierge, laundry/dry cleaning.

Parador Nacional de Salamanca. Teso de la Feria, 2, 37008 Salamanca. ☎ **923-19-20-82.** Fax 923-19-20-87. 108 units. A/C MINIBAR TV TEL. 15,000 ptas. ($100.50) double; 23,000 ptas. ($154.10) suite. AE, DC, MC, V. Free parking outside, 1,000 ptas. ($6.70) garage.

Situated just across the Tormes River, this multilevel parador with a modern facade opened in the early 1980s. It sits less than a mile south of the historic center of town. It's a fine choice, but isn't as special as some of Spain's other paradors (the public areas are looking a bit worn, for example). Each of the well-furnished and comfortable midsize bedrooms has two or three framed lithographs, a mirador-style balcony, and a hair dryer.

Dining: The restaurant is formal and a bit stuffy, but serves a respectable regional and international cuisine.

Amenities: On-site are a garden, a parking garage, and an outdoor swimming pool. Room service, concierge, dry cleaning/laundry.

MODERATE

Hotel las Torres. Plaza Mayor, 26 (at the intersection of calle Concejo), 37002 Salamanca. ☎ **923-21-21-00.** Fax 923-21-21-01. 44 units. A/C MINIBAR TV TEL. 11,200–14,000 ptas. ($75.05–$93.80) double; 15,000 ptas. ($100.50) suite. AE, DC, MC, V. Parking 1,250 ptas. ($8.40).

Well maintained and dignified, with a congenial staff, this hotel occupies an enviable position near the northwestern corner of Plaza Mayor. A recent restoration of a historic monument, the hotel may look a little seedy, but it's not. It has a narrow reception area sheathed with polished marble. The modern, comfortable rooms, though not overly large, are well upholstered and contain excellent beds. Each contains a well-designed bathroom accented with marble and tile, a safe, and, in many cases, views over the plaza. There's an unpretentious restaurant on the premises. Additional seating spills over beneath the arcades of the plaza, allowing indoor-outdoor dining and lots of opportunities for people-watching.

INEXPENSIVE

Hostal Laguna. Consuelo, 19, 37001 Salamanca. ☎ **923-21-87-06.** 13 units (6 with bathroom). 3,530 ptas. ($23.65) double without bathroom; 4,800 ptas. ($32.15) double with bathroom. MC, V.

This unpretentious hotel lies in the center of the historic core of Salamanca, close to both cathedrals and next to the Torre del Clavero. It is also near Plaza Mayor and the university. Its facade is traditional, with distinctive balustrades. The interior has been recently renovated, making for spartan but large, comfortable, and clean doubles. Each comes with a simple but good bed, either a twin or double. A few units have a cramped bathroom with shower stalls.

Hostal Mindanao. Paseo de San Vicente, 2, 37007 Salamanca. ☎ and fax **923-26-30-80.** 33 units. 3,600–3,900 ptas. ($24.10–$26.15) double. No credit cards.

In a nondescript modern building that dates from the early 1980s, this unpretentious hostal is especially popular with students and, from time to time, their visiting parents. The small bedrooms have tiny private bathrooms or showers, but absolutely no frills other than a comfortable place to sleep. No meals are served, but numerous cafes are nearby, making a trek out for morning coffee relatively painless. The hotel lies along the southwestern edge of the busy traffic peripheral ringing the town center and is within a 12-minute walk of Plaza Mayor. Parking is available along the street.

WHERE TO DINE

✪ **Chez Victor.** Espoz y Mina, 26. ☎ **923-21-31-23.** Reservations required. Main courses 2,000–3,500 ptas. ($13.40–$23.45). AE, DC, MC, V. Tues–Sun 2–3:30pm, Tues–Sat 9–11:30pm. Closed Aug. CONTINENTAL.

Set within the historic center of town, this is the most glamorous restaurant around. Its food is easily the best in town, as the owner/chef Victoriano Salvador spent some 15 years in France learning and perfecting his innovative cuisine. He returned home to open this restaurant, which won the only star Michelin has ever granted to a Salamanca restaurant. Amid a monochromatic and deliberately understated modern decor, you'll enjoy dishes prepared with market-fresh ingredients.

Specialties include freshly prepared fish—perhaps sea wolf in black squid sauce, broiled turbot in a hot vinaigrette sauce, or, even better, bluefin tuna steak in sesame seeds. Try the veal medallions in lemon sauce, and, if it's offered, ribs of pork stuffed with prunes and served with a honey-mustard sauce. Despite the modernity of the cuisine, the portions are ample and well suited to Spanish tastes.

Restaurant Chapeau. Gran Via, 20. ☎ **923-26-57-95.** Reservations recommended. Main courses 2,100–3,000 ptas. ($14.05–$20.10); fixed-price menu 3,200 ptas. ($21.45). AE, DC, MC, V. Daily 1–4pm and 8:30pm–midnight. INTERNATIONAL.

Set on the main street of Salamanca, within a stone-sided building originally erected around 1900, this is a well-managed, socially prominent restaurant that has hosted most of the political and business dignitaries of town at one time or another. A tactful and uniformed staff works hard to present a medley of dishes that cater to conservative Castilian tastes as well as to more international kinds of palates. Within a high-ceilinged dining room, you're likely to find fish imported from the coast of Cantabria, including hake, sole, and mullet, that are either baked, fried, roasted, or added as the main components of a savory roster of stews and soups. Meat dishes include grilled, roasted, and stewed versions of veal, pork, beef, and chicken, any of which might be preceded with salads, pastas, soups, or an Iberian version of *carpaccio* (raw, thin-sliced beef) drizzled with olive oil and fresh herbs.

Río de la Plata. Plaza del Peso, 1. ☎ **923-21-90-05.** Reservations recommended. Main courses 1,000–5,000 ptas. ($6.70–$33.50); menú del día 2,500 ptas. ($16.75). MC, V. Tues–Sun 1:30–3:30pm and 8pm–12:30am. Closed July. CASTILIAN.

This tiny basement restaurant, 2 blocks south of Plaza Mayor on a small side square formed by the junction of Plaza Poeta Iglesia and calle San Justo, has thrived since 1958. The kitchen uses fresh ingredients, preparing a traditional but simple *cocida castellana* (Castilian stew), house-style sole, roast baby goat, many varieties of fish, and pungently flavored sausages. Although a modest place, good-quality ingredients go into the dishes served. The linen is crisply ironed and the service usually impeccable. On a wintry night in Salamanca, this is one of the most inviting places in the city, with its cozy dark wood and fireplace. Locals fill up the place every night, which is endorsement enough.

SALAMANCA AFTER DARK

Don't expect a huge variety of nightlife options; this is a small-scale university town with an emphasis on undergraduate shenanigans. Your best bet is a stroll around the Plaza Mayor, where you'll pass cafes and bars that seem to lend themselves to lingering or loitering, depending on your point of view. You might also wander onto such neighboring medieval streets as the calle de Bordedores, calle San Vicente, calle Rua Mayor, and calle Varillas, any of which offer tucked away spots for a quick caffeine or alcohol fix. Two Salamanca discos of particular note include **Disco Morgana,** calle Iscar Peyra (no phone); and its better-established, more historic competitor, **Camelot,** calle Bordadores (no phone). The latter occupies the site of a stone-sided monastery whose occupants 400 years ago would undoubtedly have been horrified at the goings-on within premises that long ago echoed only with prayer and plainsong. And for a more modern spin on Salamanca's nightlife, head for the **Pub Rojo y Negro,** calle Espoz y Mina (no phone), where bouts of karaoke are interspersed with chatter, wine, whisky, and foaming mugs of Spanish beer.

AN EASY SIDE TRIP TO ALBA DE TORMES

Admirers of St. Teresa may want to make the 11-mile (18km) pilgrimage southeast of Salamanca to visit the medieval village of Alba de Tormes. Follow highway C-510. Cross a bridge with 22 arches spanning the Tormes River. Head between the Iglesia de San Pedro and the Basilica de Santa Teresa to Plaza de Santa Teresa, where you will come upon the **Convento de las Carmelitas,** Plazuela de Santa Teresa (☎ **923-30-00-43**), and the **Iglesia de Santa Teresa,** Plaza de Santa Teresa, 4. The church is a combination of Gothic, Renaissance, and baroque styles. The marble vault over the altar contains the ashes of Spain's most beloved saint, St. Teresa of Ávila, who died here in 1582. One of the two reliquaries flanking the altar is said to contain her arm; the other is said to hold the remains of her heart. Opposite the entrance door in the rear of the church is a grating through which you can look at the cell in which she died. Pope John Paul II visited Alba de Tormes in 1982 on the occasion of the 400th anniversary of St. Teresa's death. Admission is free. The complex is open daily 10am to 1:30pm and 4 to 7:30pm, Sunday 10am to 2pm; donations requested.

3 Zamora

40 miles (64km) N of Salamanca, 148 miles (238km) NW of Madrid

Little known to North American visitors, Zamora (pronounced Tha-*mor*-a) is the quintessential city of Old Castile, blending ancient and modern, but noted mainly for its Romanesque architecture. In fact, Zamora is often called a "Romanesque museum." A medieval frontier city, it rises up starkly from the Castile flatlands, a reminder of an era of conquering monarchs and forgotten kingdoms.

You can explore Zamora's highlights in about 4 hours. Stroll along the main square, dusty Plaza Canovas; cross the arched Romanesque bridge from the 1300s; and take in at least some of the Romanesque churches for which the town is known, many of which date from the 12th century. The cathedral is the best example, but others include **Iglesia de la Magdalena,** rua de los Francos, and **Iglesia de San Ildefonso,** calle Ramos Carrión. You might also want to look at **Iglesia de Santa María la Nueva,** Plaza de Santa María, and **Iglesia de Santiago el Burgo,** calle Santa Clara.

The crowning achievement, however, at the far west end of Zamora, is the **cathedral** San Salvador, Plaza Castillo o Pio XII. It is topped by a gold-and-white Eastern-looking dome. Inside, you'll find rich hangings, interesting chapels, two 15th-century Mudéjar pulpits, and intricately carved choir stalls. Later architectural styles, including Gothic, have been added to the original Romanesque features, but this indiscriminate mixing of periods is typical of Spanish cathedrals. Inside the cloister, the Museo de la Catedral features ecclesiastical art, historical documents, church documents, and an unusual collection of "Black Tapestries" dating from the 1400s. The cathedral is free but admission to the museum costs 300 ptas. ($2) for adults. The cathedral can generally be visited throughout the day. The museum is open April through September Tuesday to Saturday 11am to 2pm and 5 to 8pm, Sunday 11am to 2pm, and Monday 5 to 8pm. Off-season hours are Tuesday to Saturday 9am to 2pm and 4 to 6pm and Sunday 11am to 2pm.

ESSENTIALS

GETTING THERE   There are four trains to and from Madrid every day and two to and from La Coruña (the trips take 3 and 6 hours, respectively). The railway station is at calle Alfonso Peña (☎ **980-52-11-10**), about a 15-minute walk from the edge of the old town. Follow Avenida de las Tres Cruces northeast of the center of town. One-way fare from Madrid to Zamora is 3,200 ptas. ($21.45).

Thirteen to 21 bus connections a day from Salamanca make this the easiest way to get in and out of town. Travel time between the cities is an hour. There are seven buses a day from Madrid; the trip takes 3½ hours and costs 2,135 ptas. ($14.30) one-way. The town's bus station lies a few paces from the railway station, at calle Alfonso Peña, 3 (☎ **980-52-12-81**).

Zamora is at the junction of eight different roads and highways. Most of the traffic from northern Portugal into Spain comes through Zamora. Highways headed north to León, south to Salamanca, and east to Valladolid are especially convenient. From Madrid, take the A-6 superhighway northwest toward Valladolid, cutting west on the N-VI and west again at the turnoff onto 122.

VISITOR INFORMATION   The **tourist information office** is at calle Santa Clara, 20 (☎ **980-53-18-45**). Open Monday through Friday from 9am to 2pm and 5 to 7pm, Saturday and Sunday from 10am to 2pm and 5 to 8pm.

SPECIAL EVENTS   Holy Week, the week before Easter, in Zamora is a celebration known throughout the country. Street processions, called *pasos,* are among the most spectacular in Spain. If you plan to visit at this time, make your hotel reservations well in advance.

WHERE TO STAY

Hostal Chiqui. Benavente, 2, 49002 Zamora. ☎ **980-53-14-80.** 14 units. 4,000–5,300 ptas. ($26.80–$35.50) double. No credit cards.

If you're looking for a bargain and don't mind a few minor inconveniences, try this simple second-floor pension. The guest rooms are spartan but clean, with no frills. No breakfast is served, but cafes are within walking distance. Chiqui lies behind the post office in the northwest section of the old town, near a corner of busy calle Santa Clara.

✪ **Hostería Real de Zamora.** Cuesta de Pizarro, 7, 49027 Zamora. ☎ and fax **980-53-45-45.** 19 units. MINIBAR TV TEL. 9,975 ptas. ($66.85) double. Rates include breakfast. AE, DC, MC, V.

The most charming small hotel in town, sporting walls that date from the 1400s, occupies the long-ago headquarters of Zamora's dreaded Inquisition. (Before that, ironically, this was the site of a Jewish-owned building reputed to have been the home of the explorer Pizarro.) Today, the outstanding historical features of the building include a medieval reservoir, a patio perfect for enjoying a cup of tea or coffee, and a verdant garden that lies along the city's medieval fortifications. An excellent example of a tastefully modernized aristocratic villa, it stands a few steps to the west of the northern embankment of the city's most photographed bridge, the Stone Bridge. The medium-size rooms contain simple but solid furnishings, including good beds, and offer safety-deposit boxes. The well-maintained bathrooms are equipped with hair dryers. If you drive to the hotel, you'll have to rely on street parking.

Dining: The restaurant Pizarro, with the air of a baronial private dining room, offers three-course fixed-price meals. Adjacent to it is the Restaurante Hostería Real, offering basically the same menu and a bar.

Amenities: 24-hour room service, laundry, baby-sitting.

✪ **Parador Turístico de Zamora.** Plaza de Viriato, 5, 49001 Zamora. ☎ **980-51-44-97.** Fax 980-53-00-63. 52 units. A/C MINIBAR TV TEL. 15,000–17,000 ptas. ($100.50–$113.90) double; 17,500–20,000 ptas. ($117.25–$134) suite. AE, DC, MC, V. Parking 1,000 ptas. ($6.70).

The site of this parador has always held a legendary role in Zamora. Originally fortified as an *Alcazaba* by the Moors during their occupation of Zamora, it was later expanded into a palace during the late Middle Ages. Most of that original monument was demolished and rebuilt upon its ancient foundations in 1459 by the Count of Alva y Aliste, and today the structure retains the severe, high-ceilinged dignity of its 15th-century Gothic form. Renovated by the Spanish government in the late 1960s, it is today one of the most beautiful paradors in Spain, and obviously the best and most tranquil place to stay in town.

Set 2 blocks south of Plaza Mayor, near the junction of Plaza de Viriato and calle Ramos Carrión, the parador is richly decorated with medieval armor, antique furniture, tapestries, and potted plants. In winter, glass partitions close off a large inner patio centered around an antique well; baronial fireplaces provide much-appreciated warmth. Midsize bedrooms are white walled, well maintained, and tastefully decorated with conservative furniture, including beds with firm mattresses. The tidy bathrooms are equipped with hair dryers.

Dining: The sumptuous but rustic dining room has a view of the swimming pool and surrounding countryside. There's also a cozy bar.

Amenities: Room service, laundry/valet, baby-sitting, pool, and a gym with sauna.

WHERE TO DINE

París. Avenida de Portugal, 14. ☎ **980-51-43-25.** Reservations recommended. Main dishes 1,400–2,200 ptas. ($9.40–$14.75); menú del día 1,800 ptas. ($12.05). AE, DC, MC, V. Mon–Sat 1–6pm and 8pm–midnight. SPANISH/INTERNATIONAL.

This elegantly decorated, air-conditioned restaurant is known for its fish, often made with a regionally inspired twist. Well-prepared specialties include vegetable flan, braised oxtail, Zamora-style clams, and a delectable hake. Dishes, of course, change with the seasons. Most critics rate this restaurant number one in town. It is on the main traffic artery (Avenida de Portugal) that funnels traffic south to Salamanca.

Serafín. Plaza Maestro Haedo, 10. ☎ **980-53-14-22.** Main courses 900–2,800 ptas. ($6.05–$18.75); fixed-price menus 1,850–3,000 ptas. ($12.40–$20.10). AE, DC, MC, V. Daily 1–4:30pm and 8:30pm–midnight. SPANISH.

At the northeast edge of the old town, about a block south of the busy traffic hub of Plaza Alemania and Avenida de Alfonso IX, this air-conditioned haven with an attractive bar makes a relaxing retreat from the sun. The specialties change with the season but might include seafood soup Serafín, paella, fried hake, Iberian ham, and a savory *cocido* (stew).

ZAMORA AFTER DARK

Calle Los Herreros, also called calle de Vinos, contains more bars per square foot than any street in Zamora—about 16 of them in all. Each is willing to accommodate a stranger with a leisurely glass of wine or beer and a selection of tapas. Calle Los Herreros is a narrow street at the southern end of the old town, about 2 blocks north of the Duero River, within the shadow of the Ayuntamiento Viejo (Old Town Hall), 1 block south of Plaza Mayor.

4 León

203 miles (327km) NW of Madrid, 122 miles (196km) N of Salamanca

Once the leading city of Christian Spain, this old cathedral town was the capital of a centuries-old empire that declined after uniting with Castile. León today is the gateway from Old Castile to the northwestern routes of Galicia. It is a sprawling city, but nearly everything of interest to visitors—monuments, restaurants, and hotels—can be covered on foot, once you arm yourself with a good map.

Once the heartbeat of a great kingdom, today León is a sleepy provincial city off the beaten track. But its wealth of old monuments, its top-notch accommodations, and a certain regal quality in the air still make the town feel like a capital.

Outlying mountain villages offer their own architectural gems, fine ski runs, and tasty concoctions of local trout and meat. Also, the region is particularly renowned for its soft-spoken and pristine Castilian accent. In sum, León is an excellent place to experience the tranquillity of the Spanish heartland, as well as an obligatory stop for students of medieval architecture.

ESSENTIALS

GETTING THERE   León has good rail connections to the rest of Spain—11 trains daily arrive from Madrid. The station, Estación del Norte, Avenida de Astorga, 2 (☎ 987-27-02-02), lies on the western bank of the Bernesga River. Cross the bridge near Plaza de Guzmán el Bueno. The rápido train from Madrid takes 5 hours, the TALGO only 4. A one-way ticket from Madrid ranges from 3,200 to 3,700 ptas. ($21.45 to $24.80), but travelers should be aware that there are many different types of tickets, which change regularly.

Most of León's buses arrive and depart from the Estación de Autobuses, Paseo Ingeniero Saenz de Miera (☎ 987-21-10-00). Three to five buses per day link León with Zamora and Salamanca, and there are 11 per day from Madrid (trip time: 4½ hours). A one-way ticket on a direct regular bus from Madrid is 2,600 ptas. ($17.40), rising to 4,200 ptas. ($28.15) for the *supra* (comfortable) service.

León lies at the junction of five major highways coming from five different regions of Spain. From Madrid's periphery, head northwest on the N-VI superhighway toward La Coruña. At Benavente, bear right onto the N-630.

VISITOR INFORMATION   The tourist information office is at Plaza de Regla, 4 (☎ 987-23-70-82). Open Monday through Friday from 9am to 1:30pm and 5 to 7pm, Saturday and Sunday from 10am to 2pm and 4 to 8pm.

EXPLORING THE TOWN

✪ Catedral de León (Santa Maria de Regla). Plaza de Regla. ☎ 987-87-57-70. Admission to cathedral free; cloisters and museum 500 ptas. ($3.35). Cathedral daily 8:30am–1:30pm and 4–7pm; cloisters and museum Mon–Sat 9:30am–1:30pm and 4–7pm. Bus: 4.

The usual cathedral elements are virtually eclipsed here by the awesome **stained-glass windows**—some 125 in all (plus 57 oculi), the oldest dating from the 13th century. They are so heavy they have strained the walls of the cathedral. Look for a 15th-century altarpiece depicting the Entombment in the Capilla Mayor, as well as a Renaissance trascoro by Juan de Badajoz. The nave dates from the 13th and 14th centuries; the Renaissance vaulting is much later. Almost as interesting as the stained-glass windows are the cloisters, dating in part from the 13th and 14th centuries and containing faded frescoes and Romanesque and Gothic tombs; some capitals are carved with starkly lifelike scenes. Visitors can also tour a museum containing valuable art and artifacts, including a Bible from the 10th century, notable sculptures, and a collection of romantic images of the Virgin Mary. The cathedral is on the edge of the old city, 7 blocks east of the town's most central square, Plaza de Santo Domingo.

Luminous in León

In the church-building sweepstakes of the Middle Ages, every Gothic cathedral vied to distinguish itself with some superlative trait. Milan Cathedral was the biggest, Chartres had the most inspiring stained-glass windows, Palma de Majorca had the largest rose window, and so on.

Structurally speaking, the boldest cathedral was at León. This edifice set the record for the highest proportion of window space, with stained-glass windows soaring 110 feet to the vaulted ceiling, framed by the slenderest of columns, occupying 18,000 square feet, or almost all the space where you'd expect the walls to be.

The roof is held up not by walls but by flying buttresses on the exterior. Inside, the profusion of light and the illusion of weightlessness astonish even medievalists. The architects Juan Pérez and Maestro Enrique, who designed the cathedral in the 13th century, were, in effect, a premonition of Mies van der Rohe, 7 centuries before the age of steel girders draped with plate-glass curtain walls.

Panteón y Museos de San Isidoro. Plaza San Isidoro, 4. ☎ **987-22-96-08.** Admission 400 ptas. ($2.70). Sept–June, Mon–Sat 10am–1:30pm and 4–6:30pm, Sun 10am–1:30pm; July–Aug, Mon–Sat 9am–2pm and 3–8pm, Sun 9am–2pm. Bus: 4 or 9.

This church, just a short walk northwest of the cathedral, was dedicated to San Isidoro de Sevilla in 1063 and contains 23 tombs of Leonese kings. One of the first Romanesque buildings in León and Castile, it was embellished by Ferdinand I's artists. The columns are magnificent, the capitals splendidly decorated, and the vaults are covered with murals from the 12th century. Unique in Spain, the Treasury holds rare finds—a 10th-century Scandinavian ivory, an 11th-century chalice, and an important collection of 10th- to 12th-century cloths from Asia. The library contains many ancient manuscripts and rare books, including a Book of Job from 951, a Visigothic Bible, an 1162 Bible, plus dozens of miniatures.

SHOPPING

Something about the city's antique architecture seems to encourage the acquisition of old-time handcrafts made from time-honored material like terra-cotta, stone, copper, wrought-iron, and leather. Plaza de la Catedral and the streets that radiate outward from it are particularly rich in battered, overcrowded kiosks that inventory this type of artifact, and part of the fun of a trip within the city's historic core involves acquiring several pieces of it. For a more up-to-date roster of shopping options, consider a quick march through the vast stacks within Léon's biggest department store, **Corte Inglés,** Fray Luis de Leon 21 (☎ **987-26-31-00**). Inside, look for men's and women's clothing, books and gift store items, and hints of the high-fashion priorities of cities as far away as Barcelona and Madrid.

WHERE TO STAY

Guzmán El Bueno. López Castrillón, 6, 24003 León. ☎ **987-23-64-12.** 26 units. 5,200 ptas. ($34.85) double. No credit cards. Walk up calle Generalísimo from Plaza de Santo Domingo, turn left onto calle de Cid; López Castrillón is a pedestrian-only street, branching off to the right.

The most inexpensive accommodation we recommend in León is the no-frills Guzmán El Bueno, on the second floor of a centrally located boardinghouse. In all, it's a safe destination, widely known among international student travelers, who are drawn to its low prices. Some rooms have phones; all are clean with decent beds. Be warned in advance that the staff speaks only Spanish. Parking is available along the streets within walking distance of the hotel.

Hotel Alfonso V. Padre Isla, 1, 24002 León. ☎ **987-22-09-00.** Fax 987-22-12-44. E-mail: alfonov@lesein.es. 57 units. A/C MINIBAR TV TEL. 16,850 ptas. ($112.90) double; 26,750 ptas. ($179.25) suite. AE, DC, MC, V.

Although we infinitely prefer the parador, this hotel in the heart of the city is less expensive and is famed for its classicism and contemporary decor. The pre-Franco hotel has been dramatically modernized with a stunning sculpture-filled lobby that rises seven wavy floors to a glass roof. The rooms, mostly medium in size, are a study in postmodernism, each fitted with French windows, excellent soundproofing, and firm beds with luxury mattresses, plus tiled bathrooms with plush towels and hair dryers.

Dining/Diversions: The restaurant attracts some of the leading business leaders of the community. It is known for its natural dishes using the finest produce in the area. Tables are spaced far enough apart so you don't hear others' conversations. The bar is an international rendezvous point.

Amenities: Room service, concierge, laundry/dry cleaning.

Hotel Quindós. Gran Vía de San Marcos, 38, 24002 León. ☎ **987-23-62-00.** Fax 987-24-22-01. 96 units. TV TEL. 10,900 ptas. ($73.05) double. AE, DC, MC, V. Parking 1,000 ptas. ($6.70) nearby. Bus: 4 or 9.

This rather functional hotel has been tastefully decorated with modern paintings, which spruce it up considerably. The snug, comfortable, and well-maintained rooms are a good value, each fitted with a firm mattress and a small but efficient tiled bathroom. The hotel offers two restaurants, one with menus typical of Old Castile, another more elegant dining room serving an international cuisine. You can, for example, enjoy fish of the day baked in an oven, sirloin with onion jelly, and marinated pigeon. The Quindós lies 3 blocks south of Plaza de San Marcos, in the central commercial district in the northwest quadrant of the old town.

☉ Parador San Marcos. Plaza de San Marcos, 7, 24001 León. ☎ **987-23-73-00.** Fax 987-23-34-58. 260 units. MINIBAR TV TEL. 21,500 ptas. ($144.05) double; 50,500 ptas. ($338.35) suite. AE, DC, MC, V. Free parking.

This 16th-century former monastery with its celebrated plateresque facade is one of the most spectacular hotels in Spain. The government has remodeled it at great expense, installing extravagant authentic antiques and quality reproductions as well as improving the facade. Before its monastery days, the old "hostal" used to put up pilgrims bound for Santiago de Compostela in the 12th century. The parador also contains a church with a scallop-shell facade and an archaeological museum. The good-size guest rooms are sumptuous, each with luxury mattresses and a bathroom equipped with plush towels and a hair dryer. The parador is located northwest of the cathedral on the outskirts of the old town, on the east bank of the Bernesga River.

Dining: The hotel restaurant serves adequate Spanish and regional cuisine, including breakfast, and lunch and dinner from 12:30 to 2pm and 9:30 to 12:30pm.

Amenities: Room service, concierge, baby-sitting, laundry and dry cleaning service, and conference rooms.

WHERE TO DINE
Alborada. Condesa de Sagasta, 24. ☎ **987-22-19-12.** Reservations recommended. Main courses 1,400–1,900 ptas. ($9.40–$12.75); menú del día 1,300 ptas. ($8.70). AE, MC, V. Tues–Sun 1–4pm and 8:30pm–midnight. Bus: 4 or 9. SPANISH.

This contemporary restaurant much favored by local residents lies outside the city center, a 15-minute walk northwest of the cathedral adjacent to the Parador San

Marcos. Within a modern monochromatic interior, the owner supervises the preparation of fresh fish and meat dishes that are loosely based on French and Spanish models. Signature dishes include *lubina al horno* (oven baked whitefish), fillet steak with pepper, hake casserole, and roast duck in orange sauce. A long wine list is available, and the room is air-conditioned.

Casa Pozo. Plaza San Marcelo, 15. ☎ **987-22-30-39.** Reservations recommended. Main courses 1,500–2,300 ptas. ($10.05–$15.40); fixed-price menus 1,425 ptas. ($9.55). AE, DC, MC, V. Mon–Sat 12:30–4pm and 8–11:45pm. Closed Christmas. Bus: 4 or 9. SPANISH.

Located 2 blocks south of the busy traffic hub of Plaza Santo Domingo and across from city hall, this unpretentious restaurant is a long-enduring favorite with locals who appreciate its unassuming style and flavorful cuisine. Habitués call owner Gabriel del Pozo Alvarez "Pin," and he's the reason behind the success of the place. Specialties, all made from fresh ingredients, include peas with salty ham, shrimp with asparagus, *estofados* (stews), roast pork or lamb laden with herbs and spices, and a delicate smothered sole. Twelve varieties of fresh fish are available and the restaurant offers an excellent selection of Rioja wines.

Mesón Leonés del Racimo de Oro. Caño Badillo, 2. ☎ **987-25-75-75.** Reservations required. Main courses 1,500–2,500 ptas. ($10.05–$16.75). AE, DC, MC, V. Wed–Sat 1:45–4pm and 9pm–midnight, Sun 1:45–4pm. CASTILIAN.

Behind Plaza Mayor and beside the cathedral, this bodega is housed in a structure from the early 1700s, and even it was built on older foundations. As such, it is one of the two or three oldest inns in León, and a lot of food and wine have been consumed on this site over the centuries. The building is what the Spanish call a *mesón típico* (house built in the regional style), and its tables overlook a patio. The food is consistently good, with the owner specializing in a regional cuisine—*mollejas con rabo de toro* (sweet meats with oxtail), for example, or *merluza* (hake) house style. You might begin with an appetizer of Serrano ham or clams, then follow with one of the roast meats, such as roast suckling lamb cooked in a wood-fired clay oven. The service is attentive.

LEÓN AFTER DARK

Few other cities in Spain evoke the mystery of the Middle Ages like León. To best appreciate the old-fashioned eloquence of the city, wander after dark around the Plaza Mayor, the edges of which are peppered with simple cafes and bars. None is particularly different from its neighbor, but overall, the effect is rich, evocative, and wonderfully conducive to conversation and romance. Our favorite of the lot is the **Bar Universale,** Plaza Mayor (no phone), which serves tapas, sherries, wines, and beers in a setting that's particularly evocative and mellow. And if your taste involves going out dancing, consider everybody's favorite León disco, **Tropicana,** calle José Maria Fernandez 56 (☎ **987-25-70-35**). It's open nightly except Monday as a bar, and cranks up the recorded music beginning at 10pm to a huge crowd of dance-a-holics.

5 Valladolid

125 miles (201km) NW of Madrid, 83 miles (133km) SE of León

From the 13th century until its eventual decay in the early 17th century, Valladolid was a royal city and an intellectual center that attracted saints and philosophers. Isabella and Ferdinand were married here; Philip II was born here; and Columbus died here on May 19, 1506, broken in spirit and body after Isabella had died and Ferdinand refused to reinstate him as a governor of the Indies.

Valladolid is bitterly cold in winter, sweltering in summer. Today, after years of decline the city is reviving economically and producing, among other things, flour, ironware, and cars. Consequently, it's polluted and noisy, and many of the old buildings have been replaced by utilitarian ones, although there are still many attractions remaining.

From the tourist office (see below), you can pick up a map that marks all the major monuments of Valladolid. These attractions can be covered on foot, although you may want to take a taxi to the two most distant points recommended: the Museo Nacional de Escultura and the Museo Oriental.

ESSENTIALS

GETTING THERE   Flights to Valladolid land at Vallanubla Airport, Highway N-601 (☎ **983-56-04-14** or 983-56-01-62), a 15-minute taxi ride from the center of town. Aviaco routes daily flights to and from Barcelona and Madrid.

Valladolid is well serviced by 14 daily trains to and from Madrid (trip time: 3 to 4½ hours). A one-way fare costs 1,800 to 3,200 ptas. ($12.05 to $21.45). Other cities with train links to Valladolid include Salamanca (10 trains per day) and Burgos (16 trains per day). The train station (Estación del Norte), calle Recondo, s/n by the Plaza Colon (☎ **983-20-02-02**), is about 1 mile south of the historic center of town, 1 block southwest of Campo Grande park.

The bus station lies within an 8-minute walk of the railway station, at Puente Colgante (☎ **983-23-63-08**), at the southern edge of town. There are more than a dozen buses every day to and from Madrid, 2¼ hours away. Eight buses per day arrive from Zamora (trip time: 1¼ hours), and 3 buses per day from Burgos (1½ hours).

Valladolid lies at the center of the rectangle created by Burgos, León, Segovia, and Salamanca and is connected to each with good highways. From Madrid, driving time is about 2¼ hours. Take superhighway A-6 northwest from Madrid, turning north on 403.

VISITOR INFORMATION   The **tourist information office** is at calle de Santiago 19 (☎ **983-35-18-01**). Hours are Monday through Friday from 9am to 2pm and 5 to 9pm, Saturday and Sunday from 10am to 2pm and 3 to 8pm.

SEEING THE SIGHTS

✪ **Museo Nacional de Escultura (National Museum of Sculpture).** Colegio de San Gregorio, calle Cadenas de San Gregorio, I. ☎ **983-26-79-77.** Admission 400 ptas. ($2.70) adults, 200 ptas. ($1.35) students, free for children under 18 and adults over 65. Tues–Sat 10am–2pm and 4–6pm, Sun 10am–2pm.

Located near Plaza de San Pablo, the museum displays a magnificent collection of gilded polychrome sculpture, an art form that reached its pinnacle in Valladolid. The figures were first carved from wood, then painted with consummate skill and grace to assume lifelike dimensions. See especially, the works by Alonso Berruguete (1480–1561), son of Pedro, one of Spain's great painters. From 1527 to 1532 the younger Berruguete labored over the altar of the Convent of San Benito—a masterpiece now housed here. In particular, see his *Crucifix with the Virgin and St. John* in Room II and his *St. Sebastian and the Sacrifice of Isaac* in Room III. Works by Juan de Juni and Gregorio Fernández are also displayed.

After visiting the galleries, explore the two-story cloisters. The upper level is florid, with jutting gargoyles and fleurs-de-lis. See the chapel where the confessor to Isabella I (Fray Alonso de Burgos) was buried—and be horrified by the gruesome sculpture *Death*.

Cathedral. Calle Arrive, 1. ☎ **983-30-43-62.** Free admission to Cathedral ; museum, 350 ptas. ($2.35). Cathedral and museum Tues–Fri 10am–1:30pm and 4:30–7pm, Sat–Sun 10am–2pm.

In 1580 Philip II commissioned Juan de Herrera, architect of El Escorial, to construct this monument in the city where he was born. When Philip died in 1598, work came to a stop for 18 years. Alberto Churriguera resumed construction, drawing up more flamboyant plans, especially for the exterior, in an unharmonious contrast to the severe lines of his predecessor. The classical, even sober, interior conforms more with Herrera's designs. A highlight is the 1551 altarpiece in the main apsidal chapel, the work of Juan de Juni. Art critics have commented that his polychrome figures seem "truly alive." The cathedral is in the heart of the city, east of Plaza Mayor and north of Plaza de Santa Cruz.

Iglesia de San Pablo. Plaza San Pablo, 4. ☎ **983-35-17-48.** Free admission. Daily 7:30–9:30am, 12:30–2pm, and 7–9:30pm.

Once a 17th-century Dominican monastery, San Pablo, with its Isabelline-Gothic facade, is very impressive. Flanked by two towers, the main entrance supports levels of lacy stone sculpture. The church lies 6 blocks north of the cathedral, 1 block south of busy Avenida Santa Teresa. Mass is held daily, with eight masses on Sunday.

Museo Oriental. Paseo de Filipinos, 7. ☎ **983-30-68-00.** Admission 400 ptas. ($2.70), free for children 9 and under. Mon–Sat 4–7pm, Sun and holidays 10am–2pm.

Located in the Royal College of the Augustinian Fathers, near Campo Grande park, the museum has 14 rooms: 10 Chinese and 4 Filipino. It has the best collection of Asian art in Spain, with bronzes from the 7th century B.C. to the 18th century A.D., wooden carvings, 100 fine porcelain pieces, paintings on paper and silk from the 12th century to the 19th, and ancient Chinese coins, furniture, jade, and ivory. In the Filipino section, ethnological and primitive art is represented by shields and arms. Eighteenth-century religious art can be admired in extraordinary ivories, embroideries, paintings, and silversmiths' work. Popular art of the 19th century includes bronzes, musical instruments, and statuary.

Casa de Cervantes. Calle del Rastro, s/n. ☎ **983-30-88-10.** Admission 400 ptas. ($2.70); free on Sun. Tues–Sat 9:30am–3:30pm, Sun 10am–3pm.

Now a museum, this house was once occupied by Miguel de Cervantes, author of *Don Quixote,* who did much of his writing in Valladolid and who remained here for the last years of his life. Behind its white walls, the house is simply furnished, as it was in his day. It lies half a block south of the cathedral, 2 blocks north of the city park, Campo Grande.

WHERE TO STAY

Enara. Plaza de España, 5, 47001 Valladolid. ☎ **983-30-02-11.** Fax 983-30-03-11. 24 units. TV TEL. 6,400 ptas. ($42.90) double. AE, MC, V. Closed Dec 24–25.

Located about a quarter mile south of the cathedral, near the junction of Avenida 2 de Mayo and Paseo Miguel Iscar, Enara is arguably the best inexpensive accommodation in Valladolid. Its central location is backed up by contemporary, pleasantly furnished guest rooms, which are small but offer good comfort because of the fine beds and the immaculately kept bathrooms. The decoration is in the typical Castilian style with some antiques. There is no restaurant, but a continental breakfast is offered, and you'll be near many low-cost dining rooms and cafes. Originally built in the 19th century as a private house, it was converted into a hotel in the mid-1970s. Two of its three stories are devoted to simple but well-maintained rooms, and the ground floor contains the breakfast area. Parking is available along the Plaza de España.

Felipe IV. Calle de Gamazo, 16, 47004 Valladolid. ☎ **983-30-70-00.** Fax 983-30-86-87. 131 units. A/C MINIBAR TV TEL. 15,300 ptas. ($102.50) double; 26,000 ptas. ($174.20) suite. AE, DC, MC, V. Parking 1,000 ptas. ($6.70).

When it was built, the Felipe IV was one of the grandest hotels in the city, although the Meliá (see below) has now usurped that position. Each of its midsize bedrooms is modernized, guaranteeing its ranking as one of Valladolid's solidly acceptable establishments. A garage provides parking for motorists. The hotel is south of the busy traffic hub of Plaza de Madrid, a few blocks north of the rail station, near the eastern edge of the city park, Campo Grande. It attracts many business travelers, as a visit to the hotel dining room at night will reveal. A standard Spanish cuisine is served—nothing special.

Hotel Meliá Parque. Joaquin Garcia Morato, 17, 47007 Valladolid. ☎ **800/336-3542** in the U.S., or 983-22-00-00. Fax 983-47-50-29. 178 units. A/C TV TEL. 15,500 ptas. ($103.85) double; 24,500 ptas. ($164.15) suite. AE, DC, MC, V. Parking 1,700 ptas. ($11.40).

Completed in 1982, this modern chain hotel lies 2 blocks west of the rail station on the city outskirts. It's popular with business travelers unwilling to negotiate the labyrinth of Valladolid's central streets. Although an acceptable choice in every way, it is not as luxuriously appointed or as comfortable as the Olid Meliá (see below). The good-size guest rooms are comfortable and functionally furnished with no surprises and few disappointments. It also provides special rooms and facilities for people with disabilities. The hotel has a restaurant featuring average Castilian meals.

Hotel Olid Meliá. Plaza San Miguel, 10, 47003 Valladolid. ☎ **800/336-3542** in the U.S., or 983-35-72-00. Fax 983-33-68-28. 221 units. A/C MINIBAR TV TEL. 18,300 ptas. ($122.60) double; 28,900–42,800 ptas. ($193.65–$286.75) suite. AE, DC, MC, V. Parking 2,200 ptas. ($14.75).

Set in the heart of the historic zone, about 5 blocks northwest of the cathedral, this is a modern hotel whose original construction in the early 1970s has been upgraded throughout the public rooms with a postmodern gloss. The good-size rooms are the most comfortable in town, filled with heavy Iberian furniture that seems to suit the hotel's neighborhood. Each unit comes with a firm mattress on a comfortable bed, plus an immaculately tiled bathroom with a hair dryer.

Dining: There's an in-house restaurant floored with cool slabs of polished stone, as well as a bar.

Amenities: 24-hour room service, laundry, baby-sitting; there is a hairdresser/barber on the premises, as well as a gym.

WHERE TO DINE

✪ **La Fragua.** Paseo de Zorilla, 10. ☎ **983-33-87-85.** Reservations recommended. Main courses 1,900–2,500 ptas. ($12.75–$16.75). AE, DC, MC, V. Mon–Sun 1:30–4pm, Mon–Sat 9–midnight. Closed Aug. CASTILIAN.

You'll enjoy beautifully prepared Castilian dishes, the best in town, amid rustic decor at this restaurant just north of the rail station across busy Paseo de Zorilla. You might begin with spicy sausage, followed by beef, chicken, or lamb, each carefully seasoned and served in generous portions. A wide variety of fish is imported daily, and the huge wine list offers many regional vintages, one of which the steward will choose for you if you request it. Dessert could include a cheese tart or a melt-in-your-mouth chocolate truffle. Owner Antonio Garrote proudly displays his culinary diplomas.

Mesón Cervantes. Rastro, 6. ☎ **983-30-61-38.** Reservations recommended. Main courses 2,000–3,000 ptas. ($13.40–$20.10). AE, DC, MC, V. Mon–Sat 1:30–4pm and daily 9pm–midnight. Closed Aug. SPANISH/INTERNATIONAL.

Opened in 1973, this restaurant is regarded by some fans as the finest in the city. The owner, Alejandro, works the dining room and is capably complemented in the kitchen by his wife, Julia. Neighborhood residents favor this place for its lack of pretension and its delectable cuisine. Two particular favorites are sole with pine nuts and seasonal river crabs. Many other fish dishes, including hake and monkfish, are available. Roast suckling pig and roast lamb are also popular. Other specialties include peppers stuffed with crabmeat; tender veal scaloppini "Don Quixote," served with a piquant sauce; and *arroz con liebre* (herb-laden rice studded with chunks of roasted wild rabbit, in season). The restaurant stands beside the Casa de Cervantes, half a mile south of the cathedral.

Mesón Panero. Marina Escobar, 1. ☎ **983-30-70-19.** Reservations required. Main courses 1,500–2,500 ptas. ($10.05–$16.75); fixed-price menu 4,500 ptas. ($30.15). AE, DC, MC, V. Daily 1:30–4pm and 9pm–midnight; July–Aug, closed Sun. CASTILIAN/FRENCH.

The chef of this imaginative restaurant, Angel Cuadrado, can turn even the most austere traditional Castilian recipes into sensual experiences. Set near the water, this 1960s establishment lures diners with fresh fish, including a succulent brochette of sole and hake with fresh asparagus. One weekly favorite is *cocida castellana,* the famous regional stew. Roast lamb and suckling pig are also available, plus a selection of well-chosen wines. The Mesón Panero is near the Casa de Cervantes, just a short walk from the tourist office.

VALLADOLID AFTER DARK

There are no great clubs to recommend after dark in Valladolid. But that doesn't mean that the city isn't a lively, bustling place when darkness falls. Instead of grand clubs, it becomes a town of bars and pubs. **Calle del Paraíso** is in itself a virtual street of bars, with action overflowing later on to the pubby **Plaza del San Miguel.** Just enter the pub or bar that looks the most amusing with the most convivial crowd, and chances are you won't go wrong. Most of these pubs and bars cater to a younger crowd, often from the university. If you're 30 or older, you might want to patronize one of the cafes along **calle de Vincente Meliner,** especially those near Plaza Dorado.

6 Burgos

150 miles (242km) N of Madrid, 75 miles (121km) NE of Valladolid

Founded in the 9th century, this Gothic city in the Arlanzón River valley lives up to its reputation as the "cradle of Castile." Just as the Tuscans are credited with speaking the most perfect Italian, so the citizens of Burgos, with their distinctive lisp ("El Theed" for "El Cid"), supposedly speak the most eloquent Castilian.

El Cid Campeador, Spain's greatest national hero immortalized in the epic *El Cantar de Mío Cid,* is forever linked to Burgos. He was born near here, and his remains lie in the city's grand cathedral.

Like all the great cities of Old Castile, Burgos declined seriously in the 16th century, only to be revived later. In 1936, during the Civil War, the right-wing city was Franco's Nationalist army headquarters.

Today, Burgos no longer enjoys its historical glory, but is a provincial city along the meseta, or plateau, of Spain. Dry as a desert and burning hot during the summer days, it comes alive at night and is filled with smoky cafes and dance clubs. Most of the bars, frequented by students, are in the area around the cathedral. Many of them don't start to party seriously until after 10pm, so it's a late-night town.

ESSENTIALS

GETTING THERE Burgos is well connected to Madrid (eight trains daily make the 3½-hour trip), Barcelona (12 trains daily, 8- to 9-hour trip), the French border (nine trains daily), and Valladolid (16 trains daily). Depending on the train, one-way fares from Madrid range from 3,400 ptas. ($22.80); from Barcelona, 5,000 ptas. ($33.50); and from Valladolid, 1,500 ptas. ($10.05). The Burgos railway station is at the terminus of Avenida de Conde Guadalhorce, half a mile southwest of the center. To get here, head for the major traffic hub in Plaza Castilla, then walk due south across the Arlazón River. For train information or a ticket, call ☎ 947-20-91-31.

About 12 to 17 buses a day make the 3-hour trip up from Madrid, and two or three buses per day make the 7½-hour trip from Barcelona. A one-way fare from Madrid costs 1,955 ptas. ($13.10) or 4,900 ptas. ($32.85) from Barcelona. The bus depot in Burgos is at calle Miranda (☎ 947-28-88-55). Calle Miranda intersects the large Plaza de Vega, due south of (and across the river from) the cathedral.

Burgos is well connected to its neighbors by a network of highways, but its routes to and from Barcelona (6 hours away) are especially wide and modern. The road from Barcelona changes its name several times, from the A-2 to the A-68 to the E-4, but it is a superhighway all the way. From Madrid, follow the N-I north for about 3 hours; the highway is fast but less modern than the road from Barcelona.

VISITOR INFORMATION The tourist information office is at Plaza Alonso Martínez, 7 (☎ 947-20-18-46). Open Monday through Friday from 9am to 2pm and 5 to 7pm, Saturday and Sunday from 10am to 2pm and 5 to 8pm.

EXPLORING THE TOWN

✪ **Catedral de Santa María.** Plaza de Santa María. ☎ 947-20-47-12. Admission to chapels, cloisters, and treasury 400 ptas. ($2.70) adults; 250 ptas. ($1.70) students, seniors; 100 ptas. (65¢) children under 14. Daily 9:30am–1pm and 4–7pm.

Begun in 1221, this cathedral was one of the most celebrated in Europe. Built in diverse styles, predominantly flamboyant Gothic, it took 300 years to complete. Ornamented 15th-century bell towers flank the three main doorways by John of Cologne. The 16th-century Chapel of Condestable, behind the main altar, is one of the best examples of Isabelline-Gothic architecture, richly decorated with heraldic emblems, a sculptured filigree doorway, figures of apostles and saints, balconies, and an eight-sided star stained-glass window.

Equally elegant are the two-story 14th-century cloisters, filled with fine Spanish Gothic sculpture. The cathedral's tapestries, including one well-known Gobelin, are rich in detail. In one of the chapels you'll see an old chest linked to the legend of El Cid—it was filled with gravel and used as collateral by the warrior to trick money-lenders. The remains of El Cid himself, together with those of his wife, Doña Ximena, lie under Santa María's octagonal lanternlike dome. Finally, you may want to see the elaborate 16th-century Stairway of Gold in the north transept, the work of Diego de Siloé.

The cathedral is across the Arlazón River from the railway station, midway between the river and the Citadel.

Monasterio de las Huelgas. Calle Compás de Adentro. ☎ 947-20-16-30. Admission 650 ptas. ($4.35) adults, 250 ptas. ($1.70) students, children. Oct–Mar, Tues–Sun 1am–1:15pm, 3:30–5:15pm; Apr–Sept, Tues–Sat 10:30am–1:15pm, and 3:30–5:45pm. Sun 10:30am–2:15pm.

This cloister outside Burgos has seen a lot of action. Built in the 12th century in a richly ornamented style, it was once a summer place for Castilian royalty, as well as a retreat for nuns of royal blood. Inside, the Gothic church is built in the shape of a Latin cross. Despite some unfortunate mixing of Gothic and baroque, it contains much of interest—notably some 14th- and 17th-century French tapestries. The tomb of the founder, Alfonso VIII, and his queen, the daughter of England's Henry II, lies in the Choir Room.

Thirteenth-century doors lead to the cloisters, dating from that century and blending Gothic and Mudéjar styles. Despite severe damage to the ceiling, the remains of Persian peacock designs are visible. The beautiful Chapter Room contains the standard of the 12th-century Las Navas de Tolora (war booty taken from the Moors), whereas the Museo de Ricas Telas is devoted to 13th-century costumes removed from tombs. These remarkably preserved textiles give a rare look at medieval dress.

The monastery is a mile off the Valladolid Road (the turnoff is clearly marked). From Plaza Primo de Rivera in Burgos, buses for Las Huelgas leave every 20 minutes.

SHOPPING

A city as old and historic as Burgos is bound to be chockablock with emporiums selling almost infinite volumes of ceramics, wood carvings, and artifacts that include fireplace bellows crafted from leather, wood, and brass or copper. Many of these shops line the edges of the city's most central square, Plaza Mayor, and the streets radiating outward from it. Two in particular are especially worthwhile and contain an appealing mixture of old and new artifacts inside. Consider **Antiguedades Javor,** Plaza Santiago s/n (☎ **947-23-51-60**), and its most visible competitor, **Antiguedades La Flora,** calle Huerto del Rey 6 (☎ **947-26-71-36**).

WHERE TO STAY
EXPENSIVE

✪ **Landa Palace.** Carretera Madrid-Irun (at km 236), 09001 Burgos. ☎ **947-20-63-43.** Fax 947-12-46-76. 39 units. A/C TV TEL. 23,000–30,000 ptas. ($154.10–$201) double; 33,000–35,000 ptas. ($221.10–$234.50) suite. MC, V. Free parking.

One of the greatest hotels of Castile, a member of Relais & Châteaux, this hotel lies some 2 miles (3km) south of Burgos on N-I. A romantic getaway, it is in a handsomely restored castle from the 1300s with later additions. Pilgrims once stopped here en route to Santiago de Compostela in Galicia, but they wouldn't recognize the grandeur of the place today. Decorated with tasteful antiques, the lobby sets the tone with its white marble and ornate coffered ceiling. Bedrooms are spacious and cozily inviting with antique decorations and tile floors. Marble bathrooms are state of the art with all the extras, including plush towels and hair dryers. Although parts of the hotel look a little worn, the graciousness of the staff compensates.

Dining: A poolside dining terrace is in the back of the hotel, serving some of the finest food in the area.

Amenities: Laundry and dry-cleaning service, room service, concierge, baby-sitting, currency exchange desk.

MODERATE

Hotel Almirante Bonifaz. Vitoria, 22-24, 09004 Burgos. ☎ **947-20-69-43.** Fax 947-20-29-19. 79 units. MINIBAR TV TEL. 17,200 ptas. ($115.25) double; 20,000 ptas. ($134) triple. AE, DC, MC, V. Parking 1,200 ptas. ($8.05).

Solidly comfortable, modern, and decorated with a contemporary kind of efficiency, this hotel attracts many of the city's visiting businesspeople, who appreciate its low-key charm and central location. The hotel lies 2 blocks east of the also recommended Condestable Hotel, near the river, within the commercial heart of town. All but a few of the midsize rooms are air-conditioned, and all have private bathrooms with hair dryers.

Dining: À la carte Castile-inspired Spanish meals are served in each of the hotel's three restaurants, the most glamorous of which is Los Sauces. There's also a bar.

Amenities: Room service (available from 7am to 10pm), laundry service, baby-sitting, car rentals, business center.

Hotel del Cid. Plaza de Santa María, 8, 09003 Burgos. ☎ **947-20-87-15.** Fax 947-26-94-60. 50 units. TV TEL. 16,000 ptas. ($107.20) double; 19,500 ptas. ($130.65) suite. AE, DC, MC, V. Parking 1,000 ptas. ($6.70).

Built in 1983 by the Alzaga family, which still owns and operates it, this establishment stands in front of the cathedral and beside their restaurant (recommended below). The restaurant is better known than the hotel, which grew up on the site of one of the first printing presses in Spain. The hotel is decorated like a 15th-century house, but it boasts 20th-century amenities, including extralarge beds and private bathrooms with hair dryers in all its guest rooms, which were refurbished in 1992.

Dining: The well-respected restaurant, Mesón del Cid, serves Spanish and regional cuisine, much to the delight of its frequently returning diners.

Amenities: Room service, concierge, and laundry and dry-cleaning service.

Hotel Fernán González. Calera, 17, 09002 Burgos. ☎ **947-20-94-41.** Fax 947-27-41-21. 84 units. A/C MINIBAR TV TEL. 16,750 ptas. ($112.25) double; 19,350 ptas. ($129.65) triple. DC, MC, V. Parking 1,000 ptas. ($6.70).

Across the Arlanzón River from the soaring bulk of the cathedral, a half block west of Plaza de Vega, this appealing and unusual hotel incorporates a scattering of Iberian antiques and architectural oddities into its modernized decor. Built in the 1970s, it was last renovated in 1994. Several of the sitting rooms contain grandly vaulted ceilings and noble columns; others are efficiently tiled and streamlined, filled with contemporary leather-covered armchairs and chrome-and-glass tables. The good-size guest rooms are cozy, conservative, and comfortable, with quality beds and tiled bathrooms.

The hotel's dining room serves traditional Spanish as well as international cuisine at lunch and dinner. Bar service is available throughout the several lounges and sitting areas of the street level. There's also a late-night disco.

✪ **Hotel Rice.** Avenida Reyes Católicos, 30, 09005 Burgos. ☎ **947-22-23-00.** Fax 947-22-35-50. E-mail: hotelrice@hotelrice.com. 50 units. A/C MINIBAR TV TEL. 14,300 ptas. ($95.80) double; 18,600 ptas. ($124.60) triple. AE, DC, MC, V.

This hotel half a mile north of the center is the town's leading boutique hotel. On the first five floors of a pink 11-floor structure, it is imbued with charm, grace, and character, almost like a London town house. Once you enter the British-style lobby, you'll feel snug, cozy, and comfortable, taking in the Queen Anne chairs, the marble surfaces, the antique cabinets, and the elegant fabrics. The bedrooms have elegant touches with luxury mattresses and the best bathrooms in Burgos, all in marble with large tubs, plush towels, pedestal sinks, and hair dryers. The restaurant serves an international cuisine, and the bar is one of our favorite meeting points in the city. With its grand piano, it often provides entertainment.

INEXPENSIVE

Hotel España. Paseo del Espolón, 32, 09003 Burgos. ☎ **947-20-63-40.** Fax 947-20-13-30. 69 units. TV TEL. 8,000 ptas. ($53.60) double; 10,000 ptas. ($67) triple. MC, V. Closed Dec 20–Jan 20.

The best budget choice in town lies a 5-minute walk southeast of the cathedral and a block south of Plaza Mayor, on a leafy promenade filled with sidewalk cafes and Castilians taking early evening strolls. The small guest rooms lack style and imagination but are completely comfortable nonetheless, with good beds and tidy bathrooms. The management is helpful to visitors. When the España is full, they have been known to call around to other hostelries for stranded tourists.

Hotel Norte y Londres. Plaza de Alonso Martínez, 10, 09003 Burgos. ☎ **947-26-41-25.** Fax 947-27-73-75. 50 units. TV TEL. 8,400–10,150 ptas. ($56.30–$68) double. AE, MC, V. Parking 1,000 ptas. ($6.70).

On a pleasant square a short walk northeast of the cathedral, this hotel has traces of faded grandeur with its leaded stained-glass windows and crystal chandeliers. The building dates from the early 20th century; it was converted into a hotel in the 1950s and has flourished ever since. Rooms are of good size, with basic furnishings, good beds, and large bathrooms equipped with yesteryear's finest plumbing. Breakfast is the only meal served.

WHERE TO DINE

The restaurants in the heart of Burgos, surrounding the cathedral, usually feature prices that soar as high as a Gothic spire. Every menu contains the roast lamb and suckling pig known throughout the area, or you might order *entremeses variados,* an appetizer sampler of many regional specialties.

Casa Ojeda. Vitoria, 5. ☎ **947-20-90-52.** Reservations required. Main courses 1,800–3,000 ptas. ($12.05–$20.10). AE, DC, MC, V. Daily 1:15–4:30pm, Mon–Sat 9–11:30pm. BURGALESE.

This top-notch restaurant combines excellent Burgos fare, cozy decor, attentive service, and moderate prices. Moorish tiles and low ceilings set an inviting ambience that's enhanced by intimate nooks, old lanterns and fixtures, and intricate trelliswork. Upstairs the restaurant is divided into two sections: one overlooking the street and the other, the Casa del Cordón, where Ferdinand and Isabella received Columbus after his second trip to America (1497). The cookery is the best in town. À la carte dishes include roast lamb, Basque-style hake, sole Harlequin, and chicken in garlic. A house specialty is *alubias con chorizo y mirocilla* (small white beans with spicy sausages).

Mesón de los Infantes. Calle Corral de los Infantes. ☎ **947-20-59-82.** Reservations recommended. Main courses 750–2,200 ptas. ($5.05–$14.75); fixed-price menu 1,700 ptas. ($11.40). AE, DC, MC, V. Daily noon–4:30pm and 8pm–midnight. CASTILIAN/BASQUE.

Just below the gate leading into the Plaza de Santa María, this restaurant serves good food amid elegant Castilian decor. Many of the chef's specialties are based on recipes in use in Castile for centuries. The roast suckling pig is everybody's favorite, and you can also order *cocido madrileño,* assorted shellfish, river crabs Burgalese style, and beef tail with potatoes. Kidneys are sautéed in sherry, and a wide list of game is often featured, including hare, partridge, rabbit, and pigeon. Grills and roasts are also crowd-pleasers.

Rincón de España. Nuño Rasura, 11. ☎ **947-20-59-55.** Reservations recommended. Main courses 1,200–2,800 ptas. ($8.05–$18.75); fixed-price menus 1,500–3,000 ptas. ($10.05–$20.10). AE, DC, MC, V. Daily 1–4pm and 8pm–midnight; closed Tues night in winter. SPANISH.

This restaurant, about 1 block southwest of the cathedral, draws many discerning visitors. You can eat in a rustic dining room or outdoors under a large awning closed off by glass when the weather threatens. The restaurant offers *platos combinados,* as well as a more extensive à la carte menu. Some special dishes include black pudding sausage with peppers, barbecued lamb cutlets with potatoes, and roast chicken with sweet peppers. The food here is good, the portions are large, and the vegetables are fresh.

BURGOS AFTER DARK

If you ask a local resident about where he or she prefers to go out dancing, you're likely to hear, "There's no disco in this very small town. Whenever we want to dance, we head for Madrid or Barcelona." Personally, we just head for the bars around the Plaza

Mayor, or even better, those along calle Vittoria. Two of the best of these include **Casa Ogeda,** calle Vittoria 5 (☎ **947-20-90-52**); and the **Cafeteria Milan,** calle Vittoria 21 (☎ **947-20-61-78**), both of which mingle liquor and conviviality pretty nicely.

A SIDE TRIP TO SANTO DOMINGO DE LA CALZADA

Some 42 miles (67.5km) east of Burgos, and easily visited on a day trip, lies Santo Domingo de la Calzada. The crowning achievement of the town, which grew as a stopover for pilgrims en route to Santiago de Compostela, is the 13th-century **cathedral** (☎ **941-34-00-33**), a national landmark. For the most part Gothic in style, it nevertheless contains a hodgepodge of architectural elements—Romanesque chapels, a Renaissance choir, and a freestanding baroque tower. St. Dominic, for whom the city is named, is buried in the crypt. A centuries-old legend is attached to the cathedral: Supposedly a rooster stood up and crowed after it had been cooked to protest the innocence of a pilgrim who had been accused of theft and sentenced to hang. To this day, a live cock and hen are kept in a cage up on the church wall, and you can often hear the rooster crowing at mass. The cathedral is open Monday to Saturday from 10am to 6pm and 4 to 7pm on Sunday to avoid the masses. It costs 250 ptas. ($1.70) for adults, 100 ptas. (65¢) for children. Sunday is free for everyone. Motorists can reach Santo Domingo de la Calzada by following either of the traffic arteries paralleling the river, heading east from Burgos Cathedral until signs indicate N-120.

6 Extremadura

This remote westernmost region of Spain has always been known as "the land beyond the River Douro." It extends from the Gredos and Gata mountain ranges all the way to Andalusia, and from Castile to the Portuguese frontier. With its varied landscape, Extremadura has plains and mountains, meadows with holm and cork oaks, and fields of stone and lime. Spanish Extremadura (not to be confused with the Portuguese province of Estremadura) includes the provinces of Badajoz and Cáceres.

The world knows Extremadura best as the land of the conquistadors. Famous sons included Cortés, Pizarro, Balboa, and many others less well known but also important, such as Francisco de Orellana and Hernando de Soto. Many of these men were driven from their homeland by economic necessity, finding it hard to make a living in this dry, sun-parched province. Some sent back money to their native land to finance the building of mansions and public structures that stand today as monuments to their long-ago adventures in the Americas.

Many of Extremadura's older civilizations have left enduring monuments as well, including the Roman ruins in Mérida, Arab ruins found in Badajoz, and medieval palaces in Cáceres.

Extremadura is a popular destination for outdoor fun. Spaniards come here to hunt, to enjoy the fishing and water sports popular in the many reservoirs in the region, and to experience horseback riding along ancient trails. Because summer is intensely hot here, spring and fall are the best times to visit.

1 Guadalupe

117 miles (188km) W of Toledo, 140 miles (225km) SW of Madrid

Guadalupe lies in the province of Cáceres, and sits 1,500 feet above sea level. The village has a certain beauty and a lot of local color. Everything of interest lies within a 3-minute walk from the point where buses deposit you, at Avenida Don Blas Perez, also known as Carretera de Cáceres.

Around the corner and a few paces downhill is the Plaza Mayor, which contains the Town Hall (where many visitors go to ask questions in lieu of a tourist office).

The village is best visited in spring, when the balconies of its white-washed houses burst into bloom with flowers. Wander at your leisure

Extremadura

Guarda N620 E80 Ciudad Rodrigo Tamames Sierra de Peña de Francia ↑ Alba

CASTILLA Y LEON

526 Sequeros N630 N110

Sierra de Gata E803

PORTUGAL Hoyos El Barco

N110 Sierra de Gredos

Plasencia Jaraíz Jarandilla C501

Coria Río Tiétar Talavera →

Castelo Branco Ceclavín N630 Navalmoral V CASTILLA LA MANCHA

Alcántara E90 Río Tajo

Río Tajo Garrovillas 524

V

N521 Arroyo Cáceres Trujillo Guadalupe

Valencia de Alacántara N521 Sierra de Guadalupe Montes de Toledo

Alburquerque C401 Río Guadiana

N523 Sierra de San Pedro Alcuéscar

V

Elvas Mérida Medellín N430 N430

E90 V Don Benito Puebla de Alcocer

Badajoz N630

Olivenza Castuera

N432 E803 C413

Villanueva del Fresno Zafra Los Santos Sierra del Pedroso Hinojosa del Duque

Jerez de los Caballeros Fregenal de la Sierra E102 N432

Río Guadiana

PORTUGAL

ANDALUSIA

SPAIN
★ Madrid

Extremadura

0 ____ 25 mi
0 ____ 25 km

Legend
Airport ✈

through the twisting, narrow streets, some no more than alleyways. The buildings are so close together that in summer you can walk in the shade of the steeply pitched sienna-colored tile roofs. Celebrated for its shrine to the Virgin, Guadalupe is packed with vendors and is a major outlet of the religious-souvenir industry.

GETTING THERE

There is one bus every day to and from Madrid's Estación Sur, a 3-hour ride away. The road is poor, but the route through the surrounding regions is full of savage beauty. In Guadalupe the buses park a few paces uphill from the Town Hall. Phone **Empresa La Sepulvedana,** Madrid (☎ **927-530-48-00**), for schedules.

One narrow highway goes through Guadalupe. Most maps don't give it a number; look on a map in the direction of the town of Navalmoral de la Mata. From Madrid, take the narrow, winding C-401 southwest from Toledo, turning north in the direction of Navalmoral de la Mata after seeing signs for Navalmoral de la Mata and Guadalupe. Driving time from Madrid is between 3½ and 4½ hours, depending on how well you fare with the bad roads.

WHAT TO SEE & DO

Except for a handful of your basic souvenir shops around the Plaza Mayor, don't expect a lot of particularly interesting shopping in Guadalupe. Two exceptions to this rule are the small but personalized **Cacharro Tienda,** Plaza Mayor 12 (no phone), with an unusual collection of brass, copper, and iron; and the gift shop within the Hotel Lujuan, calle Gregorio Lopez 19 (☎ **927-36-71-70**).

Real Monasterio de Santa María de Guadalupe. Plaza de Juan Carlos, 1. ☎ **927-36-70-00.** Admission to museum and sacristy 300 ptas. ($2) adults, 100 ptas. (65¢) children 7–14, free for children 6 and under. Apr–Oct daily 9:30am–1pm and 3:30–7pm; off-season daily 9:30am–1pm and 3:30–6:30pm.

In 1325, a farmer searching for a stray cow reportedly spotted a statue of the Virgin in the soil. In time, this statue became venerated throughout the world, honored in Spain by Queen Isabella, Columbus, and Cervantes. Known as the Dark Virgin of Guadalupe, it is said to have been carved by St. Luke. A shrine was built to commemorate the statue, and tributes poured in from all over the world, making Guadalupe one of the wealthiest foundations in Christendom. You can see the Virgin in a small alcove above the altar.

The church is noted for the wrought-iron railings in its naves and a magnificently decorated sacristy with eight richly imaginative 17th-century masterpieces by Zurbarán. Be sure to see the museum devoted to ecclesiastical vestments and to the choir books produced by 16th-century miniaturists. The 16th-century Gothic cloister is also flamboyant, with two galleries. The pièce de résistance is the stunning Mudéjar cloister, with its brick-and-tile Gothic-Mudéjar shrine dating from 1405 and a Moorish fountain from the 14th century.

WHERE TO STAY

Hospedería Real Monasterio. Plaza Juan Carlos, 1, 10140 Guadalupe. ☎ **927-36-70-00.** Fax 927-36-71-77. 47 units. A/C TEL. 7,750 ptas. ($51.95) double; 21,000 ptas. ($140.70) suite. MC, V. Closed Jan 12–Feb 12.

Once a way station for pilgrims visiting the shrine, the Hospedería used to provide lodging for a small donation. Times have changed, but the prices remain moderate at this two-star hotel in the center of town, which is the second best place to stay in town after the parador, and a whole lot cheaper. Since the place is installed in an antique

Land of the Conquistadors

It's estimated that some 15,000 Extremeños (from a total population of 400,000) went to seek gold in the New World. The most fabled of these adventurers were: Hernán Cortés (from Medellín) in Mexico; Francisco Pizarro (from Trujillo) in Peru; Vasco Núñez de Balboa (from Jerez de los Caballeros) in Panama, where he first sighted the Pacific Ocean; Hernando de Soto (from Barcarrota) in Florida and beyond, discovering the Mississippi River; and Francisco Orellana (also from Trujillo) in Ecuador and the Amazon.

Thanks to these conquistadors, the names of Extremaduran villages are sprinkled through the Americas, as exemplified by the Guadalupe Mountains (Texas), Albuquerque (New Mexico), Trujillo (Peru), Mérida (Mexico), and Medellín (Colombia).

Because Extremeños faced such a hard time making a living in the harsh land of their birth, they often turned elsewhere to seek their fortune. One of the reasons for the poverty was that huge ranches were owned by absentee landlords, as many still are even today. These ranches are called *latifundios,* and often farmers and their families live on these ranches, paying the owners for the privilege of grazing a few goats or growing some slight crops in the dry climate. A system of *mayorazgo* (still in effect) granted all the family property to the eldest son. The other sons, called secundinos, were left penniless, and often chose to set sail for the New World to seek their gold.

Many of the conquistadors died or else stayed in the New World, but others who had grown rich there returned to the land of their birth and built magnificent homes, villas, and ranches, many of which still stand today.

Bernal Díaz, who joined the Cortés expedition to Mexico, put the situation very bluntly. "We came here to serve God and the king," he wrote, "and to get rich."

monastery, the accommodations come in various shapes and sizes, but each is tastefully furnished and fitted with amenities such as firm mattresses and well-maintained bathrooms with stall showers. There is a bar and the regional meals served in the restaurant are generally good. Top off a meal with a home-brewed licor de Guadalupe.

Parador Nacional Zurbarán. Marqués de la Romana, 12, 10140 Guadalupe. ☎ **927-36-70-75.** Fax 927-36-70-76. 40 units. A/C MINIBAR TV TEL. 15,000 ptas. ($100.50) double; 16,500 ptas. ($110.55) suite. AE, DC, MC, V. Parking 900 ptas. ($6.05).

Located in a scenic spot in the center of the village, the area's most luxurious accommodation is housed in a 16th-century building with a beautiful garden. Queen Isabella once stayed here, and the place often saw meetings between royal representatives and explorers, who signed their contracts here before setting out for the New World. The house is named after Francisco de Zurbarán, the great 17th-century painter who was born in the nearby town of Fuente de Cantos. There is a Zurbarán painting in one of the salons, along with ancient maps and engravings—many of them valuable works of art. Bedrooms are comfortable and partially decorated with reproduction medieval furnishings. Most of the accommodations are quite spacious, and all of the units contain excellent beds with firm mattresses and beautifully tiled bathrooms with plush towels and hair dryers.

Dining: The attractive restaurant serves good regional food at both lunch and dinner. Try such local dishes as herb-flavored roast kid or pork Mudéjar style.

Amenities: Swimming pool, bar, garage, and tennis court.

WHERE TO DINE

Both of the hotels recommended above also have good restaurants.

Mesón el Cordero. Alfonso Onceno, 27. ☎ **927-36-71-31.** Reservations recommended. Main courses 1,600–2,100 ptas. ($10.70–$14.05); fixed-price menu 1,500 ptas. ($10.05). AE, DC, MC, V. Tues–Sun 1–4pm and 7–11pm. Closed Feb 1–15. SPANISH.

Miguel and Angelita run Guadalupe's best independent restaurant, named for their specialty, *asado de cordero* (roast lamb flavored with garlic and thyme). The couple has operated this restaurant for more than 20 years and enjoys a devoted local following, which is recommendation enough. You might begin with another of their specialties, sopa guadalupanas, then follow with partridge "from the countryside" if you have a taste for game. The house dessert is a creamy custard, flan casero.

2 Trujillo

152 miles (245km) SW of Madrid, 28 miles (45km) E of Cáceres

Dating from the 13th century, the walled town of Trujillo is celebrated for the colonizers and conquerors born here. Among the illustrious natives were Francisco Pizarro, the conqueror of Peru, whose family palace on Plaza Mayor was built with gold from the New World, and Francisco de Orellana, the founder of Guayaquil, Equador, and the first European to explore the Amazon. Other Trujillano history-makers were Francisco de las Casas, who accompanied Hernán Cortés in his conquest of Mexico and founded the city of Trujillo in Honduras; Diego García de Paredes, who founded Trujillo in Venezuela; Nuño de Chaves, founder of Santa Cruz de la Sierra in Bolivia; and several hundred others whose names are found throughout maps of North, Central, and South America. There is a saying that 20 American countries were born here.

Celts, Romans, Moors, and Christians have inhabited Trujillo over the centuries. The original town, lying above today's modern one, was built on a granite ledge on the hillside. It is centered on the Plaza Mayor, one of the artistic landmarks of Spain. A Moorish castle and a variety of 16th- and 17th-century palaces, manor houses, towers, churches, and arcades encircle the plaza and overlook a bronze equestrian statue of Pizarro by American artists Mary Harriman and Charles Runse. Steep, narrow streets and shadowy little corners evoke the bygone times when explorers set out from here on their history-making adventures.

ESSENTIALS

GETTING THERE There are nine buses per day to and from Madrid (trip time: 3½ or 4½ hours, depending on whether it's local or *expreso*). There are also six buses running daily from Cáceres, 45 minutes away, and six from Badajoz. A one-way ticket from Madrid to Trujillo costs 1,980 ptas. ($13.25); from Cárceres, 395 ptas. ($2.65); and from Badajoz, 1,210 ptas. ($8.10). Trujillo's bus station, calle Marqués Albayda (☎ 927-32-12-02), lies on the south side of town on a side street that intersects with calle de la Encarnación.

Trujillo lies at a network of large and small roads connecting it to Cáceres, via the N-521, and both Lisbon and Madrid, via the N-V superhighway. Driving time from Madrid is around 4 hours.

VISITOR INFORMATION   The **tourist information office,** Plaza Mayor (☎ **927-32-26-77**), is open April through October daily from 9am to 2pm and 5 to 7pm, off-season daily from 9am to 2pm and 4 to 6pm.

EXPLORING THE PLAZA & BEYOND

In the heart of Trujillo, the ✪ **Plaza Mayor** is one of the outstanding architectural sights in Extremadura. A statue honoring Francisco Pizarro, who almost single-handedly destroyed the Inca civilization of Peru, dominates it. The statue is an exact double of one standing in Lima. Many of the buildings on this square were financed with wealth brought back from the New World.

The most prominent structure on the square is the **Ayuntamiento Viejo (Old Town Hall),** with three tiers of arches, each tier squatter than the one below.

Iglesia de San Martín stands behind the statue dedicated to Pizarro. This granite church, originally from the 15th century, was reconstructed in the 16th century in Renaissance style. Inside are an impressive nave, several tombs, and a rare 18th-century organ still in working condition.

While you are on the square, observe the unusual facade of the **Casa de las Cadenas,** a 12th-century house draped with a heavy chain, a symbol that Philip II had granted the Orellana family immunity from heavy taxes.

You can then visit the **Palacio de los Duques de San Carlos,** a 16th-century ducal residence turned into a convent. Ring the bell to gain entry any time daily from 9am to 1pm and 3 to 7pm. A donation of at least 100 ptas. (65¢) is appreciated, and a resident will show you around; appropriate dress (no shorts or bare shoulders) is required. The facade has Renaissance sculptured figures, and the two-level courtyard inside is even more impressive.

Palacio de la Conquista, also on the square, is one of the most grandiose mansions in Trujillo. Originally constructed by Hernán Pizarro, the present structure was built by his son-in-law to commemorate the exploits of this explorer, who accompanied his half-brother, Francisco, to Peru.

The stores that ring the Plaza Mayor have the town's best shopping; they stock stonework, leather, brass, copper, and ironwork. The best is **Bazar Sant'Olaria,** Plaza Mayor 37 (☎ **927-32-01-70**), which stocks a selection of the best of virtually everything produced within the region. Handcrafted wood carvings are available from a small-scale artisan, **Domingo Pablos Barquillo,** Plazuela de San Judas 3 (☎ **927-32-10-66**), whose intensely detailed effigies of saints and characters from Spanish literature are nothing short of charming.

Iglesia de Santa María. Calle de Ballesteros. No phone. Admission 100 ptas. (65¢). Daily 10am–2pm and 4:30–7:30pm.

This Gothic building is the largest church in Trujillo, having been built over the ruins of a Moorish mosque. Ferdinand and Isabella once attended mass in this church, with its outstanding Renaissance choir. Its proudest treasure is an altar retablo with two dozen panels painted by Fernando Gallego. Also here is the tomb of Diego García de Paredes, the "Samson of Extremadura," who is said to have single-handedly defended a bridge against an attacking French army with only a gigantic sword. To reach the church, go through the gate of the Plaza Mayor at Puerta de San Andrés, and take calle de las Palomas through the old town.

Castillo. Crowning the hilltop. Free admission. Dawn to dusk; many visitors find it most dramatic at sunset.

Constructed by the Arabs on the site of a Roman fortress, this castle stands at the summit of the granite hill on which Trujillo was founded. Once at the castle, you can climb its battlements and walk along the ramparts, enjoying a panoramic view of the austere countryside of Extremadura. Later, you can go below and see the dungeons. It is said that the Virgin Mary appeared here in 1232, giving the Christians renewed courage to free the city from Arab domination.

WHERE TO STAY

Las Cigüeñas. Avenida de Madrid, s/n, Carretera N-V, 10200 Trujillo. ☎ **927-32-12-50.** Fax 927-32-13-00. 78 units. A/C MINIBAR TV TEL. 10,500 ptas. ($70.35) double; 15,000 ptas. ($100.50) suite. AE, DC, MC, V. Free parking.

Located just east of the town center, and convenient if you're driving, this is the second-best place to stay in Trujillo. It doesn't have the charm of the parador (see below), but it's cheaper. The hotel was built in two different three-story sections in 1971, with a major enlargement in 1983. A roadside hotel with a garden, it offers functional but clean and comfortable rooms, which, though generally small, are still equipped with firm mattresses and well-organized private bathrooms covered in tile and equipped with shower stalls. Its restaurant specializes in regional cuisine, and there is also a bar. You'll find Las Cigüeñas on the main highway from Madrid, about a mile before Trujillo.

✪ **Parador Nacional de Trujillo.** Calle de Santa Beatriz de Silva, 10200 Trujillo. ☎ **927-32-13-50.** Fax 927-32-13-66. 45 units. A/C MINIBAR TV TEL. 15,500 ptas. ($103.85) double; 17,500 ptas. ($117.25) suite. AE, DC, MC, V. Parking in garage 900 ptas. ($6.05).

Housed in the 1533 Convent of Santa Clara, this centrally located parador, about 1 block south of Avenida de la Coronación, is a gem of Trujillo-style medieval and Renaissance architecture that's been faithfully restored since it was converted into a parador in 1984. The beautifully decorated guest rooms, once nuns' cells, have canopied beds and spacious marble bathrooms with hair dryers and plush towels. The gardens and fruit trees of the Renaissance cloister are inviting, and there is a swimming pool in the courtyard of a new section that blends with the original convent architecture. You can have breakfast in the old refectory and dinner in what was once a long, vaulted chapel. Try the *caldereta extremena*, a stew made with lamb or baby goat.

WHERE TO DINE

Both hotels recommended above also have good restaurants serving regional cuisine.

Mesón la Troya. Plaza Mayor, 10. ☎ **927-32-13-64.** Reservations recommended. Fixed-price menu 2,000 ptas. ($13.40). MC, V. Daily 1–4:30pm and 8:45pm–midnight. EXTREMADURAN.

Locals and visitors alike are drawn to this centrally located restaurant featuring the regional cuisine of Extremadura and doing the province proud. Have a dry sherry in the bar designed to resemble the facade of a Spanish house. This cozy provincial theme also flows into the dining rooms, with their white walls (decorated with ceramic plates), potted plants, and red tiles. Few people leave hungry after devouring the set menu, with its more than ample portions; food items change daily. Local dishes include *prueba de cerdo* (garlic-flavored pork casserole) and *carne con tomate* (beef cooked in tomato sauce). A table is always reserved for the village priest, who comes here for breakfast, lunch, and dinner and has done so for more than 27 years.

Pizarro. Plaza Mayor, 13. ☎ **927-32-02-55.** Reservations recommended. Main courses 900–2,000 ptas. ($6.05–$13.40); *menú del día* 1,300 ptas. ($8.70). AE, DC, MC, V. Wed–Sun 1:30–4pm and 8:30–10:30pm. EXTREMADURAN.

Locals cite this centrally located hostal as the best place to go for regional Extremaduran cookery. Built in 1864, the inn is set on the town's main square and named for its famous son. The same family has owned and operated the place since 1919.

Regional wines accompany meals that invariably include ham from acorn-fed pigs. You might begin with asparagus with mayonnaise sauce, then follow with *asado de cordero* (roast lamb flavored with herbs and garlic) or Roman-style fried *merluza* (hake). The kitchen's game specialty is *estofado de perdices* (partridge casserole).

3 Cáceres

185 miles (298km) SW of Madrid, 159 miles (256km) N of Seville

A national landmark and the capital of Extremadura, Cáceres is encircled by old city walls and has several palaces and towers, many financed by gold sent from the Americas by the conquistadors.

One of six cities in Spain designated as World Heritage Sites by UNESCO, Cáceres was founded in the 1st century B.C. by the Romans as Norba Caesarina, but its present-day name is derived from Alcazares, meaning fortified citadel. After the Romans, it was settled by all the cultures that have made the south of Spain the unique cultural melting pot of influences it is today. The contemporary city offers a unique blend of the traces these successive invaders left behind.

ESSENTIALS
GETTING THERE   Cáceres has the best rail connections in the province, with five trains per day from Madrid. Trip time ranges from 4 to 5 hours, and a one-way ticket costs from 3,400 to 4,000 ptas. ($22.80 to $26.80). There is also one train per day from Lisbon; the trip time is 4½ hours and a one-way fare is 4,475 ptas. ($30). One train per day also runs from Seville, taking 4 hours and costing 2,300 ptas. ($15.40).

The station in Cáceres is on Avenida Alemania (☎ **927-23-37-61**), near the main highway heading south (Carretera de Sevilla). A green-and-white bus shuttles passengers about once an hour from the railway and bus stations (across the street from one another; board the shuttle outside the bus station) to the busiest traffic junction in the new city, Plaza de América. From there it's just a 10-minute walk to the edge of the old town.

Bus connections to Cáceres are more frequent than railway connections. From the city bus station (☎ **927-23-25-50**), on the busy Carretera de Sevilla, about a half mile south of the city center, buses arrive and depart for Madrid and Seville (one every 2 to 3 hours); transit by bus to Madrid takes 5 hours; transit by bus to Seville takes 4½ hours). There's also bus transport to Guadalupe (one per day); Trujillo (six or seven a day); Mérida (two a day); Valladolid (three a day); and Córdoba (two a day). Many travelers opt to walk the short distance from the Caceres bus station to the city center.

Driving time from Madrid is about 5 hours. Most people approach Cáceres from eastern Spain via the N-V superhighway until they reach Trujillo. Here, they exit onto the N-521, driving another 28 miles (45km) west to Cáceres.

VISITOR INFORMATION   The **tourist information office,** Plaza Mayor, 20 (☎ **927-24-63-47**), is open Monday through Friday from 9am to 2pm and 4 to 6:15pm, Saturday and Sunday from 9:30am to 2pm.

EXPLORING THE OLD CITY
The modern city lies southwest of the *barrio antiguo,* **Cáceres Viejo,** which is enclosed by massive **ramparts.** The heart of the old city lies between Plaza Santa María and, a few blocks to the south, Plaza San Mateo. **Plaza Santa María** is an irregularly shaped, rather elongated square. On each of its sides are the honey-brown facades of buildings once inhabited by the nobility. On a casual stroll through the city's cobblestone streets, your attention will surely be drawn at first to the walls that enclose the old upper

town. These are a mixture of Roman and Arab engineering, and their state of preservation is excellent. About 30 towers remain from the city's medieval walls, all of them heavily restored. Originally much taller, the towers reflected the pride and independence of their builders; when Queen Isabella took over, however, she ordered them cut down to size. The largest tower is at Plaza del General Mola. Beside it stands the Estrella Arco (Star Arch), constructed by Manuel Churriguera in the 18th century. To its right you'll see the Torre del Horno, a mud-brick adobe structure left from the Moorish occupation.

On the far side of Plaza Santa Maria rises the **Catedral de Santa María,** which is basically Gothic in style, although many Renaissance embellishments have been added. Completed some time in the 1500s, this is the cathedral of Cáceres and it contains the remains of many conquistadors. It has three Gothic aisles of almost equal height and a carved retablo at the high altar dating from the 16th century. (Insert coins to light it up.)

La Casa de los Toledo-Montezuma was built by Juan Cano de Saavedra with money from the dowry of his wife, the daughter of Montezuma. The house is set into the northern corner of the medieval ramparts, about a block to the north of Plaza de Santa María. It is now a public records office.

The **Plaza Mayor** is remarkably free from most of the blemishes and scarring effects that city planning and overregulation have made so common in other historically important sites. Passing through **El Arco de la Estrella (Arch of the Star),** you will then catch the most advantageous angle of Santa María Cathedral.

Some of the most appealing shops in Cáceres lie on the streets radiating outward from the Plaza Mayor, with a particularly good selection of artifacts along either side of the **calle Pintores.** One better-than-expected establishment is **Mansabora,** Plaza San Juan, s/n (☎ **927-21-18-84**), nestled into a battered-looking building near the Meliá Hotel and selling an assortment of silver jewelry, North African artifacts, and ceramics from Spain and Portugal.

Cuesta de la Compañía leads to Plaza San Mateo and the 14th-century **Iglesia de San Mateo,** which has a plateresque portal and a rather plain nave—except for the plateresque tombs, which add a decorative touch.

Two adjoining plazuelas near here embody the old flavor of Cáceres. At the first of these, the **Plaza de las Veletas,** on the site of the old Alcázar, is the **Casa de las Veletas** (Weather Vane House; ☎ **927-24-72-34**), which houses a provincial archaeological museum with priceless prehistoric and roman pieces, along with a famous *alijibe* (Arab well). Its baroque facade, ancient Moorish cistern, five naves with horseshoe arches, and patio and paneling from the 17th century have been preserved. The museum displays Celtic and Visigothic remains, Roman and Gothic artifacts, and a numismatic collection. Admission is 200 ptas. ($1.35), and the museum is open Tuesday to Saturday from 9:30am to 2:30pm, and Sunday from 10am to 2:30pm. At the second plazuela, **San Pablo,** sits the **Casa de las Cigueñas (storks),** the only palace whose tower remains intact, despite an order by Queen Isabella at the turn of the 15th century to reduce the height of all such strategic locations for military reasons. The building now serves as a military headquarters and is not open to the public.

You'll probably notice lots of storks nesting on most of the rooftops and bell towers in the town. This is a revealing sign of how Cáceres has managed to preserve not only its landmarks but also an environmentally sound balance between people and nature.

The **Church of Santiago** was begun in the 12th century and restored in the 16th century. It has a *reredos* carved in 1557 by Alonso de Berruguete and a 15th-century figure of Christ. The church lies outside the ramparts, about a block to the north of Arco de Socorro. To reach it, exit the gate, enter Plaza Socorro, then walk down calle Godoy. The church is on your right.

If you want to see a more modern face of the region, and shop for housewares and fashion while you're at it, drive 15 minutes west of the town center to the **Centro Comercial Ruta de la Plata,** Carretera Portugal, where you'll find a scattering of boutiques, plus a number of simple snack bars and cafes.

WHERE TO STAY

Hotel Alcántara. Avenida Virgen de Guadalupe, 14, 10001 Cáceres. ☎ **927-22-39-00.** Fax 927-22-39-04. 67 units. A/C MINIBAR TV TEL. 11,200–13,000 ptas. ($75.05–$87.10) double; 16,000 ptas. ($107.20) suite. AE, DC, MC, V. Parking 1,000 ptas. ($6.70).

Located in the commercial center of town, this seven-story blandly modern building opened in 1966, and has been renovated at least twice since. Though its heyday has long past, it is convenient for exploring the old town. Guest rooms are comfortably furnished and well maintained, albeit a bit small but with good beds. The hotel restaurant serves a traditional menú del día for 1,800 to 2,800 ptas. ($12.05 to $18.75).

Hotel Extremadura. Avenida Virgen de Guadalupe, 5, 10001 Cáceres. ☎ **927-22-16-00.** Fax 927-21-10-95. 67 units. A/C TV TEL. 10,000 ptas. ($67) double. AE, DC, MC, V. Parking 900 ptas. ($6.05).

Angular but comfortable, this clean, simple 1960s hotel offers straightforward rooms. They're a bit boxy and functionally furnished but are well maintained and reasonably comfortable, with good beds and immaculate tiled baths with stall showers. Located about half a mile southwest of the historic center in a bustling commercial district, it offers air-conditioned relief from the heat, as well as a much-appreciated swimming pool. Prices are fair for what you get. The hotel's restaurant, Alazán, serves Spanish and international food, and there is also a bar. There is a surprising number of amenities, including room service (available from 7am to midnight), laundry, concierge, an in-house tour operator/travel agent, and car rentals.

✪ **Meliá Cáceres.** Plaza San Juan, 11, 10003 Cáceres. ☎ **927-21-58-00.** Fax 927-21-40-70. 86 units. A/C MINIBAR TV TEL. 20,300 ptas. ($136) double. AE, DC, MC, V.

The Meliá hotel chain continues to show up the government parador system by opening superior lodgings in towns long dominated by a parador. Although the Parador de Cáceres is fine in every way, the Meliá is superior in both service and amenities. This converted Renaissance palace is located just south of the Plaza del Général Mola, by the entrance to the old town. Its bedrooms are better appointed, sunnier, and more spacious than those at the parador. Bathrooms are roomy and contain hair dryers. Everything is tastefully converted, and there is lots of exposed stone, along with indirect lighting and sleek modern furnishings.

Dining: The cuisine is also superior to that at the parador; you get international dishes along with some of the better regional specialties of the Extremadura plain.

Amenities: Concierge, laundry/dry cleaning, room service.

✪ **Parador de Cáceres.** Calle Ancha, 6, 10001 Cáceres. ☎ **927-21-17-59.** Fax 927-21-17-29. 31 units. A/C MINIBAR TV TEL. 16,500 ptas. ($110.55) double; 25,000 ptas. ($167.50) suite. AE, DC, MC, V. Free parking on streets, garage parking 1,300 ptas. ($8.70).

This state-operated parador lies within what was originally a palace in the 15th century. Built in a severe, somewhat austere style, it enjoys a tranquil location and a well-scrubbed, durable format of exposed stone, white plaster, and tile or stone floors. Pristine white corridors lead to dignified bedrooms, outfitted in a starkly appealing combination of white walls and dark-grained, somewhat bulky furniture inspired by the austere decorative traditions of Extremadura. All the modern amenities have been installed here, including luxury mattresses and excellent bathrooms with plush towels, toiletries, and hair dryers. Suits of armor adorn some of the public areas, giving the place a vaguely feudal feel, but the patios that open onto masses of potted plants and flowers are quite welcoming.

Dining: The restaurant serves a good regional cuisine. There's also a bar and cafeteria catering to general sightseers; it's open daily from 11:30am to 11:30pm and is the most convenient place in town to stop in for snacks at odd hours.

Amenities: Room service, laundry/dry cleaning, concierge.

WHERE TO DINE

The cuisine offered at the parador and at many other places in Cáceres affords a novel experience to even seasoned travelers. You might try the famous *cuchifrito,* a suckling pig stewed in pepper, orange, and vinegar sauce, or the *caldereta de cordero,* lamb with pepper and almonds. A more daring choice would be *jabalí la carcereña,* a wild boar dish marinated in red wine and herbs. The most characteristic dessert of all of Extremadura is *técula mécula,* an ancient example of the region's marzipan confectionery, which, like most things in Cáceres, has been passed down from one generation to the next for centuries.

✪ **Atrio.** Avenida de España, 30. ☎ **927-24-29-28.** Reservations recommended. Main courses 5,500–7,000 ptas. ($36.85–$46.90). DC, MC, V. Daily 1:30–4pm, Mon–Sat 9pm–midnight. SPANISH/CONTINENTAL.

Atrio serves the finest cuisine in the entire province. Even hard-to-please Michelin grants this place a star. Situated in a shopping mall cul-de-sac, the inside decor is elegant and somewhat unusual for this part of Spain—all streamlined and sleek in white and sunflower yellow. The chef steers a skillful course between rich, regional flavors and continental fare. The menu changes frequently to take advantage of the best of the various seasons. Prices can go much higher than those indicated above if truffles are added to your dish. Service is the finest in the area—in all, it's a professional and deluxe operation that comes as a surprise in such a provincial city.

El Figón de Eustaquio. Plaza San Juan, 12. ☎ **927-24-81-94.** Reservations recommended. Main courses 1,000–4,000 ptas. ($6.70–$26.80); fixed-price menus 1,700–2,800 ptas. ($11.40–$18.75). AE, DC, MC, V. Daily 1:30–4pm and 8pm–12:30am. EXTREMADURAN.

El Figón, a pleasant place serving local cuisine, has been satisfying locals since 1948. You'll notice the four Blanco brothers who run the place doing practically everything. This includes preparing the amazingly varied dishes—for example, honey soup, *solomillo* (fillet of beef), and trout Extremaduran style (covered in ham), as well as typical Spanish specialties. The air-conditioned interior has a rustic decor. El Figón lies west of the western ramparts of the old city, near the intersection of Avenida Virgen de Guadalupe and Plaza San Juan.

CACERES AFTER DARK

Don't expect swinging nightlife in this small, dusty border town, since part of its charm comes from its relative isolation. Your best bet is to stroll past the bars and cafes of the Plaza Mayor, the calle Sergio Sanchez, or the Avenida de España, many of which seem to come alive only during the cool of the evening. The town's most hopping disco is **Aquario,** Avenida de España, 2 (☎ **927-222-06-14**). Everyone in town seems to pull up a chair at the **Gran Café**, San Pedro Alcantara (☎ **927-24-99-97**), in the early evening.

4 Mérida

44 miles (71km) S of Cáceres, 35 miles (56km) E of Badajoz

Mérida, founded in 25 B.C., is at the crossroads of the Roman roads linking Toledo and Lisbon and Salamanca and Seville. At one time the capital of Lusitania (the Latin name for the combined kingdoms of Spain and Portugal), Mérida was one of the most splendid cities in Iberia, ranking as a town of major importance in the Roman Empire; in fact, it was once called a miniature Rome. Its monuments, temples, and public works make it the site of some of the finest Roman ruins in Spain, and, as such, it is the tourist capital of Extremadura. Old Mérida can be covered on foot—in fact, that is the only way to see it. Pay scant attention to the dull modern suburb across the Guadiana River, which skirts the town with its sluggish waters.

ESSENTIALS

GETTING THERE   Trains depart and arrive from the RENFE station on the calle Cardero (☎ **924-31-81-09**), about half a mile north of the Plaza de España. Each day there are four trains to and from Cáceres (trip time: 1 hour), five trains to and from Madrid (4 hours), one to and from Seville (3 hours), and 7 to and from Badajoz (1 hour). On a regular train a one-way ticket from Madrid costs 2,840 ptas. ($19.05); on the faster TALGO train the one-way fare is 4,000 ptas. ($26.80).

The bus station is on Avenida de la Libertad (☎ **924-37-14-04**), near the train station. Every day, there are three buses to and from Madrid (5½ hours), six to eight buses to and from Seville (3 hours), two to and from Cáceres (2 hours), and 5 to 10 to Badajoz (1 hour). From Mérida to Madrid, the fare is 2,720 ptas. ($18.20); Mérida to Seville, 1,695 ptas. ($11.35); Mérida to Cáceres, 675 ptas. ($4.50); Mérida to Badajoz, 610 ptas. ($4.10).

To drive here, take the N-V superhighway from Madrid or Lisbon. Driving time from Madrid is approximately 5 hours; from Lisbon, about 4½ hours. Park in front of the Roman theater and explore the town on foot.

VISITOR INFORMATION   The **tourist information office** is at Pedro María Plano (☎ **924-31-53-53**). Open April through October Monday through Friday from 9am to 1:45pm and 5 to 7pm, Saturday 9:15am to 1:45pm. Off-season hours are Monday through Friday from 9am to 2pm and 4 to 6pm, Saturday and Sunday from 9:15am to 1:45pm. Those are the official hours but don't expect the staff to interpret them too literally.

EXPLORING MÉRIDA

The **Roman bridge** over the Guadiana was the longest in Roman Spain—about half a mile—and consisted of 64 arches. It was constructed of granite under either Trajan or Augustus, then restored by the Visigoths in 686. Philip II ordered further refurbishment in 1610; work was also done in the 19th century. The bridge crosses the river south of the center of Old Mérida, its length increased because of the way it spans two forks of the river, including an island in midstream. In 1993, it was restored and turned into a pedestrian walkway. A semicircular suspension bridge for cars was constructed to carry the heavy traffic and save the bridge for future generations. Before the restoration and change, this bridge served as a main access road into Mérida, witnessing transportation evolve from hooves and feet to trucks and automobiles.

Another sight of interest is the old hippodrome, or **Circus Maximus,** which could seat about 30,000 spectators for chariot races. The Roman masonry was carted off to use in other buildings, and today the site looks more like a parking lot. Excavations have uncovered rooms that may have housed gladiators. The site of the former circus lies at the end of Avenida Extremadura, on the northeastern outskirts of the old town, about half a mile north of the Roman bridge and a 10-minute walk east of the railway station.

The **Arco Trajano (Trajan's Arch)** lies near the heart of the Old Town, beside calle Trajano, about a block south of the Parador Vía de la Plata. An unadorned triumphal arch, it measures 16 yards high and 10 yards across.

The **Acueducto de los Milagros** is the most intact of the town's two remaining Roman aqueducts; this one brought water from Proserpina, 3 miles (5km) away. From the aqueducts, water was fed into two artificially created lakes, Cornalvo and Proserpina. The aqueduct is northwest of the old town, lying to the right of the road to Cáceres, just beyond the railway tracks. Ten arches still stand.

The latest monument to be excavated is the **Temple of Diana** (dedicated to Caesar Augustus). Squeezed between houses on a narrow residential street, it was converted in the 17th century into the private residence of a nobleman, who used four of the original Corinthian columns in his architectural plans. The temple lies at the junction of calle Sagasta and calle Romero Léal in the center of town.

While in the area, you can also explore the 13th-century **Iglesia de Santa María la Mayor,** Plaza de España. It has a 16th-century chapel and is graced with Romanesque and plateresque features. It stands on the west side of the square.

Teatro Romano. José Ramón Melida, s/n. ☎ **924-31-25-30.** Admission 600 ptas. ($4) adults (includes admission to Anfiteatro Romano), free for children. Daily 9am–1:45pm and 5–6:45pm.

This Roman theater, one of the best-preserved Roman ruins in the world, was built by Agrippa (Augustus's son-in-law) in 18 B.C. to house an audience of 6,000 people. Modeled after the great theaters of Rome, it was constructed by dry-stone methods, a remarkable achievement. During the reign of Hadrian (2nd century A.D.), a tall stage wall was adorned with statues and colonnades. Behind the stage, visitors today can explore excavations of various rooms. From the end of June to early July, they can also enjoy a season of classical plays.

Anfiteatro Romano. Calle José Ramón Melida, s/n. ☎ **924-31-25-30.** Admission included in Teatro Romano ticket (see above). Daily 9am–1:45pm and 5–6:45pm.

At the height of its glory, in the 1st century B.C., the amphitheater could seat 14,000 to 15,000 spectators. Chariot races were held here, along with gladiator combats and mock sea battles, for which the arena would be flooded. Many of the seats were placed dangerously close to the bloodshed. You can visit some of the rooms that housed the wild animals and gladiators waiting to go into combat.

✪ **Museo Nacional de Arte Romano.** Calle José Ramón Melida, 2. ☎ **924-31-16-90.** Admission 500 ptas. ($3.35) adults, 400 ptas. ($2.70) students, free for children. Tues–Sat 10am–1:45pm and 5–7pm, Sun 10am–2pm.

Located in a modern building adjacent to the ancient Roman amphitheater, to which it is connected by an underground tunnel, this museum is acclaimed as the greatest repository of Roman artifacts in Spain. Not only does it contain more than 30,000 artifacts from Augusta Emerita, capital of the Roman province of Lusitania, but it also incorporates part of a Roman road, discovered in the early 1980s during the construction of the building. Many of the museum's sculptures came from the excavations of the Roman theater and amphitheater. You'll see displays of mosaics, figures, pottery, glassware, coins, and bronze objects. The museum is built of red brick in the form of a Roman basilica.

Alcazaba. Plaza de España. ☎ **924-31-73-09.** Admission 600 ptas. ($4). Apr–Sept, Mon–Sat 9am–2pm and 5–7:15pm, Sun 9am–2pm; Oct–Mar, Mon 9am–1pm, Tues–Sat 9am–1pm and 3–6pm.

On the northern bank of the Guadiana River, beside the northern end of the Roman bridge (which it was meant to protect), stands the Alcázar, also known as the Conventual or the Alcazaba. Built in the 9th century by the Moors, who used fragments left over from Roman and Visigothic occupations, the square structure was later granted to the Order of Santiago.

Museo Arqueológico de Arte Visigodo. Plaza de España. ☎ **924-30-01-06.** Free admission. July–Sept, Tues–Sat 10am–2pm and 5–7pm, Sun 10am–2pm; Oct–June, Tues–Sat 10am–2pm and 4–6pm, Sun 10am–2pm.

In front of Trajan's Arch is this archaeological museum, housing a treasure trove of artifacts left by the conquering Visigoths. Look especially for the two statues of Wild Men in one of the alcoves.

WHERE TO STAY

Hotel Emperatriz. Plaza de España, 19, 06800 Mérida. ☎ **924-31-31-11.** Fax 924-31-33-05. 42 units. A/C TV TEL. 12,500 ptas. ($83.75) double. AE, DC, MC, V. Free parking nearby.

A former 16th-century palace, the Emperatriz housed a long line of celebrated guests in its day, from Kings Philip II and III of Spain to Queen Isabella of Portugal and Charles V, the Holy Roman Emperor. Its intricate tiled gallery foyer is in the Moorish style. All the guest rooms are functionally furnished and comfortable, but try to get one facing the plaza for an unusual view of the storks' nests built on the eaves and cornices of the surrounding buildings. Many of the rooms have grown seedy over the years, though others have been renovated (request one of the restored rooms). Late-night noise can be a problem.

The restaurant serves many intriguing Extremaduran specialties, including a soothing gazpacho made with white garlic and *tencas fritas* (fried tench), a typical fish of the region. Later you can visit the Emperatriz's nightclub and bar. A garden stands in the center of this good-value three-star hotel, located in the center of town, just north of the ruins of the Alcazaba. Parking is available along the street.

Nova Roma. Súarez Somonte, 42, 06800 Mérida. ☎ **924-31-12-61.** Fax 924-30-01-60. 55 units. A/C TV TEL. 12,425 ptas. ($83.25) double. AE, DC, MC, V. Parking 1,500 ptas. ($10.05).

Lacking the charm of the Parador Vía de la Plata (see below), the 1991 Nova Roma wins hands down for those with more modern taste. Clean, comfortable, and functionally furnished, it is a good value for this heavily frequented tourist town. Bedrooms range from small to medium, and each comes with firm mattresses and a compact tiled bathroom with shower stall. The hotel also runs a reasonably priced restaurant offering a menú del día for 1,400 ptas. ($9.40) with many regional dishes. The Nova Roma is west of the Teatro Romano and north of Plaza de Toros (bullring).

✪ **Parador Vía de la Plata.** Plaza de la Constitución, 3, 06800 Mérida. ☎ **924-31-38-00.** Fax 924-31-92-08. 82 units. A/C MINIBAR TV TEL. 16,500 ptas. ($110.55) double; 28,000 ptas. ($187.60) suite. AE, DC, MC, V. Parking 1,100 ptas. ($7.35).

This parador is in the heart of town, on the Plaza de la Constitución, in the former Convento de los Frailes de Jesus (dating from the 16th century). Though it has had a long and turbulent history and was once a prison, a salon has been installed in the cloister, and a central garden is studded with shrubbery and flowers. Old stone stairs lead to the bedrooms, which come in various shapes and sizes, each beautifully kept and furnished. Mattresses and bathrooms are luxurious, the best in town. Each unit comes with a hair dryer and plush towels. In the 1960s two dictators met here: Franco of Spain and Salazar of Portugal.

Dining: The parador has an excellent restaurant, serving both regional and national dishes and cafeteria.

Amenities: In addition to its bar and garage, the parador has a pool, sauna, and gym.

Tryp Medea. Avenida de Portugal, s/n, 00800 Mérida. ☎ **924-37-24-00.** Fax 924-37-30-20. 126 units. A/C MINIBAR TV TEL. 15,400–17,000 ptas. ($103.20–$113.90) double; 19,500 ptas. ($130.65) triple. AE, DC, MC, V. Garage parking 900 ptas. ($6.05) or free in the street. Bus: 4 or 6.

Located a 15-minute walk west of the town's historic center, on the opposite bank of the Guadiana River, this hotel opened in 1993 and immediately ranked among the finest hotels in the area. A member of the nationwide Tryp chain, the four-story hotel employs large amounts of white marble within its lobby and bedrooms. Lots of mirrors, stylish postmodern furniture crafted from locally made wrought iron, and numerous modern accessories decorate the rooms, many of which offer views over the historic core of Mérida. Ranging from small to medium, each unit is well appointed, with firm mattresses and tidily arranged private bathrooms.

Dining: There's a bar and a formal restaurant, El Encenar (named after a type of tree indigenous to Extremadura), serving both international and regional specialties.

Amenities: On the premises is an outdoor swimming pool, a health club/gymnasium, squash courts, a sauna, and a helpful multilingual staff.

WHERE TO DINE

In addition to the listings below, all the hotels recommended above have good restaurants.

Briz. Félix Valverde Lillo, 5. ☎ **924-31-93-07.** Main courses 1,000–2,000 ptas. ($6.70–$13.40); fixed-price menu 1,350 ptas. ($9.05). MC, V. Mon–Sat 1–4pm and 9pm–midnight. EXTREMADURAN.

There is almost universal agreement, even among the locals, that the set menu at Briz represents the best value in town—not only reasonable in price but also very filling. Briz is known for its Extremaduran regional dishes, and has been feeding locals since 1949. Main dishes include heavily flavored lamb stew and *perdiz* in salsa (a gamy partridge casserole), which might be preceded by an appetizer of peppery sausage mixed into a medley of artichokes. Peppery veal steak and fried fillet of goat are other specialties. Strong, hearty wines accompany the dishes. You'll find Briz across from the post office.

Restaurante Nicolás. Félix Valverde Lillo, 13. ☎ **924-31-96-10.** Reservations recommended. Main courses 1,200–1,800 ptas. ($8.05–$12.05); fixed-price menu 2,000 ptas. ($13.40). AE, DC, MC, V. Daily noon–5pm, Mon–Sat 8:30pm–midnight. SPANISH.

Transformed from an old, run-down house in 1985, Nicolas ranks as the most charming restaurant in town. If the lower dining room isn't to your liking, you'll find seating upstairs, as well as a pleasant garden for outdoor meals. Menu specialties are made with care from fresh ingredients. You might enjoy roast baby goat, carefully seasoned roast lamb, and flavorful concoctions of sole, salmon, and monkfish. Roast partridge is the game specialty. Nicolás is located opposite the post office.

5 Badajoz

57 miles (92km) SW of Cáceres, 39 miles (63km) E of Mérida, 254 miles (409km) SW of Madrid

The capital of Spain's largest province, Badajoz stands on the banks of the Guadiana River near the once turbulent Portuguese border. A Moorish fortress and an old

Roman bridge are but two reminders of the past. Sightseeing here is lackluster, but Badajoz does have some local color, provided mainly by its huge ramparts and its narrow medieval streets. Its fortified site is best appreciated if you drive to Badajoz from the north. Park outside and walk into town; along the way you'll pass the 13th-century Gothic cathedral.

ESSENTIALS

GETTING THERE   Four trains daily arrive from Madrid (trip time: 5 to 8 hours). Eight trains per day arrive from Mérida (1½ hours), and three from Cáceres (2½ hours). The railway station is situated at the terminus of Carolina Coronado in Badajoz (☎ 924-27-11-70), a 15-minute walk northwest of the center of town.

From Madrid, 10 buses daily make the 4-hour trip; from Seville, there are 5 daily buses (4½ hours). From Mérida, there are 8 buses daily (45 minutes). The bus station (☎ 924-25-86-61) is at Carretera de Valverde, about a half mile south of town. Take bus no. 3 from the bus station to the Plaza de España, in the center of town.

Badajoz sits astride the superhighway N-V, which connects Madrid with Lisbon. The E-803 links it with Seville. Driving time from Madrid is around 4 hours; from Seville the time is about 3½ hours.

VISITOR INFORMATION   The **tourist information office,** Plaza de la Libertad, 3 (☎ 924-22-27-63), is open Monday through Friday from 9am to 2pm and 4 to 6pm, Saturday and Sunday from 9am to 2pm.

WHERE TO STAY

Gran Hotel Zurbarán. Paseo Castelar, s/n, 06001 Badajoz. ☎ **924-22-37-41.** Fax 924-22-01-42. 213 units. A/C MINIBAR TV TEL. 18,375 ptas. ($123.10) double; 28,300 ptas. ($189.60) suite. AE, DC, MC, V. Parking 1,000 ptas. ($6.70).

Set above the heavy ramparts that flank the southern bank of the River Guadiana, this modern but slightly dated four-star hotel enjoys one of the most scenic positions in town, overlooking the welcome and verdant Parque de Castelar. The public rooms are decorated with lots of metal trim and a kind of 1970s-era pizzazz, and the guest rooms are comfortably equipped and have been recently remodeled. Most accommodations are medium in size, and each comes with comfortable beds fitted with fine linen and quality mattresses. Bathrooms are small but neatly organized tub and shower combos. The service is attentive.

Dining/Diversions: An in-house restaurant serves à la carte meals. There is also a bar and a disco.

Amenities: Concierge, laundry, room service, baby-sitting, outdoor pool, tennis courts, large garden with stately trees and flowers, in-house news kiosk and bookstore, shopping arcade.

Hotel Lisboa. Avenida de Elvas, 13, 06006 Badajoz. ☎ **924-27-29-00.** Fax 924-27-22-50. 176 units. A/C TV TEL. 8,000 ptas. ($53.60) double. MC, V. Parking 800 ptas. ($5.35).

One of Badajoz's major hotels, this eight-floor establishment is located about a half mile west of the town center, near the access roads of traffic coming in from Lisbon. Built in 1978, and appealing to many business travelers en route between Madrid and Lisbon, it offers uncomplicated modern rooms with conservative furnishings, and an efficient staff. Even though rooms are cramped, the hotel is a great value considering the low prices charged. Beds are comfortable, and bathrooms, just barely big enough for the job, have shower stalls and adequate towels. The hotel contains a bar, a garage, and an economical restaurant.

Hotel Río. Adolfo Diaz Ambrona, 13, 06006 Badajoz. ☎ **924-27-26-00.** Fax 924-27-38-74. 93 units. A/C MINIBAR TV TEL. 11,390 ptas. ($76.30) double; 14,500 ptas. ($97.15) suite. AE, DC, MC, V. Free parking. Bus: Urbano no. 2 or 8.

Located near a bridge on the highway connecting Lisbon and Madrid, the Hotel Río offers views of a eucalyptus grove and the river. Amenities include an outdoor pool, a parking garage, bingo, a disco pub/restaurant, and a garden. The small and functional guest rooms are comfortably furnished and well maintained. The hotel attracts many of the Portuguese who come over for the night for a taste of Spain.

WHERE TO DINE

✪ **Aldeberán.** Avenida de Elvas, s/n, Urbanización Guadiana. ☎ **924-27-42-61.** Reservations recommended. Main courses 2,200–2,850 ptas. ($14.75–$19.10); fixed-price menu 4,800 ptas. ($32.15). AE, DC, V. Mon–Sat 1:30–3:45 and 9–11:45pm. SPANISH/ EXTREMADURAN.

Established in 1990 within a modern building overlooking the river, on the highway about a mile west of Badajoz's center, Aldeberán is the best restaurant in the entire area. It prides itself on its Extremaduran origins, having adopted the name of a race of local bulls. Although a range of fish and meat dishes are offered, the menu features succulent pork dishes prepared from *pata negra* (black-footed) pigs, one of the specialties of the region. Offerings include *solomillo ibérico,* a tender pork fillet carefully seasoned and usually served with spinach; portions of wafer-thin cured ham, served au naturel or flavorfully mixed into salads of very fresh greens; hake in green sauce; and several different preparations of sole and monkfish. A signature dessert is ripe peaches flambéed in honey sauce and served with mint-flavored crème fraîche.

Mesón el Tronco. Calle Muñoz Torrero, 16. ☎ **924-22-20-76.** Reservations recommended. Main courses 1,250–2,700 ptas. ($8.40–$18.10); fixed-price menu 1,250 ptas. ($8.40). DC, MC, V. Tues–Sat 9am–4pm, Tues–Sat 7pm–midnight. EXTREMADURAN.

You might not suspect an attractive restaurant exists here when you encounter the popular bar near the front door, but the excellent tapas hint at the delicacies available in the back room. The owner offers traditional Extremaduran dishes, as well as a changing repertoire of daily specials. Menu items include gazpacho, *cocido* (stew) of the region, and lamb cutlets, all at affordable prices and served in air-conditioned comfort. Mesón el Tronco is in the center of town, 2 blocks west of the cathedral.

SIDE TRIPS FROM MÉRIDA & BADAJOZ

Jerez de los Caballeros makes an interesting journey from either Badajoz (46½ miles [75km] south on the N-432) or Mérida (61½ miles [99km] southwest on the N-360). It's a small town of white houses clustered on a hillside, with the cathedral on the summit. The birthplace of Balboa, the first European to discover the Pacific, is nearby—a modest whitewashed house at Capitán Cortés, 10. A statue honors the explorer in one of the town's small squares. Jerez de los Caballeros, with many belfries and towers, including the **Torre Sagrienta (Bloody Tower),** takes its name, traditions, and ambience from the Caballeros del Templo (Knights Templars), who were given the town after it was taken from the Moors in 1230.

Medellín, 25 miles (40km) east of Mérida and 62 miles (100km) east of Badajoz, is the little town where Hernán Cortés, conqueror of Mexico, was born. From the approach you'll see the old whitewashed buildings on the opposite side of the Guadiana River, with the ruins of medieval Medellín Castle dominating the skyline. A 17th-century stone bridge crosses the river into the town, where you'll find a monument to Cortés in the main cobblestoned plaza. From either Mérida or Badajoz, take the N-V superhighway heading to Madrid; exit at the C-520, the road into Medellín.

6 Zafra

38 miles (61km) S of Mérida, 107 miles (172km) N of Seville

One of the most interesting stopovers in Lower Extremadura, the white-walled town of Zafra is filled with old Moorish streets and squares. The 1457 castle of the dukes of Feria, the most important in the province, boasts both a sumptuous 16th-century Herreran patio and the Sala Dorada, with a richly paneled ceiling. The place is now a government parador (see below). You'll want to spend time on the central square, the arcaded 18th-century Plaza Mayor, and its satellite, the 16th-century Plaza Vieja (Old Square). These are the two most important sights in Zafra, along with the Nuestra Señora de la Candelaria, a church with nine panels by Zurbarán, displayed on the retablo in a chapel designed by Churriguera. The church, constructed in the Gothic-Renaissance style, has a redbrick belfry. Admission is free and it's open Monday through Friday from 10:30am to 1pm and 7 to 8:30pm and Sunday from 11am to 12:30pm.

ESSENTIALS

GETTING THERE   Five buses a day arrives from Mérida; a one-way ticket costs 600 ptas. ($4). For schedules, call ☎ **924-55-00-07.**

Zafra lies at the point where the highway from Seville (E-803) splits, heading east to Mérida and Cáceres and west to Badajoz. Driving there is easy. From Mérida to Zafra, allow an hour; from Seville, about 2½ hours. There's also a direct road from Córdoba.

VISITOR INFORMATION   The **tourist information office** is at Plaza de España, 30 (☎ **924-55-10-36**), open Monday through Friday from 11am to 2pm and 6 to 8pm, Saturday from 11am to 1:30pm.

WHERE TO STAY & DINE

Huerta Honda. López Asme, 32, 06300 Zafra. ☎ **924-55-41-00.** Fax 924-55-25-04. 40 units. A/C MINIBAR TV TEL. 9,200 ptas. ($61.65) double; 12,500 ptas. ($83.75) apt; 20,000 ptas. ($134) suite. AE, MC, V.

From the modern, recently renovated bedrooms of this hotel in front of the Plaza del Alcázar, you'll get views of the citadel and the old town. Living space here is a bit tight, but the beds are good and the bathrooms immaculately kept. There's a disco, as well as a garden and a pretty patio for midafternoon drinks. Under the same management, at no. 36 on the same street, is the restaurant Barbacana, a well-recommended regional dining room, offering French and Basque cuisine. Meals cost from 3,800 to 4,000 ptas. ($25.45 to $26.80).

Parador Hernán Cortés. Plaza Corazón de María, 7, 06300 Zafra. ☎ **924-55-45-40.** Fax 924-55-10-18. 45 units. A/C MINIBAR TV TEL. 15,000 ptas. ($100.50) double; 25,000 ptas. ($167.50) suite. AE, DC, MC, V. Free parking along the Plaza Corazón de María.

This government-run parador, located in a restored castle near the Plaza de España, is named after Cortés, who stayed here with the dukes of Feria before his departure for the New World. The castle was originally built in 1457, on a square plan with four round towers. The interior, beautiful but restrained, contains the chapel of the Alcázar, with an octagonal Gothic dome. In addition to being decorated in splendid taste, the Hernan Cortés is quite comfortable, boasting a patio, a garden, and a swimming pool. Though not the finest parador in Extremadura, the bedrooms here are medium in size or even spacious, and all the furnishings are sturdy and comfortable, especially the firm mattresses. Bathrooms are fairly roomy and equipped with hair dryers and plush towels. The magnificent-looking dining room offers regional meals from 3,500 ptas. ($23.45). A bar and a large lounge are also on the premises.

7

Andalusia

This once-great stronghold of Muslim Spain is rich in history and tradition, containing some of the country's most celebrated sightseeing treasures: the world-famous Mezquita (mosque) in Córdoba, the Alhambra in Granada, and the great Gothic cathedral in Seville. It also has many smaller towns just waiting to be discovered—Úbeda, castle-dominated Jaén, gorge-split Ronda, sherry-producing Jerez de la Frontera, and the gleaming white port city of Cádiz. Give Andalusia at least a week and you'll still have only skimmed the surface of its many offerings.

This dry, mountainous region also embraces the Costa del Sol (Málaga, Marbella, and Torremolinos), a popular coastal strip that is covered separately in the following chapter. Go to the Costa del Sol for beach resorts, nightlife, and relaxation; visit Andalusia for its architectural wonders and beauty.

Crime alert: Anyone driving south into Andalusia and the Costa del Sol should be wary of thieves. Daylight robberies are commonplace, especially in Seville, Córdoba, and Granada. It is not unusual for a car to be broken into while tourists are enjoying lunch in a restaurant. Some establishments have hired guards (a service for which you should tip, of course). Under no circumstances should you ever leave passports and traveler's checks unguarded in a car.

1 Jaén, Baeza & Úbeda

International tourists discovered the province of Jaén, with three principal cities—Jaén, the capital; Baeza; and Úbeda—in the 1960s. For years, visitors whizzed through Jaén on the way south to Granada or bypassed it altogether on the southwest route to Córdoba and Seville. But the government has improved the province's hotel outlook with excellent paradors, which now provide some of the finest accommodations in Andalusia.

JAÉN
60 miles (97km) E of Córdoba, 60 miles (97km) N of Granada, 210 miles (338km) S of Madrid

In the center of Spain's major olive-growing district, Jaén is sandwiched between Córdoba and Granada and has always been a gateway between Castile and Andalusia. Christian forces gathered here in 1492 before marching on Granada to oust the Moors.

Andalusia

Mediterranean Sea

N322
N324
Úbeda
Linares
Bailén
Baeza
Mancha Real
N323
Jaén
E902
N323
NIV
N324
E5
Córdoba
Río Guadajoz
Castro
Montilla
N331
Lucena
Sierra Morena
Sierra de los Santos
Cazalla
Lora
Río Guadalquivir
Seville
E803
N630
N433
N435
Sierra Aracena
Valverde del Camino
N431
A49
E1
Huelva
Sanlúcar de Barrameda
Golfo de Cádiz
COSTA DE LA LUZ
Cádiz
NIV
E5
Jerez de la Frontera
E5
N340
Arcos de la Frontera
N342
N333
A4
Utrera
N334
A92
NIV
N333
Marchena
Écija
Río Genil
Palma
Osuna
Morón
Sierra de Morón
Olvera
C341
Ronda
Sierra Bermeja
N340
Marbella
Fuengirola
Bahía de Málaga
Málaga
N340
Montes de Málaga
Sierra de Almijara
Nerja
Salobreña
E15
N323
GR420
Granada
Santa Fe
N342
Loja
A92
N321
Antequera
Sierra de Yeguas
Campillos
N342
N334
Estepa
Alcalá la Real
Mon-efrío
N432
Sierra Harana
N324

25 mi
25 km
0
0

Legend
✈ Airport

Jaén's bustling modern section is of little interest to visitors, but **the Moorish old town,** where narrow cobblestoned streets hug the mountainside, is reason enough to visit. A hilltop castle, now converted into a first-rate parador, dominates the city. On a clear day you can see the snow-covered peaks of the Sierra Nevada.

The city of Jaén is at the center of a large province of 5,189 square miles (13,491 sq. km), framed by mountains: the Sierra Morena to the north, the Segura and Cazorla ranges to the east, and those of Huelma, Noalejo, and Valdepeñas to the south. To the west, plains widen into the fertile Guadalquivir Valley and the landscape is rugged and irregular. Jaén province comprises three well-defined districts: the Sierra de Cazorla, a land of wild scenery; the plains of Bailén, Ajona, and Arjonilla, filled with wheat fields, vineyards, and old olive trees; and the valleys of the tributaries of the Guadalquivir.

ESSENTIALS

GETTING THERE   It's easier to leave Jaén than it is to get here. Trains to Jaén run only from south to north. Northbound trains—including four daily to Madrid's Atocha Railway Station—arrive and depart from Jaén's RENFE station on the Paseo de la Estación (☎ **953-27-02-02**), north of the center of town. The trip to Madrid takes 4 to 5 hours, depending on the type of train. If you're traveling from north to south, however, it isn't quite so easy. Most southbound trains from Madrid, and all trains heading south to Seville and the rest of Andalusia, stop only at a larger railway junction that lies inconveniently in the hamlet of Espeluy, 22 miles (35.5km) to the north. From Espeluy, trains are sometimes funneled a short ride to the east, to the railway junction midway between Linares (31 miles [50km] from Jaén) and Baeza (the Estación de Linares—Baeza). Consult the Jaén tourist office or the railway station for advice on your particular routing.

The bus terminal is at Plaza Coca de la Piñera (☎ **953-25-50-14**), 1 block south of the central Parque de la Victoria. Either directly or after a transfer at Baeza, 30 miles (48km) to the north, buses travel 13 times a day to Granada (1½ hours away), 10 times to Úbeda (30 minutes), four times to Málaga (3 hours), and 10 times to Baeza (1 hour).

Four important highways, plus several provincial roads, converge on Jaén from four directions. From Madrid, follow the N-IV (E-5) to N-323 (E-902).

VISITOR INFORMATION   The **tourist information office** is at calle Arquitecto Bergés, 1 (☎ **953-22-27-37**). Open April through October, Monday through Friday from 8:30am to 2:30pm; Saturday 10:30am to 1pm; off-season, Monday through Friday from 8:30am to 2:30pm, Saturday 10am to 12:30pm.

EXPLORING JAÉN

Jaén produces some of the most appealing pottery in the south of Spain, as well as some of the most intricately crafted baskets. You'll find outlets for the stuff all over the city's historic core, but two stores whose inventories are particularly well chosen include **Peñalver,** calle Bernabe Soriano, 17 (☎ **953-24-34-15**) and **Antanyo,** calle Virgen de la Capilla, 7 (☎ **953-24-37-35**).

Catedral de Santa María. Plaza de la Catedral. ☎ **953-23-42-33.** Free admission to cathedral; museum 100 ptas. (65¢). Cathedral daily 8:30am–1pm and 4:30–8pm (closes at 7pm in winter); museum Sat–Sun 11am–1pm. Bus: 8, 10, 16.

The formality and grandeur of Jaén's cathedral stand witness to the city's importance in days gone by. Begun in 1555 and completed in 1802, it is a honey-colored blend of Gothic, baroque, and Renaissance styles, but mainly Renaissance. A huge dome dominates the interior, with its richly carved choir stalls. The cathedral museum contains an important collection of historical objects in two underground chambers, including paintings by Ribera. The cathedral stands southwest of the Plaza de la Constitución.

Iglesia de la Magdalena. Calle de la Magdalena. ☎ **953-25-60-19.** Free admission. Daily 6am–8pm.

Of the many churches worth visiting in Jaén, La Magdalena is the oldest and most interesting. This Gothic church was once an Arab mosque.

Museo Provincial. Paseo de la Estación, 29. ☎ **953-25-06-00.** Admission 250 ptas. ($1.70). Tues 3–8pm, Wed–Sat 9am–8pm, Sun 9am–3pm.

The Provincial Museum's collection includes Roman mosaics, a Mudéjar arch, and many ceramics from the early Iberian, Greek, and Roman periods. On the upper floor is an exhibition of Pedro Berruguete paintings, including *Christ at the Column.* Look also for the Paleo-Christian sarcophagus from Martos. The museum lies between the bus and train stations.

Centro Cultural Palacio de Villardompardo. Plaza de Santa Luisa de Marillac, s/n. ☎ **953-23-62-92.** Free admission. Tues–Fri 9am–8pm (closes at 7pm in winter), Sat–Sun 9:30am–2:30pm. You must go on foot: In the old quarter of Jaén, follow signs indicating either Baños Arabes or Barrio de la Magdalena.

This is a three-in-one attraction, including some former Arab baths (known as *hamman*), a Museo de Artes y Costumbres Populares (folk art and crafts), and a Museo Internacional de Arte Naif (with works by self-taught artists from all over the world). The hours (see above) are the same for all three attractions, and none charge admission.

Underneath the palace, which lies near calle San Juan and the Chapel of St. Andrew (San Andrés), are the former Arab baths. These represent some of the most important Moorish architecture from the 11th century ever discovered in Spain—in fact, they are the most significant ruins of Arab baths in the country. You can visit a warm room, a hot room, and a cold room—the latter having a barrel vault and 12 star-shaped chandeliers. Later you can go upstairs to see the folk art and the Naif collection that opened in 1990.

WHERE TO STAY

Hotel Condesable Iranzo. Paseo de la Estacion, 32, 23008 Jaén. ☎ **953-22-28-00.** Fax 953-26-38-07. 165 units. A/C MINIBAR TV TEL. 8,250–10,300 ptas. ($55.30–$69) double; 12,000 ptas. ($80.40) suite. AE, DC, MC, V. Parking: 1,100 ptas. ($7.35).

No hidden old-fashioned Andalusian charm here—what you see is what you get in this large 12-floor hotel, which occupies an entire corner of the main square. The building is no beauty, but it is well located, has a good view of the castle and the mountains, and has a wide range of facilities. In the public areas the decor is a shiny combination of marble, glass, and wood. The midsize rooms are functional and comfortable—a good deal for the low price. Apart from various convention rooms, the hotel has four reception areas, two coffee bars, a disco that stays open until 4am, and two restaurants, which serve very reasonably priced meals with a *menú del día* at 2,300 ptas. ($15.40).

Hotel Europa. Plaza de Belén, 1, 23001 Jaén. ☎ **953-22-27-00.** Fax 953-22-26-92. 37 units. A/C TV TEL. 8,805 ptas. ($59) double; 11,450 ptas. ($76.70) triple. Rates include continental breakfast. AE, DC, MC, V. Parking: 825 ptas. ($5.55).

In the commercial and historical center of Jaén, this little hotel is a winner following its massive renovation, which brought everything up to date. Although the avantgarde decor is a little severe, it manages to be cozy and contemporary at the same time.

The medium-size rooms have been spruced up, with firm new mattresses and sparkling clean bathrooms. The hotel has a coffee bar but no restaurant.

✪ **Parador Castillo de Santa Catalina.** Castillo de Santa Catalina, 23000 Jaén. ☎ **953-23-00-00.** Fax 953-23-09-30. 45 units. A/C MINIBAR TV TEL. 17,500 ptas. ($117.25) double. AE, DC, MC, V. Free parking. Follow Carretera al Castillo y Neveraol.

Three miles (4.8km) to the east on the hill overlooking the city, this castle is one of the government's showplace paradors, and staying here is reason enough to visit Jaén. In the 10th century the castle was a Muslim fortress, surrounded by high protective walls and approached only by a steep, winding road. The castle is still reached by the same road; visitors enter through a three-story-high baronial hallway, and a polite staff shows them to their balconied and midsize rooms (doubles only), tastefully furnished and comfortable, with spick-and-span tile bathrooms equipped with hair dryers.

Dining: Dining at the castle is quite dramatic—the high-vaulted restaurant looks like a small cathedral with its wrought-iron chandeliers and stone arches, plus a raised hearth and a collection of copper kettles and ceramics. On either side of the lofty room, arched windows open onto either a terrace or a fabulous view of town. Lunch or dinner here includes typical Jaén dishes—usually made with the olives for which the area is famous—and regional wine.

Amenities: Room service, concierge, baby-sitting, dry cleaning/laundry.

Xauen. Plaza Deán Mazas, 3, 23001 Jaén. ☎ **953-24-07-89.** Fax 953-19-03-12. 35 units. A/C TV TEL. 7,000 ptas. ($46.90) double. MC, V. Parking 500 ptas. ($3.35).

This family run hotel stands a block west of Plaza de la Constitución. The handcrafted detailing of the building and its central location make it an attractive choice, though it's certainly modest. The small guest rooms are simply furnished but comfortable, with good beds and immaculate baths. Breakfast is served daily. If you're driving, you might have to park far away from the entrance.

WHERE TO DINE

Consider a meal in the luxurious hilltop parador commanding a view of Jaén (see above). It's one of the loveliest spots in the area.

Mesón Rio Chico. Calle Nueva, 12. ☎ **953-24-08-02.** Reservations recommended. Main courses 1,500–2,500 ptas. ($10.05–$16.75). AE, DC, MC, V. Tues–Sun noon–3:30pm and 9–11:30pm. ANDALUSIAN.

Charming, intimate, and serving authentic regional cuisine, this restaurant has been around since 1962 within a simple modern building in the heart of Jaén. Menu items include strongly flavored, earthy versions of hake, beefsteak, roasted pork, and chicken. Because there's room for only 45 diners at a time, it's important to reserve in advance. In spite of its informality and simplicity, many locals claim this is their favorite dining room in town, even though many recipes and dishes haven't been changed since the 1960s.

Nelson. Pasaje de la Estación, 33. ☎ **953-22-92-01.** Reservations required. Main courses 900–2,000 ptas. ($6.05–$13.40). AE, DC, MC, V. Mon–Sat 1:30–4:30pm and 8pm–midnight. Closed weekends in Aug. SPANISH.

On a pedestrian walkway near the railway station, Plaza de las Batallas, and the Museo Provincial, this restaurant relies on fresh produce and the gruff charm of the owners, the Ordóñez brothers, José and Salvador. An impressive array of tapas greets you at the bar, where you can pause for predinner drinks. In the air-conditioned dining room, full meals might include such specialties as roast goat baked with savory spices, fillet steak grilled in olive oil and garlic, escabeche of fish, hake stewed with eels, and grilled lamb chops. Although the cooking is only standard, very fresh ingredients are used.

BAEZA
28 miles (45km) NE of Jaén, 191 miles (307km) S of Madrid

Historic Baeza (known to the Romans as Vilvatia), with its Gothic and plateresque buildings and cobblestoned streets, is one of the best-preserved old towns in Spain. At twilight, lanterns hang on walls of plastered stone, flickering against the darkening sky and lighting the narrow streets. The town had its heyday in the 16th and 17th centuries, and in the Visigothic period was the seat of a bishop.

ESSENTIALS
GETTING THERE   The nearest important railway junction, receiving trains from Madrid and most of Andalusia, is the Estación Linares-Baeza (☎ **953-65-02-02**), 8½ miles (14km) west of Baeza's center. For information about which trains arrive there, refer to the section on Jaén, above.

There are 10 buses a day to Úbeda; the ride is 15 minutes long, costing 100 ptas. (65¢) one way. From Jaén, there are seven buses per day (trip time: 1 hour), costing 445 ptas. ($3) one way. For more information, call ☎ **953-74-04-68.**

Baeza lies east of the N-V, the superhighway linking Madrid with Granada. Highway 321/322, which runs through Baeza, links Córdoba with Valencia.

VISITOR INFORMATION   The **tourist information office** is at Plaza del Pópulo (☎ **953-74-04-44**). Open Monday through Friday from 9am to 2:30pm, and Saturday 10am to 12:30pm.

EXPLORING BAEZA
Entering Baeza from Jaén, you'll approach the main square, **Plaza del Pópulo,** a two-story open colonnade, and a good point to begin exploring. The buildings here date in part from the 16th century and one of the most interesting houses the tourist office (see above), where you can obtain a map to help guide you through the town. Look for the fountain containing four half-effaced lions, the Fuente de los Leones, which may have been brought here from the Roman town of Cantulo.

Head south along the Cuesta de San Gil to reach the Gothic and Renaissance **cathedral,** Plaza de la Fuente de Santa María (no phone), constructed in the 16th century on the foundations of an earlier mosque. Look for the Puerta de la Luna (Moon Door), in Arab-Gothic style, and in the interior, remodeled by Andrés de Vandelvira and his pupils, the carved wood and the brilliant painted *rejas* (iron screens). The Gold Chapel is especially outstanding. The cathedral is open daily from 10:30am to 1pm and 4 to 7pm; admission is free.

After leaving the cathedral, continue up the Cuesta de San Felipe to the **Palacio de Jabalquinto,** a beautiful example of civil architecture in the flamboyant Gothic style, built by Juan Alfonso de Benavides, a relative of King Ferdinand. Its facade is filled with interesting decorative elements, and there is a simple Renaissance-style courtyard with marble columns. Inside, two lions guard the stairway, heavily decorated in the baroque style.

WHERE TO STAY & DINE
On the outskirts of town, toward Úbeda, the **Hotel Juanito,** Plaza del Arca del Agua, s/n, 23400 Baeza (☎ **953-74-00-40;** fax 953-74-23-24), is more famous for its restaurant (see below), but it also rents 35 very affordable rooms. They're small and unpretentious but clean and comfortable.

Casa Juanito. In the Hotel Juanito, Plaza del Arca del Agua, s/n. ☎ **953-74-00-40.** Reservations required Fri–Sat. Main courses 3,500–4,500 ptas. ($23.45–$30.15). MC, V. Daily 1–4pm, Tues–Sat 8–11pm. Closed Nov 1–15. ANDALUCIAN.

Owners Juan Antonio and Luisa Salcedo serve regional specialties from Andalusia and La Mancha. Devotees of the lost art of Jaén cookery, they revive ancient recipes in their frequently changing suggestions for the day. The hotel owners also run a small olive oil outlet and use only their own produce when cooking. Game is served in season, and many vegetable dishes are made with ham. Among the savory and well-prepared menu items are *habas* (beans), fillet of beef with tomatoes and peppers, partridge in pastry crust, and codfish house style.

El Sali. Pasaje Cardenal Benavides, 15. ☎ **953-74-13-65.** Reservations not required. Main courses 950–2,500 ptas. ($6.35–$16.75); fixed-price menu 1,600 ptas. ($10.70). AE, DC, MC, V. Daily 1–4pm, Thurs–Tues 8:30–11:30pm. Closed Sept 20–Oct 15. SPANISH/ANDALUSIAN.

This restaurant is set in a modern building erected in the 1980s in the town center, adjacent to Plaza del Pópulo. In air-conditioned comfort diners enjoy what many locals regard as the most reasonable set menu in town, and in the summer diners can sit on a terrace that overlooks the city's Renaissance monuments. The owners serve not only the cuisine of Andalusia but also certain dishes from around Spain. They are known for their fresh vegetables, as exemplified by *la pipirana,* a cold medley of vegetables with tuna, accented with boiled eggs, fresh tomatoes, onions, and spices (only in summer). The atmosphere is relaxed, the service cordial and the portions generous. You won't leave feeling hungry or overcharged.

ÚBEDA

6 miles (10km) NE of Jaén, 194 miles (312km) S of Madrid

A former stronghold of the Arabs and often called the "Florence of Andalusia," Úbeda is a Spanish National Landmark filled with golden-brown Renaissance palaces and tile-roofed whitewashed houses. The best way to discover Úbeda's charm is to wander its narrow cobblestone streets.

The government long ago created a parador here in a renovated ducal palace—you might stop for lunch if you're not pressed for time. Allow time for a stroll through Úbeda's shops, which specialize in leather craft goods and esparto grass carpets.

The palaces and churches of the city are almost endless. You might begin your tour at the centrally located **Plaza de Vázquez de Molina,** which is flanked by several mansions, including the Casa de las Cadenas, now the Town Hall. The mansions have been decaying for centuries, but many are now finally being restored.

ESSENTIALS

GETTING THERE   The nearest train station is the **Linares-Baeza station** (☎ **953-65-02-02**). For information on trains to and from the station, refer to the Jaén section (see above).

There are 15 buses daily to Baeza, less than 6 miles (9.6km) away, and to Jaén. Seven buses per day go to the busy railway station at Linares-Baeza, where a train can take you virtually anywhere in Spain. Bus service to and from Córdoba, Seville, and Granada is also available. Úbeda's bus station lies in the heart of the modern town, on calle San José (☎ **953-75-21-57**), where signs will point you on a downhill walk to the *zona monumental.*

To drive here, turn off the Madrid-Córdoba road and head east for Linares, then on to Úbeda, a detour of 26 miles (42km). The turnoff is at the junction with Route 322.

VISITOR INFORMATION   The **tourist information office** is at Avenida Cristo Rey, 2 (☎ **953-75-08-97**). Open Monday through Friday from 9am to 2:30pm, Saturday from 11am to 2pm.

EXPLORING ÚBEDA

Iglesia El Salvador. Plaza de Vázquez de Molina. No phone. Free admission. Daily 9am–1pm and 5–7pm.

One of the grandest examples of Spanish Renaissance architecture, this church was designed in 1536 by Diego de Siloé. The richly embellished portal is mere window dressing for the wealth of decoration inside the church, including a sacristy designed by Andréas de Vandelvira and a single nave with gold-and-blue vaulting. The many sculptures and altarpieces and the spectacular rose windows are of special interest.

Iglesia de San Pablo. Plaza 1 de Mayo. No phone. Free admission. Daily 9am–1pm and 7–9pm.

This church, in the center of the old town, is almost as fascinating as the Iglesia El Salvador. The Gothic San Pablo is famous for its 16th-century south portal in the Isabelline style and for its chapels.

Hospital de Santiago. Calle Santiago. ☎ **953-75-08-42**. Admission 225 ptas. ($1.50). Mon–Fri 8am–3pm and 3:30–10pm, Sat 8am–3pm.

On the western edge of town off the calle del Obispo Coros stands the Hospital of Santiago, completed in 1575 and still in use today. Built by Andrés de Vandelvira, "the Christopher Wren of Úbeda," over the years it has earned a reputation as the "Escorial of Andalusia." Today the hospital is a cultural venue, hosting concerts and also containing a minor modern art museum.

Iglesia de Santa María de Los Reales Alcázares. Arroyo de Santa María. ☎ **953-75-07-77**. Free admission. Daily 9am–1pm and 5–7pm.

Another intriguing Úbeda church is Santa María de los Reales Alcázares, on the site of a former Arab mosque. The cloisters, with their fan vaulting, are Gothic; the interior, with its tiled and painted ceiling, blends the Gothic and Mudéjar styles. Also inside the church you'll find a gruesome statue of a mutilated Christ. Santa María is in the center of town, opposite the Ayuntamiento (Town Hall).

WHERE TO STAY

Hotel Consuelo. Avenida Ramón y Cajal, 12, 23400 Úbeda. ☎ **953-75-08-40**. Fax 953-75-68-34. 48 units. A/C MINIBAR TV TEL. 5,500 ptas. ($36.85) double; from 7,500 ptas. ($50.25) suite. MC, V. Parking 750 ptas. ($5.05).

If price is the most important item on your agenda, head for this comfortable and utilitarian three-story building across from the Instituto Ensenanza Media. Built in the late 1960s and renovated in 1991, the hotel doesn't serve breakfast, so you'll have to head out for coffee at one of the nearby cafes. The small guest rooms are little more than basic but are clean and comfortable. The somewhat cramped bathrooms have stall showers.

Hotel la Paz. Calle Andalucía, 1, 23400 Úbeda. ☎ **953-75-21-46**. Fax 953-75-08-48. 50 units. A/C TV TEL. 5,800–6,800 ptas. ($38.85–$45.55) double. AE, DC, MC, V. Parking 1,000 ptas. ($6.70).

Set on a sharply angled street corner in the heart of the commercial district opposite a statue to a military hero, this seven-story hotel contains comfortably unpretentious rooms. Each is decorated in a simplified Iberian style of dignified wood furniture, with either pure white or papered walls. The hotel was built in 1971 and renovated in 1994 with new mattresses and rejuvenated plumbing. The street-level El Olivo restaurant opens directly onto the sidewalk and does a thriving business with the local community. There's also a simple snack restaurant for coffee and drinks, plus a bar. Services include laundry and baby-sitting.

✪ **Parador Nacional del Condestabe Dávalos.** Plaza de Vázquez de Molina, 1, 23400 Úbeda. ☎ **953-75-03-45.** Fax 953-75-12-59. 32 units. A/C MINIBAR TV TEL. 18,000–21,000 ptas. ($120.60–$140.70) double; 23,000 ptas. ($154.10) suite. AE, DC, MC, V.

In the heart of town on the most central square, near the Town Hall, stands this 16th-century palace turned parador, which shares an old paved plaza with the Iglesia El Salvador and its dazzling facade. The formal entrance to the Renaissance palace leads to an enclosed patio, encircled by two levels of Moorish arches, where palms and potted plants stand on the tile floors. The guest rooms, doubles only, are nearly two stories high, with beamed ceilings and tall windows. Antiques and reproductions adorn the rooms, and the beds are comfortable, the bathrooms immaculate.

Dining: Before lunch or dinner, stop in at the low-beamed wine cellar, with its stone arches, provincial stools and tables, and giant kegs of wine. Dinner is served in a tastefully decorated ground-floor room, where a costumed staff serves traditional Spanish dishes.

Amenities: Concierge, laundry/dry cleaning, massages, newspaper delivery, room service.

WHERE TO DINE

Parador Restaurante Nacional del Condestabe Dávalos. Plaza de Vázques de Molina. ☎ **953-75-03-45.** Reservations recommended. Main courses 1,800–2,700 ptas. ($12.05–$18.10). Menú del parador 3,500 ptas. ($23.45); tasting menu 6,300 ptas. ($42.20) for two persons. AE, DC, MC, V. Daily 1:30–4pm and 8:30–11pm. SPANISH/ANDALUSIAN.

This parador is the best place to dine for miles around. Though the cuisine here isn't the most creative, it's all made with market-fresh ingredients, prepared for the most part from recipes handed down through the decades. The menu is wide ranging, too, with varied choices in all categories. Fish is the most limited offering, which is natural given that Jaén is so far inland. Start with a really typical dish of the area such as cold soup with almonds, most delightful on a hot day. Partridge appears three times on the appetizer list, as it is a local favorite: stuffed green peppers with partridge, an unusual combination of stewed partridge with plums, and, finally, a refreshing salad with marinated partridge. The best fish dish, in our view, is grilled monkfish in a saffron sauce, although the grilled sole with garlic and an apple vinegar sauce is also enticing. Meat eaters might be tempted by the regional dishes such as oxtail in red wine sauce or stewed kid with pine nuts. The menú del parador is a good bet, including not only an appetizer but fish or meat for a main course, plus dessert. For the adventurous palate, the tasting menu for two showcases four typical regional dishes nightly.

2 Córdoba

65 miles (105km) W of Jaén, 260 miles (419km) SW of Madrid

Ten centuries ago Córdoba was one of the greatest cities in the world, with a population of 900,000. The capital of Muslim Spain, it was Europe's largest city and a cultural and intellectual center. This seat of the Western Caliphate flourished with public baths, mosques, a great library, and palaces. Later, greedy hordes passed through, sacking the city, tearing down ancient buildings, and carting off many art treasures. Despite these assaults, Córdoba still retains traces of its former glory—enough to challenge Seville and Granada as the most fascinating city in Andalusia.

Today this provincial capital is known chiefly for its mosque, but it abounds with other artistic and architectural riches, especially its lovely homes. The old Arab and Jewish quarters are famous for their narrow streets lined with whitewashed houses boasting flower-filled patios and balconies, and it's perfectly acceptable to walk along gazing into the courtyards. This isn't an invasion of privacy: The citizens of Córdoba take pride in showing off their patios as part of the city's tradition. And don't forget to bring along a good pair of walking shoes, as the only way to explore the monumental heart of the city is on foot.

Córdoba has recently joined the ranks of UNESCO's World Heritage sites, so you'll want to spend at least a couple of days here.

ESSENTIALS

GETTING THERE   Córdoba is a railway junction for routes to the rest of both Andalusia and Spain. There are about 22 TALGO and AVE trains daily between Córdoba and Madrid (1½ to 2 hours). Other, slower trains (*tranvías*) take 5 to 8 hours for the same transit. There are also 25 trains from Seville every day (1½ hours). The main railway station is on the town's northern periphery, at Avenida de América, 130, near the corner of Avenida de Cervantes. For information, call ☎ 957-49-02-02. To reach the heart of the old town from the station, head south on Avenida de Cervantes or Avenida del Gran Capitán. While you're staying in Córdoba, if you want to buy a ticket or to get departure times and prices, you can go to the RENFE office at Ronda de los Tejares, 10 (☎ 957-47-58-54).

There are several different bus companies serving Córdoba, each of which maintains a separate terminal. The town's most important bus terminal is at calle Diego Serrano, 14, a block south of Avenida Medina Azahara, 29 (☎ 957-23-64-74), on the western outskirts of town (just west of the gardens beside Paseo de la Victoria). The bus company there is called Alsina Graells Sur.

From the bus terminal operated by Empresa Bacoma, Avenida de Cervantes, 22 (☎ 957-45-64-14), a short walk south of the railway station, there are three buses per day to and from Seville (a 2-hour and 3-hour trip, respectively) and five daily buses to Jaén (3 hours). Buses arrive here from Madrid (5½ hours).

Córdoba lies astride the N-IV (E-5) connecting Madrid with Seville. Don't think of entering the complicated maze of streets in the old town with a car, though. You'll inevitably get lost and find no place to park. There are two small public parking lots outside the old town, one on calle Robledo, the other on calle Aeropeurto. Both are well positioned, well marked, and easy to find.

VISITOR INFORMATION   The **tourist information office** is at calle Torrijos, 10 (☎ 957-47-12-35). Open Monday through Saturday from 9:30am to 8pm and Sunday from 9am to 2pm.

EXPLORING THE CITY

Among the many sights is Córdoba's **Roman bridge (Puente Romano),** believed to date from the time of Augustus. It's hardly Roman anymore because none of its 16 supporting arches are original. The sculptor Bernabé Gómez del Río erected a statue of St. Raphael in the middle of the bridge in 1651. The Roman bridge crosses the Guadalquivir River about 1 block south of the Mezquita.

The **Plaza de Toros** on Grand Vía del Parque stages its major **bullfights** in May, although fights are also presented at other times of the year. Watch for local announcements. Most hotels will arrange tickets for you, ranging in price (in general) from 1,000 to 2,000 ptas. ($6.70 to $13.40). Call ☎ 957-41-49-99 for information.

✪ **Mezquita-Catedral de Córdoba.** Calle Cardenal Herrero, s/n. ☎ **957-47-05-12.** Admission 750 ptas. ($5.05) adults, 375 ptas. ($2.50) children under 13. May–Sept, daily 10am–7pm; Oct–Apr, daily 10am–6pm.

Dating from the 8th century, the Mezquita was the crowning Muslim architectural achievement in the West, rivaled only by the mosque at Mecca. It is a fantastic labyrinth of red-and-white peppermint-striped pillars. To the astonishment of visitors, a cathedral now sits awkwardly in the middle of the mosque, disturbing the purity of the lines. The 16th-century cathedral, a blend of many styles, is impressive in its own right, with an intricately carved ceiling and baroque choir stalls. Additional ill-conceived annexes later turned the Mezquita into an architectural oddity. Its most interesting feature is the mihrab, a domed shrine of Byzantine mosaics that once housed the Koran.

After exploring the interior, stroll through the Courtyard of the Orange Trees, which has a beautiful fountain. The hardy can climb a 16th-century tower built here on the base of a Moorish minaret to catch a panoramic view of Córdoba and its environs.

The Mezquita is south of the train station, just north of the Roman bridge.

✪ **Alcázar de los Reyes Cristianos.** Amador de los Ríos, s/n. ☎ **957-42-01-51.** Admission 425 ptas. ($2.85) adults, 150 ptas. ($1) children. May–Sept, Tues–Sat 10am–2pm and 6–8pm, Sun 10am–2pm; Oct–Apr, Tues–Sat, 9:30am–3pm and 4:30–6:30pm, Sun 9:30am–3pm. Gardens illuminated May–Sept 10pm–1am. Bus: 3 or 12.

Commissioned in 1328 by Alfonso XI (the "Just"), the Alcázar of the Christian Kings is a fine example of military architecture. Ferdinand and Isabella governed Castile from this fortress on the river as they prepared to reconquer Granada, the last Moorish stronghold in Spain. Columbus journeyed here to fill Isabella's ears with his plans for discovery.

Located 2 blocks southwest of the Mezquita, this quadrangular building is notable for powerful walls and a trio of towers—the Tower of the Lions, the Tower of Allegiance, and the Tower of the River. The Tower of the Lions contains intricately decorated ogival ceilings that are the most notable example of Gothic architecture in Andalusia.

The beautiful gardens, illuminated at night, and the Moorish baths are celebrated attractions. The Patio Morisco is another lovely spot, its pavement decorated with the arms of León and Castile. A Roman sarcophagus is representative of 2nd- and 3rd-century funeral art and the Roman mosaics are also outstanding—especially a unique piece dedicated to Polyphemus and Galatea.

Sinagoga. Calle de los Judíos. ☎ **957-20-29-28.** Admission 75 ptas. (50¢). Tues–Sat 10am–2pm and 3:30–5:30pm, Sun 10am–1:30pm. Bus: 3 or 12.

In Córdoba you'll find one of Spain's few remaining pre-Inquisition synagogues, built in 1350 in the Barrio de la Judería (Jewish Quarter), 2 blocks west of the northern wall of the Mezquita. The synagogue is noted particularly for its stucco work; the east wall contains a large orifice where the Tabernacle was once placed (inside, the scrolls of the Pentateuch were kept). After the Jews were expelled from Spain, the synagogue was turned into a hospital, until it became a Catholic chapel in 1588.

Museo de Bellas Artes de Córdoba. Plaza del Potro, 1. ☎ **957-47-33-45.** Admission 250 ptas. ($1.70) adults, free for children 11 and under. Tues 3–8pm, Wed–Sat 9am–8pm, Sun and public holidays 9am–3pm. Bus: 3, 4, 7, or 12.

As you cross the Plaza del Potro to reach the Fine Arts Museum, notice the fountain at one end of the square. Built in 1557, it shows a young stallion with forelegs raised, holding the shield of Córdoba.

Housed in an old hospital on the plaza, the Fine Arts Museum contains medieval Andalusian paintings, examples of Spanish baroque art, and works by many of Spain's important 19th- and 20th-century painters, including Goya. The museum is east of the Mezquita, about a block south of the Church of St. Francis (San Francisco).

Museo de Julio Romero de Torres. Plaza del Potro. ☎ **957-49-19-09.** Admission 425 ptas. ($2.85) adults, 210 ptas. ($1.40) children under 18, free for adults over 75. Free on Tues. Oct–Apr, Tues–Sat 10am–2pm and 5–7pm; May–Sept, Tues–Sat 10am–2pm and 6–8pm, Sun 9:30am–3pm.

Across the patio from the Fine Arts Museum, this museum honors Julio Romero de Torres, a Córdoba-born artist who died in 1930. It contains his celebrated *Oranges and Lemons,* and other notable works such as *The Little Girl Who Sells Fuel, Sin,* and *A Dedication to the Art of the Bullfight.* A corner of Romero's Madrid studio has been reproduced in one of the rooms, displaying the paintings left unfinished at his death.

Museo Municipal de Arte Táurino. Plaza de las Bulas (also called Plaza Maimónides). ☎ **957-20-10-56.** Admission 425 ptas. ($2.85), free for children under 18. May–Sept, Tues–Sat 10:30am–2pm and 6–8pm, Sun 9:30am–3pm; Oct–Apr, Mon–Sat 10am–2pm and 5–7pm, Sun 9:30am–3pm. Bus: 3 or 12.

Memorabilia of great bullfights are housed here in the Jewish Quarter in a 16th-century building, inaugurated in 1983 as an appendage to the Museo Municipal de Arte Cordobesas. Its ample galleries recall Córdoba's great bullfighters with suits of lights, pictures, trophies, posters, even stuffed bulls' heads. You'll see a wax likeness of

Manolete in repose and the blood-smeared uniform of El Cordobés—both of these famous matadors came from Córdoba. The museum is located about a block north-west of the Mezquita, midway between the mosque and the synagogue.

Torre de la Calahorra. Avenida de la Confederación, Puente Romano. ☎ **957-29-39-29.** Admission to museum, 500 ptas. ($3.35) adults, 400 ptas. ($2.70) children; multimedia pre-sentation, 650 ptas. ($4.35) adults, 550 ptas. ($3.70) children. May–Sept, daily 10am–2pm and 4:30–8:30pm; Oct–Apr, daily 10am–6pm; multivisión, 11am, noon, 3pm, 4pm. Last tour is 1 hour before closing time. Bus: 16.

The Tower of Calahorra stands across the river at the southern end of the Roman bridge. Commissioned by Henry II of Trastamara in 1369 to protect him from his brother, Peter I, it now houses a town museum where visitors can take a self-guided tour with headsets. One room houses wax figures of Córdoba's famous philosophers, including Averro and Maimónides. Other rooms exhibit a miniature model of the Alhambra, at Granada, complete with water fountains; a miniature Mezquita; and a display of Arab musical instruments. Finally, you can climb to the top of the tower for some panoramic views of the Roman bridge, the river, and the cathedral/mosque.

✪ **Museo Arqueológico Provincial.** Plaza Jerónimo Paz, 7. ☎ **957-47-40-11.** Admission 250 ptas. ($1.70). Tues 3–8pm, Wed–Sat 9am–8pm, Sun and public holidays 9am–3pm.

Córdoba's Archaeological Museum, 2 blocks northeast of the Mezquita, is one of the most important in Spain. Housed in a palace dating from 1505, it displays artifacts left behind by the various peoples and conquerors who have swept through the province. There are Paleolithic and Neolithic items, Iberian hand weapons and ceramics, and Roman sculptures, bronzes, ceramics, inscriptions, and mosaics. Espe-cially interesting are the Visigothic artifacts. The most outstanding collection, how-ever, is devoted to Arabic art and spans the entire Muslim occupation. Take a few minutes to relax in one of the patios, with its fountains and ponds.

Palacio Museo de Viana. Plaza de Don Gome, 2. ☎ **957-48-01-34.** Palace admission 400 ptas. ($2.70); patios 200 ptas. ($1.35). June–Sept, Thurs–Tues 9am–2pm; Oct–May, Thurs–Sat and Mon–Tues 10am–1pm and 4–6pm, Sun 10am–2pm. Closed June 1–15.

The public has seldom had access to Córdoba's palaces, but that's changed with the opening of this museum. Visitors are shown into a carriage house, where the elegant vehicles of another era are displayed. Note the intricate leather decoration on the car-riages and the leather wall hangings, some of which date from the period of the Recon-quest; there's also a collection of leather paintings. You can wander at leisure through the garden and patios. The palace lies 4 blocks southeast of Plaza de Colón on the northeastern edge of the old quarter.

A NEARBY ATTRACTION

Conjunto Arqueológico Madinat Al-Zahra. Carretera Palma de Río, km 8. ☎ **957-32-91-30.** Admission 250 ptas. ($1.70). June 16–Sept 15, Tues–Sat 10am–1:30pm and 6–8:30pm, Sun 10am–1:30pm; Sept 16–Sept 30 and May 1–June 15, Tues–Sat 10am–2pm and 6–8:30pm, Sun 10am–2pm. Oct 1–Apr 30, Tues–Sun 10am–2pm and 4–6:30pm, Sun 10am–2pm. Bus: A bus leaves from the station on calle de la Bodega, but it lets you off about 2 miles (3km) from the site.

This palace, a kind of Moorish Versailles just outside Córdoba, was constructed in the 10th century by the first caliph of Andalus, Abd ar-Rahman III. He named it after the favorite of his harem, nicknamed "the brilliant." Thousands of workers and animals slaved to build this mammoth pleasure palace, said to have contained 300 baths and 400 houses. Over the years the site was plundered for building materials; in fact, it might have been viewed as a quarry for the entire region. Some of its materials, so it is claimed, went to build the Alcázar in Seville. The Royal House, rendezvous point for the ministers, has been reconstructed. The principal salon remains in fragments, though, so you have to imagine it in its majesty. Just beyond the Royal House lie the ruins of a mosque constructed to face Mecca. The Berbers sacked the place in 1013.

SHOPPING
In Moorish times Córdoba was famous for its leather, known as "cordwainer." Highly valued in 15th-century Europe, this leather was studded with gold and silver ornaments, then painted with embossed designs (*guadamaci*). Large panels of it often served in lieu of tapestries. Today the industry has fallen into decline, and the market is filled mostly with cheap imitations. You might want to seek out the following shop, especially if you're interested in Córdoban handcrafts: **Artesanía Andaluza,** Tomás Conde, 3 (no phone), near the bullfight museum, features a vast array of Córdoban handcrafts, especially filigree silver from the mines of Sierra Morena and some excellently crafted embossed leather, a holdover from the Muslim heyday. Lots of junk is mixed in with the good stuff, though, so beware.

Arte Zoco, Calle de los Judios, s/n (no phone), is the largest association of craftspeople in Córdoba. Established in the Jewish Quarter as a business cooperative in the mid-1980s, it assembles on one site the creative output of about a dozen artisans whose media include leather, wood, silver, crystal, terra-cotta, and iron. About a half dozen of the artisans maintain their studios on the premises, so you can visit and check out the techniques and tools they use to pursue their crafts. You'll find everything from new, iconoclastic, and avant-garde designs to well-made pieces that honor centuries-old traditions. Of special interest is the revival of the *Califar* pottery first introduced to Córdoba during the regimes of the Muslim caliphs. The shop is open Monday through Friday from 9:30am to 8pm, Saturday and Sunday from 9:30am to 2pm. The workshops and studios of the various artisans open and close according to the whims of their occupants, but are usually maintained Monday through Friday from 10am to 2pm and 5:30 to 8pm.

Libreria Seferad, Calle Romero, 4 (☎ 957-29-88-95), set across from Córdoba's oldest synagogue, is a cubbyhole-sized place selling articles that hark back to the Sephardic culture of medieval Europe. You'll find tapes of Sephardic music and chants, pottery fashioned into traditional Sephardic designs, filigreed silver ornaments, and reference works to Ladino, the medieval Iberian dialect spoken by Jews throughout the Diaspora. Inventory is limited, and hours are erratic, usually Monday through Friday from 10:30am to 8:30pm.

Angel López-Obrero and his two skilled sons run **Meryan,** Calleja de Las Flores, 2 (☎ 957-47-59-02), on one of the most colorful streets in the city. In this 250-year-old building you can see the artisans plying their craft, and though most items must be custom-ordered, there are some ready-made pieces for sale, including cigarette boxes, jewel cases, attaché cases, book and folio covers, and ottoman covers. Open Monday through Friday from 9am to 8pm and Saturday from 9am to 2pm.

Córdoba also has a branch of Spain's major department store, **El Corte Inglés,** at Ronda de los Tejares, 32 (☎ 957-47-02-67). At least some of the staff speaks English. It's open Monday through Saturday from 10am to 10:30pm.

STAYING ACTIVE
The best golf is found 5½ miles (9km) north of town at **Club de Golf Los Villares,** Vía Avenida del Brilliante (☎ 957-35-02-08). This is an excellent 18-hole golf course that's also a bit of a resort, with tennis courts and a swimming pool, along with a restaurant. Nonmembers are welcome to use the facilities, after making a reservation.

The best horseback riding is at the **Club Hipico (Riding Club),** at Carretera Santa María de Trassiera (☎ 957-27-16-28), which grants temporary membership.

WHERE TO STAY

At the peak of its summer season, Córdoba has too few hotels to meet the demand, so reserve as far in advance as possible.

EXPENSIVE

✪ **El Conquistador Hotel.** Magistral González Francés, 15, 14003 Córdoba. ☎ **957-48-11-02.** Fax 957-47-46-77. 102 units. A/C MINIBAR TV TEL. 19,000 ptas. ($127.30) double; from 23,100 ptas. ($154.75) suite. AE, DC, MC, V. Parking 1,950 ptas. ($13.05). Bus: 12.

Built centuries ago as a private villa, this first-class three-story hotel was tastefully renovated in 1986 into one of the most attractive in town, with triple rows of stone-trimmed windows and ornate iron balustrades. It sits opposite an unused rear entrance to the Mezquita. The marble-and-granite lobby opens into an interior courtyard filled with seasonal flowers, a pair of splashing fountains, and a symmetrical stone arcade. The quality, size, and comfort of the rooms—each with a black-and-white marble floor and a private bathroom—have earned the hotel four government-granted stars. Bathrooms are well maintained and equipped with toiletries, a hair dryer, and plush towels.

Amenities: There is no restaurant, but a coffee shop and a bar serve snacks and drinks. Baby-sitting, room service, laundry/valet, garage, sauna, solarium, car-rental facilities.

Hotel Gran Capitán. Avenida de América, 5, 14008 Córdoba. ☎ **957-47-02-50.** Fax 957-47-46-43. 94 units. A/C MINIBAR TV TEL. 16,750 ptas. ($112.25) double. AE, DC, MC, V. Parking 1,750 ptas. ($11.75).

Set about ⅔ mile north of the Mezquita, on a broad avenue near the railway station, this efficiently modern hotel is a member of the Tryp chain. Its good-size bedrooms are comfortably furnished in a contemporary international style, with tightly sound-proofed windows and contemporary tile bathrooms, equipped with hair dryers.

Dining/Diversions: The restaurant, La Reja, serves local and international food as part of its three-course, fixed-price lunches and dinners. There's also a bar.

Amenities: 24-hour room service, laundry, concierge, baby-sitting, car rentals, sauna, and a pool.

Hotel Meliá Córdoba. Jardines de la Victoria, 14004 Córdoba. ☎ **800/336-3542** in the U.S., or 957-29-80-66. Fax 957-29-81-47. 147 units. A/C MINIBAR TV TEL. 17,000 ptas. ($113.90) double; 20,500 ptas. ($137.35) suite. AE, DC, MC, V. Parking 2,000 ptas. ($13.40). Bus: 12.

Originally built in 1955 in one of Córdoba's most desirable locations, the Meliá was the first of the town's modern hotels, filling what was regarded as a serious lack of hotel accommodations. Today it's the most visible and prominent hotel in town, especially since a major renovation in 1991 improved much of its infrastructure, although a lack of effective soundproofing lets a lot of extra noise into the bedrooms. Meliá offers a very large lobby, enough distractions and amenities to please most tastes, and an enviable setting at the southwestern tip of the city's best-known park. Its distinguishing feature is its flower-filled terrace. The midsize rooms, all with private bathrooms, are cool, contemporary, and comfortable, often with balconies and views over nearby fountains. However, many of them are a bit too dark for our tastes. The cathedral, the historic district, and the modern commercial heart of Córdoba all lie within easy walking distance.

Dining/Diversions: The Palace restaurant serves international food in gracefully modern surroundings. An adjacent bar does an active business with the city's business community.

Amenities: Laundry/valet, concierge, room service (available from 10am to midnight), car rentals, shopping, boutiques, outdoor swimming pool, barber shop.

✪ **Parador Nacional de la Arruzafa.** Avenida de la Arruzafa, 33, 14012 Córdoba. ☎ **957-27-59-00.** Fax 957-28-04-09. 96 units. A/C MINIBAR TV TEL. 17,500–20,000 ptas. ($117.25–$134) double; 21,500 ptas. ($144.05) suite. AE, DC, MC, V. Free parking.

Lying 2½ miles (4km) outside town in a suburb called El Brillante, this parador, named after an Arab word meaning "palm grove," offers the conveniences and facilities of a luxurious resort hotel at reasonable rates. Occupying the site of a former caliphate palace, it's one of the finest paradors in Spain, with both a view and a swimming pool. The spacious guest rooms have been furnished with fine dark-wood pieces, and some have balconies for eating breakfast or relaxing over a drink. All have private bathrooms equipped with hair dryers.

Dining: The restaurant serves regional specialties, which include *salmorejo* (a chilled vegetable soup that's a variation of gazpacho), stewed oxtail, and a local cake called *pastel cordobés.*

Amenities: The government staff is a bit sleepy, but the hotel offers room service, laundry/valet, baby-sitting, swimming pool, tennis court.

MODERATE

Hotel Residencia El Califa. Lope de Hoces, 14, 14004 Córdoba. ☎ **800/528-1234** in the U.S. and Canada, or 957-29-94-00. Fax 957-29-57-16. www.bestwestern.com. 70 units. A/C TV TEL. 13,000 ptas. ($87.10) double; 16,400 ptas. ($109.90) suite. AE, MC, V. Bus: 12.

Attracting mainly a Spanish clientele, this centrally located hotel lies a short walk northwest of the Mezquita. Although rather impersonal and a bit austere, it is generally a good value. Built in 1974, it rises three floors and is serviced by two elevators. Inside, the hotel has russet-colored marble floors, velour wall coverings, a spacious lounge, and a TV that seems to broadcast non-stop soccer matches. Upstairs, midsize guest rooms are reasonably comfortable and furnished in a functional modern style. The mattresses are excellent with efficiently organized private bathrooms with shower stalls. In lieu of a restaurant, the hotel maintains a snack bar and also a bar. Parking is available along the street.

Sol Inn Gallos. Medina Azahara, 7, 14005 Córdoba. ☎ **800/336-3542** in the U.S., or 957-23-55-00. Fax 957-23-16-36. 115 units. A/C TV TEL. 11,200–12,500 ptas. ($75.05–$83.75) double; 15,700 ptas. ($105.20) triple. AE, DC, MC, V.

Half a block from a wide, tree-shaded boulevard on the western edge of town, this aging 1970s hotel stands eight floors high, crowned by an informal roof garden. The hotel is a favorite of both groups and commercial travelers. The comfortable but small guest rooms have many extra comforts, such as balconies, firm mattresses, and neatly organized private bathrooms with hair dryers. An outdoor swimming pool awaits you to jump in on a hot Andalusian day. The hotel also offers a restaurant, a drinking lounge, and a spacious public lobby.

INEXPENSIVE

Hostal El Triunfo. Corregidor Luís de la Cerda, 79, 14003 Córdoba. ☎ **957-47-55-00.** Fax 957-48-68-50. 50 units. A/C TV TEL. 7,000 ptas. ($46.90) double; 8,100 ptas. ($54.25) triple. AE, DC, MC, V. Parking 2,000 ptas. ($13.40). Bus: 12.

Opposite the mosque, a block from the northern bank of the Guadalquivir River, this is a real find—a simple hotel with a formal entranceway, a pleasant white-walled lounge, and comfortable, well-furnished rooms that come with good beds plus tiny bathrooms with shower stalls. Built in the late 1970s, El Triunfo was renovated in

1992 and offers polite and efficient service. The three-floor hotel has no elevator; its only other drawback is that the bells of the Mezquita may make it difficult to sleep.

Hotel Albacusis. Calle Buen Pastor, 11, 14003 Córdoba. ☎ **957-47-86-25.** 15 units. A/C TEL. 9,950 ptas. ($66.65) double. MC, V. Parking 1,900 ptas. ($12.75).

You'll find this small family hotel in the very heart of old Córdoba, in the maze of tiny streets and alleys that was the Jewish quarter, close to the restored synagogue just a few minutes' walk from the cathedral/mosque. The three-story building goes back hundreds of years, and the present management has completely renovated the interior without spoiling its original charm. Neutral colors help maintain a calm atmosphere. All rooms have more than adequate bathrooms. They also have shuttered windows opening onto a large interior courtyard and are consequently sheltered from the street noise. There's a reception room and bar inside, but during the long Andalusian summer season, guests prefer to have breakfast and relax on the large interior patio, which is adorned with two large trees, vines, and flower pots.

Hotel González. Manríquez, 3, 14003 Córdoba. ☎ **957-47-55-85.** Fax 957-47-62-19. 17 units. A/C TV TEL. 9,850 ptas. ($66) double; 12,600 ptas. ($84.40) triple. MC, V. Parking 2,000 ptas. ($13.40).

Within walking distance of the major monuments of Córdoba, the González is a clean, decent hotel but not a lot more. The midsize guest rooms are well kept, functionally furnished, and comfortable, with good beds fitted with firm mattresses and well-kept bathrooms equipped with hair dryers. In the hotel's excellent restaurant you can sample both regional and national specialties. Readers have praised the staff's attitude. One claimed, "They solve problems like magicians, take your car to the parking lot and back, and even teach you Spanish."

Hotel Riviera. Plaza de Aladreros, 5, 14001 Córdoba. ☎ **957-47-30-00.** Fax 957-47-60-18. 30 units. A/C TV TEL. 5,300–6,300 ptas. ($37.10–$44.10) double; 7,000–8,000 ptas. ($49–$56) triple. AE, DC, V. Parking 1,200 ptas. ($8.40).

The genial owner of this modern hotel is likely to be behind the reception desk when you arrive. His establishment is set on a triangular plaza in a commercial section of town a short walk south of the train station. It offers very clean no-frills accommodations and, while no meals are served, many cafes are within walking distance.

Hotel Selu. Calle Eduardo Dato, 7, 14003 Córdoba. ☎ **957-47-65-00.** Fax 957-47-83-76. 105 units. A/C MINIBAR TV TEL. 7,000–11,400 ptas. ($46.90–$76.40) double. AE, DC, MC, V. Parking 1,260 ptas. ($8.45).

In a commercial part of town near Paseo de la Victoria, the four-story Selu was constructed in 1969, and renovated in 1991. The staff is helpful and the public rooms are attractive, with masses of plants, dozens of velvet-covered armchairs, and a huge photograph of the Moorish columns of the Mezquita. The hotel contains functional rooms that are not special in any way but are reasonably comfortable with fine beds. There's an in-house parking garage. Only breakfast is served.

Los Omeyas. Calle Encarnacion, 17, 14003 Córdoba. ☎ **957-49-22-67.** Fax 957-49-16-59. 36 units. A/C TV TEL. 7,000–8,500 ptas. ($46.90–$56.95) double; 9,000–10,000 ptas. ($60.30–$67) triple; 10,500–11,500 ptas. ($70.35–$77.05) quadruple. AE, DC, MC, V. Parking 1,500 ptas. ($10.05).

If you want to stay in the very heart of Córdoba, you couldn't be better located than this hotel, lying nestled in a tangle of streets in what was the Jewish quarter. The name comes from the Umayyad dynasty who ruled the Muslim empire of al-Andalus. Although recently refurbished, the Arab tradition is still clearly visible in its white marble and lattice work. The hotel is naturally lit by a central colonnaded patio furnished with tables, and there is also a salon and Arab-style bar. Though in no way grand, the rooms are extremely comfortable, tastefully decorated, have complete bathrooms, and those on the top floor offer a panoramic view of the ancient tower of the Mosque/Cathedral, which is literally round the corner.

WHERE TO DINE

By all means, shake free of your hotel for at least one meal a day in Córdoba. The restaurants are not just places at which to have a quick bite but may combine food with flamenco—so make an evening of it.

EXPENSIVE

✪ **La Almudaina.** Plaza de los Santos Mártires, 1. ☎ **957-47-43-42.** Reservations required. Main courses 3,000–5,000 ptas. ($21–$35); fixed-price menus 3,000 ptas. ($21). AE, DC, MC, V. Daily noon–5pm; Mon–Sat 8:30pm–midnight. Closed Sun in July–Aug. Bus: 12. SPANISH/FRENCH.

The owners of this historic restaurant near the Alcázar deserve as much credit for their renovations of a decrepit 15th-century palace as they do for the excellent cuisine produced in their bustling kitchen. Fronting the river in the old Jewish Quarter, La Almudaina is one of the most attractive eateries in Andalusia, where you can dine in one of the lace-curtained salons or on a glass-roofed central courtyard. Specialties include salmon crepes; a wide array of fish, such as hake with shrimp sauce; and meats, such as pork loin in wine sauce. For dessert, try the not-too-sweet chocolate crepe. The cuisine's success is in its use of very fresh ingredients that are deftly handled by the kitchen and not overcooked or overspiced.

MODERATE TO INEXPENSIVE

Ciro's. Paseo de la Victoria, 19. ☎ **957-29-04-64.** Reservations recommended. Main courses 1,900–2,500 ptas. ($13.30–$17.50); fixed-price menu 2,600 ptas. ($18.20). AE, DC, MC, V. Daily 1–5pm and 8pm–midnight. Closed Sun in summer. ANDALUSIAN.

Once a simple cafeteria, Ciro's has been transformed into an accommodating, comfortably air-conditioned restaurant. The proprietors mix good service with modern and Andalusian-style cuisine. The menu includes dishes such as a salmon-and-anchovy pudding, stuffed sweet peppers, hake in shrimp sauce, veal in red wine, and an array of dessert sorbets. Ciro's lies directly south of the rail station, about a quarter of a mile northwest of the Mezquita.

El Blasón. José Zorrilla, 11. ☎ **957-48-06-25.** Reservations recommended. Main courses 1,800–2,600 ptas. ($12.60–$18.20). AE, DC, MC, V. Daily noon–4:30pm and 8pm–midnight. ANDALUSIAN.

Established in the late 1980s within a relatively modern building near the Gran Teatro that's been accessorized to commemorate old Andalusia, this is a well-recommended restaurant where the tab, without wine, rarely exceeds 5,000 ptas. ($35). You'll dine within any of four separate rooms, each of which evokes the mid–19th century, thanks to formal crystal chandeliers and a scattering of antiques. Especially appealing is an enclosed patio, where ivy creeps up walls and the noises from the city outside are muffled. Cuisine is well prepared and in some cases described in terms that verge on the poetic. Examples include "salmon with oranges from the mosque," and "goose thigh in fruited wine." Braised oxtail is always a good bet here, as well as any of the roasted lamb dishes that emerge from ovens redolent with the scent of olive oil and herbs.

✪ **El Caballo Rojo.** Cardinal Herrero, 28, Plaza de la Hoguera. ☎ **957-47-53-75.** Reservations required. Main courses 1,600–3,000 ptas. ($11.20–$21). AE, DC, MC, V. Daily 1–4:30pm and 8pm–midnight. Bus: 12. SPANISH.

This restaurant is the most popular in Andalusia, and except for the Almudaina (see above), it remains the best in Córdoba, although often overrun by tourists. The place has a noise level no other restaurant here matches, but the skilled waiters seem to cope with all demands. Within walking distance of the Mezquita in the old town, it is down a long open-air passageway flanked by potted geraniums and vines. Stop in the restaurant's popular bar for a predinner drink, then take the iron-railed stairs to the upper dining room, where a typical meal might include gazpacho, a main dish of chicken, then ice cream and sangría. (The ice cream, incidentally, is likely to be homemade pistachio.) Try a variation on the usual gazpacho—almond-flavored broth with apple pieces. In addition to Andalusian dishes, the chef offers both Sephardic and Mozarabic specialties, an example of the latter being monkfish prepared with pine nuts, currants, carrots, and cream. Real aficionados come here for the *rabo de toro* (stew made with the tail of an ox or a bull). The cookery is robust and flavorsome.

El Churrasco. Romero, 16. ☎ **957-29-08-19.** Reservations required. Main courses 1,400–2,800 ptas. ($9.80–$19.60); fixed-price menu 3,500–7,000 ptas. ($24.50–$49). AE, DC, MC, V. Daily 2–5:30pm and 7:45pm–midnight. Closed Aug. Bus: 12. SPANISH.

Housed in an ancient stone-fronted building in the Jewish Quarter just northwest of the Mezquita, El Churrasco serves elegant meals in five different dining rooms on two floors. You'll pass a bar and an open grill before reaching a ground-floor dining room that resembles a Moorish courtyard, with rounded arches and a splashing fountain. Upstairs, more formal rooms display the owner's riveting collection of paintings. You can enjoy such specialties as grilled fillet of beef with whiskey sauce, succulent roast lamb, grilled salmon, and monkfish in a pine-nut sauce—all accompanied by good service—but the signature dish here is the charcoal-grilled pork loin.

Restaurante Da Vinci. Plaza de Los Chirinos, 6. ☎ **957-47-75-17.** Reservations required. Main courses 1,300–1,900 ptas. ($9.10–$13.30); menú del día 1,600 ptas. ($11.20). V. Daily 1:30–4:30pm and 8pm–midnight. ITALIAN/INTERNATIONAL.

Situated in a quiet neighborhood a block off the city's main boulevard, calle Cruz Conde, this is a good value restaurant. Before heading into the dining room stop for a drink in the comfortable bar near the entrance, where many guests order from a selection of tempting tapas. Both the cuisine and the decor are a blend of Andalusian, international, and Italian influences, arranged in a curious but pleasing mishmash. Menu items include roast meats (veal, pork, beefsteak, and lamb), a variety of pastas and salads, and many kinds of fish and seafood, especially hake, monkfish, squid, and salmon. This is standard Andalusian fare, with no innovation and little flair, but it's still good.

CÓRDOBA AFTER DARK

Nighttime fun in the oldest part of Córdoba usually means visiting several tapas bars surrounding the Mezquita. Foremost among these is **Casa Pepe,** calle Romero 1 (☎ 957-20-07-44), an atmospheric old hideaway in an antique building, where many generations have lifted a glass before you. It's open daily from 1 to 4pm, and like most of the other places, reopens from 8pm to 1am. Nearby is **Casa Salinas,** Puerto de Almodovar, s/n (no phone), offering glasses of sherry and plates of tapas. **Bar El Juramento,** calle Juramento, 6 (no phone), is old-fashioned enough to be cozy, and crowded enough to be convivial. The oldest *bodega* in Córdoba (established around 1812) is the **Casa Miguel,** Plaza Cirino, 7 (no phone). And for a bar where discussions about the relative merits of Andalusian bullfighters always seem more passionate than anywhere else in town, head for **Bar Circolo Taurino,** calle Manuel Maria Arcona, 1 (☎ 957-48-18-62). Small, cramped, and loaded with memorabilia from bullfights past, it lies near Plaza Colón. Looking for a particularly flavorful platter of thin-sliced Serrano ham? Head for a historic cellar near the Plaza del Potro: the **Bodega Campos,** calle Lineros, 32 (no phone), where you'll be joined by locals.

La Canoa, Pasaje Ronda Los Tejares, 18–20 (☎ 957-47-17-61), has a rustic interior decorated with wine-barrel tables and Carthusian cellar decor. A glass of wine or beer here will be more of a rapid pick-me-up than something to linger over for hours. You can order a ration of Serrano ham or a hefty platter of cheese if you're hungry. La Canoa, located between the Plaza de Colón and the Paseo de la Victoria, is open Monday through Saturday from noon to 4pm and 8pm to midnight. It's closed for 2 weeks in August.

Push back a thick curtain to enter the dimly lit **Casa Rubio,** Puerta de Almodóvar, 5 (☎ 957-29-00-64), where you'll find a gruff but accommodating welcome at the rectangular bar or in one of a pair of rooms partially covered with Andalusian tiles. We like the leafy inner courtyard, where iron tables and a handful of chairs wobble only slightly on the uneven flooring. Casa Rubio is open Thursday through Tuesday from 8am to 3pm and 8pm to midnight.

The city's most popular flamenco club is **El Cardenal,** calle Torijos, 12 (☎ 957-48-31-12). Shows are presented at 10:30pm every Tuesday to Saturday, with a cover charge of 2,800 ptas. ($19.60), a price that includes the first drink. For more formal entertainment, check out the listings at the city's theatrical grande dame, the turn-of-the-century **Gran Teatro de Córdoba,** Avenida Gran Capitán, 3 (☎ 957-48-02-37), site of most of the ballet, opera, chamber-music, and symphony performances in town. If your preferred entertainment medium happens to be rock and roll, punk rock, or loud electronically amplified bands, chances are high that they'll be presented within the circa 1960s **Teatro de la Axaquia,** Avenida Menandez Piral, s/n (☎ 957-47-20-00). Set about a mile from the town center, it's the site of most of the large-scale pop music concerts of the region, and as such, sometimes draws spectators from throughout Andalusia.

If you want to shake your booty, head for Córdoba's most popular disco, **Disco Plato,** calle Gongera, 10 (☎ 957-48-52-46). Nothing old-fashioned here—it's a modern setting with lots of space devoted to a bar and a dance floor. This place attracts a broad age group, and won't make a visitor in his or her mid-40s feel out of place. It's open Wednesday to Saturday from 10:30pm to dawn, charging 700 ptas. ($4.90) entrance for men (women usually enter free). The price includes the first drink and after that beers cost around 250 ptas. ($1.75) each. A younger crowd hits the dance floor to the sounds of salsa, merengue, Spanish pop, and U.S. disco classics from the 1980s at **Disco Cahira,** calle Conde de Roblado, s/n (no phone), which holds court nightly after 11pm within a busy commercial neighborhood of modern Córdoba.

3 Seville

341 miles (549km) SW of Madrid, 135 miles (217km) NW of Málaga

Sometimes a city becomes famous simply for its beauty and romance. Seville (Sevilla in Spanish), the capital of Andalusia, is such a place. In spite of its sultry heat in summer and its many problems, such as high unemployment and street crime, it remains one of the most charming Spanish cities.

Don Juan and Carmen—aided by Mozart and Bizet—have given Seville a romantic reputation. Because of the acclaim of *Don Giovanni* and *Carmen,* not to mention *The Barber of Seville,* debunkers have risen to challenge this reputation. But if a visitor can see only two Spanish cities in a lifetime, they should be Seville and Toledo.

All the images associated with Andalusia—orange trees, mantillas, lovesick toreros, flower-filled patios, and castanet-rattling gypsies—come to life in Seville. But it's not just a tourist city; it's a substantial river port, and it contains some of the most important artistic works and architectural monuments in Spain.

Unlike other Spanish cities, Seville has fared rather well under most of its conquerors—the Romans, Arabs, and Christians. Rulers from Pedro the Cruel to Ferdinand and Isabella held court here. When Spain entered its 16th-century golden age, Seville funneled gold from the New World into the rest of the country, and Columbus docked here after his journey to America.

Be warned, however, that driving here is a nightmare: Seville was planned for the horse and buggy rather than for the car, and nearly all the streets run one way toward the Guadalquivir River. Locating a hard-to-find restaurant or a hidden little square will require patience and luck.

ESSENTIALS

GETTING THERE Seville's Aeropuerto San Pablo, calle Almirante Lobo (☎ 95-467-29-81), is served by **Iberia** (☎ 901/333-111 toll free within Spain), which flies several times a day to and from Madrid (and elsewhere via Madrid). It also flies several times a week to and from Alicante, Grand Canary Island, Lisbon, Barcelona, Palma de Majorca, Tenerife, Santiago de Compostela, and (once a week) Zaragoza. The airport lies about 6 miles (9.6km) from the center of the city, along the highway leading to Carmona.

Train service into Seville is now centralized into the Estación Santa Justa, Avenida Kansas City, s/n (☎ 95-454-02-02 for information and reservations, or 95-454-03-03 for information). Buses C1 and C2 take you from this train station to the bus station at Prado de San Sebastián, and bus EA runs to and from the airport. The high-speed AVE train has reduced travel time from Madrid to Seville to 2½ hours. The train makes 17 trips daily, with a stop in Córdoba. Sixteen trains a day connect Seville and Córdoba; the AVE train takes 45 minutes and a TALGO takes 1½ hours. Three trains a day run to Málaga, taking 3 hours; there are also three trains per day to Granada (4 hours).

Although Seville confusingly has several satellite bus stations servicing small towns and nearby villages of Andalusia, most buses arrive and depart from the city's largest bus terminal, on the southeast edge of the old city, at Prado de San Sebastián, calle José María Osborne, 11 (☎ 95-441-71-11). Several different companies make frequent runs to and from Córdoba (2½ hours), Málaga (3½ hours), Granada (4 hours), and Madrid (8 hours). For information and ticket prices, call Alsina Graells at ☎ 95-441-88-11. A newer bus station is at **Plaza de Armas** (☎ 95-490-80-40), but it usually services destinations beyond Andalusia, including Portugal.

Several major highways converge on Seville, connecting it with all the rest of Spain and Portugal. During periods of heavy holiday traffic, the N-V (E-90) from Madrid through Extremadura—which, at Mérida, connects with the southbound N630 (E-803)—is usually less congested than the N-IV (E-5) through eastern Andalusia.

VISITOR INFORMATION The **tourist information office,** Oficina de Información del Turismo, Avenida de la Constitución, 21B (☎ 95-422-14-04), is open Monday through Saturday from 9am to 7pm, Sunday and holidays from 10am to 2pm.

SPECIAL EVENTS The most popular times to visit Seville are during the April Fair—the most famous *feria* in Spain, with bullfights, flamenco, and folklore on parade—and during Holy Week, when wooden figures called *pasos* are paraded through streets by robed penitents. See the Calendar of Events in chapter 2, and contact the tourist office for more information.

Seville

FAST FACTS   The **American Express** office in Seville is in the Hotel Inglaterra, Plaza Nueva, 7 (☎ **95-421-16-17**), open Monday through Friday from 9:30am to 1:30pm and 4:30 to 7:30pm, Saturday from 10am to 1pm.

Most banks in Seville are open Monday through Friday from 9am to 2pm and on Saturday from 9am to noon. (Always conceal your money before walking out of a bank in Seville.) Shops are generally open Monday through Saturday from 9:30am to 1:30pm and 4:30 to 8pm. Most department stores are open Monday through Saturday from 10am to 8pm.

There's a **U.S. Consulate** at Paseo de las Delicias, 7 (☎ **95-423-18-85**), open Monday through Friday from 10am to 1pm and 2 to 4:30pm. The **consulate of the United Kingdom** is at Plaza Nueva, 8B (☎ **95-422-88-75**), open Monday through Friday from 8am to 3pm.

For medical emergencies, go to the **Hospital Universitario y Provincial,** Avenida Doctor Fedriani, s/n (☎ **95-455-74-00**). The **police station** is located on Avenida Paseo de las Delicias (☎ **95-461-54-50**).

You can do laundry at **Lavandería Robledo,** calle Sánchez Bedoya, 18 (☎ **95-421-81-32**), which is open Monday through Friday from 10am to 2pm and 5 to 8pm and Saturday from 10am to 2pm.

The **post office** is at Avenida de la Constitución, 32 (☎ **95-421-95-85**). Hours are Monday through Friday from 8:30am to 8:30pm, Saturday from 9:30am to 2pm.

With massive unemployment, the city has been hit by a crime wave in recent years. María Luisa Park is especially dangerous, as is the highway leading to Jerez de la Frontera and Cádiz. Dangling cameras and purses are especially vulnerable. Don't leave cars unguarded with your luggage inside. Regrettably, some daring attacks are made when passengers stop for traffic signals—as they are in U.S. cities.

If you need a cab, call **Tele Taxi** at ☎ **95-462-22-22** or **Radio Taxi** at ☎ **95-458-00-00.** Cabs are metered and charge 52 ptas. (35¢) per kilometer.

SEEING THE SIGHTS

The only way to explore Seville is on foot, with a good map in hand—but remember to be alert to muggers.

THE TOP ATTRACTIONS

✪ **Catedral.** Plaza del Triunfo, Avenida de la Constitución. ☎ **95-421-49-71.** Admission (including visit to Giralda Tower) 700 ptas. ($4.90) adults, 200 ptas. ($1.40) children and students. Daily 11am–5pm.

The largest Gothic building in the world, and the third-largest church in Europe after St. Peter's in Rome and St. Paul's in London, this church was designed by builders with a stated goal—that "those who come after us will take us for madmen." Construction began in the late 1400s and took centuries to complete.

Built on the site of an ancient mosque, the cathedral claims to contain the remains of Columbus, with his tomb mounted on four statues.

Works of art abound, many of them architectural, such as the 15th-century stained-glass windows, the iron screens (*rejas*) closing off the chapels, the elaborate 15th-century choir stalls, and the Gothic reredos above the main altar. During Corpus Christi and Immaculate Conception observances, altar boys with castanets dance in front of the high altar. In the Treasury are works by Goya, Murillo, and Zurbarán as well as a touch of the macabre in a display of skulls.

After touring the dark interior, emerge into the sunlight of the Patio of Orange Trees, with its fresh citrus scents and chirping birds.

Sightseeing Tip

Shorts and T-shirts are not allowed in the cathedral. Remember to dress appropriately before you set out, so you're not turned away.

Giralda Tower. Plaza del Triunfo. Admission included in admission to cathedral (above). Same hours as cathedral (above).

Just as Big Ben symbolizes London, La Giralda conjures up Seville. This Moorish tower, next to the cathedral, is the city's most famous monument. Erected as a minaret in the 12th century, it has seen later additions, such as 16th-century bells. To climb it is to take the walk of a lifetime. There are no steps—you ascend an endless ramp. If you can make it to the top, you'll have a dazzling view of Seville. Entrance is through the cathedral.

✪ **Alcázar.** Plaza del Triunfo, s/n. ☎ **422-71-63.** Admission 600 ptas. ($4.20). Oct–Mar, Tues–Sat 9:30am–6pm, Sun 9:30am–2:30pm; Apr–Sept, Tues–Sat 9:30am–8pm, Sun 9:30am–6pm.

Pedro the Cruel built this magnificent 14th-century Mudéjar palace, north of the cathedral. It is the oldest royal residence in Europe still in use today: On visits to Seville, King Juan Carlos stays here. From the Dolls' Court to the Maidens' Court through the domed Ambassadors' Room, it contains some of the finest work of Sevillian artisans. In many ways, it evokes the Alhambra at Granada. Ferdinand and Isabella, who at one time lived in the Alcázar and influenced its architectural evolution, welcomed Columbus here on his return from America. On the top floor, the Oratory of the Catholic Monarchs has a fine altar in polychrome tiles made by Pisano in 1504.

The well-kept gardens, filled with beautiful flowers, shrubbery, and fruit trees, are alone worth the visit.

EL PARQUE DE LOS DESCUBRIMIENTOS (DISCOVERY PARK)

Isla de la Cartuja. ☎ **95-446-16-16.** Admission 3,300 ptas. ($23.10) adults, 2,300 ptas. ($16.10) children. June 20–Sept 12, Mon–Thurs 11am–9pm, Fri–Sun 11am–midnight. Sept 13–Nov 2, daily 11am–midnight. Nov 3–June 19, Mon–Thurs 11am–9pm, Fri–Sun 11am–11pm. Bus C2 from city center.

On the 540-acre island of La Cartuja in the Guadalquivir River, site of Expo '92, the government opened a theme park in 1993. Eight new bridges now join the island to Seville. The theme park itself takes up 168 acres of the site and incorporates some of the more acclaimed attractions at Expo. Among them are the Pavilion of Navigation, tracing the history of maritime exploration from its beginnings to the present; the Pavilion of Nature, containing flora and fauna from all over the world; and eight other pavilions, representing the autonomous regions of Spain.

Puerto de Indias is the re-creation of a 15th-century port, with small shops and evocative taverns, along with silversmiths, cobblers, welders, and other tradespersons. Replicas of Christopher Columbus's ships the *Niña, Pinta,* and *Santa María* are docked here. The Children's Park offers a host of entertainment, including puppet shows and water slides.

The audiovisual offerings are said to equal or top those of any theme park in the world. The computer-controlled Digital Planetarium, for example, housed in the Pavilion of the Universe, is the only one of its kind in the world—images are projected onto a 60-foot dome, taking viewers on a ride through the universe.

Buses, cable cars, a monorail, catamarans, trolley cars, and rowboats are some of the transportation available to haul visitors around. Other facilities and attractions include concerts, plays, dance clubs, two parades and a circus daily, a laser-sound show with fireworks, 12 food stalls, 15 family restaurants, 7 tapas bars, and two deluxe restaurants.

Hospital de la Santa Caridad. Calle Temprado, 3. ☎ **95-422-32-32.** Admission 400 ptas. ($2.80). Mon–Sat 9:30am–1:30pm and 3:30–6pm, Sun 9am–1pm.

This 17th-century hospital is intricately linked to the legend of Miguel Manara, portrayed by Dumas and Mérimée as the scandalous Don Juan. It was once thought that he built this institution to atone for his sins, but this has been disproved. The death of Manara's beautiful young wife in 1661 caused such grief that he retired from society and entered the "Charity Brotherhood," burying corpses of the sick and diseased as well as condemned and executed criminals. Today the members of this brotherhood continue to look after the poor, the old, and invalids who have no one else to help them.

Nuns will show you through the festive orange-and-sienna courtyard. The baroque chapel contains works by the 17th-century Spanish painters Murillo and Valdés-Leál. As you're leaving the chapel, look over the exit door for the macabre picture of an archbishop being devoured by maggots.

Torre del Oro. Paseo de Cristóbal Colón. ☎ **95-422-24-19.** Admission 100 ptas. (70¢). Free on Tues. Tues–Fri 10am–2pm, Sat–Sun 11am–2pm.

The 12-sided Tower of Gold, dating from the 13th century, overlooks the Guadalquivir River. Originally it was covered with gold tiles, but someone long ago made off with them. Recently restored, the tower has been turned into a maritime museum, Museo Náutico, displaying drawings and engravings of the port of Seville in its golden heyday.

Casa de Pilatos. Plaza Pilatos, 1. ☎ **95-422-50-55.** Admission, museum 1,000 ptas. ($7); patio and gardens 500 ptas. ($3.50). Museum daily 10am–2pm and 4–6pm; patio and gardens daily 9am–7pm.

This 16th-century Andalusian palace of the dukes of Medinaceli recaptures the splendor of the past, combining Gothic, Mudéjar, and plateresque styles in its courtyards, fountains, and salons. According to tradition, this is a reproduction of Pilate's House in Jerusalem. Don't miss the two old carriages or the rooms filled with Greek and Roman statues. The collection of paintings includes works by Carreño, Pantoja de la Cruz, Sebastiano del Piombo, Lucas Jordán, Batalloli, Pacheco, and Goya. The palace lies about a 7-minute walk northeast of the cathedral on the northern edge of Barrio de Santa Cruz, in a warren of labyrinthine streets whose traffic is funneled through the nearby calle de Aguilas.

Archivo General de Indias. Avenida de la Constitución, s/n. ☎ **95-421-12-34.** Free admission. Mon–Fri 10am–1pm.

The great architect of Philip II's El Escorial, Juan de Herrera, was also the architect of this building next to the cathedral, originally the Lonja (Stock Exchange). Construction on the Archivo General de Indias lasted from 1584 to 1646. In the 17th century it was headquarters for the Academy of Seville, which was founded in part by the great Spanish artist Murillo.

In 1785, during the reign of Charles III, the building was turned over for use as a general records office for the Indies. That led to today's Archivo General de Indias, said to contain some four million antique documents, even letters exchanged between patron Queen Isabella and explorer Columbus (he detailing his discoveries and impressions). These very rare documents are locked in air-conditioned storage to keep them from disintegrating. Special permission has to be acquired before examining some of them. Many treasure-hunters come here hoping to learn where Spanish galleons laden with gold went down off the coasts of the Americas. On display in glass cases are fascinating documents in which the dreams of the early explorers come alive.

✪ **Museo Provincial de Bellas Artes de Sevilla.** Plaza del Museo, 9. ☎ **95-422-18-29.** Admission 250 ptas. ($1.75), free for students. Tues 3–8pm; Wed–Sat 9am–8pm; Sun 9am–3pm. Bus: 21, 24, 30, or 31.

This lovely old convent off calle de Alfonso XII houses one of the most important Spanish art collections. A whole gallery is devoted to two paintings by El Greco, and works by Zurbarán are also on exhibit; however, the devoutly religious paintings of the Seville-born Murillo are the highlight. An entire wing is given over to macabre paintings by the 17th-century artist Valdés-Leál. His painting of John the Baptist's head on a platter includes the knife—in case you didn't get the point. The top floor, which displays modern paintings, is less interesting.

More Attractions

✪ **BARRIO DE SANTA CRUZ**   What was once a ghetto for Spanish Jews, who were forced out of Spain in the late 15th century in the wake of the Inquisition, is today the most colorful district of Seville. Near the old walls of the Alcázar, winding medieval streets with names like *Vida* (Life) and *Muerte* (Death) open onto pocket-sized plazas. Flower-filled balconies with draping bougainvillea and potted geraniums jut out over this labyrinth, shading you from the hot Andalusian summer sun. Feel free to look through numerous wrought-iron gates into patios filled with fountains and plants. In the evening it's common to see Sevillians sitting outside drinking icy sangría under the glow of lanterns.

Although the district as a whole is recommended for sightseeing, seek out in particular the **Casa de Murillo (Murillo's House),** Santa Teresa, 8 (☎ **95-421-75-35**). Bartolomé Esteban Murillo, the great Spanish painter known for his religious works, was born in Seville in 1617. He spent his last years in this house in Santa Cruz, dying in 1682. Five minor paintings of the artist are on display. The furnishings, although not owned by the artist, are period pieces. Admission is 250 ptas. ($1.75), and the house is open Tuesday through Saturday 10am to 2pm and 6 to 8pm. The house is currently closed for renovations; check its status with the tourist office before heading here.

To enter the Barrio Santa Cruz, turn right after leaving the Patio de Banderas exit of the Alcázar. Turn right again at Plaza de la Alianza, going down calle Rodrigo Caro to Plaza de Doña Elvira. Use caution when strolling through the area, particularly at night; many robberies have occurred here.

PARQUE MARÍA LUISA   This park, dedicated to María Luisa, sister of Isabella II, was once the grounds of the Palacio de San Telmo. The palace, whose baroque facade is visible behind the deluxe Alfonso XIII Hotel, today houses a seminary. The former private royal park is now open to the public.

Running south along the Guadalquivir River, the park attracts those who want to take boat rides, walk along paths bordered by flowers, jog, or go bicycling. The most romantic way to traverse it is by rented horse and carriage, but this can be expensive, depending on your negotiation with the driver.

In 1929 Seville was to host the Spanish American Exhibition, and many pavilions from other countries were erected here. The worldwide depression put a damper on the exhibition, but the pavilions still stand.

Exercise caution while walking through this park as many muggings have been reported.

PLAZA DE AMÉRICA Another landmark Sevillian square, Plaza de América represents city planning at its best: Here you can walk through gardens planted with roses, enjoying the lily ponds and the fountains and feeling the protective shade of the palms. And here you'll find a trio of elaborate buildings left over from the world exhibition that never materialized—in the center, the home of the government headquarters of Andalusia; on either side, two minor museums worth visiting only if you have time to spare.

The **Museo Arqueológico Provincial,** Plaza de América, s/n (☎ **95-423-24-01**), contains many artifacts from prehistoric times and the days of the Romans, Visigoths, and Moors. It's open Tuesday through Sunday from 10am to 2:30pm. Admission is 250 ptas. ($1.75) for adults and free for students and children. Buses 30, 31, and 34 go there. Nearby is the **Museo de Artes y Costumbres Populares,** Plaza de América, s/n (☎ **95-423-25-76**), displaying folkloric costumes, musical instruments, Cordoban saddles, weaponry, and farm implements that document the life of the Andalusian people. It's open Tuesday through Saturday from 9am to 2:30pm, but closed on holidays. Admission is 250 ptas. ($1.75) for adults and free for children and students.

PLAZA DE ESPAÑA The major building left from the exhibition at the Parque María Luisa (see above) is a half-moon-shaped structure in Renaissance style, set on this landmark square of Seville. The architect, Anibal González, not only designed but also supervised the building of this immense structure; today it is a government office building. At a canal here you can rent rowboats for excursions into the park, or you can walk across bridges spanning the canal. Set into a curved wall are alcoves, each focusing on characteristics of one of Spain's 50 provinces, as depicted in tile murals.

REAL FÁBRICA DE TABACOS When Carmen waltzed out of the tobacco factory in the first act of Bizet's opera, she made its 18th-century original in Seville world famous. This old tobacco factory was constructed between 1750 and 1766, and 100 years later it employed 10,000 cigarreras, of which Carmen was one in the opera. (She rolled cigars on her thighs.) In the 19th century, these tobacco women made up the largest female workforce in Spain. Many visitors arriving today, in fact, ask guides to take them to "Carmen's tobacco factory." The building, the second largest in Spain and located on calle San Fernando near the city's landmark luxury hotel, the Alfonso XIII, is still here. But the Real Fábrica de Tabacos is now part of the Universidad de Sevilla. Look for signs of its former role, however, in the bas reliefs of tobacco plants and Indians over the main entrances. You'll also see bas reliefs of Columbus and Cortés. Then you can wander through the grounds for a look at student life, Sevillian style. The factory is directly south of the Alcázar gardens.

BULLFIGHTS

From Easter until late October, some of the best bullfighters in Spain appear at the **Maestranza** bullring, on the Paseo de Colón (☎ **95-422-35-06**). One of the leading bullrings in Spain, the stadium attracts matadors whose fights often receive television and newspaper coverage throughout Iberia. Unless there's a special festival going on, bullfights (*corridas*) occur on Sunday. The best bullfights are staged during April Fair celebrations. Tickets tend to be pricey, and should be purchased in advance at the ticket office (*despacho de entradas*) on calle Adriano, beside the Maestranza bullfight stadium. You'll also find many unofficial kiosks selling tickets placed strategically along the main shopping street, calle Sierpes. However, they charge a 20% commission for their tickets—a lot more if they think they can get it.

SHOPPING

ART   One of the most respected galleries in Seville, **Rafael Ortíz,** Marmolles, 12 (☎ 95-421-48-74), specializes in contemporary paintings, usually from Iberian artists. Exhibitions change frequently, and because of the canniness of this emporium's judgments, inventories sell out quickly. It's open Monday through Saturday from 10am to 1:30pm and 4:30 to 8pm.

BOOKS   The **English Bookshop,** Eduardo Dato, 36 (☎ 95-465-57-54), is the kind of place where you can find tomes on gardening, political discourse, philosophy, and pop fiction, all gathered into one cozy place. Open Monday through Saturday from 10am to 1:45pm and 4:30 to 8:30pm.

Set conveniently close to Seville's university, **Libreria Vértice,** San Fernando, 33 (☎ 95-421-16-54), stocks books in a polyglot of languages. Inventory ranges from the esoteric and professorial to Spanish romances of the soap-opera genre. Open Monday through Saturday from 10am to 1:30pm and 4:30 to 8:30pm.

CERAMICS   In the town center, near the cathedral, **El Postigo,** Arfe, s/n (☎ 95-456-00-13), has a wide selection of Andalusian ceramics. Some of the pieces are much, much too big to fit into your suitcase; others—especially the hand-painted tiles—make charming souvenirs that can easily be transported. Open Monday through Saturday from 10am to 2pm, Monday through Friday from 5 to 8pm.

Near the town hall, **Martian,** Calle Sierpes, 74 (☎ 95-421-34-13), sells a wide array of painted tiles and ceramics: vases, plates, cups, serving dishes, and statues, all made in or near Seville. Many of the pieces exhibit ancient geometric patterns of Andalusia. Other floral motifs are rooted in Spanish traditions of the 18th century. Open Monday through Saturday from 10am to 1:30pm and 4:30 to 8:30pm.

DEPARTMENT STORES   **El Corte Inglés,** Plaza Duque, 10 (☎ 95-422-09-31), is the best of the several department stores clustered in Seville's commercial center. It features multilingual translators and rack after rack of every conceivable kind of merchandise for the well-stocked home, kitchen, and closet. If you're in the market for the brightly colored feria costumes worn by young girls during Seville's holidays, there's an impressive selection of the traditional regional fashion, along with all the latest designer fashions for everyday. Open Monday through Saturday from 10am to 9pm.

Marks & Spencer, Plaza Duque, 6 (☎ 95-456-36-56), is the Seville branch of a gigantic chain of middle-of-the-road department stores based in England. It caters to British expatriates and retirees based in the hills around Seville, so expect conservative, well-made clothes. Open Monday through Saturday from 10am to 9pm.

FANS   Carmen fluttered her fan and broke hearts. You can, too, if you pick up a traditional Andalusian fan at **Casa Rubio,** Sierpes, 56 (☎ 95-422-68-72). It stocks one of the city's largest selections, from the austere and dramatic to the florid and fanciful. Open Monday through Saturday from 10am to 1:45pm and 5 to 8pm.

Impressions

Seville doesn't have an ambiance. It is ambiance.

—James A. Michener

Seville is a pleasant city, famous for oranges and women.

—Lord Byron

FASHION   See also "Department Stores," above. **Iconos,** Avenida de la Constitución (☎ 95-422-14-08), is a small, idiosyncratic boutique loaded with fashion accessories that can be used by everyone from teenage girls to mature women. Silk scarves, costume jewelry, and an assortment of T-shirts with logos lettered in varying degrees of taste—it's all here. Open Monday through Saturday from 10am to 2pm, Monday through Friday from 5 to 8pm.

Head for **Nicole Miller,** Albareda, 16 (☎ 95-456-36-14), for chic outfits from this internationally successful designer. Open Monday through Saturday from 10am to 2pm, Monday through Friday from 5 to 8pm. More sleek, upscale fashions are available from **Victorio & Lucchino,** Sierpes, 87 (☎ 95-422-79-51). Open Monday through Saturday from 10am to 2pm, Monday through Friday from 5 to 8pm.

For traditional regional costumes, try **Perdales,** Cuna, 23 (☎ 95-421-37-09), which outfits many of the region's professional flamenco performers. Much of its merchandise is akin to couture; other items are less expensive and sold off the rack. Open Monday through Saturday from 10am to 2pm, Monday through Friday from 5 to 8pm.

GIFTS   **Artesania Textil,** Sierpes, 70 (☎ 95-456-28-40), specializes in the nubby and rough textiles that reflect the earthiness of contemporary Spanish art. Weavings—some using linen, others the rough fibers of Spanish sheep—are the specialty here. Examples include place mats, tablecloths, blankets, shawls, and wall hangings. Open Monday through Saturday from 10am to 2pm, Monday through Friday from 5 to 8pm.

Souvenirs of the city, T-shirts, hammered wrought-iron whatnots, and ceramics are available at **Matador,** Avenida de la Constitución, 28 (☎ 95-422-62-47). Open Monday through Saturday from 10am to 2pm, Monday through Friday from 5 to 8:30pm.

More upscale gifts, such as crystal and art objects, can be found at **Venecia,** Cuna, 51 (☎ 95-422-99-94). Open Monday through Saturday from 10am to 2pm, Monday through Friday from 5 to 8:30pm.

JEWELRY   **Joyero Abrines,** Sierpes, 47 (☎ 95-427-84-55), is the kind of place where grooms have bought engagement and wedding rings for their brides for generations, and where generations of girlfriends have selected watches and cigarette lighters for the hombres of their dreams. There's another branch of this well-known store at calle de la Asunción, 28 (☎ 95-427-42-44). Both are open Monday through Saturday from 10am to 2pm, Monday through Friday from 5 to 8:15pm.

MUSIC   There's a **Virgin Megastore** at Sierpes, 81 (☎ 95-421-21-11), offering the latest sounds from across Europe and North America while also stocking some traditional regional music. It also sells computer games (having brought Nintendo to Andalusia) and a limited roster of books. Open Monday through Friday from 10am to 2pm, Saturday from 10am to 9pm.

RIDING GEAR   If you're passionately interested in horses (or know someone who is), **Arcab,** Paseo Cristobal Colon, 8 (☎ 95-456-14-21), can provide an array of Andalusian-style riding costumes, harnesses, saddles, bridles, and buckles that will make you and your mount feel like direct descendants of the conquistadors. Open Monday through Friday from 10am to 2pm, Saturday from 10am to 9pm.

WHERE TO STAY

During Holy Week and the Seville Fair, hotels often double, even triple, their rates. Price increases are often not announced until the last minute. If you're going to be in Seville at these times, arrive with an ironclad reservation and an agreement about the price before checking in.

VERY EXPENSIVE

✪ **Hotel Alfonso XIII.** San Fernando, 2, 41004 Sevilla. ☎ **800/221-2340** in the U.S. and Canada, or 95-422-28-50. Fax 95-421-60-33. www.ittsheraton.com. 148 units. A/C MINIBAR TV TEL. 48,000–64,000 ptas. ($336–$448) double; 90,000–115,000 ptas. ($630–$805) suite. AE, DC, MC, V. Parking 2,250 ptas. ($15.75).

Set at the southwestern corner of the gardens that front Seville's famous Alcázar, in the historic heart of town, this five-story rococo building is one of the three or four most legendary hotels in Spain and is the premier address in Seville. Built as an aristocratic shelter for patrons of the Ibero-American Exposition of 1929 and named after the then-king of Spain, it reigns as a superornate and superexpensive bastion of glamour. Built in the Mudéjar/Andalusian revival style, its rooms and hallways glitter with hand-painted tiles, acres of marble and mahogany, antique furniture embellished with intricately embossed leather, and a spaciousness nothing short of majestic.

Dining/Diversions: The San Fernando restaurant offers Italian and continental cuisine. A lobby bar features midday coffee amid potted palms and memorials to another age, its blue, white, and yellow tiles reflecting the colors of Seville.

Amenities: 24-hour room service, laundry/valet, concierge, car rentals with or without drivers, baby-sitting, a spectacular garden, outdoor pool, tennis courts, shops, arcade-enclosed courtyard with potted flowers and splashing fountain.

Hotel Tryp Colón. Canalejas, 1, 41001 Sevilla. ☎ **95-422-29-00.** Fax 95-422-09-38. E-mail: hotel@tryp.es. 228 units. A/C MINIBAR TV TEL. 33,600–42,000 ptas. ($235.20–$294) double; 82,050–117,200 ptas. ($574.35–$820.40) suite. AE, DC, MC, V. Parking 2,200 ptas. ($15.40).

Set about a quarter mile northwest of the Giralda and about two blocks southeast of the Fine Arts Museum (Museo Provincial de Bellas Artes), this hotel is the closest rival in prestige and architectural allure to the legendary Alfonso XIII (see above). Originally built around the turn of the century and overhauled in 1988, it retains such features as a massive stained-glass dome stretching over the lobby, baronial stair-cases, formal service, and all the niceties of an expensive hotel. The rooms, all with private bathrooms, are conservative and traditional, although some are in need of a refurbish.

Dining/Diversions: El Burladero restaurant serves lunches and dinners (see "Where to Dine," below). There's also a bar favored by visiting bullfighters, journalists, and politicians.

Amenities: 24-hour room service, concierge, baby-sitting, laundry/valet, sauna, car-rental facilities, shopping boutiques.

EXPENSIVE

Hotel Inglaterra. Plaza Nueva, 7, 41001 Sevilla. ☎ **95-422-49-70.** Fax 95-456-13-36. 116 units. A/C TV TEL. Jan–Mar and May–Dec 18,000–22,000 ptas. ($126–$154) double; Apr 21,000–23,000 ptas. ($147–$161) double. AE, DC, MC, V. Parking 1,500 ptas. ($10.50).

Established in 1857 and since modernized into a comfortably glossy seven-story con-temporary design, this eminently respectable and rather staid hotel lies a 5-minute walk southwest of the cathedral, occupying one entire side of a palm-fringed plaza. Much of its interior is sheathed in acres of white or gray marble, and the furnishings include ample use of Spanish leather and floral-patterned fabrics. Despite their moder-nity, the rooms nonetheless evoke old-fashioned touches of Iberian gentility. The best rooms lie on the fifth floor.

Dining/Diversions: One floor above street level, overlooking the mosaic pave-ments of Plaza Nueva, the hotel's sunny restaurant serves well-prepared fixed-price meals from a frequently changing international menu. There's also an in-house cock-tail lounge favored by local businesspeople.

Amenities: 24-hour room service, laundry/valet service, concierge, baby-sitting, car-rental facilities, business center.

Hotel Meliá Sevilla. Doctor Pedro de Castro, 1, 41004 Sevilla. ☎ **800/336-3542** in the U.S., or 95-442-15-11. Fax 95-442-16-08. 366 units. A/C MINIBAR TV TEL. 20,300 ptas. ($142.10) double; from 30,000 ptas. ($210) suite. AE, DC, MC, V. Parking 1,350 ptas. ($9.45).

Located a short walk east of the Plaza de España, near the Parque María Luisa, this is the most elegant, tasteful, and international of the modern skyscraper hotels of Seville. It opened in 1987 and rises 11 floors. It incorporates acres of white marble as well as several dozen shopping boutiques and private apartments into its L-shaped floor plan. Guest room decor is contemporary and comfortable, and each unit offers a private bathroom, though rooms at the back lack views. The Meliá was a favorite of the planners of the massive Expo, which transformed the face of both Seville and Andalusia. The hotel lacks the personal touch provided by the staff at Alfonso XIII, but its rooms are superior to those at the Inglaterra.

Dining/Diversions: The Giralda Restaurant serves three-course fixed-price lunches and dinners. There's also a large and stylish piano bar, Corona, plus an informal coffee shop, Las Salinas.

Amenities: 24-hour room service, laundry, baby-sitting, business center, car rentals, outdoor swimming pool with a section reserved for children, sauna, arcade of shops and boutiques, several flowering outdoor terraces.

✪ **Principe de Asturias Plaza Hotel Sevilla.** Isla de la Cartuja, 41018 Sevilla. ☎ **95-446-22-22.** Fax 95-446-04-28. 295 units. A/C MINIBAR TV TEL. Mon–Thurs 21,000–30,000 ptas. ($147–$210) double; 65,000 ptas. ($455) suite. Fri–Sun 14,500 ptas. ($101.50) double; 35,000 ptas. ($245) suite. AE, DC, MC, V. Parking 1,500 ptas. ($10.50).

Named after the son and designated heir of King Juan Carlos, Don Felipe de Borbón, Principe de Asturias (his title is something akin to Britain's Prince of Wales), this hotel was built expressly to house the surge of visitors at the Seville Expo of 1992. The only hotel located on the former site of Expo itself, facing the Guadalquivir River, it lies a 5-minute taxi ride from the center of Seville. The location seems a bit isolated and sad now that the excitement of Expo is long gone and as a consequence the hotel is often underbooked. It was designed in three hypermodern ring-shaped modules, each four stories tall and all interconnected by passageways leading to the public rooms. This five-star luxury hotel was reserved during Expo for visiting dignitaries and heads of state. Its designers intended its perpetual use, at the end of the party, as one of the city's most visible hotels—sort of a modern-day counterpart to the Alfonso XIII (which was designed for use by dignitaries during Seville's International Exposition of 1929).

Dining/Diversions: The Restaurante Colón serves gourmet versions of regional cuisine. The lobby bar and the Cartura Bar offer soothing libations, sometimes to live piano music.

Amenities: 24-hour room service, concierge, laundry/valet, limousine pickups, baby-sitting, business center, conference facilities, outdoor swimming pool, in-house florist, shops, currency exchange, car rentals, multilingual TV channels, health club with sauna, massage, gymnasium, squash courts.

MODERATE

Bécquer. Calle Reyes Católicos, 4, 41001 Sevilla. ☎ **95-422-89-00.** Fax 95-421-44-00. 118 units. A/C TV TEL. 13,000 ptas. ($91) double. AE, DC, MC, V. Parking 1,400 ptas. ($9.80). Bus: 21, 24, 30, or 31.

A short walk from the action of the Seville bullring (Maestranza) and only 2 blocks from the river, Bécquer lies on a street of cafes where you can order tapas and drink

Andalusian wine. The Museo Provincial de Bellas Artes also lies nearby. Built in the 1970s, the hotel was enlarged and much renovated in the late 1980s. It occupies the site of a mansion and retains many objets d'art rescued before the building was demolished. Guests register in a wood-paneled lobby before being shown to one of the bedrooms, which are functionally furnished, well kept, and reasonably comfortable—in all, a good value in a pricey city. All have private bathrooms. Only breakfast is served, but you'll find a bar and lounge, as well as a garage.

Hotel Alcázar. Menéndez y Pelayo, 10, 41004 Sevilla. ☎ **95-441-20-11.** Fax 495/442-16-59. 100 units. A/C TV TEL. 13,500–17,000 ptas. ($94.50–$119) double. Rates include breakfast. AE, DC, MC, V. Parking 1,000 ptas. ($7).

On the wide and busy Bulevar Menéndez y Pelayo, across from the Jardines de Alcázon, this pleasantly contemporary hotel is sheltered behind a facade of brown brick. Built in 1964, the hotel was last renovated in 1991. Slabs of striated gray marble cool the reception area in the lobby, next to which you'll find a Spanish restaurant and bar. Above, three latticed structures resemble a trio of *miradores*. The medium-size guest rooms have functional modern furniture and private bathrooms.

Hotel América. Jesús del Gran Poder, 2, 41002 Sevilla. ☎ **95-422-09-51.** Fax 95-421-06-26. 100 units. A/C MINIBAR TV TEL. 11,000 ptas. ($77) double; 12,000 ptas. ($84) triple. AE, DC, MC, V. Parking 1,125 ptas. ($7.90) nearby.

Built in 1976 and partially renovated in 1994, this hotel offers rather small rooms but keeps the place spick-and-span. Superior features include wall-to-wall carpeting and, in winter, individual heat control that works. Relax in the TV lounge or order a drink in the Duque Bar. Near the hotel is a parking garage for 600 cars. There isn't a major restaurant, but the América does offer a tearoom, snack bar, and cafeteria that serves regional and international cuisine. The hotel is set on the northern side of the Plaza del Duque. One of Spain's major department stores, El Corte Inglés, opens onto the same square.

✪ Hotel Doña María. Don Remondo, 19, 41004 Sevilla. ☎ **95-422-49-90.** Fax 95-421-95-46. 69 units. A/C TV TEL. Jan–Feb and July–Aug 13,000 ptas. ($91) double; Mar–June and Sept–Dec 18,000–26,000 ptas. ($126–$182) double. AE, DC, MC, V. Parking 2,000 ptas. ($14).

Staying at this four-star, four-story hotel is a worthwhile investment, partly because of the tasteful Iberian antiques in the stone lobby and upper hallways. Also, its location a few steps from the cathedral creates a dramatic view from the Doña María's rooftop terrace. An ornate neoclassical entryway is offset with a pure white facade and iron balconies, which hint at the building's origin in the 1840s as a private villa. Amid the flowering plants on the upper floor, you'll find a swimming pool ringed with garden-style lattices and antique wrought-iron railings. Each of the one-of-a-kind rooms offers a private bathroom and is well furnished and comfortable, although some are rather small. A few have four-poster beds, others a handful of antique reproductions. Light sleepers might find the noise of the church bells jarring. Breakfast is the only meal served.

✪ Residencia y Restaurante Fernando III. San José, 21, 41001 Sevilla. ☎ **95-421-77-08.** Fax 95-422-02-46. 157 units. A/C TV TEL. 12,500 ptas. ($87.50) double. AE, DC, MC, V. Parking 1,500 ptas. ($10.50).

You'll find the Fernando III on a narrow, quiet street at the edge of the Barrio de Santa Cruz, near the northern periphery of the Murillo Gardens. Its vast lobby and baronial dining hall are reminiscent of a luxurious South American hacienda. The building is modern, constructed around 1970 with marble and hardwood detailing, and is sparsely furnished with leather chairs, plants, and wrought-iron accents. Many of the accommodations—medium in size, comfortably furnished, and well maintained—offer balconies filled with cascading plants; all have private bathrooms. There is a TV salon as well as a paneled bar. The hotel's restaurant features regional Andalusian cuisine on its menu.

INEXPENSIVE

Hostal Goya. Mateus Gago, 31, 41004 Sevilla. ☎ **95-421-11-70.** Fax 95-456-29-88. 20 units (10 with bathroom). Jan–Mar and May–Dec 5,990 ptas. ($41.95) double without bathroom; 6,400 ptas. ($44.80) double with bathroom. Apr 7,000 ptas. ($49) double without bathroom; 8,000 ptas. ($56) double with bathroom. No credit cards.

Its location in a narrow-fronted town house in the oldest part of the barrio is one of the Goya's strongest virtues. The building's gold-and-white facade, ornate iron railings, and picture-postcard demeanor are all noteworthy. Rooms are cozy and simple, without phones or TVs. Guests congregate in the marble-floored ground-level salon, where a skylight floods the couches and comfortable chairs with sunlight. No meals are served. Reserve well in advance. Parking is often available along the street.

Hotel Ducal. Plaza de la Encarnación, 19, 41003 Sevilla. ☎ **95-421-51-07.** Fax 95-422-89-99. 51 units. A/C TEL. 6,250–10,500 ptas. ($43.75–$73.50) double. AE, DC, MC, V. Parking 1,800 ptas. ($12.60) nearby.

In this fairly modern hotel the guest rooms are modest but comfortable, with provincial and utilitarian furnishings and central heating for those Sevillian winters. A continental breakfast can be brought to your room, but no other meals are served. The location, near El Corte Inglés department store, is handy to many specialty shops.

Residencia Murillo. Calle Lope de Rueda, 7–9, 41004 Sevilla. ☎ **95-421-60-95.** Fax 95-421-96-16. 57 units. TEL. 6,200–7,800 ptas. ($43.40–$54.60) double; 7,700–9,800 ptas. ($53.90–$68.60) triple. AE, DC, MC, V. Parking 2,000 ptas. ($14) nearby.

Tucked away on a narrow street in the heart of Santa Cruz, the old quarter, the Residencia Murillo (named after the artist who used to live in this district) is almost next to the gardens of the Alcázar. Inside, the lounges harbor some fine architectural characteristics and antique reproductions; behind a grilled screen is a retreat for drinks. Many of the rooms we inspected were cheerless and gloomy, so have a look before checking in. Like all of Seville's hotels, the Murillo is in a noisy area.

You can reach this residencia from the Menéndez y Pelayo, a wide avenue west of the Parque María Luisa, where a sign will take you through the Murillo Gardens on the left. Motorists should try to park in Plaza de Santa Cruz. Then walk 2 blocks to the hotel, which will send a bellhop back to the car to pick up your suitcases. If there are two in your party, station a guard at the car, and if you're going out at night, call for an inexpensive taxi to take you instead of strolling through the streets of the old quarter—it's less romantic but a lot safer.

ACCOMMODATIONS NEARBY

✪ **Hacienda Benazuza.** Calle Virgen de las Nieves, s/n, 41800 Sanlúcar la Major, Seville. ☎ **95-570-33-44.** Fax 95-570-3410. 44 units. A/C MINIBAR TV TEL. 35,000–42,000 ptas. ($245–$294) double; 45,000–124,000 ptas. ($315–$868) suite. AE, DC, MC, V. Free parking. Closed July 15–Aug 31. From Seville, follow the signs for Huelva and head south on the A-49 highway, exiting at exit no. 6.

Set on a hillside above the agrarian hamlet of Sanlúcar la Mayor, 12 miles (19km) south of Seville, this legendary manor house is surrounded by 40 acres of olive groves and its own farmland. Its ownership has been a cross section of every major cultural influence that has swept through Andalusia since the Moors laid its foundations in the

10th century. After the Catholic conquest of southern Spain, the site became a much-feared stronghold of the fanatically religious *Caballeros de Santiago.*

In 1992 the property was bought by Basque-born entrepreneur Rafael Elejabeitia, who, after spending many millions of pesetas, transformed it into one of Andalusia's most charming hotels. Careful attention was paid to preserving the ancient Moorish irrigation system, whose many reflecting pools nourish the gardens. All but a few of the bedrooms lie within the estate's main building, and each is individually furnished with Andalusian antiques and Moorish trappings, representative of the original construction.

Dining/Diversions: The most formal of the hotel's three restaurants is La Alquería, where first-class service and Andalusian and international cuisine culminate in surprise menus. El Patio is an indoor-outdoor affair overlooking the estate's redbrick patio and palm trees. (Both of the above serve lunch and dinner daily, and are open to nonresidents who reserve in advance.) A lunch buffet beside the swimming pool, where everyone seems to show up in bathing suits and jewelry, is offered in La Alberca.

Amenities: Laundry, 24-hour room service, and a concierge well trained to procure almost anything; tennis courts with a resident pro, paddle tennis courts, golf range, billiard room, outdoor pool. A minimuseum of Andalusian agriculture lies within an antique building originally designed as an olive press. Many other sporting options lie within driving distance, and can be arranged by the concierge staff.

WHERE TO DINE
VERY EXPENSIVE

✪ **Egaña Oriza.** San Fernando, 41. ☎ **95-422-72-11.** Reservations required. Main courses 2,700–5,900 ptas. ($18.90–$41.30); fixed-price menus 5,200–9,600 ptas. ($36.40–$67.20). AE, DC, MC, V. Restaurant Mon–Fri 1:30–3:30pm, Mon–Sat 9–11:30pm; bar daily 9am–midnight. Closed Aug. BASQUE/INTERNATIONAL.

Seville's most stylish and best restaurant is set within the conservatory of a restored mansion adjacent to the Murillo Gardens. Much of its reputation stems from its role as one of the few game specialists in Andalusia—a province otherwise devoted to seafood. The restaurant was established by Basque-born owner and chef José Mari Egaña, who managed to combine his passion for hunting with his flair for cooking. Many of the ingredients that go into the dishes presented on the menu were trapped or shot within Andalusia, a region whose potential for sports shooting is underutilized, according to Sr. Egaña. The view from the dining room encompasses a garden and a wall that formed part of the fortifications of Muslim Seville.

The availability of many specialties depends on the season, but might include ostrich carpaccio, gazpacho with prawns, steak with foie gras in grape sauce, casserole of wild boar with cherries and raisins, quenelles of duck in a potato nest with apple puree, stewed mountain sheep cooked with figs, rice with stewed thrush, and woodcock flamed in Spanish brandy. The wine list provides an ample supply of hearty Spanish reds to accompany these dishes. Dessert might feature a chocolate tart slathered with freshly whipped cream. Sr. Egaña's wife, Mercedes, runs the establishment's two-story dining room.

La Isla. Arfe, 25. ☎ **95-421-26-31.** Reservations recommended. Main courses 5,000–6,000 ptas. ($35–$42). AE, DC, MC, V. Daily 1–5pm and 8pm–midnight. Closed Aug. SPANISH/ANDALUSIAN.

Set within two large dining rooms designed in Andalusian fashion (thick plaster walls, tile floors, and taurine memorabilia), this air-conditioned restaurant was established shortly after World War II and has done a thriving business ever since. Its seafood is trucked or flown in from either Galicia, in northern Spain, or Huelva, one of

Andalusia's major ports, and is almost always extremely fresh. Menu items include *merluza a la primavera* (hake with young vegetables), *solomillo a la Castellana* (grilled beefsteak with strips of Serrano ham), chicken croquettes, and shellfish soup. The restaurant lies a short walk from the cathedral, within a very old building erected, the owners say, on foundations laid by the ancient Romans.

EXPENSIVE TO MODERATE

Casa Robles. Calle Álvarez Quintero, 58. ☎ **95-421-31-50.** Reservations recommended. Main courses 1,200–2,200 ptas. ($8.40–$15.40); fixed-price menus 4,800–10,500 ptas. ($33.60–$73.50). AE, DC, MC, V. Daily 1–4:30pm and 8pm–1am. ANDALUSIAN.

Praised by local residents as well as visitors, this restaurant began its life as an unpretentious bar and bodega in 1954. Over the years, thanks to a staff directed by owner-chef Juan Robles and his children, it developed into a courteous and bustling restaurant scattered over two floors of a building a short walk from the cathedral. Amid an all-Andalusian decor, you can enjoy such dishes as fish soup in the Andalusian style, *lubina con naranjas* (whitefish with Sevillana oranges), hake baked with strips of Serrano ham, and many kinds of fresh fish. The dessert list is long, diverse, and very tempting.

El Burladero. In the Hotel Tryp Colón, Canalejas, 1. ☎ **95-422-29-00.** Reservations recommended. Main courses 2,000–4,000 ptas. ($14–$28); fixed-price menus 4,100–4,500 ptas. ($28.70–$31.50). AE, DC, MC, V. Daily 1:30–4:30pm and 9pm–midnight. Closed Aug. CONTINENTAL.

Set within one of Seville's most prominent hotels, this restaurant is awash with the memorabilia and paraphernalia of the bullfighting trade. The interior wall tiles were removed from one of the pavilions at the 1929 Seville World's Fair, and the photographs adorning the walls are a veritable history of bullfighting. (The restaurant, incidentally, is named after the wooden barricade—*el burladero*—behind which bullfighters in an arena can escape from the charge of an enraged bull.) The restaurant boasts a popular bar, where a wide assortment of Sevillanos meet and mingle before their meals.

Menu specialties include upscale interpretations of local country dishes, with an attractive mix of items from other regions of Spain as well. Examples include *bacalao al horno con patatas* (baked salt cod with potatoes and saffron sauce); roasted shoulder of lamb stuffed with a deboned bull's tail and served in a richly aromatic sauce; clams with white kidney beans; a local version of *cocido,* a boiled amalgam of sausages, meats, chickpeas, and vegetables; and a stew of eel meat heavily laced with garlic and spices. Dishes from other parts of Europe might include truffled fillet steak in puff pastry, duck liver, and salmon cooked in lemon-flavored dill sauce.

✪ **Enrique Becerra.** Gamazo, 2. ☎ **95-421-30-49.** Reservations recommended. Main courses 1,900–2,400 ptas. ($13.30–$16.80). AE, DC, MC, V. Mon–Sat 1–5pm and 8pm–midnight. ANDALUSIAN.

This is a cozy, snug retreat in a whitewashed house with wrought-iron window grilles near the cathedral, and its home-cooked dishes are among the city's finest. The restaurant takes its name from its owner, a smart and helpful host, who installed it in a late-19th-century building. This popular tapas bar and Andalusian dining spot offers an intimate setting and a hearty welcome that leaves you with the feeling that your business is really appreciated. While perusing the menu, you can sip dry Tío Pepe and nibble herb-cured olives with lemon peel. The gazpacho here is among the city's best, and the sangría is served ice cold. Specialties include hake real, sea bream Bilbao style, and a wide range of meat, fish, and vegetarian dishes. The wine list is one of the best in Seville.

Food on the Run

Directly east of the cathedral, **Cervecería Giralda,** calle Mateus Gago, 1 (☎ 95-422-74-35), is one of the least expensive dining spots near the cathedral, Alcázar, and Giralda Tower. It draws locals and tourists alike. You can make a meal from the selection of tapas, ranging from 225 to 275 ptas. ($1.60 to $1.95), or order one of the *platos combinados* (combination plates), ranging from 800 to 1,300 ptas. ($5.60 to $9.10). The place is open daily 9am to midnight.

On the same street, **Pizzeria El Artesano,** calle Mateus Gago, 9 (☎ 95-421-38-58), also lures in customers near the cathedral. Here the feature is an Andalusian version of pizza costing 525 to 725 ptas. ($3.70 to $5.10). Daily hours are noon to midnight.

Lying on the opposite side of the Guadalquivir, away from the throngs of tourists, is the Barrio de Triana. This used to be its own little village community until Seville burst its seams and absorbed it. It still is the place to go to escape the high prices on the cathedral side of the river.

El Puerto, Betis, s/n (☎ 95-427-17-25), stands next door to the famed Río Grande restaurant. It has a multilevel alfresco terrace opening onto the river. You can get fresh seafood here, but the special buy is the chef's *cubierto* (menu of the house), costing 1,500 ptas. ($10.50); tapas range from 200 to 725 ptas. ($1.40 to $5.10). At the cafeteria bar, you serve yourself; inside is an inexpensive restaurant with waiter service. It's open Tuesday through Sunday; lunch is served from 1 to 4pm and dinner from 8pm to midnight (it's closed in January); bus: 41 or 42.

Another way to enjoy quick meals is to eat at one of the tapas bars recommended below under "Seville After Dark." Portions, called *raciones,* are usually generous, and many tourists on the run often eat standing at the bar, making a full meal out of two orders of tapas.

La Albahaca. Plaza de Santa Cruz, 12. ☎ **95-422-07-14.** Reservations recommended. Main courses 2,600–3,000 ptas. ($18.20–$21); fixed-price menus 4,500–5,500 ptas. ($31.50–$38.50). AE, DC, MC, V. Mon–Sat noon–4pm and 8pm–midnight. BASQUE/FRENCH.

Located on a prominent square in the Barrio de Santa Cruz, this restaurant with an open-air terrace offers a limited but savory menu that has become a favorite of locals. Specialties include a salad of carpaccio of codfish with fresh asparagus and herbs, seafood soup, shellfish bisque, grilled lamb chops, partridge braised in sherry, salmon wrapped in parchment, and chocolate pudding for dessert. The restaurant is in a manor home built in 1929.

Río Grande. Calle Betis, s/n. ☎ **95-427-39-56.** Reservations required. Main courses 1,600–5,000 ptas. ($11.20–$35); fixed-price menu 2,750 ptas. ($19.25). AE, DC, MC, V. Daily 1–5pm and 8pm–1am. Bus: 41 or 42. ANDALUSIAN.

This classic Sevillian restaurant is named for the Guadalquivir River, which its panoramic windows overlook. It sits against the bank of the river near Plaza de Cuba in front of the Torre del Oro. Some diners come here just for a view of the city monuments. A meal might include stuffed sweet pepper *flamenca,* fish-and-seafood soup seaman's style, the chef's fresh salmon, chicken-and-shellfish paella, bull tail Andalusian, and garlic chicken. You can also have a selection of fresh shellfish that's brought in daily. Large terraces contain a snack bar, the Río Grande Pub, and a bingo room. You can often watch sports events on the river in this pleasant (and English-speaking) spot.

✪ **Taverna del Alabardero.** Calle Zaragoza, 20. 41001 Seville. ☎ **95-456-06-37.** Fax 95-456-36-66. Reservations recommended. Main courses 1,600–2,800 ptas. ($11.20–$19.60). AE, DC, MC, V. Daily 1–3:30pm and 8pm–midnight. Closed Aug. Bus: 13, 25, 26. ANDALUSIAN.

One of Seville's most prestigious and well-recommended restaurants occupies a 19th-century town house near Plaza Nueva, 3 blocks from the cathedral. Famous as the dining venue of virtually every politician and diplomat who visits Seville, it has recently hosted the king and queen of Spain, the king's mother, the Spanish president and members of his cabinet, and dozens of well-connected but merely affluent visitors. Amid a collection of European antiques and oil paintings, you'll dine in any of two main rooms or three private ones, and perhaps precede your meal with a drink or tapas within the building's flowering patio. There's a garden in back with additional tables. Menu items include spicy peppers stuffed with pulverized thigh of bull, an Andalusian fish (*urta*) set on a compote of aromatic tomatoes with coriander, a fillet of cod-fish with essence of red peppers, and Iberian beefsteak with foie gras and green peppers.

On the premises are seven comfortable bedrooms outfitted in the Andalusian style, each with its own Jacuzzi and air-conditioning, minibar, TV, and telephone. Doubles cost 18,000 ptas. ($126) throughout most of the year, including breakfast, except during Holy Week and *feria,* when the price rises to 30,000 ptas. ($210). Hint: If you want to just drop into this place for a look, the bar within the patio serves tapas and drinks throughout the day from 8am until 1am.

INEXPENSIVE

Hostería del Laurel. Plaza de los Venerables, 5. ☎ **95-422-02-95.** Reservations recommended. Main courses 850–2,500 ptas. ($5.95–$17.50). AE, DC, MC, V. Daily noon–4pm and 7:30pm–midnight. ANDALUSIAN.

Located in one of the most charming buildings on tiny, difficult-to-find Plaza de los Venerables in the labyrinthine Barrio de Santa Cruz, this hideaway restaurant has iron-barred windows stuffed with plants. Inside, amid Andalusian tiles, beamed ceilings, and more plants, you'll enjoy good regional cooking. Many diners stop for a drink and tapas at the ground-floor bar before going into one of the dining rooms. The hostería is attached to a three-star hotel.

Pizzeria San Marco. Calle Mesón de Moro, 6. ☎ **95-421-43-90.** Reservations recommended. Main courses 650–1,250 ptas. ($4.55–$8.75). MC, V. Tues–Sun 1:30–4:30pm and 8:30pm–12:30am. ITALIAN.

Though the name may sound like this is a fast-food joint, this is actually a well-managed restaurant with sit-down service and bilingual waiters. Pizza is only one of the many items featured on the menu; most people opt for pasta, salmon salad, duck in orange sauce, osso bucco, chicken Parmesan, and several forms of scallopini. There's also a congenial corner for drinking, named Harry's Bar in honor of grander role models in Venice and elsewhere.

Despite the allure of the food, the real interest of the place is its setting. It lies within what was originally, more than 1,000 years ago, an Arab bathhouse. Its interior reminds some visitors of a secularized mosque, despite the presence of a modern wing added around 1991 in anticipation of increased business from Seville's Expo celebration. The establishment lies within the Barrio de Santa Cruz, on an obscure side street running into calle Mateus Gago.

La Raza. Isabel la Católica, 2. ☎ **95-423-38-30.** Reservations recommended. Main courses 1,200–2,300 ptas. ($8.40–$16.10). AE, DC, MC, V. Daily noon–5pm and 8pm–midnight. ANDALUSIAN.

A terrace restaurant in Parque María Luisa, La Raza is known both for its setting and for its tapas. Begin with gazpacho, then go on to one of the meat dishes, or perhaps an order of the savory paella. On Friday and Saturday there is often music to entertain guests, many of whom are American and Japanese tourists.

SEVILLE AFTER DARK

When the sun goes down, think sherry, wine, and tapas. After a couple of drinks have got you going, you might venture to a flamenco club, or possibly even try to learn the intricate steps of one of southern Spain's most addictive dances, La Sevillana.

DRINKS & TAPAS

You might begin your evening by enjoying the cool breeze that blows from the nearby river onto the outdoor terrace at **Bar Capote,** Paseo Cristóbal Colón (no phone), open every night at 10pm between June and October (and closed the rest of the year). It's most active around midnight, and continues in full force until at least 4am. There's no live music, but the crowds can get thick here. Entrance is free, and bottled beer costs 250 ptas. ($1.75) each.

Tapas are said to have originated in Andalusia, and the old-fashioned **Casa Román,** Plaza des los Venerables (☎ **95-421-64-08**), looks as if it has been dishing them up since day one, though it's actually been around only since 1934. Definitely include this place on your *tasca* hopping through the old quarter. At the deli counter in front you can make your selection; you might even pick up the fixings for a picnic in the Parque María Luisa. Casa Román is in the Barrio de Santa Cruz. It's open Monday through Friday from 9am to 3pm and 5:30pm to 12:30am, Saturday and Sunday from 10am to 3pm and 6:30pm to 12:30am. Tapas are priced from 550 ptas. ($3.85).

El Rinconcillo, Gerona, 40 (☎ **95-422-31-83**), has a 1930s ambience, partly because of its real age and partly because of its owners' refusal to change one iota of the decor—this has always been one of the most famous bars in Seville. Actually, it may be the oldest bar in Seville, with a history going back to 1670. Amid dim lighting, heavy ceiling beams, and iron-based, marble-topped tables, you can enjoy a beer or a full meal along with the rest of the easygoing clientele. The bartender will mark your tab in chalk on a well-worn wooden countertop. El Rinconcillo is especially known for its salads, omelettes, hams, and selection of cheeses. Look for the art nouveau tile murals. El Rinconcillo is at the northern edge of the Barrio de Santa Cruz, near the Santa Catalina Church. It's open Thursday through Tuesday from 1pm to 2am. A complete meal will cost around 3,000 ptas. ($21).

The best seafood tapas in town are served at **La Alicantina,** Plaza del Salvador, 2 (☎ **95-422-61-22**), amid a glazed-tile decor typical of Seville. Both the bar and the sidewalk tables are always filled to overflowing. The owner serves generous portions of clams marinara, fried squid, grilled shrimp, fried codfish, and clams in béchamel sauce. La Alicantina, located about 5 blocks north of the cathedral, is open daily from 11:30am to 3:30pm and 7:30 to 11:30pm. Tapas range upward from 300 ptas. ($2.10).

At the northern end of Murillo Gardens, opening onto a quiet square with flower boxes and an ornate iron railing, **Modesto,** Cano y Cueto, 5 (☎ **95-441-68-11**), also serves fabulous seafood tapas. The bar is air-conditioned, and you can choose your appetizers just by pointing. Upstairs there's a good-value restaurant, offering a meal for 2,000 ptas. ($14), including such dishes as fried squid, baby sole, grilled sea bass, and shrimp in garlic sauce. Modesto is open daily from 8pm to 2am. Tapas are priced from 500 ptas. ($3.50).

Our favorite bar in town is undoubtedly ✪ **Abades,** Calle Abades, 1 (☎ **95-422-56-22**), where a converted mansion in the Barrio de Santa Cruz has been turned into something resembling a living room in a luxurious movie set. In the heart of the Jewish ghetto, it evokes the style of the Spanish Romantic era. The house dates from the 19th century, when it was constructed around a central courtyard with a fountain, and it became notorious as a love den in Franco's era. Drinks and low-key conversations are the style here, and though you might spot the occasional celeb, you'll see lots of folks in jeans enjoying the comfort of the sofas and wicker armchairs. The ingredients of the special house drink called *aqua de Sevilla* are a secret, but we suspect sparkling white wine, pineapple juice, and eggs (the whites and yolks mixed in separately, of course). Classical music is played in the background. Take a taxi to get here at night, as it might not be safe to wander late along the narrow streets of the barrio. In summer, it's open daily from 9pm to 4am; in winter, hours are daily from 8pm to 2:30am.

FLAMENCO

When the moon is high in Seville and the scent of orange blossoms is in the air, it's time to wander the alleyways of Santa Cruz in search of the sound of castanets. Or take a taxi, to be on the safe side.

Consider a visit to **Club Los Gallos,** Plaza de Santa Cruz, 11 (☎ **95-421-69-81**), a well-managed and reputable nightclub where male and female performers stamp, clap, and exude rigidly controlled Iberian passion on a small stage in front of appreciative observers. A cover charge of 3,500 ptas. ($24.50) includes the first drink, after which beer costs around 300 ptas. ($2.10) each. No meals are served, and advance reservations are a good idea.

Its leading competitor, charging roughly the same prices with more or less the same program, is **El Arenal,** calle Rodo, 7 (☎ **95-421-64-92**), where you'll sit at tiny, cramped tables with barely enough room to clap—but you will, because of the smoldering emotions conveyed in the performances here.

In central Seville on the riverbank between two historic bridges, **El Patio Sevillano,** Paseo de Cristóbal Colón, 11 (☎ **95-421-41-20**), is a showcase for Spanish folk song and dance, performed by exotically costumed dancers. The presentation includes a wide variety of Andalusian flamenco and songs, as well as classical pieces by composers such as Falla, Albéniz, Granados, and Chueca. From March through October, there are three shows nightly, beginning at 7:30pm, 10pm, and 11:45pm. There are only two shows from November through February, beginning nightly at 7:30 and 10pm. Drinks cost from 500 to 1,000 ptas. ($3.50 to $7). Admission, including one drink, is 3,800 ptas. ($26.60).

DANCING THE SEVILLANA

Flamenco is danced in solitary grandeur, but everyone joins in with the communal but complicated dance steps of the *sevillana.* The best place to check it out is **El Simpecao,** calle Bertis, s/n (no phone). Beginning at 11pm every night of the year, recorded music presents four distinctly different facets of the complicated and old-fashioned dance steps in which dozens of everyday folk strut their Andalusian style in a way you'll rarely see outside of Spain. The setting is modern and just a wee bit battered. Entrance is free; bottled beer costs from around 300 ptas. ($2.10) each.

DANCE CLUBS

If you're interested in the latest dance tunes, Seville's most popular club is **Disco Antigüedades,** calle Argote de Molina (no phone). Set about 2 blocks north of the cathedral within a much-renovated antique building, it opens nightly at 11pm, charging around 650 ptas. ($4.55) entrance, which includes the price of the first drink. Expect lots of salsa and merengue in addition to more international fare from across Europe and the United States.

GAY BARS

Seville has a large gay and lesbian population, much of it composed of foreigners, including Americans, Germans, and British, and of Andalusians who fled here for a better life, escaping smaller, less tolerant towns and villages. Gay life thrives in such bars as **Isbiliyya Café-Bar,** Paseo de Colón (☎ 95-421-04-60), which is usually open in summer daily from 7pm to 3am. The bar is found across the street from the Puente Isabel II bridge, near Bar Capote. Outdoor tables are a magnet in summer. A very similar bar, also with outdoor tables, is **To Ca Me,** calle Reyes Católicas, 25 (☎ 95-422-22-97), which hosts a mainly gay crowd, although many straights show up as well. Its video jukebox and blue neon lighting keep the joint jumping, but only on Friday and Saturday from 9pm to 5am. Another option on the gay scene is **Poseidon,** calle Marqués de Parades, 30 (☎ 95-421-31-92). This bar and dance club—mercifully air-conditioned in summer—draws not only a mixed crowd but an assortment of ages, although most patrons tend to be under 30. It jumps Thursday to Saturday from 10:30pm to 5am.

THE PERFORMING ARTS

To keep abreast of what's happening in the arts and after dark in Seville, pick up a copy of the free monthly leaflet *El Giraldillo,* or consult the listings in the local press, *Correo de Andalucía, Sudoeste, Nueva Andalucía,* or *ABC Sevilla.* Everything is listed here, from jazz venues to classical music concerts and from art exhibits to dance events. You can also call a cultural hot line at ☎ 010 to find out what's happening. Most of the staff at the other end speaks English.

Keep an eye out for classical concerts that are sometimes presented in the cathedral of Seville, the church of San Salvador, and the Conservatorio Superior de Música at Jesús del Gran Poder. Variety productions, including some plays for the kids, are presented at **Teatro Alameda,** Crédito (☎ 95-438-83-12). The venerable **Teatro Lope de Vega,** Avenida María Luisa (☎ 95-423-45-46), is the setting for ballet performances and classical concerts, among other events. Near Parque María Luisa, this is the leading stage of Seville, but knowledge of Spanish is necessary.

It wasn't until the 1990s that Seville got its own opera house, but **Teatro de la Maestranza,** Paseo de Colón, 22 (☎ 95-422-65-73), quickly became one of the world's premier venues for operatic performances. Naturally, the focus is on works inspired by Seville itself, including Verdi's *La Forza del destino* or Mozart's *Marriage of Figaro.* Jazz, classical music, and even the quintessentially Spanish *zarzuelas* (operettas) are also performed here. The opera house may only be visited during performances. Tickets (which vary in price, depending on the event staged) can be purchased daily from 10am to 2pm and from 5 to 8pm at the box office in front of the theater.

SIDE TRIPS FROM SEVILLE
CARMONA

An easy hour-long bus trip from the main terminal in Seville, Carmona is an ancient city dating from Neolithic times. Twenty-one miles (34km) east of Seville, it grew in power and prestige under the Moors, establishing ties with Castile in 1252.

Surrounded by fortified walls, Carmona has three Moorish fortresses—one a parador and, the other two, the **Alcázar de la Puerta de Córdoba** and **Alcázar de la**

The Legacy of al-Andalus

The Moors who once occupied Andalusia—notably Seville, Granada, and Córdoba—left more than such architectural treasures as the Giralda Tower in Seville, the great mosque in Córdoba, and the Alahambra in Granada. Their intellectual and cultural legacy still influence modern life, not only in Spain, but throughout the Western world.

The celebrated Arab princesses and sultans with their harems are long gone, encountered today only in the tales of Washington Irving and others. Yet from the year 711 A.D., the Moors (Muslims who were an ethnic mixture of Berbers, Hispano-Romans, and Arabs) occupied southern Spain for nearly 8 centuries and turned it into a seat of learning. It was a time of soaring achievements in philosophy, medicine, and music.

Moorish rule brought the importation of the eggplant and the almond, as well as the Arabian steed—not to mention such breakthroughs in academia as astronomy (including charting the positions of the planets) and a new and different view of Aristotle. Arab numerals replaced the more awkward Roman system, and from the Arabs came the gift of algebra. Ibn Muadh of Jaén wrote the first European treatise on trigonometry.

Such intellectual giants emerged as the Córdoba-born Jewish philosopher Maimónides. It is said that Columbus evolved his theories about a new route to the East after hours and hours of studying the charts of Idrisi, an Arabian geographer who drew up a world map as early as 1154. Arabs relied upon the compass as a navigational aid long before its use among Portuguese explorers.

Córdoba desired to shine brighter than Baghdad as a center of science and the arts. In time it attracted Abd ar-Rahman II, who introduced the fifth string to the Arab lute, leading to the development of the six-string guitar. He also ordained the way food should be eaten at mealtimes, a legacy that lives to this day. Before, everybody just helped himself randomly to whatever had been prepared; but he devised a method where courses were served in a regimented order, ending with dessert, fruit, and nuts. Today, Andalusian chefs are reviving many of the old recipes from the Arab cupboard, such as lamb cooked with honey.

Arab poetry may have inspired the first ballads sung by European troubadours, which had an enormous impact on later Western literature. Also, many Spanish words today have their origins in the Arabic language, including *alcázar* for fortress, *arroz* for rice, *naranja* for orange, and *limón* for lemon.

The Moors brought an irrigation system to Andalusia, which increased crop production; many of today's systems follow those 1,000-year-old channels. And paper first arrived in Europe through Córdoba.

Although the fanatical Isabella la Católica may have thrown a fit at the heretical idea, it was really a trio of peoples who shaped modern Spain as a nation: the Jews, the Christians, and most definitely the Arabs. The Arabs and the Jews may have been ousted by Isabella and Ferdinand at the close of the 15th century, but their influence still lingers.

Puerta de Sevilla. The top attraction is **Seville Gate,** with its double Moorish arch, opposite St. Peter's Church. Note too, **Córdoba Gate** on calle Santa María de Gracia, which was attached to the ancient Roman walls in the 17th century.

The town itself is a virtual national landmark, filled with narrow streets, white-washed walls, and Renaissance mansions. **Plaza San Fernando** is the most important square, with many elegant 17th-century houses. The most important church is dedicated to **Santa María** and stands on the calle Martín López. You enter a Moorish patio before exploring the interior with its 15th-century white vaulting.

In the area known as Jorge Bonsor (named for the original discoverer of the ruins) there's a **Roman amphitheater** as well as a **Roman necropolis** containing the remains of 1,000 families that lived in and around Carmona 2,000 years ago. Of the two important tombs, the Elephant Vault consists of three dining rooms and a kitchen. The other, the Servilia Tomb, was the size of a nobleman's villa. On site is a **Museo Arquelógico** (☎ 95-414-08-11), displaying artifacts found at the site. From April through October hours are Tuesday through Saturday from 9am to 2pm and 4 to 6pm; off-season, Tuesday through Friday from 10am to 2pm, Saturday and Sunday from 10am to 2pm. Admission is 250 ptas. ($1.70).

If you're driving to Carmona, exit from Seville's eastern periphery onto the N-V superhighway, following the signs to the airport, then to Carmona on the road to Madrid. The Carmona turnoff is clearly marked.

Where to Stay & Dine

✪ **Casa de Carmona.** Plaza de Lasso, 1, 41410 Carmona (Sevilla). ☎ **95-419-10-00,** or 212/686-9213 for reservations within North America. Fax 95-414-37-52. www.casadecarmona. com. E-mail: reservations@casadecarmona.com. 30 units. A/C MINIBAR TV TEL. 23,000– 27,000 ptas. ($154.10–$180.90) double; 90,000 ptas. ($603) suite. Add about 30% for Feria de Sevilla and Easter (Semana Santa). AE, DC, MC, V. Free parking.

One of the most elegant and intimate hotels in Andalusia, this plushly furnished hide-away was originally built as the home of the Lasso family during the 1500s. Several years ago, a team of entrepreneurs added the many features required for a luxury hotel, all the while retaining the marble columns, massive masonry, and graceful proportions of the building's original construction. The most visible public room still maintains vestiges of its original function as a library. Each good-size bedroom is a cozy enclave of opulent furnishings, with a distinct decor theme inspired by ancient Rome, medieval Andalusia, or Renaissance Spain. All the immaculately kept and tiled bathrooms are equipped with hair dryers.

Dining: On the premises is an outdoor restaurant whose culinary inspiration derives from modern interpretations of Andalusian and international cuisine, with meals served daily from 1 to 4pm and from 9 to 11:30pm and priced from around 4,000 ptas. ($26.80) each.

Amenities: Set at the edge of the village, the hotel offers an outdoor swimming pool with a flowery terrace, an inner courtyard covered against the midsummer heat with canvas awning, and a small exercise room. Concierge, room service, laundry/dry cleaning, newspaper delivery, baby-sitting, currency exchange.

ITÁLICA

Lovers of Roman history will flock to **Itálica** (☎ 95-599-73-76), the ruins of an ancient city 5½ miles (9km) northwest of Seville, on the major road to Lisbon, near the small town of Santiponce.

After the battle of Ilipa, Publius Cornelius Scipio Africanus founded Itálica in 206 B.C. Two of the most famous of Roman emperors, Trajan and Hadrian, were born here. Indeed, master builder Hadrian was to have a major influence on his hometown. In his reign the **amphitheater,** the ruins of which can be seen today, was among the largest in the Roman Empire. Lead pipes that carried water from the

Guadalquivir River still remain. A small museum displays some of the Roman statuary found here, although the finest pieces have been shipped to Seville. Many mosaics, depicting beasts, gods, and birds are on exhibit, and others are constantly being discovered. The ruins, including a Roman theater, can be explored for 250 ptas. ($1.70). The site is open April through September, Tuesday through Saturday, from 9am to 6:30pm and on Sunday from 9am to 3pm. From October through March, it's open Tuesday through Saturday from 9am to 5:30pm and on Sunday from 10am to 4pm.

If you're driving, exit from the northwest periphery of Seville, following the signs for highway E-803 in the direction of Zafra and Lisbon. But if you don't have a car, take the bus marked "Calle de Santiponce" leaving from calle Marqués de Parada near the railway station in Seville. Buses depart every hour for the 30-minute trip.

4 Jerez de la Frontera

54 miles (87km) S of Seville, 368 miles (592km) SW of Madrid, 21 miles (34km) NE of Cádiz

The charming little Andalusian town of Jerez made a name for itself in England for the thousands of casks of golden sherry it shipped there over the centuries. Nearly 3,000 years old, Jerez is nonetheless a modern, progressive town with wide boulevards, although it does have an interesting old quarter. Busloads of visitors pour in every year to get free drinks at one of the bodegas where wine is aged and bottled.

The name of the town is pronounced Her-*ez* or Her-*eth,* in Andalusian or Castilian, respectively. The French and the Moors called it various names, including Heres and Scheris, which the English corrupted to Sherry.

ESSENTIALS

GETTING THERE   Iberia and Avianco offer flights to Jerez every Monday through Friday from Barcelona and Zaragoza; daily flights from Madrid; and several flights a week to and from Valencia, Tenerife, Palma de Majorca, and Grand Canary Island. No international flights land at Jerez. The airport at Ctra. Jerez-Sevilla lies about 7 miles (11km) northeast of the city center (follow the signs to Seville). Call ☎ 956-15-00-00 for information.

Trains from Madrid arrive daily. A ticket from Madrid to Jerez on the TALGO costs 7,600 to 8,800 ptas. ($50.90 to $58.95), and the trip takes 4½ hours. The railway station in Jerez is at Plaza de la Estación (☎ 956-34-23-19), at the eastern end of calle Medina.

Bus connections are more frequent than train connections, and the location of the bus terminal is also more convenient. You'll find it on calle Cartuja, at the corner of calle Madre de Díos, a 12-minute walk east of the Alcázar. About 17 buses arrive daily from Cádiz (1 hour away) and 3 per day travel from Ronda (2¾ hours). Seven buses a day arrive from Seville (1½ hours). Phone ☎ 956-34-52-07 for more information.

Jerez lies on the highway connecting Seville with Cádiz, Algeciras, Gibraltar, and the ferryboat landing for Tangier, Morocco. There's also an overland road connecting Jerez with Granada and Málaga.

VISITOR INFORMATION   The **tourist information office** is at calle Larga, 39 (☎ 956-33-11-50). To reach it from the bus terminal, take calle Medina to calle Honda and continue along as the road turns to the right. The English-speaking staff can provide directions, transportation suggestions, open hours, and so on for any bodega you might want to visit. You will also be given a map pinpointing the location of various bodegas. Open April through October, Monday through Friday from 9am to 2pm and 5 to 8pm, Saturday from 9am to 2pm; off-season, Monday through Saturday from 8am to 3pm and 5 to 7pm, Saturday.

EXPLORING THE AREA
✪ TOURING THE BODEGAS

Jerez is not surrounded by vineyards, as you might expect. Instead, the vineyards lie to the north and west of Jerez, within the "Sherry Triangle" marked by Jerez, Sanlúcar de Barrameda, and El Puerto de Santa María (the latter two towns on the coast). This is where top-quality *albariza* soil is found, the highest quality containing an average of 60% chalk, which is ideal for the cultivation of grapes used in sherry production, principally the white *Palomino de Jerez*. The ideal time to visit is September. However, visitors can count on the finest in hospitality year-round, since Jerez is widely known for the warm welcome it bestows.

There must be more than 100 bodegas in and around Jerez where you can not only see how sherries are made, bottled, and aged, but also get free samples. Among the most famous producers are Sandeman, Pedro Domecq, and González Byass, the maker of Tío Pepe.

On a typical visit to a bodega, you'll be shown through several buildings in which sherry and brandy are manufactured. In one building, you'll see grapes being pressed and sorted; in another, the bottling process; in a third, thousands of large oak casks. Then it's on to an attractive bar where various sherries—amber, dark gold, cream, red, sweet, and velvety—can be sampled. If either is offered, try the very dry La Ina sherry or the Fundador brandy, one of the most popular in the world.

Warning: These drinks are more potent than you might expect!

Most bodegas are open Monday through Friday only, from 10:30am to 1:30pm. Regrettably, many of them are closed in August, but many do reopen by the third week of August to prepare for the wine festival in early September.

Of the dozens of bodegas you can visit, the most popular are listed below. Some of them charge an admission fee and require a reservation.

A favorite among British visitors is **Harveys of Bristol,** calle Arcos, 57 (☎ 956-15-10-02), which doesn't require a reservation. An English-speaking guide leads a 2-hour tour year-round, except for the first 3 weeks of August. Visit Monday through Friday for tours at noon, costing 300 ptas. ($2).

You'll definitely want to visit **Williams & Humbert Limited,** Nuño de Cañas, 1 (☎ 956-34-45-39), which offers tours at noon and 1:30pm Monday through Friday, charging 300 ptas. ($2). Their premium brands include the world-famous Dry Sack Medium Sherry, Canasta Cream, Fino Pando, and Manzanilla Alegría, in addition to Gran Duque de Alba Gran Reserva Brandy. It is wise to reserve in advance.

Another famous name is **González Byass,** Manuel María González, 12 (☎ 956-34-00-00); admission is 500 ptas. ($3.35), and reservations are required. Tours depart at 10am, 11am, noon, and 1pm Monday through Friday. Equally famous is **Domecq,** calle San Ildefonso, 3 (☎ 956-35-70-00), requiring a reservation but charging no admission. Tours depart at 10am, 11am, and noon Monday through Friday.

Since many people go to Jerez specifically to visit a bodega, August or weekend closings can be very disappointing. If this happens to you, make a trip to the nearby village of **Lebrija,** about halfway between Jerez and Seville, 8½ miles (14km) west of the main highway. Lebrija, a good spot to get a glimpse of rural Spain, is a local wine-making center where some very fine sherries originate. At one small bodega, that of Juan García, you are courteously escorted around by the owner. There are several other bodegas in Lebrija, and the local citizens will gladly point them out to you. It's all very casual, and much more informal than the bodegas of Jerez.

THE DANCING HORSES OF JEREZ

A rival of sorts to Vienna's famous Spanish Riding School is the **Escuela Andaluza del Arte Ecuestre (Andalusian School of Equestrian Art),** Avenida Duque de Abrantes, 11 (☎ 956-30-77-98). In fact, the long, hard schooling that brings horse and rider into perfect harmony originated in this province. The Viennese school was started with Hispano-Arab horses sent from this region, the same breeds you can see today. Every Thursday at noon, crowds come to admire the Dancing Horses of Jerez as they perform in a show that includes local folklore. Numbered seats sell for 2,400 ptas. ($16.10), with unnumbered seats going for 1,500 ptas. ($10.05). When performances aren't scheduled, you can visit the stables and tack room, observing as the elegant horses are being trained. Hours are Monday to Wednesday and Friday from 11am to 1pm, costing 450 ptas. ($3). Bus 18 goes here.

WHERE TO STAY
EXPENSIVE TO MODERATE

Hotel Avenida Jerez. Avenida Alcalde Álvaro Domecq, 10, 11405 Jerez de la Frontera. ☎ **956-34-74-11.** Fax 956-33-72-96. www.nh-hoteles.es. E-mail: nh@nh-hoteles.es. 95 units. A/C MINIBAR TV TEL. 14,000 ptas. ($93.80) double; 26,000 ptas. ($174.20) suite. AE, DC, MC, V. Parking 1,500 ptas. ($10.05).

Set very close to the commercial heart of Jerez, this hotel occupies a modern balconied structure of seven stories and is the best hotel within Jerez itself, although Montecastillo (see below) on the outskirts is a serious challenger. Inside, cool floors of polished stone, leather armchairs, and a variety of potted plants create a restful haven. The good-size rooms are discreetly contemporary and decorated in neutral colors, with big windows, comfortable beds, and private bathrooms equipped with hair dryers.

Dining/Diversions: The hotel maintains a pleasant and unpretentious cafeteria providing coffee-shop-style snacks and platters of Spanish food. There's also a bar.

Amenities: Room service (available daily from 7am to 11pm), baby-sitting, concierge, laundry/valet, car-rental desk.

Hotel Royal Sherry Park. Avenida Alcalde Álvaro Domecq, 11 Bis, 11405 Jerez de la Frontera. ☎ **956-30-30-11.** Fax 956-31-13-00. www.travelcom.es/sherry. E-mail: sherry@travelcom.es. 170 units. A/C MINIBAR TV TEL. 16,750–18,250 ptas. ($112.25–$122.30) double; 25,725–29,400 ptas. ($172.35–$197) suite. AE, DC, MC, V. Free parking.

Especially noted for its setting within a palm-fringed garden and for its large swimming pool, whose tiled edges attract many sun-loving residents, this is one of the best modern hotels in Jerez. Located on a wide and verdant boulevard north of the historic center of town, it contains a marble-floored lobby, efficiently modern public rooms, and fairly standard but comfortable bedrooms, each with a private tiled bathroom. The uniformed staff lays out a copious breakfast buffet and serves drinks at several hideaways, both indoors and within the garden.

Dining/Diversions: El Abaco Restaurant, which spills over onto an outdoor terrace, serves flavorful international cuisine. A bar with a good selection of sherries and whiskeys lies nearby.

Amenities: Room service (available daily from 8am to midnight), laundry/valet, concierge, baby-sitting, outdoor swimming pool, car rentals, shopping boutiques.

Montecastillo. Carretera N-342, 11406 Jerez de la Frontera. ☎ **956-15-12-00.** Fax 956-15-12-09. 120 units. A/C MINIBAR TV TEL. 19,000–26,000 ptas. ($127.30–$174.20) double; 62,500–125,000 ptas. ($418.75–$837.50) suite. AE, DC, MC, V. Free parking.

Giving Hotel Avenida Jerez serious competition is this deluxe country club found in the rolling hills of the sherry *campiña,* or wine country. The most tranquil retreat in the area, it has bedrooms with scenic-view balconies overlooking a Jack Nicklaus–designed 18-hole golf course. Just a 10-minute ride from the center of Jerez, the hotel is elegantly furnished and professionally run. The spacious guest rooms are decorated in a provincial French style with elegant fabrics, beautiful linens, and large beds fitted with quality mattresses. The marble bathrooms are also elegant with plush towels, toiletries, and hair dryers.

Dining: At the Montecastillo restaurant, favorite regional meals are combined with traditional Spanish and international dishes for some of the best cuisine in the area.

Amenities: Room service, laundry/dry cleaning, baby-sitting. In addition to the golf course, there are swimming pools and a sauna. Horseback riding and tennis are available nearby, and there are paddle tennis facilities at the adjacent and exclusive Montecastillo Country Club.

INEXPENSIVE

Hotel Ávila. Calle Ávila, 3, 11140 Jerez de la Frontera. ☎ **956-33-48-08.** Fax 956-33-68-07. 32 units. A/C TV TEL. 6,400–6,900 ptas. ($42.90–$46.25) double. AE, DC, MC, V. Parking 600–1,000 ptas. ($4–$6.70) nearby.

One of the better bargains in Jerez, the Ávila is a modern, three-story building, erected in 1968 and renovated in 1987. It lies near the post office and Plaza del Arenal in the commercial center of town. Inside, its rooms are clean, comfortable, and well maintained, although not special in any way. The beds, however, are quite comfortable, and the bathrooms well maintained and equipped with shower stalls.

Hotel Serit. Higueras, 7, 11402 Jerez de la Frontera. ☎ **956-34-07-00.** Fax 956-34-07-16. E-mail: hotelsedit@redicon.es. 35 units. A/C TV TEL. 7,000–8,000 ptas. ($46.90–$53.60) double. AE, DC, MC, V. Parking 1,000 ptas. ($6.70).

The modern three-star Hotel Serit, near Plaza de la Angustias, offers rooms that are functionally furnished and comfortable at a good price. Ranging in size from small to medium, rooms are equipped with firm mattresses resting on good Spanish beds, and small but well-maintained private bathrooms, each with a shower stall and a hair dryer. There's a pleasant bar downstairs, plus a modern breakfast lounge. Laundry and room service are provided.

WHERE TO DINE

El Bosque. Alcalde Álvaro Domecq, 26. ☎ **956-18-08-80.** Reservations required. Main courses 2,500–4,500 ptas. ($16.75–$30.15). AE, DC, MC, V. Mon–Sat 1:30–5pm and 8:30pm–2am. SPANISH/INTERNATIONAL.

Less than a mile northeast of the city center, the city's most elegant restaurant was established just after World War II. A favorite of the sherry-producing aristocracy, it retains a strong emphasis on bullfighting memorabilia, which make up most of the decoration.

Order the excellent *rabo de toro* (bull's-tail stew) if you want to dine like a true native. You might begin with a soothing Andalusian gazpacho, then try one of the fried-fish dishes, such as hake Seville style. Rice with king prawns and baby shrimp omelettes are deservedly popular dishes. Occasionally, Laguna duck in honey with chestnuts and pears is a feature. Desserts are usually good, including the pistachio ice cream.

Gaitán. Calle Gaitán, 3. ☎ **956-34-58-59.** Reservations recommended. Main courses 975–2,375 ptas. ($6.55–$15.90), fixed-price menu 2,100 ptas. ($14.05). AE, DC, MC, V. Daily 1–4:30pm , Mon–Sat 1–4:30pm, 8:30–11:30pm. ANDALUSIAN.

Juan Hurtado, who has won acclaim for the food served here, owns this small restaurant near Puerta Santa María. Surrounded by walls displaying celebrity photographs, you can enjoy such Andalusian dishes as garlic soup, various stews, duck à la Sevillana, and fried seafood. One special dish is lamb cooked with honey, based on a recipe so ancient it dates from the Muslim occupation of Spain. For dessert, the almond tart is a favorite.

Restaurante Tendido 6. Calle Circo, 10. ☎ **956-34-48-35.** Reservations required. Main courses 450–2,000 ptas. ($3–$13.40). AE, DC, MC, V. Mon–Sat 1–4pm and 8pm–midnight. SPANISH.

This combination restaurant and tapas bar has loyal clients who come from many walks of life. The chef creates a dignified regional cuisine that includes grilled rump steak, fish soup, and a wide array of Spanish dishes, including Basque and Castilian cuisine. There's nothing really exciting here, but the long-tested recipes are filled with flavor and the place is a good value. The Tendido is on the south side of Plaza de Toros.

SIDE TRIPS FROM JEREZ DE LA FRONTERA
MEDINA SIDONIA

This survivor of the Middle Ages is one of the most unspoiled hillside villages of Spain, about 29 miles (46.5km) east of Cádiz and 22 miles (35.5km) southeast of Jerez de la Frontera. Motorists from Jerez should follow the 440 southeast.

A village that time forgot, Medina Sidonia has cobblestoned streets, tile-roofed white buildings dotting the hillside, a Gothic church, a Moorish gate, and steep alleyways traveled by locals on donkeys. The Arab influence is everywhere, and the surrounding countryside is wild and seldom visited. The pockets of fog that sometimes settle over the land will make you think you're on the Yorkshire moors.

From Medina Sidonia, it's a 2½-hour drive to the port city of Algeciras, or you can take the Jerez road back to Seville.

✪ ARCOS DE LA FRONTERA

Twenty miles (32km) east of Jerez de la Frontera, this old Arab town, now a National Historic Monument, was built in the form of an amphitheater. Sitting on a rock and surrounded by the Guadalete River on three sides, it contains many houses that have been hollowed out of this formation. From the old city, there's a high-in-the-clouds view that some visitors consider without rival on the Iberian Peninsula.

The city is filled with whitewashed walls and narrow winding streets that disappear into steps. It holds a lot of historical interest and has a beautiful lake complete with paddleboats and a Mississippi riverboat.

The most exciting attraction is the **view from the principal square,** the Plaza del Cabildo, a rectangular esplanade overhanging a deep river cleft. You can see a Moorish castle, but it is privately owned and cannot be visited by the public. You can, however, visit a church on the main square, the **Iglesia de Santa María,** constructed in 1732 with a blend of Gothic, Renaissance, and baroque styles. Its western front, and its most outstanding architectural achievement, is in plateresque style. The second major church of the town, **Iglesia de San Pedro,** standing on the northern edge of the old barrio (quarter), at the far end of the cliff, is known for its 16th- and 18th-century tower. This church, which grew up on the site of a Moorish fortress, owns art works by Zurbarán and Murillo, among others. Check with the tourist office (see below) about gaining admission to these churches, as they are often closed for security reasons. Several art thefts have occurred in the area.

Even if you don't succeed in gaining entrance to the churches, it is reason enough to visit Arcos merely to wander its alleys and view its ruins from the Middle Ages. If you have to return to wherever you're going for the night, stay at least long enough to have a drink in the patio of the parador (recommended below) and take in the monumental view.

There is no train service to this little bit of paradise, but you can take a bus from Jerez de la Frontera, Seville, or Cádiz. Motorists from Jerez should follow the 342 east until they see the turnoff for Arcos.

The **tourist information office** is at Plaza del Cabildo (☎ **956-70-22-64**), open Monday through Friday from 9am to 2pm and 5 to 7pm, Saturday from 9am to 2pm, and Sunday from 11am to 2pm.

WHERE TO STAY & DINE

Parador de Arcos de la Frontera. Plaza del Cabildo, 11630 Arcos de la Frontera. ☎ **956-70-05-00.** Fax 956-70-11-16. 24 units. A/C MINIBAR TV TEL. 17,500 ptas. ($122.50) double. AE, DC, DISC, MC, V. Free parking.

The best place to stay is this government-run parador, in a restored palace in the heart of the old quarter. Built in the 1700s, it was the palace and government seat of the king's magistrate (*corregidor*) in Arcos. From the balconies, there are views of the Valley of Guadalete with its river, plains, and farms. In good weather you can take your meals (try the pork with garlic) on one of these balconies; lunch or dinner costs 3,500 ptas. ($23.45). The decor consists of tiles and antiques. The good-size rooms are handsomely furnished and beautifully maintained; perhaps you'll be assigned the one where Charles de Gaulle once stayed. Bathrooms are tiled and efficiently organized, each one equipped with a hair dryer.

5 Cádiz

76 miles (122km) S of Seville, 388 miles (625km) SW of Madrid

The oldest inhabited city in the Western world, founded in 1100 B.C., this now modern, bustling Atlantic port is a kind of Spanish Marseilles, a melting pot of Americans, Africans, and Europeans who are docking or passing through. The old quarter teems with local characters, little dives, and seaport alleyways. But despite its thriving life, the city does not hold major interest for tourists, except for the diverse cultural strains that have helped shape it. Phoenicians, Arabs, Visigoths, Romans, and Carthaginians all passed through Cádiz and left their cultural imprints. Throughout the ages this ancient port city has enjoyed varying states of prosperity, especially after the discovery of the New World.

At the end of a peninsula, Cádiz separates the Bay of Cádiz from the Atlantic, so from numerous sea walls around the town, you have views of the ocean. It was here that Columbus set out on his second voyage.

ESSENTIALS

GETTING THERE   Trains arrive from Seville (taking 2 hours), Jerez de la Frontera (40 minutes), and Córdoba (5 hours). The train station is located on Avenida del Puerto (☎ **956-25-43-01**), on the southeast border of the main port.

If you're taking a bus from Madrid, you'll probably have to transfer in Seville. Buses arrive in Cádiz at two separate terminals. From Seville (12 per day; 2 hours), Jerez de la Frontera (6 per day; 1 hour), Málaga, Córdoba, and Granada, buses arrive at the Estación de Comes terminal, Plaza de la Hispanidad, 1 (☎ **956-22-42-71**), on the north side of town, a few blocks west of the main port. Far less prominent is the terminal run by the Transportes Los Amarillos, Avenida Ramón de Carranza, 31 (☎ **956-28-58-52**), several blocks to the south, which runs frequent buses to several nearby towns and villages, most of which are of interest only for local residents and workers.

Driving from Seville, the A-4 (also called E-5), a toll road, or N-IV, a toll-free road running beside it, will bring you into Cádiz.

VISITOR INFORMATION   The **tourist information office** is at Calderón de la Barca, 1 (☎ **956-21-13-13**). Open Monday through Friday from 9am to 7pm, Saturday from 10am to 1pm.

EXPLORING CÁDIZ

Despite being one of the oldest towns in Europe, Cádiz has few remnants of antiquity. It is still worth visiting, however, especially to wander through the old quarter, which retains a special charm.

Plaza de San Juan de Dios is the ideal place to sit at a sidewalk cafe and people-watch in the shadow of the neoclassical **Isabellino Ayuntamiento** (Town Hall), with its outstanding chapter house. The **Oratorio de San Felipe Neri,** Santa Inés (☎ **956-21-16-12**), where the Cortés (Parliament) met in 1812 to proclaim its constitution, has an important Murillo (*Conception*) and a history museum. Admission is free, and it's open August through June, daily from 8:30 to 10am and 7:30 to 9:45pm. The **Hospital de Mujeres** (Women's Hospital) has a patio courtyard dating from 1740 and a chapel with El Greco's *Ecstasy of St. Francis.*

Museo de Cádiz. Plaza de Mini, s/n. ☎ **956-21-22-81.** Admission 250 ptas. ($1.70), free Sun. Tues 2:30–8pm, Wed–Sat 9am–8pm, Sun 9:30am–2:30pm.

This museum, now fully restored, contains one of Spain's most important Zurbarán collections, as well as paintings by Rubens and Murillo (including the latter's acclaimed picture of Christ). The archaeology section displays Roman, Carthaginian, and Phoenician finds; and ethnology exhibits include pottery, baskets, textiles, and leather works.

Catedral de Cádiz. Plaza Catedral. ☎ **956-28-61-54.** Free admission to Cathedral; museum 500 ptas. ($3.35) adults, 200 ptas. ($1.35) children. Tues–Sat 10am–12:30pm.

This magnificent 18th-century baroque building by architect Vicente Acero has a neoclassical interior dominated by an outstanding apse. The tomb of Cádiz-born composer Manuel de Falla lies in its splendid crypt; music lovers from all over the world come here to pay their respects. Haydn composed *The Seven Last Words of Our Savior on the Cross* for this cathedral. The treasury/museum contains a priceless collection of Spanish silver and embroidery, and paintings by Spanish, Italian, and Flemish artists.

WHERE TO STAY

Cádiz has a number of inexpensive accommodations, some of which are quite poor. However, for a moderate price you can afford some of the finest lodgings in the city. Note that rooms are scarce during the February carnival season.

Parador Hotel Atlántico. Duque de Nájera, 9, 11002 Cádiz. ☎ **956-22-69-05.** Fax 956-21-45-82. 159 units. A/C MINIBAR TV TEL. 12,000–15,000 ptas. ($80.40–$100.50) double; 18,500–33,000 ptas. ($123.95–$221.10) suite. AE, DC, MC, V. Parking 1,500 ptas. ($10.05) for garage.

Actually a modern resort hotel, this national parador is built on one of the loveliest beaches of the Bay of Cádiz, at the western edge of the old town. It is clearly the outstanding choice for accommodations here, dwarfing the competition. The white six-story building has a marble patio, a salon decked out in rattan and cane, and spacious rooms that feature balconies with tables and chairs for relaxed ocean viewing. More than half of the rooms were renovated in 1995, when all the mattresses were renewed and the plumbing restored. Palm trees surround the Atlántico's swimming pool. The hotel also boasts a bar and a dining room known for its superb Andalusian cuisine, particularly the seafood.

Regio 1. Ana de Viya, 11, 11009 Cádiz. ☎ **956-27-93-31.** Fax 956-27-91-13. 44 units. A/C TV TEL. 8,000–9,500 ptas. ($53.60–$63.65) double. AE, DC, MC, V. Parking in garage 500 ptas. ($3.35).

Built in 1978, this aging hotel rises six stories and is about a block inland from the harbor and Paseo Marítimo. The small rooms are simple but airy and comfortable— nowhere near the equal of the Atlántico (see above), but then its prices are much more reasonable. Breakfast is the only meal served. The overflow from this hotel is sometimes directed to the hotel's slightly more expensive twin, the superior Regio 2 (see below).

Regio 2. Avenida Andalucía, 79, 11008 Cádiz. ☎ **956-25-30-08.** Fax 956-25-30-09. 45 units. A/C TV TEL. 9,500 ptas. ($63.65) double. AE, DC, MC, V. Parking 500 ptas. ($3.35).

Business was successful enough in the late 1970s to justify the construction of this five-story twin of an already existing hotel, the Regio 1 (see above). Run by the same management, and sharing some of their staff and amenities in common, it was built in 1981, about 200 yards from its twin. It offers air-conditioning in each of its simple but pleasant rooms, which are more comfortable and in better shape than those of Regio 1 (see above). Both hotels are a very short walk from the ocean. The Regio 2 operates a cafeteria serving *platos combinados* (combination plates) daily.

WHERE TO DINE

El Faro. Calle San Félix, 15. ☎ **956-21-10-68.** Reservations recommended. Main courses 1,200–2,200 ptas. ($8.05–$14.75); fixed-price menu 3,500 ptas. ($23.45). AE, DC, MC, V. Daily 1–4:30pm and 8:30pm–midnight. SEAFOOD.

Unless you're a devotee of seafood, this might not be your preferred restaurant in Cádiz. There's only a limited selection of meat with the main emphasis on the array of fresh fish and shellfish available in its large dining room. (There's an additional, much smaller room to the side, usually reserved for groups of locals.) Established in 1964, and the favorite restaurant of many visitors, El Faro occupies the white-walled premises of one of the simple houses near the harbor front in Cádiz's oldest neighborhood. Menu items include fried lamb chops and beefsteak and a long list of seafood, such as seafood soup, roulades of sole with spinach, hake with green sauce, monkfish with strips of Serrano ham, and lobster.

CÁDIZ AFTER DARK

Most dance clubs around Cádiz come and go with the seasons, but **La Boîte,** Edificio Isecotel, Paseo Marítimo, s/n (☎ **956-26-13-16**), has stayed alive longer than many of its competitors, attracting a large crowd of Andalusian youth and other revelers with recorded music and air-conditioning. In the old town on an avenue running alongside Playa de la Victoria, it's open nightly from 10:30pm to 6am. There is a one-drink minimum but no cover; a beer costs 500 ptas. ($3.35).

6 Costa de la Luz

Isla Cristina, one of the coast's westernmost cities, lies 34 miles (55km) W of Huelva, 403 miles (649km) SW of Madrid; Tarifa, at the opposite end of the coast, lies 59 miles (95km) SE of Cádiz, 429 miles (691km) SW of Madrid

West of Cádiz, near Huelva and the Portuguese frontier, lies the rapidly developing Costa de la Luz (Coast of Light), which hopes to pick up the overflow from Costa del

Sol. The Luz coast stretches from the mouth of the Guadiana River, forming the boundary with Portugal, to Tarifa Point on the Straits of Gibraltar. Dotting the coast are long stretches of sand, pine trees, fishing cottages, and lazy whitewashed villages. The Huelva district forms the northwestern half of Costa de la Luz. The southern half stretches from Tarifa to **Sanlúcar de Barrameda,** the spot from which Magellan, in 1519, embarked on his voyage around the globe. Columbus also made this the home port for his third journey to the New World. Sanlúcar today is widely known in Andalusia for its local sherry, Manzanilla, which you can order at any of the city's wine cellars (bodegas). If you make it to Sanlúcar, you'll find the **tourist information office** at Calzada de Ejército, Paseo Marítimo (☎ **956-36-61-10**), just 1 block inland from the beach. It's open Monday through Friday from 10am to 11am and 6 to 8pm, Saturday and Sunday from 11am to 1pm. Do not count on a great deal of guidance, however. To travel between the northern and southern portions of Costa de la Luz, you must go inland to Seville, since no roads go across the Coto Doñana and the marshland near the mouth of the Guadalquivir.

ESSENTIALS

GETTING THERE   Huelva, the coast's most prominent city, is serviced by trains from Seville, 2 hours away. If you're going on to Portugal from here, you can take a bus to Ayamonte, where you can board a ferry to the gateway of Vila Real de Santa Antonio, the beginning of Portugal's Algarve coast.

Buses run several times a day from Seville, where connections can be made to all parts of Spain. From Huelva, about eight buses a day depart for Ayamonte and the Portuguese frontier.

Huelva is easily reached by car in about an hour from Seville, 55 miles (88.5km) to the east, via a broad and modern highway, the E-01.

VISITOR INFORMATION   The **tourist information office** is in Huelva at Avenida de Alemania, 12 (☎ **959-25-74-03**), open Monday through Friday from 8:30am to 7:30pm, Saturday from 9am to 2pm.

EXPLORING THE AREA

At **Huelva,** a large statue on the west bank of the river commemorates the departure of Christopher Columbus on his third voyage of discovery. About 4½ miles (7.2km) up on the east bank of the Tinto River, a monument marks the exact spot where his ships were anchored while they were being loaded with supplies before departure.

South of Huelva is the **Monasterio de la Rábida,** Palos de la Frontera (☎ **959-35-04-11**), in whose little white chapel Columbus prayed for success on the eve of his voyage. Even without its connections to Columbus, the monastery would be worth a visit for its paintings and frescoes. A guide will show you around the Mudéjar chapel and a large portion of the old monastery, which is open Tuesday through Sunday, 10am to 1pm and 4 to 6:15pm. Admission is free, but donations are accepted. The monastery lies on the east bank of the Tinto. Take bus number 1 from Huelva.

WHERE TO STAY & DINE

Accommodations are severely limited along Costa de la Luz in summer, so it's crucial to arrive with a reservation. You can stay at a government-run parador east of Huelva in Mazagón (see below) or in Ayamonte, near the Portuguese frontier. Where you are unlikely to want to stay overnight is in the dreary industrial port of Huelva itself.

Ayamonte was built on the slopes of a hill on which a castle stood. It is full of beach high-rises, which, for the most part, contain vacation apartments for Spaniards in July and August. Judging by their license plates, most of these visitors come from Huelva,

Seville, and Madrid, so the Costa de la Luz is more Spanish in flavor than the overrun and more international Costa del Sol.

Ayamonte has clean, wide, sandy beaches and the waves, for the most part, are calm. Portions of the beaches are even calmer because of sandbars some 55 to 110 yards from the shore, which become virtual islands at low tide. The nearest beaches to Ayamonte are miles away at Isla Canela and Moral.

Parador Nacional Costa de la Luz. El Castillito, 21400 Ayamonte. ☎ **959-32-07-00.** Fax 959-32-07-00. 53 units. A/C MINIBAR TV TEL. 11,500–15,000 ptas. ($77.05 $100.50) double; 17,000–23,000 ptas. ($113.90–$154.10) suite. AE, DC, MC, V. Free parking. From the center of Ayamonte, signs for the parador will lead you up a winding road to the hilltop, about ½ mile (1km) southeast of the center.

The leading accommodation in Ayamonte, this parador opened in 1966 and was completely renovated in 1991. Commanding a sweeping view of the river and the surrounding towns along its banks—sunsets are memorable here—the parador stands about 100 feet above sea level on the site of the old castle of Ayamonte. Built in a severe modern style, with Nordic-inspired furnishings, it numbers among its facilities a swimming pool, a garden, central heating, a dining room, and a bar. Most rooms are medium in size, and each is comfortably appointed, with good beds and tidy bathrooms, each equipped with a hair dryer. Good regional meals cost from 3,200 ptas. ($21.45). Try, if it's featured, *raya en pimiento* (stingray with red pepper); *calamar relleno* (stuffed squid) is another specialty.

Parador Nacional Cristóbal Colón. Carretera de Matalascañas, s/n, 21130 Mazagón. ☎ **959-53-63-00.** Fax 959-53-62-28. 44 units. A/C MINIBAR TV TEL. 16,500–19,000 ptas. ($110.55–$127.30) double; 22,000–24,000 ptas. ($147.40–$160.80) suite. AE, DC, MC, V. Free parking. Exit from Magazón's eastern sector, following the signs to the town of Matalascañas. Take the coast road (Highway 442) to the parador.

One of the best accommodations in the area is 14 miles (24km) from Huelva and 3½ miles (6km) from the center of Mazagón. A rambling 1960s structure, the parador has comfortable and spacious guest rooms with balconies and terraces overlooking a tranquil, expansive garden and pine groves that slope down to the white-sand beach of Mazagón. Swimmers and sunbathers can also enjoy the large pool, and there are tennis courts. The dining room features two menús del día, at 3,700 ptas. ($24.80) and a children's menu at 1,500 ptas. ($10.05).

7 Ronda

63 miles (101km) NE of Algeciras, 60 miles (97km) W of Málaga, 91 miles (147km) SE of Seville, 367 miles (591km) S of Madrid

This little town, high in the Serranía de Ronda Mountains (2,300 feet above sea level), is one of the oldest and most aristocratic places in Spain. The main tourist attraction is a 500-foot **gorge,** spanned by a Roman stone bridge, Puente San Miguel, over the Guadelevín River. On both sides of this hole in the earth are cliff-hanging houses, which look as if, with the slightest push, they would plunge into the chasm.

Ronda is an incredible sight. The road here, once difficult to navigate, is now a wide highway with guard rails. The town and the surrounding mountains were legendary hideouts for bandits and smugglers, but today the Guardia Civil has just about put an end to that occupation.

The gorge divides the town into an older part, the Moorish and aristocratic quarter, and the newer section south of the gorge, built principally after the Reconquest. The old quarter is by far the more fascinating; it contains narrow, rough streets and buildings with a marked Moorish influence (watch for the minaret). After the lazy resort living of Costa del Sol, make a side excursion to Ronda; its unique beauty and refreshing mountain air are a tonic.

Ronda is great for the explorer. Local children may attach themselves to you as guides. For a few pesetas it might be worth it to hire one, since it's difficult to weave your way in and out of the narrow streets.

ESSENTIALS

GETTING THERE   There are three trains daily from Málaga (2 hours), three per day from Seville (3½ hours), and three per day from Granada (3 hours). Most rail routes into Ronda require a change of train in the railway junction of Bobadilla, several miles to the northeast. Ronda's railway station lies in the western edge of the new city, on the Avenida Andalucía (☎ **95-287-16-73**).

The main bus company in Ronda is Los Amarillos, which runs daily bus service from both Málaga and Seville. Buses arrive and depart from the bus station on the western edge of the new town, at Plaza Concepcion Garcia Redonda, 2 (☎ **95-218-7061**). To Málaga, there are six buses a day Monday through Friday and four on weekends. To Seville, there are five buses a day Monday through Friday, three on Saturday, and four on Sunday.

Five highways converge on Ronda from all parts of Andalusia. All five head through mountainous scenery, but the road south to Marbella, through the Sierra Palmitera, is one of the most winding and dangerous.

VISITOR INFORMATION   The **tourist information office** is at Plaza de España, 1 (☎ **95-287-12-72**), open Monday through Friday from 9am to 2pm and 4 to 7pm, Saturday and Sunday 10am to 3pm.

EXPLORING RONDA

The still-functioning **Baños Árabes** are reached from the turnoff to Puente San Miguel. Dating from the 13th century, the baths have glass roof-windows and hump-shaped cupolas. They are generally open Tuesday through Sunday from 9am to 2pm and 4 to 6pm. Admission is free, but you should tip the caretaker who shows you around.

Palacio de Mondragón, El Campillo (☎ **95-287-84-50**), was once the private home of one of the ministers to Charles III. Flanked by two Mudéjar towers, it now has a baroque facade. Inside are Moorish mosaics. Open Monday through Friday from 10am to 7pm and Saturday and Sunday from 10am to 3pm; admission is 250 ptas. ($1.70), but free for children under 14.

The **Casa del Rey Moro,** Marqués de Parada, 17, is misnamed as this House of the Moorish King was actually built in the early 1700s. However, it is believed to have been constructed over Moorish foundations. The interior is closed, but from the garden you can take an underground stairway, called La Mina, which leads you to the river, a distance of 365 steps. Christian slaves cut these steps in the 14th century to guarantee a steady water supply in case Ronda came under siege.

On the same street you'll see the 18th-century **Palacio del Marqués de Salvatierra** (☎ **95-287-12-06**). Still inhabited by a private family, this Renaissance-style mansion is open for guided tours, operating every 30 minutes, provided that half a dozen people are present. It's open Monday through Wednesday and Friday and Saturday from 11am to 2pm and 4 to 7pm, Thursday and Sunday from 11am to 2pm. Admission is 400 ptas. ($2.70).

Ronda has the oldest bullring in Spain. Built in the 1700s, **Plaza de Toros** is the setting for the yearly Goyesque Corrida in honor of Ronda native son Pedro Romero, one of the greatest bullfighters of all time. If you want to know more about Ronda bullfighting, head for the **Museo Taurino** (☎ 95-287-41-32), reached through the ring. It is open June through September, daily from 10am to 8pm; October through May, daily 10am to 6pm. Admission is 300 ptas. ($2).

Exhibits document the exploits of the noted Romero family. Francesco invented the killing sword and the muleta, and his grandson, Pedro (1754–1839), killed 5,600 bulls during his 30-year career. Pedro was the inspiration for Goya's famous Tauromaquia series. There are also exhibits devoted to Cayetano Ordóñez, the matador immortalized by Hemingway in *The Sun Also Rises*.

A NEARBY ATTRACTION: PREHISTORIC CAVE PAINTINGS

Near Benaoján, **Cueva de la Pileta** (☎ 95-216-72-02), 15½ miles (25km) southwest of Ronda, plus a 1¼-mile (2km) hard climb, has been compared to the Caves of Altamira in northern Spain, where prehistoric paintings were discovered toward the end of the 19th century. In a wild, beautiful area known as the Serranía de Ronda, José Bullón Lobato, grandfather of the present owners, discovered this cave in 1905. More than a mile in length and filled with oddly and beautifully shaped stalagmites and stalactites, the cave was found to contain five fossilized human skeletons and two animal skeletons.

In the mysterious darkness, prehistoric paintings have been discovered, depicting animals in yellow, red, black, and ocher, as well as mysterious symbols. One of the highlights of the tour is a trip to the chamber of the fish, containing a wall painting of a great black seal-like creature about 3 feet long. This chamber, the innermost heart of the cave, ends in a precipice that drops vertically nearly 250 feet.

In the valley just below the cave lives a guide who will conduct you around the chambers, carrying artificial light to illuminate the paintings. Plan to spend at least an hour here. Tours are given daily from 10am to 1pm and 4 to 5pm. Admission, including the 1-hour tour, is 800 ptas. ($5.35) adults, 500 ptas. ($3.35) children.

You can reach the cave most easily by car from Ronda, but those without private transport can take the train to Benaoján. The cave, whose entrance is at least 4 miles (6.5km) uphill, is located in the rocky foothills of the Sierra de Libar, midway between two tiny villages: Jimera de Libar and Benaoján. The valley that contains the cave is parallel to the valley holding Ronda, so the town of Ronda and the cave are separated by a steep range of hills, requiring a rather complicated detour either to the south or north of Ronda, then a doubling back.

WHERE TO STAY
EXPENSIVE TO MODERATE

✪ **Parador de Ronda.** Plaza de España, 29400 Ronda. ☎ **95-287-75-00.** Fax 95-287-81-88. 78 units. A/C MINIBAR TV TEL. 15,000–18,500 ptas. ($100.50–$123.95) double; 20,000–25,000 ptas. ($134–$167.50) suite. AE, DC, MC, V. Parking 1,200 ptas. ($8.05).

When this parador opened in 1994, it surpassed the Reina Victoria (see below) to become the finest accommodation in the area. It sits on a high cliff overlooking the Tajo, a fantastic gorge that cuts a swath more than 500 feet deep and 300 feet wide through the center of this mountain town. Stretching along the edge of the gorge to a bridge, Puente Nuevo, built over the Tajo in 1761, the parador is surrounded by a footpath with scenic overlooks, offering views of the gorge and the torrents of the Guadalevín River below. The parador fronts the old food market and the original Town Hall on the town's most historic square. The good-size guest rooms are beautifully furnished, often opening onto views of the rugged peaks that surround Ronda. Each accommodation comes with an immaculately kept and tiled bathroom, equipped with a hair dryer.

Dining/Diversions: Overlooking the gorge, the parador dining room (open to the pubic) features a typically regional cuisine of almond soup, gazpacho, wild game dishes—whatever's good and fresh in any season. There is also a bar-cafeteria.

Amenities: Room service, laundry, baby-sitting; the grounds include a swimming pool.

✪ **Hotel Reina Victoria.** Paseo Dr. Fleming, 25, 29400 Ronda. ☎ **95-287-12-40.** Fax 95-287-10-75. 89 units. A/C TV TEL. 17,000 ptas. ($113.90) double; 23,000 ptas. ($154.10) suite. AE, DC, MC, V. Free parking.

On the eastern periphery of town, a short walk from the center, this country-style hotel was built in 1906 by an Englishman in honor of his recently departed monarch, Queen Victoria. It's near the bullring, with terraces that hang right over a 490-foot precipice. Hemingway frequently visited the hotel, but the Reina Victoria is known best as the place where poet Rainer Maria Rilke wrote *The Spanish Trilogy.* His third-floor room has been set aside as a museum, with first editions, manuscripts, photographs, and even a framed copy of his hotel bill. A life-size bronze statue of the poet stands in a corner of the hotel garden.

Rooms are big, airy, and comfortable, some with complete living rooms containing sofas, chairs, and tables. Many also have private terraces with garden furniture. The beds are sumptuous, and the bathrooms boast all the latest improvements.

Dining here can be recommended, as the food is well prepared. The hotel also contains an outdoor pool and a well-stocked bar.

INEXPENSIVE

Hostal Residencia Royal. Virgen de la Paz, 42, 29400 Ronda. ☎ **95-287-11-41.** Fax 95-287-81-32. 29 units. A/C TEL. 5,000 ptas. ($33.50) double. AE, DC, MC, V. Parking 1,000 ptas. ($6.70).

An adequate stopover for those who want to spend the night in the modern section of town, the Residencia Royal stands near the old bull arena. Each of the basic and small guest rooms is reasonably comfortable; units in the rear, however, tend to be noisy. No breakfast is served; guests head out to a cafe for their morning caffeine.

Hotel Don Miguel. Villanueva, 8. ☎ **95-287-77-22.** Fax 95-287-83-77. 19 units. A/C TV TEL. 9,500 ptas. ($63.65) double. AE, DC, MC, V. Parking 750 ptas. ($5.05). Closed Jan 10–24.

From the narrow street leading to it, this hotel presents a severely dignified white-fronted facade very similar to that of its neighbors. From the back, however, the hotel looks out over the river gorge of a steep ravine, adding drama to those rooms overlooking it. Set a few steps east of Plaza de España, and composed of several interconnected houses, it offers a vine-strewn patio above the river, a warmly modernized interior accented with exposed brick and varnished pine, and small, simple but comfortable rooms, each with a firm mattress. The restaurant, Don Miguel, is recommended separately (see below).

Hotel Residencia Polo. Mariano Soubirón, 8, 29400 Ronda. ☎ **95-287-24-47.** Fax 95-287-24-49. 33 units. A/C TV TEL. 6,750–9,500 ptas. ($45.25–$63.65) double. AE, DC, MC, V. Parking 1,400 ptas. ($9.40).

The Polo is a professionally run hotel in the commercial, modern heart of Ronda near a large shopping arcade. Its accommodations are pleasantly, though not elegantly, decorated and maintained. Rooms are spacious, with even the closets and private bathrooms large enough for your needs. The hotel has a bar and restaurant and also offers room service.

WHERE TO DINE

Don Miguel Restaurant. Plaza de España, 3. ☎ **95-287-10-90.** Reservations not required. Main courses 1,500–2,200 ptas. ($10.05–$14.75); menú del día 2,300 ptas. ($15.40). AE, DC, MC, V. Daily 12:30–4pm and 8–11pm. Closed Jan 10–24. ANDALUSIAN.

At the end of the bridge, facing the river, this restaurant offers diners views of the upper gorge. It has enough tables set outside on two levels to seat 300 people, and in summer this is a bustling place. The food is good, the rest rooms are clean, and the waiters are polite and speak enough English to get by. There is also a pleasant bar for drinks and tapas. Try one of the seafood selections or the house specialty, stewed bull's tail. The also recommended Hotel Don Miguel (see above) runs the restaurant.

Mesón Santiago. Marina, 3. ☎ **95-287-15-59.** Reservations required. Main courses 1,500–2,000 ptas. ($10.05–$13.40); fixed-price menus 1,200–1,600 ptas. ($8.05–$10.70). MC, V. Daily 10am–5pm. SPANISH.

Santiago Ruíz Gil operates one of the best inexpensive restaurants in Ronda, serving lunch only. A three-course menú del día, with bread and wine, is not a bad deal, considering the price. If you order from the *especialidades de la casa,* count on spending more. Try the *caldo de cocido,* a savory stew with large pieces of meat cooked with such vegetables as garbanzos and white beans, almost a meal in itself. You might also like the tongue cooked in wine and served with potato salad. All the servings are generous. The more expensive à la carte menu is likely to include partridge, lamb, mountain trout, and regional meats. Fresh asparagus and succulent strawberries are also available in season. Mesón Santiago is located near Plaza del Socorro.

Pedro Romero. Virgen de la Paz, 18. ☎ **95-287-11-10.** Reservations required on day of corrida. Main courses 1,000–2,000 ptas. ($6.70–$13.40). AE, DC, MC, V. Daily 12:30–4pm and 8–11pm. SPANISH/ANDALUSIAN.

Named after famed bullfighter Pedro Romero, this restaurant attracts aficionados of that sport. In fact, it stands opposite the bullring and gets extremely busy on bullfighting days, when it's almost impossible to get a table. While seated under a stuffed bull's head, surrounded by photographs of young matadors, you might begin your meal with the classic garlic soup, then follow with a well-prepared array of meat or poultry dishes.

8 Granada

258 miles (415km) S of Madrid, 76 miles (122km) NE of Málaga

This former stronghold of Moorish Spain, in the foothills of the snowcapped Sierra Nevada range, is full of romance and folklore. Washington Irving (*Tales of the Alhambra*) used the symbol of this city, the pomegranate (*granada*), to conjure up a spirit of romance. In fact, the name probably derives from the Moorish word Karnattah. Some historians have suggested that it comes from Garnatha Alyehud, the name of an old Jewish ghetto.

Washington Irving may have helped publicize the glories of Granada to the English-speaking world, but in Spain the city is known for its ties to another writer: Federico García Lorca. Born in 1898, this Spanish poet and dramatist, whose masterpiece was *The House of Bernarda Alba,* was shot by soldiers in 1936 in the first months of the Spanish Civil War. During Franco's rule García Lorca's works were banned in Spain, but happily that situation has changed and he is once again honored in Granada, where he grew up.

Granada lies 2,200 feet above sea level, sprawls over two main hills, the Alhambra and the Albaicín, and is crossed by two rivers, the Genil and the Darro.

Cuesta de Gomérez is one of the most important streets in Granada. It climbs uphill from Plaza Nueva, the center of the modern city, to the Alhambra. At Plaza Nueva the east-west artery, calle de los Reyes Católicos, goes to the heart of the 19th-century city and the towers of the cathedral. The main street of Granada is the Gran Vía de Colón, the principal north-south artery.

Calle de los Reyes Católicos and the Gran Vía de Colón meet at the circular Plaza de Isabel la Católica, graced by a bronze statue of the queen offering Columbus the Santa Fé agreement, which granted the rights to the epochal voyage to the New World. Going west, calle de los Reyes Católicos passes near the cathedral and other major sights in the downtown section of Granada. The street runs to Puerta Real, which is the commercial hub of Granada, with many stores, hotels, cafes, and restaurants.

ESSENTIALS

GETTING THERE Iberia flies to Granada once or twice daily from Barcelona and Madrid, several times a week from Palma de Majorca, three times a week from Valencia, and every Thursday from Tenerife in the Canary Islands. Granada's airport lies 10 miles (16km) west of the center of town; dial ☎ **958-24-52-00.** A convenient Iberia ticketing office lies 2 blocks east of the cathedral, at Plaza Isabel la Católica, 2 (☎ **958-22-75-92**). A shuttle bus departs several times daily, connecting this office with the airport, costing 425 ptas. ($2.85) one way.

Two trains connect Granada with Madrid's Atocha Railway Station daily (taking 5 hours). Many connections to the rest of Spain are funneled through the railway junction at Bobadilla, a 2-hour ride to the west. The train station is at Avenida Andaluces (☎ **958-27-12-72**).

Most buses pull into the station on the fringe of Granada at Carretera de Madrid. **Alsina Graells** (☎ **958-18-50-10**) is the most useful company here, offering six buses per day from Córdoba (3 hours), 12 per day from Jaén (1½ hours), nine per day from Madrid (5 hours), 15 from Málaga (2 hours), and six from Sevilla (3 hours).

Granada is connected by superhighway to Madrid, Málaga, and Seville. Many sightseers prefer to make the drive from Madrid to Granada in 2 days, rather than 1. If that is your plan, Jaén makes a perfect stopover.

VISITOR INFORMATION The **tourist information office** is at Plaza de Mariana Pineda, 10 (☎ **958-22-66-88**), open Monday through Friday from 9am to 7pm, Saturday from 10am to 2pm.

EXPLORING GRANADA

Try to spend some time walking around Old Granada. Plan on about 3 hours to see the most interesting sights.

Puerta de Elvira is the gate through which Ferdinand and Isabella made their triumphant entry into Granada in 1492. It was once a grisly place, with the rotting heads of executed criminals hanging from its portals. The quarter surrounding the gate was the Arab section (*morería*), until all the Arabs were driven out of the city after the Reconquest.

One of the most fascinating streets in Granada is **calle de Elvira,** west of which the Albaicín, or old Arab quarter, rises on a hill. In the 17th and 18th centuries, many artisans occupied the shops and ateliers along this street and those radiating from it. Come here if you're looking for antiques.

The most-walked street in Granada is **Carrera del Darro,** running north along the Darro River. It was discovered by the Romantic artists of the 19th century; many of their etchings (subsequently engraved) of scenes along this street were widely circulated, doing much to spread the fame of Granada throughout Europe. You can still find some of these old engravings in the musty antiques shops. Carrera del Darro ends at **Paseo de los Tristes (Avenue of the Sad Ones),** so named for the funeral corteges that used to go by here on the way to the cemetery.

On calle de Elvira stands the **Iglesia de San Andrés,** begun in 1528, with its Mudéjar bell tower. Much of the church was destroyed in the early 19th century, though several interesting paintings and sculptures remain. Another old church in this area is the **Iglesia de Santiago,** constructed in 1501 and dedicated to St. James, patron saint of Spain. Built on the site of an Arab mosque, it was damaged in the 1884 earthquake that struck Granada. The church contains the tomb of architect Diego de Siloé (1495–1563), who did much to change the face of Granada.

Despite its name, the oldest square in Granada is **Plaza Nueva,** which, under the Muslims, was the site of the bridge of the woodcutters. The Darro River was covered over here, but its waters still flow underneath the square (which in Franco's time was named Plaza del General Franco). On the east side of the Plaza Nueva is the 16th-century **Iglesia de Santa Ana,** built by Siloé. Inside its five-nave interior you can see a Churrigueresque reredos and coffered ceiling.

The *corrida* isn't really very popular here, but if you want to check out a bullfight anyway, they're usually limited to the week of the Fiesta de Corpus Christi from May 29 to June 6 or the Día de la Cruz (Day of the Cross) observed on May 3. There is also a fight on the last Sunday in September. The **Plaza de Toros,** the bullring, is on Avenida de Doctor Olóriz, close to the soccer stadium. On the day of the fight, tickets can be purchased in the center of town on calle Escudo del Carmen in back of the city hall from 5 to 9pm. For more information, call ☎ 958-77-24-51.

✪ **Alhambra.** Palacio de Carlos V. ☎ **958-22-09-12.** Comprehensive ticket, including Alhambra and Generalife (below), 750 ptas. ($5.05); Museo Bellas Artes 250 ptas. ($1.70); Museo Hispano-Musulman 250 ptas. ($1.70); illuminated visits 750 ptas. ($5.05). Mar–Oct, daily 9am–7:45pm, floodlit visits daily 10pm–midnight; Nov–Feb, daily 9am–5:45pm, floodlit visits daily 8–10pm. Bus: 2.

Later enriched by Moorish occupants into a lavish palace, the Alhambra was originally constructed for defensive purposes on a hilltop's rocky outcropping above the Darro River. The modern city of Granada was built across the river from the Alhambra, about half a mile from its western foundations.

When you first see the Alhambra, you may be surprised by its somewhat somber exterior. You have to walk across the threshold to discover the true delights of this Moorish palace. Tickets are sold in the office next to the uncompleted palace of the Hapsburg king Charles V. Enter through the incongruous 14th-century Gateway of Justice. Most visitors do not need an expensive guide but will be content to stroll through the richly ornamented open-air rooms, with their lacelike walls and their courtyards with fountains. Many of the Arabic inscriptions translate as "Only Allah is conqueror."

The most-photographed part of the palace is the Court of Lions, named after its highly stylized fountain. This was the heart of the palace, the most private section, where the sultan enjoyed his harem. Opening onto the court are the Hall of the Two Sisters, where the favorite of the moment was kept, and the Gossip Room, a factory of intrigue. In the dancing room in the Hall of Kings, entertainment was provided nightly to amuse the sultan's party. Eunuchs guarded the harem but apparently not very well—one sultan, according to legend, beheaded 36 Moorish princes here because one of them was suspected of having been intimate with his favorite.

You can see the room where Washington Irving lived (in the chambers of Charles V) while he was compiling his *Tales of the Alhambra.* The best known tale is the legend of Zayda, Zorayada, and Zorahayda, the three beautiful princesses who fell in love with three captured Spanish soldiers outside "La Torre de las Infantas."

Irving credits the French with saving the Alhambra for posterity, but in fact they were responsible for blowing up seven of the towers in 1812, and it was a Spanish soldier who cut the fuse before more damage could be done. When the duke of Wellington arrived a few years later, he chased out the chickens, the gypsies, and the transient beggars who were using the Alhambra as a tenement and set up housekeeping here himself.

Charles V may have been horrified when he saw the cathedral in the middle of the great mosque at Córdoba, but he is responsible for architectural meddling here, building a Renaissance palace at the Alhambra—which, although quite beautiful, is terribly out of place. Today it houses the **Museo Bellas Artes en la Alhambra** (☎ 958-22-48-43), open Tuesday through Saturday from 9am to 2pm. Of minor interest, it displays mostly religious paintings and sculpture dating from the 1500s to the present. It also shelters the **Museo Hispano-Musulman en la Alhambra** (☎ 958-22-62-79), devoted to Hispanic-Muslim art and open Tuesday through Saturday from 9am to 2:30pm.

Note: Because of the overwhelming crowds, there is a chance you may not be admitted to the Alhambra, as the government is forced to limit the number of people who can enter. Your best bet is to go as early as possible, but, even then, some people arriving at 10am may not be admitted until 1:30pm. If you arrive after 4pm, it is unlikely you'll get in at all.

Many visitors opt for a taxi or the bus to the Alhambra. But some hardy souls enjoy the uphill climb from the cathedral, Plaza de la Lonja (signs indicate the winding roads and the steps that lead to the Alhambra). If you decide to walk, enter the Alhambra via the Cuesta de Gomérez, which, although steep, is the quickest and shortest pedestrian route. It begins at Plaza Nueva, about 4 blocks east of the cathedral, and goes steeply uphill to Puerta de las Granadas, the first of two gates to the Alhambra. The second, another 200 yards uphill, is Puerta de la Justicia, which accepts 90% of the touristic visits to the Alhambra. Beware of self-styled guides milling around the parking lot; they may just be interested in picking your pocket.

✪ **Generalife.** Alhambra, Cerro de Sol. ☎ **958-22-09-12.** Comprehensive ticket, including Alhambra and Generalife, 750 ptas. ($5.05), see above. For hours see the Alhambra, above. Exit from the Alhambra via Puerta de la Justicia, then circumnavigate the Alhambra's southern foundations until you reach the gardens of the summer palace, where Paseo de los Cipreses quickly leads you to the main building of the Generalife.

The sultans used to spend their summers in this palace (pronounced hay-nay-rahl-*ee*-fay), safely locked away with their harems. Built in the 13th century to overlook the Alhambra, the Generalife's glory is its gardens and courtyards. Don't expect an Alhambra in miniature: The Generalife was always meant to be a retreat, even from the splendors of the Alhambra. This palace was the setting for Irving's story of the prince locked away from love.

✪ **Catedral and Capilla Real.** Plaza de la Lonja, Gran Vía de Colón, 5. ☎ **958-22-29-59.** Admission to cathedral 300 ptas. ($2); chapel 300 ptas. ($2). Cathedral and chapel daily 10:30am–1:30pm and 3:30–6:30pm (open 4–7pm in winter).

This richly ornate Spanish Renaissance cathedral, with its spectacular altar, is one of the country's architectural highlights, acclaimed for its beautiful facade and gold-and-white decor. It was begun in 1521 and completed in 1714. Behind the cathedral (entered separately) is the flamboyant Gothic Royal Chapel, where the remains of Queen Isabella and her husband, Ferdinand, lie. It was their wish to be buried in recaptured Granada, not Castile or Aragón. The coffins are remarkably tiny—a reminder of how short they must have been. Accenting the tombs is a wrought-iron grill, itself a masterpiece. Occupying much larger tombs are the remains of their daughter, Joanna the Mad, and her husband, Philip the Handsome. The cathedral lies in the center of Granada, off two prominent streets, the Gran Vía de Colón and the calle de San Jerónimo. The Capilla Real abuts the cathedral's eastern edge.

Albaicín. Bus: 7 to calle de Pagés.

This old Arab quarter, on one of the two main hills of Granada, doesn't belong to the city of 19th-century buildings and wide boulevards. It, and the surrounding gypsy caves of Sacromonte, are holdovers from an older past. The Albaicín once flourished as the residential section of the Moors, even after the city's reconquest, but it fell into decline when the Christians drove them out. This narrow labyrinth of crooked streets escaped the fate of much of Granada, which was torn down in the name of progress. Fortunately, it has been preserved, as have its cisterns, fountains, plazas, whitewashed houses, villas, and the decaying remnants of the old city gate. Here and there, you can catch a glimpse of a private patio filled with fountains and plants, a traditional elegant way of life that continues.

Monasterio Cartuja. Camino de Alfacar, s/n. ☎ **958-16-19-32.** Admission 350 ptas. ($2.35). Daily 10am–1pm and 4–7pm (closes at 6pm in winter). Bus: 8 from cathedral.

This 16th-century monastery, off the Albaicín on the outskirts of Granada, is sometimes called the "Christian answer to the Alhambra" because of its ornate stucco and marble and the baroque Churrigueresque fantasy in the sacristy. Its most notable paintings are by Bocanegra, its outstanding sculpture by Mora. The church of this Carthusian monastery was decorated with baroque stucco in the 17th century and its 18th-century sacristy is an excellent example of latter-day baroque style. Napoléon's armies killed St. Bruno here, and La Cartuja is said to be the only monument of its kind in the world. Sometimes one of the Carthusian monks will take you on a guided tour.

Casa-Museo Federico García Lorca. Virgen Blanca, 6, Fuentevaqueros. ☎ **958-51-64-53.** Admission 200 ptas. ($1.35). Oct 7–Mar 31, 10am–7pm, 4-6pm; Apr 1–June 30, 10am–1pm, 5–7pm; July 1–Sept 30, 10am–1pm, 6–8pm.

Poet and dramatist Federico García Lorca spent many happy summers with his family here at their vacation home. He had moved to Granada in 1909, a dreamy-eyed schoolboy, and he was endlessly fascinated with its life, including the Alhambra and the gypsies, whom he was later to describe compassionately in his *Gypsy Ballads*. The house is decorated with green trim and grillwork and filled with family memorabilia, including furniture and portraits. You can look out at the Alhambra from one of its balconies. Visitors may inspect the poet's upstairs bedroom and see his oak desk, stained with ink. Look for the white stool that he carried to the terrace to watch the sun set over Granada. The house is in the Fuentevaqueros section of Granada, near the airport.

Casa-Museo de Manuel de Falla. Antequeruela Alta, 11. ☎ **958-22-94-21.** Admission 250 ptas. ($1.70). Apr–Sept, daily 9am–3pm; Oct–Mar, daily 10am–4pm.

The famous Spanish composer Manuel de Falla, known for his strongly individualized works, came to live in Granada in 1919, hoping to find a retreat and inspiration. He moved into a *carmen* (local dialect for a small white house) just below the Alhambra, and in time befriended García Lorca. In 1922, on the grounds of the Alhambra, they staged the Cante Jondo Festival, the purest expression of flamenco. Today visitors can walk through the gardens of the man who wrote such works as *Nights in the Gardens of Spain* and see his collection of handcrafts and ceramics, along with other personal memorabilia.

Baños Arabes. Carrera del Darro, 31. ☎ **958-22-23-39.** Free admission. Tues–Sat 10am–2pm.

The Moors called these the "baths of the walnut tree." Among the oldest buildings still standing in Granada, and among the best-preserved Muslim baths in Spain, they predate the Alhambra. Visigothic and Roman building materials are supposed to have gone into their construction, and it is remarkable that they escaped destruction during the reign of the Reyes Católicos (Ferdinand and Isabella).

Casa de Castril. Museo Arqueológico, Carrera del Darro, 41. ☎ **958-22-56-40.** Admission 250 ptas. ($1.70). Tues–Sat 10am–2pm. Bus: Neptuno-Albaicín.

This building has always been one of the most handsome Renaissance palaces in Granada. The plateresque facade of 1539 has been attributed to Diego de Siloé. In 1869 it was converted into a museum with a collection of minor artifacts found in the area.

SHOPPING

The **Alcaicería,** once the Moorish silk market, is next to the cathedral in the lower city. The narrow streets of this rebuilt village of shops are filled with vendors selling the arts and crafts of Granada province. For the souvenir hunter, the Alcaicería offers one of the most splendid assortments in Spain of tiles, castanets, and wire figures of Don Quixote chasing windmills. Lots of Spanish jewelry can be found here, comparing favorably with the finest Toledan work. For the window-shopper, in particular, it makes a pleasant stroll.

Artesanía Albaicín (Tienda Eduardo Ferrer Lucena), Calle del Agua, 19 (☎ 958-27-90-56), is a standout in the Arab Quarter for intricately tooled Andalusian leather. The inventory includes useful items (purses, wallets, briefcases, coasters for those glasses of sherry you'll be consuming after your return home) as well as some truly odd items. The shop is open daily from noon to 2pm and 5:30 to 8:30pm.

Casa Ferrer (Tienda Eduardo Ferrer Castillo), Cuesta de Gomérez, 30 (☎ 958-22-18-32), is the granddaddy of music stores in Andalusia. Founded in 1875 by an ancestor of the present owner, it stocks an elegant assortment of Spanish guitars, each a handcrafted work of aesthetic and musical art. Depending on its resonance and degree of ornamentation, guitars range in price from 40,000 to 400,000 ptas. ($268 to $2,680). Open Monday through Saturday from 8:45am to 1:30pm, Monday through Friday from 4:30 to 8:30pm.

At **Tejidos Artistocos Fortuny,** Plaza Fortuny, 1 (☎ 958-22-43-27), you can buy curtains, knotted carpets, nubby-textured draperies, tablecloths, place mats, and fabrics. Much of the merchandise is handwoven. Open Monday through Friday from 10am to 2pm and 5 to 8:30pm.

OUTDOOR PURSUITS

The tourist office (see above) will provide you with a map for hikes through the **Parque de Invierno,** Granada's most popular outdoor recreation and picnic area.

Some trail maps follow the original route of the Muslims or of the snow carriers who brought ice from the mountains to the Alhambra before electricity was invented. To reach the park, take bus number 2 beyond the Alhambra to the Cementerio stop. You'll find the entrance to the park at the cemetery here.

The slopes at **Solynieve** (☎ **958-24-91-00**) offer some of the best skiing in Spain. This is the southernmost ski resort on the European continent, located some 20 miles (32km) from the heart of Granada and reached along a mountain road. Solynieve climbs to a height of 11,000 feet and has snow all year. The up-to-date facilities include chairlifts and cable cars.

WHERE TO STAY
VERY EXPENSIVE

✪ **Parador Nacional de San Francisco.** Alhambra, 18009 Granada. ☎ **800/343-0020** in the U.S., or 958-22-14-40. Fax 958-22-22-64. 36 units. A/C MINIBAR TV TEL. 33,000–39,500 ptas. ($221.10–$264.65) double. AE, DC, MC, V. Free parking. Bus: 3.

This most famous parador in Spain—and the hardest to get into—is set within the grounds of the Alhambra. It's housed in an old brick building with a new annex. The decor is tasteful and the place evokes a lot of history and a rich Andalusian ambience. The parador itself is within a former convent founded by the Catholic monarchs immediately after they conquered the city in 1492. Before that, the building was part of the Muslim complex that included the Alhambra Palace and a mosque built in the middle of the 1300s by Caliph Yusuf I. The bodies of Ferdinand and Isabella were once placed here until their tombs could be readied in the cathedral. One side of the parador opens onto its own lovely gardens and the other fronts the Alhambra itself. From its terrace, you will have views of the Generalife gardens and the Sacromonte caves. Accommodations are generally roomy and comfortable, receiving their last renovation in 1992. Tile bathrooms with such extras as hair dryers add to the allure, and housekeeping is excellent. Try for a room in the older section, which is furnished with antiques; rooms in the more modern wing are less inspired.

Dining: See "Where to Dine" for the parador's restaurant recommendation.
Amenities: Concierge, currency exchange, room service, laundry service.

EXPENSIVE TO MODERATE

Hotel Alhambra Palace. Peña Partida, 2, 18009 Granada. ☎ **958-22-14-68.** Fax 958-22-64-04. 130 units. A/C MINIBAR TV TEL. 21,500 ptas. ($144.05) double; 32,000 ptas. ($214.40) suite. AE, DC, MC, V. Free parking. Bus: destination Alhambra.

Evoking a Moorish fortress, complete with a crenellated roofline, a crowning dome, geometric tile work, and a suggestion of a minaret, this legendary hotel is a good choice. The best known of Granada's hotels, it was built in 1910 in a sort of Mudéjar Revival style in a shady, secluded spot, midway up the slope toward the Alhambra. The private rooms don't live up to the drama of the public areas. Try for a room with a balcony opening onto a view of the city of Granada The court rooms are less desirable because they lack double glazing and are subject to noise at night. Many rooms are spacious and quite comfortable, whereas a few are small and need some restoration. Frankly, whether you love or hate this hotel will depend on your room assignment—some are excellent, some a bit seedy. But there's nothing like this Moorish palace in all of Granada.

Dining/Diversions: The dining room, decorated Arabian Nights style, serves a standard international and Andalusian cuisine, with a glassed-in dining terrace. Have a drink in the bar with its panorama over Granada.

Amenities: Concierge, room service, dry cleaning/valet, twice-daily maid service, baby-sitting, secretarial service, valet parking.

✪ Hotel América. Real de la Alhambra, 53, 18009 Granada. ☎ **958-22-74-71.** Fax 958-22-74-70. 14 units. TEL. 15,500 ptas. ($103.85) double; 18,100 ptas. ($121.25) suite. AE, DC, MC, V. Closed Dec–Feb. Parking nearby 1,500 ptas. ($10.05). Bus: 2.

Located within the ancient Alhambra walls, this is one of the small hotels of Granada. Walk through the covered entryway of this former villa into the shady patio that's lively yet intimate, with large trees, potted plants, and ferns. Other plants cascade down the white plaster walls and entwine with the ornate grillwork. The living room of this homey little retreat is graced with a collection of regional decorative objects; some of the rooms have Andalusian reproductions. Although small, each room is comfortably furnished and well maintained with compact bathrooms with shower stalls. Garden chairs and tables are set out for home-cooked Andalusian meals. The menu is changed every day depending on what was fresh and good at the market that day. If a guest would like to dine in, dinner costs 2,200 ptas. ($14.75) per person. No meals are served on Sunday.

Hotel Carmen. Acera del Darro, 62, 18009 Granada. ☎ **958-25-83-00.** Fax 958-25-64-62. 283 units. A/C MINIBAR TV TEL. 16,000–20,000 ptas. ($107.20–$134) double; 30,000–75,000 ptas. ($201–$502.50) suite. AE, DC, MC, V. Parking 2,000 ptas. ($13.40).

Located about half a mile south of the cathedral on a wide boulevard central to the city's business district, this 1992 hotel offers good service and clean and decent accommodations, each with its own balcony and private bathroom. Many of the rooms are quite small, and the decor is traditional though lackluster. Nonetheless, beds are comfortable and bathrooms well maintained with mainly tub and shower combos. There is lots of polished marble and comfortable sofas scattered throughout a variety of public rooms devoted to reading, card playing, or socializing.

Dining/Diversions: There's a dignified modern restaurant here that serves three-course fixed-price lunches and dinners, as well as a shiny cafeteria for drinks, snacks, and coffee-shop-style food. The Bar Inglés serves drinks amid hardwood paneling, leather upholstery, and patterned fabrics.

Amenities: Laundry, concierge, baby-sitting, room service. Disco, car rentals, business center, shopping boutiques, outdoor swimming pool.

Hotel Granada Center. Avenida Fuentenueva, s/n, 18002 Granada. ☎ **958-20-50-00.** Fax 958-28-96-96. 172 units. A/C MINIBAR TV TEL. 20,500 ptas. ($137.35) double; 60,000 ptas. ($402) suite. AE, DC, MC, V. Parking 1,800 ptas. ($12.05).

One of the most recommendable modern hotels in Granada opened in 1992 adjacent to the university. Its seven-story design allowed its architects to create a marble-floored, glass-covered atrium at its center, where elevators rise in glass cages and potted plants and armchairs are bathed in natural light from above. The midsize rooms are comfortable, monochromatically decorated in neutral beige and earth tones, with ample use of postmodern furniture and slabs of polished stone, especially in the bathrooms.

Dining: Al Zafal, the hotel's restaurant, serves adequate Andalusian and international fare; however, the service could be greatly improved.

Amenities: Room service, laundry and dry-cleaning service, conference rooms, in-house garage, baby-sitting, and currency exchange.

Hotel Meliá Granada. Angel Ganivet, 7, 18009 Granada. ☎ **800/336-3542** in the U.S., or 958-22-74-00. Fax 958-22-74-03. 197 units. A/C MINIBAR TV TEL. 16,900 ptas. ($113.25) double; 20,000 ptas. ($134) suite. AE, DC, MC, V. Parking 1,700 ptas. ($11.40).

A modern and efficient place run by the Meliá chain, about 5 blocks southeast of the Ayuntamiento (Town Hall), this hotel offers comfort with welcomed air-conditioning throughout both the public and guest rooms. Furnished with either extrawide twin or double beds, the rooms are fairly standardized, with well-chosen carpets, art on the walls, and private bathrooms, equipped with phones and hair dryers. One floor is devoted to executive rooms, where guests receive extra pampering. If you don't get a room with a terrace, you haven't missed much, as the views are hardly interesting. Rooms opening onto the street are double-glazed, and some accommodations are for persons with disabilities. The street level is punctuated with old-fashioned arcades, but once inside, you'll find a glossy and contemporary world of clean comfort, soothing monochromes, and efficient service.

Dining/Diversions: The restaurant Mulhacen, featuring international cuisine, serves fixed-price lunches and dinners. There's also a bar.

Amenities: 24-hour room service, concierge, laundry service, plus a sauna and health club, hairdresser/barber, car-rental desk, shopping boutiques.

Hotel Princesa Ana. Constitución, 37, 18014 Granada. ☎ **958-28-74-47.** Fax 958-27-39-54. 61 units. A/C MINIBAR TV TEL. 17,500 ptas. ($117.25) double; 33,000 ptas. ($221.10) suite. AE, DC, MC, V. Parking 1,300 ptas. ($8.70).

Set midway between the railway station and the Plaza de Toros, about 1½ miles (2.5km) northwest of the Alhambra, this balconied five-story hotel welcomes guests into an interior sheathed with marble and decorated in tones of soft pink and white. Although it has been surpassed by newer four-star hotels since its construction in 1989, it maintains an allure for foreign visitors and business travelers. The good-size rooms evoke a British aura, with their dark wood furnishings; the tile bathrooms with dual sinks are well maintained. Each comes with a hair dryer.

Dining/Diversions: On the premises is an intimate bar, plus a restaurant (La Princesa Ana) and an uncomplicated cafeteria.

Amenities: Room service, concierge, currency exchange.

Hotel Rallye. Camino de Ronda, 107, 18003 Granada. ☎ **958-27-28-00.** Fax 958-27-28-62. 80 units. A/C MINIBAR TV TEL. 16,900 ptas. ($113.25) double; 19,500 ptas. ($130.65) suite. AE, DC, MC, V. Parking 1,400 ptas. ($9.40). Bus: 11.

Local residents designate this as one of the best hotels in town, and a relatively good value for the price. Originally built as a three-star hotel in 1964, it was thoroughly upgraded into a four-star format in 1990, and today rises five light-green stories above the neighborhood that surrounds it. It lies within a 15-minute walk of the cathedral, on the northern perimeter of Granada's urban center. Midsize rooms are comfortable and well maintained, with light-green and white color schemes. The in-house restaurant, the Rallye, serves well-prepared meals.

Hotel Residencia Cóndor. Constitución, 6, 18012 Granada. ☎ **958-28-37-11.** Fax 958-28-38-50. 104 units. A/C TV TEL. 15,000 ptas. ($100.50) double. AE, DC, MC, V. Parking 1,300 ptas. ($8.70). Bus: 1, 3, 6, 8, 9, 10, or 11.

The attractive design of this hotel helps make it one of Granada's best in its price range. It's in the center of town, a 5-minute walk from the Alhambra and the cathedral. Many of the small- to medium-size rooms have terraces, and all have light-grained contemporary furniture. The compact tiled bathrooms are equipped with hair dryers. The hotel's restaurant serves both Spanish and international cuisine, and there's also a cafeteria for snacks. Room service is 24 hours a day.

Hotel Saray. Tierno Galván, s/n, 18006 Granada. ☎ **958-13-00-09.** Fax 958-12-91-61. 213 units. A/C MINIBAR TV TEL. 19,500 ptas. ($130.65) double; 52,500–115,000 ptas. ($351.75–$770.50) suite. Rates include breakfast. AE, DC, MC, V. Parking 1,300 ptas. ($8.70).

Just a 10-minute walk south of Granada's historic center, this nine-story hotel offers views of the Sierra Nevada range from some of its upper floors. Built in 1991, it maintains carefully designed rooms whose color scheme varies from one floor to another, incorporating terra-cottas and Andalusian blues and oranges. Rooms are moderate in size for the most part but fairly standard and ordinary, although comfortable, with bedside controls, firm mattresses, mirrored closets, and private safes along with tiled bathrooms with phones and hair dryers.

Dining/Diversions: There's a bar near the reception area, which is sheathed, like many of the other public areas, with pale orange-pink marble, and a lobby-level restaurant, the Saray.

Amenities: The hotel maintains its own outdoor swimming pool for use during the midsummer months. Room service, laundry/dry cleaning, baby-sitting, concierge.

INEXPENSIVE

Hotel Guadalupe. Avenida de los Alixares, s/n, 18009 Granada. ☎ **958-22-34-23.** Fax 958-22-37-98. www.eel.es/guadalupe/default.htm. 58 units. A/C TV TEL. 8,000–11,800 ptas. ($53.60–$79.05) double. AE, DC, MC, V. Parking 1,300 ptas. ($8.70). Bus: 2.

This four-story building, set beside an inclined road leading up to the Alhambra, stands just above the older and more famous Washington Irving Hotel. It was built in 1969, but with its thick stucco walls, rounded arches, and jutting beams, it seems older. The last renovation was in 1993. The comfortably furnished but rather small rooms overlook the Alhambra. The compact tiled bathrooms have adequate shelf space and are equipped with a hair dryer. There's a fifth-floor à la carte restaurant, plus a pleasant bar in the lobby.

Macía Plaza. Plaza Nueva, 4, 18010 Granada. ☎ **958-22-75-36.** Fax 958-22-75-33. 44 units. TV TEL. 8,000 ptas. ($53.60) double. AE, DC, MC, V. Parking 1,300 ptas. ($8.70).

An attractive 1970s hotel at the bottom of the hill leading to the Alhambra, the Macía is a real bargain for what should be a three-star hotel. All the small guest rooms are functionally but still comfortably furnished with good beds and tidy but tiny bathrooms with shower stalls. About half have air-conditioning. Breakfast is the only meal served. Parking is available along the street.

WHERE TO DINE
EXPENSIVE TO MODERATE

Carmen de San Miguel. Plaza de Torres Bermejas, 3. ☎ **958-22-67-23.** Reservations recommended. Main courses 2,000–3,100 ptas. ($13.40–$20.75); 3-course menú del día 3,725–6,025 ptas. ($24.95–$40.35). AE, DC, DISC, MC, V. Mon–Sat 1:30–4pm and 8:30–11:30pm. INTERNATIONAL.

Set on the sloping incline leading up to the Alhambra, this likable restaurant offers spectacular views over the city center. Proud of its glassed-in dining room and patio-style terrace whose banks of flowers are changed seasonally, the restaurant serves specialties that include *rabo de toro* (stewed oxtail), an array of such fish dishes as grilled hake and well-seasoned zarzuela (seafood stew), and a (*paletilla de cordero*) shoulder of lamb stuffed with pine nuts and herbs. The food, although good, doesn't quite match the view. The wines are from throughout the country, with a strong selection of Riojas.

Parador Nacional San Francisco. Real de la Alhambra. ☎ **958-22-14-40.** Reservations unaccepted. Main courses 3,000–4,000 ptas. ($20.10–$26.80); fixed-price menu 3,700 ptas. ($24.80). AE, DC, MC, V. Daily 1–4pm and 8:30–11pm. Bus: 2. SPANISH.

Even if you can't afford to stay at this luxurious parador (see "Where to Stay," above), the most famous in Spain, consider taking a meal here. The dining room is spacious, the service is polite, and you gaze upon the rose gardens and a distant view of the Generalife. The set menu at lunch, which changes daily, is repeated in the evening, although you can always order à la carte. At this 16th-century convent built by the Reyes Católicos, you get not only atmosphere, but also a cuisine that features regional dishes of Andalusia and Spanish national specialties. Lunch is the preferred time to dine here, because the terrace overlooking the palace is open then. A light outdoor lunch menu of sandwiches and salads can be ordered on the à la carte menu if you don't want to partake of the heavy major Spanish repast in the heat of the day. The cuisine is competent in every way, although at no point rising to any culinary achievement. Ingredients are fresh and deftly handled by kitchen staff members who prefer to stick to tried-and-true Spanish recipes that have been perfected over the years. When in doubt, order the Andalusian specialties instead of the Spanish national dishes, as most of the chefs are Andalusian and seem more familiar with and better at this style of regional cookery.

Restaurante Cunini. Plaza de la Pescadería, 14. ☎ **958-25-07-77.** Reservations recommended. Main courses 1,200–3,000 ptas. ($8.05–$20.10); fixed-price menu 2,400 ptas. ($16.10). AE, DC, MC, V. Tues–Sun noon–4pm and 8pm–midnight. SEAFOOD.

The array of seafood specialties served at Cunini, perhaps 100 selections, extends even to the tapas served at the long stand-up bar. Many guests move on, after a drink or two, to the paneled ground-floor restaurant, where the cuisine reflects the whole of Spain. Meals often begin with soup—perhaps *sopa sevillana* (with ham, shrimp, and whitefish). Also popular is a deep fry of small fish called a *fritura Cunini*, with other specialties including rice with seafood, *zarzuela* (seafood stew), smoked salmon, and grilled shrimp. Plaza de la Pescadería is adjacent to the Gran Vía de Colón, just below the cathedral.

✪ **Ruta del Valleta.** Carretera Vieja de la Sierra Nevada, km 5.5, Cenés de la Vega. ☎ **958-48-61-34.** Reservations recommended. Main courses 1,000–5,900 ptas. ($6.70–$39.55); fixed-price menus 5,500 ptas. ($36.85) without wine. AE, DC, MC, V. Daily 1–4pm, Mon–Sat 8pm–midnight. ANDALUSIAN.

Despite its origins in 1976 as an unpretentious roadhouse restaurant, this place rapidly evolved into what is usually acclaimed as the best restaurant in or around Granada. It lies within the hamlet of Cenés de la Vega, about 3½ miles northwest of Granada's center, and contains six dining rooms of various sizes, each decorated with a well-planned mixture of English and Andalusian furniture and accessories. (These include a worthy collection of hand-painted ceramics from the region, many of which hang from the ceilings.)

Its owners are a pair of Granada-born brothers, Miguel and José Pedraza, who direct the impeccable service rituals. Menu items change with the season, but are likely to include roast suckling pig; roasted game birds such as pheasant and partridge, often served with Rioja wine sauce; preparations of fish and shellfish, including monkfish with Andalusian herbs and strips of Serrano ham; fillet steak in a morel-studded cream sauce; and a dessert specialty of frozen rice pudding on a bed of warm chocolate sauce. The wine list is said to be the most comprehensive in the region.

INEXPENSIVE

Chikito. Plaza del Campilio, 9. ☎ **958-22-33-64.** Reservations recommended. Main courses 1,000–2,700 ptas. ($6.70–$18.10); fixed-price menu 1,950 ptas. ($13.05). AE, DC, MC, V. Thurs–Tues 1–4pm and 8–11:30pm. Bus: 1, 2, or 7. SPANISH.

Chikito sits across the street from the famous tree-shaded square where García Lorca met with other members of El Rinconcillo (The Little Corner), a dozen young men considered the best and the brightest in the 1920s, when they brought a brief but dazzling cultural renaissance to their hometown. The cafe where they met has now changed its name, but it's the same building. The present-day Chikito is both a bar and a restaurant. In fair weather, guests enjoy drinks and snacks on tables placed in the square; in winter they retreat inside to the tapas bars. There is also a complete restaurant facility, offering *sopa sevillana,* shrimp cocktail, Basque hake, baked tuna, oxtail, *zarzuela* (seafood stew), grilled swordfish, and Argentine-style veal steak. Regrettably, this literary shrine has barely civil waiters, who obviously lack patience with newcomers. You may want to skip dinner here and settle only for tapas and a glass of sherry at the bar.

La Nueva Bodega. Cetti Merriem, 9. ☎ **958-22-59-34.** Reservations recommended. Platos combinados 925 ptas. ($6.20); main courses 1,000–1,900 ptas. ($6.70–$12.75); fixed-price menus 950–1,300 ptas. ($6.35–$8.70). AE, DC, MC, V. Daily noon–midnight. IBERIAN.

This place seems to be everyone's favorite inexpensive restaurant in Granada. You can enjoy both cafeteria and restaurant service and even order food at the bar, which is cheaper than sitting at a table. The restaurant and cafeteria specialize in *platos combinados* (combination plates). This doesn't mean that you get everything on one plate. You might be served chicken soup, followed by an omelette, then swordfish Milanese style, along with bread and a simple dessert. In addition, the restaurant offers fixed-price menus that are both filling and well prepared. Specialties are from not only Andalusia but all of Iberia, including Portugal.

Mesón Antonio. Ecce Homo, 6. ☎ **958-22-95-99.** Main courses 1,000–2,000 ptas. ($6.70–$13.40). AE, MC, V. Mon–Sat 2–3:30pm and 9–10:30pm. Closed June–Sept. SPANISH.

This appealing and unpretentious restaurant, established in 1980, is one floor above street level in an unassuming 1740s house, whose address is a bit hard to find. (The narrow street on which it's found lies a few steps from the landmark Campo del Príncipe.) You'll traverse a communal patio before climbing a flight of stairs to reach the simply decorated dining room. All of the specialties served here are prepared in wood-burning ovens. These might include roasted lamb in local herbs, zarzuela (seafood stew), several different versions of steaks, and such vegetables as fresh asparagus and roasted leeks au gratin.

Polinario. Real de la Alhambra, 3. ☎ **958-22-29-91.** Reservations recommended. Luncheon buffet 1,350 ptas. ($9.05). MC, V. Daily 9am–4pm; bar daily 9am–7pm. Bus: 2. SPANISH.

Although its food is usually somewhat ordinary, this simple restaurant is one of only three restaurants within the walled confines of the Alhambra. (Another is the dining room within the local parador, which, while preferable, is also more expensive.) The Polinario enjoys an enviable position within a very old building across from the Palace of Carlos V, and, as such, does a thriving lunch business every day with participants of organized tours. By the end of a hot day, the luncheon buffet might be a bit fatigued, but the Spanish cooking is adequate, and usually includes a selection of salads, soups, meats, and desserts.

Restaurant Mirador de Moraima. Calle Pianista Garcia Carillo, 2. ☎ **958-22-82-90.** Reservations recommended. Main courses 1,300–2,300 ptas. ($8.70–$15.40). AE, MC, V. Mon–Sat 1:30–3:30pm and 8:30–11:30pm. ANDALUSIAN/ SPANISH.

Facing the Alhambra, within a solidly built antique house that has witnessed the arrival and departure of thousands of diners since it was established in 1988, this is a large, rambling, and well-recommended restaurant with a half-dozen dining rooms and three separate outdoor terraces. The hardworking staff prepares large quantities of such dishes as roasted goat in wine sauce, slabs of beefsteak with a sauce of aromatic herbs, several different preparations of codfish, grilled Spanish sausages, and roasted lamb. Any meal might begin with a bowl of gazpacho. Don't expect subtlety or big-city sophistication here—what you'll get is generous portions of good cooking and a deeply entrenched pride in the region's rural traditions.

Restaurant O Caña. Plaza de Realejo 7. ☎ **958-25-64-70.** Reservations not necessary. Main courses 700–2,000 ptas. ($4.70–$13.40); fixed-price menu 900 ptas. ($6.05). AE, DC, MC, V. Daily 1–4pm and 7:45–11:45pm. SPANISH.

Set behind a mosaic-sheathed facade, within an antique building in Granada's Jewish Quarter, this recommended site has a long and highly appealing bar near its entrance, a salon where you might be tempted to sit down before a meal with a glass of sherry, and a well-managed dining room. Here portions are generous, well flavored, and authentic to the old-time traditions of Andalusia. Since it was established in 1905, the site has turned out endless versions of its specialties (bull's tail, grilled *solomillo* of beef-steak, Spanish sausages, grilled breast of duck, and endless amounts of suckling pig and roasted lamb). It has earned the loyalty of several generations of local families, many of whom arrive en masse to dine together, especially on Sundays.

Restaurante Sevilla. Calle Oficios, 12. ☎ **958-22-12-23.** Reservations recommended. Main courses 1,100–3,200 ptas. ($7.35–$21.45); fixed-price menu 2,500 ptas. ($16.75). AE, DC, MC, V. Daily 1–4pm, Mon–Sat 8–11pm. SPANISH/ANDALUSIAN.

Attracting a mixed crowd of all ages, the Sevilla is definitely *típico*, with an upbeat elegance. In the past, you might have seen El Cordobés (when he was Spain's leading bullfighter), Brigitte Bardot, or even Andrés Segovia dining here. Even before them, the place had been discovered by García Lorca, a patron in the 1930s, and Manuel de Falla. Our most recent meal here included gazpacho, Andalusian veal, and caramel custard, plus bread and the wine of Valdepeñas. To break the gazpacho monotony, try *sopa virule,* made with pine nuts and chicken breasts. For a main course, we recommend the *cordero a la pastoril* (lamb with herbs and paprika). The best dessert is bananas flambé. You can dine inside, where it is pleasantly decorated, or have a meal on the terrace. Sevilla also has a bar. You'll find the place in the center of town opposite the Royal Chapel, near Plaza Isabel la Católica.

GRANADA AFTER DARK
DRINKS & TAPAS

A good place to begin your nightlife wanderings is along the **Campo del Principe,** where at least seven old-fashioned tapas bars do a rollicking business during the cool of the evening. Our favorite among these is **La Esquinita,** Campo del Principe, s/n (☎ **958-22-71-06**). Small, atmospheric, and sometimes claustrophobic, it serves a clientele that mostly eats standing up, sometimes spilling into the street, rather than sitting at any of the trio of small tables. A specialty tapas dish here is a *ración* of fried fish that tastes absolutely sublime when accompanied by wine or cold beer.

Another good spot on the same street, which is bathed in an atmospheric and antique-looking patina of its own, is **Casa Paco,** Campo del Principe, s/n (no phone). Each of the tapas bars within this review opens around noon every day but becomes really appealing between 9pm and around 3am.

A perennial favorite, set directly in front of the cathedral, is **El Bodegas Castañera,** calle Almiraceros, s/n (☎ **958-22-97-06**). Inside, rows of antique wine barrels and exposed masonry evoke many generations of wine connoisseurs, whose ranks you'll be tempted to join thanks to the fact that virtually nothing has been changed within this place in several generations.

Another contender for your bar business is **Casa Henrique,** calle Acero de Darro, s/n (no phone), an old-fashioned masonry-sided hole-in-the-wall lined with antique barrels of wine and sherries. Its specialty tapas consist of thin-sliced Serrano ham and heaping platters of mussels steamed with herbs and white wine.

One of the most especially sought-after tapas bars in Granada (at least by us) is **Casa Vino del Agua,** calle Algibe de Trillo (☎ **958-22-43-56**), a small, well-maintained bar with an adjoining restaurant, set within a small garden in the heart of the Albaicín. Everyone agrees that the cooling nighttime breezes show off this convivial spot to its best advantage. Don't expect full-fledged platters, as its strength revolves around small-scale portions of cheeses, pates, and salads, which go especially well with glasses of wine and beer.

An equally historic spot that's graced with a verdant patio loaded with plants and shrubs, is **Bar Pilar del Toro,** calle Hospital de Santa Ana, 12 (☎ **958-22-38-47**), that's set near Granada's cathedral and the Plaza Nueva. A more modern, larger bar is **Bar Torcuato,** calle Pages, 31 (no phone). Its even larger competitor, **La Gran Taverna,** Plaza Nueva, 12 (☎ **958-22-88-46**), is a modern, bustling, and irreverent site that attracts coffee- and wine-tasters, as well as lovers of sliced Serrano ham, fondues, and liqueurs throughout the day and evening. Another site with a more modern, yet firmly traditional, decor, is **Bar Europa II,** calle Elvira, 1 (no phone); and there is a roughly equivalent site nearby, **Bar La Mancha,** calle Joaquin Corta, 10 (☎ **958-22-89-68**).

THE GYPSY CAVES OF SACROMONTE

These inhabited gypsy caves are the subject of much controversy. Admittedly, they are a tourist trap, one of the most obviously commercial and shadowy rackets in Spain. Still, the caves are a potent-enough attraction, if you follow some rules.

Once thousands of gypsies lived on the "Holy Mountain," so named because of several Christians martyred here. However, many of the caves were heavily damaged in the floodlike rains of 1962, forcing hundreds of the occupants to seek shelter elsewhere. Nearly all the gypsies remaining are in one way or another involved with tourism. (Some don't even live here—they commute from modern apartments in the city.)

When evening settles over Granada, loads of visitors descend on these caves near the Albaicín, the old Arab section. In every cave you'll hear the rattle of castanets and the strumming of guitars, while everybody in the gypsy family struts his or her stuff. Popularly known as the *zambra,* this is intriguing entertainment only if you have an appreciation of the grotesque. Whenever a gypsy boy or girl comes along with genuine talent, he or she is often grabbed up and hustled off to the more expensive clubs. Those left at home can be rather pathetic in their attempts to entertain.

One of the main reasons for going is to see the caves themselves. If you're expecting primitive living, you may be in for a surprise—many are quite comfortable, with conveniences like telephones and electricity. Often they are decorated with copper and ceramic items—and the inhabitants need no encouragement to sell them to you.

If you want to see the caves, you can walk up the hill by yourself. Your approach will already be advertised before you get here. Attempts will be made to lure you inside one or another of the caves—and to get money from you. Alternatively, you can book an organized tour, arranged by one of the travel agencies in Granada. Even at the end of one of these group outings—with all expenses theoretically paid in advance—there is likely to be an attempt by the cave dwellers to extract more money from you. As soon as the *zambra* ends, hurry out of the cave as quickly as possible. Many readers have been critical of these tours.

During the *zambra,* refuse to accept a pair of castanets, even if offered under the friendly guise of having you join in the fun. If you accept them, the chances are that you'll later be asked to pay for them. Buying anything in these caves is not recommended. Leave your jewelry at your hotel, and don't take more money than you're prepared to lose.

A visit to the caves is almost always included as part of the morning and (more frequently) afternoon city tours offered every day by such companies as **Grana Vision** (☎ **958-13-58-04**). Night tours of the caves (when the caves are at their most eerie, most evocative, and, unfortunately, most larcenous) are usually offered only to those who can assemble 10 or more persons into a group. This might have changed by the time of your visit, so phone a reputable tour operator, such as Grana Vision, to learn if any newly developed options are available.

FLAMENCO

The best flamenco show in Granada is staged at **Jardines Neptuno,** calle Arabial, s/n (☎ **958-25-11-12**), nightly at 10:15pm. The acts are a bit racy, even though they have been toned down considerably for today's audiences. In addition to flamenco, performers attired in regional garb do folk dances and give guitar concerts. The show takes place in a garden setting. There's a high cover charge of 3,800 ptas. ($25.45), but it includes a drink that you can nurse all evening. It's best to take a taxi here.

DANCE CLUBS

If you eventually tire of bodega-crawling, you might be tempted as the night progresses to go dancing in either of the town's two most popular discos. The more crowded and convivial of the two, and the one that's best suited to a wide mixture of ages, is **Granada 10,** calle Carcel Baja, 10 (☎ **958-22-40-01**). Open from 12:30pm until 5am nightly, it charges 700 ptas. ($4.70) entrance, a price that includes the first drink. Beer costs 250 ptas. ($1.70). Your other choice is a relatively new locale that has housed a series of (now defunct) discos. At press time, its name was **Meeting Point,** Plaza de Gracia, s/n (no phone). Set at the edge of the old city, it caters more to clients under 25 than its somewhat more dignified competitor. It plays a sometimes alluring mix of South American salsa and merengue, mixed liberally with Spanish pop music and mainstream U.S. disco classics from the '80s.

GAY BARS

Granada has a number of bars, many of which are not exclusively gay but draw a mixed crowd of locals and foreigners. Two of the best bets include **Al Pie de la Vela,** calle del Darro, 35 (☎ **958-22-85-39**), which is a cruisy bar attracting a mostly male clientele of mixed ages, although the 18-to-28 set seems to predominate. The club is open nightly from 9:30pm to 4am. Another local favorite is **Versus,** Carrera del Darro, 25 (☎ **958-22-69-03**), with its gorgeous interior. It lies beside the old Arab baths. In addition to its beautiful bar, Spanish cuisine is served here. The venue attracts both gays and straights of mixed ages. It's open nightly from 9pm to 4am.

The Costa del Sol 8

The mild winter climate and almost-guaranteed summer sunshine have made this razzle-dazzle stretch of Mediterranean shoreline a year-round attraction. From the harbor city of Algeciras, it stretches east to the port city of Almería. Sandwiched in between is a steep, rugged coastline set against the Sierra Nevada. You'll find poor to fair beaches, sandy coves, whitewashed houses, olive trees, lots of new apartment houses, fishing boats, golf courses, souvenir stands, fast-food outlets, and widely varied populations—both human and vegetable.

This coastal strip, quite frankly, no longer enjoys the chic reputation it had in Franco's day. It is overbuilt and spoiled, although you can still find pockets of posh (including Puerto Banús, with its yacht-clogged harbor). One advantage of the area is that, thanks to European Community money, it is easier to get around than ever before. The infamous N-340 highway from Málaga to Estepona has become a fast, safe six-lane road. In days of yore, it was the most dangerous highway in Spain.

The coast is probably even better for **golf** than for beaches. The best resorts are **Los Monteros** (☎ 95-277-17-00), in Marbella, which is the leading course; **Parador de Golf** (☎ 95-238-12-55), between Málaga and Torremolinos; **Hotel Atalaya Park** in Estepona (☎ 95-288-90-00); and **Golf Hotel Guadalmina,** also in Marbella (☎ 95-288-22-11). To learn more, pick up a copy of the monthly magazine *Costa Golf* at any newsstand. Many golfers prefer to play a different course at every hotel. Usually, if you notify your hotel reception desk a day in advance, a staff member will arrange a playing time.

Waterskiing and windsurfing are available in every resort, and all types of boats can be rented from various kiosks at all the main beaches. You don't have to search hard for these outfitters—chances are they'll find you.

From June through October the coast is mobbed, so make sure you have a reservation in advance. And keep in mind that October 12 is a national holiday—visitors should make doubly sure of their reservations. At other times, innkeepers are likely to roll out the red carpet.

Many restaurants close around October 15 for a much-needed vacation. Remember, too, that many supermarkets and other facilities are closed on Sunday.

1 Algeciras

422 miles (679km) S of Madrid, 82 miles (132km) W of Málaga

Not really a destination in and of itself, Algeciras is the jumping-off point for Africa—it's only 3 hours to Tangier, in Morocco. If you're planning an excursion, there's an inexpensive baggage storage depot at the ferry terminal. Algeciras is also a base for day trips to **Gibraltar.** For information, check with the Gibraltar Tourist Office, 158 Main St., Gibraltar (☎ **956-77-49-82**). It's open Monday through Friday 10am to 6pm, Saturday 10am to 2pm. If you don't have time to visit "the Rock," you can at least see it from Algeciras—it's only 6 miles (10km) away.

ESSENTIALS

GETTING THERE & DEPARTING   The local RENFE office is at calle Juan de la Cierva (☎ **956-63-02-02**). From Madrid, three **trains** daily make the 6-hour trip; the fare is 4,500 ptas. ($30.15). From Málaga, there are three trains daily; the fare is 2,015 ptas. ($13.50). The trip takes 5½ hours and runs along most of the Costa del Sol, including Marbella and Torremolinos. Trains leave Seville (6 hours) and Granada (5½ hours) three times a day. From either city, the fare is 2,950 ptas. ($19.75).

Various independent **bus companies** serve Algeciras. Empresa Portillo, Avenida Virgen de Carmen, 15 (☎ **956-65-10-55**), 1½ blocks to the right when you exit the port complex, runs nearly a dozen buses a day along the Costa del Sol to Algeciras from Málaga. It also sends two buses a day to Córdoba (6 hours) and two buses a day to Granada (5 hours). To make connections to or from Seville, use Empresa La Valenciana, Viajes Koudubia, calle Juan de la Cierva, 5 (☎ **956-60-34-00**). Six buses a day go to Jerez de la Frontera, and eleven to Seville. **Transporres Generales Comes,** Hotel Octavio, calle San Bernardo, 1 (☎ **956-65-34-56**), sells tickets to **La Línea,** the border station for the approach to Gibraltar.

Most visitors in Algeciras plan to cross to Tangier, Morocco. **Ferries** leave every hour on the hour daily from 8am to 10pm. A Class A ticket costs 4,500 ptas. ($30.15) per person, a Class B ticket 3,200 ptas. ($21.45). To transport a **car** costs at least 9,900 ptas. ($66.35) per vehicle, and cars aren't transported in stormy weather. Discounts are available: 20% for EurailPass holders, 30% for InterRail pass holders, and 50% for children. The price of tickets is the same at the dozens of travel agencies scattered throughout the town; don't bother shopping around. There is no central number to call for ferry information.

The **Carretera de Cádiz** (E-15/N-340) runs from Málaga west to Algeciras. If you're driving south from Seville (or Madrid), take highway N-IV to Cádiz, then connect with the N-340/E-5 southwest to Algeciras.

VISITOR INFORMATION   The **tourist information office,** at Juan de la Cierva (☎ **956-57-26-36**), is open Monday through Friday 9am to 2pm.

WHERE TO STAY

Hotel Alarde. Alfonso XI, 4, 11201 Algeciras. ☎ **956-66-04-08.** Fax 956-65-49-01. 78 units. A/C TV TEL. 8,600 ptas. ($57.60) double. AE, DC, MC, V. Parking 1,000 ptas. ($6.70).

If you want to get away from the tacky, noisy port area, consider this three-star hotel near the Parque María Cristina. It's a central location in a quiet commercial section of town. The small double rooms have balconies and Andalusian-style furnishings, including beds with firm mattresses. The hotel also has a snack bar, restaurant, and laundry. The restaurant, open daily, serves a good-value international and regional fixed-price menu. During our most recent stay, we were impressed with both the staff and the inviting atmosphere.

Hotel Al-Mar. Avenida de la Marina, 2, 11201 Algeciras. ☎ **956-65-46-61.** Fax 956-65-45-01. www.eel.es/etursa/etursa. 192 units. A/C TV TEL. 9,600 ptas. ($64.30) double; from 11,000 ptas. ($73.70) suite. Rates include breakfast. AE, DC, MC, V. Parking 800 ptas. ($5.35).

The three-star Al-Mar is one of the best choices in town, with better rooms than the Alarde. It stands near the port, where the ferries embark for Ceuta and Tangier. The large hotel boasts blue-and-white Sevillian and Moorish decor, as well as three restaurants, a handful of bars, and lots of verdant hideaways. The midsize guest rooms are well maintained, furnished in a Andalusian style, with good beds and tiled baths. A fourth-floor drawing room provides a panoramic view of the Rock.

Hotel Octavio. San Bernardo, 1, 11207 Algeciras. ☎ **956-65-27-00.** Fax 956-65-28-02. 77 units. A/C MINIBAR TV TEL. 15,000–40,000 ptas. ($100.50–$268) double. AE, DC, MC, V. Parking 1,400 ptas. ($9.40).

Beaches: The Good, the Bad & the Ugly

We'd like to report that the Costa del Sol is a paradise for swimmers. Surprisingly, it isn't, although it was the allure of beaches that originally put the "sun" in the Costa del Sol, beginning in the 1950s.

The worst beaches—mainly pebbles and shingles—are found at Nerja, Málaga, and Almuñécar. Moving westward, you encounter the gritty, grayish sands of Torremolinos. The best beaches here are at El Bajondillo and La Carihuela (which borders an old fishing village). Another good stretch of beach is along the meandering strip between Carvajal, Los Boliches, and Fuengirola. In addition, two good beaches—El Fuerte and La Fontanilla—lie on either side of Marbella. However, all these beaches tend to be overcrowded, especially in July and August when mama and papa take the kids to the beach from the hinterlands. Crowding is worst on Sundays from May through October, when beaches are overrun with family picnickers as well as sunbathers.

All public beaches in Spain are free, and you shouldn't expect changing facilities. There might be a cold shower on the major beaches, but that's it.

Although it's not sanctioned or technically allowed by the government, many women, especially those from France, go topless on the beaches. Nudity is common on some of the less frequented beaches, although it is against the law; if you indulge, you will be subject to arrest by the civil guard. Many bathers flout the law and go nude anyway, but it's not advised. If you want to bare it all, head for the Costa Natura, about 2 miles (3km) west of Estepona. This is the site of the only official nudist colony along the Costa del Sol.

Conveniently located in the center of town near the railway station, the Octavio is our second choice after the Reina Cristina (and it's more affordable). It's decorated with reproductions of English antiques, which contrast sharply with the building's angular modern exterior. The good-size guest rooms are nicely furnished and well maintained, with excellent beds and tiled bathrooms. An American-style bar serves international drinks, and room service is available daily from 8am to 11pm.

Hotel Reina Cristina. Paseo de la Conferencia, 11207 Algeciras. ☎ **956-60-26-22.** Fax 956-60-33-23. 170 units. AC TV TEL. 22,000 ptas. ($147.40) double; from 45,000 ptas. ($301.50) suite. AE, DC, MC, V. Free parking.

In its own park on the southern outskirts of the city (a 10-minute walk south of the rail and bus stations), this is the town's leading hotel. A Victorian building accented with turrets, ornate railings, and a facade appropriately painted with pastels, the Reina Cristina offers its guests (many of whom are British) a view of the faraway Rock of Gibraltar. On the premises are a small English-language library and a semitropical garden held in place with sturdy retaining walls. The comfortable, high-ceilinged guest rooms have excellent furnishings, including comfortable beds and tiled baths.

Dining: La Parilla is the more formal à la carte restaurant, and the Andalucía is buffet style. There's also a bar.

Amenities: Room service (7am to midnight), laundry and valet, concierge, babysitting, sauna, indoor and outdoor swimming pools, tennis courts.

WHERE TO DINE

Because Algeciras is not distinguished for its restaurants, many visitors dine at their hotels instead of taking a chance at the dreary little spots along the waterfront.

La Capilla. Calle Murillo, s/n. ☎ **956-65-28-00.** Reservations recommended. Main courses 1,550-3,950 ptas. ($10.40–$26.45). MC, V. Mon–Sat 2–4:30pm and 9pm–midnight. SPANISH.

In a deconsecrated chapel in Algeciras's historic core, this restaurant provides a soothing and (usually) cool respite from the city's dust, noise, and heat. There's room for only about 50 diners in one large and one small dining room, and the menu incorporates Spain's most popular dishes. Expect hearty soups, grilled beefsteak or entrecôte, pork chops, chicken breasts, Spanish sausages, and veal. Fish is fresh and flavorful, with a special emphasis on hake, swordfish, squid, octopus, red snapper, mullet, and cod.

2 Tarifa

14 miles (22km) W of Algeciras, 443 miles (713km) S of Madrid, 61 miles (98km) SE of Cádiz

Instead of heading east from Algeciras along the Costa del Sol, we'd suggest a visit west to Tarifa. The old Moorish town is the southernmost point in Europe. After leaving Algeciras, the roads climb steeply, and the drive to Tarifa is along one of Europe's most splendid coastal routes. In the distance you'll see Gibraltar, the straits, and the green hills of Africa—in fact, you can sometimes get a glimpse of houses in Ceuta and Tangier on the Moroccan coastline.

Named for the Moorish military hero Tarik, Tarifa has retained more of its Arab character than any other town in Andalusia. Narrow cobblestoned streets lead to charming patios filled with flowers. The main square is the Plaza San Mateo.

Two factors have inhibited the development of Tarifa's beautiful 3-mile (5km) white beach, the Playa de Lances: It's still a Spanish military zone, and the wind blows almost half the time. For windsurfers, though, the strong western breezes are unbeatable. Tarifa is filled with shops that rent windsurfing equipment and give advice about the best locales.

Many visitors also come to see Tarifa's historical artifacts and wander its crumbling ramparts. The **Castle of Tarifa,** site of a famous struggle in 1292 between Moors and Christians, dominates the town. The castle was held by Guzmán el Bueno ("the Good"). When Christians captured his 9-year-old son and demanded surrender of the garrison, Guzmán tossed the Spanish a dagger, saying he preferred "honor without a son, to a son with dishonor." The execution was carried out. Sadly, the castle is not open to the public.

GETTING THERE

From Algeciras, **Transporres Generales Comes,** calle San Bernardo, 1 (☎ **956-65-34-56**), under the Hotel Octavio, runs several buses daily to Tarifa. The trip takes 30 minutes and costs 215 ptas. ($1.45).

To drive, take the Cádiz highway, N-340/E-5, west from Algeciras.

WHERE TO STAY & DINE

Hotel Balcón de España. La Peña, 2, carretera Cádiz-Málaga, km 77, 11380 Tarifa. ☎ **956-68-43-26.** Fax 956-68-04-72. E-mail: balcones@cherrytel.es. 38 units. TEL. 8,200–12,300 ptas. ($54.95–$82.40) double. AE, MC, V. Closed Oct 20–Apr 1. Free parking.

A surrounding park adds welcome calm at the Balcón de España, located 5 miles (8km) north of Tarifa. Although relatively modest, it's the best place to stay in the area. The hotel offers midsize, well-kept accommodations, an outdoor pool, tennis courts, and access to a nearby riding stable. Some guests prefer to stay in outlying bungalows. In the restaurant, meals are served daily from 1 to 4pm and 8 to 11pm.

Mesón de Sancho. Carretera Cádiz-Málaga, km 94, 11380 Tarifa. ☎ **956-68-49-00.**
Fax 956-68-47-21. 45 units. TV TEL. 6,400–8,150 ptas. ($42.90–$54.60) double. AE, DC,
MC, V. Free parking.

Ten miles (16km) southwest of Algeciras and 6½ miles (10.5km) northeast of Tarifa
on the Cádiz road stands this informal hacienda-style inn, where you can swim in a
pool surrounded by olive trees and terraces. The small rooms are furnished in modest
but contemporary style, with steam heating in the cooler months. In the provincial
dining room, where window walls overlook the garden, a complete lunch or dinner
goes for 2,000 ptas. ($13.40).

3 Estepona

53 miles (85km) W of Málaga, 397 miles (639km) S of Madrid, 28½ miles (46km) E of
Algeciras

A town of Roman origin, Estepona is a budding beach resort, less developed than Marbella or Torremolinos and more likable for that reason. Estepona contains an interesting
15th-century parish church, with the ruins of an old aqueduct nearby (at Salduba). Its
recreational port is an attraction, as are its **beaches:** Costa Natura, km 257 on the
N-340, the first legal nude beach of its kind along the Costa del Sol; La Rada, 2 miles
(3km) long; and El Cristo, only 600 yards long. After the sun goes down, stroll along
the Paseo Marítimo, a broad avenue with gardens on one side, beach on the other.

In summer, the cheapest places to eat in Estepona are the *merenderos,* little dining
areas set up by local fishers and their families right on the beach. Naturally, they feature seafood, including sole and sardine kebabs grilled over an open fire. You can usually order a fresh salad and fried potatoes; desserts are simple.

After your siesta, head for the tapas bars. You'll find most of them—called *freidurías*
(fried-fish bars)—at the corner of the calle de los Reyes and La Terraza. Tables spill
onto the sidewalks in summer, and *gambas a la plancha* (shrimp) are the favorite (but
not the cheapest) tapas to order.

ESSENTIALS

GETTING THERE   The nearest rail links are in Algeciras. However, Estepona is on
the bus route from Algeciras to Málaga. If you're driving, head east from Algeciras
along the E-5/N-340.

VISITOR INFORMATION   The **tourist information office** is at Avenida San
Lorenzo, 1 (☎ **95-280-20-02**). It's open Monday through Friday 9am to 5pm.

WHERE TO STAY

Atalaya Park Golf Hotel & Resort. Carretera de Cádiz, km 168.5, 29688 Estepona.
☎ **95-288-90-00.** Fax 95-288-90-02. www.atalaya-park.es. E-mail: hotel@atalaya-park.es.
469 units. A/C MINIBAR TV TEL. 25,000–33,000 ptas. ($167.50–$221.10) double; 32,000–
46,000 ptas. ($214.40–$308.20) suite. Rates include breakfast. AE, DC, MC, V. Free parking.

Located midway between Estepona and Marbella, this modern resort complex attracts
sports and nature lovers. It's in a tranquil beachside location amid 20 acres of subtropical gardens. The hotel is among the largest, most opulent, and most expensive in
and around Estepona. Its spacious rooms, furnished in elegant modern style, are well
maintained and inviting. Guests have complementary use of the hotel's extensive
sports facilities. Many guests from northern Europe check in and almost never leave
the grounds.

Dining/Diversions: The hotel's three restaurants serve Spanish and international
food. Several bars are scattered throughout the property, and there is a dance club.

Amenities: Baby-sitting, concierge, laundry and valet, room service (breakfast only), sauna, health club, solarium, indoor and outdoor swimming pools, car-rental facilities, boutiques, tennis, water-sports center. Two 18-hole golf courses are nearby.

Buenavista. Avenida de España, 180, 29680 Estepona. ☎ **95-280-01-37.** Fax 95-280-55-93. 38 units. A/C TV. 4,500–6,600 ptas. ($30.15–$44.20) double. AE, MC, V.

This comfortable if modest little five-story residencia beside the coastal road opened in the 1970s. The tiny guest rooms are likely to be noisy in summer because of heavy traffic nearby. Beds are comfortable, and the little tiled bathrooms have shower stalls. Buses from Marbella stop nearby.

✪ **Las Dunas.** Urbani La Boladilla Baja-Noreste, Ctra. de Cádiz, km 163.5, 29689 Estepona. ☎ **95-279-43-45.** Fax 95-279-48-25. www.las-dunas.com. E-mail: lasdunas@las-dunas.com. 73 units. A/C MINIBAR TV TEL. 25,000–40,000 ptas. ($167.50–$268) double; 40,000–65,000 ptas. ($268–$435.50) 2-bedroom suite. Free parking.

One of the great hotels of the Costa del Sol and a member of the "Leading Hotels of the World," Las Dunas attracts fashionable Europeans pursuing the pampered life. Site of a world-class spa, and one of the area's newest resorts, the five-star hotel is a 3-story building constructed in a U-shape, evocative of a gigantic hacienda. The hotel stands in the midst of gardens and fountains; regrettably, the beach nearby is mediocre. Suites outnumber standard doubles, and most units have furnished balconies overlooking the Mediterranean. All are sumptuously comfortable, with luxury mattresses, fine furnishings, and elegant fabrics. The roomy baths have plush towels, hair dryers, and deluxe toiletries.

Dining/Diversions: The Lido restaurant is among the most elegant on the coast. Heinz Winkler, a Michelin-starred German chef, supervises the superb cuisine. The bistro, East Meets West, serves European and Asian food, and there's a piano bar with nightly entertainment.

Amenities: Spa treatments (specialties include thalassotherapy and ionized oxygen treatments), beauty treatments, room service, concierge, library, game room, pool, whirlpool, sauna. The staff makes arrangements for golf.

WHERE TO DINE

Costa del Sol. Calle San Roque, 23. ☎ **95-280-11-01.** Main courses 750–2,000 ptas. ($5.05–$13.40); fixed-price menus 850–2,500 ptas. ($5.70–$16.75); menú especial 1,775 ptas. ($11.90). AE, MC, V. Tues–Sun 8am–3pm and 8–10:30pm. TRADITIONAL ENGLISH.

Recently renovated by its new owners, the Bowens, the Costa del Sol has undergone a complete identity change. The menu caters to a large community of expatriate and traveling Brits, homesick for such dishes as fish-and-chips, steak-and-ale pie, and peppered Ulster pork. The traditional Sunday roast is always a winner. For dessert, try the apple pie or the treacle tart.

4 San Pedro de Alcántara

43 miles (69km) W of Málaga, 42½ miles (68km) E of Algeciras

Situated between Marbella and Estepona, this interesting village contains **Roman remains** that have been officially classified as a national monument. In recent years it has been extensively developed as a resort suburb of Marbella. It now offers some good hotel selections, the best of which is listed below.

To get here, you can take a bus (they leave from Marbella every 30 minutes) or drive on the E-15 west from Marbella.

WHERE TO STAY

Golf Hotel Guadalmina. Hacienda Guadalmina, carretera de Cádiz, 29670 San Pedro de Alcántara. ☎ **95-288-22-11.** Fax 95-288-22-91. www.spa.es/hotel_guadalmina. 70 units. A/C MINIBAR TV TEL. 27,090–32,650 ptas. ($181.50–$218.75) double.

At this large, country club–type resort, the first tee and the 18th green are next to the hotel. The golf course is open to both guests and non-guests. This is an informal place, like a private world on the shores of the Mediterranean. The resort is 50 yards from the beach, 8 miles (13km) east of Marbella, and 1¼ miles (2km) from the center of San Pedro de Alcántara. You reach it by a long driveway from the coastal road. The spacious guest rooms, which open onto the pool/recreation area and the sea, are attractively decorated in traditional Spanish style.

Dining: The hotel offers two excellent dining choices. One is a lunch-only, reed-covered poolside terrace overlooking the golf course and the sea, the other an interior room in the main building, with a sedate clubhouse aura. Informality and good food reign.

Amenities: In addition to the golf course, two seawater swimming pools attract those seeking the lazy life, while the tennis courts appeal to the more energetic.

5 Puerto Banús

5 miles (8km) E of Marbella, 486 miles (782km) S of Madrid

A favorite resort for international celebrities, this coastal village was created almost overnight in the traditional Mediterranean style. It's a dreamy place, the personification of what a Costa del Sol fishing village should look like, but rarely does. Yachts can be moored nearly at your doorstep. Along the harbor front you'll find an array of expensive bars and restaurants. Wandering through the quiet backstreets, you'll pass archways and patios with grilles.

To reach the town, you can take one of 15 buses that run daily from Marbella, or drive east from Marbella along the E-15.

WHERE TO STAY

Hotel Marbella-Dinamar. Urbanización Nueva Andalucía, carretera de Cádiz, km 175, 29660 Puerto Banús. ☎ **95-281-05-00.** Fax 95-281-23-46. 116 units. A/C MINIBAR TV TEL. 16,900–27,000 ptas. ($113.25–$180.90) double. AE, DC, MC, V. Free parking.

Distinctly Moorish in feel, this striking, exotic resort celebrates the Arab domination of what is today Spanish Andalusia. Just 400 yards from both the beach and the borders of Puerto Banús's congested center, it was built around 1980. It has stark white walls, soaring arches, and a central courtyard with a large, abstractly shaped swimming pool. The midsize guest rooms each have simple furniture and two large beds; they look out on either the palm trees beside the pool or the sea. The resort offers two tennis courts (which are floodlit at night), and an indoor swimming pool. Guests have easy access to the casino at the neighboring Plaza Andalucía hotel and to one of the best all-around golf courses along the Costa del Sol. Perhaps best of all, the diversions of Puerto Banús lie within a 3-minute walk.

WHERE TO DINE

Dalli's Pizza Factory. Muelle de Rivera. ☎ **95-281-86-23.** Reservations not accepted. Pastas 795–1,450 ptas. ($5.35–$9.70); meat platters 1,495–2,500 ptas. ($10–$16.75). AE, MC, V. Daily 1–3:30pm and 7pm–1am. PASTA.

The lighthearted, California-inspired philosophy at Dalli's offers a new way to save pesetas in high-priced Puerto Banús. Its specialty is pasta, pasta, and more pasta—served with a portion of garlic bread and a carafe of house wine, it's a great bargain. In a setting that's a cross between high-tech and art deco, you can order nutmeg-flavored ravioli with spinach filling, *penne all'arrabbiata,* lasagna, and several kinds of spaghetti. More filling are chicken cacciatore and scallopini of chicken and veal. These are served with—guess what?—pasta as a side dish. The owners, incidentally, are a trio of Roman-born brothers who were reared in England and educated in California.

Don Leone. Muelle Ribera, 45. ☎ **95-281-17-16.** Reservations recommended. Main courses 1,150–3,400 ptas. ($7.70–$22.80). AE, MC, V. Year-round daily 8pm–2am; late Sept to late June also daily 1–4pm. Closed Nov 21–Dec 21. INTERNATIONAL.

Many residents in villas around Marbella drive to this luxuriously decorated dockside restaurant for dinner, and it gets crowded at times. Begin with the house minestrone, then follow with pasta in Bolognese or clam sauce; lasagna is also a regular treat. Meat specialties include veal parmigiana and roast baby lamb, and the fish dishes are also worth a try, especially the *frita mista del pescados* (mixed fish fry). The food is competently prepared with fresh ingredients, although at times it fails to capture authentic Spanish flavor. The wine list is one of the best along the coast.

La Taberna del Alabardero. Muelle Benabola, A2. ☎ **95-281-27-94.** Reservations required. Main courses 2,100–3,500 ptas. ($14.05–$23.45). AE, DC, MC, V. Daily 1–4pm and 8pm–midnight. INTERNATIONAL.

This restaurant, the best in the port, lies directly on the harbor, within full view of the hundreds of strolling pedestrians. You can dine inside, but you might have more fun at one of the dozens of outdoor tables. The only hints of upper-crust status are immaculate napery, well-disciplined waiters, and discreet twinkle of expensive jewelry among the blue jeans or formal attire of the fashionable clientele. An armada of private yachts bobs at anchor a few feet away. The cuisine, although good, seems secondary to the see-and-be-seen set that hangs out here. Meals might include crepes stuffed with chunks of lobster and crayfish, hake and small clams served in a Basque-inspired green sauce, fillet of duck's breast with green peppercorns or orange sauce, and a wide assortment of desserts.

Red Pepper. Muelle Ribera. ☎ **95-281-21-48.** Reservations recommended. Main courses 2,500–8,000 ptas. ($16.75–$53.60). AE, DC, MC, V. Daily noon–1 or 3am. GREEK/INTERNATIONAL.

Run by an exuberant band of Cypriot expatriates, Red Pepper offers an array of Greek and international dishes in a sunny, sparsely furnished dining room. Selections include Hellenic chicken soup, moussaka, a variety of well-seasoned grilled meats, lots of fish, calf's liver, and lamb on a skewer in the Greek fashion. King prawns and lobster, priced by the gram, are the most expensive main courses. A selection of Greek and Spanish wines usually accompany full meals. You'll find the place in the center of Paseo Marítimo.

6 Marbella

37 miles (59km) W of Málaga, 28 miles (45km) W of Torremolinos, 50 miles (80km) E of Gibraltar, 47 miles (76km) E of Algeciras, 373 miles (600km) S of Madrid

Though it's packed with tourists, and only slightly less popular than Torremolinos, Marbella is still the nicest resort along the Costa del Sol, with some of the regions' best upscale resorts coexisting beside budget hotels. Despite the hordes, Marbella remains a pleasant Andalusian town at the foot of the Sierra Blanca. Traces of the past survive in its palatial town hall, medieval ruins, and ancient Moorish walls. Marbella's most charming area is the **old quarter,** with narrow cobblestone streets and Arab houses, centered around the Plaza de los Naranjos.

The biggest attractions in Marbella, however, are **El Fuerte** and **La Fontanilla,** the two main beaches. There are other, more secluded beaches, but you need your own transportation to get there.

A long-ago visitor, Queen Isabella, was said to have exclaimed *"¡Que mar tan bello!"* ("What a beautiful sea!"), and the name stuck.

ESSENTIALS

GETTING THERE   Twenty buses run between Málaga and Marbella daily. Three buses each come from Madrid and Barcelona.

If you're driving, Marbella is the first major resort as you head east on the N-340/E-15 from **Algeciras.**

VISITOR INFORMATION   The **tourist information office** at Glorieta de la Fontanilla, s/n (☎ **95-277-14-42**), is open Monday through Friday 9:30am to 8pm, Saturday 9:30am to 2pm. Another tourist office is on Plaza de los Naranjos (☎ **95-282-35-50**); it keeps the same hours.

SHOPPING

Some other Andalucian village might inspire you to buy handcrafts (particularly pottery, wood carvings, or wrought iron), but Marbella's international glamour might incite so much insecurity about your wardrobe that you'll want to rush out to accessorize. Should you suddenly feel underdressed, head for the old town. The cornucopia of fashion outlets includes, among many top European designers, every Hollywood starlet's favorite emporium, **Versace,** in the Centro Commercial Benabola, 8, Puerto Banús (☎ **95-281-02-96**).

If art is your passion, tour the art galleries that pepper the town. You'll spot high-rolling investors picking up a contemporary treasure as part of a holiday shopping spree. Two of Marbella's most appealing art galleries lie in the old town: the **Galleria d'Arte Van Gestel,** Plaza de los Naranjos, 11 (☎ **95-277-48-19**), and **Galleria H,** calle 3D (☎ **95-281-12-60**). And if your search for fine art carries over to **Puerto Banús,** consider an overview of the contemporary artwork displayed at the **Sammer Gallery,** Jardines del Puerto, Local 3-A (☎ **95-281-29-95**).

On Saturday morning forget the shops and head with the locals to **Nueva Andalucía flea market**. Everything is likely to be on sale, from Spanish leather goods to local pottery and embroideries.

WHERE TO STAY

Because the setting is ideal, some of the best hotels along the Costa del Sol are in Marbella.

VERY EXPENSIVE

Gran Meliá Don Pepe. Finca Las Merinas, 29600 Marbella. ☎ **800/336-3542** in the U.S., or 95-277-03-00. Fax 95-277-99-54. www.solmelia.es. 185 units. A/C MINIBAR TV TEL. 35,000–45,000 ptas. ($234.50–$301.50) double; 95,000–110,000 ptas. ($636.50–$737) suite. AE, MC, V. Free parking.

The Meliá Don Pepe occupies 6 acres of prize-winning tropical gardens and lawns between the coastal road and the sea. It sits on a broad artificial beach set back from the road. The good-size, well-furnished guest rooms, with tiled bathrooms and wall-to-wall carpeting, face either the sea or the Sierra Blanca range. The latter rooms can be noisy. The facilities are so vast that you could spend a week here and not use them all.

Marbella

Accommodations
El Rodeo **4**
Hotel Munich **3**
Hotel El Castillo **11**
Hotel El Fuerte **1**
Residencia Finlandia **5**
Residencia Lima **6**
Residencia San Cristóbal **7**

Dining
Balcón de la Virgen **10**
La Pescera **8**
Mesón del Museo **9**
Santiago **2**

Dining/Diversions: The hotel has lounges, bars, and restaurants. La Farola grill serves international cuisine.

Amenities: 24-hour room service, laundry and valet, baby-sitting, three swimming pools, tennis courts, health club, Swedish sauna, Turkish baths, boutiques, yacht harbor, golf course.

✪ **Marbella Club.** Bulevar Príncipe Alfonso von Hohenlohe, s/n, 29600 Marbella. ☎ **800/448-8355** in the U.S., or 95-282-22-11. Fax 95-282-98-84. www.marbellaclub.com. E-mail: hotel@marbellackeb.com. 130 units. A/C MINIBAR TV TEL. 25,500–55,500 ptas. ($170.85–$371.85) double; 41,000–77,000 ptas. ($274.70–$515.90) suite; 120,000–250,000 ptas. ($804–$1,675) bungalow. AE, DC, MC, V. Free parking.

Until a few equally chic hotels were built along the Costa del Sol, the snobbish Marbella Club reigned almost without equal as the exclusive hangout of aristocrats and tycoons. Established in 1954, the resort sprawls over a landscaped property that slopes from its roadside reception area down to the beach. Composed of small, ecologically conscious clusters of garden pavilions, bungalows, and small-scale annexes (none of which are higher than two stories), the Marbella sits amid some of the loveliest gardens along the coast.

Hotel rooms along the Costa del Sol don't come much better than these varied and spacious choices, often with canopy beds and always with luxurious mattresses. Most of the bathrooms are roomy and clad in marble, with dual basins, plush towels, and hair dryers. Rooms also have private balconies or terraces. The clientele is discreet, international, elegant, and appreciative of the resort's small scale and superb service.

Dining: The Marbella Club Restaurant moves from indoor shelter to an outdoor terrace according to the season (see "Where to Dine," below). There's a bar in the garden nearby.

Amenities: 24-hour room service, baby-sitting, laundry and valet, massage, excellent concierge service. There are two swimming pools and a beach with a lunch restaurant. Golf can be arranged nearby. Tennis courts at the Marbella Club's twin resort, Puente Romano, 2 minutes away.

✪ **Puente Romano.** Carretera de Cádiz, km 177, 29600 Marbella. ☎ **800/448-8355** in the U.S., or 95-282-09-00. Fax 95-277-57-66. www.puenteromano.com. E-mail: hotel@puenteromano.com. 226 units. A/C MINIBAR TV TEL. 32,000–53,000 ptas. ($214.40–$355.10) double; 40,000–67,000 ptas. ($268–$448.90) suite. AE, MC, V. Free parking. By car, take the E-15 2½ miles (4km) west of Marbella.

This hotel was originally built as a cluster of vacation apartments, which influenced the attention to detail and the landscaping that surrounds it. In the early 1970s, a group of entrepreneurs transformed it into one of the most unusual hotels in the south of Spain. Although it sits close to the frenetic coastal highway midway between Marbella and Puerto Banús, and some critics have dismissed it as "more flash than class," it still enjoys a loyal following.

Inside the complex, arbor-covered walkways pass cascading water, masses of vines, and a subtropical garden. Each of the spacious Andalusian-Mediterranean-style accommodations is a showcase of fabrics, accessories, and furniture. Units have marble bathrooms, electronic safes, and semisheltered balconies with flowers.

Dining/Diversions: Three of the indoor/outdoor bars and restaurants overlook a terra-cotta patio bordered at one end by the stones of a reconstructed Roman bridge, the only one of its kind in southern Spain. There is also a nightclub.

Amenities: 24-hour room service, laundry and valet, baby-sitting; free-form swimming pool with edges bordered by trees, vines, and a waterfall. Sandy beach with water sports, tennis courts, boutiques, gym, sauna, solarium.

EXPENSIVE

Andalucía Plaza. Urbanización Nueva Andalucía, 29660 Apartado, 21, Nueva Andalucía Marbella. ☎ **95-281-20-00.** Fax 95-281-09-96. 410 units. A/C MINIBAR TV TEL. 21,500–28,000 ptas. ($144.05–$187.60) double; from 30,900 ptas. ($207.05) suite. Rates include American breakfast. AE, DC, MC, V.

Built in 1972, the six-story Andalucía Plaza resort complex is showing its age, but it offers more of a Spanish atmosphere than some other pricey choices. On the mountain side of the coastal road between Marbella and Torremolinos, it consists of twin buildings linked by a reception lounge and formal gardens. On the sea side is the hotel's beach club. The public rooms are spacious and decorated in bold, brassy style. The equally luxurious guest rooms have spacious bathrooms and reproduction furnishings in the classic Castilian manner, including twin beds with firm mattresses. The beach is on a 300-plus-foot strip of sand, 4 miles (6km) west of the center of Marbella and a 10-minute walk from Puerto Bánus.

Dining/Diversions: The Córdoba restaurant serves upscale international meals. The Bar Toledo, primarily a watering hole, offers light snacks and suppers. There's also a casino (see "Marbella After Dark," below).

Amenities: Limited room service, concierge, baby-sitting, laundry. Beach club with adjacent sunbathing terraces, tennis courts, two saunas, indoor and outdoor swimming pools, golf course. At the 1,000-berth marina ½ mile away, the hotel will arrange charters for deep-sea fishing.

Don Carlos. Jardines de las Goldondrinas, carretera de Cádiz, km 192, 29600 Marbella. ☎ 95-283-11-40. Fax 95-283-34-29. www.hotel-doncarlos.com. E-mail: don-carlos@ vnet.es. 240 units. A/C MINIBAR TV TEL. 18,500–36,500 ptas. ($123.95–$244.55) double; 32,000–110,000 ptas. ($214.40–$737) suite. AE, DC, MC, V. Free parking.

One of the most dramatic hotels on the coast, the Don Carlos rises on a set of angled stilts above a pine forest. Between the hotel and its manicured beach, the best in Marbella, are 130 acres of award-winning gardens. With cascades of water and thousands of subtropical plants, they require a full-time staff of 22 gardeners. There's far more to this hotel than the modern tower that rises above the eastern edge of Marbella. Its low-lying terraces and elegant eating and drinking facilities attract high-powered conferences from throughout Europe, as well as diners from along the Mediterranean coast. Each of the roomy accommodations has lacquered furniture, and bathrooms boast honey-colored marble and hair dryers. The hotel also offers the finest tennis in the area.

Dining/Diversions: You can dine beside an oversized swimming pool or in La Pergola, where ficus and potted palms decorate hundreds of lattices. A hideaway, Los Naranjos, has a sun-flooded atrium and live piano music. Meals, including elaborate buffets, are served here and in the beachfront cabana. The most popular bar offers English-inspired decor, a panoramic sea view, plenty of sofas, a dance floor, and a musical trio.

Amenities: 24-hour room service, laundry, baby-sitting, three swimming pools, use of five golf courses nearby, saunas, gym, 11 tennis courts. Water sports (extra charge).

Los Monteros. Carretera de Cádiz, km 187, 29600 Marbella. ☎ **95-277-17-00.** Fax 95-282-58-46. www.losmonteros.com. E-mail: monteros@ctv.es. 170 units. A/C MINIBAR TV TEL. 24,200–31,900 ptas. ($162.15–$213.75) double; from 35,200 ptas. ($235.85) suite. Rates include breakfast. AE, DC, MC, V. Free parking.

Los Monteros, located 400 yards from a beach and 4 miles (6km) east of Marbella, is one of the most tasteful resort complexes along the Costa del Sol. Situated between the coastal road and its private beach, it attracts those seeking intimacy and luxury. Its many small public rooms are Andalusian and Japanese in style. There are salons with open fireplaces, a library, and terraces. The midsize guest rooms are brightly decorated, with light-colored lacquered furniture, large marble bathrooms, and terraces.

Dining/Diversions: The hotel has a bar and four restaurants that open onto flower-filled patios, gardens, and fountains. Grill El Corzo is one of the finest grill rooms along the coast. There's soft, romantic music nightly, and the cuisine is a pleasing combination of French and Spanish.

Amenities: 24-hour room service, baby-sitting, laundry and valet. Guests can use the nearby 18-hole golf course, Río Real, free. Several swimming pools, beach club with heated indoor pool, 10 tennis courts, 5 squash courts, riding club and school, fully equipped gymnasium with sauna, massage, and Jacuzzi.

MODERATE

Hotel El Fuerte. Avenida del Fuerte, s/n, 29600 Marbella. ☎ **800/448-8355** in the U.S., or 95-286-15-00. Fax 95-282-44-11. 263 units. A/C MINIBAR TV TEL. 17,800–23,800 ptas. ($119.25–$159.45) double; from 33,600 ptas. ($225.10) suite. Rates include breakfast. AE, DC, MC, V. Parking 650 ptas. ($4.35).

This is the largest and most recommendable hotel in the center of Marbella. Directly on the waterfront, El Fuerte has a balconied angular facade and consists of two six-story towers. Originally built in 1957, it was last renovated in 1994. Catering to a sedate clientele of northern Europeans, it offers a palm-fringed swimming pool across the street from a sheltered lagoon and a wide-open beach. The hotel also has a handful of terraces, some shaded by flowering arbors, which are perfect hideaways for a quiet drink. The midsize guest rooms are contemporary, with piped-in music, terraces, and twin beds with firm mattresses.

The hotel has a coffee shop and a restaurant. The facilities for leisure activities include the pool, a floodlit tennis court, a health club, and a squash court.

INEXPENSIVE

El Rodeo. Victor de la Serna, s/n, 29600 Marbella. ☎ **95-277-51-00.** Fax 95-282-33-20. 100 units. A/C TV TEL. 8,000–14,000 ptas. ($53.60–$93.80) double. AE, DC, MC, V.

Even though this modern hotel stands just off the main coastal road of Marbella, within walking distance of the bus station, the beach, and the old quarter, it is quiet and secluded. The facilities in the seven-story structure include a swimming pool, terrace, sunbathing area, solarium, and a newly renovated piano bar where many guests and locals gather. Elevators whisk you to the sunny, spacious second-floor lounges with country furnishings; there's also a bar with tropical bamboo chairs and tables. Continental breakfast is served in the cheerful breakfast room. The midsize guest rooms are functional, with several shuttered closets, lounge chairs, and white desks. The hotel is year-round; peak season and rates run June through October.

Hostal El Castillo. Plaza San Bernabé, 2, 29600 Marbella. ☎ **95-277-17-39.** 25 units. 4,500–5,000 ptas. ($30.15–$33.50) double. MC, V. Free parking.

At the foot of the castle in the narrow streets of the old town, this small hotel opens onto a minuscule triangular area used by the adjoining convent and school as a playground. There's a small, covered courtyard, and the simple second-floor guest rooms have only inner windows. The spartan rooms are scrubbed clean and have white-tile bathrooms. No morning meal is served, and only a little English is spoken.

Hostal Munich. Calle Virgen del Pilar, 5, 29600 Marbella. ☎ **95-277-24-61.** 18 units. TEL. 4,250 ptas. ($28.50) double. No credit cards.

Set back from the street and shielded by banana and palm trees, this unassuming three-story lodging is just a short walk from the water and the bus station. Some guest rooms have balconies; all are simply furnished but well kept, with good beds. The homey lounge is warm and inviting.

Residencia Finlandia. Finlandia, 12, 29600 Marbella. ☎ and fax **95-277-07-00.** 11 units. TEL. 5,800–6,900 ptas. ($38.85–$46.25) double. AE, DC, MC, V.

The slightly tattered 1970s Finlandia is only a 5-minute walk from the center of the old quarter, and 200 yards from the beach. In the Huerta Grande, a peaceful residential section, it's clean and well run. Guest rooms are spacious but rather plain, with contemporary furnishings. Your bed will be turned down at night.

Residencia Lima. Antonio Belón, 2, 29600 Marbella. ☎ **95-277-05-00.** Fax 95-286-30-91. 64 units. TEL. 12,000 ptas. ($80.40) double. AE, DC, MC, V.

Tucked away in a residential area, right off the N-340/E-15 and near the sea, the Lima is more secluded than other hotels nearby. The modern eight-story structure features plain guest rooms with Spanish provincial furnishings and private balconies.

Residencia San Cristóbal. Ramón y Cajal, 3, 29600 Marbella. ☎ **95-277-12-50.** Fax 95-286-20-44. 97 units. A/C TV TEL. 9,000–11,600 ptas. ($60.30–$77.70) double. MC, V.

In the heart of Marbella, 200 yards from the beach, this 1960s five-story hotel has long, wide terraces and flower-filled window boxes. The small, somewhat tattered guest rooms have walnut headboards, individual overhead reading lamps, and room dividers separating the comfortable beds from the small living areas. Each room has a private terrace—a perfect spot to enjoy breakfast.

A NEARBY PLACE TO STAY

✪ **El Castillo de Monda.** Monda 29110, Málaga. ☎ **095-245-71-42.** Fax 095-245-73-36. www.costadelsol.spa.es/hotel/monda. E-mail: mondas@spa.es. 28 units. A/C TV TEL. 15,000–32,000 ptas. ($100.50–$214.40) double. AE, MC, V. Free parking.

In 1996, a group of entrepreneurs transformed the crumbling ruins of an 8th-century Moorish fortress into the showplace of a sleepy village 7½ miles (12km) north of Marbella. El Castillo de Monda adds a soothing note of calm and quiet to a region that grows glitzier by the year. The ceiling beams came from a demolished convent in Barcelona, the thousands of glazed tiles from the outfit that's been manufacturing the historically accurate accessories for the restoration of the Alhambra. Guest rooms are beautifully maintained, generous in size, and traditionally furnished. The restaurant occupies a cool, high-ceilinged dining room.

WHERE TO DINE
EXPENSIVE

✪ **El Portalón.** Carretera de Cádiz, km 178. ☎ **95-282-78-80.** Reservations recommended. Main courses 1,800–3,200 ptas. ($12.05–$21.45). AE, DC, MC, V. Daily 1pm–12:30am. SPANISH/INTERNATIONAL.

This is one of Marbella's most stylish, sophisticated dining enclaves. It's staff is one of the most urbane and international in town, serving clients from throughout Europe with aplomb and obvious pride. Menu selections include some time-honored Iberian dishes, such as suckling lamb and pig slowly roasted in a wood-burning oven, grilled meats, and impeccably fresh fish imported daily. Calorie-conscious, low-fat dishes are like those you might expect to find at a California spa—lobster salad, grilled sea bass with a julienne of fresh vegetables, and entrecôte of beef with fresh vegetables and red wine sauce (served on the side if you request). A recent addition is an art deco–style pavilion called the "vinoteca," which serves an excellent selection of wines from all over Spain.

The restaurant lies about a mile west of town, beside the road leading to Puerto Banús, across from the beach, and adjacent to the entrance to the Marbella Club.

✪ **La Hacienda.** Urbanización Hacienda Las Chapas, carretera de Cádiz, km 193. ☎ **95-283-12-67.** Reservations recommended. Main courses 2,200–3,200 ptas. ($14.75–$21.45); fixed-price menu 6,815 ptas. ($45.65). AE, DC, MC, V. Summer, daily 8:30–midnight; winter, Wed–Sun 1–3:30pm and 8:30–11:30pm. Closed Nov 15–Dec 20. INTERNATIONAL.

La Hacienda, a tranquil choice 8 miles (13km) east of Marbella, serves some of the best food along the Costa del Sol. In cooler months you can dine in the rustic tavern before an open fireplace. In fair weather, meals are served on a patio partially encircled by open Romanesque arches. The chef is likely to offer foie gras with lentils, lobster croquettes (as an appetizer), and roast guinea hen with cream, minced raisins, and port. The flavorful food is prepared with the freshest ingredients and presented with style. An iced soufflé finishes the meal nicely.

✪ **Marbella Club Restaurant.** In the Marbella Club, Bulevar Príncipe Alfonso von Hohen-lohe, s/n. ☎ **95-282-22-11.** Reservations recommended. Lunch buffet 7,000 ptas. ($46.90); dinner main courses 3,300–8,500 ptas. ($22.10–$56.95). AE, DC, MC, V. Daily 1:30–4pm; summer daily 9pm–12:30am, winter daily 8:30–11:30pm. INTERNATIONAL.

Our favorite meals here have been whenever the staff moves the action onto the terrace in good weather. Lunch is traditionally an overflowing buffet served in the beach club. Dinners are served amid blooming flowers, flickering candles, and the strains of live music—perhaps a Spanish classical guitarist, a small chamber orchestra playing 19th-century classics, or a South American vocalist. Menu items, inspired by European cuisines, change with the season. You might begin with beef carpaccio or lobster salad delicately flavored with olive oil. Specialties include one of the coast's most savory paellas, and tender veal cutlets from Ávila.

Villa Tiberio. Carretera de Cádiz, km 178.5. ☎ **95-277-17-99.** Reservations recommended. Main courses 1,500–2,900 ptas. ($10.05–$19.45). AE, DC, V. Mon–Sat 7:30pm–12:30am. ITALIAN.

Villa Tiberio's proximity to the upscale Marbella Club (a 5-minute walk away) ensures a flow of visitors from that elite hotel. In what was originally built as a private villa during the 1960s, it serves the most innovative Italian food in the region, and attracts the many north European expatriates living nearby. Appetizers include thinly sliced smoked beef with fresh avocados and oil-and-lemon dressing, and *fungi fantasia* (a large wild mushroom stuffed with seafood and lobster sauce). Especially tempting is the *pappardelle alla Sandro*—large flat noodles studded with chunks of lobster, tomato, and garlic. Other versions come with cream, caviar, and smoked salmon. Main dishes include sea bass with cherry tomatoes, basil, and black truffle oil; duck baked with orange and Curaçao liqueur; and *osso bucco* (braised veal shanks).

MODERATE

Balcón de la Virgen. Remedios, 2. ☎ **95-277-60-92.** Reservations recommended. Main courses 875–2,195 ptas. ($5.85–$14.70). AE, DC, MC, V. Daily 7pm–midnight. Closed Tues Nov–May. SPANISH.

In an antique house in the historic core of old Marbella, this restaurant is named after a 200-year-old statue of the Virgin that adorns a wall niche surrounded by flowers and vines. A short walk from the Plaza de los Naranjos, it's popular because of its good food, attentive service, and reasonable prices. The menu—derived mostly from Andalusia and, to a lesser degree, the rest of Spain—features Málaga-style meat stew, baked hake with olive oil and herbs, marinated swordfish, roasted pork, and grilled fillets of beef.

Hostería del Mar. Cánovas del Castillo, 1. ☎ **95-277-02-18.** Reservations recommended. Main courses 1,500–2,100 ptas. ($10.05–$14.05). AE, MC, V. Mon–Sat 1–4pm and 7:30pm–midnight. MEDITERRANEAN.

Consistently good, the Hostería del Mar's cuisine is known throughout the region for being both delicious and unusual. In the dining room, you'll sit beneath decorative ceiling beams and eat off hand-painted porcelain. In summer, there are tables on a tree-shaded patio. Delectable meals might include calves' sweetbreads in mustard sauce, clams stuffed with ratatouille, roast duck with roasted-fig and-cassis sauce, Catalan-style shrimp with chicken, and a casserole of monkfish with white wine sauce, clams, and fresh asparagus. The sumptuous desserts include a selection of cold soufflés. The restaurant is at the beginning of the bypass road that runs beside the Hotel Meliá Don Pepe.

Mesón del Museo. Plaza de los Naranjos, 11. ☎ **95-282-56-23.** Reservations recommended. Main courses 2,250–5,000 ptas. ($15.10–$33.50). AE, DC, MC, V. Mon–Sat 7:30–11pm. Closed Sun Dec 23–May 1, July–Aug. FRENCH.

Mesón del Museo is on the upper floor of an 18th-century building that contains one of the oldest art and antique galleries in Marbella. The dining room is decorated with Iberian accessories and Andalusian antiques. A new chef has recently shifted the menu's focus to French dishes. Try delicious fried Camembert, followed by fillet of sole stuffed with langostines in a champagne sauce. A selection of French and Spanish wines complements the menu.

Santiago. Duque de Ahumada, 5. ☎ **95-277-43-39.** Reservations required. Main courses 800–12,000 ptas. ($5.35–$80.40). AE, DC, MC, V. Daily 1–5pm and 7pm–1am. SEAFOOD/INTERNATIONAL.

As soon as you enter Santiago, the bubbling lobster tanks give you an idea of what's in store. The decor, the tapas bar near the entrance, and the summertime patio join with fresh fish dishes to make this one of the most popular eating places in town. On our most recent visit, we arrived early for lunch and found that the mussels for our mussels marinara were just being delivered. Savory fish soup is well prepared and well spiced. Follow with a generous serving of sole in champagne, or grilled or sautéed turbot. On a hot day, the seafood salad, garnished with lobster, shrimp, and crabmeat and served with a sharp sauce, is especially recommended. In addition to seafood, the menu offers many meat dishes. For dessert, we suggest a serving of Manchego cheese.

INEXPENSIVE

La Pescera. Plaza de la Victoria, s/n. ☎ **95-286-14-04.** Reservations recommended Thurs–Sat night. Main courses 890–3,360 ptas. ($5.95 $22.50). AE, DC, MC, V. Daily 1–3:30pm and 7:30–11pm. ANDALUSIAN.

Beside a historic square in the heart of old Marbella, this is a bustling, well-managed restaurant. It has twin dining rooms, a loyal local clientele, and a reputation for serving well-prepared fish and seafood. There's a worthwhile roster of meat dishes, such as grilled steaks and pork fillets, but most diners opt for fish. Specialties range from working-class dishes such as *bacalao frito* (fried codfish) to more esoteric versions of shellfish and crayfish—kept alive and healthy until the last moment in big on-site holding tanks.

A NEARBY PLACE TO DINE

El Refugio. Carretera de Ojén, C-337. ☎ **95-288-10-00.** Main courses 650–2,250 ptas. ($4.35–$15.10); fixed-price menu 3,750 ptas. ($25.15). AE, DC, MC, V. Daily 1–4pm and 8–10:30pm. SPANISH.

A Marbella Tasca Crawl

To really rub shoulders with the locals and experience a taste of Spain, take your meals in the tapas bars. You can eat well in most places, and Marbella boasts more hole-in-the-wall tapas bar than virtually any other resort town in southern Spain. Even if you set out with a specific place in mind, you'll likely be waylaid en route by a newer, older, bigger, smaller, brighter, or more mysterious joint you want to try. That's half the fun.

Prices and hours are remarkably consistent: The coffee house that opens at 7am will switch to wine and tapas when the first patron asks for it (sometimes shortly after breakfast), then continue through the day dispensing wine, sherry, and more recently, bottles of beer to accompany the food. On average, tapas cost 200 to 1,000 ptas. ($1.35 to $6.70) per *ración*, though some foreign visitors configure them into *platos combinados*.

Tapas served along the Costa del Sol are principally Andalusian in origin, with an emphasis on seafood. The most famous plate, *fritura malagueña*, consists of fried fish based on the catch of the day. Sometimes *ajo blanco*, a garlicky local version of gazpacho, is served, especially in summer. Fried squid or octopus is another favorite, as are little Spanish-style herb-flavored meatballs. *Tortilla* (an omelette, often with potatoes) is the most popular egg dish. Other well-known tapas selections include pungent tuna, grilled shrimp, *piquillos rellenos* (red peppers stuffed with fish), *bacalao* (salt cod), and mushrooms sautéed in olive oil and garlic.

Tapas bars line many of the narrow streets of Marbella's historic core, with rich pickings around La calle del Perral and, to a somewhat lesser extent, calle Miguel Cana. In August especially, when you want to escape wall-to-wall people and the heat and noise of the old town, head for one of the shoreline restaurants and tapas bars called *chiringuitos*. All serve local specialties, and you can order a full meal, a snack, tapas, or a drink. Our favorites include **Los Sardinales,** Playa de los Alicates (☎ **952-83-70-12**), which serves some of the best sangría in the area. You might return later for a succulent seafood dinner. Another favorite hangout is **Chiringuito La Pesquera,** Marbellamar Playa (☎ **952-77-03-38**), where you can order a plate of fresh grilled sardines.

If the summer heat has you down, retreat to the Sierra Blanca, just outside Ojén. Motorists come here to enjoy both the mountain scenery and the cuisine at El Refugio, up in the hills 9 miles (15km) north of Marbella. Meals are served in a rustic dining room, with an open terrace for drinks. Specialties include spicy regional sausages, roast pork, roast chicken, grilled steaks, and in season, local pheasant. The lounge has an open fireplace and comfortable armchairs.

MARBELLA AFTER DARK

There's more international wealth hanging out in the watering holes of Marbella, and a wider choice of glam (or pseudoglam discos), than you'll find virtually anywhere else in the south of Spain. Foremost among these is the chic **Oliva Valer,** in the Hotel Puente Romano, C.N. 340, km 177 (☎ **95-282-09-00**). A worthwhile, very stylish alternative, is **O! Marbella,** C.N. 340, km 192 (☎ **95-283-54-77**), adjacent to the Hotel Don Carlos. For a nightclub with a bit of Italian flair, consider **La Notte,** "Las Lomas" de Marbella Club (☎ **95-282-60-24**), where people often come for an after-dinner drink from the upscale restaurant La Méridiana, nearby.

If you're in the heart of historic Marbella, enjoy a night in the bodegas and taverns of the old town. One that's conveniently located adjacent to one of the town's widest thoroughfares is **Bodega La Venensia,** Pasoa del Duca Ahumada (no phone). Its wide choice of sherries, wines, and tapas welcomes lots of chattering patrons. In the old town, you might check out **Bar El Estrecha,** calle San Lazaro, s/n (no phone) or its nearby competitor, **Bar Mattutte,** in the calle Arte, s/n (no phone). One with a particularly large assortment of wines is **Vinacoteca,** in the calle Peral, s/n (no phone). Dedicated to the inventory of as many Spanish wines as possible, it provides the opportunity to compare the vintages produced in the surrounding region.

The best flamenco club in town is **Ana María,** Plaza del Santo Cristo, 4-5 (☎ **95-277-56-46**). We think it's simultaneously the most authentic place, and the safest for foreign visitors with a limited knowledge of Spanish. The long, often-crowded bar area sells tapas, wine, sherry, and a selection of more international libations. On the stage, singers, dancers, and musicians performs flamenco and popular songs. This is late-night entertainment—the doors don't open till 11pm, and the crowd really gets going between midnight and 4am. It's closed November to March. Drink prices start at 1,300 ptas. ($8.70); the cover charge is 2,600 ptas. ($17.40).

Six miles (10km) west of Marbella, near Puerto Banús, **Casino Marbella,** Andalucía Plaza, Urbanización Nueva Andalucía (☎ **95-281-40-00**), this casino is on the lobby level of the Andalucía Plaza resort complex (see above). Unlike the region's competing casino, at the Hotel Torrequebrada, the Marbella does not offer cabaret or nightclub shows. The focus is on gambling, in which mobs of visitors from northern Europe engage with abandon. Individual games include French and American roulette, blackjack, punto y banco, craps, and chemin de fer.

You can dine before or after gambling in the Casino Restaurant, a few steps above the gaming floor. Meals go for about 3,800 ptas. ($25.45) per person, including wine. Jackets are not required for men, but shorts and T-shirts will be frowned on. The casino is open daily from 8pm to 4 or 5am. There's a cover charge of 600 ptas. ($4); a passport is required for admission.

7 Fuengirola & Los Boliches

20 miles (32km) W of Málaga, 64½ miles (104km) E of Algeciras, 356½ miles (574km) S of Madrid

The fishing towns of Fuengirola and Los Boliches lie halfway between the more famous resorts of Marbella and Torremolinos. The promenade along the water stretches some 2½ miles (4km). Less developed Los Boliches lies just half a mile from Fuengirola.

These towns don't have the facilities or drama of Torremolinos and Marbella. Except for two major luxury hotels, however, Fuengirola and Los Boliches are cheaper, and that has attracted hordes of budget-conscious European tourists.

The ruins of **San Isidro Castle** can be seen from a promontory overlooking the sea. The **Santa Amalja, Carvajal,** and **Las Gaviotas beaches** are broad, clean, and sandy. Everybody goes to the big **flea market** at Fuengirola on Tuesdays.

ESSENTIALS

GETTING THERE   From Torremolinos, take the Metro at La Nogalera station (under the RENFE sign). Trains depart every 30 minutes. The fare is 250 ptas. ($1.70).

Fuengirola is on the main Costa del Sol bus route from either Algeciras in the west or Málaga in the east.

If you're driving from Marbella, take the N-340/E-15 east from Marbella.

VISITOR INFORMATION The **tourist information office,** Avenida Jesús Santos Reino, 6 ☎ 95-246-74-57), is open Monday through Friday 9:30am to 2pm and 5 to 8pm, Saturday 10am to 1pm.

WHERE TO STAY

✪ **Byblos Andaluz.** Urbanización Mijas Golf, 29640 Fuengirola. ☎ **95-246-02-50.** Fax 95-247-67-83. 144 units. A/C MINIBAR TV TEL. 29,000–42,000 ptas. ($194.30–$281.40) double; 44,500–190,000 ptas. ($298.15–$1,273) suite. AE, DC, MC, V. Free parking.

This luxurious resort, with excellent recreational facilities, is in a golf club setting 3 miles (5km) from Fuengirola and 6 miles (10km) from the beach. The grounds contain a white minaret, Moorish arches, tile-adorned walls, and an orange-tree patio inspired by the Alhambra grounds. The large rooms and suites are elegantly and individually designed and furnished in Roman, Arabic, Andalusian, and rustic styles. Private sun terraces and lavish bathrooms add to the comfort.

Dining: Choices include Le Nailhac, which serves French food, and El Andaluz, with its regional and Spanish specialties.

Amenities: The resort's two 18-hole Robert Trent Jones golf courses, tennis courts, spa facilities, gymnasium, and two outdoor swimming pools bask in the Andalusian sunshine. The health spa is in a handsome classic structure, Mijas Thalasso Palace. Laundry and valet, baby-sitting, room service, sauna, solarium, three indoor pools.

Florida. Paseo Marítimo, s/n, 29640 Fuengirola. ☎ **95-247-61-00.** Fax 95-258-15-29. 116 units. TV TEL. 9,500–11,500 ptas. ($63.65–$77.05) double. AE, DC, MC, V.

In the semitropical garden in front of the Florida, guests can enjoy refreshments under a wide, vine-covered pergola. During the summer there is live music and flamenco shows. Most of the small guest rooms have balconies overlooking the sea or mountains, although furnishings and decor are a bit bleak and severe. The floors are tile, and plastic furniture abounds, particularly in the lounge. It's a 10-minute walk from the train station.

Hostal Sedeño. Don Jacinto, 1, 29640 Fuengirola. ☎ **95-247-47-88.** 34 units. 3,700–5,300 ptas. ($24.80–$35.50) double. No credit cards.

The Sedeño is 3 minutes from the beach, in the heart of town. Its modest lobby leads to a larger lounge furnished with antiques and reproductions. You pass a small open courtyard where stairs lead to the second- and third-floor guest rooms. They're small and basic, with balconies that overlook a small garden with fig and palm trees, plus a terrace. There is no restaurant (not even breakfast is served), but there is a cafe, and many restaurants and cafes nearby.

Las Pirámides. Paseo Marítimo, 29640 Fuengirola. ☎ **95-247-06-00.** Fax 95-258-32-97. www.costadelsol.spa.es/hotel/piramide/index.htm. E-mail: piramides@vnet.es. 316 units. A/C MINIBAR TV TEL. 15,000-21,500 ptas. ($100.50–$144.05) double; 18,000–23,500 ptas. ($120.60–$157.45) suite. Rates include breakfast. AE, MC, V. Parking 1,000 ptas. ($6.70).

This resort, a favorite of northern Europeans and tour groups, consists of two 10-story towers capped with pyramidal roofs. It's a citylike compound, about 50 yards from the beach, with just about every kind of diversion: flamenco shows on the large patio, a cozy bar and lounge, traditionally furnished sitting rooms, a coffee shop, a poolside bar, and a gallery of boutiques and tourist facilities, such as car-rental agencies. All the good-size guest rooms have slick modern styling, as well as terraces. There is room service, as well as laundry/valet services and baby-sitting.

WHERE TO DINE

Casa Vieja. Avenida de Los Boliches, 27, Fuengirola. ☎ **95-266-44-67.** Reservations recommended. Fixed-price 4-course menu 3,000 ptas. ($20.10). MC, V. Tues–Sat 7:30-10:45pm (last orders). FRENCH.

Inside the thick stone walls of a cottage built in the 1870s for a local fisherman, this restaurant lies on the main street of Los Boliches, a short walk east of the center of Fuengirola. It recently underwent extensive renovations, gaining a covered garden where there's year-round outside dining, as well as a blues and jazz cocktail bar. The new owners, David (who can help you select a wine) and Bernard, have gone to great lengths to create a soft, romantic ambience. The extensive menu contains one sumptuous option after another. For starters, try warm goat's cheese salad with honey vinaigrette, or sea bass and salmon terrine. Follow with beef carbonnades falmandes, fish duo with white butter sauce, or pork fillet with caramelized mustard sauce. For desserts, don't pass up the signature chocolate fondant.

Don Pé. De la Cruz, 17 (off the Avenida Ramón y Cajal), Fuengirola. ☎ **95-247-83-51.** Reservations recommended. Main courses 1,350–3,000 ptas. ($9.05–$20.10). V. Mon–Sat 7pm–midnight. CONTINENTAL.

In hot weather, Don Pé patrons dine in the courtyard, where the roof can be adjusted to allow in light and air. In cold weather, a fire on the hearth illuminates the heavy ceiling beams and rustic accessories. The menu features a selection of game dishes, including medallions of venison, roast fillet of wild boar, and duck with orange sauce. The ingredients are imported from the forests and plains of Andalusia.

El Paso. Calle Francisco Cano, 39, Los Boliches. ☎ **95-247-50-94.** Reservations recommended. Main courses 1,200–2,200 ptas. ($8.05–$14.75). MC, V. Daily 7pm–midnight (12:30am in summer). MEXICAN.

This 150-year-old building was originally the hamlet's largest plant for the canning of the local fleet's catch of sardines. Today, the stonework has been reconfigured with splashing fountains and decorative tiles into the resort's premier Mexican restaurant. You can order from a wide selection of Mexican beers and tequilas at the long and convivial bar area, or head into either of two dining rooms for such New World specialties as *chimichangas, tortillas, burritos, frijoles, fajitas,* and *guacamole.* Any of the barbecued meats make a savory main course.

La Cazuela. Calle Miguel Márquez, 8, Fuengirola. ☎ **95-247-46-34.** Reservations recommended. Main courses 975–1,900 ptas. ($6.55–$12.75). MC, V. Daily 6:30–11:30pm. SPANISH/INTERNATIONAL.

South of the center of Fuengirola, at the edge of the road leading off to Marbella, this cozy restaurant has flourished since the 1970s. Its longtime owner, Francisco Calle, outfits his dining rooms with hand-painted, Spanish-style porcelain. The house specialty is a tender chicken Kiev, which fans cite as even better than the tasty fillets of grilled beef, grilled prawns with garlic, homemade pâtés, and crayfish. A worthy beginning for any meal is the cheese crepes.

La Langosta. Calle Francisco Cano, 1, Los Boliches. ☎ **95-247-50-49.** Main courses 1,390–3,390 ptas. ($9.30–$22.70); fixed-price menus 1,290–1,990 ptas. ($8.65–$13.35). AE, DC, MC, V. Mon–Sat 7pm–midnight. Closed Dec–Jan. SPANISH/SEAFOOD.

Just a stone's throw from Fuengirola, La Langosta is one of the most-recommended restaurants in the area. The stylish two-story art deco dining room is a welcome relief from the ever-present Iberian rustic style of so many other restaurants in the region. The menu features a variety of seafood (the place is just 2 blocks in from the beach), as well as Spanish dishes that include gazpacho Andaluz and prawns *al ajillo* (in olive oil and garlic). Lobster is prepared thermidor style, or virtually any way you want; among the beef offerings is an especially succulent version of chateaubriand. The staff seems particularly well trained and helpful.

8 Mijas

18½ miles (30km) W of Málaga, 363 miles (584km) S of Madrid

Just 5 miles (8km) north of coastal road N-340/E-15, this village is known as "White Mijas" because of its marble-white Andalusian-style houses. Mijas is at the foot of a mountain range near the turnoff to Fuengirola, and from its lofty height—1,476 feet (443m) above sea level—you get a panoramic view of the Mediterranean.

Celts, Phoenicians, and Moors preceded today's intrepid tourists to Mijas. The town itself, rather than a specific monument, is the attraction. The easiest way to get around its cobblestoned streets is to rent a burro taxi. If you consider Mijas overrun with souvenir shops, head for the park at the top of Cuesta de la Villa, where you'll see the ruins of a **Moorish fortress** dating from 833. If you're in town for a fiesta, you'll be attending events in the country's only square bullring.

There's frequent bus service to Mijas from the terminal at Fuengirola, 30 minutes away. To drive from Fuengirola, take the Mijas road north.

WHERE TO STAY

✪ **Hotel Mijas.** Urbanización Tamisa, 2, 29650 Mijas. ☎ **95-248-58-00.** Fax 95-248-58-25. 103 units. TV TEL. 13,500–14,500 ptas. ($90.45–$97.15) double; 26,750–28,750 ptas. ($179.25–$192.65) suite. AE, DC, MC, V. Free parking.

One of the most charming hotels on the Costa del Sol was built in the 1970s on steeply sloping land in the center of town. The four-story, Andalusian-inspired block of white walls, wrought-iron accents, and flowering terraces is sun flooded and comfortable throughout. There are sweeping views over the Mediterranean from most of the public areas and the somewhat tiny but still comfortable guest rooms. The staff is tactful and hardworking. There's a tavern and a lounge that has live music on some evenings. The hotel has tennis courts, a swimming pool, sauna, gymnasium, boutique, facilities for lawn bowling, a hairdresser, and a barber. There is no elevator.

WHERE TO DINE

Club El Padrastro. Paseo del Compás. ☎ **95-248-50-00.** Reservations recommended. Main courses 1,300–2,900 ptas. ($8.70–$19.45); fixed-price menus 1,500–8,000 ptas. ($10.05–$53.60). AE, DC, MC, V. Daily 11am–11pm. INTERNATIONAL.

Part of the fun of dining at the town's best restaurant is getting there. You go to the cliff side of town and, if you're athletic, walk up 77 steps; if you're not, take the elevator to the highest point. El Padrastro serves international cuisine on its covered terraces with panoramic views of the coast. You can choose whether to eat inexpensively (stick with the regional dishes) or elaborately (break the bank and go for the chateaubriand with a bottle of the best Spanish champagne).

Restaurante El Capricho. Los Caños, 5. ☎ **95-248-51-11.** Reservations recommended. Main courses 1,400–2,100 ptas. ($9.40–$14.05); fixed-price lunch 1,200 ptas. ($8.05). AE, DC, MC, V. Thurs–Tues noon–4pm and 7–11pm. Closed Nov 15–Dec 15. INTERNATIONAL.

El Capricho, draws a large English-speaking clientele, and the varied menu is geared to their tastes. Appetizers include prawn cocktail, Serrano ham, omelettes, soups, and salads. Among the main dishes are sole, grilled swordfish, chicken Kiev, steak

Stroganoff, and flambéed meats. You might prefer the excellent paella Mijeña. Desserts range from flambéed concoctions to baked Alaska. The wine list offers good choices, including the house Rioja. The building, a former private home in the town center, dates from the 1850s.

9 Torremolinos

9 miles (14km) W of Málaga, 76 miles (122km) E of Algeciras, 353 miles (568km) S of Madrid

This Mediterranean beach resort is the most famous in Spain. It's known as a melting pot for international visitors, mostly Europeans and Americans. Many relax here after a whirlwind tour of Europe—the living is easy, the people are fun, and there are no historical monuments to visit. Once a sleepy fishing village, Torremolinos has been engulfed in a cluster of cement-walled resort hotels. Prices are on the rise, but it remains one of Europe's vacation bargains.

ESSENTIALS

GETTING THERE   The nearby Málaga airport serves Torremolinos, and frequent trains also run from the terminal at **Málaga.** For train information, call ☎ **95-238-57-64.** Buses run frequently between Málaga and Torremolinos; call ☎ **95-238-24-19** for schedules.

If you're driving, take the N-340/E-15 west from Málaga or the N-340/E-15 east from Marbella.

VISITOR INFORMATION   The **tourist information office** is at Plaza de las Comunidades Autónomas (☎ **95-237-19-09**). It's open daily from 8am to 3pm.

WHERE TO STAY
VERY EXPENSIVE

Meliá Costa del Sol. Paseo Marítimo, 11, 29620 Torremolinos. ☎ **800/336-3542** in the U.S., or 95-238-66-77. Fax 95-238-64-17. www.solmelia.es. 540 units. A/C TV TEL. 11,300-23,900 ptas. ($75.70–$160.15) double; 28,900-40,500 ptas. ($193.65–$271.35) suite. AE, DC, MC, V. Free parking.

There are two Meliá hotels in Torremolinos, both operated by a popular Spanish hotel chain. This one is more centrally located; the other Meliá is more luxurious. The mid-size guest rooms are modern and well maintained, and each has a private safe, firm mattress, and tiled bathroom. However, the hotel is popular with package-tour groups, so you may not feel a part of things if you're here alone.

Dining/Diversions: The hotel food, although competently prepared, is not the reason to stay here. It includes the usual array of Spanish and regional dishes, plus dinner buffets and a health food menu. Once a week there's a free flamenco show for guests, and on the other 6 nights a pianist entertains dancing couples.

Amenities: Swimming pool, thalassotherapy center (for medicinal seawater treatments), shopping arcade, hairdresser.

Meliá Torremolinos. Carlota Alessandri, 109, 29620 Torremolinos. ☎ **800/336-3542** in the U.S., or 95-238-05-00. Fax 95-238-05-38. 281 units. A/C TV TEL. 11,300–17,100 ptas. ($75.70–$114.55) double; from 18,100 ptas. ($121.25) suite. AE, DC, MC, V. Closed Nov–Mar. Free parking.

This is the more luxurious of the two Meliá hotels at the resort, but farther removed from the center. This hotel has deliberately lowered its official rank from five stars to four, which means you can enjoy the better amenities and service at lower prices. The six-story hotel, which stands in its own gardens, is on the western outskirts of town, on the road to Cádiz. Guest rooms range from small to spacious. Many contain minibars; all have marble bathrooms and are well furnished and maintained.

Dining/Diversions: The hotel serves standard cuisine and has a number of bars. Flamenco shows are occasionally presented.

Amenities: Swimming pool, tennis courts, room service (breakfast only).

Sol Élite Aloha Puerto. Calle Salvador Allende, 45, 29620 Torremolinos. ☎ **800/ 336-3542** in the U.S., or 95-238-70-66. Fax 95-238-57-01. 430 units. A/C MINIBAR TV TEL. 14,400–19,600 ptas. ($96.50–$131.30) double. Rates include buffet breakfast. AE, DC, MC, V. Parking available on street.

Heralded as one of the most modern hotels along the Costa del Sol when it was built in 1972, this now-aging choice stands on the seashore in the residential suburb of El Saltillo. It's on the southwestern edge of Torremolinos, beside the coastal road leading to Marbella. Away from the noise of the town center, it offers spacious rooms, all defined by the hotel as minisuites. Each faces the sea, the Benalmádena marina, or the beach, and each contains a separate sitting area. Parking may be difficult to find along the street.

Dining/Diversions: There are two restaurants and four bars. The most popular lunch option is a poolside buffet that includes an all-you-can-eat medley of meats, salads, and seafood. Spanish evenings at El Comodoro bar last well into the early morning.

Amenities: Two swimming pools (one is heated). Concierge, laundry and dry cleaning, room service, baby-sitting, conference rooms, boutiques.

Sol Élite Don Pablo. Paseo Marítimo, s/n, 29620 Torremolinos. ☎ **95-238-38-88.** Fax 95-238-37-83. 443 units. A/C MINIBAR TV TEL. 14,444–20,222 ptas. ($96.75–$135.50) double. Rates include buffet breakfast. AE, DC, MC, V.

One of the most desirable hotels in Torremolinos, Don Pablo is in a modern building a minute from the beach, surrounded by its own garden and playground areas. The surprise is the glamorous interior, which borrows heavily from Moorish palaces and medieval castle themes. Arched-tile arcades have splashing fountains, and the grand staircase features niches with life-size stone statues of nude figures. The comfortably furnished guest rooms have sea-view terraces, and bathrooms have hair dryers and tub-and-shower combos.

Dining/Diversions: The buffet-only restaurant offers some of the most generous spreads along the coast. They include both Andalusian specialties and international dishes. Several places serve drinks. The full day and night entertainment program includes dancing at night to a live band, and a disco.

Amenities: Fitness classes.

MODERATE

Don Curro. Sancha de Lara, 7, 29015 Málaga. ☎ **95-222-72-00.** Fax 95-221-59-46. 118 units. A/C MINIBAR TV TEL. 8,250–15,460 ptas. ($55.30–$103.60) double; 11,700–16,140 ptas. ($78.40–$108.15) suite. AE, DC, MC, V.

The most traditional hotel in Málaga, Don Curro has classic decor that gives it character and atmosphere, unlike most of its competitors. The old Casa Curro, built in 1933 in the center of town (and rebuilt in 1965), was the origin of the present hotel. The lounges set the tone; in winter you can sit in an upholstered chair enjoying an open fireplace. Guest rooms are streamlined and often done in art deco style. Most are medium in size to spacious, with luxury mattresses and elegantly tiled bathrooms. The hotel also has on-site cafeteria and an elegant bar.

Hotel Cervantes. Calle las Mercedes, s/n, 29620 Torremolinos. ☎ **95-238-40-33.** Fax 95-238-48-57. 397 units. A/C TV TEL. 11,000-14,000 ptas. ($73.70–$93.80) double. Rates include breakfast. Full board 4,900 ptas. ($32.85) per person. AE, DC, MC, V.

The four-star Cervantes is a 7-minute walk from the beach. It has a garden and is adjacent to a maze of patios and narrow streets of boutiques and open-air cafes. The self-contained facilities include a sun terrace, a sauna, massage, two pools (one covered and heated), hairdressers, a gift shop, a TV and video lounge, a card room, and games, such as billiards, table tennis, and darts. The guest rooms have modern furniture, piped-in music, safes, TVs, and spacious terraces; many have balconies with views of the sea.

Also on the premises are a restaurant, a bar with live music and entertainment, and a coffee shop. In midsummer this hotel is likely to be booked with tour groups from northern Europe.

Hotel Las Palomas. Carmen Montes, 1, 29620 Torremolinos. ☎ **95-238-50-00.** Fax 95-238-64-66. 300 units. TEL. 7,750–11,300 ptas. ($51.95–$75.70) double. AE, DC, MC, V.

Built at the height of Torremolinos's construction boom (1968), this well-managed hotel is one of the town's most attractive, surrounded by carefully tended gardens. Located near the coastal road, it's a 1-minute walk from the beach and a 10-minute walk south of the center of town. It has Andalusian decor in the public and guest rooms, and a clientele of repeat visitors who hail mostly from France, Belgium, and Holland. Each of the midsize rooms contains a private balcony, a tiled bathroom, and furniture inspired by southern Spain. There's no air-conditioning, but many guests compensate by opening windows and balcony doors to catch the sea breezes. The hotel boasts a sauna, three swimming pools (one reserved for children), entertainment throughout the day and early evening, a handful of shops, a hairdresser, and an unending series of lunch and dinner buffets.

Sidi Lago Rojo. Miami, 1, 29620 Torremolinos. ☎ **95-238-76-66.** Fax 95-238-08-91. 144 units. A/C TV TEL. 11,095–13,279 ptas. ($74.35–$88.95) double. AE, DC, MC, V.

In the heart of the fishing village of La Carihuela, Sidi Lago Rojo is its finest place to stay. It stands only 150 feet from the beach and has its own gardens, swimming pool, sunbathing terraces, and refreshment bar. Built in the 1970s, and renovated at least once since then, it offers studio-style guest rooms (doubles only), tastefully decorated with contemporary Spanish furnishings and tile bathrooms. All rooms have terraces with views; some have minibars. In the late evening there is disco dancing. The hotel also has a good restaurant.

INEXPENSIVE

Hostal Los Jazmines. Avenida de Lido, 6, 29620 Torremolinos. ☎ **95-238-50-33.** Fax 95-237-27-02. 85 units. TV TEL. 5,400–6,600 ptas. ($36.20–$44.20) double. AE, DC, MC, V.

Located on one of the best beaches in Torremolinos, Hostal Los Jazmines faces a plaza at the foot of the shady Avenida del Lido. Sun-seekers will find it replete with terraces, lawns, and an irregularly shaped swimming pool. The small guest rooms (all doubles) seem a bit impersonal, but they have their own little balconies and compact bathrooms. From here it's a good hike up the hill to the town center. Meals are served alfresco or inside the appealing dining room.

Hotel El Pozo. Casablanca, 4, 29620 Torremolinos. ☎ **95-238-06-22.** Fax 95-238-71-17. 28 units. TV TEL. 6,420–8,025 ptas. ($43–$53.75) double. DC, MC, V.

This hotel isn't for light sleepers—it's in one of the liveliest sections of town, a short walk from the train station. It's usually filled with budget travelers, including many students from northern Europe. The lobby-level bar has professional French billiards, heavy Spanish furniture, and a view of a small courtyard. From your window or terrace you can view the promenades below. The small guest rooms are furnished in a simple, functional style—nothing special, but the price is right.

Miami. Aladino, 14, 29620 Torremolinos. ☎ **95-238-52-55.** 27 units. TEL. 4,800–7,500 ptas. ($32.15–$50.25) double. No credit cards. Free parking.

The Miami, near the Carihuela section, might remind you of a 1920s Hollywood movie star's home. High walls and private gardens surround the swimming pool. Fuchsias and bougainvillea climb over the rear patio's arches. A tile terrace is used for sunbathing and refreshments. The country-style living room contains a walk-in fireplace, and the compact guest rooms are furnished in traditional and comfortable style. Each has a balcony. Breakfast is the only meal served.

NEARBY PLACES TO STAY

Where Torremolinos ends and Benalmádena-Costa to the west begins is hard to say. Benalmádena-Costa is packed with hotels, restaurants, and tourist facilities.

✪ Hotel Torrequebrada. Carretera de Cádiz, km 220, 29630 Benalmádena. ☎ **95-244-60-00.** Fax 95-244-27-46. www.torrequebrada.com. E-mail: reservas@torrequebrada.com. 340 units. A/C MINIBAR TV TEL. 34,200–37,700 ptas. ($229.15–$252.60) double; from 39,300 ptas. ($263.30) suite. Discounts for stays of 5 or more days. Rates include breakfast. AE, DC, MC, V. Free parking.

In the late 1980s this became one of the largest five-star luxury hotels along the Costa del Sol. Three miles (5km) west of Torremolinos, it opens onto its own beach and offers a wide range of facilities and attractions. You'll find one of the largest casinos in Europe, and a world-class golf course. The hotel is furnished in muted Mediterranean colors, with both antique and modern furniture. The spacious, handsomely furnished rooms occupy two 11-story towers. All accommodations have large terraces with sea views, plus private safes and tiled bathrooms with plush towels.

Dining/Diversions: A specialty restaurant, Café Royal, overlooks the gardens and the sea; it enjoys a five-fork rating for its international cuisine. Adjacent to the garden, and overlooking the sea, the Pavillion provides buffet and cafeteria service throughout the day. A flamenco show is presented at 10:30pm Tuesday through Saturday. Guests gather in a piano bar at night, or roll the dice in the huge casino.

Amenities: Outstanding golf course, pools, health club, tennis courts, and nine levels of underground parking. Room service, laundry and dry cleaning, baby-sitting.

Tritón. Avenida António Machado, 29, 29491 Benalmádena-Costa. ☎ **95-244-32-40.** Fax 95-244-26-49. E-mail: hotel_triton@spa.es. 373 units. A/C MINIBAR TV TEL. 17,500–24,500 ptas. ($117.25–$164.15) double; from 39,000 ptas. ($261.30) suite. Rates include breakfast. AE, DC, MC, V. Free parking.

Less than 2 miles (3km) north of Torremolinos, the Tritón is a Miami Beach–style resort colony in front of the Benalmádena-Costa marina. It features a high-rise stack of midsize guest rooms as well as an impressive pool and garden area. Surrounding the swimming pool are subtropical trees and vegetation, plus thatched sunshade umbrellas. All the rooms have well-maintained tile bathrooms and wide windows opening onto sun balconies. Among the public rooms are multilevel lounges and two wood-paneled bars.

Dining/Diversions: The main restaurant presents a three-tiered display of hors d'oeuvres, fruits, and desserts. There's a barbecue grill and a luncheon terrace. The bar features music with an orchestra in July and August.

Amenities: Swimming pool, Swedish sauna, tennis courts, room service, dry cleaning and laundry, concierge.

WHERE TO DINE

The cuisine in Torremolinos is more American and continental European than Andalusian. The hotels often serve elaborate four-course meals, but you may want to sample more casual local offerings. A good spot to try is the food court **La Nogalera,** the major gathering place located between the coast road and the beach. Head down the calle del Cauce to this compound of modern whitewashed Andalusian buildings. Open to pedestrian traffic only, it's a maze of passageways, courtyards, and patios for eating and drinking. You can find anything from sandwiches to Belgian waffles to scrambled eggs to pizza.

AT LA NOGALERA

El Gato Viudo. La Nogalera, 11. ☎ **95-238-51-29.** Main courses 800–1,900 ptas. ($5.35–$12.75). AE, DC, MC, V. May–Oct, daily 1–4pm and 6–11:30pm; Nov–Apr, Thurs–Tues 1–4pm and 6–11:30pm. SPANISH.

El Gato Viudo has been a tradition with local diners for almost 40 years. Simple and amiable, this old-fashioned tavern occupies the street level and cellar of a building off calle San Miguel, and offers sidewalk seating. The menu includes such good dishes as grilled fish; marinated hake; roasted pork, steak, and veal; calamari with spicy tomato sauce; grilled shrimp; and shellfish or fish soup. The atmosphere is informal, and the staff is accustomed to coping with diners from virtually everywhere.

Golden Curry. Calle Guetaria, 6, La Nogalera, Bloque 6. ☎ **95-237-48-55.** Main courses 500–1,000 ptas. ($3.35–$6.70). AE, DC, MC, V. Sat–Thurs 1–4pm, daily 7pm–midnight. INDIAN.

One floor above street level, in the commercial heart of Torremolinos, this restaurant specializes in traditional Mogul dishes of India, adapted and altered to suit British tastes. The two chefs and the Calcutta-born owner all worked in Indian restaurants in London before emigrating to Spain, and many patrons are Brits on holiday. Menu items include chicken Madras, chicken in onion sauce, lamb slow-cooked in spices and served with lentils, and succulent prawns. The best of the vegetarian offerings arrive as an array of small dishes.

AT LA CARIHUELA

If you want to get away from the high-rises and honky-tonks, head to nearby La Carihuela. In the old fishing village on the western outskirts of Torremolinos, you'll find some of the best bargain restaurants. Walk down a hill toward the sea to reach the village.

Casa Juan. Calle Mar, 14, La Carihuela. ☎ **95-238-41-06.** Reservations recommended. Main courses 800–2,800 ptas. ($5.35–$18.75). AE, DC, MC, V. Tues–Sun 12:30–4:30pm and 8pm–midnight. Closed Dec. SEAFOOD.

In a modern-looking building in old-timey La Carihuela, this seafood restaurant lies about a mile west of Torremolinos's center. Menu items include selections from a lavish display of fish and shellfish prominently positioned near the entrance. You might try *mariscada de mariscos* (shellfish), a fried platter of mixed fish, codfish, kebabs of meat or fish, or paella. Of special note is *lubina a la sal*—sea bass packed in layers of roughly textured salt, broken open at your table and deboned in front of you. When the restaurant gets busy, as it often does, the staff is likely to rush around hysterically—something many local fans think adds to its charm.

El Roqueo. Calle del Carmen, 35, La Carihuela. ☎ **95-238-49-46.** Reservations recommended. Main courses 1,400–2,200 ptas. ($9.40–$14.75); fixed-price menu 1,300 ptas. ($8.70). AE, DC, MC, V. Wed–Mon noon–4pm and 8pm–midnight. Closed Nov 1–Dec 8. SEAFOOD.

In the heart of the village, El Roqueo, established in 1975, is the perfect place for a seafood dinner near the sea. Begin with savory sopa de mariscos (shellfish soup). Then try a specialty of the chef, a delectable fish baked in rock salt; you can also order grilled sea bass or shrimp. Top everything off with soothing caramel custard. Some of the more expensive fish courses are priced by the gram, so order carefully.

AT PLAYAMAR

El Vietnam del Sur. Playamar, Bloque, 9. ☎ **95-238-67-37.** Reservations required. Main courses 700–1,200 ptas. ($4.70–$8.05). AE, DC, MC, V. Sat–Sun and holidays 1–4pm, daily 7pm–1am. Closed Jan. VIETNAMESE.

The inexpensive food here is good for sharing. Begin with spring rolls, served with mint and a spicy dipping sauce. The chef's specials include fried stuffed chicken wings, and beef with rice noodles. The wine list is short and moderately priced. The restaurant, in the Playamar section near the beach, has an outdoor dining terrace.

AT LOS ALAMOS

Frutos. Carretera de Cádiz, km 228, Urbanización Los Alamos. ☎ **95-238-14-50.** Reservations recommended. Main courses 800–2,200 ptas. ($5.35–$14.75); fixed-price menu 2,000 ptas. ($13.40). AE, DC, MC, V. Daily 1–4pm; Mon–Sat 8pm–midnight. SPANISH/ INTERNATIONAL.

Malagueños frequent this place in droves, drawn by good old-style cooking. The cuisine is Spanish with a vengeance. Portions are large and service hectic. Diners enjoy the day's catch, perhaps *rape* (monkfish), angler fish, or the increasingly rare *mero* (grouper). Also available are garlic-studded leg of lamb and oxtail prepared in a savory ragout. Frutos is next to the Los Alamos service station, 1¼ miles (2km) from the town center.

AT BENALMÁDENA-COSTA

✪ **Mar de Alborán.** Alay, 5. ☎ **95-244-64-27.** Reservations recommended. Main courses 1,200–3,000 ptas. ($8.05–$20.10); menú del día 4,200 ptas. ($28.15). AE, DC, MC, V. Sun and Tues–Fri 1:30–4pm, Tues–Sat 8:30–midnight. Closed Dec 22–Jan 22. BASQUE/ ANDALUSIAN.

This restaurant's elegantly airy decor seems appropriate for its location near the sea, just a short walk from the resort's Puerto Marina. It serves the specialties of both Andalusia and the Basque region of northern Spain. Menu items change with the season. They might include cold terrine of leeks; Basque *piperadda* in puff pastry; *piquillos rellenos* (red peppers stuffed with pulverized fish in a sweet pepper sauce), or *bacalao* (salt cod) "Club Ranero," served with garlic and red-pepper cream sauce. You can also try *kokotxas,* the Basque national dish of hake cheeks in green sauce with clams; anglerfish with prawns; or foie gras served with sweet Málaga wine and raisins. The restaurant's game dishes (available in season) are renowned. Dessert might be a frothy version of peach mousse with puree of fruit and dark-chocolate sauce.

TORREMOLINOS AFTER DARK

Torremolinos has more nightlife than any other spot along the Costa del Sol. The earliest action is always at the bars, which are lively most of the night, serving drinks and tapas. Sometimes it seems that in Torremolinos there are more bars than people, so you shouldn't have trouble finding one you like. Note that some bars are open during the day as well.

We like the **Bar Central,** Plaza Andalucía, Bloque, 1 (☎ 95-238-27-60), for coffee, brandy, beer, cocktails, limited sandwiches, and pastries, served indoors or on a large, French-style covered terrace. It's a good spot to meet people. Prices begin at 150 ptas. ($1) for a beer, 450 ptas. ($3) for a hard drink. Open Monday through Saturday 8am to 11:30pm (later in summer).

In the very center of town, **Joyeria Kohinoor,** San Miguel, 30 (☎ 95-238-32-40), is for bullfight aficionados. Kegs of beer, stools, and the terrace in the main shopping street make it a perfect spot for a before-dinner sherry or an after-dinner beer. Prices for table service begin at 350 ptas. ($2.35) for a pitcher of beer or sangría. Open daily 10am to 10pm in winter, 10am to 2am in summer.

La Bodega, San Miguel, 40 (☎ 95-238-73-37), relies on its colorful clientele and the quality of its tapas to draw customers, who seem to rank this place above the dozens of other tascas in this popular tourist zone. You'll be fortunate to find space at one of the small tables because many consider the bar food plentiful enough for a satisfying lunch or dinner. Once you begin to order—platters of fried squid, pungent tuna, grilled shrimp, tiny brochettes of sole—you might not be able to stop. Most tapas cost 200 to 750 ptas. ($1.35 to $5.05). A beer costs 185 ptas. ($1.25), a hard drink at least 400 ptas. ($2.70). Open daily 12:30pm to midnight.

Ready to dance off all those tapas? **El Palladium,** Palma de Mallorca (☎ 95-238-42-89), a well-designed nightclub in the town center, is one of the most convivial in Torremolinos. Strobes, spotlights, and a sound system (described as loud and distortion-free) set the scene. There's even a swimming pool. Expect to pay 350 ptas. ($2.35) or more for a drink; cover is 1,000 ptas. ($6.70), including one drink after 11pm. Open from 11pm to 6am.

Gay men and women from throughout northern Europe are almost always in residence in Torremolinos; if you want to meet some of them, consider a drink or two at **Abadia,** La Nogalera 9 (no phone). Other options, all around La Nogalera, include **Contactos,** La Nogalera 204 (no phone) which does not get busy till well after 10pm, and **Morbos,** La Nogalera 113 (no phone), which is open till 5am. The most popular gay disco in town is the **Tension,** La Nogalera 524 (no phone), which plays popular dance music for a very cruisy crowd.

One of the Costa del Sol's major casinos, **Casino Torrequebrada,** carretera de Cádiz, Benalmádena-Costa (☎ 95-244-25-45), is on the lobby level of the Hotel Torrequebrada (see above). It has tables devoted to blackjack, chemin de fer, punto y banco, and two kinds of roulette. The casino is open daily 8am to 4am. The nightclub offers a flamenco show year-round, at 11pm on Thursday, Friday, and Saturday nights; in midsummer, there might be more glitz and more frequent shows (ask when you get there or call). Nightclub acts begin at 10:30pm (Spanish revue) and 11:30pm (Las Vegas revue). The restaurant is open nightly 8:30pm to 11pm. Casino admission is 600 ptas. ($4); with one drink, both shows, casino and cabaret/nightclub admission, it's 4,500 ptas. ($30.15); with dinner, it's 8,800 ptas. ($58.95). Bring your passport to be admitted.

10 Málaga

340 miles (547km) S of Madrid, 82 miles (132km) E of Algeciras

Málaga is a bustling commercial and residential center whose economy does not depend exclusively on tourism. Its chief attraction is the mild off-season climate. Summer can be sticky.

Málaga's most famous citizen was Pablo Picasso, born in 1881 at Plaza de la Merced, in the center of the city. The artist unfortunately left little of his spirit—and only a small selection of his work—in his birthplace.

ESSENTIALS

GETTING THERE   Travelers from North America must transfer for Málaga in Madrid or Barcelona. From within Europe, some airlines (including British Airways from London) offer nonstop flights to Málaga. **Iberia** has frequent service, and even more flights offered through its affiliate airlines, which include **Binter, Viva,** and **Aviaco.** Flights can be booked through Iberia's reservations line (☎ **800/772-4642** in the U.S. or 902-40-05-00 in Spain).

At least five **trains** a day serve Málaga from Madrid. The trip takes around 4 hours. Three trains a day connect the Andalusian city of Seville with Málaga, a 3-hour run. For ticket prices and rail information in Málaga, call RENFE (☎ **95-221-31-22**).

Buses from all over Spain arrive at the terminal on the Paseo de los Tilos, behind the RENFE offices. Buses run to all the major Spanish cities, including Madrid (8 buses per day), Córdoba (5 per day), and Seville (10 per day). From Madrid, the trip is 7 hours; from Barcelona, 17 hours; from Valencia, 12 hours. Call ☎ **95-235-00-61** in Málaga for bus information.

From the resorts in the west (such as Torremolinos and Marbella), you can drive east along the N-340/E-15 to Málaga. If you're in the east at the end of the Costa del Sol (Almería), take the N-340/E-15 west to Málaga, with a stopover at Nerja.

VISITOR INFORMATION   The **tourist information office** is at Pasaje de Chinitas, 4 (☎ **95-221-34-45**). It's open Monday through Friday 9am to 1pm.

SPECIAL EVENTS   The most festive time in Málaga is the first week in August, when the city celebrates its reconquest by Ferdinand and Isabella in 1487. The big **feria** (fair) is an occasion for parades and bullfights. A major tree-shaded boulevard, **Paseo del Parque,** is transformed into a fairground featuring amusements and restaurants.

EXPLORING MÁLAGA

Unlike the rest of the Costa del Sol, Málaga has several historical sites of interest to the average visitor.

Alcazaba. Plaza de la Aduana, Alcazabilla. ☎ **95-221-60-05.** Admission to museum 30 ptas. (20¢). Museum Tues–Fri 9:30am–1:30pm and 5–8pm, Sat 10am–1pm, Sun 10am–2pm. Bus: 4, 18, 19, or 24.

The remains of this ancient Moorish palace are within easy walking distance of the city center, off Paseo del Parque. Plenty of signs point the way up the hill. The fortress was erected in the 9th or 10th century, although there have been later additions and reconstructions. Ferdinand and Isabella stayed here when they reconquered the city. The Alcazaba now houses an archaeological museum, with exhibits of cultures ranging from Greek to Phoenician to Carthaginian. With government-planted orange trees and purple bougainvillea making the grounds even more beautiful, the view overlooking the city and the bay is among the most panoramic on the Costa del Sol.

Málaga Cathedral. Plaza Obispo. ☎ **95-221-59-17.** Admission 200 ptas. ($1.35). Mon–Sat 10am–12:45pm and 4–6:30pm. Closed holidays. Bus: 14, 18, 19, or 24.

This 16th-century Renaissance cathedral in Málaga's center, built on the site of a great mosque, suffered damage during the Spanish Civil War. However, it remains vast and impressive, reflecting changing styles of interior architecture. Its most notable attributes

Don't Be a Victim

Málaga has one of the highest crime rates in Spain. The most common complaint is purse snatching, with an estimated 75% of the crimes committed by juveniles. Stolen passports are also a problem. Keep your wits about you.

are the richly ornamented choir stalls by Ortiz, Mena, and Michael. The cathedral has been declared a national monument.

Castillo de Gibralfaro. Cerro de Gibralfaro. Free admission. Daylight hours. Microbus: H, leaving hourly from cathedral.

On a hill overlooking Málaga and the Mediterranean are the ruins of an ancient Moorish castle-fortress of unknown origin. It is near the government-run parador, and might easily be tied in with a luncheon visit.

Warning: Do not walk to Gibralfaro Castle from town. Readers have reported muggings along the way, and the area around the castle is dangerous. Take the bus from the cathedral.

Museo de Bellas Artes. Calle San Agustín, 8. ☎ **95-221-83-82**. Admission 200 ptas. ($1.35). Mon–Fri 10am–1:30pm and 4–7pm, Sat 10am–1:30pm. Bus: 4, 18, 19, or 24.

Behind the cathedral, this former Moorish palace houses a modest collection of paintings, including a gallery devoted to native son Pablo Picasso. It also displays works by Murillo, Ribera, and Morales, along with Andalusian antiques, mosaics, and sculptures.

Picasso House-Museum. Plaza de la Merced. ☎ **95-221-50-05**. Free admission. Mon–Sat 10am–2pm and 5pm-8pm, Sun 11am-2pm.

A well-told tale concerns the birth of Picasso: In October 1891, when the artist was born, he was unable to draw breath until his uncle blew cigar smoke into his lungs. Whether this rather harsh entry into the world had any effect on his work is mere speculation. What cannot be denied is the effect he was to have on the world. His place of birth is a 5-story building in the heart of Málaga's historic quarter, where he spent the first 17 months of his life. The house is now more of a museum, with about 200 works on display. The museum also mounts monthly exhibitions featuring avant-garde movements from Picasso's time.

SHOPPING

The region around Málaga produces artfully rustic pottery, which makes a worthwhile souvenir. A handful of highly appealing outlets are scattered throughout the city's historic core. The best include **Almazul,** calle Beatas, 53 (☎ **95-221-28-43**); **Fina,** calle Coronel, 4 (no phone), on a small street near the calle San Juan; and **Los Artesanos**, Cister, 13 (☎ **95-260-45-44**). Outside the town limits, the most comprehensive collection of ceramics and pottery can be found at **La Vistillas,** Carretera Mijas, km 2 (☎ **95-45-13-63**), about 1¼ miles (2km) from Málaga's center.

WHERE TO STAY

For such a large city in a resort area, Málaga has a surprising lack of hotels. Book well in advance, especially if you want to stay in a parador.

EXPENSIVE

Málaga Palacio. Cortina del Muelle, 1, 29015 Málaga. ☎ **95-221-51-85**. Fax 95-221-51-85. 230 units. A/C MINIBAR TV TEL. 16,500–19,750 ptas. ($110.55–$132.35) double; 27,500 ptas. ($184.25) suite. AE, DC, MC, V. Parking 1,000 ptas. ($6.70) nearby. Bus: 4, 18, 19, or 24.

The leading hotel in the town center, the Palacio opens onto a tree-lined esplanade near the cathedral and the harbor. The 1960s building was constructed flatiron style; it rises 15 stories and is crowned by an open-air swimming pool and refreshment bar. Most of the balconies offer views of the port, and down below you can see horses pulling turn-of-the-century carriages. The midsize guest rooms are traditionally furnished and contain firm beds and tiled bathrooms. The street-floor lounges mix antiques with more modern furnishings.

Dining: There's no restaurant on-site, but many dining options lie within walking distance. The cafeteria serves breakfast.

Amenities: Room service (breakfast only), concierge, baby-sitting, hairdresser for women and men, boutiques, laundry and dry cleaning. Facilities for sports, including golf and tennis, are nearby.

Parador de Málaga-Gibralfaro. Monte Gibralfaro, 29016 Málaga. ☎ **95-222-19-02.** Fax 95-222-19-04. 38 units. A/C MINIBAR TV TEL. 17,500-19,000 ptas. ($117.25–$127.30) double. AE, DC, MC, V. Free parking. Take the coastal road, Paseo de Reding, which becomes Avenida Casa de Pries and then Paseo de Sancha. Turn left onto Camino Nuevo and follow the small signs.

Restored in 1994, this is one of Spain's oldest, more tradition-laden paradors. It enjoys a scenic location high on a plateau near an old fortified castle. Overlooking the city and the Mediterranean, it has views of the bullring, mountains, and beaches. Originally a famous restaurant, the parador has been converted into a fine hotel with two dining rooms. The guest rooms have private entrances, living-room areas, and wide glass doors opening onto private sun terraces. The medium-size rooms are tastefully decorated with modern furnishings and reproductions of Spanish antiques.

Dining: The hotel restaurant serves adequate Spanish fare.

Amenities: Room service, concierge, currency exchange, swimming pool, laundry and dry cleaning.

Tryp Guadalmar. Urbanización Guadalmar, Carretera de Cádiz, km 238, 29080 Málaga. ☎ **95-223-17-03.** Fax 95-224-0385. www.tryp.es. E-mail: trypguadalmar@sel.es. 195 units. A/C MINIBAR TV TEL. 15,500–19,100 ptas. ($103.85–$127.95) double; 26,250 ptas. ($175.90) suite. Children under 12 half price in parents' room. AE, DC, MC, V. Free parking.

Drenched in sunlight, this 9-story modern hotel sits across from a private beach 2 miles (3km) west of the center of Málaga. It benefited from a radical renovation in 1996 and a takeover by the well-respected Tryp chain. Accommodations are spacious, airy, and simply furnished, with chairs and tables appropriate to a beach resort, and each has a private sea-view balcony. You're likely to get heavy doses of families with children at this hotel. An air of anonymity prevails as the staff struggles with constant exposure to the comings and goings of large numbers of vacationers.

Dining/Diversions: The restaurant, La Bodega, has a view of the sea. For dancing, head for La Corrida, the hotel's bar, which features live music.

Amenities: Baby-sitting, laundry and dry cleaning, children's playground, indoor and outdoor pools.

MODERATE

Hotel Los Naranjos. Paseo de Sancha, 35, 29016 Málaga. ☎ **95-222-43-19.** Fax 95-222-59-75. 41 units. A/C MINIBAR TV TEL. 15,600 ptas. ($104.50) double; 19,600 ptas. ($131.30) suite. AE, DC, MC, V. Parking 1,500 ptas. ($10.05). Bus: 11.

The Hotel Los Naranjos is one of the more reasonably priced choices in the city. It's a well-run, well-maintained hotel 1 mile from the heart of town on the eastern side of Málaga, past the Plaza de Toros (bullring). It is near the best beach in Málaga, the Baños del Carmen. The hotel offers midsize guest rooms in contemporary style. Some bathrooms have showers, not tubs. The public rooms are decorated in typical Andalusian style, with colorful tiles and ornate wood carving. Breakfast (which costs extra) is the only meal served.

Parador Nacional del Golf. Carretera de Málaga, Apartado, 324, 29080 Torremolinos, Málaga. ☎ **95-238-12-55.** Fax 95-238-89-63. 60 units. A/C MINIBAR TV TEL. 17,500 ptas. ($117.25) double. AE, DC, MC, V. Free parking.

A tasteful resort hotel created by the Spanish government, this hacienda-style parador is flanked by a golf course on one side and the Mediterranean on another. It's less than 2 miles (3.2km) from the airport, 6½ miles (10.5km) from Málaga, and 2½ miles (4km) from Torremolinos. Each guest room has a private balcony with a view of the golfing greens, the circular swimming pool, or the water. Some units have Jacuzzis. The furnishings are attractive, and the beds excellent. Long tile corridors lead to the air-conditioned public rooms: graciously furnished lounges, a bar, and a restaurant.

INEXPENSIVE

El Cenachero. Barroso, 5, 29001 Málaga. ☎ **95-222-40-88.** 14 units. TV. 5,300–5,400 ptas. ($35.50–$36.20) double. No credit cards. Bus: 15.

Opened in 1969, this modest little hotel is 5 blocks from the park near the harbor. The nicely carpeted guest rooms are simply and functionally furnished; half have showers, the rest have full bathrooms. No meals are served.

Hostal Residencia Carlos V. Cister, 10, 29015 Málaga. ☎ **95-221-51-20.** Fax 95-221-51-29. 50 units. TV TEL. 7,100–8,100 ptas. ($47.55–$54.25) double. AE, DC, MC, V. Parking 1,400 ptas. ($9.40). Bus: 15 from the rail station.

This hotel is in a central location near the cathedral, with an interesting facade decorated with wrought-iron balconies and *miradores*. The lobby is fairly dark, but this remains a reliable, conservative choice. An elevator will take you to your small room, furnished in a no-frills style, but well maintained.

Hostal Residencia Derby. San Juan de Díos, 1, 29015 Málaga. ☎ **95-222-13-01.** 17 units, 12 with bathroom. TEL. 3,800 ptas. ($25.45) double with sink; 4,500 ptas. ($30.15) double with bathroom. No credit cards. Bus: 7, 9, 12, 14, 15, 16, 17.

The Derby is a real find. A fourth-floor boarding house, it's in the heart town, on a main square directly north of the train station. Some of the rather basic, cramped rooms have excellent views of the Mediterranean and the port of Málaga. Most units have a shower, not a tub. No breakfast is served.

A LUXURIOUS PLACE TO STAY NEARBY

✪ **La Bobadilla.** Finca La Bobadilla, 18300 Loja (Granada), Apartado 144. ☎ **958/32-18-61.** Fax 958/32-18-10. www.la-bobadilla.com. E-mail: info@la-bobadilla.com. 60 units. A/C MINIBAR TV TEL. 34,000–48,500 ptas. ($227.80–$324.95) double; 58,000–107,000 ptas. ($388.60–$716.90) suite. AE, DC, MC, V. Free parking. From the Málaga airport, follow signs toward Granada, but at km 175 continue through the village of Salinas. Take road marked SALINAS/RUTE; after 2 miles (3km), follow signposts for hotel to the entrance.

An hour's drive northeast of Málaga, La Bobadilla is the most luxurious retreat in southern Spain. It is a secluded oasis in the foothills of the Sierra Nevada near the town of Loja, which is 44 miles (71km) north of Málaga. La Bobadilla is a 13-mile (21km) drive from Loja.

The hotel complex is built like an Andalusian village, a cluster of whitewashed *casas* constructed around a tower and a white church. Every casa has a roof terrace and a balcony overlooking the olive-grove-studded district. Each sumptuous accommodation is individually designed, from the least expensive doubles to the most expensive King's Suite (which has plenty of room for bodyguards). The hotel caters to a pampered coterie of international guests, and the service is perhaps the finest in Spain.

The hotel village stands on a hillside, on 1,750 acres of private, unspoiled grounds. If you get bored in this lap of luxury, you can always drive to Granada, an hour away.

Should you decide to marry your companion at the resort, the chapel has a 30-foot-high organ with 1,595 pipes.

Dining/Diversions: Even the king of Spain has dined at La Finca, which serves Spanish and international cuisine. El Cortijo specializes in regional cuisine. Concerts, featuring flamenco, are presented on Friday and Saturday nights.

Amenities: Laundry and valet, 24-hour room service, massage, baby-sitting; two tennis courts, horseback riding, archery, outdoor swimming pool, heated indoor swimming pool, Jacuzzis, Finnish sauna, Turkish steam bath, fitness club, bicycles, beauty salon.

WHERE TO DINE
EXPENSIVE

Café de Paris. Vélez Málaga, 8. ☎ **95-222-50-43.** Reservations required. Main courses 1,400–2,950 ptas. ($9.40–$19.75); menú del día 3,000 ptas. ($20.10). AE, DC, MC, V. Mon–Sat 1–4pm and 8pm–midnight. Closed July 1–15. Bus: 13. FRENCH/SPANISH.

Café de Paris, Málaga's best restaurant, is in La Malagueta, the district surrounding the Plaza de Toros (bullring). Proprietor and chef de cuisine José García Cortés worked at many important dining rooms before carving out his own niche. Some critics have suggested that the chef's cuisine is beyond the average Malagueño's taste, or at least pocketbook—particularly the caviar, game (including partridge), and foie gras.

Much of Cortés's cuisine has been adapted from classic French dishes to please the Andalusian palate. Menus change frequently, reflecting both the chef's imagination and the availability of produce in the Málaga markets. You might be served crepes gratinée filled with baby eels, or local whitefish baked in salt (it doesn't sound good but is excellent). Stroganoff is made not with the usual beef but with ox meat. Save room for the creative desserts, such as citrus-flavored sorbet made with champagne, or custard apple mousse.

MODERATE

El Chinitas. Moreno Monroy, 4. ☎ **95-221-09-72.** Main courses 1,000–2,800 ptas. ($6.70–$18.75). AE, DC, MC, V. Daily 1–4pm and 8pm–midnight. SPANISH.

In the heart of Málaga, a short walk from the tourist office, this is one of the most established restaurants in town. Many regular patrons follow a ritual: They consume a round of tapas and drinks at the associated Bar Orellana next door (which maintains the same hours, without the midafternoon closing), then head to Chinitas for a meal. The place is often filled with local residents, which is a good sign. The menu changes but might include a mixed fish fry, grilled red mullet, shrimp cocktail, grilled sirloin, or shellfish soup. The service is both fast and attentive.

Las Trevedes. In El Corte Inglés Department Store, Andalucía 4. ☎ **95-230-00-00.** Main courses 1,500–2,800 ptas. ($10.05–$18.75); buffet 3,800 ptas. ($26.60). AE, DC, MC, V. Mon–Sat 1–4:30pm. Bus: 15. SPANISH.

Although it originated to lure shoppers into Málaga's best department store, this restaurant quickly developed a clientele of its own. On the sixth floor of El Corte Inglés, the local branch of the national chain, it offers a buffet table of salads and hot and cold meats and fish, as well as à la carte service. The setting is dignified and comfortable, with a well-trained staff. You might try green peppers stuffed with shellfish, fillet of pork in pepper-cream sauce, or several kinds of brochettes, and order from a long list of wines.

Parador de Málaga-Gibralfaro. Monte Gibralfaro. ☎ **95-222-19-02.** Main courses 1,800–2,400 ptas. ($12.05–$16.10); fixed-price menu 3,700 ptas. ($24.80). AE, DC, MC, V. Daily 1–4pm and 8:30–11pm. Microbus: H, by the cathedral. SPANISH.

This government-owned restaurant, on a mountainside high above the city, is especially notable for its view. You can look down into the heart of the Málaga bullring, among other sights. Meals are served in the attractive dining room or under the arches of two wide terraces, which provide views of the coast. Featured dishes include hors d'oeuvres parador—your entire table covered with tiny dishes of tasty tidbits. Two other specialties are an omelette of *chanquetes*, tiny whitefish popular in this part of the country, and chicken Villaroi.

Parador Nacional del Golf. Carretta de Málaga, Apartado 324, Málaga. ☎ **95-238-12-55.** Main courses 1,800–2,300 ptas. ($12.05–$15.40); fixed-price menu 3,500 ptas. ($23.45). AE, DC, MC, V. Daily 1:30–4pm and 8:30–11pm. SPANISH.

This government-owned restaurant has an indoor/outdoor dining room that opens onto a circular swimming pool, golf course, and private beach. The interior room, furnished with reproductions of antiques, has a refined country-club atmosphere. Before-lunch drinks at the sleek modern bar tempt golfers, among others, who then proceed to the covered terrace for their Spanish meals.

Refectorium. Calle Cervantes, 8. ☎ **95-221-89-90.** Reservations recommended on weekends and at bullfights. Main courses 800–2,000 ptas. ($5.35–$13.40). AE, DC, MC, V. Daily 1–5pm and 9pm–12:30am. SPANISH.

Located behind the Málaga bullring, this place becomes hectic during any bullfight. It fills with aficionados and often, after the fight, with the matadors. But you can dine here anytime, especially when the pace is less frantic. The cuisine has an old-fashioned flair, and the servings are generous. The typical soup of the Málaga area is *ajo blanco con uvas* (cold almond soup flavored with garlic and garnished with big muscatel grapes). For a classic opener, try a plate of garlic-flavored mushrooms seasoned with bits of ham. The fresh seafood is a delight, including *rape* (monkfish) and angler fish; lamb might be served with a saffron-flavored tomato sauce. Desserts are like Mama made, including rice pudding.

INEXPENSIVE

La Manchega. Marín García, 4. ☎ **95-222-21-80.** Main courses 685–1,360 ptas. ($4.60–$9.10); fixed-price menu 1,200 ptas. ($8.05). No credit cards. Daily 11am–midnight. Bus: 7 or 9. SPANISH.

This crowded, popular tavern and restaurant has thrived since 1954. The 1920s building sits on a popular pedestrian-only street in Málaga's downtown commercial zone. La Manchega offers sidewalk tables, a ground-floor bar with tile walls, and a decorator's attempt to create an indoor Andalusian courtyard. A *salon comedor* offers additional space on an upper floor. Menu items include peppery fish soup, shrimp omelettes, Málaga-style soup, beans with Serrano ham, snails, eels, and a full selection of seafood, including grilled shrimp, hake, monkfish, clams, and mussels.

Mesón Danes (Faarup). Barroso, 7. ☎ **95-222-74-42.** Main courses 775–1,785 ptas. ($5.20–$11.95); menú del día 995 ptas. ($6.65). AE, DC, MC, V. Mon–Sat 11am–4:30pm and 7pm–midnight. Closed Aug. Bus: 15. DANISH/SPANISH.

Here you can enjoy low-cost Danish and Spanish snacks, including soup, fish, and meat. The cheapest menú del día represents one of the best food values in Málaga. Mesón Danes is near the harbor and city center.

MÁLAGA AFTER DARK

The fun of nightlife in Málaga is wandering (though a few destinations do stand out). More than just about any other city in the region, Málaga offers night owls the chance to stroll a labyrinth of inner-city streets, drinking wine at any convenient tasca, and talking with friends and new acquaintances.

We suggest that you start out along the town's main thoroughfare, **calle Larios,** which runs adjacent to the city's port. Off calle Larios, you can gravitate to any of the tascas, discos, and pubs lining the edges of the **calle Granada.** Of particular interest, in terms of the fun and atmosphere you're likely to find inside, are **Bar Pimpil,** calle Granada, s/n (no phone), and **La Posada,** calle Granada, s/n (no phone).

We'll let you in on a secret. If you want to eat well and cheaply, do as the locals do and head for either or both of the taverns below. Although nothing is refined, the food is some of the finest in Málaga, and some of the least expensive. You can easily fill up on two or three orders of tapas because portions are extremely generous.

The entrance to **Bar Loqüeno,** Marín García, 12 (☎ 95-222-30-48), is behind a wrought-iron-and-glass door, which leads into a stucco-lined room decorated in a local tavern style with a vengeance. There are enough hams, bouquets of garlic, beer kegs, fish nets, and sausages to feed an entire village for a week. However, there's hardly enough room to stand, and you'll invariably be jostled by a busy waiter shouting "Calamari!" to cooks in the back kitchens.

La Tasca, Marín García, 1-6 (between calle Larios and calle Nueva; ☎ 95-222-20-82), is not the place to go if you're looking for a quiet, mellow spot where no one ever raises a voice. The most famous bar in Málaga, this is a hole-in-the-wall; but it has style, conviviality, and a large staff crowded behind the bar to serve the sometimes-strident demands of practically everyone in Málaga, many of whom bring their children. Try the *croquetas* (croquettes) and the pungent shish kebabs laced with garlic and cumin. If you see an empty seat, try to commandeer it politely. Otherwise you'll stand in what might be awestruck observation of the social scene around you. Tapas and beer are very cheap. Open daily from noon to 4pm and 8pm to midnight.

Nearby, an all-pedestrian street, **calle Compagnía,** and a square, **Plaza Uncibaj,** are home to simpler tascas. Completely unpretentious (and in some cases without any discernable name), they serve glasses of wine and tapas similar to those available from their neighbors.

Looking for art history? As part of your tasca crawl, head for the **Plaza de la Merced,** where at least one simple bar accents the square that contains the birthplace of Pablo Picasso. (At press time the site was closed for renovation; it almost certainly will not reopen during the lifetime of this edition.) Two popular dance bars are **Saloma,** calle Luis de Valazquez, s/n; and **Cosa Nuestra,** calle Las Lazcano, 5. Don't even think of heading to either before 11pm, but once you're there, the music will probably continue till at least 4am.

11 Nerja

32 miles (51km) E of Málaga, 104 miles (167km) W of Almería, 340 miles (547km) S of Madrid

Nerja is known for its good beaches and small coves, its seclusion, its narrow streets and courtyards, and its whitewashed flat-roofed houses. Nearby is one of Spain's greatest attractions, the Cave of Nerja (see below).

At the mouth of the Chillar River, Nerja gets its name from the Arabic word *narixa,* meaning "bountiful spring." Its most dramatic spot is the **Balcón de Europa,** a palm-shaded promenade that juts out into the Mediterranean. The walkway was built in 1885 in honor of a visit from the Spanish king Alfonso XIII in the wake of an earthquake that had shattered part of nearby Málaga. The phrase "Balcón de Europa" (Balcony of Europe) is said to have been coined by the king during one of the speeches he made in Nerja praising the beauty of the panoramas around him. To reach the best beaches, head west from the Balcón and follow the shoreline.

ESSENTIALS

GETTING THERE   At least 10 buses per day make the 1½-hour trip from Málaga. From Almería, 4 buses a day make the 3-hour trip. Call the bus station, calle San Miguel, 3 (☎ 95-252-15-04), for information and schedules.

If you're driving, head along the N-340/E-15 east from Málaga or take the N-340/E-15 west from Almería.

VISITOR INFORMATION   The **tourist information office** is at Puerta del Mar, 2 (☎ 95-252-15-31). It's open Monday through Friday 10am to 2pm and 5:30 to 8:30pm, Saturday 10am to 1pm.

SPECIAL EVENTS   A **cultural festival** takes place here in July. In the past it has drawn leading artists, musicians, and dancers from around the world, including Yehudi Menuhin, Maya Plisetskaya, and the Bolshoi Ballet.

EXPLORING THE CUEVA DE NERJA

The most popular outing from Málaga and Nerja is to the ✪ **Cueva de Nerja** (Cave of Nerja), Carretera de Maro, s/n (☎ 95-252-96-35). Scientists believe this prehistoric stalactite and stalagmite cave was inhabited from 25,000 to 2000 B.C. It lay undiscovered until 1959, when a handful of boys found it by chance. When fully opened, it revealed a wealth of treasures left from the days of the cave dwellers, including Paleolithic paintings. These depict horses and deer, but as of this writing they are not open to the public. The archaeological museum in the cave contains a number of prehistoric artifacts. You can walk through stupendous galleries where ceilings soar to a height of 200 feet.

The cave is in the hills near Nerja. From here you get panoramic views of the countryside and sea. The cave is open daily from 10am to 2pm and from 4pm to 6:30pm. Admission is 650 ptas. ($4.35) for adults, 350 ptas. ($2.35) for children 6 to 12, free for children under 6. Buses to the cave leave from Muelle de Heredia in Málaga hourly from 7am until 8:15pm. Return buses are also hourly until 8:15pm. The journey takes about 1 hour.

WHERE TO STAY

EXPENSIVE

Hotel Mónica. Playa de la Torrecilla, s/n, 29780 Nerja. ☎ **95-252-11-00.** Fax 95-252-11-62. 235 units. A/C MINIBAR TV TEL. 18,000–24,000 ptas. ($120.60–$160.80) double. AE, DC, MC, V. Free parking.

Viewed from the air, Hotel Mónica looks something like a three-pronged propeller. At ground level, it has North African arches and green-and-white panels. The four-star hotel opened in 1986 in an isolated beachfront location about a 10-minute walk from the Balcón de Europa.

The glistening white marble in the lobby is highlighted with elaborately detailed cast-iron balustrades, curved marble staircases, and bas-reliefs, paintings, and sculptures. Some of the stairwells even contain oversize copies, set in tiles, of Claude Monet's beach scenes. The comfortable, good-size guest rooms have private balconies and tiled bathrooms.

Dining: Both restaurants have outdoor terraces or patios and serve standard international and Andalusian cuisine.

Amenities: A curved swimming pool is built into a terrace a few feet above the beach. Room service, baby-sitting, concierge, laundry and dry cleaning.

✪ Parador Nacional de Nerja. Calle Almuñecar, 8, Playa de Burriana-Tablazo, 29780 Nerja. ☎ **95-252-00-50.** Fax 95-252-19-97. 73 units. A/C MINIBAR TV TEL. 15,000–20,500 ptas. ($100.50–$137.35) double. AE, DC, MC, V. Free parking.

This government-owned hotel is on the outskirts of town, a 5-minute walk from the center. The modern design incorporates beamed ceilings, tile floors, and hand-loomed draperies. On the edge of a cliff, the hotel centers around a flower-filled courtyard with a splashing fountain. The spacious guest rooms are furnished in understated but tasteful style, and bathrooms are equipped with hair dryers and toiletries.

Dining: The restaurant serves international and Spanish meals.

Amenities: Social life centers on the large swimming pool and tennis courts. An elevator runs to the sandy beach below.

MODERATE

Hotel Balcón de Europa. Paseo Balcón de Europa, 1, 29780 Nerja. ☎ **95-252-08-00.** Fax 95-252-44-90. 111 units. A/C TV TEL. 11,900–17,100 ptas. ($79.75–$114.55) double; 16,100–26,500 ptas. ($107.85–$177.55) suite. AE, DC, MC, V. Parking 900 ptas. ($6.05).

Occupying the best position in town, at the edge of the Balcón de Europa, this 1970s hotel offers guest rooms with private balconies overlooking the water and the rocks. At a private beach nearby, parasol-shielded tables offer a place for a peaceful vista. The comfortable, midsize guest rooms have modern furniture, including firm beds, and marble floors. There's a private garage a few steps away.

Guests can dine at the fourth-floor restaurant Azul, which offers a panoramic view, or at the beach restaurant, Nautico. An international menu is served. The Nautico serves lunch and dinner in summer, lunch only in winter. The facilities include a sauna, health club, and solarium; the services include baby-sitting, laundry, and room service.

INEXPENSIVE

Cala-Bela. Puerta del Mar, 8, 29780 Nerja. ☎ **95-252-07-00.** Fax 95-252-07-04. 9 units. 5,000–6,500 ptas. ($33.50–$43.55) double. MC, V.

Originally built as a private house in 1895, and much modernized since, this well-positioned hotel lies only a 1-minute walk from the Balcón de Europa. Its guest rooms open onto the sea. They may be small, but what a view! The lounge is charming. The food in the seafront dining room is good—even if you're not staying at the hotel, you may want to give the restaurant a try. Try the fillet of pork in sherry sauce, the chef's paella, grilled crayfish, or trout with cream.

Hostal Mena. El Barrio, 15, 29780 Nerja. ☎ **95-252-05-41.** 12 units. TV. 3,500–5,500 ptas. ($23.45–$36.85) double. No credit cards.

This century-old little residencia sits near the Balcón de Europa. It's a charming place, with hundreds of blue-and-white Andalusian tiles lining the back walls of the central hallway. The small guest rooms are plain and functional, with good beds. The family that runs the hostal is very helpful. No meals are served.

Hostal Miguel. Almirante Ferrándiz, 31, 29780 Nerja. ☎ **95-252-15-23.** Fax 95-252-65-35. E-mail: hostal_miguel@hotmail.com. 9 units. 4,000–6,000 ptas. ($26.80–$40.20) double. MC, V.

The family-run Miguel is a pleasant, unpretentious inn whose simply furnished, somewhat small rooms have been renovated to add more Andalusian flavor. They're in a 19th-century building with iron-rimmed balconies, on a quiet back street about a 3-minute walk from the Balcón de Europa, and across from the well-known Pepe Rico Restaurant. Breakfast is the only meal served, usually on a lovely roof terrace with a view of the mountains and sea.

WHERE TO DINE

Casa Luque. Plaza Cavana, 2. ☎ **95-252-10-04.** Reservations required. Main courses 1,500–2,600 ptas. ($10.05–$17.40); tasting menu 2,950 ptas. ($19.75). AE, DC, MC, V. Daily 11am–4pm and 7–11:30pm. ANDALUSIAN.

With its impressive canopied and balconied facade, Casa Luque, near the heart of town, looks like a dignified private villa. The interior has an Andalusian courtyard, and in summer there is a sea-view terrace. Dishes are tasty and helpings quite filling—you'll find good value here. Meals change according to the season and might include Andalusian gazpacho, shoulder of ham, *osso bucco* (braised veal shank), pork fillet, hot-pepper chicken Casanova, or grilled meats. The limited selection of fish includes grilled Mediterranean grouper.

El Colono. Granada, 6. ☎ **95-252-18-26.** Reservations required. Wed and Fri, flamenco shows with fixed-price menus 2,995–3,995 ptas. ($20.05–$26.75); other nights, fixed-price lunch and dinner 1,195 ptas. ($8). No credit cards. Tues–Sun 8pm–midnight. Closed Nov 15–Dec 20. ANDALUSIAN/FRENCH.

A family place for a night of Spanish fun—that's El Colono, near the Balcón de Europa, a 3-minute walk from the main bus stop at Nerja. Guitar music and flamenco dancing are the entertainment highlights, and you can also dine here in a tavern atmosphere, enjoying set menus that feature local specialties. If you just want a glass of wine, you can still enjoy the shows (three per evening, from 8pm until "the wee hours").

Pepe Rico Restaurant. Almirante Ferrándiz, 28. ☎ **95-252-02-47.** Reservations recommended. Main courses 1,400-2,300 ptas. ($9.40–$15.40); fixed-price menu 1,500 ptas. ($10.05) at lunch, 3,500 ptas. ($23.45) at dinner. DC, MC, V. Wed–Mon 12:30–3pm and 7–11pm. Closed Dec 10–20 and Jan 10–Feb 17. INTERNATIONAL.

Established in 1966, Pepe Rico is one of Nerja's finest places for food. It's in a white building with grille windows and little balconies. The rooms open onto a large rear balcony overlooking a flower-filled courtyard. Dining is in a tavern room with plaster walls and ivy vines that creep in from the patio, where you can order meals alfresco.

The specialty of the day, which might be a Spanish, German, Swedish, or French dish, ranges from almond-and-garlic soup to duck in Málaga wine. The impressive list of hors d'oeuvres includes Pepe Rico salad, smoked swordfish, salmon mousse, and prawns *pil-pil* (with hot chile peppers). Main dishes include fillet of sole Don Pepe, roast leg of lamb, prawns Café de Paris, and steak dishes. Considering the quality of the food, the prices are reasonable.

Restaurante de Miguel. Pintada, 2. ☎ **95-252-29-96.** Reservations recommended. Main courses 1,400–2,200 ptas. ($9.40–$14.75); fixed-price menu 2,400 ptas. ($16.10). MC, V. Daily 8pm–midnight. Closed Feb and 2 Mondays each month. INTERNATIONAL.

This restaurant is the best in town. Established in 1986 by the son of a Nerja resident, at first it drew only local families hoping for their friend to succeed. Since then, mostly because of the excellent food, the place has attracted a devoted crowd of foreign visitors and expatriate residents of the Costa del Sol. It sits in the center of town near the busiest traffic intersection, behind a plate-glass aquarium loaded with fresh lobsters, fish, and shellfish. Its small air-conditioned interior is one of the most upscale places in Nerja, with white marble floors, elegant crystal and porcelain, and crisp white napery. The menu lists a full array of well-prepared international dishes, including cream of shrimp soup flavored with cognac, tournedos with goat-cheese sauce, and sea bass with Pernod and fennel. There's a wide selection of beef and steak dishes, and concoctions composed from the cornucopia of fish from the aquarium.

Restaurante Rey Alfonso. Paseo Balcón de Europa, s/n. ☎ **95-252-09-58.** Reservations recommended. Main courses 700–1,900 ptas. ($4.70–$12.75). MC, V. Thurs–Tues 11am–4pm and 7–11pm. Closed Nov. SPANISH/INTERNATIONAL.

Few visitors to the Balcón de Europa realize that they're standing directly above one of the most unusual restaurants in town. The restaurant's menu and decor don't hold many surprises, but the close-up view of the crashing waves makes dining here worthwhile. Have a drink at the bar if you don't want a full meal. Specialties include a well-prepared *paella valenciana*, Cuban-style rice, five preparations of sole (from grilled to meunière), several versions of tournedos and entrecôte, beef Stroganoff, crayfish in whisky sauce, and crêpes suzette for dessert. You enter from the bottom of a flight of stairs that skirts the rocky base of a late-19th-century *miradora* (viewing station), which juts seaward as an extension of the town's main square.

Valencia & the Costa Blanca 9

Spain's third-largest city, Valencia—celebrated for oranges and paella—lies in the midst of a *huerta,* a fertile crescent of an alluvial plain that's irrigated by a system built centuries ago. The area is a bread basket of Spain, a place where "the soil never sleeps."

For such a major city, Valencia is relatively unexplored by tourists, even though it has some rewarding treasures, including a wealth of baroque architecture, fine museums, and good cuisine, and a proud if troubled history.

The Costa Blanca (White Coast) begins rather unappealingly at Valencia but improves considerably as it winds its way south toward Alicante. The overbuilt route is dotted with fishing ports and resorts known chiefly to Spanish and other European vacationers. The success of **Benidorm** began in the 1960s, when the fishing village was transformed into an international resort. **Alicante,** the official capital of the Costa Blanca, enjoys a reputation as a winter resort because of its mild climate. **Murcia** is inland, but it's on the main road to the Costa del Sol, so hordes of motorists pass through it.

1 Valencia

218 miles (351km) SE of Madrid, 224 miles (361km) SW of Barcelona, 404 miles (650km) NE of Málaga

Valencia's charms—or lack thereof—have been much debated. Some who claim that the city where El Cid faced the Moors is one of the most beautiful on the Mediterranean. Many more write it off as drab, provincial, and industrial. The truth lies somewhere in between.

Set in the midst of orange trees and rice paddies, Valencia has a reputation as a romantic city that seems justified more by its past than by its present looks. Hidden between modern office buildings and monotonous apartment houses, remnants of that illustrious past do remain. However, floods and war have been cruel to Valencia, forcing Valencianos to tear down buildings that today would be architectural treasures.

Valencia also has a strong cultural tradition. Its most famous son was writer Vicente Blasco Ibáñez, best known for his novel about bullfighting, *Blood and Sand,* and for his World War I novel, *The Four Horsemen of the Apocalypse.* Both were filmed twice in Hollywood, with Rudolph Valentino starring in the first version of each. Joaquín Sorolla, the famous Spanish impressionist, was another native of Valencia. You can see his works at a museum dedicated to him in Madrid.

ESSENTIALS

GETTING THERE   **Iberia** flies to Valencia from Barcelona, Madrid, Málaga, and many other cities. There are also flights between Palma de Majorca and Valencia. You'll land 9 miles (14.5km) southwest of the city; bus no. 15, which leaves hourly, will take you into the city (150 ptas./$1). For flight information, contact the Iberia Airlines office, calle Paz, 14 (☎ **96-352-75-52**).

Trains run to Valencia from all parts of Spain. The Estación del Norte (North Station), calle Xàtiva 24, is close to the heart of the city, making it a convenient arrival point. Its information office, calle Renfe (☎ **96-352-02-02**), is open daily 7am to 9pm. From Barcelona, 11 trains—both the *TALGO* (which takes 4 hours and is more expensive) and the *rápido* (6 hours)—arrive daily. Eleven trains daily connect Madrid to Valencia—the *TER* (5 hours and more expensive) and the *rápido* (7½ hours). From Málaga, on the Costa del Sol, the trip takes 9 hours.

Buses arrive at Valencia's Estació Terminal d'Autobuses, Avenida de Menéndez Pidal, 15 (☎ **96-349-72-22**), about a 30-minute walk northwest of the city's center. Take bus no. 8 from the Plaza del Ayuntamiento. Thirteen buses a day, at least one every hour, run from Madrid (5 hours away), 10 buses from Barcelona (5 hours), and 5 buses from Málaga (11 hours).

You can take a **ferry** to and from the Balearic Islands (see chapter 18). Ferries to Palma de Majorca take 6 hours. Ferries leave Valencia for Ibiza at midnight Thursday through Tuesday from June 15 to September 15. Travel agents in Valencia sell tickets, or you can buy them from the Transmediterránea office at the port, Estació Marítima (☎ **96-367-06-44**), on the day of your departure. To reach the port, take bus no. 4 or 19 from the Plaza del Ayuntamiento.

The easiest route if you're driving is the express highway (E-15) south from Barcelona. You can also use a national highway, E-901, from Madrid, which lies northwest of Valencia. From Alicante, take the E-15 express highway north. If you're coming from Andalusia, the roads are longer, more difficult, and not connected by express highways. You can drive from Málaga north to Granada and cut across southeastern Spain on the 342, which links with the 340 into Murcia. From there, take the road to Alicante for an easy drive into Valencia. The Barcelona-Valencia toll is 3,000 ptas. ($20.10).

VISITOR INFORMATION   The **tourist information office** is at Plaza del Ayuntamiento, 1 (☎ **96-351-04-17**). It's open Monday through Friday 8:30am to 2:15pm and 4:15 to 6pm, Saturday 9am to 12:45pm.

GETTING AROUND   Most local buses leave from Playa del Ayuntamiento, 22. You can buy tickets at any newsstand. The one-way fare is 110 ptas. (75¢), and a 10-ride booklet sells for 695 ptas. ($4.65). Bus no. 8 runs from Playa del Ayuntamiento to the bus station at Avenida Menéndez Pidal. A bus map is available at the EMT office, calle En Sanz, 4. It's open Monday through Friday 8am to 3:30pm. For bus information, call ☎ **96-352-83-99.**

If you need a taxi, call ☎ **96-370-33-33** or 96-357-13-13.

SPECIAL EVENTS   The *Fallas de San José,* honoring the arrival of spring, is held in March (dates vary). It is a time for parades, street dancing, fireworks, and bullfights. Neighborhoods compete to see who can erect the most intricate and satirical papier-mâché effigy, or *ninot.* Some 300 ninots then appear in the street parades. The festival ends with *la nit del foc,* or "fire night," when effigies are burned. Historically, this inferno was to exorcise social problems and bring luck to farmers in the coming summer.

FAST FACTS   The local **American Express** representative is **Duna Viajes,** calle Cirilo Amorós, 88 (☎ **96-374-15-62**). It's open Monday through Friday 10am to 2pm and 5pm to 8pm, Saturday 9am to 2pm.

The Costa Blanca

Sagunto

234

Requena

Valencia

To
Majorca →

NIII   E901

N322

La
Albufera

To
Ibiza →

Casas Ibáñez

N332

N330

N340

E15
A7

Játiva

N430

N430

N340

N430

Almansa

Alcoy

N330

Seco River

N344

E15
A7

Benidorm

N332

N301

A7

Alicante

E15

Elche

E15
A7

Mula

Murcia

N332

E15

N340

SPAIN

★ Madrid

N301

Costa
Blanca

Totana

N332

Cartagena

| 0 | 100 mi |
| 0 | 100 km |

N

The **U.S. Consular Agency** is at calle Paz, 6 (☎ **96-351-69-73**); it's open Monday through Friday 10am to 1pm.

In a medical emergency, call ☎ **091** or 092, or go to the **Hospital Clínico Universitario,** Avenida Blasco Ibáñez, 17 (☎ **96-386-26-00**).

Don't be surprised if you see signs in a language that's not Spanish or Catalán. It is *valenciano,* a dialect of Catalán. Often you'll be handed a "bilingual" menu in Castilian Spanish and in *valenciano.* Many citizens of Valencia are not caught up in this cultural resurgence, and view the promotion of the dialect as possibly damaging to the city's economic goals. Most street names appear in valenciano.

The self-service **Lavandería El Mercat,** Plaza del Mercado, 12 (☎ **96-391-20-10**), is open Monday through Friday 10am to 2pm and 4:40 to 8:30pm, Saturday 10am to 1:30pm.

The local **telephone office** at Plaza del Ayuntamiento, 24 (☎ **96-003**), is open Monday through Saturday 9am to 11pm. Making a long-distance call here is much cheaper than making one from your hotel room.

EXPLORING VALENCIA

Corridas (**bullfights**) are staged for a week during the *fallas* observances in the summer (see "Spain Calendar of Events" in chapter 2). Today, locals seem more interested in soccer than in bullfighting. Nevertheless, one of the largest rings in Spain lies adjacent to the rail station at calle de Xátiva, 28 (☎ **96-351-93-15**).

Catedral (Seu). Plaza de la Reina. ☎ **96-391-81-27**. Admission to cathedral free; to Miguelete 200 ptas. ($1.35); to Museo de la Catedral 200 ptas. ($1.35). Cathedral daily 7:30am–1pm and 4:30–8:30pm; Miguelete Mon–Sat 10am–12:30pm and 4:30–7:30pm, Sun 10am–1pm and 5–7:30pm; Museo de la Catedral Mon–Sat 10am–1pm and 4–6pm. Bus: 9, 27, 70, or 71.

For 500 years, this cathedral has claimed to possess the Holy Grail, the chalice Jesus used at the Last Supper; it's on display in a side chapel. The subject of countless legends, the Grail was said to have been used by Joseph of Arimathea to collect Jesus' blood as it fell from the cross. It looms large in Sir Thomas Malory's *Morte d'Arthur,* Tennyson's *Idylls of the King,* and Wagner's *Parsifal.*

Although this 1262 cathedral represents a number of styles, including Romanesque and baroque, Gothic predominates. Its huge arches have been restored, and in back is a handsome domed basilica. It was built on the site of a mosque torn down by the Catholic monarchs.

After seeing the cathedral, you can scale an incomplete 155-foot-high Gothic tower—known as **Miguelete** (or Micalet in local dialect). It affords a panoramic view of the city and the fertile *huerta* beyond. Or visit the **Museo de la Catedral,** where works by Goya and Zurbarán are on exhibit.

Palau de la Generalitat. Caballeros, 2. ☎ **96-386-34-61**. Free admission. Mon–Fri 9am–2pm. Bus: 5.

In the old aristocratic quarter of Valencia, this Gothic palace, built in the 15th and 16th centuries, is one of the most fascinating edifices in Spain. It has two square towers (one constructed as recently as 1952), carved wooden ceilings and galleries, and frescoes. It now serves as the headquarters of the regional government (Generalitat).

La Lonja de la Seda. Plaza del Mercado. ☎ **96-391-36-08**. Free admission. Tues–Fri 9am–1:30pm and 5–7pm, Sat–Sun 9am–1:30pm. Closed holidays. Bus: 4, 7, 27, 60, or 81.

The former silk exchange, completed in 1498, is the most splendid example of secular Gothic architecture in Spain. A beautiful building, La Lonja has twisted spiral columns inside, and stained-glass windows.

Valencia

Casa Museo José Benlliure ④
Catedral ⑨
Instituto Valenciano de Arte Moderno ⑩
Jardín Botánico ⑤
Jardines del Real ①
La Lonja de la Seda ⑪
Museo San Pio ②
Museo Nacional de Cerámica ⑫
Museo Taurino ⑭
Palacio de la Generalitat ⑧
Plaza de Toros ⑬
San Nicolás ⑦
Torres de Quart ⑥
Torres de Serranos ③

Legend
Church ✝
Information ⓘ

SPAIN
★ Madrid
● Valencia

Museu San Pío (Museu Sant Píus V). San Pío V, 9. ☎ **96-393-20-46.** Free admission. Tues–Sat 10am–2:15pm and 4–7:30pm, Sun 10am–2:15pm. Bus: 1, 5, 6, 8, 11, 18, 26, 29, 36, and 79. Metro: Alameda.

This treasure house of paintings and sculptures, which stands on the north bank of the Turia River, contains a strong collection of Flemish and native Valencian art. Of particular note are those by the 14th- and 15th-century Valencian "primitives." The most celebrated painting is a 1640 self-portrait by Velázquez, and a whole room is devoted to Goya. Other artists exhibited include Bosch, Morales, El Greco (*St. John the Baptist*), Ribera, Murillo, Pinturicchio, and Sorolla. Of special interest is a salon displaying the works of contemporary Valencian painters and an important sculpture by Mariano Benlliure. The ground-floor archaeological collection encompasses early Iberian, Roman (including an altar to a pagan emperor), and early Christian finds.

✪ **Instituto Valencia de Arte Moderno (IVAM).** Calle Guillém Castro, 118. ☎ **96-386-30-00.** Admission 350 ptas. ($2.45) adults, free for children. Julio González Center, Tues–Sun 10am–7pm; Center del Carmen, Tues–Sun 11am–2:30pm and 4:30–7pm. Bus: 5.

This giant complex consists of two sites: an ultramodern building and a 13th-century former convent. Its opening gained Valencia prime status among the world's art capitals.

The **Julio González Center** is named for the avant-garde Spanish artist whose paintings, sculptures, and drawings form the nucleus of the permanent collection. Much influenced by Picasso, González was a pioneer in iron sculpture. His work in turn exerted a profound influence on the American sculptor David Smith, among others.

The other site is the nearby **Center del Carmen,** the old convent, with cloisters from the 14th and the 16th centuries. It contains three halls devoted to changing exhibits of contemporary art. Permanent displays include works of Ignacio Pinazo, whose paintings and drawings mark the beginning of modernism in Valencia.

The institute is on the western edge of the old quarter, near the Torres de Quart.

Ciudad de las Artes y de las Ciencias (City of the Arts and Sciences). Monte Olivete. ☎ **902-10-00-31.** L'Hemisferic Tues–Fri 11am–8:30pm; Sat 11am–3pm and 5–11pm; Sun 11am–3pm and 5–8:30pm. Other venues Sun and Tues–Thurs 11am–9:30pm, Fri–Sat 11am–11pm. Admission to L'Hemisferic Tues–Fri 1,000 ptas. ($6.70) adults; 700 ptas. ($4.70) children, students, seniors; Sat–Sun and holidays 1,000 ptas. ($6.70). Prices for other sections not available at press time. Bus: 13, 14, or 15 to Centro Comercio de Saler.

In a bid to rival Seville's Expo and Barcelona's redeveloped port, Valencia recently unveiled what has been billed as "the largest urban complex in Europe for cultural, educational, and leisure expansion." It's in the southern part of the city, on a 90-acre site in a carefully landscaped park of lush greenery and peaceful lagoons. Started 10 years ago, it should be complete by 2000.

The point of the complex is to make learning fun. The state-of-the-art educational center consists of four main buildings: L'Hemisferic, L'Oceanografic, the Palacio de las Artes, and the Museum de las Ciencias.

L'Hemisferic: Designed by award-winning architect Santiago Calatrava, this building offers the public a range of documentaries and an exploration of the universe. The laser show (with changing programs) runs on an 900-square-foot concave IMAX screen, with the soundtrack in four languages, and six-channel stereo.

L'Oceanografic: Twenty acres of the complex are dedicated to an amazing arrangement of lagoons and leisure pavilions. They re-create marine habitats from every ocean. There is a dolphinarium for aquatic shows, and a miniport for playing with remote-controlled boats. Submarine glass walkways connect the areas, and there is an underwater restaurant.

Palacio de las Artes: A seemingly weightless 150-foot-high glass and metal construction contains one outdoor and two indoor auditoriums. All three have the latest technology for the performance of plays, opera, and music.

Museo de las Ciencias: This enormous building houses an interactive museum where visitors are encouraged to look and touch. It has an information center that's networked to educational resources, and an exhibition center for high-technology companies.

BEACHES, BULLFIGHTING & MORE

BEACHES   The beaches to the north and south of the port, Playa de la Punta and Playa de Levante, are too polluted for swimming. To go to the beach, head south in the direction of **El Saler,** where you'll find cleaner waters.

BOATING   **Club Náutico Valencia,** Camí del Canal, 91 (☎ **96-367-90-11**), has a sailing school that rents boats for scuba diving, fishing, and snorkeling. It also maintains a full yacht service facility.

GOLF   There are four major golf courses in the area. One of the best is **Golf El Saler** at the Parador Luis Vives (☎ **96-161-03-84**), 11 miles (18km) south of Valencia in a panoramic setting of pine dunes. Another good course is the **Club de Campo del Bosque,** Carretera Godelleta, km 4.1, Chiva (☎ **96-180-41-42**), 2½ miles (4km) from Valencia. Or try the **Club de Golf Escorpión at Bétera** (☎ **96-160-12-11**), 12 miles (19km) northwest en route to Liria. All three are 18-hole courses. There's a nine-hole course, the **Manises Golf Club** (☎ **96-152-38-04**), on the Carretera Riba Roja, km 4 at Manises, 7½ miles (12km) west of Valencia.

SHOPPING

There are fewer souvenir shops and tourist facilities in workaday Valencia than in any other Spanish city its size. Instead, you're likely to find everyday reality in the form of middle-brow department stores and food and wine emporiums. The best shopping streets include the **Plaza Ayuntamiento, calle Don Juan de Austria, calle Colon,** and the streets thereabouts. For a peek at what aging Valencian *duennas* are storing in their cellars and attics, head for the *rastro* (flea market) in the Avenida de Suecia, near the soccer stadium, beginning around 8:30am every Sunday. The city's largest department store, **El Corte Inglés,** calle Pintor Sorolla (☎ **96-351-24-44**), sells a wide array of everything you might need, including local handcrafts, crystal and porcelain, and other luxury items.

Valencia is home to some of Spain's best pottery. The region produces Lladró porcelain, Manises stoneware, and glassware. Local craftspeople take pride in their *azuelejos*—brightly colored ceramic tiles, first developed during the Muslim occupation of Andalusia.

One worthy detour is to **Manises,** 5½ miles (9km) west of Valencia. It's known as a center for Valencian ceramics and for its *azulejos.* As a pottery center, Manises dates from the Middle Ages. Representatives from all the major kingdoms of Europe came here to purchase the wares, which are characterized by their distinctive blue-and-white patterns. The town is packed with ceramics factories and retail outlets. From the center of Valencia, several buses run frequently to Manises. The tourist office will give you a bus schedule.

Another good stop for the serious shopper is nearby **Paterna,** about 4 miles (6km) northwest of Valencia off C-234 (it's signposted all the way). It has dozens of pottery stores, with prices far below those in the center of Valencia.

Continuing farther north to the province of Castellón, you'll find the towns of **Alcora** and **Onda.** They're justly celebrated for their pottery, much of which is reasonably priced because the "middleperson" is often eliminated. In addition to pottery, several shops in Onda sell some of the best-crafted azulejos in this part of Spain. **Alcora** is 12 miles (19km) northwest of Castellón de la Plana along the C-232; **Onda,** 9 miles (15km) west along the C-223.

In the city of Valencia itself, head for **Lladró,** calle Poeta Querol, s/n (☎ **96-351-1625**), where prices are consistent with those at other retail outlets. Or seek out the shop adjacent to the factory, **Casa de Lladró,** carretera de Alborraya, s/n, in the suburb of Tavernas Blancas (☎ **96-185-01-77**), 3 miles north of the city center. The factory retail outlet sells slightly damaged or irregular pieces, at lower prices. To visit the factory, call 1 month in advance.

WHERE TO STAY

In July and August, when Valencia can be uncomfortably hot and humid, some hoteliers will significantly lower prices if business is slow. It never hurts to ask.

EXPENSIVE

Hotel Astoria Palace. Plaza Rodrigo Botet, 5, 46002 Valencia. ☎ **96-352-67-37.** Fax 96-352-80-78. 203 units. A/C MINIBAR TV TEL. 18,900–27,000 ptas. ($126.65–$180.90) double; 22,000–32,000 ptas. ($147.40–$214.40) junior suite. AE, DC, MC, V. Parking 1,500 ptas. ($10.05) nearby. Bus: 9, 10, 27, 70, or 71.

On a small, charming square in the heart of town, this modern business hotel contains some of the best-furnished public and private rooms in Valencia. A favorite of such Spanish stars as opera singer Montserrat Caballé, bullfighter Manuel Benítez ("El Cordobés"), and an impressive roster of writers and politicians, the Astoria is plush, well managed, and appealing. Many of the tastefully furnished guest rooms overlook a statue of Grecian maidens and swans in the square outside. The highest prices are for three premium floors, which have a private lounge and separate check-in. Each of the tiled bathrooms is equipped with a hair dryer. The hotel is 5 short blocks south of the cathedral.

Dining/Diversions: The Vinatea restaurant serves regional and international three-course fixed-price lunches and dinners. There's also a bar.

Amenities: 24-hour room service, laundry and limousine service, concierge, baby-sitting; car rentals, boutiques, gym, Jacuzzi.

Hotel Reina Victoria. Barcas, 4, 46002 Valencia. ☎ **96-352-04-87.** Fax 96-352-27-21. www.husa.es. E-mail: hreinavictoriavalencia@husa.es. 97 units. A/C MINIBAR TV TEL. 14,000–21,000 ptas. ($93.80–$140.70) double. Weekend prices include breakfast. AE, DC, MC, V. Parking 1,600 ptas. ($10.70). Bus: 4, 7, or 27.

Although it has lost some of its charm and luster in recent years, the Reina Victoria has a reputation as the most architecturally glamorous hotel in Valencia. Built in 1913, the hotel has welcomed many distinguished guests, including Alfonso XIII and Queen Victoria (its namesake), Dalí, Manolete, Picasso, Falla, Garcia Lorca, and Miró. Bristling with neoclassical detailing and wrought-iron accents, it overlooks the flower gardens and fountains of Valencia's central square, the Plaza del País Valenciano. Rooms range from small to medium in size (only a few are really spacious), and have first-class mattresses and private safes. The bathrooms, though tiny, contain both a tub and a shower. The hotel lies in the heart of town, a 5-minute walk from the railway station.

Dining: The Bar Inglés is a popular rendezvous, and the hotel's restaurant, El Levant, serves international food in a dignified setting. There's also a cafeteria-style restaurant.

Amenities: Concierge, laundry and dry cleaning, room service, baby-sitting, business services, conference rooms, boutiques.

Meliá Rey Don Jaime. Avenida de Baleares, 2, 46023 Valencia. ☎ **800/336-3542** in the U.S., or 96-337-50-30. Fax 96-337-15-72. 319 units. A/C MINIBAR TV TEL. 12,850–26,400 ptas. ($86.10–$176.90) double; 50,000 ptas. ($335) suite. AE, DC, MC, V. Parking 1,350 ptas. ($9.05). Bus: 19, 41, 89, or 90.

A respected member of one of Spain's largest hotel chains, the Meliá towers over the urban landscape about half a mile southeast of the cathedral. Many guests appreciate the hotel's proximity to the convention and concert hall (Palau de la Música) midway between the Old Town and the port. The stylish public rooms are sheathed in marble, rough stone, and tile work, whereas the guest rooms are sunny, well-maintained enclaves of contemporary style. The best units—more spacious and better furnished— are on the third floor. However, all rooms come with fine mattresses, private safes, and hair dryers. Many of the accommodations on the upper floors open onto panoramic views of the port and the sea.

Dining: The Restaurante Christina serves international cuisine. The richly paneled bar, with leather sofas and armchairs, evokes a private club in England.

Amenities: 24-hour room service, laundry and valet, concierge, baby-sitting, business center, car-rental kiosk, solarium, rooftop swimming pool.

MODERATE

✪ **Hotel Consul del Mar.** Avenida del Puerto, 39, 46021 Valencia. ☎ **96-362-54-32**. Fax 96-362-16-25. 40 units. A/C TV TEL. 12,000–17,000 ptas. ($80.40–$113.90) double. AE, DC, MC, V. Parking 1,200 ptas. ($8.05). Bus: 1, 2, or 4.

This hotel occupies a meticulously renovated 19th-century structure. The building, once known as an *antigua casa señorial*, retains much of the old architectural decoration. Guest rooms are good-size and often furnished with antiques, including the beds. Each has a luxury mattress and a private safe-deposit box; bathrooms have hair dryers, hydromassage baths, and deluxe toiletries. The hotel, whose facade is beautifully lit at night, also has a good restaurant, room service, laundry, and dry cleaning.

Hotel Inglés. Marqués de Dos Aguas, 6, 46002 Valencia. ☎ **96-351-64-26**. Fax 96-394-02-51. 63 units. A/C MINIBAR TV TEL. 20,000 ptas. ($134) double. AE, DC, MC, V. Parking 2,000 ptas. ($14). Bus: 6, 9, 11, 31, or 32.

This turn-of-the-century hotel, the former palace of the Duke and Duchess of Cardona, has aged well. In the heart of old Valencia, it stands opposite another Churrigueresque palace. Guest rooms vary in size, and most overlook the tree-lined street. They offer comforts such as sofa beds with fine linens, and immaculately kept bathrooms equipped with plush towels and hair dryers. Ask for a room with a view of one of the city's many palaces. The lounge and dining room have chandeliers, gilt mirrors, provincial armchairs, and murals. The service is discreet and polite.

Hotel Villacarlos. Avenida del Puerto, 60, 46023 Valencia. ☎ **96-337-50-25**. Fax 96-337-50-74. 51 units. A/C MINIBAR TV TEL. Mon–Thurs 14,500 ptas. ($97.15) double, Fri–Sun 8,500 ptas. ($56.95) double. AE, DC, MC, V. Parking 1,600 ptas. ($10.70). Bus: 19.

Located close to the river, the hotel is within easy walking distance of most of the city's monuments. Following Barcelona's lead, Valencia has been keen to adopt the new, and the Hotel Villacarlos is a prime example. The hotel has a simple postmodern facade that makes the reception area's bright orange decor all the more surprising. Abstract paintings in orange and blue (the hotel's color scheme) adorn the walls—remember your sunglasses if you have a headache. In the guest rooms, blue and orange are kept to a minimum. There's cable TV and good air-conditioning. The furniture is functional and new, including comfortable beds and full-length mirrors. Bathrooms are well stocked.

The restaurant offers menús del día for 2,500 to 3,000 ptas. ($16.75 to $20.10) at lunch, and a buffet in the evening.

INEXPENSIVE

Hostal Residencia Bisbal. Pie de la Cruz, 9, 46001 Valencia. ☎ **96-391-70-84.** Fax 96-392-37-37. 15 units. 4,000–5,000 ptas. ($26.80–$33.50) double. No credit cards. Parking 1,900 ptas. ($12.75). Bus: 8, 27, 29, or 81.

Conveniently located in the old city, this husband-and-wife operation has simply furnished rooms. They're a bit small, but tidy and comfortable, with good beds. No meals are served, but you'll find many bars and restaurants nearby. The English-speaking staff is very helpful.

Sorolla. Convento de Santa Clara, 5, 46002 Valencia. ☎ **96-352-33-92.** Fax 96-352-14-65. 50 units. A/C TV TEL. 10,200 ptas. ($68.35) double. AE, DC, MC, V. Parking nearby 1,700 ptas. ($11.40). Bus: Any route from the rail station.

In the city center, this six-story hotel built in the 1960s is named after Valencia's most famous artist. The guest rooms have narrow balconies and compact, utilitarian furnishings, including good beds. Comfort, not style, is the key. No meals are served.

WHERE TO DINE
EXPENSIVE

Eladio. Calle Chiva, 40. ☎ **96-384-22-44.** Reservations recommended. Main courses 1,600–3,200 ptas. ($10.70–$21.45). AE, DC, MC, V. Mon–Sat 1–4pm and 8–11:30pm. Closed Aug. SPANISH/INTERNATIONAL.

Borrowing from culinary models he learned during his apprenticeship in Switzerland, Eladio Rodríguez prepares flavorful cuisine based on seasonal ingredients. The menu changes daily, depending on what is fresh and available. Some diners particularly praise his shellfish and fish from his native Galicia, which might include hake, monkfish, or sea wolf, prepared as simply or as elaborately as you want. Many order them grilled simply over charcoal and served with garlic butter sauce. Noteworthy dishes include octopus and ragout of shellfish, anglerfish, and salmon. Pastries, prepared by Eladio's wife, Violette, make a suitable finish. The setting is calm and pleasant.

✪ **Oscar Torrijos.** Calle Dr Sumsi, 4. ☎ **96-373-29-49.** Reservations required. Main courses 1,600–3,500 ptas. ($10.70–$23.45); menú de gourmet 1,500 ptas. ($10.05); tasting menu 5,000 ptas. ($33.50). AE, DC, MC, V. Mon–Sat 1–4pm and 9–11:30pm. Closed Aug 15– Sept 15. Metro: Calle Colon. MEDITERRANEAN/INTERNATIONAL.

This stellar restaurant serves the best cuisine in Valencia. The menu follows a philosophy described as Mediterranean by the owner and chef, Oscar Torrijos. His food displays his knowledge of French and German cooking, which he acquired while working for many years in Switzerland. His years abroad also taught him the importance of good lighting and soft illumination. Specialties include rice dishes (for which Valencia is famous), in particular paella. Rice with rape and artichokes is excellent, as is rice with king prawns. Fish from the Mediterranean and the Atlantic features heavily on the menu. Señor Torrijos also makes delicious foie gras. Wine buffs should note that there are some 25,000 quality bottles in his cellar. The restaurant is centrally located in the Barrio Carmen.

MODERATE

El Gourmet. Calle Taquígrafo Martí, 3. ☎ **96-395-25-09.** Reservations recommended. Main courses 1,900–3,800 ptas. ($12.75–$25.45); fixed-priced menu 2,550 ptas. ($17.10). AE, DC, MC, V. Mon–Sat 1–4pm and 9–11:30pm. Closed 1 week at Easter and Sat–Sun in Aug. SPANISH/INTERNATIONAL.

This restaurant has long been known as an honest establishment where well-trained waiters serve good-quality, reasonably priced food. Set in the center of Valencia, it offers such dishes as hake with clams, partridge with herbs in puff pastry, oxtail stew, fried fillets of veal or pork, scrambled eggs with eggplant and shrimp, and seasonal vegetables.

Palace Fesol. Hernán Cortés, 7. ☎ **96-352-93-23.** Reservations recommended. Main courses 1,500–3,000 ptas. ($10.05–$20.10). AE, DC, MC, V. Mon–Sun 1–4pm, Tues–Sat 9–11:30pm. Closed Sat–Sun June 15–Sept 15. Bus: 5. Metro: Colon. MEDITERRANEAN.

In the years after World War I, the Palace Fesol became famous for its namesake specialty, lima beans. Today, many more excellent dishes grace the menu at the "bean palace," with typical Valencian paella high on the list at lunch. You can also order several chicken dishes served with rice (included under the general name *paella* because they are cooked in paella pans). Dinner selections include *zarzuela de mariscos* (shellfish medley), grilled red mullet and baby hake, baby lamb cutlets, and chateaubriand. Photos of film stars, bullfighters, and other celebrities line the walls. The restaurant is cooled by old-fashioned ceiling fans and decorated with beamed ceilings, lanterns, and a hand-painted tile mosaic.

INEXPENSIVE

✪ **El Plat.** Ciscar, 3. ☎ **96-374-12-54.** Reservations recommended. Main courses 1,500–4,000 ptas. ($10.05–$26.80). AE, MC, V. Tues–Sun 1–3:30pm and Tues–Sat 9–11pm. Closed Easter week. SPANISH/INTERNATIONAL.

If you want a taste of the dish that brought Valencia its culinary fame, El Plat will deliver. The local media hail it as "El Rey del Arroz" (Rice King), because it features a variation of the city's most famous dish, paella, every day. The daily versions of *arroz* keep the menu fresh and ever changing. Other choices include typical Spanish fare of meat and fish dishes. The decor reflects the location—whitewashed walls and displays of local art create a bright environment that serves as a constant reminder that you are on the "white coast." The service is helpful and friendly, and the atmosphere festive.

Patos. Calle del Mar, 28. ☎ **96-392-1522.** Reservations recommended. Main courses 800–1,800 ptas. ($5.35–$12.05). Fixed-price lunch 1,421 ptas. ($9.50); fixed-price dinner 1,675 ptas. ($11.20). MC, V. Daily 1–4pm and 8:30–midnight. Bus: El Carte Inglés. SPANISH.

In a slightly battered turn-of-the century town house, this restaurant in the town center has thrived since the early 1980s. At least part of its reputation derives from its daily preparations of *patos* (duck), which is better here than anywhere else in town. Expect pressed and grilled versions with orange, cherry, or herb sauce, usually accompanied by fresh vegetables and potatoes. There are two dining rooms plus an outdoor terrace that overlooks a garden. Other choices include pizza, pasta, steak, grilled pork loin, and such desserts as flan and freshly baked pastries.

VALENCIA AFTER DARK

Where you go at night in Valencia depends on when you visit. The best area in the cooler months is in the center, in the historic **Barrio Carmen.** Valencia is famous for its *marcha* (nightlife) and for its bohemian bars. The **Calle Alta** is a good street to start your "tasca crawl" or to bar-hop.

An evening out in Valencia might also involve a series of tasca crawls that focus on the historic core around the **Plaza de Ayuntamiento.** Some of the most evocative tascas don't even have clear signs—your best bet involves hopping in and out of whichever appeals to you. Among our favorites, a short walk from Town Hall and Valencia's tourism office, are the **Bar Canovas,** Plaza de Canovas del Castillo, s/n (no phone), and the **Bar Zaena,** calle Antiguo Reino de Valencia, s/n (no phone).

The Disappearing Barracas

The orchard lands around Valencia once held hundreds of *barracas,* shedlike farm buildings where workers lived. These symbols of life in the area are now disappearing. Barracas are built of mud mixed with rice husks and strengthened with reeds to form whitewashed walls. The ground plan is rectangular, and a cross tops the front wall. The steep, saddle-back roof provides easy drainage of scarce (though torrential) rainwater and shelter from the summer heat.

The lower rooms of the structure are laid out in rows, and the top room (*andana*) is used for storage or for raising silkworms. A smaller *barraca,* used as a kitchen or for stables, is often attached. Barracas can still be seen in and around Valencia at El Saler, at El Palma, and in the areas of Fuente San Luis and La Punta. The tourist office in Valencia will locate these areas on a map for you.

Other interesting but disappearing forms of architecture are found in the area around Alicante known as La Marina Alta. You can see two very typical house types: the *riu-rau* and the *naia.* Both have porticos of semicircular, usually whitewashed arches and very low springers. The riu-rau's arched porticocs are used as drying places for raisins, whereas those of the naia are the setting for family life.

Another longtime local favorite is **Barcas,** Barcas, 7 (☎ **96-352-12-33**), among banks and office buildings in the heart of town, directly north of the Estación del Norte. It serves drinks and tapas (including small servings of paella) at the stand-up bar. You could conceivably stop here for your first cup of coffee at 7am and for your final "nightcap" at 1am. In the evening there is often live music. The establishment is more popular as a bar than as a restaurant. It's open daily from 7am to 1am. Drink prices start at 450 ptas. ($3), and tapas cost 300 to 1,200 ptas. ($2 to $8.05).

In summer the emphasis switches to the beach, Playa de Malvarrosa. Valencia is hot and steamy, and the cooling night breezes blowing in from the sea are especially welcome. From teens to 40-somethings, people congregate around open-air bars. They play music, often have dance floors, and are open from late May through September. Drinks usually cost 500 to 800 ptas. ($3.35 to $5.35). There are also discos in this part of town, one of which is the **Disco Caballito de Mar,** calle Eugenia Vines, 22 (☎ **96-371-07-64**). These are more expensive, and drinks are several hundred pesetas more than in the open-air bars.

Valencia is Spain's third-biggest city and, after Madrid and Barcelona, the country's biggest gay center. Most of the action is in the historic center in the **Barrio Carmen,** particularly along calle Quart. Valencia is a progressive, liberal city, and visitors need have no fear about being "out" on the street. For more information, interested parties can stop in at or call the **Lambda organization.** It has a **coffee shop,** calle Salvador Giner, 9 (☎ **96-391-20-84**), where the staff is very helpful. There are many venues, clubs, bars, coffee shops, saunas, hotels, and restaurants from which to choose. The best publication for what's happening when is Madrid-based *Shanghai,* distributed free in gay establishments.

The latest offering on the club scene is **Le Goulou,** calle Quart, 30 (no phone), which opens nightly at 10pm and closes at 3am. The long-established **Venial,** calle Quart, 26 (☎ **96-391-73-56**), is a few doors down. It opens at 11pm and closes at 2:30am Sunday to Thursday, and at 6:30am on Friday and Saturday, when there is a charge of 1,200 ptas. ($8.05) with a drink included.

If you want to forget dancing and concentrate on late-night naughtiness, head to **La Guerra**, calle Quart, 47 (☎ 96-391-36-75). It has five action-packed floors, a labyrinth, and the latest Californian "movies" nightly from 8pm to 3am.

As in many cities, gay men have to some degree elbowed lesbian interests out of the way, but Valencianas are fighting back. Women wanting a boy-free zone can try **Donna Donna,** calle Portal Valldigna, 2 (no phone), open Thursday to Sunday from 6pm to 2am. The lesbian disco **Mogambo,** Sangre, 2 (no phone), is more mixed and attracts a youngish crowd. Entry is 1,200 ptas. ($8.05), which covers one drink. Mogambo is open Thursday to Sunday from 11pm to 4am. As in the rest of Spain, the night starts late, and 10pm is considered quite early. At this time, one of the best places to go is the **Café de la Seu,** calle Santo Caliz, 7 (☎ 96-391-57-15). All shades of pinkdom can have a relaxing drink for 300 to 600 ptas. ($2 to $4) from 8pm to 2am, Tuesday to Sunday.

On the cultural front, **Palau de la Música,** Paseo de la Alameda, 30 (☎ 96-337-50-20), is a contemporary concert hall in a dried-out bed of the Turia River, between the Aragón and Angel Custudio bridges. Opened in 1987, it occupies a sort of Hispano-Muslim venue, with palm trees, "temples," and reflecting pools. Call to find out the day's program or ask at the tourist office (see "Essentials," above). Details of major concerts are also published in the newspapers. Ticket prices vary.

For additional ideas, consult a recent copy of *Que y Donde*, a magazine available at any news kiosk for around 200 ptas. ($1.35).

SIDE TRIPS FROM VALENCIA
LA ALBUFERA

Eleven miles (17.7km) south of Valencia lies La Albufera, a land of rice paddies and reed beds. The largest wetland along Spain's Mediterranean coast, it was called "an agreeable lagoon" in the writings of Pliny the Elder. Sand dunes separate the fresh-water from the saltwater.

La Albufera has been declared a national park. Its lake is home to some 250 species of waterfowl, including a European version of the endangered flamingo. It abounds with such fish as mullet, tench, and eel, still caught by ancient traps. You can rent an *albuferenc* (flat-bottomed boat) from local fishers, but make sure to negotiate prices beforehand. As you go about the lake, you can see barracas, whitewashed houses with thatched and steeply pitched roofs (see box, "The Disappearing Barracas"). Some of these structures, on stilts, can be reached only by boat.

La Albufera is famed for giving the world paella, and nearly all the restaurants in the area serve the classic dish. Try **Raco de l'Olla,** carretera de El Palma, s/n (☎ 96-162-01-72), 8 miles (13km) south of Valencia on the El Saler road near the turnoff to El Palma. The restaurant opened in the 1960s and has served paella to thousands of visitors from around the world. Most of the year it is open only for lunch, Tuesday through Sunday 11am to 6pm. In July and August it is also open 9pm to midnight from Monday to Saturday. Meals cost 3,500 to 4,000 ptas. ($23.45 to $26.80); American Express and Visa cards are accepted. It's also customary to stop in the town of **El Palma** to order a plate of *alli al pebre* (garlic-flavored eels) before heading north to Valencia or south to Alicante.

SAGUNTO

Another popular excursion is to Sagunto, 15½ miles (25km) north of Valencia. It's accessible by bus or rail. Sagunto is known for holding out against Hannibal's conquering Carthaginian soldiers for 9 months in 219 B.C. The Iberians set themselves on fire rather than surrender. In time, the Romans discovered the town, and later the Visigoths and the Muslims overran it.

Its **Roman ruins** today are just that: ruins. But it makes an interesting stopover. In the 2nd century A.D. it had an amphitheater that seated 8,000. (Theatrical performances are still staged in the remains.) It also has an old **Acrópolis/*castillo*** (castle); the remains of its Moorish walls and ramparts stretch for about ½ mile.

The best place for food is near the castle: **L'Armeler,** calle Subida del Castillo, 44 (☎ **96-266-43-82**). Meals cost 3,800 to 5,000 ptas. ($25.45 to $33.50) with wine. The restaurant is open Tuesday through Saturday 1:30 to 4pm and 9:30 to 11:30pm. It serves French and Spanish food in the ambience of a *vieja mansión* (old mansion). Try one of the splendid pâtés, salmon casserole, or beef fillet with truffle sauce. The terrace provides a fine view.

2 Benidorm

27 miles (43km) NE of Alicante, 84 miles (135km) S of Valencia

Before tourists discovered its 3½ miles (6km) of beaches, Benidorm was a tiny fishing village. But now summer vacationers pour in, and a new concrete hotel seems to be built every day. With its heavy northern European influence, Benidorm has become the most overrun beach town east of Torremolinos. It has both ardent fans and determined detractors.

According to an 1890s guidebook, Benidorm was a "very tranquil place where drunkenness was unknown." What a change had come over the resort by the 1970s and 1980s, when it attracted a rowdy, beer-drinking crowd. Today some 180,000 people a day visit the long beach strip.

After the bad press of the past, city officials are trying to clean up Benidorm and make it more of an upmarket (rather than package-tour) destination. The Aiguera Park and its amphitheater exemplify the change. It offers such free cultural activities as dancing, jazz, soul music, and even a Russian choir.

Despite efforts to upgrade its image, Benidorm still has high-rises and economical package tourists. In winter pensioners from all over Europe, even Russia, fill the villas and small hotels. In summer, however, the place takes on a much more youthful aura. The resort has two fine white-sand beaches.

ESSENTIALS

GETTING THERE   From Alicante, there are hourly train departures for Benidorm. Buses from Valencia and Alicante leave almost hourly, too.

If you're driving, take the E-15 expressway south from Valencia or north from Alicante. The one-way toll from Alicante to Benidorm is 700 ptas. ($4.70); the one-way toll from Valencia to Benidorm is 1,500 ptas. ($10.05).

VISITOR INFORMATION   The **tourist information office** is at Avenida Martínez Alejos, 16 (☎ **96-585-32-24**). It's open Monday through Saturday 10am to 2pm and 5 to 8pm.

WHERE TO STAY

Make sure you reserve in advance between mid-June and September. If you arrive without a reservation, you'll be out of luck. During this time hotel managers often slap the full-board requirement onto their rates. To beat this, book one of the rare residencias, which serve breakfast only.

Don Pancho. Avenida del Mediterráneo, 39, 03500 Benidorm. ☎ **96-585-29-50.** Fax 96-586-77-79. 252 units. A/C MINIBAR TV TEL. 13,800–20,300 ptas. ($92.45–$136) double. AE, DC, MC, V.

One of the best hotels in Benidorm, Don Pancho is a high-rise a short distance from the beach. Each of the well-furnished, well-maintained guest rooms opens onto a small balcony. The midsize rooms are doubles, and can be rented for single use. The tiled bathrooms have hair dryers. Facilities include a swimming pool and a lighted tennis court.

Gran Hotel Delfín. Playa de Poniente (La Cala), 03500 Benidorm. ☎ **96-585-34-00.** Fax 96-585-71 54. 90 units. A/C MINIBAR TV TEL. 15,200–19,300 ptas. ($101.85–$129.30) double. AE, DC, MC, V. Closed Nov–Mar. Free parking.

About 2 miles (3km) west of the center of town, away from the traffic-clogged mayhem that sometimes overwhelms the center of Benidorm, this 1960s hotel lies beside the very popular Poniente Beach. It is the resort's finest hotel, catering to a sun-loving crowd of vacationers who appreciate its airy spaciousness and lack of formality. Guest rooms are sparsely decorated, with masonry floors and much-used furniture, some in a darkly stained Iberian style. Nonetheless, the accommodations are quite comfortable and the tiled bathrooms well maintained.

The in-house restaurant, El Delfín, serves a fixed-price menú del día for 2,800 ptas. ($18.75). There are also two bars, one of which serves drinks near the pool. There is an outdoor swimming pool in a large garden, and tennis courts.

Hotel Brisa. Avenida de Madrid, 31, Playa de Levante, 03500 Benidorm. ☎ and fax **96-585-54-00.** 75 units. A/C TV TEL. July 15–Sept 16,000 ptas. ($107.20) double; Oct–June 15 12,600 ptas. ($84.40) double. Summer rates include half board; off-season rates include breakfast. MC, V.

Just across from one of the town's most popular beaches, this hotel is a five-story modern building with a swimming pool and a small garden. The sunny guest rooms, simply furnished with sturdy furniture, have good beds and tile floors. This is very much a beach hotel, where many guests bring uncomplicated wardrobes, and in some cases their children, in anticipation of lazy days on the beach. There's a bar on the premises, and an airy, sun-flooded dining room. Many summer guests are from northern Europe.

Hotel Canfali. Plaza de San Jaime, 5, 03500 Benidorm. ☎ **96-585-08-18.** Fax 96-585-00-66. 39 units. TV TEL. 5,300–14,900 ptas. ($35.50–$99.85) double. Rates include full board. No credit cards.

A seaside villa between the Playa de Levante and the Playa de Poniente, the Canfali is one of the best small hotels in town. Originally built in 1950, it was enlarged in 1992. Its position is a scene-stealer—on a low cliff at the end of the esplanade, with a staircase winding down to the beach. The best rooms have balconies with sea views. Although the hotel is spacious and comfortable, its decor is undistinguished, its guest rooms functional. Terraces overlook the sea, a perfect spot for morning coffee.

Hotel Cimbel. Europa, 1, 03500 Benidorm. ☎ **96-585-21-00.** Fax 96-586-06-61. 140 units. A/C MINIBAR TV TEL. 12,100-21,500 ptas. ($81.05–$144.05) double. AE, DC, MC, V. Parking 1,325 ptas. ($8.90). Bus: 1, 2, 3, 4, or 5.

On one of the most popular beaches in town, this hotel especially appeals to sun worshipers, who step from the lobby practically onto the sand. There's also a swimming pool. The small guest rooms are functionally furnished but comfortable, with good beds and hair dryers. The hotel restaurant's menú del día, for 2,800 ptas. ($18.75), often features fresh catches. **Bar Hall,** a nighttime gathering spot, has a terrace. Also on the premises are a disco, a cafeteria, and safe-deposit boxes.

WHERE TO DINE

Pérgola. Acantillado-Edificio Coblanca, 10, calle Hamburgo, Rincón de Loix. ☎ **96-585-38-00.** Reservations recommended. Main courses 1,250–2,475 ptas. ($8.40–$16.60). MC, V. Tues–Sun 1–3:30pm and 8pm–midnight. SPANISH/INTERNATIONAL.

Of the many buildings along the sea at the Playa de Levante, this is the one nearest the center of Benidorm. Established in 1979, it offers a sweeping view over the bay, an airy, stylish interior, and a flower-strewn terrace for warm-weather lunches and dinners. Skillfully prepared choices include seafood crepes with clams, a combination platter of hake and salmon drizzled with crabmeat sauce, stuffed crabs, stewed codfish with garlic confit, duck breast with pears, and rack of beef with mustard sauce.

Tiffany's. Avenida del Mediterráneo, 51. ☎ **96-585-44-68.** Reservations recommended. Main courses 2,100–2,500 ptas. ($14.05–$16.75). AE, DC, MC, V. Daily 7:30pm–midnight. Closed Jan 7–Feb 7. SPANISH/INTERNATIONAL.

Tiffany's, one of the town's better restaurants, has attracted visitors since the 1970s. Meals are served with well-rehearsed dignity. A live pianist plays occasionally. The food offerings change with the seasons and the availability of the ingredients. Your meal might include a roulade of fillet of sole stuffed with caviar and shrimp, tournedos Tiffany (with foie gras and truffles), a fish or veal dish, and a dessert of homemade chocolate éclairs with warm chocolate sauce.

BENIDORM AFTER DARK

The best nightclub in the region is the **Benidorm Palace, Carretera de Diputación,** s/n, Rincón de Loix (☎ **96-585-16-60**). The cover (including one drink) is a steep 3,000 to 5,500 ptas. ($20.10 to $36.85), but the place features the latest music, a large dance floor, and the biggest stage in Europe (130 feet wide). The stage fills with 50 international artists, often entertaining an audience of 1,500. Shows have ranged from "Hurrah for Hollywood" to Russian dancers. Always count on glamorous dancing women as part of the show. There are expansive bars and ample seating. It's open Tuesday through Saturday from 9pm to 2am; shows start at 10:30pm. Drinks cost 500 ptas. ($3.35).

The **Casino Royal Palm,** Carretera Nacional, 332, km 114 (☎ **96-589-07-00**), offers gambling in a modern building surrounded by the rolling hills of the Costa Blanca. Most visitors come to try their hand at roulette (French and American), blackjack, and *boules*. An on-site restaurant, Costa Blanca, serves à la carte Spanish meals from 3,000 ptas. ($20.10) per person every evening from 9pm to 2am. The casino is open nightly from 8pm to 4am. It's about 4½ miles (7km) from Benidorm, beside the highway to Alicante. Casino admission is 600 ptas. ($4); a passport is required for admission.

3 Alicante

50 miles (80km) N of Murcia, 25 miles (40km) S of Benidorm, 107 miles (172km) S of Valencia, 259 miles (417km) SE of Madrid

Alicante, capital of the Costa Blanca, is popular in both summer and winter. Many consider it the best all-around city in Spain. As you amble about its esplanades, you almost feel as if you were in Africa: Women in caftans and peddlers hawking carvings from Senegal or elsewhere often populate the waterfront.

San Juan, the largest beach in Alicante, lies a short distance from the capital. It's lined with villas, hotels, and restaurants. The bay of Alicante has two capes, and on the bay is **Postiguet Beach.** The bay stretches all the way to the **Cape of Santa Pola,** a town with two good beaches, a 14th-century castle, and several seafood restaurants.

ESSENTIALS

GETTING THERE   Alicante's **Internacional El Altet Airport** (☎ **96-691-90-00**) is 12 miles (19.3km) from the city. There are usually as many as six daily flights from

Madrid, about three flights per week from Seville, and three weekly from Barcelona. Three flights arrive weekly from Ibiza and Málaga (on the Costa del Sol). Thirteen buses daily connect the city to the airport; the fare is 125 ptas. (85¢). The Iberia Airlines ticket office (☎ 96-691-91-00) is at the airport.

Five **trains** a day make the 3-hour trip from Valencia. Five trains a day come from Barcelona (11 hours), and six a day from Madrid (9 hours). The RENFE office is at the Estación Término, Avenida Salamanca (☎ 96-592-02-02).

Different **bus** lines from various parts of the coast converge at the terminus, calle Portugal, 17 (☎ 96-513-07-00). There is almost hourly service from Benidorm (see above) and from Valencia (4 hours). Buses also run from Madrid, a 5- to 6-hour trip.

To drive here, take the E-15 expressway south along the coast from Valencia. The expressway and N-340 run northeast from Murcia.

Transmediterránea runs 3 **ferries** a day to and from Ibiza (3 hours). Call the office in Valencia (☎ 96-367-06-44) for tickets and information. Flebasa, Estacion Marítima, Puerto de Denia (☎ 96-578-40-11), offers service to Ibiza (7 hours) daily, and to Formentera (10 hours) twice weekly.

VISITOR INFORMATION The **tourist information office** is at Explanada d'Espanya, 2 (☎ 96-520-00-00). It's open Monday through Friday 10am to 8pm, Saturday 10am to 2pm and 3 to 8pm.

FAST FACTS For medical assistance, go to the **Hospital General,** calle Maestro Alonzo (☎ 96-590-89-99). In an emergency, dial ☎ 091; to reach the city police, call ☎ 96-514-22-22.

EXPLORING ALICANTE

With its wide, palm-lined avenues, this town was made for walking—and that's just what you'll do! The magnificent **Explanada d'Espanya,** extending around part of the yacht harbor, includes a great promenade of mosaic sidewalks under the palms. All the boulevards are clean and lined with unlimited shopping options. At Alicante's leading department store, El Corte Inglés, you can find bargains without being trampled by mobs, as in Madrid. Alicante is known for its parks, gardens, and lines of palm trees, and it boasts several old plazas, some paved with marble.

High on a hill, the stately **Castell de Santa Bárbara** (☎ 96-526-31-31) towers over the bay and provincial capital. The Greeks called the fort Akra Leuka (White Peak). Its original defenses, erected by the Carthaginians in 400 B.C., were later used by the Romans and the Arabs. The fortress's grand scale is evident in its moats, drawbridges, tunneled entrances, guard rooms, bakery, cisterns, underground storerooms, hospitals, batteries, powder stores, barracks, high breastworks, deep dungeons, and the Matanza Tower and the Keep. From the top of the castle there's a panoramic view over land and sea. The castle is accessible by road or elevator (board at the Explanda d'Es-panya). Admission by elevator is 400 ptas. ($2.70). In summer it's open daily 10am to 7:30pm; in winter, daily 9am to 6:30pm.

It is also possible to drive to the top. A paved road off Avenida Vasquez de Mella leads directly to a parking lot beside the castle. If you drive, admission is free.

On the slopes of the Castillo de Santa Bárbara behind the cathedral is the **Barrio de Santa Cruz.** Forming part of the **Villa Vieja** (the old quarter), it is a colorful section with wrought-iron window grilles, banks of flowers, and a view of the entire harbor.

Alicante isn't all ancient. Facing the Iglesia Santa Maria is the **Museu Colecció Art del Segle XX,** Plaza de Santa Maria, 3 (☎ 96-514-07-68). Housed in the city's oldest building, it contains modern art. Constructed as a granary in 1685, the restored building features works by Miró, Calder, Cocteau, Vasarély, Dalí, Picasso, and Tàpies. Other notable artists include Braque, Chagall, Giacometti, Kandinsky, and Zadkine.

You'll also see a musical score by Manuel de Falla. The museum was formed in 1977 with the donation of a private collection by the painter and sculptor Eusebio Sempere, whose works are also on display. It is open May through September, Tuesday through Saturday 10:30am to 1:30pm and 6 to 9pm; October through April, Tuesday through Saturday 10am to 1pm and 5 to 8pm. Admission is free.

SHOPPING

Despite the hurly-burly of tourism that unfolds around you at almost every street corner, there are many worthwhile shopping opportunities. Some of the best involve handmade artifacts—ceramics, hand-tooled leather, wood carvings, ornamental boxes, candleholders, and small-scale mosaics. One of the best all-purpose shops is **Fran Holuba,** calle Jaime Segarra 16, (☎ 96-524-45-95), which carries examples of each of the major artisanal forms described above. A shop specializing only in ceramics is **Albarado,** calle Moreno, 6 (☎ 96-526-47-62), a few paces from the beach. For modern (not religious) sculpture crafted from wood and such stones as marble, head for the studio of **Pedro Soriano,** Plaza San Antonio, 2 (☎ 96-520-78-54). Its leading competitor is **Ibáñez Bernabeu,** calle Sipreses, 56 (☎ 96-528-08-53). Ibáñez Bernabeu will sell you an unusual sculpture off its showroom floor or commission a replica of whatever you like (if you have the time and the power to articulate your artistic vision). Appointments must be made by telephone before visiting. For general merchandise, head for the town's largest department store, **El Corte Inglés,** Avenida Maison Nave, 53 (☎ 96-592-50-01).

WHERE TO STAY
EXPENSIVE

Hotel Meliá Alicante. Playa de El Postiguet, 03001 Alicante. ☎ **800/336-3542** in the U.S., or 96-520-50-00. Fax 96-520-47-56. 545 units. A/C MINIBAR TV TEL. 21,250 ptas. ($142.40) double; 30,000 ptas. ($201) suite. Weekend room rates include breakfast. AE, DC, MC, V. Parking 1,800 ptas. ($12.05).

Built in 1973 on a spit of landfill jutting into the Mediterranean, this massive hotel almost dwarfs every other establishment in town. Midsize guest rooms are painted in clear, sunny colors and have balconies, usually with sweeping panoramas of sailboats in the nearby marina or over the beach. The public rooms are contemporary, with lots of marble. The hotel is midway between the main harbor and the very popular El Postiguet beach.

Dining/Diversions: Two restaurants serve à la carte meals. There is also a bar near the pool, an indoor bar with a piano player, and a *sala de fiestas* for drinking, conversation, and dancing.

Amenities: Concierge, laundry, 24-hour room service, baby-sitting, outdoor swimming pools.

Hotel Tryp Gran Sol. Rambla Méndez Núñez, 3, 03002 Alicante. ☎ **800/272-8674** in the U.S., or 96-520-30-00. Fax 96-521-14-39. www.tryp.net. 123 units. A/C MINIBAR TV TEL. 18,900 ptas. ($126.65) double; 25,000 ptas. ($167.50) suite. AE, DC, MC, V. Parking 1,000 ptas. ($6.70).

In the heart of the tourist zone, a block from the beachfront Paseo Marítimo, this 1970 hotel towers above most of the buildings in town. A member of the widely known Tryp chain, it offers simple guest rooms with unimaginative but comfortable furnishings. Bathrooms have tile or marble accents and hair dryers. One-third of the rooms were recently renovated.

Dining/Diversions: The Ramblas Restaurant and a popular bar are on the 26th floor, where big windows offer sweeping views of the town and coastline.

Amenities: Room service (until midnight), laundry, concierge, baby-sitting, car rentals, reading room, game room, TV room, meeting facilities.

MODERATE

Hotel Residencia Leuka. Calle Segura, 23, 03004 Alicante. ☎ **96-520-27-44.** Fax 96-514-12-22. 108 units. A/C MINIBAR TV TEL. Mon–Thurs 9,150 ptas. ($61.30) double, Fri–Sun 5,950 ptas. ($39.85) double. AE, DC, MC, V. Parking 1,000 ptas. ($6.70). Bus: 22.

The Leuka is best booked for the weekend, when it offers good value and is free of packs of businesspeople. Although it's about a 15-minute walk from the sea, it is close to the station and two of the city's main thoroughfares. Guests have easy access to almost all destinations by bus. The 10-story building has an anonymously ugly 1970s facade. However, all the rooms have good-size balconies, and units above the third floor offer wonderful views of the castle. Guest rooms are quite plain, but spacious and reasonably comfortable. The bar serves a three-course menú del día at lunch for 1,450 ptas. ($9.70); one-course platos combinados cost 1,000 to 1,200 ptas. ($6.70 to $8.05) at night.

Sol Inn Hotel. Calle Gravina, 9, 03002 Alicante. ☎ **96-521-07-00.** Fax 96-521-09-76. www.solmelia.es. E-mail: sol.alicante@solmelia.es. 66 units. A/C MINIBAR TV TEL. Mon–Thurs 10,300 ptas. ($69) double, Fri–Sun 8,800 ptas. ($58.95) double. Weekend rates include breakfast. AE, DC, MC, V. Parking 1,000 ptas. ($6.70). Bus: 21.

True to its name, this three-star hotel is decorated in sunny hues. The reasonable, no-frills hotel is on a narrow street 30 yards from the Mediterranean and a short stroll from the historic castle. The comfortable rooms are decorated in a basic fashion but are spacious enough, and all have hair dryers. There is a bar downstairs, and many restaurants and bars nearby.

INEXPENSIVE

Hotel Residencia San Remo. Navas, 30, 03001 Alicante. ☎ **96-520-95-00.** Fax 96-520-96-68. 27 units. A/C TV TEL. 6,000–7,000 ptas. ($40.20–$46.90) double. AE, DC, MC, V. Bus: B.

A white-plaster seven-floor building, the San Remo offers small, unpretentious rooms. Some have balconies, and all have good beds and tiny tiled bathrooms with shower stalls. Breakfast is the only meal served. The welcome is warm, and the price is right. Room service is provided from 8am to 2pm and 7 to 9pm.

Portugal. Calle Portugal, 26, 03003 Alicante. ☎ **96-592-92-44.** 16 units, 8 with bathroom. 3,400–3,800 ptas. ($22.80–$25.45) double with sink; 4,200–4,500 ptas. ($28.15–$30.15) double with bathroom. No credit cards. Parking 1,200 ptas. ($8.05).

The two-story Portugal is 1 block from the bus station, about 4 blocks from the railway station, and a 3-minute walk from the harbor. The small accommodations, furnished in tasteful modern style, are immaculate but rather basic. Guests in accommodations with private bathrooms will find their units a bit cramped but serviceable. For those who share, the corridor bathrooms are adequate.

WHERE TO DINE

The characteristic dish of Alicante is rice, served in many different ways. The most typical sauce is aioli, a kind of mayonnaise made from oil and garlic. Dessert selections are the most varied on the Costa Blanca; *turrón de Alicante* (Spanish nougat) is the most popular.

Delfín. Explanada d'Espanya, 12. ☎ **96-521-49-11.** Reservations recommended. Main courses 2,200–2,800 ptas. ($14.75–$18.75); menú del día 5,000 ptas. ($33.50). AE, DC, MC, V. Daily 1–4pm and 8pm–midnight. MEDITERRANEAN.

On the town's most visible promenade, this restaurant has an upstairs dining room with views over the harbor and yacht basin. The service is discreet and attentive, the ingredients fresh, and the dishes flavorful. Specialties might include smoked salmon on toast with a gratin of shrimp, fillet of beef grilled with a goat-cheese topping, sauté of sweetbreads flavored with foie gras and strips of duck meat, crepes stuffed with seafood, or paella. An array of tempting pastries rolls from table to table on a trolley.

La Dársena. Muelle del Puerto (Explanada d'Espanya). ☎ **96-520-75-89.** Reservations required at lunch. Main courses 1,300–2,000 ptas. ($8.70–$13.40); fixed-price menu 4,200 ptas. ($28.15). AE, DC, MC, V. Mon–Sun 1–4pm, Tues–Sat 8:30–11pm. SPANISH.

Paella is the best choice at this popular place overlooking the harbor. Some 20 other rice dishes are also commendable—for example, *arroz con pieles de bacalao* (rice with dried codfish). Try crab soup flavored with Armagnac, or a tart made with tuna and spinach.

Nou Manolín. Calle Villegas, 3. ☎ **96-520-0368.** Reservations recommended. Main courses 1,800–3,000 ptas. ($12.05–$20.10); menú del día 3,800 ptas. ($25.45). AE, DC, MC, V. Daily 1–4pm and 8:30pm–midnight. REGIONAL/SPANISH.

When he established it in 1972, the founder of this restaurant named it after an almost-forgotten neighborhood bar (El Manolín), which his grandfather had maintained before the Spanish Civil War. Nou Manolín's street level contains a busy bar area, but diners usually gravitate to the upstairs dining room, where tiled walls and uniformed waiters contribute to the ambience of an elegant *tasca*. Menu items include many kinds of fish cooked in a salt crust, as well as a delectable paella, several kinds of stew, fresh shellfish, and a wide selection of Iberian wines.

Restaurante El Jumillano. César Elquezábal, 64. ☎ **96-521-17-64.** Reservations recommended. Main courses 1,500–2,600 ptas. ($10.05–$17.40). AE, DC, MC, V. Mon–Sat 1–4pm and 8pm–midnight, Sun noon–4pm. Closed Sun July–Sept. Bus: D or F. SPANISH.

This was a humble wine bar when it opened in 1936 near the old city. The original wine-and-tapas bar is still going strong, but the food has improved immeasurably. Today the original owner's sons (Juan José and Miguel Pérez Mejías) offer a cornucopia of succulent food, including fresh fish laid out in the dining room on the sun-bleached planks of an antique fishing boat. Many menu items derive from locally inspired recipes. The specialties include a "festival of canapés," slices of cured ham served with fresh melon, shellfish soup with mussels, Alicante stew, pig's trotters, a savory fillet of beef seasoned with garlic, and a full gamut of grilled hake, sea bass, and shellfish.

ALICANTE AFTER DARK

A town devoted to the pursuit of hot times, Alicante never seems to lack for a bar. You can find alcohol and socializing at almost any time of the day or night. One of the town's densest concentrations of watering holes lies adjacent to the port. Night owls wander from one bar to the next along the length of the **Muelle del Puerto** (a stretch of pavement that's also known as the Explanada d'Espanya). There are at least 20 nightspots that rock through the night. Three of the most popular and visible are **Bar Potato; Casa Yum-Yum,** where tapas are consumed with something approaching vigor; and **Mesón del Puerto.** Their addresses are all Muelle del Puerto, s/n, and they have no phones. Also consider the bar at one of our favorite restaurants, **La Dársena** (see above), even if you don't wish to dine.

Alternatively, consider walking through the narrow streets of Alicante's **Casco Antiguo.** Streets particularly rich in bodegas and tavernas include **calle Laboradores, calle Cien Fuegos,** and the **Plaza Santa Face.** We usually prefer to wander aimlessly through this district, popping in and out wherever we feel most comfortable. If you want to plan ahead, consider **El Mesón,** in the calle Labradores, 23; **La Tapería,** Plaza Santa Face, s/n; and **El Pote Gallego,** Plaza Santa Face, s/n. Again, no phones.

Alicante also has a well-established and relatively large gay scene for a city of its size. The numbers swell in July and August, with tourists from the rest of Spain and Madrid in particular. For information, contact the Lambda organization, calle Doctor Santa Oblaya, 7 in the San Blas area (☎ **96-513-26-10**). It's open Wednesday 7 to 9pm, Saturday 7 to 10pm.

The evening starts at one of several bars. A popular haunt is **Monecristo** (☎ **96-512-31-89**), Calle Ab-El-Hamet, 1, which is open daily from 8:15pm to 3am. Another, **Missing** (☎ **96-521-67-28**), calle Gravina, 4, is open daily from 9pm to 3:30am. The bar and club **El Jardineto,** calle Baron de Finestat (no phone), operates from 11pm to 3am Sunday to Thursday, until 5 or 6am on Friday and Saturday.

4 Elche

13 miles (21 km) SW of Alicante, 35 miles (56km) NE of Murcia, 252 miles (406km) SE of Madrid

Sandwiched between Alicante and Murcia, the little town of Elche is famous for its age-old mystery play, lush groves of date palms, and shoe- and sandal-making.

On August 14 and 15 for the last 6 centuries, the ✪ **Misteri d'Elx** (**Mystery of Elche**) has celebrated the Assumption of the Virgin. It is reputedly the oldest dramatic liturgy in Europe. Songs are performed in an ancient form of Catalán. Admission is free, but it's hard to get a seat unless you book in advance through the tourist office (see below). The play takes place at the Church of Santa María, which dates from the 17th century.

Unless you visit at the time of the mystery play, the town's date palms hold the most appeal. The 600,000-tree palm forest is unrivaled in Europe. It's said that Phoenician (or perhaps Greek) seafarers originally planted the trees. The Moors created the irrigation system that maintains the palms 1,000 years ago. Stroll through the **Huerto del Cura** (**Priest's Grove**), open daily from 9am to 6pm, to see the palm garden and collection of tropical flowers and cacti. In the garden, look for the **Palmera del Cura** (Priest's Palm), from the 1840s, with seven branches sprouting from its trunk. In the grove you will see one of the most famous ladies of Spain, *La Dama de Elche.* This is a replica—the original 500 B.C. limestone bust, discovered in 1897, is on display in the National Archaeological Museum in Madrid.

ESSENTIALS

GETTING THERE   The central train station is the Estación Parque, Plaza Alfonso XII. Trains arrive almost hourly from **Alicante.** Call ☎ **96-545-62-54** for schedules.

The bus station (☎ **96-545-58-58**) is at Avenida de la Libertat. Buses travel between **Alicante** and Elche on the hour.

Take the N-340 highway from Alicante and proceed southwest if you're driving.

VISITOR INFORMATION   The **tourist information office** is at Passeig de l'Estació (☎ **96-545-38-31**). It's open Monday through Friday 10:30am to 2pm and 4 to 6pm, Saturday and Sunday 10:30am to 1:30pm.

WHERE TO STAY

✪ **Huerto del Cura.** Porta de La Morera, 14, 032003 Elche. ☎ **96-545-80-40.** Fax 96-542-19-10. 86 units. A/C MINIBAR TV TEL. Mon–Thurs 17,850 ptas. ($119.60) double, Fri–Sun 10,000 ptas. ($67) double; July 26–Sept 5 12,000 ptas. ($80.40) double. AE, DC, MC, V. Parking 1,275 ptas. ($8.55).

Staying here is a unique experience. Huerto del Cura stands in the so-called Priest's Grove, and you'll have panoramic views of the palm trees from your room. The privately owned parador consists of a number of immaculately kept cabins in the grove. Each is well furnished and roomy, with comfortable mattresses and efficiently organized, tiled bathrooms. Service is impeccable. A swimming pool under the palms separates the cabins from the main hotel building. A tennis court, sauna, solarium, and cafeteria are on the grounds. There is an attractive bar and a high-quality dining room, Els Capellans.

WHERE TO DINE

Parque Municipal. Paseo Alfonso XIII, s/n. ☎ **96-545-34-15.** Reservations recommended. Main courses 1,500–2,000 ptas. ($10.05–$13.40); fixed-price menu 1,300 ptas. ($8.70). MC, V. Daily 1–4pm and 8–11pm. INTERNATIONAL.

A large open-air restaurant and cafe in the middle of a public park, the Parque Municipal is a good place to go for decent food and relaxed service. Many regional dishes appear on the menu; try one of the savory rice dishes as a main course, followed by "cake of Elche." Two specialties are paella and Mediterranean sea bass, sailor's style.

Restaurante La Finca. Partida de Perleta, 1-7. ☎ **96-545-60-07.** Reservations recommended. Main courses 2,000–3,000 ptas. ($13.40–$20.10); fixed-price menus 4,500–6,500 ptas. ($30.15–$43.55). AE, DC, MC, V. Daily 1–5pm; Tues–Sat 8:30pm–midnight. MEDITERRANEAN.

In the countryside near the Elche football stadium, 3 miles (5km) south of town along the carretera de El Alted, La Finca opened in 1984. Its good food has attracted customers ever since. The menu changes frequently, based on the season and what's fresh. Both fish and meat are prepared in creative ways, although time-tested recipes are used as well. Try tuna-stuffed peppers, or veal kidneys with potatoes. Chocolate mousse might be available for dessert.

5 Murcia

52 miles (83km) SW of Alicante, 245 miles (409km) SE of Madrid, 159 miles (256km) SW of Valencia

This ancient Moorish city of sienna-colored buildings is an inland provincial capital on the main road between Valencia and Granada. It lies on the Segura River.

ESSENTIALS

GETTING THERE   From Alicante, 9 to 17 **trains** daily make the 1½-hour trip. From Barcelona (7 to 10 hours), there are three trains daily; from Madrid (4 to 5 hours), three or four trains daily. From the Estació del Carmen, calle Industria, s/n (☎ 968-25-21-54), take bus no. 11 to the heart of the city.

   Buses arrive at calle San Andrés (☎ 968-29-22-11), behind the Museo Salzillo. The information window is open daily from 7am to 10pm. There's frequent service from Granada (4 to 5 hours), Cádiz (12½ hours), Córdoba (9 hours), Valencia (3¾ hours), and Seville (7 to 9 hours).

   If you're driving, take the N-340 southwest from Alicante.

VISITOR INFORMATION   The **tourist information office** is at calle San Cristobal (☎ 968-36-61-00). It's open Monday through Friday 9:30am to 2pm, Saturday 5 to 7:30pm.

SPECIAL EVENTS   Murcia's **Holy Week celebration,** from Palm Sunday to Easter Sunday, is an ideal time to visit. Its processions are spectacular, with about 3,000

people taking part, and some sculptures of Salzillo (see below) are carried through the streets. Musicians blow horns so big they have to be carried on wheels.

EXPLORING MURCIA

Although it suffered much from fire and bombardment during the Spanish Civil War, the city abounds in grand 18th-century houses.

The principal artistic treasure is the **cathedral,** Plaza Cardenal Belluga (☎ 968-21-63-44), a bastardized medley of Gothic, baroque, and Renaissance styles. Begun in the 1300s, its bell tower was built in four different periods by four different architects. You can climb the tower for a view of Murcia and the enveloping *huerta* (plain). Capilla de los Vélez, off the ambulatory, is the most interesting chapel. You can see works by the famous local sculptor, Francisco Salzillo (1707–83), as well as the golden crown of the Virgen de la Fuensanta, patron of Murcia. Off the north transept, the museum of the cathedral contains such relics as Salzillo's polychrome wood sculpture of the penitent St. Jerome. You can visit daily from 10am to 1pm and 5 to 7pm. Admission is free, but it costs 250 ptas. ($1.70) to visit both the museum and the bell tower.

The other major sight is the **Museo de Salzillo,** San Andrés, 1 (☎ 968-29-18-93). The son of an Italian sculptor father and a Spanish mother, Francisco Salzillo won fame with his sculptures in polychrome wood. This museum displays his finest work, plus many terra-cotta figurines based on biblical scenes. It is open Tuesday through Saturday 9:30am to 1pm and 4 to 7pm, Sunday 11am to 1pm. Admission is 250 ptas. ($1.70).

Another attraction is the **Museo de Arqueología,** calle Gran Vía Alfonso, X El Sabio, 7 (☎ 968-23-46-02), one of the best in Spain. Through artifacts—mosaics, pottery fragments, Roman coins, ceramics, and other objects—it traces life in Murcia province from prehistoric times. The two most important collections are devoted to objects from the Hispano-Moorish period of the 12th to the 14th centuries and to Spanish ceramics of the 17th and 18th centuries. Hours in July and August are Monday through Friday 9am to 1:30pm; September through June, Monday through Friday 9am to 2pm and 5 to 8pm, Saturday 11am to 2pm. Admission is 75 ptas. (50¢).

WHERE TO STAY

Hotel Conde de Floridablanca. Princesa, 18, 30002 Murcia. ☎ **968-21-46-26.** Fax 968-21-32-15. 97 units. A/C MINIBAR TV TEL. 8,500 ptas. ($56.95) double. AE, DC, MC, V. Parking 1,200 ptas. ($8.05). Bus: 2, 5, 6, or 11.

Rising from the center of the Barrio del Carmen, near the cathedral, this hotel is ideally situated for exploring the old city. Originally built in 1972, it was thoroughly renovated and enlarged in 1992. The building is attractively decorated in conservative modern style, with comfortable and appealing midsize guest rooms. Guests have the use of a safe. The hotel serves breakfast, and a bar and restaurant offer dinner and drinks.

Hotel Hispano 1. Calle Trapería, 8, 30001 Murcia. ☎ **968-21-61-52.** Fax 968-21-68-59. 46 units. TEL. 5,000 ptas. ($33.50) double. AE, DC, MC, V. Bus: 2, 5, 6, or 11.

An older version of Hispano 2 (see below), run by the same people, this good-value hotel is still reliable after all these years. It stands right next to the cathedral. The well-kept guest rooms are functional and homey, but a bit small, although the beds are firm. The hotel restaurant serves regional cuisine.

Hotel Hispano 2. Calle Radio Murcia, 3, 30001 Murcia. ☎ **968-21-61-52.** Fax 968-21-68-59. 35 units. A/C MINIBAR TV TEL. 7,500–10,000 ptas. ($50.25–$67) double. AE, DC, MC, V. Parking 1,000 ptas. ($6.70). Bus: 2, 5, 6, or 11.

The older Hispano 1 (see above) proved so successful that the owners inaugurated this property in 1976. The comfortable furnished guest rooms are superior to those at the older sibling. The family-run restaurant next door, Hispano, offers well-prepared and reasonably priced regional food and tapas.

Hotel Meliá 7 Coronas. Paseo de Garay, 5, 30000 Murcia. ☎ **800/336-3542** in the U.S., or 968-21-77-72. Fax 968-22-12-94. 153 units. A/C MINIBAR TV TEL. 20,000 ptas. ($134) double. AE, DC, MC, V. Parking 1,500 ptas. ($10.05). Bus: 2, 5, 6, or 11.

A member of the well-recommended nationwide chain, this is the finest hotel in town. The angular 1971 building offers comfortable midsize guest rooms and a cool, refreshing terrace with bar service and a legion of flowering plants. The restaurant serves à la carte Spanish and French cuisine. There's also a bar. The hotel is within a 15-minute walk east of the cathedral, near the gardens abutting the northern edge of the Río Segura.

Residencia Rincón de Pepe. Calle de Apóstoles, 34, 30007 Murcia. ☎ **968-21-22-39.** Fax 968-22-17-44. 148 units. A/C MINIBAR TV TEL. 12,500–14,200 ptas. ($83.75–$95.15) double. AE, DC, MC, V. Parking 1,450 ptas. ($9.70).

This modern hotel hidden on a narrow street in the heart of the old quarter is attached to a well-known restaurant, Rincón de Pepe (see below). It has a good-size lounge and a new casino, as well as a bar. The small to medium-size guest rooms are up-to-date, with many built-in conveniences.

A NEARBY RESORT

✪ **Hyatt Regency La Manga.** Los Belones, 30385 Cartagena, Murcia. ☎ **800/223-1234** or 968-33-12-34. Fax 968-33-12-35. www.lamanga.hyatt.com. 249 units. A/C MINIBAR TV TEL. 41,300–44,800 ptas. ($276.70–$300.15) double; 63,000–160,000 ptas. ($422.10–$1,072) suite; 19,400–22,800 ptas. ($130–$152.75) studio apt.; 23,000–38,800 ptas. ($154.10–$259.95) 1- to 3-bedroom apt. AE, DC, MC, V. Free parking.

One of the best resorts in Spain is away from the coast, near the eastern part of Andalusia. Nestled on 1,400 acres (the grounds are larger than the land controlled by the Principality of Monaco), it's the only resort in Europe with three championship golf courses. It also features a comprehensive array of sports facilities. The decor is inspired by the aristocratic private villas of Andalusia. Families usually opt for one of the functional four-star apartments in the airy Los Lomos complex. Fifty apartments (as well as about 20 time-share units not accessible to the public) make up a re-creation of an Andalusian pueblo. Couples and clients staying for a week or less tend to gravitate toward the luxurious doubles. The grand five-star accommodations occupy the resort's architectural showcase, the Príncipe Felipe, named for the son of King Juan Carlos.

Dining/Diversions: The Ampola restaurant has views over the golf courses. Other dining venues include La Cala, a Mexican restaurant; Luigi's, an Italian pizza and pasta restaurant; and a jazz bar, Andaie. There's also a sandwich shop.

Amenities: Baby-sitting, 24-hour room service, hairdressing, laundry and valet, concierge. Health and fitness club, children's camp with facilities for supervision and baby-sitting, four outdoor swimming pools and sundeck. Tennis center with 18 courts (14 lighted), golf and tennis pro shops. A beach with water-sports facilities and kiosks is 10 minutes away by shuttle bus.

WHERE TO DINE

Acuario. Plaza Puxmaria, 1. ☎ **968-21-99-55.** Reservations recommended. Main courses 1,500–2,000 ptas. ($10.05–$13.40); fixed-price menu 3,000 ptas. ($20.10). AE, DC, MC, V. Mon–Sat 1–4pm and 8:30pm–midnight. Closed 2 weeks in Aug. Bus: 2, 5, 6, or 11. REGIONAL/INTERNATIONAL.

This restaurant near the cathedral allows you to dine in air-conditioned comfort. Since it opened in 1987, it has been known for excellent Murcian cuisine and its selection of international dishes. You might begin with pâté of salmon, following with *merluza* (hake) in sherry sauce, a tender tournedos, or the chef's specialty, eggplant cooked with Serrano ham and mushrooms. If it's available, the lemon soufflé is delectable.

✪ **Rincón de Pepe.** Plaza de Apóstoles, 34. ☎ **968-21-22-39.** Reservations recommended. Main courses 1,800–4,500 ptas. ($12.05–$30.15). AE, DC, MC, V. Daily noon–4pm; Mon–Sat 8pm–midnight. Closed Aug. Bus: 3, 4, or 8. SPANISH/INTERNATIONAL.

Many visitors won't leave town without going to this culinary landmark. Established in the mid-1920s, it's the best restaurant in town. You can spend a lot or a little, depending on what you order. Specialties change frequently, and the menu varies seasonally. You might enjoy pig's trotters and white beans, spring lamb kidneys in sherry, or white beans with partridge. Shellfish selections include Carril clams, a platter of assorted grilled seafood and fish, and grilled red prawns. Among the meat and poultry specialties are roast spring lamb Murcian style, and duck in orange sauce.

10 Barcelona

Blessed with rich and fertile soil, an excellent harbor, and a hard-working population, Barcelona has always prospered. When Madrid was still a dusty Castilian backwater, Barcelona was a powerful, diverse capital, influenced more by the Mediterranean empires that conquered it than by the cultures of the arid Iberian plains to the west. Carthage, Rome, and Charlemagne-era France overran Catalonia, and each left an indelible mark on the region's identity.

The Catalan people have clung fiercely to their unique culture and language, both of which Franco systematically tried to eradicate. But Catalonia has endured, becoming a semiautonomous region of Spain (with Catalán its official language). And Barcelona, the region's lodestar, has truly come into its own. The city's most powerful monuments open a window onto its history: the intricately carved edifices of the medieval Gothic Quarter; the curvilinear *modernisme* (Catalan art nouveau) that inspired Gaudí's Sagrada Familia; and the seminal surrealist works of Picasso and Miró, in museums that mark Barcelona as a crucial incubator for 20th-century art.

As if those attractions weren't enough, Barcelona is on the doorstep of some of Europe's great playgrounds and vacation retreats. The Balearic Islands lie to the east, the Costa Brava to the north, the Penedés wine country to the west, and to the south, the Roman city of Tarragona, the monastery at Montserrat, and such Costa Dorada resort towns as Sitges.

Despite its allure, Barcelona grapples with problems common to many major cities—the increasing polarization of rich and poor, a rising tide of drug abuse, and an escalating crime rate, mostly in theft. But in reaction to a rash of negative publicity, city authorities have, with some degree of success, brought crime under control, at least within the tourist zones.

A revitalized Barcelona eagerly prepared for and welcomed thousands of visitors as part of the 1992 Summer Olympic Games. But the action didn't end when the last medal was handed out. Barcelona turned its multimillion-dollar building projects into permanently expanded facilities for sports and tourism. Its modern $150 million terminal at El Prat de Llobregat Airport can accommodate 12 million passengers a year, and ever-pragmatic Barcelona races to the 21st century with a restructuring program called "Post Olympic." The city is fast emerging as one of the hottest tourist cities in Europe.

Landmark buildings and world-class museums fill the historic city. They include Antoni Gaudí's famed Sagrada Familia, the Museu Picasso, the Gothic cathedral, and Les Rambles, the famous tree-lined promenade that cuts through the heart of the old quarter.

An array of nightlife (Barcelona is a *big* bar town) and shopping possibilities, plus nearby wineries, ensure that you'll be entertained round the clock. It makes for some serious sightseeing; you'll need plenty of time to take it all in—in fact, more time than it takes to see Madrid.

1 Catalonian Culture

Barcelona (which was described in the Middle Ages as "the head and trunk of Catalonia") has always thrived on contact and commerce with countries beyond Spain's borders. From its earliest days, the city has been linked more closely to France and the rest of Europe than to Iberia. Each of the military and financial empires that swept through Catalonia left its cultural imprint.

LANGUAGE   Catalonia lies midway between France and Castilian Spain. The province is united by a common language, **Catalán.** The region's linguistic separation is arguably the single most important element in its people's streak of independence.

Modern linguists attribute the earliest division of Catalán from Castilian to two phenomena. The first was the cultural links and trade ties between ancient Barcina and the neighboring Roman colony of Provence, which shaped the Catalán tongue along Provençal and Languedocian models. The second major event was the invasion of the eastern Pyrenees by Charlemagne in the late 800s, and the designation of Catalonia as a Frankish march (buffer zone) between Christian Europe and Moorish-dominated Iberia.

Though Catalán is closely related to Castilian Spanish, even those travelers who are fluent in Spanish are occasionally confronted with unfamiliar words in Barcelona. Don't be surprised if maps or brochures have addresses in Castilian, but then you find signs in Catalán on the street.

ARCHITECTURE   Like many other cities in Spain, Barcelona claims its share of Neolithic dolmens and ruins from the Roman and Moorish periods. Monuments survive from the Middle Ages, when the Romanesque solidity of no-nonsense barrel vaults (sometimes with ribbing), narrow windows, and fortified design were widely used.

In the 11th and 12th centuries, religious fervor swept through Europe, and pilgrims began to flock to Barcelona on their way west to Santiago de Compostela, bringing with them French building styles and the need for new and larger churches. The style that emerged, called Catalonian Gothic, had softer lines and more elaborate ornamentation than traditional gothic. Appropriate for both civic and religious buildings, it called for ogival (pointed) arches, intricate stone carvings, large interior columns, exterior buttresses, and vast rose windows set with colored glass. One of Barcelona's

Impressions

Although the great adventures that befell me there occasioned me no great pleasure, but rather much grief, I bore them the better for having seen the city [Barcelona].
—Don Quixote

purest and most-loved examples of this style is the Church of **Santa María del Mar,** north of the city's harbor.

The Barcelona that visitors best remember, however, is the Barcelona of *modernisme,* an art nouveau movement that, from about 1890 to 1910, put the city on the architectural map. A highly articulate school of Catalan architects blended pre-Raphaelite voluptuousness and Catalonian romanticism, heavily laced with a yearning for the curved lines and organic forms easily recognized in nature.

The movement's most famous architect was Antoni Gaudí. The chimneys of his buildings look like half-melted mounds of chocolate twisted into erratic spirals; his horizontal lines flow over vertical supports. Some of Gaudí's most distinctive creations include Casa Milá, Casa Batlló, Parc Güell, and the landmark Temple Expiatori de la Sagrada Familia (left incomplete).

Other modernist architects of this era looked for inspiration to medieval models, particularly the fortified castles and sculpted gargoyles and dragons of the 12th-century Barcelonan counts. Examples include Domènech i Montaner and Puig i Cadafalch, whose elegant mansions and concert halls seemed perfectly suited to the enlightened, sophisticated prosperity of the 19th-century Catalonian bourgeoisie. A 19th-century economic boom neatly coincided with the profusion of geniuses who suddenly emerged in the building business. Entrepreneurs who had made their fortunes in the fields and mines of the New World commissioned some of the beautiful and elaborate villas in Barcelona and nearby Sitges.

Initiated in 1858, the expansion of Barcelona into the northern **Eixample district** laid the groundwork, as it were, for the *modernisme* architects' designs. The gridlike pattern of streets in the Eixample was intersected with broad diagonals. Although opposed by local landowners and never endowed with the detail of its original design, it provided a carefully planned, elegant path in which a growing city could showcase its finest buildings.

A city competition conducted in the late 1850s was to decide the final architect to draw up the plans for the Eixample. Antoni Rovira won the competition and produced a radical plan. The apartment buildings, which surrounded park areas, were to be democratically occupied—"by the people of Barcelona." The plan was never carried out. The Spanish Ministry of Works approved a rectangular grid plan devised by Ildefons Cerdà, and Catalan officials felt that Madrid centralism had quashed their grand new scheme. The gardens in Cerdà's more conservative plan were never built, and the property passed to greedy landlords who constructed more buildings. Ruthless property speculation came immediately after work on the Eixample began in 1860. This dramatic story of failed hopes and dreams is told in Eduardo Mendoza's novel *The City of Marvels* and Robert Hughes's *Barcelona.*

Consistent with the general artistic stagnation in Spain during the Franco era (1939–75), the 1950s saw a tremendous increase in the number of anonymous housing projects around the periphery of Barcelona. Since the death of Franco, a cultural renaissance has ensued: New and more creative designs for buildings are again being executed.

ART From the cave paintings discovered at Lérida to several true giants of the 20th century—Picasso, Dalí, and Miró—Catalonia has had a long and significant artistic tradition. It is the Spanish center of plastic arts.

The first art movement to attract attention in Barcelona was **Catalonian Gothic sculpture,** which held sway from the 13th to the 15th centuries and produced such renowned masters as Bartomeu and Pere Johan. Sculptors working with Italian masters brought the Renaissance to Barcelona, but few great Catalonian legacies remain from this period. The rise of baroque art in the 17th and 18th centuries saw Catalonia filled with several impressive examples, but nothing worth a special pilgrimage.

In the neoclassical period of the 18th century, Catalonia, and particularly Barcelona, arose from an artistic slumber. Art schools opened and foreign painters arrived, exerting considerable influence. The 19th century produced many Catalonian artists who followed the general European trends of the time without forging any major creative breakthroughs.

The 20th century brought renewed artistic ferment in Barcelona, as reflected by the arrival of Málaga-born Pablo **Picasso**. (The Catalan capital today is the site of a major Picasso museum.) The great surrealist painters of the Spanish school, Joan **Miró** (who also has an eponymous museum in Barcelona) and Salvador **Dalí** (whose fantastical museum is along the Costa Brava, north of Barcelona), also came to the Catalonian capital.

Many Catalan sculptors also achieved acclaim in this century, including Casanovas, Llimon, and Blay. The Spanish Civil War brought cultural stagnation, yet against all odds many Catalan artists continued to make bold statements. Antoni Tàpies was one of the principal artists of this period (one of the newest museums in Barcelona is devoted to his work). Among the various schools formed in Spain at the time was the neofigurative band, which included such artists as Váquez Díaz and Pancho Cossio.

Today, at the end of the 20th century, many Barcelona artists are making major names for themselves, and their works are sold in the most prestigious galleries of the Western world. Outstanding among these is **Susana Solano,** who ranks among the most renowned names in Spanish contemporary art. In her metal sculptures and installations, she creates what one critic called "spatial objects which combine rigorously geometrical structures with sensually flowing shapes and material qualities."

MUSIC & DANCE   The counts of Barcelona, we are told, were great music lovers, and the Catalan appreciation of music continues to this day. Richard Strauss dedicated the musical center, the Palau de la Música Catalana, in 1908.

In addition to importing the great talents of Europe, the people of Catalonia also create music. Many of their own artists and composers, most prominently Pablo Casals, have earned international acclaim.

But few artistic traditions enjoy the renown of the *sardana,* the national dance. This is truly a street dance, accompanied by *coblas* (brass bands). You can perform a *sardana* almost anywhere and at any time, provided you get some like-minded people to join you. Age doesn't matter—everybody joins in the spontaneous outburst. The dance's roots are unknown. Some claim that it originated on a Greek island and was brought to Barcelona by seafarers; others say it came from the Italian island of Sardinia, which would at least account for its name.

To see this dance, go to the Plaça de Sant Jaume in the Barri Gòtic on Sunday at noon. It's a group dance with participants forming a ring. Any number can participate; the ring just gets bigger. Joining hands, the dancers raise their arms and dance in repetitive rhythms in complete silence. Catalans view the dance as a statement of their national identity. It has also represented peaceful resistance to oppression—they danced it during the dreaded Franco era.

2 Orientation

ARRIVING

BY PLANE   Most travelers to Barcelona fly to Madrid and change planes there, though there are direct flights to Barcelona on TWA and Delta. Iberia offers many daily shuttle flights between Barcelona and Madrid—at 15-minute intervals during peak hours on weekdays—plus service from Valencia, Granada, Seville, and Bilbao. Generally cheaper than Iberia, both **Air Europa** (☎ 93-298-33-28) and **Spanair** (☎ 93-298-33-62) run shuttles between Madrid and Barcelona. Shuttle schedules depend on demand, with more frequent service in the early morning and late afternoon. For more information on flying into Madrid, refer to "Getting There," in chapter 2.

The airport, **El Prat de Llobregat,** 08820 Prat de Llobregat (☎ 93-298-38-38), lies 7½ miles (12km) southwest of the city. The route to the center of town is carefully signposted. A train runs between the airport and Barcelona's Estació Central de Barcelona-Sants every day from 6:14am (the first airport departure) to and 10:13pm (from Sants) or 10:43pm (the last city departure). The 21-minute trip costs 305 ptas. ($2.05) Monday through Friday, 350 ptas. ($2.35) Saturday and Sunday. If your hotel lies near Plaça de Catalunya, you might opt for an Aerobús. It runs daily every 15 minutes between 5:30am and midnight from the airport and 11:15pm from the Plaça de Catalunya. The fare is 475 ptas. ($3.20). A taxi from the airport into central Barcelona costs approximately 3,000 to 3,500 ptas. ($20.10 to $23.45).

BY TRAIN   A train called the **Barcelona-TALGO** provides rail service between Paris and Barcelona in 11½ hours. For many other routes from the rest of Europe, you change trains at Port Bou, on the French-Spanish border. Most trains issue seat and sleeper reservations.

Trains arrive at the **Estació de França,** Avenida Marqués de L'Argentera (metro: Barceloneta, L3), from points throughout Spain as well as from international cities. From Madrid there are four TALGOS trains per day that make the trip in 7 hours, and two night trains that take 9½ hours; from Seville, there are two trains daily making the 12-hour trip; and from Valencia, there are 11 trains daily making the 3½-hour trip. There are express night trains to and from Paris, Zurich, Milan, and Geneva.

The modernized 1929 station has a huge screen with updated information on train departures and arrivals, personalized ticket dispatching, a passenger attention center, a tourism information center, showers, internal baggage control, a first-aid center, and centers for hotel reservations and car rentals. It is much more than a departure point: The station also has an elegant restaurant, a cafeteria, a book-and-record store, a jazz club, and even a disco. Estació de França is steps from Ciutadella Park, the zoo, and the port, and is near Vila Olímpica.

RENFE also has a terminal at **Estació Central de Barcelona-Sants,** Plaça de Països Catalanes (metro: Sants-Estació).

For general RENFE information, call ☎ 93-490-02-02.

BY BUS   Bus travel to Barcelona is possible but not popular—it's pretty slow. Barcelona's Estació del Nord is the arrival and departure point for **Enatcar** (☎ 93-245-25-28) buses to and from southern France and Italy. Enatcar also operates 21 buses per day to and from Madrid (trip time: 7½ hours) and 9 buses per day to and from Valencia (4½ hours). A one-way ticket from Madrid costs 3,200 ptas. ($21.45); from Valencia, 2,900 ptas. ($19.45).

Linebús (☎ 93-265-07-00) offers six trips a week to and from Paris. **Julià Via,** carrer Viriato (☎ 93-490-40-00), operates four buses a week to and from Frankfurt and another four per week to and from Marseille.

For bus travel to the beach resorts along the Costa Brava (see chapter 12), go to **Sarfa,** Estació del Nord (☎ 93-265-11-58). Trip time is usually 1 hour, 20 minutes.

BY CAR   From **France** (the usual European road approach to Barcelona), the major access route is at the eastern end of the **Pyrenees.** You have a choice of the express highway (**E-15**) or the more scenic coastal road. But be warned: If you take the coastal road in July and August, you will often encounter bumper-to-bumper traffic. You can also approach Barcelona via **Toulouse.** Cross the border into Spain at **Puigcerdá** (where there are frontier stations), near the principality of Andorra. From there, take the N-152 to Barcelona.

From **Madrid,** take the **N-2** to Zaragoza, then the **A-2** to El Vendrell, followed by the **A-7** motorway to Barcelona. From the **Costa Blanca** or **Costa del Sol,** follow the **E-15** north from Valencia along the eastern Mediterranean coast.

BY FERRY   Transmediterránea, Moll Sant Bertran, s/n (☎ **93-295-91-00**), operates daily trips to and from the Balearic islands of Majorca (trip time: 8 hours) and Minorca (9 hours). In summer, it's important to have a reservation as far in advance as possible.

VISITOR INFORMATION

Barcelona has two types of tourist offices. The local government office deals with Spain in general and Catalunya in particular, with basic information about Barcelona. This organization has an office at the airport, **El Prat de Llobregat** (☎ **93-478-47-04**), which you'll pass as you clear customs. Summer hours are Monday through Saturday 9:30am to 8:30pm; off-season hours are Monday through Saturday 9:30am to 8pm; year-round, it's open Sunday 9:30 to 3pm. There is another large office in the center of Barcelona at the **Palau de Rubert,** Passeig de Gràcia, 107 (☎ **93-238-40-40**), where there are often exhibitions. It is open daily 10am to 7pm.

The other organization, the **Oficina de Informació de Turisme de Barcelona,** Plaça de Catalunya, 17-S (☎ **93-304-34-21** or 906-30-12-82 from inside Spain), deals exclusively with the city of Barcelona. The staff can help you make hotel reservations in person and by telephone (☎ **93-304-34-34**). This is also where you can obtain detailed information about the city and the Barcelona card for tourist discounts. The office is open daily 9am to 9pm. The same organization has an office at the **Estació Central de Barcelona-Sants** (Sants railway station), Plaça Päisos Catalanes (no phone; metro: Sants-Estació). In summer it is open daily 8am to 8pm; off-season, Monday through Friday 8am to 8pm, Saturday and Sunday 8am to 2pm.

CITY LAYOUT

MAIN SQUARES, STREETS & ARTERIES   **Plaça de Catalunya** (Plaza de Cataluña in Spanish) is the city's heart; the world-famous **Rambles** (Ramblas) are its arteries. Les Rambles begins at the Plaça Portal de la Pau, with its 164-foot-high monument to Columbus and a panoramic view of the port, and stretches north to the Plaça de Catalunya. Along this wide promenade you'll find bookshops and newsstands, stalls selling birds and flowers, and benches or cafe tables and chairs, where you can sit and watch the passing parade.

At the end of the Rambles is the **Barri Xinés** (Barrio Chino or Chinese Quarter). It has long enjoyed notoriety as a haven of prostitution and drugs, populated in Jean Genet's *The Thief's Journal* by "whores, thieves, pimps, and beggars." Still a dangerous district, it is best viewed during the day, if at all.

Off the Rambles lies **Plaça Reial** (Plaza Real), the most harmoniously proportioned square in Barcelona. Come here on Sunday morning to see the stamp and coin collectors peddle their wares.

The major wide boulevards of Barcelona are the **Avinguda** (Avenida) **Diagonal** and **Passeig** (Paseo) **de Colom,** and an elegant shopping street, the **Passeig de Gràcia.**

A short walk from the Rambles will take you to the **Passeig del Moll de la Fusta,** a waterfront promenade developed in the 1990s. It's home to some of the best (but

The Barcelona Card

An ideal way to appreciate Barcelona better and save money at the same time is with the Barcelona card. It's definitely a bargain if you will stay in the city for more than an afternoon and do any sightseeing at all. For 24 hours it costs 2,500 ptas. ($16.75) for adults, 2,000 ptas. ($13.40) for children 6 to 15. For 48 hours it is 3,000 ptas. ($20.10) for adults, 2,500 ptas. ($16.75) for children; for 72 hours, 3,500 ptas. ($23.45) and 3,000 ptas. ($20.10).

The card offers visitors many advantages. The 24-hour card covers 10 free journeys on the metro or bus, and the 48- and 72-hour cards offer unlimited travel on all public transport. Cardholders receive 25% discounts on the Tombbus (which runs along the best shopping route in central Barcelona) and the Tibibus (to the Fun Fair on Mount Tibidabo). On airport and tourist buses, fares are reduced by 15%.

Culture vultures who hold the card can get discounts of 30% to 50% in 28 museums. Eleven theaters and shows grant a 10% to 25% discount, which also applies at 16 leisure and night venues. Barcelona is famous for its designers, whose work ranges from clothes to ceramics. With this card you get a 12% discount at 23 leading stores. Finally, there is an 8% discount in 11 restaurants. The cards specify where they can be used. They're for sale at the tourist offices at the airport, at Sants station, and in the Plaça de Catalunya (see "Visitor Information," above).

not the cheapest) restaurants in Barcelona. If you can't afford the prices, come here at least for a drink in the open air and a view of the harbor.

To the east is the old port, **La Barceloneta,** which dates from the 18th century. This strip of land between the port and the sea has traditionally been a good place for seafood.

Barri Gòtic (Barrio Gótico or Gothic Quarter) lies east of the Rambles. This is the site of the city's oldest buildings, including the cathedral.

North of Plaça de Catalunya, the **Eixample** unfolds. An area of wide boulevards, in contrast to the labyrinthine Gothic Quarter, it contains two major roads that lead out of Barcelona, the Avinguda Diagonal and Gran Vía de les Corts Catalanes. Another major neighborhood, working-class **Gràcia,** lies north of the Eixample.

Montjuïc, one of the city's mountains, begins at Plaça d'Espanya, a traffic rotary, beyond which are Barcelona's famous fountains. Montjuïc was the setting for the principal events of the 1992 Summer Olympic Games. The other mountain is **Tibidabo,** in the northwest, which boasts great views of the city and the Mediterranean. It contains an amusement park.

FINDING AN ADDRESS/MAPS   Finding a Barcelona address can be a problem. The city abounds with long boulevards and a complicated maze of narrow, twisting streets. Knowing the street number, if there is one, is essential. The designation s/n (*sin número*) means that the building has no number. It's crucial to learn the cross street if you're seeking a specific address.

The rule about street numbers is that there is no rule. On most streets, numbering begins on one side and runs up that side until the end, then runs in the opposite direction on the other side. Number 40 might be opposite 408. But there are many exceptions. Sometimes street numbers on buildings in the older quarters have been obscured by the patina of time.

Arm yourself with a good map before setting out. Free maps from tourist offices and hotels aren't adequate, because they don't label the little streets. The best map for exploring Barcelona, published by **Falk,** is available at most bookstores and newsstands, such as those found along the Rambles. This pocket map includes all the streets, with an index of how to find them.

Neighborhoods in Brief

Barri Gòtic This section rises to the north of Passeig de Colom, with its **Columbus Monument.** Its eastern border is a major artery, Via Laietana, which begins at La Barceloneta at Plaça d'Antoni López and runs north to Plaça d'Urquinaona. Les Rambles forms the western border of the Gothic Quarter, and on the northern edge is the Ronda de Sant Pere, which intersects with **Plaça de Catalunya** and the **Passeig de Gràcia.** The heart of this medieval quarter is the **Plaça de Sant Jaume,** which was a major crossroads in the old Roman city. Many of the structures in the old section are ancient, including the ruins of a Roman temple dedicated to Augustus. Antique stores, restaurants, cafes, museums, some hotels, and bookstores fill the area today. It is also the headquarters of the **Generalitat,** seat of the Catalan government.

Les Rambles Also commonly known as **La Rambla.** The most famous promenade in Spain, ranking with Madrid's Paseo del Prado, it was once a drainage channel. These days, street entertainers, flower vendors, news vendors, cafe patrons, and strollers flow along its length. The gradual 1-mile descent toward the sea has often been called a metaphor for life, because its bustling action combines cosmopolitanism and crude vitality.

Les Rambles actually consists of five sections, each a particular *rambla*—Rambla de Canaletes, Rambla dels Estudis, Rambla de Sant Josep, Rambla dels Caputxins, and Rambla de Santa Mònica. The shaded pedestrian esplanade runs from the Plaça de Catalunya to the port—all the way to the Columbus Monument. Along the way you'll pass the **Gran Teatre del Liceu,** on Rambla dels Caputxins, one of the most magnificent opera houses in the world until it caught fire in 1994 and had to be rebuilt. Miró did a sidewalk mosaic at the Plaça de la Boquería. During the stagnation of the Franco era, this street grew seedier and seedier. But the opening of the Ramada Renaissance hotel and the restoration of many buildings have brought energy and hope for the street.

Barri Xinés Despite the name ("Chinese Quarter"), this isn't Chinatown—historians are unsure how the neighborhood got its name. For decades it's had an unsavory reputation. Franco outlawed prostitution in 1956, but apparently no one ever told the denizens of this district of narrow, often murky, old streets and dark corners. Petty thieves, drug dealers, and purse-snatchers are just some of the neighborhood characters. Nighttime is dangerous, so exercise caution; still, most visitors like to take a quick look to see what all the excitement is about. Just off Les Rambles, the area lies primarily between the waterfront and carrer de l'Hospital. Although it has a long way to go, Barri Xinés is undergoing tremendous change that began before the '92 Olympics. An urban renewal program has led to the destruction of some of the seedier parts of the barrio. The opening of the **Museu d'Art Contemporani** at Plaça dels Angels has led to a revitalization of the area and the opening of a lot more art galleries. The official name Barcelona has given to this district is **El Raval.**

Barri de la Ribera Another neighborhood that stagnated for years but is now well into a renaissance, the Barri de la Ribera is adjacent to the Barri Gòtic, going east to

Passeig de Picasso, which borders the Parc de la Ciutadella. The centerpiece of this district is the **Museu Picasso,** housed in the 15th-century Palau Agüilar, Montcada, 15. Numerous art galleries have opened around the museum, and the old quarter is fashionable. Many mansions in this area were built during one of Barcelona's major maritime expansions, principally in the 1200s and 1300s. Most of these grand homes still stand along **carrer de Montcada** and other nearby streets.

La Barceloneta & the Harbor Front   Although Barcelona has a long seagoing tradition, its waterfront was in decay for years. Today, the waterfront promenade, **Passeig del Moll de la Fusta,** bursts with activity. The best way to get a bird's-eye view of the area is to take an elevator to the top of the Columbus Monument in Plaça Portal de la Pau.

Near the monument were the **Reials Drassanes,** or royal shipyards, a booming place during Barcelona's maritime heyday in the Middle Ages. Years before Columbus landed in the New World, ships sailed around the world from here, flying the traditional yellow-and-red flag of Catalonia.

To the east lies a mainly artificial peninsula, **La Barceloneta** (Little Barcelona). Formerly a fishing district dating mainly from the 18th century, it's now filled with seafood restaurants. The blocks here are long and surprisingly narrow—architects planned them that way so that each room in every building fronted a street. Many bus lines terminate at the Passeig Nacional, site of the **Barcelona Aquarium**.

The Eixample   To the north of the Plaça de Catalunya lies the Eixample, or Ensanche, the section of Barcelona that grew beyond the old medieval walls. This great period of enlargement (*eixample* in Catalán), came mainly in the 19th century. Avenues form a grid of perpendicular streets, cut across by a majestic boulevard— **Passeig de Gràcia,** a posh shopping street ideal for leisurely promenades. The area's main traffic artery is **Avinguda Diagonal,** which links the expressway and the heart of the congested city.

The Eixample was the center of Barcelona's *modernisme* movement, and it possesses some of the most original buildings any architect ever designed. Gaudí's Sagrada Familia is one of the major attractions.

Montjuïc & Tibidabo   Montjuïc, called Hill of the Jews after a Jewish necropolis there, gained prominence in 1929 as the site of the World's Fair and again in 1992 as the site of the Summer Olympic Games. Its major attractions are the Joan Miró museum, the Olympic installations, and the **Poble Espanyol** (Spanish Village), a 5-acre site constructed for the World's Fair. Examples of Spanish art and architecture are on display against the backdrop of a traditional Spanish village. Tibidabo (1,650 feet) is where you should go for your final look at Barcelona. On a clear day you can see the mountains of Majorca (the largest and most famous of the Balearic Islands), some 130 miles away. Reached by train, tram, and cable car, Tibidabo is the most popular Sunday excursion in Barcelona.

Pedralbes   Pedralbes is where wealthy Barcelonans live, some in stylish blocks of apartment houses, others in 19th-century villas behind ornamental fences, still others in stunning *modernisme* structures. Set in a park, the **Palau de Pedralbes** (Avinguda Diagonal, 686) was constructed in the 1920s as a gift from the city to Alfonso XIII, the grandfather of King Juan Carlos. The king abdicated and fled in 1931, and never made much use of the palace. Today it has a new life, housing a museum of carriages and a group of European paintings called the **Colecció Cambó.**

Vila Olímpica   This seafront property contains the tallest buildings in the city. The revitalized site, in the post–Olympic Games era, is the setting for numerous imported-car showrooms, designer clothing stores, restaurants, and business offices. The "village" was where the athletes lived during the 1992 games. A miniature city is taking shape, complete with banks, art galleries, nightclubs, bars, and even pastry shops.

3 Getting Around

To save money on public transportation, buy a card that's good for 10 trips. **Tarjeta T-1**, for 795 ptas. ($5.35), is good for the metro and the bus. **Tarjeta T-2**, for 625 ptas. ($4.40), covers everything but the bus.

Passes (*abonos temporales*) are available at **Transports Metropolita de Barcelona,** Plaça de la Universitat. It's open Monday through Friday 8am to 7pm, Saturday 8am to 1pm.

To save money on sightseeing tours during the summer, ride on **Bus Turistic,** which passes by 24 of the most popular sights. You can get on and off the bus as you please, and the price also covers the Tibidabo funicular and the Montjuïc cable car and funicular. Tickets, which may be purchased on the bus or at the tourist office at Plaça de Catalunya, cost 1,800 ptas. ($12.05) for 1 day, 2,300 ptas. ($15.40) for 2 days.

BY SUBWAY   Barcelona's metro system consists of five main lines; it crisscrosses the city more frequently and with greater efficiency than the bus network. Two commuter trains run between the city and the suburbs. Service operates Monday through Friday 5am to 11pm, Saturday 5am to 1am, and Sunday and holidays 6am to 1am. The one-way fare is 145 ptas. (95¢). Each metro station entrance is marked with a red diamond. The major station for all subway lines is **Plaça de Catalunya.**

BY BUS   Some 50 bus lines traverse the city, and as always, you don't want to ride them at rush hour. The driver issues a ticket as you board at the front. Most buses operate daily from 6:30am to 10pm; some night buses go along the principal arteries from 11pm to 4am. Buses are color-coded—red ones cut through the city center during the day, and yellow ones do the job at night. The one-way fare is 145 ptas. (95¢).

BY TAXI   Each yellow-and-black taxi bears the letters SP (*servicio público*) on its front and rear. A lit green light on the roof and a "LIBRE" sign in the window indicate that the taxi is free to pick up passengers. The basic rate begins at 300 ptas. ($2). Check to make sure you're not paying the fare of a previously departed passenger; taxi drivers have been known to "forget" to turn back the meter. Each additional kilometer in the slow-moving traffic costs 110 to 120 ptas. (75¢ to 80¢). Supplements might also apply—150 ptas. ($1) for a large suitcase that is placed in the trunk, for instance. Rides to the airport sometimes carry a supplement of 300 ptas. ($2). For a taxi, call ☎ **93-330-08-04.**

BY CAR   Driving in congested Barcelona is frustrating and potentially dangerous. Besides, it's unlikely that you'd ever find a place to park. Try other means of getting around. Save your car rentals for excursions and for when you're ready to move on.

All three of the major U.S.-based car-rental firms are represented in Barcelona, both at the airport and (except for Budget) downtown. The longest hours and some of the most favorable rates are at the airport office of **Budget** (☎ **93-298-35-00**), open daily 7am to midnight, without a midday break.

Avis, carrer de Casanova, 209 (☎ **93-209-95-33**), is open Monday through Friday 8am to 1pm and 4 to 7pm, Saturday 8am to 1pm. **Hertz** is at Tuset, 10 (☎ **93-217-80-76**); it's open Monday through Friday 8am to 2pm and 4 to 7pm, Saturday 9am to 1pm. Hertz and Avis are closed on Sunday except in the airport, where they are open from 7am to midnight daily. This forces clients of those companies to trek out to the airport to pick up or return their cars; however, after-hours arrangements can be made.

Remember that it's usually cheaper and easier to arrange your car rental before leaving the United States. For more information on car rentals in Spain, refer to "Getting Around," in chapter 2.

FUNICULARS & RAIL LINKS At some point in your journey, you may want to visit Tibidabo or Montjuïc (or both). A train called **Tramvía Blau** (Blue Streetcar) goes from Plaça Kennedy to the bottom of the funicular to Tibidabo. It operates every 15 to 20 minutes from 9:05am to 9:35pm on weekends only. The fare is 300 ptas. ($2) one way, 450 ptas. ($3) round-trip. During the week, buses run from the Plaça Kennedy to the bottom of the funicular from approximately 7am to 9:30pm daily. The bus costs 145 ptas. (95¢) one way.

At the end of the run, you can go the rest of the way by funicular to the top, at 1,650 feet, for a stunning panoramic view of Barcelona. The funicular operates only when the funfair at Tibidabo is open. Opening times vary according to the time of year and the weather conditions. As a rule, the funicular starts operating 20 minutes before the Fun Fair opens, then every half an hour. During peak visiting hours, it runs every 15 minutes. The fare is 300 ptas. ($2) one way, 400 ptas. ($2.70) round-trip.

The **Tibibus** (☎ 93-211-79-42) goes from the Plaça de Catalunya, in the center of the city, to Tibidabo from June 24 to September 15, Tuesday through Sunday, and on every weekend out of season. It runs every 30 minutes from 10:30am to 6:30pm and sometimes 8:30pm, depending on when the park closes. The one-way fare is 270 ptas. ($1.80). To reach Montjuïc, the site of the 1992 Olympics, take the **Montjuïc funicular** (☎ 93-318-70-74). It links with subway line 3 at Paral.lel. The funicular operates from June 13 to September 30 daily from 11am to 10pm. In winter it operates daily from 10:45am to 8pm. The round-trip fare is 600 ptas. ($4).

A **cable car** linking the upper part of the Montjuïc funicular with Castell de Montjuïc is in service in winter, daily from 11:15am to 6:30pm (until 7:30pm on weekends). The one-way fare is 400 ptas. ($2.70); the round-trip fare is 600 ptas. ($4) for adults, 500 ptas. ($3.35) for children. From June 28 to September 15 and holidays it operates Monday through Friday 11:15am to 8pm, until 9pm on weekends.

The **Montjuïc telèferic** (cable car) runs from Barceloneta to Montjuïc. Service from June 20 through September 15 is daily 10:30am to 7pm, and noon to 5pm in winter. The fare is 1,000 ptas. ($6.70) one way, 1,200 ptas. ($8.05) round-trip.

Fast Facts: Barcelona

American Express   The office is at Passeig de Gràcia, 101 (☎ 93-217-00-70; metro: Diagonal), near the corner of carrer del Rosselló. It's open Monday through Friday 9:30am to 6pm, Saturday 9am to noon.

Consulates   For information on embassies, refer to chapter 2, "Fast Facts: Spain." The **U.S. Consulate,** Reina Elisenda, 23 (☎ 93-280-22-27; train: Reina Elisenda), is open Monday through Friday 9am to 12:30pm and 3 to 5pm. The **Canadian Consulate,** Passeig de Gràcia, 77, 3rd floor (☎ 93-215-07-04; metro: Passeig de Gràcia), is open Monday through Friday 10am to noon. The **U.K. Consulate,** Avinguda Diagonal, 477 (☎ 93-419-90-44; metro: Hospital Clinic), is open Monday through Friday 9:30am to 1:30pm and 4 to 5pm. The **Australian Consulate** is at Gran Vía Carlos III, 98, ninth floor (☎ 93-330-94-96; metro: María Cristina), and is open Monday through Friday 10am to noon.

Barcelona Metro

Currency Exchange   Most banks will exchange currency Monday through Friday from 8:30am to 2pm and—in the downtown area, except in the summer—on Saturday from 8:30am to 1pm. A major *oficina de cambio* (exchange office) is at the Estació Central de Barcelona-Sants, the principal rail station. It's open Monday through Saturday 8:30am to 10pm, Sunday 8:30am to 2pm and 4:30 to 10pm. Exchange offices at Barcelona's airport, El Prat de Llobregat, are open daily 6:30am to 11pm.

Dentist   Call the **Clínica Dental Beonadex,** Passeig Bonanova, 69, 3rd floor (☎ **93-418-44-33**), for an appointment. It's open Monday 3 to 9pm, Tuesday through Friday 8am to 3pm.

Doctors   See "Hospitals," below.

Drugstores   The most centrally located one is **Farmacia Manuel Nadal i Casas,** Rambla de Canaletes, 121 (☎ **93-317-49-42**; metro: Plaça de Catalunya). It's open daily from 9am to 1:30pm and 4:30 to 10pm. Pharmacies take turns staying open late at night. Those that aren't open post the names and addresses of pharmacies in the area that are.

Emergencies   Fire, ☎ **080**; police, ☎ **092**; ambulance, ☎ **061.**

Eyeglasses   Complete service is provided by **Optica 2000,** Santa Anna, 2 (☎ **93-302-12-47**; metro: Plaça de Catalunya), near Plaça de Catalunya. It's open Monday through Saturday 10:30am to 2pm and 4:30 to 8pm.

Hospitals   Barcelona has many hospitals and clinics, including **Hospital Clínic,** and **Hospital de la Santa Creu i Sant Pau,** at the intersection of carrer Cartagena and carrer Sant Antoni Maria Claret (☎ **93-291-90-00**; metro: Hospital de Sant Pau).

Internet Cafe   **El Café de Internet,** Avenida de las Corts Catalanes, 656 (☎ **34-93-412-1915**; e-mail: JordiCarcellaChoia@sevicom.es), is open daily 9am to midnight.

Laundry   Ask at your hotel for the self-serve laundry nearest you, or try one of the following. **Lavandería Brasilia,** Avinguda Meridiana, 322 (☎ **93-352-72-05**; metro: Plaça de Catalunya), is open Monday through Friday 9am to 1:30pm and 4 to 8pm, Saturday 10am to 7pm. Also centrally located is **Lavandería Yolanda,** carrer Carma, 114 (☎ **93-329-43-68**; metro: Liceu, at Les Rambles). It is open Monday through Friday 9am to 1:30pm and 4 to 8pm, Saturday 9am to 1:30pm.

Newspapers/Magazines   *The International Herald-Tribune* is sold at major hotels and nearly all the news kiosks along Les Rambles. Sometimes you can also buy *USA Today* or one of the London newspapers, such as the *Times.* Barcelona's leading daily newspapers, which often list cultural events, are *El Periódico* and *La Vanguardia.*

Police   In an emergency, call ☎ **092.**

Post Office   The main post office is at Plaça d'Antoni López (☎ **93-318-38-31**; metro: Jaume I). It's open Monday through Saturday 8:30am to 9:30pm for sending letters and telegrams, Sunday 9am to 2pm for letters and 8am to 10pm for telegrams.

Safety   Be particularly careful with cameras, purses, and wallets, all favorite targets of thieves and pickpockets in Barcelona, and particularly on the world-famous Rambles. The southern part of Les Rambles, near the waterfront, is the most dangerous section, especially at night. Proceed with caution.

Taxis   See "Getting Around," earlier in this chapter.

Telephone   Dial ☎ **1003** for information in Barcelona. For elsewhere in Spain, dial ☎ **1009.** Most local calls cost 25 ptas. (15¢). Hotels impose surcharges on phone calls, especially long distance, either in Spain or abroad. There is no longer a central telephone office, but calls can be made in comfort and security from phone centers on Les Rambles.

Transit Information   For general RENFE (train) information, dial ☎ **93-490-02-02.** For airport information, call ☎ **93-298 38-38.**

4 Accommodations

Barcelona's hotel options have never been better or more plentiful. It may be one of the most expensive cities in Spain, but prices at Barcelona's first-class and deluxe hotels are completely in line with those in other major European cities—and they even look reasonable when stacked up against the prices in Paris and London. A favorable U.S. dollar exchange rate also makes prices more affordable.

Safety is an important factor when choosing a hotel. Some of the least expensive hotels are not in good locations. A popular area for budget-conscious travelers is the **Barri Gòtic** (Gothic Quarter), in the heart of town. You'll live and eat less expensively here than in any other part of Barcelona. But you should be careful when returning to your hotel late at night.

More modern, but also more expensive, accommodations can be found north of the Barri Gòtic in the **Eixample district,** centered around the metro stops Plaça de Catalunya and Universitat. Many buildings are in the *modernisme* style, from the first 2 decades of this century—and sometimes the elevators and plumbing are of the same vintage. The Eixample is a desirable and safe neighborhood, especially along its wide boulevards. Noise is the only problem you might encounter.

Farther north, above the Avinguda Diagonal, you'll enter the **Gràcia** area, where you can enjoy distinctively Catalan neighborhood life. The main attractions are a bit distant but reached easily by public transportation.

Many of Barcelona's hotels were built before the invention of the automobile, and even those that weren't rarely found space for a garage. When parking is available at the hotel, the price is indicated; otherwise, the hotel staff will direct you to a garage. Expect to pay upwards of 2,000 ptas. ($13.40) for 24 hours, and if you do have a car, you might as well park it and leave it there, because we'd never recommend driving around the city.

CIUTAT VELLA

The Ciutat Vella (Old City) forms the monumental center of Barcelona, taking in Les Rambles, Plaça de Sant Jaume, Via Laietana, Passeig Nacional, and Passeig de Colom. Its older structures contain some of the city's best hotel bargains. Most of the glamorous, and more expensive, hotels are in Sur Diagonal (see below).

VERY EXPENSIVE

✪ **Le Meridien Barcelona.** Les Rambles, 111, 08002 Barcelona. ☎ **800/543-4300** in the U.S., or 93-318-62-00. Fax 93-301-77-76. 205 units. A/C MINIBAR TV TEL. 36,000 ptas. ($241.20) double; from 46,000 ptas. ($308.20) suite. AE, DC, MC, V. Parking 2,000 ptas. ($13.40). Metro: Liceu or Plaça de Catalunya.

This is the finest hotel in the old town, as the roster of famous guests (such as Michael Jackson) will surely attest. It's superior in both amenities and comfort to its two closest rivals in the area, the Colón and the Rivoli Ramblas (note that it's more

Barcelona Accommodations

BARCELONA

Avenida Palace **9**
Barcelona Hilton **3**
Claris **7**
Duques de Bergard **14**
Granvía **11**
Hostal Levante **24**
Hostal Neutral **8**
Hotel Arts **27**
Hotel Astoria **5**
Hotel Colón **22**
Hotel Condes
   de Barcelona **6**
Hotel Continental **16**
Hotel Cortés **15**
Hotel Derby/
   Hotel Gran Derby **2**
Hotel Hespería **1**
Hotel Lleó **12**
Hotel Meliá
   Barcelona Sarriá **3**
Hotel Princess Sofia **3**
Hotel Regencia Colón **21**
Hotel Rivoli Ramblas **20**
Hotel San Agustín **23**
Hotel Suizo **26**
Hotel Wilson **4**
Meridien Barcelona **18**
Mesón Castilla **13**
Montecarlo **19**
Rey Juan Carlos I **3**
Rialto **25**
Ritz **10**
Turín **17**

TIBIDABO ↑   **1**

Avinguda de Madrid

Carrer del Vallespir
Carrer de
Berlin
Carrer de Numància
Carrer de la Infanta Carlota Joaquim
Carrer de Còrseg
Carrer de Rossello
Carrer de Provença
Avinguda de Roma
Carrer de Sant Antoni
Carrer de Sants de la Creu Coberta
Carrer de Tarragona
Carrer d'Entrença
Carrer de Rocafort
Carrer de Calabria
Carrer de Viladomat
Carretera de la Bordeta
Pià de
la Pau
Carrer de Sant Fructuós
Plaça de
Espanya
Gran Vía de les Corts Catalanes
Carrer de Sepulveda
Av. de Marqus de Comillas
Av. de la Riena
Maria Cristina
Avinguda de Parallel
Carrer de Floridablanca
Carrer de Tamarit
Carrer de Mansc
Carrer del
Parlamen
Avinguda de
l'Estadi
Estadi
Olímpic
MONTJUÏC
Avinguda de Miramar
Parc d'Atraccions
de Montjuïc
Passeig de Josep Carner

2

3 **Plaça de Francesc Macia**

Carrer de Buenos Aires   4

Carrer de Londres

Travessera de Gràcia

Carrer de Paris   5

Avinguda Diagonal

Travessera de Gràcia

Carrer de Còrsega

Av. de Sant Antoni Maria Claret

Carrer de la Industria

EIXAMPLE

Carrer de Rossello

Carrer de Provença   6

Carrer de Mallorca

Carrer de Balmes

Ramble de Catalunya

Passeig de Gràcia

Carrer de Pau Claris

Carrer de Valencia   7

Avinguda Diagonal

Carrer d'Aragó

Carrer de Girona

Carrer de Bailèn

Passeig de Sant Joan

Carrer de Napols

Carrer de Sicilia

Carrer del   8   Consell   de Cent

Carrer de la Diputació

Gran Vía de les Corts Catalanes   9

Carrer de R. de Llúcia

del Bruc

Plaça de Tetuan

Carrer de Roger de Flor

Carrer de Comte Borrell

Carrer del Comte d'Urgell

Carrer de Villarroel

Carrer de Casanova

Carrer de Muntaner

Carrer d'Aribau

10   11

Ronda de Sant Antoni

Carrer de Pelai

12   Ronda Universitat

13   14   **Plaça de Catalunya**

Plaça Urquinaona

Carrer

Carrer de Casp

Carrer d'Ausias Marc

Ronda de Sant Pere

Carrer d'Ali Bei

Carrer de Ribes

Carrer de Sardenya

Passeig de Carles I

Ronda Sant Pau

RAVAL

17   16   15

18   19   La Rambla   Av. Portal de l'Angel

20

Carrer de Hospital

Avinguda de la Catedral

21

22

Via Laietana

23

BARRI GÒTIC

Carrer de Sant Pau

Carrer de Ferran   24   25   26   Carrer de la Princesa

Carrer Nou de   la Rambla

La Rambla

Avinguda de les Drassanes

Carrer Ample

Carrer de Comerc

Passeig de Picasso

Passeig de Lluis Companys

LA RIBERA

Passeig de Pujades

Parc de la Ciutadella

Carrer de Wellington

Plaça Portal de la Pau   Passeig de Colom   Mull de la Fusta

Avinguda d'Icàvia

BARCELONETA

Port Nou

Villa Olímpica →

27

0 ———— 1/4 mi
0 ———— 1/4 km

N

expensive than either of these choices, though). Originally built in 1956, it's a medley of artful pastels and tasteful decorating. Guest rooms are spacious and comfortable, with extralarge beds, heated bathroom floors, on-command movies, hair dryers, and two phones in each room. All rooms have double-glazed windows, but that doesn't fully block out noise from Les Rambles. The Renaissance Club, an executive floor popular with businesspeople, provides extra amenities.

Dining/Diversions: The chic lobby bar, open daily from 7pm to 2am, has live piano music. The main restaurant, Le Patio, serves fine continental and Catalan cuisine.

Amenities: 24-hour room service, laundry, concierge, baby-sitting, business center, rooms for people with disabilities. Small gym nearby.

EXPENSIVE

Hotel Colón. Avinguda de la Catedral, 7, 08002 Barcelona. ☎ **800/845-0636** in the U.S., or 93-301-14-04. Fax 93-317-29-15. E-mail: colon@nexus.es. 148 units. A/C MINIBAR TV TEL. 25,500–40,000 ptas. ($170.85–$268) double; from 45,000 ptas. ($301.50) suite. AE, DC, MC, V. Bus: 16, 17, 19, or 45.

The Colón is an appropriate choice if you plan to spend a lot of time exploring Barcelona's medieval neighborhoods. Blessed with what might be the most dramatic location in the city, opposite the main entrance to the cathedral, this hotel sits behind a dignified neoclassical facade graced with carved pilasters and ornamental wrought-iron balustrades. Inside, you'll find conservative and slightly old-fashioned public rooms, a helpful staff, and good-size guest rooms filled with comfortable furniture. Despite recent renovations, they retain an appealingly dowdy charm. Each room comes with a hair dryer, a private safe, and a first-rate firm mattress. Not all rooms have views, and units in back are quieter. Sixth-floor rooms with balconies overlooking the square are the most desirable. Some of the lower rooms are rather dark.

Dining: The hotel maintains two well-recommended restaurants, the Grill (for continental specialties) and Carabela.

Amenities: 24-hour room service, laundry and valet, limousine, concierge, baby-sitting.

Rivoli Ramblas. Les Rambles, 128, 08002 Barcelona. ☎ **93-302-66-43.** Fax 93-317-50-53. E-mail: rivoli@alba.mssl.es. 87 units. A/C MINIBAR TV TEL. 31,500 ptas. ($211.05) double; from 85,000 ptas. ($569.50) suite. Rates include breakfast. AE, DC, MC, V. Metro: Plaça de Catalunya or Liceu.

Behind a dignified art deco town house on the upper section of the Rambles, a block south of the Plaça de Catalunya, this recently renovated hotel incorporates many fine examples of avant-garde Catalan design in its stylish interior. The Colón has more tradition and style, and the Meridien more modern comfort; this is choice number three in the old town. The minimalist public rooms glisten with polished marble. Guest rooms are carpeted, soundproofed, and elegant, but rather cramped. Guest rooms have safe-deposit boxes, VCRs, radios, and TVs with satellite hookups.

Dining/Diversions: Le Brut Restaurant serves regional, Spanish, and international dishes. The Blue Moon cocktail bar features piano music. A rooftop terrace, suitable for coffee or drinks, offers a view over the rooftops of one of Barcelona's most architecturally interesting neighborhoods.

Amenities: Room service, baby-sitting, concierge, laundry and valet, small health club and fitness center, sauna, solarium, car rentals, boutiques.

MODERATE

✪ **Duques de Bergara.** Bergara, 11. ☎ **93-301-51-51.** Fax 93-317-34-42. 149 units. A/C MINIBAR TV TEL. 24,900 ptas. ($166.85) double; 32,900 ptas. ($220.45) triple. AE, DC, MC, V. Public parking nearby 3,000 ptas. ($20.10). Metro: Plaça de Catalunya.

This upscale hotel occupies an 1899 town house built for the Duke of Bergara. In 1998, the original five-story structure more than doubled in size with the addition of a new seven-story tower. Guest rooms throughout have the same conservative, traditional comforts. Each unit has large, comfortable beds with first-rate mattresses, elegant fabrics, and good lighting. The roomy marble bathrooms are equipped with plush towels and hair dryers. Public areas contain most of the paneling, stained glass, and decorative accessories originally installed by modernisme architect Emilio Salas i Cortes, a professor of the movement's greatest luminary, Gaudí. In the reception area, look for stained-glass panels containing the heraldic coat of arms of the building's original occupant and namesake, the duke of Bergara.

On the premises are a restaurant, El Duc (see "Where to Dine," below), a bar and cafe one floor above the lobby, and an outdoor swimming pool that's generally a hopping social scene in the afternoon and early evening.

Hotel Lleó. Carrer de Pelai, 22-24, 08001 Barcelona. ☎ **93-318-13-12.** Fax 93-412-26-57. www.hotel-lleo.es. E-mail: reservas@hotel-lleo.es. 76 units. A/C MINIBAR TV TEL. 20,000 ptas. ($134) double. AE, DC, MC, V. Parking 3,500 ptas. ($23.45) nearby. Metro: Plaça de Catalunya or Universitat.

Solid, well run, and conservative, this hotel occupies an 1840s building on a busy commercial street in a centrally located neighborhood. Completely renovated in 1992 (in time for the Olympics), it offers streamlined, comfortable guest rooms. Each has a lock-box and functional furniture, including good beds. The medium-size bathrooms are tiled and equipped with hair dryers. There's a restaurant. This is a good, standard choice, but not a lot more.

Hotel Regencia Colón. Sagristans, 13-17, 08002 Barcelona. ☎ **93-318-98-58.** Fax 93-317-28-22. 55 units. A/C MINIBAR TV TEL. 16,000 ptas. ($107.20) double; 19,500 ptas. ($130.65) triple. AE, DC, MC, V. Metro: Plaça de Catalunya or Urquinaona.

This stately stone six-story building stands directly behind the pricier Hotel Colón—both lie in the shadow of the cathedral. The Regencia Colón attracts tour groups, and that's because it's a good value for Barcelona. The formal lobby seems a bit dour, but the well-maintained rooms are comfortable and often roomy, albeit worn. Rooms are insulated against sound, and 40 of them have full bathrooms with tubs (the remainder have showers only). All have comfortable beds and piped-in music. The hotel's location at the edge of the Barri Gòtic is a plus.

Montecarlo. Les Rambles, 124, 08002 Barcelona. ☎ **93-412-04-04.** Fax 93-318-73-23. E-mail: montecarlobcn@abaforum.es. 74 units. A/C MINIBAR TV TEL. 16,400–23,000 ptas. ($109.90–$154.10) double; 25,500 ptas. ($170.85) triple. AE, DC, MC, V. Parking 2,000 ptas. ($13.40). Metro: Plaça de Catalunya.

This hotel, beside the promenade of the Rambles, was built around 200 years ago as an opulent private home. In the 1930s, it was transformed into the comfortably unpretentious hotel you'll find today. It offers a level of comfort superior to that at such competitors as the Lleó (see above). Each of the midsize guest rooms is efficiently decorated and comfortable. Double-glazed windows help keep out some of the noise. Public areas include some of the building's original accessories, with carved doors, a baronial fireplace, and crystal chandeliers.

INEXPENSIVE

Granvía. Gran Vía de les Corts Catalanes, 642, 08007 Barcelona. ☎ **93-318-19-00.** Fax 93-318-99-97. 50 units. A/C MINIBAR TV TEL. 12,500 ptas. ($83.75) double. AE, DC, MC, V. Parking 2,300 ptas. ($15.40). Metro: Plaça de Catalunya.

A grand hotel on one of the most fashionable boulevards in Barcelona, the Granvía has public rooms that reflect the opulence of the 1860s—chandeliers, gilt mirrors, and

French provincial furniture—and a grand balustraded staircase. It's your best choice if you want to feel like royalty but not pay a king's ransom. Although the traditional guest rooms contain interesting antique reproductions, they are comfortable rather than luxurious. Expect fancifully shaped headboards and pastel-colored chenille bedspreads, along with upholstery that needs refreshing. Rooms vary in shape and size. The courtyard, graced with a fountain and palm trees, holds tables for alfresco drinks; in the garden room off the courtyard, continental breakfast (1,300 ptas./$8.70) is served. Centrally heated in the winter, the hotel has one drawback: street noise, which might disturb light sleepers.

Hotel Continental. Rambla de Canaletes, 138, 08002 Barcelona. ☎ **93-301-25-70.** Fax 93-302-73-60. www.hotelcontinental.com. E-mail: hotel_continental@seker.es. 35 units. MINIBAR TV TEL. 9,700–12,500 ptas. ($65–$83.75) double; 14,900 ptas. ($99.85) triple; 16,900 ptas. ($113.25) quad. Rates include buffet breakfast. AE, DC, MC, V. Metro: Plaça de Catalunya.

This hotel occupies the upper two floors of a commercial building in a safe section of the upper Rambles. The flowery, slightly faded reception area is accented with 19th-century statues. The small to midsize rooms are pleasant and modern; 10 have semicircular balconies overlooking the Rambles. Though the decor in some rooms seems to shout "Laura Ashley gone mad," everything is comfortable. Amenities include safe-deposit boxes and hair dryers. The buffet breakfast is served daily from 6am to noon.

Hotel Cortés. Santa Ana, 25, 08002 Barcelona. ☎ **93-317-91-12.** Fax 93-302-78-70. 43 units. TV TEL. 9,820 ptas. ($65.80) double. Rates include breakfast. AE, DC, MC, V. Metro: Plaça de Catalunya.

A short walk from the cathedral, the Cortés was built around 1910 and, like many of its competitors, thoroughly renovated in time for the 1992 Olympics. It competes effectively with the Continental. Midsize to small guest rooms are scattered over five floors. About half overlook a quiet central courtyard, the other half open onto the street. On the ground floor, the unpretentious restaurant and bar serves breakfast.

Hotel San Agustín. Plaça de San Agustín, 3, 08001 Barcelona. ☎ **93-318-16-58.** Fax 93-317-29-28. 76 units. A/C TV TEL. 14,000 ptas. ($93.80) double; 17,500 ptas. ($117.25) triple; 20,000–24,000 ptas. ($134–$160.80) quad; 28,000 ptas. ($187.60) 2-room family unit. Rates include breakfast. AE, DC, MC, V. Metro: Liceu.

This tastefully renovated five-story hotel stands in the center of the old city, near the covered produce markets overlooking the brick walls of an unfinished Romanesque church. The small guest rooms are comfortable and modern, with such amenities as piped-in music, safe-deposit boxes, and tiled bathrooms with hair dryers. Some units are equipped for persons with disabilities. The hotel also runs a good restaurant that serves reasonably priced meals.

✪ Mesón Castilla. Valldoncella, 5, 08002 Barcelona. ☎ **93-318-21-82.** Fax 93-412-40-20. 56 units. A/C TEL. 13,600 ptas. ($91.10) double. V. Parking 2,000 ptas. ($13.40). Metro: Plaça de Catalunya or Universitat.

This two-star hotel, a former apartment building, has a Castilian facade with a wealth of art nouveau detailing. Owned and operated by the Spanish hotel chain HUSA, the Castilla is charming and well maintained, and it certainly has a fantastic location, right in the center of the city, close to Les Rambles. Its nearest rival is the Regencia Colón, to which it is comparable in atmosphere and government ratings. It is far superior to the Cortés and the Continental. The midsize rooms are comfortable—beds have ornate Catalan-style headboards—and some open onto large terraces. The tiled bathrooms are equipped with hair dryers. Breakfast is the only meal served, but it is a fine buffet, with ham, cheese, and eggs.

Rialto. Ferran, 40-42, 08002 Barcelona. ☎ **93-318-52-12.** Fax 93-318-53-12. 190 units. A/C MINIBAR TV TEL. 16,100 ptas. ($107.85) double. AE, DC, MC, V. Parking nearby 2,500 ptas. ($16.75). Metro: Jaume I.

One of the best choices in the Barri Gòtic, this hotel is part of the Gargallo chain. The three-star Rialto is furnished with Catalan flair and style. It offers well-maintained and comfortably furnished guest rooms with small, tiled bathrooms. There is a cafeteria.

Turín. Carrer Pintor Fortuny, 9-11, 08001 Barcelona. ☎ **93-302-48-12.** Fax 93-302-10-05. www.hotelturin@icab.es. 60 units. A/C TV TEL. 13,900 ptas. ($93.15) double; 16,500 ptas. ($110.55) triple. AE, DC, MC, V. Parking 2,000 ptas. ($13.40). Metro: Plaça de Catalunya.

This neat, well-run, three-star hotel is in a terra-cotta grillwork building in a shopping district. It offers small, streamlined accommodations with balconies, plus tiled bathrooms with hair dryers. The restaurant specializes in grilled meats and fresh fish. The Turín is a safe choice, comparable to the Lleó, but in its price range inferior in atmosphere to the Mesón Castilla.

SUR DIAGONAL
VERY EXPENSIVE

✪ **The Claris.** Carrer de Pau Claris, 150, 08009 Barcelona. ☎ **800/888-4747** in the U.S., or 93-487-62-62. Fax 93-215-79-70. www.derbyhotels.es. E-mail: info@derbyhotels.es. 120 units. A/C MINIBAR TV TEL. Mon–Thurs 40,900 ptas. ($274.05) double; from 50,000 ptas. ($335) suite. Fri–Sun 26,000 ptas. ($174.20) double; from 32,500 ptas. ($217.75) suite. Fri–Sun rates include breakfast. AE, DC, MC, V. Parking 2,250 ptas. ($15.10). Metro: Passeig de Gràcia.

One of the most unusual hotels built in Barcelona since the 1930s, this postmodern lodging is the only five-star deluxe property in the city center. It incorporates vast quantities of teak, marble, steel, and glass with the historically important facade of a landmark 19th-century building (the Verdruna Palace). Although we prefer the Ritz (see below), many hotel critics hail the Claris as the city's top choice. Opened in 1992 (in time for the Olympics), it's a seven-story structure with a swimming pool and garden on its roof. There's a small museum of Egyptian antiquities from the owner's collection on the second floor. The blue-violet guest rooms contain state-of-the-art electronic accessories as well as unusual art objects—Turkish kilims, English antiques, Hindu sculptures, Egyptian stone carvings, and engravings. The spacious rooms are among the most opulent in town, with wood marquetry and paneling, custom furnishings, private safes, and some of the city's most sumptuous beds, with deluxe mattresses and fine linen. Bathrooms are roomy and filled with thick towels, deluxe toiletries, and generous shelf space. If money is no object, book one of the 20 individually designed duplex units.

Dining: The Restaurante Claris serves Catalan meals in the Ampurdán style. The restaurant sponsored by the international emporium Caviar Caspa serves light but elegant lunches and suppers. Sturgeon eggs from many distributors accompany smoked meats, smoked fish, and bubbly wines.

Amenities: Laundry and valet, baby-sitting, room service, swimming pool, sauna, currency exchange.

Hotel Princesa Sofía. Plaça de Pius XII, 4, 08028 Barcelona. ☎ **93-330-71-11.** Fax 93-330-76-21. www.interconti.com. E-mail: barcelona@interconti.com. 500 units. A/C MINIBAR TV TEL. 38,000–48,000 ptas. ($254.60–$321.60) double; from 70,000 ptas. ($469) suite. AE, DC, MC, V. Parking 2,600 ptas. ($17.40). Metro: Palau Reial or María Cristina.

ⓘ Family-Friendly Hotels

Hotel Colón *(see p. 374)*   Opposite the cathedral in the Gothic Quarter, this hotel has been compared to a country home. Families ask for, and often get, spacious rooms.

Hotel Hespería *(see p. 381)*   At the northern edge of the city, this hotel has gardens and a safe neighborhood setting. Rooms are large enough to hold an extra bed.

Hotel Princesa Sofía *(see p. 377)*   Although primarily a business hotel, the Princesa Sofía has excellent baby-sitting and two pools (one indoor, one outdoor). It's ideal for the business traveler and his or her family.

About 2 miles (3km) northwest of Barcelona's historic center, the bustling high-rise Princesa Sofía is the city's busiest, most business-oriented modern hotel. It's much better than the Hilton. Although it opened as a five-star hotel, its new four-star government rating is more accurate. The hotel was built in 1975 and renovated in the early 1990s. Packed with glamorous touches, the Princesa Sofía hosts dozens of daily conferences and social events. Guest rooms contain comfortable traditional furniture, often with a vaguely British feel. Rooms, usually midsize, are well appointed, with private safes, thick carpeting, and king-size beds with quality mattresses. The tiled bathrooms contain thick towels, hair dryers, and dual marble vanities.

Dining/Diversions: Le Gourmet restaurant serves lackluster continental and Catalan meals. L'Empordá is slightly less expensive, and the coffee shop, El Snack 2002, is open until midnight. There's also a bar, and a branch of Régine's disco.

Amenities: 24-hour room service, laundry and valet, concierge, baby-sitting. In-house Iberia Airlines branch, boutique, barber and hairdresser, car rentals. Amply equipped gym and health club, sauna, indoor and outdoor swimming pools. Extensive conference and meeting facilities, an unusually well-managed business center offering translation (English and French) and secretarial services.

✪ Hotel Ritz. Gran Vía de les Corts Catalanes, 668, 08010 Barcelona. ☎ **93-318-52-00.** Fax 93-318-01-48. www.ritzbcn.com. E-mail: ritz@ritzbcn.com. 125 units. A/C MINIBAR TV TEL. 38,000–43,000 ptas. ($254.60–$288.10) double; 45,000–175,000 ptas. ($301.50–$1,172.50) suite. AE, DC, MC, V. Parking 3,500 ptas. ($23.45). Metro: Passeig de Gràcia.

Acknowledged by many as the finest, most prestigious, and most architecturally distinguished hotel in Barcelona, the art deco Ritz was built in 1919. Richly remodeled during the late 1980s, it has welcomed more millionaires, famous people, and aristocrats (and their official and unofficial consorts) than any other hotel in northeastern Spain. One of the finest features is the cream-and-gilt neoclassical lobby, where afternoon tea is served to the strains of a string quartet. The sumptuous guest rooms are as formal, high-ceilinged, and richly furnished as you'd expect. Some have Regency furniture, bathrooms accented with mosaics, and bathtubs inspired by those in ancient Rome. You get all the luxuries here: elegant fabrics, deluxe mattresses, plush towels, hair dryers, and private safes.

Dining/Diversions: The elegant Restaurante Diana serves French and Catalan cuisine (see "Where to Dine," below). In the elegantly paneled Bar Parilla, music from a grand piano will soothe your frazzled nerves.

Amenities: 24-hour room service, laundry, limousine service, concierge, baby-sitting, business center, car rentals, shopping kiosks and boutiques.

Rey Juan Carlos I. Avinguda Diagonal, 661, 08028 Barcelona. ☎ **800/448-8355** in the U.S., or 93-448-08-08. Fax 93-364-32-64. www.hilton.com. 432 units. A/C MINIBAR TV TEL. 44,000 ptas. ($294.80) double; 70,000 ptas. ($469) suite. Occasional weekend discounts. AE, DC, MC, V. Free parking. Metro: Zona Universitària.

Named for the Spanish king who attended its opening and has visited several times, this five-star hotel competes effectively against the Ritz, Claris, and Hotel Arts. Opened just before the Olympics, it rises 17 stories at the northern end of the Diagonal, in a wealthy neighborhood known for corporate headquarters, banks, and upscale stores. Note that it's a bit removed, however, from many of Barcelona's top attractions. The design includes a soaring inner atrium with glass-sided elevators. Midsize to spacious guest rooms contain many electronic extras, conservatively comfortable furnishings, and oversized beds. Many have views over Barcelona to the sea. Thoughtful touches include good lighting, adequate work space, spacious closets, and blackout draperies, plus marble bathrooms with plush towels and hair dryers.

Dining/Diversions: The hotel's most elegant restaurant is Chez Vous, a glamorous and panoramic locale with impeccable service and French and Catalan meals. Saturday night, a dinner dance offers a live orchestra accompanied by a set-price menu. The Café Polo serves an endless series of buffets at lunch and dinner.

Amenities: 24-hour room service, laundry, concierge staff, swimming pool, health club, jogging track, men's and women's hairdresser, car-rental facilities, business center.

EXPENSIVE

Avenida Palace. Gran Vía de les Corts Catalanes, 605 (at Passeig de Gràcia), 08007 Barcelona. ☎ **93-301-96-00.** Fax 93-318-12-34. 160 units. A/C MINIBAR TV TEL. 29,000 ptas. ($194.30) double; 48,000–69,000 ptas. ($321.60–$462.30) suite. AE, DC, MC, V. Metro: Plaça de Catalunya or Passeig de Gràcia.

In an enviable 19th-century neighborhood filled with elegant shops and apartment buildings, this hotel lies behind a pair of mock-fortified towers. Despite its relative modernity (it dates to 1952), it evokes an old-world sense of charm, partly because of the attentive staff, scattering of flowers and antiques, and 1950s-era accessories that fill its well-upholstered public rooms. Guest rooms are solidly traditional and quiet, and some are set aside for nonsmokers. The soundproofed rooms range from midsize to spacious, with private safes, wide comfortable beds, and mostly wood furnishings. Bathrooms are well equipped, with dual basins, hair dryers, and heat lamps.

Dining/Diversions: El Restaurante Candelabro serves lunch and dinner Monday through Friday. The bar and lounge contains a scattering of interesting antiques.

Amenities: Concierge, translation and secretarial services, currency exchange, hairdresser and barber, room service, express checkout, baby sitting.

Hilton Barcelona. Diagonal, 589, 08014 Barcelona. ☎ **800/445-8667** in the U.S. and Canada, or 93-495-77-77. Fax 93-495-77-00. www.hilton.com. E-mail: rm_barcelona@hilton.com. 286 units. A/C MINIBAR TV TEL. 32,000–36,000 ptas. ($214.40–$241.20) double; 40,000–95,000 ptas. ($268–$636.50) suite. AE, DC, MC, V. Parking 3,000 ptas. ($20.10). Metro: María Cristina.

First opened in 1990, this five-star property stands in a desirable location on one of the most famous and elegant boulevards in town. Opposite the gates to the Barcelona fairgrounds (and beyond that, to the Olympic Stadium), this is a huge seven-floor corner structure, topped with a massive tower. It hides sleek public spaces behind a rather lackluster white marble facade. Most guest rooms are fairly large and finely equipped, although none is set aside for nonsmokers. Furnishings are standard Hilton, with suitable amenities such as private safes. Bathrooms are also well accessorized, with large mirrors and hair dryers.

Dining/Diversions: The Restaurant Cristal Garden serves well-prepared international and Spanish menus in a relaxed but polished setting. A bar and lounge lies nearby.

Amenities: 24-hour room service, laundry and valet, concierge, translation and secretarial services, express checkout, limousine service, baby-sitting. The hotel maintains a cooperative relationship with a well-equipped health club ½ mile away. Tennis courts are a mile away, and the hotel can arrange golf at a course 16 miles away. Boutiques and a news kiosk are on the premises.

○ **Hotel Condes de Barcelona.** Passeig de Gràcia, 73-75, 08008 Barcelona. ☎ 93-488-22-00. Fax 93-467-47-85. www.condesdebarcelona.com. E-mail: cbhotel@condesdebarcelona.com. 183 units. A/C MINIBAR TV TEL. 28,000 ptas. ($187.60) double; 55,000–65,000 ptas. ($368.50–$435.50) suite. AE, DC, MC, V. Parking 2,000 ptas. ($13.40). Metro: Passeig de Gràcia.

Off the architecturally splendid Passeig de Gràcia, this four-star hotel, originally a private villa (1895), is one of Barcelona's most glamorous. Business was so good it opened a 74-room extension across the street (Carrer Majorca), which regrettably lacks the flair of the original. It boasts a unique neomedieval facade, influenced by Gaudí's modernisme movement. The curved lobby-level bar and restaurant add a touch of art deco. All the comfortable midsize guest rooms contain marble bathrooms, reproductions of Spanish paintings, and soundproofed windows. Some rooms are already beginning to show post-Olympic wear and tear.

Dining/Diversions: the restaurant serves lunch and dinner daily. The cafe features regional dishes. Guests also enjoy the piano bar.

Amenities: Laundry, baby-sitting, room service, outdoor swimming pool.

Hotel Meliá Barcelona Sarrià. Avinguda Sarrià, 50, 08029 Barcelona. ☎ 800/336-3542 in the U.S., or 93-410-60-60. Fax 93-321-51-79. 314 units. A/C MINIBAR TV TEL. 30,500 ptas. ($204.35) double; 40,000–180,000 ptas. ($268–$1,206) suite. AE, DC, MC, V. Parking 2,450 ptas. ($16.40). Metro: Hospital Clínic.

One block from the junction of the Avinguda Sarría and the Avinguda Diagonal, in the heart of the business district, this five-star hotel originally opened in 1976. Some rooms were renovated in the early to mid-1990s, but others look a bit worn. It offers comfortably upholstered and carpeted guest rooms done in neutral international modern style. They have wide beds with firm mattresses. A member of the Meliá chain, the hotel caters to both the business traveler and the vacationer.

Dining/Diversions: The restaurant serves Catalan and international dishes, and the cocktail bar has piano music 6 nights a week.

Amenities: 24-hour room service, concierge, laundry and valet, executive floor, private parking, baby-sitting. Business center, one of the best-equipped health clubs in Barcelona.

MODERATE

Hotel Derby/Hotel Gran Derby. Carrer Loreto, 21-25 and 28, 08029 Barcelona. ☎ 93-322-32-15. Fax 93-410-08-62. www.derbyhotels.es. E-mail: info@derbyhotels.es. 151 units. A/C MINIBAR TV TEL. Hotel Derby 22,000 ptas. ($147.40) double; Grand Derby 25,000 ptas. ($167.50) junior suite. AE, DC, MC, V. Parking 2,250 ptas. ($15.10). Metro: Hospital Clínic.

These twin hotels lie in a tranquil neighborhood about 2 blocks south of the busy intersection of the Avinguda Diagonal and Avinguda Sarría. The Derby offers 111 conventional hotel rooms; the Gran Derby, across the street, contains 40 junior suites. Many suites have small balconies overlooking a flowered courtyard. The larger Derby contains the drinking, dining, and entertainment facilities. A team of English-inspired designers imported a British aesthetic, and the pleasing results include well-oiled hardwood panels, soft lighting, and comfortably upholstered armchairs. Less British in feel than the public rooms, midsize guest rooms and suites are outfitted with simple furniture in a variety of decorative styles. All are comfortable and quiet.

Although the hotel does not have a restaurant, its unpretentious coffee shop, the Times, serves Spanish, British, and international food. The Scotch Bar, an upscale watering hole, has won several awards for the diversity of its cocktails.

INEXPENSIVE

✪ **Hotel Astoria.** París, 203, 08036 Barcelona. ☎ **93-209-83-11.** Fax 93-202-30-08. www.derbyhotels.es. E-mail: info@derbyhotels.es. 117 units. A/C MINIBAR TV TEL. 20,200 ptas. ($135.35) double. AE, DC, MC, V. Parking nearby 1,800 ptas. ($12.05). Metro: Diagonal.

One of our favorite hotels, and an excellent value, the Astoria is near the upper part of the Rambles and the Diagonal. It has an art deco facade that makes it appear older than it is. The high ceilings, geometric designs, and brass-studded detail in the public rooms could be Moorish or Andalusian. The comfortable midsize guest rooms are soundproofed; half have been renovated, with slick louvered closets and glistening white paint. The more old-fashioned units have warm textures of exposed cedar and elegant, pristine modern accessories. For an American-style buffet breakfast (1,400 ptas./$9.40), the Astoria is one of the best bets in town. Its offers eggs, bacon, juice, fried potatoes, even pancakes, and a lot more.

NORTE DIAGONAL
MODERATE

Hotel Hespería. Los Vergós, 20, 08017 Barcelona. ☎ **93-204-55-51.** Fax 93-204-43-92. www.hoteles-hesperia.es. 134 units. A/C MINIBAR TV TEL. 21,000 ptas. ($140.70) double. AE, DC, MC, V. Parking 1,750 ptas. ($11.75). Metro: Tres Torres.

This hotel on the northern edge of the city, a 10-minute taxi ride from the center, sits amid the verdant gardens of one of Barcelona's most pleasant residential neighborhoods. Built in the late 1980s, the hotel was renovated before the 1992 Olympics. You'll pass a Japanese rock garden to reach the stone-floored reception area, with its adjacent bar. Sunlight floods the monochromatic guest rooms (all doubles—prices for singles are the same). Most rooms are medium-size, and all emphasize comfort and convenience. Beds have quality mattresses and fine linen; bathrooms have a generous assortment of good-size towels. The uniformed staff offers fine service. The restaurant serves regional cuisine.

INEXPENSIVE

Hotel Wilson. Avinguda Diagonal, 568, 08021 Barcelona. ☎ **93-209-25-11.** Fax 93-200-83-70. www.husa.es. E-mail: depcomcen@husa.es. 57 units. A/C MINIBAR TV TEL. 17,000 ptas. ($113.90) double; 24,000 ptas. ($160.80) suite. Parking 2,000 ptas. ($13.40). AE, DC, DISC, MC, V. Metro: Diagonal.

This comfortable hotel in an architecturally rich neighborhood is a member of the national HUSA chain. The small lobby isn't indicative of the rest of the building. The second floor opens into a large, sunny coffee shop, bar, and TV lounge. The guest rooms are well kept, generally spacious, and furnished in traditional style. Amenities include private safes and hair dryers. Laundry service is available.

VILA OLÍMPICA
VERY EXPENSIVE

Hotel Arts. Carrer de la Marina, 19-21, 08005 Barcelona. ☎ **800/241-3333** in the U.S., or 93-221-10-00. Fax 93-221-10-70. www.ritzcarlton.com. 482 units. A/C MINIBAR TV TEL. 35,000–45,000 ptas. ($234.50–$301.50) double; 60,000 ptas. ($402) suite. AE, DC, MC, V. Parking 3,200 ptas. ($21.45). Metro: Ciutadella-Vila Olímpica.

Managed by the Ritz-Carlton chain, this hotel occupies 33 floors of one of the tallest buildings in Spain, and one of Barcelona's only skyscrapers. (The upper floors of the 44-floor postmodern tower contain the private condominiums of some of the country's most gossiped-about aristocrats and financiers.) The hotel is about 1½ miles southwest of Barcelona's historic core, near the sea and the Olympic Village. Its decor is contemporary and elegant. The spacious, well-equipped guest rooms have built-in furnishings, generous desk space, private safes, and large, sumptuous beds with deluxe mattresses and quality linen. Clad in pink marble, the deluxe bathrooms have fluffy robes, Belgian towels, hair dryers, dual basins, and separate phones. Views take in the skyline and the Mediterranean. The young staff is polite and hardworking, the product of months of Ritz-Carlton training. The Japanese retailer Sogo operates the upscale cluster of luxury boutiques next door.

Dining: The Newport Room pays homage to new American and New England cuisine; Café Veranda is an airy indoor/outdoor restaurant; and Goyesca serves Spanish food and shellfish.

Amenities: 24-hour room service, laundry, excellent concierge staff, fitness center, outdoor pool, business center.

5 Dining

If money is no object, in Barcelona you'll find some of the grandest culinary experiences in Europe. Diverse Catalan cuisine reaches its pinnacle in Barcelona, and many of the finest dishes feature fresh seafood. But you don't get just Catalan fare—the city is also rich in the cuisines of all the major regions of Spain, including Castile and Andalusia. Because of Barcelona's proximity to France, many of the finer restaurants also serve French or French-inspired dishes.

On the other end of the spectrum, finding an affordable restaurant in Barcelona is easier than finding an inexpensive, safe hotel. There are sometimes as many as eight restaurants and tapas bars on a block. Reservations are seldom needed, except in the most expensive and popular places. The **Barri Gòtic** offers the cheapest meals. There are also many budget restaurants in and around the **carrer de Montcada,** site of the Picasso museum. Dining rooms in the **Eixample** tend to be more formal and expensive, but less adventurous.

CIUTAT VELLA
EXPENSIVE

✪ **Agut d'Avignon.** Trinitat, 3 (at carrer d'Avinyó). ☎ **93-302-60-34.** Reservations required. Main courses 1,800–5,000 ptas. ($12.05–$33.50). AE, DC, MC, V. Daily 1–4:30pm and 9pm–12:30am. Metro: Jaume I or Liceu. CATALAN.

One of our favorite restaurants in Barcelona is in a tiny alleyway near the Plaça Reial. The city's restaurant explosion has toppled Agut d'Avignon from its lofty position, but it's still going strong after 40 years and has a dedicated following. It attracts politicians, writers, journalists, financiers, industrialists, and artists—and even the king and cabinet ministers, along with visiting dignitaries. Since 1983, Mercedes Giralt Salinas and her son, Javier Falagán Giralt, have run the restaurant. A small 19th-century vestibule leads to the multilevel dining area, which has two balconies and a main hall; it evokes a hunting lodge. You might need help translating the Catalán menu. The traditional specialties are likely to include acorn-squash soup served in its shell; fisherman's soup with garlic toast; haddock stuffed with shellfish; sole with *nyoca* (a medley of nuts); large shrimp with aioli; duck with figs; and fillet beef steak in sherry sauce.

Casa Leopoldo. Sant Rafael, 24. ☎ **93-441-30-14.** Reservations required. Main courses 1,500–5,500 ptas. ($10.05–$36.85); fixed-price menu 5,250 ptas. ($35.20). AE, DC, MC, V. Tues–Sun 1:30–4pm; Tues–Sat 9–11pm. Closed Aug and Easter week. Metro: Liceu. SEAFOOD.

An excursion through the somewhat seedy streets of the Barri Xinés is part of the Casa Leopoldo experience. At night it's safer to come by taxi. This colorful restaurant, founded in 1939, serves some of the freshest seafood in town to its loyal clientele. There's a popular stand-up tapas bar in front, and two dining rooms. Specialties include eel with shrimp, barnacles, cuttlefish, seafood soup with shellfish, and deep-fried inch-long eels.

Quo Vadis. Carme, 7. ☎ **93-302-40-72.** Reservations recommended. Main courses 1,250–3,500 ptas. ($8.40–$23.45); menú del día 3,750 ptas. ($25.15). DC, MC, V. Mon–Sat 1:15–4pm and 8:30–11:30pm. Metro: Liceu. SPANISH/CONTINENTAL.

Elegant and impeccable, this is one of the finest restaurants in Barcelona. In a century-old building near the open stalls of the Boquería food market, it was established in 1967 and has done a discreet but thriving business ever since. The four paneled dining rooms exude conservative charm. Personalized culinary creations include a ragout of seasonal mushrooms; fried goose liver with prunes; fillet of beef with wine sauce; and a variety of grilled or flambéed fish. There's a wide choice of desserts made with seasonal fruits imported from all over Spain.

✪ **Restaurant Hoffmann.** Argenteria, 74-78. ☎ **93-319-58-89.** Reservations recommended. Main courses 2,000–4,500 ptas. ($13.40–$30.15); fixed-price lunch (includes wine and coffee) 4,800 ptas. ($32.15); tasting menu 7,500 ptas. ($50.25). AE, DC, MC, V. Mon–Fri 1:30–3:30pm and 9–11:30pm. Metro: Jaume I. CATALAN/FRENCH/INTERNATIONAL.

This restaurant in the Barri Gòtic has suddenly become one of the most famous in Barcelona, partly because of its creative cuisine, partly because of its close association with a respected school that trains employees for Catalonia's hotel and restaurant industry. The culinary and entrepreneurial force behind it is Mey Hoffmann, the child of a German father and Catalan mother. Her restaurant overlooks the facade of one of Barcelona's most beloved Gothic churches, Santa María del Mar. In good weather, three courtyards also hold tables. Menu items change every 2 months and often include French ingredients. Examples include a superb *fine tarte* with deboned sardines; foie gras wrapped in puff pastry; baked John Dory with new potatoes and ratatouille; a ragout of crayfish with green risotto; succulent pigs' feet with eggplant; and rack of lamb with grilled baby vegetables. Especially flavorful, if you appreciate beef, is a fillet steak cooked in Rioja and served with shallot confit and potato gratin. Fondant of chocolate makes a worthy dessert.

MODERATE

Brasserie Flo. Jonqueras, 10. ☎ **93-319-31-02.** Reservations recommended. Main courses 1,500-3,600 ptas. ($10.05–$24.10); fixed-price menu 3,000 ptas. ($20.10). AE, DC, MC, V. Mon–Thurs 1–4pm and 8:30pm–midnight, Fri–Sun 1–4pm and 8:30pm–1am. Metro: Urquinaona. FRENCH/INTERNATIONAL.

A group of Frenchmen opened this restaurant in 1982 in a former textile factory. It is as close as Barcelona gets to an Alsatian brasserie. The spacious art deco dining room is palm-filled and air-conditioned. Begin with fresh foie gras. The specialty is a large plate of *choucroute* (sauerkraut) served with a steamed ham hock. Also good are shrimp in garlic, salmon tartare with vodka, black rice, and stuffed sole with spinach. The familiar fare is solid, satisfying, and filling.

Barcelona Dining

Plaça de
Francesc Macia

Travessera de Gràcia

Carrer de Buenos Aires

Carrer de Londres

Carrer de Paris

Avinguda Diagonal

Carrer de Còrsega

Travessera de Gràcia

Av. de Sant Antoni Maria Claret

Carrer de la Industria

EIXAMPLE

Carrer de Rossello

Carrer de Provença

Carrer de Roger de Flor

Avinguda Diagonal

Carrer de Balmes

Rambla de Catalunya

Passeig de Gracia

Carrer de Pau Claris

Carrer de Mallorca

Carrer de Valencia

Carrer d'Aragó

Carrer de Girona

Carrer de Bailèn

Passeig de Sant Joan

Carrer de Napols

Carrer de Sicilia

Carrer de Comte Borrell

Carrer del Comte d'Urgell

Carrer de Villarroel

Carrer de Casanova

Carrer de Muntaner

Carrer d'Aribau

Carrer del   Consell

de Cent

Carrer de la Diputació

Carrer de R. de Llúcia

Carrer del Bruc

Plaça de
Tetuan

Gran Vía de les Corts Catalanes

Carrer de Sardenya

Ronda de Sant Antoni

Ronda Universitat

Plaça
Catalunya

Ronda de Pelai

Plaça
Urquinaona

Carrer de Casp

Carrer d'Ausias Marc

Ronda de Sant Pere

Carrer d'Ali Bei

Carrer de Ribes

Passeig de Carles I

RAVAL

La Rambla

Av. Portal
del Angel

Avinguda de
la Catedral

Via Laietana

Carrer de Hospital

Ronda Sant Pau

Carrer de Sant Pau

BARRI GOTIC

Carrer de Ferran

Carrer de la Princesa

Passeig de Picasso

Passeig de
Lluís Companys

Carrer de Comerç

Passeig de Pujades

Parc de la
Ciutadella

Carrer de Wellington

Carrer Nou de   la Rambla

Avinguda de les Drassanes

La Rambla

LA RIBERA

Carrer Ample

Plaça Portal
de la Pau

Passeig de Colom

Moll de la Fusta

Avinguda d'Icàvia

BARCELONETA

Port Nou

Villa Olímpica →

Can Culleretes. Quintana, 5. ☎ **93-317-64-85.** Reservations recommended. Main courses 1,000–2,000 ptas. ($6.70–$13.40); menú del día 2,100 ptas. ($14.05). MC, V. Tues–Sun 1:30–4pm, Tues–Sat 9–11pm. Closed 3 weeks in July. Metro: Liceu. Bus: 14 or 59. CATALAN.

Founded in 1786 as a *pastelería* (pastry shop) in the Barri Gòtic, the oldest Barcelona restaurant retains many original architectural features. All three dining rooms are decorated in Catalan style, with tile dadoes and wrought-iron chandeliers. The well-prepared food features authentic dishes of northeastern Spain, including sole Roman style, *zarzuela a la marinera* (shellfish medley), cannelloni, and paella. From October to January, special game dishes, including *perdiz* (partridge), are available. Signed photographs of celebrities, flamenco artists, and bullfighters who have visited decorate the walls.

Can Pescallunes. Carrer Magdalenas, 23. ☎ **93-318-54-83.** Reservations required for lunch. Main courses 1,800–2,500 ptas. ($12.05–$16.75). MC, V. Mon–Fri 1–3:30pm and 8:30–10:30pm. Metro: Urquinaona. FRENCH/CATALAN.

With the look, feel, and menu of a French bistro, this reasonably priced 10-table restaurant is a short walk from the cathedral. In 1980 it opened in this turn-of-the-century building; an elaborate street lantern marks the entrance. The specials change daily. Flavorful specialties include *rape* (monkfish) with clams and tomatoes, smooth vichyssoise, chateaubriand with béarnaise sauce, sole cooked in cider, steak tartare, and dessert crepes with Cointreau.

Egipte. Les Rambles, 79. ☎ **93-317-74-80.** Reservations recommended. Main courses 1,200–2,500 ptas. ($8.05–$16.75); fixed-price menus 1,100–2,000 ptas. ($7.35–$13.40). AE, DC, MC, V. Daily 1–4pm and 8pm–midnight. Metro: Liceu. CATALAN/SPANISH.

A neighborhood favorite, this tiny place behind the central marketplace jumps day and night. The excellent menu includes spinach vol-au-vent (traditionally served with an egg on top), *lengua de ternera* (tongue), and the signature *berengeras* (stuffed eggplant). The local specialty is codfish in cream sauce. The ingredients are fresh, and the price is right. Expect hearty market food and a total lack of pretension.

Els Quatre Gats. Montsió, 3. ☎ **93-302-41-40.** Reservations required Sat–Sun. Main courses 1,200–3,000 ptas. ($8.05–$20.10); fixed-price menu (Mon–Sat) 1,500 ptas. ($10.05). AE, MC, V. Daily 1–4pm; Mon–Sat 7:30pm–midnight. Cafe daily 8am–2am. Metro: Plaça de Catalunya. CATALAN.

A Barcelona legend since 1897, the "Four Cats" (in Catalan slang, "just a few people") was a favorite of Picasso, Rusinyol, and other artists, who once hung their works on its walls. On a narrow cobblestoned street in the Barri Gòtic near the cathedral, the fin-de-siècle cafe was the setting for poetry readings by Joan Maragall, piano concerts by Isaac Albéniz and Ernie Granados, and murals by Ramón Casas. It was a base for members of the modernisme movement and figured in the city's intellectual and bohemian life.

Today the restored bar is a popular meeting place. The fixed-price meal is one of the better bargains in town, considering the locale. The unpretentious style of Catalan cooking is called *cuina de mercat* (based on whatever looked fresh at the market). The constantly changing menu reflects the seasons. No hot food is served on Sunday.

La Cuineta. Paradis, 4. ☎ **93-315-01-11.** Reservations recommended. Main courses 2,000–3,200 ptas. ($13.40–$21.45); fixed-price menu 3,200 ptas. ($21.45). AE, DC, MC, V. Daily 1–4pm and 8pm–midnight. Metro: Jaume I. CATALAN.

This restaurant near the center of the Catalan government is a culinary highlight of the Barri Gòtic. Decorated in typical regional style, it favors local cuisine. The fixed-price menu is a good value, or you can order à la carte. The most expensive appetizer is *bellota* (acorn-fed ham), but we suggest a market-fresh Catalan dish, such as *favas* (broad beans) stewed with *butifarra*, a tasty, spicy local sausage.

○ **Los Caracoles.** Escudellers, 14. ☎ **93-302-31-85.** Reservations required. Main courses 1,500–8,000 ptas. ($10.05–$53.60). AE, DC, MC, V. Daily 1pm–midnight. Metro: Drassanes. CATALAN/SPANISH.

In a labyrinth of narrow cobblestoned streets, Los Caracoles is the port's most colorful and popular restaurant—and it has been since 1835. It has won acclaim for its spit-roasted chicken and for its namesake, snails. A long, angular bar is up front, with a two-level restaurant in back. You can watch the busy preparations in the kitchen, where dried herbs, smoked ham shanks, and garlic bouquets hang from the ceiling. In summer, tables spill outside. The excellent food features all sorts of Spanish and Catalan specialties. Everybody from Richard Nixon to John Wayne has stopped in, and Salvador Dalí was a devoted patron. Today's clientele may not be as legendary, but hordes keep coming to dine. Tourists often make this their number-one restaurant stop in Barcelona, but it is no tourist trap—Los Caracoles delivers the same aromatic and robust food it always has. If you avoid the fresh shellfish dishes, you'll find most offerings are at the lower end of the price scale.

INEXPENSIVE

Biocenter. Pintor Fortuny, 25. ☎ **93-301-45-83.** Main courses 625–1,000 ptas. ($4.20–$6.70); fixed-price menu 1,125 ptas. ($7.55). No credit cards. Bar Mon–Sat 9am–5pm; food Mon–Sat 1–5pm. Metro: Plaça de Catalunya. VEGETARIAN.

This is the largest and best-known vegetarian restaurant in Barcelona, the creation of Catalonia-born entrepreneur Pep Cañameras, who is likely to be directing the service from behind the bar. Vegetarians or not, patrons congregate over drinks in the front room. Some stay for meals in one of two ground-floor dining rooms, amid paintings and artwork by the owner and his colleagues. There's a salad bar, an array of vegetarian casseroles, soups (such as gazpacho or lentil), and a changing selection of seasonal vegetables.

○ **El Duc.** In the Duques de Bergara, Bergara 11. ☎ **93-301-51-51.** Reservations recommended. Main courses 1,000–2,000 ptas. ($6.70–$13.40). Fixed-price menu (Mon–Fri only) 2,500 ptas. ($16.75). AE, DC, MC, V. Daily 1–4pm and 8–11pm. Metro: Plaça de Catalunya.

On the lobby level of the hotel (see above), this well-managed restaurant serves food a lot better than the fare at other hotel dining rooms. Adjacent to the Plaça de Catalunya, it offers a conservative roster of flavorful dishes. They include prawn cocktails, goose-liver pâté, magret of duckling in fruit sauce, tenderloin of beef "Café de Paris," grilled entrecôte, fried fish, Asturian hake, and large prawn served with a gratin

Calling All Chocoholics!

Established in 1930, **Dulcinea,** Via Petrixol, 2 (☎ **93-302-68-24**), is the most famous chocolate shop in Barcelona. The specialties are *melindros* (sugar-topped soft-sided biscuits), and the regulars who flock here love to dunk them into the very thick hot chocolate—so thick, in fact, that drinking it feels like eating a melted chocolate bar. A cup of hot chocolate with cream costs 400 ptas. ($2.70), and a *ración* of *churros* (a deep-fried pastry), which is dipped in the hot chocolate, goes for 125 ptas. (85¢); no credit cards. Dulcinea is open daily from 9am to 1pm and 4:30 to 9pm; closed in August. Take the Metro to Liceu.

of scallops. Ingredients are fresh, and the chefs are more than competent: They add flavor to every dish without destroying the natural taste. For such an elegant enclave, prices are extremely reasonable.

Garduña. Morera, 17. ☎ **93-302-43-23.** Reservations recommended. Main courses 1,000–3,800 ptas. ($6.70–$25.45). Fixed-price lunch 1,100–1,500 ptas. ($7.35–$10.05); fixed-price dinner 1,500 ptas. ($10.05). AE, DC, MC, V. Mon–Sat 1–4pm and 8pm–midnight. Metro: Liceu. CATALAN.

This is the most famous restaurant in Barcelona's covered food market, La Boquería. Originally conceived as a hotel, it has concentrated on food since the 1970s. Battered, somewhat ramshackle, and a bit claustrophobic, it's fashionable with an artistic set that might have been designated as bohemian in an earlier era. It's near the back of the market, so you'll pass endless rows of fresh produce, cheese, and meats before you reach it. You can dine downstairs, near a crowded bar, or a bit more formally upstairs. Food is ultrafresh—the chefs certainly don't have to travel far for the ingredients. You might try "hors d'oeuvres of the sea," cannelloni Rossini, grilled hake with herbs, *rape* (monkfish) *marinera,* paella, brochettes of veal, fillet steak with green peppercorns, seafood rice, or a *zarzuela* (stew) of fresh fish with spices.

Nou Celler. Princesa, 16. ☎ **93-310-47-73.** Reservations required. Main courses 750–1,800 ptas. ($5.05–$12.05); fixed-price menus 1,000–1,300 ptas. ($6.70–$8.70). AE, MC, V. Sun–Fri 8am–midnight. Closed June 15–July 15. Metro: Jaume I. CATALAN/SPANISH.

Near the Picasso Museum, this establishment is perfect for a bodega-type meal or just a cup of coffee. Country artifacts hang from the beamed ceiling and plaster walls. The back entrance, at Barra de Ferro, 3, is at the quieter end of the place, where dozens of original artworks make up a collage. The dining room offers such Franco-era food as fish soup, Catalan soup, *zarzuela* (a medley of seafood), paella, hake, and other classic dishes.

Pitarra. Avinyó, 56. ☎ **93-301-16-47.** Reservations required. Main courses 1,000–2,000 ptas. ($6.70–$13.40); fixed-price lunch 1,200 ptas. ($8.05). AE, DC, MC, V. Mon–Sat 1–4pm and 8:30–11pm. Closed August 3–30. Metro: Liceu. CATALAN.

Founded in 1890, this restaurant in the Barri Gòtic was named after the 19th-century Catalan playwright who lived and wrote in the back room. Try grilled fish chowder or a Catalan salad, followed by grilled salmon or squid Málaga style. Valencian paella is another specialty. The cuisine does not even pretend to be imaginative but strictly adheres to time-tested recipes—"the type of food we ate when growing up," in the words of one diner.

SUR DIAGONAL
VERY EXPENSIVE

Beltxenea. Majorca, 275. ☎ **93-215-30-24.** Reservations recommended. Main courses 2,500–5,500 ptas. ($16.75–$36.85); tasting menu 6,900 ptas. ($46.25). AE, DC, MC, V. Mon–Fri 1:30–4pm, Mon–Sat 8:30–11:30pm. Closed 2 weeks in Aug. Metro: Passeig de Gràcia. BASQUE/FRENCH.

In a building originally designed in the late 19th century as an apartment building, this restaurant in the Eixample celebrates Basque cuisine. The Basques are noted as the finest chefs in Spain, and this is indeed grand cuisine. It's served here in one of the most elegantly and comfortably furnished restaurants in Barcelona. Schedule a meal for a special night—it's worth the money. The menu might include hake fried with garlic or garnished with clams and served with fish broth. Roast lamb, grilled rabbit, and pheasant are well prepared and succulent, as are the desserts. There's dining outside in the formal garden during the summer.

✪ **La Dama.** Diagonal, 423. ☎ **93-202-06-86.** Reservations required. Main courses 3,000–4,000 ptas. ($20.10–$26.80); fixed-price menus 6,500–9,000 ptas. ($43.55–$60.30). AE, DC, MC, V. Daily 1:30–3:30pm and 8:30–11:30pm. Metro: Provença. CATALAN/ INTERNATIONAL.

This is one of the few restaurants in Barcelona that deserves, and gets, a Michelin star. In one of the grand 19th-century buildings for which Barcelona is famous, this stylish and well-managed restaurant serves a clientele of local residents and civic dignitaries. You take an art nouveau elevator (or the sinuous stairs) up one flight to reach the dining room. Specialties include salmon steak served with vinegar derived from *cava* (sparkling wine) and onions, cream of potato soup flavored with caviar, a salad of cray-fish with orange-flavored vinegar, an abundant platter of autumn mushrooms, and succulent preparations of lamb, fish, shellfish, beef, goat, and veal. The building, designed by Manuel Sayrach, lies 3 blocks west of the intersection of Avinguda Diag-onal and Passeig de Gràcia.

✪ **Jaume de Provença.** Provença, 88. ☎ **93-430-00-29.** Reservations recommended. Main courses 1,950–7,000 ptas. ($13.05–$46.90). AE, DC, MC, V. Tues–Sun 1–4pm; Tues–Sat 9–11:30pm. Closed Easter week, Aug. Metro: Entença. CATALAN/FRENCH.

A few steps from the Estació Central de Barcelona-Sants railway station, at the western end of the Eixample, this is a small, cozy restaurant with rustic decor. It is the only restaurant along the Diagonal that can compare to La Dama. Named after its owner and chef, Jaume Bargués, it features modern interpretations of traditional Catalan and southern French cuisine. Examples include gratin of clams with spinach, a salad of two different species of lobster, foie gras and truffles, and pigs' trotters with plums and truffles. Or you might order crabmeat lasagna, cod with saffron sauce, sole with mush-rooms in port-wine sauce, or an artistic dessert specialty of orange mousse.

EXPENSIVE

Can Isidre. Les Flors, 12. ☎ **93-441-11-39.** Reservations required. Main courses 2,000–5,000 ptas. ($13.40–$33.50). AE, DC, MC, V. Mon–Sat 1:30–4pm and 8:30–11:30pm. Closed Sat–Sun June–Aug. Metro: Paral.lel. CATALAN.

In spite of its seedy location (take a cab at night!), this is perhaps the most sophisti-cated Catalan bistro in Barcelona. Opened in 1970, it has served King Juan Carlos and Queen Sofía, Julio Iglesias, and the famous Catalan band leader, Xavier Cugat. Isidre Gironés, helped by his wife, Montserrat, is known for his fresh cuisine. The food is beautifully prepared and served. Try spider crabs and shrimp, a gourmand salad with foie gras, sweetbreads with port and flap mushrooms, or carpaccio of veal Harry's Bar style. The selection of Spanish and Catalan wines is excellent.

Restaurante Diana. In the Hotel Ritz, Gran Vía de les Corts Catalanes, 668. ☎ **93-318-52-00.** Reservations recommended. Main courses 2,000–3,900 ptas. ($13.40–$26.15); fixed-price lunch menu Mon–Fri 3,575 ptas. ($23.95); fixed-price dinner menu Mon–Fri and fixed-price menu Sat–Sun 4,750 ptas. ($31.85). AE, DC, MC, V. Daily 1:30–4pm and 8–11pm. Metro: Urquinaona. INTERNATIONAL.

At least part of the allure of dining here is the chance to visit the most legendary hotel in Barcelona. On the lobby level of the Ritz, the restaurant is filled with French fur-nishings and accessories. The well-trained staff serves such dishes as seafood salad fla-vored with saffron; fillets of sole layered with lobster; filet mignon braised in cognac, cream, and peppercorn sauce; turbot in white-wine sauce; and a wide array of delec-table desserts. The cuisine is of a high international standard, although the restaurant doesn't quite reach the sublime culinary experience of La Dama or Jaume de Provença.

(†) Family-Friendly Restaurants

Dulcinea *(see p. 387)*   This makes a great refueling stop any time of the day—guaranteed to satisfy any chocoholic.

Poble Espanyol *(see p. 403)*   A good introduction to Spanish food. All the restaurants in the "Spanish Village" serve comparable food at comparable prices—let the kids choose what to eat.

INEXPENSIVE

Ca La María. Tallers, 76. ☎ **93-318-89-93.** Reservations recommended Sat–Sun. Main courses 950–1,600 ptas. ($6.35–$10.70). AE, DC, MC, V. Mon–Sun 1:30–4pm, Tues–Sat 8:30–11pm. Metro: Universitat. CATALAN.

This small (18 tables) blue-and-green-tiled bistro is on a quiet square opposite a Byzantine-style church near the Plaça de la Universitat. Look for the constantly changing daily specials. This is not a place for haute cuisine. A bit battered-looking, the restaurant serves endearingly homelike food—if you grew up in a family of Catalan cooks. The dishes are often surprisingly tasty—try baby squid with onions and tomatoes, anglerfish with burned garlic, or veal sirloin cooked to order.

El Caballito Blanco. Mallorca, 196. ☎ **93-453-10-33.** Main courses 900–3,900 ptas. ($6.05–$26.15). AE, MC, V. Tues–Sun 1–3:45pm, Tues–Sat 9–10:45pm. Closed Aug. Metro: Hospital Clínic. SEAFOOD/INTERNATIONAL.

This Barcelona standby, famous for seafood, has long been popular with the locals. The fluorescent-lit dining area does not offer much atmosphere, but the food is good, varied, and relatively inexpensive (unless you order lobster). The "Little White Horse," in the Passeig de Gràcia area, features a huge selection, including monkfish, mussels marinara, and shrimp with garlic. If you don't want fish, try the grilled lamb cutlets. Several different pâtés and salads are offered. There's a bar to the left of the dining area.

NORTE DIAGONAL
VERY EXPENSIVE

✪ Botafumeiro. Gran de Gràcia, 81. ☎ **93-218-42-30.** Reservations recommended for dining rooms. Main courses 3,000–6,000 ptas. ($20.10–$40.20). AE, DC, MC, V. Daily 1pm–1am. Metro: Enrique Quiroga. SEAFOOD.

Although the competition is strong, this classic *marisquería* consistently puts Barcelona's finest seafood on the table. Much of the allure comes from the attention of the white-jacketed staff. If you like, you can eat at the bar. If you do venture to the rear, you'll find a series of attractive dining rooms noted for the ease with which business deals seem to be arranged during the lunch hour. International businesspeople often rendezvous here. The king of Spain is sometimes a patron.

Menu items include ultrafresh seafood prepared in a glistening modern kitchen that's visible from parts of the dining room. The establishment prides itself on its fresh and saltwater fish, clams, mussels, lobster, crayfish, scallops, and several varieties of crustaceans that you may never have seen before. Stored live in holding tanks or in enormous crates near the entrance, many of the creatures are flown in every day from Galicia, home of owner Moncho Neira. With the 100 or so fish dishes, the menu lists only four or five meat dishes, including three kinds of steak, veal, and a traditional version of pork with turnips. The wine list offers a wide array of cavas from Catalonia and highly drinkable choices from Galicia.

EXPENSIVE

✪ **Neichel.** Pedralbes, 16. ☎ **93-203-84-08.** Reservations required. Main courses 2,300–3,800 ptas. ($15.40–$25.45). AE, MC, V. Mon–Fri 1:30–3:30pm; Mon–Sat 8:30–11pm. Closed holidays and Aug. Metro: Palau Reial or María Cristina. FRENCH/MEDITERRANEAN.

Alsatian-born Jean Louis Neichel, this restaurant's owner and operator, has been called "the most brilliant ambassador French cuisine has ever had within Spain." He serves a clientele whose credentials might best be described as stratospheric. Neichel is almost obsessively concerned with gastronomy—the savory presentation of some of the most talked-about preparations of seafood, fowl, and sweets in Spain.

Your meal might include a "mosaic" of foie gras with vegetables, strips of salmon marinated in sesame and served with *escabeche* (vinaigrette) sauce, or slices of raw and smoked salmon stuffed with caviar. The prize-winning terrine of sea crab floats on a lavishly decorated bed of cold seafood sauce. Move on to escalope of turbot served with *coulis* (puree) of sea urchins, fricassee of Bresse chicken served with spiny lobsters, sea bass with a mousseline of truffles, Spanish milk-fed lamb served with the juice of Boletus mushrooms, or rack of lamb gratinéed in an herb-flavored pastry crust. The selection of European cheeses and the changing array of freshly made desserts are nothing short of spectacular.

Reno. Tuset, 27. ☎ **93-200-91-29.** Reservations required. Main courses 1,200–3,500 ptas. ($8.05–$23.45). AE, DC, MC, V. Sun–Fri 1–4pm; Sun–Sat 8:30–11:30pm. Metro: Diagonal. CATALAN/FRENCH.

One of the finest and most enduring haute cuisine restaurants in Barcelona, Reno sits behind sidewalk-to-ceiling windows, hung with fine-mesh lace to shelter diners from prying eyes on the octagonal plaza outside. The impeccably mannered staff is formal but not intimidating. The seasonal specialties show a French influence. They might include partridge simmered in wine or port sauce, a platter of assorted fish smoked on the premises, hake with anchovy sauce, or fillet of sole stuffed with foie gras and truffles or grilled with anchovy sauce. An appetizing array of pastries wheels from table to table on a cart. Dessert might also be crepes flambéed at your table.

Roig Robí. Séneca, 20. ☎ **93-218-92-22.** Reservations required. Main courses 2,000–4,500 ptas. ($13.40–$30.15); fixed-price menu 6,800 ptas. ($45.55). AE, DC, MC, V. Mon–Fri 1:30–4pm; Mon–Sat 9–11pm. Metro: Diagonal. CATALAN.

This restaurant—the name means "ruby red" (the color of a perfectly aged Rioja) in Catalán—serves excellent food from an imaginative kitchen. A warm welcome keeps patrons coming back. Although we're not as excited about this restaurant as we once were, it does remain one of the city's most dependable choices. Order an aperitif at the L-shaped oak bar, then head down a long corridor to a pair of flower-filled dining rooms. In warm weather, glass doors open onto a verdant walled courtyard. Menu items include fresh beans with pine-nut sauce, hake al Roig Robí, fresh mushroom salad with green beans and fresh tomatoes, and shellfish from Costa Brava. Monkfish comes with clams and onion confit, ravioli stuffed with spring herbs, and chicken stuffed with foie gras. Cockscomb salad is available but may be too adventuresome for many palates.

✪ **Via Veneto.** Ganduxer, 10. ☎ **93-200-72-44.** Reservations required. Main courses 2,200–4,000 ptas. ($14.75–$26.80). AE, DC, MC, V. Mon–Fri 1:15–4pm, Mon–Sat 8:45pm–midnight. Closed Aug 1–20. Metro: La Bonanova. INTERNATIONAL.

Consistently well-prepared cuisine attracts diners to this conservatively decorated restaurant a short walk from the Plaça de Francesc María. The kitchen is always inventing imaginative Catalan recipes based on fresh local ingredients. It offers such

Quick Bites & Picnic Fare

Café Viena, Rambla, 115 (☎ 93-317-14-92; metro: Plaça de Catalunya), is Barcelona's most elegant fast-food place. Waiters in Viennese vests serve croissants with Roquefort for breakfast, then toasted ham sandwiches, hamburgers with onions, and pasta with tomato sauce. Meals cost 300 to 1,200 ptas. ($2 to $8.05). Open Monday through Saturday 8:30am to 1am, Sunday 9am to midnight.

The best place in Barcelona for picnic fixings is **Mercat de la Boquería,** in the center of the Les Rambles (metro: Liceu). In the old marketplace, you'll jostle with butchers and fishmongers in bloodied smocks and see people selling cheeses and sausages. Much of the food is uncooked, but hundreds of items are prepared; you can even buy a bottle of wine or mineral water.

Now for where to have your picnic. In the heart of Barcelona is the **Parc de la Ciutadella** (see "Parks & Gardens," below). It's in the southeast section of the district known as the Barri de la Ribera, site of the Picasso Museum. After lunch, take the kids to the zoo, then go out on the lake in a rented rowboat.

It's more scenic to picnic in **Montjuïc,** site of several Olympic events. After your picnic, you can enjoy the amusement park, take in the Miró museum, or walk through the Poble Espanyol, a re-created Spanish village.

---

dishes as tartare of fresh fish with caviar, roasted salt cod with potatoes, and veal kidney with truffle sauce. Loin of roast suckling pig comes with seasonal baby vegetables, and fillet steak is served in a brandy, cream, and peppercorn sauce. There's a wide array of wines. Dessert might be a richly textured combination of melted chocolate, cherries, Armagnac, and vanilla ice cream.

MOLL DE LA FUSTA & BARCELONETA
EXPENSIVE

✪ **Can Costa.** Passeig Don Joan de Borbò, 70. ☎ **93-221-59-03.** Reservations recommended. Main courses 2,000–5,000 ptas. ($13.40–$33.50). AE, MC, V. Daily 12:30–4pm; Mon–Sat 8–11:30pm. Metro: Barceloneta. SEAFOOD.

One of the oldest seafood restaurants in this seafaring town is Can Costa, an emporium of fish and shellfish whose big windows overlook the water. Established in the late 1930s, it has two busy dining rooms, a practiced staff, and an outdoor terrace. Fresh seafood prepared according to traditional recipes rules the menu. It includes the best baby squid in town—sautéed in a flash so that it has a nearly grilled flavor, almost never overcooked or rubbery. A log-standing chef's specialty *fideuá de peix,* a relative of the classic Valencian shellfish paella, with noodles instead of rice. Desserts are made fresh daily.

Can Majó. Almirante Aixada, 23. ☎ **93-221-54-55.** Reservations recommended. Main courses 1,800–3,500 ptas. ($12.05–$23.45); fixed-price menu 6,000 ptas. ($40.20). AE, MC, V. Tues–Sun 1:30–4:30pm and 9–11:30pm. Metro: Barceloneta. SEAFOOD.

In the old fishing quarter of Barceloneta, Can Majó attracts many people from fancier areas, who come here for a great seafood dinner. The Suárez-Majó family operates the business where their grandmother first opened a bar. Start with *entremeses* (hors d'oeuvres), for which you can select barnacles, oysters, prawns, whelks, clams, and crab—whatever was caught that day. The clams with white beans are recommended.

The classic vegetable gazpacho comes with fresh mussels and shrimp. Or try a house specialty, *pelada* (Catalán for paella).

Ramonet. Carrer Maquinista, 17. ☎ **93-319-30-64.** Reservations recommended. Main courses 2,300–3,950 ptas. ($15.40–$26.45); fixed-price menus 4,600–7,000 ptas. ($30.80–$46.90). AE, DC, MC, V. Daily 10am–4pm and 8pm–midnight. Usually closed Aug 10–Sept 10. Metro: Barceloneta. SEAFOOD.

In a Catalan-style villa near the seaport, this rather expensive restaurant has served a large variety of fresh seafood since 1763. The front room, with stand-up tables for seafood tapas, beer, and regional wine, is often crowded. In the two dining rooms, you can choose from a variety of seafood—shrimp, hake, and monkfish are almost always available. Other specialties include pungent anchovies, grilled mushrooms, black rice, braised artichokes, tortilla with spinach and beans, and mussels "from the beach."

MODERATE

El Túnel. Ample, 33–35. ☎ **93-315-27-59.** Reservations recommended for lunch. Main courses 1,200–2,200 ptas. ($8.05–$14.75). MC, V. Tues–Thurs 6pm–midnight; Fri–Sat 6pm–1:30am. Closed Aug. Metro: San Jaume. SPANISH.

This long-established restaurant serves delectable fish soup, cannelloni with truffles, kidney beans with shrimp, roast kid, fish stew, and fillet of beef with peppers. The food is uncomplicated but delicious. The service is eager, the wine cellar extensive. El Túnel lies close to the general post office.

7 Portes. Passeig d'Isabel II, 14. ☎ **93-319-30-33.** Reservations required. Main courses 3,000–4,500 ptas. ($20.10–$30.15). AE, DC, MC, V. Daily 1pm–midnight. Metro: Barceloneta. SEAFOOD.

This is a lunchtime favorite for businesspeople (the Stock Exchange is across the way) and an evening favorite for many in-the-know diners who have made it their preferred restaurant in Catalonia. Festive and elegant, it's been going since 1836. Regional dishes include fresh herring with onions and potatoes, a different paella daily (sometimes with shellfish, for example, or with rabbit), and a wide array of fresh fish. You might order succulent oysters, or an herb-laden stew of black beans with pork or white beans with sausage. Portions are enormous. The restaurant's name means "Seven Doors," and it really does have seven doors. Waiters wear the long white aprons of the belle epoque era.

WEST OF TIBIDABO

La Balsa. Infanta Isabel, 4. ☎ **93-211-50-48.** Reservations required. Main courses 2,000–3,200 ptas. ($13.40–$21.45); fixed-price lunch 3,000 ptas. ($20.10); fixed-price dinner 6,500–7,000 ptas. ($43.55–$46.90). AE, MC, V. Tues–Sat 2–3:30pm; Mon–Sat 9–11:30pm. Closed Easter week. No buffet in Aug. INTERNATIONAL.

On the uppermost level of a circular tower that was built as a cistern, La Balsa offers a view over most of the surrounding cityscape. To reach it, you climb to the structure's original rooftop. You're likely to be greeted by owner and founder Mercedes López. Food emerges from a cramped but well-organized kitchen several floors below. (The waiters are reputedly the most athletic in Barcelona, because they must run up the stairs carrying steaming platters.) The restaurant serves such dishes as a *judías verdes* (salad of broad beans) with strips of salmon in lemon-flavored vinaigrette, stewed veal with wild mushrooms, a salad of warm lentils with anchovies, and pickled fresh salmon with chives. Undercooked magret (breast) of duck is served with fresh, lightly poached foie gras, and baked hake (flown in from Galicia) is prepared in squid-ink sauce. The restaurant lies 1¼ miles north of the city's heart—you'll need a taxi—in the Tibidabo district, close to the Science Museum (Museu de la Ciència). It's often booked several days in advance.

OUR FAVORITE TASCAS

The bars listed below are known for their tapas; for more recommendations, refer to the "Barcelona After Dark" section, below.

Alt Heidelberg. Ronda Universitat, 5. ☎ **93-318-10-32.** Tapas 250–750 ptas. ($1.70–$5.05); combination plates 1,000–1,450 ptas. ($6.70–$9.70). MC, V. Mon–Fri 8am–1:30am, Sat–Sun noon–2am. Metro: Universitat. GERMAN/TAPAS.

A Barcelona institution since the 1930s, Alt Heidelberg serves German beer on tap, a good selection of German sausages, and Spanish tapas. You can also order full meals—sauerkraut garni is a specialty.

Bar del Pi. Plaça Sant Josep Oriol, 1. ☎ **93-302-21-23.** Tapas 250–550 ptas. ($1.70–$3.70). No credit cards. Mon–Fri 9am–11pm, Sat 9:30am–10pm, Sun 10am–10pm. Metro: Liceu. TAPAS.

One of the most famous bars in the Barri Gòtic, this establishment lies midway between two medieval squares opening onto the church of Pi. Tapas are limited; most visitors come to drink coffee, beer, or wine. You can sit inside at one of the cramped bentwood tables, or stand at the crowded bar. In warm weather, take a table beneath the single plane tree on the landmark square. The plaza usually draws an interesting group of young bohemian sorts and travelers.

Bar Turò. Tenor Viñas, 1. ☎ **93-200-69-53.** Tapas 300–1,300 ptas. ($2–$8.70). MC, V. Sun–Thurs 9am–1am, Fri–Sat 9am–3am. Metro: Maria Cristina. TAPAS.

In an affluent residential neighborhood north of the old town, Bar Turò serves some of the best tapas in town. In summer you can sit outside or retreat to the narrow confines of the bar. You select from about 20 kinds of tapas, including Russian salad, fried squid, and Serrano ham.

Bodega la Plata. Mercè, 28. ☎ **93-315-10-09.** Tapas 200–1,000 ptas. ($1.35–$6.70). No credit cards. Mon–Sat 10am–11pm. Metro: Barceloneta. TAPAS.

Established in the 1920s, La Plata is one of a trio of famous bodegas on this narrow medieval street. It occupies a corner building whose two open sides allow aromatic cooking odors to permeate the neighborhood. This bodega contains a marble-topped bar and overcrowded tables. The culinary specialty is *raciones* (small plates) of deep-fried sardines—head and all. You can make a meal with two servings, coupled with the house's tomato, onion, and fresh anchovy salad.

Bodegueta. Rambla de Catalunya, 100. ☎ **93-215-48-94.** Tapas from 200 ptas. ($1.35). No credit cards. Mon–Sat 8am–1:45am, Sun 7pm–1:30am. Metro: Diagonal. TAPAS.

Founded in 1940, this old wine tavern specializes in Catalan sausage. Wash it all down with inexpensive Spanish wines. Beer costs 150 to 300 ptas. ($1 to $2); wine goes for 150 ptas. ($1).

Casa Alfonso. Rogre de Lluria, 6. ☎ **93-301-97-83.** Tapas 1,200–2,500 ptas. ($8.05–$16.75). No credit cards. Mon–Tues 9am–10pm, Wed–Sat 9am–1am. Metro: Urquinaona. TAPAS.

Spaniards love their ham, which comes in a great many forms. The best of the best is *Jamon Jabugo*, the only one sold at this traditional establishment. Entire hams hang from steel braces. They're taken down, carved, and trimmed before you into paper-thin slices. This particular form of cured ham, generically called *jamon serrano*, comes from pigs fed acorns in Huelva, in deepest Andalusia. Devotees of all things porcine will ascend to piggy-flavored heaven.

Casa Tejada. Tenor Viñas, 3. ☎ **93-200-73-41.** Tapas 325–2,500 ptas. ($2.20–$16.75). MC, V. Daily 9am–2am. Metro: Muntaner. TAPAS.

Covered with rough stucco and decorated with hanging hams, Casa Tejada (established in 1964) offers some of Barcelona's best tapas. Arranged behind a glass display case, they include such dishes as marinated fresh tuna, German-style potato salad, ham salad, and five preparations of squid (including one that's stuffed). For variety, quantity, and quality, this place is hard to beat. There's outdoor dining in summer.

La Jarra. Mercè, 9. ☎ **93-315-17-59.** Tapas 300–500 ptas. ($2–$3.35). No credit cards. Thurs–Tues 11:30am–1am. Metro: Barceloneta. TAPAS.

Established in the 1950s, La Jarra occupies a tile-covered L-shaped room. It's somewhat bleak, but residents claim it is one of the most authentic tapas bars in the old town. You can order a ración (portion) of marinated mushrooms or well-seasoned artichokes Rioja style, but the culinary star is the ever-present haunch of *jamón canario* (Canary Island ham). It's carved while you watch into lean, succulent morsels served with boiled potatoes, olive oil, and lots of salt. It resembles roast pork in flavor and appearance.

Las Campanas (Casa Marcos). Mercè, 21. ☎ **93-315-06-09.** Tapas 125–1,250 ptas. (85¢–$8.40). No credit cards. Thurs–Tues 12:30am–4pm and 7pm–2am. Metro: Jaume I. TAPAS.

From the street (there's no sign), Las Campanas looks like a storehouse for cured hams and wine bottles. Patrons flock to the long, stand-up bar for chorizo, pinioned between two pieces of bread. Sausages are usually eaten with beer or red wine. The place opened in 1952, and nothing has changed since. A tape recorder plays nostalgic favorites, from Edith Piaf to the Andrews Sisters.

Rey de la Gamba. Joan de Borbò, 48-53. ☎ **93-221-75-98.** Tapas 500–10,000 ptas. ($3.35–$67). MC, V. Daily 11am–1am. Metro: Barceloneta. SHELLFISH.

The "King of Prawns" could also be called the House of Mussels, since it sells more of that shellfish. In the 18th-century fishing village of Barceloneta, this place packs them in, especially on weekends. A wide array of seafood accompanies cured ham—the combination is a tradition.

6 Seeing the Sights

THE TOP ATTRACTIONS

One of Barcelona's greatest attractions is not a single sight but an entire neighborhood, the ✪ **Barri Gòtic (Gothic Quarter).** This is the old aristocratic quarter, parts of which have survived from the Middle Ages. Spend at least 2 or 3 hours exploring its narrow streets and squares, which continue to form a vibrant, lively neighborhood. Start by walking up the carrer del Carme, east of Les Rambles. A nighttime stroll takes on added drama, but exercise caution—safety is an issue here. The buildings, for the most part, are austere and sober, the cathedral being the crowning achievement. Roman ruins and the vestiges of 3rd-century walls add further interest. This area is intricately detailed and filled with many attractions that are easy to miss. To guide you, we've outlined a walking tour, later in this section; see page 00.

✪ **La Sagrada Familia.** Majorca, 401. ☎ **93-207-30-31.** Admission (includes video) 800 ptas. ($5.35). Elevator to the top (about 200 feet) 200 ptas. ($1.35). Daily, Nov–Feb 9am–6pm; Mar and Sept–Oct, 9am–7pm; Apr and Aug, 9am–8pm. Metro: Sagrada Familia.

Gaudí's incomplete masterpiece is one of the country's more idiosyncratic creations—if you have time to see only one Catalan landmark, make it this one. Begun in 1882 and incomplete at the architect's death in 1926, this incredible cathedral—the Church of the Holy Family—is a bizarre wonder. The languid, amorphous structure embodies

Barcelona Attractions

Plaça de
Francesc Macia

Carrer de Buenos Aires

Carrer de Londres

Carrer de Paris

Carrer de Còrsega

Travessera de Gràcia

Avinguda Diagonal

Travessera de Gràcia

Av. de Sant Antoni Maria Claret

Carrer de la Industria

EIXAMPLE

Carrer de Rossello

Carrer de Provença

Avinguda Diagonal

Carrer del Comte d'Urgell

Carrer de Villarroel

Carrer de Casanova

Carrer de Muntaner

Carrer d'Aribau

Carrer de Balmes

Rambla de Catalunya

Passeig de Gracia

Carrer de Pau Claris

Carrer de Mallorca

Carrer de Valencia

Carrer d'Aragó

Carrer de Girona

Carrer de Bailén

Passeig de Sant Joan

Carrer de Roger de Flor

Carrer de Napols

Carrer de Sicilia

Carrer del Consell

de Cent

Carrer de la Diputació

Gran Vía de les Corts Catalanes

Carrer de R. de Llúcia

Carrer del Bruc

Plaça de
Tetuan

Ronda de Sant Antoni

Carrer de Pelai

Ronda Universitat

Plaça de
Catalunya

Plaça
Urquinaona

Carrer de Casp

Carrer d'Ausias Marc

Carrer de Sardenya

RAVAL

La Rambla

Av. Portal
de l'Angel

Ronda de Sant Pere

Carrer d'Ali Bei

Carrer de Ribes

Passeig de Carles I

Carrer de Hospital

Avinguda de
la Catedral

Via Laietana

Passeig de
Lluís Companys

Passeig de Pujades

BARRI
GOTIC

Carrer de Sant Pau

Carrer de Ferran

Carrer de la Princesa

Carrer de Comerc

Passeig de Picasso

Parc de la
Ciutadella

Carrer de Wellington

Carrer Nou de la Rambla

LA RIBERA

Avinguda de
Drassanes

La Rambla

Carrer Ample

Plaça Portal

Passeig de Colom

Moll de la Fusta

de la Pau

Avinguda d'Icàvia

BARCELONETA

Port Nou

Villa Olímpica →

0   1/4 mi
0   1/4 km

the essence of Gaudí's style, which some have described as Art Nouveau run wild. Admission includes a 12-minute video on Gaudí's religious and secular works. Work continues on the structure, but without any sure idea of what Gaudí intended. Some say that the cathedral will be completed by the mid–21st century.

✪ **Catedral de Barcelona.** Plaça de la Seu, s/n. ☎ **93-315-15-54.** Admission to cathedral free; to museum 100 ptas. (65¢). Cathedral daily 8am–1:30pm and 4–7:30pm; cloister museum daily 10am–1pm and 4–7pm. Metro: Jaume I.

Barcelona's cathedral is a celebrated example of Catalonian Gothic architecture. Construction began at the end of the 13th century and was nearly completed in the mid–15th century (the west facade dates from the 19th century). The three naves, cleaned and illuminated, have splendid gothic details. With its large bell towers, blending of medieval and Renaissance styles, beautiful cloister, high altar, side chapels, sculptured choir, and gothic arches, it ranks as one of the most impressive cathedrals in Spain. Vaulted galleries in the cloister, enhanced by forged iron grilles, surround a garden of magnolias, medlars, and palm trees. The historian Cirici called this place the loveliest oasis in Barcelona. The cloister, illuminated on Saturdays and fiesta days, also contains a museum of medieval art. Its most notable work is the 15th-century *La Pietat* of Bartolomé Bermejo. At noon on Sunday you can see the *sardana*, a Catalonian folk dance, performed in front of the cathedral.

✪ **Museu Picasso.** Montcada, 15-19. ☎ **93-319-63-10.** Admission 700 ptas. ($4.70) adults, 400 ptas. ($2.70) students and people under 25, free for children under 13. Tues–Sat 10am–8pm, Sun 10am–3pm. Metro: Jaume I.

Two old palaces on a medieval street contain this museum of the work of Pablo Picasso(1881–1973). He donated some 2,500 of his paintings, engravings, and drawings to the museum in 1970. Picasso was particularly fond of Barcelona, where he spent much of his youth. In fact, some of the paintings were done when he was only 9. One portrait, dating from 1896, depicts his stern aunt, Tía Pepa. Another, completed when Picasso was 16, depicts *Science and Charity* (his father was the model for the doctor). Many works, especially the early paintings, show the artist's debt to van Gogh, El Greco, and Rembrandt; a famous series, *Las Meninas* (1957), is said to "impersonate" the work of Velázquez (if you've just been to the Prado in Madrid, or are about to go, this is a particularly interesting comparison). The *La Vie* drawings from the blue period are perhaps the most interesting. His notebooks contain many sketches of Barcelona scenes. Because the works are arranged in rough chronological order, you can get a wonderful sense of Picasso's development, and watch as he discovered a trend or had a new idea, mastered it, grew bored with it, and then was off to something new. You'll also learn that Picasso was a master portraitist and did many traditional representational works before his flights of fancy took off.

Museu Nacional d'Art de Catalunya. Palau Nacional, Parc de Montjuïc. ☎ **93-423-71-99.** Admission 800 ptas. ($5.35) adults, 400 ptas. ($2.70) youths 7–20, free for children under 7. Tues–Wed and Fri–Sat 10am–7pm, Thurs 10am–9pm, Sun 10am–2:30pm. Metro: Espanya.

This museum, which recently underwent massive renovations, is the major depository of Catalan art. The National Art Museum of Catalonia is perhaps the most important center for Romanesque art in the world. More than 100 pieces, including sculptures, icons, and frescoes, are on display. The highlight is the collection of murals from various Romanesque churches. The frescoes and murals are displayed in apses much like those in the churches in which they were found. They're in sequential order, providing the viewer with a tour of Romanesque art from its primitive beginnings to the more advanced, late Romanesque and early Gothic eras.

⚫ Frommer's Favorite Barcelona Experiences

A Walk Through the Barri Gòtic. You'll pass through 15 centuries of history in one labyrinthine district.

Watching the Sardana. The national dance of Catalonia is performed at noon on Sunday at the Plaça de San Jaume, in front of the cathedral.

A Trip to the Top of Montjuïc. Barcelona spreads out at your feet. This stop will provide enough amusement to fill 3 days.

Soaking Up Designer Bar Culture. Bars of all shapes and sizes are the chic places to go at night—Barcelona has more than any other city in Spain. Catalan design is paramount.

Drinking Cava in a Xampanyería. Enjoy a glass of bubbly, Barcelona style. The wines are excellent, and Catalans swear that their *cavas* taste better than French champagne.

A Tour of Barcelona's Harbor. Stroll from the pier in front of the Columbus Monument to the breakwater.

Exploring the Museu Picasso. Examine the evolution of the world's greatest 20th-century artist from the age of 9.

Marveling at La Sagrada Familia. Gaudí's "sand-castle cathedral" is a testimony to the architect's talent and religious belief.

A Visit to Poble Espanyol. Artificial village, to be sure, but it gives you a chance to see the architecture of all of Spain without leaving Barcelona.

Fundació Joan Miró. Plaça de Neptú, Parc de Montjuïc. ☎ **93-329-19-08.** Admission 800 ptas. ($5.35) adults, 450 ptas. ($3) students, free for children under 15. June–Sept, Tues–Wed and Fri–Sat 10am–8pm, Thurs 10am–9:30pm, Sun 10am–2:30pm; Nov–May, Tues–Wed and Fri–Sat 11am–7pm, Thurs 10am–9:30pm, Sun 10am–2:30pm. Bus: 61 at Plaça d'Espanya.

Born in 1893, Joan Miró was one of Spain's greatest artists, known for his whimsical abstract forms and brilliant colors. Some 10,000 works by the Catalan surrealist, including paintings, graphics, and sculptures, are collected here. The building has been greatly expanded in recent years, following the design of Catalan architect Josep Lluís Sert, a close friend of Miró's. An exhibition in a modern wing charts (in a variety of media) Miró's artistic evolution, from his first drawings at the age of 8 to his last works. The museum frequently mounts temporary exhibitions of contemporary art.

Parc Güell. At end of carrer de Llarrard. ☎ **93-424-38-09.** May–Sept, daily 10am–9pm; Oct–Apr, daily 10am–6pm. Bus 24, 25, 31, or 74.

Gaudí began this idiosyncratic park as a real-estate venture for a friend, the well-known Catalan industrialist Count Eusebi Güell, but it was never completed. Although only two houses were constructed, it makes for an interesting excursion. The city took over the property in 1926 and turned it into a public park. One of the houses, **Casa-Museu Gaudí,** carrer del Carmel, 28 (☎ 93-219-38-11), contains models, furniture, drawings, and other memorabilia of the architect. (Ramón Berenguer, not Gaudí, designed the house.) Admission is 300 ptas. ($2.10). Open daily 10am to 8pm.

Gaudí completed several of the public areas, which today look like a surrealist Disneyland, complete with a mosaic pagoda and a lizard fountain spitting water. Gaudí had planned to make this a model community of 60 dwellings, arranged somewhat like a Greek theater. A central grand plaza was built above a market, as well as an undulating bench decorated with ceramic fragments. The bizarre Doric columns of the would-be market are hollow, part of Gaudí's drainage system.

IF YOU HAVE MORE TIME

Museu Barbier-Mueller Art Precolombí. Carrer de Montcada, 12-14. ☎ **93-310-45-16.** Admission 500 ptas. ($3.35) adults, 250 ptas. ($1.70) students, free for children under 12. Free to all first Sat of every month. Tues–Sat 10am–8pm, Sun and holidays 10am–3pm. Metro: Jaume I. Bus: 14, 17, 19, 39, 40, 45, or 51.

Inaugurated by Queen Sofia in 1997, this is one of the most important collections of pre-Columbian art in the world. In the restored Palacio Nadal, which was built during the Middle Ages, the collection contains almost 6,000 pieces of tribal and ancient art. Josef Mueller (1887–1977) acquired the first pieces by 1908. Pre-Columbian cultures created religious, funerary, and ornamental objects of great stylistic variety with relatively simple means. Stone sculpture and ceramic objects are especially outstanding. For example, the Olmecs, who settled on the Gulf of Mexico at the beginning of the first millennium B.C., executed notable monumental sculpture in stone and magnificent figures in jade. Many exhibits focus on the Mayan culture, the most homogenous and widespread of its time, dating from 1000 B.C. Mayan artisans mastered painting, ceramics, and sculpture. Note also the work by the pottery makers of the Lower Amazon, particularly those from the island of Marajó.

Museu Frederic Marès. Plaça de Sant Iú, 5-6. ☎ **93-310-58-00.** Admission 300 ptas. ($2) adults, free for children under 12. Tues and Thurs 10am–5pm; Wed, Fri, and Sat 10am–7pm; Sun 10am–2pm. Metro: Jaume I. Bus: 17, 19, or 45.

One of the biggest repositories of medieval sculpture in the region is the Frederic Marès Museum, located just behind the cathedral. It's in an ancient palace with impressive interior courtyards, chiseled stone, and soaring ceilings, an ideal setting for the hundreds of polychrome sculptures. The sculpture section dates from pre-Roman times to the 20th century. In the same building is the Museu Sentimental, a collection of everyday items that help to illustrate life in Barcelona during the past 2 centuries. The ticket price includes admission to both museums.

Center of Contemporary Culture of Barcelona (CCCB). Montalegre, 5. ☎ **93-306-41-00.** Admission 600 ptas. ($4) adults, 400 ptas. ($2.70) students and adults over 65, free for children under 16. Tues, Thurs–Fri 11am–2pm and 6–8pm; Wed and Sat 11am–8pm; Sun 11am–7pm. Metro: Plaça de Catalunya or Universitat.

In the Ciutat Vella, the Center of Contemporary Culture of Barcelona focuses on the city. It explores Barcelona's culture, history, and present role as a modern European city.

L'Aquarium de Barcelona. Port Vell. ☎ **93-221-74-74.** Admission 1,400 ptas. ($9.40) adults, 950 ptas. ($6.35) children 4–12 and students, free for children under 4. June–Aug daily 9:30am–11pm, Sept daily 9:30am–9:30pm, Oct–May daily 9:30am–9pm. Metro: Drassanes or Barceloneta.

One of the most impressive testimonials to sea life anywhere opened in 1996 in Barcelona's Port Vell, a 10-minute walk from the bottom of the Rambles. The largest aquarium in Europe, it contains 21 glass tanks positioned along either side of a wide curving corridor. Each tank depicts a different marine habitat, with emphasis on everything from multicolored fish and corals to seagoing worms to sharks. The highlight is a huge "oceanarium" representative of the Mediterranean as a self-sustaining ecosystem. You view it from the inside of a glass-roofed, glass-sided tunnel that runs along its entire length, making fish, eels, and sharks appear to swim around you.

Museu Marítim. Avinguda de las Drassanes, s/n. ☎ **93-318-32-45.** Admission 800 ptas. ($5.35) adults, 400 ptas. ($2.70) children 7–17 and seniors, free for children under 7. Tues–Sat 10am–7pm. Closed holidays. Metro: Drassanes. Bus: 14, 18, 36, 38, 57, 59, 64, or 91.

In the former Royal Shipyards (Drassanes Reials), this 13th-century gothic complex was used to construct ships for the Catalano-Aragonese rulers. The most outstanding exhibition is a reconstruction of *La Galería Real* of Don Juan of Austria, a lavish royal galley. Another special exhibit features a map by Gabriel de Vallseca that belonged to explorer Amerìgo Vespucci.

Museu de la Ciència (Science Museum). Teodor Roviralta, 55. ☎ **93-212-60-50.** Admission to museum and planetarium, 750 ptas. ($5.05) adults, 650 ptas. ($4.35) children under 17. Museum only 500 ptas. ($3.35) adults, 350 ptas. ($2.35) children. Planetarium only 250 ptas. ($1.70). Tues–Sun 10am–8pm. Bus: 17, 22, 58, or 73.

The Museu de la Ciència of the La Caixa Foundation is one of the most popular in Barcelona. More than 500,000 people visit annually. Its modern design and hands-on activities have made it the most important science museum in Spain and a major cultural attraction.

Visitors can touch, listen to, watch, and participate in a variety of hands-on exhibits. From the beauty of marine life to the magic of holograms, the museum introduces a world of science. Watch the earth turn beneath the Foucault Pendulum; ride on a human gyroscope; hear a friend whisper from 65 feet (20m) away; feel an earthquake; or use the tools of a scientist to examine intricate life forms with microscopes and video cameras.

More than 300 exhibits explore the wonders of science, from space travel to life sciences. In the "Optics and Perception" exhibits, visitors interact with prisms, lenses, and holograms, and walk inside a kaleidoscope. In the "Living Planet" area, baby sharks swim, a tornado swirls, and plants magically change their form when touched.

In the "Mechanics" exhibit, visitors can lift an 88-pound (40kg) weight with little effort. The use of lasers and musical instruments provides a fun way to learn about sound and light waves. Throughout the exhibits, there are computers to help you delve deeper into various topics. Visitors can also walk inside a submarine and make weather measurements in a working weather station. For those who want to explore new worlds, there are planetarium shows where the beauty of the night sky surrounds the audience.

To reach the museum, ride the bus from Plaça de Catalunya all the way to Avinguda del Tibidabo. Then follow the signs for 2 blocks, turning left onto carrer Teodor Roviralta, where you'll see the museum. The building is at the southern foothills of Tibidabo, reached by following Avinguda del Tibidabo.

Fundació Antoni Tàpies. Aragó, 255. ☎ **93-487-03-15.** Admission 500 ptas. ($3.35) adults, 300 ptas. ($2) students, free for children under 11. Tues–Sun 11am–8pm. Metro: Passeig de Gràcia.

When it opened in 1990, this became the third Barcelona museum devoted to the work of a single artist. In 1984 the Catalan artist Antoni Tàpies set up a foundation bearing his name, and the city of Barcelona donated an ideal site: the old Montaner i Simon publishing house, near the Passeig de Gràcia in the 19th-century Eixample district. One of the city's landmark buildings, the brick-and-iron structure was built between 1881 and 1884 by that exponent of Catalan art nouveau, architect Lluís Domènech i Montaner. The core of the museum is a collection of works by Tàpies (most contributed by the artist), covering stages of his career as it evolved into abstract expressionism. Here you can see the entire spectrum of media in which he worked:

painting, assemblage, sculpture, drawing, and ceramics. His associations with Picasso and Miró are apparent. The largest of the works is on top of the building: a controversial gigantic sculpture, *Cloud and Chair*, made from 9,000 feet of metal wiring and tubing.

Museu d'Art Modern. Plaça d'Armes, Parc de la Ciutadella. ☎ **93-319-57-28.** Admission 500 ptas. ($3.35) adults, 250 ptas. ($1.70) youths 8–21, free for children under 8. Tues–Sat 10am–7pm, Sun 10am–2:30pm. Closed Jan 1, Dec 25. Metro: Arc de Triomf. Bus: 14, 16, 17, 39, 40, 41, 51, 57, 59, or 64.

This museum shares a wing of the Palau de la Ciutadella with the Catalan parliament. Constructed in the 1700s, it was once used as an arsenal. It later became a royal residence before being turned into a museum early in this century. Its collection of art focuses on the early 20th century and features the work of Catalan artists, including Martí Alsina, Vayreda, Casas, Fortuny, and Rusiñol. The collection also encompasses some 19th-century Romantic and neoclassical works, as well as modernisme furniture (including designs by architect Puig i Cadafalch).

Monestir de Pedralbes. Baixada del Monestir, 9. ☎ **93-203-92-82.** Admission 400 ptas. ($2.70) adults, 250 ptas. ($1.70) students and seniors over 64, free for children under 13. Tues–Sun 10am–2pm. Metro: Reina Elisenda. Bus: 22, 63, 64, 75, or 114.

One of the oldest buildings in Pedralbes (the city's wealthiest residential area) is this monastery, founded in 1326 by Elisenda de Montcada, queen of Jaume II. Still a convent, the establishment is also the mausoleum of the queen, who is buried in its gothic church. Walk through the cloisters, with nearly two dozen arches on each side, rising three stories high. A small chapel contains the chief treasure of the monastery, murals by Ferrer Bassa, who was the major artist of Catalonia in the 1300s.

This monastery was a minor attraction until 1993, when 72 paintings and 8 sculptures from the famed Thyssen-Bornemisza collection went on permanent display. Among the outstanding works of art are Fra Angelico's *The Virgin of Humility* and 20 paintings from the early German Renaissance period. Italian Renaissance paintings range from the end of the 15th century to the middle of the 16th century. They include works by Dosso Dossi, Lorenzo Lotto, Tintoretto, Veronese, and Titian. Such old masters as Rubens, Zurbarán, and Velázquez represent the baroque era.

Museu Arqueològic. Passeig de Santa Madrona, 39-41, Parc de Montjuïc. ☎ **93-423-21-49.** Admission 400 ptas. ($2.70) adults, 300 ptas. ($2) students, free for children. Tues–Sat 9:30am–7pm, Sun 10am–2:30pm. Metro: Espanya. Bus: 55.

The Museu Arqueològic occupies the former Palace of Graphic Arts, built for the 1929 World's Fair. It reflects the long history of this Mediterranean port city, beginning with prehistoric Iberian artifacts. The collection includes articles from the Greek, Roman (glass, ceramics, mosaics, bronzes), and Carthaginian periods. Some of the more interesting relics were excavated in the ancient Greco-Roman city of Empúries in Catalonia; other parts of the collection came from the Balearic Islands.

Museu d'Art Contemporani de Barcelona. Plaça dels Angels, 1. ☎ **93-412-08-10.** Admission 750 ptas. ($5.05) adults, 500 ptas. ($3.35) students, free for children. Tues–Sat 11am–7:30pm, Sun 10am–3pm. Metro: Plaça de Catalunya.

A soaring white edifice in the once-shabby but rebounding Raval district, the Museum of Contemporary Art is to Barcelona what the Pompidou Center is to Paris. Designed by the American architect Richard Meier, the building is a work of art, manipulating sunlight to offer brilliant, natural interior lighting. On display in the 74,000 square feet of exhibit space is the work of modern luminaries such as Tápies, Klee, Miró, and many others. The museum has a library, bookshop, and cafeteria.

Museu de les Arts Decoratives. Palau Reial de Pedralbes, Avinguda Diagonal, 686. ☎ **93-280-50-24.** Admission 400 ptas. ($2.70). Free 1st Sun of every month. Tues–Sat 10am–7pm, Sun and holidays 10am–3pm. Metro: Palau Reial. Bus: 7, 63, 67, 68, or 75.

In a beautiful park, this palace was constructed as a municipal gift to King Alfonso XIII. He didn't make much use of it, however—he was forced into exile in 1931. Today it houses a collection of objets d'art, furniture, jewelry, and glassware from the 14th century to the present. More than 200 pieces, all of Spanish origin, are on display.

Museu Egipci de Barcelona. Calle València, 284. ☎ **93-488-01-88.** Admission 700 ptas. ($4.70) adults, 500 ptas. ($3.35) students and children. Mon–Sat 10am–2pm and 4–8pm, Sun 10am–2pm. Guided tours Sat. Closed holidays. Metro: Passeig de Gràcia.

Spain's only museum dedicated specifically to Egyptology contains more than 250 pieces from the personal collection of founder Jordi Clos (the owner of the Hotel Claris). On display are sarcophagi, jewelry, hieroglyphics, sculptures, and artwork. Exhibits focus on ancient Egyptians' everyday life, including education, social customs, religion, and food. The museum has its own lab for restorations. A library with more than 3,000 works is open to the public.

Museu d'Història de la Ciutat. Plaça del Rei. ☎ **93-315-11-11.** Admission (includes multimedia show) 700 ptas. ($4.70) adults, 500 ptas. ($3.35) children and students. Tues–Sat 10am–2pm and 4–8pm, Sun 10am–2pm. Bus: 16, 17, 19, 22, or 45.

Connected to the Royal Palace (see below), this museum traces the history of the city, from its early days as a Roman colony to its role in the 1992 Summer Olympics. The museum is in a 15th-century mansion, the Padellás House. Many exhibits date from Roman days, with much else from medieval times.

Palau Reial (Royal Palace). Plaça del Rei. ☎ **93-315-11-11.** Admission 700 ptas. ($4.70). Summer, Tues–Sat 10am–8pm; off-season, Tues–Sat 10am–2pm and 4–8pm; year-round Sun 10am–2pm. Bus: 16, 17, 19, 22, or 45.

The former palace of the counts of Barcelona, this later became the residence of the kings of Aragón. It is believed that Isabella and Ferdinand received Columbus here when he returned from his first voyage to the New World. Here, some say, the monarchs got their first look at a Native American. The Saló del Tinell, a banquet hall with a wood-paneled ceiling held up by half a dozen arches, dates from the 14th century. Rising five stories above the hall is the Torre del Reí Martí, a series of porticoed galleries.

Poble Espanyol. Marqués de Comillas, Parc de Montjuïc. ☎ **93-325-78-66.** Admission 950 ptas. ($6.35) adults, 525 ptas. ($3.50) children 7–14, free for children under 7. Audiovisual hall free. Mon 9am–8pm, Tues–Thurs 9am–2am, Fri–Sat 9am–4am, Sun 9am–midnight Metro: Espanya.

In this re-created Spanish village, built for the 1929 World's Fair, various regional architectural styles are reproduced. From the Levant to Galicia, 115 life-size reproductions of buildings and monuments represent the 10th through the 20th centuries. At the entrance, for example, stands a facsimile of the gateway to the walled city of Ávila. The center of the village has an outdoor cafe where you can sit and have drinks. Numerous shops sell provincial crafts and souvenir items, and in some of them you can see artists at work, printing fabric and blowing glass. Since the 1992 Olympics, the village has offered 14 restaurants, one disco, and eight musical bars. In addition, visitors can see an audiovisual presentation about Barcelona and Catalonia. Many families delight in the faux Spanish atmosphere, but the more discriminating find it a bit of a tourist trap—overly commercialized and somewhat cheesy. It's a matter of personal taste. You'll find lots of mediocre places to eat here.

Mirador de Colón. Portal de la Pau. ☎ **93-302-52-24.** Admission 250 ptas. ($1.70) adults, 150 ptas. ($1) children 4–12, free for children under 4. Sept 25–March, Mon–Fri 10am–2pm and 3:30–6:30pm, Sat–Sun and holidays 10am–6:30pm; Apr-May, Mon–Fri 10am–2pm and 3:30–7:30pm, Sat–Sun 10am–7:30pm. June–Sept 24, daily 9am–8:30pm. Closed Jan 1, Jan 6, Dec 25–26. Metro: Drassanes. Bus: 14, 18, 36, 57, 59, or 64.

This monument to Christopher Columbus was erected at the Barcelona harbor on the occasion of the Universal Exhibition of 1888. It consists of three parts, the first being a circular structure, raised by four stairways (19½ feet wide) and eight iron heraldic lions. On the plinth are eight bronze bas-reliefs depicting Columbus's principal feats. (The originals were destroyed; these are copies.) The second part is the base of the column, consisting of an eight-sided polygon, four sides of which act as buttresses; each side contains sculptures. The third part is the 167-foot column, which is Corinthian in style. The capital boasts representations of Europe, Asia, Africa, and America—all linked together. Finally, over a princely crown and a hemisphere recalling the newly discovered part of the globe, is a 25-foot-high bronze statue of Columbus—pointing, ostensibly, to the New World—by Rafael Ataché. Inside the iron column, an elevator ascends to the *mirador*. From here, a panoramic view of Barcelona and its harbor unfolds.

MORE ARCHITECTURAL HIGHLIGHTS

Architecture enthusiasts will find a wealth of fascinating sights in Barcelona. Primary among them, of course, are the fantastical creations of Antoni Gaudí and his modernisme cohorts.

Casa Milà. Passeig de Gràcia, 92. ☎ **93-484-59-80.** Metro: Diagonal.

Commonly called La Pedrera, Casa Milà is the most famous apartment complex in Spain. Antoni Gaudí's imagination went wild when he planned its construction; he even included vegetable and fruit shapes in his sculptural designs. Controversial and much criticized upon its completion, today it stands as a classic example of modernisme architecture. The entire building was restored in 1996. The ironwork around the balconies forms an intricate maze, and the main gate has windowpanes shaped like turtle shells. Phantasmagorical chimneys known in Spanish as *espantabrujas* (witch-scarers) fill the rooftop. From the rooftop, you'll also have a view of Gaudí's unfinished cathedral, La Sagrada Familia. The Espai Gaudí (Gaudí Space) in the attic has an intriguing multimedia display of the controversial artist's work. Tours of the famous rooftops are available daily from 10am to 8pm, with tours in English Monday through Friday at 6pm, Saturday and Sunday at 11am. Admission and a tour cost 600 ($4) for adults, 350 ptas. ($2.35) for students, free for children under 12.

Casa Amatller. Passeig de Gràcia, 41 ☎ **93-216-01-75.** Metro: Passeig de Gràcia.

Constructed in a cubical design, with a Dutch gable, this building was created by Puig i Cadafalch in 1900. It stands in sharp contrast to its neighbor, the Gaudí-designed Casa Batlló (see below). The architecture of the Casa Amatller, imposed on an older structure, is a vision of ceramic, wrought iron, and sculptures. The structure combines grace notes of Flemish Gothic—especially on the finish of the facade—with elements of Catalan architecture. The gable outside is in the Flemish style. Inside, visitors may view the original gothic revival interior, now the headquarters of the Institut Amatller d'Art Hispanic. Admission is free, but donations are welcome. You must phone ahead to schedule a visit. The interior is open on Thursday at 10am, 11am, and noon.

Casa Batlló. Passeig de Gràcia, 43. ☎ **93-488-06-66.** Mon–Fri 10am–4pm. Metro: Passeig de Gràcia.

Next door to the Casa Amatller, Casa Batlló was designed by Gaudí in 1905. Using "sensuous" curves in iron and stone, the architect gave the facade a lavish baroque exuberance. The balconies have been compared to "sculpted waves." The upper part of the facade evokes animal forms, and delicate tiles spread across the design. The downstairs building is the headquarters of an insurance company. Many tourists walk inside for a view of Gaudí's interior, which is basically as he designed it. This is a place of business, so be discreet. At press time, the building was undergoing renovations and was scheduled to reopen in mid-2000. Call ahead to confirm.

Casa Lleó Morera. Passeig de Gràcia, 35. No phone. Metro: Passeig de Gràcia.

Between the carrer del Consell de Cent and the carrer d' Aragó stands one of the most famous buildings of the modernisme movement. It is one of the trio of structures called the Mançana de la Discòrdia (Block of Discord), an allusion to the mythical judgment of Paris. Three of Barcelona's most famous modernisme architects, including Gaudí, competed with their works along this block. Florid Casa Lleó, designed by Domènech i Montaner in 1905, was revolutionary in its day. That assessment still stands. The building is private, and the interior is closed to the public.

Casa de la Ciutat/Ayuntamiento. Plaça de Sant Jaume. ☎ **93-402-70-00.** Metro: Jaume I.

Constructed at the end of the 14th century, the building that houses the municipal government is one of the best examples of gothic civil architecture in the Catalan-Mediterranean style. Across the landmark square from the Palau de la Generalitat, it has been endlessly renovated and changed. Behind a neoclassical facade, the building has a splendid courtyard and staircase. Its major architectural highlights are the 15th-century Salón de Ciento (Room of the 100 Jurors) and the black marble Salón de las Crónicas (Room of the Chronicles). The Salón de Ciento, in particular, represents a medley of styles. You can enter the building on Sunday from 10am to 2pm or by special arrangement.

OLYMPIC MEMORIES

Galería Olímpica. Passeig Olimpic, s/n, lower level. ☎ **93-426-06-60.** Admission 400 ptas. ($2.70). Apr–Sept, Tues–Sat 10am–2pm and 4–8pm, Sun 10am–2pm; Oct–Mar, Tues–Sat 10am–1pm and 4–6pm, Sun 10am–2pm. Metro: Espanya. Bus: 9 or 13.

An enthusiastic celebration of the 1992 Olympic Games in Barcelona, this is one of the few museums in Europe exclusively devoted to sports and statistics. Exhibits include photos, costumes, and memorabilia, with heavy emphasis on the events' pageantry, the number of visitors who attended, and the fame the events brought to Barcelona. Of interest to statisticians, civic planners, and sports buffs, the gallery contains audiovisual information about the building programs that prepared the city for the onslaught of visitors. There are also conference facilities, an auditorium, video recordings of athletic events, and archives. In the cellar of the Olympic Stadium's southeastern perimeter, the museum is most easily reached by entering the stadium's southern gate (Porta Sud).

BULLFIGHTING

Catalans do not pursue this art form, or sport, with as much fervor as Castilians do. Nevertheless, you may want to attend a *corrida* in Barcelona. Bullfights are held from April through September, usually on Sunday at 6:30pm at Plaça de Toros Monumental, Gran Vía de les Corts Catalanes (☎ **93-245-58-04**). Buy tickets in advance from the office at Muntaner, 24 (☎ **93-453-38-21**). Tickets cost 1,800 to 6,500 ptas. ($12.05 to $43.55).

PARKS & GARDENS

Barcelona isn't just museums; much of its life takes place outside, in its unique parks and gardens. See the entry on Parc Güell under "The Top Attractions," above.

Tibidabo Mountain, north of the port, offers the finest panoramic view of Barcelona. A funicular takes you up 1,600 feet to the summit. The ideal time to visit this summit (the culmination of the Sierra de Collserola) is at sunset, when the city lights are on. At the time of the Olympics, an 850-foot communications tower, Mirador Torre de Collserola, was built. Although attacked by traditionalists for destroying the natural beauty of the mountain, Torre de Collserola offers the most panoramic views in all of Catalonia. It costs 500 ptas. ($3.35) to go up the tower. From Plaça de Catalunya, take bus no. 58 to Avinguda del Tibidabo, where you can board a special bus to the funicular. Hop aboard to scale the mountain. The funicular runs daily when the park is open, starting 20 minutes before the Fun Fair. The fare is 300 ptas. ($2) one way, 400 ptas. ($2.70) round-trip.

In the southern part of the city, the mountain park of **Montjuïc** has splashing fountains, gardens, outdoor restaurants, and museums, making for quite an outing. The re-created Spanish village, the Poble Espanyol, and the Joan Miró museum are also in the park. (See individual listings, above, for information.) There are many walks and vantage points for viewing the Barcelona skyline.

The park was the site of several Olympic events. An illuminated fountain display, the **Fuentes Luminosas,** is on view at Plaça de la Font Magica, near the Plaça d'Espanya. It runs from 8 to 11pm every Saturday and Sunday from October through May, 9pm to midnight on Thursday, Saturday, and Sunday from June through September.

To reach the top, take bus no. 61 from Plaça d'Espanya or the Montjuïc funicular. The funicular is open from June 13 to September 30 daily from 11am to 10pm. In winter it operates daily from 10:45am to 8pm. The round-trip fare is 600 ptas. ($4).

Parc de la Ciutadella, Avinguda Wellington, s/n (☎ **93-225-67-80**), gets its name (Park of the Citadel) because it is the site of a former fortress. After Philip V won the War of the Spanish Succession (Barcelona was on the losing side), he got his revenge: He ordered that the "traitorous" residential suburb be leveled. In its place rose a citadel. In the mid–19th century it, too, was leveled, though some architectural evidence survives in a governor's palace and an arsenal. Today lakes, gardens, and promenades fill most of the park, which also holds a **zoo** (see "Especially for Kids," below) and the **Museu d'Art Modern** (see "More Attractions," above). Gaudí contributed to the monumental fountain in the park when he was a student; the lampposts are also his. The park is open daily from 8am to 9pm. Admission is free. To reach the park, take the metro to Ciutadella.

Parc de Joan Miró, near the Plaça de Espanya, is dedicated to one of Catalonia's most famous artists. It dates to the 1990s and occupies an entire block. One of Barcelona's most popular parks, it is often called Parc de l'Escorxador (slaughterhouse), a reference to its former occupant. Its main features are an esplanade and a pond from which a giant sculpture by Miró, *Woman and Bird,* rises. Palm, pine, and eucalyptus trees, as well as playgrounds and pergolas, complete the picture. To reach the park, take the metro to Espanya. It is open throughout the day.

ESPECIALLY FOR KIDS

The Catalan people have great affection for children, and although many of the attractions of Barcelona are for adults, an array of amusements is designed for the young—and the young at heart.

Children from 3 to 7 have their own place at the **Museu de la Ciència,** Teodor Roviralta, 55 (☎ **93-212-60-50**). "Clik del Nens" is a science playground. Children walk on a giant piano, make bubbles, lift a hippopotamus, and enter an air tunnel. They observe, experiment, and examine nature in an environment created just for them. Special 1-hour guided sessions take place daily. (See "More Attractions," above.)

At the **Poble Espanyol,** Marqués de Comillas, Parc de Montjuïc (☎ **93-325-78-66**), kids find a Spanish version of Disneyland. Frequent fiestas enliven the place, and it's fun for everybody, young and old. (See "More Attractions," above.)

Parc Zoologic. Parc de la Ciutadella. ☎ **93-225-25-06.** Admission 1,500 ptas. ($10.05) adults, 950 ptas. ($6.35) students and children, free for children under 3. Summer, daily 9:30am–7:30pm; off-season, daily 10am–5pm. Metro: Ciutadella.

Modern, with barless enclosures, this ranks as Spain's top zoo. One of the most unusual attractions is the famous albino gorilla Snowflake (Copito de Nieve), the only one of its kind in captivity in the world. The main entrances to the Ciutadella Park are on the Passeig de Pujades and Passeig de Picasso.

Parc d'Atraccions (Tibidabo). Plaça Tibidabo, 3-4, Cumbre del Tibidabo. ☎ **93-211-79-42.** Ticket for all rides 2,400 ptas. ($16.10) adults, 600 ptas. ($4) adults over 64, free for children under 5. May to mid-June, Wed–Sun noon–8pm; mid-June to Sept, Tues–Sun noon–8pm; off-season, Sat–Sun and holidays 11am–8pm. Transit: Bus no. 58 to Avinguda del Tibidabo to Tramvía Blau, then take funicular.

On top of Tibidabo, this park combines tradition with modernity—rides from the beginning of the century complete with 1990s novelties. In summer the place takes on a carnival-like atmosphere.

ORGANIZED TOURS

Pullmantur, Gran Vía de les Corts Catalanes, 635 (☎ **93-317-12-97;** metro: Plaça de Catalunya), offers a number of tours and excursions with English-speaking guides. For a preview of the city, you can take a morning tour. They depart from the company's terminal at 9:30am, and take in the cathedral, the Gothic Quarter, Les Rambles, the monument to Columbus, and the Spanish Village and the Olympic Stadium. Tickets cost 4,575 ptas. ($32.05). An afternoon tour leaves at 3:30pm and visits some of the most outstanding architecture in the Eixample, including Gaudí's Sagrada Familia, Parc Güell, and a stop at the Picasso Museum. This tour costs 4,750 ptas. ($31.85).

Pullmantur also offers several excursions outside Barcelona. The daily tour of the monastery of Montserrat includes a visit to the Royal Basilica to view the famous sculpture of the Black Virgin. This tour, which costs 6,000 ptas. ($40.20), departs at 9:30am and returns at 2:30pm to the company's terminal. A full-day Girona–Figueres tour includes a visit to Girona's cathedral and its Jewish quarter, plus a trip to the Dalí museum. This excursion, which costs 12,145 ptas. ($81.35), leaves Barcelona at 9am and returns at approximately 6pm. Call ahead—a minimum number of participants is required or the tour isn't conducted.

Another company that offers tours of Barcelona and the surrounding countryside is **Juliatours,** Ronda Universitat, 5 (☎ **93-317-64-54**). Itineraries and prices are similar to Pullmantur's. One tour, the "Visita Ciudad Artística," focuses on the city's artistic significance. The tour also passes Casa Lleó Morera, designed in 1905 by Domènech i Montaner in a floral modernist mode, and takes in many of Gaudí's brilliant buildings, including the Casa Milá (La Pedrera) and La Sagrada Familia. Also included is a visit to the Museu Picasso or Museu d'Art Modern, depending on the day of your tour. This tour, which leaves at 3:30pm and returns at 6:30pm, costs 4,700 ptas. ($31.50).

Walking Tour
The Gothic Quarter

Start: Plaça Nova.
Finish: Plaça de la Seu.
Time: 3 hours.
Best Times: Any sunny day.
Worst Times: Monday through Saturday from 7 to 9am and 5 to 7pm, because of traffic.

Begin at the:

1. **Plaça Nova.** In the shadow of the cathedral, this is the largest open-air space in the Gothic Quarter and the usual site of the Barcelona flea market. Opening onto this square is the Portal del Bisbe, a gate flanked by two round towers—remnants of the ancient Roman wall that once stood here. From Plaça Nova, climb the narrow asphalt-covered street (carrer del Bisbe) between the massive walls. On your right, notice the depth of the foundation, which indicates how much the city has risen since the wall was constructed.

   At the approach of the first street, carrer de Santa Llúcia, turn left, noticing the elegant simplicity and Romanesque facade of the corner building, the:

2. **Capilla de Santa Llúcia** (☎ **93-315-15-54**). The chapel's solid, graceful portal and barrel-vaulted interior were completed in 1268. Open daily from 9am to 1pm and 4 to 7pm.

   Continue down carrer de Santa Llúcia a few paces, noticing the:

3. **Casa de L'Ardiaca** (Archdeacon's House). Constructed in the 15th century as a residence for Archdeacon Despla, the gothic building has sculptural reliefs with Renaissance motifs. In its cloisterlike courtyard are a fountain and a palm tree. Notice the mail slot, where five swallows and a turtle carved into stone await the arrival of important messages. Since 1919 this building has been home to the **Museu d'Historia de la Ciutat (City History Museum).** As you exit the Archdeacon's House, continue in the same direction several steps until you reach the:

4. **Plaça de la Seu.** From this square in front of the main entrance to the **Catedral de Barcelona** (see "The Top Attractions," above), you can stand and admire the facade of Mediterranean Gothic architecture. On each side of Plaça de la Seu, you can see the remains of Roman walls. After touring the cathedral, exit through the door you entered and turn right onto carrer dels Comtes, admiring the gargoyles along the way. After about 100 paces, you'll approach the:

5. **Museu Frederic Marés,** on Plaça de Sant Iú. On the lower floors are Punic and Roman artifacts, but most of the museum is devoted to the works of the Catalan sculptor. Exit through the same door you entered and continue your promenade in the same direction. You'll pass the portal of the cathedral's side, where the heads of two abstract angels flank the throne of a seated female saint. A few paces farther, notice the stone facade of the:

6. **Arxiu de la Carona d'Aragó.** This is the archives building of the crown of Aragón. Formerly called Palacio del Lugarteniente (Deputy's Palace), this gothic building was the work of Antonio Carbonell. On some maps it also appears as the Palacio de los Virreyes (Palace of the Viceroys). The palace contains medieval and royal documents. Enter its courtyard, admiring the century-old grapevines. Then climb the 11 monumental steps to your left, facing a modern

Walking Tour—The Gothic Quarter

0   50 y
0   50 m

Plaça Nova

Avinguda Catedral

Plaça de Antoni Maura

start here ☆ ❶

Carrer de

Plaça de la Seu

† ❷ ❸ ❹

Carrer del Bisbe

la Tapineria

❺ ☆ ❽ finish here

Via Laietana

Sant Honorat

Catedral

†

Carrer de

la Pietat

Comtes

dels

❻

Plaça del Rei

Plaça de Ramón Berenguer el Gran

❽

Paradís

Carrer

❼

⓬

Carrer

del

Carrer de la Tapineria

Carrer

⓫

Carrer de

del

Arlet

Carrer de la Llibreteria

Baixada de la Llibreteria

Plaça de Sant Jaume

❾

JAUME 1 Ⓜ

Carrer de   Sant   Jaume I

Carrer de la Ciutat

Carrer de

Carrer Daguería

Carrer del Sots-Tinent Navarro

Via Laietana

Casa de la Ciutat

Carrer d'Hércules

†

⓾

Plaça de Sant Just

Plaça de Emili Vilanova

Palma de Sant Just

Carrer del Lledó

Legend

Church †

Metro Ⓜ

BARCELONA

Gothic Quarter

❶ Plaça Nova
❷ Capilla de Santa Llúcia
❸ Casa de L'Ardiaca
❹ Plaça de la Seu
❺ Museu Frederic Marés
❻ Arxiu de la Corona d'Aragó
❼ Plaça del Rei

❽ Casa del Canonge
❾ Plaça de Sant Jaume
⓾ Plaça de Sant Just
⓫ Carrer de la Tapineria
⓬ Plaça de Ramón Berenguer el Gran
⓭ Roman Walls

bronze sculpture by a Catalan artist. It represents, with a rather abstract dateline and map, the political history and imperial highlights of Catalonia.

As you exit the courtyard, you'll find yourself back on carrer dels Comtes. Continue in the same direction, turning left at the intersection of Baixada de Santa Clara. This street, in 1 short block, brings you to one of the most famous squares of the Gothic Quarter:

7. **Plaça del Rei.** The Great Royal Palace, an enlarged building that was originally the residence of the counts of Barcelona, stands at the bottom of this square. Here at the King's Square you can visit both the **Palau Reial** and the **Museu d'Història de la Ciutat** (see "More Attractions," above). On the right side of the square stands the **Palatine Chapel of Santa Agata,** a 14th-century Gothic temple that is part of the Palau Reial. In this chapel is preserved the altarpiece of the Lord High Constable, a 15th-century work by Jaume Huguet.

Retrace your steps up Baixada de Santa Clara, crossing carrer dels Comtes, and continue straight to carrer de la Pietat, which skirts the semicircular, massively buttressed rear of the cathedral. With the buttresses of the cathedral's rear to your right, pass the 14th-century:

8. **Casa del Canonge** (House of the Canon), opening onto carrer Arzobispo Iru-rita. This Gothic building was restored in 1929; escutcheons from the 15th and 16th centuries remain. Notice the heraldic symbols of medieval Barcelona on the stone plaques—twin towers supported by winged goats with lion's feet. On the same facade, also notice the depiction of twin angels. The building is a women's training school, the Escola Professional per a la Doña.

Continue walking along carrer de la Pietat, which makes a sudden sharp left. Notice the carved *Pietà* above the Gothic portal leading into the rear of the cathedral. Continue walking straight. One block later, turn left onto carrer del Bisbe and continue downhill. Your path will lead you beneath one of the most charming bridges in Spain. Carved into lacy patterns of stonework, it connects the Casa del Canonge with Palau de la Generalitat.

Continue walking until carrer del Bisbe opens into:

9. **Plaça de Sant Jaume.** In many ways, this plaza is the political heart of Catalan culture. Politicians and bureaucrats intent on Catalonian government affairs race across this square, constructed at what was once a major junction of two Roman streets. On Sunday at noon you can witness the *sardana,* the Catalonian national dance. Many bars and restaurants stand on side streets leading from this square. Standing in the square, with your back to the street you just left (carrer del Bisbe), you'll see, immediately on your right, the Doric portico of the **Palau de la Gener-alitat,** the parliament of Catalonia. It has a large courtyard and open-air stairway, along with twin arched galleries. Construction on this exquisite Catalonian Gothic work began in the era of Jaume I. A special feature is the Chapel of St. George, constructed in flamboyant Gothic style between 1432 and 1435 and enlarged in 1620 with the addition of vaulting and a cupola with hanging capitals. The back of the building encloses an orangery courtyard begun in 1532. In the Salón Dorado, the Proclamation of the Republic was signed. The palace bell tower houses a carillon that plays both old and popular music each day at noon. Across the square are the Ionic columns of the **Casa de la Ciutat/Ayuntamiento,** the Town Hall of Barcelona (see "More Architectural Highlights," above).

With your back to carrer del Bisbe, turn left onto the narrow, ancient carrer de la Llibreteria. Two thousand years ago, this was one of the two roads that marked the Roman center of town. Walk uphill on carrer de la Llibreteria for about 1½ blocks.

☕ **TAKE A BREAK**   **Mesón del Café,** Llibreteria, 16 (☎ **93-315-07-54**), founded in 1909, specializes in coffee and cappuccino. It is one of the oldest coffeehouses in the neighborhood. Some regulars perch on stools at the bar and order breakfast. Coffee costs 115 ptas. (75¢), cappuccino 260 ptas. ($1.75). The cafe is open Monday to Saturday from 7am to 11pm.

Retrace your steps along carrer de la Llibreteria and enter the Plaça de Sant Jaume. Facing the Town Hall, take the street that parallels its left side, carrer de la Ciutat. Note the elegant stonework on the building's side, carved in a style radically different from the neoclassical facade. At the first left, turn onto carrer d'Hercules, and follow it for 1 block until you enter the quiet, somewhat faded beauty of:

10. **Plaça de Sant Just.** The entrance to the Eglésia dels Sants Just i Pastor dominates the square. Above the entrance portal, an enthroned Virgin is flanked by a pair of protective angels. The Latin inscription hails her as "Virgo Nigra et Pulchra, Nostra Patrona Pia" (Black and Beautiful Virgin, Our Holy Patroness). This church dates from the 14th century, although work continued into the 16th. Some authorities claim that the church—in an earlier manifestation of the present structure—is the oldest in Barcelona. Visiting hours are erratic; the doors are usually closed except during Sunday mass.

    Opposite the facade of the church, at Plaça de Sant Just, 4, is an aristocratic town house covered with faded but elegant frescoes of angels cavorting among garlands—an example of the artistry, taste, and wealth of a bygone era. With your back to the Virgin, turn right onto the narrow cobblestoned street, carrer del Lledo, which begins at the far end of the square. One short block later, turn left onto Baixada de Cassador. As you descend the steep slope of this narrow street, notice the blue-and-white covering of the House of the Blue Tiles at the bottom of the hill.

    Turn left onto carrer del Sots Tinent Navarro. The massive gray stone wall rising on your left is the base of an ancient Roman fort. Note the red bricks of a 13th-century palace on top of the Roman wall. The solitary Corinthian column rising from the base is another reminder of Barcelona's Roman past.

    Continue on to Plaça d'Emili Vilanova. Near the top of the Roman wall, note the pair of delicate columns of a gothic window. Continue another block to the cross street, carrer Jaume I. Cross it and approach Plaça de l'Angel. Continue walking to the:

11. **Carrer de la Tapineria.** For centuries, Catalonia has been the center of Spain's footwear industry. In medieval times, this was the street of the shoemakers. In fact, the industry is so entrenched that there is even a museum devoted to antique footwear, the **Museu del Calçat,** Plaça Sant Felip Neri, 5 (☎ **93-301-45-33**), open Tuesday through Sunday from 11am to 2pm. Admission is 200 ptas. ($1.35).

    In 1 short block carrer de la Tapineria leads to:

12. **Plaça de Ramón Berenguer el Gran.** An equestrian statue dedicated to the hero (1096–1131) is ringed with the gravel of a semicircular park. It sits in front of the walls of the ancient Roman fort and, nearby, a gothic tower.

    Traverse the park, crossing in front of the equestrian statue, until you again reach the edge of the Roman wall as you head toward the park's distant end. Here carrer de la Tapineria leads you on a path paralleling the ancient:

13. **Roman Walls.** These are among Barcelona's most important treasures. The walls, known as *Las Murallas* in Spanish, were constructed between A.D. 270 and 310.

The walls followed a rectangular course, and were built so that their fortified sections would face the sea. By the 11th and 12th centuries, Barcelona had long outgrown their confines. Jaume I ordered the opening of the Roman Walls, and the growth that ensued virtually destroyed them, except for the foundations you see today.

Continue your promenade, turning left at the narrow Baixada de la Canonja. A short walk down this cobblestoned alleyway will return you to **Plaça de la Seu,** not far from where you began.

7 Active Pursuits

AN OUTSTANDING FITNESS CENTER   The city's main fitness center lies adjacent to the Olympic Stadium, in an indoor-outdoor complex whose main allure is its two beautifully designed swimming pools. Built for the 1992 Summer Olympics, the facility contains a health club and gym. It's open to the public for 1,300 ptas. ($8.70) for a full day's pass. For the address and hours, see the Piscina Bernardo Picornell listing in "Swimming," below.

GOLF   One of the city's best courses, **Club de Golf Vallromanas,** Afueras, s/n, Vallromanas, Barcelona (☎ **93-572-90-64**), is 20 minutes north of the center by car. Nonmembers who reserve tee times in advance are welcome to play. The greens fees is 7,000 ptas. ($46.90) on weekdays, 14,000 ptas. ($93.80) on weekends. The club is open Wednesday through Monday 9am to 8:30pm. Established in 1972, it is the site of Spain's most important golf tournament.

Reial Club de Golf El Prat, El Prat de Llobregat (☎ **93-379-0278**), is a prestigious club that allows nonmembers to play under two conditions: They must have a handicap issued by the governing golf body in their home country, and they must prove membership in a golf club at home. The club has two 18-hole par-72 courses. Greens fees are 12,380 ptas. ($82.95) on weekdays, 24,840 ptas. ($166.45) on weekends. From Barcelona, follow Avinguda Once de Septiembre past the airport to Barrio de San Cosme. From there follow the signs along carrer Prat to the golf course.

SWIMMING   Most city residents head to the beaches near the Vila Olímpica or Sitges when they feel like swimming. If you're looking for an uncrowded pool, you'll find one at the **Esportiu Piscina DeStampa,** carrer Rosich, s/n, in the Hospitalet district (☎ **93-334-56-00**). It's open Monday through Friday 8am to 10pm; Saturday 10am to 2pm and 4 to 8pm; and Sunday 10am to 2pm. Monday through Friday admission is 345 ptas. ($2.30); Saturday and Sunday, it's 400 ptas. ($2.70).

A much better choice, however, allows you to swim where some Olympic events took place, at **Piscina Bernardo Picornell,** Avinguda de Estadi, 30-40, on Montjuïc (☎ **93-423-40-41**). Adjacent to the Olympic Stadium, it incorporates two of the best swimming pools in Spain (one indoors, one outdoors). Custom built for the Olympics, they're open to the public Monday through Friday 7am to midnight, Saturday 7am to 9pm, and Sunday 7am to 4pm. Admission costs 1,300 ptas. ($8.70) and allows full use throughout the day of whichever pool is open, plus the gymnasium, the sauna, and the Jacuzzis. Bus no. 61 makes frequent runs from the Plaça d'Espanya.

8 Shopping

For fashion and style, Barcelonans look more to Paris and their own sense of design than to Madrid. *Moda joven* (young fashion) is all the rage.

If your time and budget are limited, you may want to patronize Barcelona's major department store, **El Corte Inglés,** for an overview of Catalan merchandise at reasonable prices. Barcelona is filled with boutiques, but clothing is expensive, even though the city has been a textile center for centuries.

Markets (see below) are very popular and are suitable places to search for good buys.

THE SHOPPING SCENE

If you're a window shopper, stroll along the **Passeig de Gràcia** from the Avinguda Diagonal to the Plaça de Catalunya. Along the way, you'll see some of the most elegant and expensive shops in Barcelona, plus an assortment of splendid turn-of-the-century buildings and cafes, many with outdoor tables. Another prime spot is the **Rambla de Catalunya** (upper Rambles).

Another shopping expedition is to the **Mercat de la Boquería,** Rambla, 101 (☎ 93-318-25-84), near carrer del Carme. Here you'll see a wide array of straw bags and regional products, along with a handsome display of the food you're likely to eat later: fruits, vegetables (artfully displayed), breads, cheeses, meats, and fish. Vendors sell their wares Monday through Saturday from 8am to 8pm.

In the **old quarter,** not far from Plaça de Catalunya, the principal shopping streets are all five Rambles, plus carrer del Pi, carrer de la Palla, and Avinguda Portal de l'Angel, to cite some major thoroughfares. Moving north in the **Eixample** are Passeig de Catalunya, Passeig de Gràcia, and Rambla de Catalunya. Even farther north, **Avinguda Diagonal** is a major shopping boulevard. Other prominent shopping streets include Bori i Fontesta, via Augusta, carrer Muntaner, Travessera de Gràcia, and carrer de Balmes.

In general, shopping hours are Monday through Saturday from 9am to 8pm. Some smaller shops close from 1:30 to 4pm.

The **American Visitors Bureau,** Gran Vía, 591 (☎ 93-301-01-50), between Rambla de Catalunya and carrer de Balmes, will pack and ship your purchases and gifts, and even handle excess luggage and personal effects. The company also operates a travel agency that books flights and hotel accommodations. It's open Monday through Friday 9am to 1pm and 4 to 7pm, Saturday by appointment only.

Watch for sales (*rebajas* or *rebaixes* in Catalán) in mid-January, late July, and August. Stores getting rid of their winter or summer stock often offer heavy discounts.

SHOPPING A TO Z

Prices in Barcelona tend to be slightly lower than those in London, Paris, and Rome.

You'll find stylish, attractively designed **clothing and shoes. Decorative objects** are often good buys. In the city of Miró, Tàpies, and Picasso, **art** is a major business and the reason gallery owners from around the world visit. You'll find dozens of galleries, especially in the Barri Gòtic and around the Picasso Museum. Barcelona is also noted for its **flea markets,** where good purchases are always available if you search hard enough.

Antiques abound, but rising prices have put many of them beyond the means of the average shopper. However, the list below includes some shops where you can at least look. Most shoppers from abroad settle happily for handcrafts, and the city is rich in offerings, ranging from pottery to handmade furniture. Barcelona has been in the business of creating and designing **jewelry** since the 17th century, and its offerings and prices are of the widest possible range.

What follows is only a limited selection of some of the hundreds of shops in Barcelona.

ANTIQUES

El Bulevard des Antiquaris. Passeig de Gràcia, 55. No central phone. Metro: Passeig de Gràcia.

This 70-unit complex, just off one of the town's most aristocratic avenues, has a huge collection of art and antiques assembled in a series of boutiques. There's a cafe-bar on the upper level. Summer hours are Monday through Friday 9:30am to 8:30pm; winter hours, Monday 4:30 to 8:30pm, Tuesday through Saturday 10:30am to 8:30pm. Some boutiques keep shorter hours.

Sala d'Art Artur Ramón. Palla, 23. ☎ **93-302-59-70.** Metro: Jaume I.

One of the finest antiques and art dealers in Barcelona can be found at this three-level emporium. Set on a narrow flagstone-covered street near Plaça del Pi (the center of the antique district), it stands opposite a tiny square, the Placeta al Carrer de la Palla. The store, which has been operated by four generations of men named Artur Ramón, contains everything from Romanesque works to Picassos. Prices are high, as you'd expect, for items of quality and lasting value. Open Monday through Saturday 10am to 1:30pm and 5 to 8pm.

Urbana. Còrsega, 258. ☎ **93-218-70-36.** Metro: Hospital Sant Pau.

Urbana sells an array of architectural remnants (usually from torn-down mansions), antique furniture, and reproductions of brass hardware. There are antique and reproduction marble mantelpieces, wrought-iron gates and garden seats, even carved wood fireplaces with the modernisme look. It's an impressive, albeit costly, array of merchandise. Open Monday through Friday 10am to 2pm and 5 to 8pm.

BOOKS

LAIE. Pau Claris, 85. ☎ **93-318-17-39.** Metro: Plaça de Catalunya or Urquinaona.

The best selection of English-language books, including travel maps and guides, is at LAIE, a block from the Gran Vía de les Corts Catalanes. It's open Monday through Friday 10am to 9pm, Saturday 10:30am to 9pm. The bookshop has an upstairs cafe with international newspapers and a little terrace. It serves breakfast, lunch (salad bar), and dinner. The cafe is open Monday through Saturday 9am to 1am. The shop also schedules cultural events, including art exhibits and literary presentations.

CAMERAS

Casa Arpí. Les Rambles, 38-40. ☎ **93-301-74-04.** Metro: Liceu.

This is one of the most famous camera shops in Spain. A multilingual staff will guide you to the best buys in new and used cameras, including familiar brand-name products. The firm also does quality processing in 24 to 48 hours. Open Monday through Saturday 9:30am to 2pm and 4 to 8pm.

DEPARTMENT STORES

El Corte Inglés. Plaça de Catalunya, 14. ☎ **93-302-12-12.** Metro: Plaça de Catalunya.

One of two local representatives of the largest and most glamorous department store chain in Spain, this branch sells a wide variety of merchandise. It ranges from Spanish handcrafts to high-fashion items, from Catalan records to food. The store also has restaurants and cafes and offers consumer-related services, such as a travel agent. It has a department that will mail your purchases home. Open Monday through Saturday 10am to 9:30pm. El Corte Inglés has two other Barcelona locations: Av. Diagonal, 617-619 (☎ **93-419-28-28;** metro: María Cristina), and Av. Diagonal, 471 (☎ **93-419-20-20;** metro: María Cristina).

DESIGNER HOUSEWARES

Vinçón. Passeig de Gràcia, 96. ☎ **93-215-60-50.** Metro: Diagonal.

Fernando Amat's Vinçón is the best in the city, with 10,000 products—everything from household items to the best in Spanish contemporary furnishings. Its mission is to purvey good design, period. Housed in the former home of artist Ramón Casas—a contemporary of Picasso's during his Barcelona stint—the showroom is filled with the best Spain has. The always-creative window displays alone are worth the trek: Expect *anything*. Open Monday through Saturday 10am to 2pm and 4:30 to 8:30pm.

FABRICS & WEAVINGS

Coses de Casa. Plaça de Sant Josep Oriol, 5. ☎ **93-302-73-28.** Metro: Jaume I.

Appealing fabrics and weavings are displayed in this 19th-century store, called simply "Household Items." Many are hand-woven in Majorca, their boldly geometric patterns inspired by Arab motifs of centuries ago. The fabric, for the most part, is 50% cotton, 50% linen; much of it would make excellent upholstery material. Open Monday through Friday 9:30am to 1:30pm and 4:30 to 8pm, Saturday 10am to 2pm and 5 to 8pm.

FASHION

Antonio Miró. Consejo de Ciento, 349. ☎ **93-487-06-70.** Metro: Passeig de Gràcia.

This shop is devoted exclusively to the clothing design of Miró, without the Groc label (see below). It carries fashionable men's and women's clothing. Before buying anything at Groc, survey the wares at this store, which seems even more stylish.

Groc. Rambla de Catalunya, 100. ☎ **93-215-74-74.** Metro: Plaça de Catalunya.

One of the most stylish shops in Barcelona, Groc is expensive but filled with high-quality men's and women's apparel made from the finest natural fibers. The men's store is downstairs, the women's store one flight up. Open Monday through Saturday 10am to 2pm and 4 to 8:30pm (the men's department stays open all day). August hours are Monday through Friday 11am to 2pm and 5 to 8pm.

GALLERIES

Art Picasso. Tapinería, 10. ☎ **93-310-49-57.** Metro: Jaume I.

Here you can get good lithographic reproductions of works by Picasso, Miró, and Dalí, as well as T-shirts emblazoned with the masters' designs. Tiles often carry their provocatively painted scenes. Open Monday through Saturday 10am to 8pm, Sunday 10am to 3pm.

Sala Parés. Petritxol, 5. ☎ **93-318-70-20.** Metro: Plaça de Catalunya.

Established in 1840, this is a Barcelona institution. The Maragall family recognizes and promotes the work of Spanish and Catalan painters and sculptors, many of whom have gone on to acclaim. Paintings are displayed in a two-story amphitheater, with high-tech steel balconies supported by a quartet of steel columns evocative of Gaudí. Exhibitions of the most avant-garde art in Barcelona change about every 3 weeks. Open Monday through Saturday 10:30am to 2pm and 4:30 to 8:30pm.

GIFTS

Beardsley. Petritxol, 12. ☎ **93-301-05-76.** Metro: Plaça de Catalunya.

Named after the Victorian English illustrator, this store is on the same street where the works of Picasso and Dalí were exhibited before they became world famous. The wide array of gifts, perhaps the finest selection in Barcelona, includes a little bit of everything—dried flowers, writing supplies, silver dishes, unusual bags, and lots more. Open Monday through Friday 9:30am to 1:30pm and 4:30 to 8pm, Saturday 10am to 2pm and 5 to 8:30pm.

Bon Original Shop. Plaça de Catalunya, 17-S. ☎ **93-307-31-23.** Metro: Plaça de Catalunya.

At the tourist offices, this shop sells a variety of articles inspired by Barcelona. It stocks a representative range of products, including textiles, ceramics, jewelry, stationery, gift items, and travel-related gear.

LEATHER

Loewe. Passeig de Gràcia, 35. ☎ **93-216-04-00.** Metro: Passeig de Gràcia.

Barcelona's biggest branch of this prestigious Spanish leather-goods chain is in one of the best-known modernisme buildings in the city. Everything is top-notch, from the elegant showroom to the expensive merchandise to the helpful salespeople. The company exports its goods to branches throughout Asia, Europe, and North America. Open Monday through Saturday 9:30am to 2pm and 4:30 to 8pm.

MARKETS

El Encants antique market is held every Monday, Wednesday, Friday, and Saturday in Plaça de les Glóries Catalanes (metro: Glóries). Go any time during the day to survey the selection.

Coins and postage stamps are traded and sold in **Plaça Reial** on Sunday from 10am to 2pm. It's off the southern flank of Les Rambles (metro: Drassanes).

A book and coin market is held at the Ronda Sant Antoni every Sunday from 10am to 2pm (metro: Universitat).

MUSIC

Casa Beethoven. Les Rambles, 97. ☎ **93-301-48-26.** Metro: Liceu.

This store, established in 1920, carries the most complete collection of sheet music in town. The collection naturally focuses on the works of Spanish and Catalan composers. Music lovers might make some rare discoveries. Open Monday through Friday 9am to 8pm, Saturday 9am to 1:30pm and 5 to 8pm.

PORCELAIN

Kastoria 2. Avinguda Catedra, 6-8. ☎ **93-310-04-11.** Metro: Plaça de Catalunya.

This large store near the cathedral is an authorized Lladró dealer, and stocks a big selection of the famous porcelain. It also carries many kinds of leather goods, including purses, suitcases, coats, and jackets. Open Monday through Saturday 10am to 7pm, Sunday 10am to 2pm.

POTTERY

Artesana i Coses. Placeta de Montcada, 2. ☎ **93-319-54-13.** Metro: Jaume I.

Here you'll find pottery and porcelain from every major region of Spain. Most of the pieces are heavy and thick-sided—designs in use in the country for centuries. Open Monday through Saturday 10am to 2pm and 4 to 8pm.

Itaca. Carrer Ferran, 26. ☎ **93-301-30-44.** Metro: Liceu.

Here you'll find a wide array of handmade pottery from Catalonia and other parts of Spain, plus Portugal, Mexico, and Morocco. The merchandise has been selected for its basic purity, integrity, and simplicity. Open Monday through Friday 10am to 2pm and 4:30 to 8pm, Saturday 10am to 8:30pm.

SHOPPING CENTERS & MALLS

The landscape has exploded since the mid-1980s, with the construction of several American-style shopping malls. Some are too far from the city's historic core to be convenient for most foreign visitors, but here's a description of some of the city's best.

Centre Comercial Barcelona Glories. Avinguda Diagonal, 208. ☎ **93-486-04-04.** Metro: Glories.

Built in 1995, this is the largest shopping center in downtown Barcelona, a three-story emporium of the good life. It's based on California models but crammed into a distinctly urban neighborhood. It has more than 100 shops, some posh, others much less so. Although there's a typical shopping-mall anonymity to some aspects of this place, you'll still be able to find almost anything you might have forgotten while packing. Open Monday through Saturday 10am to 10pm.

Diagonal Center (Lilla Diagonal). Avinguda Diagonal, 557. ☎ **93-444-00-00.** Metro: María Cristina.

This two-story mall contains stores devoted to luxury products, as well as a scattering of bars, cafes, and simple but cheerful restaurants favored by office workers and shoppers. It has about half the number of shops the Centre Comercial Barcelona Glories (see above) offers. Built in the early 1990s, it even has an area devoted to video games, where teenagers can make as much electronic noise as they want while their guardians shop. Open Monday through Saturday 10am to 9pm.

Maremagnum. Moll d'Espanya, s/n. ☎ **93-225-81-00.** Metro: Drassanes.

The best thing about this place is its position adjacent to the waterfront on Barcelona's historic seacoast; it's also well suited to outdoor promenades. Built in the early 1990s near the Columbus Monument, it contains a handful of shops that sell touristy items, and lots of cafes, bars, and places to sit. You might get the idea that only a few of the people who come here are interested in shopping.

Poble Espanyol. Marqués de Comillas, Parc de Montjuïc. ☎ **93-325-78-66.** Metro: Espanya, then take free red double-decker bus to Montjuïc, or bus no. 13 (145 ptas./95¢).

This is not technically a shopping mall but a "village" (see "More Attractions," above). It has about 35 stores selling typical folk crafts from every part of Spain: glassware, leather goods, pottery, paintings, carvings, and so forth. Store hours vary, but you can visit any time during the day.

STRAW PRODUCTS

La Manual Alpargatera. Avinyó, 7. ☎ **93-301-01-72.** Metro: Jaume I or Liceu.

In addition to its large inventory of straw products, such as hats and bags, this shop is known mainly for its footwear. Espadrilles (*alpargatas* in Spanish), or basic rope-soled shoes (said to be 1,000 years old), are made on the premises. Some Catalans only wear espadrilles when performing the *sardana,* their national dance. To find the shop, turn off Les Rambles at carrer Ferran, walk 2 blocks, and make a right. Open Monday through Saturday 9:30am to 1:30pm and 4:30 to 8pm.

UMBRELLAS

Julio Gómez. Rambla de Sant Josep, 102-104 (also called Rambla de las Flors). ☎ **93-301-33-26.** Metro: Liceu.

For more than a century, Julio Gómez has rung up umbrella sales here. In a workshop out back, women labor over the unique umbrellas or lace-trimmed silk or cotton parasols. There are also Spanish fans, walking sticks capped with silver, and other memorabilia. It all adds up to an evocative piece of shopping nostalgia. Open Monday through Saturday 9:30am to 1:30pm and 4 to 8pm.

9 Barcelona After Dark

Barcelona comes alive at night, and the array of nighttime diversions is staggering. There is something to interest almost everyone and to fit most pocketbooks. The **funicular ride** to Tibidabo and the illuminated **fountains** of Montjuïc are especially popular, and fashionable **clubs** operate in nearly every major district of the city. For families, the **amusement parks** are the busiest venues.

Locals sometimes opt for an evening in the *tascas* (taverns) or pubs, perhaps settling for a bottle of wine at a cafe, an easy and inexpensive way to spend an evening people-watching. Serious drinking in pubs and cafes begins by 10 or 11pm. But for the most fashionable bars and discos, Barcelonans delay their entrances until at least 1am.

Your best source of local information is a little magazine called *Guía del Ocio,* which previews "La Semana de Barcelona" (This Week in Barcelona). It's in Spanish, but most of its listings will probably be comprehensible. Almost every news kiosk along Les Rambles carries it.

Nightlife begins for many Barcelonans with a **promenade** (*paseo*) along Les Rambles in the early evening, usually from 5 to 7pm. Then things quiet down a bit until a second surge of energy brings out the crowds again, from 9 to 11pm. After that the esplanade clears out quite a bit, but it's always lively.

If you've been scared off by press reports about Les Rambles between the Plaça de Catalunya and the Columbus Monument, know that the area's really been cleaned up in the past decade. Still, you will feel safer along the Rambla de Catalunya, in the Eixample, north of the Plaça de Catalunya. This street and its offshoots are lively at night, with many cafes and bars. During the Franco era, the center of club life was the cabaret-packed district near the south of Les Rambles, but the area is known for nighttime muggings—use caution if you go there.

Cultural events are also big in the Catalonian repertoire, and old-fashioned **dance halls** survive in some places. Although **disco** has waned in some parts of the world, it is still going strong in Barcelona. Decaying movie houses, abandoned garages, and long-closed vaudeville theaters have been taken over and restored as nightlife venues.

Flamenco isn't the rage here that it is in Seville and Madrid, but it still has its devotees. The city is also filled with **jazz** aficionados. Best of all, the old tradition of the **music hall** with vaudeville lives on.

In the summer you'll see plenty of free entertainment—everything from opera to monkey acts—just by walking the streets. The Rambles is a particularly good place to watch.

THE PERFORMING ARTS

Culture is deeply ingrained in the Catalan soul, and the performing arts are strong. In fact, some take place on the street, especially along Les Rambles. Crowds often gather around a singer or a mime. A city square will suddenly come alive on Saturday night with a spontaneous festival "tempestuous, surging, irrepressible life and brio," is how the writer Rose MacCauley described it.

Long a city of the arts, Barcelona experienced a cultural decline during the Franco years, but now it is filled once again with the best opera, symphonic, and choral music. At the venues listed here, unless otherwise specified, ticket prices depend on the event.

CLASSICAL MUSIC

Palau de la Música Catalana. Sant Francesc de Paula, 2. ☎ **93-268-10-00.** Box office Mon–Sat 10am–9pm.

In a city chock-full of architectural highlights, this one stands out. In 1908 Lluís Domènech i Montaner, a Catalan architect, designed this structure, using stained glass, ceramics, statuary, and ornate lamps, among other elements. It stands today, restored, as a classic example of modernisme. Concerts and leading recitals take place here.

THEATER

Theater is presented in the Catalán language and therefore will not be of interest to most visitors. For those who do speak the language, or perhaps are fluent in Spanish (even then, though, you're unlikely to understand much), here are some recommendations.

✪ **Gran Teatre del Liceu.** Rambla dels Caputxins. ☎ **93-485-99-00.** Metro: Liceu.

This monument to belle epoque extravagance, a 2,700-seat opera house, is one of the grandest theaters in the world. It was designed by the Catalan architect Josep Oriol Mestves. On January 31, 1994, fire gutted the opera house, shocking Catalonians, many of whom regarded this place as the citadel of their culture. The government immediately vowed to rebuild, and the new Liceu was scheduled to open in October 1999, well before the millennium deadline set by the cultural czars.

Mercat de Los Flors. Lleida, 59. ☎ **93-426-18-75.** Tickets 1,500–3,000 ptas. ($10.05–$20.10). Metro: Espanya.

Housed in a building constructed for the 1929 International Exhibition at Montjuïc, this is the other major Catalan theater. Peter Brook first used it as a theater for a 1983 presentation of *Carmen*. The theater focuses on innovators in drama, dance, and music, as well as European modern dance companies. The 999-seat house also has a restaurant overlooking the city rooftops.

Teatre Lliure. Montseny, 47. ☎ **93-218-92-51.** Tickets 2,000–2,500 ptas. ($13.40–$16.75) Tues–Thurs; 2,500–3,000 ptas. ($16.75–$20.10) Fri–Sun. Metro: Fontana.

This self-styled free theater is the city's leading Catalán-language playhouse. Once a workers' union, the building has been the headquarters of a theater cooperative since 1976. Its directors are famous in Barcelona for their bold presentations, including works by Bertolt Brecht, Luigi Pirandello, Jean Genêt (who wrote about Barcelona), and even Molière and Shakespeare. New dramas by Catalan playwrights are also presented. The house seats 200 to 350.

Teatre Nacional de Catalunya. Plaça de les Arts, 1. ☎ **93-306-57-00.** Tickets 3,200–3,700 ptas. ($21.45–$24.80). Closed Aug. Metro: Monumental.

Josep María Flotats heads this major company. The actor-director trained in the tradition of theater repertory, working in Paris at Théâtre de la Villa and the Comédie Française. His company presents both classic and contemporary plays.

FLAMENCO

El Tablao de Carmen. Poble Espanyol de Montjuïc. ☎ **93-325-68-95.** Dinner and show 7,800 ptas. ($52.25); drink and show 4,200 ptas. ($28.15).

This club presents a highly rated flamenco cabaret in the re-created village. You can go early and explore the village, and even have dinner. This place has long been a tourist favorite. The club is open Tuesday through Sunday from 8pm to past midnight— around 1am on weeknights, often until 2 or 3am on weekends, depending on business.

The first show is always at 9:30pm; the second show is at 11:30pm on Tuesday, Wednesday, Thursday, and Sunday, and midnight on Friday and Saturday. Reservations are recommended.

Los Tarantos. Plaça Reial, 17. ☎ **93-318-30-67.** Cover (includes 1 drink) 1,500 ptas. ($10.05). Metro: Liceu.

Established in 1963, this is the oldest flamenco club in Barcelona, with a rigid allegiance to the tenets of Andalusian flamenco. Its roster of artists changes regularly. They often come from Seville or Córdoba, stamping out their well-rehearsed passions in ways that make the audience appreciate the arcane nuances of Spain's most intensely controlled dance idiom. No food is served. The place resembles a cabaret theater, where up to 120 people at a time can drink, talk quietly, and savor the nuances of a dance that combines elements from medieval Christian and Muslim traditions. Each show lasts around 1¼ hours. Shows are Monday through Saturday at 10pm and midnight.

Tablao Flamenco Cordobés. Les Rambles, 35. ☎ **93-317-66-53.** Dinner and show 7,800 ptas. ($52.25); 1 drink and show 4,200 ptas. ($28.15). Closed Jan. Metro: Drassanes.

At the southern end of Les Rambles, a short walk from the harbor front, you'll hear the strum of the guitar, the sound of hands clapping rhythmically, and the haunting sound of the flamenco, a tradition here since 1968. Head upstairs to an Andalusian-style room where performances take place with the traditional *cuadro flamenco*—singers, dancers, and guitarist. Cordobés is said to be the city's best flamenco showcase. From November through March (except 1 week in December), the show with dinner begins at 8:30pm, the show without dinner at 10pm. April through October and December 25 through December 31, four shows are offered nightly with dinner, at 8pm and 9:45pm; without dinner at 9:30pm and 11:15pm. Reservations are required.

THE CLUB & MUSIC SCENE
CABARET
Arnau. Avinguda del Parallel, 60. ☎ **93-329-21-04.** Cover (includes 1 drink) from 2,000 ptas. ($13.40). Metro: Parallel.

A veteran of the many changes that have affected the worlds of cabaret and entertainment since its heyday in the 1970s, this place has managed to keep up with the times and the demands of the marketplace. Shows mingle touches of Catalan folklore with glitz and glitter, hints of family nostalgia, and doses of melodrama. Two shows are presented Wednesday through Sunday, at 10:30pm. Drink prices start at 700 ptas. ($4.70).

Espai Barroc. Carrer Montcada, 20. ☎ **93-310-06-73.** Cover (includes 1 drink) 2,500 ptas. ($16.75). Metro: Jaime I.

One of Barcelona's most culture-conscious nightspots occupies some of the showplace rooms of the Palau Dalmases, a stately palace in the Barri Gòtic. In a room lined with grand art objects, you can listen to recorded opera arias and sip glasses of beer or wine. The most appealing night is Thursday—beginning at 11pm, 10 singers perform a roster of arias from assorted operas, one of which is invariably *Carmen.* Since its establishment in 1996, the place has thrived. Almost everyone around the bar apparently has at least heard of the world's greatest operas, and some can even discuss them more or less brilliantly. Open Tuesday through Sunday, 8pm to 2am.

Luz de Gas. Carrer de Muntaner, 246. ☎ **93-209-77-11.** Cover (includes 1 drink) 2,000 ptas. ($13.40). Bus: 7, 15, 33, 58, or 64.

This theater and cabaret has the hottest Latino jazz on weekends. On weeknights, there is cabaret. The place is an art nouveau delight, with colored glass lamps and enough voluptuous nudes to please Rubens. The club was once a theater, and its original seating has been turned into different venues, each with its own bar. The lower two levels open onto the dance floor and stage. If you'd like to talk, head for the top tier, which has a glass enclosure. Call to see what the lineup is on any given night: jazz, pop, soul, rhythm and blues, salsa, bolero, whatever.

DANCE CLUBS & DISCOS

Bikini. Deu i Mata, 105. ☎ **93-322-00-05.** Cover 1,000–3,000 ptas. ($6.70 $20.10). Metro: Les Corts.

In the basement of a commercial-looking shopping center is this wide-ranging nightlife compound, with at least two venues for dancing in every conceivable genre (including funk, indie, rock-and-roll, and golden-oldie music). There's a separate room for Puerto Rican salsa (the owners refer to it as a "salsoteca"), and a large area devoted to emerging musical groups. The venue changes every night of the week, and has even been known to include sophisticated adaptations of conventional tango music. Open Monday through Thursday 7pm to 4:30am, Friday and Saturday 7pm to 6am.

Up and Down. Numancia, 179. ☎ **93-280-29-22.** Cover (includes 1 drink) 1,000–2,000 ptas. ($6.70–$13.40). Metro: María Cristina.

The chic atmosphere here attracts elite Barcelonans of all ages. The more mature patrons, specifically the black-tie, postopera crowd, head for upstairs, leaving the downstairs section to loud music and "flaming youth." Up and Down is the most cosmopolitan disco in Barcelona, with impeccable service, sassy waiters, and a welcoming atmosphere. Technically, this is a private club—you can be turned away at the door. The restaurant is open Monday through Saturday 10pm to 2am, and prices for meals run 3,500 ptas. ($23.45) and up. The disco is open Tuesday through Saturday midnight to 6am. Drinks in the disco cost 1,400 ptas. ($9.40) for a beer, at least 1,900 ptas. ($12.75) for a hard drink.

JAZZ & BLUES

Barcelona Pipa Club. Plaça Reial, 3. ☎ **93-302-47-32.** Cover (includes 1 soft drink or beer) 1,000 ptas. ($6.70). Metro: Liceu.

If you find the Harlem Jazz Club (see below) small, wait until you get to the "Pipe Club." Long beloved by jazz aficionados, this is for true devotees. Ring the buzzer and you'll be admitted (at least we hope you will), then climb two flights up in a rundown building. This is hardly a trendy nighttime venue. Five rooms are decorated with displays or photographs of pipes (naturally Sherlock Holmes gets in on the act). Depending on the performer, music ranges from New Orleans jazz to Brazilian rhythms. The club and its comfortable bar are open daily 10pm to 5am; jazz is featured Thursday through Sunday.

Jamboree. Plaça Reial, 17. ☎ **93-301-75-64.** Cover (includes 1 drink) 1,500–2,000 ptas. ($10.05–$13.40). Metro: Liceu.

In the heart of the Barri Gòtic, this has long been one of the city's premier venues for good blues and jazz, though it doesn't feature jazz every night. Sometimes a world-class performer will appear here, but most likely it'll be a younger group. The crowd knows its stuff and seems to demand only the best talent. On our last visit, we were entertained by an evening of Chicago blues. Or you might find that a Latin dance band has been scheduled. Open daily 11pm to 5am; shows begin at midnight.

Harlem Jazz Club. Comtessa de Sobradiel, 8. ☎ **93-310-07-55.** 1-drink minimum. No cover. Closed Aug. Metro: Jaume.

On a nice street in the Ciutat Vella, this is one of Barcelona's oldest and finest jazz clubs. It's also one of the smallest, with just a handful of tables. No matter how many times you've heard "Black Orpheus" or "The Girl from Ipanema," they always sound new again here. Music is viewed with a certain reverence; no one talks when the performers are on. Live jazz, blues, tango, Brazilian music—the sounds are always fresh. Open Tuesday to Thursday and Sunday 8pm to 4am, until 5am Friday and Saturday. Live music begins at 10:30pm on Tuesday to Thursday and Sunday, and 11:30pm on Friday and Saturday. The second set is at midnight (1am on Friday and Saturday).

A DANCE HALL

La Paloma. Tigre, 27. ☎ **93-301-68-97.** Cover 800 ptas. ($5.35). Metro: Universitat.

Those feeling nostalgic may want to drop in on Barcelona's most famous dance hall. Remember the fox-trot? The mambo? If not, learn about them here, along with the tango, the cha-cha, and the bolero. Live orchestras provide the music. The ornate old hall is open from Wednesday through Sunday. "Matinees" are from 6 to 9:30pm; night dances are from 11:30pm to 5am. Drink prices start at 1,000 ptas. ($6.70).

THE BAR SCENE

In addition to the bars listed below, we recommend several tapas bars (see "Dining," above).

BARS & PUBS

Coctelería Boadas. Carrer Taller, 1 (at Les Rambles). ☎ **93-318-95-92.** Metro: Plaça de Catalunya.

At least part of the fun at this bustling cocktail bar derives from trying to remember the parade of famous patrons who have come here since the place was established in 1933. The art deco setting might remind you of swinging old Havana—where the founder got his start before moving back to his family's home turf. Many patrons order Hemingway's favorite drink, a *mojito* (the Cuban rum equivalent of a mint julep). Open Monday through Saturday noon to 2am (till 3am on Friday and Saturday).

El Born. Passeig del Born, 26. ☎ **93-319-53-33.** Metro: Jaume I.

Facing a rustic-looking square, this former fish store has been cleverly converted. There are a few tables near the front, but our preferred spot is the inner room, decorated with rattan furniture and modern paintings. The music might be anything from Louis Armstrong to classic rock and roll. The upstairs buffet serves dinner. The room is somewhat cramped, but you'll find a simple, tasty collection of fish, meat, and vegetable dishes, all carefully laid out. A full dinner without wine costs around 2,500 to 4,000 ptas. ($16.75 to $26.80). Beer and wine are quite cheap. Open Monday through Saturday 6pm to 3am.

Café Bar Padam. Rauric, 9. ☎ **93-302-50-62.** Metro: Liceu.

The clientele and decor here are modern and hip. The bar, which attracts many gay patrons, is on a narrow street in the Ciutat Vella, about 3 blocks east of the Rambla dels Caputxins. The only color in the black-and-white rooms comes from fresh flowers and modern paintings. Jazz is sometimes featured. Open Monday through Saturday 7pm to 2am.

Cocktail Bar Boadas. Tallers, 1. ☎ **93-318-95-92.** Metro: Plaça de Catalunya.

This intimate, conservative bar is usually filled with regulars. Established in 1933, it lies near the top of Les Rambles. Many visitors stop in for a predinner drink and snack before wandering to one of the district's many restaurants. It stocks a wide array of

Caribbean rums, Russian vodkas, and English gins, and the skilled bartenders know how to mix them all. The place is especially well known for its daiquiris. Open daily noon to 2am (till 3am on Friday and Saturday).

Dirty Dick's. Taberna Inglesa, Carrer Marc Aureli, 2. ☎ **93-200-89-52.** Metro: Muntaner.

An English-style pub in a residential part of town, Dirty Dick's has lots of dark paneling and exposed brick, with banquettes for quiet conversation. If you sit at the bar, you'll be faced with a tempting array of tiny sandwiches that taste as good as they look. The pub is at the crossing of Vía Augusta, a main thoroughfare through the district. Open daily 6pm to 2:30am.

Otto Zutz Club. Carrer Lincoln, 15. ☎ **93-238-07-22.** Cover 2,000 ptas. ($13.40). Metro: Passeig de Gràcia or Fontana.

With one of the most carefully planned neoindustrial decors in Spain, this nightspot is the last word in hip. It's a magnet for the city's artists and night people. Facetiously named after a German optician, it sits behind an angular facade that reminds some visitors of a monument to a mid–20th-century megalomaniac. Originally built to house a textile factory, the building contains a labyrinth of metal staircases decorated in shades of blue, highlighted with endless spotlights, and warmed with lots of exposed wood. Open Tuesday through Saturday 11pm to 5am—but don't even think of showing up before midnight.

Pub 240. Aribau, 240. ☎ **93-209-09-67.** Cover 2,500 ptas. ($17.50).

This elegant bar, which bears no resemblance to a traditional pub, consists of three sections: a bar, a small amphitheater, and a lounge for talking and listening to music. Rock and South American folk music play, and the place is jammed almost every night. Open daily 7pm to 5am.

Zig-Zag Bar. Platón, 13. ☎ **93-201-62-07.** Metro: Muntaner.

Favored by actors, models, cinematographers, and photographers, this bar claims to have inaugurated Barcelona's trend toward high-tech minimalism in its watering holes. It's owned by the same entrepreneurs who developed the state-of-the-art Otto Zutz Club (see above). Open Monday through Thursday 10pm to 2:30am, Friday and Saturday 10pm to 3am.

CHAMPAGNE BARS

The Catalans call their own version of sparkling wine *cava*. In Catalán, champagne bars are called *xampanyerías*. The Spanish wines are often excellent, and some consider them better than their French counterparts. With more than 50 Spanish companies producing cava, and each bottling up to a dozen grades of wine, the best way to learn about Spanish champagne is to visit the vineyard or to sample the products at a *xampanyería*.

Champagne bars usually open at 7pm and stay open into the wee hours of the morning. They serve tapas, ranging from caviar to smoked fish to frozen chocolate truffles. Most establishments sell only a limited array of house *cavas* by the glass, and more esoteric varieties by the bottle. You'll be offered a choice of *brut* (slightly sweeter) or *brut nature*. The most acclaimed brands include Mont-Marçal, Gramona, Mestres, Parxet, Torello, and Recaredo.

Xampanyería Casablanca. Bonavista, 6. ☎ **93-237-63-99.** Metro: Passeig de Gràcia.

Someone had to fashion a champagne bar after the Bogart-Bergman film, and this is it. It serves four kinds of house cava by the glass, plus a good selection of tapas, especially pâtés. Open Sunday through Thursday 6:45pm to 2:30am, Friday and Saturday until 3am.

Xampú Xampany. Gran Vía de los Corts Catalanes, 702. ☎ **93-265-04-83.** Metro: Girona.

At the corner of the Plaça de Tetuan, this *champanería* offers a variety of hors d'oeuvres in addition to wine. Abstract paintings, touches of high tech, and bouquets of flowers break up the pastel color scheme. Open daily 6pm to 3:30am.

A Bit of Nostalgia

Bar Pastis. Carrer Santa Mònica, 4. ☎ **93-318-79-80.** Metro: Drassanes.

Valencianos Carme Pericás and Quime Ballester opened this tiny bar just off the southern end of Les Rambles in 1947. They made it a shrine to Edith Piaf, and her songs still play on an old phonograph in back of the bar. The decor consists mostly of paintings by Ballester, who had a dark, rather morbid vision of the world. You can order four kinds of pastis in this dimly lit "corner of Montmartre." Outside the window, check out the view—usually a parade of transvestite hookers. The crowd is likely to include almost anyone, especially people who used to be called bohemians. There's live music Sunday and Tuesday at 11:30pm. Open Monday through Thursday 7:30pm to 2:30am, Friday, Saturday and Sunday until 3am.

Els Quatre Gats. Montsió, 3. ☎ **93-302-41-40.** Metro: Urquinaona.

In 1897 Pere Romeu and three of his friends, painters Ramón Casas, Santiago Rusiñol, and Miguel Utrillo, opened a cafe for artists and writers at the edge of the Barri Gòtic. Early on, they staged a one-man show for a young artist, Pablo Picasso. He didn't sell a single painting, but did stick around to design the art nouveau menu cover. The cafe folded in 1903, becoming a private club and art school and attracting Joan Miró.

In 1978 two Catalans reopened the cafe in the Casa Martí, a building designed by Josep Puig i Cadafalch, one of the leading architects of modernisme. The cafe displays works by major modern Catalan painters, including Tàpies. You can drink coffee, taste wine, eat a full meal (see "Where to Dine," above)—and even try, if you dare, potent *Marc de Champagne,* an eau-de-vie distilled from the local cava. Open Monday through Saturday 8am to midnight, Sunday 6pm to midnight.

Gay & Lesbian Bars

Arena Classic. Diputació, 233. No phone. Cover Thurs–Fri 600 ptas. ($4), Sat and holidays 1,000 ptas. ($6.70). Metro: Universitat.

Attracting a crowd of gay men and lesbians, this club successfully combines '70s and '80s dance music to keep you moving and grooving till the wee hours. Thursdays there's a special party organized by a local lesbian group. Open Thursday through Saturday 11pm to 4am.

El Convento. Carrer Bruniquer, 59 (Plaça Joanic). No phone. Cover (includes 1 drink) 1,000 ptas. ($6.70). Metro: Joanic.

This may be like no other disco you've ever seen. It's decorated like a church, with depictions of the Virgin Mary and even candles adding to the ecclesiastical atmosphere. But the clientele consists mainly of young gay males in a party mood. The club often presents shows and organized parties. A novelty, to say the least. Open daily midnight to 5am.

New Chaps. Avinguda Diagonal, 365. ☎ **93-215-53-65.** Metro: Diagonal.

Gay Barcelonans refer to this saloon-style watering hole as Catalonia's premier leather bar. In fact, the dress code usually is leather of a different stripe: more boots and jeans than leather and chains. Behind a pair of swinging doors evocative of the old American West, Chaps contains two different bar areas. Open daily 9pm to 3am (until 3:30am on Friday and Saturday).

Metro. Sepúlveda, 185. No phone. Cover 1,000 ptas. ($6.70). Metro: Universitat.

One of the most popular gay discos in Barcelona, Metro attracts a diverse crowd—from young fashion victims to more rough-and-ready macho types. One dance floor plays contemporary house and dance music, and the other traditional Spanish music mixed with Spanish pop. This is a good opportunity to watch men of all ages dance the "Sevillanas" together in pairs with a surprising degree of grace. One interesting feature appears in the bathrooms, where videos have been installed in quite unexpected places. Open daily midnight to 5am.

Punto BCN. Muntaner, 63-65. No phone. Metro: Eixample.

Barcelona's largest gay bar attracts a mixed crowd of young trendies and foreigners. Always crowded, it's a good base to start out your evening. With every drink you receive free entry to Arena, Arena Classic (see above), and Arena VIP. There is a very popular happy hour on Wednesday from 6 to 9pm. On Friday and Saturday there are lots of surprises and giveaways. Open daily 6pm to 2:30am.

Satanassa. Carrer Aribau, 27. No phone. Cover (includes 1 drink) 1,000 ptas. ($6.70) Fri–Sat; no cover Sun–Thurs. Metro: Universitat.

This is a staple on Barcelona's gay circuit. It has a dance floor, provocative art, and a clientele whose percentage of gay women has greatly increased in the past several years. Open daily 11pm to 3am.

MORE ENTERTAINMENT

MOVIES   Recent releases from Paris, New York, Rome, Hollywood, and even Madrid come quickly to Barcelona, where an avid audience often waits in long lines for tickets. Most foreign films are dubbed into Spanish or Catalán, unless the listing indicates VO (*versió original,* or original version). Movie listings are published in *Guía del Ocio,* available at any newsstand along Les Rambles.

If you're a movie buff, the best time to be in Barcelona is June and early July for the annual film festival.

A CASINO   Between the coastal resorts of Sitges and Villanueva, about 25 miles (40km) southwest of Barcelona and 2 miles (3km) north of Sitges, stands the **Gran Casino de Barcelona,** Sant Pere (San Pedro) de Ribes (☎ **93-893-36-66**). Catalonia's major casino, it is in a 19th-century villa and attracts restaurant clients as well as gamblers. A set menu in the restaurant (reservations recommended) costs 5,000 ptas. ($33.50), and drinks go for around 800 ptas. ($5.35). For admission to the casino, you'll pay 550 ptas. ($3.70) and must show your passport. The casino is open year-round Sunday through Thursday 5pm to 4am, Friday and Saturday until 5am.

9 Side Trips from Barcelona

The major day trips, such as those to the monastery of Montserrat and the resorts along the Costa Brava, are covered in chapters 11 and 12. If you have a day to spare, you might also want to consider the following.

PENEDÉS WINERIES: HOME OF *CAVA*

From the Penedés wineries comes the famous *cava,* Catalan champagne, which can be sampled in Barcelona's champagne bars. You can see where the wine originates by journeying 25 miles (40km) from Barcelona, on highway A-2, to Exit 27. There are also daily trains to Sant Sadurní d'Anoia, home to 66 cava firms. Trains depart from Barcelona Sants.

The firm best equipped to receive visitors is **Codorníu** (☎ 93-818-32-32), the largest producer of *cava*, with some 40 million bottles a year. Public transportation is unreliable, so try to visit by cart. It is sometimes possible to get a taxi from the station at Sant Sadurní d'Anoia.

Groups of at least four are welcome at Codorníu. It's not necessary to make an appointment before showing up. Tours are presented in English, among other languages, and take 1½ hours; they visit some of the 10 miles (16km) of underground cellars by electric cart. Take a sweater, even on a hot day. A former pressing section has been turned into a museum, with exhibits of winemaking instruments through the ages. The museum is in a building designed by the great modernisme architect Puig i Cadafalch—one reason King Juan Carlos has declared the plant a national historic and artistic monument.

The tour ends with a *cava* tasting. Tours are conducted Monday through Friday throughout the day. The ideal time for a visit is for the autumn grape harvest. Admission is free Monday through Friday, Saturday and Sunday 200 ptas. ($1.35).

CARDONA: A CATALAN CASTLE VILLAGE

Another popular excursion from Barcelona is to Cardona, 60 miles (97km) northwest. Take the N-11 west, then go north on Route 150 to Manresa. Cardona lies 20 miles (32km) northwest of Manresa along Route 1410.

The home of the dukes of Cardona, the town is known for its canonical church, **Sant Vicenç de Cardona,** inside the walls of the castle. The church was consecrated in 1040. The great Catalan architect Josep Puig i Cadafalch wrote, "There are few elements in Catalan architecture of the 12th century that cannot be found in Cardona, and nowhere better harmonized." The church reflects the Lombard style of architecture. The castle (now a parador; see below) was the most important fortress in Catalonia.

WHERE TO STAY & DINE

Parador Nacional Duques de Cardona. Castillo de Cardona, s/n, 08261 Cardona. ☎ **93-869-12-75.** Fax 93-869-16-36. 54 units. A/C TV TEL. 15,000–17,500 ptas. ($100.50–$117.25) double; 19,000 ptas. ($127.30) suite. AE, DC, MC, V.

Sitting atop a cone-shaped mountain that towers 330 feet above Cardona, this restored castle opened as a four-star parador in 1976. Once the seat of Ludovici Pio (Louis the Pious) and a stronghold against the Moors, it was later expanded and strengthened by Guifré el Pilós (Wilfred the Hairy). In the 9th century it belonged to Charlemagne's nephew Don Ramón Folch. The massive fortress proved impregnable to all but the inroads of time, and several ancient buildings in this hilltop complex have been restored and made part of the parador.

The spacious accommodations, some with minibars, have canopy beds and woven bedspreads and curtains. The guest rooms command panoramic views. The public rooms are decorated with antique furniture, tapestries, and paintings of various periods. The bar is in a former dungeon, and meals are served in the stone-arched medieval dining room where the counts once ate. A complete meal of regional dishes costs 3,500 ptas. ($23.45). Try the Catalan bouillabaisse, accompanied by wines whose taste would be familiar to the Romans. Food is served daily from 1 to 4pm and 8 to 10:30pm.

THE ABELLO MUSEUM

The recently opened **Abello Museum,** carrer Berenguer, 122, Mollet del Valls (☎ 93-593-80-70), is 12 miles (19km) from Barcelona. Follow the Autopisto 17, and turn off at the Mollet exit. The trip takes about 20 minutes. By public transportation, the CA5 train to Mollet departs from the Sants railway station in Barcelona.

The Abello Museum's collection is one of the most important in Spain. It houses works by its namesake, the Catalan artist Joan Abello, and pieces dedicated to him by his friends Salvador Dalí, Pablo Picasso, and Joan Miró. The museum also contains 19th- and 20th-century paintings and sculptures, Catalan art, Romanesque and Baroque carvings, Asian art, bullfighting memorabilia, furniture, ceramics, and glass. Admission is 300 ptas. ($2) for adults, 150 ptas. ($1) for students and children. It is open Tuesday through Friday 11am to 2pm and 4 to 8pm; Saturday 11am to 8pm; Sunday 11am to 3pm.

THE PABLO CASAL MUSEUM

The recently opened **Pablo Casal Museum,** calle Santa Anna, 2 (☎ **977-665-684**), is in the house where the famous cellist was born in 1878 and spent the first 11 years of his life. The museum is in El Vendrall, 50 miles (80km) south of Barcelona. By car, take the A7 to Carra-Ruga, then follow signs south.

The exhibits include general memorabilia of Casal's youth and home life. Of particular note is a photograph of the young musician wearing a sailor suit, as well as the piano where his father, a musician, gave lessons. Also interesting is the museum's re-creation of an authentic late-19th-century Catalan village home. Admission is free. It is open daily 11am to 1pm, Monday through Saturday 5 to 7pm.

11 Catalonia

From Barcelona you can take several noteworthy 1-day excursions. The most popular is to the Benedictine monastery of **Montserrat,** northwest of Barcelona. To the south, the Roman city of **Tarragona** has been neglected by visitors but is particularly interesting to those who appreciate ancient history. Beach lovers should head for the resort town of **Sitges.**

About six million people live in Catalonia, and twice that many visit every year. It is one of Europe's playgrounds, with its beaches along the **Costa Brava** (see chapter 12) and the **Costa Dorada,** centered around Sitges. Tarragona is the capital of its own province, and Barcelona, of course, is the political, economic, and cultural center of Catalonia (see chapter 10).

The province of Catalonia forms a triangle bordered by the French frontier to the north, the Mediterranean Sea to the east, and the province of Aragón to the west. The northern coastline is rugged, whereas the Costa Dorada is flatter, with miles of sandy beaches as well as a mild, sunny climate.

Pilgrims may go to Montserrat for its scenery and religious associations, and history buffs to Tarragona for its Roman ruins, but just plain folks head to the Costa Dorada for fun. This seashore, named for its strips of golden sand, extends along the coastlines of Barcelona and Tarragona provinces. Avid beachcombers sometimes traverse the entire coast.

One popular stretch is **La Maresme,** extending from Río Tordera to Barcelona, a distance of 40 miles (64.5km). Allow at least 2½ hours to cover it without stops. The Tarragonese coastline extends from Barcelona to the Ebro River, a distance of 120 miles (193km); a trip along it will take a whole day. Highlights along this coast include Costa de Garraf, a series of creeks skirted by the corniche road after Castelldefels, Sitges, and Tarragona. One of the most beautiful stretches of the coast is **Cape Salou,** lying south of Tarragona in a setting of pinewoods.

We'll begin our tour through this history-rich part of Catalonia by going not along the coast, but rather inland to the Sierra de Montserrat, which has more spectacular views than any location along the coast. Wagner used it as the setting for his opera *Parsifal.* The serrated outline made by the sierra's steep cliffs led the Catalonians to call it *montserrat* (sawtooth mountain). Today it remains the religious center of Catalonia. Thousands of pilgrims annually visit the town's monastery, with its Black Virgin.

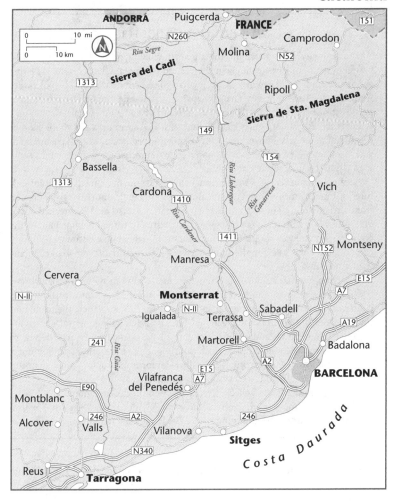

The **Monestir de Poblet** in Tarragona is the other major monastery of Catalonia. It, too, is a world-class attraction.

1 Montserrat

35 miles (56km) NW of Barcelona, 368 miles (592km) E of Madrid

The monastery at Montserrat, which sits atop a 4,000-foot mountain 7 miles (11km) long and 3½ miles (5.5km) wide, is one of the most important pilgrimage spots in Spain. It ranks alongside Zaragoza and Santiago de Compostela. Thousands travel here every year to see and touch the medieval statue of La Moreneta (The Black Virgin), the patron saint of Catalonia. Many newly married couples flock here for her blessing.

Avoid visiting on Sunday, if possible, as thousands of locals pour in, especially if the weather is nice. Remember that the winds blow cold up here even in summer, so

A Journey to Andorra

You may never have heard of the tiny principality of Andorra, sandwiched between Spain and France high in the eastern Pyrenees. Charlemagne gave this country its independence in 784, and with amused condescension, Napoléon let Andorra keep its autonomy. The principality is now ruled by two co-princes, the president of France and the Spanish archbishop of La Seu d'Urgell.

Less than 200 square miles (322 sq km) in size, Andorra is a storybook land of breathtaking scenery—cavernous valleys, snowcapped peaks, rugged pastureland, and deep gorges. It's long been popular for summer excursions and, more recently, as a winter ski resort as well.

Because of its isolation, Andorra retained one of the most insular peasant cultures in Europe until as late as 1945. But since the 1950s, tourists have increased from a trickle to a flood—12 million every year, in fact. This has wreaked havoc on Andorra's traditional way of life and has virtually turned a huge part of the country into one vast shopping center. Andorrans live almost entirely on monies earned from their tax-free shopping, along with the thriving ski market in the winter months.

Some suggest that Andorra has ruined its mountain setting with urban sprawl because taxis, crowds, and advertising have transformed the once-rustic principality into a busy center of trading and commerce. At first glance, the route into the country from Spain looks like a used-car lot, and its mile-long traffic jams are legendary. New hotels and hundreds of shops have opened in the past decade to accommodate the French and Spanish pouring across the frontiers to buy duty-free merchandise. A magazine once called Andorra "Europe's feudal discount shopping center." In addition, gasoline is cheap here.

Warning: Border guards check very carefully for undeclared goods.

Most people make their base in the capital, Andorra-la-Vella (in Spanish, Andorra-la-Vieja) or the adjoining town, Les Escaldes, where there are plenty of

visitors should take along warm sweaters, jackets, or coats. In winter, thermal underwear might not be a bad idea.

ESSENTIALS

GETTING THERE   The best and most exciting way to go is via the Catalan railway, **Ferrocarrils de la Generalitat de Catalunya** (Manresa line), with five trains a day leaving from the Plaça d'Espanya in Barcelona. The central office is at Plaça de Catalunya, 1 (☎ 93-205-15-15). The train connects with an aerial cable way (Aeri de Montserrat), which is included in the fare of 1,785 ptas. ($11.95) round-trip.

The train, with its funicular tie-in, has taken over as the preferred means of transport. However, a long-distance bus service is provided by **Autocars Julià** in Barcelona. Daily service from Barcelona to Montserrat is generally operated, with departures near Estació Central de Barcelona-Sants, Plaça de Països Catalanes. One bus makes the trip at 9am, returning at 5pm; the round-trip ticket costs 1,400 ptas. ($9.40). Contact the Julià company at carrer Viriato (☎ 93-490-40-00).

To drive here, take the **N-2** southwest of Barcelona toward Tarragona, turning west at the junction with the **N-11.** The signposts and exit to Montserrat will be on your shops, bars, and hotels. Shuttles run between the towns, but most shoppers prefer to walk. Most of the major hotels and restaurants are on the main street of Andorra-la-Vella (Avinguda Meritxell) or on the main street of Les Escaldes (Avinguda Carlemany). French francs and Spanish pestas. may be used interchangeably, and hotel, restaurant, and shop prices are quoted in both currencies.

But unless you've come just to shop, you will want to leave the capital for a look at this tiny principality. Two nearby villages, La Massana and Ordino, can be visited by car or by bus (leaving about every 30 minutes from the station in Andorra-la-Vella). Buses cross the country from south to north and vice versa. The drive to Andorra will take you through some of the finest mountain scenery in Europe, with a backdrop of peaks, vineyards, and rushing brooks. From Barcelona, drive via Puigcerda to La Seu d'Urgell. From here on the C-145, it's a quick 6 miles (10km) to the border of this autonomous principality, one of the world's smallest countries.

Although no one ever accused the Pyrenees of being more dramatic than the Alps, they are, in fact, far more rugged. The climate of dry air is brisk in winter, and some of Europe's best skiing can be found within this tiny country. There is abundant snow from November lasting (usually) through April. Pas de la Casa-Grau Roig is the oldest resort, located just within the French border. Along with a slalom course, it has 18 trails for advanced skiers, plus some tame slopes for neophytes, along with 25 lifts. The largest complex, however, is Soldeu-El Tarter, with 28 slopes (some designed for children) and a 7½-mile cross-country course. There are also 22 ski lifts. The resort of Pals feature 20 trails, 14 lifts, and a forest slalom course. Arinsal offers 25 slopes serving both the experienced skier and the beginner. But the most beautiful and dramatic resort of all is Ordino Arcalis, with 11 lifts and 16 slopes. Many British visitors flock here in winter, as Andorran ski packages, in general, are far more reasonable than those offered in either Switzerland or Austria.

right. From the main road, it's 9 miles (14.5km) up to the monastery through eerie rock formations and dramatic scenery.

VISITOR INFORMATION   The **tourist information office** is at Plaça de la Creu (☎ **93-835-02-51**). Open daily 10am to 1:45pm and 3 to 5:30pm.

EXPLORING MONTSERRAT

One of the monastery's noted attractions is the 50-member ✪ **Escolanía,** one of the oldest and most renowned boy's choirs in Europe, dating from the 13th century. At 1pm daily you can hear them singing *Salve Regina* and the *Virolai* (hymn of Montserrat) in the basilica. The basilica is open daily from 8 to 10:30am and noon to 6:30pm. Admission is free. To view the Black Virgin, a statue from the 12th or 13th century, enter the church through a side door to the right.

At the Plaça de Santa María you can also visit the **Museu de Montserrat** (☎ **93-835-02-51**), known for its collection of ecclesiastical paintings, including works by Caravaggio and El Greco. Modern Spanish and Catalan artists are also represented (see Picasso's early *El Viejo Pescador,* dating from 1895). Works by Dalí and such French impressionists as Monet, Sisley, and Degas are also shown. The collection of ancient artifacts is quite interesting, and make sure to look for the crocodile mummy, which is at least 2,000 years old. The museum is open Monday to Friday 10am to 6pm, Saturday and Sunday 9:30am to 6:30pm, charging 500 ptas. ($3.35) for adults and 300 ptas. ($2) for children and students.

The 9-minute **funicular ride** to the 4,119-foot-high peak, Sant Jeroni, makes for a panoramic trip. The funicular operates about every 20 minutes in April through October, daily from 10am to 6:40pm. The cost is 900 ptas. ($6.05) round-trip. From the top, you'll see not only the whole of Catalonia but also the Pyrenees and the islands of Majorca and Ibiza.

You can also make an excursion to **Santa Cova (Holy Grotto),** the alleged site of the discovery of the Black Virgin. The grotto dates from the 17th century and was built in the shape of a cross. You go halfway by funicular but must complete the trip on foot.

The chapel is open April through October, daily from 9am to 6:30pm; off-season hours are daily 10am to 5:30pm. The funicular operates from April through October only, every 15 minutes daily from 10am to 7pm, at a cost of 350 ptas. ($2.35) round-trip.

WHERE TO STAY & DINE

Few people spend the night here, but most visitors will want at least one meal. If you don't want to spend a lot, purchase a picnic in Barcelona or ask your hotel to pack a meal.

Abat Cisneros. Plaça de Monestir, 08199 Montserrat. ☎ **93-877-77-01.** Fax 93-877-77-24. 56 units. TV TEL. 5,100–10,000 ptas. ($34.15–$67) double. AE, DC, MC, V. Parking 450 ptas. ($3).

On the main square of Montserrat, this is a well-maintained modern hotel with few pretensions and a history of family management dating from 1958. The small rooms are simple and clean, each equipped with a comfortable bed, and the tiled bathrooms come with hair dryers. The in-house restaurant offers fixed-price meals for around 2,500 ptas. ($16.75) per person. Many regional dishes of Catalonia are served. The hotel's name is derived from a title given to the head of any Benedictine monastery during the Middle Ages.

2 Tarragona

60 miles (97km) S of Barcelona, 344 miles (554km) E of Madrid

The ancient Roman port city of Tarragona, on a rocky bluff above the Mediterranean, is one of the grandest, but most neglected, sightseeing centers in Spain. Despite its Roman and medieval remains, it is merely the second modern city of Catalonia.

The Romans captured Tarragona in 218 B.C., and during their rule the city sheltered one million people behind its 40-mile-long (64km) city walls. One of the four capitals of Catalonia when it was an ancient principality, and once the home of Julius Caesar, Tarragona today consists of an old quarter filled with interesting buildings, particularly the houses with connecting balconies. The upper walled town is mainly medieval, the town below newer.

In the new town, walk along Ramble Nova, a wide and fashionable boulevard that is the main artery of life. Running parallel with Ramble Nova to the east is the Ramble Vella, which marks the beginning of the old town. The city has a bullring, good hotels, and even beaches. The Romans were the first to designate Tarragona a resort town.

After seeing the attractions listed below, cap off your day with a stroll along the Balcó del Mediterráni (the Balcony of the Mediterranean), where the vistas are especially beautiful at sunset.

ESSENTIALS

GETTING THERE   Daily, 30 to 40 trains make the 1½-hour trip to and from the Barcelona-Sants station. Five trains per day make the 8-hour trip from Madrid. In Tarragona, the RENFE office is in the train station, Plaza Pedrera, s/n (☎ **977-24-02-02**).

From Barcelona, there are 10 buses per day to Tarragona (1½ hours); from Valencia 9 buses (3½ hours), and from Alicante 6 buses (6½ hours). Call ☎ **977-22-20-72** in Tarragona for more information.

To drive, take the **A-2** southwest from Barcelona to the **A-7,** then take the **N-340.** The route is well marked. This is a fast toll road. The one-way cost of the toll road from Barcelona to Tarragona is 1,200 ptas. ($8.05).

VISITOR INFORMATION   The **tourist information office** is at Fortuny, 4 (☎ **977-23-34-15**). It's open Monday through Friday from 9am to 3pm and 4 to 7pm, Saturday from 9am to 2pm.

EXPLORING THE TOWN

✪ **Amfiteatre Romà.** Parc del Milagro. ☎ **977-24-25-79.** Admission 475 ptas. ($3.20). June–Sept, Tues–Sun 10am-1:30pm and 4–5pm Bus: 1.

At the foot of Miracle Park and dramatically carved from a cliff that rises from the beach, the Roman amphitheater recalls the days in the 2nd century when thousands of Romans gathered here for amusement.

Catedral. Plaça de la Seu. ☎ **977-23-86-85.** Admission to cathedral and museum 300 ptas.($2). Mar 16–June 30, daily 10am–12:30pm and 4–6:45pm; July 1–Oct 15, daily 10am–7pm; Oct 16–Nov 15, daily 10am–12:30pm and 3–6pm; Nov 16–Mar 15, daily 10am–1:45pm. Bus: 1.

Situated at the highest point of Tarragona is this 12th-century cathedral, whose architecture represents the transition from Romanesque to Gothic. It has an enormous vaulted entrance, fine stained-glass windows, Romanesque cloisters, and an open choir. In the main apse, observe the altarpiece of St. Thecla, patron of Tarragona, carved by Pere Joan in 1430. Two flamboyant doors open into the chevet. The east gallery is the Museu Diocesà, with a collection of Catalan art.

Museu Nacional Arqueològic. Plaça del Rei, 5. ☎ **977-23-62-09.** Admission 400 ptas. ($2.70). June 1–Sept 30, Tues–Sat 10am–8pm, Sun 10am–2pm. Off-Season, Tues–Sat 10am–1:30pm and 4–7pm, Sun 10am–2pm. Bus: 8.

Overlooking the sea, the Archaeology Museum houses a collection of Roman relics— mosaics, ceramics, coins, silver, sculpture, and more. The outstanding attraction here is the *Head of Medusa*, with its penetrating stare.

✪ **Museu Necròpolis.** Paleocristians, Avinguda de Ramón y Cajal, 80. ☎ **977-251515.** Admission to Necròpolis plus museum 400 ptas. ($2.70). June 1–Sept 30, Tues–Sat 10am–8pm, Sun and holidays 10am–2pm; off-season, Tues–Sat 10am–1:30pm and 4–7pm, Sun and holidays 10am–2pm. Bus: 4.

This is one of the most important burial grounds in Spain, used by the Christians from the 3rd through the 5th centuries. It stands outside town next to a tobacco factory whose construction led to its discovery in 1923. While on the grounds, visit the Museu Paleocristià, which contains a number of sarcophagi and other objects discovered during the excavations.

Passeig Arqueològic. Plaça del Pallol. ☎ **977-24-57-96.** Admission 420 ptas. ($2.95). Oct–May, Mon–Sat 10am–1pm and 3–7pm, Sun and holidays 10am–2pm; June–Sept, Mon–Sat 9am–8pm, Sun and holidays 10am–2pm. Bus: 1.

At the far end of Plaça del Pallol, an archway leads to this half-mile walkway along the ancient ramparts, built by the Romans on top of cyclopean boulders. The ramparts have been much altered over the years, especially in medieval times and in the 1600s. There are scenic views from many points along the way.

SHOPPING

You'll find a scattering of handcraft shops throughout Tarragona's historic core, with a particularly dense concentration along the Ramble Nova. (Its central section is an all-pedestrian zone.) Any of them might provide a handcrafted souvenir of your visit. But for the densest concentration in town of shops and boutiques, head for the **Centro Commercial Parc Central,** on the Avinguda Roma. Although the main focus here revolves around a supermarket, the site also contains at least 40 shops selling whatever you'd need in terms of clothing, sundries, and household goods.

NEARBY THEME PARK THRILLS

A 10-minute ride from the heart of Barcelona, **Port Aventura Amusement Park,** Port Aventura (☎ **902-20-22-20**), is the biggest theme park in Spain. Universal Studios has acquired a prime stake in it and plans to make it even larger postmillennium. On a vast 2,000 acres, it will be expanded to become the largest entertainment center in Europe. Since its inauguration in 1995, it has already become one of the Mediterranean's favorite family destinations.

The park is a microcosm of five distinct worlds, with full-scale re-creations of classic villages ranging from Polynesia to Mexico, from China to the old American West. It also offers a thrilling variety of roller coaster and white-water rides, all centered on a lake on which you can travel via the deck of a Chinese junk.

Over the coming years Universal will expand the site, including, of course, a mammoth replica of a Hollywood studio lot. The park is open daily: March 26 to June 19, 10am to 8pm; June 20 to September 13, 10am to midnight; September 14 to January 11, 10am to 8pm. Admission costs 4,100 ptas. ($27.45) for adults, 3,100 ptas. ($20.75) for children. Nighttime admission goes for 2,500 ptas. ($16.75) for adults or 1,900 ptas. ($12.75) for children. The fee includes all shows and rides.

Some 50% of the trains on the Barcelona-Sitges-Tarragona line stop at Port Aventura. From Barcelona, the trip takes 1½ hours, a one-way fare costing 150 ptas. ($1). A taxi from the center of Tarragona costs 1,900 ptas. ($12.75) one-way.

WHERE TO STAY
EXPENSIVE

Hotel Imperial Tarraco. Paseo de las Palmeras/Rambla Vella, 43003 Tarragona. ☎ **977-23-30-40.** Fax 977/21-65-66. E-mail: imperial@ finet.fut.es. 170 units. A/C MINIBAR TV TEL. 10,000–25,000 ptas. ($67–$167.50) double; 22,000–35,000 ptas. ($147.40–$234.50) suite. AE, DC, MC, V. Free parking. Bus: 1.

Located about ¼ mile south of the cathedral, atop an oceanfront cliff whose panoramas include a sweeping view of both the sea and the Roman ruins, this hotel is the finest in town. Designed in the form of a crescent, it has guest rooms that may angle out to sea and almost always include small balconies. The accommodations, all with private bathrooms, are furnished with uncomplicated modern furniture and are a bit plain. However, all the beds are comfortable with fine linens and good mattresses.

The public rooms contain lots of polished white marble, Oriental carpets, and leather furniture. The staff responds well to the demands of both traveling businesspeople and art lovers on sightseeing excursions.

The hotel contains both a bar and a restaurant. Some Catalonian regional dishes are featured, and there is a menú del día for 3,999 ptas. ($26.80), although the food is rather standard. You'll also find an outdoor pool, tennis courts, and a pleasant garden.

MODERATE TO INEXPENSIVE

Hotel Astari. Vía Augusta, 95, 43003 Tarragona. ☎ **977-23-69-00.** Fax 977-23-69-11. E-mail: astari@tinet.fut.es. 83 units. TV TEL. 8,900 ptas. ($59.65) double. AE, DC, MC, V. Parking 900 ptas. ($6.05). Bus: 9.

In-the-know travelers in search of peace and quiet on the Mediterranean come to the Astari, which opened its doors back in 1959 and was last renovated in 1992. This five-story resort hotel on the Barcelona road offers fresh and airy, but rather plain, accommodations. Most rooms are small but each comes with a good bed and a well-maintained private bathroom with a hair dryer. Other features of the hotel include a swimming pool and a solarium. The Astari has long balconies and terraces, one favorite spot being the outer flagstone terrace with its umbrella tables set among willows, orange trees, and geranium bushes. There is a cafeteria as well as a cocktail lounge. This is the only hotel in Tarragona with garage space for each guest's car.

Hotel Lauria. Rambla Nova, 20, 43004 Tarragona. ☎ **977-23-67-12.** Fax 977-23-67-00. 72 units. A/C TV TEL. 9,500–10,000 ptas. ($63.65–$67) double. AE, DC, MC, V. Parking 1,000 ptas. ($6.70). Bus: 1.

Set less than half a block north of the town's popular seaside promenade (Passeig de les Palmeres), beside the tree-lined Rambla, this straightforward three-star hotel offers unpretentious, functional, and clean rooms, each of which has been recently modernized. Rooms range from small to medium in size, and each tiled bathroom is equipped with a hair dryer. For years considered the leading hotel of town, until the arrival of some newcomers, it still draws a loyal clientele of repeat visitors. The rooms in back open onto a view of the sea, a garden, and the hotel's swimming pool. Only the public rooms are air-conditioned. The ground floor contains an informal pizzeria.

Hotel Urbis. Carrer Reding, 20 bis, 43001 Tarragona. ☎ **800/528-1234** in the U.S. and Canada, or 977-24-01-16. Fax 977-24-36-54. E-mail:urbis@tinet.fut.es. 44 units. A/C MINIBAR TV TEL. 8,000–12,000 ptas. ($53.60–$80.40) double. Rates include buffet breakfast. AE, DC, DISC, MC, V. Parking 1,200 ptas. ($8.05). Bus: 3.

The rooms at this hotel off the Plaça de Corsini are three-star quality and much improved in recent years, with such added amenities as safes. Each is fitted with a double or twin bed with a comfortable mattress, and the tiled bathrooms have recently been renewed. The hotel also offers a restaurant with an English menu. The nearby tourist office will give you a map for exploring Tarragona.

Nuría. Vía Augusta, 217, 43007 Tarragona. ☎ **977-23-50-11.** Fax 977-24-41-36. 61 units. TV TEL. 7,000–9,500 ptas. ($46.90–$63.65) double. MC, V. Closed Nov–Mar. Parking 975 ptas. ($6.55). Bus: 1 or 9.

Built near the beach in 1967, this five-floor modern hotel offers neat, pleasant and well-kept though bland rooms, most with balconies. Accommodations are small but neatly arranged, each coming with a tiled bathroom with a hair dryer. You can dine in the sunny restaurant, where the specialty is romesco, a kind of *zarzuela* (seafood medley).

WHERE TO DINE

Barquet. Gasometro, 16. ☎ **977-24-00-23.** Reservations recommended. Main courses 2,500–5,000 ptas. ($16.75–$33.50); menú del día 1,300 ptas. ($8.70). AE, DC, MC, V. Mon–Sat 1–3:30pm and 8–11pm. Closed Aug. CATALAN/SEAFOOD.

In the center of town, within a 5-minute walk of the cathedral, this restaurant specializes in seafood and shellfish prepared in the Catalan style. It was established in 1950 in the cellar of a relatively modern building and today is run by the third generation of its original owners. Within a pair of nautical-themed dining rooms you can enjoy such dishes as *sopa de pescados* Tarragona style, *romesco* (ragout) of sea bass with herbs, a local assemblage of fried finned creatures identified for many hundreds of years as *fideos rossejats,* and several different preparations of sole and hake. If you're not interested in seafood, a choice of grilled veal, chicken, or beef is also offered. The list of Spanish and Catalan wines will complement any meal here. The staff is well-trained, polite, and proud of their Catalan antecedents.

Cafetería Arimany. Rambla Nova, 43–45. ☎ **977-23-79-31.** Reservations not necessary. Main courses 1,200–2,200 ptas. ($8.05–$14.75); fixed-price menu 1,550 ptas. ($10.40). AE, DC, MC, V. Daily 8am–midnight in winter and 8am–7pm in summer. Bus: 1. CATALAN/INTERNATIONAL.

When this central and popular cafeteria opens its doors at 8am, visitors and locals alike pour in for breakfast. Others come back for lunch, and some finish with a good-value dinner. You can eat here inexpensively or for more money, depending on your appetite. The shrimp in garlic oil is outstanding. Try the fresh fish of the day, based on the local catch, or perhaps squid cooked Roman style. The dessert specialty is "Pau Casals," named after a native Catalonian, the late, great cellist Pablo Casals. It is a chocolate cake served with a hot chocolate sauce. Another bakery specialty is *maginet* (a sugar cookie with nuts), the typical cookie of Tarragona.

Sol-Ric. Vía Augusta, 227. ☎ **977-23-20-32.** Reservations not necessary. Main courses 1,800–4,900 ptas. ($12.05–$32.85); fixed-price menu 1,600 ptas. ($10.70). AE, MC, V. Tues–Sat 1–4pm, Tues–Sun 8:30–11pm. Closed mid-Dec to mid-Jan. CATALAN/INTERNATIONAL.

Many guests remember the service here long after memories of the good cuisine have faded. Dating from 1859, the place has a rustic ambience, replete with antique farm implements hanging from the walls. There is an outdoor terrace as well as a central fireplace, usually blazing in winter. The chef prepares oven-baked hake with potatoes, tournedos with Roquefort, seafood stew, and several exotic fish dishes, among other specialties.

TARRAGONA AFTER DARK

Rambla Nova contains a handful of sleepy-looking bars, any of which might serve a cup of coffee or bottle of beer throughout the day and evening.

There's a little more action at the convivial **Club Nautico,** Passeig Marítimo, s/n (no phone), where tapas, wines, and drinks are served to an often crowded room that overlooks the sea. Similar bars in the town's medieval core include **Bar Anticuario,** carrer Santa Ana, s/n (no phone).

You might also try **Cucudrulus,** carrer del Protectorado/Pau de Protectorat, s/n (no phone), which is a pub with heavy English overtones, an international crowd, and a knack for presenting emerging rock and roll bands of varying degrees of talent. At **Bar Poetes,** carrer Sant Llorenç, 15 (no phone), live bands sometimes perform in a cellar located a very short walk from the cathedral.

Concerts and theatrical productions are staged in the city's cultural centerpiece, the **Teatro Metropol,** Rambla Nova, 46 (☎ **977-25-09-23**). Because of the language

The Beaches of Costa Dorada

Running along the entire coastline of the province of Tarragona, for some 131 miles (212km) from Cunit as far as Les Cases d'Alcanar, there is a series of excellent beaches and impressive cliffs, along with beautiful pine-covered headlands. In the city of Tarragona itself there is El Milagre beach, and a little farther north can be found the beaches of L'Arrabassade, Savinosa, dels Capellans, and the Llarga. At the end of the latter stands La Punta de la Mora, which has a 16th-century watchtower. The small towns of Altafulla and Torredembarra, both complete with castles, stand next to these beaches and are the location of many hotels and urban developments.

Farther north again are the two magnificent beaches of Comarruga and Sant Salvador. The first is particularly cosmopolitan, whereas the second is more secluded. Lastly come the beaches of Calafell, Segur, and Cunit, all with modern tourist complexes. You'll also find the small towns of Creixell, Sant Vicenç de Calders, and Clarà, which have wooded hills in the background.

South of Tarragona, the coastline forms a wide arc that stretches for miles and includes La Piñeda beach. El Recó beach fronts the Cape of Salou where, in among its coves, hills, and hidden-away corners, many hotels and residential centers are located. The natural port of Salou is nowadays a center for international tourism.

Continuing south toward Valencia, you next come to Cambrils, a maritime town with an excellent beach and an important fishing port. In the background stand the impressive Colldejou and Llaberia Mountains. Farther south are the beaches of Montroig and L'Hospitalet, as well as the small town of L'Ametlla de Mar with its small fishing port.

After passing the Balaguer massif, the traveler eventually reaches the delta of the River Ebro, a wide lowland area covering more than 300 miles (500km), opening like a fan into the sea. This is an area of rice fields, crisscrossed by branches of the River Ebro and by an enormous number of irrigation channels. There are also some lagoons that, because of their immense size, are ideal as hunting and fishing grounds. Moreover, there are some beaches over several miles in length and others in small, hidden-away estuaries. Two important towns in the region are Amposta, located on the River Ebro itself, and Sant Carles de la Ràpita, a 19th-century port town favored by King Carlos III.

The Costa Dorada extends to its most southwesterly point at the plain of Alcanar, a large area given over to the cultivation of oranges and other similar crops. Its beaches, along with the small hamlet of Les Cases d'Alcanar, mark the end of the Tarragona section of the Costa Dorada.

problem, you might skip theatrical events presented in Catalán, in favor of some of the musical and dance presentations.

SIDE TRIPS FROM TARRAGONA

If you rent a car, you can visit two attractions within a 30- to 45-minute drive from Tarragona. The first stop is the **Monestir de Poblet,** Plaça Corona d'Aragó, 11, E-43448 Poblet (☎ **977-7-02-54**), 29 miles (46.5km) northwest of Tarragona, one of the most intriguing monasteries in Spain. Its most exciting features are the oddly designed tombs of the old kings of Aragón and Catalonia. Constructed in the 12th and 13th centuries and still in use, Poblet's cathedral-like church reflects both Romanesque and Gothic architectural styles. Cistercian monks still live here, passing their days writing, studying, working a printing press, farming, and helping to restore the building, which suffered heavy damage during the 1835 revolution. Admission to the monastery costs 500 ptas. ($3.35) for adults and 300 ptas. ($2) for children 13 and under and students. From March to October, it's open daily 10am to 12:30pm and 3 to 6pm. From November to February, it's open daily 10am to 12:30pm and 3 to 5:30pm. Except for Monday, when no guide service is available, visits to the monastery are usually configured as part of tours, mostly in Spanish but with occasional English translations. These depart at 75-minute intervals throughout the monastery's opening hours.

About 3 miles (4.8km) farther, you can explore an unspoiled medieval Spanish town, **Montblanch.** At its entrance, a map pinpoints the principal artistic and architectural treasures—and there are many. Walk, don't drive, along the narrow, winding streets.

3 Sitges

25 miles (40km) S of Barcelona, 370 miles (596km) E of Madrid

Sitges is one of the most popular resorts of southern Europe, the brightest spot on the Costa Dorada. It is especially crowded in summer, mostly with affluent young northern Europeans, many of them gay. For years the resort largely drew prosperous middle-class industrialists from Barcelona, but those staid days have gone; Sitges is as swinging today as Benidorm and Torremolinos down the coast, but nowhere near as tacky.

Sitges has long been known as a city of culture, thanks in part to resident artist, playwright, and Bohemian mystic Santiago Rusiñol. The 19th-century modernismo movement began largely at Sitges, and the town remained the scene of artistic encounters and demonstrations long after the movement waned. Sitges continued as a resort of artists, attracting such giants as Salvador Dalí and poet Federico García Lorca. The Spanish Civil War (1936–39) erased what has come to be called the "golden age" of Sitges. Although other artists and writers arrived in the decades to follow, none had the name or the impact of those who had gone before.

ESSENTIALS

GETTING THERE   RENFE runs trains from Barcelona-Sants to Sitges, a 40-minute trip, costing 305 ptas. ($2.05). Call ☎ **93-490-02-02** in Barcelona for information about schedules. Four trains leave Barcelona per hour.

Sitges is a 45-minute drive from Barcelona along the **C-246,** a coastal road. An express highway, the **A-7,** opened in 1991. The coastal road is more scenic, but it can be extremely slow on weekends because of the heavy traffic, as all of Barcelona seemingly heads for the beaches.

VISITOR INFORMATION   The **tourist information office** is at Carrer Sínis Morera, 1 (☎ **93-894-42-51**). Open June through September 15, daily from 9am to 9pm; September 16 through May, Monday through Friday from 9am to 2pm and 4 to 6:30pm, Saturday from 10am to 1pm.

SPECIAL EVENTS   The **Carnaval** at Sitges is one of the outstanding events on the Catalan calendar. For more than a century, the town has celebrated the days before the beginning of Lent. Fancy dress, floats, feathered outfits, and sequins all make this an exciting event. The party begins on the Thursday before Lent with the arrival of the king of the Carnestoltes and ends with the Burial of a Sardine on Ash Wednesday. Activities reach their flamboyant best on Sant Bonaventura, where gay people hold their own celebrations.

We'll Have a Gay Old Time

Along with Ibiza, Key West, and Mikonos, Sitges has established itself firmly on the "A" list of gay resorts. It's a perfect destination for those who want a ready-made combination of beach and bars, all within a few minutes walk of each other. It also works well as a temporary, calmer alternative to Barcelona, which is 20 minutes away by train, and so is great for a day trip or a few days out of the city. Off-season, it's pretty quiet on the gay front apart from the carnival in February when hordes of gays and lesbians descend from Barcelona and then the party really begins.

Summer, however, is pure hedonistic playtime, and the town draws the boys in from all over Europe. Sitges is never going to tax the intellect, but it might well exhaust the body. There is a gay beach crammed with the usual overload of muscles and summer accessories in the middle of the town in front of the Passeig Maritim. The other beach is nudist and is farther out of town between Sitges and Vilanova. The best directions would be to go as far as the Atlantida disco and then follow the train track to the farther of the two beaches. The woods next to it are unsurprisingly packed with playful wildlife with short hair and deep tans.

FUN ON & OFF THE BEACH

The old part of Sitges used to be a fortified medieval enclosure. The castle is now the seat of the town government. The local parish church, called *La Punta* (The Point) and built next to the sea on top of a promontory, presides over an extensive maritime esplanade, where people parade in the early evening. Behind the side of the church are the Museu Cau Ferrat and the Museu Maricel (see below).

Most people are here to hit the beach. The beaches have showers, bathing cabins, and stalls; kiosks rent motorboats and water-sports equipment. Beaches on the eastern end and those inside the town center are the most peaceful—for example, **Aiguadoiç** and **Els Balomins. Playa San Sebastián, Fragata Beach,** and the **"Beach of the Boats"** (below the church and next to the yacht club) are the area's family beaches. A young, happening crowd heads for the **Playa de la Ribera,** to the west.

All along the coast women can and certainly do go topless. Farther west are the most solitary beaches, where the scene grows more racy, especially along the **Playas del Muerto,** where two tiny nude beaches lie between Sitges and Vilanova i la Geltrú. A shuttle bus runs between the cathedral and Golf Terramar. From Golf Terramar, go along the road to the club L'Atlántida, then walk along the railway. The first beach draws nudists of every sexual persuasion, and the second is almost solely gay. Be advised that lots of action takes place in the woods in back of these beaches.

MUSEUMS

Beaches aside, Sitges has some choice museums, which really shouldn't be missed.

Museu Cau Ferrat. Carrer del Fonollar. ☎ **93-894-03-64.** Admission 500 ptas. ($3.35) adults, 250 ptas. ($1.70) students, free for children under 16; combination ticket for 3 museums listed 800 ptas. ($5.35) adults, 400 ptas. ($2.70) students and children. June 22–Sept 10, Tues–Sat 9:30am–2pm and 4–9pm, Sun 9:30am–2pm; Sept 11–June 21, Tues–Fri 9:30am–2pm and 4–6pm, Sat 9:30am–2pm and 4–8pm, Sun 9:30am–2pm.

The Catalan artist Santiago Rusiñol combined two 16th-century cottages to make this house, where he lived and worked and which upon his death in 1931 he willed to Sitges along with his art collection. More than anyone else, Rusiñol made Sitges a popular resort. The museum collection includes two paintings by El Greco and several small Picassos, including *The Bullfight.* A number of Rusiñol's works are also on display. See the box on Rusiñol and his house/museum below.

Museu Maricel. Carrer del Fonallar. ☎ **93-894-03-64.** Admission 500 ptas. ($3.35) adults, 250 ptas. ($1.70) students, free for children under 16; admission included in combination ticket (see Museu Cau Ferrat, above). June 21–Sept 11, Tues–Sat 9:30am–2pm and 4–8pm, Sun 9:30am–2pm; Sept 12–June 20, Tues–Fri 9:30am–2pm and 4–6pm, Sat 9:30am–2pm and 4–8pm, Sun 9:30am–2pm.

Opened by the king and queen of Spain, Museu Maricel contains art donated by Dr. Jesús Pérez Rosales. The palace, owned by American Charles Deering when it was built right after World War I, is made up of two parts connected by a small bridge. The museum has a good collection of Gothic and Romantic paintings and sculptures, as well as many fine Catalan ceramics. There are also three noteworthy works by Santiago Rebull and an allegorical painting of World War I by José María Sert.

Museu Romàntic ("Can Llopis"). Sant Gaudenci, 1. ☎ **93-894-29-69.** Admission 500 ptas. ($3.35) adults, 250 ptas. ($1.70) students, free for children under 16; admission included in combination ticket (see above). June 21–Sept 11, Tues–Sat 9:30am–2pm and 4–8pm, Sun 9:30am–2pm; Sept 12–June 20, Tues–Fri 9:30am–2pm and 4–6pm, Sat 9:30am–2pm and 4–8pm, Sun 9:30am–2pm.

This museum re-creates the daily life of a Sitges land-owning family in the 18th and 19th centuries. The family rooms, furniture, and household objects are most interesting. You'll also find wine cellars, and an important collection of antique dolls (upstairs).

WHERE TO STAY

In spite of a building spree, Sitges just can't handle the large numbers of tourists who flock here in July and August. By mid-October just about everything—including hotels, restaurants, and bars—slows down considerably or closes altogether.

EXPENSIVE

Hotel Calípolis. Avinguda Sofia, 2-4, 08870 Sitges. ☎ **93-894-15-00.** Fax 93-894-07-64. 170 units. A/C MINIBAR TV TEL. 17,440–21,400 ptas. ($116.85–$143.40) double; 29,425–41,105 ptas. ($197.15–$275.40) suite. AE, DC, MC, V. Parking 2,000 ptas. ($13.40).

This 11-story hotel fits in a gently undulating curve against the resort's beachfront and seaside promenade. The good-size rooms contain expansive balconies, individual safes, satellite TV hookups, marble-sheathed bathrooms, and a comfortably conservative decor of contemporary furniture. Most offer sea views; the remainder offer views of the mountains.

Dining/Diversions: The hotel restaurant includes a flowering outdoor terrace and offers formal service with both international and Catalonian specialties. There's also a bar.

Amenities: Concierge, baby-sitting, car rentals, excursions to nearby tennis courts and golf courses, horseback riding, sailing, and trips to nearby historic monasteries can be arranged. The parking lot is available only during the congested summer months; the lot closes when street parking becomes available again in the fall.

Meliá Gran Sitges. El Puerto de Aiguadolç, 08870 Sitges. ☎ **800/336-3542** in the U.S., or 93-811-08-11. Fax 93-894-90-34. 307 units. A/C MINIBAR TV TEL. Mon–Thurs 22,500 ptas. ($150.75) double; Fri–Sun 15,000 ptas. ($100.50) double; 32,500 ptas. ($217.75) suite throughout week. Weekend rates include breakfast. AE, DC, MC, V. Parking 1,300 ptas. ($8.70).

Designed with steeply sloping sides, reminiscent of a pair of interconnected Aztec pyramids, this hotel was built in 1992 as housing for spectators and participants in the Barcelona Olympics. Angled to curve around two sides of a large swimming pool and set a few yards from the beach, the hotel contains a white-marble lobby with what feels

Rusiñol: The Enigmatic Figure of Modernismo

Cau Ferrat was the home and studio of artist and writer Santiago Rusiñol. Born in Barcelona in 1861, he was one of the most enigmatic figures of *modernismo,* or Catalan art nouveau, a literary and artistic trend that represented a spiritualist reaction to 19th-century positivism. He died in Aranjuez in 1931.

On return from a trip to Italy in 1892, he bought a couple of terraced fisher's cottages that had been built on the edge of a rocky coastline. Then he commissioned the architect Francesc Rogent to build a new house on the ground where the cottages stood.

Rusiñol described Cau Ferrat as a "refuge for those whose heart no longer feels the warmth it needs, a place to rest the spirit that has become weary from the toil of life, a hermitage near the sea for those injured by indifference and a hostel for the pilgrims of Holy Poetry."

Today, the collection at Cau Ferrat that arouses most interest is the painting and drawing collection. Works by the most outstanding artists of the modernismo period can be seen here—such artists as Ramón Casas, Aleix Clapés, Pere Ferran, Joan Llimona, Arcadi Mas i Fontdevila, Isidre Nonell, Dario de Regoyos, Miquel Utrillo, and Ignacio Zuloaga. There are also works by younger artists such as Herman Anglada i Camarasa and Picasso. Rusiñol's work is represented by a wide range of styles, from realism to symbolism.

Cau Ferrat is a treasure chest containing a large number of private objects, objects that are inseparable from the private and social life of its creator. There are portraits of friends Casellas, Eleonora Duse, Casas, Utrillo, and Benito Pérez Galdós.

The Catalan writer Josep Pla defined Rusiñol as a "man who was horrified by industrial civilization, who postulated freedom in all domains, who tended to replace reality by literature and reason by sentiments, fascinated by nature and gardens, who searched for vagrancy and melancholy, sentimental expression, who valued the inaccessible, death and nihilism, dreams and indecision."

An outstanding painter and a renowned satirical writer, novelist, and dramatist, Rusiñol lived in Paris when impressionism made its appearance. In his own artwork he employed many elements of impressionism as far as technique, light, and color were concerned. However, he portrayed his own private and lyrical world. Rusiñol considered painting to be a spiritual language that transmitted his poetry rather than a medium that reflected the real world.

---

like the largest window in Spain, overlooking a view of the mountains. Each midsize room is outfitted in shades of blue, includes many of the electronic amenities you'd expect and comes with a large, furnished veranda for sunbathing. Each of the immaculately kept tiled bathrooms come with a hair dryer. Many guests at this hotel are here to participate in any of dozens of conferences and conventions held frequently within the establishment's battery of high-tech convention facilities. It's about a 15-minute walk east of the center of Sitges, near the access roads leading to Barcelona.

Dining/Diversions: The in-house restaurant, Morai, offers international and Catalonian cuisine with attentive service. The hotel also has two bars.

Amenities: Concierge, baby-sitting, barber shop, room service, and safety security boxes.

MODERATE

El Galeón. Sant Francesc, 44, 08870 Sitges. ☎ **93-894-06-12.** Fax 93-894-63-35. 74 units. AC, TV TEL. 6,700–11,200 ptas. ($44.90–$75.05) double. Rates include breakfast. MC, V. Closed Oct 20–Apr. Parking 1,500 ptas. ($10.05).

A leading three-star hotel only a short walk from both the beach and the Plaça d'Espanya, this well-styled hostelry blends a bit of the old Spain with the new. The small public rooms feel cozy, whereas the good-size guest rooms, accented with wood grain, have a more streamlined aura. Each comes with a comfortable bed, plus a well-maintained private bathroom with a shower stall. The hotel has a swimming pool and a patio in the rear.

Hotel Romàntic de Sitges. Carrer de Sant Isidre, 33, 08870 Sitges. ☎ **93-894-83-75.** Fax 93-894-81-67. 60 units. TEL. 9,300–10,950 ptas. ($62.30–$73.35) double. Rates include breakfast. AE, MC, V. Closed Nov–Mar 15.

Made up of three beautifully restored 19th-century villas, this hotel lies only a short walk from both the beach and the train station. The romantic bar is an international rendezvous, and the public rooms are filled with artworks. You can have breakfast either in the dining room or in the garden filled with mulberry trees. Rooms range in size from small to medium, and each is well maintained with good beds and tiled bathrooms. Overflow guests are housed in a nearby annex, the Hotel de la Renaixença.

Hotel Platjador. Passeig de la Ribera, 35, 08870 Sitges. ☎ **93-894-50-54.** Fax 93-811-03-84 60 units. A/C TV TEL. 7,400–13,400 ptas. ($49.60–$89.80) double. Rates include breakfast. MC, V. Closed Nov–Apr.

One of the best hotels in town, the Platjador, on the esplanade fronting the beach, has comfortably furnished and recently restored guest rooms, all with private bathrooms and many with big French doors opening onto balconies and sea views. There is also a swimming pool. The dining room, facing the beach, is known for its good cuisine, including gazpacho, paella, fresh fish, and flan for dessert.

INEXPENSIVE

Hotel El Cid. San José, 39 bis, 08870 Sitges. ☎ **93-894-18-42.** Fax 93-894-6335. 77 units. 5,200–8,400 ptas. ($34.85–$56.30) double. Rates include continental breakfast. MC, V. Closed Nov–May.

El Cid's exterior suggests Castile and inside, appropriately enough, you'll find beamed ceilings, natural stone walls, heavy wrought-iron chandeliers, and leather chairs. The same theme is carried out in the rear dining room and in the pleasantly furnished rooms, which, though small, are still quite comfortable, with fine beds and linens. Breakfast is the only meal served. The hotel has a top-floor swimming pool and solarium. El Cid lies off the Passeig de Vilanova in the center of town.

Hotel Subur. Passeig de la Ribera, s/n, 08870 Sitges. ☎ **93-894-00-66.** Fax 93-894-69-86. 96 units. A/C MINIBAR TV TEL. 11,600 ptas. ($77.70) double. Rates include breakfast. AE, DC, MC, V. Parking 1,200 ptas. ($8.05).

The first hotel built in Sitges (in 1916), the Subur was later torn down and reconstructed in 1960 and last renovated in 1992. Today, as always, it occupies a prominent position in the center of town on the seafront. Its small rooms are well furnished, with balconies opening onto the Mediterranean. The dining room, decorated with fine woods, offers a bountiful table of both regional and international dishes, and there is a menú del día for guests only for 2,000 ptas. ($13.40). The hotel remains open year-round, even during the cooler months.

Sitges Park Hotel. Carrer Jesús, 16, 08870 Sitges. ☎ **93-894-02-50.** Fax 95-894-08-39. www.el-garrafinet/sitgesparkhotel. 85 units. A/C TV TEL. 7,300–11,000 ptas. ($48.90–$73.70) double. AE, DC, MC, V. Closed Dec–Feb.

Outside, the Sitges Park has an 1880s redbrick facade. Inside, past the desk, a beautiful garden with palm trees and a swimming pool awaits. This was once a private villa, owned by a family that made its fortune in Cuba. Rooms come in various shapes and sizes, but each is well furnished with good beds, plus a well-kept private bathroom clad in tiles. You'll find a good restaurant downstairs, and you can have your coffee or drinks indoors or outdoors at the cafe/bar, surveying the landmark Catalan tower on the premises. The hotel is about 50 yards from the bus station.

WHERE TO DINE
EXPENSIVE

El Velero. Passeig de la Ribera, 38. ☎ **93-894-20-51.** Reservations required. Main courses 1,750–4,950 ptas. ($11.75–$33.15); fixed-price menu 3,000 ptas. ($20.10). AE, DC, MC, V. Daily 1:30–4pm and 8:30–11:30pm. SEAFOOD.

This is one of the leading restaurants of Sitges, occupying a position along the beachfront promenade. The most desirable tables are found on the glass greenhouse terrace, opening onto the esplanade, although there is a more glamorous restaurant inside. Try a soup such as clam and truffle or whitefish, followed by a main dish such as paella marinara (with seafood) or supreme of salmon in pine-nut sauce.

MODERATE

Chez Jeanette. Sant Pau, 23. ☎ **93-894-00-48.** Reservations recommended. Main courses 1,000–2,650 ptas. ($6.70–$17.75); menú del día 1,675–1,850 ptas. ($11.20–$12.40). AE, DC, V. Daily 7–11:30pm, Sat–Sun 1–4pm. Closed Dec 20–Jan 15. INTERNATIONAL.

A Frenchwoman named Jeanette established a Catalan-style restaurant here in 1975. She has since died, but her culinary tradition continues. Patrons flock to the rustic atmosphere created by textured stucco walls and a regional tavern decor. Set back on a restaurant-flanked street a short walk from the beach, it draws both straight and gay clients. From the standard menu, you can order such dishes as onion soup, *rape* (monkfish) with whisky, and entrecôte with Roquefort sauce. There are also several *platos del día.* The chef is proudest of his *parilla pescada,* a mixed grill of fresh fish from the Mediterranean.

✪ Els Quatre Gats. Sant Pau, 13. ☎ **93-894-19-15.** Reservations recommended. Main courses 3,000–4,500 ptas. ($20.10–$30.15); menú del día 2,200 ptas. ($14.75). AE, DC, MC, V. Thurs–Tues 1–4pm and 8–11pm. Closed Nov–Mar. CATALAN.

When it was established in the early 1960s as a bar and cafe, it adopted the name of one of Catalonia's most historic cafes, Els 4 Gats, a Barcelona hangout that had been a favorite of Picasso. By 1968 the newcomer was firmly established as one of the leading restaurants in Sitges, serving a well-received *cocina del mercado,* based on whatever was fresh and available that day in the local markets. In a setting accented with paintings and varnished paneling, you can enjoy fresh grilled fish, garlic soup, lamb cutlets with local herbs, roast chicken in wine sauce, and veal kidneys in sherry sauce. Set on a side street near the sea, the restaurant is a few steps from the beachfront Passeig de la Ribera.

Fragata. Passeig de la Ribera, 1. ☎ **93-894-10-86.** Reservations recommended. Main dishes 2,500–3,200 ptas. ($16.75–$21.45). AE, DC, MC, V. Daily 1–4:30pm and 8:30–11:30pm. SEAFOOD.

Although its simple interior offers little more than well-scrubbed floors, tables with crisp napery, and air-conditioning, some of the most delectable seafood specialties in town are served here, and hundreds of loyal customers come to appreciate the fresh, authentic cuisine. Specialties include seafood soup, a mixed grill of fresh fish, codfish salad, mussels marinara, several preparations of squid and octopus, plus some flavorful meat dishes, such as grilled lamb cutlets.

La Masía. Passeig Vilanova, 164. ☎ **93-894-10-76.** Reservations required. Main courses 1,450–2,950 ptas. ($9.70–$19.75); menú del día 1,500 ptas. ($10.05). AE, DC, MC, V. Daily 1–4pm and 8:30–11:30pm. CATALAN.

A provincial decor complements the imaginative regional specialties for which this place has been known since 1972. They include several preparations of codfish, roast suckling lamb well seasoned with herbs, *pollo ajillo* (garlic chicken, a regional dish), a wide array of fresh fish and shellfish, and monkfish with aioli—the chef's pride. Every Catalonian's favorite dessert is *crema Catalana* (caramel pudding). If you prefer to dine outdoors, you can sit in the pleasant garden adjacent to the main dining room.

Mare Nostrum. Passeig de la Ribera, 60. ☎ **93-894-33-93.** Reservations required. Main courses 2,250–2,400 ptas. ($15.10–$18.75). AE, DC, MC, V. Thurs–Tues 1–4:30pm and 8–11pm. Closed Dec 15–Feb 1. SEAFOOD.

This landmark restaurant was established in 1950 within what had been a private home built in the 1890s. It has flourished ever since. The dining room has a waterfront view, and in warm weather tables are placed outside. The menu includes a full range of seafood dishes, among them grilled fish specialties and steamed hake with champagne. The fish soup is particularly delectable. Next door, the restaurant's cafe serves ice cream, milk shakes, sandwiches, a selection of tapas, and three varieties of sangría, including one with champagne and fruit.

Oliver's. Isla de Cuba, 39. ☎ **93-894-35-16.** Reservations required. Main courses 1,650–2,200 ptas. ($11.05–$14.75). MC, V. Sat–Sun 1–4pm, Tues–Sun 8:30pm–11:30. CATALAN/INTERNATIONAL.

On the northern fringe of the old town, directly south of the Plaça de Maristany, this angular bistro-style establishment is decorated like a regional tavern with local paintings. It is a good choice for dinner, unless you insist on being on the beachfront esplanade, 5 minutes away. The wines are reasonably priced, and the seafood is excellent—look for the chef's daily specials. Also try the grilled salmon, entrecôte flavored with herbs of Provence, grilled goat cutlets, or a daily soup prepared with fresh ingredients.

SITGES AFTER DARK

One of the best ways to pass an evening in Sitges is to walk the waterfront esplanade, have a leisurely dinner, then retire at about 11pm to one of the open-air cafes for a nightcap and some serious people-watching. Few local dives can compete with the scene taking place on the streets.

If you're straight, you may have to hunt to find a bar that isn't predominantly gay. There are so many gay bars, in fact, that a map is distributed pinpointing their locales. Nine of them are concentrated on **Carrer Sant Bonaventura** in the center of town, a 5-minute walk from the beach (near the Museu Romàntic). If you grow bored with the action in one place, you just have to walk down the street to find another. Drink prices run about the same in all the clubs.

Mediterráneo, Sant Bonaventura, 6 (no phone), is the largest gay disco and bar. It sports a formal Iberian garden and sleek modern styling. And upstairs in this restored

1690s house just east of the Plaça d'Espanya, there are pool tables and a covered terrace. On summer nights, the place is filled to overflowing.

Other gay bars include **Bourbon's,** Sant Bonaventura, 13 (☎ **93-894-33-47**), which appeals to a predominately youngish crowd, and **El Candil,** Carrer de la Carreta, 9 (no phone), where the age range is wider and which has a dark room and video shows. **El Horno,** Joan Tarrida, 6 (☎ **93-894-09-09**), with slight leather overtones that grow more prominent as the night progresses, opens earlier, at 5:30pm, and also features videos and a dark room.

Another of the town's most popular and crowded nightspots, with DJs spinning the latest dance hits, is **Ricky's Disco,** Sant Pau, 25 (☎ **93-894-96-81**), which charges a cover of 1,200 ptas. ($8.05). This place caters to an international mix of gay and straight visitors. It's set back from the beach on a narrow street noted for its inexpensive restaurants and folkloric color.

Trailer, Angel Vidal, 36 (no phone), is a large, extremely popular club and the best place to end the night. It closes at 5:30am, and the entry cost of 1,500 ptas. ($10.05) includes the price of a drink.

12

Girona & the Costa Brava

The Costa Brava, the so-called wild coast, is a 95-mile (153km) stretch of coastline—the northernmost Mediterranean seafront in Spain—that begins north of Barcelona at Blanes and stretches toward the French border. Visit this area in May, June, September, or October and avoid July and August, when tour groups from northern Europe book virtually all the hotel rooms.

Undiscovered little fishing villages along the coast long ago bloomed into resort towns. **Tossa de Mar** is the most delightful of these. **Lloret de Mar** is also immensely popular but too commercial and overdeveloped for many tastes. The most unspoiled spot is remote **Cadaqués.** Some of the smaller villages also make excellent stops.

If you want to visit the Costa Brava but simply cannot secure a room in high season, consider taking a day trip by car from Barcelona or booking one of the daily organized tours that leave from that city. Allow plenty of time for driving. In summer the traffic jams can be fierce, and the roads between towns difficult and winding.

If you visit the coast in summer without a hotel reservation, you'll stand a fair chance of getting a room in Girona, the capital of the province and one of the most interesting medieval cities in Spain.

1 Girona

60 miles (97km) NE of Barcelona, 56 miles (90km) S of the French city of Perpignan

Founded by the Romans, Girona is one of the most important historical sites in Spain. Later, it became a Moorish stronghold. Later still, it reputedly withstood three invasions by Napoléon's troops (1809). For that and other past sieges, Girona is often called "The City of a Thousand Sieges."

Split by the Onyar River, this sleepy medieval city attracts crowds of tourists darting inland from the Costa Brava for the day. For orientation purposes, go to the ancient stone footbridge across the Onyar. From here, you'll have the finest view. Bring good walking shoes, as the only way to discover the particular charm of this medieval city is on foot. You can wander for hours through the **Call,** the labyrinthine old quarter, with its narrow, steep alleyways and lanes and its ancient stone houses, which form a rampart chain along the Onyar. Much of Girona can be appreciated from the outside, but it does contain some important attractions you'll want to see on the inside.

Girona & the Costa Brava

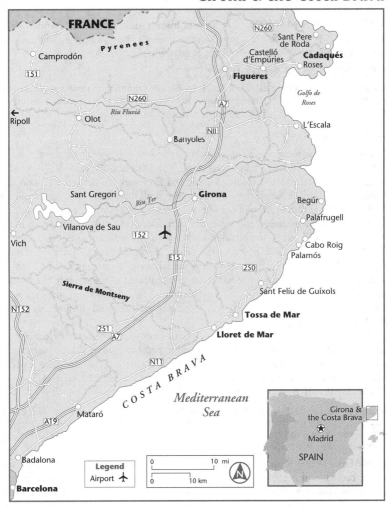

ESSENTIALS

GETTING THERE   More than 26 trains per day run between Girona and Barcelona from 6:08am to 9:26pm, including two TALGOS. Trip time is 1 to 2 hours, depending on the train. Trains arrive in Girona at the Plaça Espanya (☎ **972-20-70-93** for information).

From the Costa Brava, you can take one of the SARFA buses (☎ **972-20-17-96** in Girona) to Girona. Three per day depart from Tossa de Mar (see below). Barcelona Bus (☎ **972-20-24-32** in Girona) also operates express buses between Girona and Barcelona at the rate of 6 to 13 per day, depending on the season and demand.

From Barcelona or the French border, drivers connect with the main north-south route (A-7), taking the turnoff to Girona. From Barcelona, take the A-2 north to reach the A-7.

VISITOR INFORMATION The **tourist information office** is at **Rambla de la Libertat** (☎ **972-22-65-75**). Open Monday through Friday from 8am to 8pm, Saturday from 8am to 2pm and 4 to 8pm, Sunday from 9am to 2pm.

EXPLORING THE MEDIEVAL CITY

Catedral. Plaça de la Catedral. ☎ **972-21-44-26.** Free admission to cathedral; cloister and museum 400 ptas. ($2.70). Cathedral, daily 9am–1pm and during cloister and museum visiting hours; cloister and museum, July–Sept, Tues–Sat 10am–8pm, Sun 10am–2pm; Oct–Feb, Tues–Sat 10am–2pm and 4–6pm, Sun 10am–2pm; Mar–June, Tues–Sat 10am–2pm and 4–7pm, Sun 10am–2pm.

Girona's major attraction is its magnificent cathedral, reached by climbing a 17th-century baroque staircase of 90 steep steps. The 14th-century cathedral represents many architectural styles, including Gothic and Romanesque, but it is most notably Catalan baroque. The facade that you see as you climb those long stairs dates from the 17th and 18th centuries; from a cornice on top rises a bell tower crowned by a dome with a bronze angel weathervane. Enter the main door of the cathedral and go into the nave, which, at 75 feet, is the broadest in the world of Gothic architecture.

The cathedral contains many works of art, displayed for the most part in its museum. Its prize exhibit is a tapestry of the Creation, a unique piece of 11th- or 12th-century Romanesque embroidery depicting humans and animals in the Garden of Eden. The other major work displayed is one of the world's rarest manuscripts—the 10th-century *Códex del Beatus,* which contains an illustrated commentary on the Book of the Apocalypse.

From the cathedral's Chapel of Hope, a door leads to a Romanesque cloister from the 12th and 13th centuries, with an unusual trapezoidal layout. The cloister gallery, with a double colonnade, has a series of biblical scenes that are the prize jewel of Catalan Romanesque art. From the cloister you can view the 12th-century Torre de Carlemany (Charlemagne's Tower).

Museu d'Art. Pujada de la Catedral, 12. ☎ **972-20-38-34.** Admission 300 ptas. ($2) adults, 225 ptas. ($1.50) for students and adults over 65, free for children. Mar–Sept, Tues–Sat 10am–7pm (June–Aug, Wed hours are 10am–2pm), Sun 10am–2pm; Oct–Feb, Tues–Sat 10am–6pm, Sun 10am–2pm. Closed Jan 1, Jan 6, Easter Sun, and Dec 25–26.

Located in a former Romanesque and Gothic Episcopal palace (Palau Episcopal) next to the cathedral, this museum displays artworks spanning 10 centuries (once housed in the old Diocesan Museum and the Provincial Museum). Stop in the throne room to view the altarpiece of Sant Pere of Púbol by Bernat Martorell and that of Sant Miguel de Crüilles by Lluís Borrassa. Both of these works, from the 15th century, are exemplary pieces of Catalan Gothic painting. The museum is also proud of its altar stone of Sant Pere de Roda, which dates from the 10th and 11th centuries; this work in wood and stone, depicting figures and legends, was once covered in embossed silver. The 12th-century *Crüilles Timber* is a unique piece of Romanesque polychrome wood. *Our Lady of Besalù,* from the 15th century, is one of the best Virgins carved in alabaster.

Banys Arabs. Carrer Ferran el Catôlic. ☎ **972-21-32-62.** Admission 200 ptas. ($1.35). Apr–Sept, Mon–Sat 10am–7pm, Sun 10am–2pm; Oct–Mar, Tues–Sun 10am–2pm. Closed Jan 1, Jan 6, Easter Sun, and Dec 25–26.

These 12th-century Arab baths, an example of Romanesque civic architecture, are found in the old quarter of the city. Visit the *caldarium* (hot bath), with its paved floor, and the *frigidarium* (cold bath), with its central octagonal pool surrounded by pillars that support a prismlike structure in the overhead window. Although the Moorish baths were heavily restored in 1929, they give you an idea of what the ancient ones were like.

Museu Arqueològic. Sant Pere de Galligants, Santa Llúcia, 1. ☎ **972-20-26-32.** Admission 300 ptas. ($2) adults, 225 ptas. ($1.50) children and students. Tues–Sat 10am–1pm and 4:30–7pm, Sun 10am–1pm.

Housed in a Romanesque church and cloister from the 11th and 12th centuries, this museum illustrates the history of the country from the Paleolithic to the Visigothic periods, using artifacts discovered in nearby excavations. The monastery itself ranks as one of the best examples of Catalan Romanesque architecture. In the cloister, note some Hebrew inscriptions from gravestones of the old Jewish cemetery.

Museu d'História de la Ciutat. Carrer de la Força. ☎ **972-22-22-29.** Free admission. Tues–Sat 10am–2pm and 5–7pm, Sun 10am–2pm.

Housed in the old 18th-century Capuchin Convent de Sant Antoni, this collection dates from the time of Puig d'en Roca (Catalonia's oldest prehistoric site) to the present. It includes Girona's (and Spain's) first electric streetlights. Additional displays of tools, technical materials, and the accoutrements of passing lifestyles make up a kind of municipal resume. From the original Capuchin convent, there remains the cemetery used for drying corpses before mummifying them (one of three of this type left in the world).

Església de Sant Feliu. Pujada de Sant Feliu. ☎ **972-20-14-07.** Free admission. Daily 9–10:30am, 11:30am–1pm, and 4–6:30pm. Holidays 4–6:30pm.

This 14th-to 17th-century church was built over what may have been the tomb of Feliu of Africa, martyred during Diocletian's persecution at the beginning of the 4th century. Important in the architectural history of Catalonia, the church has pillars and arches in the Romanesque style and a Gothic central nave. The bell tower—one of the Girona skyline's most characteristic features—has eight pinnacles and one central tower, each supported on a solid octagonal base. The main facade of the church is baroque. The interior contains some exceptional works, including an altarpiece from the 16th century and an alabaster *Reclining Christo* from the 14th century. Notice the eight pagan and Christian sarcophagi set in the walls of the presbytery, the two oldest of which are from the 2nd century A.D. One shows Pluto carrying Persephone off to the depths of the earth.

SHOPPING

Consistent with its role as an international seaside resort, Girona contains a network of shops that cater to everything from sportswear to formal wear. The most appealing, and densely inventoried, shopping street is the **carrer Santa Clara,** one of whose most visible shops is **Adolfo Domínguez,** carrer Santa Clara, 36 (☎ 972-22-29-61), whose inventories of men's and women's clothing derives from Spain and the rest of Europe. For men's and women's sportswear, try **Tommy,** Rambla Llibertat, 28 (☎ 972-22-36-93); or its almost-adjacent neighbor specializing only in women's clothing, **Casual,** Rambla Llibertat, s/n (no phone). Finally, consider **Zara,** Carrer Joán Maragall, s/n (☎ 972-22-13-05), as a stylish but very affordable emporium for both men and women.

If handcrafts appeal to you, consider a 20-mile eastward trek from Girona to the hamlet of **La Bispal,** which is set more or less midway between Girona and the town of Palamos. (From Girona, follow the signs pointing to Palamos.) Here, rows of simple shops display and sell the output of dozens of artisans who labor to produce sturdy, artfully rustic ceramics, some of which are too bulky to ship, others which can be packed and carried as part of your carry-on luggage. But if a hot and dusty trek outside of Girona doesn't appeal to you, you can acquire an impressive selection of La Bispal's ceramics at somewhat more expensive prices at a Girona-based branch of one of La Bispal's most visible producers, **Vila Clara,** Vallesteries, 40 (☎ 972-22-37-78).

WHERE TO STAY
MODERATE

Costabella. Avinguda de França, 61, 17007 Girona. ☎ **972-20-25-24.** Fax 972-20-22-03. 46 units. A/C MINIBAR TV TEL. 9,900–12,900 ptas. ($66.35–$86.45) double. AE, DC, MC, V. Free parking.

Built in the 1960s and renovated in 1989 and again in 1999, this hotel lies about 2 miles (3km) north of Girona's center, beside the N-11 highway leading to Figueres, near the town's largest hospital. The midsize rooms are comfortable, outfitted in pastel colors, and conservatively modern, each fitted with good beds and tiled bathrooms. The in-house restaurant serves fixed-price meals, and breakfast is a generous buffet.

Hotel Sol Girona. Carrer Barcelona, 112, 17003 Girona. ☎ **800-336-3542** in the U.S., or 972-24-32-32. Fax 972-24-32-33. 113 units. A/C MINIBAR TV TEL. 14,500 ptas. ($97.15) double; 20,900 ptas. ($140.05) suite. AE, DC, MC, V. Parking 1,300 ptas. ($8.70).

A short drive southwest of Girona's historic center, in an industrial and commercial neighborhood with heavy traffic, this member of the widely known Sol chain is the most prestigious hotel in town, a position it has maintained since it opened in 1989. A favorite of both businesspeople and visiting art lovers, it offers calm, quiet, and tastefully comfortable midsize accommodations, many with king-size beds and all with elegant bathrooms amply stocked with toiletries.

The hotel lies immediately adjacent to one of Girona's largest shopping malls, which provides lots of diversions. The in-house restaurant, **Espai,** serves international and continental cuisine, and there is an adjacent bar. Services include a concierge, laundry, baby-sitting, and 24-hour room service.

Hotel Ultonia. Avinguda Jaume I, 22, 17001 Girona. ☎ **972-20-38-50.** Fax 972-20-33-34. 45 units. A/C MINIBAR TV TEL. 9,900–12,000 ptas. ($66.35–$80.40) double. AE, DC, MC, V. Parking 800 ptas. ($5.35) nearby.

A three-star hotel just a short walk from the Plaça de la Independència, the Ultonia was restored in 1993 and is now better than ever. Ever since the late 1950s it has been a favorite with business travelers, but today it attracts more tourists, as it lies close to the historical district. Rooms are compact and furnished in modern style with functional but comfortable beds. Double-glazed windows keep out the noise. Some of the rooms opening onto the avenue have tiny balconies. In just 8 to 12 minutes, you can cross the Onyar into the medieval quarter. Guests enjoy a breakfast buffet in the morning, but no other meals are served.

Novotel Girona. Carretera del Aeropuerto, 17457 Riudellots de la Selva (Girona). ☎ **800/ 221-4542** in the U.S., or 972-47-71-00. Fax 972-47-72-96. www.novotel.com. 81 units. A/C MINIBAR TV TEL. 11,500–14,000 ptas. ($77.05–$93.80) double; 14,000–16,000 ptas. ($93.80–$107.20) suite. Children under 16 free in parents' room. AE, DC, MC, V. Free parking. Take exit 8 from the A-7 motorway, signposted a few miles west of the Girona city center.

Low-slung, modern and set within a sunny, tree-dotted park, this member of a French chain offers some of the most consistently reliable accommodations and best values in the region. Located beside the A-7 motorway, just south of the Girona airport and a short drive west of the city center, Novotel Girona offers comfortable and efficient midsize rooms with soundproofed windows, large writing tables, and a simple modern decor much appreciated by both families and businesspeople.

The clean and modern restaurant Le Grill serves à la carte meals daily from 6am to 3am. There's also a bar. Room service is offered from 6am to midnight daily, plus there's a concierge and laundry service. Car rentals can be arranged at the hotel, and guests enjoy the outdoor pool set within a garden and the tennis court.

INEXPENSIVE

Condal. Joan Maragall, 10, 17002 Girona. ☎ and fax **972-20-44-62.** 38 units. 5,350–6,350 ptas. ($35.85–$42.55) double. AE, MC, V.

Located near the rail and bus stations west of the old town, this third-class 1960s hotel is, in the words of one frequent visitor, "aggressively simple." As such, it's recommended to bargain hunters only. The lounge and reception area are small; there is no elevator; and no meals (not even breakfast) are served—but these are minor concerns. The small rooms are clean and functional, and some of them open onto pleasant views. Each comes with a comfortable bed. The attendants speak only a little English, but they are more than willing to try.

Hotel Peninsular. Carrer Nou, 5, 17001 Girona. ☎ **972-20-38-00.** Fax 972-21-04-92. 45 units. TV TEL. 6,000 ptas. ($40.20) double. AE, DC, MC, V. Parking 750 ptas. ($5.05) nearby.

Devoid of any significant architectural character, this one-star hotel provides clean but uncontroversial accommodations in a location near the cathedral and the river. The small rooms, which benefited from a 1990 renovation, are scattered over five different floors. The hotel is better for short-term stopovers than for prolonged stays. No meals other than breakfast are served, but 24-hour room service is available.

A NEARBY PLACE TO STAY

✪ **Hostal de la Gavina.** Plaça de la Rosaleda, 17248 S'Agaro (Girona). ☎ **972-32-11-00.** Fax 972-32-15-73. E-mail: Gavina@iponet.es. 73 units. A/C MINIBAR TV TEL. 22,500–39,500 ptas. ($150.75–$264.65) double; 33,500–99,000 ptas. ($224.45–$663.30) suite. AE, DC, MC, V. Closed Nov–Apr. Parking 1,600 ptas. ($10.70) garage, free outside.

Since its establishment in the early 1980s, the Hostal de la Gavina has attracted some of the most glamorous people in the world, including King Juan Carlos, Elizabeth Taylor, and a host of celebrities from northern Europe. It lies on a peninsula jutting seaward from the center of S'Agaro, within a thick-walled Iberian villa that was originally built as the private home of the Ansesa family (the owners of the hotel) in 1932. The public rooms, the main restaurant, and most of the accommodations are contained within the resort's main building, which has been much enlarged and modified since its original construction. The rooms are spacious and the most sumptuous in the area, with elegant appointments, deluxe fabrics, plush towels, toiletries, luxury mattresses, and hair dryers. Many of the paneled public rooms are enclaves of taste and style. A large and very modern swimming pool is a short walk away, above the town's public beach. Adjacent to the pool is a beach house, containing a Jacuzzi, a handful of boutiques, and a daytime restaurant.

Dining/Diversions: The daytime restaurant is **Las Conchas,** which serves fresh salads, brochettes, and light platters beside the pool. More formal evening meals are served in the main building, in the **Candlelight Restaurant,** which features well-prepared international specialties and an outdoor patio. There are also two bars.

Amenities: 24-hour room service, hairdresser, massage, laundry/valet, concierge, 2 tennis courts, paddle tennis courts, 2 bars, masses of well-tended gardens, Jacuzzi, swimming pool.

WHERE TO DINE

Bronsoms. Sant Francesc, 7. ☎ **972-21-24-93.** Reservations recommended. Main courses 900–1,850 ptas. ($6.05–$12.40); fixed-price menu 975 ptas. ($6.55). AE, MC, V. Tues–Sun 1–4pm and 8–11:30pm. CATALAN.

Set in the heart of the old town, within an 1890s building that was originally a private home, this restaurant is one of the most consistently reliable in Girona. The subject of praise from newspapers as far away as Madrid, it has been under its present management since 1982, perfecting the art of serving a Catalan-based *cocina del mercado*—that is, cooking with whatever market-fresh ingredients are available each day. The frequently ordered house specialties include fish paella, *arroz negre* (black rice, tinted with squid ink and studded with shellfish), white beans and several preparations of Iberian ham.

✪ **El Cellar de Can Roca.** Carret Taiala, 40 (☎ **972-22-21-57**). Reservations recommended. Main courses 1,600–3,800 ptas. ($10.70–$25.45); fixed-price menus 3,800–6,000 ptas. ($25.45–$40.20). AE, DC, MC, V. Tues–Sat 1–4pm and 9–11pm. CATALAN.

Located just 1¼ miles (2km) from the center of Girona, El Cellar de Can Roca is the best of the new spate of restaurants appearing in Girona, and represents the success of the campaign to transform Girona into one of the more fashionable and lively cities in Spain. Run by three young brothers, the restaurant is small and intimate, consisting of only 12 tables. The interior is modern in appearance, with earthy tones. The cuisine is an interesting combination of traditional Catalan dishes creatively transformed into contemporary Mediterranean fare. Start with an avocado purée, and for dessert you can't pass up the mandarin orange sorbet with pumpkin compote.

GIRONA AFTER DARK

Central Girona has a good number of tapas bars and cafes, some of which don't have easily distinguishable names. Many of them are scattered along **La Rambla,** around the edges of the keynote **Plaça de Independencia,** and within the antique boundaries of the **Plaça Ferrán el Católic.** Moving at a leisurely pace from one to another is considered something of an art form in the sultry heat of Girona's early evenings. Some animated tapas bars in the city center include **Bar de Tapes,** carrer Barcelona, 13, (☎ **972-41-01-64**), near the railway station; and **Tapa't,** Plaça de l'Oli (no phone), which is noteworthy for its old-timey, old-fashioned charm. Also appealing for its crowded conviviality and its impressive roster of shellfish and seafood tapas is **Bar Boira,** Plaça de Independencia, 17 (☎ **972-20-30-96**).

Beginning around 11pm, you might want to drop into one or another of the town's discos, the most popular of which includes **Disco/Sala de Fiestas Platea,** carrer Reial de Fontclara, s/n (☎ **972-22-72-88**). Set within the city's oldest core, it's open Wednesday to Sunday beginning at 11pm. (Be warned in advance that your greatest difficulty will involve finding the place; the street that contains it lies on a narrow alleyway just behind Girona's main post office.) Newer, with less of a track record but a rapidly evolving style that appeals to everyone between the ages of 23 and around 45 who likes to dance, is **Discoteca 7 Artes,** carrer Sant'Narcis, s/n (no phone), which is open Wednesday to Saturday from 11pm until at least 4am.

Despite the appeal of the above-mentioned sites, one of the most appealing things to do in Girona after dark, at least between June and September, is to cross to the opposite side of the river into the verdant precincts of the **Parque de la Devesa.** This park is an artfully landscaped terrain of stately trees, flowering shrubs, kiosk-style refreshment stands, and open-aired bars which in some cases have disco music and patrons dancing on wooden decks. One of the most appealing of these is **Disco Glops,** Parque de la Devesa (no phone), which rocks and rolls in the open-air every Wednesday evening from around 10:30pm till dawn. Entrance is free; beer costs around 225 ptas. ($1.50).

2 Lloret de Mar

62 miles (100km) S of the French border, 42 miles (68km) N of Barcelona

Although it has a good half-moon-shaped sandy beach, Lloret is neither chic nor sophisticated, and most of the people who come here are tourists on package tours and

Europeans looking for an inexpensive vacation. The competition for cheap rooms is fierce.

Lloret de Mar has grown at a phenomenal rate from a small fishing village with just a few hotels to a bustling resort with more hotels than anyone can count. And more keep opening up, although there are never enough in July and August. The accommodations are typical of those in other Costa Brava towns, running the gamut from impersonal modern box-type structures to vintage whitewashed, flowerpot-adorned buildings on the narrow streets of the old town. There are even a few pockets of posh, including the Hotel Roger de Flor (see below). The area has rich vegetation, attractive scenery, and a mild climate.

ESSENTIALS

GETTING THERE   From Barcelona, take a train to Blanes, then take a bus 5 miles (8km) to Lloret.

If you drive, head north from Barcelona along the A-19.

VISITOR INFORMATION   The **tourist information office** is at Plaça de la Vila, 1 (☎ 972-36-47-35). Open daily from 9am to 1pm and 4 to 8pm.

WHERE TO STAY

Many of the hotels—particularly the three-star establishments—are booked solidly by tour groups. Here are some possibilities if you reserve in advance.

Hotel Excelsior. Passeig Mossèn Jacinto Verdaguer, 16, 17310 Lloret de Mar. ☎ **972-36-61-76.** Fax 972-37-16-54. 44 units. TV TEL. July–Sept (including obligatory half board), 8,180 ptas. ($54.80) per person; Oct–June (including breakfast), 3,400–4,025 ptas. ($22.80–$26.95) per person double. AE, DC, MC, V. Closed Oct 31–Apr 1. Parking 1,000 ptas. ($6.70).

This well-managed three-star hotel attracts a beach-oriented clientele from Spain and northern Europe, many of whom have returned every summer since the hotel opened in 1978. The Excelsior sits almost directly on the beach, rising six floors above the esplanade, and contains an elevator. All but a handful of the rooms offer either frontal or lateral views of the sea, and some have TVs. The furniture is modern but uninspiring. The hotel frequently renews its mattresses and its rooms. Mediterranean food in the restaurant, Les Petxinea, is well prepared, and clients seem generally content with the services provided. There is also a restaurant offering, simple, buffet style meals. During midsummer, half-board is obligatory.

Hotel Marsol. Passeig Jacint Verdaguer, 7, 17310 Lloret de Mar. ☎ **972-36-57-54.** Fax 972-37-22-05. 100 units. A/C MINIBAR TV TEL. 7,500–12,600 ptas. ($50.25–$84.40) double. Rates include breakfast. AE, DC, MC, V.

Completely refurbished and vastly improved in 1992, this medium-size hotel opens directly onto beachfront action. Its chief drawing card is its rooftop swimming pool along with sauna and solarium. Favored by an essentially European clientele, it offers sleekly modern but small rooms, each with satellite TV, air-conditioning, radio, personal safe, good beds, soundproof windows, and minibar. Occupying the ground floor is a cafeteria serving drinks and snacks, plus a restaurant, Els Dofins, overlooking a palm-shaded plaza.

✪ **Hotel Roger de Flor.** Turó de l'Estelat, s/n, 17310 Lloret de Mar. ☎ **972-36-48-00.** Fax 972-37-16-37. E-mail: rogerdeflor@nexo.es. 95 units. TV. 13,000–24,000 ptas. ($87.10–$160.80) double; 30,000–38,000 ptas. ($201–$254.60) suite. AE, DC, MC, V. Free parking.

This much-enlarged older hotel, some of which is reminiscent of a dignified private villa, is a pleasant diversion from the aging and unimaginative slabs of concrete filling other sections of the resort. Set at the eastern edge of town, the hotel offers some of the most pleasant and panoramic views of any hotel. Potted geraniums, climbing masses of bougainvillea, and evenly spaced rows of palms add elegance to the combinations of new and old architecture. The midsize rooms are high-ceilinged, modern, and filled with excellent furnishings, including quality mattresses and fine linens. The public rooms contain plenty of exposed wood and spill out onto a partially covered terrace, which functions as a centerpiece for the dining and drinking facilities.

Dining/Diversions: The modern and panoramic L'Estelat restaurant, near an airy and comfortable bar, serves international food.

Amenities: Room service (offered from 8am to 10:30pm), laundry, concierge, baby-sitting, car rentals, shopping boutique, outdoor swimming pool filled with pumped-in seawater set within the garden, tennis courts, billiard room, and a card lounge.

✪ **Hotel Santa Marta.** Playa de Santa Cristina, 17310 Lloret de Mar. ☎ **972-36-49-04.** Fax 972-36-92-80. 78 units. A/C MINIBAR TV TEL. 18,000–30,000 ptas. ($120.60–$201) double; 28,000–48,000 ptas. ($187.60–$321.60) suite. July–Sept full board is recommended for 11,000 ptas. ($73.70). AE, DC, MC, V. Closed Dec 23–Jan 31. Free parking.

This tranquil hotel, a short walk above a crescent-shaped bay favored by swimmers, is nestled amid a sun-flooded grove of pines. The spacious rooms offer private balconies overlooking either the sea or a pleasant garden, and about two-thirds contain minibars, TVs, and air-conditioning. Both the public rooms and the bedrooms are attractively paneled and filled with traditional furniture, including excellent beds. The hotel's seaside neighborhood is quiet but desirable, about 1½ miles (2km) west of the commercial center of town.

Dining/Diversions: The Restaurante Santa Marta is recommended separately below. An airy bar is nearby.

Amenities: Laundry/valet, concierge, baby-sitting, car-rental kiosk, solarium, limited room service.

WHERE TO DINE

El Trull. Cala Canyelles, s/n. ☎ **972-36-49-28.** Reservations not necessary. Main courses 1,500–5,350 ptas. ($10.05–$35.85); fixed-price menus 1,650 ptas. ($11.05). AE, DC, MC, V. Daily 1–4pm and 8–11:30pm (till midnight on weekends). SEAFOOD.

Since its establishment in 1975, this restaurant has attracted hordes of Spanish clients who appreciate the beautiful scenery of the 2-mile (3km) trek north of Lloret into the nearby hills. Set in the modern suburb of Urbanización Playa Canyelles and known for its enduring popularity, El Trull positions its tables within view of a well-kept garden and a (sometimes crowded) swimming pool. The food is some of the best in the neighborhood. Menu items focus on seafood, and include fish soup; a fish stew heavily laced with lobster; many variations of hake, monkfish, and clams; and an omelette "surprise." (The waiter will tell you the ingredients if you ask.)

Restaurante Santa Marta. In the Hotel Santa Marta, Playa de Santa Cristina. ☎ **972-36-49-04.** Reservations recommended. Main courses 3,000–3,500 ptas. ($20.10–$23.45); fixed-price menu 6,000 ptas. ($40.20). AE, DC, MC, V. Daily 1:30–3:30pm and 8:30–10:30pm. Closed Dec 23–Jan 31. INTERNATIONAL/CATALAN.

Set within a previously recommended 40-year-old hotel lying about 1½ miles (2km) west of the commercial center of town, this pleasantly sunny enclave offers well-prepared food and a sweeping view of the beaches and the sea. Menu specialties vary with the seasons but might include pâté of wild mushrooms in a special sauce, smoked salmon with hollandaise on toast, medallions of monkfish served with a mousseline of garlic, a ragout of giant shrimp with broad beans, a fillet of beef Stroganoff, and a regionally inspired cassolette of chicken prepared with cloves.

LLORET DE MAR AFTER DARK

Casino Lloret de Mar. Carrer Esports, 1. ☎ **972-36-65-12.** Admission 550 ptas. ($3.70).

Games of chance include French and American roulette, blackjack, and chemin de fer, among others. There is a restaurant, buffet dining room, bar boîte, and dance club, along with a swimming pool. Drinks range from 600 to 1,000 ptas. ($4 to $6.70). The casino lies southwest of Lloret de Mar, beside the coastal road leading to Blanes and Barcelona. Drive or take a taxi at night and bring your passport for entry. Hours are Monday through Friday from 5pm to 4pm and Saturday and Sunday from 5pm to 4:30am. (The casino closes 30 minutes later in summer.)

Hollywood. Carrer Esports, 5. ☎ **972-36-74-63.**

This dance club at the edge of town is the place to be and be seen. Look for it on the corner of carrer Girona. It's open nightly from 10pm to 5am, and drinks cost from 800 ptas. ($5.35).

3 Tossa de Mar

56 miles (90km) N of Barcelona, 7½ miles (12km) NE of Lloret de Mar

This gleaming white town, with its 12th-century walls and labyrinthine old quarter, fishing boats, and fairly good sands, is perhaps the most attractive base for a Costa Brava vacation. It seems to have more joie de vivre than its competitors. The battlements and towers of Tossa were featured in the 1951 Ava Gardner and James Mason movie *Pandora and the Flying Dutchman,* which is still sometimes shown on late-night television.

In the 18th and 19th centuries Tossa survived as a port center, growing rich on the cork industry. But that declined in the 20th century, and many of its citizens emigrated to America. Yet in the 1950s, thanks in part to the Ava Gardner movie, tourists began to discover the charms of Tossa and a new industry was born.

To experience these charms, walk through the 12th-century walled town, known as **Vila Vella,** built on the site of a Roman villa from the 1st century A.D. Enter through the Torre de les Hores.

Tossa was once a secret haunt for artists and writers—Marc Chagall called it a blue paradise. It has two main beaches, **Mar Gran** and **La Bauma.** The coast near Tossa, north and south, offers even more possibilities.

As one of few resorts to have withstood exploitation and retained most of its allure, Tossa enjoys a broad base of international visitors—so many, in fact, that it can no longer shelter them all. In spring and fall, finding a room may be a snap, but in summer it's next to impossible unless reservations are made far in advance.

ESSENTIALS

GETTING THERE   Direct bus service is offered from Blanes and Lloret. Tossa de Mar is also on the main Barcelona-Palafruggel route. Service from Barcelona is daily from 7:40am to 7:10pm, taking 1½ hours. For information call ☎ **972-30-42-36** or 972-34-09-03.

Drive north from Barcelona along the **A-19.**

VISITOR INFORMATION   The **tourist information office** is at Avinguda El Pelegrí, 25 (☎ 972-34-01-08). Open April through October, Monday through Saturday from 9am to 9pm, Sunday 10am to 1pm; off-season, Monday through Friday from 10am to 1pm and 4 to 7pm, Saturday from 10am to 1pm.

WHERE TO STAY
VERY EXPENSIVE

Grand Hotel Reymar. Platja de Mar Menuda, 17320 Tossa de Mar. ☎ **972-34-03-12.** Fax 972-34-15-04. 166 units. A/C MINIBAR TV TEL. 13,800–29,200 ptas. ($92.45–$195.65) double; 20,000–49,000 ptas. ($134–$328.30) per person in suite. Rates include breakfast. AE, DC, MC, V. Closed Nov–Apr. Parking 1,200 ptas. ($8.05).

A triumph of engineering—the hotel occupies a very unusual position on a jagged rock above the edge of the sea—this gracefully contoured building was constructed in the 1960s and renovated in the early 1990s. Located a 10-minute walk southeast of the historic walls of the old town, the Reymar offers several levels of expansive terraces ideal for sunbathing away from the crowds below, plus a wide variety of indoor/outdoor dining and drinking areas. Each of these has big windows, expansive views, and a clientele devoted to relaxing in the streaming sunlight. Each good-size room has a balcony, a sea view, a safety-deposit box, a TV with satellite reception, a marble-covered bathroom, and a combination of modern wood-grained and painted furniture.

Dining/Diversions: The hotel contains four restaurants (one open in midsummer only) and at least four bars scattered amid the terraces and beachfronts. There's also a dance club.

Amenities: limited hour room service, laundry/valet, concierge, baby-sitting, outdoor swimming pool, Jacuzzi, solarium, car rentals, children's playground, tennis courts.

MODERATE

Mar Menuda. Platja de Mar Menuda, 17320 Tossa de Mar. ☎ **800/528-1234** or 972-34-10-00. Fax 972-34-00-87. 50 units. 13,054 ptas. ($87.45) double with breakfast; 17,120 ptas. ($114.70) double including half-board July 16–Aug 21. AE, DC, MC, V. Closed Nov–Dec. Parking 1,200 ptas. ($8.05) garage, free on street.

This rustically decorated Mediterranean-style hotel offers a pool, tennis courts, a garden, and a big parking lot. A restaurant serves competently prepared meals. The small rooms are pleasant and comfortably furnished, all with private bathrooms and 10 with air-conditioning, minibars, TVs, and phones (naturally these are booked first).

INEXPENSIVE

Hotel Cap d'Or. Passeig de Vila Vella, 1, 17320 Tossa de Mar. ☎ and fax **972-34-00-81.** 11 units. 8,000–9,000 ptas. ($53.60–$60.30) double. MC, V. Closed Nov–Mar.

Perched on the waterfront on a quiet edge of town, this 1790s building, originally a fish store, nestles against the stone walls and towers of the village castle. Built of rugged stone itself, the Cap d'Or is like an old country inn and seaside hotel combined. It is both neat and well run. Rooms come in different shapes and sizes, but are decently maintained, each with a good bed and a small tiled bathroom with a shower stall. The old-world dining room, with its ceiling beams and ladder-back chairs, has a pleasant sea view. Although the hotel is a bed-and-breakfast, it does have a terraza on the promenade offering tapas, salads, pizzas and ice-cream.

Hotel Diana. Plaça de Espanya, 6, 17320 Tossa de Mar. ☎ **972-34-18-86.** Fax 972-34-18-86. 21 units. 8,700–12,400 ptas. ($58.30–$83.10) double. AE, DC, MC, V. Closed Nov–Apr.

Set back from the esplanade, this two-star hotel is a former villa designed in part by students of Gaudí. It boasts the most elegant fireplace on the Costa Brava. The inner patio—with its towering palms, vines and flowers, and fountains—is almost as popular with guests as the sandy front yard beach. The spacious rooms contain fine traditional furnishings; many open onto private balconies.

Hotel Neptuno. La Guardia, 52, 17320 Tossa de Mar. ☎ **972-34-01-43.** Fax 972-34-19-33. 124 units. June–Sept 4,700 ptas. ($31.50) per person double; off-season (including breakfast), 2,800 ptas. ($18.75) per person double. Rates include breakfast. AE, DC, MC, V. Closed Nov–Mar. Free parking.

The popular Neptuno sits on a quiet residential hillside northwest of Vila Vella, somewhat removed from the seaside promenade and the bustle of Tossa de Mar's inner core. The hotel, originally built in the 1960s, was renovated and enlarged in the late 1980s. Inside, antiques are mixed with modern furniture, creating a personalized decor; the beamed-ceiling dining room is charming, and the bedrooms are tastefully lighthearted, modern, and sunny, each fitted with a good bed and a small, tiled bathroom. A small swimming pool with its own terraced garden has a view of the sloping forest next door. This place is a longtime favorite with northern Europeans, who often book it solid during July and August.

Hotel Tonet. Plaça de l'Església, 1, 17320 Tossa de Mar. ☎ and fax **972-34-02-37.** 36 units. June–Sept, 8,550 ptas. ($57.30) double; off-season, 6,150 ptas. ($41.20) double. Rates include breakfast. AE, DC, MC, V. Parking 1,500 ptas. ($10.05) nearby.

Established in the early 1960s, in the earliest days of the region's tourist boom, this simple family run pension is one of the resort's oldest. Renovated since then, it lies on a central plaza surrounded by narrow streets. It maintains the ambience of a country inn, with upper-floor terraces where guests can relax or have breakfast amid potted vines and other plants. There's a somewhat sleepy bar on the premises where tapas and snacks are served, and a simple dining room for clients taking half board. The small rooms are rustically simple, with wooden headboards and furniture. Tonet maintains its own brand of well-entrenched Iberian charm.

Hotel Vora la Mar. Avinguda de La Palma, 14, 17320 Tossa de Mar. ☎ **972-34-03-54.** Fax 972-34-11-03. 60 units. TEL. 5,675–8,950 ptas. ($38–$59.95) double. AE, DC, MC, V. Closed Nov–Apr. Free parking 5 min. from hotel; 1,000 ptas. ($6.70) garage parking nearby.

Located on a quiet street a block away from the beach, this hotel was built in the 1950s and renovated in the 1970s. It has an outdoor cafe, a garden, and a dining room. The terrazzo-floored bedrooms are comfortable, but rather small, many with balconies. The furnishings are a little tired, but the mattresses still have life and comfort in them.

WHERE TO DINE

Bahía. Passeig del Mar, 19. ☎ **972-34-03-22.** Reservations recommended. Main courses 1,125-3,975 ptas. ($7.55–$26.65); menú del día 885–3,425 ptas. ($5.95–$22.95). AE, DC, MC, V. Daily 1–4:30pm and 7:30–11:30pm. CATALAN.

Set adjacent to the sea, Bahía is a well-known restaurant with a much-awarded chef and a history of feeding hungry vacationers since 1953. Menu favorites are for the most part based on time-honored Catalan traditions and include *simitomba* (a grilled platter of fish), Brandade of cod fish, baked monkfish, and an array of grilled fish—including *salmonete* (red mullet), *dorada* (John Dory), and *calamares* (squid)—depending on what's available from local fisherfolk. (Most fish served here are caught locally.)

�‍✪ **Can Tonet.** Plaça de l'Església, 2. ☎ **972-34-05-11.** Reservations not necessary. Main courses 775–3,200 ptas. ($5.20–$21.45); menú del día 1,350–2,575 ptas. ($9.05–$17.25). AE, DC, MC, V. Daily noon–4pm and 6–11pm. CATALAN.

Perched beside one of the most secluded, charming squares of the old town, this restaurant occupies what was originally built in the 1600s as a dormitory for local field hands. Established in 1979, Can Tonet has been one of the best-valued and most-popular restaurants in Tossa de Mar ever since, known for its Catalan cuisine and fresh seafood. It has an extensive menu that includes paella, Tossa crayfish, grilled shrimp, and *zarzuela* (fish stew). Diners can eat at outside cafe tables or in the tavernlike dining room with its old beams and brass chandeliers.

✪ **Es Molí.** Carrer Tarull, 5. ☎ **972-34-14-14.** Reservations recommended. Main courses 1,200–3,500 ptas. ($8.05–$23.45); fixed-price menus 2,250–4,500 ptas. ($15.10–$30.15). AE, DC, MC, V. Daily 1–3:30pm and 7:30–11:30pm. Closed Dec 1–Apr 1. CATALAN.

The best and most beautiful restaurant in Tossa is located behind the church, set in the courtyard of a stone-walled windmill built in 1856. You'll dine beneath one of three arcades, each facing a three-tiered fountain. There is also a cluster of iron tables near the garden for those who prefer the sunlight. Among the specialties are an elaborately presented platter of local grilled fish, a delightful sole amandine, fisher's cream soup, salad Es Molí (garnished with seaweed), hazelnut cream soup, hake and shrimp in garlic sauce, crayfish flambéed with Calvados, and a long list of well-chosen wines. The impeccably dressed waiters serve with a flourish.

TOSSA DE MAR AFTER DARK

In Tossa de Mar's fast-changing nightlife, there is little stability or reliability. However, one club that's been in business for a while is the **Ely Club,** carrer Bernat, 2 (☎ **972-34-00-09**). Fans from all over the Costa Brava come here to dance to up-to-date tunes. Daily hours are 10pm to 5am between March 15 and October 15, only. It is closed otherwise. In July and August there is a one-drink minimum. Beer starts at 500 ptas. ($3.35), and whisky drinks start at 1,000 ptas. ($6.70). The Ely Club is in the center of town between the two local cinemas.

4 Figueres

136 miles (219km) N of Barcelona, 23 miles (37km) E of Girona

At the heart of Catalonia, Figueres once played a role in Spanish history. Philip V wed Maria Luisa of Savoy here in 1701 in the church of San Pedro, thereby paving the way for the War of the Spanish Succession. But that historical fact is nearly forgotten today: The town is better known as the birthplace of surrealist artist Salvador Dalí in 1904.

There are two reasons for visiting Figueres: one of the best restaurants in Spain and the Dalí Museum.

ESSENTIALS

GETTING THERE   RENFE has hourly train service between Barcelona and Figueres. All trains between Barcelona and France stop here.

It's better and faster to take the train if you're coming from Barcelona. But if you're in Cadaqués (see section 5), there are five daily SARFA buses making the 45-minute trip.

Figueres is a 40-minute drive from Cadaqués. Take the excellent north-south highway, the A-7, either south from the French border at La Jonquera or north from Barcelona, exiting at the major turnoff to Figueres.

VISITOR INFORMATION   The **tourist information office** is at the Plaça del Sol (☎ 972-50-31-55). The office is open June 21 through September, Monday through Saturday from 8:30am to 8pm; October until Easter, Monday through Friday 8:30am to 3pm; and Easter until June 20, Monday through Friday 8:30am to 3pm and 4:30 to 8pm, Saturday 9am to 1pm.

VISITING THE DALÍ MUSEUM

○ **Teatre Museu Dalí** Plaça de Gala-Dalí, 5. ☎ **972-51-17-96.** Admission 1,000 ptas. ($6.70) adults, 800 ptas. ($5.35) students and adults over 65, free for children under 9. July–mid-Sept, daily 9am–7:45pm; mid-Sept–June, Tues–Sun 10:30am–5:45pm. Visits available various nights in July and Aug; call for information.

The internationally known Dalí was as famous for his surrealist and often erotic imagery as he was for his flamboyance and exhibitionism. At the Figueres museum, located in the center of town beside the Rambla, you'll find his paintings, watercolors, gouaches, charcoals, and pastels, along with graphics and sculptures, many rendered with seductive and meticulously detailed imagery. His wide-ranging subject matter encompassed such repulsive issues as putrefaction and castration. You'll see, for instance, *The Happy Horse,* a grotesque and lurid purple beast that the artist painted during one of his long exiles at Port Lligat. A tour of the museum is an experience. When a catalog was prepared, Dalí said with a perfectly straight face, "It is necessary that all of the people who come out of the museum have false information."

For additional insights into the often bizarre aesthetic sensibilities of Spain's most famous surrealist, consider a 25-mile trek from Figueres eastward along highway C-252, following the signs to Parlava. Within the village of Púbol, whose permanent population almost never exceeds 200, you'll find the **Castell de Púbol,** carrer Gala Salvador Dał, s/n (☎ **972-48-82-11**). Stately and severely dignified, dating from 1000, it was partially ruined when bought by Dalí as a residence for his estranged wife, Gala, in 1970, on the condition that he would come only when she invited him. (She almost never did.) After her death in 1982, Dalí moved in for a 2-year stint, moving on to other residences in 1984 after his bedroom mysteriously caught fire one night. Quieter, more serious, and much less surrealistically flamboyant than the houses in Port Lligat and Figueres, the castle is noteworthy for its severe Gothic and Romanesque dignity, and for furniture and decor that follow the tastes of the surrealist master. (Don't expect a lot of paintings—that is the specialty of the museum at Figueres.) Between June 15 and September 15, the castle is open daily from 10:30am to 7:30pm. Between March 13 and June 14, and from September 16 to November 1, it's open Tuesday through Sunday from 10:30am to 5:30pm. It's closed in winter. Entrance costs 700 ptas. ($4.70) for adults, 500 ptas. ($3.35) for students, and free for children under 9.

WHERE TO STAY

Emporda. Antigua Carretera de Francia, s/n (N-II), 17600 Figueres. ☎ **972-50-05-62.** Fax 972-50-93-58. www.hotelemporda.com. E-mail: hotelemporada@hotelemporada.com. 42 units. A/C TV TEL. 10,550–11,400 ptas. ($70.70–$76.40) double; 14,000–17,000 ptas. ($93.80–$113.90) suite. AE, DC, MC, V. Parking 1,200 ptas. ($8.05).

Although the restaurant is a gastronomic landmark (see "Where to Dine," below), the hotel associated with it provides reasonably priced accommodations for those passing between France and Spain, usually on business. It does not lie near the beach, it does not have a pool, and although the midsize rooms are comfortable and distinguished, it is not designed as a place for long-term sojourns. It has three floors of rooms.

The Mad, Mad World of Salvador Dalí

Salvador Dalí (1904–89) became one of the leading exponents of surrealism, depicting irrational imagery of dreams and delirium in a unique, and meticulously detailed, style. Famous for his eccentricity, he was called "outrageous, talented, relentlessly self-promoting, and unfailingly quotable." At his death at age 84, he was the last survivor of the three famous enfants terribles of Spain (the poet García Lorca and the filmmaker Luís Buñuel were the other two).

For all his international renown, Dalí was born in Figueres, and he died in Figueres. Most of his works are in the eponymous Theater-Museum there, built by the artist himself around the former theater where his first exhibition was held. Dalí was also buried in the Theater-Museum, next door to the church that witnessed both his christening and his funeral—the first and last acts of a perfectly planned scenario.

Salvador Felipe Jacinto Dalí i Domènech, the son of a highly respected notary, was born on May 11, 1904, in a house on carrer Monturiol in Figueres. In 1922 he registered at the School of Fine Arts in Madrid and went to live at the prestigious Residencia de Estudiantes. There, his friendship with García Lorca and Buñuel had a more enduring effect on his artistic future than his studies at the school. As a result of his undisciplined behavior and the attitude of his father, who clashed with the Primo de Rivera dictatorship over a matter related to elections, the young Dalí spent a month in prison.

In the summer of 1929, the artist René Magritte, along with the poet Paul Éluard and his wife, Gala, came to stay at Cadaqués, and their visit caused sweeping changes in Dalí's life. The young painter became enamored of Éluard's wife; Dalí left his family and fled with Gala to Paris, where he became an enthusiastic member of the surrealist movement. Some of his most famous paintings— *The Great Masturbator, Lugubrious Game,* and *Portrait of Paul Éluard*—date from

---

Hotel Bon Retorn. Carretera Nacional IIA, km 3, 17600 Figueres. ☎ **972-50-46-23.** Fax 972-67-39-79. 50 units. A/C MINIBAR TV TEL. 7,000–8,000 ptas. ($46.90–$53.60) double; 9,500–10,500 ptas. ($63.65–$70.35) suite. DC, MC, V. Parking 900 ptas. ($6.05). Take a taxi from the rail station or take A-17 to exit (Figueres south) and head toward town on Carretera Nacional IIA.

Located near the edge of the national highway, 1½ miles (2.5km) south of Figueres, this family owned hotel features a large and relaxing bar, a children's garden, and a sunny restaurant with an outdoor terrace. The hotel also has a private enclosed garage. The small rooms are rustically furnished and comfortable, each with a good bed. Some rooms contain minibars.

Hotel Pirineos. Ronda de Barcelona, 1, 17600 Figueres. ☎ **972-50-03-12.** Fax 972-50-07-66. 55 units. A/C TV TEL. 7,720 ptas. ($51.70) double. Rates include breakfast. AE, DC, MC, V. Parking 1,000 ptas. ($6.70).

This pleasant hotel, near the main road leading to the center of town, is a 5-minute walk from the Dalí Museum. The hotel's restaurant takes up most of the ground floor, and there's also a bar. Many of the comfortable but small rooms have balconies, but furnishings are rather plain, although the beds are good.

his life at Portlligat, the small Costa Brava town where he lived and worked off and on during the 1930s.

Following Dalí's break with the tenets of the surrealist movement, his work underwent a radical change, with a return to classicism and what he called his mystical and nuclear phase. He became one of the most fashionable painters in the United States, and seemed so intent on self-promotion that the surrealist poet André Breton baptized him with the anagram "Avida Dollars." Dalí wrote a partly fictitious autobiography entitled *The Secret Life of Salvador Dalí* and *Hidden Faces,* a novel containing autobiographical elements. These two short literary digressions earned him still greater prestige and wealth, as did his collaborations in the world of the cinema (such as the dream set for Alfred Hitchcock's *Spellbound,* 1945) and in those of the theater, opera, and ballet.

On August 8, 1958, Dalí and Gala were married according to the rites of the Catholic church in a ceremony performed in the strictest secrecy at the shrine of Els Àngels, just a few miles from Girona.

During the 1960s, Dalí painted some very large works, such as *The Battle of Tetuán.* Another important work painted at this period is *Perpignan Railway Station,* a veritable revelation of his paranoid-critical method that relates this center of Dalí's mythological universe to his obsession with painter Jean-François Millet's *The Angelus.*

In 1979 Dalí's health began to decline, and he retired to Portlligat in a state of depression. When Gala died, he moved to Púbol, where, obsessed by the theory of catastrophes, he painted his last works, until suffering severe burns in a fire that nearly cost him his life. Upon recovery he moved to the Torre Galatea, a building that he had bought as an extension to the museum in Figueres. Here he lived for 5 more years, hardly ever leaving his room, until his death in 1989.

WHERE TO DINE

Durán. Carrer Lasauca, 5, 17600 Figueres. ☎ **972-50-12-50.** Fax 972-50-26-09. Reservations required. Main courses 925–5,925 ptas. ($6.20–$39.70); fixed-price menus 2,400–3,725 ptas. ($16.10–$24.95). AE, DC, MC, V. Daily 12:45–4pm and 8:45–11:30pm. CATALAN.

This popular place for a top-notch meal in the provinces also had Dalí as a loyal patron. You might start with the Catalan salad, made with radishes, boiled egg, ham pâté, tuna fish, tomato, and fresh crisp salad greens. Other specialties include steak with Roquefort, *zarzuela* (fish stew), and *filetes de lenguado à la naranja* (sole in orange sauce). Like the Emporda (see below), the Durán specializes in game. Try, if it's available, the grilled rabbit on a plank, served with white wine. The french fries here, unlike those in most of Spain, are crisp and excellent. Finish off with a rich dessert or at least an espresso.

You can also stay at the Durán, in one of its 65 well-furnished rooms, each with private bathroom, air-conditioning, TV, and phone. A double goes for 9,200 ptas. ($61.65).

✪ **Emporda.** Antigua Carretera de Francia, s/n (N-II). ☎ **972-50-05-62.** Reservations required. Main courses 2,500–4,000 ptas. ($16.75–$26.80); fixed-price menu 4,900 ptas. ($32.85). AE, DC, MC, V. Daily 12:45–3:30pm and 8:30–10:30pm. CATALAN.

A stop at this restaurant just might provide you with your finest meal in Catalonia. (See "Where to Stay," above, for its hotel recommendation.) Don't judge the place by its appearance, which is ordinary if not institutional-looking; there's nothing ordinary about the cuisine, as all the food-loving French who cross the border to dine here will tell you. This family run restaurant, half a mile north of the center of town, also gained a reputation early on among U.S. military personnel in the area for subtly prepared game and fish dishes. Salvador Dalí (who wrote his own cookbook) and Josep Pla, perhaps the country's greatest 20th-century writer, were fans. The appetizers are the finest along the Costa Brava, including such selections as duck foie gras with Armagnac, warm pâté of rape (monkfish) with garlic mousseline, and fish soup with fennel. The outstanding fish and seafood dishes include cuttlefish in Catalan sauce, supreme of sea bass with flan made with fennel and anchovy, and a brochette of grilled baby squids in vinaigrette. Among the meat selections are the chef's special *lieure à la royale* (hare), beef fillet in red-wine sauce with onion marmalade, and goose in a delectable mushroom sauce.

5 Cadaqués

122 miles (196km) N of Barcelona, 19 miles (31km) E of Figueres

This little village is still unspoiled and remote, despite the publicity it received when Salvador Dalí lived in the next door village of Lligat in a split-level house surmounted by a giant egg. The last resort on the Costa Brava before the French border, Cadaqués is reached by a small winding road, twisting over the mountains from Rosas, the nearest major center. When you get to Cadaqués, you really feel you're off the beaten path. The village winds around half a dozen small coves, with a narrow street running along the water's edge. This street has no railing, so exercise caution.

Scenically, Cadaqués is a knockout: crystal-blue water; fishing boats on the sandy beaches; old whitewashed houses; narrow, twisting streets; and a 16th-century parish up on a hill.

ESSENTIALS

GETTING THERE   Two to five buses per day run from Figueres to Cadaqués. Trip time is 1¼ hours. The service is operated by SARFA (☎ 972-25-87-13).

VISITOR INFORMATION   The **tourist information office** is at Cotxe, 2 (☎ 972-25-83-15). It's open Monday through Saturday from 10:30am to 1pm and 4 to 7pm.

WHERE TO STAY

Hostal S'Aguarda. Carretera de Port Lligat, 28, 17488 Cadaqués. ☎ **972-25-80-82.** Fax 972-25-87-56. 28 units. A/C TV TEL. 6,500–9,550 ptas. ($43.55–$64) double. MC, V. Closed Nov. Free parking.

Situated on the road winding above Cadaqués on the way to Port Lligat, this hostal has a panoramic view of the village's harbor and medieval church. Each of the modern, airy accommodations opens onto a flower-decked terrace. The rooms have tile floors and simple furniture, each with a comfortable bed. A swimming pool, solarium, and tennis courts are located on the hotel grounds.

Hotel Playa Sol. Platja Planch, 3, 17488 Cadaqués. ☎ **972-25-81-00.** Fax 972-25-80-54. www.playasol.com. 50 units. A/C TV TEL. 12,900–19,900 ptas. ($86.45–$133.35) double. AE, DC, MC, V. Closed Jan–Feb. Parking 950–1,300 ptas. ($6.35–$8.70).

Located in a relatively quiet section of the port along the bay, this 1950s hotel has, arguably, the best view of the stone church at the distant edge of the harbor. The balconied building is constructed of brick and terra-cotta tiles. The small rooms are comfortably furnished; 25 are air-conditioned. The hotel doesn't have an official restaurant, but it does offer lunch over the summer from June 15 to September 15. There is also a large verdant garden and an outside swimming pool.

Hotel Port Lligat. Salvador Dalí, 17488 Cadaqués. ☎ **972-25-81-62.** Fax 972-25-86-43. 30 units. TEL. 8,300–9,500 ptas. ($55.60–$63.65) double. Rates include breakfast. MC V. Closed Nov; Dec–Feb open weekends only.

Many visitors find the relative isolation of this hotel—at the end of a winding gravel road a half mile outside Cadaqués—its most alluring feature. The terrace overlooks an idyllic harbor and an unusual house once occupied by Salvador Dalí. The gallery adjoining the reception lobby features a changing series of surrealist paintings. Also on the premises are a swimming pool with cabanas and a snack bar. The airy rooms, all doubles, have tile floors, exposed wood, good beds, tiled bathrooms, and balconies.

WHERE TO DINE

Don Quijote. Caridad Seriñana, 5. ☎ **972-25-81-41.** Reservations recommended. Main courses 800–2,400 ptas. ($5.35–$16.10); fixed-price menus 2,000–4,700 ptas. ($13.40–$31.50). MC, V. Daily noon–4pm and 7pm–midnight. Closed Nov–Mar. CATALAN.

Located on the road leading into the village, this intimate bistro has a large vine-covered garden in front. You can dine either inside or alfresco. The well-prepared à la carte specialties include lamb chops, pepper steak, *zarzuela* (seafood stew), and gazpacho. The Don Quijote cup, a mixed dessert, is the best way to end a meal.

Es Trull. Port Ditxos, s/n. ☎ **972-25-81-96.** Reservations recommended. Main courses 1,500-3,000 ptas. ($10.05–$20.10); fixed-price menus 1,400–2,000 ptas. ($9.40–$13.40). AE, DC, MC, V. Daily 12:30–4pm and 7–11pm. Closed Nov–Easter. SEAFOOD.

On the harborside street in the center of town, this cedar-shingled cafeteria is named for the ancient olive press that dominates the interior. A filling fixed-price meal is served. According to the chef, if it comes from the sea and can be eaten, he will prepare it with that special Catalan flair. You might try mussels in a marinara sauce or grilled hake. Rice dishes are also a specialty, not only paella, but also "black rice" colored with squid ink and rice with calamari and shrimp. Natural baby clams are yet another dining delight.

۞ La Galiota. Carrer Narciso Monturiol, 9. ☎ **972-25-81-87.** Reservations required. Main courses 1,800–2,600 ptas. ($12.05–$17.40); fixed-price menu 2,000–5,000 ptas. ($13.40–$33.50). AE, DC, MC, V. Daily 1:30–3:30pm and 8:30–10:30pm. Closed Nov–May. CATALAN/FRENCH.

Dozens of surrealist paintings, including some by Dalí, adorn the walls of this award-winning restaurant, the finest in town. Located on a sloping street below the cathedral, the place has a downstairs sitting room and a dining room converted from what was a private house. The cuisine is not at all pretentious. The chef's secret is in selecting only the freshest of ingredients and preparing them in a way that enhances their natural flavors. The roast leg of lamb, flavored with garlic, is a specialty. The menu changes with the season but always features the best of French and Catalan fare. The marinated salmon is excellent, as are the sea bass and the sole with orange sauce.

CADAQUÉS AFTER DARK

L'Hostal. Paseo, 8A. ☎ **972-25-80-00.**

This distinctive place has attracted some of the most glamorous names of the art and music worlds. Some music critics have called it the second-best jazz club in Europe, and it certainly rates as the best club along the coast. It's a Dixieland bar par excellence, run by the most sophisticated entrepreneurial team in town. Habitués still remember when Salvador Dalí escorted Mick Jagger here, much to the delight of Colombian writer Gabriel García Márquez. In fact, the bar's logo was designed by Dalí himself. Heightening the ambience are the dripping candles, the high ceilings, and the heavy Spanish furniture. The best music is usually performed late at night. Open daily from 11am to 5am. Entrance is free. Beer costs from 500 to 800 ptas. ($3.35 to $5.35); whisky, 850 to 1,000 ptas. ($5.70 to $6.70).

Aragón 13

Landlocked Aragón, along with Navarre, forms the northeastern quadrant of Spain. It is an ancient land, composed of three provinces: Zaragoza; remote Teruel, which is farther south; and Huesca, in the north as you move toward the Pyrenees. These are also the names of the provinces' three major cities.

Most of Aragón constitutes terra incognita for the average tourist—which is unfortunate, since it is one of the most history-rich regions of the country. You can visit it as an extension of your trip to Castile, to the west, or as a segment of your trek through Catalonia, to the east. Huesca, close to the mountains, is ideal for a summer visit—unlike most of Aragón, especially the fiercely hot southern section, which has Spain's worst climate. Winter is often bitterly cold, but spring and autumn are ideal.

Aragón is known best for two former residents: Catherine of Aragón, who foolishly married Henry VIII of England, and Ferdinand of Aragón, whose marriage to Isabella, queen of Castile and León in the 15th century, led to the unification of Spain.

Aragón also prides itself on its exceptional Mudéjar architecture and on its bullfighting tradition. In September many villages in the region have their own festivals, when bulls run through the streets. What they don't have is the good promotion that Hemingway gave the festival at Pamplona, in the neighboring province of Navarre. On the other hand, they aren't plagued with wine-drunk tourists—the curse of the Pamplona festival. In folklore, Aragón is known for the jota, a bounding, leaping dance performed by men and women since at least the 1700s.

Aragón's capital, Zaragoza, is the most-visited destination because it lies on the main route between Madrid and Barcelona. If you're driving from Madrid to Barcelona (or vice versa), make a detour to Zaragoza. If you get interested in Aragón while there, stick around to explore this ancient land.

1 Zaragoza

200 miles (322km) NE of Madrid, 190 miles (306km) W of Barcelona

Zaragoza (pronounced Tha-ra-*go*-tha) lies halfway between Madrid and Barcelona. This provincial capital, the seat of the ancient kingdom of Aragón, is a bustling, prosperous, commercial city of wide boulevards and arcades.

Zaragoza has not one, but two, cathedrals and, like Santiago de Compostela in Galicia, was a major pilgrimage center. According to legend, the Virgin Mary appeared to St. James, patron saint of Spain, on the banks of the Ebro River and ordered him to build a church there.

Zaragoza lies in the center of a rich *huerta,* or plain. Its history dates from the Romans, who called it Caesar Augusta. Today, Zaragoza is a city of more than three-quarters of a million people, just less than 75% of the entire population of Aragón.

The 40,000 students at the University of Zaragoza have livened up this once-staid city. Cafes, theaters, restaurants, music bars, and tascas have boomed in recent years, and more monuments have been restored and opened to the public.

ESSENTIALS

GETTING THERE   Aviaco has direct flights to Zaragoza from Madrid and Barcelona. From the airport in Zaragoza, you can get a bus to the Plaza de San Francisco. The Iberia office in Zaragoza is at calle Bilbao, 11 (☎ **976-21-82-56**).

Eight trains arrive daily from Barcelona and 8 from Madrid. The trip takes 4½ hours from Barcelona and 3½ to 5 hours from Madrid. The RENFE office in Zaragoza is at calle San Clemente, 13 (☎ **976-28-02-02**), just off Paseo de la Independencia.

There is one direct bus a day running between Zaragoza and Barcelona (7 hours away).

Zaragoza is easily reached on the E-90 (A-2) east from Madrid or west from Barcelona.

VISITOR INFORMATION   The **tourist information office** is at Torreón de la Zuda—Glorieta Pio XII (☎ **976-39-35-37**), next to the Roman wall. Open Monday through Friday 8:30am to 2:45pm and 3:30 to 8pm, Saturday and Sunday from 10am to 1:30pm.

SPECIAL EVENTS   One of the city's big festivities is the **Fiesta de la Virgen del Pilar,** held the week of October 12, with top-name bullfighters, religious processions, and general merriment.

SEEING THE SIGHTS

Basilica de Nuestra Señora del Pilar. Plaza de las Catedrales. ☎ **976-39-74-97.** Free admission to cathedral; museum 150 ptas. ($1). Cathedral, daily 6am–9:30pm; museum, daily 9am–2pm and 4–6pm. Bus: 22 or 23.

This 16th- and 17th-century basilica on the bank of the Ebro River is in an almost Oriental style with its domes and towers. Thousands of the faithful travel here annually to pay homage to the tiny statue of the Virgin del Pilar in the Holy Chapel. The name of the cathedral, El Pilar, comes from the pillar upon which the Virgin is supposed to have stood when she asked Santiago (St. James) to build the church.

During the second week of October, the church is a backdrop for an important festival devoted to Our Lady of the Pillar, with parades, bullfights, fireworks, flower offerings, and street dancing. Also of interest within the church are frescoes painted by Goya, who was born nearby.

You can also visit the Museo del Pilar, which houses the jewelry collection used to adorn the Pilar statue, as well as sketches by Goya and other artists, including Bayeu. Much of the collection is ancient, including an 18th-century ivory horn.

La Seo del Salvador. Plaza de la Seo. ☎ **976-29-12-38.** Museum admission 250 ptas. ($1.70). Museum, daily 10am–2pm and 4–8pm. Bus: 21, 22, 29, 32, 35, 36, 43, 44, or 45.

This Gothic-Mudéjar church, built between 1380 and 1550, is more impressive than El Pilar (see above). It has a rich baroque and plateresque facade and is a particularly fine example of Aragonese Gothic architecture. Among its more important features are

Aragón

0　　　　　25 mi
0　　　　　25 km

FRANCE

Pamplona　　Anso　　　Torla　Parque Nacional　Vielha
Pyrenees
Sierra de
Tendeñera
N330
Hecho　　Biescas　　　Valle de Ordesa
Sierra Solana
Sierra Ferrera
Jaca　　　　　Benasque
N240
Castejón　Pont de
de Sos　Suert
Ainsa
Sos del ⑤
Rey Católico
N330　　139
127
E7　　Sierra de Guarda
A15
Sádaba　　　　　　　　　　Graus
Ejea de
los Caballeros　　Huesca　　　Benabarre
E804
Tudela　　　　　　　　　N240　　Barbastro
Río Ebro
N113
N230
A68　　　N330
E7　　　　　Sariñena
②
Tarazona　Borja　　　　　　　　Lérida
Río Duero
Zaragoza ①
Parque Natural　　　　　Fraga
Dehesa del Moncayo
N234　　　　　　　　　　A2
E90
Calatayud　　N330
③
Cariñena
E90　　　　220
N210　　　Belchite　　Caspe
Hijar
Daroca　　　　　　　N232
④ Nuévalos
Sierra del Cucalón
202
Calamocha　　Montalbán　　N211
Molina　N211　N330　　　　　　Tortosa
de Aragón
N420
Sierra Palomera
Sierra del Pobo
Villafranca
del Cid
Maestrazgo
A7
Albarracín　　　　　　　　E15
Sierra de Gúdar
Balearic Sea
Teruel　↘ To Mora de Rubielos

Aragón

★
Madrid

SPAIN

Calatayud ③
Nuévalos/Piedra ④
Sos del Rey Católico ⑤
Tarazona ②
Zaragoza ①

the main altar and a fine collection of French and Flemish tapestries from the 15th to the 17th centuries, which are housed in the adjacent museum. The baroque cupolas in the Temple of Pilar were decorated by Goya and Bayeu.

Palacio de la Aljafería. Aljafería, calle Los Diputados. ☎ **976-28-95-28.** Admission 300 ptas. ($2) adults; 150 ptas. ($1) students, free 11 and under. Tues–Sat 10am–2pm and 4–8pm, Sun 10am–2pm. Bus: 21 or 33.

This most unusual sight, a Moorish palace in Aragón, has been restored by the parliament and preserved as a national monument. Reminiscent of Cordoban architecture, it was built in the 11th century for Moorish kings but has seen considerable alterations and additions since then, particularly when Ferdinand and Isabella lived here.

Museo de Zaragoza. Plaza de los Sitios, 6. ☎ **976-22-21-81.** Admission 500 ptas. ($3.35). Tues–Sun 9am–2pm. Bus: 30, 35, or 40.

This museum is installed in a 1908 building that has 10 ground-floor rooms devoted to exhibits from the prehistoric to the Muslim period. The Roman legacy (rooms 4 to 8) has sculptures (the head of Augustus), mosaics, and ceramics. The fine arts section includes paintings by Goya (room 20); you see his self-portrait there. In the next room you'll find his drawings *Los Caprichos* (*The Whims*). Also displayed is a Goya portrait of Carlos IV and his wife. The museum lies directly north of Paseo de Marino Moreno.

Museo Camón Aznar. Espoz y Mina, 23. ☎ **976-39-73-28.** Admission 100 ptas. (65¢). Tues–Fri 9:15am–2:15pm and 6–9pm, Sat 10am–2pm and 6–9pm, Sun 8am–2pm. Bus: 22 or 23.

Occupying a Renaissance palace 1 block from El Pilar (see above), this museum has three floors and 23 rooms filled with artwork. On the second floor is a sketch of María Sarmiento that Velzquez made for his masterpiece *Las Meninas* (*The Maids of Honor*), which hangs in the Prado in Madrid. The Bayeu brothers (Francisco and Ramón) are represented by several works, as is Goya. His collection includes an important self-portrait, a version of his *Los Caprichos* (*The Whims*), *La Tauromaquia* (*The Tauromachy*), *Los Desastres de la Guerra* (*The Disasters of War*), and *Los Disparates* (*The Follies*).

Museo Pablo Gargallo. Plaza de San Felipe, 3. ☎ **976-39-20-58.** Free admission. Tues–Sat 10am–2pm and 5–9pm, Sun 10am–2pm. Bus: 22 or 23.

The museum honors sculptor Pablo Gargallo, born in Maella in 1881. It is installed in a beautiful Aragonese Renaissance-style palace (1659) that was declared a national monument in 1963. Gargallo, influential in the art world of the 1920s, is represented by 100 original works, ranging from *Dr. Petit's Fireplace* (1904) to *Great Prophet,* a bronze piece from 1933. The museum is located in the center, a 5-minute walk south of El Pilar.

WHERE TO STAY
EXPENSIVE

Boston. Camino de las Torres, 28, 50008 Zaragoza. ☎ **976-59-91-92.** Fax 976-59-74-10. 313 units. A/C MINIBAR TV TEL. 17,600 ptas. ($117.90) double; 25,000–29,000 ptas. ($167.50–$194.30) suite. AE, DC, MC, V. Parking 1,850 ptas. ($12.40). Bus: 29.

Set in the heart of Zaragoza's modern business district, a 15-minute walk from the medieval neighborhoods that most visitors want to explore, this eight-story hotel was opened in 1992. Named in honor of Boston, Massachusetts, where the building's architect earned his degree, it's the city's best hotel and one of the tallest buildings in town. Many of its public areas are sheathed in layers of beige marble, occasionally accented with wood paneling. Throughout, the style is ultramodern, even futuristic, strongly infused with postmodern design and American ideas. Rooms are the town's finest—usually spacious, with all the modern comforts such as luxury mattresses and plush towels; each tiled bathroom is equipped with a hair dryer.

Dining: The in-house restaurant, Niagara, is one floor below the lobby level and serves filling fixed-price meals.

Amenities: Health club with sauna, 24-hour room service, concierge.

Hotel Palafox. Calle Casa Jiménez, s/n. 50004 Zaragoza. ☎ **976-23-77-00.** Fax 976-23-47-05. www.sendanet.es/soasa/hza/hoza26.htm. E-mail: palafoxsendanet.es. 184 units. A/C MINIBAR TV TEL. 19,500–22,600 ptas. ($130.65–$151.40) double; 24,000 ptas. ($160.80) suite. AE, MC, V. Parking 1,700 ptas. ($11.40). Bus: 22.

One of the top hotels in town, the Palafox looks somewhat like an apartment house. It was inaugurated in 1982 and rates five stars. A favorite of business travelers, it frequently hosts local events such as fashion shows. The mid-size rooms have sleek traditional styling (often leather armchairs) and are well maintained and comfortable, with quality beds and neatly organized tiled bathrooms.

Dining: The hotel restaurant, Puerto Sanco, serves a traditional Aragonese cuisine.

Amenities: A rooftop swimming pool is the place to be during the long, hot summer. Sauna, massage, 24-hour room service.

MODERATE

Gran Hotel. Joaquín Costa, 5, 50001 Zaragoza. ☎ **976-22-19-01.** Fax 976-23-67-13. 134 units. A/C MINIBAR TV TEL. 15,900 ptas. ($106.55) double; from 19,500 ptas. ($130.65) suite. AE, DC, MC, V. Parking 1,800 ptas. ($12.05).

Located half a mile south of the cathedral, behind one of the most beautiful Hispano–art deco facades in town, this hotel is the most historic and the most charming in Zaragoza, and a good value. Established by King Alfonso XIII in 1929, the Gran offers a domed rotunda for conversation and an array of formal public rooms and conference facilities with crystal chandeliers and classic furniture. Bedrooms have been restored into a neutral, traditional international style, yet they retain the high ceilings and spaciousness of their original design, as well as occasional touches of art deco. A favorite of the business community, the hotel offers excellent service. Hemingway and one of his biographers, A. E. Hotchner, stayed at the Gran when they were in Zaragoza.

The hotel's restaurants include the very elegant La Ontina, where three-course fixed-price lunches and dinners are served daily. Current newspapers are available along with the drinks served in the bar, an enclave that some visitors consider their favorite spot. There are lots of hideaways for quiet drinks and conversation. Other perks include 24-hour room service, laundry, and a concierge.

Rey Alfonso I. Calle Coso, 17-19, 50003 Zaragoza. ☎ **976-39-48-50.** Fax 976-39-96-40. 117 units. A/C MINIBAR TV TEL. 9,800–15,000 ptas. ($65.65–$100.50) double. AE, DC, MC, V. Parking 1,300 ptas. ($8.70). Bus: 22.

This clean, efficient place is a favorite with businesspeople, who prefer its location in the commercial heart of town. A prominent arcade marks the entrance. The hotel has a popular countertop-service snack bar and, in the basement, a comfortably modern restaurant. A helpful crew of veteran, good-natured doormen helps visitors with their luggage. The small rooms are furnished with comfortable modern furniture, especially the beds.

✪ Vía Romana. Calle de Don Jaime, 1, 50001 Zaragoza. ☎ **976-39-82-15.** Fax 976-29-05-11. 66 units. A/C MINIBAR TV TEL. 13,500 ptas. ($90.45) double. AE, DC, MC, V. Parking 1,300 ptas. ($8.70) nearby.

This is a real find, lying in the old quarter adjacent to Plaza del Pilar and behind a statue dedicated to Goya. A three-star hotel that is welcoming and comfortable, Vía

Romana is in a superb location, especially if you want to cover the town on foot. The hotel has been beautifully restored, with a well-trained staff and inviting midsize rooms with good furnishings and comfortable beds, plus immaculately kept tiled bathrooms. For some reason, this hotel always seems fully booked in October but you can make a reservation easily during other months. A snack bar/cafeteria is a convenient stopover if you're rushed, but the kitchen staff prepares tasty meals, both regional and international, in its more formal dining room as well. Room service, concierge, dry cleaning, and laundry are some extra features.

INEXPENSIVE

Don Yo. Juan Bruil, 4-6, 50001 Zaragoza. ☎ **976-22-67-41.** Fax 976-21-99-56. 181 units. A/C MINIBAR TV TEL. 8,100 ptas. ($54.25) double. AE, DC, MC, V.

Of course, we had to check this place out because of its intriguing name. Right in the center of town at the Plaza de Aragón and Plaza de la Independencia, it is a favorite among local journalists, and draws a large repeat clientele among the business communities of Madrid and Barcelona. The hotel is graced with quiet and personal service, though it is not strong on atmosphere. The medium-size rooms are well furnished, not particularly stylish, but well maintained and relaxing, with especially good beds. For comfort and good value, Don Yo is an appealing choice. The hotel's Dona Talverna is a fine choice for a meal, both regional specialties and international dishes prepared with a certain flair. Room service, concierge, dry cleaning, and laundry are available.

Hotel Sauce. Calle Espoz y Mina, 33, 50003 Zaragoza. ☎ **976-39-01-00.** Fax 976-39-85-97. E-mail: sauce@svalero.es. 40 units. A/C TV TEL. 10,100 ptas. ($67.65) double. AE, MC, V. Parking 1,500 ptas. ($10.05). Bus: 22.

Lying in the historic and artistic old town right off calle de Don Jaime I, this is as one of the best bargains in a high-priced city. The decor is cozy, the staff helpful. The recently refurbished guest rooms are small but comfortably furnished and well maintained with good beds.

Ramiro I. Coso, 123, 50001 Zaragoza. ☎ **976-29-82-00.** Fax 976-39-89-52. 104 units. A/C MINIBAR TV TEL. 10,900–12,500 ptas. ($73.05–$83.75) double. AE, DC, MC, V. Parking 1,600 ptas. ($10.70). Take calle San Vincente de Paul south from the west end of the Cathedral. After 4 blocks, follow calle San Jorge west for 1 block to reach the hotel.

If you don't care about style and just want a comfortable place to sleep at a moderate price, head for the Ramiro I. It's an older establishment with much comfort although it seems to need more staff. A three-star hotel at the edge of the old town, it offers small rooms that are contemporary and functional, often booked by businesspeople, and, surprisingly, by very few tourists. There's an in-house restaurant as well as a bar.

WHERE TO DINE

Gurrea. San Ignacio de Loyola, 14. ☎ **976-23-31-61.** Reservations recommended. Main courses 2,200–2,800 ptas. ($14.75–$18.75); fixed-price menu 4,500–5,000 ptas. ($30.15–$33.50). AE, DC, MC, V. Daily 1–3:30pm, Mon–Sat 9–11:30pm. SPANISH/INTERNATIONAL.

This is a landmark in Zaragoza, committed to maintaining its reputation for good service, an attractive setting, and a time-honored cuisine. It's a favorite of the business crowd at lunchtime, and it's a good place to seal the deal. Quality ingredients are fashioned into delectable dishes, which are beautifully presented. Menu items might include goose-meat terrine, duck with orange sauce, chateaubriand with foie-gras, hake served with fruit sauce, venison meatballs (in season) with truffles, wild mushrooms with goose liver, and filet mignon in curry sauce—plus a killer array of desserts.

La Mar. Plaza Aragón, 12. ☎ **976-21-22-64.** Reservations recommended. Main courses 1,500–2,800 ptas. ($10.05–$18.75); fixed-price menu 5,000 ptas. ($33.50). AE, DC, MC, V. Mon–Sat 1:30–4pm and 9–11:30pm. SEAFOOD.

This is one of the top seafood restaurants in town. Service is leisurely, but if you're in the mood for a prolonged meal, the menu will include a full range of seasonal vegetables, peppers stuffed with seafood mousse, *dorada* cooked in a salt crust, baked sea bream, turbot with clams, grilled hake or monkfish, grilled squid, shellfish soup or shellfish rice. If you're not in the mood for fish, try the grilled beefsteak with several kinds of sauces.

La Rinconada de Lorenzo. Calle La Salle, 3. ☎ **976-55-51-08.** Reservations required. Main courses 3,000–4,000 ptas. ($20.10–$26.80); fixed-price menu 2,500 ptas. ($16.75). AE, DC, MC, V. Daily noon–4pm and 8–11:45pm. Bus: 40 or 45. ARAGONESE.

One of the best in town, this restaurant offers unusual dishes such as fried rabbit with snails. Oven-roasted lamb or lamb hock can be ordered in advance, but lamb skewers are always available. The chef prepares several versions of *migas* (fried bread crumbs) flavored with a number of different ingredients, including grapes and ham. Giant asparagus spears are often served. Even though Zaragoza is inland, fresh fish is always on the menu: hake, grilled sole, sea bream, and salmon, for example. Veal is featured on the menu with wild boar and veal ribs, as well as veal meatballs served in a bean stew. Desserts are all homemade, including rice pudding, chocolate mousse with cream, and fig ice cream with nuts. Regional red, white, and rosé wines make fine accompaniments.

Los Borrachos. Paseo de Sagasta, 64. ☎ **976-27-50-36.** Reservations recommended. Main courses 1,800–2,900 ptas. ($12.05–$19.45); tasting menu 4,500 ptas. ($30.15). AE, DC, MC, V. Daily 12:45–3:45pm and 8:45–11:45pm. SPANISH/FRENCH.

Solid, dignified, and committed to preserving an old-fashioned kind of service, this restaurant occupies a formal set of dining rooms in a location near the heart of town. Menu items may include a combination platter of hake with lobster, wild boar with wine sauce, fillet of beef with a pepper-cognac sauce, roasted pheasant or rabbit, and an asparagus mousse accented with strips of Serrano ham. This restaurant's name, incidentally, translates as "The Drunkards," and was taken from the characters in a famous Velásquez painting.

ZARAGOZA AFTER DARK

Zaragoza seems sleepy and low-key until after around 11pm, when things perk up a bit. A good place to begin an evening's bar and pub crawl is the Plaza Santa Cruz, site of one of the city's most stylish bars, **Café Praga** (no phone) and its more relaxed and funky neighbor, **Embajada de Jamaica** (no phone), which will tempt you with party-colored drinks. A particularly animated bar belongs to a restaurant, the **Club Nautico,** Plaza Pilar (no phone), which overlooks the muddy waters of the Ebro River.

A popular hangout near the Plaza del Pilar is **Casa Amadico,** Jordán de Urriés, 3 (☎ 976-29-10-41), where local government and business types congregate after work for tasty seafood tapas. Temptations include oysters, smoked salmon, lobster, and Serrano ham. It's open Tuesday through Sunday from 1 to 4pm and 7pm to midnight, and closed in August. Another tapas bar worth a look is **Casa Luís,** Romea, 8 (☎ 976-29-11-67), whose array of shellfish tapas includes oysters, shrimp, and razor clams in little bundles. It's open year-round daily from noon to 5pm and 8pm to midnight. A glass of wine costs 100 ptas. (65¢), and the selection of tapas ranges from 100 to 600 ptas. (65¢ to $4).

A disco that doesn't even begin to function until most of the others have closed is **Discoteca Kit,** calle Fernando el Católico, 70 (no phone), which begins to rock and roll around 6am. An outfit with more reasonable hours that begin around 11pm, and with the added benefit of an outdoor terrace where people dance under the moon and stars, is **Broadway,** calle Miguel Servet, 193 (☎ **976-41-67-40**). Another option is **Café Hispano,** Camino de las Torres, 42 (☎ **976-22-21-61**), a bar where singers (either professional or members of the crowd who've just gotta sing) croon danceable and drinkable songs.

If you just want to bar-hop and try different tascas, most of which aren't even identified with individual signs, consider a promenade along the calle Dr. Cerrada (near Plaza Pamplona), the nearby calle Dr. Casas, or calle La Paz, where neighborhood residents usually duck inside at regular intervals for a quick fix of wine or sherry.

SIDE TRIPS FROM ZARAGOZA

Goya aficionados (male ones only) can visit the **Cartuja de Aula Dei** (☎ **976-71-49-34**), a 16th-century Carthusian monastery 7 miles (11km) north of Zaragoza in Montañana. The young Goya, an Aragonese, completed one of his first important commissions here in 1774, a series of 11 murals depicting scenes from the lives of Christ and Mary. During the Napoleonic invasion, the murals suffered badly but have since been restored. Only men are admitted to this strictly run Carthusian community. The monastery is open on the last Saturday of every month only from 9am to 3pm. Call ahead to arrange a time. From Zaragoza, bus number 28 departs about every half hour to the site (trip time: 20 minutes), with a one-way ticket costing 80 ptas. (55¢). Catch the bus at the stop near the Roman walls. You can also drive; take E-90 east out of town and follow the signs for Montañana.

Goya fans of both genders can also go south from Zaragoza to the little village of **Fuendetodos,** where the artist was born in 1746. A small two-room cottage in the village (not his actual birthplace, however) was restored in 1985 and turned into a museum, **Casa de Goya,** Zuloaga, 3 (☎ **976-14-38-30**). You're shown transparencies of his most important works. It is open Tuesday through Sunday from 11am to 2pm and 4 to 7pm. Admission is 300 ptas. ($2). Take the N-330 south to the town of Muel, then go 11 miles south (18km) to Villanueva del Huerve. Bear east on the A-220 and continue for 5 miles (8km) to Fuendetodos. From Zaragoza, Autobuses Samar Buil, calle Borao, 13 (☎ **976-43-43-04**) carry passengers to the village.

2 Tarazona

54½ miles (88km) W of Zaragoza, 182 miles (293km) NE of Madrid

To call this town the "Toledo of Aragón" may be a bit much, but it does deserve the name "Mudéjar City." Lying about halfway along the principal route connecting Zaragoza to the province of Soria, it is laid out in tiers above the quays of the Queiles River. Once the kings of Aragón lived here, and before that the city was known to the Romans. You can walk through the old barrio with its tall facades and narrow medieval streets.

ESSENTIALS

GETTING THERE   From Zaragoza, four buses leave daily for Tarazona (1½ hours away). If you're driving, head west from Zaragoza along the A-68, connecting with the N-122 to Tarazona.

VISITOR INFORMATION   The **tourist information office** is at calle Iglesias, 5 (☎ **976-64-00-74**). Hours are Monday through Friday from 9am to 1:30pm and 4:30 to 7pm; Saturday and Sunday 10am to 1pm and 4 to 7pm.

EXPLORING TARAZONA

Tarazona's major attraction is its Gothic **cathedral,** begun in 1152 but essentially reconstructed in the 15th and 16th centuries. However, the Aragonese Mudéjar style is still much in evidence, especially as reflected in the lantern tower and belfry. The dome resembles that of the old cathedral in Zaragoza.

The town is also known for its 16th-century **Ayuntamiento (Town Hall),** which has reliefs across its facade depicting the retaking of Granada by Ferdinand and Isabella. The monument stands on Plaza de España in the older upper town, on a hill overlooking the river. Take the Ruta Turística from here up to the church of Santa Magdalena, with a Mudéjar tower that forms the chief landmark of the town's skyline; its mirador opens onto a panoramic view. Continuing up the hill, you reach **La Concepción,** another church with a narrow brick tower.

WHERE TO STAY & DINE

Brujas de Bécquer. Teresa Cajal, 30, 50500 Tarazona. ☎ **976-64-04-00** or 976-64-04-04. Fax 976-64-01-98. 57 units. A/C TV TEL. 4,800–6,600 ptas. ($32.15–$44.20) double. AE, DC, MC, V. Parking garage 700 ptas. ($4.70).

Half a mile southeast of town, beside the road leading to Zaragoza, you'll find this unpretentious modern hotel, which was built in 1972 and renovated 20 years later. Rooms are modest but comfortable, although the beds are good with firm mattresses. The dining room serves fixed-price meals for 1,100 ptas. ($7.35) each, every day from 1 to 4pm and 8 to 10:30pm. Reservations are almost never needed. The hotel, incidentally, was named in honor of a 19th-century Seville-born patriot and poet (Gustavo Adolfo Bécquer) who praised the beauties of Aragón in some of his writing.

3 Calatayud

53 miles (85km) W of Zaragoza, 146 miles (235km) NE of Madrid

The Romans founded this town only to abandon it some time during the 2nd century, and it wasn't until the arrival of the Muslims in the 8th century that it was repopulated. The Moors were routed in 1120 by the conquering Catholic forces, who allowed some of the inhabitants to stay. But they were made virtual slaves and forced to live in a *morería* (Moorish ghetto). Some of the Moorish influence can still be seen in the town. Many 14th- and 15th-century church towers in Calatayud are reminiscent of minarets.

ESSENTIALS

GETTING THERE   Calatayud lies on the main rail line linking Madrid to Zaragoza. There are 12 trains a day from Madrid, 9 from Zaragoza, and 3 from Barcelona. There are three to four buses a day from Zaragoza (1¼ hours away). Calatayud is on the E-90 linking Madrid with Zaragoza.

VISITOR INFORMATION   The **tourist information office** is at Plaza del Fuerte, s/n (☎ **976-88-63-22**). Open Monday through Friday from 9am to 5pm.

EXPLORING CALATAYUD

The major attraction of Calatayud is **Santa María la Mayor,** calle de Opispo Arrué, a brick church built in Aragonese style, with an ornate plateresque-Mudéjar facade and an exceptionally harmonious octagonal belfry. Nearby, on the calle Datao, **Iglesia de San Pedro de los Francos** is the leaning tower of Calatayud. This is a fine example of the Mudéjar style.

A walk along calle Unión leads to **La Parraguía de San Andrés,** with an elegant and graceful Mudéjar belfry.

Strike a path through the old Moorish quarter up the hill to the ruins of the castle that dominated Qal'at Ayyub (the old Arab name for the town). Once you're there, a panoramic view unfolds.

East of Calatayud, excavations continue to uncover the **Roman city of Bibilis,** lying on the Mérida-Zaragoza highway. It was the birthplace of Roman satirist Martial (ca. A.D. 40–104).

WHERE TO STAY & DINE

Hotel Calatayud. Autovia de Aragón Salida, km 237, 50300 Calatayud. ☎ **976-88-13-23.** Fax 976-88-54-38. 63 units. A/C TV TEL. 8,920 ptas. ($59.75) double. AE, DC, MC, V.

Of a lackluster lot, this low-slung, modern hotel is your best bet in town. Set about a mile (1.6km) east of Calatayud, on the N-II highway to Zaragoza, the hotel contains acceptable rooms with simple furnishings, plus good beds and well-maintained private baths. It also offers a garden and a popular restaurant and bar, the only air-conditioned areas in the entire building.

4 Nuévalos/Piedra

73 miles (118km) W of Zaragoza, 143 miles (230km) E of Madrid

The town of Nuévalos, with its one paved road, isn't much of a lure, but thousands of visitors from all over the world flock to the **Monasterio de Piedra,** called the garden district of Aragón (see review below).

GETTING THERE

From Madrid, train connections reach Alhama de Aragón. Take a taxi from there to the monastery.

From Zaragoza, head southwest on the N-II through Calatayud. At the little town of Ateca, take the left turnoff, which is marked for Nuévalos and the Monasterio de Piedra, and drive for 14 miles (22.5km). If you're driving from Madrid, take the N-II and turn east at the spa town of Alhama de Aragón.

TOURING THE MONASTERY

In Nuévalos, the major attraction is the ✪ **Monasterio de Piedra** (☎ 976-84-90-11). *Piedra* means rock in Spanish, and after the badlands of Aragón, you expect bleak, rocky terrain. Instead, you have a virtual Garden of Eden, with a 197-foot waterfall. It was here in 1194 that Cistercian monks built a charter house on the banks of the Piedra River. The monks are long gone, having departed in 1835, and their former quarters have been reconstructed and turned into a hotel (see below).

Two pathways, marked in either blue or red, meander through the grounds and views are offered from any number of levels. Tunnels and stairways, dating from the 19th century, are the work of Juan Federico Mutadas, who created the park here. Slippery steps lead down to an iris grotto, just one of many quiet, secluded retreats. It is said that the original monks inhabited the site because they wanted a "foretaste of paradise." To be honest, they were also escaping the court intrigues at the powerful Monestir de Poblet in Tarragona province. The monastery at Piedra lies only 2 miles (3.2km) from the hillside village of Nuévalos. You can wander through the monastery grounds daily from 9am to 8pm in summer (closed at 5pm in winter) for an admission charge of 1,000 ptas. ($6.70) for adults, 550 ptas. ($3.70) for children.

WHERE TO STAY & DINE

Monasterio de Piedra. 50201 Nuévalos. ☎ **976-84-90-11.** Fax 976-84-90-54. TEL. 10,500–11,235 ptas. ($70.35–$75.25) double. AE, DC, MC, V.

This is one of the showplaces of Aragón. The grounds include a swimming pool, tennis courts, and, naturally, a garden, with little log bridges and masses of flowering plants and trees. The beautifully maintained rooms (all doubles), which you should reserve well in advance, have phones but no other amenities. Some open onto terraces.

Dining: A meal in the great hall is a medieval event. The room has been tastefully decorated and is a perfect backdrop for the fine Aragonese fare. Meals start at 2,500 ptas. ($17.50), and service is daily from 8 to 11am, 1 to 4pm, and 9 to 11pm. On weekends, the dining room can get crowded.

5 Sos del Rey Católico

262 miles (422km) N of Madrid, 37 miles (60km) SW of Pamplona

In northern Aragón, Sos del Rey Católico formed one of the Cinco Villas of Aragón, stretching along a 56-mile (90km) frontier with Navarre. These villages, in the far-distant part of northern Aragón, also included Tauste, Ejea, Uncastillo, and Sabada. Despite their small size, they were raised to the status of towns by Philip V, who was grateful for their assistance and loyalty in the War of Spanish Succession (1701–13).

The most visited town is Sos del Rey Católico, so named because it was the birth-place of Ferdinand, the Catholic king, in 1452. He entered the world's history books after his marriage to Isabella of Castile and León. Locals will point out the Palacio de Sada, where the future king is said to have been born. The town is more interesting than its minor monuments, and you can explore it at will, wandering its narrow cobbled streets and stopping at any place that attracts your fancy. The kings of Aragón fortified this village on the Navarre border with a thick wall. Much of that medieval character has been preserved—enough so that the village has been declared a national monument.

GETTING THERE

From Zaragoza to Sos, a 2¼-hour ride away, there is a daily bus at 6:30pm, returning at 7am the next morning.

To drive from Zaragoza, take the N-330 to Huesca. Continue on N-330 to Jaca, then bear west on the N-240 towards Pamplona. Turn south at the cutoff to Sanguesa.

WHERE TO STAY & DINE

Parador Fernando de Aragón. Sianz de Vicuña, 1, 50680 Sos del Rey Católico. ☎ **948-88-80-11.** Fax 948-88-81-00. 65 units. A/C MINIBAR TV TEL. 12,500–15,000 ptas. ($83.75–$100.50) double. AE, DC, MC, V. Closed Jan–Feb. Parking 1,000 ptas. ($6.70).

This member of the government-owned parador network is unusual because of the care that was taken to blend a six-story building into its medieval setting. Built in 1975 on much older foundations, it's composed mostly of stone and wood timbers, with lots of interior paneling and antique-looking accessories. Despite its location in the heart of the village, sweeping views open from some of the windows onto the nearby countryside. Coming in various shapes and sizes, each accommodation is well maintained and beautifully furnished, with quality beds and immaculately kept private bathrooms with plush towels. Hearty Aragonese food is served in the restaurant, where the menús del día costs 3,500 ptas. ($23.45). Service is daily from 1 to 4pm and from 8:30 to 10:30pm.

14 Navarre & La Rioja

The ancient land of Navarre (*Navarra* in Spanish, *Nafarroa* in Basque) shares an 81-mile (130km) frontier with France, with nine crossing points. This province with a strong Basque tradition is an important link between Iberia and the rest of the continent.

As a border region, Navarre has seen its share of conflicts, and to this day the remains of lonely castles and fortified walled towns bear witness to that. But somehow this kingdom, one of the most ancient on the peninsula, has managed to preserve its own government and identity. Romans, Christians, Muslims, and Jews have all left their stamp on Navarre, and its architecture is as diverse as its landscape. It is also a province rich in folklore. Pagan rites were blended into Christian traditions to form a mythology that lives even today in Navarre's many festivals. Dancers and singers wear the famous red berets; the jota is the most celebrated folk dance; and the best-known sport is *pelota*—sometimes called jai alai in other parts of the world.

Navarre is also rich in natural attractions, though most foreign visitors miss them when they visit just for the **Fiesta de San Fermín** in July, to see the running of the bulls through the streets of Pamplona, Navarre's capital and major city. Even if you do visit just for the festival, try to explore some of the panoramic Pyrenean landscape.

Adjoining Navarre is La Rioja, the smallest region of mainland Spain—bordered not only by Navarre but also by Castile and Aragón. Extending along the Ebro River, this province has far greater influence than its tiny dimensions would suggest, because it is one of the most important wine-growing districts in Europe. The land is generally split into two sections: Rioja Alta, which gets a lot of rainfall and has a mild climate, and Rioja Baja, which is much hotter and more arid, more like Aragón. The capital of the province, Logroño, a city of some 200,000, links the two regions.

The most visited towns are **Logroño** and **Haro,** the latter known for its wineries. **Santo Domingo de la Calzada** was a major stop on the ancient pilgrims' route on the way to Santiago de Compostela, while **Nájera** once served as capital for the kings of Navarre. Now little more than a village, it lies along the Najerilla River.

1 Pamplona (Iruña)

56 miles (90km) SE of San Sebastián, 239 miles (385km) NE of Madrid, 104 miles (167km) NE of Zaragoza

In 1927, Ernest Hemingway wrote *The Sun Also Rises;* his descriptions of the running of the bulls made Pamplona known throughout the world. The book's glamour remains undiminished for the crowds who read it and then rush off to Pamplona to see the *encierros* during the Fiesta de San Fermín. Attempts to outlaw this world-famous ceremony have failed so far, and it remains a superstar attraction, particularly among bullfighting aficionados. The riotous festival usually begins on July 6 and lasts through the 14th. Fireworks and Basque flute concerts are only some of the spectacles that give added color to the fiesta. The wine flows and people party nonstop for the duration. Those who want to know they'll have a bed after watching the *encierro* should reserve a year in advance at one of the city's handful of hotels or boarding houses or stay in San Sebastián or some other neighboring town and visit Pamplona during the day.

But Pamplona is more than just a city where an annual festival takes place. Long the most significant town in Spain's Pyrenean region, it was also a major stopover for those traveling either of two frontier roads: the Roncesvalles Pass or the Velate Pass. Once a fortified city, it was for centuries the capital of the ancient kingdom of Navarre.

In its historic core, the Pamplona of legend lives on, but the city has been engulfed by modern real-estate development. The saving grace of new Pamplona is La Taconera, a spacious green swath of fountain-filled gardens and parkland, lying west of the old quarter, where you will see students from the University of Navarre.

Pamplona became the capital of Navarre in the 10th century. Its golden age was during the reign of Charles III (called "the Noble"), who gave it its cathedral, where he was eventually buried. Over the years the city has been the scene of many battles, with various factions struggling for control. Those who lived in the old quarter, the Navarrería, wanted to be allied with Castile, whereas those on the outskirts favored a French connection. Obviously, Castile eventually won out, although some citizens of Navarre today want Pamplona to be part of a newly created country of the Basque lands.

ESSENTIALS

GETTING THERE   Pamplona is the air hub of the Navarre region. The city is served by two weekday Aviaco flights from both Madrid and Barcelona; international connections can be made from either city. Arrivals are at Aeropuerto de Noaín (☎ 948-31-71-82), 4 miles (6km) from the city center and accessible only by taxi, about 1,200 ptas. ($8.05).

Three **trains** a day arrive from Madrid (trip time: 5 to 6 hours) and two to three from Barcelona (7 to 9 hours). Pamplona also has three daily train connections from San Sebastián to the north (1¾ hours) and four to seven daily from Zaragoza to the south (2 to 3 hours). For information, call ☎ 948-13-02-02.

Buses connect Pamplona with several major Spanish cities: four per day from Barcelona (6 hours), five to seven per day from Zaragoza (3½ hours), and nine per day from San Sebastián (1½ hours). Instead of being able to call for information, you'll have to consult the bulletin board's list of destinations at the **Estación de Autobuses** (☎ 948-22-38-54) at calle Conde Oliveto (corner of calle Yanguas y Miranda). Nearly 20 privately owned bus companies converge here, and it's a mass of confusion.

Pamplona

MAGDALENA

N-121

Parque de la Media Luna

Media Luna

Pza. Dña. Blanca de Navarra

Pza. del Conde Rodezno

Calle Aoiz

Río Arga

Parque de la Tejera

Calle Aratar

Calle Olite

Av. de la Baja Navarra

Calle Amaya

20 ENSANCHE

Castillo de Maillé

Calle Tablas Iturrama

Calle Eco.

Bergamín

Parque de San Domingo

C. Carmen

Calle Dormitaleria

Calle Hemingway

Calle Dormitaleria

4

3

Av. Carlos

Paulino

Pza. de la Cruz

Calle Sangüesa

Estadio Larrabide

Pza. de los Burgos

Calle Estafeta

Mercaderes

Cortes de Navarra

i

Av. de San Ignacio

Pza. de Príncipe de Viana

Padre Calatayud

Dr. Huarte

Av. de Zaragoza

Comedias

2

Pza. de San Domingo

Sto. Domingo

i

Biblioteca

Pza. de San Francisco

1er ENSANCHE

Calle Oliveto

Tudela

Miranda

Pza. de los Fueros

Paseo de Sarasate

San Antón

Zapatería

Bosquecillo

Descalzos

C. Oliveto

Yanguas

San Lorenzo

Pza. de Recoletos

Taconera

Navas de Talosa

Calle Moret

Av. de Ejército

Parque de Taconer

Calle Mayor

Ciudadela

Río Arga

Av. de Guipuzcoa

Recta de

Parque Larraina

Cuesta de la Reina

Calle San Roque

Pza. de Juan XXIII

Av. de Bayona

Av. de Undax

Monasterio

Av. Pío XII

Vuelta

del

Castillo

Av. de Sancho Fuerte

ITURRAMA

SAN JUAN DONIBANE

1/2 mi

1/2 km

0

0

Catedral 3
Museo de Navarra 1
Plaza de Toros 4
Plaza del Castillo 2

The A-15 Navarra national highway begins on the outskirts of Pamplona and runs south to join A-68, midway between Zaragoza and Logroño. N-240 connects San Sebastián with Pamplona.

VISITOR INFORMATION The **tourist information office** is at Duque de Ahumada, 3 (☎ 948-22-07-41). Open Monday through Friday from 10am to 2pm and 4 to 7pm, Saturday and Sunday from 10am to 2pm.

EXPLORING PAMPLONA

The heart of Pamplona is **Plaza del Castillo,** formerly the bullring, built in 1847. Today it is the seat of the autonomous provincial government. This elegant tree-lined paseo becomes a virtual communal bedroom during the Festival of San Fermín.

The narrow streets of the old quarter extend from three sides of the square. The present bullring, **Plaza de Toros,** lies just east and south of this square alongside the Paseo Hemingway. Running parallel to the east of the square is **calle Estafeta,** a narrow street that is the site of the running of the bulls. With its bars and tascas, it attracts university students and is lively all year, even without a festival. During the festival it is the most frequented place in town next to the Plaza del Castillo. The bulls are also run through the barricaded streets of Santo Domingo and Mercaderes.

Catedral. Curia. ☎ **948-22-56-79.** Free admission to cathedral; museum, 500 ptas. ($3.35). July 1–Sept 15, daily 10am–7pm. Off-season, daily 8:30am–1:30pm and 4–7pm.

The most important sight in Pamplona is the cathedral, dating from the late 14th century on the site of a former Romanesque basilica. The present facade, a mix of neoclassical and baroque, was the work of Ventura Rodríguez, architect to Charles III. The interior is Gothic, with lots of fan vaulting. In the center is the alabaster tomb of Charles III and his Castilian wife, Queen Leonor; it was done in 1416 by Flemish sculptor Janin de Lomme. The 14th- and 15th-century Gothic cloisters are a highlight of the cathedral. The Barbazán Chapel, off the east gallery, is noted for its vaulting. The Museo Diocesano, housed in the cathedral's refectory and kitchen, displays religious objects, spanning the era from the Middle Ages to the Renaissance.

Museo de Navarra. Cuesta de Santa Domingo, s/n. ☎ **948-42-64-92.** Admission 300 ptas. ($2). Tues–Sat 9:30am–2pm and 5–7pm, Sun 11am–2pm.

The major museum of Pamplona is housed in a 16th-century hospital, the Nuestra Señora de la Misericordia, located close to the river. It has rich collections of both Roman artifacts, including some 2nd-century mosaics, and Romanesque art, plus an important Goya portrait of the Marqués de San Adrián. Gothic and Renaissance paintings are on the second floor. Murals from the 13th century are another highlight.

ATTENDING A PELOTA MATCH

While in Pamplona, you might want to head about 3½ miles (6km) outside of town to **Frontón Euskal–Jai Berri** (☎ 948-33-11-59), along the Avenida de Francia, to check out a professional *pelota* (jai alai) match. Game times are Tuesday, Saturday, and Sunday at 4pm and on regional and national holidays. Four matches are usually played on game days, and tickets can be purchased at any time during the sets. Admission to the bleachers is 1,600 to 1,800 ptas. ($10.70 to $12.05). We'd recommend leaving the betting to the experts.

SHOPPING

You'll find lots of handcrafts of Navarese culture in kiosks scattered through the old city, but for a particularly well-inventoried outlet, head for **Echeve,** calle Estafeta, 47 (☎ 948-22-28-34), which sells such handcrafted items as vests, ceramics, hats,

The Running of the Bulls

Beginning at noon on July 6 and continuing nonstop through July 14, the ❂ **Fiesta de San Fermín** is one of the most popular events in Europe, drawing thousands of tourists, who overtax the severely limited facilities of Pamplona.

Get up early (or don't go to bed in the first place), since the bulls run every day at 8am sharp. To watch, be in position behind the barricades along the calle Estafeta no later than 6am. Only the able-bodied and sober should plan to run. Women are officially not permitted to run, although many defy this ban each year.

There simply aren't enough beds or bullfight tickets to go around, and scalpers have a field day. Technically, tickets for a good seat in the ring go on sale at 8pm the night before the *corrida,* and tickets for standing room go on sale at 4pm on the day of the bullfight. But all of the tickets are sold out, and since it is impossible to obtain them through a travel agent beforehand, tourists have to use scalpers.

The fiesta draws half a million visitors, many of whom camp in the city parks. Temporary facilities are set up, but there are never enough beds. Hotel reservations should be confirmed *at least* 6 months beforehand. If you look respectable, some *Pamplónicos* may rent you a room. Be aware, however, that they may gouge you for the highest price they think you're willing to pay, and your room may turn out to be a dirty floor shared with others in a slumlike part of the city. The tourist office will not make any recommendations during the festival—you're basically on your own. Many young visitors sleep on the grounds of the Ciudadela and Plaza Fueros traffic ring, but you could be mugged. Longtime visitors to Pamplona advise that it's better to sleep in a group, on top of your belongings, and during the day, when it's safer than under cover of darkness. If you can't find a room, check your valuables at the bus station on the calle Conde Oliveto (where there are also showers—free, but cold).

As for bars and restaurants, ignore all of the times given below. Most establishments operate around the clock at this time.

Warning: Some people go to the festival not to watch the bulls but to pick pockets. And don't take needless risks, such as leaping from the building in the hope that friends below will catch you. Many people do this each year, and not all are caught.

woodcarvings, and *botas* (wine skins) which locals use to squirt wine, with great dexterity, into their open mouths. A roughly equivalent competitor is **Tienda Anel,** calle Comedias, 7 (☎ **948-22-44-38**), which sells wine skins, neckerchiefs, and wide belts known as gerrikos, which are favored by weight lifters and sports enthusiasts who feel a twinge in their backs whenever they're called upon to perform heavy-duty lifting.

If you're looking for fashion or accessories, head for a boutique called **Zara,** Avenida Carlos III, no. 7 (☎ **948-22-75-04**), which is closed on Monday, or explore the aisles of Pamplona's biggest department store, **Unzu,** calle Mercaderes, 3 (☎ **948-20-91-00**).

WHERE TO STAY

During the Festival of San Fermín, prices are three to four times higher than those listed below. In some instances, a hotel will commit itself to prices it will charge at *Fiesta* (the original name of *The Sun Also Rises* when it was first published in Britain). Other owners charge pretty much what they think they can get, and they can get a lot.

Therefore, agree on the price when making a reservation, if you've been able to get a reservation in the first place. At other times of the year, Pamplona is a reasonably priced tourist destination.

EXPENSIVE

Avenida. Zaragoza, 5, 31003 Pamplona. ☎ **948-24-54-54.** Fax 948-23-23-23. 27 units. MINIBAR TV TEL. 15,500–28,500 ptas. ($103.85–$190.95) double. AE, DC, MC, V. Parking 1,100 ptas. ($7.35).

One of the best inns in town, this small, well-run place opened in 1989. The midsize guest rooms are well furnished and maintained; some are even better than the inn's three-star rating suggests. Furnishings tend toward the sleek and modern, and local watercolors add a warm touch. Sixteen units are air-conditioned.

Dining: Full lunches and dinners are served in the restaurant Leyre, known for its regional cuisine. From Monday to Friday a menú del día is available at 1,500 ptas. ($10.05) and another on the weekend at 2,800 ptas. ($18.75). There's also a cafeteria on the premises, serving snacks and drinks daily from 7am to 11pm.

Hotel Sancho Ramírez. Calle Sancho Ramírez, 11, 31008 Pamplona. ☎ **948-27-17-12.** Fax 948-17-11-43. 86 units. A/C MINIBAR TV TEL. 14,500–25,000 ptas. ($97.15–$167.50) double. AE, DC, MC, V. Parking 1,200 ptas. ($8.05). Bus: 7.

Half mile south of the town center and built in 1981 (last renovated in 1990), the Sancho Ramírez has quickly stolen business away from its older competitors. Each of the reasonably priced units has a streamlined and contemporary decor; some contain minibars, and all the tiled bathrooms are equipped with hair dryers. Rooms are outfitted in a conservatively contemporary decor. It's not a particularly exciting hotel, rather bland and angular. The hotel restaurant serves regional cuisine.

Hotel Tres Reyes. Jardines de la Taconera, s/n, 31001 Pamplona. ☎ **800/448-8355** in the U.S., or 948-22-66-00. Fax 948-22-29-30. www.hotel3reyes.com. E-mail: hotel3reyes@abc. ibernet.com. 168 units. A/C MINIBAR TV TEL. 20,000 ptas. ($134) double; 37,000 ptas. ($247.90) suite. AE, DC, MC, V. Parking 1,500 ptas. ($10.05) indoors; free outside.

A short walk west of the old town, just 2 blocks north of the ancient citadel, this is one of the finest hotels in town, surpassed only by Iruña Park. Modern, with a cement-balconied 10-story facade that curves around a pleasant garden, it provides tasteful and airy rooms with contemporary furnishings, lots of sunlight, and private bathrooms equipped with hair dryers. Many have balconies, and all are welcome refuges from the intensity of the local festivities.

Dining/Diversions: The Grill Tres Reyes serves well-prepared Basque and Navarre cuisine. There's also a bar and an inexpensive cafeteria.

Amenities: 24-hour room service, laundry, concierge, baby-sitting, daily exercise classes, car rentals; shopping boutiques; health club with sauna, gymnasium, squash courts, and massage facilities; heated outdoor swimming pool.

Iruña Park Hotel. Ronda Ermitagaña, s/n, 31008 Pamplona. ☎ **800/448-8335** in the U.S., or 948-17-32-00. Fax 948-17-23-87. 225 units. A/C MINIBAR TV TEL. 19,400 ptas. ($130) double; 33,000 ptas. ($221.10) suite. AE, DC, MC, V. Parking 1,650 ptas. ($11.05).

A short walk west of the Parque de la Ciudadela, behind a facade of mirrored glass and white masonry, this is the largest and best hotel in town, and often the site of conventions. A large staff maintains the blandly furnished but comfortable rooms, some suitable for persons with disabilities. All the beds have quality mattresses, and the amenities include private safes and hair dryers. The public rooms are modern and glossy, with deep armchairs and big windows.

Dining/Diversions: The Royal Restaurant serves regional and international cuisine. There's also a bar.

Amenities: Room service (daily from 8am to 11pm), concierge, baby-sitting, laundry, car rentals, sauna, solarium, business center.

MODERATE

Hotel Leyre. Leyre, 7, 31002 Pamplona. ☎ **948-22-85-00.** Fax 948-22-83-18. www.webs.navarra.net/hleyre. E-mail: hleyre@cmn.navarra.net. 55 units. MINIBAR TV TEL. 15,100 ptas. ($101.15) double. AF, DC, MC, V. Parking 1,200 ptas. ($8.05). Bus: 11.

Conveniently located in the town center, a few steps from the bus station, the Leyre was built around 1965 and renovated in 1996. It's been consistently popular with bull breeders and with matadors and their fans. The small rooms are comfortable but simple, with sturdy furniture such as good beds and high ceilings. A restaurant and a popular bar are on the premises.

La Perla. Plaza del Castillo, 1, 31001 Pamplona. ☎ **948-22-77-06.** Fax 948-21-15-66. 67 units. 9,000–15,000 ptas. ($60.30–$100.50) double; 21,000 ptas. ($140.70) suite. AE, DC, MC, V.

Opened in 1880 and last renovated long ago, this is not exactly the most outstanding hotel in town. But during the festival it becomes *the* place to stay, because it opens onto the main square of Pamplona and overlooks calle Estafeta, the straightaway of the *encierro* through which the bulls run. The small guest rooms are often furnished with an old-fashioned flair, and in days of yore they sheltered everybody from Ernest Hemingway to U.S. Sen. Henry Cabot Lodge.

Maisonnave. Nueva, 20, 31001 Pamplona. ☎ **948-22-26-00.** Fax 948-22-01-66. www.hotelmaisonnave.es. E-mail: informacion@hotelmaisonnave.es. 138 units. A/C MINIBAR TV TEL. 11,900 ptas. ($79.75) double. AE, DC, MC, V. Parking 1,200 ptas. ($8.05). Bus: 5, 9, or 10.

Located in the historic old town of Pamplona, west of the Plaza del Castillo and within easy walking distance of the tascas and restaurants, this place is solidly booked for the fiesta. You must reserve at least 6 months in advance—and even then, say a prayer. The small rooms have been completely renovated, each well furnished, well maintained, and comfortably though blandly standardized. The hotel also offers a Navarrese restaurant serving a regional and Spanish national cuisine on the first floor. On the sixth floor is another dining room, the Elmirador, with elaborate windows that expose the scenery of Pamplona.

Residencia Eslava. Plaza Virgen de la O, 7, or calle Recoletas, 20, 31001 Pamplona. ☎ **948-22-22-70.** Fax 948-22-51-57. www.hotel-eslava.com. E-mail: correo @hotel-eslava.com. 28 units. TV TEL. 9,500 ptas. ($63.65) double. AE, DC, MC, V. Bus: 9.

Located right off Plaza de Recoletas, a 10-minute walk from the bus station, this renovated hotel manages to combine the spirit of old and new Spain. Its small living room resembles the drawing room of a distinguished Spanish house. All the average-size guest rooms are tastefully decorated; some have balconies with views of the city walls and the balconies beyond. All come with comfortable beds and tiled bathrooms. A cellar lounge offers drinks.

WHERE TO DINE
EXPENSIVE

✪ **Hartza.** Juan de Labrit, 19. ☎ **948-22-45-68.** Reservations recommended. Main courses 3,000–4,000 ptas. ($20.10–$26.80). AE, DC, MC, V. Tues–Sun 1:30–3:30pm, Tues–Sat 9–11:30pm. Closed Aug and 10 days at Christmas. REGIONAL/INTERNATIONAL.

One of the oldest bodegas in town, a popular restaurant has flourished at this location near the bullring since the 1870s. Even though it doesn't have a Michelin star, it manages to give Josetxo and Europa (see below) serious competition. The chef's touch is delicate, and although Hartza doesn't attempt as many dishes as Josetxo, what it does is sublime and inventive. There's a summer garden for outdoor dining, plus a street-level bar. The portions are generous (but expensive); specialties change with the seasons but might include a well-seasoned vegetable soup, stuffed peppers, tournedos, hake and eel, and a selection of regional cheeses. The interior is air-conditioned during the hottest summer months.

✪ **Josetxo.** Plaza Príncipe de Viana, 1. ☎ **948-22-20-97.** Reservations recommended on weekends. Main courses 2,200–4,000 ptas. ($14.75–$26.80). AE, DC, V. Mon–Sat 1–3:30pm and 9–11pm. Closed Holy Week and Aug. BASQUE.

The finest and grandest restaurant in town, Josexto is run by a civic-minded local family with more than 30 years' experience in the restaurant trade. The chef has a magic combination: inventiveness and a solid technique, backed up by the very freshest ingredients. Specialties vary with the seasons but might include cream-of-crabmeat soup, puff pastry stuffed with shellfish, lobster salad, a panaché (medley) of fresh vegetables with Serrano ham, sea bass cooked in white wine, variations of goose pâté, and several rabbit and trout dishes. Dessert might be a chocolate truffle tart layered with orange-flavored cream. The restaurant lies beside a busy traffic circle, 4 blocks south of the Plaza del Castillo.

MODERATE

Alhambra. Calle Bergamín, 7. ☎ **948-24-50-07.** Reservations recommended. Main courses 2,500–3,000 ptas. ($16.75–$20.10). AE, DC, MC, V. Mon–Sat 1–3pm and 9–11:30pm. REGIONAL/SPANISH.

One of the best-known and most stable restaurants in Pamplona, and just a 15-minute walk from the cathedral, Alhambra was established shortly after World War II. Since 1985, it has been directed by a well-trained group of new owners, and in 1995 the restaurant was renovated and enlarged. Set within two paneled dining rooms, it features a complete selection of local wines and regional specialties, including carefully deboned sardines, grilled and served with truffles; grilled fillet of hake with local herbs; and selected cuts of fillet steak with sauces made from local mushrooms and garlic.

✪ **Europa.** Calle Espoz y Mina, 11. ☎ **948-22-18-00.** Reservations recommended. Main courses 2,600–3,200 ptas. ($17.40–$21.45); menú del día 3,250 ptas. ($21.80). AE, DC, MC, V. Mon–Sat 1–3:30pm and 9–11pm. SPANISH.

Located in the center of Pamplona near the Plaza del Castillo, this is, along with Josetxo (see above), the best restaurant in the entire region. Both have Michelin stars, which are rarely doled out in this part of Europe. Known for its creative interpretations of regional recipes, the restaurant occupies several intimate, recently renovated dining rooms within what was originally built in the 1930s as a private house. The chef and culinary artist is Pamplona-born Pilar Idoate, who prepares a seasonal menu. Examples include baked potatoes stuffed with truffles and minced crayfish, roulades of sole with mountain herbs, fillet steaks with Roquefort dressing, and such game dishes as venison and pheasant. Desserts include an orange mousse with a *marquesa de chocolate*.

INEXPENSIVE

Erburu. Calle San Lorenzo, 19. ☎ **948-22-51-69.** Reservations recommended. Main courses 650–2,500 ptas. ($4.35–$16.75); fixed-price menu 1,300 ptas. ($8.70). AE, DC, V. Tues–Sun 10am to midnight. Closed 1 week in July. REGIONAL.

There's absolutely nothing fancy or artificial about this restaurant, which has been serving well-conceived, old-fashioned food for the past 30 years. It contains only 45 seats, staffed by a crew that seems to have been here since virtually the day the place opened. Many of the regular clients don't even ask for a menu, opting instead for platters of good tasting food they've been served countless times in the past. Examples include snails in garlic sauce; braised oxtail; steaming bowlfuls of kale and potato soup; hake in garlic-flavored green sauce; and several kinds of beef, pork, and chicken. Dessert might be an old time portion of flan, accompanied, according to your wishes, with fresh fruit and/or ice cream.

PAMPLONA AFTER DARK

In a city famous for the way bulls run through its streets, there's something consistent about the local habit of wandering through the city's streets, particularly within the historic *casco antiguo.* Two streets in particular, **calle San Nicolas** and **calle de Jarauta,** are lined with tascas, bars, bodegas, and pubs. Lots of them don't even have signs, so just wander and drop in and out of whichever strikes your fancy.

One particularly atmospheric bar is **Mesón de la Navarrería,** calle el Navarrería, 15 (no phone). Amid a patina built up by years of cigarette smoke and spilled beer, it evokes old-time Navarre. A newer contender is Celtic import **O'Connor's Irish Pub,** Paseo Sarasate, s/n (no phone), where pints of Guinness and recorded Irish ballads enliven the old town.

Looking for a dance club to let off some late-night steam? Head for Pamplona's most popular disco, **Reverendos,** Monastero de Velate, 5 (☎ **948-26-15-93**), where twenty- and thirtysomethings dance, flirt, and drink till all hours. The cover charge costs 1,000 ptas. ($6.70), which includes the price of a drink.

Dating from 1888, the art deco **Café Iruña,** Plaza del Castillo, 44 (☎ **948-22-20-64**), has an outdoor terrace that's popular in summer. The winter crowd is likely to congregate around the bar, ordering combination plates and snacks in addition to drinks. The place thrives as a cafe/bar daily from 8am to 1am; however, it becomes more of a restaurant during the lunch hour. Platters of hot food are served to many of the local office workers and day laborers. The menú del día is 1,350 ptas. ($9.05), and a full lunch, served daily from 1 to 3:30pm, costs from 1,500 to 2,000 ptas. ($10.05 to $13.40). Beer goes for 170 ptas. ($1.15) at the bar, slightly more at a table.

Cafetería El Molino, Bayona, 13 (☎ **948-25-10-90**), centrally located in the commercial Barrio San Juan, doubles as a popular tapas bar. Late in the evening, the action really heats up. The huge assortment of tapas includes fried shrimp, squid, anchovies, fish croquettes, and Russian salad. Most tapas don't exceed 175 ptas. ($1.15), although some of the more expensive ones go for 350 ptas. ($2.35). Open Monday through Saturday from 8am to 1am and Sunday from 9am to 1am.

2 Olite

27 miles (43km) S of Pamplona, 229 miles (369km) N of Madrid

A historical city, Olite sits in a rich agricultural belt with a Mediterranean climate of short winters and long hot summers. Cornfields and vineyards, along with large villages, pepper the countryside. It is also the center of a winemaking industry carried on by cooperative cellars. These wine merchants hold a local festival each year from September 14 to 18.

ESSENTIALS

GETTING THERE   Two to four trains per day from Pamplona run to Olite, taking 35 minutes one way. For rail information, call ☎ **948-70-06-28.**

Rustic Lodgings in the Navarre Countryside

If you have some time to spend in the area, consider a rental at one of the government-sponsored rustic home stays, ranging from rooms in old farmhouses in the mountains to simple lodgings in homes in small hamlets in the region. Sometimes fully equipped apartments in the region are available. In nearly all cases, these lodgings are extremely reasonable in price and very affordable to families who'd like to experience the great outdoors in this often neglected part of Spain. Called *casas rurales,* the lodgings are documented in detail in a helpful guide called *Guía de Alojamientos de Turismo Rural.* These guides are distributed free at any of the tourist offices in Navarre, including the one at Pamplona. For reservations, call the office at ☎ **948-22-93-28,** where some members of the staff speak English.

Two bus companies, Conda (☎ **948-82-03-42**) and La Tafallesa (☎ **948-70-09-79**), run from Pamplona to Olite at the rate of 6 to 12 per day. The trip takes 45 minutes.

By car, take the A-15 expressway south from Pamplona.

VISITOR INFORMATION   The **tourist information office** is at Plaza Carlos II el Noble, s/n (☎ **948-71-24-34**). It's open Monday through Friday from 10am to 2pm and 4 to 7pm, Saturday and Sunday from 10am to 2pm.

EXPLORING OLITE

In the 15th century, this Gothic town was a favorite address of the kings of Navarre. Charles III put Olite on the map, ordering that the **Palacio Real,** Plaza Carlos III el Noble, be built in 1406. The towers and lookouts make visiting it an adventure. From April through September, hours are daily from 10am to 2pm and 5 to 8pm; October through March, daily 10am to 6pm. Admission is 350 ptas. ($2.35) for adults, 200 ptas. ($1.35) for children.

Next to the castle stands a Gothic church, **Iglesia de Santa María la Real,** with a splendid 12th-century doorway decorated with flowers.

WHERE TO STAY & DINE

Parador Príncipe de Viana. Plaza de los Teobaldos, 2, 31390 Olite. ☎ **948-74-00-00.** Fax 948-74-02-01. 43 units. A/C MINIBAR TV TEL. 17,500 ptas. ($117.25) double. AE, DC, MC, V.

This state-run parador in the center of town lies within one of the wings of the Palacio Real (see above). Surrounded by watchtowers, thick walls, and massive buttresses, the building is one of the most impressive sights in town. Only 12 accommodations, however, lie within the parador's medieval core, and these go for a premium over their very comfortable counterparts, which lie in a new wing, added to the castle in 1963 when it became a parador. Regardless of their location within the compound, the rooms are dignified and quite comfortable, each with quality mattresses.

Dining: Even if you're visiting just for the day, consider a meal here, which might include grilled ribs, rabbit with snails, or other regional offerings. Meals cost from 3,500 ptas. ($23.45). The restaurant is open daily from 1 to 4pm and 8:30 to 11pm.

SIDE TRIPS TO UJÚE & A HISTORIC MONASTERY

High up on a mountain of the same name, **Ujúe,** a short drive east along a secondary road from Olite, seems plucked from the Middle Ages. Built as a defensive town, it has cobbled streets and stone houses clustered around its fortress **Church of Santa**

María, dating from the 12th to the 14th century. The heart of King Charles II ("the Bad") was placed to rest here. The church towers open onto views of the countryside, extending to Olite in the west and the Pyrenees in the east.

On the Sunday after St. Mark's Day (April 25), Ujúe is an important pilgrimage center for the people of the area, many of whom, barefoot and wearing tunics, carry large crosses. They come to Ujúe to worship Santa María, depicted on a Romanesque statue dating from 1190. It was plated in silver in the second half of the 15th century.

If you have a car, you might also check out the **Monasterio de la Oliva,** 21 miles (34km) south of Olite. It was founded by King García Ramírez in 1164 and is an excellent example of Cistercian architecture. This monastery, one of the first to be constructed by French monks outside of France, once had great influence; today the most notable feature is its 14th-century Gothic cloisters. The church, which dates from the late 12th century, is even more impressive than the cloisters. It has a distinguished portal and two rose windows. Pillars and pointed arches fill its interior. From April to September, it's open daily from 9am to 8pm; October to March, daily from 9am to 6pm.

3 Tudela

52 miles (84km) S of Pamplona, 196 miles (316km) N of Madrid

In the center of the food belt of the Ribera or Ebro Valley, the ancient city of Tudela, with a population of only 30,000, is the second largest in Navarre. Situated on the right bank of the Ebro, it had a long history as a city where Jews, Arabs, and Christians lived and worked together. The Muslims made it a dependency of the caliphate at Córdoba, a period of domination that lasted until 1119. The city had a large Moorish quarter, the morería, and many old brick houses are in the Mudéjar style. King Sancho VII ("the Strong"), who defeated the Saracens, chose Tudela as his favorite residence in 1251. It has been a bishopric since the 18th century.

ESSENTIALS

GETTING THERE   Tudela lies on the southern rail line south of Pamplona. Two RENFE trains pass through here, one connecting La Rioja to Zaragoza via Castejón de Ebro. Another train links Zaragoza to Vitoria-Gasteiz via Pamplona. For more information and schedules (subject to change), call ☎ **948-82-06-46.**

Conda buses (☎ **948-82-03-42**) go to Tudela from Pamplona at the rate of six to nine per day (trip time: 1 hour).

Take A-15 south from Pamplona, if you're driving.

VISITOR INFORMATION   The **tourist information office** is at Plaza Viejal (☎ **948-882-15-39**), open Monday through Friday from 10am to 2pm and 4 to 7pm, Saturday and Sunday from 10am to 2pm.

TOURING THE CATHEDRAL

Begin your exploration at the central Plaza de los Fueros, from where you can wander through a maze of narrow alleys laid out during the Moorish occupation.

At the square called Plaza Vieja, visit Tudela's most important monument, **Catedral de Santa Ana,** open Tuesday through Saturday from 9am to 1pm and 4 to 7pm, Sunday from 9am to 1pm. Constructed in the 12th and 13th centuries, it has an outstanding work of art on its facade, the Doorway of the Last Judgment, with about 120 groups of figures. Creation is depicted, but the artisans were truly inspired in showing the horrors of hell. The church contains many Gothic works of art, such as choir stalls from the 1500s. Several chapels are richly decorated, including one dedicated to Our

Lady of Hope, with masterpieces from the 15th century. The main altar contains an exceptional *retablo* painted by Pedro Díaz de Oviedo. The small but choice cloisters are the highlight of the tour, however, and cost 100 ptas. (65¢) to enter. Dating from the 12th and 13th centuries, they contain many Romanesque arches. Capitals on the columns include scenes from the New Testament.

WHERE TO STAY & DINE

Hotel Tudela. Avenida Zaragoza, 60, 31500 Tudela. ☎ **948-41-08-02.** Fax 948-41-09-72. 50 units. A/C MINIBAR TV TEL. 8,300 ptas. ($55.60) double. AE, DC, MC, V. Parking 1,275 ptas. ($8.55).

Directly in front of the bullring (Plaza de Toros), this hotel was built in the 1930s and tripled in size by 1992. Today, with five floors, it's the best hotel in town, modern and functional, with a polite and helpful staff. Rooms, though a bit boxy and standardized, are nevertheless comfortable with firm mattresses and well-maintained private bathrooms.

Dining: The in-house restaurant is one of the best in the city. It draws a lively crowd, especially before and after bullfights, and serves well-prepared food. It offers typical fresh products of the Ribera region, along with some magnificent fish and grilled meat. Try the omelette with codfish or the baked monkfish. You can also order beefsteak, followed by homemade pastries and desserts. And sample such wines as Viña Magaña. You can dine in air-conditioned comfort and find parking on the premises. Reservations are recommended. Main courses range from 1,800 to 2,200 ptas. ($12.05 to $14.75); a bargain fixed-price menu can be had for 1,390 ptas. ($9.30). Lunch is served daily; dinner is served Monday through Saturday.

Morase. Paseo de Invierno, 2, 31500 Tudela. ☎ **948-82-17-00.** Fax 948-82-17-04. 7 units. A/C MINIBAR TV TEL. 7,900 ptas. ($52.95) double. AE, DC, MC, V. Closed Aug 1–7. Parking 600 ptas. ($4).

Not only is this one of the best places to stay in town, but it's also a leading restaurant. First built in 1963, it's small but very comfortable. The midsize guest rooms are modern and well maintained, each with a firm mattress.

Dining: The finest dining room in town, the Morase is a special delight when the first of the asparagus comes in, as the region's product is praised by gastronomes all over Spain. The specialties sound conventional but are well prepared, including a *pastel* of vegetables and hake baked with garlic. The lamb from Navarre is delectable, as is roast pork with herbs or red peppers stuffed with puree of seafood. Set on the bank of the Ebro, the restaurant offers a garden, an air-conditioned dining room, and adequate parking. Reservations are recommended. Main courses run 1,400 to 2,200 ptas. ($9.40 to $14.75), or you can opt for a menú del día for 2,500 to 3,500 ptas. ($16.75 to $23.45). Lunch is served daily, dinner Monday to Saturday.

4 Sangüesa

253 miles (407km) N of Madrid, 29 miles (47km) SE of Pamplona

Sangüesa stands on the left bank of the Aragón River, at the Aragonese frontier. If after visiting the town you want to spend the night in the area, drive 9 miles (14.5km) across the border south to Sos del Rey Católico, one of the most charming towns of Aragón; it features an excellent parador. A monumental town in its own right, Sangüesa can also serve as a base for a number of excursions in the area, including visits to some of Navarre's major attractions, such as the monastery at Leyre and Javier Castle.

Long known to the Romans, Sangüesa was later involved in the battle against Muslim domination in the 10th century. It has seen many wars, including occupation by supporters of Archduke Charles of Austria in 1710 and many a skirmish during the Carlist struggles of the 19th century. On several occasions it has been the seat of the parliament of Navarre. Pilgrims crossing northern Spain to Santiago de Compostela stopped at Sangüesa.

ESSENTIALS

GETTING THERE   Two to three buses bound for Sangüesa leave from Pamplona daily; the trip takes 45 minutes one way. For information, call ☎ **948-87-02-09.**

If you're driving from Pamplona, take secondary road N-240 to Sangüesa.

VISITOR INFORMATION   The **tourist information office** is at calle Alfonso el Batallador, 20 (☎ **948-87-03-29**). It's open Monday through Friday from 10am to 2pm and 4 to 7pm, Saturday and Sunday from 10am to 2pm.

VISITING THE CHURCHES

The **Iglesia de Santa María** stands at the far end of town beside the river. Begun in the 12th century, it has a doorway from the 12th and 13th centuries that is one of the outstanding works of Romanesque art. The south portal, filled with remarkably carved sculptures, is Santa María's most outstanding feature. The vestry contains a 4½-foot-high processional monstrance from the 15th century.

The nearby **Iglesia de Santiago** is a late traditional Romanesque structure from the 12th and 13th centuries. It has a battlement-type tower and contains an impressive array of Gothic sculpture, discovered under the church only in 1964. Look for the bizarre statue of St. James atop a big conch.

WHERE TO STAY & DINE

Yamaguchy. Carretera de Javier, s/n, 31400 Sangüesa, ☎ **948-87-01-27.** Fax 948-87-07-00. www.interbook.net. E-mail: yamaguchy@interbook.net. 41 units. TV TEL. 7,100 ptas. ($47.55) double. AE, DC, MC, V. Free parking.

The best place to stay among extremely limited choices is this hotel ¼ mile (.4km) outside town on the road to Javier. In summer, its most attractive feature is its swimming pool. The small rooms are functional and modern, clean, and comfortable, each with a good bed.

Meals ranging from 3,000 ptas. ($20.10) are available daily from 1 to 3:30pm and 8 to 11pm and there is a menú del día for 1,675 ptas. ($11.20). The many Navarrese dishes served include lamb stew and steak. You can also sample some of the award-winning red and rosé wines from local wine cellars.

SIDE TRIPS TO LEYRE & JAVIER CASTLE
LEYRE

The **Monasterio de San Salvador of Leyre** (☎ **948-88-40-11**) is 10 miles (16km) east of Sangüesa, perched on the side of a mountain of the same name, overlooking the Yesa Dam. Of major historic and artistic interest, the main body of the monastery was constructed between the 11th and the 15th centuries on the site of a primitive pre-Romanesque church; in time, it became the spiritual center of Navarre. Many kings, including Sancho III, made it their pantheon. Its crypt, consecrated in 1057, ranks as one of the country's major works of Romanesque art.

When the church was reconstructed by the Cistercians in the 13th century, they kept the bays of the old Romanesque church. The outstanding and richly adorned 12th-century west portal is called the Porta Speciosa, and is covered with intricate carvings. In one section Jesus and his disciples are depicted atop mythical creatures. Some of the other artistic treasures of this once-great monastery are displayed at the Museo de Navarra in Pamplona.

When Navarre joined with Aragón, the power of Leyre declined. Finally, in the 19th century, the monastery was abandoned. It wasn't until 1954 that a Benedictine order came here and began the difficult restoration.

The monastery lies 2½ miles (4km) from Yesa, which itself is on N-240, the major road linking Pamplona, Sangüesa, and Huesca. Take the N-240 into Yesa, then follow an uphill road marked LEYRE, 2½ miles (4km) to reach the monastery. Visits are possible Monday through Friday from 10:30am to 2pm and 4 to 7pm, Sunday from 10:30 to 11:15am, 1 to 2pm, and 4 to 7pm. Admission is 225 ptas. ($1.50) for adults and 50 ptas. (35¢) for children.

At Leyre, you'll also find one of the most unusual accommodations in Navarre, the **Hospedería,** Monasterio de Leyre, 31410 Leyre (☎ **948-88-41-00**). This two-star inn with 32 rooms (all with private bathroom and phone) was created from the annexes constructed by the Benedictines in the 1700s. Guest rooms open onto views of the Yesa Reservoir. The rate is 8,600 ptas. ($57.60) for a double room, and parking is free. The hotel restaurant serves good Navarrese food in a rustic setting. Breakfast costs 750 ptas. ($5.05) and dinner averages 1,500 ptas. ($10.05). The restaurant is open daily from 8:30 to 10am, 1 to 3:30pm, and 8 to 10:30pm. The Hospedería is closed December 10 through March 1.

JAVIER CASTLE

The second major excursion possible in the area is to **Castillo de Javier** (☎ **948-88-40-00**), 5 miles (8km) from Sangüesa. The castle dates from the 11th century, but owes its present look to restoration work carried out in 1952. Francisco Javier (Xavier), patron of Navarre, was born here on April 7, 1506. Along with Ignatius Loyola, he founded the order of the Society of Jesus (the Jesuits) in the mid–16th century. The castle houses a magnificent 13th-century crucifix, and thousands of the faithful congregate at Javier on 2 consecutive Sundays in March. This is the most popular pilgrimage in Navarre. Known as the Javierada, it pays homage to Francisco Javier, who was canonized in 1622.

During your visit to the castle, visit the oratory, the guard chamber, the great hall, and the saint's bedroom. The castle is teeming with interesting art, including a 15th-century fresco called the *Dance of Death*. To get to the castle, take N-240 to Yesa, then follow an unmarked road that's signposted CASTILLO DE JAVIER. It's open daily from 9am to 1pm and 4 to 7pm. Admission is free, but donations are requested.

For food and lodging, go to the tranquil **Hotel El Mesón,** Explanada, 31411 Javier (☎ **948-88-40-35;** fax 948-88-42-26), right in the center of the hamlet of Javier, on the same unmarked road the castle is on. Management rents eight comfortably furnished rooms, but the hotel is closed December 15 through February. Doubles go for 6,200 ptas. ($41.55), and parking is free. The hotel's restaurant offers the best food in the area, with a fixed-price menu going for 1,950 ptas. ($13.05).

5 Logroño

205 miles (330km) N of Madrid, 57 miles (92km) W of Pamplona

The capital of the province of La Rioja, Logroño is also the major distribution center for the area's wines and agricultural products. Because La Rioja is so small, Logroño could serve as your base for touring all the major attractions of the province. Although much of Logroño is modern and dull, it does have an old quarter known to the pilgrims crossing this region to visit the tomb of St. James at Santiago de Compostela.

ESSENTIALS

GETTING THERE   There are four daily RENFE trains from Barcelona (trip time: 7 hours) and one per day from Madrid (5¼ hours). From Bilbao in the north, two to three trains arrive per day (3 hours). For information, call ☎ **941-24-02-02.**

Five buses arrive daily from Pamplona (trip time: 2 hours) and 4 to 5 from Madrid (5 hours). For information, call ☎ **941-23-59-83.**

Take N 111 southwest from Pamplona by car or A-68 northwest from Zaragoza.

VISITOR INFORMATION   The **tourist office** is at Paseo del Príncipe de Vergara (☎ **941-26-06-65**). Open June through October, Monday through Saturday from 10am to 2pm and 4:30 to 7:30pm, Sunday from 10am to 2pm; November through May, Monday through Friday from 9am to 2pm.

EXPLORING LOGROÑO

Catedral de Santa María de la Redonda, Plaza del Mercado (☎ **941-25-76-11**), has vaulting from the 1400s, although the baroque facade dates from 1742. Inside, you can visit its 1762 Chapel of Our Lady of the Angels, built in an octagonal shape with rococo adornments. Constructed on top of an earlier Romanesque church, today's cathedral is known for its broad naves and twin towers. It's open daily from 8am to 1pm and 6 to 8:30pm.

From the square on which the cathedral sits, walk up calle de la Sagasta until you reach the 12th-century **Iglesia de Santa María de Palacio,** on Marqués de San Nicolás, once part of a royal palace. The palace part dates from 1130, when Alfonso VII offered his residence to the Order of the Holy Sepulchre. Most of what he left is long gone, of course, but there is still a pyramid-shaped spire from the 13th century.

Walk through the heart of Logroño, exploring the gardens of the broad **Paseo del Espolón.** In the late afternoon, all the residents turn out for their paseo.

While in Logroño, you can visit the **Bodegas Olarra,** Polígono Independencia de Cantabria, s/n (☎ **941-23-52-99**), open Monday through Friday from 9am to 1pm and 3 to 7pm; closed August 3 to 31. Reserve in advance for a tour. It produces wines under the Otonal and Olarra labels.

WHERE TO STAY

Hotel Murrieta. Marqués de Murrieta, 1, 26005 Logroño. ☎ **941-22-41-50.** Fax 941-22-32-13. www.pretur.es. E-mail: hotels@pretur.es. 111 units. MINIBAR TV TEL. 10,700 ptas. ($71.70) double. AE, MC, V. Parking 1,450 ptas. ($9.70).

At the western border of the historic part of town, a block north of the Gran Vía, is this 1980s hotel offering midsize, comfortable, pristine rooms at a relatively good value. The public rooms, all modernized in the early 90s, are outfitted with colored marble, deep carpeting, and tasteful upholstery. Room service is available from 7:30am to midnight; other extras include laundry, baby-sitting, and car rentals.

Efficient and unpretentious, the Murrieta restaurant serves both regional and Spanish food, along with an appealing collection of Rioja wines. Uncomplicated à la carte lunches and dinners are served in the hotel's cafeteria.

La Numantina. Calle Sagasta, 4, 26001 Logroño. ☎ and fax **941-25-14-11.** 29 units. TEL. 5,350 ptas. ($35.85) double. AE, MC, V. Closed Dec 22–Jan 7.

This rather simple hotel, one of the best bargains in town, lies on a street central to both the historic core and the commercial district. Its small and basic rooms are clean and reasonably comfortable, each with a good bed. No breakfast is served, but you can buy pastries at a shop across the street.

A Special Event

About a third of all Rioja wine production comes from the Najerilla River's valleys. From September 15 to 30, the **Wine Harvest Festival** takes place throughout the region of La Rioja. Barefoot locals stomp upon grapes spilling from oak casks, and area vineyards showcase their wares. Other activities include dances, parades, music, and bullfights.

✪ **Meliá Confort Los Bracos.** Bretón de los Herreros 29, 26001 Logroño. ☎ **941-22-66-08.** Fax 941-22-67-54. 62 units. A/C MINIBAR TV TEL. 15,700 ptas. ($105.20) double. AE, DC, MC, V. Parking 1,725 ptas. ($11.55).

This landmark four-star hotel is the finest in town, according to many wine merchants who journey here frequently on business. The town's toniest address offers an elegant reception hall and the most helpful staff in town. The street on which it sits is one of the best known within the city and, although it used to lie outside the walls, Logroño has now caught up with it. The midsize rooms are handsomely furnished though rather monotonous in style. Room service, dry cleaning, laundry, and a concierge are among some of the creature comforts. Although its dining possibilities are limited to a somewhat dull cafeteria, many good restaurants and cafes lie within an easy walk.

WHERE TO DINE

Asador La Chata. Carnicerías, 3. ☎ **941-25-12-96.** Reservations required. Main courses 900–2,200 ptas. ($6.05–$14.75); fixed-price menu 3,000 ptas. ($20.10). AE, DC, MC, V. Daily 1:30–4pm, Wed–Sat 9–11pm. REGIONAL.

Founded in 1821 and occupying a building close to the town's cathedral, this delightful dining choice exudes a sense of Old Navarre. Its tactful owners define it as an asador, which means that it specializes in wood-roasted meat dishes, in this case in the style of the region. Lunch is an everyday event, and much patronized by workers in the local wine trade, but dinner is served only 4 evenings a week. Because of the establishment's small size (only 60 seats), advance reservations are essential. Within the wood-paneled dining room, ringed with artifacts of the wine trade, you can enjoy the two house specialties: fresh asparagus prepared with strips of locally cured ham, and *cabrito asado* (roast baby goat with herbs). Meats are succulently tender.

Casa Emilio. Pérez Galdós, 18. ☎ **941-25-88-44.** Reservations recommended. Main courses 1,800–2,500 ptas. ($12.05–$16.75); menú del día 3,000 ptas. ($20.10). AE, DC, MC, V. Mon–Sat 1:30–4pm and 9–11:30pm. Closed Aug. REGIONAL.

An ample bar greets you as you enter Casa Emilio, which serves primarily roasts, especially goat and beef. In air-conditioned comfort, you can also enjoy peppers stuffed with codfish or baked hake. From the well-stocked wine cellar come some of the finest Rioja wines. Casa Emilio lies south of the old town, directly west of the major boulevard, Vara de Rey.

6 Haro

223 miles (359km) N of Madrid, 30 miles (48km) NE of Logroño

Center of the wine tours of the Rioja Alta district, the region around Haro has been compared to Tuscany. Come here to taste the wine at the bodegas, as international wine merchants do all year long (but especially after the autumn harvest).

ESSENTIALS

GETTING THERE   Four to five RENFE trains (☎ 941-31-15-97) run daily from Logroño (trip time: 1 hour one-way). There are also four to five connections per day from Zaragoza; the trip takes 3½ hours one-way.

Five to six buses per day run to Haro from Logroño. Trip time is 45 minutes to 1 hour one way.

By car, follow the A-68 expressway (south of Logroño) northwest to the turnoff for Haro.

VISITOR INFORMATION   The **tourist information office** is at Plaza Monseñor Florentino Rodríguez, s/n (☎ 941-30-33-66). It is open Monday through Saturday from 10am to 2pm and 4:30 to 7:30pm, Sunday from 10am to 2pm.

SPECIAL EVENTS   Every June 29, the **Battle of Wine** erupts. It's an amusing, mock-medieval brawl in which opposing teams splatter each other with wine skins filled with the output from local vineyards.

EXPLORING HARO & VISITING THE BODEGAS

The town itself deserves a look before you head for the bodegas. Its old quarter is filled with mansions, some from the 16th century; the most interesting ones lie along **calle del Castillo.** At the center of the old quarter is the major architectural landmark of the town, the **Iglesia de San Tomás,** Plaza de la Iglesia. Distinguished by its wedding-cake tower and plateresque south portal, the 16th-century church has a Gothic interior.

You could spend at least 3 days touring the wineries in town, but chances are that a few visits will satisfy your curiosity. **Bodegas Muga,** Barrio de la Estación, s/n (☎ 941-31-04-98), near the rail station, offers tours (usually in Spanish) of its wine cellars. A tour in English is offered Monday through Friday at 11am.

Finally, pay a visit to **Rioja Alta,** avenida Vizcaya, s/n (☎ 941-31-03-46), not far from Muga. It's open Monday through Friday from 8:30am to 1:30pm and 4 to 6pm (closed from mid-August to mid-September). Visits must be arranged in advance.

If you arrive in Haro in August or the first 2 weeks in September, when many of the bodegas are closed, settle instead for drinking wine in the tascas that line the streets between Parroquia and Plaza de la Paz. After a night spent there, you'll forget all about the bodega tours. Some of the finest wines in Spain are sold at these tascas, along with tapas—all at bargain prices.

WHERE TO STAY

Iturrimurri. Carretera N-124, km 41, s/n, 26200 Haro. ☎ **941-31-12-13.** Fax 941-31-17-21. E-mail: h iturri@eniac.es. 52 units. A/C MINIBAR TV TEL. 11,000 13,500 ptas. ($73.70–$90.45) double. AE, DC, MC, V. Free parking.

Half a mile southeast of the city on the highway, this is the second choice hotel in Haro. The small but comfortable rooms are attractively furnished, many with impressive views. There is an animated cafeteria, as well as a large dining room serving regional meals accompanied by Rioja wines. Ample parking facilities are also provided. In summer, the garden and the swimming pool are compelling reasons to stay here.

Los Agustinos. Calle San Agustín, 2, 26200 Haro. ☎ **941-31-13-08.** Fax 941-30-31-48. 62 units. A/C TV TEL. 12,800 ptas. ($85.75) double; 24,400 ptas. ($163.50) suite. AE, DC, MC, V. Parking 900 ptas. ($6.05).

A former Augustinian convent has been turned into a four-star hotel in the center of Haro. Since its restoration and reopening in 1990, it has become the most desirable place to stay in a town that has always had too few accommodations. Owned by a

Basque chain of hotels, it lies in a "zone of tranquillity" (pedestrian zone). The rooms are well appointed and comfortable, each equipped with a good bed. The tidily arranged private bathrooms are equipped with hair dryers. The restaurant serves good-tasting regional meals, accompanied by selections from a well-stocked cellar of Rioja wines.

WHERE TO DINE

Beethoven I, II, y III. Santo Tomás, 3-5, ☎ **941-31-11-81.** Reservations required in summer. Main courses 1,800–2,200 ptas. ($12.05–$14.75); fixed-price menus 2,000–5,000 ptas. ($13.40–$33.50). MC, V. Daily 1:30–4pm and 9–11:30pm. REGIONAL/BASQUE.

The premier restaurant of Haro, located in the center of town, is actually three restaurants in one, each standing beside each other. Each offers good food and value. One of them is a large old house where a bar has been installed. Have a drink here, then perhaps move next door to sample the more modern dining rooms at Beethoven II or III. They're justifiably famous for their platters of wild mushrooms, which owner Carlos Aquirre raises himself. Try the stuffed fillet of sole, vegetable stew, or wild pheasant, finishing off with an apple tart. The interiors are air-conditioned. The wine cellars are among the finest in the area.

Terete. Arana, 17. ☎ **941-31-00-23.** Reservations recommended. Main courses 3,000–4,000 ptas. ($20.10–$26.80); fixed-price menu 1,600 ptas. ($10.70). MC, V. Tues–Sun 1:15–4pm, Tues–Sat 8:30–11pm. Closed July 1–15 and Oct 15–31. REGIONAL.

This place has been an *horno asado* (restaurant specializing in roasts) since 1867 and is beloved by locals for its roast suckling pig. The service is discreet, the food savory and succulent—the kitchen has had a long time to learn the secrets of roasting meats. The dishes are all prepared according to traditional regional recipes. When the fresh asparagus comes in, that is reason enough to dine here. The local peaches in season make the best dessert. Naturally, the finest of Rioja wines are served. Terete is located in the center of Haro.

The Basque Country 15

The Basque people are the oldest traceable ethnic group in Europe. Their language, called Euskera (also spelled Euskara), predates any of the commonly spoken Romance languages, and its origins, like that of the Basque race itself, are lost in obscurity. There are many competing theories. One commonly posited is that the Basques descended from the original Iberians, who lived in Spain before the arrival of the Celts some 3,500 years ago. Conqueror after conqueror, Roman to Visigoth to Moor, may have driven these people into the Pyrenees, where they stayed and carved out a life for themselves—filled with tradition and customs practiced to this day.

The region is called Euskadi, which in Basque means "collection of Basques." In a very narrow sense it refers to three provinces of Spain: Guipúzcoa (whose capital, **San Sebastián,** the number-one sightseeing destination in Euskadi, features La Concha, one of Spain's best-loved and most popular stretches of sand), Viscaya (whose capital is the industrial city **Bilbao**), and Alava (with its capital at **Vitoria**). But to Basque nationalists, who dream of forging a new nation that will one day unite all the Basque lands, Euskadi also refers to the northern part of Navarre and three provinces in France, including the famed resort of Biarritz.

The three current Basque provinces occupy the eastern part of the Cantabrian Mountains, between the Pyrenees and the valley of the Nervión. They maintained a large degree of independence until the 19th century, when they finally gave in to control from Castile, which continued to recognize their ancient rights and privileges until 1876.

Geographically, the Basque country straddles the western foothills of the Pyrenees, so the Basque people live in both France and Spain—but mostly in the latter. During the Spanish Civil War (1936–39), the Basques were on the Republican side and were defeated by Franco. Oppression during the Franco years has led to deep-seated resentment against the policies of Madrid.

The Basque separatist movement, ETA (Euskadi ta Askatasuna, or Basque Nation and Liberty), and the French organization Enbata (Ocean Wind) engaged, unsuccessfully, in guerrilla activity in 1968 to secure a united Basque state. On July 10, 1997, an event occurred that (again) brought world attention to the ETA. A 29-year-old Basque politician, Miguel Ángel Blanco, vanished from his home in the town of Ermua in the province of Viscaya. The kidnappers, all members of ETA, were protesting against the jailing of Basque prisoners in the

Canary Islands instead of in one of the Basque provinces. The central government has consistently refused to cave in to this demand that has been made on a number of occasions before. When ETA members learned that the government once again was refusing their demands, they fatally shot Miguel Ángel in the head. This led to an outpouring of protests among ordinary Basques themselves who shouted "*Basta ya*"— enough already. Thousands and thousands of people in the Basque provinces and throughout Spain took to the streets against the ETA. The consensus of the protesters seemed to be that violence and murder were not the way to achieve their long-desired autonomy. Still, many Basque nationalists fervently wish that the Basque people could be united into one autonomous state instead of being divided between France and Spain.

The Basque language is a riddle that has puzzled linguists and ethnologists for years; its grammar, syntax, and vocabulary are unrelated to those of any other European language. Depending on the dialect spoken, the language is known as Euskera, Uskara, or Eskuara. Although on the wane since the beginning of this century, the Basque language is now enjoying a modest renaissance; it is taught in schools and autonomous television stations in the Basque Country broadcast in the language.

Basques wear a *boina,* a beret of red, blue, or white woolen cloth as a badge of pride and a political statement. You may see nationalist graffiti as you travel, slogans such as *Euskadi Ta Askatasuna* ("Basques Nation & Liberty") painted everywhere. Though the separatist movement is still simmering, you'll find most of the people friendly, hospitable, and welcoming. Politics rarely intrudes on vacationers in this beautiful corner of Spain.

1 San Sebastián (Donostia)

13 miles (21km) W of the French border, 300 miles (483km) N of Madrid, 62 miles (100km) E of Bilbao

San Sebastián (Donostia in the Basque language) is the summer capital of Spain, and here the belle epoque lives on. Ideally situated on a choice spot on the Bay of Biscay, it is surrounded by green mountains. From June to September, the population swells as hundreds of Spanish bureaucrats escape the heat and head for this regional capital. A tasteful resort, it has few of the tawdry trappings associated with major beachfront cities. It is also an ideal excursion center for trips to some of the Basque country's most fascinating towns.

Queen Isabella II put San Sebastián on the map as a tourist resort when she spent the summer of 1845 there. In time it became the summer residence of the royal court. On July 8, 1912, Queen María Cristina inaugurated the grand hotel named after her, and the resort became very fashionable. In what is now the city hall, built in 1887, a casino opened, and European aristocrats gambled in safety here during World War I.

San Sebastián is the capital of the province of Guipúzcoa, the smallest in Spain, tucked in the far northeastern corner bordering France. It is said that Guipúzcoa has preserved Basque customs better than any other province. Half of the *donostiarras*— residents of San Sebastián—speak Euskera. The city is also a major seat of Basque nationalism, so be advised that protests, sometimes violent, are frequent.

San Sebastián contains an old quarter, **La Parte Vieja,** with narrow streets, hidden plazas, and medieval houses, but it is primarily a modern city of elegant shops, wide boulevards, sidewalk cafes, and restaurants.

La Concha is the city's most famous beach—especially in July and August it seems as though half the population of Spain and France spends its days under striped canopies when not dashing into the refreshingly cool waters of the bay. The

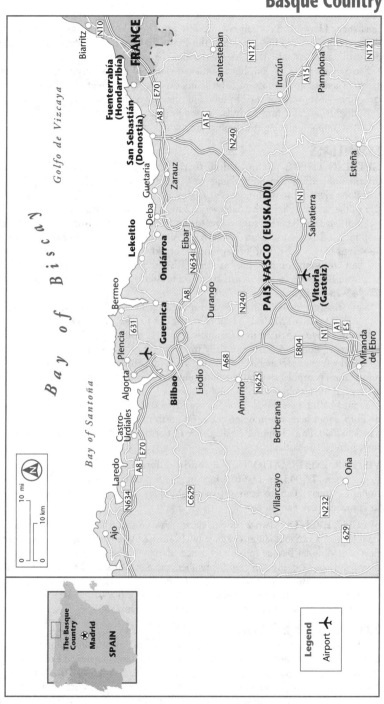

shell-shaped La Concha is half-encircled by a promenade, where crowds mill during the evening. The adjoining beach is the **Playa de Ondarreta.** The climate here is decidedly more Atlantic than Mediterranean.

San Sebastián has a good, but insufficient choice of hotels in summer, plus many excellent restaurants, most of which are expensive. Its chief drawback is over-crowding—it is overpopulated in July, and there are no beds to be had in August.

Bullfights, art and film festivals, sporting events, and cultural activities keep San Sebastián hopping during the summer season.

ESSENTIALS

GETTING THERE   From Madrid, **Iberia Airlines** (☎ 943-64-12-67 for flight information) offers two daily flights to San Sebastián, plus one daily flight from Barcelona. The domestic airport is at nearby Fuenterrabía. From Fuenterrabía buses run to the center of San Sebastián every 12 minutes from 7:48am to 10pm.

From Madrid, **RENFE** runs trains to the French border at Irún, many of which stop in San Sebastián (a 6- to 7-hour trip). An overnight train from Paris to Madrid also stops in San Sebastián, just in time for breakfast (and San Sebastián's cafes serve the best croissants south of the Pyrenees). RENFE also provides overnight train ser-vice from Barcelona to San Sebastián and on to Bilbao. For RENFE information, call ☎ 943-28-30-89.

San Sebastián is well linked by a bus network to many of Spain's major cities, although if you're in Madrid, it's more convenient to take a train. Nine to 29 buses a day connect San Sebastián to Bilbao (trip time: 1¼ hours); 3 daily buses arrive from Barcelona (7 hours); 5 buses run daily from Pamplona (1½ hours). These routes are covered by several private bus companies. The tourist office (see below) distributes an information pamphlet outlining various routes, the companies that service these runs, and telephone numbers to call for schedules.

From Madrid, take the N-1 toll road north to Burgos, then follow A-1 to Miranda de Ebro. From here, continue on the A-68 north to Bilbao and then the A-8 east to San Sebastián. From Pamplona, take the A-15 north to the N-1 route, which will lead right into San Sebastián.

VISITOR INFORMATION   The **tourist information office** is at calle Reina Regente, s/n (☎ 943-48-11-66). Open June to September, Monday to Saturday 8am to 8pm, Sunday 10am to 1pm; off-season, Monday to Friday 9am to 2pm and 3:30 to 7pm, Saturday 8am to 8pm.

SPECIAL EVENTS   Two weeklong events draw visitors from around the world. In mid-August, San Sebastián stages its annual carnival, **Aste Nagusia,** a joyous celebra-tion of traditional Basque music and dance, along with fireworks, cooking competi-tions, and sports events. In mid-September, the San Sebastián **International Film Festival** draws luminaries from America and Europe. The actual dates of these festi-vals vary from year to year, so check with the tourist office (see above). Also, in the second half of July, San Sebastián hosts a jazz festival, **Jazzaldia.**

EXPLORING & ENJOYING SAN SEBASTIÁN

San Sebastián means beach time, excellent Basque food, and strolling along the Paseo de la Concha. The monuments, such as they are, can easily be viewed before lunch.

The **Museo de San Telmo,** Plaza Zuloaga, 1 (☎ 943-42-49-70), housed in a 16th-century Dominican monastery, contains an impressive collection of Basque arti-facts dating from prehistoric Iberian times. The museum also includes works by Zuloaga (*Torreillos en Turégano,* for example), golden age artists such as El Greco and Ribera, and a large number of Basque painters. Standing in the old town at the base of Monte Urgull, the museum is open Tuesday through Saturday from 10:30am to 1:30pm and 4 to 7pm, Sunday 10am to 2pm. Admission is 350 ptas. ($2.35) adults, 200 ptas. ($1.35) students and children.

The wide promenade **Paseo Nuevo** almost encircles Monte Urgull, one of the two mountains between which San Sebastián is nestled (**Monte Igueldo** is the other one). A ride along this promenade opens onto panoramic vistas of the Bay of Biscay. The paseo comes to an end at the **Palacio del Mar,** Muelle, 34 (☎ **943-44-00-99**), an oceanographic museum and aquarium. Like most cutting-edge aquariums, it boasts a mesmerizing collection of huge tanks containing myriad marine species. A transparent underwater walkway allows an entire 360° view of sharks, rays, and other fish as they swim around you. A maritime museum upstairs presents a fascinating synopsis of mankind's precarious relationship with the sea down through the ages through historical displays of fishing gear, naval artifacts, and marine fossils. Here you can also see the skeleton of the last whale caught in the Bay of Biscay, in 1878. The museum is open July to May, daily from 10am to 1:30pm and 3 to 7pm, and June, daily 10am to 10pm. Admission is 700 ptas. ($4.70) for adults, 350 ptas. ($2.35) for children ages 5 to 12, and free for children 4 and under.

Other sights include **El Palacio de Miramar,** which stands on its own hill opening onto La Concha. In the background is the residential district of Antiguo. Queen María Cristina, after whom the grandest hotel in the north of Spain is named, opened this palace in 1893, but by the turbulent 1930s it had fallen into disrepair. The city council took it over in 1971 and renovations continue. You can visit daily in summer from 9am to 9:30pm and daily in winter from 10am to 5pm. Because you can't go inside the palace, you must settle for a look at the lawns and gardens. The palace stands on land splitting the two major beaches of San Sebastián: **Playa de la Concha** and **Playa de Ondarreta.**

Another palace of interest is the **Palacio de Ayete,** which was constructed by the duke of Bailéen in 1878 and became the summer home of King Alfonso XIII and his queen, María Cristina, until their own Palacio Miramar (see above) was completed. With 250,000 square feet of parkland, the palace also served as the summer home of Franco from 1940 until 1975. The residence remains closed to the public, but you can wander through the beautiful grounds daily in summer from 10am to 8:30pm or in off-season daily from 10am to 5pm. To reach it, take bus number 19 to Ayete from Plaza de Guipúzcoa.

Finally, to get the best view of the city take the funicular to the top of **Monte Igueldo,** where from a gazebo you get a panoramic view of the bay and the Cantabrian coastline. From June 25 through September 25, the funicular runs Monday through Friday from 10am to 9pm and on Saturday and Sunday from 10am to 10pm. Off-season service is daily from 11am to 8pm. A round-trip fare costs 170 ptas. ($1.15). It's also possible to drive up. In spring, the air is scented with honeysuckle.

SHOPPING

Your immersion into Basque culture will probably prompt you to buy some of the handcrafts and accessories from the region. Two of the best outlets for them include **Txapela,** calle Puerto, s/n (☎ 943-42-02-43), and **Arriluzea,** calle 31 de Augusto, 13 (☎ 943-42-56-66). Both sell souvenirs and rough cotton shirts for which the Basques are famous. And if you're just looking for a *boina* (beret), or any other form of headgear, consider a visit to the venerable shelves of San Sebastián's oldest hat manufacturer, **Ponsol,** calle Narrica, 4 (☎ 943-42-08-76). For virtually anything else within the city, try the length of the city's most congested shopping district, **Paseo de Muelle,** where dozens of merchants hawk everything from T-shirts to cameras and film.

WHERE TO STAY

If you book well in advance, you'll find many good hotel values, but in season most hoteliers may insist that you take at least half-board (breakfast plus one main meal).

VERY EXPENSIVE

✪ **Hotel María Cristina.** Oquendo, 7, 20004 San Sebastián. ☎ **800/221-2340** in the U.S., or 943-42-49-00. Fax 943-42-39-14. www.luxury.collection.com. E-mail: hmc@ittsheraton. com. 136 units. A/C MINIBAR TEL. 29,500–57,000 ptas. ($197.65–$381.90) double; 45,000–185,000 ptas. ($301.50–$1,239.50) suite. AE, DC, MC. Parking 2,900 ptas. ($19.45).

One of the most spectacular belle epoque hotels in Spain, enviably positioned in the heart of town midway between the bay and Río Urumea, this is the town's top hotel. Set behind a facade of chiseled stone and ornate ironwork, the Cristina opened in 1912 and was once the preferred hotel of virtually every titled aristocrat in France and Spain who came here. Today the clientele is likely to include movie stars, film directors, and a crowd of newly monied moguls; this is where the glitterati stay during San Sebastián's film festival.

It was richly remodeled in 1987. The public rooms are opulent with ormolu, Cuban mahogany, acres of onyx and exotic marbles, and rosewood marquetry. The spacious guest rooms are appropriately lavish, with luxury beds, bathrooms, and furnishings. Amenities include extraplush towels and hair dryers.

Dining/Diversions: The main dining room, the restaurant Easo, serves Basque and international food in three-course, fixed-price lunches and dinners. The hotel also contains one of the most beautiful bars in town, the Gritti, with occasional piano music.

Amenities: 24-hour room service, baby-sitting, laundry/valet, concierge, car rentals (with or without driver), business center.

EXPENSIVE

Hotel de Londres y de Inglaterra. Zubleta, 2, 20007 San Sebastián. ☎ **943-42-69-89.** Fax 943-42-00-31. www.paisvasco.com/hotel/londres. E-mail: h.londres@paisvasco.com. 145 units. A/C MINIBAR TV TEL. 19,800–21,500 ptas. ($132.65–$144.05) double; 23,000–28,000 ptas. ($154.10–$187.60) suite. AE, DC, MC, V. Parking 1,800 ptas. ($12.05) nearby.

Beside the northern edge of the town's most popular beach, Playa de la Concha, this venerable 19th-century hotel is one of the most stylish in town. It's not as plush as the María Cristina, but then again, it's significantly more affordable. Views from many of the balconies encompass the beach and a handful of rocky offshore islands. The traditional-style public rooms contain deep armchairs and big windows. Completely renovated in the past few years, the hotel has comfortably conservative and good-size guest rooms with a vaguely English decor, individual safes, and modern marble bathrooms with hair dryers.

Dining/Diversions: Serving both Basque and international cuisine is La Brasserie Mari Galant. A bar is adjacent to it, and there's also the street-level Swing Bar.

Amenities: Room service (from 1 to 4pm and 8:30 to 11pm), laundry/valet, concierge, baby-sitting, in-house tour operator/travel agent, car rentals, cafeteria, and bingo parlor.

MODERATE

Hotel San Sebastián. Avenida Zumalacárregui, 20, 20008 San Sebastián. ☎ **943-21-44-00.** Fax 943-21-72-99. 94 units. MINIBAR TV TEL. 14,000–18,000 ptas. ($93.80–$120.60) double; 24,000–26,500 ptas. ($160.80–$177.55) suite. AE, DC, MC, V. Parking 1,400 ptas. ($9.40). Bus: 5.

Located only a short distance from Ondarreta beach, near the edge of the city on the main road to Bilbao, this modern hotel has a swimming pool in a pleasant garden, as well as an informal restaurant, a disco, two bars, and one coffee bar. The small rooms are comfortable and attractively furnished, each with a firm mattress and a tidily kept tiled bathroom. The place is a serviceable but not exciting stopover.

Monte Igueldo. Paseo del Faro, 134, Monte Igueldo, 20008 San Sebastián. ☎ **943-21-02-11.** Fax 943-21-50-28. 125 units. TV TEL. 16,500–18,000 ptas. ($110.55–$120.60) double; 22,000–24,000 ptas. ($147.40–$160.80) triple. Extra bed 5,500 ptas. ($38.50). AE, DC, MC, V. Free parking. Bus: Igueldo.

This first-class hotel is perched like a castle on the top of the mountain overlooking San Sebastián, only a 10-minute drive from the center of town. The public rooms, bedrooms, and pool terrace all boast panoramic views of the Cantabrian coast. Each of the streamlined, modern rooms has a private balcony. Furnishings are standardized but reasonably comfortable; each room has a firm mattress and an immaculately kept bathroom clad in tiles. Ample parking is provided. A restaurant serves Spanish and international cuisine; there is also a bar on the premises.

Niza. Zubieta, 56, 20007 San Sebastián. ☎ **943-42-66-63.** Fax 943-42-66-63. www.adegi.es/hotelniza. E-mail: niza@adego.es. 41 units. TV TEL. 13,700–15,900 ptas. ($91.80–$106.55) double. AE, MC, V. Parking 1,000 ptas. ($6.70) nearby. Bus: 5 or 6.

This charming little hotel, which opens onto the Playa de la Concha, has real character and a location near the beach and the esplanade. It has modern furnishings in the small bedrooms and antiques in the public lounges. The petit salon, for example, contains an Oriental rug, Directoire chairs, a tall grandfather clock, and a rosewood breakfront. In direct contrast are the rather basic rooms, with wooden headboards, white walls, and wall-to-wall carpeting. There's a pizzeria in the cellar, plus a bar overlooking the sea.

INEXPENSIVE

Codina. Avenida Zumalacárregui, 21, 20008 San Sebastián. ☎ **943-21-22-00.** Fax 943-21-25-23. 77 units. TV TEL. July–Sept (including half board), 10,000 ptas. ($67) double; Oct–June, 8,800 ptas. ($58.95) double. AE, DC, MC, V. Parking 1,000 ptas. ($6.70). Bus: 5, 25.

Set within an attractive and upscale residential district, less than 250 yards from one of San Sebastián's two most popular beaches (Playa Undaretta), this six-story, modern-looking hotel was originally built in the mid-1960s. Each of the comfortably furnished, compact rooms has a view of the bay and simple, summery, virtually indestructible furniture, including good beds. On the side of the hotel that faces the busy avenida Zumalacárregui, you'll find a popular cafe and bar that serves a traditional Basque cuisine.

Hostal Bahía. Calle San Martín, 54B, 20007 San Sebastián. ☎ **943-46-92-11.** Fax 943-46-39-14. 59 units. TV TEL. 7,900–10,900 ptas. ($52.95–$73.05) double. Rates include breakfast. DC, MC, V. Parking 1,500 ptas. ($10.05). Bus: 5, 6, 7, 8, or 9.

A good-value hotel just 1 block from the beach near a string of other hotels, the Bahía features guest rooms of varying sizes: Some are large enough to contain sofas and armchairs; others fall into the cubicle category. Each comes with a firm mattress and a tidy little bathroom with a shower stall. Many North Americans stay at the hostal and take public transportation to Pamplona for the running of the bulls.

Hotel Parma. Paseo de Salamanca, 10, 20003 San Sebastián. ☎ **943-42-88-93.** Fax 943-42-40-82. www.atenet.es/hagi/parma/index.htm. 27 units. TEL. 9,300–15,300 ptas. ($62.30–$102.50) double. AE, DC, MC, V. Parking 1,800 ptas. ($12.05). Bus: 5, 6, 8, 9, 21, or 28.

This modern, clean hotel in the center of town has beautiful views of the ocean. The Parma has up-to-date but small rooms cozily furnished in wood, with good, modern bathrooms with a shower stall. There is also a downstairs snack bar as well as a pleasant TV lobby, with armchairs and sofas. Breakfast is the only meal served.

WHERE TO DINE
EXPENSIVE

✪ **Akelare.** Paseo del Padre Orkolaga, 56. ☎ **943-21-20-52.** Reservations strongly recommended. Main courses 2,500–5,500 ptas. ($16.75–$36.85); tasting menu 9,500 ptas. ($63.65). AE, DC, MC, V. Tues–Sun 1–3:30pm, Tues–Sat 8:30–11pm. Closed Jan 2–Mar 7 and from Sept 27–Oct 13. BASQUE.

A visit to Akelare is a must for serious foodies. Owner/chef Pedro Subijana won the 1983 National Prize for Gastronomy, awarded to the best chef in Spain. His preparations have influenced a generation of chefs and defined, perhaps more than any other, the entire philosophy of *la nueva cocina vasca* (modern Basque cuisine). Established in 1974, the restaurant lies on the western edge of San Sebastián, within a hexagonal villa originally built as a catering hall for weddings and christenings. Inside, a sweeping view through large windows encompasses the mists and raging currents of the Bay of Biscay far below. The plushly upholstered modern decor, with its hospitable fireplace, is an appropriate foil for dishes inspired by the Basque *caseríos* (farmsteads).

The perfect beginning to any meal here is puff pastry filled with fillets of anchovies, accompanied by a glass of chilled *fino* sherry. Traditional dishes might include fish cooked on a griddle with garlic and parsley; beans accompanied by bacon, chorizo, and pork ribs; baked rice with clams; or a special *marmitako* (fisherman's stew). More innovative are the snails with watercress sauce; boiled cabbage stuffed with duck meat and served with puree of celery; a warm salad of bonito fish served with a basil, lemon, chervil, and vinegar sauce; and fillet of duck with an assortment of exotic seasonal mushrooms. On occasion, Subijana may venture into the dining room to gauge the reaction to his inventions and to offer advice about the day's menu. The name of the restaurant, incidentally, translates from the Basque as "Witches' Sabbath."

✪ **Arzak.** Alto de Miracruz, 21. ☎ **943-28-55-93.** Reservations required. Main courses 2,800–4,900 ptas. ($18.75–$32.85); fixed-price menu 10,800 ptas. ($72.35) excluding drinks. AE, DC, MC, V. Tues–Sun 1–3:30pm, Tues–Sat 8:30–11:30pm. Closed June 15–July 3 and Nov 5–30. BASQUE.

One of the most famous restaurants in the Basque world (an honor it shares with Ake-lare; see above), this legendary establishment occupies the lavishly renovated child-hood home of owner/chef Juan Mari Arzak. Well known in San Sebastián for his role in preparing a meal for Queen Elizabeth II of Britain (for which he later received an invitation to Buckingham Palace), Arzak combines staples of the Basque culinary legacy with many new creations of his own and is in the forefront of new Basque cui-sine. Begin with a selection of fresh oysters or, even more elegant, natural foie gras. Crayfish is regularly featured as an appetizer, as is the chef's special *sopa de pescado* (fish soup). For a main course, consider *merluza* (hake) in a vinaigrette with onions and small squid. On the back of the menu is a list of classic dishes that have won the most praise among visitors since the restaurant's opening—everything from stuffed sweet peppers with a fish mousse to pheasant or partridge. For dessert, the orange flan with cream might just be the best version you've ever had. The restaurant is on the main road leading from the center of town to the French border.

Casa Nicolasa. Calle Aldamar, 4. ☎ **943-42-17-62.** Reservations required. Main courses 2,600–4,450 ptas. ($17.40–$29.80); menú del chef 6,100 ptas. ($40.85). AE, DC, MC, V. Mon–Sat 1–3:30pm, Tues–Sat 8:30–11:30pm. Closed Jan 21–Feb 13. BASQUE.

Members of all-male eating clubs (a Basque tradition begun in the 19th century) have assured us that Casa Nicolasa serves the best cuisine at San Sebastián. That would be difficult to prove, especially in a city where international food critics have rated Arzak and Akelare even higher (see above).

In the heart of the resort, at the edge of the old town by the Mercado la Brecha, the restaurant features a refined cuisine and impeccable service. Diners are made to feel like guests being served by a proper butler. Master chef José Juan Castillo, greatly aided by his gracious wife, Ana María, seems to believe that gastronomy should be elevated to a high art—and he does that convincingly here.

Many of the dishes served here have stood the test of time; others reflect the free-reign culinary imagination of the 1990s. The foie gras is homemade and is the smoothest, albeit the most expensive, way to begin a meal here. *Rape* (monkfish) is prepared in various creative ways and, we have found, is one of the most satisfying main courses. Save room for dessert, as the pastry selections are one of the outstanding features of the kitchen. When business is at its peak in August and September, the restaurant is likely to open Monday night for dinner as well.

✪ **Martín Berasategui.** Loidi Kalea, 4, Lasarte. ☎ **943-36-64-71.** Reservations required. Main courses 2,000–3,750 ptas. ($13.40–$25.15); tasting menu 8,500 ptas. ($56.95). MC, V. Tues–Sat 8:30–11pm. Closed 2 weeks at Christmas. BASQUE.

Just when you thought the dining situation in San Sebastián couldn't stand any more starred chefs, along comes Martín Berasategui, with a cuisine that has excited food critics throughout Europe. Trained by his mother, who cooked for local fishers for a small fee, Berasategui opened his restaurant on the outskirts of town, and the world has literally flocked to his door ever since.

His cuisine is subtle and pure, and he uses butter and cream for desserts only. The hors d'oeuvres are among the best we've ever sampled in the region—everything from a curl of cider-marinated mackerel with fried anchovies in olive oil to morsels of rare tuna belly grilled over wooden charcoal. Starters include the rich-sounding lobster soup with barnacles. For a main dish, opt for such delectable choices as hake with baby clams or a refreshing gazpacho of *langostinos*. If you try one of the "tasting menus," you'll get a summation of Berasategui's cuisine—perhaps pan-seared lambs' brains surrounded by baby salad greens and a fat and juicy slice of duck liver. The chef's attention to detail is terrific. For example, for a *porrusalda* (soup) made with, among other ingredients, fresh sea eel and ribbons of smoked eel, Berasategui collects the moisture the eels give off when smoked and mixes it back into the savory broth.

✪ **Panier Fleuri.** Paseo de Salamanca, 1. ☎ **943-42-42-05.** Reservations required. Main courses 2,300–4,500 ptas. ($15.40–$30.15); fixed-price menu 5,800 ptas. ($38.85). AE, DC, MC, V. Thurs–Tues 1–3:30pm, Mon–Tues and Thurs–Sat 8:30–11pm. Closed June 1–24 and Dec 24–31. BASQUE/INTERNATIONAL.

Yet another celebrated restaurant in San Sebastián, this citadel of cuisine serves Basque dishes with a definite French flavor and flair, typical of the resort of Biarritz across the border in France. A third generation of the Fombedilla family of chefs has had a long time to perfect their cuisine and their special offerings. Service is discreet and elegant, and diners here have a chance to learn why Basque food preparation is regarded as among the finest in Europe. The setting alone is rewarding, in a formal dining room opening onto the pounding surf at the mouth of the Urumea River.

The chef, Tatus Fombellida, has won the National Prize for Gastronomy in Spain, and critics of San Sebastián cuisine claim she's better than ever. Her *faisan* (pheasant) and *becada asada* (roast woodcock) have been hailed as among the finest game dishes at the resort. Another delectable offering is sole baked with spinach and presented with a fresh hollandaise sauce, similar to what you might find in one of the better restaurants of Florence. Finish off this rich fare with a lemon sorbet with champagne.

Even better known than the cuisine here is the wine cellar, which contains many vintage bottles. The wine steward will guide you through an often perplexing selection, including mellow versions of such wines as Remelluri, Barón de Oña, and Viña Albina.

MODERATE

Juanito Kojua. Puerto, 14. ☎ **943-42-01-80.** Reservations required. Main courses 1,750–5,500 ptas. ($11.75–$36.85); fixed-price menus 2,500–3,100 ptas. ($16.75–$20.75). AE, DC, MC, V. Daily 1–3:30pm, Mon–Sat 8:30–11:30pm. BASQUE/SEAFOOD.

This little seafood restaurant in the old town, off Plaza de la Constitución, has no decor to speak of, but it has become famous throughout Spain. There's always a wait, but it's worth it. There are two dining areas on the main floor, behind a narrow bar (perfect for an appetizer while you're waiting for your table), plus one downstairs—both air-conditioned in summer. Specialties may include paella, half a *besugo* (sea bream), rape (monkfish) *l'americana,* and *lubina* (sea bass). The meats are good, too, but it's best to stick to the fresh fish dishes.

✪ **Urepel.** Paseo de Salamanca, 3. ☎ **943-42-40-40.** Reservations required. Main courses 1,500–3,400 ptas. ($10.05–$22.80). AE, DC, MC, V. Mon and Wed–Sat 1–3:30pm, Mon and Wed–Sat 8:30–11pm. Closed at Easter for Holy Week, July 1–23, and Dec 24–Jan 6. BASQUE/INTERNATIONAL.

Standing close to one of its major competitors, the equally rewarding Panier Fleuri (see above), Urepel lies near the mouth of the Urumea River, at the edge of the old town. Its interior is not as elegant as the establishments reviewed above, but fans of this place aren't bothered by that at all. They're here for the food.

The chef demands impeccable ingredients to concoct a menu of traditional Basque fare, and serves only the freshest and best produce along with the finest cuts of meat and "harvests of the sea." The Basque palate, at least according to legend, is the most discriminating in Spain, and few complaints are heard here. The restaurant is the domain of Tomás Almandoz, one of the outstanding chefs in the north of Spain. Seafood dominates the menu and is deftly handled by the kitchen staff. The fish is often served with delicate sauces, and the main courses are made even better by an emphasis on fresh and perfectly prepared vegetables. Rape, *dorada,* and *cigalas* (crayfish) are likely to turn up on the menu. You can also order goose or duck, somewhat rare in San Sebastián. One specialty is *pato de caserio filleteado a la naranja* (regional-style duck flavored with oranges).

One local food critic got so carried away with the dessert cart and its presentation that she claimed, "It would take Velázquez to arrange a pastry so artfully"—an indication of how highly regarded this place is. We prefer it in the evening instead of at midday, when many of the tables are reserved by local businesspersons and government officials.

INEXPENSIVE

La Oka. San Martín, 46. ☎ **943-46-38-84.** Main courses 750–1,400 ptas. ($5.05–$9.40); fixed-price menu 1,400 ptas. ($9.40). AE, MC, V. Daily 1–3:30pm, Fri–Sat 8:30–11pm. BASQUE.

Don't come to La Oka, near the beach in the center of town, looking for glamour. Come for an inexpensive self-service cafeteria experience. Some critics, in fact, rate it the best self-service cafeteria in Spain. The diners represent a cross section of the city's office workers. The Basque cooking here is hearty and plentiful, and you can also order a very good Valencia-style paella.

SAN SEBASTIÁN AFTER DARK

The best evening entertainment in San Sebastián is to go **tapas tasting** in the old quarter of town. Throughout the rest of Spain this is known as a tapeo, or tapas crawl. In San Sebastián it's called a *poteo-ir-de-pinchos,* or searching out morsels on toothpicks. Groups of young people often spend their evenings on some 20 streets in the old town, each leading toward Monte Urgull, the port, or La Brecha marketplace. Alameda del Bulevar, the "popular grove," is the most upscale of these streets; calle Fermín Calveton, one of the most popular. You'll find plenty of these places on your own, but here are some to get you going.

Bar Asador Ganbara, calle San Jerónimo, 21 (☎ **943-42-25-75**), is decorated with a flair in light-colored wood and is a tapas lover's delight. The dishes are well prepared, using market-fresh ingredients. Try the house specialty and the chef's pride: small melt-in-your-mouth croissants filled with cheese, egg, bacon, and Serrano ham. Also sample the spider crab and prawns with mayonnaise. Tapas run 150 to 250 ptas. ($1 to $1.70); drinks from 175 to 600 ptas. ($1.15 to $4). In addition to its bar service, the establishment also runs a restaurant in a separate section, offering a fixed-price menu at 2,950 ptas. ($19.75). The bar is open Tuesday through Sunday from 11am to 3:15pm and Tuesday through Saturday 6 to 11:45pm. The restaurant is open Tuesday through Sunday from 1 to 3:30pm and Tuesday through Saturday 8 to 11:15pm. Calle San Jerónimo runs at right angles to calle Fermín Calveton.

The tasty tapas served at **Casa Alcalde,** Mayor, 19 (☎ 943-42-62-16), just a 5-minute walk from the Parque Alderdi Eder, are thinly sliced ham, cheese, and shell-fish dishes. The different varieties are all neatly displayed, and priced from 175 to 225 ptas. ($1.15 to $1.50). You can also have full meals in a small restaurant at the back, for 3,000 to 4,500 ptas. ($20.10 to $30.15). It's open daily from 10am to 11pm.

The variety of tapas and wines offered at **Casa Valles,** Reyes Católicos, 10 (☎ 943-45-22-10), seems endless. Go to hang out with the locals and feast on tid-bits guaranteed to spoil your dinner. Most tapas cost 150 ptas. ($1), with a beer going for 200 ptas. ($1.35). Casa Valles is in the center of town behind the cathedral. Open daily from 8:30 to 11:30pm (closed the last 2 weeks of June and the last 2 weeks of December).

Many locals say that **La Cepa,** 31 de Agosto, 7-9 (☎ 943-42-63-94), located on the northern edge of the old town, serves perhaps the best tapas in town, and the Jabugo ham is one proof of this claim. Try the grilled squid or the salt-cod-and-green-pepper omelette. You can also order dinner here—a daily changing menu that costs 3,000 ptas. ($20.10). Tapas begin at 175 ptas. ($1.15) but could go up to 1,900 ptas. ($12.75) for a small portion of Jabugo ham. A glass of wine costs 100 ptas. (65¢). It's open daily from 11am to midnight.

Delectable tapas can also be found at **Aloña/Berri,** Berminghan, 24, Nuevo Gros (☎ 943-290-818), where you can feast on the delights of silky salt cod brandade, pigeon in pastry, and anchovies in red pepper cream from 150 ptas. ($1). At **Oñatz,** Urdaneta, 22 (☎ 943-455-547), they serve the city's most exquisite morsels, none better than a "haystack" of foie gras and apples. You can go on to the mussel and garlic flan or braised oxtail. At the family run **Bar Juli,** Viteri, 27, Renteria (☎ 943-512-887), Igor, a graduate of Arzak (see above), lures and satisfies the most demanding palates of San Sebastián. Try his sushilike tuna salad and what have been called "the best seafood *croquetas* on the northern shore of Spain." Tapas cost from 150 to 350 ptas. ($1 to $2.35).

In most of the Basque country, the tapas-eating ritual is different from the rest of Spain. A platter of tapas, or more correctly called pinchos, such as stuffed anchovies is placed out on the bar. Patrons spear the tasty morsels with toothpicks, and when they're done, servers tally up the toothpicks to determine how much is owed. A pale dry white wine, known as xacoli, is usually consumed chilled in a plain highball glass to accompany tapas such as eels with parsley, garlic, and virgin olive oil.

San Sebastián has other nightlife possibilities, but they dim when compared to a tapeo. Nevertheless, if disco isn't too retro for you, head for **Kabutzia,** Muelle (no phone), where a cover and one drink costs 2,000 ptas. ($13.40). The club opens at 8pm, with variable closing times, depending on business. The best live jazz is found at the jazz gallery, **Altxeri Galeria,** calle Reina Regente, 2 (☎ 943-42-29-31), where a cover charge may or may not be imposed, depending on the group. It's open Sunday through Thursday from 5pm to 1:30am and Friday and Saturday 5pm to 3:30am.

San Sebastián's only venue for gambling is the **Casino de San Sebastián,** Mayor, 1 (☎ 943-42-92-15). The casino requires minimum bets of between 250 and 500 ptas. ($1.70 and $3.35) for the roulette tables, and 250 ptas. ($1.70) for the blackjack tables. Entrance costs 625 ptas. ($4.20) per person, and requires the presentation of an identity card with a photograph or a passport. Jackets and neckties for men are not required. From September 16 to June 14, the casino is open daily from 6:30pm to 3am (until 4am on Saturday and holidays), and between June 15 and September 15, it's open daily from 6:30pm to 4am (till 5am on Saturday and on holidays).

SIDE TRIPS FROM SAN SEBASTIÁN

One of the reasons for coming to San Sebastián is to use it as a base for touring the sur-rounding area. Driving is best because bus connections are awkward or nonexistent.

PASAI DONIBANE

On the east bank of a natural harbor 6½ miles (10.5km) from San Sebastián, Pasai Donibane—formerly known by its Spanish name, Pasajes de San Juan—is one of the most typical of Basque fishing villages. Many visitors come here to dine. The village, with its codfish-packing factories, is on a sheltered harbor; fishing boats are tied up at the wharf. The architecture is appealing: five- and six-story balconied tenement-like buildings in different colors.

Victor Hugo lived here in the summer of 1846 (it hasn't changed much since) at building number 63 on the narrow main street, San Juan.

In summer, don't take a car into the village. Parking is difficult, the medieval streets are one-way, and the wait at traffic signals is long because all southbound traffic has to clear the street before northbound motorists have the right of way.

A bus leaves every 15 minutes from the calle Aldamar in San Sebastián for **Pasajes de San Pedro,** Pasai Donibane's neighboring fishing village. From here, it's possible to walk to Pasai Donibane. Buses head back to San Sebastián from Pasajes de San Pedro at a quarter to the hour all day long.

Where to Dine

Txulotxo. San Juan, 82, Pasai Donibane. ☎ **943-52-39-52.** Reservations recommended. Main courses 1,200–2,000 ptas. ($8.05–$13.40); menú del día 2,000 ptas. ($13.40). AE, V. Wed–Mon 1:30–4:30pm, Wed–Sat and Mon 8:30–11:30pm. Closed Dec. BASQUE.

Right on the waterfront, this old stone building with a glass-enclosed dining room overlooking the harbor is one of the most authentic and typical of Basque restaurants. The house specialties are made from fish delivered daily. For openers, try the *sopa de pescado* (fish soup) or a mixture of *entremeses variados* (hors d'oeuvres). Although pasta dishes are featured, most diners opt for one of the good-tasting seafood selections, per-haps hake in green sauce or perfectly grilled shrimp. The grilled monkfish with clams and shrimp is also done to perfection. There are new specialties worth the palette, including brochettes and *crepes de txangurro.*

LOYOLA

Surrounded by mountain scenery, Loyola, 34 miles (55km) southwest of San Sebastián, is the birthplace of St. Ignatius, the founder of the Jesuits. He was born in 1491, died in 1556, and was canonized in 1622. The sanctuary at Loyola is the most visited attraction outside San Sebastián.

There are large pilgrimages to Loyola for the annual celebration on St. Ignatius Day, July 31. The activity is centered at the **Monasterio de San Ignacio de Loyola,** an immense structure built by the Jesuits in the 1700s around the Loyola family manor house near Azpeitia. An International Festival of Romantic Music is held here during the first week of August.

The **basilica** is the work of Italian architect Fontana. Surrounded by a 118-foot-high cupola by Churriguera, it is circular in design. From 12:30 to 3:30pm daily, visitors can enter the **Santa Casa,** site of the former Loyola manor house, with its 15th-century tower. The rooms in which the saint was born and in which he convalesced have been converted into richly decorated chapels. At the entrance you can rent a tape detailing Loyola's life, and dioramas are shown at the end of the tour.

Six buses a day leave from Plaza Guipúzcoa, 2, San Sebastián, for Loyola (the first departing at 8:30am and the last at 8pm). Buses return about every 2 hours.

2 Fuenterrabía (Hondarribía)

14 miles (23km) E of San Sebastián, 317 miles (510km) N of Madrid, 11 miles (18km) W of St-Jean-de-Luz (France)

A big seaside resort and fishing port, Fuenterrabía (Hondarribía in Basque) lies near the French frontier, and for that reason has been subject to frequent attacks over the centuries. In theory, it was supposed to guard access to Spain, but sometimes it hasn't performed that task too well.

ESSENTIALS

GETTING THERE   Fuenterrabía does not have a train station, but it is serviced by the station in nearby Irún (☎ 943-61-67-08 for information). Buses depart Irún's Plaza de San Juan for Fuentarrabía at 10- to 15-minute intervals. Irún is the end of the line for trains in northern Spain. East of Irún, you must board French trains.

Buses run every 15 minutes from Plaza Guipúzcoa in San Sebastián to Fuenterrabía, 1 hour away. Call ☎ 943-64-13-02 for information.

By car take A-8 east to the French border, turning toward the coast at the exit sign for Fuenterrabía.

VISITOR INFORMATION   The **office of tourism** at calle Javier Ugarte, 6 (☎ 943-64-54-58), is open July and August daily 10am to 8pm; Off-season Monday through Friday 9am to 1:30pm and 4 to 6:30pm, Saturday 10am to 2pm.

EXPLORING FUENTERRABÍA & ENVIRONS

The most interesting part of town is the **medieval quarter** in the upper market. Some of the villas here date from the early 17th century. The fishing district, in the lower part of town, is called **La Marina:** old homes, painted boats, and marine atmosphere attract many visitors. Because restaurants in Fuenterrabía tend to be very expensive, you can fill up here on seafood tapas in the many taverns along the waterfront. The beach at Fuenterrabía is wide and sandy, and many prefer it to the more famous ones at San Sebastián.

Wander for an hour or two around the old quarter, taking in the calle Mayor, calle Tiendas y Pampinot, and calle Obispo. The **Castillo de Carlos V,** standing at the Plaza de las Armas, has been turned into one of the smallest and most desirable paradors in Spain (see below). It's hard to get a room here unless you reserve well in advance, but you can visit the well-stocked bar over the entrance hall.

Sancho Abarca, a king of Navarre in the 10th century, is supposed to have founded the original castle that stood on this spot though the present look owes more to

Charles V in the 16th century. You can still see the battle scars on the castle that date from the time of the Napoleonic invasion of Spain.

The most impressive church in the old quarter is the **Iglesia de Santa María,** a Gothic structure that was vastly restored in the 17th century and given a baroque tower. The proxy wedding of Louis XIV and the Infanta María Teresa took place here in June 1660.

If you have a car, you can take some interesting trips in the area, especially to **Cabo Higuer,** a promontory with panoramic views, reached by going 2½ miles (4km) north. Leave by the harbor and beach road. You can see the French coast and the town of Hendaye from this cape.

You can also head west out of town along the **Jaizkibel Road,** which many motorists prefer at sunset. After going 3 miles (5km), you'll reach the shrine of the Virgin of Guadalupe, where another panoramic view unfolds. From here, you can see the French Basque coast. Even better views await if you continue along to the Hostal Jaizkibel. If you stay on this road, you will come to the little fishing village of Pasai Donibane (see "Side Trips from San Sebastián" above), 11 miles (18km) away.

WHERE TO STAY

✪ **Hotel Pampinot.** Kale Nagusia, 3, 20280 Fuenterrabía. ☎ **943-64-06-00.** Fax 943-64-51-28. 8 units. TV TEL. 13,000–16,500 ptas. ($87.10–$110.55) double; 17,000–20,000 ptas. ($113.90–$134) suite. AE, DC, MC, V. Closed Nov.

If the walls here could talk, they would probably reveal more tales than those of any other hotel in the region. Originally built as an aristocratic mansion in 1587, it housed the Infanta María Teresa for a night as she headed toward France to marry the Sun King, Louis XIV. Today, it presents a richly textured stone facade with Renaissance detailing and heraldic symbols to one of the most historic and quiet streets of the old town. Inside, an antique sense of elegance is conveyed by beamed ceilings, exposed stonework, parquet flooring, and ornate ironwork. The midsize guest rooms are traditional and charming, with a mixture of antique and reproduction furniture, including good beds with firm mattresses. Each of the immaculately kept tiled bathrooms comes with a hair dryer. Parking is available along the street only.

Dining: Although breakfast is the only meal served, the staff can direct you to a choice of nearby eateries.

Amenities: Laundry, concierge, baby-sitting, car rentals.

Jáuregui. Zuloaga, 5, 20280 Fuenterrabía. ☎ **943-64-14-00.** Fax 943-64-44-04. www.adegi.es/hjauregui. E-mail: jauregui@adegi.es. 53 units. MINIBAR TV TEL. 8,900–11,600 ptas. ($59.65–$77.70) double for single use; 11,250–14,525 ptas. ($75.40–$97.30) double; 14,450–26,075 ptas. ($96.80–$174.70) apt. AE, MC, V. Parking 1,000 ptas. ($6.70).

Opened in 1981 in the center of the old village, this is a good choice for moderately priced accommodations. The modern interior boasts comfortable accessories, and the hotel also has a garage—a definite plus, since parking in Fuenterrabía is virtually impossible. Each of the small rooms is well furnished and maintained; thoughtful extras include a hair dryer in each bathroom, a safe in every room, and a shoeshine machine on each floor. Only breakfast is served.

Parador de Hondarribía. Plaza de Armas, 20280 Fuenterrabía. ☎ **943-64-55-00.** Fax 943-64-21-53. www.parador.es. 36 units. TEL. 15,000–19,000 ptas. ($100.50–$127.30) double. AE, DC, MC, V. Free parking.

This beautifully restored 10th-century castle, situated on a hill in the center of the old town, was once used by Emperor Charles V as a border fortification. The building itself is impressive, and so are the taste and imagination of the restoration: Antiques, old weapons, and standards hang from the high-vaulted ceilings. Some of the comfortable provincial-style rooms open onto the Bay of Biscay. Units range from small to medium in size, and each is well equipped with firm mattresses plus hair dryers in the tiled bathrooms. Breakfast is the only meal served. Parking is available out front. It's best to reserve a room here well in advance.

WHERE TO DINE

✪ **Ramón Roteta.** Villa Alnara. ☎ **943-64-16-93.** Reservations recommended. Main courses 2,200–3,200 ptas. ($14.75–$21.45). AE, MC, V. Tues–Sun 1:15–3:30pm and Tues–Sat 8:30–11pm. From June–Sept Tues–Sun 1:15-11pm. BASQUE.

Named after its owner and founder, this attractively furnished restaurant is one of Europe's most consistently respected purveyors of traditional Basque cuisine. Contained within what was originally a 1920s private villa, it lies on the southern outskirts of town, near the local parador and the city limits of Irún. Menu specialties include a terrine of green vegetables and fish served with red-pepper-flavored vinaigrette, baked sea crabs with tiny potatoes and onions, fresh pasta with seafood, and the dessert specialty, a mandarin-orange tart flavored with rose petals. The villa is surrounded by a pleasantly unstructured garden which can be appreciated from a table on the terrace.

Sebastián. Mayor, 7. ☎ **943-64-01-67.** Reservations required. Main courses 1,400–2,900 ptas. ($9.40–$19.45); fixed-price menus 5,000–6,500 ptas. ($33.50–$43.55). AE, DC, DISC, MC, V. Tues–Sun 1–3:30pm, 8:30–11:30pm. Closed Nov. BASQUE.

Lying within the oldest district of Fuenterrabía, close to the castle, this restaurant offers modern cuisine, well presented and using top-notch ingredients appropriate to the season. The two floors of the restaurant feature thick masonry walls, among which are scattered an array of 18th-century paintings. Try one of the specialties: foie gras of duckling Basque style, terrine of fresh mushrooms, or medallions of sole and salmon with seafood sauce.

3 Ondárroa

30 miles (48km) W of San Sebastián, 38 miles (61km) E of Bilbao, 265 miles (427km) N of Madrid

Ondárroa is described as a *pueblo típico,* a typical Basque fishing village. It is also the area's largest fishing port. Lying on a spit of land, it stands between a hill and a loop of the Artibay River. Laundry hangs from the windows of the little plant-filled balconied Basque houses, and most of the residents are engaged in canning and fish salting, if not fishing. The local church looks like a ship's prow at one end. Around the snug harbor you'll find many little places to drink and dine after taking a stroll through the village. From San Sebastián, Ondárroa is serviced by buses that run along the Costa Vasca.

If you're driving, head west from San Sebastián along the coastal road.

WHERE TO DINE

Restaurante Penalty. Eribera, 32. ☎ **94-683-00-00.** Reservations required. Main courses 1,800–3,000 ptas. ($12.05–$20.10). AE, MC, V. Thurs–Tues 1:30–3:30pm and 8:30–10:30pm. Closed Dec–Jan. SEAFOOD.

This small restaurant with a limited number of tables stands at a crossroads at the edge of town. Meals might include a house recipe for hake that is simply heavenly, plus other fish specialties. The *sopa de pescado* (fish soup) invariably makes a good choice for a beginning to a fine meal.

4 Lekeitio

38 miles (61km) W of San Sebastián, 37 miles (60km) E of Bilbao, 280 miles (451km) N of Madrid

This unspoiled but talked-about Basque fishing village is most often visited on a day trip. There are those who consider it "more authentic" than Ondárroa. Situated at the foot of Mount Calvario, Lekeitio opens onto a deeply indented bay. Queen Isabella II first gave the town prominence when she spent time here in the 19th century. Fishing may have diminished in recent years, but Lekeitio is still home to some of the Basque coast's trawlers. The island of San Nicolás converts the bay into a naturally protected harbor, a phenomenon that led to the village's growth. Note the 15th-century church guarding the harbor. Three tiers of flying buttresses characterize this monument, which has a baroque belfry. Go inside to the third south chapel, off the right nave, to see a remarkable altarpiece, *The Road to Calvary,* which was erected in a flamboyant Gothic style.

A beach lies across from the harbor, but the one at Carraspio, farther along the bay, is considered safer.

ESSENTIALS

GETTING THERE   Seven buses a day connect Lekeitio with Bilbao (45 minutes away), and four buses a day run from San Sebastián (1½ hours away).

Driving from Ondárroa, take the coastal road northwest along the Costa Vasca.

SPECIAL EVENTS   The town is noted for its festivals, including the **feast day of Saints Peter and Paul** on June 29, at which a *Kaxarranca,* a Basque folk dance, takes place. A dancer leaps about on top of a trunk carried through the streets by some hearty Basque fishers. Even better known is the controversial Jaiak San Antolín, or **goose festival,** on September 1 to 8. A gruesome custom, it involves hanging live geese in the harbor. Youths leap from rowboats to grab the greased necks of the geese. Both youth and goose are dunked into the water, using a system of pulleys, until the youth cries uncle or the neck of the goose is wrenched off. Unless your tastes run to the macabre, you might want to skip this one. The candlelit march through the streets, with everyone dressed in white, does not mourn the unfortunate geese but signals the end of the festival.

WHERE TO DINE

Restaurante Egaña. Santa Catalina, 4. ☎ **94-684-01-03.** Reservations not necessary. Main courses 950–1,600 ptas. ($6.35–$10.70); Tues–Fri menú del día 1,000–1,350 ptas. ($6.70–$9.05). AF, MC, V. Tues–Sun 1–4pm and 8–11pm and July–Sept 1am–11pm. SEAFOOD.

Fans of Basque seafood can get their fill in this spacious, breezy dining room on the upper side of the village. The portions are large and generous, and the price is right. The place is unfussy and unpretentious: You are here to eat without frills. The menu depends on the catch of the day—try the Basque-style hake.

5 Guernica

266 miles (428km) N of Madrid, 52 miles (84km) W of San Sebastián

The subject of Picasso's most famous painting (returned to Spain from the Museum of Modern Art in New York and now displayed at the Reina Sofía Museum in Madrid), Guernica, the spiritual home of the Basques and the seat of Basque nationalism, was destroyed in a Nazi air raid on April 26, 1937, during the Spanish Civil

War. It was the site of a revered oak tree, under whose branches Basques had elected their officials since medieval times. No one knows how many died during the 3½-hour attack—estimates range from 200 to 2,000. The bombers reduced the town to rubble, but a mighty symbol of independence was born. Though activists around the world attempted to rally support for the embattled Spanish Republicans, governments everywhere, including that of the United States, left the Spaniards to fend for themselves, refusing even to supply them with arms.

The town has been attractively rebuilt, close to its former style. The chimes of a church bell ring softly, and laughing children play in the street. In the midst of this peace, however, you'll suddenly come upon a sign: "Souvenirs . . . Remember."

The former Basque parliament, **Casa de Juntas (or Juntetxea),** is the principal attraction in town. It contains a historical display of Guernica and is open daily from 10am to 2pm and 4 to 7pm in summer (to 6pm in winter). Admission is free. Outside are the remains of the ancient communal oak tree, symbol of Basque independence; it was not uprooted by Hitler's bombs. From the train station, head up the calle Urioste.

GETTING THERE

From Bilbao, trains run five times daily to Guernica. Trip time is 50 minutes. Call ☎ **94-625-11-82** for schedules.

Vascongados, at Estación de Amara in San Sebastián, runs buses to Bilbao, with connections to Guernica. Inquire at the station or call ☎ **94-625-50-13** for schedules. From Bilbao, CAV, calle Hurtado de Amézaga (☎ **94-423-78-60**), operates 28 buses per day to Guernica Monday through Friday and five buses per day on the weekends. The trip time is 45 minutes.

From Bilbao, head east along the A-8 superhighway; cut north on the 6315 and follow the signs for Guernica. From San Sebastián, drive west along A-8, and cut north on the 6315. A more scenic, but slightly longer, route involves driving west from San Sebastián on the A-8, and branching off on the coastal road to Ondárroa. Continue on as the road turns south and follow the signs to Guernica.

A NEARBY PLACE TO DINE

Asador Zaldua. Sabino Arana, 10. ☎ **94-687-08-71.** Reservations required in summer. Main courses 1,600–2,400 ptas. ($10.70–$16.10); menú del día 3,500 ptas. ($23.45). AE, MC, V. Daily 1:30–3:30pm, Mon–Sat 8:30–11pm and Nov–May Fri–Sat 8:30–11pm only. Closed Dec 20–Jan 5. BASQUE.

Most of the specialties served here come from the blazing grill, whose turning spits are visible from the dining room. A wide array of seafood and fish is also available, some dishes baked to a flaky goodness in a layer of rock salt. The lobster salad alone is worth the trip here. The restaurant is 5½ miles (9km) north of the center of town on the road to Bermeo.

6 Bilbao

246 miles (396km) N of Madrid, 62 miles (100km) W of San Sebastián

Bilbao, Spain's sixth-largest city and biggest port, has been described as an "ugly, gray, decaying, smokestack city," and so it is—in part. But it has a number of interesting secrets to reveal, as well as good cuisine, and as a rail hub it serves as a center for exploring some of the best attractions in the Basque country. Most of the city's attractions can be viewed in a day or two. Many visitors flock here only to see the new and controversial $100 million Guggenheim Museum, designed by American architect

Bilbao

Basílica de Begoña **6**
Catedral de Santiago **3**
Euskal Arkeología **4**
Museo de Bellas Artes **2**
Museo Guggenheim **1**
San Nicolás **5**

Universidad de Deusto

BEGOÑA

Virgen de Begoña **6**

Itxmik Vilariño

Calzadas de Malloña

CASCO VIEJO **4**

SIETE CALLES **3**

Jardines Víctor

Torre Cint.

BILBAO LA VIEJA
(OLD BILBAO)

Monte de Mirravilla

1/2 mi
1/2 km

Campo de Malloña

Esperanza

Sendeja

Navarra

Puente del Arenal

5

Hurtado de Amézaga

Urquijo

Pza. de Zabálburu

Alameda

Autonomía

de

López de Haro

Ledesma

Río Nervión

Muelle de Urbitarte

Paseo Campo de Volantín

Alameda de Mazarredo

Iparragirre

Larreategui

Elcano

Alameda de Recalde

Alameda de San Mamés

Ercilla

Pza. de Frederico Moyúa

C. de Iparraguirre

C. de Gordoniz

Lersundi

Barraincúa

Alhumaguerra

C. de Henao

Alameda de Recalde

Colón de

Juan

Máximo Aguirre

Ercilla

Pza. Indaucho

Urquijo

C. de Bolívar

Simón Bolívar

Alameda de Mazarredo

Elcano

2

Arias

Gran Vía de Don Diego

Alameda de Doctor Areilza

Alameda de

C. de Rodríguez

Licenciado Poza

Av. Universidades

Muelle de Everest Churruca

1

Parque de Doña Casilda de Iturrízar

Ribera de Botica Vieja

Puente de Deusto

Av. de Sabino Arana

513

Frank Gehry and called "the beast" by some locals because of its bizarre shape. From afar, it resembles a gargantuan sculpture, with a "tumbling boxes" profile and a 430-foot-long "ship gallery."

Bilbao is the industrial hub of the north and the political capital of the Basques. Shipping, shipbuilding, and steelmaking have made it prosperous so there is no shortage of bankers or industrialists in Bilbao. Its commercial heart, bursting with sky-scrapers and sky cranes, hums with activity. Among cities of the Basque region, it has the highest population (around 450,000); the metropolitan area, including the sub-urbs and many surrounding towns, is home to over one million inhabitants.

Bilbao has a wide-open feeling, extending more than 5 miles (8km) across the valley of the Nervión River, one of Spain's most polluted waterways. Many buildings wear a layer of grime. Some visitors compare Bilbao to the sooty postindustrial sprawl of an English port town. However, the extravagant Guggenheim museum is cast as a symbol of Basque economic revival, and locals hope it will lead to a revitalization of their city. Bilbao was badly hit by the 1970s economic crisis, leading to a closure of shipyards and steelworks. It has benefited greatly from a $1.5 billion reconversion grant, of which the Guggenheim project is one of the main beneficiaries. Signs of revitalization are also in the flashy new Metro system designed by Sir Norman Foster of England and a new airport terminal, the work of Santiago Calatrava, the Spanish architect. In addition, many owners of local buildings are removing layers of accumulated grime to beautify their properties.

Bilbao was established by charter June 15, 1300, which converted it from a village (*pueblo*), ruled by local feudal duke Don Diego López de Haro, into a city. Aided by water power and the transportation potential of the Nervión River, it grew and grew, most of its fame and glory coming during the industrial expansion of the 19th cen-tury. Many of the city's grand homes and villas for industrialists were constructed at that time, particularly in the wealthy suburb of Neguri. The most famous son of Bilbao was Miguel de Unamuno, the writer and educator more closely associated with Salamanca.

ESSENTIALS

GETTING THERE   Bilbao Airport (☎ 94-486-93-00) is 5 miles (8km) north of the city, near the town of Erandio. Flights arrive from Madrid, Barcelona, Alicante, Arrecife, Fuenteventura, Las Palmas, Málaga, Palma, Santiago de Compostela, Sevilla, Tenerife, Valencia, Vigo, Brussels, Frankfurt, Lisbon, London, Milan, Paris, and Zurich. Iberia's main booking office in Bilbao is at Ercilla, 20 (☎ 94-424-10-94); it's open Monday through Friday from 8:30am to 1:30pm and 3 to 6pm.

From the airport into town, take red bus A3247 to the heart of the city for 140 ptas. (95¢).

The RENFE Station, Estación de Abando (☎ 94-423-86-23), is on the Hurtado de Amézaga, just off the Plaza de España, in Bilbao. From here, you can catch short-distance trains within the metropolitan area of Bilbao and long-distance trains to most parts of Spain. Two trains per day run to and from Madrid (trip time: 6 hours on the afternoon train, 7 hours on the night train). Two trains per day run to and from Barcelona (11 hours), and one train per day goes to and from Galicia (12 hours). There are also two night trains per week to and from the Mediterranean Coast: one toward Alicante and Valencia (daily during the summer months) and the other toward Málaga (three times a week in the summer).

PESA, calle Hurtado de Amézaga (☎ 94-424-88-99), at the Estación Abando, operates more than a dozen buses per day to and from San Sebastián (trip time: 1¼ hours). ANSA, calle Autonomía, 17 (☎ 94-444-31-00), has nine buses per day from

Madrid (trip time: 5 hours). It also has four buses per day to and from Barcelona (7 hours). If you'd like to explore either Lekeitio or Guernica (see section 5, above) by bus, use the services of CAV, Plaza Encarnación, 7 (☎ **94-454-05-44**). Seven buses per day go to Lekeitio Monday through Saturday and two on Sunday. Trip time is 45 minutes. Ten buses run each weekday to Guernica (trip time: 45 minutes). On weekends, only five buses per day go to Guernica.

Bilbao lies beside the A-8, linking the cities of Spain's northern Atlantic seacoast to the western edge of France. It is connected by superhighway to both Barcelona and Madrid.

VISITOR INFORMATION   The **Bilbao Tourist Office** is at Plaza Arriaga, s/n (☎ **94-479-57-60**). It's open Monday through Friday from 9am to 2pm and 4 to 7:30pm, Saturday from 9am to 2pm, and Sunday from 10am to 2pm. The Post Office is at Alameda de Urquijo, 19 (☎ **94-422-05-48**), and is open Monday through Friday from 8:30am to 8:30pm, Saturday from 9:30am to 2pm.

SPECIAL EVENTS   Festivals often fill the calendar, the biggest and most widely publicized being **La Semana Grande,** dedicated to the Virgin of Begoña and lasting from mid-August until early September. During the celebration, the Nervión River is the site of many flotillas and regattas. July 25 brings the festival of Bilbao's patron saint, **Santiago (St. James),** and July 31 is the holiday devoted to the region's patron saint, **St. Ignatius.**

EXPLORING BILBAO

The **River Nervión** meanders through Bilbao, whose historic core was built inside one of its loops, with water protecting it on three sides. Most of the important shops, banks, and tourist facilities lie within a short walk of the **Gran Vía,** running east-west through the heart of town. The old quarter lies east of the modern commercial center, across the river.

THE TOP ATTRACTIONS

✪ **Guggenheim Museum.** Muella Evaristo Churruca, 1. ☎ **94-423-27-99.** Admission 800 ptas. ($5.35) adults, 400 ptas. ($2.70) seniors and students, free for children 12 and under. Tues–Sun 11am–8pm. Closed Jan 1 and Dec 25. Bus: 1, 10, 13, or 18.

The newest and biggest attraction in Bilbao is the Guggenheim Museum, at the inter-section of the bridge called Puente de la Salve and the Nervión River. The 349,000-square-foot colossus is the focal point of a $1.5 billion redevelopment plan for the city. The internationally acclaimed Frank Gehry design features a 165-foot-high atrium—more than 1½ times the height of the rotunda of Frank Lloyd Wright's Guggenheim Museum in New York. Stretching under the aforementioned bridge and incorporating it in its design, the museum reanimates the promenade with its towering roof, remi-niscent of a blossoming metallic flower. The museum, which opened in fall 1997, is devoted to American and European art of the 20th century, featuring the works of such renowned artists as Kandinsky, Mondrian, Picasso, Ernst, Pollock, Lichtenstein, Oldenburg, Serra, and others.

The Guggenheim is not an encyclopedic museum like the Met in New York. It is conceived in 19 galleries to provide "chapters" of but not the whole story of modern art, from Braque to Picasso to Damien Hirst. Artwork lent by the Guggenheim in New York and Venice will rotate, and Bilbao will also host temporary exhibitions trav-eling here from New York.

Although some disgruntled Basque locals still call the museum "the colossal Cali-fornian cauliflower" or "a cheese factory," many architectural critics from around the world, including Paul Goldberger of the *New York Times,* have hailed Frank Gehry's unique structure as the first great building of the 21st century, even though conceived and constructed in the waning years of the 20th century. The structure is said to have been inspired by the Fritz Lang film classic *Metropolis,* and is viewed as a homage to Bilbao's industrial past and a commitment to its future. The massive museum is clad in shimmering titanium, which many observers find sexy and unmistakably elegant. The building takes up 24,000 square meters in the former dockyards beside the Nervión River, and about half of that space is devoted to the exhibition halls, connected by ramps and surrounding a central, glassed-in atrium that is impressive in size, the equivalent of a 17-story building. The museum has virtually abolished right angles and flat walls. As one critic put it, "it was as if Gehry were working in pastry rather than concrete or steel."

✪ **Museo de Bellas Artes.** Plaza del Museo, 2. ☎ **94-439-60-60.** Admission 400 ptas. ($2.70) adults, 200 ptas. ($1.35) seniors, students, and children. Free Wed. Tues–Sat 10am–1:30pm and 4–7:30pm, Sun 10am–2pm.

This is another one of Spain's important art museums, containing both medieval and modern works, including paintings by Velázquez, Goya, Zurbarán, and El Greco. Among the works of non-Spanish artists are *The Money Changers* by the Flemish painter Quentin Massys and *The Lamentation Over Christ* by Anthony van Dyck. In its modern wing, the museum contains works by Gauguin, Picasso, Léger, Sorolla, and the American Mary Cassatt. The gallery is particularly strong in 19th- and 20th-century Basque artists, the foremost of which is the modern sculptor Eduardo Chillida, who created a massive piece entitled *Monument to Iron.* If you tire of looking at the art, you can walk in the English-inspired gardens around the museum, which lies 4 blocks south of the old quarter.

Museo a Euska/Museo Vasco. Cruz, 4. ☎ **94-415-54-23.** Admission 300 ptas. ($2) adults, 150 ptas. ($1) children and students, free for children under 10. Tues–Sat 10:30am–1:30pm and 4–7pm, Sun 10:30am–1:30pm.

Devoted to Basque archaeology, ethnology, and history, this museum is in the center of the old quarter, south of calle Esperanza Ascao. It is housed in a centuries-old Jesuit cloister. Some of the exhibits showcase Basque commercial life during the 16th century. You see everything from ship models to shipbuilding tools, along with reconstructions of rooms illustrating political and social life. Basque gravestones are also on view. In addition, you'll see the equipment used to play the popular Basque game of *pelota.*

EXPLORING THE CASCO VIEJO (OLD QUARTER)

Despite the fact that Bilbao was established around 1300, it is curiously scarce in medieval monuments. It does have an intriguing old quarter, however, located on the east side of Nervión River and the site of its most interesting bars and restaurants. The custom is to go here at night and bar-hop, ordering small cups of beer or wine. A small glass of wine is called a *chiquiteo.*

The old quarter of Bilbao is connected to the much larger modern section on the opposite bank by four bridges. A few paces north of the old quarter's center lie the graceful arches, 64 in all, enclosing Plaza Nueva, also called Plaza de los Martires, completed in 1830.

The entire barrio has been declared a national landmark. It originally defined an area around seven streets, but it long ago spilled beyond that limitation. Its most important church is the **Iglesia de San Nicolás.** Behind this church you'll find an elevator on calle Esperanza Ascao, which, if working, carries sightseers to the upper town. You can also climb 64 steps from Plaza Unamuno. From here it's a short walk to the **Basílica de Begoña,** built largely in the early 1500s. Inside the dimly lit church, there is a brightly illuminated depiction of the Virgin, dressed in long, flowing robes. She is the patroness of the province. Also displayed are some enormous paintings by Luca Giordano.

While in the old town, you might also visit the **Catedral de Santiago,** Plaza Santiago, which was originally built in the 14th century, then restored in the 16th century after a fire. The cathedral's facade was later rebuilt in the 19th century. On Sundays you might also take in the flea market, starting at 8am, on the streets of the old quarter.

To reach the old town on foot, the only way to explore it, take the Puente del Arenal from the Gran Vía, the main street of Bilbao.

WHERE TO STAY
EXPENSIVE

Gran Hotel Ercilla. Ercilla, 37-39, 48011 Bilbao. ☎ **94-470-57-00.** Fax 94-443-93-35. 350 units. A/C MINIBAR TV TEL. Mon-Thurs 21,500 ptas. ($144.05) double, Fri–Sun 13,750 ptas. ($92.15); 43,675 ptas. ($292.60) suite. AE, DC, MC, V. Parking 1,800 ptas. ($12.05).

Soaring high above the buildings surrounding it and located in the heart of Bilbao's business district, this is a tastefully decorated bastion of attentive service and good living. Midsize to spacious guest rooms are conservative and comfortably furnished, each with luxurious mattresses and roomy bathrooms with plush towels and hair dryers. Completely renovated in 1989 and 1990, the Ercilla is one of Bilbao's most desirable hotels, usually the preferred choice of Spanish politicians, movie stars, and journalists away from home.

Dining/Diversions: The restaurant, Bermeo, specializing in Basque cuisine, is known as one of the best restaurants in Bilbao (see "Where to Dine," below). Adjacent to it is an American-inspired bar (with an English-inspired decor) providing a peaceful haven with richly grained hardwood paneling. There is also an informal and stylishly modern snack bar, the Ercilla (open daily from 7am to 2am), plus a high-tech, high-energy disco, the Bocaccio.

Amenities: 24-hour room service, concierge, laundry/valet, baby-sitting, business center, car rental, safety-deposit boxes, boutiques.

✪ **Hotel López de Haro.** Obispo Orueta, 2-4, 48009 Bilbao. ☎ **94-423-55-00.** Fax 94-423-45-00. 53 units. A/C MINIBAR TV TEL. 22,500–28,125 ptas. ($150.75–$188.45) double; 35,000–43,750 ptas. ($234.50–$293.15) suite. AE, DC, MC, V. Parking 2,100 ptas. ($14.05).

Behind a discreet facade of chiseled gray stone and filled with English touches, this 6-story elegant 1990 hotel features marble flooring, hardwood paneling, and a uniformed staff. The comfortable midsize guest rooms each contain flowered or striped upholstery, a modern bathroom with a hair dryer, and wall-to-wall carpeting or hardwood floors.

Dining/Diversions: The hotel has two restaurants, one of which, Club Náutico, is recommended below in "Where to Dine." Both provide gracious havens for good food and service. A luxurious English-inspired cocktail bar, called The Ambigú, lies nearby.

Amenities: 24-hour room service, laundry/valet, limousines available, concierge, baby-sitting, car rentals.

MODERATE

Avenida. Zumalacárregui, 40, 48007 Bilbao. ☎ **94-412-43-00.** Fax 94-411-46-17. 116 units. TV TEL. 12,950 ptas. ($86.75) double. Rates include breakfast. AE, MC, V. Free parking. Metro: Santutxu.

For those who want to be away from the center, and don't mind a bus or taxi ride or two, this is a welcoming choice. It lies in the Barrio de Begoña, near one of the major religious monuments of Bilbao, the Basílica de Begoña. The five-story hotel was built in the late 1950s and its small rooms, furnished in a sober, functional modern style, are well kept and maintained. The hotel has a restaurant and snack bar and a helpful staff. During special fairs in Bilbao, rates increase by at least 10%.

INEXPENSIVE

Roquefer. Lotería, 2-4, 48005 Bilbao. ☎ **94-415-07-55.** 18 units (6 with bathroom). 4,000 ptas. ($26.80) double without bathroom, 5,000 ptas. ($33.50) double with bathroom. No credit cards. Parking 1,000 ptas. ($6.70).

If you'd like to stay in the old quarter and avoid the high prices of business hotels, this is a very basic choice, suitable if your main concern is only a place to lay your head. The small rooms are simple and furnished in a functional style, each with a good bed. You'll be in the center of the tasca and restaurant district for nighttime prowls. To reach the hotel, take the bridge, Puente del Arenal, across the river to the old town.

WHERE TO DINE
EXPENSIVE

✪ **Bermeo.** In the Gran Hotel Ercilla, Ercilla, 37. ☎ **94-470-57-00.** Reservations required. Main courses 1,975–3,675 ptas. ($13.25–$24.60); fixed-price menu 5,650 ptas. ($37.85). AE, DC, MC, V. Sun–Fri 1–3:30pm, Mon–Sat 8:30–11:30pm. BASQUE.

One of the best hotel restaurants in all of Spain and one of the finest representatives of Basque cuisine anywhere in the world, Bermeo caters to a clientele of the Basque world's most influential politicians, writers, and social luminaries. Contained within the modern walls of one of Bilbao's tallest hotels, the restaurant is decorated with richly conservative glowing wood panels, crisp linens, and copies of 19th-century antiques. The service from the uniformed and formal staff is impeccable. Menu items change with the seasons but might include a salad of lettuce hearts in saffron dressing with smoked salmon, homemade foie gras scented with essence of bay leaves, fresh thistles sautéed with ham, five preparations of codfish, stewed partridge with glazed shallots, and fillets of duckling with green peppercorns. For dessert, try the truffled figs or a slice of bilberry pie with cream.

✪ **Club Náutico.** In the Hotel López de Haro, Obispo Orueta, 2. ☎ **94-423-55-00.** Reservations recommended. Main courses 2,000–5,000 ptas. ($13.40–$33.50); fixed-price menus 5,000–10,500 ptas. ($33.50–$70.35). AE, DC, MC, V. Mon–Fri 1–3:30pm, Mon–Sat 8:30–11:30pm. BASQUE/FRENCH.

One of the top restaurants in the Basque world, the elegantly decorated Club Náutico lies within a previously recommended hotel. The chef, Alberto Velez, is the former protégé of Alberto Zuluaga, who ran the kitchen here for years and was one of the most publicized culinary luminaries of northern Spain. The restaurant offers formal tables set with some of the finest china, crystal, and silverware available. Menu specialties include succulent local artichokes stuffed with foie gras, poached eggs with beluga caviar and oyster sauce, lobster sautéed with artichokes and balsamic vinegar, baked sea bass with béarnaise sauce, sautéed scallops with truffle sauce, and roast beef with a puree of radishes. A superb selection of Spanish and international wines is available by either the glass or the bottle.

Guría. Gran Vía de López de Haro, 66. ☎ **94-441-57-80.** Reservations required. Main courses 1,800–4,600 ptas. ($12.05–$30.80); fixed-price menus 5,800–8,700 ptas. ($38.85–$58.30). AE, DC, MC, V. Mon–Sat 1–4pm and 9pm–midnight. Closed last week of July and first week of Aug. BASQUE.

One of the most venerable restaurants of Bilbao, the air-conditioned Guría is expensive—and worth it, say its fans. The chef shows care and concern for his guests, serving only market-fresh ingredients. He is celebrated for his bacalao (codfish), which he prepares many ways. Try the sea bass with saffron or loin of beef cooked in sherry as an alternative. A slightly caloric but divine dessert is *espuma de chocolat.*

Guría lies on the southern edge of one of the most monumental traffic arteries in town, 6 blocks west of Bilbao's most prominent square, Plaza de Federico Moyúa, 1 block south of the sprawling Parque de Dr. Casilda Ituriza. Inside you'll find a modern decor of exposed, dark-stained wood, two separate dining rooms, and a monochromatic color scheme of beige and earth tones.

MODERATE

Matxinbenta. Ladesma, 26. ☎ **94-424-84-95.** Reservations required. Main courses 2,000–2,600 ptas. ($13.40–$17.40); menú del día 4,000 ptas. ($26.80). AE, DC, MC, V. Mon–Sat 1–4pm and 8–11:30pm. BASQUE.

Serving some of the finest Basque food in the city since the 1950s, this restaurant is popular for business lunches or dinners. Specialties include fresh tuna in piquant tomato sauce and a local version of ratatouille known as *piperada.* You can also order veal cutlets cooked in port wine and finish with a mint-flavored fresh-fruit cocktail. The service is excellent. Matxinbenta contains three separate dining rooms, each outfitted with modern lines, contemporary furniture, potted plants, and lots of exposed wood. Its location is 1 block north of the Gran Vía, in the center of the city, adjacent to Bilbao's most visible merchandiser, El Corte Inglés.

Restaurante Begoña. Virgen de Begoña, s/n. ☎ **94-412-72-57.** Reservations recommended. Main courses 1,800–2,900 ptas. ($12.05–$19.45). AE, MC, V. Mon–Sat 1:30–3:30pm and 8–11pm. Closed Aug. Bus: 48. BASQUE.

At this tranquil choice, near the famous Basílica de Begoña lying on the eastern bank of the river, the chef imaginatively combines classic dishes with modern ones. Specialties include stuffed onions, loin of pork, and sea bass with fine herbs. This restaurant offers good value, serving quality food at reasonable prices. The wine cellar offers prestigious vintages at competitive rates, and the service is attentive.

INEXPENSIVE

Aitxiar. Calle Maria Muñoz, 8. ☎ **94-415-09-17.** Reservations not necessary. Main courses 1,500–3,200 ptas. ($10.05–$21.45). V. Tues–Sun 9am–11pm. Metro: Plaza Unamuno. BASQUE.

Venerable and well respected for its good food, its low prices, and its utter lack of pretensions, this restaurant in the Casco Viejo serves all-Basque cuisine within two dining rooms of a house built in the 1930s. Expect a decor that includes lots of exposed stone and wood, a hardworking wait staff, strong flavors, and lots of regional and nationalistic pride. Menu items include potato soup with chunks of fresh tuna, and an array of very fresh fish hauled in that morning from nearby waters. Two of the most appealing are hake, which tastes marvelous in an herb-infused green sauce, and codfish, prepared in at least two different versions. Baby squid is a savory choice, as are the spicy sausages (*chuletas*), which taste best when consumed as an appetizer.

BILBAO AFTER DARK

Basque cuisine is the finest in Spain, featuring *pintxos* (pronounced *peen*-chohz)— tapas. The best place for tapas bars is calle Licenciado Poza, between Alameda del Doctor Areilza and calle Iparraguirre. Favorites include **Atlanta,** calle Rodríguez Arias, 28 (☎ **94-427-64-72**), famous locally for its *jamon serrano* (cured ham) sandwiches, and **Busterri,** calle Licenciado Poza, 43 (☎ **94-441-50-67**), also well known locally for its grilled anchovies and *jamon jabugo.*

During your nights in Bilbao, you might be happiest wandering through the old town's narrow alleyways, two of which (calle Pozas and calle Barrencalle) are dotted with all manner of bars, tascas, and bodegas. After a drink or two, you might opt to go out dancing, or at least visit any of three popular discos to watch how it's done in the Basque Country. Favorites include **Disco Rock Star,** Gran Vía, 89 (☎ **94-441-10-60**); **Disco-Pub Crystal,** calle Buenos Aires, 5 (no phone); and **El Palladium,** calle Iparraguirre, 11 (no phone). If you're looking for a gay bar, you'll find a scattering along the calle Barrencalle Barena, where the most popular of several nearby competitors includes the **Bar Consorcio** (no phone).

The major cultural venue in Bilbao is the **Teatro Arriaga,** Plaza Arriaga, s/n (☎ **94-416-33-33**), on the banks of the Nervión River. This is the setting for world-class opera, classical music concerts, ballet, and even zarzuelas (comic operas). Both zarzuela and opera are also performed at **Teatro Coliso Alvia,** Alameda Urquijo, 13 (☎ **94-415-39-54**). Announcements of cultural events at the time of your visit are available at the tourist office (see "Visitor Information," earlier in this section).

7 Vitoria (Gasteiz)

41 miles (66km) S of Bilbao, 71 miles (114km) SW of San Sebastián, 218 miles (351km) N of Madrid

Quiet and sleepy until the early 1980s, Vitoria was chosen as headquarters of the Basque region's autonomous government. In honor of that occasion, it revived the name *Gasteiz,* by which it was known when founded in 1181 by King Sancho of Navarre. Far more enduring, however, has been the name *Vitoria,* a battle site revered by the English. On June 21, 1813, Wellington won here against the occupying forces of Napoléon. A statue dedicated to the Iron Duke stands today on the neoclassical Plaza de la Virgen Blanca.

Shortly after its founding, the city became a rich center for the wool and iron trades, and this wealth paid for the fine churches and palaces in the medieval quarter. Many of the city's buildings are made of gray-gold stone. Local university students keep the taverns rowdy until the wee hours.

ESSENTIALS

GETTING THERE   Aeropuerto Vitoria-Foronda (☎ **945-16-35-00**) lies 5 miles (8km) northwest of the town center and has direct air links to Madrid on Iberia Airlines. For flight information, call Iberia at ☎ **945-27-40-00** daily from 7am to 11pm.

From San Sebastián, seven to nine trains daily make the 2-hour trip to Vitoria. For information, call ☎ **945-23-02-02.**

From San Sebastián, roughly four buses daily make the 1½-hour trip. Bus connections are also possible through Bilbao (8 to 12 buses daily make the 1-hour trip).

Take the E-5 north from Madrid to Burgos, cutting northwest until you see the turnoff for Vitoria. (Note that along its more northerly stretches this superhighway is identified as both E-5 and A-1.)

VISITOR INFORMATION   The **tourist information office** is at Parque de la Florida (☎ **945-13-13-21**). From June to September, hours are Monday through Friday 9am to 7pm, Saturday 10am to 7pm, and Sunday 10am to 2pm. From October to May, times are Monday to Thursday 9am to 1:30pm, and Friday 8am to 3pm.

SPECIAL EVENTS   One of the major jazz festivals in the north of Spain takes place here annually in mid-July. It's the weeklong **Festival de Jazz de Vitoria-Gasteiz.** For the big-name performers, tickets range from 500 to 2,000 ptas. ($3.35 to $13.40), but spontaneous entertainment takes place on the street, and for free, although donations are appreciated. The tourist office will supply complete details.

EXPLORING VITORIA

The most important sight in Vitoria is the **medieval district,** whose Gothic buildings were constructed on a series of steps and terraces. Most of the streets are arranged in concentric ovals and are named after medieval artisan guilds. The northern end is marked by the Catedral de Santa María, its southern flank by the Iglesia de San Miguel.

One of the most interesting streets in the barrio is **calle Cuchillaría,** which contains many medieval buildings. You can enter the courtyard at number 24, the Casa del Cordón, which was constructed in different stages from the 13th to the 16th century. Number 58, the Bendana Palace, built in the 15th century, has a fine ornate staircase set into its courtyard.

The **Catedral de Santa María** (the "old" cathedral), calle Fray Zacaras, was built in the 14th century in the Gothic style. It contains a good art collection, with paintings that imitate various schools, including those of van Dyck, Caravaggio, and Rubens, as well as several tombs carved in a highly decorated plateresque style. Santa María lies at the northern edge of the old town. This cathedral is not to be confused with the town's enormous neo-Gothic "new" cathedral on avenida Magdalena (just north of the Jardines la Florida).

The major historic square is **Plaza de la Virgen Blanca,** a short walk south of the medieval quarter. Its neoclassical balconies overlook the statue of Wellington. The square is named after the late-Gothic polychrome statue of the Virgen Blanca (the town's patron) that adorns the portico of the 13th-century **Church of San Miguel,** which stands on the square's upper edge. The 17th-century altarpiece inside was carved by Gregoria Hernández.

At **Plaza de España** (also known as Plaza Nueva), a satellite square a short walk away, the student population of Vitoria congregates to drink.

Vitoria has some minor museums, which are free. **Museo de Arqueología de Álava,** Correría, 116 (☎ **945-14-23-10**), behind a half-timbered facade, exhibits artifacts such as pottery shards and statues unearthed from digs in the area. Some of these date from Celto-Iberian days others from the Roman era. The museum is open Tuesday through Friday from 10am to 2pm and 4 to 6:30pm, Saturday from 11am to 2pm.

Museo de Bellas Artes de Álava, Palacio de Agustín, Paseo de Fray Francisco, 8 (☎ **945-23-17-77**), has a collection of several unusual weapons, a *Crucifixion* and portraits of Saints Peter and Paul by José Ribera, and a triptych by the Master of Ávila. It is open Tuesday through Friday 10am to 2pm and 4 to 6:30pm, Saturday 10am to 2pm, and Sunday 11am to 2pm.

WHERE TO STAY
EXPENSIVE

Hotel Residencia Gasteiz. Avenida Gasteiz, 45, 01009 Vitoria. ☎ **945-22-81-00.** Fax 945-22-62-58. E-mail: hoteldcgasteiz@barcelo.com. 150 units. A/C MINIBAR TV TEL. Mon–Thurs 19,000 ptas. ($127.30) double, Fri–Sun 11,000 ptas. ($73.70) double; Mon–Thurs 22,000 ptas. ($147.40) suite, Fri–Sun 13,500 ptas. ($90.45) suite. AE, DC, MC, V. Parking 1,400 ptas. ($9.40).

Located on the eastern flank of the broad, tree-lined boulevard that circumnavigates the old town, this is the most modern and solidly reliable hotel around. Built in 1982 it was completely renovated in 1994. Although not architecturally distinguished, it serves as the preferred meeting point for the city's business community, offering conservative and good-size rooms with uncomplicated furnishings and a series of comfortable (albeit not dramatic) public rooms. The tiled bathrooms are state of the art, and each is equipped with a hair dryer.

Dining/Diversions: Restaurante Artagnan, specializing in Basque and international cuisine, serves a set menu and à la carte dinners. The restaurant is closed every Sunday and from August 10 to September 10. There is also a bar (which doubles as a cafeteria during the day).

Amenities: Room service (daily from 7am to midnight), laundry, concierge, babysitting, car rentals.

MODERATE

Hotel General Álava. Gasteiz, 79, 01009 Vitoria. ☎ **945-22-22-00.** Fax 945-24-83-95. E-mail: hga@jet.es. 114 units. TV TEL. Mon–Thurs 14,900 ptas. ($99.85) double, Fri–Sun 10,500 ptas. ($70.35) double, breakfast included; 22,500 ptas. ($150.75) suite. AE, DC, MC, V. Parking 1,150 ptas. ($7.70).

Named after a local hero—a Spanish general who won an important battle against the French in 1815—this hotel is one of the best and most comfortably furnished in town. Bedrooms range from small to medium in size, each fitted with a firm mattress and coming with a small tiled bathroom with shower stalls. Built in 1975, it attracts scores of business travelers from throughout Spain. It maintains an informal restaurant, a well-managed bistro (open only Monday through Friday) which offers a menú del día for 2,000 ptas. ($13.40), and a bar. The hotel is a 10-minute walk west of the town center, near the junction of calle Chile.

INEXPENSIVE

Achuri. Rioja, 11, 01005 Vitoria. ☎ **945-25-58-00.** Fax 945-26-40-74. 40 units. TV TEL. 6,600 ptas. ($44.20) double. AE, DC, MC, V.

This attractively priced modern hotel has a welcoming style. Located a short walk from the train station, it offers tidy and comfortably furnished but small rooms and laundry service. Breakfast is the only meal available, but you'll find several places serving food in the vicinity.

Hotel Dato. Eduardo Dato, 28, 01005 Vitoria. ☎ **945-14-72-30.** Fax 945-23-23-20. 14 units. TV TEL. 5,136 ptas. ($34.40) double. AE, DC, MC, V. Parking meters on street.

Three blocks south of the southern extremity of the old town in the pedestrian zone, this hotel has firmly established itself as the best budget accommodation in town. It has modern decor and amenities but only a few rooms, so reservations are wise. Bedrooms, ranging from small to medium, are well decorated, often with quite a bit of style, and each comes with a firm mattress and an immaculately kept tiled bathroom. No breakfast is served.

WHERE TO DINE

As in Bilbao, tasca hopping before dinner with the consumption of many small glasses (*chiquiteos*) of beer or wine at many different bars and taverns is very popular and fun for visitors to Vitoria. There are a number of places on the Avenida de Gasteiz.

✪ **El Portalón.** Correría, 151. ☎ **945-14-27-55.** Reservations recommended. Main courses 1,500–3,100 ptas. ($10.05–$20.75); fixed-price menu 2,950 ptas. ($19.75). AE, DC, MC, V. Mon–Sat 1:15–3:30pm and 8:30–11:30pm. Closed Aug 10–Sept 1. BASQUE.

This is the finest and most interesting restaurant in town. It was originally built in the late 1400s as a tavern and post office near what was, at the time, one of the only bridges leading in and out of Vitoria. Rich with patina and a sense of history, the restaurant prides itself on serving extremely fresh fish from the nearby Gulf of Biscay, always prepared in traditional Basque style. Cream and butter are rarely used here. Menu items include a salad of endive with shellfish, vegetarian crepes, a traditional hake dish known as *merluza koxkera,* ragout of fish and/or shellfish, and many variations of monkfish, turbot, and eel.

Mesa. Chile, 1. ☎ **945-22-84-94.** Reservations recommended. Main courses 1,000–1,900 ptas. ($6.70–$12.75); menú de la casa 1,800 ptas. ($12.05). AE, MC, V. Thurs–Tues 1–3:30pm and 9–11:30pm. Closed Aug 10–Sept 10. BASQUE.

For price and value, this ranks as one of the most competitive and worthwhile restaurants in town. In air-conditioned comfort you can partake of a number of Basque specialties, none better than the notable *merluza* (hake), the fish so beloved by Basque chefs. Fresh fish and a well-chosen selection of meats are presented nightly. The service is attentive. The setting is solid, sober, and severely dignified, with white walls and wood trim, and tables and chairs that are stained dark in the Iberian style.

16 Cantabria & Asturias

The provinces of Cantabria and Asturias are historic lands that lay claim to attractions ranging from the fishing villages of the Cantabrian and Asturian coastlines to the Picos de Europa, a magnificent stretch of snowcapped mountains.

Cantabria was settled in prehistoric times and later colonized by the Romans. The Muslims were less successful in their invasion. Protected by the mountains, many Christians found refuge here during the long centuries of Moorish domination. Much religious architecture remains from this period, particularly Romanesque. Cantabria was once part of the Castilla y León district of Spain but is now an autonomous region with its own government.

Most tourism is confined to the northern coastal strip; much of the inland mountainous area is poor and unpopulated. If you venture away from the coast, you'll usually need a rental car, because public transport is inadequate at best. **Santander,** a rail terminus, makes the best center for touring the region; it also has the most tourist facilities. From Santander, you can get virtually anywhere in the province in a 3-hour drive.

The principality of Asturias lies between Cantabria in the east and Galicia in the west. It reaches its scenic (and topographical) summit in the **Picos de Europa,** where the first Spanish national park was inaugurated. With green valleys, fishing villages, and forests, Asturias is a land for all seasons.

The coastline of Asturias constitutes one of the major sightseeing attractions in northern Spain. Called the **Costa Verde,** it begins in the east at San Vicente de la Barquera and stretches almost 90 miles (145km) to Gijón. Allow about 6 hours to drive it without stops. The western coast, beginning at Gijón, goes all the way to Ribadeo, a border town with Galicia—a distance of 112 miles (180km). This rocky coastline, studded with fishing villages and containing narrow estuaries and small beaches, is one of the most spectacular stretches of scenery in Spain. It takes all day to explore.

Asturias is an ancient land, as prehistoric cave paintings in the area demonstrate. Iron Age Celtic tribes resisted the Romans, as Asturians proudly point out to this day. They also resisted the Moors, who subjugated the rest of Spain. The Battle of Covadonga in 722 represented the Moors' first major setback after their arrival in Iberia some 11 years previously.

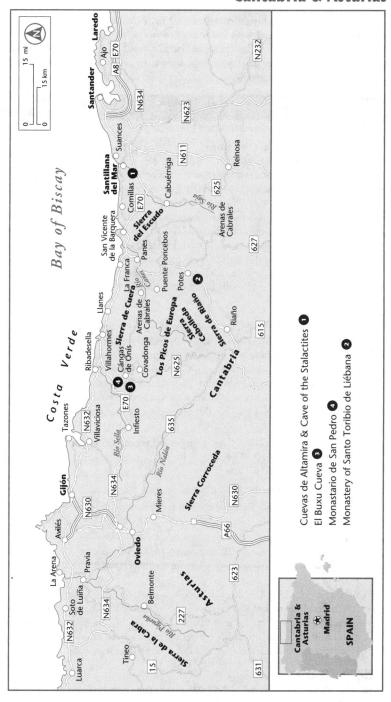

Cuevas de Altamira & Cave of the Stalactites **1**

El Buxu Cueva **3**

Monastario de San Pedro **4**

Monastery of Santo Toribio de Liébana **2**

Asturians are still staunchly independent. In 1934 Francisco Franco, then an ambitious young general, arrived with his Moroccan troops to suppress an uprising by miners who had declared an independent Socialist republic. His Nationalist forces returned again and again to destroy such Asturian cities as Gijón for their fierce resistance during the Spanish Civil War.

1 Laredo

37 miles (60km) W of Bilbao, 30 miles (48km) E of Santander, 265 miles (427km) N of Madrid

To an American, "the streets of Laredo" means the gun-slinging Old West. To a Spaniard it means an ancient maritime town on the eastern Cantabrian coast that has been turned into a major summer resort, with hundreds of apartments and villas along its 3 miles (5km) of beach. Playa de la Salvé lies to the west and Playa de Oriñón to the east.

The medieval quarter, the **Puebla Vieja,** retains the traditional atmosphere of Laredo. It was walled on orders of Alfonso VIII of Castile, who wanted to protect the town from pirate raids along the coast. The hillside **Iglesia de la Asunción,** dating from the 13th century, overlooks the harbor. It has five naves and rather bizarre capitals.

If you're driving west to Santoña, note the big monument honoring native son Juan de la Cosa, the cartographer who sailed with Columbus on his first voyage to America.

ESSENTIALS

GETTING THERE From Bilbao, head west along the coastal highway (identified at various points as either the A-8 or the E-70), and follow the signs to Laredo.

Bus service is available from both Bilbao and Santander. The station is in the town center at the avenida de José Antonio, s/n (☎ **94-260-49-67**). There are at least 20 buses per day coming into Laredo from Bilbao, and between 23 and 24 per day coming into Laredo from Santander. Travel time to Laredo from Bilbao is 40 minutes, and the one-way fare is 500 ptas. ($3.35). Travel time from Santander is 30 minutes, and the one-way fare is 435 ptas. ($2.90).

VISITOR INFORMATION The **tourist information office,** Alameda de Miramar, s/n (☎ **942-61-10-96**), is open Monday through Friday from 9am to 3pm and 4 to 8pm, Saturday from 10am to 1pm.

SPECIAL EVENTS On the last Friday of August, the annual **Battle of Flowers** draws thousands of visitors to watch bloom-adorned floats parade through the old town.

WHERE TO STAY

Risco. La Arenosa, 2, 39770 Laredo. ☎ **942-60-50-30.** Fax 942-60-50-55. 26 units. TV TEL. 10,500–15,000 ptas. ($70.35–$100.50) double. Rates include breakfast. AE, DC, MC, V. Free parking.

On a hillside overlooking Laredo, half a mile southeast of the center of town, this aging 1960s hotel opens onto impressive views of the old town and of one of the nearby beaches. It offers simple, very functionally furnished rooms, each clean and comfortable with a firm mattress. In the garden are scattered tables for food service (see the restaurant recommendation below). Ample parking is provided.

WHERE TO DINE

Camarote. Vitoria, s/n. ☎ **942-60-67-07.** Reservations recommended. Main courses 2,000–2,500 ptas. ($13.40–$16.75); fixed-price menu 2,500 ptas. ($16.75). AE, DC, MC, V. Daily 1–4pm and 9pm–midnight. Closed Jan and Sun dinner in winter. SEAFOOD.

The owner of Camarote (in the center of town) is Felipe Manjarrés, and his chef de cuisine specializes in seafood, especially fresh fish as opposed to shellfish. The decor is tasteful and attractive, and the outdoor terrace makes a pleasant alternative to the indoor dining room. The spinach with crayfish and the cheese tarts are truly excellent. Original recipes are used for salads with ham and shrimp as well as for those with tuna and fresh fruit. Try the grilled sea bream or a fillet steak Rossini.

Risco. La Arenosa, 2. ☎ **942-60-50-30.** Reservations recommended. Main courses 1,900–2,500 ptas. ($12.75–$16.75); *menús del día* 1,500–4,000 ptas. ($10.05–$26.80). AE, DC, MC, V. Daily 1–3:30pm and 8:30–11pm. SEAFOOD.

This is Laredo's most appealing restaurant, known for its innovative seafood dishes. Assisted by a battery of helpers, the chef prepares such items as marinated salmon with pink peppercorns, scrambled eggs with lobster, and peppers stuffed with minced pigs' trotters or crabmeat. For dessert, try a fresh-fruit sorbet. Some tables are set up in the garden, or you can dine in a traditional room with views of the sea. The restaurant is on the ground floor of the Risco hotel (see above). During the busy months of July and August, it remains open on Monday.

2 Santander

244 miles (393km) N of Madrid, 72 miles (116km) NW of Bilbao

Santander has always been a rival of San Sebastián, in the east, though it has never attained the premier status of that Basque resort. It did, however, become a royal residence from 1913 to 1930, after city officials presented an English-style Magdalena Palace to Alfonso XIII and his queen, Victoria Eugenia.

An ancient city, Santander was damaged by a 1941 fire, which destroyed the old quarter and most of its dwellings. It was rebuilt along original lines, with wide boulevards, a waterfront promenade, sidewalk cafes, shops, restaurants, and hotels.

Most visitors to Santander head for El Sardinero, a resort less than 1½ miles (2.4km) from the city. Buses and trolleys make the short run between the city center and **El Sardinero** both day and night. Besides hotels and restaurants, Santander has three **beaches,** Playa de Castaneda, Playa del Sardinero, and Playa de la Concha, where people stretch out under candy-striped umbrellas. If these become too crowded, take a 15-minute boat ride to **El Puntal,** a beautiful beach that is rarely crowded, even in August.

If you don't like crowds or beaches, go up to the lighthouse, a little more than 1¼ miles (2km) from El Sardinero, where the views are wide-ranging. A restaurant serves snacks both indoors and outdoors. Here, you can hike along the green cliffs or loll in the grass.

ESSENTIALS

GETTING THERE   Daily flights from Madrid and Barcelona land at Aeropuerto de Santander (☎ 942-25-10-07), a little more than 4 miles (6.5km) from the town center, accessible by taxi only, costing 1,500 ptas. ($10.05). The local office of **Iberia** is at Po. Pereda, 18 (☎ 942-22-97-00).

There are three trains daily from Madrid (5 hours away); a one-way fare costs 4,100 ptas. ($27.45). Four trains a day travel from Bilbao (3 hours). For rail information call ☎ 942-28-02-02.

Buses arrive at Plaza Estaciones (☎ 942-21-19-95). There are 24 connections a day to and from Bilbao (trip time: 3 hours), a one-way ticket costing 900 to 1,500 ptas. ($6.05 to $10.05). Six to nine buses a day arrive from Madrid (6 hours), costing from 3,255 to 4,550 ptas. ($21.80 to $30.50), depending on the bus.

N-634 continues west from Laredo to Santander, with an N-635 turnoff to reach the resort.

VISITOR INFORMATION   The **tourist information office** is at Jardines de Pereda (☎ **942-21-61-20**). Open daily from 9am to 1pm and 4 to 7pm.

SPECIAL EVENTS   The **Music and Dance Festival** in August is one of the most important artistic events in Spain (accommodations are very hard to come by during this time). Occasionally, this festival coincides with religious celebrations honoring Santiago (Saint James), the patron saint of Spain. Santander is an education center in summer as well. Courses are offered at the once-royal palace, now the Menéndez Pelayo International University. Students and teachers from North America and Europe come here to study and enjoy the area.

EXPLORING SANTANDER

Catedral. Somorrostro, s/n. ☎ **942-22-60-24.** Free admission. Daily 10am–1pm and 4–6pm.

Greatly damaged in the 1941 fire, this restored fortress-like 13th-century cathedral holds the tomb of historian/writer Marcelino Menéndez y Pelayo (1856–1912), Santander's most illustrious man of letters. The 12th-century crypt with a trio of low-slung aisles, untouched by fire, can be entered through the south portico. The Gothic cloister was restored after the fire. Roman ruins were discovered beneath the north aisle in 1983.

Museo Regional de Prehistoria y Arqueología de Cantabria. Calle Casimiro Sáinz, 4. ☎ **942-20-71-09.** Free admission. June 16–Sept 16, Tues–Sat 10am–1pm and 4–7pm, Sun 11am–2pm, Sept 17–June 15, Tues–Sat 9am–1pm and 4–7pm, Sun 11am–2pm.

This museum has some interesting artifacts discovered in the Cantabrian province—not only Roman but also some unusual prehistoric finds. Since it is unlikely that you'll be allowed to visit the Cuevas de Altamira (see section 3, later in this chapter), come here to see objects and photographs from these prehistoric caves with their remarkable paintings. Some of the items on display date from 15,000 years ago.

Museo Municipal de Bellas Artes. Calle Rubio, 6. ☎ **942-23-94-85.** Free admission. Mon–Fri 10am–1pm and 5–9pm, Sat 10am–1pm.

Located near the Ayuntamiento (Town Hall), the Municipal Museum of Fine Arts has some interesting Goya paintings, notably his portrait of Ferdinand VII, commissioned by the city, and his series of etchings called *Disasters of War.* You can also see some of his continuing series of *Caprichos* (*Whims*). See also Zurbarán's *Mystic Scene* and an array of works by Flemish, Spanish, and Italian artists, many of them contemporary.

Biblioteca Menéndez y Pelayo. Calle Rubío, 4. ☎ **942-23-45-34.** Free admission. Mon 9am–1:30pm, Tues–Thurs 9am–2pm and 4–9:30pm.

Located in the same building as the Municipal Museum is this 45,000-volume library amassed by Menéndez y Pelayo and left to Santander upon his death in 1912. Guided tours are available. Opposite the building is the Casa Museo, which displays this great man's study and shows how modestly he lived.

SHOPPING

True aficionados of pottery and the nuances of ceramics usually drive from Santander to **Santillana del Mar,** 18 miles (29km) away, where handcrafted ceramics are in great abundance.

But if you want to see a pared-down version of what's available in Santillana del Mar within the city limits of Santander, head for any of the retailers on the calle Arrabal, in the city's commercial center. One of the most promising of them is **La Muralla,** 17 calle Arrabal (no phone).

An antique gallery that's richly stocked with old furniture and paintings with rich veneers is **Fundación Marcellino Botín,** calle Pedrueca, 1 (☎ 942-22-60-72).

Ironically, many of the boutiques and stores of Santander don't lie within the city at all but within a 50-unit shopping center 2 miles from town, beside the road leading to the airport. Check out the **Centro Comercial Valle Real,** Carretera Bilbao km 2.

And if you can't find whatever it is you need anywhere else in Santander, consider an excursion through the aisles of Santander's biggest department store, **Lainz,** calle Puente, 2 (☎ 942-21-42-00).

WHERE TO STAY

Santander is loaded with good-value hotels, from its year-round city hotels to its summer villas at El Sardinero. It gets crowded, so try to reserve well in advance.

IN TOWN

Hotel Ciudad de Santander. Menéndez Pelayo, 13-15, 39006 Santander. ☎ **942-22-79-65.** Fax 942-21-73-03. www.nh-hoteles.es. E-mail: nh@nh-hoteles.es. 62 units. A/C MINIBAR TV TEL. 14,000–19,000 ptas. ($93.80–$127.30) double; 19,000–23,700 ptas. ($127.30–$158.80) suite. AE, DC, MC, V. Parking 800 ptas. ($5.35) outdoors, 1,250 ptas. ($8.40) indoors. Bus: 8.

Located about 8 blocks north of Santander's busiest seaside promenade (Paseo de Pereda) in the heart of the city's commercial heartland, this white-sided rectangular hotel was built in 1989, rising five floors. Although it is the best address within the city itself, for true luxury check into Real at El Sardinero (see below). The big-windowed lobby has marble floors, honey-colored wooden paneling, and modern accessories. The midsize rooms are monochromatic, reflecting themes similar to that of the lobby, with fully equipped bathrooms and conveniently proportioned writing desks.

Dining/Diversions: The hotel contains an informal snack bar, plus a stone-and-glass-sheathed restaurant serving three-course fixed-price lunches and dinners.

Amenities: Room service (daily 7am to midnight), laundry/valet, concierge, car rentals.

Hotel México. Calderón de la Barca, 3, 39002 Santander. ☎ **942-21-24-50.** Fax 942-22-92-38. 35 units. TV TEL. 7,800–10,500 ptas. ($52.25–$70.35) double. MC, V.

Only a block from the rail station, this is one of your best budget bets in the heart of the city, ideal for those without transportation who don't want to range far afield of the hotel, especially if they have luggage. The exterior may not be too enticing, but the atmosphere improves inside this family operated inn. Even though it's in a congested area, street noises seem at a minimum, and the midsize rooms are well cared for and comfortably furnished, each with a firm mattress. Often they are in the old-fashioned architectural style of northern Spain, with glassed-in balconies and tall ceilings. Breakfast, the only meal served, is offered in a formal room with Queen Anne chairs and oak wainscoting.

AT EL SARDINERO

✪ **Hotel Real.** Paseo Pérez Galdós, 28, 39005 Santander. ☎ **942-27-25-50.** Fax 942-27-45-73. www.intermail.es/users/realsantander. E-mail: realsantander@husa.es. 123 units. A/C MINIBAR TV TEL. 23,520–39,375 ptas. ($157.60–$263.80) double; 47,250–126,000 ptas. ($316.60 –$844.20) suite. AE, DC, MC, V. Free parking. Bus: 1, 2, 5, or 7.

Architecturally noteworthy—it was the first building in the entire region constructed of reinforced concrete—the Real was built in 1917 to house the entourage of courtiers who accompanied King Alfonso XIII on his midsummer vacations to Santander. Purchased and completely renovated by the prestigious HUSA chain in 1987, it is once again one of the most elegant hotels in northern Spain, filled with updated reminders of a more gracious age. Located about 2 miles (3km) east of the commercial center of town, near the site of the Royal Palace on a hillside above the Magdalena Beach, the Real contains richly conservative and spacious rooms, most with views of the sea and all with many comfort-inducing amenities, such as hair dryers, luxury mattresses, and plush towels.

Dining/Diversions: El Puntal restaurant serves regional and international three-course fixed-price lunches and dinners. Nearby lies a cocktail lounge accented with potted palms and high ceilings, and boasting a well-mannered staff.

Amenities: 24-hour room service, concierge, baby-sitting, laundry/valet, car rentals, golfing available nearby.

Hotel Rhin. Avenida Reina Victoria, 153, 39005 Santander. ☎ **942-27-43-00.** Fax 942-27-86-53. www.gruporhin.com. E-mail: rhin@gruporhin.com. 89 units. A/C MINIBAR TV TEL. 12,000–21,000 ptas. ($80.40–$140.70) double. AE, DC, MC, V. Parking 800 ptas. ($5.35). Bus: 1, 2, 5, or 7.

Built in the early 1970s and renovated last in 1995, this hotel has panoramic views of the city's beaches. Following massive renovation, it has improved considerably and has earned a four-star rating from the government. The midsize rooms are handsome and very comfortable, and housekeeping is fastidious. There is a cafeteria and a restaurant, both serving international cuisine, although food is not one of the reasons to stay here. Laundry service and room service are provided. Even though it is at the beach, the hotel is open year-round.

WHERE TO DINE

Most visitors to Santander dine at their hotels or boardinghouses, which sometimes offer better value for the money and more efficient service than city restaurants. For variety, however, here are a few suggestions.

IN TOWN

Bodega Cigaleña. Daoiz y Velarde, 19. ☎ **942-21-30-62.** Reservations not necessary. Main courses 1,200–2,600 ptas. ($8.05–$17.40); fixed-price menu 3,000 ptas. ($20.10). AE, DC, MC, V. Mon–Sat noon–4pm and 7:30pm–midnight. Closed June 20–July 1, Oct 20–Nov 20. Bus: 5. REGIONAL.

Popular with the young set in Santander, this Castilian bodega in the city center serves typical regional cuisine in a rustic decor—hanging hams, large wine kegs, and provincial tables. The set menu changes every day. A sample meal might be *sopa de pescado* (fish soup), shellfish paella, fruit of the season, bread, and wine. The Cigaleña offers a good choice of wines from an old Castilian town near Valladolid. Ask to see its Museo del Vino.

AT EL SARDINERO

La Sardina de Plata. Doctor Fleming, 3-4. ☎ **942-27-10-35.** Reservations required. Main courses 1,600–2,500 ptas. ($10.70–$16.75); tasting menu 5,500 ptas. ($36.85). AE, DC, MC, V. Wed–Mon 1:30–4pm, Wed–Sat and Mon 8:30pm–midnight. Bus: 1, 2, 5, or 7. SEAFOOD.

In a warren of small streets in the center of the old city, this nautically designed restaurant serves an imaginative cuisine highlighted by several delicate sauces. Menu selections might include such enticing dishes as cheese mousse, beef fillet with truffles and cognac, and a succulent fish salad. There is also an extensive wine list. The service is courteous and efficient.

SANTANDER AFTER DARK

The most exciting thing to do in the evening is to head for the gaming tables of the **Gran Casino del Sardinero,** Plaza de Italia (☎ 942-27-60-54), which has a cover charge of 500 ptas. ($3.35). It's open daily from 8pm to 4am; be sure to bring your passport for entry. In the same complex is a bar/restaurant/cafe called **Lisboa** (☎ 942-27-10-20), which is a good place to celebrate your winnings or try to forget what you've lost. It serves moderately priced meals, and some locals even drop in for breakfast. In summer it's especially crowded. It's open daily from 9am to 2am.

3 Santillana del Mar & Cuevas de Altamira

18 miles (29km) SW of Santander, 244 miles (393km) N of Madrid

THE VILLAGE OF SANTILLANA

Among the most perfectly preserved medieval villages in Europe, ✪ **Santillana del Mar,** a Spanish national landmark, was once a famous place of pilgrimage. A monastery housed the relics of St. Juliana, a martyr in Asia Minor who refused to surrender her virginity to her husband. Pilgrims, especially the *grandees* of Castile, came to worship at this site. The name Santillana is a contraction of Santa Juliana. The "del Mar" is misleading, as Santillana is not on the water but inland.

Jean-Paul Sartre called Santillana "the prettiest village in Spain," and we wouldn't want to dispute his esteemed judgment. In spite of all the tour buses, Santillana still retains its medieval atmosphere and is very much a village of dairy farmers to this day.

Wander on foot throughout the village, taking in its principal sites, including **Plaza de Ramón Pelayo** (sometimes called Plaza Mayor). Here the Parador de Santillana (see below) has been installed in the old Barreda Bracho residence.

A 15th-century tower, facing calle de Juan Infante, is known for its pointed arched doorway. A walk along calle de las Lindas (Street of Beautiful Women) may not live up to its promise, but it does include many of the oldest buildings in Santillana and two towers dating from the 14th and 15th centuries. Calle del Rio gets its name from a stream running through town to a central fountain.

ESSENTIALS

GETTING THERE   La Cantábrica (☎ 942-72-08-22) operates six buses a day from Santander but cuts back to four between September and June. Trip time is 45 minutes.

By car, take the N-611 out of Santander to reach the C-6316 cutoff to Santillana.

VISITOR INFORMATION   The tourist information office is at Plaza Mayor (☎ 942-81-82-51). Hours are daily from 9:30am to 1pm and 4 to 7pm.

EXPLORING SANTILLANA

Visit the 800-year-old cathedral, the **Colegiata de Santillana,** calle Santo Domingo, which shelters the tomb of the patron saint of the village, Juliana, and walk through its ivy-covered cloister. Other treasures include 1,000-year-old documents and a 17th-century Mexican silver altarpiece. The cathedral is open April through October, daily from 9:30am to 1pm and 4 to 7:30pm; off-season, daily from 10am to 1pm and 4 to 6pm. Admission, including entrance to the Convent of the Poor Clares, is 300 ptas. ($2).

At the other end of the main street, the 400-year-old Covento de Regina Coelí, also called the **Convent of the Poor Clares (Museo Diocesano)** (☎ 942-81-80-04), houses a rich art collection that was inspired by a Madrid art professor who encouraged the nuns to collect and restore religious paintings and statues damaged or abandoned during the Spanish Civil War. The collection is constantly expanding. It's open daily from 10am to 1pm and 4 to 8pm (closing at 6pm in winter). Admission is 150 ptas. ($1).

WHERE TO STAY

Expensive

✪ **Parador de Santillana.** Plaza de Ramón Pelayo, 8, 39330 Santillana del Mar. ☎ **942-81-80-00.** Fax 942-81-83-91. 54 units. MINIBAR TV TEL. 15,000–17,500 ptas. ($100.50–$117.25) double. AE, DC, MC, V. Free parking.

A 400-year-old former palace filled with many beautiful antiques, this parador is one of the best and most popular in Spain. The public rooms are elegantly informal. The hand-hewn plank floors, old brass chandeliers, and refectory tables with their bowls of fresh flowers enhance the atmosphere. Large portraits of knights in armor hang in a gallery. Most of the guest rooms are unusually large, with antiques and windows on two sides; many have views of a small garden. The large bathrooms contain all sorts of conveniences, including terry-cloth robes. Note that the third-floor rooms are very small. Four-course evening meals and luncheons, offering rather standard fare, are served in the great dining hall.

Moderate

Hotel Altamira. Calle Cantón, 1, 39330 Santillana del Mar. ☎ **942-81-80-25.** Fax 942-84-01-36. 32 units. A/C TV TEL. 7,000–10,850 ptas. ($46.90–$72.70) double. AE, DC, MC, V.

This three-star hotel in the center of the village is also a 400-year-old former palace; it's the best place to stay if you can't get into the government-run parador (see above). Although not as impressive as the parador, it often takes the overflow in its comfortable, well-maintained rooms, each fitted with a firm mattress on a twin or double bed. Dinner is available at two of the hotel's restaurants, El Cantón and El Racial. Both restaurants serve Castilian-inspired cuisine.

Los Infantes. Avenida L'Dorat, 1, 39330 Santillana del Mar. ☎ **942-81-81-00.** Fax 942-84-01-03. 50 units. TV TEL. 7,500–14,700 ptas. ($50.25–$98.50) double. AE, DC, MC, V. Free parking.

This three-star hotel is a comfortable choice, although not as charming as the Hotel Altamira (see above). Located in an 18th-century building on the main road leading into the village, Infantes has successfully kept the old flavor of Santillana: beamed ceilings and lounges furnished with tapestries, antiques, clocks, and paintings. The small rooms are pleasant and simple, with wall-to-wall carpeting; two have small balconies. A restaurant serves international cuisine, with dinner costing 1,500 to 2,500 ptas. ($10.05 to $16.75).

Inexpensive

Hostal-Residencia Emperador. Avenida le Dorat, 12, 39330 Santillana del Mar. ☎ **942-81-80-54.** 5 units. TV. 5,500–6,900 ptas. ($36.85–$46.25) double. No credit cards.

In the historic district, this *residencia* offers simply furnished but clean and reasonably comfortable rooms, each with a good bed. For such a modest place, the hospitality is gracious. Because of the Emperador's small size, it can be difficult to get a room from June 15 to September 1.

WHERE TO DINE

Dining isn't one of the compelling reasons to visit Santillana del Mar. Except for Los Blasones (see below), the only recommendable independent restaurant, your best bet is to dine at one of the previously recommended hotels. For atmosphere and quality of cuisine, the finest choice is Parador de Santillana (see above).

Los Blasones. Plaza de la Gándara, 8. ☎ **942-81-80-70.** Reservations recommended. Main courses 1,400–2,000 ptas. ($9.40–$13.40); fixed-price menu 2,750 ptas. ($18.45). AE, MC, V. Daily 1–4pm and 8–11:30pm. Closed Dec 10–Mar 10. REGIONAL.

Located in the center of town on the Plaza de la Gándara, this bar-restaurant, a local hangout, serves the best food in town among the independent restaurants. It's in a rustic building made of stone. Barbecue selections are featured and the chef's specialty is *solomillo al queso de Treviso* (sirloin with cheese sauce). Try also the perfectly grilled hake or the tasty stuffed peppers.

THE ALTAMIRA CAVES

About 1½ miles (2.5km) from Santillana del Mar are the ♻ **Cuevas de Altamira** (☎ **942-81-80-05**), famous for prehistoric paintings dating from the end of the Ice Age, paintings that have led those caves to be called the "Sistine Chapel of prehistoric art." The cave paintings at Altamira are ranked among the finest prehistoric paintings ever discovered. They are rivaled but not matched by similar paintings discovered at Lascaux in the Dordogne Valley in France. These ancient depictions of bison and horses, painted vividly in reds and blacks on the caves' ceilings, were not discovered until the late 19th century. Once their authenticity was established, scholars and laypersons alike flocked to see these works of art, which provide a fragile link to our remote ancestors.

Severe damage was caused by the bacteria brought in by so many visitors, so now the Research Center and Museum of Altamira allows only 20 visitors per day June through September (no children under 13) and five visitors per day October through May. Admission is 400 ptas. ($2.70). If you don't have a car, you have to walk from Santillana del Mar, as there is no bus service. From the center of Santillana signs point the way to the cave. You walk past the abandoned Iglesia de San Sebastián, then cut through the streets of the hamlet of Herrán. Signs there direct you right across a farmer's field until you reach the cave. If you wish to visit, write to this address 1 year in advance asking permission to see the main cave and specifying the number in your party and the desired date: **Centro de Investigación y Museo de Altamira,** 39330 Santillana del Mar, Cantabria, Spain (☎ **942-81-80-05**).

Reservations are not necessary for visits to the nearby **Cave of the Stalactites** and the little free museum at the site, open Monday through Saturday from 10am to 1pm and 4 to 6pm, Sunday from 10am to 1pm. Here you can see reproductions of the caves' artwork and buy color slides that show the subtleties of color employed. You'll also see pictures of what the bacteria did to these priceless paintings. To reach the area, you need to go by car or on foot because there is no bus service.

4 Los Picos de Europa

Potes: 71 miles (114km) W of Santander, 247 miles (398km) N of Madrid; Cangas de Onís: 91 miles (147km) W of Santander, 260 miles (419km) N of Madrid

These mountains are technically part of the Cordillera Cantábrica, which runs parallel to the northern coastline of Spain. In the narrow and vertiginous band known as Los Picos de Europa, they are by far at their most dramatic.

These "European Peaks" are the most famous and most legend-riddled mountains in Spain. Rising more than 8,500 feet, they are not high by alpine standards, but their proximity to the sea makes their height especially awesome. During the Middle Ages, they were passable only with great difficulty. (Much earlier, the ancient Romans constructed a north-south road whose stones are still visible in some places.) The abundance of wildlife, the medieval battles that occurred here, and the dramatically rocky heights have all contributed to the twice-told tales that are an essential part of the entire principality of Asturias.

The position of Los Picos defined the medieval borders between Asturias, Santander, and León. Covering a distance of only 24 miles (39km) at their longest point, they are geologically and botanically different from anything else in the region. Thousands of years ago, busy glaciers created massive and forbidding limestone cliffs, which today challenge the most dedicated and intrepid rock climbers in Europe.

As you're touring the majestic Picos de Europa, be on the lookout for some of the rarest wildlife remaining in Europe. On the beech-covered slopes of these mountains and in gorges laden with jasmine, you might spot the increasingly rare Asturcon. This is a shaggy and rather chubby wild horse that's so small it first looks like a toy pony. Another endangered species is the Iberian brown bear—but if you see one, keep your distance. The park is also the home of the surefooted chamois goat. Many bird watchers flock here every year to see rare birds of prey that include peregrine falcons, buzzards, and golden eagles. There are also some rare butterflies. All this wildlife is strictly protected by the government.

If you want to hike in this region, make sure you're well prepared. Many of the slopes are covered with loosely compacted shale, making good treads and hiking boots a must. Inexperienced hikers should definitely stick to well-established paths. In summer, temperatures can get hot and humid, and sudden downpours sweeping in from the frequently rainy coastline are common in any season. Hiking is not recommended between October and May, though you can drive or do the walk described in Tour 3, below, in any season.

The Picos are divided by swiftly flowing rivers into three regions: From east to west, they are Andara, Urrieles, and Cornion.

By far the best way to see this region is by car. Most drivers arrive in the region on the N-621 highway, heading southwest from Santander, or on the same highway northeast from the cities of north-central Spain (especially León and Valladolid). This highway connects many of the region's best vistas in a straight line. It also defines the region's eastern boundary. If you're driving east from Oviedo, you'll take the N-6312, in which case the first town of any importance will be Cangas de Onís.

Travel by bus is much less convenient but possible if you have lots of time and have had your fill of the rich architecture of the Spanish heartland. The region's touristic hubs are the towns of Panes and Potes, both of which have bus service (2 buses per day in summer, one per day in winter) from both Santander and León. More frequent buses (five per day) come to Potes from the coastal town of Unquera (which lies along the coastal train lines). From Oviedo, there are two buses daily to the district's easternmost town of Cangas; these continue a short distance farther southeast to Covadonga. Within the region, a small local bus runs once a day, according to an erratic schedule, along the northern rim of the Picos, connecting Cangas de Onís with Las Arenas. Frankly, bus service in this region is too time consuming for most visitors.

EXPLORING THE REGION

If you have a car, the number and variety of tours within this region are almost endless, but for the purposes of this guide, we have organized the region into three driving tours. Any of them, with their side excursions, could fill an entire day; if you're rushed and omit some of the side excursions, you'll spend half a day.

DRIVING TOUR 1—PANES TO POTES

18 miles (29km); 1 hour

Except for one optional detour, this drive extends entirely along one of the region's best roads, N-621, which links León and Valladolid to Santander. The drive is most noteworthy for its views of the ravine containing the Deva River, a ravine so steep that direct sunlight rarely penetrates it.

About two-thirds of the way to Potes, signs will point you on a detour to the village of:

1. Lebana, half a mile off the main road. Here you'll find the church of **Nuestra Señora de Lebana,** built in the 10th century in the Mozarabic style, surrounded by a copse of trees at the base of tall cliffs. Some people consider it the best example of Arabized Christian architecture in Europe, with Islamic-inspired geometric motifs. If it isn't open, knock at the door of the first house you see as you enter the village—the home of the guardian, who will unlock the church if she's around. For this, she will expect a tip. If she's not around, content yourself with admiring the church from the outside, noting its spectacular natural setting.

Continuing for about another 5 miles (8km), you'll reach the village of:

2. Potes, a charming place with well-kept alpine houses against a backdrop of jagged mountains. Two miles (3.2km) southwest of Potes, near Turiano, stands the:

3. Monastery of Santo Toribio de Liébana, dating from the 17th century. Restored to the style it enjoyed at the peak of its vast power, a transitional Romanesque, it contains what is reputed to be a splinter from the True Cross, brought from Jerusalem in the 8th century by the Bishop of Astorga. The monastery is also famous as the former home of Beatus de Liébana, the 8th-century author of *Commentary on the Apocalypse,* one of medieval Spain's most famous ecclesiastical documents. Today the building remains a functioning monastery. Ring the bell during daylight hours, and one of the brothers will let you enter if you are properly attired.

At the end of a winding and breathtakingly beautiful road to the west of Potes lies the:

4. Parador del Río Deva, where you can spend the night or just stop for lunch. The drive following the path of the Deva River for the most part will take you to:

5. Fuente-Dé. Once you're here, a *teleférico* will carry you 2,000 feet up to an observation platform above a wind-scoured rock face. In summer this cable car operates daily in July and August from 9am to 8pm; from September through June hours are daily 10am to 6pm. Round-trip fare is 1,200 ptas. ($8.05). At the top you can walk 3 miles (4.8km) along a footpath to the rustic **Refugio de Aliva** (☎ **942-73-09-99**), open between June 15 and September 15. Doubles cost 7,500 to 8,500 ptas. ($50.25 to $56.95). If you opt for just a meal or a snack at the hostal's simple restaurant, remember to allow enough time to return to the teleférico before its last trip down. If you plan on taking the next driving tour (below), then head back to Potes.

DRIVING TOUR 2—POTES TO CANGAS DE ONÍS

93 miles (150km); 4 hours

This tour includes not only the Quiviesa Valley and some of the region's most vertiginous mountain passes, but also some of its most verdant fields and most elevated pastures. You might stop at an occasional village, but most of the time you will be going through deserted countryside. Your route will take you under several tunnels and high above mountain streams set deep into gorges. The occasional belvederes along the way always deliver on their promise of panoramic views.

1. **Potes** (see "Driving Tour 1" above) is your starting point. Take N-621 southwest to Riaño. At Riaño, turn north for a brief ride on N-625. Then take a winding route through the heart of the region by driving northwest on N-637. Though it's beautiful all along the way, the first really important place you'll reach is:

2. **Cangas de Onís,** the westernmost town in the region, where you can get a clean hotel room and a solid meal after a trek through the mountains. The biggest attraction in Cangas de Onís is an ivy-covered **Roman bridge,** lying west of the center, spanning the Sella River. Also of interest is the **Capilla de Santa Cruz,** immediately west of the center. One of the earliest Christian sites in Spain (and a holy spot many centuries before that), it was originally constructed in the 8th century over a Celtic dolmen and rebuilt in the 15th century.

   A mile northwest of Cangas de Onís, beside the road leading to Arriondas, stands the:

3. **Monasterio de San Pedro,** a Benedictine monastery in the village of **Villanueva.** The church that you see was originally built in the 17th century, when it enclosed within its premises the ruins of a much older Romanesque church. Combining Baroque opulence and Romanesque simplicity, it has some unusual carved capitals showing the unhappy end of the medieval King Favila, supposedly devoured by a Cantabrian bear.

DRIVING TOUR 3—CANGAS DE ONÍS TO PANES

35 miles (56km); 1 hour

This tour travels along the relatively straight C-6312 from the western to the eastern entrance to the Picos de Europa region. A number of unusual excursions could easily stretch this into an all-day outing.

   From Cangas de Onís, heading west about 1 mile (1.6km), you'll reach the turnoff to:

1. **El Buxu Cueva.** Inside the cave are a limited number of prehistoric rock engravings and charcoal drawings, somewhat disappointingly small. Only 25 persons per day are allowed inside (respiration erodes the drawings), so unless you get there early, you won't get in. It's open Wednesday through Sunday from 10am to 2pm and 4 to 6:30pm. Admission is 200 ptas. ($1.35).

   Four miles (6.5km) east, signs point south in the direction of:

2. **Covadonga.** Revered as the birthplace of Christian Spain, it is about 6 miles (9.6km) off the main highway. A battle here in A.D. 718 pitted a ragged band of Christian Visigoths against a small band of Muslims. The resulting victory established the first niche of Christian Europe in Moorish Iberia.

   The town's most important monument is **La Santa Cueva,** a cave containing the sarcophagus of Pelayo (d. 737), king of the Visigothic Christians, and an enormous neo-Romanesque basilica, built between 1886 and 1901, commemorating the Christianization of Spain. At the end of the long boulevard that funnels into the base of the church stands a statue of Pelayo.

Return to the highway and continue east. You'll come to the village of Las Estazadas; then after another 7 miles (11km) you'll reach:

3. **Las Arenas de Cabrales** (some maps refer to it as Arenas). This is the headquarters of a cheese-producing region whose Cabrales, a blue-veined cheese made from ewes' milk, is avidly consumed throughout Spain.

Drive 3 miles (4.8km) south from Arenas, following signs to the village of:

4. **Puente de Poncebos** (shown on some maps as Poncebos). Here, the road ends abruptly (except perhaps for four-wheel-drive vehicles). This village is set several miles downstream from the source of Spain's most famous salmon-fishing river, the Cares, which flows from its source near the more southerly village of Cain through deep ravines.

Beginning at Poncebos, a footpath has been cut into the ravine on either side of the Cares River. It is one of the engineering marvels of Spain, known for centuries as **"The Divine Gorge."** It crosses the ravine many times over footbridges and sometimes through tunnels chiseled into the rock face beside the water, making a hike along the banks of this river a memorable outing. You can climb up the riverbed from Poncebos, overland to the village of Cain, a total distance of 7 miles (11km). Allow between 3 and 4 hours. At Cain, you can take a taxi back to where you left your car in Poncebos if you don't want to retrace your steps.

After your trek up the riverbed, continue your drive on to the village of:

5. **Panes**, a distance of 14 miles (22km), to the eastern extremity of the Picos de Europa.

WHERE TO STAY & DINE IN THE AREA

Accommodations are extremely limited in these mountain towns. If you're planning an overnight stop, make sure you have a reservation. Most taverns will serve you food during regular opening hours without a reservation.

IN CANGAS DE ONÍS

Hotel Aultre Naray. Km. 335 N634, Peruyes, 33547 Asturias. ☎ **98-584-08-08.** Fax 98-584-08-48. www.princast.es/asturias/alosom/casonas/aultre.htm. E-mail: aultre@hprz.es. 10 units. TV TEL. 8,000–12,000 ptas. ($53.60–$80.40) double. AE, DC, MC, V. Free parking.

A small hotel with character, this establishment, which opened in 1995, is an Asturian country house dating from 1873. Its robust masonry work is typical of the last century, and it has a beautiful stone archway in the entrance. The decoration came from an interior design workshop in Madrid, resulting in a harmonious blend of traditional architecture with current design trends. The hotel has well-furnished midsize bedrooms, each with a private tiled bathroom. Four rooms have sloping ceilings. There's also a cozy sitting room with a fireplace for guests, a bar and dining room, and a garden. The hotel is set in the foothills of the Escapa mountain range, enjoying a panoramic view of these mountains and of an oak forest on the banks of the River Sella. The area is a perfect place for fishing; hiking in the mountains and canoeing are other popular diversions.

La Palmera. Soto de Cangas. ☎ **98-594-00-96.** Main courses 1,100–3,000 ptas. ($7.35–$20.10); menú del día 1,500 ptas. ($10.05). AE, DC, MC, V. Daily 1:30–4:30pm and 8:30–11:30pm. REGIONAL.

When the weather is right you can dine outside here, enjoying some mountain air with the mountain food. Sometimes this place is overrun, but on other occasions you can have a meal in peace. The menu features game from the surrounding mountains, along with fillet of beef, lamb chops, and salmon in green sauce. Try the local mountain cheese. La Palmera lies 2 miles (3km) east of Cangas de Onís on the road to Covadonga.

IN COSGAYA

Hotel del Oso. Carretera Espinama, s/n, 39539 Cosgaya. ☎ **942-73-30-18.** Fax 942-73-30-36. 36 units. TV TEL. 7,700–8,700 ptas. ($51.60–$58.30) double. DC, MC, V. Closed Jan 7–Feb 15. Free parking. From Potes, take the road signposted to Espinama 9 miles (14.5km) south.

This well-run little hotel is located in two buildings set next to the banks of the Deva River, beside the road leading from Potes to the parador and cable car at Fuente-Dé. The place is ringed with natural beauty. Its small rooms are well furnished and maintained, and meals are taken at the Mesón del Oso (see below).

Mesón del Oso. Carretera Espinama, s/n. ☎ **942-73-30-18.** Main courses 1,200–2,400 ptas. ($8.05–$16.10). DC, MC, V. Daily 1–4pm and 9–11pm. Closed Jan 7–Feb 15. From Potes, take the route south toward Espinama 9 miles (14.5km). ASTURIAN.

Open to the public since 1981, this stone-built place is named after the bear that supposedly devoured Favila, an 8th-century king of Asturias. Here, at the birthplace of the Christian warrior King Pelayo, you can enjoy Lebaniega cuisine, reflecting the bounty of mountain, stream, and sea. The portions are generous. Try trout from the Deva River, grilled tuna, roast suckling pig, or a mountain stew called *cocida lebaniego*, whose recipe derives from local lore and tradition. Dessert might be a fruit-based tart. There's also an outdoor terrace.

IN COVADONGA

Hotel Pelayo. 33589 Covadonga. ☎ **98-584-60-61.** Fax 98-584-60-54. 45 units. TV TEL. 8,000–14,000 ptas. ($53.60–$93.80) double; 11,000–18,000 ptas. ($73.70–$120.60) suite. AE, DC, MC, V. Closed Dec 15–Feb 1. Free parking. Drive east and then south from Cangas de Onís, following the signs for Covadonga and the hotel.

There's no street address for this place, but it lies in the shadow of the large 19th-century basilica that dominates the village. The view from its windows takes in a panoramic landscape. Guests come here to enjoy the mountain air, and many pilgrims check in while visiting religious shrines in the area. The place has a somewhat dated, but nevertheless appealing, family atmosphere. The small rooms are comfortable and well furnished, each with a good bed. The facilities include a parking lot, a garden, and a restaurant offering well-prepared lunch or dinner ranging from 1,600 to 2,000 ptas. ($10.70 to $13.40).

IN FUENTE-DÉ

Parador de Fuente-Dé. At 3.5km de Espinama, 39588 Espinama. ☎ **942-73-66-51.** Fax 942-73-66-54. 78 units. MINIBAR TV TEL. 11,500–13,500 ptas. ($77.05–$90.45) double. AE, DC, MC, V. Closed Nov 15–Mar 1. Free parking. Drive 16 miles (26km) west of Potes.

The finest place to stay in the area, this government-run parador faces panoramic vistas of the Picos de Europa. Opened in 1975, it lies at the end of the major road through the Liébana region. Hunters in autumn and mountain climbers in summer often fill its attractively decorated and comfortably furnished bedrooms, which are midsize to spacious. The place has a pleasant bar, and its restaurant serves good regional cuisine, with a menú del día costing 3,200 ptas. ($21.45).

IN POTES

Restaurant Martín. Roscabao, s/n. ☎ **942-73-02-33.** Main courses 750–1,500 ptas. ($5.05–$10.05); fixed-price menu 1,000 ptas. ($6.70). AE, V. Daily 1–4:30pm and 8–11pm. Closed Jan. REGIONAL.

This family run establishment in the center of Potes is filled with regional charm and spirit. They prepare *garbanzos* (chickpeas) with bits of *chorizo* (sausage), other vegetables and the rich produce of the region, depending on the season. They also serve game from the Picos and fish from the Cantabrian coast. The dessert choices comprise more than a dozen tarts and pastries.

5 Gijón (Xixón)

294 miles (473km) N of Madrid, 119 miles (192km) W of Santander, 18 miles (29km) E of Oviedo

The major port of Asturias and its largest city is also a summer resort and an industrial center rolled into one. As a port, Gijón (pronounced hee-*hon*) is said to predate the Romans. The Visigoths came through here, and in the 8th century the Moors also wandered through the area, but none of those would-be conquerors made much of an impression.

The best part of the city to explore is the *barrio* of **Cimadevilla,** with its maze of alleys and leaning houses. This section, jutting into the ocean to the north of the new town, spills over an elevated piece of land known as Santa Catalina. Santa Catalina forms a headland at the west end of the **Playa San Lorenzo,** stretching for about 1½ miles (2km); this beach has good facilities and is sandy. After time at the beach you can stroll through the **Parque Isabel la Católica** at its eastern end.

Gijón is short on major monuments. The city was the birthplace of Gaspar Melchor de Jovellanos (1744–1811), one of Spain's most prominent men of letters, as well as an agrarian reformer and liberal economist. Manuel de Godoy, the notorious minister, ordered that Jovellanos be held prisoner for 7 years in Bellver Castle on Majorca. In Gijón his birthplace has been restored and turned into the **Museo-Casa Natal de Jovellanos,** Plaza de Jovellanos, open Tuesday through Saturday from 10am to 2pm and 4 to 8pm. Admission is free.

ESSENTIALS

GETTING THERE Gijón doesn't have an airport, but Iberia flies to the airport at Ranón, 26 miles (42km) away, a facility it shares with Oviedo-bound passengers.

Gijón has good rail links and makes a good gateway into Asturias. Three trains a day make the 6½- to 8½-hour trip from Madrid. León is a convenient rail hub for reaching Gijón because nine trains per day make the 2- to 3-hour trip between these cities. You can also take the narrow-gauge FEVE from Bilbao.

Six buses a day connect Gijón with Madrid (5½ hours away), and two buses per day run to and from Santander (4½ hours away). Four buses a day go to León (2 hours away).

From Santander in the east, drive west along the N-634. At Ribadesella, you can take the turnoff to the 632, which is the coastal road that will take you to Gijón. This is the scenic route. To save time, continue on N-634 until you reach the outskirts of Oviedo, then cut north on A-66, the expressway highway to Gijón.

VISITOR INFORMATION The **tourist information office** is at Marqués de San Esteban, 1 (☎ **98-534-60-46**). It's open Monday through Friday from 9am to 2pm and 4 to 7pm, Saturday from 9am to 2pm.

SPECIAL EVENTS The most exciting time to be in Gijón is on **Asturias Day,** the first Sunday in August. This fiesta is celebrated with parade floats, traditional folk dancing, and lots of music. But summers here tend to be festive even without a festival. Vacationers are fond of patronizing the cider taverns (*chigres*), eating grilled sardines, and joining in sing-alongs in the port-side tascas. Be aware that you can get as drunk on cider as you can on beer, maybe somewhat faster.

WHERE TO STAY
EXPENSIVE

Hernán Cortés. Fernández Vallín, 5, 33205 Gijón. ☎ **98-534-60-00.** Fax 98-535-56-45. 56 units. A/C MINIBAR TV TEL. 17,000–22,000 ptas. ($113.90–$147.40) double; 20,000–30,000 ptas. ($134–$201) suite. AE, DC, MC, V. Parking 1,250 ptas. ($8.40) nearby. Bus: 4 or 11.

About 1 block east of Plaza del 6 de Agosto, midway between Playa San Lorenzo and the harbor, this hotel named after the conquistador is one of the finest in town. Although it was recently renovated, its midsize guest rooms still retain a bit of the allure of yesteryear and provide such thoughtful extras as shoe-shine equipment. The Cortés doesn't have a restaurant, but it does offer a nighttime cafeteria for breakfast. The proprietors will serve lunch or dinner in your room from a neighboring restaurant.

✪ **Parador El Molino Viejo (Parador de Gijón).** Parque Isabel la Católica, s/n, 33203 Gijón. ☎ **800/223-1356** in the U.S., or 98-537-05-11. Fax 98-537-02-33. 40 units. A/C MINIBAR TV TEL. 15,000–19,000 ptas. ($100.50–$127.30) double. AE, DC, MC, V. Free parking. Bus: 4 or 11.

Next to the verdant confines of Gijón's most visible park, about half a mile east of the town center and an easy walk from the popular beach Playa San Lorenzo, this is the premier place to stay. Awarded four stars by the government (which also runs it), it was constructed around the core of an 18th-century cider mill. The parador is surrounded by a garden strewn with tables, beside a stream sheltering colonies of swans. It contains a marble-sheathed reception area, an unpretentious restaurant, and a cider bar that, on weekends, is quite popular with local residents. The guest rooms are somewhat cramped and surprisingly simple for a four-star hotel; however, they're tastefully restored with well-scrubbed wooden floors, thick shutters, traditional furniture, and larger-than-usual bathrooms.

MODERATE

Begoña. Carretera de la Costa, 44, 33205 Gijón. ☎ **98-514-72-11.** Fax 98-539-82-22. 250 units. TV TEL. 10,425–11,380 ptas. ($69.85–$76.25) double. AE, DC, MC, V. Parking 1,300 ptas. ($8.70). Bus: 4 or 11.

This functional modern hotel with much-appreciated parking has small rooms that are well furnished and comfortable, plus efficient chamber service to keep everything clean. Regional and national dishes, with many seafood concoctions, are served in the restaurant, where meals begin at 1,500 ptas. ($10.05). The hotel lies on the southern outskirts of the new town, 1 block north of Avenida Manuel Llaneza, the major traffic artery from the southwest.

La Casona de Jovellanos. Plaza de Jovellanos, 1, 33201 Gijón. ☎ **98-534-12-64.** Fax 98-535-61-51. 15 units. TV TEL. 6,500–12,600 ptas. ($43.55–$84.40) double; 7,000–20,000 ptas. ($46.90–$134) suite. AE, DC, MC, V. Parking nearby 1,300 ptas. ($8.70). Bus: 4 or 11.

This venerable hotel stands on the rocky peninsula that was the site of the oldest part of fortified Gijón, a short distance south of the Parque Santa Catalina. It contains only a few rooms, so reservations are imperative. The small rooms themselves are attractively furnished and well maintained, each with a comfortable bed. The hotel was built on foundations 3 centuries old. In 1794 the writer Jovellanos established the Asturian Royal Institute of Marine Life and Mineralogy here, and it was later transformed into a hotel, lying within walking distance of the beach and yacht basin.

WHERE TO DINE

Casa Justo (Chigre Asturianu). Hermanos Feigueroso, 50. ☎ **98-538-63-57.** Reservations recommended. Main courses 1,500–3,000 ptas. ($10.05–$20.10); fixed-price menus 1,200–1,500 ptas. ($8.05–$10.05). AE, DC, MC, V. Fri–Wed 1pm–1am. Closed June 15–July 1. Bus: 4 or 11. REGIONAL.

Housed within a very old cider press, for years this place has been called Chigre Asturianu, but most locals still refer to it by its old designation. Renovations have added well-designed dining rooms and kitchens to what used to be a large and drafty building. The cuisine is based primarily on fish and shellfish but with plenty of Asturian regional dishes as well. Try octopus with potatoes, grilled fresh John Dory, or veal chops. There is a full array of wines. Here, too, you can sample that Roquefort-like cheese, Cabrales, made in the Picos de Europa. Casa Justo lies south of the old town near Campo Sagrada on the road to Pola de Siero.

Casa Tino. Alfredo Truán, 9. ☎ **98-534-13-87.** Reservations recommended. Main courses 1,600–2,500 ptas. ($10.70–$16.75); menú del día 1,300 ptas. ($8.70). AE, DC, MC, V. Fri–Wed 1:15–3:30pm and 8:45–11:30pm. Bus: 4 or 11. REGIONAL.

Quality combined with quantity, at reasonable prices, is the hallmark of this restaurant, located near the police station, north of Manuel Llaneza and west of the Paseo de Begoña. Each day the chef prepares a different stew—sometimes fish and sometimes meat. The place is packed with chattering diners every evening, many of them habitués. Sample the white beans of the region cooked with pork, stewed hake, or marinated beefsteak, perhaps finishing with one of the fruit tarts.

Casa Victor. Carmen, 11. ☎ **98-534-83-10.** Reservations recommended. Main courses 2,500–3,000 ptas. ($16.75–$20.10); fixed-price menu 1,900 ptas. ($12.75). AE, DC, MC, V. Mon–Sat 1–3:30pm and 8:30–11:30pm. Closed mid-Dec to mid-Jan. Bus: 4 or 11. SEAFOOD.

Owner and sometime chef Victor Bango is a bit of a legend. He oversees the buying and preparation of the fresh fish for which this place is famous. The successful young people of Gijón enjoy the tavernlike atmosphere here, as well as the imaginative dishes—a mousse made from the roe of sea urchins, for example, is all the rage in Asturias these days. Well-chosen wines accompany such other menu items as octopus served with fresh vegetables and grilled steak. Casa Victor is located by the dockyards.

6 Oviedo (Uviéu)

126 miles (203km) W of Santander, 276 miles (444km) N of Madrid

Oviedo is the capital of Asturias. Despite its high concentration of industry and mining, the area has unspoiled scenery. Only 16 miles (26km) from the coast, Oviedo is very pleasant in summer, when much of Spain is unbearably hot. It also makes an ideal base for excursions along the Costa Verde.

A peaceful city today, Oviedo has had a long and violent history. Razed in the 8th century during the Reconquest, it was rebuilt in an architectural style known as Asturian pre-Romanesque, which predated many of the greatest achievements under the Moors. Remarkably, this architectural movement was in flower when the rest of Europe lay under the black cloud of the Dark Ages.

As late as the 1930s Oviedo was suffering violent upheavals. An insurrection in the mining areas on October 5, 1934, led to a seizure of the town by miners, who set up a revolutionary government. The subsequent fighting led to the destruction of many historical monuments. The cathedral was also damaged, and the university was set on fire. Even more destruction came during the Spanish Civil War.

ESSENTIALS

GETTING THERE   Oviedo doesn't have an airport. The nearest one is at Ranón, 32 miles (51.5km) away, which it shares with Gijón-bound passengers. Call ☎ **98-555-18-33** for information.

From Madrid, there are six trains per day. Call RENFE at ☎ **98-525-02-02** for information.

One bus per day arrives from Santander (trip time: 1 hour). Seven buses pull in daily from Madrid (6 hours). For bus schedules, call ☎ **98-528-12-00.**

From the east or west, take N-634 across the coast of northern Spain. From the south, take N-630 or A-66 from León.

VISITOR INFORMATION   The **tourist information office** is at Plaza de Alfonso II el Casto (☎ **98-521-33-85**). Hours are Monday through Friday from 9:30am to 1:30pm and 4:30 to 6:30pm, Saturday from 9am to 2pm, and Sunday from 11am to 2pm.

EXPLORING OVIEDO

Oviedo has been rebuilt into a modern city around the Parque de San Francisco. It still contains some historical and artistic monuments, however, the most important being the **cathedral** on the Plaza de Alfonso II el Casto (☎ **98-522-10-33**). The Gothic church was begun in 1348 and completed at the end of the 15th century (except for the spire, which dates from 1556). Inside is an altarpiece in the florid Gothic style, dating from the 14th and 15th centuries. The cathedral's 9th-century **Cámara Santa (Holy Chamber)** is famous for the Cross of Don Pelayo, the Cross of the Victory, and the Cross of the Angels, the finest specimens of Asturian art in the world. Admission to the cathedral is free, but entrance to the Holy Chamber is 400 ptas. ($2.70) for adults and 300 ptas. ($2) for children 10 to 15; children under 10 are free. The cathedral is open May through October, Monday through Saturday from 10am to 1pm and 4 to 7pm; November through April, Monday through Saturday from 10am to 1pm and 4 to 6pm. Take bus number 1.

Behind the cathedral, the **Museo Arqueológico,** calle San Vicente, 5 (☎ **98-521-54-05**), in a former convent dating from the 15th century, houses prehistoric relics discovered in Asturias, pre-Romanesque sculptures, a numismatic display, and old musical instruments. It's open Tuesday through Saturday from 10am to 1:30pm and 4 to 6pm, Sunday from 11am to 1pm. Admission is free.

Standing above Oviedo, on Monte Naranco, are two of the most famous examples of Asturian pre-Romanesque architecture. **Santa María del Naranco** (☎ **98-529-67-55**), originally a 9th-century palace and hunting lodge of Ramiro I, offers views of Oviedo and the snowcapped Picos de Europa. Once containing baths and private apartments, it was converted into a church in the 12th century. Intricate stonework depicts hunting scenes, and barrel vaulting rests on a network of blind arches. The open porticoes at both ends were 200 years ahead of their time architecturally. The church is open April through September, daily from 9:30am to 1pm and 3 to 7pm; October through March, daily from 10am to 1pm and 3 to 5pm. Admission is 300 ptas. ($2).

Lying about 100 yards away is **San Miguel de Lillo** (☎ **98-529-56-85**). It, too, was built by Ramiro I, as a royal chapel, and was no doubt a magnificent specimen of

Asturian pre-Romanesque until 15th-century architects marred its grace. The stone carvings that remain, however, are exemplary. Most of the sculptures have been transferred to the archaeological museum in town.

The church is open daily from 9:30am to 1pm Monday through Saturday, also from 3 to 7pm. Admission is 250 ptas. ($1.70) Tuesday through Sunday, free on Mondays. Ask at the tourist office for its 45-minute walking tour from the center of Oviedo to the churches. Also check that the churches will be open at the time of your visit.

SHOPPING

Serious shoppers know that Oviedo offers some of the best outlets in Spain for handbags and shoes. For a number of the finest boutiques, head for the intersection of Uria and Gil de Jaz. In this district and on adjoining side streets you'll find some of the country's best-known designer boutiques, selling the same merchandise that goes at far higher prices in such cities as Madrid and Barcelona. Many artisans in this district make their own products—selling, for example, a variety of calfskin goods and hand-sewn leather. You'll also come across good sales on Asturian ceramic ware.

WHERE TO STAY
EXPENSIVE

✪ **Hotel de la Reconquista.** Gil de Jaz, 16, 33004 Oviedo. ☎ **98-524-11-00.** Fax 98-524-60-11. 142 units. A/C MINIBAR TV TEL. 29,500 ptas. ($197.65) double; from 45,000 ptas. ($301.50) suite. AE, DC, MC, V. Parking 1,800 ptas. ($12.05). Bus: 1, 2, or 3.

Named after a subject dear to the hearts of the Catholic monarchs—the ejection of the Muslims from Iberia—this is one of the most prestigious hotels in Spain. Originally built between 1754 and 1777 as an orphanage and hospital, it received visits from Queen Isabella II in 1858 and a reworking of its baroque stonework during a restoration in 1958. The Reconquista was converted into a hotel in 1973 after the outlay of massive amounts of cash. Despite the growth of the city, it remains the second-largest building in Oviedo.

Today, the interior boasts a combination of modern and reproduction furniture, as well as a scattering of ecclesiastical paintings and antiques. The spacious guest rooms contain private bathrooms and are outfitted in antique styles, with views of the old town or of a series of elegantly antique interior courtyards. The hotel lies 2 blocks north of the largest park in the town center, the Campo San Francisco.

Dining/Diversions: A cafeteria/restaurant, Rey Casto, offers both regional and national dishes. In addition there is a bar, plus a lounge bar with live piano music.

Amenities: 24-hour room service, concierge, currency exchange, safe-deposit boxes, doctor on call, baby-sitting upon request, sauna, hairdresser, shopping boutiques, business center.

MODERATE

Clarín. Caveda, 23, 33002 Oviedo. ☎ **98-522-72-72.** Fax 98-522-80-18. www.hotelclarin.es. E-mail: clarin@hotelclarin.es. 47 units. MINIBAR TV TEL. 14,800 ptas. ($99.15) double. AE, MC, V. Parking 1,300 ptas. ($8.70). Bus: 1, 2, or 3.

This recently built modern hotel in the old quarter is noted for its tasteful decor, with comfortable, inviting, and well-maintained but small rooms. On the premises you'll find a cozy and well-managed cafeteria but no restaurant. The hotel stands right in the middle of the historic district within walking distance of many of the attractions.

Hotel La Gruta. Alto de Buenavista, s/n, 33006 Oviedo. ☎ **98-523-24-50.** Fax 98-525-31-41. 105 units. MINIBAR TV TEL. 11,500 ptas. ($77.05) double. AE, DC, MC, V. Free parking. Bus: 1.

In this family run hotel just outside the city limits, the small rooms are comfortably but simply furnished, many with views of the surrounding countryside. Amenities include safety-deposit boxes. Regional cuisine is served in the on-premises restaurant.

Hotel Principado. Calle San Francisco, 6, 33003 Oviedo. ☎ **98-521-77-92.** Fax 98-521-39-46. 70 units. MINIBAR TV TEL. 15,000 ptas. ($100.50) double; 17,800 ptas. ($119.25) suite. AE, DC, MC, V. Parking 1,500 ptas. ($10.05).

The well-managed Principado stands opposite the university. Guests have access to an underground public parking garage, easing the problem of parking in the center of town. The midsize rooms are comfortably furnished and well maintained. The dining room, featuring a regional menu, serves locals as well as guests. Although built in 1951, the hotel was completely renovated in 1991.

A NEARBY PLACE TO STAY

If you're driving to La Coruña and Santiago de Compostela, you may want to stop in the little town of Cornellana (Salas), 24 miles (39km) west of Oviedo on the route to Luarca.

Hotel La Fuente. Carretera N-634, 33876 Cornellana. ☎ **98-583-40-42.** 16 units. TV TEL. 6,000 ptas. ($40.20) double; 7,500 ptas. ($50.25) triple. MC, V. Free parking. Take the N-634 west to Cornellana.

This little inn, located on N-634, has a sitting room on each floor as well as a bathroom. The good-size bedrooms are simply furnished but comfortable. In the dining room overlooking the garden you can order a three-course menú del día, which costs 1,200 ptas. ($8.05). The food is hearty and generous in portion, prepared according to old recipes and using regional products whenever possible.

WHERE TO DINE

Casa Conrado. Argüelles, 1. ☎ **98-522-39-19.** Reservations required. Main courses 2,250–3,250 ptas. ($15.10–$21.80); fixed-price menu 3,700 ptas. ($24.80). AE, DC, MC, V. Mon–Sat 1–4pm and 9pm–midnight. Closed Aug. Bus: 1. REGIONAL.

Almost as solidly established as the cathedral nearby, this restaurant offers good-tasting and hearty Asturian stews, seafood platters, seafood soups, several preparations of hake, including one cooked in cider, escallops of veal with champagne, and a full range of desserts. It is a local favorite and a long-established culinary tradition. The service is attentive.

✪ **Casa Fermín.** Calle San Francisco, 8. ☎ **98-521-64-52.** Reservations recommended. Main courses 2,200–3,200 ptas. ($14.75–$21.45); menú Asturiana 2,900 ptas. ($19.45). AE, DC, MC, V. Mon–Sat 1:30–4pm and 8:30–11:30pm. Bus: 1 or 2. REGIONAL/INTERNATIONAL.

The chef here prepares the best regional cuisine in town in a building near the university and the cathedral. To order its most classic dish, ask for *fabada asturiana,* a bean dish with Asturian black pudding and Avilés ham. A tasty hake cooked in cider is another suggestion. Venison is a speciality in season (October through March). Try also the traditional Cabrales cheese of the province. The restaurant decor is in pink and granite. Although it's been around for half a century, it has a contemporary air to it because it's filled with plants and covered with skylights. Casa Fermín lies directly east of the Parque de San Francisco.

El Raitán. Trascorrales, 6. ☎ **98-521-42-18.** Reservations recommended. Menú Asturiana 3,900 ptas. ($26.15). AE, DC, MC, V. Mon–Sat 1:30–4pm and 9pm–midnight. Bus: 1. REGIONAL.

This restaurant south of the cathedral serves a set menu and bases all its dishes on regional ingredients, with meals accompanied by wines from La Rioja. A large array of well-prepared choices is available for each course. Each day the chef presents nine classic regional dishes that change with the season. The place has a tavern setting with overhead beams—atmospheric and intimate.

OVIEDO AFTER DARK

Very few of the many bars of Oviedo's old town stand out as particularly unique, so most night owls make it a point to wander from one joint to another as part of an evening's entertainment. Your best bet involves the old town neighborhoods around the Plaza del Paraguas, the Plaza da Fontán, and the Plaza Riego, each of which offers lots of unusual architecture in addition to hole-in-the-wall bars, many of which aren't identified with any discernible name. If you really want to go dancing as part of your nocturne in Oviedo, consider the town's most popular disco, **Estilo,** calle Pomarin, s/n (☎ **98-529-67-38**), where clients from the ages of 21 to around 30 rock and roll to recorded dance music, but never, ever, before midnight. It is open Thursday to Sunday.

17

Galicia

Extending above Portugal in the northwest corner of Spain, Galicia is a rain-swept land of grass and granite, much of its coastline gouged out by fjordlike inlets. It is a land steeped in Celtic tradition—in many areas its citizens, called *Gallegos,* speak their own language (not a dialect of Spanish but a separate language, *gallego,* that sounds and looks like a combination of Portuguese and Spanish). Galicia consists of four provinces: La Coruña (including Santiago de Compostela), Pontevedra, Lugo, and Ortense.

The Romans, who arrived after having conquered practically everything else in Europe, made quite an impression on the region. The Roman walls around the city of **Lugo** and the Tower of Hercules at **La Coruña** are part of that legacy. The Moors came this way, too, and did a lot of damage along the way. But finding the natives none too friendly and other battlefields more promising, they moved on.

Nothing did more to put Galicia on the tourist map than the **Camino de Santiago,** the Pilgrims' Route. It is the oldest, most traveled, and most famous route on the old continent. To guarantee a place in heaven, pilgrims journeyed to the supposed tomb of Santiago (St. James), patron saint of Spain. They trekked across the Pyrenees by the thousands, risking their lives in transit. The Camino de Santiago contributed to the development and spread of Romanesque art and architecture across Spain. Pilgrimages to the shrine lessened as medieval culture itself began its decline.

1 La Coruña

375 miles (604km) NW of Madrid, 96 miles (155km) N of Vigo

Despite the fact that La Coruña (A Coruña in Galician) is an ancient city, it does not have a wealth of historical and architectural monuments. Celts, Phoenicians, and Romans all occupied the port, and it is another of the legendary cities that claim Hercules as its founder.

The great event in the history of La Coruña occurred in 1588, when Philip II's Invincible Armada sailed from here to England. Only half of the ships made it back to Spain. The following year, Sir Francis Drake and his ships attacked the port in reprisal.

ESSENTIALS

GETTING THERE There are five flights a week from Madrid to La Coruña. Serviced only by Aviaco, the **Aeropuerto de**

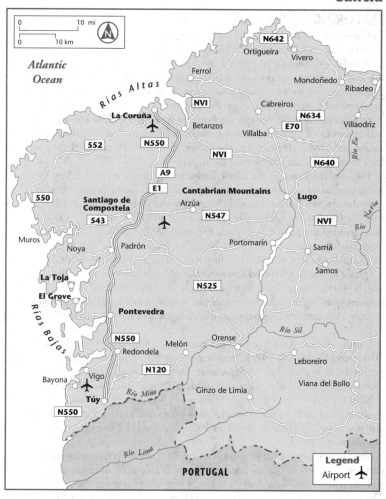

Alvedro (☎ **981-18-72-00**) is 6 miles (10km) from the heart of the city.

From Madrid (via Orense and Zamora), there is express train service two times a day (trip time: 8½ hours). Arrivals are at the **La Coruña Station** on calle Joaquín Planelles (☎ **981-15-02-02**). For the RENFE office, Calle Fonseca, 3, call **981-22-19-48.**

From Santiago, there's frequent daily bus service leaving from the station on the calle Caballeros (☎ **981-23-96-44**). Four buses a day connect Madrid and La Coruña (trip time: 8½ hours). A one-way ticket from Madrid is 4,850 ptas. ($32.50).

La Coruña is reached from Madrid by the N-VI. You can also follow the coastal highway, the N-634, which runs all the way across the northern rim of Spain from San Sebastián to the east.

VISITOR INFORMATION   The **tourist information office** is at Dársena de la Marina, s/n (☎ **981-22-18-22**). The office is open Monday through Friday 9am to 2pm and 4:30 to 6:30pm, Saturday from 10:30am to 1pm.

EXPLORING LA CORUÑA

La Coruña's old town is ideal for strolling around and stopping at any of the historic churches and mansions. **Plaza de María Pita**—named after the 16th-century Spanish Joan of Arc—divides the old town from the new. María Pita, a La Coruña housewife, was said to have spotted the approach of Drake's troops. Risking her own life, she fired a cannon shot to alert the citizens to an imminent invasion. For that act of heroism, she is revered to this day. Drake, on the other hand, is still a hated name in these parts.

You can take a stroll through the **Jardines de Méndez Núñez,** lying between the harbor and Los Cantones (Cantón Grande and Cantón Pequeño). Facing the police station and overlooking the port, the gardens are in the very center of town and make for a restful interlude during your sightseeing.

The cobbled **Plazuela de Santa Bárbara** also merits a visit—a tiny tree-shaded plaza, flanked by old houses and the high walls of the Santa Bárbara convent.

Jardín de San Carlos, reached along Paseo del Parrote, dates from 1843 and lies near the Casa de la Cultura. This garden grew up on the site of an old fortress that once guarded the harbor. It contains the tomb of Gen. Sir John Moore, who fought unsuccessfully against the troops of Napoléon. He retreated with his British forces to La Coruña, where he was shot in a final battle. These gardens are an ideal picnic spot.

Iglesia de Santa María del Campo, calle de Santa María, is a church with an elaborately carved west door from the 13th century—modeled in the traditional Romanesque-Gothic style. Beneath its rose window you'll see a Gothic portal from the 13th or 14th century. The tympanum is carved with a scene depicting the Adoration of the Magi.

Castillo de San Antón, a 16th-century fort, is now the **Museo Arqueológico e Histórico** (☎ 981-20-59-94), standing out in the bay on the southeast side of the peninsula. It is open July to September Tuesday through Saturday 11am to 9pm; October to June Tuesday through Saturday 10am to 7pm. Admission is 400 ptas. ($2.70) for adults, but free for children aged 13 and under and adults 66 and over. In addition to having a panoramic location on its own islet, it displays many unusual artifacts from La Coruña province, including a collection of pre-Roman jewelry. Take bus number 3 or 3A.

The second-largest port in Spain, La Coruña is also a popular vacation resort, so it gets very crowded in July and August. Riazor Beach, right in town, is a good, fairly wide beach, but the best one is Santa Cristina, about 3 miles (5km) outside town. There's regular round-trip bus service. The best way to go, however, is via the steamer that plies the bay.

SHOPPING

Its relative isolation from the rest of Spain seems to contribute to the perception that ceramics and handcrafts in Galicia are somehow more rustic and charming than those in territories closer to Madrid and Barcelona. You can judge for yourself by taking a 30-mile westward detour from La Coruña to the Galician hamlet of Buño. (From La Coruña, follow the signs to Carballo along C-552, then detour when you see the signs to Buño.) Although Buño contains lots of kiosks selling ceramics (virtually everyone in the hamlet is involved in some aspects of handcrafts), you can save yourself the drive by remaining in La Coruña and heading for the headquarters of a cooperative that markets Buño's production, **Alfares de Buño,** Plazuela de Los Angeles, 6 (no phone). A privately funded competitor, richly inventoried with pottery from Buño and other towns throughout Galicia, is **Obradoiro,** Plazuela de Los Angeles, 4 (no phone). The town's most visible and influential art gallery is the **Asociación de Artistas,** calle Riego de Agua, 32 (☎ 981-22-52-77). Host to dozens of exhibitions every year, it displays, solicits, markets, and publicizes the work of local artists throughout Spain and the rest of Europe.

Looking for antiques? Consider a stroll along calle Santiago, where such stores as **Antiguedades Encantes** (at no. 4, no phone) and **Antiguedades Rosa Jordan** (at no. 7, no phone) display the finery and ornaments of yesterday. Finally, if visits to the above-mentioned sites fail to produce the product you're looking for, consider a trek through the well-accessorized interior of La Coruña's largest department store, **El Corte Inglés,** calle Ramón y Cajal, 57-59 (☎ **981-29-00-11**).

WHERE TO STAY
EXPENSIVE

Hotel Finisterre. Paseo del Parrote, 20, 15001 La Coruña. ☎ **981-20-54-00.** Fax 981-20-84-62. www.hotelfinisterre.com. E-mail: info@hotelfinisterre.com. 127 units. MINIBAR TV TEL. 17,500–20,600 ptas. ($117.25–$138) double; 25,000–30,000 ptas. ($167.50–$201) suite. AE, DC, MC, V. Free parking. Bus: 1, 2, 3, or 5.

Immediately above the port, a short walk east of the tourist information office at the edge of the old town, this high-rise hotel is the finest and most panoramic in town. Bedrooms are small but comfortable, with wall-to-wall carpeting, lots of exposed wood, brightly contemporary upholstery, and private bathrooms with hair dryers and plush towels. The hotel is the preferred choice of business travelers. Although it was built in 1947, it has been remodeled many times since, the latest in 1991.

Dining/Diversions: The restaurant, Ara Solis, serves à la carte meals featuring fresh catches; there's also a bar.

Amenities: Room service, concierge, baby-sitting, laundry, tennis courts, four outdoor seawater swimming pools (two heated for year-round use, one reserved for children), garden, children's nursery, gym and health club, skating rink, sauna, ample opportunities for brisk and invigorating seafront walks, barber/hairdresser, nearby basketball court, gift shop.

MODERATE

Ciudad de La Coruña. Ciudad Residencial La Torre, Polígono de Adormideras, s/n, 15002 La Coruña. ☎ **981-21-11-00.** Fax 981-22-46-10. 132 units. MINIBAR TV TEL. 10,000–12,000 ptas. ($67–$80.40) double; 15,000–17,000 ptas. ($100.50–$113.90) suite. AE, DC, MC, V. Free parking. Bus: 3, 3A, or 5.

On the northwestern tip of the peninsula, surrounded by sea grasses and dunes, this three-star establishment is cordoned off from the apartment-house complexes that surround it by a wide swath of green. Built in the early 1980s, the hotel features a swimming pool; a big-windowed bar; a gym with sauna, whirlpool, and solarium; and a ground-floor restaurant, which serves a menú del día for 1,850 ptas. ($12.40). Each attractively modern guest room contains a kitchenette and a private bathroom. Accommodations are generally roomy and maintenance is excellent. There is also a bar-style cafeteria serving coffee, drinks, and snacks.

Hotel Atlántico. Jardines de Méndez Nuñez, s/n, 15006 La Coruña. ☎ **981-22-65-00.** Fax 981-20-10-71. 199 units. A/C MINIBAR TV TEL. 14,500–17,500 ptas. ($97.15–$117.25) double; 20,000–25,000 ptas. ($134–$167.50) suite. AE, DC, MC, V. Parking 1,500 ptas. ($10.05). Bus: 1, 2, or 3.

This convenient, comfortable hotel with a contemporary design contrasts with the lavishly ornate 19th-century park surrounding it where crowds of Galicians promenade here in fine weather. The Atlántico is in the building that also houses the city's casino, a modern restaurant, and a disco, which is open on Saturday and Sunday from 10pm to 6am. The well-furnished guest rooms are among the most appealing in town, thanks to relatively spacious dimensions and comfortably contemporary furnishings that are a cut above those within less expensive competitors. Each tiled bathroom is equipped with a hair dryer.

Residencia Riazor. Barrie de la Maza, 29, 15004 La Coruña. ☎ **981-25-34-00.** Fax 981-25-34-04. 176 units. MINIBAR TV TEL. 14,600 ptas. ($97.80) double. AE, DC, MC, V. Parking 900 ptas. ($6.05). Bus: 5, 20, or 22.

This 12-story 1960s hotel is right on the beach and was last renovated in 1993. It has a glass-enclosed lounge on the second floor and a snack bar/cafeteria. The small guest rooms are functional and lack style, but they are clean and comfortable and have private bathrooms. Room service is available until 11pm.

INEXPENSIVE

Almirante. Paseo de Ronda, 54, 15011 La Coruña. ☎ **981-25-96-00.** Fax 981-25-96-08. 20 units. TV TEL. 4,300-6,000 ptas. ($28.80–$40.20) double. AE, MC, V. Parking 700 ptas. ($4.70). Bus: 7, 14, or 14A.

There are few amenities here—just good, clean rooms, all doubles, at good prices. Both the room and bathroom dimensions are a bit skimpy, but the price is right. There is no restaurant, but a continental breakfast is served in the cafeteria. Room service is available. The location is a bonus: just 1 minute from the beach.

Hotel España. Juana de Vega, 7, 15004 La Coruña. ☎ **981-22-45-06.** Fax 981-20-02-79. 84 units. TV TEL. 6,100–8,800 ptas. ($40.85–$58.95) double. AE, DC, MC, V. Parking 1,200 ptas. ($8.05). Bus: 1, 2, or 23.

This pleasant but somewhat lackluster choice, just a few steps from the gazebos and roses of the Jardines de Méndez Núñez, has a narrow reception area, a comfortable series of long sitting rooms, and modern, simply furnished rooms. The cafeteria offers combination platters. The hotel has a bar and provides laundry service.

WHERE TO DINE

Two or so blocks from the waterfront, there are several restaurants that specialize in Galician cuisine, all with competitive prices. It's customary to go window shopping for food here. The restaurants along two of the principal streets—calle de la Estrella and calle de los Olmos—have display counters up front.

✪ **Casa Pardo.** Novoa Santos, 15. ☎ **981-28-71-78.** Reservations recommended. Main courses 1,790–2,900 ptas. ($12–$19.45); fixed-price menus 4,500–5,000 ptas. ($30.15–$33.50). AE, DC, MC, V. Mon–Sat 1:30–4pm and 9pm–midnight. GALICIAN.

Located near the Palacio de Congresos south of the old town, this restaurant is justly acclaimed as the finest dining room in the city. Under the direction of Eduardo Pardo, the restaurant offers both a traditional cuisine and innovative seafood dishes. Fresh shellfish and fish dishes, everything from oysters to salmon, are prepared here with skill. The Galician turbot is delectable. Seafood items aren't the only selections on the menu—meat and vegetable dishes are also well prepared. The kitchen seems always aware of the necessity of securing fresh ingredients both from field and shore. Patrons of this well-entrenched dining room prefer such wines as Terras Gauda and Viña Costeira. The restaurant is elegant but unstuffy. The fact that the first-rate staff is alert and informed about the graceful service rituals of old Spain makes this a subtle and relaxed, though undeniably formal, atmosphere.

✪ **El Coral.** Callejón de la Estacada, 9. ☎ **981-20-05-69.** Reservations recommended. Main courses 1,800–2,500 ptas. ($12.05–$16.75). AE, DC, MC, V. Daily 1–4pm and 9pm–midnight. Closed Sun except July 15–Sept 15. Bus: 1, 2, 5, or 17. GALICIAN/SEAFOOD/INTERNATIONAL.

This is our favorite and one of the most popular dining spots at the port. In business since 1954 it offers polite service, cleanliness, and Galician cookery prepared with distinction. This restaurant specializes in shellfish, fish, meats, and Galician wines. The chef's specialty is *turbante de mariscos* (shellfish). You might also try the *calamares rellenos* (stuffed squid). A popular main course is *lubina* (sea bass) *al horno*. A pitcher (1 liter) of Ribero wine makes a good choice, and you can also order Condados and Rioja wines. The front window forms an altar of shellfish in infinite varieties, a tapestry of crustaceans and mollusks. Inside, the atmosphere is intimate and elegant, with formally dressed waiters, crisp white linens, dark wood-paneled walls, and glittering crystal chandeliers.

Taverna Pil-Pil. Paralela a Orillamar, s/n. ☎ **981-21-27-12.** Reservations recommended. Main courses 950–1,800 ptas. ($6.35–$12.05). No credit cards. Tues–Sat 1–5pm and 8pm–12:30am. Closed Sept 15–Oct 15. Bus: 3 or 3A. GALICIAN/SPANISH.

In spite of its size, this small tavern has a fine culinary tradition and serves many elegant, moderately priced wines like the Albariño white. Host Luis Moya purchases fresh ingredients, often seafood, and handles them deftly in the kitchen. Try a mussel omelette as an appetizer, followed by one of the main courses, perhaps smoked salmon, concluding with a velvety chocolate mousse. The place is on the road leading to the Torre de Hércules.

LA CORUÑA AFTER DARK

Some of the most appealing bars in La Coruña are atmospheric holes-in-the-wall with a local clientele and a decor that has remained virtually unchanged since the end of the Spanish Civil War. A good example of this is **La Traida,** calle Torreiro, 1 (☎ 981-22-93-21), whose *empanadas* and tapas are much sought after. The place's walls are lined with posters from past bullfights, political rallies, and art exhibitions. Don't look for a sign—there isn't one, at least not one marking its entrance. Equally appealing is **Bar La Bombilla,** Torreiro, 6 (☎ 981-22-46-91), where flavorful tapas and strong red wines help a night go by faster. A roughly equivalent competitor is **Bar Yeboles,** calle Capitán Trancoso, s/n (☎ 981-20-62-20), set close to Town Hall and the Plaza Mariapita, the town's main square. If you want to go dancing after your drinks and tapas, and if it's after around 11pm, consider a run-in with the town's most appealing and most popular disco, **Disco Play Club,** Avenida Pedro Barrie de la Massa, s/n (☎ 981-25-00-63). Set on an ocean-front terrace, a few feet from the waves of Playa Riazor, it's open year-round and attracts dancers and drinkers even during the fogs of midwinter.

2 Santiago de Compostela

381 miles (613km) NW of Madrid, 46 miles (74km) S of La Coruña

All roads in Spain once led to this northwestern pilgrimage city. In addition to being the third-largest holy city of the Christian world, Santiago de Compostela is both a university town and a marketplace for Galician farmers.

But it was the medieval pilgrims who made the city famous. A pilgrimage to the tomb of the beheaded apostle, St. James, was a high point for the faithful—peasant and prince alike—who journeyed here from all over Europe, often under difficult, sometimes life-threatening, conditions.

Santiago de Compostela's link with legend began in A.D. 813, when an urn was discovered containing, it was believed, the remains of St. James. A temple was erected over the spot, but the poor saint wasn't allowed to remain in peace. In the 16th century church fathers hid the remains of the saint, fearing that they might be destroyed in raids along the coast by Sir Francis Drake, who was ravaging this part of Galicia. Somewhat amazingly, the alleged remains—subject of millions of pilgrimages from across Europe—lay relatively forgotten.

For decades no one was exactly certain where they were. Then in 1879 a workman making repairs on the church discovered what was supposed to be the remains, hidden since the 1500s. Of course, these remains were seriously questioned by skeptics as to their authenticity. To prove that this was the actual corpse of St. James, church officials brought back a sliver of the skull of St. James from Italy. They claimed that like a puzzle piece it fit perfectly into the recently discovered skeleton.

Aside from its religious connections, Santiago de Compostela, with its flagstone streets, churches, and shrines, is one of the most romantic and historic of Spain's great cities. It has been declared a national landmark. Santiago also has the dubious distinction of being the rainiest city in Spain, but the showers tend to arrive and end suddenly. Locals claim that the rain only makes their city more beautiful, and the rain-slick cobblestones might prompt you to agree.

ESSENTIALS

GETTING THERE From Madrid, Iberia has daily flights to Santiago, and there are also daily flights from Barcelona. The only international airport in Galicia is east of Santiago de Compostela at Lavacolla (☎ **981-59-74-00** for flight information), 7 miles (11km) from the center on the road to Lugo.

From La Coruña, 16 trains make the 1-hour trip daily at a cost of 500 to 575 ptas. ($3.35 to $3.85). Two trains arrive daily from Madrid. The 8-hour trip costs 4,700 to 5,600 ptas. ($31.50 to $37.50). Call ☎ **981-52-02-02** for information.

Buses leave on the hour, connecting La Coruña with Santiago (1½ hours away) and cost 650 to 820 ptas. ($4.35 to $5.50). Three buses arrive in Santiago daily from Madrid (8 to 9 hours). The trip costs 5,440 ptas. ($36.45). Phone ☎ **981-58-77-00** for schedules.

If you're driving, take the expressway highway (A-9/E-50) south from La Coruña to reach Santiago. From Madrid, N-VI runs to Galicia. From Lugo, head south along N-640.

VISITOR INFORMATION The **tourist information office** is at rúa del Villar, 43 (☎ **981-58-40-81**). Office hours are Monday through Friday 10am to 2pm and 4 to 7pm, Saturday from 11am to 2pm.

STROLLING THROUGH SANTIAGO

Santiago de Compostela's highlight is undoubtedly its storied cathedral, and you should take at least 2 hours to see it. Afterward, take a stroll through this enchanting town, which has a number of other interesting monuments as well as many stately mansions along rúa de Villar and rúa Nueva.

The ✪ **Catedral,** Plaza del Obradoiro (☎ **981-56-15-27**), begun in the 11th century, is the crowning achievement of Spanish Romanesque architecture, and, even though it actually reflects a number of styles, parts of it are spectacular. The Pórtico de la Gloria, carved by Mateo in the late 12th century, ranks among the finest produced in Europe at that time; the altar, with its blend of Gothic simplicity and baroque decor, is also extraordinary. The cathedral has three naves in cruciform shape and several chapels and cloisters. You can visit the crypt, where a silver urn contains what are believed to be the remains of the Apostle St. James. A cathedral museum displays tapestries and archaeological fragments. Next door, the **Palacio de Gelmírez** (☎ **981-57-23-00**), an archbishop's palace built during the 12th century, is another outstanding example of Romanesque architecture.

Santiago de Compostela

Casa de la Canónica **3**
Catedral **2**
Centro Galego de Arte Contemporáneo **5**
Hostal Los Reyes Católicos **1**
Monasterío de San Martín Pinario **4**
Palacio de Gelmírez **2**
Paseo de la Herradura **7**
Plaza de la Quintana **3**
Plaza de las Platerías **3**
Santa María del Sar **6**

The Pórtico de la Gloria, the work carved by Maestro Mateo in 1188, was the original entrance to the cathedral. The three arches of the portico are carved with biblical figures from the Last Judgment. In the center Christ is flanked by apostles and the 24 Elders of the Apocalypse. Below the Christ figure is a depiction of St. James himself. He crowns a carved column that also includes a depiction of Mateo at the bottom. If you observe this column you will see that a series of five deep indentations has been made by pilgrims since the Middle Ages. They have placed their hands here and worn down the pillar in gratitude to Mateo for designing it. Even today pilgrims line up here to lean forward to place their hands on the pillar and touch foreheads with Mateo.

Admission to the cathedral is free; to the cloisters, 500 ptas. ($3.35); to the Palacio de Gelmírez, 200 ptas. ($1.35). Hours for the cathedral are daily from 7am to 9pm; for the museum, July to October, Monday through Saturday 10am to 1:30pm and 4 to 7:30pm, Sunday 10am to 1:30pm and 4 to 7pm; November to June, Monday through Saturday 11am to 1pm and 4 to 6pm, Sunday 10am to 1:30pm and 4 to 7pm; for the Palacio de Gelmírez, July through September daily from 10:30am to 1:30pm and 4 to 7pm.

Most of the other impressive buildings are also on Plaza del Obradoiro, also called Plaza de España. Next door to the cathedral is **Hostal de los Reyes Católicos,** now a parador (see "Where to Stay," below), formerly a royal hospice and, in the 15th century, a pilgrims' hospice. It was designed by Enrique de Egas, Isabella and Ferdinand's favorite architect. Tourists (daily from 10am to 1pm and 4 to 7pm; ☎ **981-58-22-00** for information) may visit the cloistered courtyard with its beautiful 16th- to 18th-century fountains and the main chapel with its beamed ceiling; however, you must have a guide from the cathedral in attendance.

Monasterio de San Martín Pinario, Plaza de la Immaculada, founded in 899 and rebuilt in the 17th century, remains one of the most important monasteries in Galicia. Its large facade was built in the Compostela baroque style, with massive Doric columns. The interior has a richly ornamented Churrigueresque high altar and choir stalls that are truly works of art.

One of the most important squares in the old town is **Plaza de la Quintana,** to the left of the cathedral's Goldsmith's Doorway. This is a favorite square with students, who often perch on the flight of broad steps that connect the rear of the cathedral to the walls of a convent. The square is dominated by **Casa de la Canónica,** the former residence of the canon, which has wrought-iron window bars, lending it a rather severe appearance.

South of the square is the Renaissance-style **Plaza de las Platerías (Silversmiths' Square),** which has an elaborate fountain.

Centro Gallego de Arte Contemporáneo, rúa Valle-Inclán, s/n (☎ **981-54-66-29**), is the Galician Center of Contemporary Art, highlighting artworks from regional, national, and international artists. The center's changing exhibits display the works of contemporary artists and also it hosts retrospectives. Until the opening of this center, contemporary art had virtually no place in the city's agenda, which emphasized the ancient or the antique. Inaugurated in 1993 by Portuguese architect Álvaro Siza, the building is a stark exterior study in slabs of granite. Among the several exhibition rooms is a terrace for open-air exhibits, affording a panoramic view of the old quarter of Santiago. The admission-free museum is open Tuesday through Saturday from 11am to 8pm and Sunday from 11am to 2pm.

Farther afield, visit the Romanesque **Santa María del Sar,** on calle Castron d'Ouro, half a mile down calle de Sar, which starts at the Patio de Madre. This collegiate church is one of the architectural gems of the Romanesque style in Galicia. Its walls and columns are on a 15° slant, thought to be attributable to either a fragile foundation or an architect's fancy. Visit the charming cloister with its slender columns. The church is open Monday through Saturday 10am to 1pm and 4 to 7pm. Admission is free.

Cap off your day with a walk along **Paseo de la Herradura,** the gardens southwest of the old town, from where you'll have an all-encompassing view of the cathedral and the old city.

SHOPPING

The artfully naive blue-and-white porcelain that's a trademark of the town is available for sale at **Sargadelos,** rúa Nueva, 16 (☎ **981-58-19-05**). A competitor that stocks similar ceramics, plus a wide range of other regional handcrafts, including textiles, metalwork, woodcarvings, and a small amount of blown glass, is **Amboa,** rúa Nueva, 44 (☎ **981-58-33-59**). The best place in town to buy hammered silver, either in the form of jewelry or tableware, is **Fernando Mayer,** Plaza de las Platerías, 2 (☎ **981-58-25-36**). You can find meticulously crafted lace as well as textiles for the bathroom, dining room, and bedroom, at **Dosel,** rúa Nova, 26 (☎ **981-56-60-78**). And finally, to satisfy your hunger pangs between visits to pilgrimage sites, Santiago is home to some worthy pastry shops including **Confitería La Mora,** rúa do Vilar, 60 (☎ **981-58-10-14**).

A favorite of most tourists is tarta Santiago, a tart sold at virtually every pastry shop in the city. Also very popular is a local cheese shaped like breasts. If you'd like to sample this regional produce, one of many places selling them is **Confitería Vilas,** Rosalía de Castro, 70 (☎ **981-596-858**).

Many of the local wines, including assorted bottles of Ribeiro, Condado, and most famous of all, Albariño, are sold without fanfare in grocery stores throughout Galicia. But for a specialist in the subtleties of Galician and other Spanish wines, head for **Vinoteca Manxares de Galicia,** rúa do Franco, 25, (☎ **981-57-72-27**).

WHERE TO STAY
VERY EXPENSIVE

✪ **Hostal de Los Reyes Católicos.** Plaza de Obradoido, 1, 15705 Santiago de Compostela. ☎ **981-58-22-00.** Fax 981-56-30-94. 136 units. A/C MINIBAR TV TEL. 26,500 ptas. ($177.55) double; from 53,000 ptas. ($355.10) suite. AE, DC, MC, V. Parking 2,200 ptas. ($14.75). Bus: 4, 21, 25, 26, 33, or 34.

This former 16th-century hospice, founded by Ferdinand and Isabella, has been turned into one of the most spectacular hotels in Europe. Next to the cathedral, it also served as a resting place and hospital for pilgrims visiting the tomb of St. James. Even if you don't stay here, you should stop in and see it, but only on a guided tour (see the box below).

The hotel has four huge open-air courtyards, each with its own covered walk, gardens, and fountains. In addition, there are great halls, French grillwork, and a large collection of antiques. The Gothic chapel is the setting for weekly concerts.

There is a full range of accommodations, everything from Franco's former bedchamber to small rooms. Many of the palatial rooms have ornate canopied beds draped in embroidered red velvet. Hand-carved chests, gilt mirrors, and oil paintings, along with private bathrooms, enhance the air of luxury. Bathrooms are quite sumptuous with hair dryers, plush towels, and deluxe toiletries.

Dining/Diversions: The hotel's formal dining room, Libredon, serves both Galician and international cuisine. There is also an elegant bar.

Amenities: Room service, laundry, car rentals, hairdresser.

The World's Oldest Hotel

The oldest hotel in the world has been giving the weary bodies and souls of travelers a place of rest for nearly 5 centuries. In 1499 the Catholic kings founded the Hospital Real (Royal Hospice) in Santiago de Compostela to serve as a respite for the hundreds of thousands of pilgrims who came to pay homage to the shrine of Saint James. Known today as the **Hostal de Los Reyes Católicos,** the same structure proudly stands as the world's most ancient hotel, and certainly one of the most luxurious, offering its guests a truly unique hotel experience.

During the Middle Ages, Santiago prevailed, together with Jerusalem and Rome, as one of the three holy cities of Christendom. The cult of Santiago (Saint James), the son of Zebedee and the brother of John the Evangelist, drew hordes of pilgrims who trekked across northern Spain in search of the tomb of the saint. The route to Santiago proved long, arduous, and dangerous; the pilgrims who did arrive came weary and fatigued. Having made the pilgrimage themselves, the Catholic monarchs experienced firsthand the dearth of accommodations along the way. Hence the decision by Ferdinand and Isabella to construct monasteries and hospitals to house and protect visitors, the best effort culminating in this prominent structure.

Construction on the Hospital Real began in the 15th century and continued through the 18th century. Set on the magnificent Obradoiro Plaza, this grand edifice shares the square with the impressive cathedral of Santiago, with its blend of architectural styles. In addition to its luxury rooms, this five-star hotel boasts a concert and exhibition room surrounded by various cloisters in different styles. The hotel doorway reflects the plateresque style, and the windows display rich baroque detailing.

Architecturally, the old part of the city stopped developing in the baroque period and, as a result, its buildings exude an aura of impressive grandeur—in fact, a sense of mysticism permeates Santiago. It is fitting, then, that one of Spain's great monumental cities should be home to one of the country's most luxurious, historically significant hotels, let alone one of the world's oldest.

Hotel Araguaney. Calle Alfredo Brañas, 5, 15701 Santiago de Compostela. ☎ **981-59-59-00.** Fax 981-59-02-87. 80 units. A/C MINIBAR TV TEL. 26,000 ptas. ($174.20) double; from 33,000 ptas. ($221.10) suite. AE, DC, MC, V. Parking 1,680 ptas. ($11.25). Bus: 4, 21, 25, 26, 33, or 34.

Located in Santiago's commercial and residential zone, about 8 blocks southwest of the cathedral, this is a comfortably streamlined hotel, newly renovated and boasting some of the most up-to-date dining, drinking, and conference facilities in town. The stylish, modern rooms range from small to midsize and each is comfortably furnished with firm mattresses. All the tiled bathrooms are equipped with hair dryers. Locals cite the hotel as their most well-orchestrated modern hotel. It has one of the best and most efficient staffs in town, and persons in the area on business often prefer this up-to-date choice. Of course, as the parador is often booked, this is a viable alternative for visitors because of its location at the historic core.

Dining/Diversions: The Restaurante Luis XVI and the Restaurante Caney (O'Portón) serve fixed-price lunches and dinners. The comfortable hotel bar offers an array of international drinks and Spanish brandies. The hotel also contains one of the most frequented discos in Galicia.

Amenities: Room service (daily from 7am to 4pm and 9pm to midnight), concierge, baby-sitting, in-house tour operator, laundry/valet, large and well-maintained swimming pool, sauna, shopping boutiques, business center, car rentals.

EXPENSIVE

Hotel Compostela. Hórreo, 1, 15702 Santiago de Compostela. ☎ **981-58-57-00.** Fax 981-56-32-69. 99 units. MINIBAR TV TEL. 16,500 ptas. ($110.55) double; 21,000 ptas. ($140.70) suite for 2. AE, DC, MC, V. Bus: 10.

This hotel is conveniently located just a few short blocks from the cathedral, but it is also, unfortunately, close to the heavily trafficked city center. It has a grand granite facade, which belies the modern interior, and bedrooms filled with clean, angular, machine-made furniture. A pleasant dining room and a cafe/bar are on the premises, offering a fixed-price lunch or dinner. The hotel was completely renovated in 1995. Mattresses are firm, and the housekeeping is excellent. All the tiled bathrooms are equipped with hair dryers. Accommodations are generally roomy, although some units are quite small.

Hotel del Peregrino. Rosalía de Castro, s/n, 15706 Santiago de Compostela. ☎ **981-52-18-50.** Fax 981-52-17-77. 149 units. A/C MINIBAR TV TEL. 18,690 ptas. ($125.20) double; 22,050 ptas. ($147.75) suite. AE, DC, MC, V. Free parking. Bus: 1 or 2.

This four-star hotel at the edge of town off the main road is conveniently located if you want to avoid traffic congestion in the town's center. The hotel is comfortable, unpretentious, and unfussy, drawing lots of business travelers. It has a good restaurant serving regional cuisine, a bar and snack bar, a rear garden with a swimming pool, and a disco. The decor is restrained and tasteful, the rooms modern and well furnished. Accommodations range from small to medium in size, and each tiled bathroom comes with a hair dryer.

MODERATE

Hotel Gelmírez. Hórreo, 92, 15702 Santiago de Compostela. ☎ **981-56-11-00.** Fax 981-56-32-69. 138 units. TV TEL. 11,000 ptas. ($73.70) double. AE, DC, MC, V. Bus: 6 or 10.

This soaring concrete structure near the train station is one of the largest hotels in the region. Built in the early 1970s, it has a comfortable and pleasant interior far more attractive than its plain facade suggests. The small guest rooms are furnished in a functional modern style—nothing special, but clean and comfortable. On the premises is a bistro/cafeteria/bar offering *platos combinados* (combination plates) from 1,200 ptas. ($8.05), along with a wide array of drinks.

INEXPENSIVE

Hostal Residencia Alameda. San Clemente, 32, 15705 Santiago de Compostela. ☎ **981-58-81-00.** Fax 981-58-86-89. 20 units, 13 with private bathroom. TV TEL. 5,200 ptas. ($34.85) double without bathroom, 7,000 ptas. ($46.90) double with bathroom. AE, DC, MC, V. Parking 800 ptas. ($5.35). Bus: 10.

Located on the second floor of a 1970s building in the cathedral district, Alameda has comfortable, immaculate rooms in a very simple boardinghouse style; it was last renovated in 1997. Beds are good but the rooms are a bit cramped. The staff here is courteous and efficient. Ample adjacent parking is available. The Alameda serves breakfast only.

Hotel Maycar. Doctor Teijeiro, 15, 15701 Santiago de Compostela. ☎ **981-56-34-44.** Fax 981-58-96-93. 40 units. TV TEL. 5,900 ptas. ($39.55) double. No credit cards. Bus: 10 from train station.

This simple two-star hotel stands not far from the busy central Plaza de Galicia. The marble-trimmed lobby is unpretentious, and there is an elevator. The rooms are well maintained but very spartan. Nonetheless, each accommodation comes with a good bed, although you don't have a lot of room for your stuff. Breakfast is the only meal served.

Hotel Universal. Plaza de Galicia, 2, 15706 Santiago de Compostela. ☎ **981-58-58-00.** Fax 981-58-57-90. E-mail: hoteluniversal@ verial.es. 54 units. TV TEL. 6,300–8,000 ptas. ($42.20–$53.60) double. AE, DC, MC, V. Parking 900 ptas. ($6.05).

Located south of the Fuente de San Antonio, just outside the center of the city, this is a pleasant and comfortable hotel despite its drab 1970s concrete facade. It has a modernized lobby, and there is a TV lounge on the premises. The aging guest rooms are furnished in a simple modern style, each with a good bed. Breakfast is the only meal served.

WHERE TO DINE

Alameda. Porta Faxeira, 15. ☎ **981-58-66-57.** Reservations recommended in summer. Main courses 2,300–4,500 ptas. ($15.40–$30.15); fixed-price menu 3,000 ptas. ($20.10). AE, DC, MC, V. Daily 1–4pm and 8pm–midnight. REGIONAL.

Since 1954 a constant stream of diners, both foreign and local, indicates the popularity of this government-rated "two-fork" restaurant, located opposite the Parque de Alameda. There is a stylish cafeteria/snack bar on the ground floor, great for light meals and drinks; guests can sit at sidewalk tables in fair weather. The fare includes many Galician specialties, and the chef is noted for his paella. Start with the *caldo gallego* (Galician soup) and follow with another regional specialty, *lacón con grelos* (ham hock with greens). The *necoras* (spider crabs) are also a real gourmet delight.

La Tacita d'Juan. Hórreo, 31. ☎ **981-56-32-55.** Reservations recommended. Main courses 1,400–2,800 ptas. ($9.40–$18.75). AE, MC, V. Mon–Sat 1:15–4pm and 8:30–midnight. Closed Aug 1–15. Bus: 10. REGIONAL.

A favorite place for business lunches, 5 minutes from the train station, this restaurant offers *caldo gallego* (Galician soup), fish soup, artichokes with ham, Basque-style eels, shellfish cocktail, and a wide array of fish platters. Two special meat courses are the ham hock with greens and *fabada asturiana,* the famous stew of Asturias. The portions are generous, and the service is attentive.

Moncho Vilas. Avenida de Villagarcía, 21. ☎ **981-59-83-87.** Reservations recommended. Main courses 2,100–3,600 ptas. ($14.05–$24.10); fixed-price menu 5,000 ptas. ($33.50). AE, DC, MC, V. Daily 1:30–4:30pm and 8:30pm–midnight. Bus: 4, 21, or 25. REGIONAL.

This restaurant is located at the edge of the old quarter, on a drab street off Avenida de Donallo Romero, but it's worth seeking out. It looks like a country tavern, and, in fact, the tasca in front is one of the most popular in the area, especially with locals. It's a family run place with conscientious service. A few of the Galician dishes served here are based on meat (the fillet of beef with sherry sauce is especially good), but the real specialties are seafood creations, such as fish soup, hake, and grilled shrimp.

Restaurante Vilas. Rosalía de Castro, 88. ☎ **981-59-21-70.** Reservations required. Main courses 1,500–3,500 ptas. ($10.05–$23.45); fixed-price menu 4,000 ptas. ($26.80). AE, DC, MC, V. Mon–Sat 1–5pm and 8pm–midnight. SEAFOOD.

Located on the outskirts of the old town on the road to Pontevedra, this reliable Spanish tavern, housed in a three-story town house, has a devoted clientele, many from industry, politics, and the arts. Beyond the large bar near the entrance and display cases filled with fresh fish, you'll find the baronial stone-trimmed dining room.

A wide variety of fish is available—fresh sardines, three different preparations of salmon, a *zarzuela* (seafood stew), and eels. Two kinds of paella are served, and non-fish dishes such as partridge and rabbit are also on the menu. The restaurant was founded in 1915 as a little eating house. Back then, it was on the outskirts of town, but the place was enveloped by the city long ago. It stands on a street named after the illustrious female poet of Galicia. Today, the restaurant is run by the grandsons of the original founders.

✪ **Toñi Vicente.** Calle Rosalía de Castro, 24. ☎ **981-59-41-00.** Reservations recommended. Main courses 2,800–3,500 ptas. ($18.75–$23.45); fixed-price menu 6,900 ptas. ($46.25). AE, DC, MC, V. Mon–Sat 1:30–4pm and 9pm–midnight. Closed first 2 weeks in Jan and Aug. GALICIAN/INTERNATIONAL.

Set in the heart of town, on two floors of a building erected around 1950, this is the finest and most flamboyantly international restaurant in Santiago or for miles around. Within dining rooms accented with a neoclassical overlay and a color scheme of blue and salmon, you can enjoy the celebrated cuisine of Toñi Vicente. Menu items change with the availability of the ingredients, but are likely to include such delectable dishes as a warm seafood salad with herbs, escallops of veal with a confit of onions, turbot with chive sauce, unusual preparations of seasonal game dishes, and for dessert, a tart made with Galician pears.

SANTIAGO AFTER DARK

There's much more to do in the religious centerpiece of Galicia after dark than just pray. There are an estimated 200 bars and *cafeterías* on the rúa do Franco and its neighbor, rúa da Raiña. The pavement along those streets during crowded weekend evenings around 11pm is mobbed. You can have a lot of fun ducking into any of them, although two that are particularly convivial are **El 42,** 42 rúa do Franco (no phone); and **Bar/Cafeteria Dakar,** rúa do Franco, 13 (☎ 981-57-81-92). Two highly appealing competitors are **Pub Borriquita de Belén,** rúa San Pelayo, 22 (no phone), and its neighbor, **Bar Crechas,** rúa San Pelayo, 28 (no phone), both of which appeal to bar-hoppers thanks to occasional live music that packs clients in anytime after 10pm. Know in advance that the de rigueur method for pursuing after-dark diversion in Santiago involves hitting a roster of bars and tapas joints before midnight, and dancing the night away beginning anytime after midnight.

Two of the most likely dance options in town, both of which begin after midnight and continue until 4 or 5am, are **Disco Casting Araguaney,** rúa Montero Rios, 25 (☎ 981-59-59-00), a rock-and-roll palace in the heart of the old city; and a counterpart that begins even later (around 5am), **Disco Black,** in the Hotel del Peregrino, Rosalía de Castro, s/n (☎ 981-52-18-50).

3 Rías Altas

In Norway they're called fjords; in Brittany, abers; in Scotland, lochs; and in Galicia, *rías.* These inlets have been cut into the Galician coastline by the turbulent Atlantic pounding against its shores. Rías Altas is a relatively modern name applied to all the estuaries on the northern Galicia coast, from Ribadeo (the gateway to Galicia on the border with Asturias) to La Coruña (the big Atlantic seaport of northwest Spain). The part that begins at Ribadeo, part of Lugo province, is also called Marina Lucense. Four estuaries form the Artabro Gulf: La Coruña, Betanzoa, Ares, and Ferrol. All four converge on a single point, where the Marola crag rises.

ON THE ROAD FROM RIBADEO TO LA CORUÑA

From Ribadeo, take the corniche road west (N-634) until you reach the Ría de Foz. About 1½ miles (2.5km) south of the Foz-Barreiros highway, perched somewhat in isolation on a hill, stands the **Iglesia de San Martín de Mondoñeda,** part of a monastery that dates from 1112.

The little town of Foz is a fishing village and also a summer resort with beaches separated by a cliff. You might stop here for lunch.

From **Foz,** cut northwest along the coastal highway (C-642), going through **Burela,** another fishing village. You can make a slight detour south to **Sargadelos,** a ceramics center. You can purchase the famous Galician pottery here much more cheaply than elsewhere in Spain.

Back on the coastal road (C-642) at Burela, continue west approaching Ría de Vivero and the historic village of **Vivero.** Part of its medieval walls and an old gate, Puerta de Carlos V, has been preserved. The town has many old churches of interest, including the Gothic-style Iglesia San Francisco. Vivero is a summer resort, attracting vacationers to its beach, the Playa Covas, and makes a good lunch stop.

The road continues northwest to **Vicedo,** passing such beaches as Xillo and Aerealong. Excellent vistas of the estuary greet you, and oxen can be seen plowing the cornfields.

Driving on, you'll notice the coastline becoming more saw-toothed. Eventually you reach **Ortigueira,** a major fishing village at the head of the ría from which it takes its name. A Celtic folk festival is staged here at the end of August.

From here you can continue south along C-642 to **El Ferrol,** which used to be called El Caudillo, in honor of the late dictator Francisco Franco, who was born here and who used to spend part of his summers in this area. El Ferrol is one of the major shipbuilding centers of Spain, and since the 18th century it has also been a center of the Spanish navy. It's a grimy town, but it lies on one of the region's most beautiful rías. In spite of its parador, few tourists will want to linger at El Ferrol (also spelled O Ferrol).

From El Ferrol, C-642 continues south, passing through the small town of **Puentedeume** (also spelled Pontedeume), on the Rías Ares. Historically, it was the center of the counts of Andrade. The last remains of their 14th-century palace can be seen, along with the ruins of a 13th-century castle, rising to the east.

Shortly below Betanzos, head west along N-VI until you reach La Coruña. The entire trip from Ribadeo is roughly 150 miles (242km) and takes at least 4 hours.

WHERE TO DINE ALONG THE COAST

Nito. Playa de Area, Vivero. ☎ **982-56-09-87.** Reservations recommended. Main courses 1,600–2,800 ptas. ($10.70–$18.75); fixed-price menu 2,000 ptas. ($13.40). AE, MC, V. Daily 1–4pm and 8pm–midnight. SEAFOOD.

Established in the early 1970s, this restaurant lies in the center of the Vivero, only 100 yards from the beach, with a sweeping view of the Atlantic. It starts serving dinner early for Spain (8pm). The restaurant maintains a balance between its prices and the quality of its ingredients, and you get unpretentious but flavorful food. Shellfish, priced according to weight, is the specialty, but you can also order grilled sea bream or perhaps a house-style beefsteak. Most diners begin their meal with a bowl of *caldo gallego* (Galician soup). A full range of wines also is offered. Diners wishing to eat outside can sit on a garden-view terrace.

Exploring the Rías Altas on Two Wheels

Some of the best biking in Spain is found in the Rías Altas. Much of south and central Spain is too hot for biking. But here temperatures are generally cool, and an interesting vista unfolds at every turn. Depending on your time, stamina, and interest, the tourist office at Vivero, Avenida de Ramón Canosa (☎ **982-56-08-79**), will provide you with a map and some suggested routes.

Vivero is also the only town in Rías Altas that will rent either motorcycles or bikes. Go to **Viajes Arifran,** C. Rosalía de Castro 54 (☎ **982-56-04-97**), open Monday through Friday 9:30am to 1pm and 4 to 7pm. In July and August, the rental shop is also open on Saturday from 9:30am to 1pm. Motorcycles rent for 9,000 ptas. ($60.30) a day, with bikes going for 1,000 ptas. ($6.70).

From Vivero the most scenic route is to the west following along the 642 to Ferrol on the sea. A particularly dramatic stretch would be to head north along a secondary road when you come to the junction at the little town of Mera. Signs point north to another little town, Carino, opening onto views of Cabo Ortegal. To the east will be a sheltered body of water, Ría de Sta. Maria, and to the west the Atlantic Ocean. From Vivero you can also go inland heading south along Route 640 following the signs to the hamlet of Oral. You can also take the coastal road east from Vivero signposted Ribadeo. Ribadeo is too built up to interest most cyclists but, depending on your stamina, you can cycle to the little seaside villages of San Ciprian, Burella, and Foz.

FROM LA CORUÑA TO CAPE FISTERRA

This next drive, "to the end of the world," takes you from La Coruña to **Cape Fisterra** (called **Fisterra** or **Finisterre** on most maps). It's a 90-mile (145km) trip that will take at least 3 hours. For the ancients, Cape Fisterra was the end of the world as they knew it.

This route takes you along **A Costa da Morte** (La Costa de la Muerte; The Coast of Death), so called because of the numerous shipwrecks that have occurred here.

Leaving La Coruña, take the coastal road west (Highway 552), heading first to the road junction of **Carballo,** a distance of 22 miles (35.5km). From this little town, many of the small coastal harbors will be within an easy drive. **Malpica,** to the northwest, is the most interesting, with its own beach. An offshore seabird sanctuary exists here, and Malpica itself was a former whaling port. From Malpica, continue to the tiny village of **Corme** at Punta Roncudo. This sheltered fishing village draws summer beach fans, as there are many isolated sand dunes.

From Corme, continue along the winding roads to the whitewashed village of **Camariñas,** which stands on the ría of the same name. A road here leads all the way to the lighthouse at Cabo Vilán. Camariñas is known as a village of expert lace makers, and you'll see the work for sale at many places.

The road now leads to **Mugia** (shown on some maps as Muxia), below which stands the lighthouse at Cabo Touriñan. Continue driving south along clearly marked coastal roads that are sometimes perched precariously on cliff tops overlooking the sea. They will lead you to **Corcubión,** a village with a Romanesque church. From here, follow signs that lead you along a lonely southbound secondary road to the end of the line,

Cabo Fisterra, for a panoramic view. The sunsets from here are among the most spectacular in the world. The Roman poet Horace said it best: "The brilliant skylight of the sun drags behind it the black night over the fruitful breasts of earth."

4 Rías Bajas

After Cabo Fisterra, some of the most dramatic coastal scenery in Spain flanks coastal Highway 550, following the edge of one of the most tortuous shorelines in Europe. The four estuaries, collectively called the ✪ Rías Bajas, face the Atlantic from Cape Silleiro to Baiona to Point Louro in Muros. Two of these are in the province of Pontevedra (Ría de Pontevedra and Ría de Vigo); one is in the province of La Coruña (Ría de Muros y Noya); and one (Ría de Arousa) divides its shores between the two provinces. The 20-mile (32km) Vigo estuary is the longest, stretching from Ponte Sampasio to Baiona.

DRIVING FROM MUROS TO SANTA UXEA DE RIBEIRA

The seaside town of **Muros** has many old houses and a harbor, but **Noya** (also spelled Noia), to the southeast, is more impressive. If you don't have a car but would like to see at least one or two ría fishing villages, you can do so at either Noya or Muros: Both lie on a bus route connecting them with Santiago de Compostela. Eleven buses per day leave from Santiago heading for Noya, and nine run to Muros. Some of the tiny villages and beaches are also connected by bus routes.

If you do drive, the entire trip is only 47 miles (76km); at a leisurely pace it should take you 2 hours. Noya is known for its braided straw hats with black bands. It has a number of interesting, handsome old churches, including the 14th-century **Igrexa de Santa María** (with tombstones dating from the 10th century) and the **Igrexa de San Francisco.** A lot of good beaches lie on the northern bank of the ría near Muros. Noya is your best bet for a lunch stop.

From Noya, the coast road (Highway 550) continues west to **Porto do Son.** You can take a detour to Cabo de Corrubedo, with its lighthouse, before continuing on to Santa Uxea de Ribeira at the southern tip. Ribeira is a fishing port and a canning center. At **Santa Uxea de Ribeira** you'll see Ría de Arousa, the largest and deepest of the inlets.

From Ribeira, continue east along the southern coastal road to **A Puebla de Caramiñal.** From here, take a signposted route 6 miles (9.6km) inland into the mountains, to admire the most magnificent panorama in all of rías country—the **Mirador de la Curota,** at 1,634 feet. The four inlets of the Rías Bajas can, under the right conditions, be seen from the belvedere. In clear weather you can also view Cape Fisterra.

Back on C-550, drive as far as Padrón, where, it is claimed, the legendary sea vessel arrived bringing Santiago (St. James) to Spain. Padrón was also the home of romantic poet Rosalía de Castro (1837–85), sometimes called the Emily Dickinson of Spain. Her house, the **Casa Museo de Rosalía de Castro,** carretera de Herbrón (☎ **981-81-12-04**), is open to the public Tuesday through Sunday from 9:30am to 1:30pm. Admission is 200 ptas. ($1.35). Padrón also makes a good lunch stop.

From Padrón, follow the alleged trail of the body of St. James north along N-550 to Santiago de Compostela or take N-550 south to Pontevedra.

WHERE TO STAY & DINE

Ceboleiro II. Galicia, 15, Noya. ☎ **981-82-44-97.** Reservations not necessary. Main courses 1,400–2,000 ptas. ($9.40–$13.40). Fixed-price menu 1,400–3,500 ptas. ($9.40–$23.45). AE, DC, MC, V. Daily 1–4pm and 9pm–midnight. Closed Dec 20–Jan 15. SEAFOOD.

For about a century, this inn has provided food and accommodations to passersby. Set in the heart of Noya, it is owned and managed by three generations of the Fernández family. It offers hearty food from the sea, prepared in conservative but flavorful ways that usually correspond to the culinary traditions of Galicia and northern Portugal. The menu almost always includes several versions of hake, shellfish soup, several kinds of rice studded with fish or shellfish, pork and beef dishes, and among other desserts, an apple tart. The establishment also contains 13 simple but comfortable accommodations, each with private bathroom, TV, and telephone nearby. Doubles cost from 5,000 ptas. ($33.50). Room reservations can be made by calling ☎ **981-82-44-97.**

Chef Rivera. Enlace Parque, 7, Padrón. ☎ **981-81-04-13.** Fax 981-81-14-54. Reservations recommended. Main courses 1,000–2,400 ptas. ($6.70–$16.10); fixed-price menus 2,300–3,400 ptas. ($15.40–$22.80). AE, DC, MC, V. Daily 12:30–4pm and 8:30pm–midnight. Closed Sun night in winter. GALICIAN/SPANISH.

The name of the owner, to everyone in town, is simply El Chef. His cuisine is innovative but also based on traditional continental recipes. His wife, Pierrette, attends to service in the dining room, which resembles an English pub with its dark, warm colors and leather upholstery. Try the shellfish soup or stew or the house-style monkfish. The restaurant is known for its *pimientos de Padrón.* Tiny green peppers are sautéed with olive oil—there's nothing unusual about that; the trick is that about one in five of those peppers is hot, as in very spicy. You might finish your meal with lemon mousse. The couple also rents 20 simply furnished guest rooms, at 6,000 to 6,800 ptas. ($40.20 to $45.55) for a double.

5 Pontevedra

36 miles (58km) S of Santiago de Compostela, 521 miles (839km) NW of Madrid

An aristocratic old Spanish town on the Lérez River and the capital of Pontevedra province, the city of Pontevedra still has vestiges of an ancient wall that once encircled the town. In medieval days, the town was called Pontis Veteris (Old Bridge).

Some of the best Gallego seamen lived in Pontevedra in the Middle Ages. Sheltered at the end of the Pontevedra Ría, the city was a bustling port and foreign merchants mingled with local traders, seamen, and fishers. It was the home of Pedro Sarmiento de Gamboa, the 16th-century navigator and cosmographer who wrote *Voyage to the Magellan Straits.* In the 18th century the Lérez delta silted up and the busy commerce moved elsewhere, mainly to Vigo. Pontevedra entered a period of decline, which may account for its significant old section. Had it been a more prosperous town, the people might have torn down the ancient structures to rebuild.

The old barrio, a maze of colonnaded squares and cobbled alleyways, lies between calle Michelena and calle del Arzobispo Malvar, stretching to calle Cobián and the river. The old mansions are called *pazos,* and they speak of former marine glory, since it was the sea that provided the money to build them. Seek out such charming squares as Plaza de la Leña, Plaza de Mugártegui, and Plaza de Teucro.

ESSENTIALS

GETTING THERE   From Santiago de Compostela in the north, 16 trains per day make the 1-hour trip to Pontevedra at a cost of 575 ptas. ($3.85) one way. RENFE has an office on calle Gondomar, 3 (☎ **986-85-13-13**), where you can get information. The actual rail and bus stations (☎ **986-85-13-13** for information about transportation in the area) lie half a mile from the center on Alféreces Provisionales.

Pontevedra has good links to major Galician cities. From Vigo in the south, the bus traveling time is only half an hour if you take one of the 12 inland expresses leaving from Vigo daily. From Santiago de Compostela in the north, a bus leaves every hour during the day for Pontevedra (1 hour away).

From Santiago de Compostela, head south along N-550 to reach Pontevedra.

VISITOR INFORMATION   The **tourist information office** is at General Mola, 3 (☎ **986-85-08-14**). Open Monday through Friday from 9:30am to 2pm and 5 to 7pm, Saturday from 10am to 12:30pm.

A SPECIAL EVENT   ✪ *A Rapa das Bestas* (The Capture of the Beasts) is held every year in the beginning of July. In the hills of nearby San Lorenzo de Sabuceno, wild horses are rounded up and herded into a corral, in a ritual that evokes the Wild West. For information, contact the tourism office in Pontevedra (see above).

EXPLORING PONTEVEDRA

In the old quarter, the major attraction is the **Basílica de Santa María la Mayor,** Arzobispo Malvar, with its avocado-green patina, dating from the 16th century. This plateresque church was constructed with funds provided by the mariners' guild. Its most remarkable feature is its west front, carved to resemble an altarpiece, with a depiction of the Crucifixion at top.

Museo Provincial, Pasantería, 10 (☎ **986-85-14-55**), with a hodgepodge of everything from the Pontevedra attic, contains displays ranging from prehistoric arti-facts to a still life by Zurbarán. Many of the exhibits are maritime-oriented, and there is also a valuable collection of jewelry. Hours are Tuesday through Saturday from 10am to 2:15pm and 5 to 8:45pm. Admission is 200 ptas. ($1.35); free for European Union citizens. The museum opens onto a major square in the old town, the Plaza de Leña (Square of Wood).

The **Iglesia de San Francisco,** Plaza de la Herrería, is another church of note. Its Gothic facade opens onto gardens. It was founded in the 14th century and contains a sculpture of Don Payo Gómez Charino, noted for his part in the 1248 Reconquest of Seville, when it was wrested from Muslim domination.

Directly south, the gardens lead to the 18th-century **Capilla de la Peregrina,** Plaza Peregrina, with a narrow half-moon facade connected to a rotunda and crowned by a pair of towers. It was constructed by followers of the cult of the Pilgrim Virgin, which was launched in Galicia sometime in the 17th century.

WHERE TO STAY
MODERATE

Hotel Rías Bajas. Daniel de la Sota, 7, 36001 Pontevedra. ☎ **986-85-51-00.** Fax 986-85-51-00. 100 units. MINIBAR TV TEL. 9,000–13,800 ptas. ($60.30–$92.45) double; 11,500–15,000 ptas. ($77.05–$100.50) suite. AE, DC, MC, V. Parking 1,000 ptas. ($6.70).

On a busy street corner near Plaza de Galicia in the commercial center, this 1960s hotel is more comfortable than you might expect judging from the outside. The largest hotel in town, it is often used for community political meetings and press con-ferences. The lobby, of stone and wood paneling, has been designed to look like an English club. The midsize bedrooms are comfortable and well maintained, with pri-vate bathrooms.

The hotel doesn't have a restaurant but does offer a cafeteria. Amenities include laundry and dry-cleaning service, room service, in-room massage, baby-sitting, access to health club and nine-hole golf course.

✪ **Parador Nacional Casa del Barón.** Baron 19, s/n, 36002 Pontevedra. ☎ **986-85-58-00.** Fax 986-85-21-95. 47 units. MINIBAR TV TEL. 11,500–15,000 ptas. ($77.05–$100.50) double. AE, DC, MC, V.

The parador is located in the old quarter of Pontevedra, in a well-preserved 16th-century palace near the Basílica de Santa María la Mayor. Built on either 13th- or 14th-century foundations, this hotel became one of Spain's first paradors when it opened in 1955. The interior has been maintained very much as the old *pazo* (manor house) looked. It includes a quaint old kitchen, or *lar* ("heart"), typical of Galician country houses and furnished with characteristic items. Off the vestibule is a court-yard dominated by a large old stone staircase. Many of the accommodations, all with private bathrooms, including hair dryers, are large enough to include sitting areas; the beds are comfortable, the furnishings attractive. Many of the rooms overlook the walled-in formal garden.

Both lunch and dinner are served at the hotel restaurant. Specialty dishes, such as a casserole of shrimp with tomato sauce, are well prepared, and served daily. It is a 4-mile drive to the beach.

INEXPENSIVE

Hotel Comercio. Augusto González Besada, 3, 36001 Pontevedra. ☎ **986-85-12-17.** Fax 986-85-99-91. 60 units. TV TEL. 5,000–7,000 ptas. ($33.50–$46.90) double. MC, V. Bus: 14 or 20 from train station.

This tall hotel with its modern facade and art deco–inspired cafe and bar, is an accept-able choice in its price category. Guest rooms are fairly comfortable but only func-tional in style. Though small, the rooms contain comfortable beds with firm mattresses. A restaurant serves both lunch and dinner, with many regional specialties offered and a menú del día for 1,500 ptas. ($10.05).

Hotel Virgen del Camino. Virgen del Camino, 55, 36001 Pontevedra. ☎ **986-85-59-00.** Fax 986-85-09-00. 53 units. TV TEL. 8,500–12,000 ptas. ($56.95–$80.40) double. MC, V. Parking 1,000 ptas. ($6.70).

On a relatively quiet street off the highway C-531, at the edge of the suburbs, this bal-conied stucco hotel contains a comfortable English-style pub as well as spacious sit-ting rooms. The midsize bedrooms have wall-to-wall carpeting and private bathrooms, plus central heating in winter. The best doubles contain separate salons and sitting rooms.

A cafeteria serves fixed-price meals. There is also a laundry service on the premises and room service.

WHERE TO DINE

Casa Román. Augusto García Sánchez, 12. ☎ **986-84-35-60.** Main courses 1,500–4,000 ptas. ($10.05–$26.80); fixed-price menu 2,500 ptas. ($16.75). AE, DC, MC, V. Daily 1:30–4pm, Mon–Sat 9pm–midnight. Closed Sun night Sept–Jan. GALICIAN.

Known for the quality of its food, this well-established restaurant is on the street level of a brick apartment building in a leafy downtown development known as Campo-longo, near Plaza de Galicia. To reach the dining room, you pass through a tavern. In addition to lobster (which you can see in the window), a wide array of well-prepared fish and shellfish dishes is served here, including sea bass, squid, sole, crab, and tuna.

✪ **Doña Antonia.** Soportales de la Herrería, 4 (second floor). ☎ **986-84-72-74.** Reserva-tions required. Main courses 1,650–3,500 ptas. ($11.05–$23.45); tasting menu 4,500 ptas. ($30.15). AE, MC, V. Mon–Sat 1:30–4pm and 9–11:30pm. INTERNATIONAL.

Without question, Pontevedra's best restaurant is Doña Antonia, located under a stone arcade on one of the town's oldest streets, east of the Jardines Vincenti. You climb one flight to reach the dining room. In such a provincial town, it is surprising to come across a restaurant of such sophistication and refinement. Although a few readers have sometimes reported a disappointing meal, most diners are filled with joy at this discovery. There's a pristine freshness to the dishes prepared with fish just caught off the coast. The reward for all this culinary vigilance is a loyal clientele of contented food lovers. Menu items include baked suckling lamb, scallopini with port, rolled fillet of salmon, and kiwi sorbet.

PONTEVEDRA AFTER DARK

The cool temperatures that descend over the hot, sultry plain that surrounds Pontevedra seem to incite local residents into after-dark promenades through the old city. You'll find a random scattering of pubs and bars sprawling on either side of the streets that interconnect the Plaza Santa Maria la Mayor, in the northwestern quadrant of the town's historic core, with the very central Plaza de la Herrería. Part of the charm of the neighborhood involves stopping randomly at whatever pub or cafe appeals to you— each awakens from its slumber after around 8:30pm. By midnight on the weekends, rhythmic electronic music emanates from two of the town's most popular discos: **Equus** (☎ **986-86-40-15**), calle Loreiro Crespo, 8, and **Disco Caravas,** calle Cobian Rafinac, 6 (no phone). Disco Caravas appeals to high-energy dance freaks in their early 20s; most folks in their 30s appreciate the slightly more mature venues at Equus. Don't even think of heading off to a Pontevedra disco before midnight, as it's likely to be locked until then (though the music keeps pumping until 4am). Expect entrance charges of between 500 and 700 ptas. ($3.35 and $4.70) at both of these venues, depending on the night of the week.

6 Lugo

314 miles (506km) NW of Madrid, 60 miles (97km) SE of La Coruña

Lugo has known many conquerors. The former Celtic-Iberian settlement fell to the Romans, and centuries later the Moors used the land and its people to grow crops for them. Today, Lugo is one of the four provincial capitals of Galicia. It is generally bypassed by those taking the Pilgrims' Way to Santiago de Compostela. However, it makes a rewarding detour for a morning or afternoon of sightseeing.

ESSENTIALS

GETTING THERE   Lugo lies on the rail link with Madrid. Two trains per day arrive from La Coruña.

Lugo has bus links with most of the major towns in the northwest, including Oviedo, with one per day making the 5-hour trip, and Orense, with five per day making the 2½-hour trip.

For those driving, N-VI connects Lugo with La Coruña as well as, at some distance, Madrid.

VISITOR INFORMATION   The **tourist information office** is at Praça Maior, 27 (☎ **982-23-13-61**). It is open Monday through Friday from 9:30am to 1:30pm and 4:30 to 6pm, Saturday from 10am to 1:30pm.

STROLLING AROUND ANCIENT LUGO

Lugo, split by the Miño River, is surrounded by a thick 1¼-mile (2km) ✪ **Roman wall,** the best preserved in all of Spain. The wall is about 33 feet high and contains a total of 85 round towers; a sentry path can be approached by steps at the various town gates. Your best bet is to enter the old town at Puerto de Santiago, the most interesting of the ancient gates, and begin a most impressive promenade—what may well be one of the highlights of your tour of Galicia.

Along the way you'll come to the **cathedral,** built in 1129 and notable for its trio of landmark towers. Standing at the Plaza Santa María, it has many Romanesque architectural features, such as its nave, but it was subsequently given a Gothic overlay. Further remodeling took place in the 18th century, when many features were added, such as the *Capilla de la Virgen de los Ojos Grandes* (Chapel of the Wide-Eyed Virgin) at the east end, with a baroque rotunda. The highlight of the cathedral is a 13th-century porch at the north end, which provides shelter for a Romanesque sculpted *Jesus Christ in His Majesty.* The figure rises over a capital and seems to hang in space. At the far end of the transept rise huge wood-built altarpieces in the Renaissance style.

As you wander about—and that is far preferable to going inside the many monuments—you'll traverse the cobblestoned, colonnaded medieval streets and interesting squares of the old town, especially behind the cathedral. The 18th-century **Episcopal Palace,** called a *pazo* in Galician, faces the north side of the cathedral and opens onto Plaza Santa María. From the palace, old alleys behind it lead to a tiny nugget, **Plaza del Campo,** one of the most charming squares of Lugo, flanked with ancient houses and graced with a fountain at its core.

Or from the bishop's palace at the Plaza Santa María, you can take calle Cantones to Plaza de España, where you will see the **Ayuntamiento (Town Hall),** built in a flowery rococo style.

From the Town Hall, follow calle de la Reina north to the **Iglesia de San Francisco,** a church said to have been founded by St. Francis upon his return from a pilgrimage west to the tomb of St. James. The cloister of the church, entered at Plaza de la Soledad, s/n, has been turned into the **Museo Provincial (☎ 982-24-21-12).** Many artifacts, including sundials from Celtic and Roman days, are found in this museum, along with folkloric displays. In July and August it is open Monday through Friday from 11am to 2pm and 5 to 8pm, Saturday 10:30am to 2pm. From September through June, it is open Monday through Saturday from 10:30am to 2pm and 4:30 to 8:30pm, Sunday 11am to 2pm. Admission is free.

WHERE TO STAY
EXPENSIVE

Gran Hotel Lugo. Avenida Ramón Ferreiro, 21, 27002 Lugo. ☎ **982-22-41-52.** Fax 982-24-16-60. 168 units. A/C MINIBAR TV TEL. 16,000 ptas. ($107.20) double; 20,500 ptas. ($137.35) suite. AE, DC, MC, V. Parking 1,000 ptas. ($6.70). Bus: 1, 2, 3, or 4.

About half a mile west of the ancient city walls in a leafy residential neighborhood, this hotel is large, modern, and the best in town. Its guest rooms are conservative and comfortable, with marble and/or tile bathrooms (offering hair dryers) and restful monochromatic colors.

Dining/Diversions: The Os Marisqueiros restaurant serves regional and international three-course fixed-price lunches and dinners. Live music is sometimes performed in the Atalaya Bar, which is open Monday through Saturday from 7pm to 4am. Snack 2003 is a coffee shop/snack bar, and the adjoining La Oca is a combination pizzeria and pub.

Amenities: Room service (daily from 8am to midnight), laundry, concierge, babysitting, business center, car rentals, shopping boutiques, bingo hall, swimming pool.

MODERATE

Hotel Jorge Primeiro. La Campiña, 27923 Lugo. ☎ **982-30-32-55.** Fax 982-30-31-07. 23 units. TV TEL. 6,300–8,000 ptas. ($42.20–$53.60) double. AE, DC, MC, V. Bus: destination La Campiña.

If you're driving, this little hotel about 2 miles (3km) north of town on carretera N-640 is one of your best bets, particularly if you're arriving from neighboring Asturias. The old building has a bit of charm, and the well-maintained but small bedrooms are filled with modern comforts such as firm mattresses. You can enjoy the scenery as you dine in the hotel restaurant, which serves regional fare and a menú del día for 1,200 ptas. ($8.05).

Méndez Núñez. Raiña, 1, 27001 Lugo. ☎ **982-23-07-11.** Fax 982-22-97-38. 84 units. TV TEL. 6,500–7,500 ptas. ($43.55–$50.25) double. AE, MC, V. Parking 160 ptas. ($1.05) per hour in nearby garage. Bus: 1, 2, 3, or 4.

Just around the corner from Plaza Mayor, this hotel was built in 1888 and named in honor of a then-famous Spanish admiral who had just won an important battle against revolutionaries in Cuba. Rebuilt and modernized in 1970, the hotel is today one of the best managed in town, although not as highly rated as the Gran Hotel Lugo. Midsize bedrooms are well maintained and comfortable, each equipped with an excellent bed. No meals other than breakfast are served, but many restaurants and cafes lie within the neighborhood. The hotel is especially convenient for exploring the medieval streets of the town's old quarter.

WHERE TO DINE

Campos. Rúa Nova, 4. ☎ **982-22-97-43.** Reservations recommended. Main courses 1,400–3,000 ptas. ($9.40–$20.10); fixed-price menus 1,850–2,500 ptas. ($12.40–$16.75). AE, DC, MC, V. Daily noon–4:30pm and 7:30pm–midnight. Closed the last 2 weeks in Oct. Bus: 1, 2, 3, or 4. GALICIAN.

In the old quarter immediately adjacent to Plaza del Campo, this acclaimed restaurant is the creation of Amparo Yañez and his son, Manuel. Together, they offer imaginative combinations of fresh ingredients that are deftly prepared and much appreciated by their loyal clients. Winner of the 1995 *Gran Cocineros de Galicia* award, they feature seasonal game dishes, especially local pheasant, along with fresh fish, such as grouper with almonds. The best dessert is fresh local strawberries with honey and cream. Decor featured within the establishment's two dining rooms is one of restrained elegance, and includes a monochromatic color scheme of soft beiges, with lots of visible hardwoods, all of it set within a building that was erected around 1900.

Ferreiros. Rua Nueva, 1. ☎ **982-22-97-28.** Reservations recommended. Main courses 700–2,100 ptas. ($4.70–$14.05); menús del día 1,200–1,500 ptas. ($8.05–$10.05). MC, V. Thurs–Tues 1–4pm and 8pm–midnight. Bus: 1, 2, 3, or 4. GALICIAN.

In business since the 1920s, this longtime favorite near the cathedral must be doing something right. In fact, it offers well-prepared and old-fashioned regional fare with a certain unpretentious flair. The portions are generous, and the food is fresh. The many shellfish dishes featured are the most expensive items on the menu. You can also order a big slab of rib of beef or monkfish prepared in different ways.

Mesón de Alberto. Calle de la Cruz, 4. ☎ **982-22-83-10.** Reservations recommended. Main courses 650–2,400 ptas. ($4.35–$16.10); fixed-price menu 2,500 ptas. ($16.75). AE, DC, MC, V. Mon–Sat 1–4pm and 8pm–midnight. Bus: 1, 2, 3, or 4. GALICIAN/SPANISH.

Alberto García is the culinary star of Lugo, and with good reason. Ably assisted by his wife, Flor, he offers a well-chosen menu of imaginative fish and meat dishes and the best wine cellar in town. In style the place resembles a rustic tavern, with a stand-up bar serving tapas, plus a handful of dining tables. The overflow is directed either to a somewhat more formal dining room beside the tavern or to the second floor. Try Alberto's salad with eel and an exotic vinegar, monkfish served with a mountain cheese (Cabrales from Asturias), or beefsteak for two, prepared with his secret sauce. Mesón de Alberto stands 1 block north of the cathedral in the old quarter.

7 El Grove & La Toja

395 miles (636km) NW of Madrid, 20 miles (32km) W of Pontevedra, 45 miles (72km) S of Santiago de Compostela

A summer resort and fishing village with some 5 miles (8km) of beaches of varying quality, **El Grove** is on a peninsula west of Pontevedra. It juts out into the Ría de Arousa, a large inlet at the mouth of Ulla River. The village, sheltered from Atlantic gales because of its eastern position, has become more commercial than many visitors would like, but it is still renowned for its fine cuisine. A shellfish festival is held here every October.

La Toja (*A Toxa* in Galician), an island linked to El Grove by a bridge, is a famous spa and the most fashionable resort in Galicia, known for its sports and leisure activities. The casino and the golf course are both very popular. The island is covered with pine trees and surrounded by some of the finest scenery in Spain.

La Toja first became known for health-giving properties when, according to legend, the owner of a sick donkey left it on the island to die. The donkey recovered, and its cure was attributed to the waters of an island spring.

GETTING THERE

The train from Santiago de Compostela goes as far as Vilagarcía de Arousa; take the bus from there. For train schedules, call the station in Santiago de Compostela (☎ **981-25-02-02**) for information.

From Pontevedra, buses heading for Ponte Vilagarcía de Arousa stop at La Toja. Call the transportation information number in Pontevedra (☎ **986-85-13-13**) for details.

From Pontevedra, drive east on the 550 coastal road via Sanxenxo. From Santiago de Compostela, expressway A-9 leads to Caldas de Reis, where you turn off onto the 550, heading west to the coast.

WHERE TO STAY & DINE IN EL GROVE

Hotel Amandi. Castelao, 94, 36980 El Grove. ☎ **986-73-19-42.** Fax 986-73-16-43. 30 units. TV TEL. 7,500–,200 ptas. ($50.25–$81.75) double. Rates include breakfast. MC, V. Closed Jan.

This stylish and tasteful family run hotel is a brisk 10-minute walk from the bridge that connects El Grove with La Toja. The midsize rooms are decorated with antique reproductions; most have tiny terraces with ornate cast-iron balustrades and sea views. Breakfast is the only meal served.

La Pousada del Mar. Castelao, 202. ☎ **986-73-01-06.** Reservations required July–Aug. Main courses 1,000–2,500 ptas. ($6.70–$16.75); fixed-price menu 3,000 ptas. ($20.10). AE, DC, MC, V. Daily 1–4pm, Mon–Sat 8:30pm–midnight. Closed Dec 10–Feb 1. SEAFOOD.

This warm, inviting place near the bridge leading to La Toja is the best dining spot outside those at the hotels. At times you can watch women digging for oysters in the river in front. The chef, naturally, specializes in fish, including a wide selection of shellfish. Among the specialties are a savory soup, outstanding shellfish paella, hake Galician style, and fresh grilled salmon. For dessert, try the *flan de la casa.*

WHERE TO STAY IN LA TOJA

Hotel Louxo. 36991 Isla de la A Toxa. ☎ **986-73-02-00.** Fax 986-73-27-91. 116 units. A/C MINIBAR TV TEL. 10,300–17,500 ptas. ($69–$117.25) double. AE, DC, MC, V. Free parking.

Set on flatlands a few paces from the town's ornate casino is this modern white building, sheltered from the Atlantic winds. It offers clean, stylish, and modern accommodations. Most rooms are midsize, and each is equipped with such amenities as a private safe and a hair dryer. The many ground-floor public rooms have rows of comfortable seating areas and sweeping views over the nearby tidal flats. The hotel also serves an outstanding menu for 2,500 ptas. ($16.75), with an emphasis on fresh fish.

8 Túy (Túi)

18 miles (29km) S of Vigo, 30 miles (48km) S of Pontevedra

A frontier town first settled by the Romans, Túy is a short distance from Portugal, located near the two-tiered road-and-rail bridge (over the Miño River) that links the two countries. The bridge was designed by Alexandre-Gustave Eiffel (he also did a tower in Paris you may have heard of). If you're driving from Portugal's Valença do Minho, Túy is your introduction to Spain.

ESSENTIALS

GETTING THERE   Trains run daily for the 1½- to 2-hour trip from Vigo to Túy.
From Vigo, buses run south to Túy hourly, taking 1 hour.
If you're driving from Vigo, head south along the A-9 expressway until you see the turnoff for Túy.

VISITOR INFORMATION   The **tourist information office** is at Puente Tripes, Avenida de Portugal (☎ **986-60-17-89**), open Monday through Friday from 9am to 1pm and 4 to 6pm, Saturday from 10am to 2:30pm.

EXPLORING TÚY

The winding streets of the old quarter lead to the **Catedral,** a national art treasure that dominates the *zona monumental.* The acropolis-like cathedral-fortress, built in 1170, wasn't used for religious purposes until the early 13th century. Its principal ogival portal is exceptional. What is astounding about this cathedral is that later architects respected the original Romanesque and Gothic styles and didn't make changes in its design. If you have time, you may want to visit the Romanesque-style **Iglesia de San Bartolomé,** on the outskirts of town, and the **Iglesia de Santo Domingo,** a beautiful example of Gothic style (look for the bas-reliefs in the cloister). The latter church stands next to the Santo Domingo park. Walls built over Roman fortifications surround Túy.

WHERE TO STAY & DINE

Parador Nacional de San Telmo. Avenida de Portugal, s/n, 36700 Túy. ☎ **986-60-03-09.** Fax 986-60-21-63. 30 units. MINIBAR TV TEL. 11,500–15,000 ptas. ($77.05–$100.50) double; 15,500–20,500 ptas. ($103.85–$137.35) suite. AE, DC, MC, V. Free parking.

Advance reservations are essential if you want to stay in this elegant, fortress-style hacienda located four streets north of the Miño River crossing. Built in 1968, the inn with its cantilevered roof was designed to blend in with the architectural spirit of the province, emphasizing local stone and natural woods. Brass chandeliers, paintings by well-known *gallegos,* and antiques combined with reproductions furnish the public rooms. In the main living room are a large inglenook fireplace, a tall banjo-shaped grandfather clock, hand-knotted rugs, 18th-century paintings, hand-hewn benches, and comfortable armchairs.

The midsize bedrooms are sober in style, but comfortable, and offer views across a colonnaded courtyard to the river and hills. They are furnished with Castilian-style pieces, and the tiled bathrooms are modern.

Dining: The dignified dining room has a high wooden ceiling and tall windows that offer a fine view of the surrounding hills. Even if you are not a hotel guest, it is worth dining on the regional cuisine served here. The hors d'oeuvres, served while you wait in the bar, consist of almost a dozen tapas. The fish dishes are excellent, especially (when available) lamprey, as well as salmon, shad, and trout. There is a menú del día for 3,500 ptas. ($23.45). Homemade cakes are offered for dessert.

Amenities: Swimming pool, tennis courts.

A SIDE TRIP INTO PORTUGAL

If you have a passport you can drive south from Túy to the Portuguese town of **Valença do Minho.** You can cross the International Bridge into Portugal; border formalities usually are mild unless there is some reason to cause suspicion from the security guards. The walled battlements of Valença, many of which are still intact, are reminders of the ancient hostilities between Portugal and Spain. A narrow covered gateway across a moat takes you into the center of this walled village of cobblestone streets, ancient stone houses, pots of geraniums, wrought-iron balconies, and old street lanterns.

Incorporated into a 13th-century fortress, a government-sponsored pousada, **Pousada do São Teotónio** (no street address, but signposted; ☎ 051-82-42-42), is the best place for lunch before heading back to Túy. If you find it's difficult to get a table here (highly likely), then head for the best independent restaurant, **Fortalez,** rúa Apolinário da Fonseca, 5 (☎ 051-231-46). Both of these dining rooms specialize in a local dish, lampreys or eels. Caught fresh in the river, they are served in a spicy pepper sauce.

18 The Balearic Islands

The Balearic Islands (*Los Baleares*), an archipelago composed of the major islands of Majorca, Minorca, and Ibiza, plus the diminutive Formentera, Cabrera, and the uninhabited Dragonera, lie off the coast of Spain, between France and the coast of northern Africa. Because they're located along the Mediterranean's major shipping lanes, the islands have known many rulers and occupying forces—Carthaginians, Greeks, Romans, Vandals, and Moors. But despite a trove of Bronze Age megaliths and some fine Punic artifacts, the invaders who have left the largest imprint on Balearic culture are the hordes of sun-seeking vacationers who descend every year.

After the expulsion of the Moors by Jaume I in 1229, the islands flourished as the kingdom of Majorca. When they were integrated into the kingdom of Castile in the mid–14th century, they experienced a massive decline. The early 19th century provided a renaissance for the islands; artists such as George Sand and her lover, Chopin, and later the poet Robert Graves established the islands, especially Majorca and Ibiza, as a haven for musicians, writers, and artists (read Sand's book *A Winter in Majorca*). Gradually the artist colony attracted tourists of all dispositions.

Today the Balearics are administered by an autonomous government, *Govern Balear*. **Majorca,** the largest island, is the most commercial and tourist oriented. It has both benefited and suffered from its huge tourism boom. Many of its scenic expanses have given way to sprawling hotels and fast-food joints, although parts remain beautiful indeed. Freewheeling **Ibiza,** world-renowned for its decadent ways, attracts the international party crowd, as well as visitors who come to the island for its tamer offerings, such as white-sand beaches and sky-blue waters. The smallest of the major islands, **Minorca,** the last to succumb to the tourist invasion, is the most serene. It is less touristy than Majorca and Ibiza, and for that reason, it is now experiencing an antitourist tourist boom.

The government of the islands has finally awakened to the damage caused by overdevelopment of Majorca and Ibiza from the 1960s through the 1980s. Under new guidelines, some 35% of this island group is now safeguarded from exploitation by builders.

Very few visitors have time to explore all three islands, so you'll have to decide early which one is for you. Many vacationers include one of the Balearic Islands as an add-on to a visit to Barcelona or the Costa Brava, whereas others view them as destinations unto themselves.

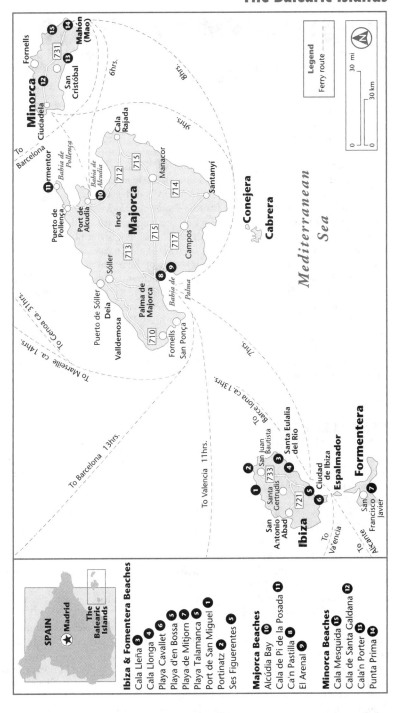

The Balearic Islands

Minorca

Fornells
731
Mahón (Mao)
San Cristóbal
Ciudadela

To Barcelona

Bahía de Pollensa
Bahía de Alcudia

Majorca

Cala Rajada
712
715
Manacor
714
Santanyí
Inca
715
717
Campos
713
Sóller
Puerto de Pollensa
Port de Alcudia
Puerto de Sóller
Deia
Palma de Majorca
Valldemosa
710
Fornells
San Ponça
Bahía de Palma

Conejera
Cabrera

Mediterranean Sea

To Genoa ca. 31hrs.
To Marseille ca. 14hrs.
6hrs.
8hrs.
9hrs.
7hrs.
Barcelona ca. 13hrs.
To Barcelona 13hrs.
To Valencia 11hrs.

Ibiza

San Juan Bautista
733
Santa Eulalia del Río
Santa Gertrudis
San Antonio Abad
721
Ciudad de Ibiza
Espalmador
San Francisco Javier

Formentera

To Valencia
To Alicante

Ibiza & Fomentera Beaches

Cala Lleña ③
Cala Llonga ④
Playa Cavallet ⑥
Playa d'en Bossa ⑤
Playa de Mitjorn ⑦
Playa Talamanca ⑤
Port de San Miguel ①
Portinatz ②
Ses Figuerentes ⑤

Majorca Beaches

Alcúdia Bay ⑩
Cala de Pi de la Posada ⑪
Ca'n Pastilla ⑧
El Arenal ⑨

Minorca Beaches

Cala Mesquida ⑮
Cala de Santa Galdana ⑫
Cala'n Porter ⑬
Punta Prima ⑭

573

1 Majorca

The largest of the Balearic archipelago, Majorca (Mallorca in Spanish) is the most popular of Spain's Mediterranean islands, drawing millions of visitors each year. One prominent tourist is King Juan Carlos, who comes with his family to their summer residence, Marivent, in Cala Mayor.

About 130 miles (209km) from Barcelona and 90 miles (145km) from Valencia, Majorca's coastline is 310 miles (500km) long. The beautiful island is an explorer's paradise in its exterior, although horribly overbuilt along certain coastal regions. The north is mountainous, while the fertile southern flatlands offer a landscape of olive and almond groves, occasionally interrupted by windmills.

The golden sands of Majorca are famous, with lovely beaches such as Ca'n Pastilla and El Arenal, although they tend to be overcrowded with sun worshippers on package tours. Tourist facilities also line the shores of Cala Mayor and Sant Agustí, both have good beaches, as is Playa Magaluf, the longest beach on the Calvía coast. Cala de San Vicente, 4 miles (6km) north of Pollença, is a beautiful beach bordered by a pine grove and towering cliffs. Sandy stretches of golden sand beaches lie between Cala Pi and Cala Murta in Formentor near the tip of the northern coast.

Majorca has much to offer—sun and surf, little harbors, hidden mountain villages, and historic sights. Brits, Americans, and Germans have all settled in, buying either homes or apartments, but the "Chopin Heights Real Estate Development" (an actual development) is a bit much! (Chopin and his mistress, George Sand, were in the legendary vanguard of the tourists to Majorca. They spent a few months on the island in 1838.)

July and August are high season for Majorca; don't even think of coming then without a reservation. It's possible to swim comfortably from June to October; after that it's too cold (except for those hardy Scandinavians and Germans used to the chilly waters).

ISLAND ESSENTIALS

GETTING THERE   At certain times of the year the trip by boat or plane can be pleasant. But in August the routes to Palma must surely qualify as the major bottleneck in Europe. Don't travel without advance reservations, and be sure you have a return plane ticket if you come in August—otherwise you may not get off the island until September!

Iberia-Aviaco (☎ 971-75-67-54) flies to Palma's Aeroport Son San Joan (☎ 971-78-90-00) from Barcelona, Valencia, and Madrid. There are daily planes from Madrid and Valencia, and several daily flights from Barcelona in summer. **Spanair** (☎ 971-74-50-20) also flies into Palma from Barcelona (up to three times a day during summer) and from Madrid, Bilbao, Minorca, Santiago de Compostela, Málaga, and Tenerife. **Air Europa** (☎ 971-17-81-00) flies to Palma from Barcelona a maximum of two times a day during peak season, and to a lesser extent, it also flies to Palma from Madrid, Minorca, Ibiza, and Seville.

British and other European travelers should really consult a travel agent and look into the available package tours, which combine airfare and accommodations; they can save you a ton of money!

Countless charter flights also make the run. Bookings are very tight in August, and delays of at least 24 hours, sometimes more, are common. If you're flying—say, Iberia—on a transatlantic flight from New York to either Madrid or Barcelona, you should have Majorca written into your ticket before your departure if you plan to visit the Balearics as part of your Spanish itinerary.

Majorca

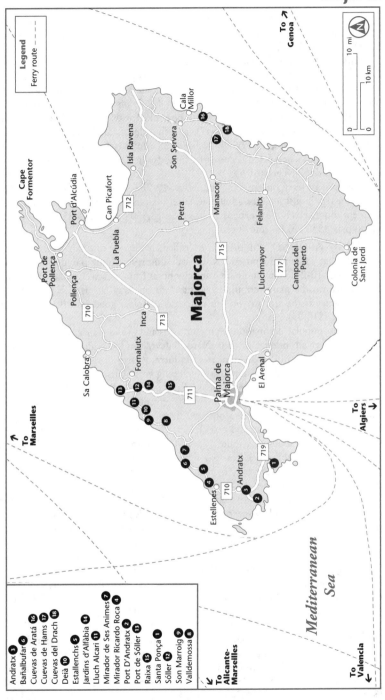

Legend
- - - Ferry route

To Genoa

10 mi
10 km

Cape Formentor

Cala Millor

Isla Ravena

Son Servera

Can Picafort

Port d'Alcúdia

712

Petra

Manacor

Felanitx

Port de Pollença

Pollença

La Puebla

710

715

717

Lluchmayor

Campos del Puerto

Colonia de Sant Jordi

Inca

713

Fornalutx

Sa Calobra

711

Palma de Majorca

El Arenal

Majorca

To Marseilles

13 12 14 15

11

10

9 8

6 7

5

4

3

719

2

Andratx

710

Estellencs

To Algiers

To Marseilles

To Alicante-Marseilles

To Valencia

Mediterranean Sea

Andratx ❸
Bañalbufar ❻
Cuevas de Aratá ❶⑥
Cuevas de Hams ⓱
Cuevas del Drach ⑱
Deià ❿
Estallenchs ❺
Jardins d'Alfàbia ⓮
Lluch Alcari ⑪
Mirador de Ses Animes ❼
Mirador Ricardo Roca ❹
Port D'Andratx ❷
Port de Sóller ⓭
Raixa ⑮
Santa Ponça ❶
Sóller ⑫
Son Marroig ❾
Valldemossa ❽

575

From the airport, bus number 17 will take you to the Plaça Espanya in the center of Palma from 7am to 11:30pm daily; the cost is 295 ptas. ($2). A metered cab costs 2,500 ptas. ($16.75) for the 25-minute drive into the city center.

Transmediterránea, Estació Marítim in Palma (☎ **971-70-73-00** for schedules), operates two to five ferries a day from Barcelona, taking 8 hours and costing from 6,735 ptas. ($45.10) for one-way passage. There are also six ferries per week from Valencia, Monday through Saturday, taking 8½ hours and costing 6,090 ptas. ($40.80) one way. In Barcelona, tickets can be booked at the Transmediterránea office at Estació Marítim (☎ **93-295-91-37**), and in Valencia at the office at Avinguda Manuel Soto Ingeniero, 15 (☎ **96-367-65-12**). Any travel agent in Spain can also book you a seat. Schedules and departure times (subject to change) should always be checked and double-checked.

A new private ferry, operated by **Buquebus** (☎ **902-41-42-42** in Spain only), now makes the trip in just 3 hours, a full hour faster than the ferry run by the Spanish government. Buquebus is more expensive, however: 18,560 ptas. ($124.35), one way, and 8,500 ptas. ($56.95) for tourist class.

GETTING AROUND   At the tourist office in Palma, you can pick up a bus schedule that explains island routes. Or call **Emprese Municipal de Transportes** (☎ **971-43-10-24**). This company runs city buses from Estació Central D'Autobus, Plaça Espanya, the main terminal. The standard one-way fare is 175 ptas. ($1.15) within Palma; at the station you can purchase a booklet good for 10 rides, costing 1,500 ptas. ($10.05).

The most popular destination routes on the island (Valldemossa, Deià, Sóller, and Port de Sóller) are offered by **Bus Nord Balear,** carrer Arxiduc Luís Salvador, 1 (☎ **971-42-71-87**) in Palma. **Autocares Mallorca,** Passeig Maritimo, 48 (☎ **971-54-56-96**), runs buses to the eastern coast, including Porto Cristo.

Ferrocarril de Sóller, carrer Eusebio Estada, 1 (☎ **971-75-20-51**), off Plaça Espanya, has train service, passing through majestic mountain scenery, to Sóller. Trains run from 8am to 7:55pm, and a one-way ticket costs 770 ptas. ($5.15). A "tourist train" leaves daily at 10:40am and costs 1,115 ptas. ($7.45) before reaching Sóller. The only thing special about this route is a 10-minute stop at Mirador del Pujol d'en Banya—a privilege for which you pay dearly. The tourist train itself, however, is a worthy sightseeing trip. Privately owned, it was constructed by orange growers early in this century and still uses the carriages of the belle epoque days.

Another train runs to Inca; it's often called "the leather express" because most passengers are on board to buy inexpensive leather goods in the Inca shops. This line is the **Servicios Ferroviarios de Mallorca,** and it too leaves from Plaça Espanya (☎ **971-75-22-45** for more information and schedules). The train ride is only 40 minutes, and departures are at the rate of 40 per day Monday through Saturday and 32 per day on Sunday. A one-way fare costs 255 ptas. ($1.70).

Contact **Belori Bike,** Edificio Pilarki, calle Maravalla, 22, Arenal (☎ **971-49-03-58**), for both bike and scooter rental. Bikes range in price from 800 to 2,400 ptas. ($5.35 to $16.10) per day, while scooters rent for 2,500 ptas. ($16.75) per day.

For a radio taxi, call ☎ **971-75-54-40** or 971-40-14-14.

If you plan to stay in Palma, you don't need a car. The city is extremely traffic clogged. Scarcity of parking is another reason not to have a car. If you'd like to take our driving tour, you can rent cars at such companies as the Spanish-owned **Atesa** at Passeig Marítim (☎ **971-78-98-96**), where rentals range from 7,200 to 13,620 ptas. ($48.25 to $91.25) per day. **Avis** at Passeig Marítimo, 16 (☎ **971-73-07-20**) is also well stocked with cars; its rates range from 8,500 to 25,500 ptas. ($56.95 to $170.85) per day. Both Atesa and Avis also maintain offices at the airport. Reservations, however, should always be made in advance, especially in summer.

PALMA DE MAJORCA

Palma, on the southern tip of the island, is the seat of the autonomous government of the Balearic Islands, as well as the center for most of Majorca's hotels, restaurants, and nightclubs. The Moors constructed Palma in the style of a Casbah, or walled city. Its roots are still visible, although obscured by the high-rise hotels that have cropped up.

Old Palma is typified by the area immediately surrounding the cathedral. Mazes of narrow alleys and cobblestone streets echo the era when Palma was one of the chief ports in the Mediterranean.

Today Palma is a bustling city, whose massive tourist industry has more than made up for its decline as a major seaport. It's estimated that nearly half the population of the island lives in Palma. Majorca attracts the largest number of visitors of any place in the Balearics. The islanders call Palma simply *Ciutat* ("City"), and it is the largest of the Balearic ports, its bay often clogged with yachts. Arrival by sea is the most impressive, with the skyline characterized by Bellver Castle and the bulk of the cathedral.

ESSENTIALS

VISITOR INFORMATION   The **National Tourist Office** is located in Palma at Plaça Reyna, 2 (☎ **971-71-22-16**). It's open Monday through Friday from 9am to 7:30pm, Saturday 10am to 1:30pm.

GETTING AROUND   In Palma, you can get around on foot (the only way, really), especially if you plan to sightsee or shop in the Old Town. Likewise, you can explore the Paseo on foot. Otherwise, you can make limited use of taxis for getting around Palma or use one of the buses that cut across the city. Out on the island, you'll have to depend mainly on buses or rented cars for transportation.

FAST FACTS   The **U.S. Consulate,** Avinguda Jaime III, 26 (☎ **971-72-26-60**), is open from 10:30am to 1:30pm Monday through Friday. The **British Consulate,** Plaça Mayor, 3 (☎ **971-71-24-45**), is open from 9am to 3pm Monday through Friday.

In case of an **emergency,** dial ☎ **112.** If you fall ill, head to the **Centro Médico,** Avenida Juan March, 8 (☎ **971-75-14-14**), a private facility.

Majorca observes the same **holidays** as the rest of Spain but also celebrates June 29, the Feast of St. Peter, the patron saint of all fishers.

The central **post office** is at carrer Constitució, 6 (☎ **902-19-71-97**). Hours are Monday through Friday 8:30am to 8:30pm, Saturday 9:30am to 2pm.

Local newsstands and tobacco shops sell phone cards valued between 500 and 2,000 ptas. ($3.35 and $13.40). They can be used in any public telephone booth, and allow you to make both domestic and international calls.

FUN ON & OFF THE BEACH

There is a beach fairly close to the cathedral in Palma, but some readers have been discouraged from swimming here because of foul-smelling, albeit covered, sewers nearby. The closest public beach is **Playa Nova,** a 35-minute bus ride from downtown Palma. Some hotels, however, have private beaches. If you head east, you reach the excellent beaches of **Ca'n Pastilla.** The beaches at **El Arenal** are very well equipped with tourist facilities and have golden sands as well. Going to the southwest, you find good but often crowded beaches at **Cala Mayor** and **Sant Agustí.**

You can swim from late June through October; don't believe the promoters who try to sell you on mild Majorcan winters in January and February—it can get downright cold. Spring and fall can be heaven sent, and in summer the coastal areas are pleasantly cooled by sea breezes.

BIKING   The best places for biking on the island are C'an Picafort, Alcúdia, and Port de Pollença, all along the north coast, because they are relatively flat. Most roads have special bike lanes on the island, as it's a popular sport here. For rentals, go to **Belori Bike,** Edificio Pilarki, calle Maravalla, 22, Arenal (☎ **971-49-03-58**). Depending on their model, and how many gears they have, pedal bikes rent for 800 to 2,400 ptas. ($5.35 to $16.10) per day.

GOLF   Majorca is a golfer's dream. The best course is the Son Vida Club de Golf, Urbanización son Vida, about 8 miles (13km) east of Palma along the Andrade highway. This 18-hole course is shared by the guests of the island's two best hotels, Arabella Golf Hotel and the Son Vida. However, the course is open to all players who call for reservations (☎ **971-79-12-10**). Greens fees are 8,500 ptas. ($56.95) for 18 holes.

HIKING   Because of the hilly terrain in Majorca, this sport is better pursued here than on Ibiza or Minorca. The mountains of the northwest, the Serra de Tramuntana, are best for exploring. The tourist office (see above) will provide you with a free booklet called *20 Hiking Excursions on the Island of Majorca,* which includes detailed maps and itineraries.

HORSEBACK RIDING   The best stables on the island are at **The Riding School of Majorca,** at km 12 on the Palma-Sóller road. Call ☎ **971-61-31-57** to make arrangements and get directions from wherever you are on the island.

TENNIS   If your hotel doesn't have a court, head for the **Club de Tenis,** carrer Sil, s/n (☎ **971-69-22-61**).

WATER SPORTS   Most beaches have outfitters who will rent you windsurfers and dinghies. The best diving operation is **Planet Escuba,** Pont Adriano (☎ **971-23-43-06**). Divers here are highly skilled and will take you to the most intriguing sights underwater if you are a qualified diver.

SHOPPING

Shopping in Palma offers handcrafts, elegant leather goods, Majorcan pearls, and fine needlework. The best shopping is on the following streets: San Miguel, carrer Sindicato, Jaume II, Jaume III, carrer Platería, Vía Roman, and Passeig des Borne, plus the streets radiating from the Borne all the way to Plaça Cort, where the city hall stands. Most shops close on Saturday afternoon and Sunday.

Elegant boudoirs throughout Europe are furnished with finely textured needlework from the famous **Casa Bonet,** Plaça Federico Chopin, 2 (☎ **971-72-21-17**), which was founded in 1860. Each of the sheets, tablecloths, napkins, and pillowcases is made in Majorca from fine linen or cotton (also, for the less expensive items, from acrylic). Many are hand-embroidered, using ancient designs and floral motifs popularized by this establishment.

Loewe, Jaime III, 1 (☎ **971-71-52-75**), offers fine leather, elegant accessories for men and women, luggage, and chic apparel for women. For funkier leather items, head for **Pink,** Avinguda Jaume III, 3 (☎ **971-72-23-33**).

Passy, Avinguda Jaume III, 6 (☎ **971-71-33-38**), offers high-quality, locally made shoes, handbags, and accessories for men and women. There's another branch at carrer Tous y Ferrer, 8 (☎ **971-71-73-38**), though it's not as well stocked.

Accommodations
Ca Sa Galesa **5**
Costa Azul **17**
Hotel Rosamar **14**
Hotel Saratoga **13**
Hotel Sol Inn
Jaimie III **12**
Hotel-Residencia
Almudaina **11**
San Lorenzo **14**

Attractions
Banys Arabs **4**
Catedral **5**
Llotja **9**
Museu d'Art Espanyol
Contemporani **1**
Palau de l'Almudaina **6**
Poble Espanyol **12**

Dining
Arroseria Sacranca **16**
Caballito del Mar
(Little Seahorse) **7**
Cellar Pagés **10**
Diplomatic **2**
Es Parlament **3**
Koldo Royo **15**
La Casita **4**
La Lubina **8**
Lonja del Pescado
(Casa Eduardo) **8**
Porto Pi **18**
Svarta Pannan **12**

Perlas Majorica, Avinguda Jaume III, 11 (☎ 971-72-52-68), is the authorized agency for the authentic Majorcan pearl. It's an elegant shop with fanciful wrought-iron gates. The pearl producers employ hundreds of artisans to make and design their stunning jewelry, and they offer a decade-long guarantee for their products. Pearls come in varied sizes and settings, of course.

SEEING THE SIGHTS

Most visitors don't spend much time exploring the historic sights in Palma, but there are a number of places to see if you've had too much sun.

Viajes Sidetours, Passeig Marítim, 16 (☎ 971-28-39-00), offers numerous full- and half-day excursions throughout Palma and the surrounding countryside. The full-day excursion to Valldemossa and Sóller takes visitors through the monastery where former island residents Chopin and his lover, George Sand, spent their scandalous winter. After leaving the monastery, the tour explores the peaks of the Sierra

Mallorquina, then makes its way to the seaside town of Sóller. A visit to the Arabian gardens of Raixa or Alfàbia is included in the 3,475 ptas. ($23.30) cost of the tour, on Wednesday only.

Another full-day tour of the mountainous western side of the island is conducted by train and boat, including a ride on one of Europe's oldest railways to the town of Sóller and the Monasterio de Lluch, as well as a boat ride between the port of Sóller and La Calobra. Daily tours cost 6,330 ptas. ($42.40). The eastern coast of Majorca is explored in the Caves of Drach and Hams tour. A concert on the world's largest underground lake (Lake Martel), tours through the caves, a stop at an olive wood works, and a visit to the Majorica Pearl Factory are all covered daily in the 5,400 ptas. ($36.20) cost. Times of departure may vary.

✪ **Catedral.** Carrer Palau Reial. ☎ **971-72-31-30.** Free admission to cathedral; museum and treasury 500 ptas. ($3.35). Mon–Fri 10am–6pm, Sat 10am–2pm. Bus: 15.

This graceful Catalonian Gothic cathedral, called La Seu, stands in the old town overlooking the seaside. It was begun during the reign of Jaume II (1276–1311) and completed in 1601. Its central vault is 144 feet high, and its columns rise 65 feet. There is a scalloped-edged, wrought-iron baldachin (canopy) by Gaudí over the main altar. The treasury contains pieces of the True Cross and relics of St. Sebastián, patron saint of Palma. Museum and cathedral hours are often subject to change; call ahead to make sure they're accepting visitors before you go.

Castell de Bellver. Between Palma and Illetas. ☎ **971-73-06-57.** Admission 260 ptas. ($1.75) adults, 150 ptas. ($1) children, students, and seniors. Sun free. Daily 8am–8pm. Museum closed Sun. Bus: 3, 4, 21, or 22.

Erected in 1309, this hilltop round castle was once the summer palace of the kings of Majorca—during the short period when there were kings of Majorca. The castle, which was a fortress with a double moat, is well preserved and now houses the Museu Municipal, which is devoted to archaeological objects and old coins. It's really the view from here, however, that is the chief attraction. In fact, the name, Bellver, means exactly that: beautiful view.

Museu d'Art Espanyol Contemporani, Fundación Juan March. Carrer Sant Miquel, 11. ☎ **971-71-35-15.** Admission 500 ptas. ($3.35) adults, 250 ptas. ($1.70) seniors and children. Mon–Fri 10am–6:30pm, Sat 10am–1:30pm.

The Juan March Foundation's Museum of Spanish Contemporary Art reopened in 1997, with a series of newly acquired modern paintings. The works represent one of the most fertile periods of 20th-century art, with canvasses by Picasso, Miró, Dalí, and Juan Gris, as well as Antoni Tàpies, Carlos Saura, Miquel Barceló, Luis Gordillo, Susana Solano, and Jordi Teixidor. A room devoted to temporary exhibits was added to the restored museum. One series, for example, featured 100 Picasso engravings from the 1930s. The oldest and best-known work in the museum is Picasso's *Head of a Woman,* from his cycle of paintings known as Les Demoiselles d'Avignon. These works form part of the collection that the Juan March Foundation began to amass in 1973.

Llotja. Passeig Sagrera. ☎ **971-71-17-05.** Free admission. Tues–Sat 11am–2pm and 5–9pm, Sun 11am–2pm. Bus: 15.

This 15th-century Gothic structure is a leftover from the wealthy mercantile days of Majorca. La Lonja (its Spanish name) was, roughly, an exchange or guild. Exhibitions here are announced in local newspapers.

Banys Arabs. Carrer Serra, 7. ☎ **971-72-15-49.** Admission 175 ptas. ($1.15). Daily 9:30am–7pm. Bus: 15.

You can spend hours exploring the narrow streets of the medieval quarter (*Barri Gòtic*) east of the cathedral. Along the way, you may want to visit these Moorish baths that date from the 10th century. The baths are the only complete remaining Moorish-constructed buildings in Palma, evoking life in the heyday of the caliphate. One room contains a dome supported by 12 columns.

Palau de l'Almudaina. Carrer Palau Reial. ☎ **971-72-71-45.** Admission 400 ptas. ($2.70) adults, 225 ptas. ($1.50) children; free on Wed. Apr–Oct, Mon–Sat 10am–2pm and 4–6:30pm; Off-season, Mon–Sat 10:30am–2pm and 4–6pm. Closed holidays. Bus: 15.

Long ago Muslim rulers erected this splendid fortress surrounded by Moorish-style gardens and fountains opposite the cathedral. During the short-lived reign of the kings of Majorca, it was converted into a royal residence that evokes the Alcázar at Málaga. Now it is one of the most popular attractions of Palma and houses a museum displaying antiques, arts, suits of armor, and Gobelin tapestries. Panoramic views of the harbor of Palma can be seen from here.

Poble Espanyol. Carrer Capitán Mesquida Veny, 39. ☎ **971-73-70-75.** Admission 800 ptas. ($5.35) adults, 700 ptas. ($4.70) children. Apr–Nov, daily 9am–8pm; Dec–Mar, daily 9am–6pm. Bus: 5.

This is a touristy collection of buildings evoking Spain in miniature and is similar to the Poble Espanyol in Barcelona. Bullfights are held in its corrida on summer Sundays. There are mock representations of such famous structures as the Alhambra in Granada, the Torre de Oro in Seville, and El Greco's House in Toledo.

Marineland. Costa d'en Blanes. ☎ **971-67-51-25.** Admission 1,900 ptas. ($12.75) adults, 1,025 ptas. ($6.85) children 3–12, free for children 2 and under. Mon–Fri 10:30am–1pm and 4–6pm; Sat–Sun 11:30am–2:30pm; 5–6:45pm. Closed 4 weeks Nov–Dec. Direct bus, marked Marineland, from Palma rail station.

Eleven miles (18km) west of Palma, just off the coast road en route to Palma Nova, this attraction offers a variety of amusements—dolphin, sea lion, and parrot shows. There's also a Polynesian pearl diving demonstration and a small zoo. You'll find a cafeteria, picnic area, and children's playground, as well as beach facilities.

WHERE TO STAY

Majorca has a staggering number of hotels, but it's still not enough to hold the crowds in August. If you go in high season, reserve well in advance.

Some of our hotel recommendations in Palma are in the El Terreno section, the heart of the local nightlife. Don't book into one of these hotels unless you like plenty of action, continuing until late at night. More conservative readers may find it unsavory. If you want peace and quiet, check our other suggestions.

Palma's suburbs, notably Cala Mayor, about 2½ miles (4km) from the center, and San Agustín, about 3 miles (5km) from town, continue to sprawl. In El Arenal, part of Playas de Palma, there is a huge concentration of hotels. The beaches at El Arenal are quite good but have a Coney Island atmosphere. We have a number of hotel recommendations in these suburbs for those who don't mind staying outside of the city center.

Very Expensive

✪ **Arabella Sheraton Golf Hotel.** Carrer de la Vinagrella, 07013 Palma de Majorca. ☎ **971-79-99-99.** Fax 971-79-99-97. www.deg.com/arabella.htm. E-mail: arabella@ arabella.es. 93 units. A/C MINIBAR TV TEL. 44,835–52,835 ptas. ($300.40–$354) double; 57,225–65,225 ptas. ($383.40–$437) suite. Rates include breakfast. AE, DC, MC, V. Parking free or 600 ptas. ($4) in garage. Bus: 7.

In 1992, the German-based Arabella chain bought this hotel, with its rolling grounds, as well as the Son Vida Hotel (which can be reached after a brisk 10-minute walk) and its 18-hole golf course. The ecology of the area surrounding the complex has been fiercely protected; it's about 3 miles (5km) northwest of the center of Palma. Don't come here expecting raucous good times on the beach; the resort is elegant and rather staid. Its focal point is a sprawling outdoor swimming pool, one of the most appealing on the island. There's no health club and no shuttle to the beach; many visitors drive to the several nearby beaches. But it does boast one of the only hotel bullrings in Spain!

The complex is low-rise, intensely landscaped, and offers views over the golf course (not of the sea) from many of its good-size bedrooms. Accommodations include white walls, dark-stained furnishings, wall-to-wall carpeting, and in all but the least expensive accommodations, a balcony or veranda.

Dining/Diversions: The Plat d'Or restaurant expects men to wear jackets and ties in the evening. The grill room, Foravila, is somewhat less formal yet very, very stylish. The three bars are staffed with an impeccably trained team used to dealing with well-heeled guests from all over the world.

Amenities: Room service, concierge, shuttle limousine to and from the airport, beauty salon/barbershop, plus complete sports facilities: golf, 5 tennis courts, minigolf, windsurfing, waterskiing, Turkish bath, sauna, whirlpool, horseback riding stables.

✪ **Casa Galesa.** Miramar, 8, 07012 Palma de Majorca. ☎ **971-71-54-00.** Fax 971-72-15-79. 12 units. A/C MINIBAR TV TEL. 28,250 ptas. ($189.30) double; 31,750–38,500 ptas. ($212.75–$257.95) suite. AE, MC, V. Closed 1 week at Christmas. Parking 1,700 ptas. ($11.40).

For generations, this 15th-century town house languished as a decaying apartment building that faced the side of the cathedral. Beginning in 1993, an entrepreneurial couple from Cardiff, Wales, restored the place, salvaging the original marble floors and stained-glass windows, sheathing the walls of the public areas with silk, and adding discreetly concealed modern amenities. Today, the setting is the most alluring in all of Palma, loaded with a worthy collection of English and Spanish antiques and paintings, and accented throughout with bouquets of flowers. Most rooms overlook an enclosed courtyard draped with potted plants and climbing vines. The rooms come in various shapes and sizes and are quite opulent with Persian rugs, antiques, plush towels, and luxury mattresses. There's no restaurant, but a hearty buffet is served each morning.

Amenities: Baby-sitting, concierge, currency exchange, laundry and dry cleaning service, room service, in-room massage, and a health club with Jacuzzi and sauna.

Hotel Son Vida. Raixa 21, 07013 Palma de Majorca. ☎ **800/223-6800** in the U.S., or 971-79-00-00. Fax 971-79-00-17. 170 units. A/C MINIBAR TV TEL. 37,000–45,000 ptas. ($247.90–$301.50) double; 71,600–134,000 ptas. ($479.70–$897.80) suite. Rates include breakfast. AE, DC, MC, V. Free parking. Bus: 7.

Set in a 13th-century castle in the Son Vida hills, on a secluded hilltop several miles from Palma, this hotel commands the most panoramic views on the island. Many rooms are also located in a modern wing, a pleasing reproduction of a Spanish hacienda. Inside, the public rooms are swathed in sumptuous fabrics, Oriental rugs, and chandeliers. Guest rooms in the new building are not quite as distinctive as those in the castle. Many rooms have private balconies or terraces. Expect spacious closets, bathrooms with touches of marble, hair dryers, deluxe toiletries, and plush towels. Most accommodations are spacious, with such amenities as two phones and private safes. All beds are wide and firm.

Dining/Diversions: The two restaurants, the Bellver and the Jardín, serve an excellent international cuisine, enhanced by an extensive wine list. A piano bar, open from 10pm to 2am, is the ideal location for an after-dinner drink.

Amenities: 24-hour room service, shuttles to town and the beach, outdoor pool, tennis courts, golf course, fitness center, covered pool, solarium, Turkish bath, whirlpool, sauna, massage.

Expensive

Sol Palas Atenea. Passeig Ingeniero Gabriel Roca, 29, 07014, Palma de Majorca. ☎ **971-28-14-00.** Fax 971-45-19-89. www.solmelia.com. 370 units. A/C MINIBAR TV TEL. 23,000 ptas. ($154.10) double; 27,500 ptas. ($184.25) suite. Rates include breakfast. AE, DC, MC, V. Parking 1,650 ptas. ($11.05). Bus: 1.

A member of the Sol chain, this modern hotel offers extensive leisure facilities for vacationers, while still catering to business travelers. It overlooks the Bay of Palma, within walking distance of the town's major restaurants and shops. Spacious guest rooms have terraces, many overlooking the harbor or Bellver Castle. Furnishings are a bit chain standardized, but each is exceedingly comfortable ranging in size from medium to spacious; all are fitted with excellently maintained tile bathrooms and wide, firm beds. An entire floor is designed for the special needs of the business traveler.

Dining/Diversions: A dining room and a cafe serve fine food. For evening entertainment you can choose from a piano bar, an outdoor terrace bar, or a nightclub.

Amenities: 24-hour room service, Club Elite floor for executives; outdoor and indoor pools, sauna, massage, Jacuzzi, solarium, beauty salon, shops.

Moderate

Hotel-Residencia Almudaina. Avinguda Jaume III, 9, 07012 Palma de Majorca. ☎ **971-72-73-40.** Fax 971-72-25-99. 78 units. A/C TV TEL. 11,875 ptas. ($79.55) double. AE, DC, MC, V. Free parking. Bus: 1 or 13.

Located on the main commercial street in Palma, this simple hotel offers comfortable, clean, basic rooms. Although small, each unit is well maintained and contains a comfortable bed with a firm mattress. Because of its location, many of the rooms are quite loud; the quietest rooms are in the rear. Some have terraces and glass doors letting in ample sunlight. The service is helpful and the Almudaina has a cafeteria.

Hotel Saratoga. Passeig Majorca, 6, 07012 Palma de Majorca. ☎ **971-72-72-40.** Fax 971-72-73-12. 187 units. A/C MINIBAR TV TEL. 14,000–20,000 ptas. ($93.80–$134) double. Rates include breakfast. AE, MC, V. Parking 1,000 ptas. ($6.70). Bus: 50 from airport.

Under the arches of an arcade beside the old city's medieval moat stands the entrance to the Hotel Saratoga. Constructed in 1962 and renovated in 1992, the hotel features bright, well-furnished guest rooms, many with balconies or terraces with views of the bay and city of Palma. The mostly midsize bedrooms have fine linens and mattresses, and each of the tiled bathrooms is well maintained. The hotel has two pools—a small wading pool in the courtyard and a large rooftop pool. The Saratoga has a dining room and a seventh-floor bar, where live music and dances are presented.

✪ **San Lorenzo.** San Lorenzo, 14, 07012 Palma de Mallorca. ☎ **971-72-82-00.** Fax 971-71-19-01. www.fehm.es/pmi/sanlorenzo. E-mail: sanlorenzo@ fehn.es. 6 units. A/C MINIBAR TV TEL. 18,000–23,000 ptas. ($120.60–$154.10) double; 29,000–31,000 ptas. ($194.30–$207.70) suite. AE, DC, MC, V.

This small, attractive hotel is set in the middle of the maze of winding streets that form the old city of Palma. The building is 18th century and the decor is a pleasant mixture of traditional Majorcan and modern. The rooms are airy, painted white, and have good-size, comfortable beds, satellite television, safes, and bathrooms that include hair dryers. All rooms have beamed ceilings and while some only have balconies, the more luxurious offer fireplaces and a private terrace. There is an indoor bar but the real bonus is a pool, surrounded by lush foliage and a sun terrace—it's perfect for relaxing after sightseeing or shopping.

Inexpensive

Costa Azul. Passeig Marítim, 7, 07014 Palma de Majorca. ☎ **971-73-19-40.** Fax 971-73-19-71. www.jehm.es/pmi/costa. E-mail: costa@arrakis.es. 126 units. A/C TV TEL. 12,700–15,750 ptas. ($85.10–$105.55) double. AE, MC, V. Bus: 3 or 21.

Head here for a bargain—despite the reasonable rates, you'll get views of the yachts in the harbor. This place isn't glamorous, but it does offer good value. A short taxi ride will deposit you at night on the Plaça Gomila in El Terreno with its after-dark diversions. Barren, well-worn rooms are clean, but furnished in very modest style, although each comes with a good bed. On the ground floor is a bar and restaurant, very Iberian in decor, offering buffet meals three times a day. A tiny pool on the third floor is heated for winter visitors who are, often booked in here on package tours from England.

Hotel Majórica. Carrer Garita, 3, 07015 Palma de Majorca. ☎ **971-40-02-61.** Fax 971-40-59-06. 153 units. A/C MINIBAR TV TEL. 9,000–21,000 ptas. ($60.30–$140.70) double. Rates include breakfast. AE, DC, MC, V. Bus: 3, 20, 21, or 22.

One of the island's older hotels, originally dating from the 1930s, the Majórica rises five floors and lies in the hills overlooking Palma Bay. It offers airy, pleasantly furnished rooms, many with views of the marina. Rooms range from small to midsize; beds, although well worn, still have some comfort in them. The food is generous, although hardly gourmet. The hotel also contains two bars plus one pool. A minibus takes guests to the beach or into the center of Palma.

Hotel Rosamar. Joan Miró, 74, 07015 Palma de Majorca. ☎ **971-73-27-23.** Fax 971-28-38-28. www.illes.balears.net/rosamar. 37 units. 6,650–6,900 ptas. ($44.55–$46.25) double. Rates include breakfast. MC, V. Bus: 3, 4, 21, or 22.

Hotel Rosamar, right on the main road in the boomtown El Terreno district, is popular with Germans and Scandinavians. Fresh, clean but small bedrooms have balconies overlooking a front patio surrounded by tall palm trees—the focus of the social life of the young, lively crowd that frequents the Rosamar. There's a stand-up bar off the lobby.

Hotel Sol Inn Jaime III. Passeig Majorca, 14B, 07012 Palma de Majorca. ☎ **971-72-59-43.** Fax 971-72-59-46. 88 units. A/C MINIBAR TV TEL. 15,000 ptas. ($100.50) double. AE, DC, MC, V. Bus: 8.

This modern hotel has a pleasant contemporary lobby, a cafeteria, and a ground-floor cafe that usually spills out onto the sidewalk. All of the small double rooms have sun terraces and basic contemporary furnishings, including good beds. The hotel stands at the end of the major shopping street of Palma.

At Illetas

This suburb of Palma lies immediately west of the center.

Hotel Bon Sol. Paseo de Illetas, 30, 07015 Illetas. ☎ **971-40-21-11.** Fax 971-40-25-59. 130 units. A/C MINIBAR TV TEL. 16,000–24,160 ptas. ($107.20–$161.85) double; 24,000–33,960 ptas. ($160.80–$227.55) suite. AE, DC, MC, V. Closed Oct. Free parking.

Set across from a beach, about 4 miles (6km) west of Palma, this four-star hotel was built in 1953 and renovated last in 1997. It charges less than hotels with similar amenities, and it's quite popular with vacationing families, who dine within the airy, somewhat spartan dining room. The core is a four-story, white-sided masonry tower, with some of the suites clustered into a simple collection of outlying villas. The hotel overlooks a garden, adjacent to the sea, with three swimming pools (two of them filled with seawater) and two tennis courts. The midsize bedrooms are larger than you might expect, efficient but comfortable and well suited to beachfront vacations.

Hotel Meliá de Mar. Paseo Illetas, 15, 07015 Calvia. ☎ **971-40-25-11.** Fax 971-40-58-52. 144 units. A/C MINIBAR TV TEL. 33,400–37,000 ptas. ($223.80–$247.90) double; 85,000–99,500 ptas. ($569.50–$666.65) suite. AE, DC, MC, V. Parking 1,500 ptas. ($10.05).

Originally built in 1964, and renovated most recently in 1998, the Meliá de Mar is one of the most comfortable (albeit expensive) hotels in Palma. This seven-story, four-star hotel is close to the beach and sports a large garden. The marble-floored lobby and light, summery furniture offer a cool refuge from the hot sun and a calm, deliberately uneventful setting that's evocative of some of the spa hotels of Central Europe. Bedrooms, mainly midsize, have many fine features, including private safes, original art, terra-cotta tiled balconies, marble or wrought-iron furnishings, excellent beds, and marble-clad bathrooms with plush towels, deluxe toiletries, hair dryers, and dual basins.

Dining/Diversions: A bar and a large, airy restaurant boast lots of space between tables and flavorful, but not particularly fussy, food.

Amenities: Swimming is available within an impressive pool, with the Mediterranean as a backdrop. The grounds have tennis and handball courts. Concierge, dry cleaning/laundry, massages, baby-sitting, currency exchange, valet parking.

At Portocolom

This hotel lies on the eastern coast, reached by going east from Palma along C-717, then cutting north at the signposted directions.

✪ **Hotel Villa Hermosa/Restaurant Vista Hermosa.** Carretera Felanitx-Portocolom, km 6, 07670 Portocolom. ☎ **971-82-49-60.** Fax 971-82-45-92. 15 units. A/C MINIBAR TV TEL. 29,980 ptas. ($200.85) double; 39,480 ptas. ($264.50) suite. Rates include breakfast. AE, DC, MC, V. From Portocolom, follow signs to roads leading northeast to Felanitx.

This is one of the most creative five-star hotels on Majorca—a 1993 adaptation of what was originally a 19th-century farm. But it's not rustic; the building and outbuildings were recently reconstructed to profit from views that soar from the high-altitude hillside. Evocative of a severe, dignified monastery, set on elaborate terraces cut into the rocky hillside, the building (which has only 10 accommodations and a quite deliberate sense of privacy) wraps around a large, heated swimming pool. Bedrooms come in various shapes and sizes and each is exceedingly well furnished, with excellent beds and immaculately kept bathrooms with plush towels.

Dining: The in-house restaurant, Vista Hermosa, is the convivial center of social life here. Even if you aren't staying, you won't be alone if you opt for a meal—it's been booked solid virtually every night for at least a year. Meals are served daily from 1 to 3:30pm and from 7 to 10:30pm. There is an à la carte menu as well as a fixed-price menu for 6,000 ptas. ($40.20). Menu items are continental and sophisticated: maigret of duck flambéed in Calvados; loin of pork with basil and bacon; and fresh salmon with a confit of tomatoes.

Amenities: Swimming pool, on-site tennis courts, a small health club, room service, concierge.

At Santa Maria

✪ **Read's Hotel.** Ca'n Moragues, 07320 Santa Maria. ☎ **971-14-02-61.** Fax 971-14-07-62. www.todoesp.es/reads. E-mail: readshotel@mail.todoesp.es. 25 units. A/C TV TEL. 17,000–38,000 ptas. ($113.90–$254.60) double; 32,000–48,000 ptas. ($214.40–$321.60) suite. Rates include breakfast. AE, DC, MC, V. Free parking.

Peacefully located in beautiful countryside, this hotel is only 11 miles from Palma on the way to Inca Alcudia. The 16th-century Majorcan villa is now run by a British family and is a favorite spot for well-heeled Northern Europeans. The building has been carefully renovated and furnished with a combination of good quality reproduction furniture as well as genuine antiques. An unspoiled view of the Tramuntana Mountains forms the backdrop to the hotel, which is surrounded by gardens. The beamed ceilings and wooden shutters add an authentically traditional touch to the bedrooms, which have all been recently refurbished and painted in a variety of subtle Mediterranean colors. They are decorated with prints of classical architecture and Turkish rugs on traditional stone floors. There are various categories of rooms and the four deluxe doubles and 10 suites have French doors opening onto terraces with stunning views. The beds are all extremely comfortable and the bathrooms well stocked with hair dryers and plush towels. Four reception rooms include the extraordinary blue room with trompe l'oeil clouds painted on the walls and what was previously the olive pressing room, the *tafona,* in which the original fittings have been preserved.

Dining: The hotel restaurant attracts foodies from Palma, and in summer diners can be served on an elevated terrace. Although a little pricey, the food is excellent and there is a special menú del día, without wine, of 7,000 ptas. ($46.90) which allows diners to choose any three dishes from the menu for the three courses. The tasting menu ranges from 9,000 to 12,000 ptas. ($60.30 to $80.40), depending on whether wine is included.

Amenities: Indoor and outdoor swimming pool, sun terrace, Jacuzzi, tennis court, horse riding, satellite television, and bar.

At Puigpunent

✪ **Gran Hotel Son Net.** 07194 Puigpunent, Majorca. ☎ **971-14-70-00.** Fax 971-14-70-01. www.sonnet.es. E-mail: son.net@jet.es. 24 units. A/C MINIBAR TV TEL. 32,000–42,250 ptas. ($214.40–$283.10) double, 95,000–123,500 ptas. ($636.50–$827.45) suite. AE, DC, MC, V. Free parking.

For those wanting a combination of total relaxation and luxury, this is the perfect destination. The 17th-century manor house is located next to a nature reserve and nestles in a lush mountain valley 9 miles (14km) from Palma. It was converted from a private residence in 1998 by David Stein, a California tycoon and art collector. The result is one of Europe's best hotels. Apart from the glorious setting, the hotel boasts works by artists such as Hockney, Stella, and Christoph, and there's even a small Chagall on the walls. A classical Majorcan aristocratic sense of decoration has been followed faithfully, with white walls, stone floors, and dark wood beams and shutters. The bedrooms are spacious, the largest being 495 feet (150m) square, and all have satellite television. The bathrooms are fully equipped with necessities such as hair dryers and also glamorous novelties such as antisteam mirrors. There are several reception rooms and an immense terrace with a seductive, curvaceous swimming pool of equally grandiose proportions. On Sunday, mass is said in the hotel's private chapel.

Dining: One of the very best features of the hotel is the Sa Tafona restaurant, which is in the old olive pressing room and which serves delicious food. Main courses range from 2,500 to 5,000 ptas. ($16.75 to $33.50), and there is a tasting menu for 7,000 ptas. ($46.90), wine extra.

Amenities: 24-hour room service, beauty salon, gym, sauna, Jacuzzi, tennis court, pool, access to the Internet.

WHERE TO DINE

The most typical main dish of Majorca is *lomo,* or pork loin, and it appears as the specialty in any restaurant offering Majorcan cuisine. *Lomo con col* is a method of preparation where the loin is enveloped in cabbage leaves and served with a sauce made with tomatoes, grapes, pine nuts, and bay leaf.

A sausage, *sabrasada,* is made with pure pork and red peppers. Paprika gives it its characteristic bright red color. *Sopas mallorquínas* can mean almost anything, but basically it is mixed greens in a soup flavored with olive oil and thickened with bread. When *garbanzos* (chickpeas) and meat are added, it becomes a meal in itself.

The best known vegetable dish is *el tumbet,* a kind of cake with a layer of potato and another of lightly sautéed eggplant. Everything is covered with a tomato sauce and peppers, then boiled for a while. Eggplant, often served stuffed with meat or fish, is one of the island's vegetable mainstays. *Frito mallorquín* might include anything, but basically is a dish of fried onions and potatoes, mixed with red peppers, diced lamb liver, "lights" (lungs), and fennel. It's zesty to say the least.

In the Balearic islands, only Majorca produces wine. But this wine isn't exported. The red wine bottled around Felanitx and Binissalem adds Franja Roja and Viña Paumina to your wine list. Most of the wine, however, comes from Spain. *Café carajillo—* coffee with cognac—is a Spanish specialty particularly enjoyed by Majorcans.

Expensive

Diplomatic. Carrer Palau Reial, 5. ☎ **971-72-64-82.** Reservations recommended. Main courses 1,800–2,600 ptas. ($12.05–$17.40); fixed-price menu 1,300 ptas. ($8.70). AE, DC, MC, V. Mon–Fri 9am–10pm, Sat 9am–5pm. Bus: 1, 3, or 15. CONTINENTAL.

In the center of Palma, near the cathedral, this restaurant is an ideal spot for just about anything, from tapas to a full meal. Its fixed-price menu is of good value, although ordering à la carte is expensive. Set in a white stuccoed medieval building with exposed beams, it offers an intimate atmosphere. Start with pâté with green peppercorns. Next try sole with almonds, steak tartare, or the filet mignon in port wine. The owner and wine connoisseur Juan Contesti will be happy to help you select a vintage from his cellar to accompany your meal.

✪ **Koldo Royo.** Avinguda Gabriel Roca, 3. ☎ **971-73-24-35.** Reservations required. Main courses 1,500–2,600 ptas. ($10.05–$17.40); fixed-price menu (lunch only) 3,600 ptas. ($24.10); tasting menu 5,800 ptas. ($38.85). AE, MC, V. Mon–Fri 1:30–3:30pm, Mon–Sat 8:30–11:30pm. BASQUE.

This is the premier place to enjoy savory Basque cuisine; if you're baffled by the unusual dishes on the menu, a staff member will assist you. This big-windowed establishment lies about ¾ mile south of Palma's cathedral, adjacent to a marina and one of the island's most popular beaches. Menu items run the gamut of Basque seafood dishes, including baked hake, tripe, lamprey eel, and roasted pork. Meal after meal, Koldo Royo serves the best food within Palma itself.

La Lubina. Muelle Viejo, s/n. ☎ **971-72-33-50.** Reservations recommended. Main courses 1,500–6,000 ptas. ($10.05 $40.20); fixed-price menu 2,200 ptas. ($14.75). AE, DC, MC, V. Daily 12:30–4pm and 8pm–midnight. Bus: 1, 4, or 21. SEAFOOD.

La Lubina's location on the old pier is responsible for the freshest seafood in Palma. Begin with an aperitif in the tiled bar and then dine in either the formal dining room or the more casual enclosed terrace. Although the menu consists mainly of seafood, La Lubina is known for its unique preparation and presentation. *Caldereta* (lobster served in an almond broth) is an excellent choice. Try the traditional Majorcan fish *en papillote* (baked in paper and encrusted with salt) or the grilled swordfish.

Lonja del Pescado (Casa Eduardo). Muelle Viejo, s/n. ☎ **971-72-11-82.** Reservations required. Main courses 1,000–4,000 ptas. ($6.70–$26.80). AE, MC, V. Tues–Sat 1–3:30pm and 8–11pm. Bus: 1 or 4. SEAFOOD.

Thriving since the 1930s, this no-frills restaurant serves the catch of the day, taken directly from the boat to the kitchen. Specialties include seafood paella and *zarzuela*

A Special Treat

Dating from 1700, **Can Juan de S'aigo,** carrer Sans, 10 (☎ 971-71-07-59), is the oldest ice-cream parlor on the island. Correspondingly elegant and old world, it serves its homemade ice creams (try the almond), pastries, cakes, *ensaimadas* (light-textured and airy specialty cakes of Palma), fine coffee, and several kinds of hot chocolate amid marble-top tables, lots of wood, beautiful tile floors, and an indoor garden with a fountain.

(a fish stew). It's also possible to get fresh lobster. The rest of the menu consists of various types of fish, most prepared in the Majorcan style.

✪ **Mediterráneo 1930.** Passeig Marítimo, 33. ☎ **971-73-03-77.** Reservations recommended. Main courses 1,700–2,500 ptas. ($11.40–$16.75); fixed-price menu 2,200 ptas. ($14.75). AE, MC, V. Daily 1–4pm and 8–11:30pm. Bus: 1. MEDITERRANEAN.

Named after the art deco, 1930s-era styling that fills its interior, this is a well-managed, artfully hip restaurant adjacent to the Hotel Meliá Victoria. One of the top two restaurants in Palma, with a sense of chic that's defined by its cosmopolitan owners Juan and Mary Martí, it contains a beige and white decor that's filled with verdant plants and art deco sculptures. The menu relies heavily on seafood, with special emphasis on fish that is slowly baked in a salt crust, a process that adds a light-textured flakiness to even the most aromatic fish. Another specialty is beefsteak cooked on a hot stone that's carried directly to your table, and then served with such sauces as béarnaise, pepper, or port.

Porto Pí. Joan Miró, 174. ☎ **971-40-00-87.** Reservations required. Main courses 1,100–2,900 ptas. ($7.35–$19.45). DC, MC, V. Mon–Sat 1–3:30pm and 7:30–11:30pm. Bus: Palma-Illetas. MODERN MEDITERRANEAN.

This restaurant, a favorite of King Juan Carlos, occupies an elegant 19th-century mansion above the yacht harbor at the west end of Palma. Contemporary paintings complement the decor, and there is also an outdoor terrace. The food has a creative Mediterranean influence. Specialties change with the season but might include house-style fish en papillote, angelfish with shellfish sauce, and quail stuffed with foie gras cooked in a wine sauce. Game is a specialty in winter.

✪ **Tristán.** Port Portals, Portals Nous. ☎ **971-67-55-47.** Reservations required. Main courses 1,500–4,200 ptas. ($10.05–$28.15). AE, DC, MC, V. Daily 1–3:30pm and 8:30–11pm. Closed mid-Nov to mid-Dec. Bus: 22. NOUVELLE CUISINE.

Several miles southwest of Palma, Tristán overlooks the marina of Port Portals. This is the finest restaurant in the Balearics, winning a coveted two stars from Michelin, a designation previously unheard of in the archipelago. The sophisticated menu varies depending on what was best in the market that day. Selections may include pigeon in rice paper, a medley of Mediterranean vegetables, or the catch of the day, usually prepared in Majorcan style. But this is mere recitation. What it doesn't prepare you for is the exceptional burst of flavor when you sample the chef's creations.

Moderate

Arroseria Sacranca. Passeig Marítim, 13. ☎ **971-73-74-47.** Reservations recommended. Main courses 950–3,000 ptas. ($6.35–$20.10). AE, DC, MC, V. Tues–Sun 1–4pm and Tues–Sat 8pm–midnight. Bus: 1. SEAFOOD.

This sophisticated, bilingual restaurant has a setting overlooking the port. Arroseria Catranca (whose name translates as "Rice Restaurant Catranca") specializes in seafood, which in many cases is mixed with rice and served in 16 different variations. The best way to appreciate its somewhat offbeat charm involves beginning a meal with either grilled baby sardines or a well-seasoned version of *buñuelos de bacalau* (minced and herb-laden codfish formed into rounded patties). Either of these might be followed with a *parillada*—an array of grilled fish and shellfish—or any of the above-mentioned rice casseroles. Two of the best of them include black rice with squid and squid ink; or a particularly succulent version with spider crabs, clams, and mussels. Other variations include vegetables, roasted goat, or hake with tomatoes and garlic.

Caballito del Mar (Little Seahorse). Passeig de Sagrera, 5. ☎ **971-72-10-74.** Reservations recommended. Main courses 1,000–5,300 ptas. ($6.70–$35.50); menú del día 1,900 ptas. ($12.75). AE, DC, MC, V. Tues–Sun 1–4pm and 7pm–midnight. Bus 5. SEAFOOD.

Although there are several outdoor tables, many guests prefer to dine inside because of the lively spirit of this popular place along the seafront. The decor is vaguely nautical, and the activity is sometimes frenzied, but that's part of its charm. The food is well prepared from fresh ingredients; specialties include a Majorcan version of bouillabaisse, a *zarzuela* (fish stew), assorted grilled fish (our favorite), oysters in season, red bream baked in salt, or sea bass with fennel. If you want something other than seafood, try the duck in orange sauce.

Es Parlament. Carrer Conquistador, 11. ☎ **971-72-60-26.** Reservations recommended. Main courses 1,000–2,600 ptas. ($6.70–$17.40). No credit cards. Mon–Sat 1–4pm and 8–11pm. Closed Aug. Bus: 15. MAJORCAN.

Es Parlament is noted for serving the island's finest paella. The chef is proud of the half-dozen paella dishes, including "blind-man's paella," made without bones or shells, and "black paella," with the added ingredient of squid ink providing both coloring and extra flavoring. The restaurant, with its belle epoque ambience, is housed in the Balearic Autonomous Parliament building.

Inexpensive

Cellar Pagés. Carrer Felipe Bauzá, 2. ☎ **971-72-60-36.** Reservations recommended. Main courses 750–1,400 ptas. ($5.05–$9.40); fixed-price menu 1,100 ptas. ($7.35). AE, DC, MC, V. Mon–Sat 1–4pm and 8:30–11pm. Bus: 15. MAJORCAN.

The set menu here can include soup, noodles, or gazpacho; steak or fish; and dessert, bread, and wine. From the à la carte menu you can select the fish of the day, which most guests prefer grilled. Other dishes include the classic kidneys in sherry or a roast chicken. Admittedly, this isn't the best cooking on the island, but the price is right. The rustic setting is cramped and intimate, with original paintings on the white stucco walls. The location is 75 yards west from the cathedral, a short walk from Plaça de la Reina.

La Casita. Joan Miró, 68. ☎ **971-73-75-57.** Reservations recommended. Main courses 900–2,500 ptas. ($6.05–$16.75); fixed-price menus 1,000–1,500 ptas. ($6.70–$10.05). AE, DC, MC, V. Tues–Sun 1–4pm, and 7pm–midnight. Closed Aug. Bus: 3. FRENCH/AMERICAN.

La Casita claims to serve French and American specialties, although the American influence is a bit hard to decipher. The ceiling fans, exposed wood, and paintings by John Winn-Morgan contribute to the ambience. À la carte dishes include French onion soup, tournedos with mushroom sauce, frogs' legs, pepper steak, and potato pancakes. For dessert, try the homemade apple pie.

Mesón Can Pedro. Carrer Rector Vives, 4. Génova. ☎ **971-40-24-79.** Reservations recommended. Main courses 625–1,900 ptas. ($4.20–$12.75). AE, DC, MC, V. Daily 1pm–1am. Bus: 4. MAJORCAN.

This restaurant has thrived since the early 1970s from a location within a hilltop suburb (Génova) overlooking Palma. A completely unpretentious local favorite, it's known for a bustling, animated atmosphere that's enhanced by odors wafting in from kitchens known for a succulent version of roasted baby lamb. Also worthwhile are T-bone steaks, roasted pork, spit-roasted chickens, spicy sausages, and different preparations of veal. One regional dish worth sampling is savory snails prepared with fennel and garlic, and served with dollops of aioli.

Svarta Pannan. Carrer Brondo, 5. ☎ **971-72-10-39.** Reservations recommended. Main courses 950–2,300 ptas. ($6.35–$15.40). AE, DC, MC, V. Mon–Fri noon–4pm and 7–10:30pm, Sat noon–4pm. Bus: 15. SWEDISH/INTERNATIONAL.

In the center of Palma, on a narrow, traffic-clogged street of the Plaça Pio XII, this restaurant caters to the culinary tastes of most of the countries of Scandinavia, serving *frikadeller* and marinated herring, as well as Wiener schnitzels and flambéed pepper steaks. Everything about it, including the lilting accent of the Swedish-born owner, is guaranteed to stave off homesickness for visiting Nordics, and the visiting Yank can even order a burger and a beer, just like he or she might have back home. Show up early as this establishment's easygoing cosmopolitanism and low prices tend to draw big crowds.

Palma After Dark

Palma is packed with bars and dance clubs. Sure, there are some fun hangouts along the island's northern tier, but for a rocking, laser- and strobe-lit club, you'll have to boogie in Palma.

Set directly on the beach, close to a dense concentration of hotels, **Tito's,** Passeig Marítimo (☎ **971-73-00-17**), charges a cover of 1,500 ptas. ($10.05), including the first drink. A truly international crowd gathers to mingle on a terrace overlooking the Mediterranean. This club is the most popular, panoramic, and appealing disco on Majorca. If you only visit one nightclub during your time on the island, this is it. Between June and September, it's open every night of the week between 11pm and at least 4am. The rest of the year, it's open only on Friday and Saturday, from 11pm to 4am.

Bar Barcelona, Carrer Apuntadores, 5 (☎ **971-71-35-57**), a popular jazz club, evokes its namesake city with its spiral staircase and atmospheric, subdued lighting. Despite its location, in the heart of Palma's busiest nightlife area, it attracts a predominately local crowd who come to enjoy the live jazz on show every night from 11pm to 3am. There is no cover charge, and drinks are reasonably priced, making this one of Palma's best values for a night out. It's open every night till 4am.

B.C.M., Avinguda Olivera, s/n, Magaluf (☎ **971-13-15-46**), is the busiest, most lighthearted, and most cosmopolitan disco in Majorca. Boasting high-tech strobe lights and lasers, this is a sprawling, three-story venue that offers a different sound system on each floor, giving you a wide variety of musical styles. If you're young, eager to mingle, and like to dance, this place is for you. The cover charge of 2,000 ptas. ($13.40) includes your first drink and entitles you to party till 4am.

Come and enjoy a Caribbean cocktail with one of Palma's more charismatic bar owners, Pasqual, who may just invite you to dance a bit of salsa at **Bodeguida del Medio,** Paseo el Mar, Cala Ratjada (no phone). The music is Latin inspired and the crowd is a mix of locals and visitors from almost everywhere. Try their delicious "mojito" cocktail, more potent than it tastes. Inside is rustic in tone, outside is more intimate and romantic with Chinese lanterns illuminating the garden, which overlooks the sea.

ABACO, carrer Sant Joan, 1 (☎ **971-71-59-11**), just might be the most opulently decorated nightclub in Spain—a cross between a harem and a czarist Russian church. The bar is decorated with a trove of European decorative arts. The place is always packed, with many customers congregating in a beautiful courtyard, which has exotic caged birds, fountains, more sculpture than the eye can absorb, extravagant bouquets, and hundreds of flickering candles. All this exoticism is enhanced by the lushly romantic music (Ravel's *Bolero*, at our last visit) piped in through the sound system. Whether you view this as a bar, a museum, or a sociological survey, be sure to go. The bar is open daily from 9pm to 2:30am, February through December only. Wandering around is free; however, drinks cost a whopping 1,500 to 2,100 ptas. ($10.05 to $14.05).

At the end of the Andraitz motorway, adjacent to the Cala Figuera turnoff, the **Casino de Majorca,** Urbanización Sol de Mallarca, s/n, Costa del Calvía (☎ **971-13-00-00**), is the place to go in search of lady luck. The cover charge is 650 ptas. ($4.35); floor show with dinner but without drinks 7,900 to 8,500 ptas. ($52.95 to $56.95); floor show without dinner but with two drinks 5,900 ptas. ($39.55). Children under 12 receive discounts of 50%. If you bring your passport, you can indulge in American or French roulette, blackjack, dice, or you can simply pull the lever on one of the many slot machines. A glittery cabaret show is styled in the fashion of Monte Carlo and accessible through a separate entrance from the section of the casino that's devoted to gambling. It's presented every Monday through Saturday at 10:30pm. You might want to precede this with dinner, which is served beginning at 8pm, although we usually prefer to dine elsewhere on the island, then arrive in time for the show at 10:30pm. The casino's gambling facilities are open Sunday through Thursday 8pm to 4am, and Friday and Saturday 8pm to 5am.

Although Majorca is generally a pretty permissive place, it doesn't have the gay scene that Ibiza does. Still, two of Palma's most noteworthy gay bars include **Sombrero,** Avenida Joan Miró, 26 (☎ **971-73-16-00**), a music pub attracting a predominately lesbian crowd, and **Baccus,** carrer Lluis Fábregas, 1 (☎ **971-45-77-89**), catering to both gays and lesbians. Both of them are open nightly from 9pm to at least 3am, and often later. Neither charges a cover and beers in both sites begin at 400 ptas. ($2.70). If you feel like dancing, the largest and most popular disco in Palma is **Black Cat**, Avenida Joan Miró, 75 (no phone), which attracts a mixed crowd of young locals as well as visitors from both Spain and the rest of the world. There are nightly shows at 3:30am. It is open daily from midnight to 6am but doesn't begin to get crowded until 2am. It is closed on Mondays over the winter. Admission is 1,000 ptas. ($6.70).

EXPLORING MAJORCA BY CAR: THE WEST COAST

Mountainous Majorca has the most dramatic scenery in the Balearics. It's best appreciated if you have your own car and can explore easily on your own. Below, we'll outline a good day-long outing of about 88 miles (142 km) that begins and ends in Palma.

Leave Palma heading west on C-719, passing through some of the most beautiful scenery of Majorca. Just a short distance from the sea rises the Sierra de Tramontana. The road passes the heavy tourist development of Palma Nova before coming to **Santa Ponça,** a town with a fishing harbor divided by a promontory. A fortified Gothic tower and a watchtower are evidence of the days when this little harbor suffered repeated raids and attacks. It was in a cove here that Jaume I's troops landed on September 12, 1229, to begin the reconquest of the island from the Muslims.

From Santa Ponça, continue along the highway, passing Paguera, Cala Fornells, and Camp de Mar, all beautiful spots with sandy coves. Between Camp de Mar and Port D'Andratx are corniche roads, a twisting journey to **Port D'Andratx.** Summer vacationers mingle with fishers in this natural port, which is set against a backdrop of pines. Once the place was a haven for smugglers.

Leaving the port, continue northeast along C-719 to reach **Andratx,** 3 miles (5km) away. Because of frequent raids by Turkish pirates, this town moved inland. Lying 19 miles (31km) west of Palma, Andratx is one of the loveliest towns on the island, surrounded by fortifications and boasting a Gothic parish church and the mansion of Son Mas.

After leaving Andratx, take C-710 north, a winding road that runs parallel to the island's jagged northwestern coast. It's the highlight of the trip; most of the road is perched along the cliff edge. It's hard to drive and pay attention to the scenery at the same time. Pine trees often shade this corniche road. Stop at the **Mirador Ricardo Roca,** for a panoramic view of a series of coves. These coves are reached only from the sea.

The road continues to **Estallenchs,** a town of steep slopes surrounded by pine groves, olive and almond trees, and fruit orchards (especially apricot). Estallenchs sits at the foot of the Galatzo mountain peak. Stop and explore some of its steep, winding streets on foot. From the town, you can also walk to the Cala de Estallenchs cove, where a spring cascades down the high cliffs.

The corniche road winds on to **Bañalbufar,** 5 miles (8km) from Estallenchs and about 16 miles (26km) west from Palma—one of the most scenic spots on the island. Set 110 yards above sea level, it seems to perch directly over the sea. ✪ **Mirador de Ses Animes,** a belvedere constructed in the 17th century, offers a panoramic view of the coastline.

Many small excursions are possible from here. You might want to venture over to **Port d'es Canonge,** reached by a road branching out from the C-710 to the north of Bañalbufar. It has a beach, a simple restaurant, and some old fishers' houses. The same road takes you inland to **San Granja,** a mansion that was originally constructed by the Cistercians as a monastery in the 13th century.

Back on C-710, continue to **Valldemossa,** the town where the composer Frédéric Chopin and the French writer George Sand spent their now-famous winter. After a visit to the **Cartuja** (Cathusian monastery), where they lived, you can wander at leisure through the steep streets of the old town. The cloister of **Ses Murteres** provides a romantic garden, and there is also a pharmacy where Chopin, who was ill a lot during that winter, spent much time. The **Carthusian Church** is from the late 18th and early 19th centuries. Goya's father-in-law, Bayeu, painted the frescoes of the dome.

Beyond Valldemossa, the road runs along cliffs some 1,300 feet high until they reach **Son Marroig,** the former residence of Archduke Luis Salvador (see below), which is actually within the town limits of Deià. He erected a small neoclassical temple on a slope overlooking the sea to give visitors a panoramic vista. Son Marroig, his former mansion, has been turned into a museum. From an arcaded balcony, you can enjoy a view of the famous pierced rock, the Foradada, rising out of the water.

By now you have reached **Deià,** where a series of small tile altars in the streets reproduces scenes from the Calvary. This was the home for many years of the English writer Robert Graves. He is buried at the **Campo Santo,** the cemetery, which you may want to visit for its panoramic view, if nothing else. Many other foreign painters, writers, and musicians have found inspiration in Deià. For living and dining, this is the choice spot on Majorca, a virtual Garden of Eden.

Continue north along the highway. You come first to **Lluch Alcari,** which Archduke Salvador considered one of the most beautiful spots on earth. Picasso retreated here for a short period in the '50s. The settlement was once the victim of pirate raids, and you can see the ruins of several defense towers.

C-710 continues to **Sóller,** just 6 miles (10km) from Deià. The urban center has five 16th-century facades, an 18th-century convent, and a parish church of the 16th

Travel Tip

If you're not driving, you can still reach Sóller aboard a turn-of-the-century narrow-gauge railroad train from Palma. It's a spectacularly scenic 3-minute ride. You can catch the train at the Palma Terminal on calle Eusebio Estada, near Plaça d'Espanya. It runs every hour on the hour from 9am to 7pm daily, and the fare is 380 ptas. ($2.55) each way. Call ☎ 971-75-20-51 for information.

and 17th centuries. It lies on a broad basin where citrus and olive trees are abundant. Many painters, including Rusiñol, settled here and found inspiration.

Travel 3 miles (5km) north on C-711 to reach the coast and **Port de Sóller,** one of the best of the natural shelters along the island. It lies at the back of a bay that is almost round. A submarine base is here today, but it is also a harbor for pleasure craft. It also has a lovely beach. The **Sanctuary of Santa Catalina** dominates one of the best views of the inlet.

Reached up a flight of stairs, **Restaurante Jaime,** carrer Archiduque Luis Salvador, 13 (☎ **971-63-90-29**), attracts both foreign visitors and the family trade. This unpretentious, family run restaurant, in business since 1964, would make a good lunch stop in high-priced Deià. Grilled meats and fresh fish are a specialty. Even if you don't want a full meal, consider stopping here for dessert, such as the almond cake with almond ice cream, before finishing your drive. Hours are Tuesday through Sunday noon to 3pm and 7 to 11pm.

After leaving the Sóller area, you face a choice. If you've run out of time, you can cut the tour in half here and head back along C-711 to Palma with two stops along the way, or you can continue north, following the C-710 and local roads, to **Cape Formentor,** where even more spectacular scenery awaits you. Among the highlights of this coastal detour: **Fornalutx,** a lofty mountain village with steep cobbled streets, Moorish-tiled roofs, and groves of almond trees; the splendid, hair-raising road to the harbor village of **Sa Calobra,** plunging to the sea one minute, then climbing arduously past olive groves, oaks, and jagged boulders; and the 13th-century **Monasterio de Lluch,** some 28 miles (45km) north of Palma, which is home to the Black Virgin of Lluch, the island's patron saint. The well-known "boys' choir of white voices" sings there daily at noon and again at twilight.

Those ending the tour at this point can head south along C-711 with a stopover at **Jardins d'Alfàbia,** carretera Palma-Sóller km 17a, former Muslim residence. This estate is located in the foothills of the sierra and includes both a palace and romantic gardens. The gardens are richly planted, and you can wander among pergolas, a pavilion, and ponds. Inside the palace you can see a good collection of Majorcan furniture and an Arabic coffered ceiling. The gardens are open June through August, Monday through Friday from 9:30am to 6:30pm, and Saturday 9:30am to 1pm; September through May, Monday through Friday from 9:30am to 5:30pm, and Saturday 9:30am to 1pm. Admission is 400 ptas. ($2.70).

From Alfàbia, the highway becomes straight and Palma lies just 11 miles (18km) away. But before reaching the capital, consider a final stop at **Raixa,** another charming place, built on the site of an old Muslim hamlet. It stands 1 mile (1.6km) outside the village of Buñola ("small vineyard"). The present building was once the estate of Cardinal Despuif, and his family, who constructed it in the Italian style near the end of the 1700s. Ruins from Roman excavations are found on the grounds. Rusiñol came here, painting the place several times. It keeps the same hours as Jardins d'Alfàbia (see above).

After Raixa, the route leads directly to the northern outskirts of Palma.

VALLDEMOSSA & DEIÀ (DEYÁ)

Valldemossa is the site of the ✪ **Cartoixa Reial,** Plaça de las Cartujas, s/n (☎ **971-61-21-06**), where George Sand and the tubercular Frédéric Chopin wintered in 1838 and 1839. The monastery was founded in the 14th century, but the present buildings are from the 17th and 18th centuries. After monks abandoned the dwelling, the cells were rented to guests, which led to the appearance of Sand and Chopin, who managed to shock the conservative locals. They occupied cells 2 and 4. The only belongings left are a small painting and a French piano. The peasants burned most of it after the couple returned to the mainland, fearing they'd catch Chopin's tuberculosis. It may be visited Monday through Saturday 9:30am to 6pm for 1,200 ptas. ($8.05) adults, free for children under 10. Off-season it shuts down an hour earlier.

It's also possible to visit the **Palau del Rei Sancho,** next door to the monastery, on the same ticket. This is a Moorish retreat built by one of the island kings. You'll be given a guided tour of the palace by a woman in Majorcan dress.

From Valldemossa, continue through the mountains following the signposts for 6½ miles (10.5km) to Deià. But before your approach to the village, consider a stopover at **San Marroig** (☎ **971-63-91-58**), at the km 26 mark on the highway. Now a museum, this was once the estate of Archduke Luis Salvador. Born in 1847, the archduke fled court life and found refuge here with his young bride in 1870. A tower on the estate is from the 1500s. Many of his personal furnishings and mementos, such as photographs and his ceramic collection, are still here. The estate is surrounded by lovely gardens, and there are many panoramic views on the property. It is open April to October, Monday through Saturday from 9:30am to 2pm and 3 to 8pm (closing at 6pm in winter). Admission is 350 ptas. ($2.35).

Set against a backdrop of olive-green mountains, **Deià (Deyá)** is peaceful and serene, with its stone houses and creeping bougainvillea. It has long had a special meaning for artists, notably Robert Graves, the English poet and novelist (*I, Claudius* and *Claudius the God*) who once lived here, until his death in 1985. He is buried in the local cemetery.

After walking through the old streets, you can stand on a rock overlooking the sea and watch the sun set over a field of silvery olive trees and orange and lemon groves. Then you'll know why painters come here to live on the slopes of a 4,000-foot mountain.

Valldemossa lacks basic services, including a tourist office. It is connected to a bus service from Palma, however. **Bus Nord Balear** (☎ 971-26-24-75) goes to Valldemossa five times daily for a one-way fare of 250 ptas. ($1.70). Buses leave from Palma at the bar at carrer Arxiduc Salvador, 1.

To reach Deià by public transportation from Palma, 17 miles (27km) away, just stay on the bus that stops in Valldemossa. If you're driving from Palma, take the carretera Valldemossa-Deià to Valldemossa; from here, you can continue on to Deià. Those with cars may want to consider one of the idyllic accommodations offered in this little Majorcan village, which has very few tourist facilities outside of the hotels.

WHERE TO STAY

Deià offers some of the most tranquil and stunning retreats on Majorca—La Residencia and Es Molí—but it has a number of inexpensive little boarding houses as well.

Expensive

✪ **Hotel Es Molí.** Carretera de Valldemossa, s/n, 07179 Deià. ☎ **971-63-90-00.** Fax 971-63-93-33. www.fehm.es/hoteles/esmoli. E-mail: esmoli@fehm.es. 87 units. A/C MINIBAR TV TEL. 25,000–29,000 ptas. ($167.50–$194.30) double; 50,400–54,400 ptas. ($337.70–$364.50) suite. Supplement for a balcony 3,600 ptas. ($24.10) per room per day.

Rates include breakfast; half board 2,500 ptas. ($16.75) extra per person per day. AE, DC, MC, V. Free parking. Closed early Nov to late Apr.

One of the best-recommended and most spectacular hotels on Majorca originated in the 1880s as a severely dignified manor house in the rocky highlands above Deià, home of the landowners who controlled access to the town's freshwater springs. In 1966 the manor house was augmented with two annexes, transforming into this luxurious four-star hotel. Bedrooms are beautifully furnished, monochromatic, and impeccably maintained, often with access to a private veranda overlooking the gardens or the faraway village. Some hardy souls make it a point to hike for 30 minutes to the public beach at Deià Bay; others wait for the shuttle bus to take them to the hotel's private beach, 4 miles (6 km) away.

Dining: The in-house restaurant, Ca'n Quet, has a stone-and-timber veranda with a view looking down the hillside (see recommendation under "Where to Dine," below).

Amenities: Room service, concierge; emphasis on multilingual, multicultural catering to clients and their needs; it also has one of the most appealing swimming pools in Majorca, fed from the freshwater springs that used to sustain the village; private beach 4 miles (6 km) from hotel; tennis court on premises.

✪ **La Residencia.** Son Moragues, s/n, 07179 Deià. ☎ **971-63-90-11.** Fax 971-63-93-70. E-mail: laresidencia@atlas-iap.es. 63 units. A/C TEL. 23,000–40,000 ptas. ($154.10–$268) double; 43,500–107,000 ptas. ($291.45–$716.90) suite. Rates include breakfast. AE, DC, MC, V. Free parking.

This is the most stylish, hip, elegant hotel on Majorca, a renowned hostelry that became even more famous in the early 1990s when it was acquired by British businessman and founder of Virgin Airlines Richard Branson. The ambience is luxurious but unpretentious at these two tawny, stone, 16th-century manor houses, surrounded by 13 acres of rocky Mediterranean gardens. Guests have included everyone from Queen Sofia and the emperor of Japan to America's rock-and-roll elite. Spacious bedrooms are outfitted with rustic antiques, terra-cotta floors, romantic-looking four-poster beds, and in some cases, beamed ceilings, all with luxurious appointments including plush towels and luxury mattresses. Open hearths, deep leather sofas, wrought-iron candelabra, and a supremely accommodating staff make this hotel internationally famous. Although it's technically defined as a four-star resort and a member of Relais & Châteaux, only the lack of such room amenities as minibars and TVs prevents it from reaching five-star status.

Dining/Diversions: The more formal of the resort's two restaurants, **El Olivo,** lies within and around an antique olive press. Its award-winning cuisine is usually concocted from fresh local ingredients. The bar evokes the private salon of an arts-conscious landowner interested in abstract and surreal paintings. A less formal Mediterranean bistro, Son Fony, operates from both beside the pool (at lunch in summer) and within a bistrolike Mediterranean area near the pool.

Amenities: Room service (8am to midnight), a concierge well versed in acquiring virtually anything, an elliptical 100-foot swimming pool lined with subtropical plants and bougainvillea; plus a tennis court. Access to the beach, less than a mile away as the crow flies, requires a winding downhill minivan ride.

Inexpensive
Hotel Costa d'Or. Lluch Alcari, s/n, 07179 Deià. ☎ **971-63-90-25.** Fax 971-63-93-47. 30 units. 9,500 ptas. ($63.65) double. Rates include breakfast. MC, V. Closed Nov–Apr 1.

This former villa, 1 mile (1.6km) north of Deià on the road to Sóller, has the best possible view of the vine-covered hills and the rugged coast beyond. Surrounded by private gardens filled with fig trees, date palms, and orange groves, this old-fashioned hotel is furnished with odds-and-ends furniture, but it's clean and comfortable. Most rooms have good views, and all come with good beds and tidy, small bathrooms. Good home-cooked meals are served in the restaurant.

WHERE TO DINE

El Olivo at La Residencia (see above) is one of the top three dining choices on the entire island, and you may opt to dine there even if you aren't a pampered guest at the hotel.

✪ **Can Costa.** Carretera Valldemossa-Deià, s/n. ☎ **971-61-22-63.** Reservations recommended. Main courses 1,000–2,000 ptas. ($6.70–$13.40). AE, DC, MC, V. Wed–Mon noon–4pm and 7:30–11pm. MAJORCAN/INTERNATIONAL.

This restaurant specializes in Majorcan cuisine but includes some international dishes to please the mostly foreign patronage. The owner has selected only the finest of wines from the island itself, which he has wisely combined with some good vintages from Rioja. The hearty regional fare includes roast pork loin with mushrooms from the fields and even thrush enveloped in cabbage. Try for a seat on the outdoor patio, with a panoramic vista of the coast.

Can Quet. Carretera de Valldemossa-Sóller. ☎ **971-63-91-96.** Reservations required. Main courses 1,800–3,000 ptas. ($12.05–$20.10). AE, MC, V. Tues–Sun 1–4pm and 8–midnight. Closed Dec–Mar. INTERNATIONAL.

This restaurant, belonging to the Hotel Es Molí (see above), is one of the most sought-after dining spots on the island. Set on a series of terraces above a winding road leading out of town, the building is well scrubbed, modern, and stylish but with an undeniably romantic air. Cascades of pink geraniums ring its terraces, and if you wander along the sloping pathways you'll find groves of orange and lemon trees, roses, and a swimming pool ringed with neoclassical balustrades.

There is a spacious and sunny bar, an elegant indoor dining room with a blazing fire in winter and alfresco dining on the upper terrace under an arbor. The food is well prepared and the portions generous. Meals can include a salad of marinated fish, terrine of fresh vegetables, fish crepes, shellfish stew, duck with sherry sauce, and an ever-changing selection of fresh fish.

Jaime. Carrer Arxiduc Luis Salvador, 13. ☎ **971-63-90-29.** Reservations recommended. Main courses 1,500–3,500 ptas. ($10.05–$23.45). AE, DC, MC, V. Mar–Oct, Tues–Sun 1–3pm and 7–10:30pm. Jan–Feb, Tues–Sun 1–3:30pm and Sat 7–10pm. Closed Nov–Dec. MAJORCAN.

Prices in Deià tend to be expensive, but this reasonably priced restaurant offers a good-quality cuisine. Local families come here to dine, mingling with the foreign visitors. They usually begin with *sopa mallorquinas* (Majorcan soup), perhaps followed with arroz brut. The specialties are always tenderloin of pork, several variations of codfish, a worthwhile roster of fresh fish based on market availability, and a dessert specialty of almond-flavored cake.

INCA

About 17 miles (27km) north of Palma is Inca, the island's second-largest city and Majorca's market and agricultural center.

Thursday is market day for farming equipment and livestock, but visitors will be more interested in the variety of low-priced leather goods—shoes, purses, jackets, and coats—sold here. In general, stores in Inca selling these leather goods are open Monday through Friday from 9:30am to 7pm and on Saturday from 9:30am to noon.

Modernization has deprived Inca of its original charm, but the parish church of Santa María la Mayor and the convent of San Jerónimo hold some interest, as does the original Son Fuster Inn, a reminder of an earlier, simpler era.

From Palma, trains (☎ 971-50-00-59) run Monday through Saturday at the rate of 40 per day and 32 on Sunday. Trip time is only 40 minutes. A round-trip ticket costs 510 ptas. ($3.40).

Inca lies on C-713, the road leading to the Pollença-Formentor region.

WHERE TO DINE

Cellar Can Amer. Carrer Paul, 39. ☎ **971-50-12-61.** Main courses 850–1,900 ptas. ($5.70–$12.75). AE, MC, V. Mon–Sat 1–5pm, and 7pm–midnight; Nov–May, Sun 1–5pm. MAJORCAN.

If you can stay for lunch or dinner, we recommend this charming spot. In this building dating from 1850, you'll find the most authentic cueva (cave) dining on the island. A container of local wine, which everyone here seems to drink, is tapped from one of the dozens of casks that line the stone walls of the vaults. The interconnected dining rooms are furnished with wooden tables and rustic artifacts. A polite staff serves large portions of Majorcan specialties, including *lechona frit* (a mélange of minced pork offal fried and seasoned), bread and vegetable soup, Majorcan codfish, thrush wrapped in cabbage leaves, and the chef's version of roast suckling pig with a bitter but tasty sauce. There is also an array of fresh seafood and fish.

PORT DE POLLENÇA/FORMENTOR

Beside a sheltered bay and between Cape Formentor to the north and Cape del Pinar to the south lies Port de Pollença, amid two hills: Calvary to the west and Puig to the east. From the town, the best views of the resort and the bay are from Calvary Chapel. The bay provides excellent waterskiing and sailing. The location is 40 miles (65km) north of Palma.

A series of low-rise hotels, private homes, restaurants, and snack bars lines the very attractive beach, which is somewhat narrow at its northwestern end but has some of the island's finest, whitest sand and warmest, clearest water. For several miles along the bay there is a pleasant pedestrian promenade. There is only one luxury hotel in the area, however, and that is out on the Formentor Peninsula.

Tons of fine white sand were imported to the beach at the southeastern end of Pollença Bay to create a broad ribbon of sunbathing space that stretches for several miles along the bay. Windsurfing, waterskiing, and scuba diving are among the water sports offered in the area.

Cabo de Formentor, "the devil's tail," can be reached from Port de Pollença via a spectacular road, twisting along to the lighthouse at the cape's end. Formentor is Majorca's fjord country—a dramatic landscape of mountains, pine trees, rock, and sea, plus some of the best beaches in Majorca. In Cape Formentor, you'll see miradores, or lookout windows, which provide panoramic views.

ESSENTIALS

GETTING THERE   Five buses a day leaving the Plaça Espanya in Palma pass through Inca and continue on to Port de Pollença.

You can continue on from Deià (see above), along C-710, or from Inca on C-713 all the way to Pollença.

VISITOR INFORMATION   The **tourist information office** (☎ 971-89-26-15), on carretera de Arta, is open May through October, Monday through Saturday from

9am to 7pm. It's closed off-season. From March to April and November another office can answer telephone queries (☎ **971-54-72-57**).

EXPLORING THE COAST

The plunging cliffs and rocky coves of Majorca's northwestern coast are a stunning prelude to Port de Pollença. The **Mirador de Colomer** provides an expansive view of the striking California-like coast that stretches from Punta de la Nau to Punta de la Troneta and includes El Colomer (Pigeon's Rock), named for the nests in its cave.

But it is the 12½-mile (20km) stretch of winding, at times vertiginous, road leading from Port de Pollença to the tip of the **Formentor Peninsula** that delivers the island's most intoxicating scenic visions. Cliffs more than 650 feet high and spectacular rock-rimmed coves embrace intense turquoise waters. About halfway along this road is the **Cala de Pi de la Posada,** where you will find the Hotel Formentor (see review below) and a lovely bathing beach. Continuing on to the end you'll come to the lighthouse at **Cabo de Formentor.**

Wednesday is **market day** in Port de Pollença, so head for the town square (there's only one) from 8am to 1pm and browse through the fresh produce, leather goods, embroidered tablecloths, ceramics, and more. Bargaining is part of the fun. Sunday is market day in the town of Pollença.

Alcúdia Bay is a long stretch of narrow, sandy beach with beautiful water backed by countless hotels, whose crowds rather overwhelm the area in peak season. The nightlife is more abundant and varied here than in Port de Pollença.

Between Port de Alcúdia and Ca'n Picafort is the **Parc Natural de S'Albufera,** carrertera Alcúdia-Artá, km 27, 07458 C'an Picafort (no phone). A wetlands area of lagoons, dunes, and canals covering some 1,975 acres, it attracts bird watchers and other nature enthusiasts. To date, more than 200 species of birds have been sighted here, among them herons, owls, ospreys, and warblers. The best times to visit are spring and fall, when migratory birds abound. Spring, too, offers a marvelous display of flora. The park is open daily, except Christmas, from October 1 to March 30 from 9am to 5pm, and from April 1 to September 30 from 9am to 7pm. Visits are free, but you must get a permit at the reception center, where all motorized vehicles must be left. Binoculars are available for rent. The reception center has further information.

In the town of Pollença, about 4 miles (6km) from Port Pollença, is an 18th-century stairway leading up to an *ermita* (hermitage). Consisting of 365 stairs, it is known as the **Monte Calvario** (Calvary), but you can also reach the top by car via carrer de las Cruces, which is lined with 10-foot-high concrete crosses.

Cala San Vicente, between Pollença and Port de Pollença, is a pleasant, small sandy cove with some notable surf. Several small hotels and restaurants provide the necessary amenities.

Various companies offer tours of Pollença Bay, and many provide glass-bottom boats for viewing the varied aquatic creatures and plants. Many of these boats leave from Port de Pollença's Estació Marítim several times daily during the summer months, with less frequent departures in winter. Your hotel concierge or the marina can provide you with a schedule.

Part of the allure of a trip to the Balearics is boating in the Mediterranean; if you're in the market to rent either a small sailing craft or a glamorous yacht that comes with a full complement of staff and crew, **Associación Provinciale d'Empresarios de Actividades Marítimas de Baleares,** Muelle Viejo, 6, in Palma (☎ **971-72-79-86**), can steer you in the right direction. Chances are that they'll direct you to either of two well-respected maritime charter companies, both based in Palma. They are

Moorings Formentor, Contramuelle, 12 (☎ 971-71-09-49), and **Alga Charter,** Plaza Jardines San Telmo, s/n (☎ 971-71-64-28). Either will lease boats of various sizes by the day, week, or month.

If you want to go windsurfing, head for **Ski Costa Calvia,** carrer Estornell, 2, Sonferrer/Calvia (☎ 971-23-03-28), which is located about 9 miles (14km) southeast of Palma.

WHERE TO STAY
In Puerto Pollença

Hotel Illa d'Or. Passeig Colón, 265, 07470 Port de Pollença. ☎ **971-86-51-00.** Fax 971-86-42-13. 120 units. A/C MINIBAR TV TEL. 12,000–26,000 ptas. ($80.40–$174.20) double; 32,000–50,000 ptas. ($214.40–$335) suite. Rates include breakfast. AE, DC, MC, V. Closed Jan 9–Feb 11. Free parking.

Originally built in 1929, and enlarged and improved several times since then, this four-story hotel sits at the relatively isolated northwestern edge of Pollença Bay—far from the heavily congested, touristed region around Palma. Decorated in a mixture of colonial Spanish and English reproductions, it offers a seafront terrace with a view of the mountains and airy, simply furnished bedrooms. Rooms are midsize to spacious, each with comfortable furnishings including good beds. There are two swimming pools on the premises, and the beach is just a few steps away. A bar and two restaurants set the scene for socializing.

Hotel Miramar. Passeig Anglada Camarasa, 39, 07470 Port de Pollença. ☎ **971-86-64-00.** Fax 971-86-40-75. 84 units. A/C TEL. 14,000–17,500 ptas. ($93.80–$117.25) double. Rates include breakfast. AE, DC, MC, V. Closed Nov–Mar.

This centrally located hotel is one of the grandly old-fashioned hostelries in town, in a desirable position across the coastal road from the beach. It has ornate front columns supporting a formal balustrade, tiled eaves, and several jardinieres. The lobby is furnished with antiques, and the formal dining room has views of the sea. Some rooms have private verandas overlooking the flower-filled courtyard in back. All the small to midsize rooms are comfortably furnished and well maintained, each with a firm bed.

Hotel Pollentia. Passeig de Londres, s/n, 07470 Port de Pollença. ☎ **971-86-52-00.** Fax 971-86-60-34. 70 units. TEL. 12,200–13,800 ptas. ($81.75–$92.45) double. Rates include breakfast. AE, DC, MC, V. Closed Dec–Mar.

This hotel is located half a mile from the commercial center of the resort, behind a screen of foliage. It's our favorite hotel in town because of its cool, airy spaciousness and the genial reception. The steps leading to the formal modern lobby are banked with dozens of terra-cotta pots overflowing with ivy and geraniums. The reception area has Majorcan glass chandeliers, and many of the well-furnished but small rooms have private terraces. Guests have access to a private terrace overlooking the Mediterranean, and the dining room offers a fine fixed-price meal of regional dishes.

In Cabo de Formentor

✪ **Hotel Formentor.** Platja de Formentor, 07470 Port de Pollença. ☎ **971-89-91-00.** Fax 971-86-51-55. www.fehm.es/pmi/formentor. E-mail: formentor@fehm.es. 127 units. A/C MINIBAR TV TEL. 35,000–52,000 ptas. ($234.50–$348.40) double; 59,000–75,000 ptas. ($395.30–$502.50) suite. Rates include breakfast; half board 7,200 ptas. ($48.25) per person extra. AE, DC, MC, V. Closed early Jan to early Mar.

Set on an isolated, sprawling, intensely manicured expanse of scrub-covered peninsula that once served as a private farm, Hotel Formentor is one of Europe's most spectacular and exclusive hotels. Far from the madding crowds of Palma, on the island's northern tip, it's elegant and unpretentious. Most of it lies within a long, low-slung three-story building that's more modern-looking than its 1920s origins would imply. It has hosted an impressive roster of guests, including a 1995 summit meeting of the heads of state for all the countries in the European Union. Stage and film stars, and even the Dalai Lama, have appeared here. Accommodations are classically modern, spacious, and supremely comfortable, with some of the more expensive units containing reproductions of Iberian antiques that include elaborately carved beds.

Dining/Diversions: Most guests prefer to dine outdoors most of the year, enjoying a regional and international cuisine on the tree-shaded terrace. There is also a full formal restaurant inside, plus a beach restaurant, ideal for lunch if you don't want to change out of your bathing suit. The cuisine is among the area's finest. A piano bar is an amusing place for a drink.

Amenities: Terrace gardens descend gracefully to the resort's private beach, although there's a pool on site. Spacious sunbathing area, hairdresser, shops, tennis coach, riding instructor, business corner, health and beauty center, concierge, dry cleaning/laundry, massages, baby-sitting, currency exchange, valet parking, room service.

WHERE TO DINE
In Port de Pollença

Stay Restaurant. Muelle Nuevo, Estació Marítima, s/n. ☎ **971-86-40-13.** Reservations recommended July–Aug. Main courses 1,720–3,500 ptas. ($11.50–$23.45); fixed-price menu 3,980 ptas. ($26.65). AE, MC, V. Daily noon–4pm and 7:30–10:30pm. SPANISH/INTERNATIONAL.

This restaurant offers a unique menu that changes about every 2 months, depending on what's available at the market. Main courses include fresh salmon fillets in a white wine sauce, roasted duck with a green peppercorn sauce, grilled fillet of beef with a sauce of foie gras de *canard* (duckling) and port wine, and our favorite, *parrillada de mariscos,* a platter of assorted grilled fish and seafood. Finish your meal with a strudel of fresh figs, almonds, and raisins smothered in a hot vanilla sauce.

In Pollença

Restaurant Clivia. Avinguda Pollentia, s/n. ☎ **971-53-46-16.** Reservations recommended. Main courses 2,000–3,000 ptas. ($13.40–$20.10). AE, DC, MC, V. Tues and Thurs–Sun 1–3pm, daily 7:30–11:30pm. Closed Nov 15–Dec 15. MALLORQUINA/SPANISH.

This is the best and most appealing restaurant in Pollença, even attracting a clientele from other districts of Majorca. The restaurant is composed of two dining rooms and an outdoor patio in a century-old house in the heart of town. It has a scattering of antique furniture and a tactful, well-organized staff that produces a limited list of meats (veal, chicken, pork, and beef) and a more appealing roster of seafood prepared with skill and finesse. Specialties depend on the availability of fish such as cod, monkfish, dorado, eel, squid, and whitefish, either baked in a salt crust or prepared as part of a succulent *parrillada* (platter) of shellfish that's among the freshest anywhere. Begin with a spicy fish soup and accompany it fresh vegetables such as asparagus or spinach. The restaurant's name derives from the variety of bright red flowers (*las clivias*) that are planted profusely beside the patio and that bloom throughout the summer.

MAJORCA'S EAST COAST: THE CAVA ROUTE
The east coast of Majorca is often called the cava route because of the caves that stud the coastline. Though there are scores, we'll include only the most important ones; other places mentioned are Manacor, where cultured Majorcan pearls are manufactured, and Petra, home of Fray Junípero Serra, founder of many California missions.

In general, the east coast of Majorca does not have the dramatic scenery of the west coast but has worthy attractions in its own right.

Leave Palma on the freeway but turn onto carretera C-715 in the direction of Manacor. About 35 miles (56km) east of Palma, you come to your first stop, Petra.

PETRA

Petra was founded by Jaume II over the ruins of a Roman settlement. This was the birthplace of Father Junípero Serra (1713–84), the Franciscan priest who founded the missions in California that eventually grew into San Diego, Monterey, and San Francisco. A statue commemorates him at the Capitol building in Washington, D.C., and you will also see a statue of Father Serra in this, his native village.

Museo Beato Junípero Serra, carrer Barracar (☎ **971-56-11-49**), gives you an idea of how people lived on the island in the 18th century. The property was bought and fixed up by the San Francisco Rotary Club, which then presented it as a gift to the citizens of Petra in 1972. The museum, which lies 500 yards from the center of the village, is open every day of the year but doesn't keep regular hours. Visits are by appointment only. Admission is free, but donations are encouraged.

MANACOR

The C-715 continues east to Manacor, the town where the famous artificial pearls of Majorca are manufactured. The trade name for the pearls is "Perlas Majorica," so avoid such knock-offs as "Majorca." You can visit the factories where the pearls are made, and purchase some if you wish. Jewelry here may be 5% to 10% cheaper than at most retail outlets in Barcelona.

The largest outlet is **Perlas Majorica,** Vía Roma, 48 (☎ **971-55-09-00**), which offers organized tours. On the road to Palma at the edge of town, it is open Monday through Friday from 9am to 1pm and 2:30 to 7pm. On Saturday and Sunday, it is open from 9:45am to 1pm. Admission is free. They'll explain how the pearls are made (from fish scales that simulate the sheen of a real pearl). Some 300 artisans work here, shaping and polishing the pearls, and they're used to being inspected by foreign visitors while at work. Perlas Majorica carry a 10-year guarantee.

CUEVAS DEL DRACH

From Manacor, take the road southeast to the sea—about 7½ miles (12km)—and the town of **Porto Cristo,** 38 miles (61km) east of Palma. Go a half mile south of town to **Cuevas del Drach (Caves of the Dragon)** (☎ **971-82-07-53**), which contain an underground forest of stalactites and stalagmites as well as five subterranean lakes, where you can listen to a concert and later go boating à la Jules Verne. The roof appears to glitter with endless icicles. Martel Lake, 581 feet long, is the largest underground lake in the world. E. A. Martel, a French speleologist who charted the then mysterious caves in 1896, described it better than anyone: "As far as the eye can see, marble cascades, organ pipes, lace draperies, pendants or brilliants, hang suspended from the walls and roof." Tours depart daily, every hour from 10am to 5pm. Admission is 1,000 ptas. ($6.70).

If you don't have a car, you can take one of the four daily buses that leave from the railroad station in Palma (inquire at the tourist bureau in Palma for times of departure). The buses pass through Manacor on the way to Porto Cristo.

CUEVAS DEL HAM

Discovered in 1906, these caves, whose name means "fish hooks," lie half a mile from Porto Cristo on the road to Manacor. **Cuevas del Ham** (☎ **971-82-09-88**) are far less impressive than the Cuevas del Drach and can be skipped if you're rushed. Tours depart every 15 minutes daily all year from 10am to 6pm, charging 1,400 ptas. ($9.40) admission for adults, but nothing for children under 12. These caves contain white stalactites and follow the course of an underground river. There is a link to the sea, so the water level inside the cave's pools rises and falls according to the tides.

CUEVAS DE ARTÁ

Near Platja de Canyamel (Playa de Cañamel on some maps), ✪ **Cuevas de Artá** (☎ 971-84-12-93) lie on a stretch of land closing Canyamel Bay to the north. They are reached by a corniche road. These caves are said to be the inspiration for the Jules Verne tale *Journey to the Center of the Earth,* published in 1864. (Verne may have heard or read about the caves; it is not known if he ever actually visited them.) Formed by seawater erosion, the caves lie about 35 yards above sea level, and some of the rooms rise about 150 feet.

You enter an impressive vestibule and immediately see walls blackened by the torches used to light the caves for early tourists in the 1800s. There follows the *Reina de las Columnas* (Queen of the Columns), rising about 72 feet tall, then a lower room whose Dante-esque appearance has led to it being called "Inferno." It is followed by a field of stalagmites and stalactites, the "Purgatory rooms," which eventually lead to the "theater" and "paradise."

The caves were once used by pirates, and centuries ago provided a haven for Spanish Moors fleeing the persecution of Jaume I. The stairs in the cave were built for Isabella II for her 1860 visit. In time, such luminaries as Sarah Bernhardt, Alexandre Dumas, and Victor Hugo arrived for the tour. Tours depart daily, every half-hour from 10am to 6pm. Admission is 1,000 ptas. ($6.70).

2 Ibiza

Ibiza (Ee-*bee*-tha) was once a virtually unknown and unvisited island; Majorca, its bigger neighbor, got all the business. But in the 1950s, Ibiza's art colony began to thrive, and in the 1960s it became the European resort most favored by the flower children. A New York art student once wrote, "Even those who come to Ibiza for the 'wrong' reason (to work!) eventually are seduced by the island's easy life. Little chores like picking up the mail from the post office stretch into day-long missions." Today, Ibiza is overrun by middle-class package-tour tourists, mainly from England, France, Germany, and Scandinavia, and it has also become a major mecca for gay travelers, making it a wild combination of chic and middle-class.

At 225 square miles, it is the third largest of the Balearic Islands. Physically, Ibiza has a jagged coastline, some fine beaches, whitewashed houses, secluded bays, cliffs, and a hilly terrain dotted with fig and olive trees. Warmer than Majorca, it's a better choice for a winter vacation, but it can be sweltering in July and August. Thousands of tourists descend on the island in summer, greatly taxing the island's limited water supply.

Ciudad de Ibiza boasts Playa Talamanca in the north and Ses Figueretes and Playa d'en Bossa in the south, two outstanding white sandy beaches. Las Salinas, in the south, near the old salt flats, also offers excellent sands. Playa Cavallet and Aigües Blanques attract the nude sunbathers. Other good beaches include Cala Bassa, Port des Torrent, Cala Tarida, and Cala Conta—all within a short bus or boat ride from San Antonio de Portmany. The long sandy cove of Cala Llonga, south of Santa Eulalia del Rio, and the white sandy beach of El Cana to the north, are sacred to Ibiza's sun worshipers. In Formentera, Playa de Mitjorn stretches 3 miles (5km) and is relatively

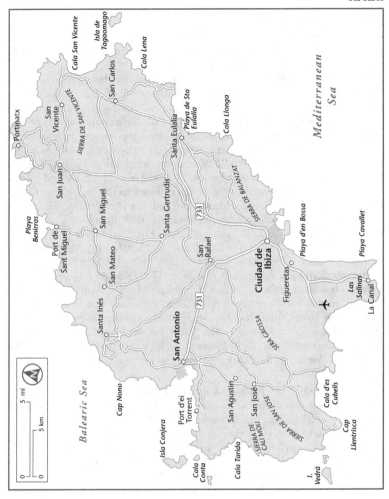

uncrowded. Set against a backdrop of pines and dunes, the pure white sand of Es Pujols is the most popular of Ibiza's beaches and deservedly so.

Many travelers still arrive dreaming of soft drugs and hard sex. Both exist in great abundance, but there are dangers. It's common to pick up the local paper and read the list of the latest group of people deported because of *irresponsibilidad económica* (no money) or *conducta antisocial* (drunk and disorderly conduct). Some young travelers, frankly, have forsaken Ibiza, taking a ferry 40 minutes away (and just 3 miles as the crow flies) to the tiny island of Formentera, where they find less harassment (although anyone looking suspicious will be noticed out here too). Formentera is the most southern of the Balearic Islands, and because of limited accommodations, restaurants, and nightlife, it is most often visited on a day trip from Ibiza.

Eivissa is the local (Catalán) name for Ibiza. Catalán is the most common language of the island, but it is a dialectal variation—called eivissenc or ibicenco. The same language is spoken on Formentera.

ISLAND ESSENTIALS

GETTING THERE   Again, as with Palma, if you come in July and August, be sure you have a return ticket and a reservation. Stories of passengers who were stranded for days in Ibiza in midsummer are legend.

Iberia (☎ 971-80-93-35) flies into **Es Codolar International Airport** (☎ 971-80-90-00), located 3½ miles (5.5km) from Ciudad de Ibiza. Four daily flights connect Ibiza with Palma de Majorca, and five flights a day arrive from Barcelona. It's also possible to take one of two daily flights from Valencia or one of three from Madrid. With the exception of charter flights winging in from virtually everywhere, Iberia is the main carrier servicing Ibiza. Its only other competitor on this route is **Air Europa** (☎ 971-80-91-91 in Ibiza), which offers flights to Ibiza from Barcelona (a maximum of two flights a day), as well as from Madrid and Palma, at intervals much less frequent than those offered aboard Iberia. The price of flights to Ibiza varies considerably because of season, promotion, and availability. Here's an indication of round-trip, coach-class fares on Iberia into Ibiza: from Barcelona, 15,000 to 33,000 ptas. ($100.50 to $221.10); from Palma, 11,000 to 18,000 ptas. ($73.70 to $120.60); from Madrid, 17,000 to 39,000 ptas. ($113.90 to $261.30). From Valencia via Palma, the fare is 15,000 to 27,000 ptas. ($100.50 to $180.90).

Transmediterránea, Avinguda B.V. Ramón (☎ 971-31-36-63), operates a ferry service to Barcelona at the rate of four per week on Monday, Wednesday, Friday, and Saturday, costing 6,050 ptas. ($40.55) for a one-way ticket. One boat per week also departs from Valencia on Thursdays, with a one-way ticket going for 6,090 ptas. ($40.80). From Palma, there are three ferries per week, on Friday, Saturday, and Sunday; it costs 3,045 ptas. ($20.40) one way. Check with travel agents in Barcelona, Valencia, or Palma regarding ferry schedules. You can also book tickets through any agent.

GETTING AROUND   If you land at Es Cordola airport outside Ciudad de Ibiza, you will find bus service for the 3½-mile (9km) ride into town. Sometimes taxis are shared. In Ciudad de Ibiza, buses leave for the airport from Avinguda Isidor Macabich, 24 (by the ticket kiosk), every hour on the hour daily from 7am to 10pm.

Once in Ibiza, you'll have to walk, but the city is compact and can be covered on foot. There are buses, however, leaving for the nearby beaches. The two main bus terminals are at Avinguda Isidor Macabich, 20 and 42.

One of the most popular means of getting around the island, especially in the south, is by a moped or bicycle. Rental arrangements can be made through **Casa Valentín,** Avinguda B.V. Ramón, Avinguda de la Paz, s/n (☎ 971-31-08-22). Mopeds cost from 1,500 ptas. ($10.05) per day.

If you'd like to rent a car, both Hertz and Avis have offices at the airport.

VISITOR INFORMATION   The **tourist information office** is located at Antonio Riquer, 2, in the port of Ciudad de Ibiza (☎ 971-30-19-00). It is open Monday through Friday 9:30am to 1:30pm and 5 to 7pm, Saturday 10:30am to 1pm. There is another office at the airport (☎ 971-80-91-18), which is open Monday through Saturday 9am to 2pm, 3 to 8pm and Sunday 9am to 2pm.

CIUDAD DE IBIZA

The island's capital, **Ciudad de Ibiza,** was founded by the Carthaginians 2,500 years ago. Today the town consists of a lively marina district around the harbor and an old town (D'Alt Vila) with narrow cobblestone streets and flat-roofed, whitewashed houses. The yacht-clogged marina and the district's main street, Vara de Rey, are constant spectacles—from old fishermen to the local Ibizan women swathed in black to ubiquitous, scantily clad tourists. The marina district is also fun to wander about with its art galleries, dance clubs, boutiques, bars, and restaurants.

Much of the medieval character of the old town has been preserved, in spite of massive development elsewhere. Many houses have Gothic styling and open onto spacious courtyards. These houses, some of which are 500 years old, are often festooned with geraniums and bougainvillea. The old quarter is entered through the Puerta de la Tablas, flanked by Roman statues.

Plaça Desamparadors, crowded with open-air restaurants and market stalls, lies at the top of the town. Traffic leaves town through the Portal Nou.

FUN ON & OFF THE BEACH

BEACHES   The most popular (and overcrowded) beaches are **Playa Talamanca** in the north and **Ses Figueretes** (also called Playa Figueretes) in the south. But you can find more remote, uncrowded spots, and don't be surprised to find a lot of nudity. The best beaches are connected by boats and buses. The remoter ones require a private car or private boat. Both Playa Talamanca and Ses Figueretes are near Ciudad de Ibiza, as is another popular beach, **Playa d'en Bossa** lying to the south.

To avoid the hordes here, keep going until you reach **Las Salinas,** near the old salt flats farther south. Here beaches include **Playa Cavallet,** one of the officially designated nudist strands (nudism doesn't always follow official designations laid down by Ibizan law).

The most horrendously overcrowded beach in Ibiza is **Playa San Antonio** at San Antonio de Portmany—if it got any worse, you'd have to stand up instead of lie down! However, a boat or bus will take you to several beaches southwest of the town, all of which are far less congested. These include **Cala Bassa, Port des Torrent, Cala Tarida, and Cala Conta.**

Santa Eulalia de Rio, site of the third major tourist development in Ibiza, has a less crowded beach, but it's also less impressive. If you stay in this east coast town, you can find a better beach at Cala Llonga in the south or at one of the beaches along the north, including **Playa d'es Caná and Cala Lleña.** These beaches are among the finest on Ibiza.

If you venture to the north coast, you'll discover more good beaches at the tourist developments of **Portinatx,** which is at the very northern tip, and at **Puerto de San Miguel,** which lies north of the small town of San Miguel. The quickest way to reach San Miguel from Ciudad de Ibiza is to go inland via Santa Gerturdis, and then north. Along the way, you'll pass Rio de Santa Eulalia, the only river in the Balearics.

HORSEBACK RIDING   This is a scenic, memorable experience. Two outfitters are **C'an Mayans,** in Santa Gertrudis (☎ **608-63-68-84**), and **Es Buig,** also in Santa Gertrudis (☎ **971-19-71-66**). The price is 1,500 ptas. ($10.05) for a 1-hour ride and an hour's class is 2,000 ptas. ($13.40).

SPORTS & FITNESS   **Ahmara Centro Deportivo,** carretera Sant Josep (km 2.7), on the road to Sant Josep (☎ **971-39-55-06**), offers the best collection of health equipment on the island, along with a swimming pool, hot tub, sauna, and even a Turkish bath with massage. There's a restaurant, grill, and bar, plus four squash courts. Badminton and indoor football are also played here. Tennis courts (and lessons) are also available. The facility's steam room continually receives praise. Sheathed with marble and lavishly carved stone columns, it's been compared to the Roman baths of yore, within a thoroughly modern, thoroughly sybaritic context.

TENNIS   In addition to the better-maintained courts at Ahmara, which were recommended above, you'll find five public tennis courts at Port San Miguel

Ciudad de Ibiza

Calle Mallorca
Avenida Ignacio Wallis
Calle Madrid
Calle Fray Vicente Nicolas
Calle Pedro Frances
C. Dipitado J. Ribas
Calle Carlos III
Calle Felipe II
Calle Carlos V
Avenida Ramon y Tur
Avenida Bme. de Rossello
Calle Madrid
Calle Abad y Lasierra
Plaza Enrique Fajarnes y Tur
C. Bme. Vicente y Ramon
Paseo Vara de Rey
C. Cayetano Soler
C. Jaime I
Calle Vincente D. Serra
C. Obispo Gonzalez Abarca
Calle Obispo Huix
Calle Juan Planells
Baluarte Puerta Nueva
Via Punica
Via Romana
Calle Castilla
Calle Catalunya
Avenida Isidoro Macabich
Calle Extremadura
Calle Canarias
Mercat Nou
Parc de la Pau
Calle Baleares
Calle Aragón
Avenida España
Calle Perez
C. I Tur
Calle de Juan Xico
Calle Murcia
Calle de Juan Ramon Jimenez
PUIG DES MOLINS
C. Pintor Sorolla
Calle Archiduque Luis Salvador
C. Navarra
Calle Ramon Muntaner
Calle Galicia
Passeig Maritim
Playa de Figueretas
Mediterranean Sea

Hotels
Cénit 4
El Corsario 12
Hostal Aragón 3
Hostal Montesol 9
Hotel Royal Plaza 2
La Ventana 15
Los Molinos 5
Sol y Brisa 8

Restaurants
El Brasero 11
El Corsario 12
El Portalón 13

Bars & Clubs
Angelo's 14
Bar Geminis 7
Bar Léon 16
Casino de Ibiza 1
Disco Anforna 10
El Divino Club 1
Montesol hotel Bar 9
Pacha 1
Rstaurant Pomelo 17
The Blue Rose 6

(☎ 971-30-19-00). It's open during daylight hours and are usually unsupervised. No appointments are necessary for access to these courts, but for information about their condition and whether there are players waiting to use them, contact the Hotel Hacienda directly.

SHOPPING

Fashion has been an important Ibiza industry since the late 1960s, when a nonconformist fashion philosophy took hold, combining elements of the traditional *pitiusa* (peasant dress) attire of the natives and the natural, free-flowing garments of the hippies who flocked here in the 1960s. In recent years Ibizan designs have become much more sophisticated and complex, but the individualistic spirit has not wavered.

At the corner of Conde Rosselón, master artisan Pedro Planells creates hand-sewn, original leather goods at **Pedro's,** Carrer Aníbal, 8 (☎ 971-31-30-26). Many items can be custom made. Pedro creates stylish accessories, as well as home furnishings in leather and silver. Well-heeled clients have included everyone from international celebrities to King Juan Carlos. Pedro's keeps conventional Spanish hours, but during the off-season hours and days vary.

The **Sandal Shop,** Plaça De Vila, 2 (☎ 971-30-54-75), sells high-quality leather goods made by a cast of local artisans. One-of-a-kind accessories, including bejeweled belts and leather bags, are designed for individual clients. Custom-made sandals can be created to suit personal fashion tastes.

A FASCINATING MUSEUM

Although Ibiza is primarily a destination for sun and fun, there's also a sightseeing attraction worth a special visit.

Museo Arqueològic de Ibiza y Formentera (Museum of Archaeology). Plaça de Catedral, 3. ☎ **971-30-12-31.** Admission 300 ptas. ($2). Winter, Tues–Sat 10am–1pm and 4–6pm, Sun 10am–2pm; Apr–Oct, Tues–Sat 10am–2pm and 5–8pm, Sun 10am–2pm. Closed holidays.

Located in Ibiza's old town, this museum in a former arsenal houses the world's most important collection of Punic remains. It contains pottery and other artifacts from prehistoric sites in Formentera and Ibiza, and Punic terra-cotta figurines and other items from the sanctuaries of Illa Plana (7th to 5th centuries B.C.) and Cuieram (4th to 2nd centuries B.C.). Also on display are vases, figurines, and other Carthaginian artifacts found in the island's burial grounds. Examples of Roman epigraphs, sculpture, and small glass bottles are included in the exhibit. Other displays include Moorish artifacts (10th to 13th centuries A.D.), various Christian wooden and stone sculptures, plus 14th- to 16th-century ceramics.

WHERE TO STAY

The chances of finding space in peak summer months are dismal, more so than in any Mediterranean resort in Spain. At other overcrowded resorts, such as those on the Costa Brava and Costa del Sol, a visitor faced with the no-vacancy sign can always press on or go inland to find a room for the night. But in Ibiza, because of infrequent transportation, a visitor without a reservation in July and August can land in a trap. You may end up sleeping on the beach on an air mattress (if the police let you; alternatively, there are camping areas), even though your pockets are bulging with pesetas.

The island is not always prepared for its hordes of international tourists. The hotels can't be built fast enough. Many of the hastily erected ones sprouting up in San Antonio de Portmany, Santa Eulalia del Rio—even on the outskirts of Ciudad de Ibiza—are more frame than picture.

Individual bookings in most establishments range from the horrifically difficult to the impossible. In many cases hoteliers don't bother to answer requests for space in summer. Armed with a nice fat contract from a British tour group, they're not interested in the plight of the stranded pilgrim. So if you're set on going to Ibiza during the summer, ***book through a package tour*** to ensure an ironclad reservation. You'll probably find a better bargain, anyway. In the less-busy months, however, using your credit card to reserve a room is enough to guarantee a hotel room upon your arrival.

In Town
In town, hotels are limited and often lack style and amenities, except for the following recommendations.

El Corsario. Carrer Ponent, 5, 07800 Ibiza. ☎ **971-30-12-48.** Fax 971-39-19-53. E-mail: elcorsario@ctv.es. 15 units. MINIBAR. 12,000–22,000 ptas. ($80.40–$147.40) double; 25,000–60,000 ptas. ($167.50–$402) suite. AE, DC, MC, V.

After your taxi deposits you near the church below, you'll have to walk the last 500 feet up a hill to reach this hotel, located within a labyrinth of cobblestone pedestrian walkways. The house was founded in 1570, and it is rumored that its terraces were built by corsairs. The modest rooms are pleasant and clean, often containing antiques. Each of the small, tiled bathrooms is equipped with a hair dryer. Some overlook an enclosed garden of trailing bougainvillea and cultivated flowers. The hotel's restaurant is one of the most romantic places to dine (see restaurant recommendations below). No parking is available.

Hostal Aragón. Carrer Aragón, 54, 07800 Ibiza. ☎ **971-30-60-60.** 6 units, with sink only. TEL. 7,500 ptas. ($50.25) double. No credit cards.

Lleo Marchuet is often cited for running one of the finest and most reasonably priced one-star hotels in town. No meals are served, but many cafes and restaurants are within walking distance. Climb one flight of stairs to enter this simple but clean environment. The small rooms are modestly furnished, but the welcome compensates. All the beds are good, and the maintenance is tidy. Arrangements can be made to accommodate families of four, and TV is available upon request.

Hostal Montesol. Vara de Rey 2. ☎ **971-31-01-61.** Fax 971-31-06-02. 55 units. A/C TV TEL. 12,700 ptas. ($85.10) double. MC, V.

Completely renovated in 1997, this old favorite has prepared itself for a new lease on life. Its proximity to the marina affords panoramic views of the sea and the small rooms are clean and comfortable, though rather sterile. Nonetheless, beds are good and have firm mattresses. This is a good bargain for Ibiza, especially if you plan to spend most of your time exploring the island and not in your room. There's an on-site cafeteria but no restaurant; however, many bistros lie outside your door.

Hotel Royal Plaza. Carrer Pedro Francés, 27-29, 07800 Ibiza. ☎ **800/528-1234** in the U.S., or 971-31-00-00. Fax 971-31-40-95. www.xpress.es/ibizanet/royal. E-mail: royalpla@ xpress.es. 117 units. A/C MINIBAR TV TEL. 13,050–22,700 ptas. ($87.45–$152.10) double; 23,650–42,250 ptas. ($158.45–$283.10) suite. AE, DC, MC, V.

Located 3 blocks from the port, this six-story modern hotel offers in-town convenience plus a casual, resortlike atmosphere. For those who wish to stay within Ciudad de Ibiza, this is the premier choice. The marble reception lobby exudes elegance. Well-appointed accommodations are midsize and carpeted; most have private terraces. Beds are firm and the bathrooms are tidily organized. The rooftop pool offers a sunbathing platform, with commanding views of the port and town of Ibiza.

During the summer months, the **Plaza Snack Bar/Restaurant** serves good meals; snacks are available daily from 11:30am to midnight and meals from 1:30 to 4pm and 8:30 to 11:30pm. The hotel's bar is open daily from 8am to 11pm.

Sol y Brisa. Avinguda B.V. Ramón, 15, 07800 Ibiza. ☎ **971-31-08-18.** 18 units, with sink only. 3,500–5,000 ptas. ($23.45–$33.50) double. No credit cards.

This is an utterly basic hostelry, clean and well maintained by helpful owners. Young people on low budgets are especially fond of this place, which attracts a lot of American students in summer (making it advisable to make a reservation as early as possible). Bedrooms are tiny, with tile floors that somehow make them seem cooler in July and August. Two courtyards are filled with plants in the old style of an *ibicenco* house.

✪ **La Ventana.** Sa Carrossa, 13, Dalt Vila, 07800 Ibiza. ☎ **971-39-08-57.** Fax 971-39-01-45. 14 units. A/C MINIBAR TV TEL. 13,900–26,000 ptas. ($93.15–$174.20) double; 33,700–40,000 ptas. ($225.80–$268) suite. AE, MC, V. Free parking.

This is a perfect name (the window) for what was once a castle and is now a hotel located on the hillside of the old city, overlooking the Mediterranean. What is more, the hotel, peaceful as it is in itself, is one of the best places to obtain tickets for clubs featuring music. The present owners have succeeded in decorating the hotel simply but very stylishly with a mixture of clever lighting, beautiful fittings, and various Asian objets d'art. The bedrooms are painted in wonderful, almost Indian colors, and have great beds with floating canopies of white net. All include bathrooms or shower stalls, have satellite television, and some even offer French doors opening onto balconies. There is a chic bar downstairs and a fantastic terrace on the roof with wide Moroccan-style sofas and an amazing view of the old city and the sea beyond. The hotel also incorporates a small, popular restaurant, which serves Mediterranean/international cuisine and is open for the summer season, from May through October. It is open daily from 7:30pm to 12:30am and main courses range from 1,200 to 3,800 ptas. ($8.05 to $25.45).

In Playa de Ses Figueretes
On the edge of town, a number of modern beach hotels have been erected that are far superior to the ones in the city. With few exceptions, most are booked solidly in summer by tour groups.

Cénit. Arxiduc Lluís Salvador, 07800 Ibiza. ☎ **971-30-14-04.** Fax 971-30-07-54. 63 units. TEL. 7,500–8,500 ptas. ($50.25–$56.95) double. AE, DC, MC, V. Closed mid-Oct through Apr.

Although way down in pecking order from Los Molinos (see below), this is still the bargain place to stay here. Circular in shape, the hotel looks like a quartered wedding cake. In the pueblo style, each floor has been staggered so as to provide a terrace for the rooms above. The small accommodations are routine but comfortable, although the beds are firm. The curved dining room, with its picture windows, is a pleasant place to enjoy a continental breakfast. The Cénit, which has a pool, is perched on a hillside a short walk from the beach.

Los Molinos. Ramón Muntaner, 60, 07800 Ibiza. ☎ **971-30-22-50.** Fax 971-30-25-04. 154 units. A/C MINIBAR TV TEL. 14,500–21,900 ptas. ($97.15–$146.75) double. AE, DC, MC, V. Free parking.

This modern resort is a favorite with snowbirds from the north of Europe. Situated less than a mile from Ibiza town, it's the finest hotel in Ses Figueretes. Nestled between the water and a medieval village, Los Molinos offers resort life combined with proximity to town. The midsize accommodations, most with private terraces facing the sea, are comfortably furnished, with safes, carpets, and twin beds pushed together European style.

Public areas include a dining room with views of the Mediterranean, two bars, and a cafe providing snacks throughout the day. The hotel has two pools (one is heated).

WHERE TO DINE

It's hard to find authentic Ibizan cuisine. The clientele and often the chefs are mainly from continental Europe, and the menu choices cater almost exclusively to their tastes.

Because of the lack of agriculture in some parts of the island, fish has always been the mainstay of the local Mediterranean diet. But budget travelers may be put off by the price of some of this fare. Once the cheapest item you could order on a menu, fish is now one of the most expensive. The fish is sautéed, baked, or broiled and might be blended in a fisher's rice, *arros à la pescadora*. *Parrillada* and *zarzuela* are two stewlike dishes containing a wide assortment of fish.

As in Majorca, pork is important in the diet. Some islanders feed figs to these animals to sweeten their meat, which is turned into such pungent cooked sausages as *sobrasadas* or *longanizas*.

A local dish, occasionally offered on some menus, is a *sofrit pages,* a stew made with three kinds of meat and poultry—chicken, pork, and lamb—then cooked with pepper, cloves, cinnamon, and garlic. One of the best seafood plates is *borrida de rajada,* crayfish in an almond sauce.

The most famous dessert is *flaó,* a kind of cheesecake to which mint and anisette are added for flavoring. *Greixonera* is a spiced pudding, and *maccarrones de San Juan* is cinnamon- and lemon-flavored milk baked with cheese.

Wines are shipped over from the mainland; however, islanders make alcohol-based herbal concoctions. These include *rumaniseta,* made from rosemary, and *frigola,* golden in color and very sweet, with a strong aroma coming from wild thyme. A rather bitter aperitif known as *balo* comes from locally grown carob. For special occasions, islanders treasure *hierbas ibicencas,* made with numerous local herbs, including anise.

El Brasero. Carrer Barcelona, Des Pasadis, 4. ☎ **971-31-14-69.** Reservations required. Main courses 2,000–2,800 ptas. ($13.40–$18.75). MC, V. Daily 8pm–midnight. Closed Oct 16–Apr 30. FRENCH.

This is one of the best-known and most popular places on the island, catering to a wide range of tastes. The cookery is robust and filled with flavor—chicken salad, grilled meats, asparagus gratiné, duckling with honey, beef fillet in hot sauce, and a steamy fish stew. There is also a sidewalk cafe section. It is elegantly decorated in a black-and-white bistro style.

El Corsario. Carrer Ponent, 5. ☎ **971-30-12-48.** Reservations required. Main courses 2,400–4,000 ptas. ($16.10–$26.80); tasting menu 14,000 ptas. ($93.80). MC, V. Daily 8pm–midnight. Closed Nov–Apr. INTERNATIONAL.

Although we've reviewed its accommodations above, the dining room, with its panoramic view, is so romantic that it deserves special mention. This 400-year-old flower-draped villa is near the hilltop fortress. Your taxi will deposit you about 500 feet down the hill in a square fronting an old church, and you must climb the slippery cobblestones to reach it. There's a stand-up bar, two pleasant dining rooms with a handful of neatly laid tables, and a view of the harbor. Menu specialties include various kinds of pasta, two different preparations of lamb, and especially fresh fish brought up from the harbor. The cookery is home style and well prepared, especially if you stick to the fish dishes.

El Portalón. Plaça dels Desamparats, 1-2. ☎ **971-30-39-01.** Reservations recommended. Main courses 800–3,950 ptas. ($5.35–$26.45). AE, DC, MC, V. Mon–Sat 12:30–3:30pm, daily 8pm–12:30am. Closed mid-Jan to mid-Feb. SPANISH/INTERNATIONAL.

Before you hit the bars (go very late, as is the fashion), dine here in the old town. Alfresco courtyard dining is a lure, as is the handsome crowd. El Portalón attracts gay as well as straight couples, usually European. The food is a combination of Spanish, Catalan, and continental. It's expensive, but worth the extra pesetas.

CIUDAD DE IBIZA AFTER DARK

In many ways, **El Divino Club,** Puerto Ibiza Nueva (☎ 971-19-01-76), is the most physically beautiful disco on Ibiza. It prides itself on the supermodels, celebs, and trendies that have graced its premises with their presence. Wear the most hip outfit you packed. The club doesn't open its doors until 11:30am; it remains open nightly until 6am but only June to September. The cover charge is 3,000 ptas. ($20.10) and up.

The crowd at the **Montesol** hotel bar, Vara de Rey, 2 (☎ 971-31-01-61), a short walk from the harbor on the main street, is likely to include expatriates, newly arrived social climbers, and Spaniards along for the view. In many ways this is the greatest circus in town, made more pleasant by the well-prepared tapas and the generous drinks. If you enjoy people-watching, sit at one of the sidewalk tables. Montesol is open daily from 8am to midnight.

Despite its age (it's one of the oldest discos on Ibiza, with a nightlife pedigree that extends back to the 1960s), **Pacha,** Avenida 8 de Agosto, s/n (☎ 971-31-36-12), a spacious split-level disco near the casino, is still hip. Made up of three separate bar areas and dance floors, it continues to attract the young and the not-so-young, the bored, the restless, and the merely jaded. In summer, overheated dancers can cool off in a swimming pool. The music, primarily droning disco and rap, evokes a pounding cadence of jackhammers. Open May through October, daily from midnight to 6am; November through April, Friday and Saturday from midnight to 6am. The cover is a painful 5,000 to 7,000 ptas. ($33.50 to $46.90).

Disco Privelege, Urbanización San Rafael (☎ 971-19-81-60), is a sprawling nightclub built to entertain 5,000, many of whom seem to rush the dance floor simultaneously. Wander from room to room, stopping wherever you feel the urge, as the interior contains more bars, semisecluded patios, and romantic trysting spots than most hotels. Dance music, however, will conspire to keep you on the floor dancing, dancing, dancing. The club is open daily June to September from midnight to 7:30am. The cover is 4,000 to 5,000 ptas. ($26.80 to $33.50), but could be as high as 7,000 to 8,000 ptas. ($46.90 to $53.60) for special events, in particular English Monday nights, when DJs are imported from London.

Ibiza's newest, most controversial, and most appealing erotic club is **The Blue Rose,** carrer Navarra, 27, Figueretas (☎ 971-39-91-37). There's a hefty cover of 5,000 ptas. ($33.50), including your first drink. It occupies what was originally established in the 1960s as the island's first disco. In 1998, amid the same black-and-white floor tiles where flower children used to tune in, turn on, and dance, California-born entrepreneur Joy Borne installed an intensely theatrical, high-class strip joint that's become one of the most popular places on an island that's obsessed with after-dark diversions. Defined as an American-style "Goddess Temple," where none of the exotic *artistes* objects to receiving an occasional bank note while she's on stage, the setting consists of a fireman's pole, equipment for some exhibitionistic acrobatics, and an area committed to exotic, tasteful nudity in a sexually provocative setting. Owned, operated, and for the most part staffed by women, it charges a hefty 5,000 ptas. ($33.50) entrance free, which includes the first drink, and from 1,200 ptas. ($8.05) for each additional cocktail. It is open every night from 11pm till 6am. Although most nights the club is filled with men watching women, Thursday nights feature male dancers performing for women from 11pm to 3am, and male dancers performing for gay patrons from 3am till closing. Most of the dancers come from northern Europe and to a lesser extent, California.

There's gambling by the sea in the modern **Casino de Ibiza,** Passeig Juan Carlos I (Passeig Marítim; ☎ **971-31-33-12**). With the usual gaming tables and slot machines, it's open nightly from 9:30pm to 4am. There's a separate room for slot machines that operate daily from 6pm to 5am. The adjoining nightclub and dining hall offer live cabaret entertainment between May and October, with shows that feature a relatively tame assortment of magicians, comedians, and pretty women in feathers and spangles whose fancy stepping begins at 9:30pm. Casino entrance is 500 ptas. ($3.35); dinner and show will run you about 7,000 ptas. ($46.90). Passport required for admission.

With the possible exception of Mykonos, few other islands in the Mediterranean cater to gay travelers as much as Ibiza. A stroll through the Ciudad Ibiza's old town reveals dozens of gay bars catering to international visitors; most are open from 9 or 10pm to 3am. Although many close and reopen with disconcerting frequency, some of the most deeply entrenched include **Disco Anfora,** carrer San Carlos, 7 (☎ **971-30-28-93**), an *haute-electronic* disco that blares away, to the dancing pleasure of a mostly gay clientele, between midnight and 6am every night in the summer. The cover charge of 1,500 ptas. ($10.05) includes the first drink. More geared toward drinking and talking than dancing is **Bar Léon,** calle de la Virgen, 3 (no phone), and its almost equivalent counterpart, **Bar Geminis,** Figueretas (no phone). Other gay sites include **Angelo's,** carrer Alfonso XII, 11 (no phone), which serves drinks beginning around 9pm every evening, and **Teatro,** calle de la Virgen, 57 (no phone), which has an outdoor bar. And if you're hungry, there's a restaurant in Ciudad Ibiza's inner core, **Restaurant Pomelo,** carrer de la Virgen (☎ **971-31-31-22**), catering to an international clientele with a huge percentage of gay patronage. The restaurant is open Easter through October, from 8pm to between 1 and 2am.

SAN ANTONIO DE PORTMANY

Known to the Romans as Portus Magnus and before that a Bronze Age settlement, this thriving town was discovered in the 1950s by foreigners and has remained popular ever since. Tourism here is "megamass." The town today goes by two names—San Antonio de Portmany for Spanish speakers or Sant Antoni de Portmany for Catalán speakers.

In summer you have as much chance of finding a room here as you would booking a reservation on the last flight to the moon if the earth were on fire. Virtually all the hotels have a direct pipeline to tour-group agencies in northern Europe, and the individual traveler probably won't get the time of day. If you're determined to stay in the area during peak travel season, your best bet is to try and arrange a package tour.

The resort, with a 14th-century parish church, is built on an attractive bay. Avoid the impossibly overcrowded narrow strip of sand at San Antonio itself. Take a ferry or bus to one of the major beaches, including Cala Gració, 1 mile (1.6km) to the north, set against a backdrop of pines, or Port des Torrent, 3 miles (5km) southwest. Cala Bassa in the south is also popular. San Antonio overlooks the Isla Conejera, an uninhabited rock island. With its hordes of visitors, San Antonio has an easygoing lifestyle, plus lots of mildly entertaining nightlife. Even if you're staying in Ibiza or Santa Eulalia, you may want to hop over for the day or evening.

But San Antonio is not for the conservative. It's not unusual to see bottomless women on the beach—and topless women in dance clubs. Note, however, that even though marijuana is common here, buying and selling it is strictly against the law.

When visiting hooligans have had too much cheap booze, San Antonio can get dangerous. In the earlier part of the evening, however, you may want to patronize one of the bars or open-air terraces around Avinguda Doctor Fleming.

ESSENTIALS

GETTING THERE   Buses leave from Ciudad de Ibiza every 30 minutes.

VISITOR INFORMATION   The **tourist information office** is at Passeig de Ses Fonts (☎ **971-34-33-63**). It's open Monday through Friday from 9:30am to 8:30pm and Saturday and Sunday from 9:30am to 1pm May through October. Off-season hours are Monday through Saturday from 9:30am to 1pm.

EXPLORING THE AREA

Throughout the day boats leave from Passeig de Ses Fonts. They will take you to Cala Bassa, a sandy beach on a thin strip, for 600 ptas. ($4) one way, or to Cala Conta, a slightly rocky beach, for 550 ptas. ($3.70). If you negotiate, they'll also take you along the coastline northwest to the far point of Portinatx. This is virtually the only way to see the coastline, since there isn't a road running along it, and most visitors agree it's the most beautiful coastline of Ibiza.

North of the waterfront, the chief attraction is **Sa Cova de Santa Agnès,** a national monument and an object of eerie devotion. This has been a place of sacred worship ever since a sailor prayed to Santa Agnès during a rough storm and was saved. The sailor, to show his gratitude, placed a figure of the saint in this dark hole. It's become a place of pilgrimage ever since, and it's open free on Monday and again on Saturday from 9am to noon.

If you have rented a car you can also explore **Cueva de Ses Fontanelles,** north of Platja Calad Salada, where faintly colorful prehistoric paintings decorate the walls.

Offshore at the popular southern beach of Cala d'Hort is the intriguing **Es Vedrá rock,** where, in times of hardship and hunger, the Ibicencos would go, at great personal risk, to gather seagull eggs for survival. A Carmelite priest once recorded mystical revelations and meetings with "unearthly beings surrounded by light" while meditating on the island. Gigantic circles of light, up to 165 feet in diameter, have allegedly emerged from the sea here at times, discouraging fishers from working the area. It is said that a strong magnetic force emanating from Es Vedrá attracts such strange phenomena. Photographers and romantics take note: After June 15 the sunrise here is especially dramatic, illuminating Es Vedrá while the surrounding hills remain in darkness.

WHERE TO STAY

The prospect of finding a room here in July and August is bleak—some Brits reserve a year in advance. British package tourists virtually occupy the crescent beach and busy harbor all during the warm months. You'll stand a better chance of finding lodgings in Ciudad de Ibiza.

Arenal Hotel. Avinguda Doctor Fleming, 16, 07820 San Antonio. ☎ **971-34-01-12.** Fax 971-34-25-65. 131 units. TEL. 6,500–14,500 ptas. ($43.55–$97.15) double. AE, DC, MC, V. Free parking.

This selection ranks among the top hotels in San Antonio de Portmany, offering value comparable to that of more expensively priced neighbors. During high season groups take over, but in October and from April to mid-May you can generally get a reservation if you write 2 weeks in advance. Off-season all you need to do is arrive.

Located at the edge of town on its own private beach, the Arenal is a four-story establishment with a swimming pool. The rooms are simple and attractive, furnished in contemporary style with comfortable beds and a balcony opening onto the sea or the little front garden lawn with palm trees.

Hotel Village. Apartado, 27, Urbanización Caló den Real (along the road to Cala Tarida), 07830 Sant Josep, Ibiza. ☎ **971-80-80-01.** Fax 971-80-80-27. 18 units. A/C MINIBAR TV TEL. 15,000–27,500 ptas. ($100.50–$184.25) double; 20,500–38,500 ptas. ($137.35–$257.95) suite. Rates include breakfast. DC, MC, V. Free parking.

Located 15 miles west of Ibiza Town, this small, elegant hotel is one of our favorite refuges on the island. Just beyond the gleaming white marble lobby sits a cozy bar, ideal for aperitifs. The midsize guest rooms, also done in white marble, have terraces, most facing the sea, but several open onto the mountains. Each room is very comfortably furnished with adequate living space, plus tidy tiled bathrooms equipped with hair dryers. A walkway leads down the hill to a rocky beach, where guests can lounge in the sun and enjoy a drink at the beachside bar. There is an elegant dining room serving international cuisine with a Spanish influence, and the hotel offers tennis courts, a fitness center, and putting green.

Les Jardins de Palerm. Apartado, 62, 07080 San José, Ibiza. ☎ **971-80-03-18.** Fax 971-80-04-53. www.bestof.org/ibiza/palerm. 9 units. TV TEL. 16,500–24,000 ptas. ($110.55–$160.80) double; 22,000–38,000 ptas. ($147.40–$254.60) suite. Rates include breakfast. AE, DC, MC, V. Closed Nov–Mar.

This intimate little hotel, located outside of the village of San José, is constructed in the style of a 17th-century hacienda. Patios and garden terraces scattered throughout the grounds are ideal locations for sunbathing, enjoying a lazy Ibiza afternoon, and getting away from the noise and bustle of the street. The small accommodations are rustic, with beamed ceilings, antiques, good beds, and ceiling fans. Each unit has its own terrace. Prices change every month—the lowest price quoted above is charged in the cool months of March, the highest tariff for the hot month of August.

Simple meals can be ordered and eaten on the terrace. A large outdoor pool is perfect for a dip in this sultry weather.

Hotel Tropical. Cervantes, s/n, 07820 San Antonio. ☎ **971-34-00-50.** Fax 971-34-40-69. 142 units. TEL. 6,400–9,000 ptas. ($42.90–$60.30) double. Rates include breakfast. AE, DC, MC, V. Closed Nov–Mar.

Located away from the port area in a commercial section of town, this hotel's garden and swimming pool are across the street from its main building. The recreation area is like a small public park with dozens of reclining chairs and some billiard tables. The hotel was built in the early 1960s with a russet- and white-marbled lobby filled with armchairs. The Tropical is rated as one of the best hotels in the center, with comfortably furnished, modernized but rather bland small to midsize bedrooms.

Pikes. Apartado, 104, 07820 San Antonio, Ibiza. ☎ **971-34-22-22.** Fax 971-34-23-12. 26 units. A/C MINIBAR TV TEL. 20,000–27,000 ptas. ($134–$180.90) double; 36,000–100,000 ptas. ($241.20–$670) suite. AE, DC, MC, V. Children under 12 must be accompanied by a parent.

Originally a *finca* (farm), this 600-year-old compound has been transformed into a luxurious playground for well-heeled travelers and celebrities from around the world. Touted for its "sophisticated informality," Pikes boasts spacious rooms with sensuous interiors, including king-size beds and oversized bathtubs. The hotel provides activities and entertainment for its guests ranging from flamenco shows to costume balls. Pikes also provides a VIP card that allows entrance to most of the area's clubs and casinos.

The hotel's restaurant serves an international cuisine in a series of intimate dining rooms. There is a poolside bar for sunbathers, and a tennis court and fitness center as well. Management will arrange boating, golfing, and horseback riding.

WHERE TO DINE

Many of Ibiza's restaurants are tucked away in quiet coves or in the countryside, so you really need a car to sample the full range of the island's culinary savoir-faire.

✪ **Cana Juana.** Carretera Sant Josep km 10, 6 miles (10km) from Ciudad Ibiza, on road to Sant Josep. ☎ **971-80-01-58.** Reservations recommended. Main courses 2,000–3,000 ptas. ($13.40–$20.10). AE, MC, V. Daily 8:30–11:30pm. Closed Nov–Dec. MEDITERRANEAN.

This 240-year-old villa has been converted into the finest restaurant on Ibiza, thanks to the dedicated efforts of owner and chef Juana Biarnes and her husband, co-owner and maître d'hôtel Michel. Before her present role, Juana was one of the first female reporters in Spain, uncovering scandals and presenting new ideas to a Spanish readership before retreating to Ibiza to perfect her cooking skills. Examples of what's available include fillets of skate that are steamed and then grilled for added crispiness and served with strips of Jabugo ham and a confit of onions. Also appealing are such Catalan specialties as codfish with spinach, raisins, and pine nuts; and an earthy but flavorful dish that every Catalan remembers from his or her childhood, *butifarra* sausage served with white beans. Other examples include a confit of canard (duckling) in the French style; baked potatoes served with truffles, and roasted *dorada* (John Dory) served with vinegar, olive oil, garlic, and baby lettuce. The restaurant's cellars contain a sophisticated roster of Spanish and European wines, with a vintage to complement virtually anything.

El Rincón de Pepe. Sant Mateu, 6. ☎ **971-34-06-97.** Reservations not necessary. Tapas 400–1,000 ptas. ($2.70–$6.70); main courses 900–1,900 ptas. ($6.05–$12.75). MC, V. Daily 11am–1:30am. Closed Nov–Easter. TAPAS.

Primarily a place for tapas and light snacks, this friendly cafe also serves a menu that includes Spanish dishes, as well as hamburgers, hot dogs, and a variety of fresh salads. The food is simple and good, the atmosphere convivial, and the bar an attractive arrangement in tile and wood.

Restaurante/Bar Rias Baixas. Carrer Ignacio Riguer, 4. ☎ **971-34-04-80.** Reservations required. Main courses 3,500–5,000 ptas. ($23.45–$33.50). AE, CB, DC, MC, V. Daily 1–4pm, 8pm–midnight. Closed Dec–Feb. GALICIAN.

This rustic air-conditioned Iberian dining room, with its stucco arches, beamed ceiling, and open fireplace, is an apt setting for the Galician specialties served here. Seafood, flown in fresh every day from northern Spain, is the restaurant's specialty— mussels, Galician clams, crabmeat soup, *caldo gallego* (Galician broth), trout meunière, and Bilbao-style eels, each accompanied by a selection of Galician wine. Good-tasting beef, pork, and veal dishes are also available.

Sa Capella. Carretera de Santa Inés 0.5km. ☎ **971-34-00-57.** Reservations recommended. Main courses 1,500–3,000 ptas. ($10.05–$20.10). MC, V. Daily 8pm–midnight. Closed Nov–Mar. MEDITERRANEAN.

This restaurant is set in a 600-year-old chapel with stone vaulting, rose windows, radiating alcoves, balconies, and chandeliers that can be lowered on pulleys from the overhead masonry. You pass beneath an arbor of magenta-colored bougainvillea and are ushered to your table by a waiter dressed in red-and-white traditional Ibizan costume. Meals are flavorful and well versed in the culinary traditions of the Mediterranean. Examples include fresh broccoli as well as exotic mushrooms with strips of Serrano ham; John Dory cooked in a salt crust; roast suckling pig in the style of Segovia; shepherd's style lamb chops served with potatoes and carrots; marinated mussels, roasted rabbit, and pepper steak. Dessert might consist of fresh-made cheesecake garnished with fresh raspberries. Partly because of its historic setting, partly because of its fine food, this dining choice has a deservedly devoted following.

THE NORTHERN COAST

The north remains largely untainted by the scourge of mass tourism, except for a handful of coves. Here you'll find some of the island's prettiest countryside, with fields of olive, almond, and carob trees and the occasional *finca* raising melons or grapes.

EXPLORING THE AREA

Off the road leading into Port de Sant Miquel (Puerto de San Miguel) is **Cova de Can Merca,** about 300 feet from the Hotel Galeón. There is a fine view of the bay from the hotel's snack bar. After a stunning descent down stairs clinging to the face of the cliff, you enter a cave that's more than 100,000 years old and forms its stalactites and stalagmites at the rate of about ¼ inch (1cm) per 100 years. A favored hiding place for smugglers and their goods in former days, today it's a beautifully orchestrated surrealistic experience—including a sound-and-light display—not unlike walking through a Dalí painting. Many of the limestone formations are delicate miniatures. The half-hour tour is conducted in several languages for groups of up to 70. From Holy Week to the end of October, tours are offered daily every half hour from 10:30am to 7:30pm. Admission is 800 ptas. ($5.35) for adults and 400 ptas. ($2.70) for children.

At the island's northern tip is **Portinatx,** a pretty series of beaches and bays now marred by a string of souvenir shops and haphazardly built hotels. For a taste of its original, rugged beauty, go past all the construction to the jagged coast along the open sea.

Every Saturday throughout the year there is a **flea market** just beyond Sant Carles (San Carlos) on the road to Santa Eulalia (you'll know where it is by all the cars parked along the road). Open from about 10am until 8 or 9pm, it offers all kinds of clothing (both antique and new), accessories, crafts, and the usual odds and ends.

If you want to escape to a lovely beach that remains a stranger to hotel construction, head for **Playa Benirras** just north of Port de Sant Miquel. An unpaved but passable road leads out to this small, calm, pretty cove, where lounge chairs are available and pedal boats are for rent. There are also snack bars and restaurants here.

A beautiful drive leads from Sant Carles (San Carlos) along the coast to Cala Sant Vicent (San Vicente).

WHERE TO STAY

Hotel offerings are more limited in the north than in the traditional pockets of tourism in the south and west. Nevertheless, the island's finest hotel, the five-star Hacienda, is here, above Na Xamena Bay. Port de Sant Miquel, Cala Sant Vicent, and Portinatx—once tranquil, seaside havens—have become increasingly pockmarked with package-tour hotels.

Hotel Galeón. Puerto de San Miguel, 07815 Sant Joan de Labritja, Ibiza. ☎ **971-33-45-34.** Fax 971-33-45-35. 189 units. 9,000–13,200 ptas. ($60.30–$88.45) double. Rates include breakfast. AE, V. Closed Nov–Apr. Free parking.

One of two hotels overlooking the little bay, this basic hotel offers simple, clean, comfortable but small guest rooms, each equipped with a good bed. Accommodations have terraces with views of the sea. Tennis courts and water sports are available. The hotel's restaurant serves a good but rather uninspired cuisine.

✪ **Hotel Hacienda.** Na Xamena, 07815 San Miguel, Ibiza. ☎ **971-33-45-00.** Fax 971-33-45-14. www.relaischateaux.fr/xamena. E-mail: htl.hacienda@vlc.servicom.es. 63 units. A/C MINIBAR TV TEL. 21,500–51,000 ptas. ($144.05–$341.70) double; 50,300–125,000 ptas. ($337–$837.50) suite. AE, DC, MC, V. Closed Nov to mid-Apr.

Located 14 miles (22km) northwest of Ciudad de Ibiza, this Moorish villa, set on a promontory overlooking Na Xamena Bay, is the top destination on Ibiza for well-heeled travelers and celebrities seeking leisure and sanctuary. Luxury, informality, privacy, and personal service—the Hacienda has it all. Public rooms are full of various cubbyholes, ideal for cozying up to a book or travel companion. Diners gather at tables beside the large outdoor pool during the warmer months. Spacious guest rooms are individualized, decorated with four-poster beds, sumptuous carpets, and balconies that overlook the Mediterranean. Many rooms have marble bathrooms and private Jacuzzis; all are equipped with hair dryers.

The hotel has an excellent terrace restaurant, **Las Cascadas,** providing panoramic vistas of the surrounding cliffs and sea. A bar offers snacks, and a pub/disco is available for evening entertainment. The Hacienda has three swimming pools (one for children), a tennis court, billiard room, bicycle rentals, horseback riding, and boat rentals, while fishing excursions are arranged on request.

SANTA EULALIA DEL RÍO

Once patronized by expatriate artists from the capital, 9 miles (14km) to the south, Santa Eulalia del Rio now attracts mostly middle-class northern Europeans.

Santa Eulalia is at the foot of the Puig de Missa, on the estuary of the only river in the Balearics. The principal monument in town is a fortress church standing on a hilltop, or *puig*. Dating from the 16th century, it has an ornate Gothic altar screen.

Santa Eulalia is relatively free of the sometimes plastic quality of San Antonio. Visitors often have a better chance of finding accommodations here than in the other two major towns.

ESSENTIALS

GETTING THERE   During the day buses run between Ciudad de Ibiza and Santa Eulalia del Rio every 30 minutes.

Seven boats a day run between Ciudad de Ibiza and Santa Eulalia del Rio. The boats run on the hour and the first leaves Ciudad de Ibiza at 10:30am and Santa Eulalia del Rio at 9:30am. The boat ride takes 45 minutes and information can be obtained at ☎ 971-33-22-51.

VISITOR INFORMATION   The **tourist information office** is at carrer Mariano Riquer Wallis (☎ **971-33-07-28**), open Monday through Friday from 9:30am to 1:30pm and 5 to 7:30pm, Saturday from 9:30am to 1:30pm. In summer the office is open from 9am to 1:30pm and 5 to 8pm Monday through Fridayriday and from 9am to 7:30pm on Saturday.

EXPLORING THE AREA

You can reach the famous northern beaches from Santa Eulalia by either bus or boat, departing from the harbor front near the boat basin. **Aigües Blanques** is one of the best beaches, lying 6 miles (10km) north. (It's legal to go nude here.) It's reached by four buses a day. A long, sandy cove, **Cala Llonga,** lies 3 miles (5km) south and is reached by 10 buses a day. Cala Llonga fronts a bevy of package-tour hotels, so it's likely to be crowded. Boats also depart Santa Eulalia for Cala Llonga every 30 minutes from 9am to 6pm. **Es Caná** is a white-sand beach, 3 miles (5km) north of town; boats and buses leave every 30 minutes from 8am to 9pm. Four buses a day also depart for **Cala Llenya** and **Cala Nova.**

WHERE TO STAY

Hotel S'Argamassa Sol. Urbanización S'Argamassa, 07182 Santa Eulalia del Rio. ☎ **971-33-00-51.** Fax 971-33-00-76. 230 units. A/C MINIBAR TV TEL. 12,500–18,000 ptas. ($83.75–$120.60) double. Rates include half board. AE, DC, MC, V. Closed Nov–Apr.

Two miles (3km) outside Santa Eulalia del Rio, near Roman ruins, the Hotel S'Argamassa is a well-run, family oriented resort. The hotel is a short walk from the beach and maintains its own small pier. All the midsize guest rooms have terraces with sea views. Accommodations are comfortable; many have been recently renovated, and each comes with a firm bed. The hotel has no restaurant, but dining options are nearby.

There is an outdoor pool, bowling alley, playground, tennis courts, and a game room. For evening entertainment, music and dancing are offered in the lounge or cocktails at the poolside bar.

Hotel Ses Estaques. Ses Estaques, 07840 Santa Eulalia del Rio. ☎ **971-33-02-00.** Fax 971-33-04-86. www.hotelestaques.com. E-mail: jmr@hotelestaques.com. 166 units. TEL. 10,900–14,900 ptas. ($73.05–$99.85) double. Rates include breakfast. AE, DC, MC, V. Closed Nov–Apr.

A much-favored hotel in this resort, close to the seashore at the edge of town, Ses Estaques is open only in the good weather months. On the walk to the private beach you will find a beautiful garden filled with roses, palms, and ivy, and the swimming pool is edged with pines and a poolside snack bar. Inside, the hotel is filled with extra touches and hideaway corners of charm. There's an aquarium in the spacious lobby, a pleasant tropical restaurant on the beach a short walk away, minigolf, and a tennis court. Each of the comfortable terrazzo-floored bedrooms has a balcony with a view of the garden or the sea. The hotel was last renovated in 1998, with new mattresses and plumbing added.

Hotel Tres Torres. Ses Estaques, s/n, 07840 Santa Eulalia del Rio. ☎ **971-33-03-26.** Fax 971-33-20-85. 114 units. A/C TV TEL. 9,400–19,000 ptas. ($63–$127.30) double; 11,000–22,000 ptas. ($73.70–$147.40) suite. Rates include half board. AE, DC, MC, V. Closed Nov–Apr.

A stylish modern hotel where many of the comfortable, mid-size, and balconied rooms overlook the two swimming pools, Hotel Tres Torres has an art gallery and a jewelry shop and a lobby filled with neo-Victorian wicker chairs. An airy and sunny dining room offers a view of the water. The hotel is usually closed in winter but may be open all year in 2000.

WHERE TO DINE

Doña Margarita. Puerto Deportiva, Santa Eulalia. ☎ **971-33-22-00.** Reservations recommended. Main courses 2,000–4,500 ptas. ($13.40–$30.15). AE, DC, MC, V. Tues–Sun 1–3:30pm and 8–11:30pm. Closed Dec–Feb. SPANISH/INTERNATIONAL.

Although one of Santa Eulalia's most venerable restaurants moved into new premises in 1998, it managed to retain the loyalty of its local clientele and the managerial skill of its owner and resident matriarch, Margarita Ribas. A modern building with big windows that overlook the yachts bobbing at anchor in the nearby marina, it offers a solidly traditional menu that includes lots of very fresh fish that are painstakingly prepared, usually with style and flair. The fish is usually served with fresh salads, and finished off with succulent desserts that are fresh-made daily, including lemon mousse with raspberries. In between, you might enjoy mussels marinara, spicy fish soup, paella, salmon with green peppercorns, calves' kidneys with fried onions, a parillada of prawns or a zarzuela of shellfish, and a changing roster of fresh fish and shellfish whose ingredients vary according to their availability in the marketplace.

✪ **El Naranjo.** Carrer San José, 31. ☎ **971-33-03-24.** Reservations required. Main courses 1,200–2,400 ptas. ($8.05–$16.10). AE, MC, V. Tues–Sun 7:30–11:30pm. Closed Nov–Feb. CONTINENTAL.

This chic nighttime rendezvous has altogether the most beautiful courtyard in town. Many refer to this place as "The Orange Tree," its name in English. The orange tree patio, with its flowering bougainvillea vines, has such appeal that many diners don't mind its out-of-the-way location (in town, several blocks from the water). If your table isn't ready when you arrive, enjoy an aperitif in the cozy bar. The menu items are beautifully prepared and served. One newspaper called the chef "an artist." Dishes include fresh fish and duckling in red-currant-and-pepper sauce. Begin with *las tres mousses* (three mousses) as an appetizer, finishing with the lemon tart for dessert.

3 Formentera

For years, Formentera was known as the "forgotten Balearic." The smallest of the archipelago, it's a 30-square-mile, flat limestone plain. In the east it is flanked by La Mola, a peak rising 615 feet, and in the west it is protected by Berberia at 315 feet.

The Romans called it Frumentaria (meaning "wheat granary"), when they oversaw it as a booming little agricultural center. But that was then. A shortage of water coupled with strong winds has allowed only meager vegetation to grow, notably some fig trees and fields of wild rosemary (which seem to be home to thousands of green lizards).

A few hearty goats live on the island, and, like Ibiza, Formentera has a salt industry. Its year-round population of 5,000 swells in summer, mostly with day-trippers from Ibiza. Limited hotels have kept development in check, and most visitors come over for the day to enjoy the beaches, where they often swim without bathing suits and sunbathe along the excellent stretches of sand. British and Germans form the majority of tourists that actually spend the night.

On the ferry ride over from Ibiza, you pass Isla Ahorcados (Hanged Men's Island), where criminals from Ibiza were once strung up, and the more reassuring Isla Espalmador, with its sandy beaches. Carry some seasickness pills, as the ferry crossing can be turbulent.

ISLAND ESSENTIALS

GETTING THERE   Formentera is serviced by up to 29 boat passages a day in summer and by about a dozen per day in winter. Boats depart from Ciudad de Ibiza, on Ibiza's southern coast, for La Savina (La Sabina), 2 miles (3km) north of the island's capital and largest settlement, Sant Francesc (San Francisco Javier). Depending on the design of the boat you select, passage across the 3-mile (5km) channel separating the islands takes between 35 minutes and 1 hour. For information on schedules, call ☎ 971-31-07-11, although it's usually easier to ask employees at virtually any hotel on the island, who are all usually well versed in the hours of ferryboats to and from Ibiza.

GETTING AROUND   As ferryboats arrive at the quays of La Sabina, taxis line up at the pier. One-way passage to such points as Es Pujols and Playa de Mitjorn costs 1,000 ptas. ($6.70) and 1,500 to 1,700 ptas. ($10.05 to $11.40), respectively, although it's always wise to negotiate or predetermine the fare before the journey begins. To call a taxi in Sant Francesc, dial ☎ 971-32-20-16; in El Pujols, ☎ 971-32-80-16; and in La Sabina, ☎ 971-32-20-02. Regardless of when and where you call for a taxi, be prepared to wait.

Car rentals can be arranged through Hertz (☎ 971-32-22-42), whose kiosk lies at La Sabina, close to where you'll disembark from the ferryboats.

If you want to enjoy seeing Formentera by a bicycle or a motor scooter, these can be rented from **Moto-Rent** in La Sabina (☎ 971-32-21-38) or in Pujols (☎ 971-32-24-88). Motor scooters rent for 1,900 ptas. ($12.75) a day, bicycles for around 500 to 1,500 ptas. ($3.35 to $10.05) a day.

VISITOR INFORMATION   The **tourist office** at Formentera is Edificio de Servicios de Puerto, 1, in Port de la Sabina (☎ **971-32-20-57**), open Monday through Friday from 10am to 2pm and 5 to 7pm, Saturday from 10am to 2pm.

HITTING THE BEACH

Beaches, beaches, and more beaches—that's why visitors come here. You can see the ocean from any point on the island. Some say the island has the best beaches in the Mediterranean —an opinion not without merit. Formentera has been declared a "World Treasure" by UNESCO, one of four places so honored because of its special character as an ecological and wildlife preserve. This implies an indirect control by UNESCO of activities that could jeopardize the island's ecological well being.

Meanwhile, day-trippers from Ibiza have fun sampling its long, sedate beaches and solitary coves before returning to Ibiza's ebullience in the evening.

The island is ringed with beaches, so selecting the one that you think will appeal to you is about the only problem you'll face—that and whether or not you should wear a bathing suit.

Playa de Mitjorn, on the southern coast, is 3 miles (5km) long; it has many uncrowded sections. This is the principal area for nude sunbathing. A few bars and hotels occupy the relatively undeveloped stretch of sand. You can make **Es Copinyars,** the name of one of the beachfronts, your stop for lunch, as it has a number of restaurants and snack bars.

At **Es Calo,** along the northern coast, west of El Pilar, there are some small boarding houses, *hostales.* From this point, you can see the lighthouse of La Mola, which was featured in Jules Verne's *Journey Round the Solar System,* and, if weather conditions are right, Majorca.

Sant Ferran serves the beach of **Es Pujols,** darling of the package-tour operators. This is the most crowded beach on Formentera, and you may want to avoid it. The beaches, however, are pure white sand, with a backdrop of dunes and pine trees. It's also a place to go windsurfing and is the site of several tourist amenities. The beach is protected by the Punta Prima headland.

Westward, **Cala Sahona** is another popular tourist spot, lying near the lighthouse on Cabo Berberia. Often pleasure vessels anchor here on what is the most beautiful cove in Formentera.

WHERE TO STAY

Accommodations are scarce, so you must arrive with an ironclad reservation should you want to spend the night or a longer time.

Club La Mola. Apartado, 23, 07871 Playa de Mitjorn, Formentera. ☎ and fax **971-32-70-69.** 349 units. A/C MINIBAR TV TEL. 16,200–31,200 ptas. ($108.55–$209.05) double. Rates include half board. AE, DC, MC, V. Closed Nov–Apr.

Located at Es Arenals, this is one of the best-equipped hotels on the island, and during the summer it is usually packed. Opening onto the longest beach on the island, La Mola is constructed in the style of a Spanish village. The good-size rooms are comfortable and well furnished, each with a firm bed and a tiled bathroom equipped with a hair dryer. Facilities include two swimming pools, tennis courts, much equipment for water sports, a gym, a garden, minigolf, and a disco. The restaurant serves Spanish and continental meals, but it's only standard fare.

Club Punta Prima. Punta Prima, 07871 Sant Ferran. ☎ **971-32-82-44.** Fax 971-32-81-28. 120 units. TV TEL. 15,200–17,500 ptas. ($101.85–$117.25) double; 16,200–20,000 ptas. ($108.55–$134) suite. Rates include half board. MC, V. Closed Nov–Apr.

Built in 1987 in a low-slung, two-story format hugging the coastline a short walk from the beach, this is the best and best-accessorized hotel on Formentera, with a loyal clientele from northern Europe, which tends to return year after year. The good-size bedrooms are comfortably furnished and well maintained, each with an excellent bed. Virtually everyone checks in here on the half-board plan, indulging in meals that are, more often than not, served as an ongoing series of buffets. Great attention has been paid to the enhancement and preservation of the site's isolated natural beauty.

Sa Volta. Apartado, 71, Sant Ferran, 07871 Es Pujols, Formentera. ☎ **971-32-81-25.** Fax 971-32-82-28. 27 units. TV TEL. 5,250–11,800 ptas. ($35.20–$79.05) double. AE, DC, MC, V.

This small hostal features good, clean but very modest rooms, and charges reasonable prices. It will have been totally renovated by 2000 with new beds added. It has a cafeteria but no restaurant. However, you are in the midst of many cafes, restaurants, and nightlife possibilities, because this is the tourist belt of Formentera. Reserve well in advance as it's hard to get a room here.

WHERE TO DINE

Es Molí del Sal. Ses Illetes (al Noroeste). ☎ **608-13-67-73** (note different area code from rest of Balearics). Reservations required. Main courses 1,700–5,500 ptas. ($11.40–$36.85). AE, MC, V. Daily 9am–11pm. Closed Nov–Apr. SPANISH/CATALAN.

This restaurant, the island's best, is in a restored windmill near the salt flats. It opens onto Platja de Ses Illetes, that slender northern tip of Formentera, the most desirable beachfront on the island. A small restaurant, it specializes in fresh fish and lobster and seems to please everybody. The cookery, although hardly spectacular, is good, simple fare prepared with fresh ingredients. The view of the sea and of Ibiza is panoramic.

4 Minorca

Minorca (also written Menorca) is one of the most beautiful islands in the Mediterranean; miles of lovely beaches have made it a longtime favorite vacation spot for Europeans.

Barely 9 miles (14.5km) wide and less than 32 miles (52km) long, its principal city is Mahón (also called Maó), population 25,000, set on a rocky bluff overlooking the great port, which was fought over for centuries by the British, French, and Spanish.

After Majorca, it is the second largest of the Spanish Balearic Islands, but it has more beaches than Majorca, Ibiza, and Formentera combined—they range from miles-long silver or golden crescents of sand to rocky bays, or calas, reminiscent of Norwegian fjords. Our favorite is Cala'n Porter, 7 miles (11km) west of Mahón. Towering promontories guard the slender estuary where this spectacular beach is found. Another of Minorca's treasures, Cala de Santa Galdana, is located 14 miles (22.5km) south of Ciudadela. Its gentle bay and excellent sandy beach afford the most scenic spot on the island. Ila d'en Colom, an island in the Mahón bay, is bordered with great beaches, but is reachable only by boat.

The beaches along 135 miles (218km) of pine-fringed coastline are the island's greatest attraction, though many are not connected by roads. Nude bathing is commonplace, although the practice is officially illegal. Golf, tennis, and sailing are available at reasonable fees, and windsurfing is offered at all major beaches.

With about 60,000 permanent inhabitants, Minorca plays host to about half a million visitors a year. But it is not overrun with tourist developments and has none of the junky excess that has plagued Ibiza and Majorca for years.

Minorca map with legend:

Attractions
- Cala'n Portet 9
- Cala Caves 2
- Cals Mesquida 2
- Cova d'en Xoroi 10
- Es Grau 1
- Església de Santa Maria la Major 4
- Naveta d'es Tudons 12
- Punta Prima 8
- Torre d'en Gaumés 11
- Trepucó 5
- Xoringuer Gin Distillery 4

Accommodations
- Hostal Reynes 4
- Hotel Capri 4
- Hotel del Almirante (Collingwood House) 3
- Biniali 7

Dining
- American Bar 4
- Bar Restaurant España 4
- Gregal 4
- Jágaro 4
- La Tropical 4
- Pilar 4
- Rocamar 6

Unlike those islands, Minorca is not utterly dependent on tourism; it has some industry, including leatherwork, costume jewelry making, dairy farming, and even gin manufacturing. Life here is quieter and more relaxed; it is not a place to go for glittering nightlife. Some clubs in Ibiza don't even open until 4 in the morning, whereas on Minorca nearly everybody, local and visitor alike, is in bed well before then.

In addition to trips to the beach, there are some fascinating things to do for those interested in history, archaeology, music, and art. Many artists live in Minorca, and exhibitions of their work are listed regularly in the local paper. The Catedral de Santa María in Mahón has one of the great pipe organs of Europe, and world-famous organists have appeared here, giving free concerts.

In the south some 1,600 archaeological sites have been found, dating from prehistoric times. Of the mysterious monuments unearthed, the most spectacular are the *taulas,* Stonehenge-type structures made from two slabs of rock forming the letter *T.* Known only on Minorca, these megalithic structures are often more than 12 feet high.

ISLAND ESSENTIALS

GETTING THERE   Minorca, lying off the eastern coast of Spain and northeast of Majorca, is reached by air or sea. The most popular method of reaching Minorca, certainly the quickest, is to fly, though you can take a ferry from mainland Spain or from the other two major Balearic Islands, Ibiza and Majorca.

It is always good to arrive with everything arranged in advance—hotel rooms, car rentals, ferry or airplane tickets. In July and August, reservations are vital, because of the limited hotel and transportation facilities.

The Minorca International Airport (☎ 902-40-05-00 for information) lies 2 miles (3km) outside the capital city of Mahón. It receives dozens of charter flights, mainly from Germany, Italy, the Scandinavian countries, and Britain. However, both **Iberia** and **Aviaco** (☎ 902-40-05-00 for information on both airlines) also operate regularly scheduled domestic flights from Barcelona, Palma de Majorca, and even Madrid.

Regular train service, which operates frequently in the summer, connects Minorca with Barcelona, Palma de Majorca, and Ibiza. From Barcelona, the journey takes 9 hours aboard moderately luxurious lines. If you're on a real budget but still want a decent night's sleep, bunk in a four-person cabin, which is about the same price as a chair in the lounge. Meals can be purchased in a self-service restaurant onboard or else brought along if you're on a strict budget.

The ferry service is operated by **Transmediterránea,** whose offices in Mahón are at Estació Marítima, along Moll (Andén) de Ponent (☎ 971-36-60-50), open from 8:30am to 1pm and 5 to 7pm Monday through Friday. Saturday hours are from 8:30am to noon, and Sunday hours from 3 to 5pm but only to receive the ferry from Valencia. However, any travel agency in Barcelona or Palma, even Ibiza, can book you a ticket; you need not go directly to one of the company's offices.

GETTING AROUND   **Transportes Menorca (TMSA),** carrer Joseph M. Quadrado, 7 (☎ 971-36-03-61), off Plaça s'Esplanada in Mahón, operates bus service around the island. The tourist office (see Mahón "Visitor Information," below) has complete bus schedules for the island.

A good local car rental company is **British Car-Hire G.B. International,** Plaça s'Esplanada in Mahón (☎ 971-36-24-32), with rentals beginning at 15,000 ptas. ($100.50) for 3 days in the high season. The Spanish-owned **Atesa** (☎ 971-36-62-13) operates a desk at the airport, charging from 7,200 ptas. ($48.25) for its cheaper models. **Avis** (☎ 971-36-15-76) also operates out of the airport, asking from 7,000 to 9,000 ptas. ($46.90 to $60.30) for its cheapest cars per day. Car-rental firms on the island will deliver a vehicle either to the airport upon your arrival or later after you check into your hotel—but you must specify in advance.

To summon a local taxi, call ☎ 971-36-12-83 or 971-36-28-91. The taxi stop is at Plaça s'Esplanada in Mahón. Typical fare—say, from Mahón to the beaches at Cala'n Porter—is 1,800 ptas. ($12.05) one-way.

To rent a bicycle, try **Just Bicicletas,** carrer Infanta, 19 (☎ 971-36-47-51), in Mahón. A 1-day bike rental costs 1,000 ptas. ($6.70).

MAHÓN (MAÓ)

Mahón and neighboring Villacarlos still show traces of British occupation in their gorgeous Georgian architecture and Chippendale reproductions. There's also Golden Farm, the magnificent mansion north of the capital, overlooking Mahón harbor, where in October 1799 Admiral Lord Nelson enjoyed a brief rest and, according to local legend, hid out with his lady love, Emma Hamilton. In truth, Nelson was here alone working on *Sketches of My Life.*

The largest city on the island, Mahón is an east-coast port. In the Minorcan language, it is called Maó. Mahón has allegedly lent its name to one of the world's most popular sauces, mayonnaise.

Mahón was built on the site of an old castle standing on a cliff overlooking one of Europe's finest natural harbors, some 3½ miles (5.5km) long. The castle and the town wall erected to dissuade pirates are long gone, except for the archway of San Roque.

The first Christian king from the mainland, Alfonso II, established a base in the harbor in 1287. It became known as **Isla del Rey** (Island of the King). When the British constructed a hospital here to tend to wounded soldiers, it was called "Bloody Island."

Since 1722, when the seat of government was moved here from Ciudadela, Mahón has been the capital of Minorca.

ESSENTIALS

GETTING THERE   From the airport (see above), you must take a taxi into Mahón, as there is no bus link. The approximate cost is 1,200 ptas. ($8.05).

Mahón is the bus transport depot for the island, with departures from Plaça s'Esplanada in the heart of town. The most popular run—six buses per day—is to Ciudadela, but there are also connections to other parts of the island. The tourist office (see "Visitor Information," below) distributes a list of schedules, and the list is also published in the local newspaper, *Menorca Diario Insular.* Tickets are purchased once you're aboard. Make sure you carry some change.

VISITOR INFORMATION   The **tourist office** is at Plaça s'Esplanada, 40 (☎ **971-36-37-90**), open May through October, Monday through Friday from 8am to 8pm, Saturday from 9am to 2pm and November through April, Monday through Friday 9am to 1pm, 5 to 7pm, Saturday 9am to 1pm.

CITY LAYOUT   The heart of Mahón is the Plaça de la Constitució, with its Town Hall from the 18th century, constructed in an English Palladian style.

Plaça s'Esplanada, seat of the tourist office and the bus departure point, is actually the main square. Here on Sundays locals gather to enjoy ice cream, the best in the Balearics. In summer, a market is held on Tuesday and Saturday from 9am to 2pm. Island artisans from all over the island sell their wares at that time. The northern boundary of the city is formed by the **Puerto de Mahón,** which has many restaurants and shops, lying along Muelle Comercial.

Mahón is not a beach town, but has some accommodations, and is the center of the best shopping and nightclubs. The closest beaches for swimming are those at **Es Grau** and **Cala Mesquida.**

Villacarlos stretches east along the port, a virtual extension of the capital, and it doesn't have beaches either. Several good restaurants line the harbor leading toward Villacarlos. When the British founded this village, now a southeast suburb of Mahón, they called it Georgetown.

FUN ON & OFF THE BEACH

BEACHES   **Cala'n Porter,** 7 miles (11km) west of Mahón, is one of the most spectacular beaches on the island. It's a sandy beach at a narrow estuary inlet protected by high promontories. Thinly scattered houses perch upon a cliff. You can drop in on a bar here during the day. **La Cova d'en Xoroi,** ancient troglodyte habitations overlooking the sea from the upper part of the cliffs, can also be visited (see below).

Going around the cliff face you'll discover more caves at **Cala Caves.** People still live in some of these caves and there are boat trips to see them from Cala'n Porter.

North of Mahón on the road to Fornells you'll encounter many beachside settlements. Close to Mahón and already being exploited is **Cala Mesquida,** one of the best beaches. To reach it turn off the road to Cala Llonga and follow the signs to "Playa."

The next fork in the road takes you to **Es Grau,** another fine beach. Along the way you see the salt marshes of S'Albufera, abundant in migrant birds. Reached by bus from Mahón, Es Grau, lying 5 miles (8km) north of Mahón, opens onto a sandy bay and gets very crowded in July and August. From Es Grau you can take a boat to **Illa d'en Colom,** an island in the bay with some good beaches. There are several bars at Es Grau for refueling.

South of Mahón is the little town of San Lluís and the large sandy beach to the east, **Punta Prima.** Patronized heavily by occupants of the local *urbanizaciones,* this beach is serviced by buses from Mahón, with six departures daily. The same buses will take you to an attractive necklace of beaches, the **Platges de Son Bou,** on the southern shore. Many tourist facilities are found here (see below).

GOLF   The only course is **Urbanizació Son Parc** (☎ 971-18-88-75), a traditional nine-hole course that recently added another nine holes.

HORSEBACK RIDING   For an equestrian tour of the island (subject to demand), call **Picadero Alaior** at ☎ 608-32-35-66 in Alaior, which is 7½ miles (12km) from Mahón on the road to Sanbu. The outfit is in front of the bridge by the beach. Both beginner and advanced riders are accommodated and an hour costs 2,000 ptas. ($13.40).

WINDSURFING & SAILING   The best spots are at Fornells Bay, which is a mile wide and several miles long. **Windsurfing Fornells** (☎ 971-37-64-00) will supply you with gear.

SHOPPING

Es Portal, Sa Ravaleta, 23 (☎ 971-36-30-36), supplies Minorca's chic men and women with fashions from such high-priced and cutting-edge names as Moschino, Versace, Christian Lacroix, Dolce & Gabbana, and Armand Basi, as well as Spanish designers. Sophisticated accessories and shoes are also available.

Looky Boutique, carrer de Ses Moreres, 43 (☎ 971-36-06-48), is Minorca's outlet for chic, elegant leather accessories, which are produced in the company's factory in Ciudadela. The shop sells exquisite handbags, shoes, and leather clothing for men and women. Other locations include a shop in Ciudadela, at José María Quadrado, 14 (☎ 971-38-19-32), and in Fornells, at Passeig Marítim, 23 (☎ 971-37-65-45).

Patricia, carrer de Ses Moreres, 31 (☎ 971-36-91-78), sells fine locally produced leather jackets, suits, skirts, and accessories. Other shops are located at Camino Santandria/Ronda Baleares (☎ 971-38-50-56).

SEEING THE SIGHTS

Most people don't take sightseeing too seriously in Mahón, as they are here mainly to enjoy the views of the port, to dine, or to shop. Even so, you may want to visit the **Església de Santa María la Major,** Plaça Constitució. The church was founded in 1287 by the Christian conqueror Alfonso III, who wanted to celebrate the Reconquest. Over the years, the original Gothic structure has been much altered, and it was rebuilt in 1772. Its has a celebrated organ with four keyboards and more than 3,000 pipes, constructed in 1810 by Johan Kyburz, a Swiss artisan. Admiral Collingwood brought it to Mahón during the Napoleonic wars. A music festival in July and August showcases the organ, whose melodic sounds can be heard even as you sit drinking in a nearby cafe.

The best way to see the changing aspect of Mahón's port involves taking an hour-long **catamaran tour.** Because part of the sailing craft's hull contains glass windows below the waterline, you'll get views of underwater life that would otherwise be possible only with a submarine. Tours begin year-round at 9:15am, then continue on the hour until 5:15pm. Departure time is not guaranteed and the boat can leave up to 30 minutes later than scheduled. The cost is 950 ptas. ($6.35) for adults, 475 ptas. ($3.20) for children under 11. Tickets for this tour are available at **Xoringuer Gin Distillery,** Moll de Ponent, 93 (☎ **971-36-21-97**).

You can also visit the **Xoriguer Gin Distillery** on the harbor front at Moll de Ponent, 93. Here giant copper vats simmer over wood-fed fires. Later, after watching the process by which the famed Minorcan gin is made, you can taste more than a dozen brews. The distillery and a store selling the products, including some potent liqueurs, is open Monday through Friday 8am to 7pm and Saturday 9am to 1pm.

SIDE TRIPS BACK IN TIME

From Mahón you can take excursions to some of the prehistoric relics in the area. One of these, marked off the Mahón-Villacarlos highway, is **Trepucó,** where you'll find both a 13-foot *taula* (huge T-shaped stone structures) and a *talayot* (circular stone tower). The megalithic monuments stand on the road to San Lluís, only about a mile from Mahón. Of all the prehistoric remains on the island, this is the easiest to visit. It was excavated by Margaret Murray and a team from Cambridge University in the 1930s.

Another legacy of prehistoric people can be visited at km 4 (a stone marker) off the Mahón-Ciudadela highway. The trail to **Talatí de Dalt** is marked. Your path will lead to this taula with subterranean caves.

Another impressive prehistoric monument is **Torre d'en Gaumés,** 9 miles (14.5km) from Mahón off the route to Son Bou (the path is signposted). You can take a bus from Mahón to Son Bou if you don't have a car. This megalithic settlement spreads over many acres, including both taulas and talayots, along with some ancient caves in which people once lived. The exact location is 2 miles (3km) south of Alayor off the road to Son Bou.

The restored **Naveta d'es Tudons** is accessible 3 miles (5km) east of Ciudadela, just to the south of the road to Mahón. This is the best-preserved and the most significant prehistoric collection of megalithic monuments on Minorca. Its naveta (a boat-shaped monument thought to be a dwelling or a burial chamber) is said to be among the oldest monuments constructed by humans in Europe. Archaeologists have found the remains of many bodies at this site, along with a collection of prehistoric artifacts, including pottery, decorative jewelry, and weapons—although these have been removed to museums. The site is more easily visited if you're staying in Ciudadela.

WHERE TO STAY

Hostal Reynes. Carrer d'es Comerc, 26, 07700 Mahón. ☎ **971-36-40-59.** 28 units. 2,700–3,200 ptas. ($18.10–$21.45) double. No credit cards.

On a quiet, narrow street in the town center near the cathedral, this is a cozy, well-maintained, family run and very inexpensive hotel. Wide hallways lead to the simple but clean bedrooms on three floors of the building. Rooms are small but nicely maintained, each with a firm mattress. Meals are served in a well-scrubbed dining room with windows overlooking the street.

Hotel Capri. Carrer Sant Esteve, 8, 07703 Mahón. ☎ **971-36-14-00.** Fax 971-35-08-53. 75 units. A/C MINIBAR TV TEL. 9,800–16,300 ptas. ($65.65–$109.20) double. AE, DC, MC, V.

If you don't stay at the more expensive and superior Hotel Port Mahón (see below), this comfortable, modern hotel, conveniently situated in the heart of Mahón, is the next best choice. Each of the simple rooms is comfortably but blandly furnished with conservative furniture, and each has a private balcony. Well managed, with a sense of stewardship that derives from its long-term ownership and administration by a local family, the hotel has a bar and a restaurant that specializes in Balearic, Spanish, and international cuisine, with particularly good pizzas. A menú del día costs 1,550 ptas. ($10.40). Unlike many hotels on the island, this one is set within the commercial core of Mahón, and as such, caters to business travelers from other parts of the Balearics and Europe, and has more of a city-oriented outlook than hotels geared only to the resort trade. There's no pool, and the nearest beach is about 3 miles (5km) away, but there are such extras as turndown service, room service from early morning until midnight, a concierge, and baby-sitting if it's arranged a half day in advance.

Hotel del Almirante (Collingwood House). Carretera de Villacarlos, s/n, 07700 Mahón. ☎ **971-36-27-00.** Fax 971-36-27-04. www.menorca.net/ualmirant. E-mail: hotel. almirante@menorca.net. 40 units. A/C TEL. 7,300–13,120 ptas. ($48.90–$87.90) double. Rates include breakfast. DC, MC, V. Closed Nov–Apr.

Originally built in the late 18th century for Admiral Collingwood, a close friend of Lord Nelson, this hotel later served as a convent, as the home of a German sculptor, and until the end of World War II, as the German embassy. Architecturally, it reflects a number of styles: Italianate, Georgian, and Minorcan.

In 1964 it was restored and enlarged into a hotel. The reception area, with its 18th-century staircase, is decorated with numerous oil paintings and, like the rest of the public rooms, successfully mixes antiques with British memorabilia. Facilities include a bar, a game room, a swimming pool, and a tennis court. Guests are housed in the main building or in one of the more modern bungalow accommodations. The rooms are a mixed bag—you don't really know what you get until the maid opens the door. But all are clean and well kept, and many rooms have terraces overlooking the Bay of Mahón. The British love it here.

Hotel Port Mahón. Avinguda Fort de L'Eau, 07701 Mahón. ☎ **971-36-26-00.** Fax 971-36-26-50. 80 units. A/C MINIBAR TV TEL. 9,000–24,000 ptas. ($60.30–$160.80) double; 20,000–38,000 ptas. ($134–$254.60) suite for 2. Rates include breakfast. AE, DC, MC, V.

Perched on a steep hillside above the harbor, this hotel looks like a large Georgian villa whose charms are largely of another era. It is, without question, the most traditional accommodation in Minorca, located in a residential neighborhood. It's one of the few large hotels that stays open all year, and half of its rooms are usually reserved for tour groups. Some guests have been coming here since the 1950s, which indicates the age level of many of the patrons.

There is a sense of calm and unhurried comfort in the airy stone-floored public areas. The bedrooms overlook the harbor, the bougainvillea-filled garden, or the quiet street outside. Each has an ornate balcony with louvered shutters and potted flowers. Elegant touches abound, like the stone cherub riding a carved snail that splashes water into a swimming pool.

The dining room, a popular spot for visitors, serves good-tasting regional and international meals daily from 1 to 3pm and 8 to 10pm.

A Nearby Place to Stay in San Lluís

✪ **Biniali.** Carretera S'Uestrà, Binibeca, 50, 07710 Sant Lluís. ☎ **971-15-17-24.** Fax 971-15-03-52. 9 units. TEL. 14,120–16,680 ptas. ($94.60–$111.75) double. AE, DC, MC, V. Closed late Oct–Easter. Free parking.

Biniali is one of the most charming hotels and restaurants in Minorca, about a mile south of San Lluís on the island's southwestern coastal road to Binibeca. The house, surrounded by English-style gardens, was originally the home of a prosperous Minorcan farmer in the 18th century. The comfortable midsize bedrooms are decorated with a scattering of antiques, seven with terraces and two with separate salons. A few of the rooms are air-conditioned, and all of them come with firm beds. There is also a small outdoor swimming pool.

Many nonresidents visit for meals. Tables are set out under an arcade, overlooking the roses and geraniums in the garden, or in one of the charmingly old-fashioned dining rooms. Specialties include fillet steak in port with truffle sauce, monkfish in a wild mushroom sauce, baked potato filled with lobster, *magret* (breast) of duck in a sweet-and-sour currant sauce, and a selection of Minorcan cheeses. The restaurant is open daily from 1:30 to 3pm and 8:30 to 11pm.

All in all, this is a retreat offering lots of peace, comfort, and quaintness within easy reach of Binibeca beach and the facilities and activities of Mahón.

WHERE TO DINE

Fish and seafood form most of the basis of the Minorcan diet. The sea harvest is abundant along the long coastline. The most elegant dish, *la caldereta de langosta,* consists of pieces of lobster blended with onion, tomato, pepper, and garlic, and flavored with an herb liqueur. This is a favorite dish of King Juan Carlos when he visits Minorca.

Shellfish paella is also popular, as is *escupinas* ("warty Venus"), a shellfish from Mahón. *Tordos con col* (thrushes with cabbage) are served in autumn. A peasant dish, *pa amb oli,* often precedes a meal. This is bread flavored with salt and olive oil and rubbed with fresh tomato.

Wine is brought in from mainland Spain, but gin is made on the island, a legacy from the days of the British occupation. You can drink the gin by itself or mix it with lemon and ice. If the latter, ask the bartender for *palloza* (pronounced pa-*yoh*-tha). Mixed with soda or lemonade, the gin drink is called a *pomada.*

Expensive

Gregal. Moll de Llevant, 306. ☎ **971-36-66-06.** Reservations recommended. Main courses 1,050–5,500 ptas. ($7.05–$36.85). AE, DC, MC, V. Daily noon–3:30pm and 7:30–11:30pm. SEAFOOD/INTERNATIONAL.

Seafood is the specialty of this small, friendly restaurant. The decor is simple; checkered tablecloths and exposed beams lend a rustic air to the interior and the catch of the day is often on display. Included on the menu are several meat and fowl dishes, most with Catalan or French influences. Along with traditional Spanish fare, a selection of international dishes appears as well. Greek specialties, including *taramosalata, moussaka,* and *dolmades,* are excellent choices.

Rocamar. Cala Fonduco, 32, 07720 Es Castell. ☎ **971-36-56-01.** Fax 971-36-52-99. Reservations recommended. Main courses 1,600–6,000 ptas. ($10.70–$40.20); fixed-price menus 2,000–4,000 ptas. ($13.40–$26.80). AE, DC, MC, V. Daily 1–3:30pm and 8–11pm. Closed Nov and Sun nights Dec–Apr. MINORCAN/INTERNATIONAL.

This restaurant is famous on Minorca—the chef has a way of making simplicity sublime. You reach it by following a narrow rutted road parallel to the harbor. The beamed and paneled restaurant on the upper floor has views overlooking the harbor. Although some locals claim the cooking was more glorious in the past, it still shines today.

Dishes might include almond soup, marinated salmon with shellfish, magret (breast) of duckling in port wine, or beef fillet with mustard sauce. Don't overlook the pleasant street-level snack bar (it's actually a restaurant in its own right). This establishment also offers 32 simple bedrooms, most of which are booked by London-based tour groups. Each has a private bathroom and TV, and breakfast is included in the rate. Rooms rent for 5,000 ptas. ($33.50) for a double.

Moderate

✪ Jàgaro. Moll de Llevant. ☎ **971-36-23-90.** Reservations recommended. Main courses 650–6,600 ptas. ($4.35–$44.20); menú del día 2,000 ptas. ($13.40). AE, DC, MC, V. Daily noon–4pm and 7pm–midnight. Closed Sun night Nov–Apr. MEDITERRANEAN.

The seafood menu here is Minorca's most eclectic and interesting. Begin with *ensalada templada con cigalitos y setas,* a mix of warm prawns and wild mushrooms served on a bed of lettuce, or Jàgaro's interpretation of gazpacho, flavored with shrimp and melon. The *mosaico de verduras,* a plate of grilled fresh vegetables is also an excellent choice. Main courses may include *carpaccio de mero* (grouper) served with a tangy green-mustard sauce, *caldereta de langosta* (lobster stew), or *ortigas* (sea anemones). Seafood offerings are extensive, although meat dishes including duck magret (breast) in orange sauce and foie gras with sweet-and-sour sauce are also very appealing. The extensive wine list assures a vintage to accompany any meal. For dessert, try one of the homemade ice creams or sorbets.

✪ Pilar. Des Forn, 61. ☎ **971-36-68-17.** Reservations recommended. Main courses 1,700–2,450 ptas. ($11.40–$16.40); fixed-price lunch 2,300 ptas. ($15.40). MC, V. Tues–Sat 1:30–3:30pm, Mon–Sat 8:30–11:30pm. Daily in Aug. Closed Dec–Jan. MINORCAN/ MEDITERRANEAN.

At this small, stylish restaurant in the center of Mahón, you'll feel you're dining in somebody's home. Even the small kitchen where owner-chef Teodoro Beurrun works culinary wonders looks more like a domestic kitchen than a restaurant kitchen. There are about half a dozen tables indoors and another half a dozen spread around the rear patio in summer. A smattering of antique furnishings and impressionistic artworks contribute to the coziness.

The menu is understandably limited, but that does not apply to the quality and care taken in preparation. The market-fresh cuisine is largely *Menorquín* with innovative variations. Based on a rigid allegiance to seasonal, high-quality, and very fresh ingredients, menu items change at least four times a year. Examples include Catalan-style blood sausage in puff pastry, served with a marmalade of onions and tomatoes; a soufflé of squid with almonds, prepared with squid ink; and veal trotters stuffed with Balearic herbs and served with a thyme-flavored honey sauce. For dessert try the homemade *pastel de nueces con chocolate* (walnut cake with chocolate).

Inexpensive

American Bar. Plaça Reial, 8. ☎ **971-36-18-22.** Main courses 700–2,000 ptas. ($4.70–$13.40); menú del día 950 ptas. ($6.35). No credit cards. Mon–Sat 6:30am–10:30pm, Sun 6:30am–2pm. MINORCAN/INTERNATIONAL.

For years, this has been the traditional international meeting place in Mahón. Many come here for drinks on its pleasant terrace, but you can also order food, eating inside or alfresco. Menu items include traditional Catalan platters (soups, stews, grilled meats), as well as pastas, salads, and American-style burgers. Dessert might include locally made ice creams, many made with fresh fruit. No one will mind if you have a drink or two too many here; if you do, you certainly won't be alone.

Bar Restaurant España. Carrer Victori, 48-50. ☎ **971-36-32-99.** Reservations recommended. Main courses 750–3,000 ptas. ($5.05–$20.10); menú del día 900 ptas. ($6.05). MC, V. Daily 1–3:30pm and 7:30–1:30pm. Closed Jan. SPANISH.

Originally established around 1938, this is one of the oldest continuously operating restaurants in Minorca, thanks to a solidly reliable clientele and well-prepared food that's served in generous portions at reasonable prices. Patrons include vacationing northern Europeans who tend to communicate with one another and the staff in English. Partly because of its cosmopolitan clientele, the menu is designed to appeal to a wide variety of palates. Examples include *cigales a la americana* (prawns in a spicy red sauce); shrimp with garlic; mussels marinara; baked fish (especially hake and cod); grilled veal and pork; and beefsteaks that are grilled and served with a decidedly Spanish flair.

La Tropical. Carrer Lluna, 36. ☎ **971-36-05-56.** Reservations not necessary. Main courses 800–2,600 ptas. ($5.35–$17.40); menú del día 1,100–3,000 ptas. ($7.35–$20.10). MC, V. Daily 8am–midnight. SPANISH/MINORCAN/INTERNATIONAL.

La Tropical is a three-in-one eatery. You can have snacks at the bar, and tapas as well as bocadillos (Spanish sandwiches) and *platos combinados* (combination plates) in the informal dining room, or full-fledged restaurant fare in the more formal dining area. The restaurant offers a good selection of Minorcan specialties, including a reasonably priced and savory fish-and-shellfish *caldereta* (stew). There is also a daily market menu and an assorted selection of Spanish and international dishes.

CIUDADELA (CIUTADELLA DE MENORCA)
27 miles (44km) W of Mahón

At the western end of the island, the town of Ciudadela has a typically Mediterranean air about it. Lining the narrow streets of the old city are noble mansions of the 17th and 18th centuries as well as numerous churches. It was the capital until 1722, when the British chose Mahón instead, largely because its harbor channel is eminently more navigable than the one at Ciudadela. Subsequently, the British built the main island road to link the two cities.

Like Mahón, Ciudadela perches high above its harbor, which is smaller than Mahón's. The seat of Minorca's bishopric, Ciudadela pontificates while Mahón administrates.

Known as Medina Minurka under the Muslims, Ciudadela retains some Moorish traces despite the 1558 Turkish invasion and destruction of the city. An obelisk in memory of the city's futile defense against that invasion stands in the pigeon-filled Plaça d'es Born (Plaza del Born), the city's main square overlooking the port.

ESSENTIALS
GETTING THERE   From the airport, you must take a taxi to Ciudadela, as there is no bus link. The cost is approximately 5,700 ptas. ($38.20) each way.

From Mahón six buses go back and forth every day. Departures are from Plaça s'Esplanada in Mahón.

VISITOR INFORMATION   The **tourist office** is at Plaça Catedral (☎ **971-38-26-93**), open Monday through Friday 8:30am to 3pm and 4:30 to 8pm, Saturday 10am to 2pm April to October.

EXPLORING CIUDADELA: THE BEACH & BEYOND
In Ciudadela, buses depart from Plaça d'Artrutx for most coastal destinations, including the best beaches. Of these, **Cala Santandria,** 2 miles (3km) to the south, is known for its white sands. This is a sheltered beach near a creek, and in the background are rock caves, which were inhabited in prehistoric times. The coves of **En Forcat, Blanes,** and **Brut** are near Ciudadela.

Cala de Santa Galdana, not reached by public transport, is the most stunning in the area, lying 14 miles (22.5km) south of Ciudadela. The bay here is tranquil and ringed with a beach of fine golden sand. Tall bare cliffs rise in the background, and the air is perfumed with the smell of pine trees. The road to this beach, unlike so many others on Minorca, is a good one.

The center of Ciudadela is **Plaça d'es Born,** site of tourist information. This was the center of life when the town was known to Jaume I. Back then Ciudadela was completely walled to protect itself from pirate incursions, which were a serious threat from the 13th century on. Much of the present look of this square, and of Ciudadela itself, is thanks to its demotion in 1722, when the capital was transferred to Mahón. For centuries that checked urban development in Ciudadela, and many buildings now stand that might probably have been torn down to make way for progress.

Plaça d'es Born looks over the port from the north. Once it was known as Plaza Generalíssimo, honoring the dictator Franco. The square was built around the obelisk that remembers the hopeless struggle of the town against the invading Turks who entered the city in 1558 and caused much destruction. On the west side of the square is the Ayuntamiento (Town Hall).

To the southwest of the square stands **Esglesia de San Francisco.** This is a 14th-century Gothic building, with some excellent carved wood altars. The town once had a magnificent opera house, Casa Salort, but that cultural note sounds no more, as it's been turned into a somewhat seedy movie theater. Another once-splendid palace, Palacio de Torre-Saura, also opens onto the square. Still owner occupied, it was constructed in the 1800s.

The **cathedral,** Plaça Pio XII, was ordered built by the conquering Alfonso III on the site of the former mosque. It is Gothic in style and fortresslike in appearance. The facade of the church, in the neoclassical style, was added in 1813. The church suffered heavy damage in 1936, during the Spanish Civil War, but has since been restored.

Ciudadela is at its liveliest at the **port,** where you'll find an array of little shops, bars, restaurants, sailboats, along with some impressive yachts in summer. **Carrer Quadrando** is another street worth walking, as it is lined with shops and arcades.

The Moorish influence still lingers in a block of whitewashed houses in the **Voltes,** lying off the Plaça s'Esplanada. In Ciudadela the local people still meet at **Plaça d'Alfons III,** the square honoring their long-ago liberator.

WHERE TO STAY
Expensive
Hotel Patricia. Passeig Sant Nicolau, 90, 07760 Ciudadela. ☎ **971-38-55-11.** Fax 971-48-11-20. 44 units. A/C MINIBAR TV TEL. 9,525–16,650 ptas. ($63.80–$111.55) double; 12,525–19,650 ptas. ($83.90–$131.65) junior suite. AE, DC, MC, V. Closed Nov–Feb. Free parking on street.

Built in 1988 this three-story is in a centrally located position that business travelers find convenient and is Ciudadela's most respected, most luxurious hotel. Set near the Plaça d'es Born, a half mile from the nearest beach (Playa de La Caleta), it has a polite and hardworking staff well versed on the island's facilities and geography. The spacious bedrooms are comfortable, carpeted, outfitted pleasantly in pastels, and have large bathrooms, equipped with hair dryers.

Dining: There's no full-fledged restaurant within this hotel, but you can get simple platters of food, coffee, beer, and wine at the in-house cafeteria.

Amenities: Room service, concierge, baby-sitting, currency exchange, conference rooms.

Moderate

Hotel Almirante Farragut. Urbanización Los Delfines, Cala'n Forcat, 07760 Ciudadela. ☎ **971-38-80-00.** Fax 971-38-81-07. 489 units. A/C TV TEL. 6,150–21,200 ptas. ($41.20–$142.05) double. Rates include breakfast. AE, MC, V. Closed Nov–Apr.

Located 3 miles (5km) outside Ciudadela, beside a small rock-lined inlet, this four-story building is one of the best hotels in the development of Los Delfines, a cluster of resort hotels initiated in the 1970s and 1980s. Public rooms are airy, large, sparsely furnished, and appropriate to the hotel's role as a warm-weather beach resort with an international clientele, often from England and Germany. Guest rooms are pleasant and standardized in both their amenities and their furnishings. Each has a balcony or terrace, usually overlooking either the rocky inlet or the open sea. Prices vary widely according to season, but lodgings that the hotel identifies as suites are nothing more than larger-than-usual double rooms.

Facilities include two saltwater pools for adults, one for children, two cafeterias, a disco, several TV and video rooms in Spanish, English, and German, two tennis courts, minigolf, shops, a salon, a supermarket, and an independently operated school for scuba divers. The hotel, incidentally, was named for U.S. Admiral Farragut, a 19th-century U.S. naval officer whose grandparents lived in one of the nearby villages.

Hotel Esmeralda. Pasaje de Sant Nicolau, 171, 07760 Ciudadela. ☎ **971-38-02-50.** Fax 971-38-02-58. 160 units. MINIBAR TEL. 10,800–21,600 ptas. ($72.35–$144.70) double. Rates include breakfast. Half board 1,600 ptas. ($10.70) extra per person. AE, DC, MC, V. Free parking. Closed Nov–Apr.

This is a respectable three-star hotel, built in the 1960s and set near the entrance to the mouth of Ciudadela's harbor. It lies within a 10-minute walk from the commercial heart of town, close to the better-accessorized Patricia Hotel, and rising three floors. The guest rooms are large but sparsely furnished, but bathrooms are big and bright and the beds are firm. In many cases, rooms have terraces and sea views. There's a pool on the premises, and the beach is within a 5-minute walk.

Inexpensive

Hostal Residencia Ciutadella. Carrer Sant Eloy, 10, 07760 Ciudadela. ☎ and fax **971-38-34-62.** 17 units. TV TEL. 5,500–8,500 ptas. ($36.85–$56.95) double; 7,500–11,500 ptas. ($50.25–$77.05) triple. Rates include breakfast. AE, MC, V.

Near Plaça d'Alfons III, on a quiet street just off the main shopping artery, this small hotel offers comfortable, convenient, but small accommodations, each with a good bed. Tiled floors and floor-length windows provide an airy atmosphere. Furniture is covered in fresh, floral fabrics. Beware, this three-story hotel has no elevator.

Hotels Cala Bona & Mar Blava. Avinguda del Mar, 14-16, 07760 Ciudadela. ☎ **971-38-00-16.** Fax 971-48-20-70. 44 units. TV TEL. 6,200–7,500 ptas. ($41.55–$50.25) double. No credit cards. Closed Nov–Mar.

These two hotels stand just a short walk from the town center, with views overlooking the little bay. Stairs lead down to a small beach, with a larger beach just 5 minutes away. Guest rooms are clean and comfortable; almost all have views facing the water. The rooms at the Mar Blava are smaller than those at the Cala Bona. The hotels share an outdoor pool, bar, and outdoor terrace. A restaurant serves snacks and light meals.

A Nearby Place to Stay

Hotel Los Cóndores Sol. Playa Santo Tomás, s/n, 07749 San Cristóbal. ☎ **971-37-00-50.** Fax 971-37-03-48. 188 units. A/C TV TEL. 9,400–15,400 ptas. ($63–$103.20) double. Rates include half board. AE, DC, MC, V. Closed late Oct to Apr 30.

This hotel gives the impression of a large, well-maintained hacienda, complete with lacy iron balconies and louvered shutters. Surrounded by lawns and flowering shrubs, it has a swimming pool, a private beach, and a sweeping view of rocky islets. Many guests make their balconies an extension of their midsize bedrooms, reading, sitting, and talking within sight of the sea. Beds are firm, the mattresses renewed as needed, and the tiled bathrooms come with hair dryers.

WHERE TO DINE

The port of Ciudadela offers a wide selection of restaurants for all palates and prices. Beyond that, there are some commendable choices in and around town.

Bar Triton. Muelle Ciutadella. ☎ **971-38-00-02.** Tapas and platos combinados 400–3,000 ptas. ($2.70–$20.10). MC, V. Daily noon–2am. TAPAS.

The best place for tapas in the port, Triton offers a wide range of snacks, including sausages, *tortillas* (Spanish omelettes), meatballs, and a dozen or so seafood tapas, among them octopus, stuffed squid, and *escupiñas* (Minorcan clams). On the wall inside are photos and illustrations of the port before it was a haven for vacationers. As in those days, fishers still make up an important part of the clientele, and you'll often find the locals engaged in a friendly afternoon game of cards.

Cas Quintu. Plaça d'Alfons III, 4. ☎ **971-38-10-02.** Reservations not necessary. Main courses 1,500–2,500 ptas. ($10.05–$16.75); fixed-price menu 1,500 ptas. ($10.05). AE, DC, MC, V. Daily 1–4:30pm and 8pm–midnight. SPANISH/MINORCAN.

One of the most solidly entrenched restaurants in town, thriving since the early 1960s from a position on an ornate square in the most historic core of town, Cas Quintu offers both indoor and outdoor tables that afford vantage points for observations of the passing crowd. You can order drinks and light food in the cafe daily from 9am to 2pm. This establishment's selection of tapas is among the best in town. Full meals are served outdoors or in one of a pair of rooms in back. Specialties include a zesty squid sautéed in butter, several different preparations of beefsteak, a perfect sole meunière, and a mixed grill of fish based on the catch of the day.

✪ **Casa Manolo.** Marina, 117. ☎ **971-38-00-03.** Reservations required in summer. Main courses 2,500–5,000 ptas. ($16.75–$33.50); off-season, fixed-price menu 3,500 ptas. ($23.45). AE, DC, MC, V. Daily 1–4:30pm and 7:30–11:30pm. Closed Sun mid-Nov to mid-Feb. SPANISH/MINORCAN.

Located at the port, across from the spot where the larger yachts anchor, Casa Manolo is a favorite of the yachting crowd. You can dine indoors in a room carved out of stone, or alfresco on the intimate terrace. King Juan Carlos has been seen here enjoying the elegant atmosphere and outstanding cuisine. The menu consists mainly of fresh seafood and lobster dishes. The specialty of the house is *arroz de pescado caldoso,* a dish resembling paella, but with more of a focus on fish. The *caldereta de langosta,* a lobster-based bouillabaisse, is one of our favorites. The hardworking and affable owner, Sra. María Postores, supervises all aspects of your dining experience.

Es Caliu Grill. Carretera Cala Blanca. ☎ **971-38-01-65.** Reservations not necessary. Main courses 1,800–2,200 ptas. ($12.05–$14.75). MC, V. May–Oct, daily 1–4pm and 7pm–midnight; off-season, Fri–Sat 7pm–midnight, Sun 1–4pm and 7pm–midnight. SPANISH.

One and a half miles (2.5km) south of Ciudadela, along the main road between Cala Santandria and Cala Blanca, Es Caliu is the place to come when you've had your fill of seafood. Specializing in grilled meats of the freshest quality, it offers lamb, veal, pork, rabbit, quail, and spit-roasted suckling pig. But beyond fine food, you get a special ambience. Above the bar hang hams and garlic braids, and off to the side are stacked wine barrels. The family style tables and benches are made of cut and polished logs. The outdoor terrace is roofed and smothered with cascading flowers; indoors there are two rustic dining areas, one with a fireplace.

Granja Colom. Plaça de s'Esplanada (Plaça Colóm), 48. ☎ **971-48-23-45.** Tapas 350 ptas. ($2.35). No credit cards. Mon– Sat 10am–10pm (depending on crowd). TAPAS.

A gathering place for locals and tourists alike, this hangout offers a variety of fresh tapas and sandwiches; you can enjoy them in the rather raucous interior or at the calmer outdoor tables. A glass of Jerez (sherry), the perfect accompaniment to tapas, costs from 150 ptas. ($1).

CIUDADELA AFTER DARK

Café El Molino, Camino de Mao, 7 (☎ 971-38-00-00), is one of our favorite bars, a hangout near the Avinguda de la Constitució. It has attracted virtually every drinker in town since it was established in 1905, within the circular premises of what was originally built as a windmill in 1794. It provides a rustic but richly international contrast to the busy square it borders, and boasts the unusual distinction of having monumental walls and vaulted ceilings that are a lot older than those of the buildings surrounding it. The clientele includes visiting foreigners and local fishers, and the mood changes from that of an early morning cafe, whose opening is timed to coincide with the departure of fishing boats, to a late-night bar. This place is earthy, regional, and brusque, yet invaluable for an insight into old-time Minorca.

CENTRAL & SOUTHERN MINORCA

Topographically and climatically, this is the more tranquil part of the island. The beaches are more accessible, and the winds blow less—as a result, tourism has taken a firmer foothold here than in the north. Santo Tomás, Cala Galdana, Platges de Son Bou, Cala Bosch, and Punta Prima are some of the focal points for travelers.

Es Mercadal, a town of several thousand inhabitants at the foot of Monte Toro, is an ensemble of white houses with grace notes of color. Among its claims to local fame are two types of almond confectionery—*carquinyols* (small, hard cookies) and *amargos* (a kind of macaroon). The place to get both is **Pastelería Villalonga Ca's Sucrer,** Plaça Constitución, 11, Es Mercadal (no phone), open Tuesday through Saturday from 9:30am to 1:30pm and 5 to 8:30pm, also open on Sunday in winter from 11am to 2pm.

From Es Mercadal, you can take a road 2½ miles (4km) up to **Monte Toro,** the island's tallest mountain at 1,170 feet, crowned with a sanctuary that is a place of pilgrimage for Minorcans. The winding road leads to a panoramic view of the island's rolling green countryside dotted with *fincas* (farm estates), trim fields, and stands of trees. From this vantage point you can also clearly see the contrast between the flatter southern part of the island and the hilly northern region. The hilltop sanctuary includes a small, simple church with an ornate gilded altar displaying the image (reportedly found nearby in 1290) of the Virgin Mare de Déu d'el Toro, the island's patron saint. In 1936 the church was destroyed, but the statue was saved from the flames and a new church built. The church is open daily from early morning to sunset; admission is free. In the courtyard of the sanctuary is a bronze monument to those Minorcans who left in the 18th century, while the island was still a British colony, to colonize Spanish settlements in North America. The large statue of Christ commemorates the dead in the Spanish Civil War. There is a snack bar with a pleasant terrace here.

Platges de Son Bou is a stunning beach scarred by two outsize hotels. Although still enchanting, the mile-long, narrow beach and clear, turquoise waters are now often crowded, even in the off-season; in July and August they're best avoided. At the eastern end of the beach just beyond the two monster hotels are the ruins of a Paleo-Christian basilica, most probably dating from the 5th or 6th century. Visible in the cliffs beyond are cave dwellings, some of which appear quite prosperous, with painted facades and shades to keep out the noonday sun.

One-half mile to the east in Cala'n Porter is a unique nightspot. Embedded in a series of caves within a sheer cliff face rising from the sea, **La Cova d'en Xoroi** (☎ **971-37-72-36**) is a conglomeration of bars, terraces, intimate nooks and crannies, and a disco floor. For sheer drama, the setting is without equal. As you walk down the entrance stairway, all magnificently unfolds before you. Then you come to the dance floor overlooking the sea at the cliff's edge—there's no window, just a railing. Prehistoric vessels were found inside these caves, which according to legend, were once the refuge of a Moor called Xoroi, who had abducted a local maid and made his home here with her and their family. You can visit this unusual spot during the day as well, from 11am to 9pm. Admission is 1,500 ptas. ($10.05) and includes one drink. In the evening, from 11pm to 4am, La Cova d'en Xoroi transforms into a disco. Admission is 1,500 ptas. ($10.05) including your first drink. Drinks cost from 900 ptas. ($6.05).

WHERE TO STAY

Most of the hotels in this area cater almost exclusively to tour groups.

✪ **Hotel Santo Tomás.** Playa Santo Tomás, 07749 Es Migjorn Gran. ☎ **971-37-00-25.** Fax 971-37-02-04. 85 units. A/C MINIBAR TV TEL. 18,000–29,000 ptas. ($120.60–$194.30) double; 23,000–34,000 ptas. ($154.10–$227.80) suite. Rates include half board. AE, DC, MC, V. Closed Nov–Apr.

One of our favorite hotels on Minorca, Santo Tomás offers the best quality and comfort on the island; it's the only four-star hotel on the beach. Public areas are airy and spacious and accommodations are comfortable, with amenities such as hair dryers and radios. Most rooms open onto a terrace that faces the sea. On the premises, guests will find a large swimming pool, surrounded by thatched umbrellas, providing shelter from the sun. A seaside bar offers refreshments, and guests may also use a minigolf course. Various water sports can be arranged.

Los Gavilanes Sol. Urbanización Cala Galdana, s/n, 07750 Ferreries. ☎ **971-15-45-45.** Fax 971-15-45-46. 364 units. A/C MINIBAR TV TEL. 9,900–22,200 ptas. ($66.35–$148.75) double; 17,900–30,200 ptas. ($119.95–$202.35) suite. Rates include breakfast. MC, V. Closed Nov–Apr. Free parking.

A large resort hotel, Gavilanes Sol is fully equipped with swimming pools, discos, restaurants, and bars. It's atop a steep slope overlooking one of the most perfect beaches in the Mediterranean, and it's surrounded by a grove of pines and palmettos. The original beauty of Cala Galdana has been substantially marred by construction, but you can enjoy the best end of its sandy, crescent-shaped beach and turquoise waters by staying here. Each of the sizable, functionally furnished rooms has a balcony, and all are equipped with a good bed. Other amenities include a hair dryer and a private safe.

Many of the clients here are on group tours from England, so the sweeping lobby-level terraces and the pub take on a British flavor. The hotel also has a restaurant, a swimming pool, and a children's playground.

WHERE TO DINE

Some of the best dining in this area is offered in the inland villages rather than along the coast. **Es Mercadal,** in particular, has a few choice restaurants.

⊙ **Ca N'Olga.** Pont Na Macarrana (near the Carrerd'es Sol), Es Mercadal. ☎ **971-37-54-59.** Reservations recommended on weekends. Main courses 1,500–2,800 ptas. ($10.05–$18.75). AE, DC, MC, V. Mar–May and Oct–Dec, Wed–Sun 1–4pm and 8–11pm; June–Sept, daily 7:45–11:30pm. Closed Jan–Feb. MINORCAN/INTERNATIONAL.

A stylish, sophisticated spot that attracts a similar clientele, Ca N'Olga is warm, winsome, and intimate. Occupying a typical white-stucco Minorcan house some 150 years old, this restaurant offers dining on a pretty outdoor patio or at a handful of indoor tables.

The eclectic menu changes frequently with the market offerings. It is likely to include quail with onion-and-sherry vinegar and osso buco. Some standard dishes that tend to appear regularly are *cap roig* (scorpion fish), *cabrito* (baby goat), some kind of fish terrine, and mussels au gratin. Among the homemade desserts you'll often find a velvety smooth fig ice cream and chestnut pudding.

Costa Sur. Playa de Santo Tomás. ☎ **971-37-03-26.** Reservations not necessary. Main courses 925–2,300 ptas. ($6.20–$15.40). MC, V. Daily 7–11pm. Closed Nov–Apr. INTERNATIONAL.

The sophisticated aspirations of Costa Sur are hampered by its rather stark decor and well-meaning but untrained staff. The well-planned menu is equally divided between seafood and meat dishes, and the house rightly prides itself on its cheese soufflé, salmon crepes, pepper steak, and *suquet de rape* (monkfish stew). It also serves a smattering of succulent pasta dishes.

Molí d'es Reco. Es Mercadal. ☎ **971-37-53-92.** Reservations recommended in summer. Main courses 815–2,700 ptas. ($5.45–$18.10); menú del día 1,500 ptas. ($10.05). AE, MC, V. Daily 1–4pm and 7–11pm. MINORCAN.

Easily spotted by the 300-year-old windmill that inspired the name of this 1982 creation, Molí d'es Reco has a pleasant outdoor patio but a rather plain indoor dining area. Overall, the place is a bit touristy, but if offers hearty Minorcan fare including stuffed eggplant, *oliaigua amb tomatecs* (a soup with tomato, onion, parsley, green pepper, and garlic), snails with spider crab, partridge with cabbage, and *calamares a la menorquina* (stuffed squid with an almond-cream sauce).

Sa Plaça. Carrer d'Enmig (also Avinguda de la Constitución), 2, Es Mercadal. ☎ **971-37-50-48.** Main courses 800–2,750 ptas. ($5.35–$18.45); fixed-price menu 1,000 ptas. ($6.70). MC, V. Daily 1–4pm and 8–10pm. MINORCAN.

Simple, unpretentious, and noted as a centerpiece of local gossip, this is a well-managed, family run bistro and cafeteria rather than a full-fledged restaurant. Within a simple and somewhat battered setting, you'll be free to order just coffee, a glass of wine, or any of 10 kinds of tapas, and seek a refuge from the searing heat outside within a low-key environment that's thoroughly and completely Minorcan in its tastes, orientation, and self-definition.

S'Engolidor. Carrer Major, 3, Es Migjorn Gran. ☎ **971-37-01-93.** Reservations recommended on weekends. Main courses 1,250–1,700 ptas. ($8.40–$11.40). MC, V. May–Oct, daily 8–11pm. Closed Dec–Apr. MINORCAN.

In the village of Es Migjorn Gran (San Cristóbal), between Es Mercadal and Santo Tomás, lies this cozy and relatively undiscovered restaurant. Except for a small sign on the door, it could be mistaken for any other house on this quiet, side street. The building dates from 1740, with sections added throughout the years. The interior is simple: stark white walls accented with various works of art. The dining area consists of several small rooms, with only a few tables each. You can also dine outdoors in one of the small patio areas; many overlook the owner's compact vegetable garden. The menu consists of various Minorcan specialties, including *olaigua*, eggplant stuffed with fish; rabbit and wild mushroom stew; and a particularly succulent version of roasted lamb. Owner José Luis maintains four very simple rooms that, although clean and cozy, contain virtually no amenities other than a private bathroom and a sense of peace and quiet. A double room, with breakfast included, costs between 4,800 and 5,000 ptas. ($32.15 and $33.50) per night, and is available only between May and October.

FORNELLS & THE NORTHERN COAST

The road leading north from Es Mercadal to Fornells runs through some of the island's finer scenery. Mass tourism hotels, so far, have not discovered this place, although there are several good dining choices. On the northern coast, the tiny town of Fornells snuggles around a bay filled with boats and windsurfers and lined with restaurants and a few shops. Built around four defense fortifications—the Talaia de la Mola (now destroyed), the Tower of Fornells at the harbor mouth, the fortress of the Island of Las Sargantanas (the Lizards) situated in the middle of the harbor, and the now-ruined Castle of San Jorge or San Antonion—Fornells today is a flourishing fishing village noted for its upscale restaurants featuring savory lobster *calderetas*.

West of Fornells is **Platja Binimella,** a beautiful beach (unofficially nudist) that's easily accessible by car. Its long, curving, sandy cove is peacefully set against undulating hills. A snack bar is the sole concession to civilization.

By far the most splendid panorama here is that from the promontory at **Cap de Cavalleria,** the northernmost tip of the island, marked by a lighthouse. Getting here requires some effort, however. At a bend in the road leading to Platja Binimella, a signpost indicates the turnoff to Cap de Cavalleria through a closed gate heading to a dirt road. The closed gate is typical of many of the roads leading to Minorca's undeveloped beaches. All the beaches in Spain, however, are public, so no one may impede access to them—although landowners may discourage visitors by making access difficult. The prevailing custom is simply to open the gate, go on through, and close it behind you. It is important that you close the gate, because often these gates keep livestock confined to certain areas. As you follow the long dirt road (negotiable in a regular car or on a motorbike) out to Cap de Cavelleria, you'll come across several more sets of gates and travel through countryside that's somewhat reminiscent of the Scottish highlands, with cultivated fields and scattered grand fincas, or farmsteads. Shortly before the lighthouse is a parking area down to the left. You'll have to pick your way across the scrub and rocks for the views. The best one is from a circular tower in ruins up to the right of the lighthouse. Now brace yourself for a vista encompassing the whole of Minorca—a symphony of dramatic cliffs and jewel-blue water.

WHERE TO STAY

Hostal S'Algaret. Plaça S'Algaret, 7, 07748 Fornells. ☎ **971-37-65-52.** 21 units. A/C TEL. 7,450–11,800 ptas. ($49.90–$79.05) double. Rates include breakfast. AE, MC, V. Closed Nov–Mar.

This is for escapists only. It's really like an unpretentious inn. It's also a bit sleepy, so don't expect a lot in the way of hotel services. But adventurous do-it-yourself types often book the modest and very simply furnished guest rooms, which are clean and reasonably comfortable. Floors are tiled, the furnishings basic but the spacious modern bathrooms are alluring. There are sizable terraces opening onto views as well. If your expectations aren't high, you might go for this one. Few will complain, either, when the reasonable bill is presented.

WHERE TO DINE

Fornells is noted for its fine seafood restaurants specializing in the Minorcan calderetas. King Juan Carlos has been known to sail in here when he wants to savor the seafood stew, and in peak summer season people call their favorite Fornells restaurant days in advance with their orders.

✪ **Es Pla.** Pasage des Pla, Fornells. ☎ **971-37-66-55.** Reservations recommended July–Aug. Main courses 750–2,600 ptas. ($5.05–$17.40); menú del día 2,600–3,000 ptas. ($17.40–$20.10) from Sept 20–June 20. AE, MC, V. Daily 1–3:30pm and 7:30pm–midnight. MINORCAN/SEAFOOD.

If any restaurant in Minorca deserves a comparison to the grand Roman watering holes of *La Dolce Vita*, it would be this one, where King Juan Carlos and his family have come to dine several times. Stylish, airy, and elegant in a way that reflects the seagoing life of the island, Es Pla has thrived here since the 1960s, on a wood-floored porch that lies only about 6 feet above the swell of the surf. Large and informal, it has a long, stainless steel bar area and an indoor-outdoor design. Menu items include a roster of perfectly prepared fish, meat, and shellfish, but the acknowledged culinary winner—and the most frequently ordered dish—is paella with crayfish.

S'Algaret. Plaça S'Algaret, 7, Fornells. ☎ **971-37-65-52.** Tapas 225–1,100 ptas. ($1.50–$7.35) per *ración* (serving); menú del día 1,600 ptas. ($10.70); platters 800–1,300 ptas. ($5.35–$8.70). AE, MC, V. Daily noon–4pm and 8–11pm. SPANISH.

Adjacent to the hostal of the same name (see above), S'Algaret is much frequented by locals and is one of the few economical alternatives for eating in Fornells (here you eat rather than dine). The restaurant is sleepy, quiet, small in scale, and unpretentious. You can nibble on good-tasting tapas, sandwiches, a varied selection of *tortillas* (Spanish omelettes), and a smattering of *platos combinados* (combination plates), the ingredients of which change daily.

Appendix A: Spain in Depth

The once-accepted adage that "Europe ends at the Pyrenees" is no longer true. Today, the two countries forming the Iberian Peninsula at the southwestern end of the continent—Spain and Portugal—are totally integrated in Europe as members of the European Union (EU), with democratic governments and vibrant economies of their own. In fact, Spain has the second fastest-growing economy in the EU; new industries and an expanding infrastructure continue to alter its ancient landscape.

Political changes adopted after the 1975 death of Gen. Francisco Franco, Europe's remaining prewar dictator, contributed to a remarkable cultural renaissance. This rebirth has transformed Spain's two largest cities—Madrid, the capital, and Barcelona—into major artistic and intellectual centers. Amid some of the world's most innovative architecture, contemporary movements in art, literature, cinema, and fashion are constantly finding new and original expression; at night the cafes and bars hum with animated discussions on politics, the economy, and society. In every aspect of urban life, a visitor feels the Spanish people's reawakened self-confidence and pride in their newfound prosperity.

These developments contrast with Spain's unhappy experiences earlier in this century, particularly during the devastating Civil War of 1936–39 and Franco's subsequent long iron-hand rule. During the Franco years, political and intellectual freedom was squelched, and Spain was snubbed by most of Europe.

Spain was previously, of course, a major world player. In the 16th century it was the seat of a great empire; the Spanish monarchy dispatched fleets that conquered the New World, returning with its riches. Columbus sailed to America and Balboa to the Pacific Ocean; Cortés conquered Mexico for glory; and Pizarro brought Peru into the Spanish fold. The conquistadors too often revealed the dark side of the Spanish character, including brutality in the name of honor and glory, but they also represented a streak of boldness and daring.

It's difficult to visit this country without recalling its golden past: Those famous "castles in Spain" really do exist. Yet many Spaniards believe that Spain isn't merely a single country but a series of nations, united the way Yugoslavia used to be. Many groups, especially the Basques, the Catalans, and the Gallegos in the northeast, are asserting their individuality in everything from culture to language. At least in the case of Basque separatists, that regional, "nationalistic" pride has taken violent turns. Castile and Andalusia, in the south, remain quintessentially Spanish. While linguistic and cultural differences are great, to the foreign visitor they will also be subtle.

As the inheritors of a great and ancient civilization dating from before the Roman Empire, Spaniards inhabit a land that is not only culturally rich but geographically varied, with wooded sierra, arid plateaus, and sandy beaches. It is this exciting variety in landscape, as well as in art, architecture, music, and cuisine, that makes Spain one of the top countries in the world to visit.

1 Spain Today

As Spain nears the millennium, tourism continues to boom. It remains the hot, hot industry. With arrivals in Spain hovering around the 45 million mark each year, Spain is one of the world's most popular destinations. Americans have become a large part of the tourist picture. Many European visitors head for the beach resorts, but Americans occupy the number one position in visits to three top Spanish cities: Madrid, Barcelona, and Seville.

No longer interested in the "lager lout" image its coastal resorts earned in the 1970s and 1980s by hosting so many cheap package tours from Britain, Spain has reached out to a more upscale visitor. Bargain Spain of the $5-a-day variety is now a distant memory, as prices have skyrocketed. The government is trying to lure visitors away from the overcrowded coasts (especially Majorca, the Costa del Sol, and the Costa Brava) and steer them to the country's less-traveled, but more historic, destinations. Government paradors and other improved tourist facilities, better restaurants, and spruced-up attractions have sent out the message.

Spain entered 1999 by coming under the euro umbrella, although Spanish pesetas will continue to circulate in the year 2000. Actually citizens will not start using the new coins and bank notes until the beginning of 2002. The peseta, which has been the Spanish monetary unit since 1868, will disappear completely on July 1, 2002.

Backers of the euro, mainly the Spanish government, have presented the new currency as the solution to many of Spanish's problems, including unemployment and deficits. Many economists in Spain remain skeptical and are watching the country's entry into the euro market with great caution. Some economists are predicting a short-term property boom, as holders of undeclared "black market" pesetas rush to invest them before they are forced to convert them into euro dollars.

Although unemployment, which remains well above 20% in Spain, continues to plague the government, progress has been made. The country's debt is some 68% of the gross domestic product. Inflation is about 2.4%, an all time low in the post-Franco era. Consumer spending remains cautious, however, since most of the new jobs being created are on short-term contracts.

Spain continues to change as it moves toward the millennium. A drug culture and escalating crime—something virtually unheard of in Franco's day—are an unfortunate sign of Spain's entry into the modern world. The most remarkable advance has been in the legal status of women, who now have access to contraception, abortion, and divorce. Sights once unimaginable are now taking place: an annual lesbian "kiss-in" at Madrid's Puerto del Sol and women officiating as governors of men's prisons. Surprising in a Catholic country, the birth rate continues to remain one of the lowest in the developed world, and the population is aging.

At least for the moment, Spain's monarchy seems to be working. England's House of Windsor might well use the Court of Borbón—presided over by King

Juan Carlos and Queen Sofia—as role models. In 1975, when the king assumed the throne after the death of Franco, he was called "Juan Carlos the Brief," implying that his reign would be short. But almost overnight he distanced himself from Franco's dark legacy and became a hardworking and serious sovereign. He staved off a coup attempt in 1981, and he and the other Spanish royals remain popular. Juan Carlos even makes do on a meager $7 million salary—less than one-tenth of what England's Queen Elizabeth is reputed to earn in a year.

The author John Hooper, in an updated version of his 1986 best-seller, *The New Spaniards,* remains optimistic about the future of Spain, in spite of its problems. He suggests Spaniards not forget that "to be true to themselves they may need to be different from others." Hooper believes that the new Spain will have arrived at adulthood "not on the day it ceases to be different from the rest of Europe, but on the day that it acknowledges that it is." Hooper was referring to the exotic, romantic, and varied faces of Spain that set it apart from other nations of Europe, ranging from flamenco to its bullfighting and its Moorish architecture to its pagan ceremonies. Nowhere—not even in Italy—is the festival and traditional, flamboyant dress more a part of annual life than in Spain, where religious processions are full of intense passion.

2 History 101

BARBARIAN INVASIONS, THE MOORISH KINGDOM & THE RECONQUEST

Dateline

- **11th century B.C.** Phoenicians settle Spain's coasts.
- **650 B.C.** Greeks colonize the east.
- **600 B.C.** Celts cross the Pyrenees and settle in Spain.
- **6th–3rd century B.C.** Carthaginians make Cartagena their colonial capital, driving out the Greeks.
- **2nd century B.C.–2nd century A.D.** Rome controls most of Iberia. Christianity spreads.
- **218–201 B.C.** Second Punic War: Rome defeats Carthage.
- **5th century** Vandals, then Visigoths, invade Spain.
- **8th century** Moors conquer most of Spain.
- **1214** More than half of Iberia is regained by Catholics.
- **1469** Ferdinand of Aragón marries Isabella of Castile.

continues

Around 200 B.C. the Romans vanquished the Carthaginians and laid the foundations of the present Latin culture. Traces of Roman civilization can still be seen today. By the time of Julius Caesar, Spain (Hispania) was under Roman law and began a long period of peace and prosperity.

When Rome fell in the 5th century, Spain was overrun, first by the Vandals and then by the Visigoths from eastern Europe. The chaotic rule of the Visigothic kings lasted about 300 years, but the barbarian invaders did adopt the language of their new country and tolerated Christianity as well.

In A.D. 711 Moorish warriors led by Tarik crossed over into Spain and conquered the disunited country. By 714 they controlled most of it, except for a few mountain regions around Asturias. For 8 centuries the Moors occupied their new land, which they called *al-Andalus,* or Andalusia, with Córdoba as the capital. A great intellectual center, Córdoba became the scientific capital of Europe; notable advances were made in agriculture, industry, literature, philosophy, and medicine. The Jews were welcomed by the Moors, often serving as administrators, ambassadors, and financial officers. But the Moors quarreled with one another, and soon the few Christian strongholds in the north began to advance south.

The Reconquest, the name given to the Christian efforts to rid the peninsula of the Moors, slowly reduced the size of the Muslim holdings, with Catholic monarchies forming in northern areas. The three powerful kingdoms of Aragón, Castile, and León were joined in 1469, when Ferdinand of Aragón married Isabella of Castile. Catholic kings, as they were called, launched the final attack on the Moors and completed the Reconquest in 1492 by capturing Granada.

That same year Columbus, the Genoese sailor, landed on the West Indies, laying the foundations for a far-flung empire that brought wealth and power to Spain during the 16th and 17th centuries.

The Spanish Inquisition, begun under Ferdinand and Isabella, sought to eradicate all heresy and secure the primacy of Catholicism. Non-Catholics, Jews, and Moors were mercilessly persecuted, and many were driven out of the country.

THE GOLDEN AGE & LATER DECLINE

Columbus's voyage to America and the conquistadors' subsequent exploration of that land ushered Spain into its golden age.

In the first half of the 16th century, Balboa discovered the Pacific Ocean, Cortés seized Mexico for Spain, Pizarro took Peru, and a Spanish ship (initially commanded by the Portuguese Magellan, who was killed during the voyage) circumnavigated the globe. The conquistadors took Catholicism to the New World and shipped cargoes of gold back to Spain. The Spanish Empire extended all the way to the Philippines. Charles V, grandson of Ferdinand and Isabella, was the most powerful prince in Europe—King of Spain and Naples, Holy Roman Emperor and lord of Germany, duke of Burgundy and the Netherlands, and ruler of the New World territories.

But much of Spain's wealth and human resources was wasted in religious and secular conflicts. First Jews, then Muslims, and finally Catholicized Moors were driven out—and with them much of the country's prosperity. When Philip II ascended the throne in 1556, Spain could indeed boast vast possessions: the New World colonies; Naples, Milan, Genoa, Sicily, and other portions of Italy; the Spanish Netherlands (modern Belgium and the Netherlands); and portions of Austria and Germany. But the seeds of decline had already been planted.

- **1492** Catholic monarchs seize Granada, the last Moorish stronghold. Columbus lands in the New World.
- **1519** Cortés conquers Mexico. Charles I is crowned Holy Roman Emperor, as Charles V.
- **1556** Philip II inherits throne and launches the Counter-Reformation.
- **1588** England defeats Spanish Armada.
- **1700** Philip V becomes king. War of Spanish Succession follows.
- **1713** Treaty of Utrecht ends war. Spain's colonies reduced.
- **1759** Charles III ascends throne.
- **1808** Napoléon places brother Joseph on the Spanish throne.
- **1813** Wellington drives French out of Spain; the monarchy is restored.
- **1876** Spain becomes a constitutional monarchy.
- **1898** Spanish-American War leads to Spain's loss of Puerto Rico, Cuba, and the Philippines.
- **1923** Primo de Rivera forms military directorate.
- **1930** Right-wing dictatorship ends; Primo de Rivera exiled.
- **1931** King Alfonso XIII abdicates; Second Republic is born.
- **1933–35** Falange party formed.
- **1936–39** Civil War between the governing Popular Front and the Nationalists led by Gen. Francisco Franco.
- **1939** Franco establishes dictatorship, which will last 36 years.
- **1941** Spain technically stays neutral in World War II, but Franco favors Germany.
- **1955** Spain joins the United Nations.

continues

- **1969** Franco names Juan Carlos as his successor.
- **1975** Juan Carlos becomes king. Franco dies.
- **1978** New, democratic constitution initiates reforms.
- **1981** Coup attempt by right-wing officers fails.
- **1982** Socialists gain power after 43 years of right-wing rule.
- **1986** Spain joins the European Community (now the European Union).
- **1992** Barcelona hosts the Summer Olympics; Seville hosts EXPO '92.
- **1996** A conservative party defeats Socialist party, ending 13-year rule. José María Aznar chosen prime minister.
- **1998** Two cultural milestones for Spain: the inauguration of the controversial Guggenheim Museum at Bilbao and the reopening of Madrid's opera house, Teatro Real.
- **1999** Spain falls under the Euro umbrella.

Philip, a fanatic Catholic, devoted his energies to subduing the Protestant revolt in the Netherlands and to becoming the standard bearer for the Counter-Reformation. He tried to return England to Catholicism, first by marrying Mary I ("Bloody Mary") and later by wooing her half sister, Elizabeth I, who rebuffed him. When, in 1588, he resorted to sending the Armada, it was ignominiously defeated; and that defeat symbolized the decline of Spanish power.

In 1700 a Bourbon prince, Philip V, became king, and the country fell under the influence of France. Philip V's right to the throne was challenged by a Hapsburg archduke of Austria, thus giving rise to the War of the Spanish Succession. When it ended, Spain had lost Flanders, its Italian possessions, and Gibraltar (still held by the British today).

During the 18th century, Spain's direction changed with each sovereign. Charles III (1759–88) developed the country economically and culturally. Charles IV became embroiled in wars with France, and the weakness of the Spanish monarchy allowed Napoléon to place his brother Joseph Bonaparte on the throne in 1808.

THE 19TH & 20TH CENTURIES

Although Britain and France had joined forces to restore the Spanish monarchy, the European conflicts encouraged Spanish colonists to rebel. Ultimately, this led the United States to free the Philippines, Puerto Rico, and Cuba from Spain in 1898.

In 1876 Spain became a constitutional monarchy. But labor unrest, disputes with the Catholic Church, and war in Morocco combined to create political chaos. Conditions eventually became so bad that the Cortés, or parliament, was dissolved in 1923, and Gen. Miguel Primo de Rivera formed a military directorate. Early in 1930 Primo de Rivera resigned, but unrest continued.

On April 14, 1931, a revolution occurred, a republic was proclaimed, and King Alfonso XIII and his family were forced to flee. Initially the liberal constitutionalists ruled, but soon they were pushed aside by the socialists and anarchists, who adopted a constitution separating church and state, secularizing education, and containing several other radical provisions (for example, agrarian reform and the expulsion of the Jesuits).

The extreme nature of these reforms fostered the growth of the conservative Falange party (*Falange española,* or Spanish Phalanx), modeled after Italy and Germany's fascist parties. By the 1936 elections, the country was divided equally between left and right, and political violence was common. On July 18, 1936, the army, supported by Mussolini and Hitler, tried to seize power, igniting the Spanish Civil War. Gen. Francisco Franco, coming from Morocco to Spain, led the Nationalist (rightist) forces in the 2 years of fighting that ravaged the country. Towns were bombed and atrocities were committed in abundance. Early in 1939, Franco entered Barcelona and went on to

Madrid; thousands of republicans were executed. Franco became chief of state, remaining so until his death in 1975.

Although Franco adopted a neutral position during World War II, his sympathies obviously lay with Germany and Italy, and Spain as a nonbelligerent assisted the Axis powers. This action intensified the diplomatic isolation into which the country was forced after the war's end—in fact, it was excluded from the United Nations until 1955.

Before his death, General Franco selected as his successor Juan Carlos de Borbón y Borbón, son of the pretender to the Spanish throne. After the 1977 elections, a new constitution was approved by the electorate and the king; it guaranteed human and civil rights, as well as free enterprise, and canceled the status of the Roman Catholic Church as the church of Spain. It also granted limited autonomy to several regions, including Catalonia and the Basque provinces, both of which, however, are still clamoring for complete autonomy.

In 1981 a group of right-wing military officers seized the Cortés and called upon Juan Carlos to establish a Francoist state. The king, however, refused, and the conspirators were arrested. The fledgling democracy overcame its first test. Its second major accomplishment—under the Socialist administration of Prime Minister Felipe González, the country's first leftist government since 1939—was to gain Spain's entry into the European Community (now Union) in 1986.

Further proof that the new Spain had been fully accepted by the international community came in 1992. Spain was designated by the European Union (EU) as the Cultural Capital of Europe for the year; but more significant, the Summer Olympics were held successfully in Barcelona and the world's fair, EXPO '92, was mounted in Seville, in Andalusia.

In March 1996, more than 78% of Spain's 32 million registered voters cast ballots and ended the 13-year rule of the scandal-plagued Socialist party of Prime Minister Felipe González. A conservative party with roots in the Franco dictatorship was swept into power, lead by José Maria Aznar, leader of the Popular party, who pledged to represent "all Spain." González took the defeat bitterly, alleging that the vote "was a step back to the fascist dictatorship of Franco."

That dire prediction has not proved accurate, as Spain forged ahead to integrate itself more fully into the European economy and took stringent measures to streamline its economy to meet the requirements necessary for that step.

In January 1999 Spain joined 10 other EU countries in adopting the euro as its new currency, although it will be going through a transitional period until January 1, 2002. Until that time, the peseta and the euro will continue to exist side by side.

3 Architecture Through the Ages

FROM THE ROMANS TO THE MOORS

Architectural roots in Spain date from the Romans, who built aqueducts and more than 12,000 miles of roads and bridges as a means of linking their assorted Iberian holdings. The greatest of these, **Via Augusta,** followed the Costa Brava, Costa Blanca, and Costa del Sol to transport armies and supplies between Cádiz and the Pyrenees.

This Hispano-Roman style involves prolific use of the vault and the arch, which you can see in such marvels as the **aqueduct at Segovia, the triumphal arch at Tarragona,** and the rectilinear carefully planned community at **Mérida** (whose Roman monuments are among the best preserved in Europe).

The Spectacle of Death

For obvious reasons, many people consider bullfighting cruel and shocking. But as Ernest Hemingway pointed out in *Death in the Afternoon:* "The bullfight is not a sport in the Anglo-Saxon sense of the word, that is, it is not an equal contest or an attempt at an equal contest between a bull and a man. Rather it is a tragedy: the death of the bull, which is played, more or less well, by the bull and the man involved and in which there is danger for the man but certain death for the bull."

When the symbolic drama of the bullfight is acted out, some believe it reaches a higher plane, the realm of art. Some people argue that it is not a public exhibition of cruelty at all, but rather a highly skilled art form that requires will to survive, courage, showmanship, and gallantry. Regardless of how you view it, the spectacle is an authentic Spanish experience and reveals much about the character of the land and its people.

The *corrida* (bullfight) season lasts from early spring until around mid-October. Fights are held in a *plaza de toros* (bullring), including the oldest ring in remote Ronda to the big-time Plaza de Toros in Madrid. Sunday is corrida day in most major Spanish cities, although Madrid and Barcelona may also have fights on Thursday.

Tickets fall into three classifications, and prices are based on your exposure to the famed Spanish sun: *sol* (sun), the cheapest; *sombra* (shade), the most expensive; and *sol y sombra* (a mixture of sun and shade), the medium-price range.

The corrida begins with a parade. For many viewers, this may be the high point of the afternoon's festivities, as all the bullfighters are clad in their *trajes de luce,* or luminous suits.

Historians cite A.D. 409 as the end of the Roman age in Iberia, the beginning of political anarchy, and the migration into Spain of thousands of immigrants (Vandals, Alans, Suevians, and Visigothic tribespeople) from Central Europe. The newcomers, recent converts to some kind of Christianity, built crude chapels and fortresses based on a mishmash of aesthetic ideals from northern Europe and Byzantium, using engineering principles copied from the ancient Romans.

Spain's Romanesque style began to develop around A.D. 800, derived from the legacy of these crude Visigothic buildings (see below). Meanwhile, a major new aesthetic was forcibly imposed upon Spain from the south.

HISPANO-MOORISH ARCHITECTURE

The Moors gained control of the Iberian Peninsula in the 8th century, and their 600-year rule left an architectural legacy that is among the most exotic and colorful in Europe. Regrettably, only a handful of *alcázares* (palaces), *alcazabas* (fortresses), and converted mosques remain intact today. Moorish buildings tended to be relatively flimsy and heavily accented with decorations. Many have collapsed (or were deliberately destroyed) in the Catholic zeal to "re-Christianize" Iberia.

The most visible traits of the Saracenic style included the use of forests of (sometimes mismatched) columns within mosques, each of which was used to

Bullfights are divided into thirds. The first is the *tercio de capa* (cape), during which the matador tests the bull with various passes and gets acquainted with him. The second portion, the *tercio de varas* (sticks), begins with the lance-carrying *picadores* on horseback, who weaken, or "punish," the bull by jabbing him in the shoulder area. The horses are sometimes gored, even though they wear protective padding, or the horse and rider may be tossed into the air by the now-infuriated bull. The picadores are followed by the *banderilleros,* whose job it is to puncture the bull with pairs of boldly colored darts.

In the final *tercio de muleta,* the action narrows down to the lone fighter and the bull. Gone are the fancy capes. Instead, the matador uses a small red cloth known as a *muleta,* which, to be effective, requires a bull with lowered head. (The picadores and banderilleros have worked to achieve this.) Using the muleta as a lure, the matador wraps the bull around himself in various passes, the most dangerous of which is the natural; here, the matador holds the muleta in his left hand, the sword in his right. Right-hand passes pose less of a threat, since the sword can be used to spread out the muleta, making a larger target for the bull. After a number of passes, the time comes for the kill, the moment of truth.

After the bull dies, the highest official at the ring may award the matador an ear from the dead bull, or perhaps both ears, or ears and tail. For a truly extraordinary performance, the hoof is sometimes added. Spectators cheer a superlative performance by waving white handkerchiefs, imploring the judge to award a prize. The bullfighter may be carried away as a hero, or if he has displeased the crowd, he may be jeered and chased out of the ring by an angry mob. At a major fight, usually six bulls are killed by three matadors in one afternoon.

support a network of horseshoe-shaped arches. These interconnected to support low, flat roofs. Some arches were scalloped, then decorated with geometric designs or calligraphic inscriptions from the Koran.

MOZARABIC ARCHITECTURE

Mozárabes were Christian Spaniards who retained their religion under the Muslim rule. They successfully blended Gothic and Moorish styles in their art and architecture. The few structures that remain intact from this period can be found in Toledo and include the **Monastery of El Cristo de la Luz,** originally built in the 900s as a mosque; a 12th-century synagogue, now the church of **Santa María de la Blanca;** and the **churches of Santiago del Arrabal and San Román.** A secular example of the style in Toledo is the **Puerto del Sol,** an ornate gate built into the walls that surround the old city. Constructed around 1200, about 150 years after Toledo's reconquest by Christian forces, it combines the distinctive Moorish horseshoe arch with feudal battlements and Christian iconography.

MUDÉAR ARCHITECTURE

Equivalent in some ways to the above-mentioned Mozárabe style (with which it is frequently confused), Mudéjar refers to the architectural and decorative style developed by Spanish Muslims living in Christian territories after the

Reconquista. A mix of Gothic and Moorish influences, it reached its peak between 1275 and 1350, made frequent use of brick instead of stone, and specialized in elaborate wood carvings that merged the Moorish emphasis on geometrics and symmetry with Christian themes. Regrettably, after the final Moorish stronghold fell to the Christians in 1492, Spanish monarchs did everything they could to purge any artistic legacy left by the Moors. Mudéjar influences, however, still cropped up in rural pockets of Spain until the middle of the 18th century, and, in some cases, even merged subtly with ornate features of the baroque.

PRE-ROMANESQUE & ROMANESQUE ARCHITECTURE

Ensconced in Asturias, feudal rulers of the Christian Visigothic tribes refined their architectural tastes. Stonework became better crafted than the crude models of the previous two centuries, and arches became more graceful. Under the rule of Alfonso the Chaste (791–842), dozens of pre-Romanesque churches were built in Oviedo, and a body believed to be that of Saint James was discovered, miraculously, in a field in Galicia. Thus was born **Santiago de Compostela** (St. James of the Field), the eventual site of a great cathedral and one of the most famous pilgrimage sites in the Christian world.

From these beginnings, and based on money and cultural influences from the floods of pilgrims pouring in from Italy, France, and other parts of Europe, a trail of Romanesque churches, shelters, monasteries, and convents sprang up across northern Spain, especially along the pilgrim route in Catalonia, Aragón, and northern Castile. The style is known for semicircular arches, small windows, crude but evocative carvings, and thick walls. It is best represented in the **church of San Gil in Zaragoza** and the **cloisters of San Pedro,** near Pamplona in the town of Estella.

SPANISH GOTHIC

This style surged across provinces adjacent to the French border (Catalonia and Navarre) beginning around 1250. By the late 1200s, churches that had been initiated in the Romanesque style (such as the **Burgos cathedral**) were completed as sometimes flamboyant Gothic monuments. During the 1300s and 1400s, bishops in León, Toledo, and Burgos even imported architects and masons from Gothic strongholds in other parts of Europe to design their cathedrals. In Spain, the Gothic style included widespread use of the ogive (high-pointed) arches and vaults, clustered pilasters, and an opening up of walls to incorporate large, usually stained-glass, windows.

THE RENAISSANCE

After the expulsion of the Moors from Iberia, and Columbus's first landings in the New World in 1492, Spain found itself caught up in a vivid, emphatic sense of its own manifest destiny. Searching for a national style of architecture, the Spanish monarchs adapted the aesthetic trends of Renaissance Italy into a "Hispanicized" style. Foremost among these was the 16th-century plateresque, which emulated in stone the finely worked forms that a silversmith might have hammered into silver plate. The style is best viewed on the exterior of the **University of Salamanca** and the **Chapel of the New Kings inside the cathedral at Toledo.**

CLASSICAL SPANISH ARCHITECTURE

The austere regime of Philip II not only welcomed but demanded a less ornate national style from the country's architects. Fervently religious and obsessively ambitious for the advancement of Spanish interests, he embraced the austere ancient Roman forms that had been revived during Italy's late Renaissance. The style's most megalomaniacal manifestation within Spain came with **Juan de Herrera's** gargantuan, brooding, and military-looking monastery and palace at **El Escorial** (1563–84) on an isolated and windswept plateau outside Madrid. Philip II considered the style an appropriate manifestation of the stern principles of the Counter-Reformation and the new Inquisition that followed.

Later during the Renaissance, Herrera's rectilinear gridirons were replaced with the curved lines of the baroque. This style was avidly embraced by the Jesuits, one of the most powerful religious orders in Spain at the time, whose austere religious bent stood in marked contrast to their flamboyant architectural tastes. The baroque style appears at its most ornate in **Andalusia,** a region enjoying a building boom at the time thanks to the wealth that poured into its ports from the gold mines of Mexico and Peru.

Ironically, baroque was the style most enthusiastically embraced by the Spanish colonies in South America. Spain's interpretation of Italian baroque architecture is sometimes referred to as Churrigueresque, after **José Churriguera** (1665–1725), designer to the kings of Spain and architect of **Salamanca's New Cathedral.** The style is characterized by its dense concentrations of busy ornamentation that often completely disguised the basic form of the building itself. An example of baroque style in Spain is the wedding-cake facade of the **Murcia cathedral.**

FROM BAROQUE TOWARD MODERN

Under the Spanish Bourbon rulers of the 18th century, the favored style embraced the baroque and neoclassical influences of aristocratic France. **El Pardo, Riofrio,** and **Aranjuez** were all built as Europeanized hideaways. Even the design of the **Royal Palace in Madrid** was modeled after Versailles.

In the 19th century the Romantic age encouraged a revolt against the ideals of balance and reason that had defined upscale European architecture during the late 1700s. Spanish architecture throughout the 19th century was torn between the value of the individual architect's eclectic, personalized, and sometimes flamboyant vision, and the inevitable reactions that swung the pendulums of public taste back toward greater restraint and symmetry. There developed a new respect for the Gothic, as many 500-year-old Gothic cathedrals were adapted or altered with neo-Gothic alterations that modern art historians sometimes view with horror.

Out of this tension emerged one of Spain's most widely recognized architectural giants, **Antoni Gaudí** (1852–1926). His idiosyncratic, organic style, called Catalan Art Nouveau, or *modernisme,* coincided neatly with the most intense building boom ever experienced within his hometown of **Barcelona.** Gaudí succeeded in fusing regional aesthetics and forms with a style that still challenges architectural thinking. He created curiously curved and sinuous, "organic-looking" buildings in protest against the rising anonymity of the industrial age and dull architecture without soul that would reach its most grotesque form in Nazi Germany long after Gaudí's death. One of the best examples of his ideas can be seen in Barcelona's **Casa Milá.**

ARCHITECTURE TODAY

Other than occasional models of genuine inspiration, such as the whimsical and surrealist buildings devised by **Salvador Dalí,** much of modern Spain's architecture is derived from the older, tried-and-true traditions. When it comes to recycling the feudal or Renaissance monuments of yesteryear, Spain has no equal, as evidenced by the country's network of historic paradors. Regrettably, some areas of modern Spain, including many neighborhoods of Madrid and long stretches of the Costa del Sol, have bristled with high-rise, concrete-and-glass apartment houses. Few boast any distinguishing features, provoking laments from traditionalists.

One example of genuine inspiration, however, is the work of **Rafael Moneo,** who lives in Madrid and has designed mainly in Spain with such exceptions as the Davis Museum and Cultural Center at Wellesley, Massachusetts, in 1993. One of his most notable designs is the **Museo Nacional de Arte Roman in Mérida.** In 1996 he won the Pritzker Architecture Prize, viewed as the Oscar for architects. The Spanish architect **Santiago Calatrava** has been hailed as one of Europe's most innovative architects, although he trained as an engineer and sculptor. He seeks to build a bridge between architecture and art. In Barcelona, his **Bach de Roda-Felipe II Bridge** spans the rail tracks that run from north to south, linking the ocean and city itself. Other projects include the **Bilbao Airport Terminal** and the **"City of Sciences" in Valencia.**

Although Spain has a lot of homegrown talent, it also turns to foreign architects, especially for flashy signature projects. The most famous example of this is **Frank Gehry's Guggenheim Museum at Bilbao,** hailed as the first great building of the 21st century. One critic said that Gehry has "repudiated Modernist sanctity, symmetry, and right-angled geometrics in his own fearless way, taking them apart and putting them back together with a rollicking, cockeyed brilliance."

4 Spanish Art

ARTISTIC ROOTS

Spanish art has always been characterized by a mixture of passion and austerity— a reflection of the country itself—that makes it one of the most unusual and riveting of national oeuvres anywhere.

Some of the best examples of prehistoric art were discovered in Spanish caves, including the hunting scenes within the **caves of Altamira and Puente Viesgo,** and the mysterious dolmens that stand like Celtic sentinels at **Antequera,** near Málaga. Equivalent dolmens (known locally as *talayots* and *navetas*) were erected on the Balearics between around 2500 and 1000 B.C.

By 1000 B.C. Spain became a crossroads of civilizations, a role it would play for the next 3,000 years. Many of the most prized artifacts in Spanish museums date from this era; the statue *The Lady of Elche,* the lions of Córdoba, and the bulls (*toros*) of Guisando all reflect the influence of **ancient Greeks and Phoenicians,** who used Spain's coast as a port of call on their trade routes. In such port cities as Cádiz, for example, rows of Phoenician sarcophagi have been unearthed.

HISPANO-MOORISH ART

Beginning in A.D. 711, when the first Moorish armies poured into Andalusia, the preconceptions of Spanish art changed forever. Forbidden by religious law to portray human or animal forms, Muslim artists restricted themselves to geometric patterns, ornate depictions of plant life, and calligraphic renderings of verses from the Koran. Their works influenced the Mozárabes, who brought these themes within a Christian context. The Moors also excelled at landscape architecture—the symmetrical placement of fountains, plants, and statues in some of the greatest gardens and pleasure pavilions ever built.

ROMANESQUE ART

Other than its architecture, the greatest artistic legacy of the Romanesque age, which began around A.D. 1000, was its sculpture. A vast number of churches and abbeys sprang up along the medieval world's most famous pilgrimage route (St. James's way across Asturias and Galicia), and each house of worship required sculpture to adorn the columns and altars. **San Juan de la Peña** was a master of the carved form, and his students branched out across the pilgrimage route, carving crude but symbolic references to apocryphal tales.

In Catalonia, aggressive merchants appropriated aesthetic ideals from Italy and France and had paintings executed on fresh plaster. Several of the most memorable of these Romanesque frescoes that remain today are credited to a mysterious painter, the **Master of Tahull,** who may have trained as far away as Byzantium. By 1300, Catalonia had been home to more than 1,000 artists, many of whom were inspired by this mysterious master.

GOTHIC ART

Beginning around 1250, as the Gothic aesthetic trickled from France into Spain, the production of painting and sculpture accelerated. Works followed religious themes, often rendered in the form of polychrome triptychs and altarpieces that stretched toward the soaring heights of a cathedral's ceiling. Many painters took their inspiration from such contemporary pre-Renaissance Italians as Giotto; others looked to France and Flanders, and the attention their painters paid to naturalistic, and sometimes stylized, detail. Eventually, the slumbering figures atop funerary sarcophagi came to resemble, in sometimes ghoulish detail, the living body of the person buried within, and decorative adornments became almost obsessive.

RENAISSANCE, BAROQUE & BEYOND

The defeat of the Muslims in 1492, and the colonialization the same year of the New World, marked the debut of the Renaissance in Spain. Choir stalls, altarpieces, funerary sarcophagi, and historical statues became commonplace throughout the newly united Spain. The popularity of gilding was a direct result of the precious metals flooding into the country from the mines of the New World. The **cathedrals of Burgos and Barcelona** and some of the chapels within the **cathedral at Granada** are fine examples of the heights to which Renaissance sculpture rose. A new technique, *estofado,* was introduced, whereby multiple colors were applied over a base of gold leaf, then rubbed or scratched to expose subtly gilded highlights in a way that prefigured the eventual rise of the baroque.

The greatest Spanish painter of the Renaissance was **El Greco** (Domenico Theotocopoulos, born in Crete in 1541; died 1614), whose interpretation of Iberian mysticism reached deeper into the Spanish soul than any painter before or since. He was well versed in classical references and trained in all the methods popular in both Italy (especially Venice) and Byzantium. His was an intensely personal vision—amplified emotion, elongated limbs, and characters that were lifted bodily, and ecstatically, toward heaven. His style, known today as mannerism, met with violent criticism and lawsuits from disgruntled patrons.

After El Greco, the leading Spanish painter was **Diego de Silva y Velázquez** (1599–1660). Appointed court painter to the vain and self-indulgent monarch Philip IV, he painted 40 portraits of Philip, and dozens of other members of the royal family. (See his famous *Las Meninas* in the Prado.) Influenced by Rubens, who urged him to travel to Italy, his craftsmanship improved to the point where he has been hailed as the single greatest painter in the lexicon of

Spanish art. Other important painters of this baroque period included **José Ribera** (1591–1652) and **Francisco de Zurbarán** (1598–1664). **Bartolomé Murillo** (1617–82) produced religious paintings that appealed, 200 years after his death, to the sentimentalism of the English Victorians.

The mantle of greatness was next passed to **Francisco de Goya y Lucientes** (1746–1828), an artist whose skill as a draftsman produced everything from tapestries to portraits of noble ladies. Rendered deaf in 1792 after a serious illness, Goya adopted a style of dark and brooding realism that many critics view as at least a century ahead of his contemporaries. In his work are vivid precursors of such future trends as romanticism and the psychological intricacies of expressionism. Victim of the political incompetencies of the Spanish regime, he was forced to flee in 1824 to Bordeaux, where he died, dejected, embittered, and broken.

MODERNISM & SURREALISM

Around the turn of the 20th century, artists of note were so frustrated by the official repression of the Spanish establishment that they emigrated, almost en masse, to Paris. Such outstanding innovators as **Joan Miró, Salvador Dalí,** and **Juan Gris** were among this group, whose names later became as closely associated with France as with Spain.

The most influential of these expatriates, of course, was **Pablo Picasso,** born in Málaga in 1881. Before the end of his extraordinary career, he would become the most famous artist of the 20th century, mastering a variety of styles and defining such major schools of art as cubism.

A divergent school, **surrealism,** was developed by Catalonia-born **Salvador Dalí.** His sometimes authentic, sometimes fraudulent commercial endeavors explored the subconscious levels of the human mind, using dream sequences whose content might have appealed to Jung and Freud.

Among the important Spanish abstract painters are **Antoni Tàpies,** a pioneer in the use of texture and geometric placement of shapes and forms, and **Juan José Tharrats.** Major sculptors include **Jorge Otieza, Eduardo Chillida** (whose abstract works bear almost no resemblance to the human form), and **Andréu Alfaro,** whose works hang in influential galleries in such cities as Barcelona and Madrid.

Born in Huesca in 1930, **Antonio Saura** began painting in 1947 and was first exhibited in 1950. He developed a technique of black-and-white outlines, always within the form of the female body. Among the younger generation, **Miguel Barceló,** born in 1957 in Majorca, has gone on to enjoy an international reputation. He spends a great amount of time in Africa, and his work has taken on many non-Western elements.

5 A Taste of Spain

Meals are an extremely important social activity in Spain, whether that means eating out late at night or having large family gatherings for lunch. Although Spain is faster paced than it once was, few Spaniards race through a meal on the way to an appointment.

The food in Spain is varied; the portions are immense, but the prices, by North American standards, are high. Whenever possible, try the regional specialties, particularly when you visit the Basque country or Galicia.

Many restaurants in Spain close on Sunday, so be sure to check ahead. Hotel dining rooms are generally open 7 days, and there's always something open in such big cities as Madrid and Barcelona or such well-touristed areas as the

Costa del Sol. Generally, reservations are not necessary, except at popular, top-notch restaurants.

MEALS

BREAKFAST   In Spain the day starts with a continental breakfast of coffee, hot chocolate, or tea, with assorted rolls, butter, and jam. Spanish breakfast might also consist of *churros* (fried fingerlike doughnuts) and hot chocolate that is very sweet and thick. However, most Spaniards simply have coffee, usually strong and black, served with hot milk: either a *café con leche* (half coffee, half milk) or *cortado* (a shot of espresso "cut" with a dash of milk). If you find it too strong and bitter for your taste, you might ask for a more diluted *café americano.*

LUNCH   The most important meal of the day in Spain, lunch is comparable to the farm-style noonday "dinner" in America. It usually includes three or four courses, beginning with a choice of soup or several dishes of hors d'oeuvres called *entremeses.* Often a fish or egg dish is served after this, then a meat course with vegetables. Wine is always part of the meal. Dessert is usually pastry, custard, or assorted fruit—followed by coffee. Lunch is served from 1 to 4pm, with "rush hour" at 2pm.

TAPAS   After the early evening stroll, many Spaniards head for their favorite *tascas,* bars where they drink wine and sample assorted tapas, or snacks, such as bits of fish, eggs in mayonnaise, or olives.

Because many Spaniards eat dinner very late, they often have an extremely light breakfast, certainly coffee and perhaps a pastry. However, by 11am they are often hungry and lunch might not be until 2pm or later, so many Spaniards have a late-morning snack, often at a cafeteria. Favorite items to order are a *tortilla* (Spanish omelette with potatoes) and even a beer. Many request a large tapa served with bread.

DINNER   Another extravaganza. A typical meal starts with a bowl of soup, followed by a second course, often a fish dish, and by another main course, usually veal, beef, or pork, accompanied by vegetables. Again, desserts tend to be fruit, custard, or pastries.

Naturally, if you had a heavy and late lunch and stopped off at a tapas bar or two before dinner, supper might be much lighter, perhaps some cold cuts, sausage, a bowl of soup, or even a Spanish omelette made with potatoes. Wine is always part of the meal. Afterward, you might have a demitasse and a fragrant Spanish brandy. The chic dining hour, even in one-donkey towns, is 10 or 10:30pm. (In well-touristed regions and hardworking Catalonia, you can usually dine at 8pm, though you still may find yourself alone in the restaurant.) In most middle-class establishments, people dine around 9:30pm.

THE CUISINE

SOUPS & APPETIZERS   Soups are usually served in big bowls. Cream soups, such as asparagus and potato, can be fine; sadly, however, they are too often made from powdered envelope soups such as Knorr and Liebig. Served year-round, chilled gazpacho, on the other hand, is tasty and particularly

Impressions

Now you have two homes.

—Traditional Spanish farewell

refreshing during the hot months. The combination is pleasant: olive oil, garlic, ground cucumbers, and raw tomatoes with a sprinkling of croutons. Spain also offers several varieties of fish soup—*sopa de pescado*—in all its provinces, and many of these are superb.

In the paradors (government-run hostelries) and top restaurants, as many as 15 tempting hors d'oeuvres are served. In lesser-known places, avoid these *entremeses,* which often consist of last year's sardines and shards of sausage left over from the Moorish conquest.

EGGS   These are served in countless ways. A Spanish omelette, a *tortilla española,* is made with potatoes and usually onions. A simple omelette is called a *tortilla francesa. A tortilla portuguesa* is similar to the American Spanish omelette.

FISH   Spain's fish dishes tend to be outstanding and vary from province to province. One of the most common varieties is *merluza* (sweet white hake). *Langosta,* a variety of lobster, is seen everywhere—it's a treat but terribly expensive. The Portuguese in particular, but some Spaniards, too, go into raptures at the mention of *mejillones* (barnacles). Gourmets relish their seawater taste; others find them tasteless. *Rape* (pronounced *rah*-pay) is the Spanish name for monkfish, a sweet, wide-boned ocean fish with a scalloplike texture. Also try a few dozen half-inch baby eels. They rely heavily on olive oil and garlic for their flavor, but they taste great. Squid cooked in its own ink is suggested only to those who want to go native. Charcoal-broiled sardines, however, are a culinary delight—a particular treat in the Basque provinces. Trout Navarre is one of the most popular fish dishes, usually stuffed with bacon or ham.

PAELLA   You can't go to Spain without trying its celebrated paella. Flavored with saffron, paella is an aromatic rice dish usually topped with shellfish, chicken, sausage, peppers, and local spices. Served authentically, it comes steaming hot from the kitchen in a metal pan called a *paellera.* (Incidentally, what is known in America as Spanish rice isn't Spanish at all. If you ask an English-speaking waiter for Spanish rice, you'll be served paella.)

MEATS   Don't expect Kansas City steak, but do try the spit-roasted suckling pig, so sweet and tender it can often be cut with a fork. The veal is also good, and the Spanish *lomo de cerdo,* loin of pork, is unmatched anywhere. Tender chicken is most often served in the major cities and towns today, and the Spanish are adept at spit-roasting it until it turns a delectable golden brown. However, in more remote spots of Spain, "free-range" chicken is often stringy and tough.

VEGETABLES & SALADS   Through more sophisticated agricultural methods, Spain now grows more of its own vegetables, which are available year-round, unlike days of yore, when canned vegetables were used all too frequently. Both potatoes and rice are a staple of the Spanish diet, the latter a prime ingredient, of course, in the famous paella originating in Valencia. Salads don't usually get the attention they do in California, and are often made simply with just lettuce and tomatoes.

DESSERTS   The Spanish do not emphasize dessert, often opting for fresh fruit. Flan, a home-cooked egg custard, appears on all menus—sometimes with a burnt-caramel sauce. Ice cream appears on nearly all menus as well. But the best bet is to ask for a basket of fruit, which you can wash at your table. Homemade pastries are usually moist and not too sweet. As a dining oddity, many restaurants serve fresh orange juice for dessert—though it's not odd at all to Spaniards.

OLIVE OIL & GARLIC   Olive oil is used lavishly in Spain, the largest olive grower on the planet. You may not want it in all dishes. If you prefer your fish grilled in butter, the word is *mantequilla.* In some instances, you'll be charged extra for the butter. Garlic is also an integral part of the Spanish diet, and even if you love it, you may find Spaniards love it more than you do and use it in the oddest dishes.

WHAT TO DRINK

WATER   It is generally safe to drink water in all major cities and tourist resorts in Spain. If you're traveling in remote areas, play it safe and drink bottled water. One of the most popular noncarbonated bottled drinks in Spain is Solares. Nearly all restaurants and hotels have it. Bubbly water is *agua mineral con gas;* noncarbonated, *agua mineral sin gas.* Note that bottled water in some areas may cost as much as the regional wine.

SOFT DRINKS   In general, avoid the carbonated citrus drinks on sale everywhere. Most of them never saw an orange, much less a lemon. If you want a citrus drink, order old, reliable Schweppes. An excellent noncarbonated drink for the summer is called Tri-Naranjus, which comes in lemon and orange flavors. Your cheapest bet is a liter bottle of *gaseosa,* which comes in various flavors. In summer you should also try a drink that we've never had outside Spain, *horchata*—a nutty, sweet milklike beverage made of tubers called *chufas.*

COFFEE   Even if you are a dedicated coffee drinker, you may find the *café con leche* (coffee with milk) a little too strong. We suggest *leche manchada,* a little bit of strong, freshly brewed coffee in a glass that's filled with lots of frothy hot milk.

MILK   In the largest cities you get bottled milk, but it loses a great deal of its flavor in the process of pasteurization. In all cases, avoid untreated milk and milk products. About the best brand of fresh milk is Lauki.

BEER   Although not native to Spain, beer (*cerveza*) is now drunk everywhere. Domestic brands include San Miguel, Mahou, Águila, and Cruz Blanca.

WINE   Sherry (*vino de Jerez*) has been called "the wine with a hundred souls." Drink it before dinner (try the topaz-colored *finos,* a dry and very pale sherry) or whenever you drop into some old inn or bodega for refreshment; many of them have rows of kegs with spigots. *Manzanilla,* a golden-colored medium-dry sherry, is extremely popular. The sweet cream sherries (Harvey's Bristol Cream, for example) are favorite after-dinner wines (called *olorosos*). While the French may be disdainful of Spanish table wines, they can be truly noble, especially two leading varieties, Valdepeñas and Rioja, both from Castile. If you're not too exacting in your tastes, you can always ask for the *vino de la casa* (wine of the house) wherever you dine. The Ampurdán of Catalonia is heavy. From Andalusia comes the fruity Montilla. There are also some good local champagnes (*cavas*) in Spain, such as Freixenet. One brand, Benjamín, also comes in individual-sized bottles.

Beginning in the 1990s, based partly on subsidies and incentives from the European Union, Spanish vintners have scrapped most of the country's obsolete wine-making equipment, hired new talent, and poured time and money into the improvement and promotion of wines from even high-altitude or arid regions not previously suitable for wine production. Thanks to irrigation, improved grape varieties, technological developments, and the expenditure of billions of pesetas, bodegas and vineyards are sprouting up throughout the country, opening their doors to visitors interested in how the stuff is grown, fermented, and bottled. These wines are now earning awards at wine competitions around the world for their quality and bouquet.

Interested in impressing a newfound Spanish friend over a wine list? Consider bypassing the usual array of Riojas, sherries, and sparkling Catalonian cavas in favor of, say, a Galician white from Rias Baixas, which some connoisseurs consider the perfect accompaniment for seafood. Among reds, make a beeline for vintages from the fastest-developing wine region of Europe, the arid, high-altitude district of Ribera del Duero, near Burgos, whose alkaline soil, cold nights, and sunny days have earned unexpected praise from wine makers (and encouraged massive investments) in the past 5 years.

For more information about these and others of the 10 wine-producing regions of Spain (and the 39 officially recognized wine-producing *Denominaciones de Origen* scattered across those regions), contact **Wines from Spain,** c/o the Commercial Office of Spain, 405 Lexington Ave., 44th Floor, New York, NY 10174-0331 (☎ **212/661-4959**).

SANGRÍA   The all-time favorite refreshing drink in Spain, sangría is a red-wine punch that combines wine with oranges, lemons, seltzer, and sugar. Be careful, however; many joints that do a big tourist trade produce a sickly sweet Kool-Aid version of sangría for unsuspecting visitors.

WHISKEY & BRANDY   Imported whiskeys are available at most Spanish bars but at a high price. If you're a drinker, switch to brandies and cognacs, where the Spanish reign supreme. Try Fundador, made by the Pedro Domecq family in Jerez de la Frontera. If you want a smooth cognac, ask for the "103" white label.

Useful Terms & Phrases

1 Basic Vocabulary

Most Spaniards are very patient with foreigners who try to speak their language. Though you may encounter several regional languages and dialects in Spain, Castillian (Castellano, or simply Español) is understood everywhere. In Catalonia they speak Catalan (the most widely spoken non-national language in Europe); in the Basque country they speak Euskerra; in Galicia you'll hear Gallego. Still, a few words in Castellano will usually get your message across with no problem.

When travelling it helps a lot to know a few basic phrases, so we've included a list of certain simple phrases in Castillian Spanish for expressing basic needs, followed by some common menu items.

ENGLISH-CASTILLIAN SPANISH PHRASES

English	Spanish	Pronunciation
Good day	Buenos días	*bway*-nohss *dee*-ahss
How are you?	¿Cómo está?	*koh*-moh ess-*tah*?
Very well	Muy bien	mwee byen
Thank you	Gracias	*grah*-see-ahss
You're welcome	De nada	day *nah*-dah
Goodbye	Adios	ah-*dyohss*
Please	Por favor	pohr fah-*vohr*
Yes	Sí	see
No	No	noh
Excuse me	Perdóneme	pehr-*doh*-ney-may
Give me	Déme	*day*-may
Where is ?	¿Dónde está . . . ?	*dohn*-day ess-*tah*?
the station	la estación	lah ess-tah-*seown*
a hotel	un hotel	oon oh-*tel*
a gas station	una gasolinera	*oon*-uh gah-so-lee-*nay*-rah
a restaurant	un restaurante	oon res-tow-*rahn*-tay
the toilet	el baño	el *bahn*-yoh
a good doctor	un buen médico	oon bwayn *may*-thee-co
the road to . . .	el camino a/hacia	el cah-*mee*-noh ah/*ah*-see-ah
To the right	A la derecha	ah lah day-*reh*-chuh

English	Spanish	Pronunciation
To the left	A la izquierda	ah lah ees-ky-*ehr*-thah
Straight ahead	Derecho	day-*reh*-cho
I would like	Quisiera	key-see-*ehr*-ah
I want	Quiero	*kyehr*-oh
to eat.	comer	ko-*mayr*
a room.	una habitación	*oon*-nuh ha-bee-tah-*seown*
Do you have?	¿Tiene usted?	tyeh-nay oos-*ted*?
a book.	un libro	oon *lee*-bro
a dictionary.	un diccionario	oon deek-seown-*ar*-eo
How much is it?	¿Cuánto cuesta?	*kwahn*-to *kwess*-tah?
When?	¿Cuándo?	*kwahn*-doh?
What?	¿Qué?	kay?
There is (Is there . . . ?)	(¿)Hay (. . . ?)	eye?
What is there?	¿Qué hay?	kay eye?
Yesterday	Ayer	ah-*yer*
Today	Hoy	oy
Tomorrow	Mañana	mahn-*yahn*-ah
Good	Bueno	*bway*-no
Bad	Malo	*mah*-lo
Better (best)	(Lo) Mejor	(loh) meh-*hor*
More	Más	mahs
Less	Menos	*may*-noss
No smoking	Se prohíbe fumar	say pro-*hee*-bay foo-*mahr*
Postcard	Tarjeta postal	tar-*hay*-ta pohs-*tahl*
Insect repellent	Rapelente	rah-pey-*yahn*-te
	contra insectos	*cohn*-trah een-*sehk*-tos

MORE USEFUL PHRASES

English	Spanish	Pronunciation
Do you speak English?	¿Habla usted inglés?	ah-blah oo-*sted* een-*glays*?
Is there anyone here who speaks English?	¿Hay alguien aquí qué hable inglés?	eye *ahl*-ghee-en kay *ah*-blay een-*glays*?
I speak a little Spanish.	Hablo un poco de español.	*ah*-blow oon *poh*-koh day ess-pah-*nyol*
I don't understand Spanish very well.	No (lo) entiendo muy bien el español.	noh (loh) ehn-tee-*ehn*-do moo-ee bee-ayn el ess-pah-*nyol*
The meal is good.	Me gusta la comida.	may *goo*-sta lah koh-*mee*-dah
What time is it?	¿Qué hora es?	kay *oar*-ah ess?
May I see your menu?	¿Puedo ver el menú (la carta)?	*puay*-tho veyr el may-*noo* (lah *car*-tah)?
The check please.	La cuenta por favor.	lah *quayn*-tah pohr fa-*vorh*
What do I owe you?	¿Cuánto lo debo?	*Kwahn*-toh loh *day*-boh?
What did you say?	¿Cómo?	*Koh*-moh?
I want (to see)	Quiero (ver)	*Key*-*yehr*-oh vehr
a room	un cuarto o una habitación (una habitación)	oon *kwar*-toh, *oon*-nuh ha-bee-tah-*seown*
for two persons.	para dos personas	*pahr*-ah doss pehr-*sohn*-as
with (without) bathroom.	con (sin) baño.	kohn (seen) *bah*-nyoh

English	Spanish	Pronunciation
We are staying here only	Nos quedamos aquí solamente . . .	nohs kay-*dahm*-ohss ah-*key* sohl-ah-*mayn*-tay
one night.	una noche.	oon-ah *noh*-chay
one week.	una semana.	oon-ah say-*mahn*-ah
We are leaving tomorrow.	Partimos (Salimos) mañana.	Pahr-*tee*-mohss (sah-*lee*-mohss) mahn-*nyan*-ah
Do you accept traveler's checks?	¿Acepta usted cheques de viajero?	Ah-*sayp*-tah oo-*sted chay*-kays day bee-ah-*hehr*-oh?
Is there a Laundromat near here?	¿Hay una lavandería cerca de aquí?	Eye *oon*-ah lah-*vahn*-day-*ree*-ah *sehr*-ka day ah-*key*?
Please send these clothes to the laundry.	Hágame el favor de mandar esta ropa a la lavandería.	*Ah*-ga-may el fah-*vhor* day mahn-*dahr ays*-tah *rho*-pah a lah lah-*vahn*-day-*ree*-ah

2 Numbers

English	Spanish	Pronunciation
1	**uno**	(*ooh*-noh)
2	**dos**	(dohs)
3	**tres**	(trayss)
4	**cuatro**	(*kwah*-troh)
5	**cinco**	(*seen*-koh)
6	**seis**	(sayss)
7	**siete**	(*syeh*-tay)
8	**ocho**	(*oh*-choh)
9	**nueve**	(*nway*-bay)
10	**diez**	(dee-ess)
11	**once**	(*ohn*-say)
12	**doce**	(*doh*-say)
13	**trece**	(*tray*-say)
14	**catorce**	(kah-*tor*-say)
15	**quince**	(*keen*-say)
16	**dieciseis**	(de-ess-ee-sayss)
17	**diecisiete**	(de-ess-ee-*syeh*-tay)
18	**dieciocho**	(dee-ess-ee-*oh*-choh)
19	**diecinueve**	(dee-ess-ee-*nway*-bay)
20	**veinte**	(*bayn*-tay)
30	**treinta**	(*trayn*-tah)
40	**cuarenta**	(kwah-*ren*-tah)
50	**cincuenta**	(seen-*kwen*-tah)
60	**sesenta**	(say-*sen*-tah)
70	**setenta**	(say-*ten*-tah)
80	**ochenta**	(oh-*chen*-tah)
90	**noventa**	(noh-*ben*-tah)
100	**cien**	(see-*en*)
200	**doscientos**	(*dos*-se-en-tos)
500	**quinientos**	(keen-ee-*ehn*-tos)
1,000	**mil**	(meal)

3 Transportation Terms

English	Spanish	Pronunciation
Airport	**Aeropuerto**	Ah-ay-row-*por*-tow
Flight	**Vuelo**	Boo-*ay*-low
Rental car	**Alquila de Autos**	Al-key-lah day autos
Bus	**Autobús**	ow-toh-*boos*
Bus or truck	**Camión**	ka-mee-*ohn*
Lane	**Carril**	kah-*rreal*
Nonstop	**Directo**	dee-*reck*-toh
Baggage (claim area)	**Equipajes**	eh-key-*pah*-hays
Luggage storage area	**Guarda equipaje**	gwar-daheh-key-*pah*-hay
Arrival gates	**Llegadas**	yay-*gah*-dahs
Originates at this station	**Local**	loh-*kahl*
Originates elsewhere;	**De Paso**	day *pah*-soh
Stops if seats available	**Para si hay lugares**	*pah-rah-see-aye-loo-gahr-ays*
First class	**Primera**	pree-*mehr*-oh
Second class	**Segunda**	say-*goon*-dah
Nonstop	**Directo**	dee-rek-to
Baggage claim area	**Recibo de Equipajes**	ray-see-boh day eh-key-*pah*-hays
Waiting room	**Sala de Espera**	*Saw*-lah day ess-*pehr*-ah
Toilets	**Aseos**	Ah-say-oos
Ticket window	**Taquilla**	tah-*key*-lah

4 Postal Glossary

English	Spanish
Airmail	Correo Aéreo
Customs	Aduana
General Delivery	Lista de Correos
Insurance (insured mail)	Seguro (correo asegurado)
Mailbox	Buzón
Money Order	Giro Postal
Parcel	Paquete
Post Office	Oficina de Correos
Post Office Box (abbreviation)	Apartado Postal
Postal Service	Correos
Registered Mail	Registrado
Rubber Stamp	Sello
Special Delivery, Express	Entrega Inmediata
Stamp	Estampilla or Timbre

Frommer's Online Directory

by Karen Pojmann and Michael Shapiro
Michael Shapiro is the author of *Michael Shapiro's
Internet Planner* (The Globe Pequot Press).

Frommer's Online Directory is a new feature designed to help you take advantage of the Internet to better plan your trip. Section 1 lists some general Internet resources that can make any trip easier, such as sites for booking airline tickets. It's not meant to be a comprehensive list—it's a discriminating selection of useful sites to get you started. In section 2, you'll find some top online guides specifically for Spain, which cover local lodging, the top attractions, and getting around.

We've awarded stars to the best sites, which are earned, not paid for (unlike some Web site rankings that are based on payment). Finally, remember this is a press-time snapshot of leading Web sites—some undoubtedly will have evolved, changed, or moved by the time you read this.

1 The Top Travel-Planning Web Sites

Among the most popular sites are online travel agencies. The top agencies, including Expedia, Preview Travel, and Travelocity, offer an array of tools that are valuable even if you don't book online. You can check flight schedules, hotel availability, car rental prices, or even get paged if your flight is delayed.

While online agencies have come a long way over the past few years, they don't *always* yield the best price. Unlike a travel agent, for example, they're unlikely to tell you that you can save money by flying a day earlier or a day later. On the other hand, if you're looking for a bargain fare, you might find something online that an agent wouldn't take the time to dig up. Because airline commissions have been cut, a travel agent may not find it worthwhile spending half an hour trying to find you the best deal. On the Net, you can be your own agent and take all the time you want.

Online booking sites aren't the only places to book airline tickets—all major airlines have their own Web sites and often offer incentives, such as bonus frequent-flyer miles or Net-only discounts, for buying online. These incentives have helped airlines capture the majority of the online booking market.

Below are the Web sites for the major airlines serving Spain. These sites offer schedules and flight booking, and most have pages where you can sign up for e-mail alerts on weekend deals.

Factoid

Far more people look online than book online, partly due to fear of putting their credit cards through on the Net. Though secure encryption has made this fear less justified, there's no reason why you can't find a flight online and then book it by calling a toll-free number or contacting your travel agent. To be sure you're in secure mode when you book online, look for a little icon of a key (in Netscape) or a padlock (Internet Explorer) at the bottom of your Web browser.

- Air Europa: **www.easyspain.com (though much of this site is in Spanish)**
- American: **www.aa.com**
- British Airways: **www.british-airways.com**
- Continental: **www.flycontiental.com**
- Delta: **www.delta-air.com**
- Iberia Airlines: **www.iberia.com**
- Qantas: **www.qantas.com**
- TWA: **www.twa.com**
- United: **www.ual.com**
- US Airways: **www.usairways.com**

WHEN SHOULD YOU BOOK ONLINE?

Online booking is not for everyone. If you prefer to let others handle your travel arrangements, one call to an experienced travel agent should suffice. But if you want to know as much as possible about your options, the Net is a good place to start, especially for bargain hunters.

The most compelling reason to use online booking is to take advantage of last-minute specials, such as American Airlines' weekend deals or other Internet-only fares that must be purchased online. Another advantage is that you can cash in on incentives for booking online, such as rebates or bonus frequent-flyer miles.

Online booking works best for trips within North America; for international tickets, it's usually cheaper and easier to use a travel agent or consolidator.

Online booking is certainly not for those with a complex international itinerary. If you require follow-up services, such as itinerary changes, use a travel agent. Though Expedia and some other online agencies employ travel agents available by phone, these sites are geared primarily for self-service.

Please remember, though: The descriptions below were true at press time, but the pace of evolution on the Net is relentless, so you'll probably find some advancements by the time you visit these sites.

LEADING BOOKING SITES

Below are listings for the top travel-booking sites. The starred selections are the most useful and best designed sites.

Cheap Tickets. **www.cheaptickets.com**
Essentials: Discounted rates on domestic and international airline tickets and hotel rooms.

Sometimes discounters such as Cheap Tickets have exclusive deals that aren't available through more mainstream channels. Registration at Cheap Tickets requires inputting a credit card number before getting started, which is one reason many people elect to call the company's toll-free number rather than booking online. One of the most frustrating things about the Cheap Tickets site is that it will offer fare quotes for a route, and later show this fare is not valid for your dates of travel (other Web sites, such as Preview, consider your dates of travel before showing what fares are available). Despite its problems, Cheap Tickets can be worth the effort because its fares can be lower than those offered by its competitors.

✪ Expedia. expedia.com

Essentials: Domestic and international flights, plus hotel and rental-car booking; late-breaking travel news, destination features, and commentary from travel experts; deals on cruises and vacation packages. Free registration is required for booking.

Expedia makes it easy to handle flight, hotel, and car booking on one itinerary, so it's a good place for one-stop shopping. Expedia's hotel search offers crisp, zoomable maps to pinpoint most properties; click on the camera icon to see images of the rooms and facilities. But like many online databases, Expedia focuses on the major chains, such as Hilton and Hyatt, so don't expect to find too many one-of-a-kind boutique hotels or B&Bs here.

Once you're registered (it's only necessary to do this once from each computer you use), you can start booking with the Roundtrip Fare Finder box on the home page, which expedites the process. After selecting a flight, you can hold it until midnight the following day or purchase online. If you think you might do better through a travel agent, you'll have time to try to get a lower price. And you may do better with a travel agent because Expedia's computer reservation system does not include all airlines. Most notably absent are some leading budget carriers, such as Southwest. (*Note:* At press time, Travelocity was the only major booking service that included Southwest.)

Expedia's World Guide, offering destination information, is a glaring weakness; it takes lots of page views to get very little information. However, Expedia compensates by linking to other Microsoft Network services, such as its Sidewalk city guides, which offer entertainment and dining advice.

Preview Travel. www.previewtravel.com

Essentials: Domestic and international flights, plus hotel and rental-car booking; Travel Newswire lists fare sales; deals on cruises and vacation packages. Free (one-time) registration is required for booking. Preview offers express booking for members, but at press time, this feature was buried below the fold on Preview's reservation page.

Preview features the most inviting interface for booking trips, though the wealth of graphics involved can make the site somewhat slow to load. Use Farefinder to quickly find the lowest current fares on flights to dozens of major cities. Carfinder offers a similar service for rental cars, but you can only search airport locations, not city pickup sites. To see the lowest fare for your itinerary, input the dates and times for your route and see what Preview comes up with.

In recent years Preview and other leading booking services have added features such as Best Fare Finder, so after Preview searches for the best deal on your itinerary, it will check flights that are a bit later or earlier to see if it might be cheaper to fly at a different time. While these searches have become quite sophisticated, they still occasionally overlook deals that might be uncovered by a top-notch travel agent. If you have the time, see what you can find online and then call an agent to see if you can get a better price.

With Preview's Fare Alert feature, you can set fares for up to three routes and you'll receive e-mail notices when the fare drops below your target amount. For example, you could tell Preview to alert you when the fare from New York to Madrid drops below $500. If it does, you'll get an e-mail telling you the current fare.

Minor quibbles: When you search for a fare or hotel (at least when we went to press), Preview launches an annoying little "Please Wait" window that gets in the way

---

Take a Look at Frommer's Site

We highly recommend Arthur Frommer's Budget Travel Online (**www.frommers.com**) as an excellent travel-planning resource. Of course, we're a little biased, but you will find indispensable travel tips, reviews, monthly vacation giveaways, and online booking.

Subscribe to Arthur Frommer's Daily Newsletter (**www.frommers.com/newsletters**) to receive the latest travel bargains and inside travel secrets in your mailbox every day. You'll read daily headlines and articles from the dean of travel himself, highlighting last-minute deals on airfares, accommodations, cruises, and package vacations. You'll also find great travel advice by checking our Tip of the Day or Hot Spot of the Month.

Search our Destinations archive (**www.frommers.com/destinations**) of more than 200 domestic and international destinations for great places to stay, tips for traveling there, and what to do while you're there. Once you've researched your trip, you might try our online reservation system (**www.frommers.com/booktravelnow**) to book your dream vacation at affordable prices.

---

of the main browser window, even when your results begin to appear. The hotel search feature is intuitive, but the images and maps aren't as crisp as those at Expedia. Also, all sorts of information that's irrelevant to travelers (such as public school locations) is listed on the maps.

Note to AOL Users: You can book flights, hotels, rental cars, and cruises on AOL at keyword: Travel. The booking software is provided by Preview Travel and is similar to Preview on the Web. Use the AOL "Travelers Advantage" program to earn a 5% rebate on flights, hotel rooms, and car rentals.

Priceline.com. www.priceline.com

Even people who aren't familiar with too many Web sites have heard about Priceline.com, which lets you "name your price" for domestic and international airline tickets. In other words, you select a route and dates, guarantee with a credit card, and make a bid for what you're willing to pay. If one of the airlines in Priceline's database has a fare that's lower than your bid, your credit card will automatically be charged for a ticket.

But you can't say when you want to fly—you have to accept any flight leaving between 6am and 10pm, and you may have to make a stopover. No frequent-flyer miles are awarded, and tickets are nonrefundable and can't be exchanged for another flight. So if your plans change, you're out of luck. Priceline can be good for travelers who have to take off on short notice (and who are thus unable to qualify for advance purchase discounts). But be sure to shop around first—if you overbid, you'll be required to purchase the ticket, and Priceline will pocket the difference.

Travelocity. www.travelocity.com

Essentials: Domestic and international flight, hotel, and rental-car booking; deals on cruises and vacation packages. Travel Headlines spotlights latest bargain airfares. Free (one-time) registration is required for booking.

Travelocity almost got it right. Its Express Booking feature enables travelers to complete the booking process more quickly than they could at Expedia or Preview, but Travelocity gums up the works with a page called "Featured Airlines." Big placards of several featured airlines compete for your attention. If you want to see the fares for *all* available airlines, click the much smaller box at the bottom of the page labeled "Book a Flight."

Some have worried that Travelocity, which is owned by American Airlines' parent company AMR, directs bookings to American. This doesn't seem to be the case—I've booked there dozens of times and have always been directed to the cheapest listed flight, for example on Tower or ATA. But this "Featured Airlines" page seems to be Travelocity's way of trying to cash in with ads and incentives for booking certain airlines. (*Note:* It's hard to blame these booking services for trying to generate some revenue. Many airlines have slashed commissions to $10 per domestic booking for online transactions, so these virtual agencies are groping for revenue streams.) There are rewards for choosing one of the featured airlines. You'll get 1,500 bonus frequent-flyer miles if you book through United's site, for example, but the site doesn't tell you about other airlines that might be cheaper. If the United flight costs $150 more than the best deal on another airline, it's not worth spending the extra money for a relatively small number of bonus miles.

On the plus side, Travelocity has some leading-edge techie tools. Exhibit A is Fare Watcher E-mail, an "intelligent agent" that keeps you informed of the best fares offered for the city pairs (round-trips) of your choice. Whenever the fare changes by $25 or more, Fare Watcher will alert you by e-mail. Exhibit B is Flight Paging: If you own an alphanumeric pager with national access that can receive e-mail, Travelocity's paging system can alert you if your flight is delayed. Finally, though Travelocity doesn't include every budget airline, it does include Southwest, the leading U.S. budget carrier.

FINDING LODGINGS ONLINE

While the services above offer hotel booking, it can be best to use a site devoted primarily to lodging; you may find properties that aren't listed on more general online travel agencies. Some lodging sites specialize in a particular type of accommodation, such as B&Bs, which you won't find on the more mainstream booking services. Other services, such as TravelWeb, offer weekend deals on major chain properties, which cater to business travelers and have more empty rooms on weekends.

All Hotels on the Web. www.all-hotels.com
Well, this site doesn't include *all* the hotels on the Web, but it does have tens of thousands of listings throughout the world. Bear in mind that each hotel listed has paid a small fee of ($25 and up) for placement, so it's not an objective list but more like a book of online brochures.

Also see Hotels and Travel on the Net (**www.hotelstravel.com**), which claims to offer discount booking on more than 100,000 hotels and other lodgings in more than 120 countries.

Hotel Reservations Network. www.180096hotel.com
Bargain on room rates at hotels in more than two dozen U.S. cities. The cool thing is that HRN prebooks blocks of rooms in advance, so sometimes it has rooms at discount rates at hotels that are "sold out." Select a city, input your dates, and you'll get a list of best prices for a selection of hotels. Descriptions include an image of the property and a locator map (to book online, click the "Book Now" button). HRN is notable for some deep discounts, even in cities where hotel rooms are expensive. The toll-free number is printed all over this site; call it if you want more options than are listed online.

InnSite. www.innsite.com
Essentials: B&B listings for inns in all 50 U.S. states and dozens of countries around the globe.

Find an inn at your destination, have a look at images of the rooms, check prices and availability, and then send e-mail to the innkeeper if you have further questions.

This is an extensive directory of B&Bs, but only includes listings if the proprietor submitted one (note: it's free to get an inn listed). The descriptions are written by the innkeepers and many listings link to the inn's own Web site, where you can find more information and images.

Places to Stay. www.placestostay.com
Mostly one-of-a-kind places in the United States and abroad that you might not find in other directories, with a focus on resorts. Again, listing is selective—this isn't a comprehensive directory, but can give you a sense of what's available at different destinations.

✪ TravelWeb. www.travelweb.com
TravelWeb lists more than 16,000 hotels worldwide, focusing on chains such as Hyatt and Hilton, and you can book almost 90% of these online. TravelWeb's Click-It Weekends, updated each Monday, offers weekend deals at many leading hotel chains. TravelWeb is the online home for Pegasus Systems, which provides transaction processing systems for the hotel industry.

LAST-MINUTE DEALS & OTHER ONLINE BARGAINS

There's nothing airlines hate more than flying with lots of empty seats. The Net has enabled airlines to offer last-minute bargains to entice travelers to fill those seats. Most of these are announced on Tuesday or Wednesday and are valid for travel the following weekend, but some can be booked weeks or months in advance. You can sign up for weekly e-mail alerts at airlines' sites (see above) or check sites such as WebFlyer (see below) that compile lists of these bargains. To make it easier, visit a site (see below) that will round up all the deals and send them in one convenient weekly e-mail. But last-minute deals aren't the only online bargains; some of the sites below can help you find value even if you can't wait until the eleventh hour.

✪ 1travel.com. www.1travel.com
Essentials: Deals on domestic and international flights, cruises, hotels, and all-inclusive resorts such as Club Med.
    1travel.com's Saving Alert compiles last-minute air deals so you don't have to scroll through multiple e-mail alerts. A feature called "Drive a little using low-fare airlines" helps map out strategies for using alternate airports to find lower fares. And Farebeater searches a database that includes published fares, consolidator bargains, and special deals exclusive to 1travel.com. *Note:* The travel agencies listed by 1travel.com have paid for placement.

BestFares. www.bestfares.com
Budget seeker Tom Parsons lists some great bargains on airfares, hotels, rental cars, and cruises, but the site is poorly organized. News Desk is a long list of hundreds of bargains, but they're not broken down into cities or even countries, so it's not easy trying to find what you're looking for. If you have time to wade through it, you might find a good deal. Some material is available only to paid subscribers.

Go4less.com. www.go4less.com
Specializing in last-minute cruise and package deals, Go4less has some eye-popping offers, such as off-peak Caribbean cruises for under $100 per day. The site has a clean design but the bargains aren't organized by destination. However, you avoid sifting through all this material by using the Search box and entering vacation type, destination, month, and price.

LastMinuteTravel.com. www.lastminutetravel.com
Travel suppliers with excess inventory distribute unsold airline seats, hotel rooms, cruises, and vacation packages through this online agency.

Handy Tip

While most people learn about last-minute weekend deals from e-mail dispatches, it can be best to find out precisely when these deals become available and check airlines' Web sites yourself at this time. To find out when bargains will be announced, check the pages devoted to these deals on airlines' Web pages. Because these offerings are limited, seats can vanish within hours (sometimes even minutes), so it pays to log on as soon as they're available. An example: Southwest's specials are posted at 12:01am Tuesdays (central time). So if you're looking for a cheap flight, stay up late and check Southwest's site at www.iflysw.com to grab the best new deals.

Moment's Notice. www.moments-notice.com
As the name suggests, Moment's Notice specializes in last-minute vacation and cruise deals. You can browse for free, but if you want to purchase a trip, you have to join Moment's Notice, which costs $25.

Smarter Living. www.smarterliving.com
Best known for its e-mail dispatch of weekend deals on 20 airlines, Smarter Living also keeps you posted about last-minute bargains on everything from Windjammer Cruises to flights to Iceland.

☺ WebFlyer. www.webflyer.com
WebFlyer is the ultimate online resource for frequent flyers and also has an excellent listing of last-minute air deals. Click on "Deal Watch" for a roundup of weekend deals on flights, hotels, and rental cars from domestic and international suppliers.

TRAVELER'S TOOLKIT

☺ Foreign Languages for Travelers. www.travlang.com
Learn basic terms in more than 70 languages and click on any underlined phrase to hear what it sounds like. (Note: Free audio software and speakers are required.)

Intellicast. www.intellicast.com
Weather forecasts for all 50 states and cities around the world.

Net Café Guide. www.netcafeguide.com
Locate Internet cafes at hundreds of locations around the globe. Catch up on your e-mail, log on to the Web, and stay in touch with the home front, usually for just a few dollars per hour.

Rail Pass Express. www.eurail.com
A good source for EurailPass information, purchasing, and deals. Also see Rick Steves's Europe Through the Back Door (www.ricksteves.com) for insider tips on EurailPasses.

☺ Subway Navigator. metro.ratp.fr:10001/bin/cities/english
An amazing site with detailed subway route maps for more than 60 cities around the world. Select a city and enter your departure and arrival points. Subway Navigator maps out your route and tells you how long the trip should take. It will even show your route on a subway map.

Trip.com: Airport Maps and Flight Status. www.trip.com
A business travel site where you can find out when an airborne flight is scheduled to arrive. Click on "Guides and Tools" to peruse airport maps for more than 40 domestic cities.

Check Your E-Mail While You're on the Road

Until a few years ago, most travelers who checked their e-mail while traveling carried a laptop, but this posed some problems. Not only are laptops expensive, they can be difficult to configure, incur expensive connection charges, and are attractive to thieves. Thankfully, Web-based free e-mail programs have made it much easier to stay in touch.

Just open an account at a free-mail provider, such as Hotmail (hotmail.com) or Yahoo! Mail (mail.yahoo.com), and all you'll need to check your mail is a Web connection, easily available at Net cafes and copy shops around the world. After logging on, just point the browser to www.hotmail.com, enter your username and password, and you'll have access to your mail.

Internet cafes have become ubiquitous, so for a few dollars an hour you'll be able to check your mail and send messages back to colleagues, friends, and family. If you already have a primary e-mail account, you can set it to forward mail to your free-mail account while you're away. Free-mail programs have become enormously popular (Hotmail claims more than 10 million members) because they enable everyone, even those who don't own a computer, to have an e-mail address they can check wherever they log on to the Web.

Visa. **www.visa.com/pd/atm/**
MasterCard. **www.mastercard.com/atm**
Find Cirrus and Plus ATMs in hundreds of cities in the United States and around the world. Both include maps for some locations and both list airport ATM locations, some with maps. Remarkably, MasterCard lists ATMs on all seven continents (there's one at Antarctica's McMurdo Station). Tip: You'll usually get a better exchange rate using ATMs than exchanging traveler's checks at banks.

Universal Currency Converter. **www.xe.net/currency**
See what your dollar or pound is worth in more than 100 other countries.

U.S. Customs Traveler Alerts. **www.customs.gov/travel/travel.htm**
Wondering what you're allowed to bring in to the United States? Check at this thorough site, which includes maximum allowance and duty fees.

2 The Top Web Sites for Spain

✪ All About Spain. **www.red2000.com**
Take a region-by-region, city-by-city photo tour of Spain online. Or check out each city-specific guide to sights, excursions, dining, nightlife, festivals, and the like. This user-friendly site also features an ample travelers' yellow pages with listings of Spain's transportation and tour operators, accommodations, restaurants, and many forms of entertainment.

Cyberspain. **www.cyberspain.com**
Whether you want to see some Picassos or get a feel for Spanish *fútbol* fanaticism, this site offers a taste of a colorful Spain. Get a quick flamenco lesson. Peek at the major cities' top tourist attractions. Try out some recipes. One drawback: Cyberspain is short on specifics, such as addresses, phone numbers, and timetables.

Tourist Office of Spain. www.okspain.org
Stake out a campsite, or find out how best to see the country from the back of a horse or the seat of a bicycle. The less rustic traveler can use this guide to make reservations at hotels and villas, explore Spain's culinary possibilities, or plan a cultural vacation.

✪ TuSpain (Your Spain). tuspain.com
Appealing to everyone from weekend museum hoppers and summer villa owners to ecotourists and language students, this site has it all. Your Spain covers real estate, arts and culture, news, embassies, residency, education programs, transportation, food and wine, museums, businesses, heritage, and translators. You can even read interviews with foreigners living in Spain.

MADRID

Madrid by All About Spain. www.red2000.com/spain/madrid
Along with facts about the history and geography of Spain's capital city, this guide gives basic information on sightseeing, monuments, museums, nightlife, fiestas, cuisine, local folklore, and day trips. The site includes a photo tour and searchable hotel and restaurant directories.

✪ Madridman. www.madridman.com
A passionate American fan of the Spanish city, Madridman is eager to help you plan a trip, offering travel tips, hotel recommendations, transportation facts, photos, museum information, and weather reports. For a multisensory experience, check out the live Madrid radio broadcasts, video clips of Spanish TV shows, audio clips of popular Spanish songs, and hour-long video tours.

Museo del Prado. museoprado.mcu.es
The art museum's site leads you by the hand through your visit, explaining how to look at a painting, showing samples of Rembrandts and Goyas, and pointing you to its 50 most important works. You can also find out about conferences, guided tours, hours, tickets, and the Prado's history online.

✪ Soft Guide Madrid. www.softguides.com/index_madrid.html
It's not much to look at, but this vast, easy-to-use site will tell you virtually everything you need to know about Madrid: how to get there, where to stay, what to eat, what to do for fun, where to shop, and so on. Big pluses: detailed city maps, information on local customs, and an ample lodging guide with breakdown of prices.

Web Madrid. www.webmadrid.com
This graphics-filled site contains a weather report, a restaurant directory, bar and disco listings, an electronic entertainment magazine, and a "Foreign Guide" with all the basics on transportation, exchange rates, and tourist offices.

OLD CASTILLE & LEÓN

Salamanca. www.geocities.com/Yosemite/Trails/7544/salaman.html
A native gives information about the history, university, monuments, architecture, weather, and nightlife of Salamanca.

ANDALUSIA

Altur: Travel and Tourism in Andalucia, Spain. www.altur.com
Looking for a relaxing sojourn in the countryside of southern Spain? Stop by this site, which directs visitors to beaches and natural areas, rural tourism, culture, and food in

the sunny provinces of Seville, Granada, Málaga, Córdoba, Cádiz, Almeria, Jaén, and Huelva. You can reserve hotel rooms and buy train or plane tickets online.

Andalucia: There's Only One. www.andalucia.org
There's more than one way to see Spain's Andalusia region. Each week, this site suggests a new travel route. Better yet, there's a searchable directory of hotels, restaurants, leisure activities, tourist services, and transportation. For an overview of the region's history, geography, and culture, check out the guide's "Touristing in Andalucia" section.

Andalucia.com. www.andalucia.com
They're a bit stingy with the photos, but the Andalucia.com folks provide a heap of information about southern Spain's outdoorsy offerings: camping, hiking, climbing, sailing, hot-air ballooning, bullfighting. For less adventurous tourists, the site covers museums, festivals, restaurants, flamenco, and the like.

Sevilla On Line. www.sol.com
Not only can you find a barber in Seville with help from this site, you can track down business conventions, hotels, bars, restaurants, museums, post offices, and city buses. Moreover, within this Seville guide is a separate directory of organizations in the Andalusia area.

THE COSTA DEL SOL

Costa del Sol: Everything Under the Mediterranean Sun. www.CostaSol.com
At this very commercial site, you can book a room, hire a car, or find package deals on golf vacations and resort holidays.

Costa Guide. www.costaguide.com
This Costa del Sol guide's tourist section points visitors to consulates and transportation schedules while providing online yellow pages of local shops and services. You can search for a restaurant by nationality, find out where the good golf courses are, and read a short history of each Costa del Sol town.

Fuengirola: Un Sol de Ciudad. www.pta.es/fuengirola
Calling Fuengirola the heart of Costa del Sol, this online brochure introduces the town's cuisine, art, culture, attractions, sports, and famous golf courses. There aren't a lot of details or interactive components, but the site does list hotels and their amenities, bus and train schedules, and useful phone numbers.

Marbella Scene: The Essence and Style of Marbella. www.marbella-scene.com
A British writer relocated in Marbella shares his impressions of the place "where Europe meets Africa" and recommends his favorite bar, restaurant, hotel, and spots for quiet contemplation. Beautiful photos are included.

Absolute Marbella. www.absolute-marbella.com
Read the current issue of this Costa del Sol magazine, which combines restaurant reviews, horoscopes, an events calendar, and a feature story. There's also an A-to-Z phone directory of local businesses.

VALENCIA & THE COSTA BLANCA

Valencia: A Virtual Trip. www.upv.es/cv/valbegin.html
For those who enjoy a walking tour, this site provides a map on which all major sites are marked. The guide also describes and shows photos of the Mediterranean city's history, festivals, cuisine, nightlife, monuments, museums, sports, business, gardens, shops, hotels, and transportation.

Benidorm. www.athenea.com/benidorm
Take a photo tour of Benidorm, a city famous for its beaches, or get the lowdown on lodging, dining, transportation, and travel agencies. If you can't make it to this little corner of Spain, you can still sample Benidorm from home through regional recipes and virtual postcards.

BARCELONA

Barcelona: A Different Point of View. members.xoom.com/barcy
A Barcelona native offers an insider's view of the city, sharing historical tidbits and observations alongside photos of oft-overlooked details. This lovely presentation reveals the emotion, the life force, the spirituality, and the sensory pleasures of Barcelona.

Barcelona Prestige. www.bcn-guide.com
This guide holds a lot of practical information like price-specific restaurant listings, museum hours, bus and subway routes, and descriptions of local shops. There's something for the dreamy cybertraveler, too: a photo tour of Barcelona's fabulous monuments.

Fundacio Joan Miró. www.bcn.fjmiro.es
If you're a modern-art lover, you won't want to miss this tribute to Miró, a Barcelona native. Along with a permanent collection of Miró's works, the foundation hosts traveling exhibits, musical programs, and activities for kids. The site gives information on hours, admission fees, and tours. A Miró biography is included.

Poble Espanyol. www.poble-espanyol.com
Duck into a little Barcelona borough. Illustrated with enticing photos, this site guides visitors to the Poble Espanyol district's architecture, galleries, Internet cafes, and convention centers. A calendar lists festivals and other events.

Some Street Scams in Barcelona. cliffs.ucsd.edu/terry/barna/scams.html
You won't be able to look at pretty pictures or make hotel reservations at this site, but you will find useful tips. This guide presents all sorts of scam scenarios and even offers descriptions of specific Barcelona con artists notorious for ripping off tourists.

Time Out: Barcelona. www.timeout.com/barcelona
As always, Time Out's guide is thorough and easily navigable. Along with weather reports, online travel booking, and a currency converter, the site provides a wealth of information on accommodations, dining, sightseeing, entertainment, kids' stuff, gay and lesbian culture, shopping, and more.

✪ Transports Metropolitans de Barcelona. www.tmb.net/weleng.htm
If the actual public transportation system in Barcelona is nearly as snazzy as its site, you're in for a treat. Amid chic, color-coded graphics and animated vehicles, you can learn how to navigate the city's bus lines and Metro (subway) system, get ticket information, read the latest TMB news, and absorb all sorts of tourist tips.

CATALONIA

✪ Castello d'Empuries. www.castellodempuries.net
A veritable multimedia extravaganza, this guide to the Spanish town features numerous video clips, a virtual-reality tour of an ancient church, and interactive maps. Lower-tech travelers can use the events calendar and photo-illustrated text, describing, in detail, Marshes National Park, the bustling Empuriabrava area, and the town's many hotels, restaurants, and tourist attractions.

Catalonia Tourism Guide. www.travelcat.com
Click on a Catalonia town listed in the margin for facts on transportation, news, events, culture, and history. For lodging, check out the guide's recommendations for two-star to five-star hotels; links take you right to their sites.

Hoteles Catalonia. www.hoteles-catalonia.es
Make reservations online to stay at a hotel in Spain's Catalonia region. The site lists three- to five-star hotels and their amenities, services, prices, and locations.

Railways of the Autonomous Government of Catalonia. www.fgc.catalunya.net
The name is a mouthful, but the site is a simply and attractively designed guide to Catalonia's transportation system. Find maps, ticket information, fares, news, a description of each train line, and customer service.

Tourism Catalonia. tourism.catalonia.net
Find out about vacation rentals, farmhouses, hostels, and other accommodations in Spain's Catalonia region. Also see what the area has to offer in the way of festivals and adventure sports. The guide's food-and-drink section includes a lesson in Catalán eating habits and a course-by-course description of the local fare.

NAVARRE & LA RIOJA

Hoteles Rurales de Navarra. www.hotelesruralesnavarra.es
A view of autumn leaves and waterfalls introduces this guide to rural lodging in Spain's Navarre region. You can make reservations online to stay in a quaint country inn. The site provides photos and a full description of each hotel as well as a brief but appealing guide to each town's attributes.

Sansol. www.arrakis.es/~melgar
This little guide to the village of Sansol shows historic works of art and architecture, plays audio clips of local musicians singing auroras, gives brief history and geography lessons, and provides a chat room.

THE BASQUE COUNTRY

Agritourism in Basque Country. www.encomix.es/nekazal
For a low-stress and low-cost vacation, take a look at this guide to rural travel in north-central Spain. The site lists accommodations by region, describes the amenities of each establishment, and gives specific prices.

San Sebastian International Film Festival. www.sansebastianfestival.com
If you time your visit right, you can catch the annual film festival in Basque country. This site lists entry requirements, schedules, ticket information, prizes, and so on. There's a section about transportation and lodging as well.

Sarean: Internet and the Basque Country. www.cd.sc.ehu.es/Sarean
Though entirely free of frills, this site virtually overflows with links. The online directory leads to Basque tour guides, individual city and village sites, activities listings, sports clubs, universities, government pages, music, and more.

GALICIA

A Coruña. www.turismocoruna.com
See the Coruña tower, where Picasso held his first exhibition. Read snippets of the beach town's history. Sample the many, multi-period art offerings. Look through a list (with some links) of 22 recommended restaurants and their prices. Find out how to get two-for-one rates on accommodations. Check out the photo gallery. Consult the online map for guidance.

Costa da Morte. www.finisterrae.com
Romp through more than two dozen coastal villages, and see their ancient artifacts, quaint hotels, and sea festivals. In this site's "tales" section, you can learn about legendary shipwrecks and local figures. Check out the lodgings segment for recommended hotels, restaurants, campsites, and rural inns.

A Guarda. www.a-guarda.eu.org
A sparse but useful guide tells you what's available in this Galician town: good food and wine, Mount Santa Tecla, festivals, mountain-biking routes, the sea, and bed-and-breakfast accommodations.

THE BALEARIC ISLANDS
Ibiza Hotels. www.ibiza-hotels.com
As the name suggests, this site lists hotels in Ibiza and offers online reservation services. Additional perks: You can rent a car, buy a ferry ticket, check the weather report, use the currency converter, and see a virtual-reality panoramic view of the Ibiza harbor.

Ibiza Night. www.ibizanight.com
A hint of English-as-a-second-language, coupled with graphics that are equal parts artful and cheesy, lend an exotic atmosphere to this site's descriptions of Ibiza's art scene, beaches, fashions, music venues, accommodations, restaurants, and other cultural offerings. For the practical traveler, Ibiza Night lists local public services and emergency phone numbers.

Guia de Formentera. www.guiaformentera.com
Along with tips on getting to the tiny island, this site gives facts on Formentera's history and geography. For biology buffs, there's a photo-illustrated guide to plant and animal life. Sun worshipers can find a map to the best beaches, complete with a legend deciphering beach signs (a blank sign indicates a nude beach).

Ciutadella de Menorca. www.infotelecom.es/ciutadella
Meander through the burial tombs, caves, and other ancient wonders of the Spanish island of Menorca under this site's guidance. A map directs visitors to the island's many beaches. A calendar lists cultural events, and special sections show the old town, stone quarries, and signs of urbanization.

Index

FROMMER'S® COMPLETE TRAVEL GUIDES

Alaska
Amsterdam
Arizona
Atlanta
Australia
Austria
Bahamas
Barcelona, Madrid & Seville
Beijing
Belgium, Holland & Luxembourg
Bermuda
Boston
Budapest & the Best of Hungary
California
Canada
Cancún, Cozumel &
    the Yucatán
Cape Cod, Nantucket & Martha's Vineyard
Caribbean
Caribbean Cruises & Ports of Call
Caribbean Ports of Call
Carolinas & Georgia
Chicago
China
Colorado
Costa Rica
Denmark
Denver, Boulder & Colorado Springs
England
Europe
Florida
France
Germany
Greece
Greek Islands
Hawaii
Hong Kong
Honolulu, Waikiki & Oahu
Ireland
Israel
Italy
Jamaica & Barbados
Japan
Las Vegas
London
Los Angeles
Maryland & Delaware
Maui
Mexico
Miami & the Keys

Montana & Wyoming
Montréal & Québec City
Munich & the Bavarian Alps
Nashville & Memphis
Nepal
New England
New Mexico
New Orleans
New York City
Nova Scotia, New Brunswick &
    Prince Edward Island
Oregon
Paris
Philadelphia & the
    Amish Country
Portugal
Prague & the Best of the Czech Republic
Provence & the Riviera
Puerto Rico
Rome
San Antonio & Austin
San Diego
San Francisco
Santa Fe, Taos &
    Albuquerque
Scandinavia
Scotland
Seattle & Portland
Singapore & Malaysia
South Africa
Southeast Asia
South Pacific
Spain
Sweden
Switzerland
Thailand
Tokyo
Toronto
Tuscany & Umbria
USA
Utah
Vancouver & Victoria
Vermont, New Hampshire
    & Maine
Vienna & the Danube Valley
Virgin Islands
Virginia
Walt Disney World & Orlando
Washington, D.C.
Washington State

FROMMER'S® DOLLAR-A-DAY GUIDES

Australia from $50 a Day
California from $60 a Day
Caribbean from $70 a Day
England from $70 a Day
Europe from $60 a Day
Florida from $60 a Day

Hawaii from $70 a Day
Ireland from $50 a Day
Israel from $45 a Day
Italy from $70 a Day
London from $85 a Day
New York from $80 a Day

New Zealand from $50 a Day
Paris from $85 a Day
San Francisco from $60 a Day
Washington, D.C.,
    from $60 a Day

FROMMER'S® PORTABLE GUIDES

Acapulco, Ixtapa &
    Zihuatanejo
Alaska Cruises & Ports of Call
Bahamas
Baja & Los Cabos
Berlin
California Wine Country
Charleston & Savannah
Chicago

Dublin
Hawaii: The Big Island
Las Vegas
London
Maine Coast
Maui
New Orleans
New York City
Paris

Puerto Vallarta, Manzanillo
    & Guadalajara
San Diego
San Francisco
Sydney
Tampa & St. Petersburg
Venice
Washington, D.C.

FROMMER'S® NATIONAL PARK GUIDES

Family Vacations in the
    National Parks
Grand Canyon

National Parks of the
    American West
Rocky Mountain

Yellowstone & Grand Teton
Yosemite & Sequoia/
    Kings Canyon
Zion & Bryce Canyon

FROMMER'S® GREAT OUTDOOR GUIDES

New England
Northern California

Southern California & Baja
Washington & Oregon

FROMMER'S® MEMORABLE WALKS

Chicago
London

New York
Paris

San Francisco
Washington D.C.

FROMMER'S® IRREVERENT GUIDES

Amsterdam
Boston
Chicago
Las Vegas

London
Los Angeles
Manhattan

New Orleans
Paris
San Francisco

Seattle & Portland
Vancouver
Walt Disney World
Washington, D.C.

FROMMER'S® BEST-LOVED DRIVING TOURS

America
Britain
California

Florida
France
Germany

Ireland
Italy
New England

Scotland
Spain
Western Europe

THE UNOFFICIAL GUIDES®

Bed & Breakfast in
  New England
Bed & Breakfast in
  the Northwest
Beyond Disney
Branson, Missouri
California with Kids
Chicago

Cruises
Disneyland
Florida with Kids
The Great Smoky &
  Blue Ridge
  Mountains
Inside Disney
Las Vegas

London
Miami & the Keys
Mini Las Vegas
Mini-Mickey
New Orleans
New York City
Paris
San Francisco

Skiing in the West
Walt Disney World
Walt Disney World
  for Grown-ups
Walt Disney World
  for Kids
Washington, D.C.

SPECIAL-INTEREST TITLES

Born to Shop: France
Born to Shop: Hong Kong
Born to Shop: Italy
Born to Shop: New York
Born to Shop: Paris
Frommer's Britain's Best Bike Rides
The Civil War Trust's Official Guide
  to the Civil War Discovery Trail
Frommer's Caribbean Hideaways
Frommer's Europe's Greatest Driving Tours
Frommer's Food Lover's Companion to France
Frommer's Food Lover's Companion to Italy
Frommer's Gay & Lesbian Europe
Israel Past & Present
Monks' Guide to California

Monks' Guide to New York City
The Moon
New York City with Kids
Unforgettable Weekends
Outside Magazine's Guide
  to Family Vacations
Places Rated Almanac
Retirement Places Rated
Road Atlas Britain
Road Atlas Europe
Washington, D.C., with Kids
Wonderful Weekends from Boston
Wonderful Weekends from New York City
Wonderful Weekends from San Francisco
Wonderful Weekends from Los Angeles

WHEREVER YOU TRAVEL, *H*ELP IS NEVER FAR AWAY.

From planning your trip to providing travel assistance along the way, American Express® Travel Service Offices are always there to help you do more.

Spain

MADRID
American Express Travel Service
Plaza de Las Cortes 2
(34) (91) 3225445

BARCELONA
American Express Travel Service
Paseo de Gracia 101
Corner Rosellon
(34) (93) 2170070

VALENCIA
Viajes Duna SI (R)
Cirilo Amoros 88
(34) (96) 3741562/3

SALAMANCA
Viajes Salamanca (R)
Plaza Mayor 24
(34) (923) 215215

MARBELLA
American Express Travel Service
Duque de Ahumada/Edf. Occidente
Loc Com 3/Complejo Marbella 2000
(34) (95) 2821494

BILBAO
Viaca (R)
Alameda Recalde 68
(34) (94) 4212049

MALAGA
Viajes Rosaleda SI (R)
Calle Especerias 14
(34) (95) 2221101

Travel

www.americanexpress.com/travel

American Express Travel Service Offices are found in central locations throughout Spain.